6TH EDITION

VILLAGE MEDICAL MANUAL

A LAYMAN'S GUIDE TO HEALTH CARE IN DEVELOPING COUNTRIES

VOLUME II

DIAGNOSIS AND TREATMENTS

Mary Vanderkooi
M.D., D.T.M. & H.

Illustrations prepared by Lawrence Ahrens

Correspondence with the author may be addressed to:

Equip, Inc.
P. O. Box 1126
Marion, NC 28752-1126
USA
www.equipministries.org
E-mail: maryvdk@ethionet.et
maryvanderkooi@yahoo.com

Information about the Missionary Medical Intensive (MMI) course, which uses this publication as the text, may be obtained from MMI, Equip, Inc., at the above address.

Published by William Carey Library
1605 E. Elizabeth Street
Pasadena, CA 91104 | www.missionbooks.org

Naomi Bradley McSwain, editorial manager
Johanna Deming, assistant editor
Rosemary Lee-Norman, copy editor
Hugh Pindur, graphic design

William Carey Library is a ministry of the
U.S. Center for World Mission
Pasadena, CA | www.uscwm.org

Library of Congress Cataloging-in-Publication Data

Vanderkooi, Mary.
Village medical manual : a layman's guide to health care in developing countries / Mary Vanderkooi ; illustrations prepared by Lawrence Ahrens. -- 6th ed.
v. cm.
Includes index.
Contents: v. 1. Principles and procedures -- v. 2. Diagnosis and treatment.
ISBN 978-0-87808-748-8 (v. 1) -- ISBN 978-0-87808-749-5 (v. 2)
1. Medicine, Popular--Handbooks, manuals, etc. 2. Community health aides--Handbooks, manuals, etc. 3. Medicine, Rural--Developing countries--Handbooks, manuals, etc. I. Title.
RC81.V37 2009
362.109172'4--dc22
2009036211

13 12 11 10 10 9 8 7 CH

PRINTED IN THE UNITED STATES OF AMERICA

M. Vanderkooi: Village Medical Manual. A Layman's Guide to Health Care in Developing Countries.

Volume I: Principles and Procedures
Volume II: Diagnosis and Treatments

Important Notice and Disclaimer

This book is intended for use only by those who are forced by location and circumstances to render medical care for which they are not professionally trained. It does not reflect the state of medical art in Western countries, and it is not to be used as a substitute for professional medical care. Please take note of the following:

1. Medicine is not an exact science. Diagnosis is largely an art learned by experience and training.
2. Only conditions that are common at least in some part of the world are included in this book.
3. Only the most common and constant symptoms are listed for each disease.
4. Only the most common diseases are listed for each symptom. Diseases that are not treatable in developing areas are not routinely listed.
5. Descriptions given for diseases will in general be correct but may not be true in certain areas of the world. How a disease manifests itself may differ according to the particular strain of the infecting organism, the environment, and the age and genetic heritage of the patient. For example, the symptoms of typhoid fever in India may be quite different from those in South America.
6. Only the most common, the safest, and lowest cost drugs are listed. More effective alternatives may be available. Every effort has been made to check and double-check the recommended doses but it is essential that doses of unfamiliar drugs be checked against another reference.
7. Only the most important precautions about drug use and possible side effects are listed. It is essential, before using drugs, to check recent information regarding safety, precautions, and side-effects. This information changes frequently. The following web addresses are useful: www.drugs.com; www.webmd.com; www.rxlist.com; www.medicinenet.com.
8. Verbal descriptions and illustrations give only a very rough approximation of how to do procedures and physical examination. They do not adequately substitute for hands-on training and experience.
9. The assumption is made that only minimal drugs and equipment are available. There are frequently better treatments where there are better facilities.
10. Only the common and less serious injuries are addressed in the injury section. Do not use these directions for obviously serious situations unless there is no other alternative. In that case, studying the principles and following those is usually more reliable than following specific directions for injuries that are similar but not the same.
11. Recommendations are made throughout the text whether a patient should be sent out to an established medical facility. These recommendations are made on the assumption that sending out would entail a considerable amount of time, expense or difficulty. For situations in which professional medical help is readily available, it should be used in all cases.
12. The disease distribution maps in Volume II give only a rough approximation of the truth. Precise, reliable information is impossible to obtain, since the distribution of diseases is continually changing. Diseases may be eliminated in some areas but may also spread and enter new areas. Maps indicating distribution of disease are notoriously contradictory and unreliable. If your location is anywhere near a shaded area or if your patient might have traveled through a shaded area at the start of the incubation period, he might have that disease. Be particularly skeptical of maps where the shading stops at political borders. Micro-organisms don't respect border controls. Be aware that in areas of civil unrest the distribution of diseases changes rapidly and unpredictably.
13. The assumption is made that the patient being treated was previously healthy, has no chronic diseases, and is on no routine medication. Many medications interact badly. In any case, if the patient is taking or will be taking more than one medication, it is imperative that potential interactions be checked. The following website is useful: www.medscape.com/druginfo/druginterchecker?src=ads.

Diagnosis and Treatment Using These Books

The following steps should be followed in attempting to diagnose and treat an ill person:

1. Carry out a patient evaluation according to the procedures outlined in Chapter 1 of Volume I.
2. Make a Problems List including:
   A. Abnormal vital signs.
   B. The patient's major symptoms.
3. Go to *Index A: Symptom Protocols,* in Volume II. For each item in your Problems List, find a Protocol in *Index A* that deals with it. From these Protocols, write down possible diagnoses for each item in the Problems List. Then try to identify one or a few diseases that could account for most or all of the observed symptoms.
4. Next go to the *Index B: Disease Index* and read about the individual diseases identified in Step 3. Some of the disease entries also make reference to *Index C: Differential Diagnosis*. *Index C* provides help for choosing between diseases that have similar or related symptoms. You should also check the *Regional Index* (*Indexes E* through *U*) for your geographical area, as it may contain special notes for the diseases on your list. Decide on this basis what is the most likely diagnosis.
5. Determine what treatment should be given. If at this stage more than one disease remains a possible diagnosis, first treat for the most probable disease, and/or the most common one in your area, and/or the one which is easiest to treat, or which uses the safest drugs. Only treat one disease at a time unless the patient is critically ill. You should have *two* goals:
   A. To make the patient better.
   B. To verify what the correct diagnosis is so you are wiser with the next, similar patient.
6. Use the Drug Index (Index D in Volume II) for detailed instructions on how to use the intended drugs. Be sure to read about any precautions, and be careful to calculate dosages correctly. Users who are mathematically challenged should review their calculations with someone more mathematically inclined.
7. Should a medical or laboratory procedure be required, refer to Appendices 1 and 2 in Volume I, which describe how to do many common procedures.

Contents: Volume I
Principles and Procedures

Contents: Volume II
Diagnosis and Treatment

Guide to Abdominal Protocols

IX. PELVIC AND RECTAL PROBLEMS 121

X. LOWER LIMB PROBLEMS.............142

Index A: Symptom Protocols

I. ABNORMAL VITAL SIGNS

PROTOCOL 1. TEMPERATURE ABNORMAL

1 A. Low Body Temperature
1B-1D. General Notes on Fevers
1 B. Mild Fevers
1 C. Remittent and Intermittent Fevers.
1 D. Sustained High Fever.

1 A. Low Body Temperature: Below 36.4°C or 97.5°F

**First check your thermometer; if two or three healthy people have low temperatures, the thermometer may be defective. Also the average body temperature does vary somewhat with the environment.

Symptomatic treatment: Before proceeding with the protocol, warm the patient. Have someone lie next to him or wrap him in warm blankets.

Is the patient an infant or elderly or does he have HEART FAILURE?

NO

YES to one or more
Check after warming the patient; he probably has trouble controlling his body temperature.

Has the patient been wet and poorly covered, exposed to cold weather, or both?

NO

YES
Consider HYPOTHERMIA; **treat immediately**.

Has the patient had prior fever or chills or both?

NO

YES
Consider MALARIA or SEPSIS.

Consider Alternatives	Characteristics
Dying patient	Blood pressure drops also; patient usually unconscious.
THYROID TROUBLE	Low thyroid: low temperature continually.
SEPSIS	Newborn or new mother or recent injury or infection.
CHOLERA	Severe, watery diarrhea, possibly vomiting also.
PLANT POISONING	Ackee[1] may drop the body temperature to subnormal.

1 B-1 D. General Notes on Fevers:

For fevers with other symptoms consider the following C Protocols: C-2: Fever plus Headache and Body Pains; C-3: Fever plus Anemia; C-5: Fever plus Jaundice; C-9: Fever plus Abdominal Pain; C-10 Fever plus Lethargy; C-13: Fever plus Back Pain.

Fever Patterns. *By "fever pattern", we mean how the body temperature changes with time.* This pattern can often be used to help diagnose the problem. The fever pattern is most helpful when fever occurs alone, that is, when there is no pain or other symptoms that can be used to diagnose the ailment or to pinpoint the part of the body causing the illness.

When trying to determine the fever pattern, do not give anti-fever medications or antibiotics which could confuse the results. Take the patient's temperature every 4-6 hours, around the clock, and write it down together with the time and date. Do this for at least 3 days in order to find the fever pattern.

Determining the fever pattern is particularly valuable when there are several people who have the same undiagnosed illness. Taking the time to do this with a few patients will enable you to better treat all the patients who have similar symptoms.

[1] Plant Poisoning, Ackee: Found in scattered areas of western Africa and the West Indies.

Listed below are various fever patterns and the most common diseases which cause them. Do not take these suggested diagnoses as absolute! Any fever pattern may be found with any disease, and your patient may be taking anti-fever medications without telling you. It is also good to know that frequently the patient will have chills when his temperature *rises,* and have sweats as it *falls*. It is most helpful to have the patient report both chills and sweats, and to take the temperature at those times in addition to regularly scheduled times.

Definitions of fever patterns:

Each of these fever patterns also can be either acute (lasting less than 2 weeks) or chronic (lasting more than 2 weeks).

1. ***Intermittent fever*** is a fever which returns to normal at least once a day on most days:
   a) With one daily return to normal: ABSCESS, MALARIA, SEPSIS.
   b) With two daily returns to normal: VISCERAL LEISHMANIASIS[1] or other rare infections.
2. ***Sustained fever*** is a fever which does not vary by more than 2.0°F (1.0°C) and does not return to normal daily: BRUCELLOSIS, SPOTTED FEVER,[2] SCARLET FEVER, ENTERIC FEVER, DRUG ERUPTION, SERUM SICKNESS, RELAPSING FEVER.
3. ***Remittent fever*** is a fever which varies by more than 2.0°F (1°C) and does not return to normal daily: Falciparum MALARIA, TUBERCULOSIS, VISCERAL LEISHMANIASIS. If the remittent fever is chronic (lasting more than 2 weeks) the diagnosis is probably TUBERCULOSIS, ENTERIC FEVER, ABSCESS, LARVA MIGRANS, HIV INFECTION, SEPSIS, AMEBAE, TRICHINOSIS, or MONONUCLEOSIS.
4. ***Relapsing fever*** might have any of the three previous daily patterns, but then the fever goes away for a matter of days before it returns.
   a) One relapse only: DENGUE FEVER,[3] LEPTOSPIROSIS, YELLOW FEVER,[4] POLIO, ARBOVIRAL FEVER (Africa).
   b) More than one relapse: RELAPSING FEVER, YELLOW FEVER, BRUCELLOSIS, DENGUE FEVER, MALARIA, RAT BITE FEVER, DRUG ERUPTION, SERUM SICKNESS.
   c) Chronic relapsing fever, lasting more than 2 weeks: VISCERAL LEISHMANIASIS, AFRICAN SLEEPING SICKNESS,[5] CHAGA'S DISEASE,[6] RELAPSING FEVER, BRUCELLOSIS, LYME DISEASE.

1 B. Mild Fever:

Definition: Mild Fevers are oral temperatures of 100-102°F (38°-39°C). (In the tropics, temperatures up to 100°F [38°C] are considered normal.)

Fevers are a common problem in the tropics; it is more efficient to look up another symptom, if there is one, than to use this Protocol. This Protocol does not list all causes of fevers, but only those that commonly occur with fever as the main or only symptom. See also the General Notes on Fevers, above.

Symptomatic treatment: Once you know the fever pattern, you can give the patient ACETAMINOPHEN or IBUPROFEN and keep him unclothed in a cool environment. Only pursue diagnosis if this treatment is unsuccessful or the fever recurs or the patient is very ill.

---

[1] Visceral Leishmaniasis: Found in scattered areas of Central and South America, Africa north of the equator, the Mediterranean area, the Indian subcontinent, eastern Europe, central Asia, and mainland China. Not present south of the equator.

[2] Spotted Fever: Not in the islands of Southeast Asia.

[3] Dengue Fever: In the Americas only near or north of the equator. In Africa only Nigeria and southern Africa. Prevalent in India, Southeast Asia, and the Pacific. Occasionally found in the Mediterranean area.

[4] Yellow Fever: South America north of Sao Paolo, central and western Africa and the Sudan.

[5] African Sleeping Sickness: Scattered areas of Africa, south of Bamako, Mali and Lake Chad; north of Lusaka, Zambia.

[6] Chaga's Disease: Found in scattered areas in the Americas.

Is the patient an infant or elderly or does he have HEART FAILURE?

NO | **YES**

Try cooling the person first; patients like this have trouble controlling their body temperature.
Consider KIDNEY INFECTION, EAR INFECTION in infants.

Does the patient have a dry mouth?

NO | **YES**

Consider DEHYDRATION; drugs and PLANT POISONING with effects like the drug ATROPINE.

Has the patient had weight loss or cough or both for a month or more?

NO | **YES**

Consider TUBERCULOSIS, HIV INFECTION, VISCERAL LEISHMANIASIS,[1] CANCER.

Does the patient have loss of appetite or yellow eyes or both?

NO | **YES**

Consider MALARIA, BRUCELLOSIS, HEPATITIS, ADDICTION to uppers, KIDNEY INFECTION, LIVER FLUKE, SYPHILIS, AMEBIC LIVER DISEASE, MUMPS, HEAT ILLNESS, INFLUENZA, LEAD POISONING, CANCER.

Is the patient extremely ill?

NO | **YES**

Consider DIPHTHERIA, or follow Protocol 1 D as if he had a high fever.

Consider Alternatives	**Characteristics**
MASTITIS	Nursing mother; sore breast(s) also.
PYOMYOSITIS	Also swelling and tenderness of muscles, usually hip or thigh.
CHICKEN POX	Older children, fever before rash, not very ill.
URINARY INFECTION	Cloudy urine, possibly some abdominal pains.
MONONUCLEOSIS	Also very tired, large neck lymph nodes, big, red tonsils.
==============	
DRUG ERUPTION	First dose or after a week on a drug; skin condition.
SERUM SICKNESS	After a bite, sting, or injection; early stage of some diseases.
TOXOPLASMOSIS	Also large neck lymph nodes, normal throat.
PLANT POISONING	Argemone oil; bad cooking oil.
LIVER FLUKE	Also liver large and tender.
FILARIASIS	Also some body swelling along with the fever.

1 C. Remittent, Intermittent and Relapsing Fevers:

Definitions: Remittent Fevers, Intermittent Fevers and Relapsing Fevers are fevers that vary by *more than* 2.0°F (1.0°C). The temperature may or may not return to normal daily.

Fevers are a common problem in the tropics; it is more efficient to look up another symptom, if there is one, than to use this Protocol. This Protocol does not list all causes of fevers, but only those that commonly occur with fever as the main or only symptom. See also the General Notes on Fevers, on page 6.

For fevers with other symptoms consider the following *Index C* Protocols: C-2, C-3, C-5, C-9, C-10, C-13.

Symptomatic treatment: Once you know the fever pattern, you can give the patient ACETAMINOPHEN or IBUPROFEN and keep him unclothed in a cool environment. Only pursue diagnosis if this treatment is unsuccessful or the fever recurs or the patient is very ill.

---

[1] Visceral Leishmaniasis: Found in scattered areas of Central and South America, Africa north of the equator, the Mediterranean area, the Indian subcontinent, eastern Europe, central Asia, and mainland China. Not present south of the equator.

Does the patient have shaking chills and drenching sweats every 1-3 days?

NO | **YES**

Regular timing: MALARIA,
Irregular timing: MALARIA, AMEBIC LIVER DISEASE, VISCERAL LEISHMANIASIS,[1] BARTONELLOSIS,[2] RELAPSING FEVER, SPOTTED FEVER,[3] KATAYAMA DISEASE, RAT BITE FEVER,[4] rarely early AFRICAN SLEEPING SICKNESS.[5]

Does the patient have pain in his upper abdomen?

NO | **YES**

Consider MALARIA, AMEBIC LIVER DISEASE, VISCERAL LEISHMANIASIS, FAMILIAL MEDITERRANEAN FEVER.[6]

Does the patient have at least two of these: cough, weight loss, diarrhea?

NO | **YES**

Consider TUBERCULOSIS, HIV INFECTION, DYSENTERY, AMEBIC LIVER DISEASE.

Consider Alternatives	Characteristics
FILARIASIS	Young or recently arrived in an affected area.
LEPTOSPIROSIS	Totally erratic fevers; red eyes, muscle pains, or both.
============	
BRUCELLOSIS	Slow onset; joint pains or back pains or headache.
TRENCH FEVER	Urban homeless, body lice, headache, shin pain.
RELAPSING FEVER	Chills and sweats are separated by less than 12 hours.
VISCERAL LEISHMANIASIS	Evening fevers; large spleen.
AFRICAN SLEEPING SICKNESS	Fevers erratic; has been in an affected area.
SERUM SICKNESS	Fevers, HIVES, headache, fatigue intermittently.
DRUG ERUPTION	First dose or else after a week with a skin rash
THALLASEMIA	Hereditary; infants; not nursing well.
TRICHINOSIS	Ate poorly cooked pork or wild carnivore meat.
TULAREMIA	Exposed to small animals or their insects.

1 D. Sustained High Fever:

Definition: A sustained fever may or may not be relapsing. The patient always has an oral temperature over 38°C/100°F and it is usually over 39°C/102°F; it may rise and fall by 2.0° F or *less*, but it never returns to normal and then becomes high again on the same day.

Fevers are a common problem in the tropics. Not all causes of fevers are listed in this Protocol, but only those that commonly present with fever as the main or only symptom. See also the General Notes on Fevers, page 6.

For fevers with other symptoms consider the following C Protocols: 2, 3, 5, 9, 10, 13.

---

[1] Visceral Leishmaniasis: Found in scattered areas of Central and South America, (mainly eastern) Africa north of the equator, the Mediterranean area, the Indian subcontinent, eastern Europe, central Asia, and mainland China.

[2] Bartonellosis: Scattered areas in Peru and adjacent border areas.

[3] Only the kind of spotted fever that occurs in the Americas.

[4] There is also an inflamed wound from an animal bite. The fever tends to be sustained for a number of days and then go away by itself for some days and then come back. Therefore, depending on when in the cycle you see the patient, it may be either sustained or up and down. This disease is rare outside of Asia.

[5] African Sleeping Sickness: Scattered areas of Africa, south of Bamako, Mali and Lake Chad; north of Lusaka, Zambia.

[6] Familial Mediterranean Fever: This affects persons of Mediterranean genetic heritage, mainly Jews, Arabs, Turks, and Armenians.

Symptomatic treatment: Once you know the fever pattern, you can give the patient ACETAMINOPHEN or IBUPROFEN and keep him unclothed in a cool environment. Only pursue diagnosis if this treatment is unsuccessful or the fever recurs or the patient is very ill.

Is the patient a child who is fussy but too young to say where he has pain?

NO

YES

Consider KIDNEY INFECTION, EAR INFECTION, ROSEOLA, SICKLE CELL DISEASE,[1] MEASLES, /// PYOMYOSITIS, OSTEOMYELITIS, MENINGITIS.

Is the patient very ill with a severe headache, SEIZURE, or loss of consciousness?

NO

YES

Consider FEBRILE SEIZURE, cerebral MALARIA, ENTERIC FEVER, MEASLES, /// ENCEPHALITIS, MENINGITIS, SEPSIS, TYPHUS, HEAT ILLNESS (stroke), TULAREMIA,[2] SPOTTED FEVER,[3] RAT BITE FEVER.[4]

Does the patient have pain along with redness, or swelling anywhere?

NO

YES

Consider CELLULITIS, STREP THROAT, MASTITIS, RHEUMATIC FEVER, DRUG ERUPTION, PYOMYOSITIS, OSTEOMYELITIS, ANTHRAX, SPOTTED FEVER, RAT BITE FEVER,[5] FAMILIAL MEDITERRANEAN FEVER.[6]

Consider alternatives	Characteristics
ENTERIC FEVER	Lethargic; abdominal pain or cough; constipation, diarrhea, or lethargy.
ROSEOLA	Children, fever unresponsive to usual cooling devices.
============	
THYROID TROUBLE	High thyroid: Also nervous, fast pulse.
LEPROSY reaction	Taking leprosy medications, rash is symmetrical.
SPOTTED FEVER	Tick-infested area, bitten by a chigger mite or consumed bad food.
TYPHUS	Bitten by flea or body louse; general aching, very ill.
MONKEY POX	Humid areas of central and west Africa; blistered rash by day four.
LASSA FEVER	Humid areas of Africa; chest pains also.
YELLOW FEVER[7]	Not immunized against this; very ill.
SICKLE CELL DISEASE	Abdominal or bone pains usual; pale or yellow.
TULAREMIA	Exposed to small animals or their insects.
SCRUB TYPHUS[8]	Bitten by a mite, gradual fever onset, light avoidance.

[1] Sickle Cell Disease: This affects Blacks of African genetic origin, mainly in Africa and the Americas. Some Indians and Arabs are also affected.

[2] Tularemia: North America, central Asia, Europe, Far East, the north coast of Africa; exposure to small animals..

[3] Spotted Fever: Not in the islands of Southeast Asia.

[4] There is also an inflamed wound from an animal bite. The fever tends to be sustained for a number of days and then go away by itself for some days and then come back. Therefore, depending on when in the cycle you see the patient, it may be either sustained or up and down. This disease is rare outside of Asia.

[5] There is also an inflamed wound from an animal bite. The fever tends to be sustained for a number of days and then go away by itself for some days and then come back. Therefore, depending on when in the cycle you see the patient, it may be either sustained or up and down. This disease is rare outside of Asia.

[6] Familial Mediterranean Fever: This affects persons of Mediterranean genetic heritage, mainly Jews, Arabs, Turks, and Armenians.

[7] Yellow Fever: South America north of Sao Paolo, Central and western Africa and the Sudan.

[8] Scrub Typhus: Indian subcontinent, Southeast Asia, central Asia, and Pacific areas.

PROTOCOL 2. BLOOD PRESSURE ABNORMAL

2 A. High Blood Pressure
2 B. Low Pulse Pressure
2 C. High Pulse Pressure
2 D. Low Blood Pressure

2 A. High Blood Pressure:

Definition: The blood pressure is equal to or greater than 140/90 in someone from a Western country; greater than 130/80 in someone from a developing country.

If the measured pressure is high, first check the size of the cuff; a small cuff on a large or obese patient may give a falsely high blood pressure reading; add 10 points to the permissible pressure if this is the case.

Is the patient a female who is 6 months or more pregnant?

NO | **YES** — **Consider** TOXEMIA.

Is the patient fearful or upset or both?

NO | **YES** — Ignore the problem for now if the pressure is less than 180/100; re-check when calm. Give a small dose of DIAZEPAM if necessary.

Consider Alternatives	Characteristics
HYPERTENSION	Usually no other symptoms or just headache.
HEART FAILURE	Short of breath, fatigued, swollen ankles, or any combination.
=============	
KIDNEY FAILURE	Usually abnormal, little, or no urine; dry, flaky skin.
ADDICTION, Uppers	History of taking some substance that keeps the patient awake.
PLANT POISONING, ephedra	History of taking this herbal remedy; also fast pulse.
THYROID TROUBLE	Also a rapid pulse, insomnia, maybe weak legs.
==============	
TETANUS	Severe muscle spasms and wild swings in blood pressure.
RABIES	Cannot swallow water or paralyzed or cannot tolerate a breeze.

2 B. Low Pulse Pressure:

Definition: *Difference between blood pressure numbers is less than 15, for example a pressure of 120/112.*
May be normal if there is a very rapid pulse; check Protocol 3 if the pulse is rapid.
Normal if there is fluid in the abdomen; check Protocol 46 A if the abdomen is swollen.

Condition	Characteristics
PERICARDITIS	Swollen neck veins, fatigue.
HEART FAILURE	Valvular or restrictive type: short of breath or swollen neck veins.
=============	
TUBERCULOSIS	Similar to PERICARDITIS, this is one cause of PERICARDITIS.
LASSA FEVER[1]	High fever, severe headache and chest pain.

[1] Lassa Fever: This occurs, mostly in epidemics, in West Africa.

2 C. High Pulse Pressure:

Definition: Difference between blood pressure numbers is over 60, for example, 90/10.

Normal if there is emotional upset, fevers, or pregnancy; may be due to old age in a Westerner. It is also normal anytime that the pulse is slow; if the pulse is slow, ignore the high pulse pressure and pursue a diagnosis for the slow pulse.

Condition	Characteristics
ANEMIA	Pale inside lower eyelid, mouth, or fingernails.
SYPHILIS, tertiary	Incubation over ten years or syphilic mother
BERIBERI	Also weakness with walking, swollen ankles, malnourished.
HEART FAILURE	Valvular type: Also an enlarged heart, usually a murmur.
EXFOLIATIVE DERMATITIS	Skin peeling off in sheets.

2 D. Low Blood Pressure:

Definition: The blood pressure is less than 90/60 in someone from a Western country; it is less than 80/50 in someone from a developing country.

Low pressures are significant if the patient has symptoms; they should be ignored if the patient feels healthy. Some ethnic groups normally have low pressures. Check the pressures of presumably healthy persons of the same age range and ethnic origin.

A common cause of low blood pressure measurements is a blood pressure cuff that is too large for the patient; standard Western adult cuffs are made for those 50 kg or over. A standard cuff on a petite person will give a pressure that is low by 10-20 points.

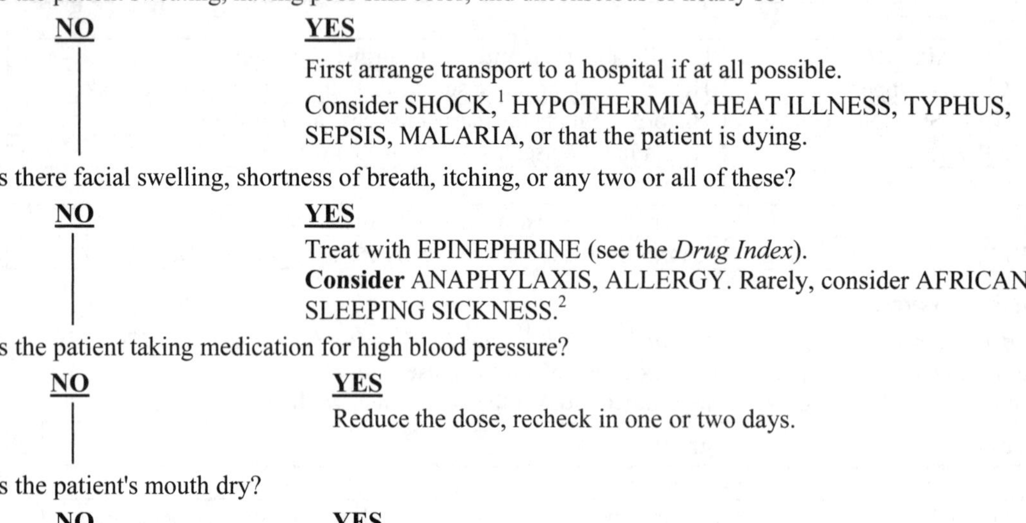

Is the patient sweating, having poor skin color, and unconscious or nearly so?
NO
YES
First arrange transport to a hospital if at all possible.
Consider SHOCK,[1] HYPOTHERMIA, HEAT ILLNESS, TYPHUS, SEPSIS, MALARIA, or that the patient is dying.
Is there facial swelling, shortness of breath, itching, or any two or all of these?
NO
YES
Treat with EPINEPHRINE (see the *Drug Index*).
Consider ANAPHYLAXIS, ALLERGY. Rarely, consider AFRICAN SLEEPING SICKNESS.[2]
Is the patient taking medication for high blood pressure?
NO
YES
Reduce the dose, recheck in one or two days.
Is the patient's mouth dry?
NO
YES
Give the person water to drink.
Consider DEHYDRATION, DIABETES.

Continued on next page.

[1] Consider the following as possible causes of SHOCK: ANAPHYLAXIS (emergency), CHOLERA, HEART ATTACK, HEMORRHAGIC FEVER, TUBAL PREGNANCY, ACUTE ABDOMEN, RELAPSING FEVER; in West Africa consider LASSA FEVER.

[2] African Sleeping Sickness: Scattered areas of Africa, south of Bamako, Mali and Lake Chad; north of Lusaka, Zambia.

(2 D. Low Blood Pressure, continued.)

Consider Alternatives	Characteristics
MALARIA	Patient has been ill with this for some time; severe falciparum.
HEART FAILURE	Short of breath, fatigued, swollen ankles or any combination.
============	
ADDICTION, Downers	History of taking some substance that causes sedation or sleep.
PLANT POISONING	Cassava or Claviceps: History of eating this.

Unusual causes are TUBERCULOSIS which affects the adrenal glands and hormonal problems which occur after childbirth. PREDNISONE may help until the person reaches a hospital.

PROTOCOL 3. PULSE ABNORMAL

3 A. Slow Pulse Without Fever
3 B. Slow Pulse Relative to a Fever
3 C. Rapid Pulse
3 D. Irregular Pulse

3 A. Slow Pulse Without Fever:

Definition: Pulse is slower than the normal ranges:

Age	Normal Pulse in beats per minute
Newborn:	100-180
1-6 months:	90-140
7-18 months	90-130
2-6 years:	80-120
7-10 years:	70-110
adult:	60-100
in athletes:	36-70

Condition	Characteristics
HEART FAILURE	Short of breath or fatigued, or both.
==============	
PLANT POISONING	Muscarine, Claviceps.
DIGITALIS (drug)	Drug effect; ignore if slightly low, decrease dosage if very slow.
PROPRANOLOL (drug)	Drug effect; ignore if slightly low, decrease dosage if very slow.
=============	
THYROID TROUBLE	Usually low body temperature, chronic fatigue.
ADDICTION	Downers; these are also sedative; the patient will be lethargic.
HYPOTHERMIA	Patient also has a low body temperature, exposed to cold environment.
CHAGA'S DISEASE[1]	Fatigued, swollen ankles, large liver or spleen.
HEART ATTACK	Patient ate a Western diet; chest, jaw, or arm pain; sweating.

3 B. Slow Pulse Relative to a Fever:

Definition: If your patient has a fever, the pulse will normally be faster. The normal range for adults will increase by about 15-18 beats for every degree Celsius above 37°, or 8-10 beats for every degree Fahrenheit above 99°. In children the rise is 21-27 beats per degree Celsius or 12-15 beats per degree Fahrenheit. Thus a 1-year-old with a temperature of 40° C will have a pulse between 151 and 211: (90 + 61 and 130 + 81 [27 x 3]; see Table in Protocol 3 A). You should be aware that it is impossible to accurately count pulses more than about 200 beats per minute.

The conditions listed below cause the patient's pulse to be abnormally slow. In an athletic person, calculate the expected pulse relative to the patient's usual pulse, not the normals for his age, since athletes' pulses normally run slow at rest, sometimes as low as 40 beats per minute for an Olympic-quality athlete. There are quite a few heart medications that will slow the pulse. These do not cause fevers but the patient may have a fever due to some other illness.

[1] Chaga's Disease: Found in scattered areas in the Americas.

(3 B. Slow Pulse Relative to a Fever, continued.)

Condition	Characteristics
ENTERIC FEVER	Lethargic; headache or abdominal pain.
DIGITALIS (drug)	A slow pulse is a normal effect of this drug.
=============	
DENGUE FEVER	Sudden onset, severe bone pain, previously healthy.
SPOTTED FEVER[1]	Sudden onset high fever, headache, red eyes.
TYPHUS	Similar to ENTERIC FEVER; history of flea, or louse bite.
SCRUB TYPHUS[2]	Scab from tick bite; rash begins on the face, seventh day.
=============	
DIPHTHERIA	The patient's pulse and respirations vary greatly from slow to fast.
YELLOW FEVER[3]	Not immunized; general aching, maybe yellow whites of eyes.
CHAGA'S DISEASE[4]	Fatigued, swollen ankles, large liver or spleen.
LASSA FEVER[5]	Sudden onset headache, fever, and chest pains.

Normal pulse rates in the presence of fever:

Temperature (°C/°F)	Child lowest normal pulse rate	Child highest normal pulse rate	Adult lowest normal pulse rate	Adult highest normal pulse rate
37.5/99.5	___ + 10= ___	___ + 13 = ___	60+7=67	100+ 9 =109
38/100.4	___ + 21= ___	___ + 27 = ___	60 + 15 = 75	100 + 18 = 118
38.5/101.3	___ + 31 = ___	___ + 40 = ___	60 + 22 = 82	100 + 27 = 127
39/102.2	___ + 42 = ___	___ + 54 = ___	60 + 30 = 90	100 + 36 = 136
39.5/103.1	___ + 52 = ___	___ + 67 = ___	60 + 37 = 97	100 + 45 = 145
40/104	___ + 63 = ___	___ + 81 = ___	60 + 45 = 105	100 + 54 = 154
40.5/104.9	___ + 73 = ___	___ + 94 = ___	60 + 52 = 112	100 + 63 = 163

3 C. Rapid Pulse:

Definition: The pulse is more rapid than the normal ranges given in Protocol 3 A, for a patient at rest. If the patient is in pain or upset, do not use this protocol; the negative emotion is probably making the pulse faster.

Is or was (recently) the patient very short of breath?

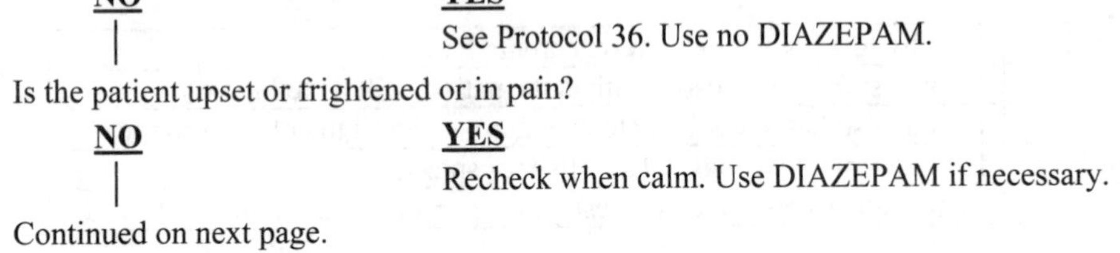

NO | **YES**
See Protocol 36. Use no DIAZEPAM.

Is the patient upset or frightened or in pain?

NO | **YES**
Recheck when calm. Use DIAZEPAM if necessary.

Continued on next page.

[1] Spotted Fever: Not in the islands of Southeast Asia.
[2] Scrub Typhus: Indian subcontinent, Southeast Asia, central Asia, and Pacific areas.
[3] Yellow Fever: South America north of Sao Paolo, Central and western Africa and the Sudan.
[4] Chaga's Disease: Scattered areas in the Americas only.
[5] Lassa Fever: Occurs in epidemics in West Africa.

(3C. Rapid Pulse, continued.)

Is the patient pale and sweaty and either unconscious or ready to faint?

NO — **YES**
Arrange transportation to the nearest hospital.
Consider SHOCK,[1] MALARIA, HYPOGLYCEMIA, SEPSIS, HEART ATTACK, RELAPSING FEVER.

Does the patient have a fever?

NO — **YES**
Fever causes a rapid pulse; recheck after the fever is gone.
Check other symptoms. **Consider** MALARIA, SEPSIS.

Is the patient's mouth dry?

NO — **YES**
Give the patient water to drink.
Consider DEHYDRATION or DIABETES, PLANT POISONING due to Datura or Jimson Weed. Also some drugs can do this.[2]

Is the patient pale (check for paleness inside lower eyelids, in mouth, and fingernails)?

NO — **YES**
Consider ANEMIA, TUBERCULOSIS, MALNUTRITION, rarely AFRICAN SLEEPING SICKNESS.[3]

Condition	**Characteristics**
HEART FAILURE	Short of breath or easily fatigued or both.
===============	
PLANT POISONING	Uppers, Cassava, Khat[4], Ephedra.
DIPHTHERIA	The patient's pulse varies greatly from very slow to very fast.
THYROID TROUBLE	High thyroid: Also insomnia, nervousness.
ADDICTION	Due to uppers or withdrawal from downers.
YELLOW FEVER[5]	Not immunized; general aching, maybe yellow eyes.
AFRICAN SLEEPING SICKNESS	Fevers and headache early; uncoordination later.
CHAGA'S DISEASE[6]	Also fatigued; swollen ankles, liver, or spleen.

3 D. Irregular Pulse:

Definition: It is impossible to predict when the next pulse will occur when you feel or listen while trying to keep time by tapping a foot or finger.

Irregular pulse may be normal in children; pulse rate usually varies with respiration.

May also be a normal (not significant) effect of caffeine and other stimulants.

(Continued on next page.)

[1] Consider the following as possible causes of SHOCK: ANAPHYLAXIS (emergency), CHOLERA, HEART ATTACK, HEMORRHAGIC FEVER, TUBAL PREGNANCY, ACUTE ABDOMEN, RELAPSING FEVER.

[2] The drugs that do this are in the general class of anticholinergics; they include some antihistamines, sedatives and anti-nausea drugs.

[3] African Sleeping Sickness: Scattered areas of Africa, south of Bamako, Mali and Lake Chad; north of Lusaka, Zambia.

[4] This is a stimulant drug, used in the Middle East and northeastern Africa.

[5] Yellow Fever: South America north of Sao Paolo, Central and western Africa and the Sudan.

[6] Chaga's Disease: Found only in scattered areas of the Americas.

(3 D. Irregular Pulse, continued.)

Condition	Characteristics
HEART FAILURE	Short of breath, severe fatigue, or swollen ankles.
RESPIRATORY INFECTION	Coughing for months or years; short of breath.
ASTHMA	Wheezing episodes come and go, get better and worse over years.
RHEUMATIC FEVER	History of red, swollen joints on both sides; maybe heart murmur.
==================	
DIGITALIS (drug)	Excess drug; stop the drug for a while.
SYPHILIS, tertiary	Incubation over 10 years or syphilic mother.
BRUCELLOSIS	Fevers off and on; joint pains or backache.
DIPHTHERIA	Also sharp pains, very swollen neck, very ill.
SEPSIS	Extremely ill; history of a recent infection.
HEART ATTACK	Western diet; chest, arm, or jaw pain, sweaty.
AFRICAN SLEEPING SICKNESS	Fevers and headache early; uncoordination later.
CHAGA'S DISEASE	Also other symptoms of HEART FAILURE.

PROTOCOL 4. RESPIRATION ABNORMAL

4 A. Slow Respiration
4 B. Irregular Respiration
4 C. Rapid Respiration

4 A. Slow Respiration:

Age	Normal Respiratory Rates
Newborn	30-50
1 y.o.	20-40
2-3 y.o.	20-30
5 y.o.	20-25
10 y.o.	17-22
Adults	12-20

Symptomatic treatment: Withdraw any sedative medication that the patient is taking.

Does the patient have sharp chest pain that is worse with breathing?

NO | **YES**
See Protocol 35B. Use IBUPROFEN to treat the pain.

Is there weakness or paralysis of one or more limbs or a drooping face?

NO | **YES**
Consider STROKE, DIPHTHERIA, or POLIO, rarely PLANT POISONING due to Botulism, RABIES.

Is the patient having general body spasms?

NO | **YES**
First arrange transport to the nearest hospital. **Consider** TETANUS, SEIZURES, rarely PLANT POISONING due to Strychnine.

Is the patient obviously laboring hard to breathe, *or* is he unconscious?

Neither | **YES to either or both**
First arrange transport to the nearest hospital if possible. Have the patient sit up during transportation if he is conscious.
Consider ASTHMA, RESPIRATORY FAILURE.

Consider alternative	Characteristics
ADDICTION	Due to downers or withdrawal from uppers.

(this may also be due to one-time drug usage of downers, without true addiction.)

4 B. Irregular Respiration:

Does the patient have pain aggravated by breathing?

NO | **YES**

YES: Due to the pain; diagnose the cause from Protocol 35 or 39. Treat the pain with IBUPROFEN.

Does the patient sigh frequently?

NO | **YES**

YES: **Consider** DEPRESSION, STRESS.

Is the patient very ill or unconscious?

NO | **YES**

YES: First arrange transport to the nearest hospital, if possible. **Consider** cerebral MALARIA, BRAIN DAMAGE, HEART FAILURE, MENINGITIS, ENCEPHALITIS, STROKE, head injury, ALTITUDE SICKNESS, SEPSIS. The patient may be dying.

Conditions	Characteristics
HEART FAILURE	Alternate fast and slow or absent respiration.
STROKE	Like HEART FAILURE; usually paralysis also.
===============	
KIDNEY FAILURE	Like HEART FAILURE; urine tests are abnormal.
DIPHTHERIA	The patient's pulse and respiration varies greatly from slow to fast.

This may also be due to poisons or drugs, especially those having the side-effect of drowsiness.

4 C. Rapid Respiration:

Age	Normal Respiratory Rates
Newborn	30-50
1 y.o.	20-40
2-3 y.o.	20-30
5 y.o.	20-25
10 y.o.	17-22
Adults	12-20

As a simple rule, the following children's normal upper limits may be remembered: 0-1 year, 50 breaths/minute; 1-3 years, 40 breaths per minute; over 3 years, 30 breaths/minute. Rates faster than these usually indicate pneumonia.

See SHORTNESS OF BREATH: Protocol 36 and also Protocol C-4: Shortness of breath.

Rapid respiration without the patient's feeling short of breath may be due to HEAT ILLNESS, DIABETES, KIDNEY FAILURE, SEPSIS, or ADDICTION. It may also be due to fear or sexual arousal.

II. WHOLE BODY PROBLEMS

PROTOCOL 5. PROBLEMS OF ALERTNESS, AWARENESS, SLEEP

5 A. Lethargy, Apathy, Excessive Sleep.
5 B. Sustained Unconsciousness or Coma.
5 C. Fainting With Momentary Loss of Consciousness.
5 D. Day and Night Reversal.
5 E. Hyperactivity, Insomnia, Irritability.
5 F. Confusion, Decreased Mental Functioning

5 A. Lethargy, Apathy, Excessive Sleep:

Definition: The patient sleeps excessively but he can be awakened and is able to get up and move. He can object to or resist treatment if he chooses to do so.

(Also see *Index C*, Protocols C-3, C-10)

Is the patient pale and sweaty?

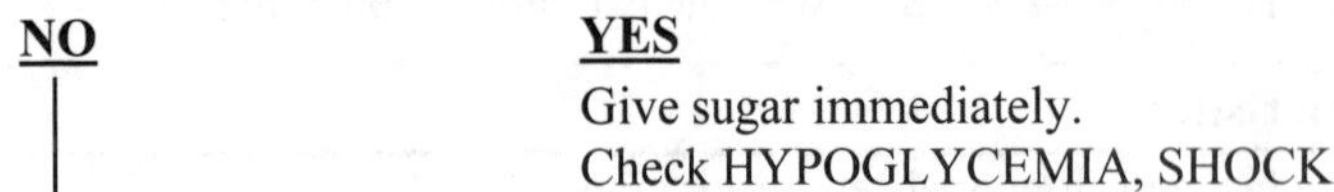

NO | **YES**
Give sugar immediately.
Check HYPOGLYCEMIA, SHOCK.

Does the patient have DIABETES, or fast respiration, DEHYDRATION, and vomiting?

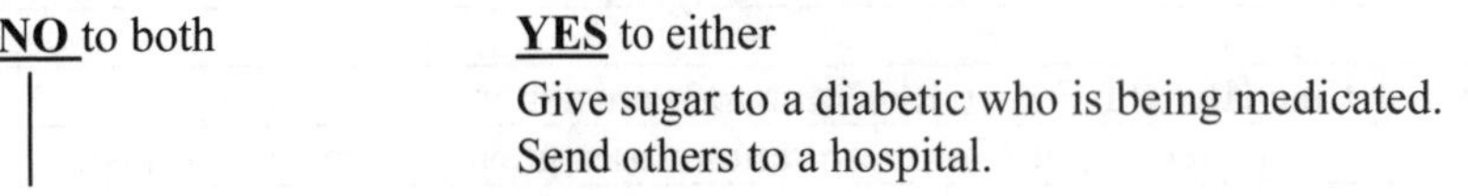

NO to both | **YES** to either
Give sugar to a diabetic who is being medicated.
Send others to a hospital.

Has part of the body been jerking or twitching?

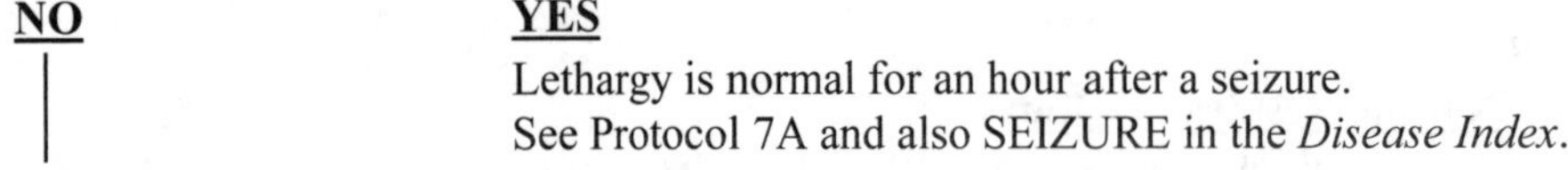

NO | **YES**
Lethargy is normal for an hour after a seizure.
See Protocol 7A and also SEIZURE in the *Disease Index*.

Is the problem of sudden onset and related to some injury or abdominal pain?

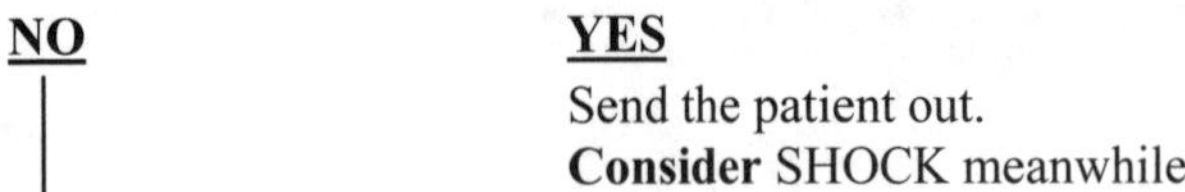

NO | **YES**
Send the patient out.
Consider SHOCK meanwhile.

Is the patient's pulse or respiration grossly abnormal?

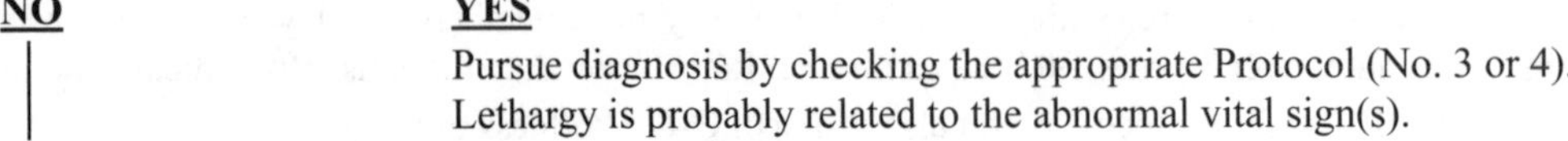

NO | **YES**
Pursue diagnosis by checking the appropriate Protocol (No. 3 or 4).
Lethargy is probably related to the abnormal vital sign(s).

Has the patient either recently taken sedative drugs or is he depressed?

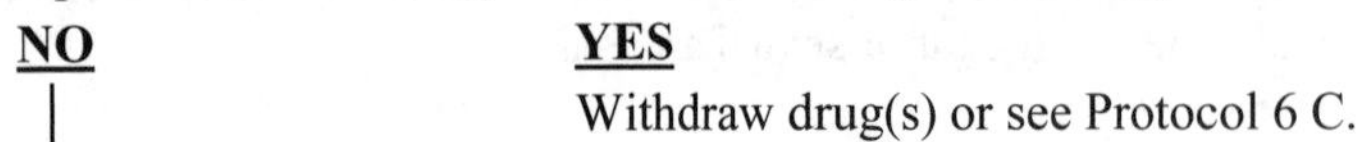

NO | **YES**
Withdraw drug(s) or see Protocol 6 C.

Does the patient have general weakness[1] or fatigue?

NO | **YES**
See Protocol 8 A.

Continued on next page.

[1] Weakness means that the person cannot exert muscle power at any time. Fatigue means that he can exert muscle power after he has rested a while but cannot sustain physical activity for a long time. Both are different than lethargy or sleepiness. Lethargy implies that the person is not aware of his environment; he likes to sleep too much. A person can be lethargic without being weak; perhaps he prefers to sleep, but he could get up and move something heavy if he wanted. He can also be weak or fatigued but be perfectly wide awake and therefore not lethargic.

(5 A. Lethargy, Apathy, Excessive Sleep, continued.)

Does the patient have a high fever, *or* Did he have one recently?

NO | **YES** to either

See Protocol C-10 A.

Is the patient pale: (check lower eyelids, mouth, and fingernails)?

NO | **YES**

Consider MALARIA, ANEMIA, MALNUTRITION, rarely AFRICAN SLEEPING SICKNESS,[1] SPRUE.

Consider alternatives: Also see Protocol C-10B

Condition	Fever	Onset	Other Characteristics
DEHYDRATION	Maybe	Variable	Very dry mouth.
ZINC DEFICIENCY	No	Days/weeks	Hot and dry climate or sweating.
MALNUTRITION	No	Days/weeks	Skinny upper arms, thin hair.
DEMONIZATION	No	Variable	A curse was put on the patient.
*STROKE	Unusual	Rapid	Weak or paralyzed.
*AFRICAN SLEEPING SICKNESS	Maybe	Over weeks	Clumsy or HEART FAILURE.
*HYPOTHERMIA	Low temp	Over hours	Exposure to cold or wet.
ADDICTION	No	Weeks/years	History of drug use or abuse.
*RESPIRATORY FAILURE	Maybe	Variable	Patient blue, breathing poorly.
*CARBON MONOXIDE POISONING	No	Minutes/hours	Exposure to fumes.
LIVER DISEASE	Unusual	Days/weeks	Yellow eyes, big belly or both.
BRUCELLOSIS	Maybe	Weeks/months	Pastoral area, joint pains.
PLANT POISONING(Ackee,[2] Cassava, Claviceps, Datura, Lolism,[3] Margosa oil,[4] Nicotine, Valerian)	No	Minutes/hrs.	Took plant in question.
KATAYAMA DISEASE	Episodic	Recurrent[5]	ALLERGY with fevers.
RADIATION ILLNESS	No	Variable	History of radiation exposure.
PELLAGRA	No	Weeks/months	Diarrhea or rash on exposed skin.
SCHISTOSOMIASIS JAPONICUM[6]	Unusual	Months/years	Exposed to water with snails, Asia/Pacific.

Chronic diseases such as HEART FAILURE, KIDNEY FAILURE, TUBERCULOSIS, VISCERAL LEISHMANIASIS,[7] and THYROID TROUBLE, can cause these symptoms when death is near.

[1] African Sleeping Sickness: Scattered areas of Africa, south of Bamako, Mali and Lake Chad and north of Lusaka, Zambia.

[2] Plant Poisoning, Ackee: Found in scattered areas of western Africa and the West Indies.

[3] Plant Poisoning: Lolism: Found only in the African, Mediterranean, and Middle Eastern areas.

[4] Plant Poisoning: Margosa Oil: A yellow oil used as an ethnic medicine worldwide, by persons from the Indian subcontinent.

[5] Each episode can come on fast, over hours to a day. There is usually an interval of days to weeks between episodes, with each episode lasting for days. The time pattern may, however, vary.

[6] Schistosomiasis Japonicum: In areas of mainland China, the Philippines, parts of the Celebes, the upper Mekong, and the Thai-Malaysia border.

[7] Visceral Leishmaniasis: Found in scattered areas of Central and South America, Africa north of the equator, the Mediterranean area, the Indian subcontinent, eastern Europe, central Asia, and mainland China.

5 B. Sustained Unconsciousness or Coma:

Anything that can cause lethargy, apathy, and excessive sleeping as described in Protocol 5 A can also cause sustained unconsciousness (coma). Those diseases listed in 5 A with an asterisk (*) are the most likely causes.

Also see Protocols C-10 A: Fever plus Lethargy or C-10 B: Lethargy or Confusion without a Fever.

5 C. Fainting With Momentary Loss of Consciousness:

Symptomatic treatment: Have the patient lie down. Then check his vital signs.

Did the patient experience an injection or an insect sting within the last hour?

NO | **YES**: **Consider** ANAPHYLAXIS, ALLERGY; treat immediately!

Is the patient pale and sweaty even when lying down?

NO | **YES**: Give sugar to the patient if his blood pressure is normal.
Treat for SHOCK if his blood pressure is low.

Is the patient emotionally upset, or has he been standing for a long time?

NO | **YES**: Have the patient lie down; he'll be fine.

Did the fainting occur after coughing or urinating with a very full bladder?

NO | **YES**: Have the patient lie down; he'll be fine.

Is any part of the patient's body jerking or twitching?

NO | **YES**: See Protocol 7 A.

Are the patient's hands cramped but not jerking or twitching?

NO | **YES**: **Consider** HYPERVENTILATION, rarely TETANUS.

Consider alternatives	**Characteristics**
ANEMIA	Pale inside lower eyelid or inside mouth or on fingernails.
DEHYDRATION	The patient is thirsty, his tongue is dry, or both.
HEAT ILLNESS	Exercising while not acclimatized, infants, and elderly.
=============	
Head injury	Should be obvious from history or looking at the patient's head.
ALTITUDE SICKNESS	Recent ascent, also headache or short of breath or both.
HEART FAILURE	Patient has an irregular pulse or a heart murmur.
STROKE	Weak in one or more limbs, or has trouble talking.

5 D. Day and Night Reversal:

Definition: The patient sleeps excessively during the day and is awake at night. There is no obvious cause like night-shift work.

Consider alternatives	**Other Characteristics**
Old age	Awakens early, frequently naps.
DEPRESSION	Awakens early and cannot sleep again.
ATTENTION DEFICIT DISORDER	Either hyperactive or has a racing brain with a slower body.
STRESS	Trouble falling asleep or like DEPRESSION.
JET LAG	After an east or west flight over six or more time zones, lasts up to 2 weeks.
DEMONIZATION	Occult involvement or someone put a curse on the patient.

Continued on next page.

(5 D. Day and Night Reversal, continued.)

==============	
SYPHILIS, tertiary	Headache, fatigue, irritability; incubation >10 yrs or syphilic mother.
AFRICAN SLEEPING SICKNESS[1]	Headaches, itching rash or large nodes, maybe HEART FAILURE.
TYPHUS	Fevers also, and quite sick; bitten by flea or louse.

5 E. Hyperactivity, Insomnia, Irritability:

Definition: The patient is awake more than is normal; he sleeps very little if at all.

This Protocol assumes no day and night reversal (see preceding Protocol).

See Protocol 6 B if there is nervousness or Protocol 6 A for bizarre behavior.

Is the patient six months or more pregnant?

NO | YES: **Consider** TOXEMIA.

Is the patient very ill with a high fever?

NO | YES: **Consider** MALARIA, HEAT ILLNESS (stroke), TYPHUS, BRUCELLOSIS, THYROID TROUBLE, BARTONELLOSIS,[2] ENCEPHALITIS, MENINGITIS, RABIES.

Is the patient going through changes or a hard time in his life?

NO | YES: **Consider** STRESS, DEPRESSION, ATTENTION DEFICIT DISORDER, DEMONIZATION.

Conditions	**Other Characteristics**
Drug side-effect	Stimulants or uppers in most; sedatives in the hyperactive.[3]
HEAT ILLNESS (exhaustion)	Very old or very young or exercising and not acclimatized.
ATTENTION DEFICIT DISORDER	Hyperactivity or adjustment problems since childhood.
ENTEROBIASIS	Insomnia or irritability because of an itchy rectum at night.
ALCOHOLISM	History of heavy or regular drinking, now withdrawing.
ADDICTION	Withdrawal from downers, drug effect of uppers.
============	
BRUCELLOSIS	Fevers off and on, joint pains, feeling rotten for weeks.
RABIES	Discomfort with swallowing liquids or a breeze blowing over skin.
THYROID TROUBLE	Weakness walking up stairs also, high thyroid.
AFRICAN SLEEPING SICKNESS	Uncoordinated or history of the disease, previously treated.
PLANT POISONING	Margosa oil,[4] Khat,[5] Mushrooms.
RADIATION ILLNESS	History of recent radiation exposure.

[1] African Sleeping Sickness: Scattered areas of Africa, south of Bamako, Mali and Lake Chad and north of Lusaka, Zambia.

[2] Bartonellosis: Scattered areas in Peru and adjacent border areas.

[3] People who have ATTENTION DEFICIT DISORDER sometimes become hyperactive with sedative drugs.

[4] Margosa oil: This is a yellow oil, used as an ethnic medicine worldwide, by persons from the Indian subcontinent.

[5] Khat: This is a stimulant, used in the Middle East and eastern Africa.

5F. Confusion, Decreased Mental Functioning:

Definition: One might think of this as recent-onset stupidity whereby a normally intelligent person suddenly cannot remember recent events and does not seem to understand simple concepts although he appears to be wide awake (not lethargic or unconscious). He is walking, talking, and caring for himself normally. Usually recent memory is the first to lapse; the person knows his childhood address but doesn't remember what he ate for breakfast that morning. Then a sense of time goes—he doesn't know the date—then place—he doesn't know where he is—and finally he does not recognize persons.

Decreased mental functioning: See Protocol C-10.

This may also arise from Alzheimer's Disease, which is decreased mental functioning without another reason. It can also arise from any illness that affects the brain such as CANCER originating elsewhere in the body.

PROTOCOL 6. PROBLEMS OF EMOTIONS AND BEHAVIOR

6 A. Bizarre Behavior
6 B. Nervousness
6 C. Depression

Definition: *The patient's behavior is abnormal by the criteria of the culture of the patient.* Behavior and emotions may seem unusual by Western criteria and still be normal within the context of another culture.

6 A. Bizarre Behavior:

Definition: *Unusual behavior that cannot be classified as simple lethargy or hyperactivity.* An example would be talking to a parking meter. Consider cultural differences; only a person from the same culture can judge behavior to be bizarre. See Protocol 5 A or 5 E if the behavior is also either lethargic or hyperactive.

The main problem is to distinguish between bizarre behavior due to *medical* causes from that due to *mental* causes. Clues that there is a *medical* cause: of the following list, the patient must have (1), together with either (2) or (3), and either (4) or (5). This protocol focuses on medical causes of bizarre behavior.

(1) Patient cannot pay attention.
(2) Starts suddenly, minutes to a day.
(3) Changes over hours to days.
(4) Patient doesn't make sense in talking.
(5) Lethargic or hyperactive.

Is the patient 6 months or more pregnant or delivered within the past week?

NO | **YES**
Consider TOXEMIA.

Does the patient have a high fever, a headache, or both?

NO | **YES to either or both**
Consider cerebral MALARIA, HEAT ILLNESS, HIV INFECTION, TYPHUS, MENINGITIS, ENCEPHALITIS, ENTERIC FEVER, PLAGUE, BARTONELLOSIS,[1] RABIES.

Does the patient eat a poor or unbalanced diet?

NO | **YES**
Consider BERIBERI, PELLAGRA, ALCOHOLISM, LIVER FAILURE, CIRRHOSIS.

Does the patient have joint or back pains?

NO | **YES**
Consider HIV INFECTION, BRUCELLOSIS, RHEUMATIC FEVER, AFRICAN SLEEPING SICKNESS.[2]

Continued on next page.

---

[1] Bartonellosis: Occurs only in Peru and adjacent border areas.

[2] African Sleeping Sickness: Scattered areas of Africa, south of Bamako, Mali and Lake Chad and north of Lusaka, Zambia.

(6 A. Bizarre Behavior, continued.)

Conditions	Fever	Other Characteristics
ZINC DEFICIENCY	No	Sweating or hot, dry climate; not acclimatized.
DEPRESSION	No	Suicidal speech is common.
DEMONIZATION	No	Variable; foul speech is common.
HIV INFECTION	Usual	Weight loss, diarrhea, other similar cases.
=============		
LIVER FAILURE	Maybe	Abnormal bleeding, maybe fluid in abdomen.
SYPHILIS, tertiary	No	Incubation over 10 yrs or syphilic mother.
MENTAL ILLNESS	No	Recurrent, first time under age 25.
ADDICTION: Alcohol, Outers	No	ALCOHOLISM or withdrawal; hallucinogen drugs.
===============		
ENCEPHALITIS	Maybe	Severe headache; usually some weakness also.
SCHISTOSOMIASIS JAPONICUM[1]	No	Also a large liver and distended abdomen.
PLANT POISONING	No	Claviceps, Jimson weed, Margosa oil,[2] Mushrooms.
AFRICAN SLEEPING SICKNESS	Maybe	Large nodes in back of neck or HEART FAILURE.
ALTITUDE SICKNESS	No	Recent ascent, high altitude, severe headache.
RABIES	Maybe	Discomfort with breeze or swallowing liquid.

6 B. Nervousness:

Definition: The patient appears to be continually in a heightened state of awareness, as if he or she were in a threatening situation when there is no threat.

Symptomatic treatment: If the cause is definable and temporary, it is legitimate to treat with DIAZEPAM. However, this should not be done over a long time because of danger of ADDICTION.

STRESS can cause this. Also ALCOHOLISM, ADDICTION: Uppers (stimulants) or withdrawal from downers, THYROID TROUBLE, LIVER FAILURE. Often accompanies ATTENTION DEFICIT DISORDER, which is common in Westerners. If the patient has a high fever, consider PLAGUE (rare). Also see Protocol 5 E.

This is common in people who sense that they are dying; spiritual counseling is appropriate. Patients commonly sense they are dying before their physicians are aware of the seriousness of their conditions.

6 C. Depression:

Definition: The patient appears to be sad or grieving out of proportion to any recent losses in his life.

Symptomatic treatment: Antidepressant medication should only be given by a physician who must follow the patient closely. It takes 2 weeks for such medication to begin working. If the cause is temporary and definable, such as a death in the family, it is unwise to give any symptomatic treatment as it delays or aborts the normal grieving process.

With ***recent travel,*** consider culture shock or JET LAG. If the patient is ***not otherwise ill***, see DEMONIZATION or DEPRESSION. With a ***slow pulse or low blood pressure***, consider THYROID TROUBLE, ADDICTION. Depression with a ***fever or a history of fever,*** consider HIV INFECTION, DENGUE FEVER,[3] TUBERCULOSIS, BRUCELLOSIS, ENTERIC FEVER, TYPHUS, ARBOVIRAL FEVER (Sand fly fever type). Depression with a ***rash:*** PELLAGRA. Depression with ***diarrhea***: HIV INFECTION, PELLAGRA or SPRUE.[4] Consider ALCOHOLISM in someone who drinks regularly or in binges.

---

[1] Schistosomiasis Japonicum: Found in areas of mainland China, the Philippines, parts of the Celebes, the upper Mekong, and the Thai-Malaysia border.

[2] Plant Poisoning: Margosa Oil: This is a yellow oil used as a folk medicine by Indians (from India) worldwide.

[3] Depression can last for years with DENGUE FEVER.

[4] Sprue: In the Americas only near or north of the equator. In Africa only Nigeria and southern Africa. Prevalent in India and Southeast Asia. It is occasionally found in the Mediterranean area.

PROTOCOL 7. ABNORMAL BODY MOVEMENT

7 A. Seizures
7 B. Spasms, Jerking, Twitching.
7 C. Gait Problems.
7 D. Trembling .
7 E. Uncoordination.

7 A. Seizures:

Definition: *The patient has regular, rhythmic, gross abnormal movement of his whole body or one or more parts of his body*. Either his eyes are rolled back and he is unconscious, or else the abnormal movement starts in one hand or foot and progresses up that limb and possibly crosses to the other side. If the patient is conscious and the seizure does not have a progressive pattern, see Protocol 7 B.

Symptomatic treatment: Keep the patient from hurting himself. Do not put your fingers in his mouth. Time the seizure with a watch. See SEIZURE in the *Disease Index*, and Chapter 4 of Volume I.

Is the patient a newborn?

NO

YES
It is likely that the seizures are due to some birth injury. **Consider** HYPOGLYCEMIA, TETANUS, MENINGITIS, or jaundice of the newborn (Chapter 7 of Vol. I). Send the patient to a hospital but first give sugar.

Is the patient being treated for DIABETES or is he sweaty or both?

NO

YES
Give him sugar immediately; treat other disease(s) if necessary. See HYPOGLYCEMIA.

Is the patient supposed to be taking medication for EPILEPSY?

NO

YES
Give him more. He probably forgot to take it, or gained weight without increasing the dose, or he has STRESS.

Is the patient very ill with a high fever?

NO

YES
Consider cerebral MALARIA, HEAT ILLNESS, FEBRILE SEIZURE, ///MENINGITIS, ENCEPHALITIS, SEPSIS, RABIES.

Is the patient 6 months or more pregnant or recently delivered?

NO

YES
Consider TOXEMIA.

Conditions	Fever	Other Characteristics
ADDICTION	No	Withdrawal from downers (sedatives).
ALCOHOLISM	No	Withdrawing after drinking heavily or regularly.
DEMONIZATION	No	Foul/blasphemous speech or disrupts worship.
STROKE	No	Some weakness or paralysis also.
HYPERVENTILATION	No	Rapid breathing; numb, cramped hands.
CYSTICERCOSIS	No	Ate insufficiently cooked pork.
=============		
LIVER FAILURE	Unusual	Abnormal bleeding, maybe fluid in abdomen.
SYPHILIS, tertiary	No	Incubation >10yrs or syphilic mother.
WHOOPING COUGH	No	Patient has severe, persistent coughing.

Continued on next page.

(7 A. Seizures, continued.)

=================		
PLANT POISONING	No or low	Ackee,[1] Margosa oil,[2] Claviceps, or Cassava.
SCHISTOSOMIASIS JAPONICUM[3]	No	Swollen abdomen, large liver; Asia.
RADIATION ILLNESS	No	History of radiation exposure.
RABIES	Maybe	Either paralysis or spasms with swallowing.

Rarely may be due to AMEBIC LIVER DISEASE, PARAGONIMIASIS,[4] BRUCELLOSIS, or LARVA MIGRANS in adults, RICKETS in babies. This can also be caused by head injury, electric shock and by any condition in which the brain is deprived of oxygen, such as near-drowning. See BRAIN DAMAGE.

7 B. Spasms, Jerking, Twitching:

Definition: *Irregular, sudden muscle contractions that are or appear to be involuntary.* Distinguish this from Protocol 7D (Trembling) and from Protocol 7A (Seizures). Trembling is regularly rhythmic, not forceful and fine whereas twitching and jerking is irregular in rhythmn. Seizures are regularly rhythmic and forceful.

Does the patient have hiccups?

NO

YES

Consider PNEUMONIA, ENCEPHALITIS, KIDNEY FAILURE, AMEBIC LIVER DISEASE, TUBERCULOSIS, CANCER, BRAIN DAMAGE if this persists. CHLORPROMAZINE may help if ordinary home remedies fail.

Does this happen only when the patient is falling asleep?

NO

YES

This is normal.

Is the patient unconscious?

NO

YES

see Protocol 7A.

Conditions	Characteristics
HYPERVENTILATION	Feels short of breath or history of rapid breathing.
DEMONIZATION	No fever; pattern does not fit any known illness.
Vomiting	Late consequence, if severe and persistent. See Protocol 47.
Diarrhea	Severe watery diarrhea with DEHYDRATION. See Protocol 56.
Night cramps[5]	Painful spasms of calf muscles, relieved by standing.
CHLORPROMAZINE (drug)	Spasms of facial muscles, maybe neck muscles.
=================	
LIVER FAILURE	Hands flap when arms are held out with fingers spread wide.
POLIO	Cold or diarrhea followed by muscle spasms and weakness.
TETANUS	All muscles contracted, hard, very visible.
RICKETS	History of no or very poor sun exposure.

Continued on next page.

[1] Plant Poisoning: Ackee: Found in scattered areas of western Africa and the West Indies.

[2] Plant Poisoning: Margosa Oil: A yellow oil used by persons from the Indian subcontinent, worldwide.

[3] Schistosomiasis Japonicum: In areas of mainland China, the Philippines, parts of the Celebes, the upper Mekong, and the Thai-Malaysian border.

[4] Paragonimiasis: Mainly in Asia and Southeast Asia, occasionally western Africa, rarely the Americas, India, and Pacific.

[5] Low doses of QUININE at bedtime can be quite helpful, if the patient is not pregnant.

(7 B. Spasms, Jerking, Twitching, continued.)

ANTACID overdose	Large amounts or for a long time; like HYPERVENTILATION.
PLANT POISONING	Due to Strychnine (homicidal) or to Lathyrism.[1]
RABIES	Throat spasms with drinking or with a breeze on the face.
KIDNEY FAILURE	Urine too much or too little, or abnormal dipstick.

These symptoms can also be caused by head injury, electric shock and by any condition in which the brain or spinal cord is deprived of oxygen for a period of time, such as near-drowning. See BRAIN DAMAGE and CEREBRAL PALSY.

7 C. Gait Problems:

If the patient has back or leg pain (protocols 63 or 60) or if he has back or leg weakness (protocols 64 or 62), then his gait will necessarily be abnormal. If this is the case, also check those protocols.

Limping may be caused by pain in hips, legs, or feet. If there is no obvious cause for the pain from the history or examination, probably the pain is due to birth injury or PYOMYOSITIS, OSTEOMYELITIS, or bone TUBERCULOSIS in children. SLIPPED DISC or ARTHRITIS of one hip is more likely in adults. Also consider BRUCELLOSIS.

Dragging one foot may be due to STROKE, an old head injury, BRAIN DAMAGE, or a complication of POLIO, DIPHTHERIA, or AFRICAN SLEEPING SICKNESS.[2]

Waddling may be due to pregnancy, fluid in the abdomen, overweight, RICKETS in adults. Many hip problems which cause limping, if present on both sides, will cause waddling.

Wide-based gaits are caused by BERIBERI, any muscular weakness, SYPHILIS (tertiary), spinal TUBERCULOSIS, DEMONIZATION. A person who is uncoordinated might maintain balance with a wide-based gait.

Staggering, lurching, twisting gaits with gross uncoordination:

With a fever: ENTERIC FEVER, AFRICAN SLEEPING SICKNESS, (rarely) PLAGUE.

Recent onset: Alcohol intoxication, PLANT POISONING: Datura, Lolism,[3] ADDICTION.

Long-lasting: BRAIN DAMAGE from any cause, SYPHILIS (tertiary), BERIBERI, AFRICAN SLEEPING SICKNESS, CEREBRAL PALSY.

Crab walk is walking purposely bow-legged on the sides of the feet. This is caused by YAWS or any pain in the big toe side of the feet.

High-stepping gaits are from LEPROSY, BERIBERI, SYPHILIS (tertiary), or ANEMIA (nutritional). This is normal when learning or relearning to walk. It can also be caused by injury (to the mother) during hard labor and childbirth.[4]

Shuffling is from PARKINSON'S DISEASE or long use of major tranquilizers. If there is a fever, consider ENTERIC FEVER. It may also be a natural response to fear of falling on a slippery surface.

Stiff, spastic walking is from BERIBERI, CRETINISM, TROPICAL SPASTIC PARAPARESIS, SPINAL NEUROPATHY, PLANT POISONING: Cassava, Lathyrism, or old paralysis.

Labored walking is from heavy, usually swollen legs. See Protocol 61.

7 D. Trembling:

Definition: Regular, fine, rhythmic involuntary muscle movements. This refers to physical trembling, not just a manifestation of nervousness (Protocol 6 B). Distinguish trembling (fine, rhythmic) from spasms, jerking, and twitching which are coarse, non-rhythmic, or both (Protocol 7 B). If the patient is sweaty, give him sugar to eat; then pursue diagnosis. See HYPOGLYCEMIA. If the patient is having shaking chills, see Protocol 13.

Many different kinds of poisonings can cause tremors; if the patient has recently taken a poison or some tainted food, make him vomit if he is alert.

---

[1] Plant Poisoning, Lathyrism: Found in East Africa, the Indian area, and the Mediterranean area.

[2] African Sleeping Sickness: Scattered areas of Africa, south of Bamako, Mali and Lake Chad and north of Lusaka, Zambia.

[3] Plant Poisoning, Lolism: Found only in the African, Mediterranean, and Middle Eastern areas.

[4] In this case, the nerve that works the muscles to hold the foot out straight is damaged. As a result the foot drops down and the patient must lift the leg high to avoid hurting her toes.

There are three kinds of tremors:

- PARKINSON'S DISEASE causes trembling at rest which **decreases with movement**; AFRICAN SLEEPING SICKNESS[1] and some drugs may also cause this. The patient appears to be rolling pills between his fingers with his hands on his lap.
- Some BRAIN DAMAGE causes tremor when the patient tries to do something as well as gross uncoordination.
- Causes of action tremors (all other causes) are listed below: in this case there is trembling only when the hand is held out straight, not when it is resting. The trembling **increases with movement**.

Conditions	Other Characteristics
STRESS	Person is nervous or angry.
ADDICTION	Due to either uppers effect or downers withdrawal.
ENTERIC FEVER	High fever, onset over several days, abdominal pains or cough.
TYPHUS	Headache and body pains present before fever; appears "not there."
ALCOHOLISM	History of heavy or regular drinking; withdrawing now.
SYPHILIS, tertiary	Incubation > 10 years or syphilic mother.
LIVER FAILURE	Hands flap, arms held out in front with fingers up and spread out.
=============	
AFRICAN SLEEPING SICKNESS	Also abnormal sleep patterns, possibly HEART FAILURE also.
PLANT POISONING	Ackee,[2] Ephedra, Lolism[3]; history of eating an affected plant product.
KIDNEY FAILURE	Abnormal amount of urine or abnormal urinalysis or both.
PELLAGRA	Also a rash, diarrhea, craziness, or any combination.

7 E. Uncoordination:

Definition: The patient cannot make his hand(s) or foot/feet do what he wants them to do.

Aside from inherited clumsiness, the most common causes are ALCOHOLISM and ADDICTION. If the patient is also weak, see Protocols 8 B and 8 C. See Protocol 7 C if the problem is specifically with walking. See protocol 20 if the patient complains of dizziness. Other causes are listed below:

Condition	Other Characteristics
ATTENTION DEFICIT DISORDER	Hyperactive or else under-active body with a racing brain.
BERIBERI	Poor diet in a child, probably only rice.
BRAIN DAMAGE	CEREBRAL PALSY or a consequence of some diseases.
ENTERIC FEVER	High fever, appears withdrawn ("not there"), abdominal pains or cough.
PARKINSON'S DISEASE	Commonly an initial manifestation, initially one limb.
HIV INFECTION	Weight loss, diarrhea or both.
STROKE	There is an appearance of uncoordination because of specific weakness.
=============	
PLANT POISONING	Due to kava-kava; history of taking plant substance.

Continued on next page.

[1] African Sleeping Sickness: Scattered areas of Africa, south of Bamako, Mali and Lake Chad; north of Lusaka, Zambia.

[2] Plant Poisoning, Ackee: Found in Africa and the Americas only.

[3] Plant Poisoning: Lolism: Found in the African, Mediterranean, and Middle Eastern areas.

(7 E. Uncoordination, continued.)

DIPHTHERIA	Wound or sore throat. Unimmunized; whitish scum on the tonsils.
Injury	A head or spinal cord injury can cause uncoordination.
AFRICAN SLEEPING SICKNESS[1]	Abnormal sleep pattern, maybe craziness or HEART FAILURE.
SYPHILIS, tertiary	Incubation >10 years or syphilic mother.
RADIATION ILLNESS	History of recent exposure to radiation.
PLANT POISONING	Due to Datura; large pupils, rapid pulse, nausea.

PROTOCOL 8. WEAKNESS, PARALYSIS, FATIGUE

8 A. General Weakness or Fatigue Without Weight Loss; See Protocol 9 if there is weight loss!!
8 B. Floppy Weakness of Body Part(s)
8 C. Stiff Weakness of Body Part(s)

Definitions:

Weakness means that the person cannot exert muscle power at any time. *Paralysis* is weakness that is severe enough that the person is not able to voluntarily move the body part at all. Paralysis and weakness may be either stiff or floppy.

Fatigue means that he can exert muscle power after he has rested a while but cannot sustain physical activity for a long time. Weakness and fatigue are both different than *lethargy* or *sleepiness*.

Lethargy implies that the person is not aware of his environment; he likes to sleep too much. A person can be lethargic without being weak; perhaps he prefers to sleep, but he could get up and move something heavy. He can also be weak or fatigued but be perfectly wide awake and therefore not lethargic. For lethargy, see Protocol 5A and Protocol C-10.

8 A. General Weakness or Fatigue Without Weight Loss:

----If there is weight loss, then see Protocol 9.

**Before proceeding with this protocol, entirely undress the patient and check his entire body surface for ticks, including in his hair. If you find one, remove it (see Volume I, Appendix 10). Some ticks inject a poison which causes paralysis. The paralysis will resolve once the tick is removed. If you find one tick and remove it, don't fail to look for a second tick.

The patient is able to do his usual work only by resting frequently, or working at a much slower pace. He is awake during normal hours. This is the usual consequence of any severe illness, e.g. advanced CANCER. If the primary problem is *lethargy*, see Protocol 5A. This protocol presupposes that the problem affects the whole body and that it is a major symptom of the disease. If it is mainly or only in a specific limb or muscle group, then see Protocol 8B or 8C.

(Continued on next page.)

[1] African Sleeping Sickness: Scattered areas of Africa, south of Bamako, Mali and Lake Chad; north of Lusaka, Zambia.

(8 A. General Weakness or Fatigue Without Weight Loss, continued.)

Does the patient have a fever or a recent history of fevers?

NO

YES

Additional symptoms:

Severe chest or abdominal pains

AMEBIC LIVER DISEASE: Pain on right side, near waist.
LASSA FEVER[1]: Chest pains: center front, center back.
BARTONELLOSIS[2]: Fatigue occurs before the fever.

Joint, bone, muscle pains

BRUCELLOSIS: Slow-onset illness, back, joint pains.
RHEUMATIC FEVER: Red, swollen joints.
DENGUE FEVER: Sudden onset, severe bone pains.
SPOTTED FEVER[3]: Headache; rash is common.
LYME DISEASE: History of fever plus a rash.
TULAREMIA[4]: Contacted small animal(s) or their insects.

Fatigue without severe pain

MONONUCLEOSIS: Large neck lymph nodes, fatigability.
TOXOPLASMOSIS: Fever and severe fatigability.

Up and down fevers

MALARIA: Chills and headache.
RELAPSING FEVER: High fever, severe headache.
VISCERAL LEISHMANIASIS[5]: Huge spleen, large liver.
KATAYAMA DISEASE: Itchy skin rash plus fevers.
RAT BITE FEVER: Open bite wound or rash.
TULAREMIA[6]: Contacted small animal(s) or their insects.

Near death

SEPSIS: A previous infection became much worse.
Also see Protocols C-3: Fever plus Anemia, and/or C-10A: Fever plus Lethargy or Confusion.

Has the patient lost body fluid from vomiting, diarrhea, or a hot environment?

NO

YES

Give the patient water or ORS to drink. See Protocol 47 or 56.
Consider HEAT ILLNESS, ZINC DEFICIENCY, HEPATITIS, MALABSORPTION, SCHISTOSOMIASIS MANSONI.[7]

Continued on next page.

[1] Lassa Fever: Only in Africa.
[2] Bartonellosis: Occurs only in Peru and adjacent border areas.
[3] Spotted Fever: Not in the islands of Southeast Asia.
[4] Tularemia: North America, central Asia, Europe, Far East, the north coast of Africa; exposure to small animals..
[5] Visceral Leishmaniasis: Found in scattered areas of Central and South America, Africa north of the equator, the Mediterranean area, the Indian subcontinent, eastern Europe, central Asia, and mainland China.
[6] Tularemia: North America, central Asia, Europe, Far East, the north coast of Africa; exposure to small animals..
[7] Schistosomiasis Mansoni: Scattered areas within Africa, the Arabian Peninsula, the Caribbean, and parts of eastern South America.

(8 A. General Weakness or Fatigue Without Weight Loss, continued.)

Is the problem of sudden onset (over minutes to a day) and with no fever?

NO

YES

Check vital signs; consider SHOCK and see appropriate protocols.
Recheck the patient for ticks.

Consider DEMONIZATION, ALTITUDE SICKNESS, PLANT POISONING due to Argemone oil or Botulism, DIPHTHERIA, Snake bite,[1] HYPOGLYCEMIA, HEART ATTACK.

Condition	Characteristics
ANEMIA	Fast pulse or pale fingernails or pale mouth.
HEART FAILURE	Short of breath with lying down or swollen ankles or both.
DEMONIZATION	Caused by a curse by someone involved in witchcraft.
DEPRESSION	Early morning awakening, can't sleep again.
HOOKWORM	ANEMIA and/or stool tests positive for blood.
================	
AMEBIC LIVER DISEASE	Burning or pain, upper right abdomen or lower right chest.
AFRICAN SLEEPING SICKNESS[2]	Also large nodes in back of neck or HEART FAILURE.
SYPHILIS, tertiary	Insomnia, headache, incubation >10 yrs or syphilic mother.
KIDNEY FAILURE	Also dry, flaky skin; blood pressure high or urine abnormal.
THYROID TROUBLE	Low thyroid; also slow pulse, brittle hair.
LIVER FLUKE[3]	Also a large, tender liver; living in an affected area.
SCHISTOSOMIASIS MANSONI[4]	Bloody diarrhea or JAUNDICE or a distended abdomen.

8 B. Floppy Weakness of Body Part(s):

Definition: The patient cannot easily move his body part(s) but someone else can move them easily since they are floppy. This is paralysis if the patient cannot move the body part(s) at all.

**Before proceeding with this protocol, entirely undress the patient and check his entire body surface for ticks, including in his hair. If you find one, remove it (see Volume I, Appendix 10). Some ticks inject a poison which causes paralysis. The paralysis will resolve once the tick is removed. If you find one tick and remove it, don't fail to look for a second tick.

BRAIN DAMAGE may initially cause a floppy weakness but the weakness becomes stiff within weeks. See Protocol 8 C.

Did the weakness develop during or after an illness with a fever?

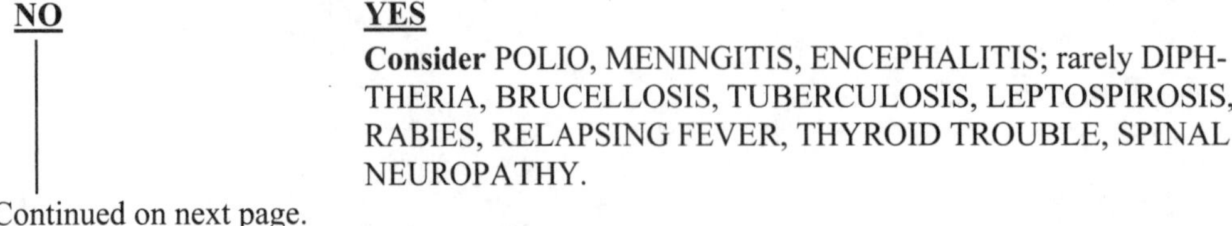

NO

YES

Consider POLIO, MENINGITIS, ENCEPHALITIS; rarely DIPHTHERIA, BRUCELLOSIS, TUBERCULOSIS, LEPTOSPIROSIS, RABIES, RELAPSING FEVER, THYROID TROUBLE, SPINAL NEUROPATHY.

Continued on next page.

[1] Occasionally a scorpion or fish bite may cause a similar effect.

[2] African Sleeping Sickness: Scattered areas of Africa, south of Bamako, Mali and Lake Chad and north of Lusaka, Zambia.

[3] Liver Fluke: Found worldwide, especially in Southeast Asia and the Far East.

[4] Schistosomiasis Mansoni: Scattered areas within Africa, the Arabian Peninsula, the Caribbean, and parts of eastern South America.

(8 B. Floppy Weakness of Body Part(s), continued.)

Condition	Onset	Characteristics
TICK PARALYSIS	Sudden	Visible tick on the patient's body; remove it.
SYPHILIS, congenital	From birth	Infant; refusal to use limb(s); pain.
STROKE	Sudden	Usually right or left side, maybe trouble talking.
BERIBERI	Weeks-months	Very poor diet (maybe rice only) or alcoholic.
CARPAL TUNNEL SYNDROME	Weeks	Starts dominant side, worse at night, middle-aged.
DEMONIZATION	Variable	Due to a curse or the involvement in witchcraft.
RICKETS	Weeks	Baby or infant is floppy; inadequate sun exposure.
============		
LEPROSY	Weeks-months	Not symmetrical, skin rash, shooting pains.
FLUOROSIS	Unknown	Neck pain, discolored teeth.
SPINAL NEUROPATHY	Varies	Also numb, tingling, bladder or bowel problems.
PLANT POISONING (Ginger-jake, Botulism, Manicheel,[1] Tobacco-cow's urine.[2])	Sudden	History of the patient exposed to the plant.
THYROID TROUBLE	Weeks	Always sleepy or trouble walking up stairs.
Spinal cord injury	Variable	History of neck injury (arms weak) or back injury.
Snake bite	Sudden	Report of an encounter with a snake.

8 C. Stiff Weakness of Body Part(s):

Definition: The patient cannot move his own limbs well and someone else cannot move them easily since they are stiff. This is **paralysis** if the patient cannot move the body part(s) at all.

The most common cause is BRAIN DAMAGE.

Did the stiff weakness develop gradually (over months) from a weakness that was first floppy?

NO

YES
See Protocol 8 B; the most common cause of stiff weakness is an old floppy weakness that became stiff.

Condition	Onset	Characteristics
BRAIN DAMAGE	Variable	Usually problems with speech or thinking also.
RICKETS	Weeks	Curved limbs in children.
SYPHILIS, tertiary	Variable	Incubation >10 yrs or syphilic mother.
PLANT POISONING	Rapid	Due to Cassava, Strychnine, or Ginger-jake.
TETANUS	Hours-days	Peculiar, pinched smile, jaw tightly shut.
SPINAL NEUROPATHY	Varies	Also numb, tingling, bowel or bladder problems.
PELLAGRA	Weeks-months	Maybe a rash, diarrhea, craziness.
TROPICAL SPASTIC PARAPARESIS	Gradual	Adults, back pain and stiff legs.
SCURVY	Unknown	Bleeding gums, doesn't eat fruits and vegetables.
TRICHINOSIS	Days	Very sore and swollen muscles, fever.

[1] Plant Poisoning: Manicheel: Found in the Americas only.

[2] This is an ethnic medicine found in some parts of Africa.

PROTOCOL 9. PROBLEMS OF FOOD INTAKE AND WEIGHT CHANGE

First check for DEHYDRATION; if present, treat that while pursing further diagnosis.

9 A. Loss of Appetite; Refusal to Eat With Weight Loss:

9 A1. Children 2 Years Old or Less:

First check the patient's vital signs: pulse, temperature, and respiratory rate. Are these reasonably normal or are they grossly abnormal?

Normal or nearly so | **Grossly abnormal**

Grossly abnormal: Make every effort to send the patient out. If this is not possible, then pursue a diagnosis according to other symptoms. Do not use a stomach tube or try to feed the patient. If he is dehydrated, then IV or intraperitoneal fluids are acceptable.

Normal or nearly so: Is the patient a very small or premature newborn, or very malnourished and under 3 months old?

NO | **YES**

YES: The patient is probably too weak to suck; see the instructions below for dealing with this. Also consider congenital SYPHILIS.

NO: Is the child 2 years old or less?

YES | **NO**, older

NO, older: See Protocol 9 A2, below.

YES: Are there other symptoms?

NO | **YES**

YES: See below, "Weight loss with other symptoms."

NO: Does the child act ill (he does not play and does not respond to his mother)?

YES | **NO, he plays and responds**

NO, he plays and responds: **Consider** that some children just decide not to eat for a while for no good reason; just watch him.

YES: Is the illness of recent onset, within the past week?

YES | **NO**

NO: **Consider** RICKETS, SCURVY, HIV INFECTION, TUBERCULOSIS, and see "Syndrome Treatment" (below).

YES: **Consider**: ERYTHEMA INFECTIOSUM, TETANUS, SEPSIS, ENTERIC FEVER, TYPHUS

Instructions for dealing with an infant too weak to suck:

Add sugar if you are using formula, then try the following in order:

1. Carefully enlarge the nipple hole if he is being bottle-fed.
2. For a breast-fed baby, have the mother exchange babies, just for one partial feeding, with a mother who has an older, very healthy child. The little one gets an easy feed and the vigorous sucking of the older baby makes the milk come better.
3. Use an eyedropper to feed the child, giving just one or two drops every 5 minutes, almost continually.
4. If the child is not short of breath or vomiting, then use a stomach tube. See Volume I, Appendix 1.

Weight loss with other symptoms:

Fever: see Protocol 1B, C, D
Shortness of breath or rapid respirations: see Protocol 36 and Index C-4
Sore mouth: see Protocol 29 B
Nausea, vomiting, or both: see Protocol 47
Diarrhea: see Protocol 56

Syndrome treatment:

Confirm whether the patient is not eating by checking a urine dipstick. If he truly is not eating, his urine will be positive for ketones.

Check for non-medical factors that might cause loss of appetite or weight: family stress, a change in available foods, or just learning to crawl, creep, or walk.

If he is willing to eat food or take a bottle offered to him, then give him food or a bottle. Try to include multivitamins and minerals.

If he is not willing to eat food or take a bottle, then consider using a stomach tube and liquid feed to put down it. See Volume I, Chapter 5 and Appendix 1.

9 A2. Children Over 2 Years Old and Adults:

Does the patient have symptoms other than loss of appetite and weight loss?

NO	YES
|	See the lists below for weight loss with other symptoms.

Confirm that food intake is deficient. Test the urine for ketones with a urine dipstick. If patient is malnourished, the urine should show positive for ketones. If no ketones, send the patient packing; he's trying to get free food.

Ketones positive in the urine: **Consider** the following, then see one of the lists below if the patient also has other symptoms:

Disease/condition	Characteristics
MALNUTRITION	Not enough food available.
DEPRESSION	Genetically thin patient, recent loss.
STRESS	Genetically thin patient, recent stress.
==================	
PELLAGRA	Diet of corn and carbohydrate only.
BERIBERI	ALCOHOLISM or a diet of white rice.
HEAT ILLNESS	Recent arrival in a hot environment.
DEMONIZATION	Curse, or involvement in occult.
ADDICTION	Use of Uppers: Amphetamine, Khat, etc.

Weight loss with other symptoms:

Feels hungry but distressing symptoms prevent eating:

Mouth or throat pain: Protocol 29
Shortness of breath: Protocol 36 and Index C, Protocol C-4.
Difficulty swallowing: Protocol 30 D
Abdominal pain: Protocols 39-45
Diarrhea: Protocol 56
Fatigue: Protocol 8 A

Does not feel hungry, not inclined to eat:

ANEMIA: see below.
DIARRHEA: see below and also Protocol 56
JAUNDICE or abdominal swelling
Abdominal pain: see below and also Protocols 39-45
Mental symptoms: see below
Nausea: see Protocol 47
Feverish: see Protocol 1-B, 1-C, 1-D

Weight loss plus anemia:

The patient is pale inside his eyelids or on his fingernails. He complains of fatigue. His pulse and possibly also his respiratory rate are faster than normal.

Condition	Characteristics
HOOKWORM	Areas with sandy soil. Stool tests positive for blood.
TUBERCULOSIS	Cough or large neck lymph nodes or history of TB exposure.
HIV INFECTION	Frequent infections; may look just like TB.
MALNUTRITION	Food availability problem or patient eats just one kind of food.
============	
BRUCELLOSIS	Back pains or joint pains, slow onset, episodes of fever.
CANCER	Lump or wound somewhere, possibly a rotten-meat body odor.
VISCERAL LEISHMANIASIS[1]	Huge spleen, large liver, fevers off and on.
AFRICAN SLEEPING SICKNESS[2]	Headaches, fevers, abnormal sleep, falls asleep eating.
KIDNEY FAILURE	Urine-like body odor, nauseated, flaky skin.
LEAD POISONING	Lead exposure from paints, herbs, or metal work; headache, low fever.

Weight loss plus diarrhea:

Condition	Characteristics
GIARDIASIS	Watery diarrhea, much gas, maybe vomiting.
HIV INFECTION	Frequent infections, sexually active, blood exposure, or ill parents.
TURISTA	Watery diarrhea in a traveler; see Protocol 56.
MALABSORPTION	Prompt diarrhea, recognizable food, right after eating.
==============	
PELLAGRA	Diet of mainly corn; maybe rash or craziness.
SPRUE[3]	Recently arrived in the area, rumbling, gassy abdomen.
CAPILLARIASIS[4]	History of eating raw fish.
INTESTINAL FLUKE[5]	History of eating raw or rare fish or water plants.

Weight loss plus jaundice or abdominal swelling:

Condition	Characteristics
HEPATITIS	Liver is tender and may be enlarged.
LIVER FAILURE	Yellow eyes, swollen abdomen, bilirubin in the urine.
MALNUTRITION	Abnormal hair, abnormal skin color, poor diet.
TUBERCULOSIS	Cough or large neck lymph nodes; TB exposure history.
==============	

Continued on next page.

[1] Visceral Leishmaniasis: Found in scattered areas of Central and South America, Africa north of the equator, the Mediterranean area, the Indian subcontinent, eastern Europe, central Asia, and mainland China.

[2] African Sleeping Sickness: Scattered areas of Africa, south of Bamako, Mali and Lake Chad and north of Lusaka, Zambia.

[3] Sprue: In the Americas only near or north of the equator. In Africa only Nigeria and southern Africa. Prevalent in India and Southeast Asia. It is occasionally found in the Mediterranean area.

[4] Capillariasis: Philippines mainly; rarely Thailand, found in Egypt with potential of spreading.

[5] Intestinal Fluke: Not in Africa south of the Sahara, or Eastern Europe. In the Americas, only in Guyana.

(Weight loss plus jaundice or abdominal swelling, continued.)

SCHISTOSOMIASIS MANSONI[1]	History of DYSENTERY common; check geography.
LEPTOSPIROSIS	Sudden-onset high fever, red eyes, general body pains.
CANCER	Abnormal lump or wound; maybe rotten-meat body odor.
SCHISTOSOMIASIS JAPONICUM[2]	Swollen abdomen, maybe also mental symptoms.
LIVER FLUKE[3]	History of eating raw or pickled fish; upper abdominal pains.
KIDNEY FAILURE	Urine abnormal in quantity or urinalysis; urine-like body odor.
VISCERAL LEISHMANIASIS[4]	Huge spleen, large liver, fevers off and on.
SPRUE[5]	Severe diarrhea, promptly whenever the person eats; sore mouth.

Weight loss with mental changes:

Consider anorexia nervosa in female offspring of Western parents. Otherwise:

Condition	Characteristics
DEPRESSION	Abnormal sleep pattern; patient genetically thin.
MALARIA	History of headache, chills, sweats, up and down fevers.
HEAT ILLNESS	Exposure to hot climates without prior acclimatization.
ENTERIC FEVER	Feverish patient, withdrawn; headache or abdominal pain common.
HIV INFECTION	Frequent infections, diarrhea.
DEMONIZATION	Due to a curse on the patient or patient involved in witchcraft.
==============	
PELLAGRA	Mainly corn diet; roughened, sun-exposed skin; diarrhea common.
BRUCELLOSIS	Fevers off and on, joint or back pains, slow-onset illness.
ADDICTION: Uppers	Stimulants decrease appetite and make the patient hyperactive.
BERIBERI	Alcoholic or poor diet; pains and weakness in legs.
AFRICAN SLEEPING SICKNESS[6]	Abnormal sleep patterns, headache, fever or history of fever.
SPRUE	Severe, watery diarrhea, depression, sore mouth.
VISCERAL LEISHMANIASIS	Huge spleen, large liver, fevers off and on, slow onset.
DENGUE FEVER	Sudden onset, severe headache, very severe bone and joint pains.
RHEUMATIC FEVER	Fevers and red, swollen joints; history of a sore throat or prior RF.
SYPHILIS, tertiary	Grandiose or stupid; incubation >10 years or syphilic mother.
CANCER	Lump or open wound somewhere or headaches.

[1] Schistosomiasis Mansoni: Scattered areas within Africa, the Arabian peninsula, the Caribbean, and parts of eastern South America.

[2] Schistosomiasis Japonicum: In areas of mainland China, the Philippines, parts of the Celebes, the upper Mekong, and the Thai-Malaysia border.

[3] Liver Fluke: Found worldwide, especially in Southeast Asia and the Far East.

[4] Visceral Leishmaniasis: Found in scattered areas of Central and South America, Africa north of the equator, the Mediterranean area, the Indian subcontinent, eastern Europe, central Asia, and mainland China. Not present south of the equator.

[5] Sprue: In the Americas only near or north of the equator. In Africa only Nigeria and southern Africa. Prevalent in India and Southeast Asia. It is occasionally found in the Mediterranean area.

[6] African Sleeping Sickness: Scattered areas of Africa, south of Bamako, Mali and Lake Chad and north of Lusaka, Zambia.

Weight loss with fever lasting more than a week:

If the fever has lasted less than a week, see Protocol 1.

Condition	Characteristics
MALARIA	Large spleen, waist pain, shoulder pain, headache, joint pains.
HEPATITIS	History of liver-toxic drugs or a tender liver.
TUBERCULOSIS	Chronic cough or large neck lymph nodes.
HIV INFECTION	Frequent infections, sexual or blood exposure.
==============	
BRUCELLOSIS	Fevers come and go, pains in lower back and pelvis.
TYPHUS	Illness before the fever; body lice or exposure to rodents.
CANCER	Lump somewhere or large lymph nodes or other symptoms.
VISCERAL LEISHMANIASIS	Very large spleen; geographically confined.
LEPTOSPIROSIS	Either red, sore eyes or severe muscle pains or both.

Unclassified problems associated with weight loss:

Condition	Characteristics
HEART FAILURE	Either short of breath or severe fatigue or both.
BERIBERI	Also burning pains in feet and leg weakness.
ENTEROBIASIS	Children who are irritable and have insomnia.
CANCER	Probably an abnormal lump or sore somewhere.
DEMONIZATION	Curse put on the patient or patient involved in the occult.
RADIATION ILLNESS	Early effect (within hours) of large-dose radiation exposure.
LIVER FLUKE	Muscle aches and/or tender, large liver.
SPOTTED FEVER[1]	High fever, headache, general muscle aching. Rash is common.

Also consider anorexia nervosa in a young, Western female.

9 B. Cravings:

Definition: The patient eats substances that are not usually considered food or else excessive and unusual amounts of food stuffs (e.g. emptying a salt shaker into his coffee and then drinking it). Usually due to pregnancy in pregnant adult females; also consider ASCARIASIS, TRICHURIASIS, HOOKWORM. Salt craving might be caused by TUBERCULOSIS.

9 C. Weight Loss With a Good Appetite:

Common in those who first arrive in the tropics; this does not need treatment but check a urine dipstick to make sure the patient does not have DIABETES or LIVER DISEASE.

This may be due to those recently arrived in a strange culture—it takes time to locate, buy, and figure out how to cook palatable food. Meantime, the person will lose weight.

May be due to an otherwise-thin mother trying to breast feed a large infant or twins; she cannot consume enough calories to support both herself and the child. Other causes are listed below:

Consider bulimia in a young, Western female.

(Continued on next page.)

[1] Spotted Fever: Not in the islands of Southeast Asia.

(9 C. Weight Loss With a Good Appetite, continued.)

Condition	Other Characteristics
ASCARIASIS	Belly pains, constipation, may pass worms.
TAPEWORM[1]	History of eating raw or rare meats.
DIABETES	Also excessive thirst and excessive urination.
ADDICTION	Patient has access to and is taking uppers.
===============	
THYROID TROUBLE	High thyroid; insomnia, a rapid pulse, and nervousness.
VISCERAL LEISHMANIASIS[2]	Large spleen, left upper belly pains, fevers.

9 D. Excessive Appetite With Constant or Increased Weight:

Normal in growing children and teenagers. Otherwise most frequently due to STRESS or DEPRESSION in those prone to overweight; to pregnancy; or to THYROID TROUBLE (low thyroid). It is normal in children who were starved and now have food available, and in diabetics who recently started treatment. It may be due to steroid drugs.

PROTOCOL 10. PROBLEMS OF FEELING AND SENSATION

10 A. Numbness And Tingling
10 B. Sharp, Shooting Pains
10 C. Aching All Over
10 D. Total Body Itching
10 E. Other Sensation Problems

10 A. Numbness And Tingling:

This may be due to an injury to a limb or a head injury. It might also be due to overuse of a limb, abnormal pressure on a nerve, or repetitive limb motions.

Stocking/glove numbness and tingling: Similar on the thumb/big toe side of the limb as on the little finger/little toe side. This might be due to DEMONIZATION or MENTAL ILLNESS but it might also be due to LYME DISEASE or HIV INFECTION and possibly some other diseases.

Neuritis pains, a special category, are felt over where nerves run under the skin, along with inability to feel well, a crawling sensation, numbness, and a feeling of pins and needles or tingling. Neuritis pains may be worse with coughing or sneezing. If this is what your patient has, consider the following: Some causative diseases are SYPHILIS, MENINGITIS, spinal TUBERCULOSIS, SHINGLES, CANCERs. It may also be due to toxins.

If your patient does not have neuritis, consider the following:

Condition	Body part(s)	Other Characteristics
HYPERVENTILATION	Around lips	Short of breath, cramped hands, rapid onset.
ISONIAZID (drug)	Limbs, symmetrical	Patient taking drugs for TB, onset over weeks.
CARPAL TUNNEL SYNDROME	Hand(s)	Starts in dominant side, worse at night, middle-age.
LEPROSY	Anywhere	Slow onset (over weeks to months), skin changes.
STROKE	Right or left side	Usually weakness also, rapid onset.
BERIBERI	Hands/feet	Pains and weakness also; poor diet.

Continued on next page.

[1] Tapeworm treatment may occur in babies who are exclusively breastfed because fingers might transmit the worm eggs.

[2] Visceral Leishmaniasis: Found in scattered areas of Central and South America, Africa north of the equator, the Mediterranean area, the Indian subcontinent, eastern Europe, central Asia, and mainland China. Not present south of the equator.

(10 A. Numbness And Tingling, continued.)

Condition	Body part(s)	Other Characteristics
PELLAGRA	Palms/soles	Also rash, diarrhea, or craziness.
===============		
SCHISTOSOMIASIS MANSONI[1]	Limbs, asymmetrical	Bloody urine, bloody stool, or swollen abdomen.
SPINAL NEUROPATHY	Genital/saddle area	Maybe problems with passing urine or stool.
ARSENIC POISONING	Hands/feet	Burning, skin changes.
ANEMIA, nutritional	Hands/feet	Pale nails, poor diet.
SLIPPED DISC	Limbs	Back pain with leg(s) or neck pain with arm(s).
DIPHTHERIA	Variable	Also sore throat or wound; large lymph nodes.
LOIASIS[2]	Anywhere	Local swelling on the same side.
RABIES	Area bitten	Also paralysis or throat spasms.
PLANT POISONING	Limbs	Due to Ergot; chest pain is common also.
TROPICAL SPASTIC PARAPARESIS	Feet	Burning pains also, stiffness of legs.
FOOD POISONING	Anywhere	Also vomiting, diarrhea; due to fish; Pacific area.

10 B. Sharp, Shooting Pains:

Definition: The patient has pains that rapidly travel away from the trunk.

Also see the definition of neuritis pains, protocol 10A. Some causative diseases are LEPROSY, SYPHILIS, MENINGITIS, spinal TUBERCULOSIS, SHINGLES, CANCERs. This may be due to toxins.

If your patient does not have neuritis pains, then consider the following:

Conditions	Other Characteristics
TUBERCULOSIS	Also neck or back pain with tenderness; fevers common.
POLIO	Also weakness or paralysis or muscle cramps.
LEPROSY	Thickened, tender nerves or skin changes.
DENGUE FEVER	Sudden onset, also severe bone pain, maybe a rash.
===============	
SCHISTOSOMIASIS MANSONI	Bloody stool or bloody urine or a swollen abdomen.
BRUCELLOSIS	Episodes of fevers, low back pains, headaches, joint pains.
SLIPPED DISC	Low back pain also if leg pain; neck pain if arm pain.
DIPHTHERIA	Also sore throat or a wound; large lymph nodes.
SYPHILIS, tertiary	Incubation >10yrs or a syphilic mother.
FLUOROSIS	Pains in the arms; neck pains also.
LOIASIS	Also swellings that come and go; only rural areas.

[1] Schistosomiasis Mansoni: Scattered areas within Africa, the Arabian Penninsula, the Caribbean, and parts of eastern South America.

[2] Loiasis: This is found only in scattered areas of humid west and central Africa.

10 C. Aching All Over:

Symptomatic treatment: Use ACETAMINOPHEN or IBUPROFEN. ASPIRIN is acceptable only in adults if you know the diagnosis and there is no contraindication to its use.

Does the patient have a high fever, or did he have a high fever within the past few days?

NO to both

YES to either

See Protocol C-2 which gives another approach to the syndrome of fever plus aching all over.

Additional symptoms:

Limb pain worse than other pain

DENGUE FEVER: Sudden onset, severe bone/joint pains.
ENTERIC FEVER: Patient withdrawn; abdominal pain.
TYPHUS: Patient appears intoxicated, very ill.
LYME DISEASE: History of discolored skin; tick bitten.
TRICHINOSIS: Also very swollen muscles.
TULAREMIA[1]: Exposed to small animals or their insects.
TRENCH FEVER: Shin pain, had body lice.

Headache worse than other pain

LEPTOSPIROSIS: Sudden onset red eyes and headache.
SPOTTED FEVER[2]: Headache always; rash common.
RELAPSING FEVER: Chills, sweats, headaches.
MALARIA: History of chills, sweats, headache.
YELLOW FEVER[3]: Not immunized; abnormal urinalysis.
RAT BITE FEVER: History of an animal bite.
TULAREMIA: Exposed to small animals or their insects.

Chest pain worse than other pain

ARBOVIRAL FEVER: Also headache; seek local lore.
BARTONELLOSIS[4]: JAUNDICE; ANEMIA also.
LASSA FEVER[5]: Cough, chest pains; occurs in epidemics.

Conditions	Fever	Characteristics
HEAT ILLNESS	Maybe	Hot environment and unacclimatized to heat.
MUSCLE STRAIN	No	Recent unaccustomed exercise.
INFLUENZA	Maybe	Mild illness; usually a group of similar cases.
HANGOVER	No	The morning after alcohol ingestion.
LICE	No	"Flu" after having body lice some time before.
================		
POLIO	Usual	Weakness of limb(s), usually legs.
RUBELLA	Low	Rash, usually children and adolescents.
TETANUS	Maybe	Muscle spasms, back and jaws.
CHOLERA	No/slight	Severe watery diarrhea, sudden onset.
LIVER FLUKE[6]	No	Liver is large, tender, or both.
CHAGA'S DISEASE[7]	Usual	Current or recent bug bite with swelling.
RABIES	Maybe	Paralyzed or throat spasms or both.

[1] Tularemia: In eastern Europe, persons exposed to small animals or their insects.
[2] Spotted Fever: Not in the islands of Southeast Asia.
[3] Yellow Fever: South America north of Sao Paolo, Central and western Africa and the Sudan.
[4] Bartonellosis: Only occurs in Peru and adjacent border areas.
[5] Lassa Fever: In Africa only.
[6] Liver Fluke: Worldwide, especially in Southeast Asia and East Asia.
[7] Chaga's Disease: Scattered areas in the Americas.

10 D. Total Body Itching:

The most common cause in almost all cultures is SCABIES but in this case there are visible itchy spots.

Visible rash: (apart from scratch marks) but it is not scabies, then see Protocol 15 A.

Deep itching with no visible rash: the problem is probably some sort of liver disease; see JAUNDICE in the *Disease Index.* Also consider ONCHOCERCIASIS,[1] KIDNEY FAILURE, ANEMIA due to iron deficiency, DIABETES, THYROID TROUBLE (low or high), BIRTH CONTROL PILLS, withdrawal from alcohol or drugs A relatively rare cause in all cultures is lymphoma, a type of CANCER. In this case there is also weight loss, fatigue, and night sweats.

Skin itching with no visible rash: consider ASCARIASIS, ONCHOCERCIASIS, SCABIES, body LICE, CHLOROQUINE (drug for MALARIA), CANCER, MALARIA (in patients with black skin), LIVER FAILURE, GALLBLADDER DISEASE, KATAYAMA DISEASE, ALLERGY, CONTACT DERMATITIS (especially caused by an allergy to soap).

10 E. Other Sensation Problems:

Conditions	Type of Problem
SYPHILIS, tertiary	Cannot tell where a limb is in space without looking;[2] the patient must watch his hand or foot in order to move it in a coordinated manner.
ANEMIA, nutritional	Similar to SYPHILIS; also fast pulse, white fingernails.[3]
LARVA MIGRANS	Patient feels a worm crawling beneath the skin.
================	
AFRICAN SLEEPING SICKNESS[4]	A tap on the shin produces severe pain after several seconds.
LOIASIS[5]	Patient feels a worm crawling beneath his skin.
ONCHOCERCIASIS	Patient feels a tingling, creeping sensation in his skin.
PELLAGRA	Burning pains; diarrhea; rough, dry rash; mental changes.
TROPICAL SPASTIC PARAPARESIS	Burning pains along with stiffness of the lower limbs.

PROTOCOL 11. POISONING

First, if applicable, see FOOD POISONING if the problem is a person's eating spoiled food containing meat. See PLANT POISONING for poisoning from plant parts or from ethnic medicines. See ARSENIC POISONING,[6] LEAD POISONING,[7] INSECTICIDE POISONING, or FLUOROSIS (from bad water) if applicable.

Note: In Western countries the standard poisoning protocol has changed from what it used to be, on account of technological advances. Since the Western technology may not be available to those who use this book, the procedures given here are based on the old methods. These should only be used in areas where the modern technology is unavailable.

(Continued on next page.)

[1] Onchocerciasis: Present in scattered area in Africa, in the Americas north of the Amazon, in Yemen and possibly in Saudi Arabia.

[2] This manifests as uncoordination that is much worse in the dark than in the light.

[3] In all races, fingernails should be a similar pink color.

[4] African Sleeping Sickness: Scattered areas of Africa, south of Bamako, Mali and Lake Chad and north of Lusaka, Zambia.

[5] Loiasis: Scattered areas in rural, humid, western and central Africa.

[6] Arsenic poisoning may be suicide/homicide though some very old antibiotics were arsenic compounds. These might still be available in developing countries. Arsenic is commonly present in herbal remedies, and is sometimes used in cancer chemotherapy.

[7] Lead poisoning is usually from paints, traditional medicines, cosmetics, or metal work. It is commonly present in ethnic cosmetics and in herbal remedies.

(Protocol 11: Poisoning, continued.)

Was the poison a corrosive such as a strong acid or base (e.g. lye), or else gasoline - kerosene type, *or* does the patient have mouth burns (chalk-white or black patches on the pink parts)?

NO to all

YES to either

Use no stomach tube, no IPECAC. Give PROMETHAZINE by injection. Give large amounts of milk or water if the patient is conscious. If he is not conscious, see the Paragraph 2 below. Send the patient out or call for help.

If the patient is alert, use Paragraph 1 (as follows). If not alert, see the instructions in Paragraph 2.

1. If and only if he is alert:

Option 1 (preferable): Have the patient drink a large amount of activated charcoal.

Option 2: Have him drink syrup of IPECAC or put down a stomach tube and pour the syrup down the tube. Follow this with warm water in either case. This will make him vomit.

2. Lethargic or unconscious patient:

Send to a hospital promptly. If the patient is unconscious because of the poison, he will probably die. Be sure to position the patient head down so if he vomits on his own, the vomit will run out rather than down his lungs. Either place a plastic airway in his mouth or stay with him to protect his airway (see Chapter 4 in Volume I).

3. Antidotes:

These are generally not available or useful. Exception: for IODINE poisoning, give a suspension of any kind of starch (e.g. flour or cornstarch in water or mashed potatoes). It will turn the iodine blue and render it harmless.

OVERDOSE CALCULATIONS: For the following medications, these are the amounts that may be lethal for an average adult:

CHLOROQUINE: 2500 mg (2.5 grams)
ACETAMINOPHEN: 7500 mg (7.5 grams).
ASPIRIN: 10,000 mg (10 grams).
IRON (Ferrous sulfate): 37,500 mg (37.5 grams).

The maximum amount possibly taken (in milligrams) can be estimated as follows:

mg possibly taken = (Maximum number of tablets missing from bottle) x (mg per tablet)

If the **mg possibly taken** is equal to or greater than the number above, the patient must be transported to a hospital while being treated with ACTIVATED CHARCOAL (preferable) or else IPECAC.

If the patient took less than the potentially lethal amount given above, then also calculate the **"mg/kg dose possibly taken":**

"mg/kg dose possibly taken" = (mg possibly taken) divided by (body weight in kilograms)

Compare to the appropriate number below (This calculation takes account of body size):

CHLOROQUINE: 50 mg/kg
ACETAMINOPHEN: 140 mg/kg
ASPIRIN: 150 mg/kg
IRON (Ferrous sulfate): 750 mg/kg

If the "mg/kg dose possibly taken" is less than this amount, you should still give charcoal or make him vomit, but there is no need to send him to a hospital (unless the patient is suicidal). If he took more, transport him to a hospital while you treat him.

PROTOCOL 12. ABNORMAL GROWTH OR DEVELOPMENT

12 A. Poor Growth
12 B. Excessive Growth
12 C. Abnormal Sexual Development
12 D. Delayed Mental Development

12 A. Poor Growth:

Does the patient have loss of appetite?

NO | **YES**
Go to Protocol 9 first, then check this protocol also.

Does the patient have a large spleen?

NO | **YES**
Consider MALARIA, SCHISTOSOMIASIS MANSONI,[1] SICKLE CELL DISEASE,[2] SCHISTOSOMIASIS JAPONICUM,[3] THALLASEMIA, VISCERAL LEISHMANIASIS.[4]

Does the patient have diarrhea or constipation or abdominal pains?

NO | **YES**
Consider GIARDIASIS, PELLAGRA, ASCARIASIS, TAPEWORM, SCHISTOSOMIASIS MANSONI, TUBERCULOSIS, HIV INFECTION, MALABSORPTION.

Is the patient an infant?

NO | **YES**
Consider RICKETS, SCURVY, TUBERCULOSIS, KIDNEY INFECTION, SYPHILIS, CRETINISM.

Conditions	Characteristics
MALNUTRITION	Poor or unbalanced diet, particularly a diet lacking in protein.
GIARDIASIS	Without symptoms or might have gas, diarrhea, or vomiting.
HIV INFECTION	MALNUTRITION even though good food is available.
ZINC DEFICIENCY	Hot weather, THALLASEMIA, or SICKLE CELL DISEASE.
TUBERCULOSIS	Cough or night sweats or child living in home with TB patient.
============	
TAPEWORM	History of eating raw or rare meats.
SCHISTOSOMIASIS HEMATOBIUM[5]	Bloody urine, now or previously; problem in the community.
SCHISTOSOMIASIS MANSONI	Large spleen, large liver, or bloody diarrhea; big belly.
RADIATION ILLNESS	Infants of mothers irradiated at or after 2 months pregnant.

[1] Schistosomiasis Mansoni: Scattered areas within Africa, the Arabian peninsula, the Caribbean, and parts of eastern South America.
[2] Sickle Cell Disease: This affects Blacks of African genetic origin, mainly in Africa and the Americas. Some Indians and Arabs are also affected.
[3] Schistosomiasis Japonicum: In areas of mainland China, the Philippines, parts of the Celebes, the upper Mekong, and the Thai-Malaysia border.
[4] Visceral Leishmaniasis: Found in scattered areas of Central and South America, Africa north of the equator, the Mediterranean area, the Indian subcontinent, eastern Europe, central Asia, and mainland China.
[5] Schistosomiasis Hematobium: Found in areas of Africa and the Middle East.

12 B. Excessive Growth:

See swelling if applicable (Protocols 34 B, 46 B, 61 D, 13 B).

Women who have DIABETES during pregnancy are likely to have very big babies.

Conditions	Characteristics
ACROMEGALY	Very coarse facial features, large bony structure.
MYCETOMA	Large foot with sores on it.
ELEPHANTIASIS, endemic	Swollen foot or feet with thick, rough skin.
FILARIASIS	Initially swelling comes and goes; geographically confined.

12 C. Abnormal Sexual Development:

Definitions:

Early sexual development, before age nine, is a serious problem that must be referred to a major medical center within a couple of weeks.

Delayed sexual development may be caused by any chronic disease such as HEART FAILURE, VISCERAL LEISHMANIASIS,[1] TUBERCULOSIS, MALNUTRITION. Also, see the list below.

Conditions	Characteristics
THALLASEMIA	Large spleen, ANEMIA.
LEPROSY	Skin is bumpy on much of the body, including ear lobes.
ZINC DEFICIENCY	Delayed growth, night blindness, fatigue.
SICKLE CELL DISEASE	Recurrent chest, abdominal, or bone pains; family history.
================	
SCHISTOSOMIASIS MANSONI[2]	Also a swollen abdomen and poor general growth.
AFRICAN SLEEPING SICKNESS[3]	Large neck lymph nodes, uncoordination, or HEART FAILURE.
SCHISTOSOMIASIS JAPONICUM[4]	Distended abdomen, possibly diarrhea or DYSENTERY.

12 D. Delayed Mental Development:

First check for deafness and CEREBRAL PALSY as these are easily mistaken for mental retardation.

Most often retardation has an obscure cause, not one listed below.

Does the patient have a history of some illness that left him/her bedridden for weeks or months?

NO — see table below.

YES — **Consider** cerebral MALARIA, MENINGITIS, ENCEPHALITIS, AFRICAN SLEEPING SICKNESS.

Conditions	Characteristics
MALNUTRITION	History of deficient food intake.
MONGOLISM	Wide set eyes, palm crease uninterrupted.
BRAIN DAMAGE	Due to any event affecting the brain, be it injury or illness.
==============	
PELLAGRA	Rash, diarrhea; usually a diet of corn.
CRETINISM	Mother of the patient had GOITER during pregnancy.
RADIATION ILLNESS	Infant of a mother irradiated at or after 2 months pregnant.

[1] Visceral Leishmaniasis: Found in scattered areas of Central and South America, Africa north of the equator, the Mediterranean area, the Indian subcontinent, eastern Europe, central Asia, and mainland China.

[2] Schistosomiasis Mansoni: Scattered areas within Africa, the Arabian Peninsula, the Caribbean, and parts of eastern South America.

[3] African Sleeping Sickness: Scattered areas of Africa, south of Bamako, Mali and Lake Chad and north of Lusaka, Zambia.

[4] Schistosomiasis Japonicum: In areas of mainland China, the Philippines, parts of the Celebes, the upper Mekong, and the Thai-Malaysia border.

PROTOCOL 13. MISCELLANEOUS WHOLE BODY PROBLEMS

13 A. Odor
13 B. Whole Body Swelling
13 C. Drenching Sweats
13 D. Chills

13 A. Odor:

Musty, moldy boots odor: TYPHUS, sometimes LIVER FAILURE, some SEPSIS, some CANCER.
Fishy, musty odor: VAGINITIS; CHOLERA (odor of the diarrhea).
Putrid sweet: SCURVY, DIPHTHERIA.
Foul, rotten odor: Poor dental hygiene, sores in mouth or throat, STREP THROAT, RESPIRATORY INFECTION due to sinusitis, SEXUALLY TRANSMITTED DISEASE, CANCRUM ORIS, RHINITIS, severe PNEUMONIA, CANCER, GANGRENE.
Medicinal odor: Due to PARALDEHYDE (drug used for SEIZURES).
Glue solvent odor (acetone-breath): MALNUTRITION, DIABETES, some SEPSIS.
Stale beer: TUBERCULOSIS involving the lymph nodes.
Ammonia or urine smell: KIDNEY FAILURE (or spilled urine which was not washed off).
Bleach-like odor: Normal odor of human semen.
Butcher shop: YELLOW FEVER[1].
Fresh feathers: RUBELLA.
Sweet: DIPHTHERIA.
Freshly baked bread: ENTERIC FEVER.

13 B. Whole Body Swelling:

Consider:

MALNUTRITION, associated with poverty or loss of appetite.
BERIBERI, associated with a white-rice diet or with ALCOHOLISM
HEART FAILURE, KIDNEY FAILURE, and LIVER FAILURE usually have onsets over days to weeks to months.
TRICHINOSIS, associated with poorly cooked meat, causes swelling with fevers and severe muscle pains.
INTESTINAL FLUKE (only the kind in the Mediterranean region) might cause this.
See Protocol C-15 to differentiate between these causes.

13 C. Drenching Sweats:

If the patient has DIABETES or an abnormal mental state, give him sugar immediately.
May be normal in children at night or menopausal women at any time of day.
With RICKETS, excessive sweating is confined to the head.
Generally any disease that causes a sudden drop of a high fever will also cause sweats. Sweating episodes also occur with MENOPAUSE. Except for the sweats associated with MENOPAUSE, it is important to find the fever pattern, if any, **before** starting symptomatic treatment. Take the patient's temperature every 2 hours around the clock for several days, noting on the record sheet when he has chills and/or sweats.

Symptomatic treatment: ACETAMINOPHEN, or IBUPROFEN; ASPIRIN in adults only.

(Continued on next page.)

[1] Yellow Fever: South America north of Sao Paolo, Central and western Africa and the Sudan.

(13 C. Drenching Sweats, continued.)

Condition	Fevers	Other Characteristics
MENOPAUSE	No	45-60 y.o. female.
ALCOHOLISM	No	Withdrawal after heavy drinking.
HYPOGLYCEMIA	No	Also trembling and mental symptoms or hungry.
MALARIA	Yes	Chills, headache; see HYPOGLYCEMIA.
HIV INFECTION	Usual	Exposure within the past 4 weeks.
AMEBIC LIVER DISEASE	Usual	Pain, right upper abdomen.
PNEUMONIA	Usual	Also a cough and quite ill, rapid onset.
TUBERCULOSIS	Usual	Cough, weight loss, or both, slow onset.
==============		
BRUCELLOSIS	Off and on	Back pains, joint pains, or both.
FILARIASIS	Off and on	Some neighbors have very swollen limb(s).
RELAPSING FEVER	Off and on	Body LICE or in a wooded area.
VISCERAL LEISHMANIASIS[1]	Off and on	Very large spleen, pain in left upper abdomen.
DENGUE FEVER	Yes	Rapid-onset, severe bone and joint pains.
PLANT POISONING	No	Ackee,[2] Muscarine, Nicotine.
INSECTICIDE POISONING	No	Heavy exposure or sensitive patient.
TETANUS	Off and On	Severe muscle spasms, variable pulse rate.
HEART ATTACK	No	Chest pain, left arm pain, or short of breath.
CANCER (lymphoma)	Maybe	Large lymph nodes, ANEMIA, weight loss.

13 D. Chills:

Definition: The patient shivers and complains of being cold when the environment is not cold.

Generally any disease that causes sudden onset of high fevers will also cause chills. Chills are most frequent when the temperature rises quickly from normal to very high. They also occur with MENOPAUSE in which case there usually is no fever. Except for the chills associated with MENOPAUSE, it is important to find the fever pattern, if any, **before** starting symptomatic treatment. Take the patient's temperature every 2 hours around the clock for at least 3-4 days, noting on the record sheet when he has chills and/or sweats.

VISCERAL LEISHMANIASIS might cause daily chills in spite of the fever never being really high.

Symptomatic treatment: ACETAMINOPHEN or IBUPROFEN; ASPIRIN in adults only.

[1] Visceral Leishmaniasis: Found in scattered areas of Central and South America, Africa north of the equator, the Mediterranean area, the Indian subcontinent, eastern Europe, central Asia, and mainland China.

[2] Plant Poisoning: Ackee: Found in scattered areas of western Africa and the West Indies.

III. SKIN PROBLEMS

PROTOCOL 14. SKIN SPOTS, LUMPS, AND BUMPS

14 A. Red Spots With a Fever:
14 A1. Red spots, not lumpy; fever plus measles-type, red rash.
14 A2. Other kinds of red rashes with fevers: Lumps, bumps, areas, white-on-red.
14 B. Red Spots, Lumps and Bumps; No Fever.
14 C. Skin Bumps, Not Red Spotted, Fever Present.
14 D. Skin Bumps, Not Red Spotted, Maybe Fever.
14 E. Skin Bumps, Not Red Spotted, No Fever.

14 A. Red Spots With a Fever:

14 A1. Red Spots, Not Lumpy; Fever Plus Measles-Type, Red Rash:

Brief differentials:

- *Rash affects the palms and soles*: Spotted Fever, Typhus, Syphilis (secondary).
- *Fever and feeling ill before the rash:* Spotted Fever, Erythema Infectiosum, Dengue Fever, Measles, Rubella (older children and adults), Tularemia.
- *Fever and rash appear together*: Rubella (small children), Meningitis.
- First "flu" symptoms, then fever, then rash: Typhus; maybe Enteric Fever.
- *Mental changes:* Spotted Fever, Meningitis, Enteric Fever, Typhus, Arboviral Fever (some kinds), Dengue Fever (depression).
- *Rash is itchy:* Seabather's eruption (very itchy); Dengue Fever; Typhus (after a while); Syphilis (in Blacks); any rash that peels is likely to be itchy at that time.
- *Body odor:* Enteric Fever (baked bread), Typhus (musty), Rubella (feathers).
- **Codes used in the following table:**

Sickness designation (How ill?): N = not sick; S = slightly sick (works at a slower than normal pace); M = moderately sick (usually in bed but gets up to care for needs); V = very sick (cannot care for own needs)

Rash designation: B = begins; S = spreads from there to --; H = heaviest; L = lightest; parts of the body not affected or lightly affected; M = maybe.

Condition; How Ill?	Rash	Who	History	Physical Exam
STREP INFECTION S to M	B: neck; S: trunk and limbs; H: skin folds; L: around eyes and mouth	Anyone, more children than adults	Sore throat only or belly pain; tongue red or red-and-white	Large, red tonsils or else a tender abdomen; redness disappears with pressure at first
SPOTTED FEVER (Americas) M to V	B: ankles, forearms, begins day 1-5; S: trunk, palms, soles	Contact with nature	Fever for 1-5 days before the rash	Maybe a little scab; spleen large and firm
SPOTTED FEVER (Eastern Hemisphere) M to V	B: limbs on day 4 or 5; H: wrists and ankles, M palms & soles	Contact with nature	Tick bite, muscle pains, vomiting, mental changes	One or more little scab(s)
TULAREMIA M to V	B: site of insect bite; S: red lumps between bite and trunk; no general rash	Children, hunters	Small mammal contact, temperate areas	Small scab with a red ring around it; large lymph nodes

Continued on next page.

(14 A1, Red Spots, Not Lumpy; Fever Plus Measles-Type, Red Rash, continued.)

ENTERIC FEVER M to V	White skin only; few; trunk only; slightly raised "freckles"	Anyone; poor sanitation	Onset over days; belly pain; headache	Appears intoxicated, abdomen tender and quiet
MENINGITIS M to V	B: pressure points S: everywhere various sizes; red, blistery, bluish	Anyone, mainly young, in epidemics	Sudden onset, severe headache; children vomit	Unconscious or stiff neck or both
RUBELLA N to M	B: face/trunk; S: face/trunk clear; H on limbs	Infants: rash and fever together[1]	Joint pains in older pts; aching all over	Body odor like feathers
SYPHILIS (secondary) N to S	B: trunk and face S: limbs; M palms soles symmetrical	Mostly sexually mature	Sexual contact 2 weeks to 6 months earlier; maybe "flu" symptoms	Variable; maybe moist "warts", maybe hair loss
MONONUCLEOSIS S to M	Unknown symmetrical	Mostly children and teenagers	Fever and profound fatigue, under 30 years old	Measles-type rash, maybe swollen tonsils, lymph nodes, or spleen
ARBOVIRAL FEVER N to V	Varies with the specific disease; seek local lore	Varies with the specific disease	Usually a flu-like illness	Varies with the specific disease
TYPHUS M to V	B: waist and armpits, 3rd to 7th day; S: trunk and limbs; L: face	Anyone, especially the poor	Mental symptoms, headache, constipated	Musty body odor; can't stick out tongue

14 A2. Other Kinds Of Red Rashes With Fevers. Lumps, Bumps, Areas, White-On-Red:

Condition; How Ill	Rash Distribution	Who gets it	History	Physical Exam
DENGUE FEVER M to V	Unknown but affects the forearms	Mostly children & expatriates; epidemics; tropical areas	Previous measles-type rash; this starts days 8-11	In Whites, skin is red with white dots on it
ERYTHEMA NODOSUM S to V	Lower legs, maybe the arms, tender to touch, color changes	Mostly young females	History of some other infection or taking some medication	Red lumps, tender, under the skin of the shins
ERYTHEMA MULTIFORME S to V	B: Limbs, symmetrical S: Anywhere, commonly near large joints	Anyone	History of some infection or taking some drug or toxin exposure	Some target-like red areas, lasts at least 7 days
SERUM SICKNESS S to V	Anywhere	Mostly Whites; from some diseases or drugs[2]	Fever plus an itchy rash resembling hives	Areas of skin are red and swollen or very pale
TULAREMIA M to V	B: site of bite; S: red lumps between bite and trunk; no general rash	Children, hunters	Small mammal contact, temperate areas	Small scab with a red ring around it; large lymph nodes

[1] Older children and adults feel ill and have a fever before the rash breaks out. In both cases the rash lasts for 3 days—hence the name, "Three-day Measles".

[2] Katayama Disease is a type of serum sickness that comes from exposure to schistosomes. Sulfa drugs are the main offenders drug-wise. There is frequently an arthritis connected to this.

14 B. Red Spots, Lumps and Bumps; No Fever:

Also consider conditions listed as being with a fever if the patient is elderly or malnourished or has waning immunity from HIV infection or cancer. In this case, conditions associated with fevers may present without the fever.

Condition	**Itching; Who?**	**Skin Only?**[1]	**Nature of the rash**
SCABIES	Much Anyone	Yes	Itching before any red spots; B: web spaces, waist, joints; S: all over; L: face; Ink rubbed on and then wiped off shows little lines between the spots.
CANDIDIASIS	Yes Sweaty	Yes	Sweaty areas: below breasts, groin, armpits. An area of red, swollen skin has satellite red dots around it.
Bedbug bites	Maybe Low-cost housing	Yes	Bedbugs may be felt but they are not seen. If many, the room may have an acrid odor. The red spots appear each morning or after naps and fade during the day. Volume I Appendix 10.
CONTACT DERMATITIS	Usually Allergic people	Yes	Spots and roughening of the skin in an area that touched some liquid or solid to which the person is allergic.
Flea bites	Maybe Animal exposure	Yes	Small, black, jumping creatures are seen occasionally. Fleas like some people and not others.
HOOKWORM, LARVA MIGRANS	Yes Soil exposure	Yes	Part(s) of the body that touched soil, usually the toe web-spaces—areas where there is poor sanitation.
LIVER FAILURE	No Trunk	No	Red spots with wiggly lines radiating out—appear like tiny red spiders.
STRONGYLOI-DIASIS	Yes! By anus	Maybe	Red, wiggly lines under the skin, near the anus or on the buttocks.
MYIASIS	Maybe Exposed skin	Yes	A countable number of discrete, large spots, maybe itch or painful, places touched by damp cloth or where a fly laid its egg and the larvae burrowed into the skin.
ONCHOCERCIASIS	Yes! Unknown	No	White skin only; also back and joint pains; maybe eye symptoms. History of being in an affected area.
SYPHILIS secondary	Maybe;[2] Whole body	No	Begins on face and trunk; spreads to limbs, possibly including palms and soles; possibly flu-like symptoms, maybe hair loss in patches; maybe a history of a painless genital ulcer.
SWIMMER'S ITCH	Yes! Whole body	Yes	After swimming in fresh water where there are water birds, bird schistosomes (worm larvae) burrow into the skin.
SEABATHER'S ERUPTION	Yes!! Everywhere	Yes	After swimming in salt water, immediate very itchy red rash, mainly clothing pressure points.
CUTANEOUS LEISHMANIASIS[3]	Minimal if any Exposed parts	No	Slow-onset skin problem, may itch or hurt but not remarkably either way; only on body parts not covered with clothing. Appearance varies; may be bumps or open sores.

[1] "Yes" means that there is no general body illness connected with the condition—no significant other symptoms or pain.

[2] Itching is common in Blacks and rare in Whites.

[3] Cutaneous leishmaniasis: Not present in the Asia and Pacific areas; otherwise scattered locations only; transmitted by sand flies.

14 C. Skin Bumps, Not Red Spotted, Fever Present:

Condition	Itch/Pain Body part	Color	Other/ Size relative to pimples (medium)
RHEUMATIC FEVER	Neither By joints	Skin	Pea-sized; recent history of symmetrical, red, swollen joints; maybe a heart murmur.
AIDS	Unknown Anywhere; 1-3 only	Blue/black/ red/skin color	Start small but becomes large, a kind of cancer that comes with advanced AIDS; commonly a cauliflower-type surface.
ERYTHEMA NODOSUM	Pain Shins and forearms	Skin or purplish	Various causative diseases; affects mostly young people; ½ to 4 cm diameter with ill-defined edges.
BRUCELLOSIS	Unknown Unknown	Skin or purplish	Gradual-onset general body pains and feeling awful; episodic fevers.
AFRICAN SLEEPING SICKNESS	Maybe pain Site of fly bite, 1-2	Dark halo, skin-color swelling	The swelling has a flat top. Geographically confined to few locations in Africa; flies that transmit this are dive-bombers.
RAT BITE FEVER	Neither Chest/arms	Purple	Look like warts; mainly Asia; history of a rat bite which may have healed initially.

14 D. Skin Bumps, Not Red Spotted, Maybe Fever:

Condition	Itch/Pain Body part	Color	Other Characteristics; Size relative to ordinary pimples)
ABSCESS	Pain Anywhere	Skin or reddish	Swollen area, tender to touch, changes slowly over days, becoming softer; large; 1-2 only.
LEPROSY lepromatous	Neither Cool parts[1]	Skin or slightly reddish	Develop slowly, innumerable bumps resembling cobblestones or bunches of tiny grapes; small to large; symmetrical.
LEPROSY tuberculoid	Neither Cool parts	Skin or lighter than skin	Rings or areas of skin; larger than pimples; not symmetrical; less than 5; maybe sharp, shooting pains.
PKDL	Neither Anywhere	Skin or slightly reddish	Same as leprosy, indistinguishable, but the patient had visceral leishmaniasis previously and was treated; small to large.
HIV INFECTION[2]	Itch Forearms[3]	Skin grayish	About 2-4 mm across, watery inside, look like small warts or molluscum contagiosum; discreet and countable; medium.
BARTONELLOSIS	Unknown Face/limbs	Purple	Only Peru and adjacent border areas; also severe joint pains; patient had a fever which dropped; skin bumps the size of pimples or larger.
YAWS	Neither Exposed skin	Off-white	Humid tropics only; cauliflower-type surface; at first one sore which heals and then many break out; mostly large.

[1] The skin bumps themselves are not painful but the patient may have sharp, shooting pains in the general area. The outer ears are almost always affected; hands and feet are commonly affected; genitals almost never are affected.

[2] Only in Black Africans, reportedly; this may happen in the early stages, before general illness.

[3] Perhaps elsewhere also.

14 E. Skin Bumps, Not Red Spotted, No Fever:

Condition	Itch/pain Body part	Color	Other Characteristics; Size relative to ordinary pimples)
Common worldwide:			
WARTS	Neither Face/limbs	Skin or grayish	Rough top; hard and dry-looking; no center hole; number varies/medium-large.
MOLLUSCUM CONTAGIOSUM	Neither Face/limbs	Skin or grayish	Just like warts but there is a center hole in each one; number varies/medium-large.
SYPHILIS	Neither Varies	Skin	Slow-growing lumps under the skin; mostly sexually mature, long incubation; large.
VARICOSE VEINS	Neither Legs	Bluish	Soft lumpy lines under the skin; disappear with raising the legs; large; legs ache.
KELOID	Neither Scar	Skin +/-	Hard, lumpy, excessive scar tissue at the site of any old injury, even very minor; large.
Uncommon worldwide, but may be locally common:			
TUNGIASIS	Both Nails/webs	Black/white	Small, spherical pea-size bumps burrow under nails; small-medium.
GUINEA WORM[1]	Both	Skin	One or few; blister top; cold relieves the pain and may break the blister; medium-large.
DONOVANOSIS	Neither	Varies	1-2 areas; scar tissue; areas with sexual contact; mainly ports and Pacific area; large.
ONCHOCERCIASIS[2]	Neither Head/trunk	Skin	Peaked bumps; insides feel lumpy; large Body itches but not the bumps.
MYCETOMA	Unknown Feet	Skin; black or colored rains	Slow-onset of swelling; looks bad but pain is minimal; arid areas only; large.
CYSTICERCOSIS	Neither Under skin	Skin	Firm, small pea-size under the skin; small to medium; history of consuming pork.
LOIASIS[3]	Pain? Anywhere	Skin	Large swellings come and go; humid central Africa only.
HYDATID DISEASE[4]	Neither Under skin	Skin	Lump feels like a water balloon; comes and stays; large.
PLANT POISONING Argemone	Unknown Unknown	Bluish	Coin-shaped and sized; bleed readily when disturbed.
TREPONARID	Itch? Exposed skin	Skin or whitish	Look like moist warts; small to large; arid tropics only, with poor sanitation.
CUTANEOUS LEISHMANIASIS[5]	Either[6] Exposed skin	Varies	One or few spots or areas, generally large; may be an area with satellite spots around; geographically confined.

[1] Guinea worm: Only scattered areas within Africa and the Middle East.
[2] Onchocerciasis: Scattered areas in Africa, the Middle East, Central America, and northern South America.
[3] Loiasis: Humid, rural, western and central Africa only.
[4] Hydatid disease: In arid tropical areas where dogs live close to people; also temperate forested areas where people gather wild foods that might be contaminated with the stool of wild animals.
[5] Cutaneous leishmaniasis: Not in the Asia or Pacific area; elsewhere present in scattered areas only.
[6] They might itch or hurt but neither the itching nor hurting is intense; it is more just irritation.

PROTOCOL 15. BLISTERING, ROUGH, SCALING, PEELING SKIN

15 A. Severe itching

15 B. Mild or No Itching

If your patient has dark skin, also see Protocol 14 A and B. A red rash in dark skin looks sandpapery.

15 A. Severe Itching:[1]

Symptomatic treatment: Calamine lotion helps but for just a little while. Try very warm water which will increase the itching—then rub the affected area vigorously with a rough Turkish towel. Thereafter put cold packs on the area. The itching will be relieved for a matter of a couple of hours. Reported alternatives are oatmeal baths, hydrocortisone cream, or chlorpromazine (by mouth).

Condition	Bisters	Flaking	Swelling	Other
SCABIES	No	Maybe	No	Very itchy; E web spaces.
CHICKEN POX	Yes	Late	No	Epidemics; E trunk; some heal while others start.
CANDIDIASIS	No	Maybe	Some	Sweaty skin; red center with red spots around.
Burns	E Yes	Usual	Usual	Itching with healing; history of a burn.
TINEA	No	Yes	Maybe	Round/oval areas or mottled.
CONTACT DERMATITIS	Maybe	Unusual	Usual	A defined area that touched something.
ECZEMA	No	Yes	Maybe	Usually hands or face; family history of allergy.
KIDNEY FAILURE	No	Yes	No[2]	High blood pressure or abnormal urine dipstick.
LIVER FAILURE	No	Yes	No[3]	Swollen abdomen or yellowish eyes.
ONCHOCERCIASIS[4]	No	Yes	Maybe	Bumps under skin; hilly areas near streams.
MONKEYPOX	Yes! Early	Late	Some	Fever; only humid central and western Africa.
DENGUE FEVER	No	Yes	Maybe	Sudden onset; severe bone pains; tropics only.
PLANT POISONING, Atriplicism	Yes	Late	Maybe	Fingers turn pale and ache; Chinese traditional medicine.
PINTA	No	Yes	Some	Americas only.
SEABATHERS ERUPTION	Maybe	Maybe	Yes	Immediately after salt water swimming.
AFRICAN SLEEPING SICKNESS[5]	No	Yes	No	Abnormal sleep pattern; weight loss; headaches.

[1] The amount of itching varies between people. Generally black skin is more itchy than white skin but there is a lot of individual variation.

[2] The skin is not swollen but the eyes, legs, and feet are.

[3] No swelling of the skin but there is general body swelling, especially the abdomen.

[4] Onchocerciasis: Scattered areas in Africa, the Middle East, Central America, and northern South America; swollen skin.

[5] African sleeping sickness: Scattered areas in Africa between 15° North and 20° South.

15 B. Mild or No Itching:[1]

Condition	Blisters	Flaking	Swelling	Other
With Blisters, usually painful:				
HERPES	Yes	Late, slight	Maybe	Mouth/genital areas; pain.
PARONYCHIA	1-2 only	No	Yes	Sides of fingernails.
GONORRHEA	Yes	Probably	Unusual	Red halos, tender.
SHINGLES	Yes	Late	Some	In a band (trunk) or an area (face).
PLANT POISONING Manicheel	Yes	Unknown	Maybe	Americas only; from a tree — exposure to any part of it.
SPOTTED FEVER/ Rickettsial pox	Yes	No	No	Mainly urban, southern Africa and northeastern Asia.
MENINGITIS	Usual	Yes	Rare	Very sick, dark discoloration.
MONKEYPOX	Yes	Late	Maybe	Fever, sick, humid Africa.
GUINEA WORM[2]	one or few	No	Some	Drank water from wells into which people step.
Maybe Blisters:				
STD	Maybe	Maybe	Occasional	Sexually exposed part(s).
IMPETIGO	Maybe	Yes	Some	Irregular areas, some yellowish crusts.
MEASLES[3]	Rare	Much	Some	Black skin peels.
GANGRENE	Maybe	Late	Usual	Skin cool, looks dead.
REITER SYNDROME	Maybe	No	Yes	Palms, soles, scalp, other.
MALNUTRITION	Unusual	Yes	Usual	Skin like peeling paint.
No Blisters:				
TINEA	No	Yes	Maybe	Round or oval areas; patient is not sick from this.
FILARIASIS	No	Maybe	Yes	Onset slow, over months; locally common.
HEAT ILLNESS	Maybe	No	Little	General, sandpapery rash; sweaty areas of body.
SYPHILIS, congenital	No	Yes	Maybe	Palms of babies born to syphilic mothers.
PELLAGRA	No	Yes!	Maybe	Symmetrical; sun-exposed.
CUTANEOUS LEISHMANIASIS[4]	No	Yes	Maybe	Unclothed skin only; usually discolored.
DONOVANOSIS	No	No	Yes	Rough swollen area, sexually exposed.
ARSENIC POISON	No	Yes	Maybe	Dry, scaly, flaky skin.
ELEPHANTIASIS, ENDEMIC	No	Maybe	Yes!	Patient walked barefoot over reddish clay soil.
EXFOLIATIVE DERMATITIS	No	Yes!	Maybe	Skin peels off in large amounts.
YAWS, tertiary	No	Yes	Yes!	Palms/soles skin very thick and splits open.

Continued on next page.

[1] The amount of itching varies between people. Generally black skin is more itchy than white skin but there is a lot of individual variation.

[2] Scattered areas within Africa and the Middle East only.

[3] White skin has red spots. Black skin has a sandpapery texture which some might interpret as tiny blisters. Asian skin with measles is somewhere between the two appearances.

[4] Cutaneous leishmaniasis: Not present in Southeast Asia or the Pacific areas; otherwise regionally variable.

(15 B. Mild or No Itching; No Blisters, continued.)

LEPROSY, tuberculoid	No	Yes	Maybe	Numbness, sharp pains.
PINTA	No	Yes	Some	Americas only.
SCURVY	No	Yes	No	Dry, rough skin with dark spots on it.
ECZEMA	No	Yes	Maybe	Family history of allergy.
KIDNEY FAILURE	No	Yes	No[1]	High blood pressure and/or abnormal urine dipstick.

PROTOCOL 16. COLOR CHANGES IN FLAT AND SMOOTH SKIN

16 A. Skin Color Lighter than Normal
16 A1. Patches of Skin Are Pale
16 A2. Whole Body Is Pale
16 B. Skin Color Darker than Normal
16 C. Reddish Skin
16 D. Other Skin Color Changes

16 A. Skin Color Lighter than Normal:

The most common cause is scar on naturally dark skin. Examples would be burns or diaper rash. The skin will heal lighter than normal; it may darken over time.

A person who is generally pale without being cool and sweaty is likely to have ANEMIA, TUBERCULOSIS or MALNUTRITION.

If the skin is pale and cool and (maybe) sweaty, see SHOCK, HEART ATTACK, PLANT POISONING due to Claviceps or Ergot. If the problem is confined to the limb(s), see FROSTBITE, GANGRENE.

16 A1. Patches of Skin Are Pale:

Condition	Itchy	Shape	Distinct[2]	Other
TINEA	Yes	Round or oval	Fairly distinct	Gradual onset.
VITILIGO	No	Very irregular	Very distinct	Symmetrical except on face; like normal fair skin.
LEPROSY tuberculoid	No	Round or irregular	Varies	Can't feel touch or can't distinguish cold & hot.
ONCHOCERCIASIS[3]	Yes	Irregular	Yes	Whole body itchy; maybe eye trouble; hilly areas.
PKDL	No	Unknown	Unknown	After treatment for VISCERAL LEISHMANIASIS.

16 A2. Whole Body Is Pale:

Condition	Characteristics
ANEMIA	Pale tongue and fingernails; either from poor diet or else from abnormal blood loss (menses, stool, or injury); rapid pulse.
TUBERCULOSIS	Slow-onset; yellowish tinge to the skin; weight loss; frequently a chronic cough.
MALNUTRITION	Poor diet, weight loss; overlaps with TB and ANEMIA. Only dark skin becomes light; Whites become dark with malnutrition.
HEMOSIDEROSIS	Grayish skin color, hereditary or from iron pots; due to excess iron.

[1] The skin is not swollen but the body is generally swollen.

[2] That is, the transition from normally-colored skin to discolored skin is at a definite line so that two observers would agree precisely where it is.

[3] Onchocerciasis: Scattered areas in Africa, the Middle East, and the Americas.

16 B. Skin Color Darker than Normal:

Condition	Characteristics
Usually no fever:	
MONGOLIAN SPOT[1]	Buttocks and back of some brown-skinned people—looks like bruising but symmetrical and doesn't change over time.
SCURVY	Diet devoid of fresh fruits and vegetables; bleeding into the skin and also bleeding gums with loose teeth.
MALNUTRITION	Generally darkened skin in Whites.
PELLAGRA	Dark discoloration with a bit of roughening; usually corn-only diet.
ARSENIC POISONING	Also numbness and tingling and weakness of limbs; homicidal or occupational or from ethnic remedies.
ONCHOCERCIASIS[2]	In Arabs with medium-dark skin; not in Blacks. There is whole-body itching.
PLANT POISONING	Argemone oil; Dark spots on the skin , especially south Asians. These spots bleed easily. There is swelling and maybe a fever.
CHAGA'S DISEASE	Scattered areas in the Americas; a swollen area of the body has a bruised appearance.
CANCER (skin)	Black discoloration, mostly in Whites; slow onset.
Fever and patient is ill:	
PLAGUE	Dark discoloration over firm, enlarged, tender lymph nodes.
HEMORRHAGIC FEVER	Very ill; bleeding into the skin causing spontaneous bruising; may be small or large areas.
GANGRENE	Usually fingers or toes; skin appears dry, dark, and dead.
MENINGITIS	Very ill; bleeding into skin which may form blisters and peel.
RELAPSING FEVER[3]	Tiny black and blue marks; fevers which last for a matter of days and then disappear.

16 C. Reddish Skin:

Reddish skin is difficult or impossible to see on very dark skin.
Also see Protocol 21 E if the face is involved.
For red areas of skin or red rings with pale centers, see Protocol 14 A.

Condition	Fever	Characteristics
ABSCESS	Maybe	Redness over a swollen, tender area below.
CELLULITIS	Maybe	Red area, warm, maybe with red streaks, large nodes.
STREP INFECTION	Usually	Fine rash; pale around lips and eyes.
ROSEOLA	Had one	Fine rash with a drop in the fever.
ERYTHEMA INFECTIOSUM	Had one	Rash develops with a drop in a fever; maybe sore joints in older patients.
DENGUE FEVER	Yes	Early: red rash on white skin; Late: white spots on red skin.
CARBON MONOXIDE POISON	No	Exposed to exhaust or fire; also headache and nausea or vomiting.
EXFOLIATIVE DERMATITIS	Maybe	Initially looks like sunburn before flaking and peeling.
LEPROSY	Maybe	Leprosy reaction during treatment or initial manifestation of leprosy in non-black skin.
FAMILIAL MEDITERRANEAN FEVER	Yes	Skin also swollen and painful, mainly or only below the knees; hereditary in people of Mediterranean genetic heritage.

[1] This is an entirely normal condition; it needs no treatment.
[2] Onchocerciasis: Scattered areas in the Americas, the Middle East, and Africa.
[3] Relapsing fever: Not present in the islands of Southeast Asia or the Pacific.

16 D. Other Skin Color Changes:

Yellow skin color: from some liver or blood problem. See JAUNDICE.
Bluish skin color: from respiratory difficulty or some poisonings.
Abnormally shiny skin: from BERIBERI or some rare diseases

PROTOCOL 17. SKIN BROKEN OPEN

17 A. Innumerable Small Holes or Raw, Disrupted Areas of Skin
17 B. One or few Well-Defined Openings in the Skin
17 B1. Body parts with sexual contact, recently or remotely
17 B2. Body parts without sexual contact

Codes used in the following tables:
Fever: M = Maybe; Y! = High; Y = Yes; N = No; U = Usually.
Itch/Pain: F = At first; L = Later; M = Maybe; Y = Yes; N = No; U = Usually; Sl = slight if any; ? = information unavailable.
Onset: H = Hours; D = Days; W = Weeks; M = Months; Y = Years; ? = unknown.
(Itching, pain, fever, and onsets might vary between patients.)

17 A. Innumerable Small Holes or Raw, Disrupted Areas of Skin:

Symptomatic Treatment: For itching see Protocol 15 A. Relieve pain by applying a dressing and elevating the sore area above the level of the heart. Oral pain medication may help also.

Condition	Part[1]	Fever	Itch	Pain	Onset	Characteristics
IMPETIGO	Head neck	N	N	Sl	H-W	Roughened, scabbed, yellowish crusts.
MYCETOMA	Feet	N	N	L	W-Y	White, black, or colored dry grains visible; area generally swollen.
TUBERCULOSIS	Head neck	U	N	N	W-M	Lumps on neck under the skin; skin opens and drains fluid that dries.
MYIASIS	Wounds	M	?	U	H-D	Maggots (short, fat 'worms') visible.
YAWS, tertiary	Feet	N	N	Y	W-M	Thick, cracking skin on soles; hard to walk.

17 B. One or Few Well-Defined Openings in the Skin:

17 B1. Body Parts With Sexual Contact, Recently Or Remotely:[2]

Condition	Fever	Itch	Pain	Onset	Characteristics
SYPHILIS primary	N	N	N	D-W	Painless round or oval ulcer with swelling below; rolled edges.
CHANCROID	N	N	Y	D?	Large groin lymph nodes; ulcer is tender to touch; maybe a halo.
DONOVANOSIS	N	N	L	W-M	Ragged edges, may smell bad, irregular shape.

Continued on next page.

[1] That is, the usual body part that is affected; there will be exceptions.

[2] A person engaging in sexual relations is most likely to develop a sore on his or her genitals. However, usually the mouth, hands, and breasts are also involved in such a relationship. These body parts can develop the sores of sexually transmitted diseases. The basic elements in choosing this part of the protocol are the types(s) of sexual activity; the exposure of the body part to sexual secretions (including saliva). Consider the time interval between that activity and the appearance of the ulcer vs. the incubation period of the disease. Thus one can have a syphilis ulcer on the lips or gonorrhea infecting the hand.

(17 B1. Body Parts With Sexual Contact, Recently Or Remotely, continued.)

Condition	Fever	Itch	Pain	Onset	Characteristics
LYMPHOGRANULOMA VENEREUM (LGV), primary/secondary	N	N	M	H-D	Small ulcer; large groin nodes with a groove down the center along the leg crease(s)
LGV tertiary	M	N	Y!	D-W	Painful abnormal holes in genitals
GONORRHEA	M	N	Y	W-Y	Painful abnormal holes in genitals; history of painful urination

17 B2. Body Parts Without Sexual Contact: [1]

Condition	Part[2]	Itch	Pain	Onset	Characteristics
No Fever:					
TROPICAL ULCER	Legs & feet	N	U	D-W	Crater, round or oval, sharp edges, generally on legs
ZINC DEFICIENCY	Old injury	M	M	D-W	Non-healing old injury
MYIASIS	Old injury	M	Y	H-D	Maggot(s) present
TUNGIASIS[3]	Nails	M	Y	H	Black/white split peas; skin touched the soil
AMEBIC SKIN ULCER	Pelvis	N	Y	D-W	Lower trunk and/or genitals; has a discharge
TUBERCULOSIS, skin	Head neck	M	N	W-M	Usually with lung TB; sometimes red-brown crusts or bumps
BURULI ULCER	Limbs	M	N	W	Ragged edges which overhang an ulcer crater; swampy areas only
CUTANEOUS LEISHMANIASIS[4]	Exposed	Sl	Sl	W	Unclothed areas of the body; slowly developing and spreading
Maybe Fever:					
ABSCESS	Old injury	N	Y	D-W	Initially warm, swollen, firm; then broke open
YAWS primary/secondary	Trunk	N	N	D-W	Off-white pus present, some raised up and some craters
DIPHTHERIA	Anywhere	N	Y	?	Blister at first; bursts open to become a skin ulcer; patient ill
CANCRUM ORIS	Face finger	N	Y	H-D	Cheek, chin, or sucked digit; black flesh, foul odor; malnourished
Fever, and patient is ill:					
SCRUB TYPHUS[5]	?	N	M	D	1-3 small black scabs; very ill
ANTHRAX	?	F	N	H-D	Black center; swelling around
TULAREMIA[6]	Bite	N	N	D	Tiny black scab by insect bite
SPOTTED FEVER[7]	?	N	N	D	Black scab(s); maybe red halo(s)
PLAGUE[8]	?	?	?	D	Small scab(s) large, tender lymph nodes with black skin over top

[1] That is, the problem is not related to sexual contact.
[2] That is, the part of the body that is usually affected; there are exceptions.
[3] Tungiasis: Parts of Africa, the Americas, and India only.
[4] Cutaneous Leishmaniasis: Not in the Asia or Pacific area; scattered areas with sanflies elsewhere.
[5] Scrub Typhus: Indian Subcontinent, Southeast Asia, central Asia, and the Pacific areas.
[6] Tularemia: Temperate areas; persons exposed to small animals or their insects.
[7] Spotted Fever: In the Americas there is likely to be one sore; in Africa and the Mediterranean areas there is likely to be multiple sores. Spotted fever in these two locations are very different diseases.
[8] Plague: Those exposed to rodents or their fleas.

PROTOCOL 18. CREATURES IN, ON, OR UNDER THE SKIN

Condition	Size/Shape	Where	Characteristics
SCABIES	Microscopic; ovals with legs	First web spaces or other soft skin;	Red, itchy spots; ink rubbed on & off leaves lines
LICE	Small commas	Hairs, head or body; seams of clothing	Small but visible; may be seen moving; eggs attached to hairs
ENTEROBIASIS	Around 0.5 cm like threads	Rectum, vagina	White color; seen moving at night or on awakening
TUNGIASIS[1]	Tiny split peas	Nails that touched soil	Black outside; white insides under or near nails
MYIASIS	Under 0.5 cm; [2]	Injuries and pink, moist parts	Look like short, fat "worms", might be seen moving
Ticks[3]	Oval; size varies	Attached to skin	Head attached to skin; oval shape
LARVA MI-GRANS	Less than 10 cm; wiggly line	Under skin that touched sand or soil	Itchy; red, line under the skin; a pen mark will show that it moves slowly
TRICHURIASIS	Coiled with tail; visible	Near the rectum	Coiled, whitish worms on the pink, moist surface
STRONGYLOI-DIASIS	Less than 10 cm; wiggly line	Buttocks, near the rec-tum	Like larva migrans; lasts hours to days, then disappear and recur later on
LOIASIS[4]	Like a small bird's egg	Under skin, anywhere	Lumps arise under the skin, then disap-pear and arise elsewhere
GUINEA WORM[5]	Long thread, around 100 cm	Legs; initially under skin	Blister which breaks open and reveals the end of a very long, skinny worm
TAPEWORM	Size of holes from a paper punch	Near rectum	Small, whitish rectangles like confetti visible; nothing that looks wormy
Leeches	Less than 5 cm; like flattened worms	Skin or mouth/throat	Long, narrow creatures attach with suc-tion cups and then swell

[1] Tungiasis: Only parts of Africa, the Americas, and India.
[2] The size and shape varies greatly from one kind to the other; see your *Regional Index*.
[3] Ticks: See Volume I, Appendix 10.
[4] Loiasis: Humid, rural western and central Africa.
[5] Guinea Worm: Scattered within Africa and the Middle East only; where there are wells into which people step to draw water.

IV. HEAD PROBLEMS

PROTOCOL 19. HEADACHE

19 A. Headache With a Fever
19 B. Headache Without Fever
Also see Protocol 21 G: Face Pain, if appropriate.

Emergency conditions:

- Instantaneous onset very severe headache
- Headache localized to one part of head, increasing severity and frequency over time
- Headache worse in the morning and with coughing or sneezing; patient vomiting or drowsy.
- Headache triggered by touching one particular spot on the temple(s).

Non-emergency conditions originating elsewhere:

- Check for tenderness in the upper neck, which may cause spasm of the muscles of the skull.
- Check the patient's vision; it us unusual, but visual problems can cause headache.
- Check for tenderness of the face, especially right below the eyes and right above the nose; see SINUSITIS.
- Check for tenderness of the skull bones. A bone problem due to infection, injury, or both can cause headache.

19 A. Headache With a Fever:

Symptomatic treatment: ACETAMINOPHEN and IBUPROFEN are appropriate once you know the fever pattern. Do not use ASPIRIN until you have a diagnosis. Do not use strong pain medications if the patient is desperately ill.

Did the patient change from healthy to very ill[1] in less than three days?

NO → (continue below)

YES → Does the patient have moderate to severe pain other than headache?

- NO → **Consider**: MALARIA, HEAT ILLNESS, MENINGITIS, ENCEPHALITIS, ARBOVIRAL FEVER, ENTERIC FEVER, RELAPSING FEVER
- YES → See *Index* C, Protocol C-2.

Has the patient been ill for two weeks or more but he still sits, talks, and eats?

NO → (continue below)

YES → Consider: MALARIA, RESPIRATORY INFECTION, SYPHILIS, KATAYAMA DISEASE, AFRICAN SLEEPING SICKNESS[2], BRUCELLOSIS.

Consider alternatives: (Illness less than 2 weeks duration, and/or bedridden)

Conditions	Fever Pattern	Other
INFLUENZA	Low usually	Recent onset, generally achy, other cases also.
MALARIA	Varies	Waist, shoulder pain common.
RESPIRATORY INFECTION	Low usually	Pain in face, center head, or behind eyes.
ENTERIC FEVER	Sustained high	Apathy; Abdominal pain or cough.

Continued on next page.

[1] Very ill means that the patient can attend to nothing around him. He cannot or will not get his own food or drink or walk to the bathroom on his own. If his house caught on fire, he would not get out.

[2] African Sleeping Sickness: Scattered areas of Africa, south of Bamako, Mali and Lake Chad and north of Lusaka, Zambia.

(19 A. Headache With a Fever, continued.)

Conditions	Fever Pattern	Other
TYPHUS	Variable	Scab from an insect bite or pain behind eyes.
LYMPHOGRANULOMA VENEREUM	Variable	Large nodes in the groin; maybe a genital sore.
FILARIASIS	Off and on	In an area where some adults have swollen limbs.
ARBOVIRAL FEVER	High	Aching muscles and a high fever.
MONKEYPOX[1]	High	Blister-rash, humid areas only, monkey contact.

19 B. Headache Without a Fever:

Symptomatic treatment: ACETAMINOPHEN and IBUPROFEN are appropriate under any circumstances. Do not use ASPIRIN until you have a diagnosis. Do not use strong pain medications if the patient is desperately ill.

Has the patient had a head injury?

NO — YES: Expect a headache for months.

Does the patient have high blood pressure?

NO — YES: **Consider** TOXEMIA, HYPERTENSION, KIDNEY FAILURE.

Is the patient at a high altitude or exposed to fire or exhaust fumes?

Both NO — YES to either: **Consider** ALTITUDE SICKNESS, CARBON MONOXIDE POISONING.

Is the pain continual or almost continual?

NO — YES: **Consider** STRESS, CANCER, KIDNEY FAILURE, DIABETES, PLANT POISONING, LEAD POISONING, FOOD POISONING, DEMONIZATION, CYSTICERCOSIS, TRICHINOSIS, PELLAGRA, BRUCELLOSIS.

Is the headache recurrent: it comes and goes with pain-free intervals?

NO — YES: **Consider** MIGRAINE, HYPERTENSION, MALARIA, CANCER.

Single episode headache, no fever or recent history of fever:

Conditions	Pain Pattern	Other
HANGOVER	Throbbing, general	Day after alcoholic intoxication.
INFLUENZA	Variable	Also general muscle aching.
DEMONIZATION	Variable	Occult involvement or due to a curse.
HEAT ILLNESS	Generalized, dull	Very hot day, patient weak, has nausea.

PROTOCOL 20. DIZZINESS

Symptomatic treatment: *If the patient is vomiting as a result of the dizziness,* PROMETHAZINE *or* HYDROXYZINE *may help. Generally bed rest in dark and quiet is helpful.*

Also see Protocol 7 E if the patient is uncoordinated; it is easy to confuse uncoordination and dizziness and they commonly occur together.

First check the patient's vital signs: pulse, respiration, and blood pressure. Seek emergency higher-level care if these are very abnormal. Only proceed if the vital signs are reasonably normal.

[1] Monkeypox: Northern D. R. Congo and adjacent Central African Republic; rarely found in western Africa.

Is the patient very ill with a high fever?

NO | **YES**

Consider MALARIA, EAR INFECTION, ENTERIC FEVER, DENGUE FEVER,[1] MENINGITIS, ENCEPHALITIS; rarely ARBOVIRAL FEVER, RELAPSING FEVER, HEMORRHAGIC FEVER, SPOTTED FEVER.[2]

Did this develop rapidly after the person took some food, drink, or medicine?

NO | **YES**

Consider ALCOHOL or STREPTOMYCIN (drug) side-effect, PLANT POISONING: Lolism,[3] Cassava, Nicotine.

Consider alternatives:

Conditions	Type	Fever	Other
ANEMIA	Weak/faint	Rare	Pale inside eyelids, mouth or nails.
ANEMIA	Off-balance	Rare	Worse with eyes closed than open; pale.
Wax in ears	Spinning or tilting	No	Can see the wax; use wax softening drops.
HEAT ILLNESS	Weak/faint	Maybe	Hot weather, nauseated, headache.
EAR INFECTION	Spinning or tilting	Usual	Red ear drum(s); had a cold before.
DEHYDRATION	Faint	No	Dry mouth, thirsty, fast pulse.
Menstruation	Weak/faint	No	Use IBUPROFEN (drug) to treat it.
HYPERVENTILATION	Faint	No	Numb by mouth, short of breath.
BRAIN DAMAGE	Unsteady	Maybe	Worse with eyes open than closed.
HEART FAILURE	Faint	Maybe	Irregular pulse or low blood pressure.
SYPHILIS, tertiary	Off balance	No	Worse with eyes closed than open.
TUBERCULOSIS	Off balance, spinning, or tilting	Maybe	Draining ear, antibiotics don't work.
AFRICAN SLEEPING SICKNESS[4]	Off balance or unsteady	No/low	Lumps on back of neck or HEART FAILURE.
STROKE	Variable	No	Weakness or paralysis, maybe high BP.

PROTOCOL 21. OTHER HEAD PROBLEMS

21 A. Hair Problems
21 B. Facial Swelling
21 C. Mongoloid Face
21 D. Skull Misshapen; Bossing
21 E. Flushed Face
21 F. Drooping of One Side of Face or Eyelid
21 G. Face Pain
21 H. Other Face and Head Problems

[1] Dengue Fever: In the Americas only near or north of the equator. In Africa only Nigeria and southern Africa. Prevalent in India, Southeast Asia, and the Pacific. Occasionally found in the Mediterranean area.

[2] Spotted Fever: Not in the islands of Southeast Asia.

[3] Plant Poisoning, Lolism: Found in the Mediterranean and Middle Eastern areas.

[4] African Sleeping Sickness: Scattered areas of Africa, south of Bamako, Mali and Lake Chad; north of Lusaka, Zambia.

21 A. Hair Problems:

Condition	Hair Problem	Other Characteristics
Lice	Creatures and eggs	Lice are barely visible; patient itching.
ZINC DEFICIENCY	Variable hair loss	Very hot or dry climate, not acclimatized.
TINEA	Loss in patches	Dry, scaly rash on bald spot.
MALNUTRITION	Color change,[1] thin	Weight loss, thin arms, maybe scaly rash.
SYPHILIS, secondary	Loss in patches	Skin in bald spot normal; fever; "flu"
TYPHUS	Loss after illness	Fever, sick for weeks; from fleas or lice.
THYROID TROUBLE	Hair thin, brittle	Tired and constipated, weight gain.
CHLOROQUINE (drug)	Premature graying	Drug for prevention of MALARIA.
VISCERAL LEISHMA-NIASIS[2]	Thinning, loss	Large spleen, weight loss.
PREDNISONE (drug)	Thinning, loss	Fat face, weight gain.
LEPROSY, lepromatous	Loss of hair rare	Europeans and Japanese-bumpy skin.
LEPROSY, lepromatous	Loss of eyebrows	Bumpy skin usually; numb fingers/toes.
LASSA FEVER[3]	Hair loss	High fever, severe pains, sudden onset.
FAVUS[4]	Bald patches	Yellow crusts after a time.
RADIATION ILLNESS	Hair loss	Recent radiation exposure.

21 B. Facial Swelling:

Symptomatic treatment: Try cold packs first; if this does not work, try a heating pad or a warm water bottle.

Is the swelling of sudden onset after an injection, insect bite, or eating something?

NO — **YES**
Consider ANAPHYLAXIS; treatment is EPINEPHINE (drug).

Is the swelling on one side only or mainly?

NO — **YES**
If the patient is a child who is not ill and the swelling is mainly around the eye, it is due to an insect bite and will heal itself.
An EYE INFECTION can cause a large lymph node in front of the ear.
The most common cause worldwide is CELLULITIS. May be MUMPS, RESPIRATORY INFECTION (sinusitis), or an ABSCESS of a tooth; rarely BURKITT LYMPHOMA, ANTHRAX, lung CANCER, CHAGA'S DISEASE,[5] HIV INFECTION in infants.

Is the patient short of breath lying down so he sits up to sleep?

NO — **YES**
Consider ALLERGY, BERIBERI, rarely HEART FAILURE, very rarely CANCER.

Continued on next page.

[1] Normally black hair becomes reddish or blond or, in some ethnic groups, it becomes straight and brittle, breaking off so it looks like a short crew cut. Normally blond hair turns darker with malnutrition.

[2] Visceral Leishmaniasis: Found in scattered areas of Central and South America, Africa north of the equator, the Mediterranean area, the Indian subcontinent, eastern Europe, central Asia, and mainland China.

[3] Lassa Fever: Found in West Africa and occurs mostly in epidemics.

[4] Favus: This occurs in the Middle East/ Mediterranean area only.

[5] Chaga's Disease: Found in scattered areas of Central and South America.

(21 B. Facial Swelling, continued.)

Is the patient very ill with a high fever?

NO

YES
Consider CELLULITIS, TYPHUS, YELLOW FEVER,[1] MONKEYPOX,[2] LASSA FEVER,[3] HEMORRHAGIC FEVER, TRICHINOSIS.

Consider Alternatives	Pattern	Other
ALLERGY	Anywhere, symmetrical	Short of breath or itchy; sudden onset.
MUMPS	By ear(s)	Some fever; maybe belly or testicle pains.
MALNUTRITION	By ears	Abnormal hair, thin upper arms.
ALCOHOLISM	By ears	History of heavy or binge drinking.
HIV INFECTION (infants)	By ear(s)	At-risk parental behavior.
KIDNEY FAILURE	Mainly eyes, mostly mornings	Abnormal urinalysis and/or high BP.
LIVER DISEASE	By ear lobes	JAUNDICE, swollen abdomen, or both.
INTESTINAL FLUKE[4]	All over	Abdominal pains common.
AFRICAN SLEEPING SICKNESS[5]	Eyelids, symmetrical	Abnormal sleep pattern or HEART FAILURE.
LEPROSY, lepromatous	Cobblestone, symmetrical	Ear lobes affected; no eyebrows.
PREDNISONE (drug side-effect)	Symmetrical, no change AM to PM	Taking drug for more than a week.
WHOOPING COUGH	Eyelids, symmetrical	Persistent cough, maybe red eyes.
PLANT POISONING	All over	Argemone oil, Atriplicism,[6] Manicheel.[7]
YAWS	Bony swelling, symmetrical, slow onset	Adults only; maybe bumps or ulcers elsewhere.

21 C. Mongoloid Face:

Definition: Low bridge of the nose, eyes set wide apart, face abnormally rounded, tongue large and may protrude; possibly appearance of retardation.

Problem	Characteristics
MONGOLISM	Retarded, continuous horizontal crease on palm.
THALLASEMIA	Hereditary, not retarded, large spleen.
CRETINISM	Retarded, very big tongue, mother had GOITER during pregnancy.

[1] Yellow Fever: South America north of Sao Paolo, central and western Africa and the Sudan.
[2] Monkeypox: Northern D. R. Congo and adjacent Central African Republic; rarely in western Africa.
[3] Lassa Fever: Found in West Africa and occurs mostly in epidemics.
[4] This kind of intestinal fluke is not in Africa, the Americas, or the Pacific areas.
[5] African Sleeping Sickness: Scattered areas of Africa, south of Bamako, Mali and Lake Chad and north of Lusaka, Zambia.
[6] Plant Poisoning, Atriplicism: Found among the Chinese in the Far East.
[7] Plant Poisoning, Manicheel: Found only in the Americas.

21 D. Skull Misshapen; Bossing:

In infants, most commonly due to the birth process; usually will correct itself. See below for bossing.

Definition: Rather than being regularly rounded, the skull is a funny shape, sticking out more on the forehead and on both sides above the ears; the shape is slightly like a clover leaf if viewed directly from the front. The following can cause bossing: This may also be simply a family trait.

Problem	Characteristics
SYPHILIS, congenital	Failure to thrive; syphilic mother.
RICKETS	Legs are bowed in or out; result of inadequate sunlight.
SICKLE CELL DISEASE[1]	Pain episodes which begin before two y.o.; pale or jaundiced or both.
THALLASEMIA	Family history, large spleen, ANEMIA.
ACROMEGALY	Large, coarse features, with large hands and feet.

21 E. Flushed Face:

Definition: White or light tan skin appears abnormally reddish. This may be caused by sunburn or any fever, especially TYPHUS, or by the following:

Problem	Characteristics
ERYTHEMA INFECTIOSUM	A fever which drops as a "slapped cheek" rash breaks out.
PLANT POISONING: Cassava	From improperly processed cassava or from cassava water.
PLANT POISONING: Betel nut	Asian women, red and black around the mouth.
ALCOHOLISM	Nose particularly red; currently or habitually intoxicated.
CARBON MONOXIDE POISONING	Exposed to fumes from fire or an engine; headache & nausea.
STREP INFECTION	Sore throat or belly pain; red face but pale around the lips.

21 F. Drooping Face or Eyelid (usually one side):

Definition: When the patient smiles one side of his mouth is markedly different than the other OR he cannot close one eye completely OR he cannot move his face at all.

Is this the consequence of a severe illness with a high fever?

NO

YES
Consider EAR INFECTION, DIPHTHERIA, MENINGITIS, ENCEPHALITIS. May be from BRAIN DAMAGE from any cause.

Consider alternatives	Characteristics
BELL'S PALSY	Cannot close one eye, sudden onset.
STROKE	Sudden onset, other weakness, unconscious, or SEIZURE.
PARKINSON DISEASE	Uncoordination, gait disturbance, usually older patient.
POLIO	History of a cold or diarrhea, other weakness, muscle cramps.
LEPROSY	One eye will not close; skin changes present, slow onset.
Head injury	History of injury or scar from an old injury.
DIPHTHERIA	Sick for weeks; also symptoms of HEART FAILURE.

[1] Sickle Cell Disease: This affects Blacks of African genetic origin, mainly in Africa and the Americas. Some Indians and Arabs are also affected.

21 G. Face Pain:

Problem	Characteristics
RESPIRATORY INFECTION (Sinusitis)	History of a stuffy nose; upper back teeth all hurt.
CELLULITIS	Redness and swelling along with a fever; maybe prior injury.
SHINGLES	Burning or shooting pain, then a blistery rash.
==================	
BRUCELLOSIS	Slow onset, up and down fevers, pain in front of ears with chewing.
Toothache	A decayed tooth should be obvious.
CANCRUM ORIS	A spontaneous wound on the lower face; malnourished child.
ANGINA	Jaw pain; possibly chest pain also, maybe pale and sweaty and faint.

21 H. Other Face and Head Problems:

Any of the problems listed under Protocol 21 F may occasionally affect both sides of the face.
A visual problem may cause an abnormal head posture in an older child or an adult.

Problem	Characteristics
TOXEMIA	Six months or more pregnant; itching of the face.
PARKINSON DISEASE	Expressionless face; peculiar, falling gait.
ALLERGY	Sneezing; itchy, runny nose; itchy eyes.
==================	
TETANUS	Tight smile due to spasms of the facial muscles.
MASTOIDITIS	Red, swollen bump(s) behind the ear(s); fever.
SYPHILIS	Open soft spot well past seven months of age.
RICKETS (infants)	Open soft spot well past seven months of age.
RICKETS (children)	Head very sweaty.
HIV INFECTION(infants)	Open soft spot well past seven months of age.

PROTOCOL 22. EYE PAIN

22 A. Eye Pain With No or Low Fever
22 B. Eye Pain Maybe With Fever
22 C. Eye Pain With Fever
22 D. Itching Eyes

22 A. Eye Pain With No or Low Fever:

**If the eyes are both painful and red, then see Protocol C-8.

Symptomatic treatment: ACETAMINOPHEN or IBUPROFEN is appropriate. Stronger pain medications such as CODEINE or NALBUPHINE may be used after diagnosis. Do not use eye anesthetic drops repeatedly to relieve pain since they will permanently blind the patient.

Types of pain designations:

FB = "foreign body"; pain like having something stuck in the eye.
Irritated = not really pain, just an annoying, scratchy feeling.
Eye motion = pain is worse when moving the eyes.

Does the patient say it feels as if something is in the eye?

NO | **YES**
Check the section on eye injuries, Chapter 9 of Volume I.
Consider KERATITIS, TRACHOMA, MYIASIS.

Is there much tearing, and the pain worse in light?

NO | **YES**
Consider XEROPHTHALMIA, LEPROSY, IRITIS, KERATITIS, PLANT POISONING due to Jimson Weed.

Continued on next page.

(22 A. Eye Pain With No or Low Fever, continued.)

Consider alternatives:

Conditions	Pain Type	Red?	Other Characteristics
MALARIA	Aching	No	Fevers, chills, headaches, waist pain.
EYE INFECTION	Irritated / burn	Yes	Pain rarely severe; more irritation.
MIGRAINE	Throbbing	No	Headache, maybe one-sided; nausea.
Eye strain	Burning	Maybe	Using eyes in poor light.
TRACHOMA	Irritated or FB	Yes	Lids misshapen or bubbles under the lid.
===============			
NAIROBI EYE	Burning eye-lids	Lids only	Brown and orange insects seen in the environment[1].
ONCHOCERCIASIS[2]	Variable	Maybe	Itching skin also; skin bumps.
LOIASIS[3]	Punch in eye	Probably	May see worm, swollen eye.
LARVA MIGRANS	Punch in eye	Probably	Swollen eye.
GLAUCOMA	Variable	Yes	Hard eyeball; nausea if rapid onset.
PINGUECULA	Irritated	Maybe	White growth, irritated with lid movement.

22 B. Eye Pain, Maybe With Fever:

**If the eyes are both painful and red, then see *Index C*, Protocol C-8.

Problem	Pain Type	Red?	Other Characteristics
CELLUITIS	Burning	No[4]	Red and/or warm to touch.
===============			
TUBERCULOSIS	IRITIS[5]	Yes	Painful bump on cornea-white border.
IRITIS	IRITIS	Yes	Fever if caused by another illness.
REITER SYNDROME	Burning	Yes	Tears, avoids light, also joint pain.
SYPHILIS, tertiary	IRITIS	Yes	Aching or sees flashing lights.
BRUCELLOSIS	Eye motion	?	Recurrent illness, joint pains, fevers.
SHINGLES	Burning	Maybe	Blister-type skin rash, one side only.
LOIASIS	Punch-like	Yes	Swelling, may see worm or his track.
CHAGA'S DISEASE[6]	Unknown	?	Swelling, one side only, from insect bite.

[1] The Nairobi Eye insects are prevalent in East Africa.

[2] Onchocerciasis: Scattered areas in Africa, the Middle East, Central America, and northern South America.

[3] Loiasis: Found in humid central Africa only

[4] Usually the whites are not red but the lids are.

[5] Pain is worse in the light and there is excessive tearing. Light shown into the other eye (provided that eye is not blind) will cause pain in the affected eye. The pain of iritis is worse when the patient attempts to change from near to far vision.

[6] Chaga's Disease: Scattered areas in the Americas.

22 C. Eye Pain With Fever:

**If the eyes are both painful and red, then see the protocol for red, painful eyes, *Index* C.

Disease	Pain Type	Fever	Other
MALARIA	Aching	Yes	Headache, chills, sweats.
MEASLES	Aching	Yes	Cough, rash, very ill.
================			
LEPTOSPIROSIS	Aching	Erratic	Aching all over, very red eyes.
RELAPSING FEVER	With light	Up/down	A kind of IRITIS; non-round pupils.
DENGUE FEVER[1]	Eye motion	High	Severe bone and joint pains.
ARBOVIRAL FEVER	Variable	High	Aching all over.
MENINGITIS	With light	High	Severe headache, stiff neck.
SPOTTED FEVER[2]	Throbbing	High	Pain worse with light; rash usual.
SCRUB TYPHUS[3]	Aching	High	Large spleen, constipated.

22 D. Itching Eyes:

Symptomatic treatment: Rinse the eyes with water or artificial tears. Do not use steroid eye ointment or drops (name ends with "-one") unless they are prescribed by a physician for the person and occasion.

Problem	Characteristics
ALLERGY	No fever; either a hot climate or other allergies.
================	
LARVA MIGRANS	Patient feels movement or a worm is visible.
KATAYAMA DISEASE	Also fever, hives, loss of appetite.
LOIASIS[4]	Initial itching becomes pain; see a worm or its track.

PROTOCOL 23. ABNORMAL EYE APPEARANCE

23 A. Red Eyes With a Fever
23 B. Red Eyes-Possible Fever
23 C. Red Eyes Without a Fever
23 D. Yellow Eyes
23 E. Swollen Eye(s)
23 F. Abnormal Whites and Corneas
23 G. Abnormal Pupils
23 H. Other Eye Abnormalities

[1] Dengue Fever: In the Americas only near or north of the equator. In Africa only Nigeria and southern Africa. Prevalent in India, Southeast Asia, and the Pacific. Occasionally found in the Mediterranean area.
[2] Spotted Fever: Not in the islands of Southeast Asia.
[3] Scrub Typhus: Indian, Asian, and Pacific areas only.
[4] Loiasis: Humid areas of west and central Africa only.

23 A. Red Eyes With a Fever:

**If the eyes are both painful and red, then see Protocol C-8.

Problem	Other Characteristics
DENGUE FEVER	Aching all over, joint and bone pains, very sudden onset.
MEASLES	Cough, spotty or sand papery rash by day three.
=============	
LEPTOSPIROSIS	Very red; erratic high fever, aching all over.
TYPHUS	Bitten by fleas or body lice; very ill, high fever.
ARBOVIRAL FEVER	Aching all over; joint pains are common.
SPOTTED FEVER[1]	Very ill, severe headache, eye pain worse with light.
HEMORRHAGIC FEVER	Whites of eyes may have bright red blood spots.
SCRUB TYPHUS[2]	Gradual onset of fever, large spleen, constipation.

23 B. Red Eyes, Possible Fever:

**If the eyes are both painful and red, then see Protocol C-8.

Problem	Other Characteristics
CELLULITIS	Redness is on lids and face; local swelling present.
GONORRHEA	Sexually active, or child of an infected adult; much pus.
================	
IRITIS	Pupil not round; key hole shape or scalloped.
GLAUCOMA	Cornea is cloudy, vision very poor.

23 C. Red Eyes Without a Fever:

**If the eyes are both painful and red, then see Protocol C-8.

Problem	Other Characteristics
ALLERGY	Eyes itchy, also runny nose.
RESPIRATORY INFECTION	Patient is congested, with an obvious cold.
ALCOHOL effect	Patient acts intoxicated or has a hangover.
EYE INFECTION	Pus or watery discharge; eyes may be stuck shut in the morning.
KERATITIS	Severe eye pain; feels as if there is something in the eye.
================	
ONCHOCERCIASIS[3]	Also very itchy skin; blindness common locally.
TRACHOMA	Bubbles underneath lids early; poor vision later.
ARSENIC POISONING	Also numbness, tingling, burning of palms and soles.
WHOOPING COUGH	Severe cough, blood-red spots on whites of eyes.
SCURVY	Blood-red spots on whites of eyes; gums bleeding also.

[1] Spotted Fever: Not in the islands of Southeast Asia.
[2] Scrub Typhus: Indian, Asian, and Pacific areas only.
[3] Onchocerciasis: Scattered areas in Africa, the Middle East, Central America, and northern South America.

23 D. Yellow Eyes:

Definition: The whites of the patient's eyes are uniformly yellow, including the part near the cornea. First see JAUNDICE in the *Disease Index* to learn about the various general causes and how to treat the symptoms. After you have worked through this protocol, then also see C-5.

Is the patient taking a medication that affects the liver[1]?

NO | **YES**: Stop the medication immediately.

Is the patient a newborn (less than 4 weeks old)?

NO | **YES**: If the yellow is intense or the patient acts ill, send him to a hospital or see Chapter 7. **Consider** SEPSIS, KIDNEY INFECTION, congenital SYPHILIS.

Does the patient have pain by his right waist area (lower chest/upper abdomen)?

NO | **YES**: **Consider** HEPATITIS, AMEBIC LIVER DISEASE, LEPTOSPIROSIS, YELLOW FEVER,[2] LIVER FLUKE.[3]

Is the problem of recent onset, with a high fever, and in a patient who had prior good health?

NO to any | **YES to all**: **Consider** MALARIA, SEPSIS, PNEUMONIA,[4] LEPTOSPIROSIS, GALLBLADDER DISEASE, BARTONELLOSIS.[5]

Has the person been ill over two weeks, either this time or recurrently?

NO | **YES**: See Protocol C-7 if there is bilirubin in the urine, either with or without urobilinogen. The diseases listed below have excessive urine urobilinogen[6] but negative bilirubin.

AFRICAN SLEEPING SICKNESS[7]: Abnormal sleep pattern.
SICKLE CELL DISEASE[8]:
Episodes of pain since early childhood.
THALLASEMIA: Hereditary ANEMIA; large spleen.
VISCERAL LEISHMANIASIS[9]: Huge spleen, large liver.
OVALOCYTOSIS: Hereditary ANEMIA; large spleen.
TROPICAL SPLENOMEGALY: Huge spleen, chronic MALARIA

Consider alternatives	Fever	Other
HEPATITIS	Low if any	Nausea, fatigue improved with jaundice.
AMEBIC LIVER DISEASE	Maybe	Burning abdominal pain, worse with walking.
GALLBLADDER DISEASE	Unusual	Light-colored stools; general itching.
MALARIA	Usually high	Headaches, chills are common.

[1] These are medications with the precaution to reduce the dose in liver disease, or with a side-effect of LIVER FAILURE.

[2] Yellow Fever: South America north of Sao Paolo, central and western Africa and the Sudan.

[3] Liver Fluke: Present worldwide, including temperate climates; common in Southeast Asia, and East Asia.

[4] Blacks and those of Mediterranean genetic origin only.

[5] Bartonellosis: Only in Peru and adjacent border areas.

[6] Almost all normal people have some urobilinogen; only 2+ to 4+ are abnormal.

[7] African Sleeping Sickness: Scattered areas of Africa, south of Bamako, Mali and Lake Chad and north of Lusaka, Zambia.

[8] Sickle Cell Disease: This affects Blacks of African genetic origin, mainly in Africa and the Americas. Some Indians and Arabs are also affected.

[9] Visceral Leishmaniasis: Found in scattered areas of Central and South America, Africa north of the equator, the Mediterranean area, the Indian subcontinent, eastern Europe, central Asia, and mainland China.

23 E. Swollen Eye(s):

Symptomatic treatment: Cool cloths or ice packs on the eyelids may decrease the swelling.

Is the patient a child who may have been bitten by an insect but is not ill?

NO — **YES**: The child will be fine; put cool cloths by the eye.

Are the eyes very itchy and tearing?

NO — **YES**: **Consider** ALLERGY.

Are the eyelids red (warm in Blacks) and swollen?

NO — **YES**: **Consider** CELLULITIS, NAIROBI EYE.[1]

Does the patient have a rash involving much or all of his body?

NO — **YES**: **Consider** KIDNEY FAILURE, MONKEYPOX,[2] MALNUTRITION.

Are the eyeballs swollen so they appear to pop out at you?

NO — **YES**: **Consider** THYROID TROUBLE, CELLULITIS, BURKITT LYMPHOMA, CANCER, rarely ABSCESS.

Consider alternatives	Characteristics
EYE INFECTION	Also pain, or red, or visible pus.
KIDNEY FAILURE	Abnormal urinalysis; eyelids swollen, soft, especially mornings.
WHOOPING COUGH	Child also has a severe, spasms of cough, maybe with vomiting.
================	
THYROID TROUBLE	Eyelids are swollen; patient fatigued, low body temperature.
PLANT POISONING	Manicheel[3] or Atriplicism.[4]
AFRICAN SLEEPING SICKNESS[5]	Headaches, abnormal sleep pattern, maybe HEART FAILURE.
CHAGA'S DISEASE[6]	One eye swollen shut; swelling lasts a week or more, feels firm.
LOIASIS[7]	Sudden onset of severe pain in eye.
TRICHINOSIS	Also swollen, sore muscles, aching all over, fevers.

[1] Nairobi Eye is caused by insects which are found in East Africa; they are brown and orange, flying, and tend to occur in large numbers at certain times of the year.

[2] Monkeypox: Northern D. R. Congo and adjacent Central African Republic; rarely found in western Africa.

[3] Plant Poisoning, Manicheel: Americas only.

[4] Plant Poisoning, Atriplicism: Chinese and in the Far East.

[5] African Sleeping Sickness: Scattered areas of Africa, south of Bamako, Mali and Lake Chad and north of Lusaka, Zambia.

[6] Chaga's Disease: Scattered areas in the Americas.

[7] Loiasis: Humid, rural western and central Africa.

23 F. Abnormal Whites and Corneas:

See Protocols 23 A-D for reddish or yellowish whites.

Is the patient a Black with grayish whites or brownish spots on the whites?

NO — **YES**: Probably normal but check XEROPHTHALMIA, PELLAGRA.

Does the patient have a skin condition affecting large areas of skin?

NO — **YES**: **Consider** LEPROSY, ONCHOCERCIASIS,[1] CHICKEN POX.

Does the patient have white growing over the cornea?

NO — **YES**: **Consider** TRACHOMA, ONCHOCERCIASIS, LEPROSY, PTERYGIUM

Consider alternatives	Characteristics
XEROPHTHALMIA	Cornea dry, maybe the white is brownish or wrinkled.
KERATITIS	Severe eye pain with a corneal surface that is not totally smooth.
=================	
PINGUECULA	White bump on the white of the eye, near the corneal edge.
TUBERCULOSIS	Bump at the white-cornea border; painful.
GLAUCOMA	The whites of the eyes may be bluish; there is pain.
LOIASIS[2]	Worm crawling over the white, or track where it had been.

23 G. Abnormal Pupils:

Definition: The pupils are either not round OR they are unequal in size (in spite of both eyes having vision) OR they do not get smaller in bright light OR they do not get larger in dim light.

Problem	Characteristics
CATARACT	White or cloudy pupil, not entirely black.
QUINNE toxicity	Pupils large, do not respond, patient blind.
PELLAGRA	Large pupils, diarrhea, rough skin rash.
PLANT POISONING	Large pupils due to Cassava, Datura, or Jimson weed.
PLANT POISONING	Small pupils due to Strychnine or Muscarine.
INSECTICIDE POISONING	Small pupils, round, also much tears, much saliva, diarrhea.
IRITIS	Small pupils, not exactly round, light sensitive.
DIPHTHERIA	Pupils small or large, will not change size.
XEROPHTHALMIA	Irregularly-shaped pupils quite late in the disease.
SYPHILIS, tertiary	Small pupils which do not respond to light or unequal pupils.
ENCEPHALITIS	Fever and other symptoms of BRAIN DAMAGE.
GLAUCOMA	Pupil(s) hazy, may not be round.
BRAIN DAMAGE	Pupil(s) either too large or too small, may not be round.
MENINGITIS	Pupil(s) either too large or too small, may not be round.

[1] Onchocerciasis: Scattered areas in Africa, the Middle East, Central America, and northern South America.

[2] Loiasis: Humid, rural western and central Africa.

23 H. Other Eye Abnormalities:

If tears spray in an infant rather than running down the cheek, the problem may correct itself or it is correctable at a modern hospital.

Dry Eyes

Old Age	Old people may have dry eyes; treat with artificial tears.
LEPROSY	Skin bumps, rash, sharp, shooting pains, or any combination.
DEHYDRATION	Mouth is also dry and skin hangs loosely on the body.
XEROPHTHALMIA	Wrinkles on the white of the eyes; corneas look dry.

Excessive tearing

ALLERGY	This is the most common cause; also itching and runny nose.
XEROPHTHALMIA	Light avoidance, maybe wrinkled whites.
EYE INFECTION	Eye pain also; if due to a virus, causes tears rather than pus.
PLANT POISONING	Due to Muscarine or Atriplicism.
INSECTICIDE POISONING	Recent exposure; also cough, runny nose.
LEPROSY	Also some skin problems and thin or absent eyebrows.

Eyelid(s) rolled in or out

TRACHOMA	Some clouding of the cornea starting on top; eyes painful.
LEPROSY	Also some skin problems and thin or absent eyebrows.

Abnormal eye movements, including crossed eyes

Crossed eyes are common in babies. They may outgrow the problem or they may need care.

BRAIN DAMAGE	Crossing is a common manifestation of brain damage.
CRETINISM	Mentally retarded; either short or deformed limbs.
LYME DISEASE	Temperate areas, history of ARTHRITIS.
SEIZURES	Eyes are rolled back and there is some jerking of the limbs.
DIPHTHERIA	Quite ill for weeks; sore throat or skin infection.
FOOD POISONING	Botulism; recently ate sausage or tainted vegetables.

Abnormality of eye closing

BELL'S PALSY	Cannot close one eye, sudden onset, face droops on one side.
LEPROSY	Like BELL'S PALSY but very gradual onset.
THYROID TROUBLE	Eyes always at least half closed or else seem to bulge out.
DIPHTHERIA	Quite ill for weeks; sore throat or skin infection.

Eyes set wide apart and prominent forehead

MONGOLISM	Patient is also mentally retarded and has a too-large tongue.
THALLASEMIA	Patient also has ANEMIA and a family history of ANEMIA.
CRETINISM	Eyes also crossed; mentally retarded, short or deformed limbs.

Abnormal substance in the eye(s)

EYE INFECTION	Some pus in the eyes which stick shut in the morning.
GONORRHEA	Much pus coming from eyes which look bloodshot.
MYIASIS	Maggots in the eyes.
XEROPHTHALMIA	White foamy stuff on the eyelids.

Eyebrows thin or absent

SYPHILIS, secondary	Also a generalized rash and fever and aching all over.
LEPROSY	Also a bumpy face and/or ear lobes or a skin rash with numbness.
THYROID TROUBLE	Due to low thyroid, loss of outer 2/3 of eyebrows.

PROTOCOL 24. LOSS OF VISION

24 A. Vision Loss With Normal Eye Appearance
24 B. Vision Loss With Abnormal Eye Appearance
24 C. Distorted Vision

24 A. Vision Loss with Normal Eye Appearance:

This is usually due to the normal effects of heredity and age; however, check below:

Has the patient consumed homemade beverage or wood alcohol within the past six hours?

NO | **YES**
The loss of vision is due to wood alcohol (methanol).
Keep the person very drunk with good alcohol (ethanol) for two days.
This must be done immediately to prevent blindness.
See ALCOHOL in the *Drug Index.*

Did the vision loss begin during the first few weeks in a hot climate?

NO | **YES**
Consider ZINC DEFICIENCY (night blindness).

Did the vision loss start while the patient took ETHAMBUTOL or QUININE or CHLOROQUINE?

NO | **YES**
Side-effect of the drug; stop the drug!

Did the problem begin with a severe illness with a high fever?

NO | **YES**
Consider all causes of BRAIN DAMAGE, both in the *Disesase Index* and in the *Regional Index*. Also consider MEASLES, ARBOVIRAL FEVER,[1] SCRUB TYPHUS.[2] May be due to QUININE (drug for MALARIA).

Does the person also have a skin condition covering a large portion of his body?

NO | **YES**
Consider LEPROSY, ONCHOCERCIASIS.[3]

Consider alternatives	**Characteristics**
SYPHILIS, tertiary	Sees or saw flashing lights and vision is distorted; maybe pain.
DIABETES	The patient is a known diabetic or he has sugar in his urine.
TOXEMIA	6 months or more pregnant; high blood pressure; swollen ankles.
==================	
GLAUCOMA	Eyeball(s) feel(s) rock hard (feel them through eyelid).
LARVA MIGRANS	History of sudden onset of severe pain.
TRICHINOSIS	History of eating raw or rare meat; aching all over.
PLANT POISONING	Nicotine, Cassava or Tobacco/cow's urine.
RADIATION ILLNESS	Infant of a mother who was irradiated after 8 weeks of pregnancy.

[1] Rift Valley Fever, which occurs in central and eastern Africa.
[2] Scrub Typhus: In the India area, Southeast and Central Asia, the Far East, and the Pacific.
[3] Onchocerciasis: Scattered areas in Africa, the Middle East, Central America, and northern South America.

24 B. Vision Loss with Abnormal Eye Appearance:

The most common cause is an old injury. If the eye is shriveled, consider XEROPHTHALMIA also.

Problem	Characteristics
KERATITIS	Bloodshot; some corneal opacities.
TRACHOMA	Eye lid(s) turn inward and scratch cornea; painful.
CATARACT	The pupil (normally black part) looks white or cloudy.
XEROPHTHALMIA	Cornea dry, whites maybe look wrinkled, “soap suds” on lids.
ONCHOCERCIASIS[1]	Itchy skin rash, bumps on the skin; blindness common locally.
QUINNE toxicity	Pupils large, do not respond, patient blind.
LOIASIS[2]	Worm visible in the eye, or a track where he had been.
IRITIS	Redness around the cornea and irregular shape to the pupil.
GLAUCOMA	Eyeballs are hard and cornea is hazy.
LEPROSY	Bumpy skin, loss of eyebrows and lashes or both, slow onset.
HERPES	Eye pain and not-totally-smooth surface of the cornea.
PTERYGIUM	Fleshy, white growth over the cornea.
PLANT POISONING	Due to Nicotine, Muscarine, or Argemone oil.

24 C. Distorted Vision:

Halos or rainbows around white lights

GLAUCOMA	Also eye pain and eyeball(s) is/are very hard.
CATARACT	The normally-black pupil looks partially or entirely white.
LEPROSY	There are also skin bumps or rash or areas of numbness.
SYPHILIS, tertiary	Was sexually active 10+ years ago or born to a syphilic mother.
ONCHOCERCIASIS	Some distortion of the cornea, "snowflakes" or lower opacities.

Doubled vision

See Protocol 23 H, as this is usually associated with crossed eyes. Also consider MIGRAINE.

Vision blurred

IRITIS	Problem has lasted a long time, with frequent eye pains.
PLANT POISONING	Due to Muscarine (a substance in mushrooms) or Jimson Weed.
FOOD POISONING	Botulism, from sausage or tainted vegetables; rare manifestation.
DIPHTHERIA	Pupils don't change size readily.

Cloudy vision

CATARACT	Pupil appears grayish or whitish rather than black.
TRACHOMA	Whitish scarring on the cornea..

Difficulty seeing in bright lights

KERATITIS	Eye pain like a foreign body stuck in the eye
LEPROSY	Also skin bumps or a rash or numbness somewhere.
SYPHILIS, tertiary	Was sexually active 10+ years ago or born to a syphilic mother.
ONCHOCERCIASIS	Some distortion of the cornea, "snowflakes" or lower opacities.

---

[1] Onchocerciasis: Scattered areas in Africa, the Middle East, Central America, and northern South America.

[2] Loiasis: Humid, rural west and central Africa.

PROTOCOL 25. HEARING LOSS

Hearing loss due to most problems cannot be treated except in a major medical center.

Does deafness run in the patient's family?

NO — **YES**: There is probably not much to do about it.

Does the patient have ringing in his ears?

NO — **YES**: **Consider** a side-effect of QUININE or ASPIRIN; may be due to a head injury, EAR INFECTION, SYPHILIS, or wax in the ear canals.[1]

Is the patient taking STREPTOMYCIN or another, similar injectable antibiotic?

NO — **YES**: Stop the drug (preferable) or reduce the dose.

Does the patient have either pain or a plugged feeling in his ears?

NO — **YES**: **Consider** wax,[1] EAR INFECTION, RESPIRATORY INFECTION, MYIASIS. See Protocol 26 for ear pain.

Did the hearing loss begin with an illness with a high fever?

NO — **YES**: **Consider** MEASLES*, LASSA FEVER*[2], TYPHUS*, EAR INFECTION, SICKLE CELL DISEASE,[3] MENINGITIS*, ENCEPHALITIS*, SCRUB TYPHUS,[4] TRICHINOSIS.

Consider alternatives	Fever	Other
Ear wax	No	Tan or dark brown wax in canals. [1]
BRAIN DAMAGE*	Maybe	Hearing loss may be a consequence of any cause of this.
CRETINISM*	No	Also poor growth, mentally retarded.
SICKLE CELL DISEASE	Maybe	Belly and limb pains, began in infancy.
SYPHILIS*	No	Sexually active 10+ years ago or born to a syphilic mother; onset age 2-25.
PLANT POISONING	No	Due to Nicotine, Cassava, Tobacco/Cow's urine (Africa).
RADIATION ILLNESS*	No	Infant of a mother irradiated after 8 weeks of pregnancy.

*Hearing not usually recovered.

PROTOCOL 26. EAR PAIN

Symptomatic treatment: ACETAMINOPHEN or IBUPROFEN is always appropriate. ASPIRIN is usually appropriate but should not be given until you have reached a diagnosis.

Problem	Fever	Other Characteristics
Wax in ears	No	Ear canals packed with wax. (See Volume I, Appendix 1.)
EAR INFECTION, MIDDLE	Usual	No change in pain with pulling on the ear.
STREP THROAT	Usual	Ears look fine; throat is abnormal.

Continued on next page.

[1] See Volume I Appendix 1 for directions on how to deal with this.

[2] Lassa Fever: Found in West Africa.

[3] Sickle Cell Disease: This affects Blacks of African genetic origin, mainly in Africa and the Americas. Some Indians and Arabs are also affected.

[4] Scrub Typhus: Indian subcontinent, Southeast Asia, central Asia, and Pacific Areas.

(Protocol 26. Ear Pain, continued.)

EAR INFECTION, EXTERNAL	Rare	Increased pain with pulling on the ear; history of recent water in the ears or a scratched ear canal.
Insect in ear	No	Patient will tell you the diagnosis.[1]
Tooth problem	Maybe	Obvious decay in a molar on the affected side.
=================		
TUBERCULOSIS	Usual	Hoarse, pain with swallowing, or draining ear.
DIPHTHERIA	Yes	Patient quite ill; leathery scum on the throat.
TYPHUS	High	Severe body aching, mentally abnormal.
BRUCELLOSIS	Erratic	Pain in the jaw joints in front of the ears.
MYIASIS	Rare	Maggots, resembling short, fat "worms" in the ear.

Any injury or skin problem can affect the outer ears or the ear canals. See Chapter 9, Volume I.

PROTOCOL 27. OTHER EAR PROBLEMS

Swelling in front of ears: Tooth ABSCESS, TYPHUS, MUMPS, LIVER DISEASE, CIRRHOSIS, CHAGA'S DISEASE,[2] HIV INFECTION in infants.

Swelling behind ear: MASTOIDITIS.

Bumps on outer ears: If firm (like the outer ear), due to LEPROSY; if hard (like pebbles), due to GOUT.

Acquired thick earlobes: Normal in those overweight; may be a late consequence of ear piercing; consider LEPROSY.

Ears itching: ALLERGY, CANDIDIASIS.

Maggots in ears: MYIASIS.

Skin of outer ears: This can have the same problems as skin elsewhere; see the Skin Protocols.

Strange-looking ears at birth: needs a major medical center.

Ringing in the ears: Old age is most common; Also consider ear wax; ASPIRIN overdose (first symptom); possibly QUININE (drug) side-effect; EAR INFECTION, MIDDLE; TUBERCULOSIS; common after head injury.

Ears feel plugged: Either due to wax or else RESPIRATORY INFECTION (a cold). Wax must be cleaned out by someone who has the use of an otoscope; wax softeners may be helpful.

Pus running out of ears: EAR INFECTION, middle or external, TUBERCULOSIS in children.

Cold, white outer ears: FROSTBITE.

PROTOCOL 28. NOSE PROBLEMS

Bloody nose: See the procedure described in Volume I, Appendix 1 to stop bleeding.

If a small amount, less than a cup of blood, it may be due to a local nose problem or a general illness such as SYPHILIS, LEPROSY, TUBERCULOSIS, CUTANEOUS LEISHMANIASIS.[3] It may also be due to dry air or nose picking. If it is more than a cupful or the patient has abnormal bleeding elsewhere or is generally ill, see below; also see Protocol C-7: Liver/Spleen Problems.

Recently ill with a high fever: DENGUE FEVER, HEMORRHAGIC FEVER, TYPHUS, DIPHTHERIA, RELAPSING FEVER,[4] ARBOVIRAL FEVER (Sand fly fever), may be due to some poisons.

Ill for quite awhile or family history of ill health or no fever: First check all causes of LIVER FAILURE, both in the main *Disesase Index* and in the *Regional Index* for your area. See Protocol C-7. Also consider SCURVY,

---

[1] The treatment is to drown the insect with cooking oil. These creatures tend to get stuck in ear wax, which acts like fly paper. As they struggle to free themselves, legs and wings tend to hit against the ear drum, causing severe pain and loud (to the patient) noise. Once the creature is dead, the normal outward flow of the ear wax will remove him from the canal. Do not try to dig the insect out yourself, though a physician who knows what he is doing might be able to do so.

[2] Chaga's Disease: Found in scattered areas of Central and South America.

[3] Cutaneous Leishmaniasis: Scattered areas in the Americas, Africa, the Mediterranean, Europe, central Asia, the Middle East, and the Indian subcontinent.

[4] Relapsing Fever: Not in the islands of Southeast Asia or the Pacific.

VISCERAL LEISHMANIASIS,[1] SICKLE CELL DISEASE,[2] THALLASEMIA, TROPICAL SPLENOMEGALY, ONYALAI.[3]

***Sneezing*:** ALLERGY, MEASLES, may be due to any irritation of the nose by dust.

Loss of smell: This may occur for no reason at all or from a RESPIRATORY INFECTION or prior injury or surgery. Otherwise ZINC DEFICIENCY, ALLERGY, DIABETES, /// LEPROSY, BRAIN TUMOR, BRAIN DAMAGE, ENCEPHALITIS, some poisons.

Runny nose (watery): RESPIRATORY INFECTION (cold), ALLERGY, MEASLES, rarely head injury (serious if due to this; send out). If the patient is quite ill, possibly DIPHTHERIA. Common in SYPHILIS in infants, acquired before birth. Consider INSECTICIDE POISONING and PLANT POISONING.

***Runny nose (pus)*:** RESPIRATORY INFECTION (sinusitis); if very sick, consider MENINGITIS. Occasionally LEPROSY, CUTANEOUS LEISHMANIASIS.[4]

Low bridge of nose: May be a family trait; otherwise MONGOLISM, CRETINISM, THALLASEMIA. If acquired later in life, may be due to LEPROSY, YAWS, or SYPHILIS (congenital or tertiary).

Wormy creatures in the nose: MYIASIS, ASCARIASIS; may be a leech (see Vol. I, Chapter 9).

Bumpy or misshapen nose: LEPROSY, YAWS, ALCOHOLISM, family trait, middle age changes. SYPHILIS in those who were sexually active 10+ years ago, or in children born to syphilic mothers.

Ulcers or boils: SYPHILIS, YAWS, TREPONARID, MYCETOMA, LEPROSY, CUTANEOUS LEISHMANIASIS, CANCER, CANCRUM ORIS.

***Congestion/stuffy nose*:** RESPIRATORY INFECTION, ALLERGY, sometimes a drug side-effect or INSECTICIDE POISONING; rarely DIPHTHERIA if the patient is very ill.

PROTOCOL 29. MOUTH AND THROAT PROBLEMS

29 A. Sore Throat:

*Suspect **epiglottitis** (inflamed epiglottis) with sudden onset of a high fever and shortness of breath, or pain with swallowing or both.* Send the person out or call for help immediately!

Sore throat plus diarrhea should be treated like STREP THROAT but with ERYTHROMYCIN rather than PENICILLIN.

Symptomatic treatment: Gargling with salt water (a teaspoon in a glass) will remarkably relieve pain. Sometimes sitting up to sleep at night will help. ACETAMINOPHEN or IBUPROFEN is always appropriate; ASPIRIN may be appropriate in adults but should not be given until you have reached a diagnosis.

(Continued on next page.)

[1] Visceral Leishmaniasis: Found in scattered areas of Central and South America, Africa north of the equator, the Mediterranean area, the Indian subcontinent, eastern Europe, central Asia, and mainland China.

[2] Sickle Cell Disease: This affects Blacks of African genetic origin, mainly in Africa and the Americas. Some Indians and Arabs are also affected.

[3] Onyalai: Only in certain parts of southern Africa.

[4] Cutaneous Leishmaniasis: Scattered areas in the Americas, Africa, the Mediterranean, Europe, central Asia, the Middle East, and the Indian subcontinent.

(29 A. Sore Throat, continued.)

Problem	Fever	Other Characteristics
RESPIRATORY INFECTION	Low if any	Stuffy or runny nose or cough, gradual onset.
STREP THROAT	Yes	Big, red tonsils, big lymph nodes, no runny nose.
Passion fruit juice	No	Can cause chronic burning throat pain.
HIV INFECTION, Sero conversion	Probably	Flu-like illness, measles-type rash, exposure history.
===============		
MONONUCLEOSIS	Yes	Large tonsils, very tired, large neck lymph nodes.
TUBERCULOSIS	Usual	Pain with swallowing over months; night sweats.
LASSA FEVER[1]	Yes	Headache, cough, chest pain; very ill.
DIPHTHERIA	Low if any	Leathery scum on tonsils; patient very ill.
RABIES	Maybe	Painful spasms of throat; cannot swallow liquids.
ARSENIC POISONING	No	Abdominal pain, numb, tingling, weak.
DENGUE FEVER[2]	High	Also severe bone and joint pains.
MONKEYPOX[3]	Yes	Also a blistered rash that breaks out all at once.
PLANT POISONING	No	Botulism usually from sausage or tainted vegetables.
TREPONARID[4]	Maybe	Children; white patches on pink inside the mouth.
FAMILIAL MEDITER-RANEAN FEVER	Yes	Hereditary, recurrent, also abdominal or joint pains.
Leech	No	Visible leech in throat. (See Volume I, Chapter 9.)

29 B. Sore Mouth:

See protocol 29 C also.

Symptomatic treatment: ACETAMINOPHEN or IBUPROFEN is always appropriate; ASPIRIN may be appropriate in adults but should not be given until you have reached a diagnosis.

Problem	Fever	Other Characteristics
HERPES	Maybe	White blisters on red base, very tender.
APHTHOUS STOMATITIS	No	Painful ulcers, red around the edges.
MEASLES	High	White spots on red base, also cough and red eyes.
CANDIDIASIS	Unusual	White scum on the surfaces in the mouth.
SYPHILIS, secondary	Maybe	White, flat areas, not painful.
REITER SYNDROME	Usual	Painful or painless ulcers; also ARTHRITIS.
TUBERCULOSIS	Maybe	Painful small ulcer(s), tip or sides of the tongue.
DONOVANOSIS	Unusual	Swollen gums, losing teeth, had genital contact.
ARSENIC POISONING	No	Abdominal pain, diarrhea, numb, tingling, weak.
TYPHUS	High	Sores inside mouth; very ill.
SHINGLES	Maybe	Blister-type rash, right or left only.
FOOD POISONING	No	Botulism, from sausage or tainted vegetables.
MALABSORPTION	No	Mouth sensitive to spicy foods, maybe sores.
PLANT POISONING	No	Manicheel[5]; also swelling of face.
Leech	No	Visible leech in mouth. (See Volume I, Chapter 9.)

[1] Lassa Fever: Found in West Africa where it usually occurs in epidemics.

[2] Dengue Fever: In the Americas only near or north of the equator. In Africa only Nigeria and southern Africa. Prevalent in India, Southeast Asia, and the Pacific. Occasionally found in the Mediterranean area.

[3] Monkeypox: Found in northern D. R. Congo and adjacent areas of Central African Republic. It is rare in West Africa.

[4] Treponarid: Arid portions of Africa, Asia, the Middle East, and the Pacific area.

[5] Plant Poisoning, Manicheel: Present in the Americas only.

29 C. Other Mouth and Throat Problems:

29 C1. Throat:

Very large tonsils: Normal in preschoolers; if red, see Protocol 29 A.

Swelling of throat: ALLERGY, ANAPHYLAXIS, ANTHRAX, ABSCESS, DIPHTHERIA, TUBERCULOSIS.

Itchy throat: ALLERGY

Hoarseness: Usually occupational in persons who use their voices too much. Common with RESPIRATORY INFECTION (croup), LARYNGITIS. Also may be due to GOITER, THYROID TROUBLE, TUBERCULOSIS, LEPROSY, DIPHTHERIA, SYPHILIS in infants, PLANT POISONING due to botulism.

Whisper voice, soft voice: Patient either has a very sore throat, is near death, or is trying to act ill, though TUBERCULOSIS may occasionally cause this. Distinguish this from LARYNGITIS when a person chooses to whisper rather than talk in a hoarse voice or cause himself pain. May sometimes be due to GOITER, DIPHTHERIA, PLANT POISONING due to botulism, or CANCER.

29 C2. Tongue:

Lengthwise cracks on tongue: SYPHILIS (tertiary), TUBERCULOSIS, CANCER.

Abnormal tongue color:

- ***White patches:*** CANDIDIASIS.
- ***Pale:*** ANEMIA.
- ***Blue:*** RESPIRATORY FAILURE, some kinds of HEART FAILURE.
- ***Deep red:*** MALNUTRITION, PELLAGRA, SCARLET FEVER, ENTERIC FEVER during the third week, CARBON MONOXIDE POISONING.
- ***Brown:*** KIDNEY FAILURE, MEASLES during the beginning.
- ***Black, furry:*** Smokers and after a person takes some antibiotics.
- ***Gray-white, furry coating***: ENTERIC FEVER during the first week, TYPHUS, SCARLET FEVER, some other illnesses with fevers. This gradually clears from the edges and the tip, leaving the tongue red.
- ***Strawberry tongue (red and white):*** STREP THROAT.

Sore tongue: STREP THROAT, PELLAGRA, ALCOHOLISM, SPRUE, MALNUTRITION, MALABSORPTION, CANDIDIASIS, ANEMIA due to lack of IRON.

Tongue ulcers: Advanced TUBERCULOSIS (small, crater-like), REITER SYNDROME, some SEXUALLY TRANSMITTED DISEASEs.

Large tongue: ALLERGY, SCURVY, ANTHRAX, CRETINISM, MONGOLISM, ACROMEGALY.

Cannot stick out tongue: TYPHUS, sometimes CANCER or an ABSCESS under the tongue.

Black on tongue and inside the mouth: may be normal with dark skin or due to PLANT POISONING: Betel nut. Also ANEMIA, or antibiotic side-effect. If very ill, tongue dry and black, consider TYPHUS.

29 C3. Mouth:

Thirst: DEHYDRATION, DIABETES, BRUCELLOSIS, PLANT POISONING: Botulism, Coral Plant,[1] Jimson Weed, side effect of some drugs.

Dark pigmented patches on pink surfaces: Normal in Blacks.

Strange taste in the mouth: RESPIRATORY INFECTION (sinusitis), DENGUE FEVER, ARSENIC POISONING, LEAD POISONING, HEARTBURN, pregnancy, side-effect of some medications.

Cannot taste: check ZINC DEFICIENCY, LEPROSY, PELLAGRA. Check if the problem is really with the sense of smell.

Rash in mouth: HERPES, MEASLES, SHINGLES, CHICKEN POX, LEPTOSPIROSIS, SYPHILIS, YAWS,[2] DIPHTHERIA, CANDIDIASIS, CARBON MONOXIDE POISONING, PELLAGRA, LASSA FEVER (Africa).

Hole in the roof of the mouth: Birth defect, YAWS, SYPHILIS (tertiary), CANCRUM ORIS, CANCER.

Painless ulcers: REITER SYNDROME, SYPHILIS, DONOVANOSIS, CANCER, other causes.

Foul breath: HALITOSIS, RHINITIS, RESPIRATORY INFECTION, CANCER, DONOVANOSIS.

Slurred speech, no fever: ALCOHOL effect, other drug side-effects, head injury, snake bite, ALTITUDE SICKNESS, STROKE, AFRICAN SLEEPING SICKNESS,[3] PLANT POISONING: Cassava or Lolism,[4] SYPHI-

---

[1] Plant Poisoning, Coral Plant: African and Middle Eastern areas.

[2] Yaws: In humid tropics only.

[3] African Sleeping Sickness: Scattered areas of Africa, south of Bamako, Mali and Lake Chad and north of Lusaka, Zambia.

[4] Plant Poisoning, Lolism: Found in the African, Mediterranean, and Middle Eastern areas.

LIS, tertiary, BRAIN DAMAGE, ADDICTION to downers, PLANT POISONING due to botulism, any severe weakness.

Slurred speech with a fever: DENGUE FEVER, cerebral MALARIA, TYPHUS, AFRICAN SLEEPING SICKNESS, RHEUMATIC FEVER, DIPHTHERIA, rarely due to PLAGUE.

Difficulty chewing: DIPHTHERIA, any mouth or tooth pain.

Excessive saliva: TETANUS, PLANT POISONING: Nicotine, Muscarine; INSECTICIDE POISONING, ADDICTION (narcotic withdrawal), PELLAGRA.

Worm crawling up into the mouth: ASCARIASIS.

29 C4. Lips:

Chapped lips: May be due to vitamin deficiency. Try taking multivitamin tablets.

Vertical cracks: SPRUE, MALNUTRITION, overdose of VITAMIN A.

Horizontal cracks: CANDIDIASIS, SYPHILIS, TREPONARID, YAWS, vitamin deficiency.

Rash on lip: DIPHTHERIA, IMPETIGO, HERPES, vitamin deficiency.

Blue around lips: RESPIRATORY FAILURE, HEART FAILURE, ANAPHYLAXIS, ALTITUDE SICKNESS.

Black and red around lips: PLANT POISONING due to Betel nut.

Splits on sides of lips: SYPHILIS, YAWS, TREPONARID, PELLAGRA, vitamin deficiency.

Sore on lip: Consider SEXUALLY TRANSMITTED DISEASE; TREPONARID (arid areas); DIPHTHERIA; HERPES; IMPETIGO.

29 C5. Teeth:

Toothache alone, upper teeth, no redness or swelling: Check for RESPIRATORY INFECTION (sinusitis). Molar pain may be due to EAR INFECTION, middle.

Toothache with redness and swelling: Use PENICILLIN or ERYTHROMYCIN for any tooth but the last molars. For the last molars, use METRONIDAZOLE. It may be necessary to pull the tooth.

Teeth falling out: Poor dental hygiene, SCURVY, DONOVANOSIS.

Malformed teeth: CRETINISM; SYPHILIS (two front upper permanent teeth); THALLASEMIA, family trait.

Delayed teething: RICKETS, HIV INFECTION.

Bleeding gums: Mouth infection (gram positive), SCURVY, poor dental hygiene, HEMORRHAGIC FEVER, VISCERAL LEISHMANIASIS,[1] LIVER FAILURE of any kind, ARSENIC POISONING, LEAD POISONING, DONOVANOSIS.

Green teeth: Late consequence of JAUNDICE in a newborn.

Swollen gums: PHENYTOIN (drug), SCURVY, SYPHILIS, tooth ABSCESS, DONOVANOSIS.

Dark discoloration of teeth: Side-effect of childhood or prenatal TETRACYCLINE (drug); FLUOROSIS.

Blue line on gums: LEAD POISONING.

29 C6. Jaw:

Swollen jaw: MUMPS, ABSCESS in a tooth, injury, BURKITT LYMPHOMA, jaw bone OSTEOMYELITIS, CANCER.

Cannot open mouth: face injury (see Volume I, Chapter 9), TETANUS if there are muscle spasms, tooth problem.

Cannot close mouth: If the jaw locks in the open position, see Volume I, Chapter 12.

Difficulty chewing: DIPHTHERIA, BRUCELLOSIS, TRICHINOSIS, not enough teeth.

Jaw pain: Dental problem, GALLBLADDER DISEASE, HEART ATTACK, HEART FAILURE. Jaw pain can be caused by jaw problems but also by disease elsewhere in the body. The nerves are wired up so that disease in one area can cause pain in another area. This is called referred pain. In the case of the jaw pain, the heart and the gallbladder are the two structures most commonly responsible for referred pain.

[1] Visceral Leishmaniasis: Found in scattered areas of Central and South America, Africa north of the equator, the Mediterranean area, the Indian subcontinent, eastern Europe, central Asia, and mainland China.

V. NECK PROBLEMS

PROTOCOL 30. NECK PAIN

30 A. Pain With Forward Motion Only
30 B. Pain With Motion Sideways
30 C. Pain Confined to One or Two Areas of the Neck
30 D. Pain With Swallowing

For pain that is the result of injury, see Neck Injury in Chapter 4 of Volume I for major injuries, or Chapter 12 of Volume I for minor injuries.

30 A. Pain With Forward Motion Only:

Definition: The patient cannot put his chin on his chest, but he can turn his head from side to side and he can look up toward the sky.

Problem	Fever	Other Characteristics
MALARIA, cerebral	High	Usually history of recent malaria.
MENINGITIS	High	Headache (adults), vomiting (children), very ill (both).
================		
STROKE	No	Sudden onset of severe headache initially.
POLIO	Yes	Muscle spasms, back pains also, weak limb(s).
ENCEPHALITIS	Usual	Similar to MENINGITIS; epidemics.
RABIES	Varies	Spasms with swallowing liquids or a breeze.
SPOTTED FEVER[1]	Yes	Severe muscle aching; rash by day 4 or 5.

30 B. Pain With Motion Sideways (maybe forward/backward also):

Symptomatic treatment: ACETAMINOPHEN or IBUPROFEN is always appropriate; ASPIRIN may be appropriate in adults but should not be given until you have reached a diagnosis.

Problem	Fever	Other Characteristics
MUSCLE STRAIN	No	History of unusual exercise or a minor accident.
TORTICOLLIS	No	Not ill, head tilted sideways, sudden onset, no injury.
ARTHRITIS	Maybe	Back of neck, warm and tender; maybe other joints also.
TUBERCULOSIS	Maybe	Pain with turning head sideways; neck bones may stick out.
==============		
BRUCELLOSIS	Off & on	Joint pains or back pains; fatigue; slow onset.
TETANUS	Unusual	All muscles very tight and visible; cannot relax.
SLIPPED DISC	No	Pain also on the thumb or little finger side of the hand.[2]

30 C. Pain Confined to One or Two Areas of the Neck:

Symptomatic treatment: ACETAMINOPHEN or IBUPROFEN is always appropriate; ASPIRIN may be appropriate in adults but should not be given until you have reached a diagnosis.

Problem	Fever	Other Characteristics
STRESS	No	Headache in back of the head or in a band around.
==============		
LEPROSY	Rare	Pains along nerves which may be swollen and tender.
ANGINA	No	Pressure-type pain also in chest and/or left arm and/or jaw.
OSTEOMYELITIS	Yes	Pain in the bones in back of the neck with tenderness also.

[1] Spotted Fever: Not in the islands of Southeast Asia.
[2] Pain that affects all fingers equally is not likely due to slipped disc.

30 D. Pain or Difficulty Swallowing:

Definition: Either the patient complains of pain with swallowing OR he says that his food gets stuck (usually temporarily) somewhere between his throat and stomach. He may have both pain and a sticking sensation.

The most common cause is something swallowed that got stuck or scratched the patient on its way down. Have the patient sit up for 24 hours and give him generous doses of crushed or injectable pain medication and tranquilizer. Send out if the problem persists after 24 hours. If this is due to a throat problem, see Protocol 29. If leeches are common in your area, consider a leech swallowed with drinking water. See Vol. I, Chapter 9.

Level refers to where the patient thinks the problem is. H is high, above the collar bones; M is medium, between the collar bones and the middle of the breast bone; L is low, below the middle of the breast bone; A is anywhere. Patients can usually localize the problem accurately.

Symptomatic treatment: ACETAMINOPHEN or IBUPROFEN is always appropriate; ASPIRIN may be appropriate in adults but should not be given until you have reached a diagnosis.

Problem	**Fever**	**Level**	**Other Characteristics**
With pain:			
PERICARDITIS	Maybe	L	Pain worse lying down, relieved by sitting.
CANDIDIASIS	No	A	White scum visible in the mouth.
HERPES	Maybe	H	Blisters in the mouth or around the mouth.
HIV INFECTION	Usual	A	Frequently associated with CANDIDIASIS or HERPES.
==============			
RABIES	Maybe	H	Rapid onset; liquids are a problem before solids.[1]
TRICHINOSIS	Yes	A	Ate raw or rare pork or game within the past month.
Maybe pain:			
CANCER	Maybe	A	Slow-onset; painless at first.
POLIO	Usual	A	Other weakness after an initial "cold" or "flu".
DIPHTHERIA	Maybe	A	Also other weakness; sore throat or wound infection.
PELLAGRA	No	?	Rough skin rash, behavior change, diarrhea, or all three.
ANTHRAX	Yes	A	Sore with a black scab; large amount of swelling.
Without pain:			
GOITER	No	H	Choking sensation lower front neck.
TUBERCULOSIS	Maybe	A	Usually a cough, weight loss, night sweats, or large neck lymph nodes.
TROPICAL SPLENOMEGALY	Unusual	L	Huge spleen; malarious area.
STROKE	No	A	Sudden or stuttering onset, other weakness.
BRAIN DAMAGE	Unusual	A	Mental changes, other weakness or sensory changes.
==============			
PLANT POISONING (Botulism)	No	A	Other weakness also, from tainted food.
LIVER FAILURE	Maybe	L	Also swollen belly with big veins on the skin.
CHAGA'S DISEASE[2]	No	A	Also constipation, maybe HEART FAILURE.

[1] Liquids are always a problem before solids. With every other cause of difficulty swallowing, solids are a problem first.

[2] Chaga's Disease: Only in scattered areas in the Americas.

PROTOCOL 31. OTHER NECK PROBLEMS

31 A. Swollen neck
31 B. Miscellaneous Neck Problems

31 A. Swollen Neck:

Is the swelling mainly lower center front, right above the breastbone?

NO — continue below.

YES — **Consider:** GOITER—there may be one or multiple swellings.

Is the swelling over a single area or is it discreet, multiple lump(s)?

Discreet lumps[1] — continue below.

Over an area — **Consider**: GOITER, ANTHRAX, MUMPS

Is the swelling visible only from the back, or from the front (also or only)?

Visible from the front: — continue below.

Visible only from the back: — **Consider**: AFRICAN SLEEPING SICKNESS,[2] LICE (head lice), RUBELLA, EAR INFECTION, IMPETIGO of the scalp, another scalp infection, MONONUCLEOSIS, SYPHILIS, CANCER

Is the throat obviously abnormal — swollen tonsils with gray or white scum on them?

NO — continue below.

YES — **Consider**: STREP THROAT, DIPHTHERIA, MONONUCLEOSIS

Has the patient had ear pain or pus coming out of his ear?

NO — **Consider**: TUBERCULOSIS, MUMPS, HIV INFECTION, CANCER

YES — **Consider**: EAR INFECTION, Tooth ABSCESS.[3]

Also consider the alternatives below:

Problem	Other large nodes[4]	Other symptoms
With Fever:		
TOXOPLASMOSIS	Maybe	Extreme fatigue, large spleen, fever.
RHEUMATIC FEVER	Maybe	Heart murmur, joint pains, or both.
HIV INFECTION, Sero conversion	Maybe	Exposure within 4 weeks, flu-like illness.
LEPROSY reaction	Yes	Patient taking medication for leprosy; fever.
PLAGUE	Maybe	Extremely tender nodes with blackened skin.
TULAREMIA[5]	Maybe	Flu-like illness; rodent or rabbit contact.

Continued on next page.

[1] Continue this protocol but also consult Protocol C-12 which details the causes of large lymph nodes in the neck and elsewhere.

[2] African Sleeping Sickness: Scattered areas of Africa, south of Bamako, Mali and Lake Chad; north of Lusaka, Zambia.

[3] There will not be pus from the ear, but if the tooth is a molar, the patient likely had ear pain.

[4] These may be found in the armpits, in the groins (leg creases), on the side of the elbows, and behind the knees.

[5] Tularemia: Temperate climates, people exposed to small animals or their insects.

(31 A. Swollen Neck, continued.)

Problem	Other large nodes[1]	Other symptoms
With Fever:		
MONKEYPOX[2]	Yes	Dense, blister-type rash; patient very ill.
SCRUB TYPHUS[3]	Usual	Also eye pain in light, fever, constipation.
BARTONELLOSIS[4]	Maybe	Also fever and joint pains.
Maybe Fever:		
CELLULITIS	No	Red or warm area of skin, head or neck.
HERPES	Maybe	Blistered or rough area of skin, head or neck.
No Fever:		
SCURVY	No	Bleeding gums; diet without fresh fruit.
CHAGA'S DISEASE[5]	Maybe	Usually swelling of one eye also.
COCCIDIOMYCOSIS[6]	Maybe	Also cough, chest pain, and fevers.
SYPHILIS	Yes	Infant or sexually active adult.

31 B. Miscellaneous Neck Problems:

Weakness: Anything that can cause upper limb weakness can also cause neck weakness; see Protocols 8 B and 8 C.

Difficulty swallowing: See Protocol 30 D.

Stiffness: Old age, previous injury, or some types of ARTHRITIS. If there is pain: see Protocol 30 A or B.

Neck arched back: See Protocol 30 A.

Swelling center front lower neck: probably GOITER or ABSCESS; rarely ANTHRAX, CANCER.

VI. UPPER LIMB PROBLEMS

PROTOCOL 32. SHOULDER PROBLEMS

32 A. Shoulder Pain
32 B. Other Shoulder Problems

Emergency conditions:

Shoulder pain after an injury to the left lower chest or upper abdomen may indicate a spleen injury which needs surgical attention.

Shoulder pain with sweating, chest pain, arm pain, and jaw pain may indicate a HEART ATTACK.

In the presence of abdominal pain, consider ACUTE ABDOMEN.

Injury: See Volume I, Chapter 12. Neck injury can cause shoulder pain. Hand and arm problems (illness or injury) can also cause shoulder pain; the listing for hand and arm pain is more complete.

Skin problems: Treat like skin problems elsewhere.

Abdominal pain also: Be aware that upper abdominal problems will manifest with shoulder pain. This is called referred pain. In this case the pain in the shoulder(s) will not increase with pushing on the painful shoulder area. The shoulder pain will likely increase with your pushing on the abdomen.

---

[1] These may be found in the armpits, in the groins (leg creases), on the side of the elbows, and behind the knees.

[2] Monkeypox: Northern D. R. Congo and adjacent border area in Central African Republic; rarely West Africa.

[3] Scrub Typhus: In the Indian subcontinent, Southeast and Central Asia, East Asia, and the Pacific area. Reportedly scrub typhus in Burma can cause huge lymph nodes so the entire neck is twice its normal diameter and the condition looks like the bull neck of DIPHTHERIA.

[4] Bartonellosis: Occurs only in Peru and adjacent border areas.

[5] Chaga's Disease: Only in scattered areas in the Americas.

[6] Coccidiomycosis: In the arid areas of Central and South America.

32 A. Shoulder Pain:

Symptomatic treatment: ACETAMINOPHEN or IBUPROFEN is always appropriate; ASPIRIN may be appropriate for adults but should not be given until you have reached a diagnosis.

Fevers and aching across shoulders in back:[1] MALARIA (left or both sides), AMEBIC LIVER (right side usually); any injured or rapidly enlarging spleen (left side only).

With movement mainly, but it also hurts when the patient relaxes his shoulders and you move them:

Without fever: SICKLE CELL DISEASE,[2] MUSCLE STRAIN, ARTHRITIS,

With fever: DENGUE FEVER,[3] RHEUMATIC FEVER, BRUCELLOSIS, OSTEOMYELITIS, BARTONELLOSIS;[4] sometimes ARTHRITIS, SICKLE CELL DISEASE, FAMILIAL MEDITERRANEAN FEVER.

One point very tender: BURSITIS.

Breathing aggravates pain: PNEUMONIA, TUBERCULOSIS, AMEBIC LIVER DISEASE, GALLBLADDER DISEASE; may be due to excessive gas (Protocol 49).

Abdominal pain present also and related to shoulder pain: Consider AMEBIC LIVER DISEASE or GALLBLADDER DISEASE on the right; consider ACUTE ABDOMEN, DENGUE FEVER, INFLUENZA, TUBAL PREGNANCY with either shoulder or both shoulders. May be due to excessive gas (Protocol 49).

Any exercise (even leg exercise) aggravates the pain but it is relieved by rest: ANGINA, SYPHILIS (tertiary), RHEUMATIC FEVER, HEART FAILURE from any cause.

Pain in a band that comes from the neck in back and goes down the arm: SHINGLES, ARTHRITIS of the spine, SLIPPED DISC, any minor injury to the neck, BRUCELLOSIS, LEPROSY, or TUBERCULOSIS of the spine, rarely FLUOROSIS, CANCER.

Muscle pains in shoulders: MUSCLE STRAIN, TRICHINOSIS, CYSTICERCOSIS. See Protocol 10 C.

32 B. Other Shoulder Problems:

One shoulder higher than the other: SCOLIOSIS.

Large lymph nodes in arm pits: FILARIASIS, SYPHILIS, CELLULITIS, ABSCESS, RHEUMATIC FEVER, LEPROSY reaction, TYPHUS, ENTERIC FEVER, ANTHRAX, TUBERCULOSIS, (rarely PLAGUE). See Protocol 34 B. Also See Protocol C-12 which deals with large lymph nodes generally.

Weak shoulders: TUBERCULOSIS of the neck bones; HIV INFECTION; PLANT POISONING: Botulism; THYROID TROUBLE; anything that can cause weak arms; see Protocols 8 B and 8 C.

Stiff shoulders: ARTHRITIS; also check similar diseases.

---

[1] Shoulders sometimes hurt, not because of a shoulder problem but because of a problem elsewhere in the body. The nerves are wired up so that pain in one part of the body is felt in another part. This is called referred pain. In the case of pain in the shoulders, the heart, the liver, the spleen, the gallbladder, the lower parts of the lungs, and the diaphragms are likely to cause referred pain.

[2] Sickle Cell Disease: This affects Blacks of African genetic origin, mainly in Africa and the Americas. Some Indians and Arabs are also affected.

[3] Dengue Fever: In the Americas only near or north of the equator. In Africa only Nigeria and southern Africa. Prevalent in India, Southeast Asia, and the Pacific. Occasionally found in the Mediterranean area.

[4] Bartonellosis: Occurs only in Peru and adjacent border areas.

PROTOCOL 33. ARM AND HAND PAIN

33 A. Muscular, Crampy Pains
33 B. Neuritis in Arms or Hands
33 C. Bone and Joint Pains
33 D. Other Kinds of Pains

Emergency conditions:

- The patient's arm is painful, pale, has numbness and tingling, feels cold, is weak, and you cannot find a pulse in it, or any three of these, he must be sent out immediately or he may lose the limb.
- Pain of sudden onset associated with chest pain, sweating, vomiting, and/or abnormal vital signs may be due to HEART ATTACK; send the patient out.

If the patient injured his head or neck, see Head And Neck Injury, either in Chapter 4 of Volume I if the injury is major, or in Chapter 12 if it is minor. If pain is due to an arm or hand injury, see Injury Section, Chapter 12 of Volume I. Treat skin problems like skin problems elsewhere. See Wound Infection section in Chapter 10 of Volume I if applicable.

33 A. Muscular, Crampy Pains

See Protocol 10 C for general aching if the patient has general body pain; or Protocol 33 D for aching that is not due to muscle cramps. See Protocol C-2 if the pain is part of an illness with fever, headache, and general body pains.

Symptomatic treatment: ACETAMINOPHEN or IBUPROFEN is always appropriate; ASPIRIN may be appropriate in adults but should not be given until you have reached a diagnosis.

Problem	**Characteristics**
MUSCLE STRAIN	Tight, aching pain, usually after unaccustomed exercise.
FILARIASIS[1]	Episodes of fever and swelling; large lymph nodes.
===============	
POLIO	Also fevers; limb weakness develops during and after aching.
CHOLERA	Muscle cramps after severe, watery diarrhea.
GANGRENE	Black or white, dead-looking, cool skin; swelling; maybe blisters.
TRICHINOSIS	Also muscle swelling; the patient looks muscular.

33 B. Neuritis in Arms or Hands:

Definition: Neuritis is nerve inflammation, causing pain that is usually sharp and shooting, though it may be burning or aching. It moves from the neck or shoulder to the arm or hand, usually either on the thumb side or little finger side. It may be accompanied by muscle cramps, weakness, numbness, or any combination of these. This may be caused by injury; see Volume I, Chapters 4 and 11-13. If it is the result of a neck problem, then there will also be pain and stiffness in the neck..

Symptomatic treatment: ACETAMINOPHEN or IBUPROFEN is always appropriate; ASPIRIN may be appropriate in adults but should not be given until you have reached a diagnosis.

Is the patient taking medication for TUBERCULOSIS, or eating a poor diet or both?

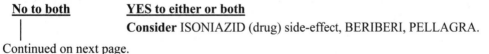

No to both	**YES to either or both**
|	**Consider** ISONIAZID (drug) side-effect, BERIBERI, PELLAGRA.

Continued on next page.

[1] Filariasis is not present everywhere; check the *Regional Notes* for your area.

(33 B. Neuritis in Arms or Hands, continued.)

Does the patient have a fever or is he very ill or both?

NO | **YES**

Consider BRUCELLOSIS, DENGUE FEVER,[1] RABIES, TUBERCULOSIS.

Consider alternatives	Characteristics
CARPAL TUNNEL SYNDROME	Numbness, tingling starts in dominant hand, from repetitive motion, middle age or older.
SYPHILIS, tertiary	10+ years after sexual contact or born of a syphilic mother.
ARSENIC POISONING	Also weakness; vocational exposure or ethnic medicine.
LEPROSY	Also skin changes: color change or rough, scaly area or bumps.
SLIPPED DISC	Usually only right or left or worse on one side; weakness common.
BRUCELLOSIS	Off-and-on fevers, fatigue, other joint or low back pains.
LOIASIS[2]	Swollen areas on arm or shoulder.

33 C. Bone and Joint Pains:

Definition: There is a deep, throbbing pain that is worse at night. It is also worse with movement regardless of whether the patient himself moves or if someone else moves the limb for him.

Symptomatic treatment: ACETAMINOPHEN or IBUPROFEN is always appropriate; ASPIRIN may be appropriate but should not be given until you have reached a diagnosis.

Has the patient had an injury?

NO | **YES**

Go to the injury section, Chapters 11-13, Volume I.

Is the problem brittle bones that break easily?

NO | **YES**

Consider SYPHILIS, THALLASEMIA, HYDATID DISEASE,[3] old age, paralysis.

Does the problem run in a family, or does it involve ANEMIA, or both?

NO to both | **YES to either or both**

Consider THALLASEMIA, SICKLE CELL DISEASE,[4] BARTONELLOSIS,[5] FAMILIAL MEDITERRANEAN FEVER.

Are one or more joints visibly red or hot, and swollen?

NO | **YES**

Consider ARTHRITIS, HIV INFECTION, RHEUMATIC FEVER, ARBOVIRAL FEVER, SICKLE CELL DISEASE, OSTEOMYELITIS, LYME DISEASE.

Continued on next page.

[1] Dengue Fever: In the Americas only near or north of the equator. In Africa only Nigeria and southern Africa. Prevalent in India, Southeast Asia, and the Pacific. Occasionally found in the Mediterranean area.

[2] Loiasis: Humid, rural central and western Africa only.

[3] Hydatid Disease: There are two kinds: one is in cattle-raising areas of the tropics where there are dogs that live close to people. The other kind is in temperate, rural areas where there are wild animals and people eat gathered, wild plant life that might be contaminated with the stool of animals.

[4] Sickle Cell Disease: This affects Blacks of African genetic origin, mainly in Africa and the Americas. Some Indians and Arabs are also affected.

[5] Bartonellosis: Only in Peru and adjacent border areas.

(33 C. Bone and Joint Pains, continued.)

Did the pains start with a feverish illness?

NO

YES

Consider:

A. Diseases listed in Protocol C-6 if there is swelling

B. Diseases listed below if there is no swelling

HEPATITIS: Joint pains, aching, loss of appetite, fatigue.

DENGUE FEVER[1]: Sudden onset severe bone/joint pains, a rash.

RELAPSING FEVER[2]: Shaking chills, severe headache.

YELLOW FEVER[3]: Not immunized; protein or bilirubin in urine.

RUBELLA: Red, spotted rash by day 3 of the ILLNESS;

ARBOVIRAL FEVER: other similar patients.

Consider alternatives	Characteristics
HEPATITIS	Recent onset; nausea or general itching also.
FILARIASIS	Community where some adults have very swollen limb(s).
================	
SYPHILIS	Joints swollen, pain worse with heat, child usually.
BARTONELLOSIS[4]	Skin bumps, especially on the non-hairy areas of the limbs.
MANSONELLOSIS PERSTANS[5]	Slow onset general bone and joint pains, maybe short of breath.

33 D. Other Kinds of Pains:

Symptomatic treatment: ACETAMINOPHEN or IBUPROFEN is always appropriate; ASPIRIN may be appropriate in adults but should not be given until you have reached a diagnosis.

Does the patient eat a very poor or unbalanced diet?

NO

YES

Consider PELLAGRA, BERIBERI, MALNUTRITION

Consider alternatives	Characteristics
HIV INFECTION	Pain in the area normally covered by gloves.
LYME DISEASE	Glove-type pains; usually ARTHRITIS also.
ARSENIC POISONING	Burning pain in palms; also abdominal pains.
ANGINA	Aching pain, maybe with chest or jaw pain; due to a heart problem.
PLANT POISONING	Claviceps or Ergot; similar to ANGINA; may cause GANGRENE.
GANGRENE	Limb(s) cool, skin darkened, cannot move the hand(s) well.
TYPHUS	Aching pain with fevers; may cause GANGRENE.
BRUCELLOSIS	Joint pains or backache or general aching with fevers.

[1] Dengue Fever: In the Americas only near or north of the equator. In Africa only Nigeria and southern Africa. Prevalent in India, Southeast Asia, and the Pacific. Occasionally found in the Mediterranean area.

[2] Relapsing Fever: Not in the islands of Southeast Asia or the Pacific.

[3] Yellow Fever: South America north of Sao Paolo, central and western Africa and the Sudan.

[4] Bartonellosis: Scattered areas in Peru and adjacent border areas.

[5] Mansonellosis Perstans: Parts of Africa (west and central) and South America (northern Argentina and north of there).

PROTOCOL 34. OTHER ARM AND HAND PROBLEMS

34 A. Abnormal Shape of Hands or Arms
34 B. Swelling - Arms, Hands, Fingers
34 C. Fingernail Problems
34 D. Abnormal Feeling and Function, Arms and Hands
34 E. Other Abnormal Appearance - Hands and Fingers

34 A. Abnormal Shape of Hands or Arms:

Broad hands with very short fingers: CRETINISM, MONGOLISM, may run in some families in persons otherwise normal.

Hand like a claw: Injury to shoulder, arm, or neck; may be due to LEPROSY or BRAIN DAMAGE.

Wrist bent, cannot straighten: LEPROSY; injury to shoulder, arm, or neck; BRAIN DAMAGE.

Crooked limbs: long-standing ARTHRITIS, old injury, birth defect, TREPONARID, SYPHILIS.

Missing limbs: old injury, birth defect, OSTEOMYELITIS,[1] LEPROSY.

Hands cramped: HYPERVENTILATION, injury.

34 B. Swelling of Arms, Hands, and Fingers:

Symptomatic treatment: Try putting cold packs or cool cloths on the hands or arms to decrease the swelling, but not if the patient has GANGRENE or snakebite. It is also good to raise the swollen part above the level of the heart, to encourage the fluid to drain out of the limb.

See Protocol C-6 for help in distinguishing the various causes of limb swelling.

Muscle swelling and soreness: CELLULITIS, ABSCESS TRICHINOSIS, CYSTICERCOSIS, PYOMYOSITIS.

Swelling generally: Injury or infection closer to the shoulder, SICKLE CELL DISEASE,[2] KIDNEY FAILURE, LEPROSY reaction, LOIASIS,[3] FILARIASIS, GANGRENE, ARSENIC POISONING, RAT BITE FEVER, MALNUTRITION, LARVA MIGRANS.

Swelling with thickened, roughened skin: FILARIASIS.

Swollen joints: ARTHRITIS, RICKETS, ARBOVIRAL FEVER, SICKLE CELL DISEASE, RHEUMATIC FEVER.

Swelling of all fingers in a child: SICKLE CELL DISEASE, (painful but not red or hot, maybe toes also), SYPHILIS (painful, may also involve long bones); TUBERCULOSIS (painless, does not involve the toes)

Swollen lymph nodes by elbows or armpits: CELLULITIS, ABSCESS, HIV INFECTION, FILARIASIS, ENTERIC FEVER, TUBERCULOSIS, /// TYPHUS, AFRICAN SLEEPING SICKNESS,[4] LEPROSY reaction, ANTHRAX, rarely TULAREMIA,[5] RAT BITE FEVER, PLAGUE, CANCER, BARTONELLOSIS.[6]

Swollen finger tips:

Severe: HEART FAILURE, TRICHURIASIS, CANCER, SEPSIS, RESPIRATORY INFECTION that has lasted for a long time, PARAGONIMIASIS,[7] FELON.

Mild: early in the course of one of the diseases above; also consider LIVER FAILURE, LIVER DISEASE, or various causes of diarrhea or DYSENTERY.

Slow-growing, hard, tender swellings in hands: TUBERCULOSIS (Africa only).

---

[1] This is a bone infection which may cause a limb to fall off.

[2] Sickle Cell Disease: This affects Blacks of African genetic origin, mainly in Africa and the Americas. Some Indians and Arabs are also affected.

[3] Loiasis: Humid, rural west and central Africa.

[4] African Sleeping Sickness: Scattered areas of Africa, south of Bamako, Mali and Lake Chad and north of Lusaka, Zambia.

[5] Tularemia: North America, central Asia, Europe, Far East, the north coast of Africa; exposure to small animals flu-like symptoms and fevers.

[6] Bartonellosis: Occurs only in Peru and adjacent border areas.

[7] Paragonimiasis: Occurs in parts of Asia and the Pacific area, rarely in Africa, India, and the Americas.

34 C. Fingernail Problems:

Fingernail appearance:

Totally white: ANEMIA.

Dark stripes or patches: Normal with dark skin.

Scooped out: In infants, ANEMIA due to iron deficiency; maybe RHEUMATIC FEVER.

Yellow: With large lymph nodes in the armpits, the fingernails may turn yellow before swelling of the arm occurs. Most common in FILARIASIS. Also due to smoking.

Shaped like an upside down saucer: See swollen fingertips, Protocol 34 B.

3/4 white, pink tips: LIVER FAILURE, CIRRHOSIS, LIVER DISEASE.

Have little bits of blood beneath: Usually due to injury; otherwise SEPSIS, TRICHINOSIS, HEMORRHAGIC FEVER, HEART FAILURE due to bad valves.

White horizontal lines: Prior illness, ARSENIC POISONING.

34 D. Abnormal Feeling and Function, Arms and Hands:

Numbness and tingling or weakness or paralysis: See Protocols 8 and 10.

Itching palms: ALLERGY; maybe FOOD POISONING due to fish in the Pacific area.

Abnormal joint motion: SYPHILIS, sometimes due to heredity.

Brittle bones, break easily: Old age, paralyzed limbs, SYPHILIS in infants, THALLASEMIA, maybe birth defect.

Stiff limbs:[1] ARTHRITIS, CRETINISM, PLANT POISONING due to Cassava, TROPICAL SPASTIC PARAPARESIS, LEPROSY, any paralysis that has lasted for long.

Spasms or cramps:[2] HYPERVENTILATION (see the illustration in Volume I, Chapter 4), any severe diarrhea, any head or neck injury, POLIO, TETANUS, TROPICAL SPASTIC PARAPARESIS, RABIES (rare).

Weakness: Any disease that can cause neuritis-type pain (Protocol 33 B); PLANT POISONING: Botulism, Ginger-jake; Snake bite; TICK PARALYSIS, ARSENIC POISONING; STROKE; DIPHTHERIA, CARPAL TUNNEL SYNDROME; sometimes side-effects of drugs; diseases listed in Protocol 8; pain in the hands and arms will cause the patient to refuse to use them and appear to be weakness.

Trembling or uncoordination: See Protocol 7 C, D, or E; also consider causes of weakness as listed above. If some muscles are weak, then the patient will be uncoordinated.

Hands very cold: Exposure to cold, GANGRENE, FROSTBITE, prior injury, SHOCK, TYPHUS.

34 E: Other Abnormal Appearance - Hands and Fingers:

Fingers rotting: CANCRUM ORIS, GANGRENE, OSTEOMYELITIS, SPOTTED FEVER.[3]

"Split peas" by finger joints: RHEUMATIC FEVER, TUBERCULOSIS, TREPONARID, YAWS.

Dark palm creases: ANEMIA, some kinds.

Dark patches of skin on the palms: Normal in Blacks.

Pale, cool fingers: PLANT POISONING: Claviceps or Atriplicism,[4] GANGRENE, TYPHUS.

Peeling skin of palms: SYPHILIS in infants, ECZEMA, sometimes TYPHUS; see Protocol A-15.

---

[1] *Stiff limbs* implies that the person has been this way for at least two months.

[2] *Spasms or cramps* implies that the problem has been of more recent onset, less than the past 2 months. In the case of hyperventilation (and perhaps diarrhea) the onset is over the past hour.

[3] Particularly Queensland Tick Typhus, listed under SPOTTED FEVER, not separately.

[4] Plant Poisoning, Atriplicism: Occurs among the Chinese in the Far East.

VII. CHEST PROBLEMS

PROTOCOL 35. CHEST PAIN

35 A. Heavy or Burning Pain in Chest
35 B. Sharp, Pleuritic Chest Pain
35 C. Chest Pain With Swallowing
35 D. Chest Wall Pain
35 E. Breast Pain

See Chapter 4 of Volume I if pain is due to an accident. If the patient is having abdominal pain or tenderness or both, see Protocol 39; the chest pain may be referred pain from the abdomen.

35 A. Heavy or Burning Pain in Chest:

Definition: Chest pain that is heavy, burning, or aching, frequently also felt in the jaw, the shoulder, or the arm, frequently accompanied by paleness and sweating. It is usually made worse with exercise, sometimes helped with rest. It is not aggravated by deep breathing or coughing or pushing on the chest wall. It is felt mainly in the front of the chest rather than the sides or back.

Symptomatic treatment: Try an ANTACID such as Maalox; if this relieves the pain, it is more likely due to a stomach than a heart problem.

Is the patient also short of breath, more so lying than sitting?

NO

YES
Consider ANGINA, HEART ATTACK, HEART FAILURE, ALTITUDE SICKNESS, SYPHILIS, tertiary; RHEUMATIC FEVER, PULMONARY EMBOLISM, CHAGA'S DISEASE.[1]

Did extreme fatigue begin with the chest pain?

NO

YES
Consider HEART FAILURE, RHEUMATIC FEVER, PERICARDITIS, LASSA FEVER.[2]

Was or is the chest pain associated with a high fever?

NO

YES
Consider RHEUMATIC FEVER, LASSA FEVER, RELAPSING FEVER,[3] BARTONELLOSIS,[4] maybe PERICARDITIS.

Consider alternatives	Characteristics
RESPIRATORY INFECTION	Coughing or congestion, with production of sputum.
DEPRESSION	Sighing, insomnia, changes in appetite.
STRESS	Sighing, insomnia, changes in appetite.
Stomach acid	Usually from lying down right after eating; treat with ANTACID.
GALLBLADDER DISEASE	Recurrent after meals; usually the right side; also in shoulder or back.
HEART FAILURE	Fatigued and/or swollen ankles and/or heart murmur.
Swallowed foreign body[5]	Anything stuck causes symptoms like a HEART ATTACK.
================	
SYPHILIS, tertiary	Ten+ years after exposure or born of a syphilic mother.
MIGRAINE	Medications used for migraine can cause this kind of pain.
PERICARDITIS	Pain goes to back; sitting and leaning forward decreases the pain.
PLANT POISONING	Claviceps or Ergot; similar to ANGINA or a HEART ATTACK.

[1] Chaga's Disease: Scattered areas within Central and South America.
[2] Lassa Fever: Found in West Africa; occurs in epidemics.
[3] Relapsing Fever: Not in the islands of Southeast Asia or the Pacific.
[4] Bartonellosis: Occurs in Peru and adjacent border areas only.
[5] Send the patient to a hospital. Do not try to have him swallow anything else.

35 B. Sharp, Pleuritic Chest Pain:

Definition: Pain is usually felt in the sides, upper front, or back of the chest, increased with deep breathing. The pain is usually sharp. It is never aggravated by touching the chest or pushing on it. A patient may take short, shallow breaths to avoid pain. He may hold his chest or bandage it tightly for pain relief. If the pain is on the right, check the patient for a tender liver; check Protocol 40 or 41 if you find one. If the pain is on the left, check for a tender spleen (Protocol 41 B).

Symptomatic treatment: ACETAMINOPHEN or IBUPROFEN is always appropriate; ASPIRIN may be appropriate in adults but should not be given until you have reached a diagnosis.

Problem	Fever	Other characteristics
PNEUMONIA	Yes	Cough, short of breath, rapid respiration.
TUBERCULOSIS	Maybe	Cough, night sweats, loss of appetite, slow onset.
AMEBIC LIVER DISEASE	Usual	Lower right side. Cough and sweating common; fatigued.
PLEURISY	Low if any	Few or no other symptoms, usually.
RESPIRATORY INFECTION	Low if any	Cough, sometimes congestion or cold symptoms.
==============		
SICKLE CELL DISEASE[1]	Probably	Ill off and on since 2 y.o.; family history.
RELAPSING FEVER	High	Fevers, sweats, headaches; body lice or tick bite.
PERICARDITIS	Maybe	Sitting and leaning forward minimizes the pain.
LASSA FEVER[2]	High	Like PERICARDITIS; epidemics in West Africa.
PULMONARY EMBOLISM	Unusual	Disabled or Westerners; short of breath.
FAMILIAL MEDITER-RANEAN FEVER	Yes	Hereditary, recurrent, abdominal or joint pains common.
HYDATID DISEASE	Unusual	Tropical areas with dogs or northern temperate forest.
PARAGONIMIASIS[3]	Maybe	Cough, worse mornings, brownish or reddish sputum.
PNEUMOTHORAX	No[4]	Sudden onset of pain and shortness of breath.
COCCIDIOMYCOSIS[5]	Yes	Cough, fatigue; may have large neck lymph nodes.

35 C. Chest Pain With Swallowing:

This is most frequently due to something swallowed that scratched the patient on its way down. If this is the case, it will usually heal within 24 hours. This may also be caused by PERICARDITIS, LASSA FEVER, (in Africa), CHAGA'S DISEASE[6] and rarely TUBERCULOSIS, PNEUMONIA, or PNEUMOTHORAX. See Protocol 30 D.

35 D. Chest Wall Pain:

Definition: Chest pain that may be of any quality (sharp, dull, burning, aching), but it is always aggravated by one of the following: deep breathing, twisting, raising the arms, or pushing on the chest. Sores on the skin are treated like any skin problem. Treat injuries. Breast pain is in Protocol 35 E.

Symptomatic treatment: ACETAMINOPHEN or IBUPROFEN is always appropriate; ASPIRIN may be appropriate in adults but should not be given until you have reached a diagnosis.

(Continued on next page.)

---

[1] This is an inherited condition affecting mainly those of African genetic heritage.

[2] Lassa Fever: Found in West Africa; occurs in epidemics.

[3] Paragonimiasis: Found in the Indian subcontinent, Asia, and the Pacific; rarely in Africa and the Americas.

[4] There is no fever unless the underlying disease that caused the pneumothorax also caused a fever. Usually a pneumothorax occurs for no good reason.

[5] Coccidiomycosis: Found in arid areas of the Americas only.

[6] Chaga's Disease: Found in scattered areas in the Americas.

(35 D. Chest Wall Pain, continued.)

Is the patient's temperature normal; he has no fever?

NO

YES, fever absent

Consider COSTAL CHONDRITIS, MUSCLE STRAIN, ARTHRITIS, SHINGLES. Maybe broken rib, tertiary SYPHILIS, RICKETS, RESPIRATORY INFECTION.

Consider alternatives	Characteristics
SHINGLES	Pain in a band, higher in back than front. Rash by day 4.
AMEBIC LIVER DISEASE	Tenderness present between the lower right ribs.
ARTHRITIS	Pain in spine or rib joints, front or back.
===============	
TRENCH FEVER	Body lice, fever, headache, severe shin pain.
SICKLE CELL DISEASE[1]	History of ill health; family history of ill health.
BRUCELLOSIS	Fevers; joint pains or sharp, shooting pains or both.
Broken rib	From a fall or coughing spells, especially elderly; or with MALNUTRITION.
TRICHINOSIS[2]	Generally sore, swollen muscles, especially chest muscles.
BARTONELLOSIS[3]	Severe pains in breast bone in front; fatigue occurs before fever.

35 E. Breast Pain:

This is normal during adolescence and milk production. Otherwise check MASTITIS, CELLULITIS, ABSCESS, TUBERCULOSIS, FILARIASIS, and (rarely) CANCER.

Symptomatic treatment: ACETAMINOPHEN or IBUPROFEN is always appropriate; ASPIRIN may be appropriate but should not be given until you have reached a diagnosis.

PROTOCOL 36. SHORTNESS OF BREATH

36 A. Shortness of Breath: Adults and Children Over Three Years Old
36 B. Shortness of Breath: Children Under Three Years Old

*****With sudden onset and patient very distressed, check for ANAPHYLAXIS and HYPERVENTILATION.** Also see Protocol C-4 for help in distinguishing the various causes of shortness of breath.

36 A. Shortness of Breath: Adults and Children Over Three Years Old:

Symptomatic treatment: Try having the patient breathe near a cool mist vaporizer or steam. Have the patient sleep sitting up; a bean bag chair[4] or lazy boy chair is best. A non-drying COUGH SYRUP[5] may be helpful.

Is the problem of sudden onset (over a minute or less)?

NO

YES

ANAPHYLAXIS, ALLERGY, ASTHMA, ///PULMONARY EMBOLISM, PNEUMOTHORAX, inhaling a foreign body: Treat immediately! Rarely, ANTHRAX, PLANT POISONING due to botulism.

Continued on next page.

[1] Sickle Cell Disease: This affects Blacks of African genetic origin, mainly in Africa and the Americas. Some Indians and Arabs are also affected.

[2] Trichinosis: The patient ate rare or raw pork or wild game within the past month.

[3] Bartonellosis: Occurs only in Peru and adjacent border areas.

[4] This is dangerous for children under 2 y.o.

[5] A non-drying cough syrup is one that does not contain any antihistamine. Read the label.

(36 A. Shortness of Breath: Adults and Children Over Three Years Old, continued.)

Is the patient breathing fast without really feeling short of breath?

NO — YES

Consider ANEMIA, DEHYDRATION, SEPSIS, STRESS, ///SHOCK, KIDNEY FAILURE, ADDICTION (uppers), or DIABETES.

Does the patient have a high fever?

NO — YES

Most likely PNEUMONIA; less likely MALARIA, ENTERIC FEVER, SICKLE CELL DISEASE,[1] TYPHUS, ANTHRAX, HIV INFECTION, DIPHTHERIA, FAMILIAL MEDITERRANEAN FEVER, rarely PLAGUE or TRICHINOSIS.

Consider Alternatives	**Fever**	**Other Characteristics**
PNEUMONIA	Usual	Cough, chest pains, chills, sweats or all of these.
MALARIA	Usual	Urobilinogen in the urine; very ill.
RESPIRATORY INFECTION	Maybe	Sick a long time. Big neck muscles from breathing.
ANEMIA	Maybe	Pale inside lower eyelids, mouth, or fingernails.
TUBERCULOSIS	Usual	Long-lasting cough with weight loss; gradual onset.
HEART FAILURE	Maybe	Worse lying than sitting, swollen ankles or fatigue.
ASTHMA	No	Harder to breathe out than in, frequently wheezing.
Abdomen distended	Maybe	Gas or fluids or pregnancy hinders breathing.
==============		
PNEUMOTHORAX	No	Sudden onset, less breath sounds on one side.
ALTITUDE SICKNESS	No	Coughing, headache, worse lying down; over 2000 m.
PULMONARY EMBOLISM	No	Debilitated or inactive person; chest pain also.
HEART ATTACK	No	Person has eaten a Western diet; chest pain, sweaty also.
SMOKE INHALATION	No	History of being by a fire.
CARBON MONOXIDE POISONING	No	History of being by a fire or an engine; headache also.
MANSONELLOSIS PERSTANS[2]	No	Also general bone and joint pains; slow onset.
PLANT POISONING	No	Muscarine, Botulism, or Nicotine.
INSECTICIDE POISONING	No	Much saliva, tears, diarrhea.

[1] Sickle Cell Disease: This affects Blacks of African genetic origin, mainly in Africa and the Americas. Some Indians and Arabs are also affected.

[2] Mansonellosis Perstans: Only in Africa (west and central) and in South America (northern Argentina and north of there).

36 B. Shortness of Breath: Children Under Three Years Old:

Newborns may have no fever with diseases that usually cause fever. The following problems are most frequent; under unusual circumstances, also consider the problems listed for older persons.

Problem	Fever	Other Characteristics
Stuffy nose	Low if any	Clean the nose or use drops.
RESPIRATORY INFECTION	Usual	Stuffy or runny nose or a barking cough.
PNEUMONIA	Usual	Moist-sounding cough; fever if over one year old.
DEHYDRATION	Maybe	Tongue or mouth or both are dry.
ANEMIA	Maybe	Pale inside lower eyelids, mouth, or fingernails.
MEASLES	High	Red eyes; very ill; rash on skin or spots in the mouth.
WHOOPING COUGH	Low	Severe coughing spells with sudden, noisy gasping.
================		
SICKLE CELL DISEASE[1]	Usual	ANEMIA, family history of ill health.
HEART FAILURE	Maybe	Swollen ankles or fatigue; better sitting than lying.
SEPSIS	Usual	Very ill, usually unconscious.

PROTOCOL 37. COUGH

37 A. Dry Cough or with White Sputum
37 B. Cough With Green or Yellow Sputum
37 C. Cough With Blood, Bloody, or Brownish Sputum

37 A. Dry Cough or with White Sputum:

Symptomatic treatment: Try having the patient breathe near a cool mist vaporizer or steam. Have the patient sleep sitting up; a bean bag chair[2] or lazy boy chair is best. A non-drying COUGH SYRUP[3] may be helpful.

Is the patient's sputum frothy?

NO

YES
Consider: ALTITUDE SICKNESS, HEART FAILURE, rarely PLAGUE. Otherwise this is saliva from the mouth, not sputum from the lungs.

Has the cough been recurrent, and present for over a month with weight loss?

NO to either

YES to both
Consider:
ASTHMA: Harder to breathe out than to breathe in.
RESPIRATORY INFECTION: History of smoke exposure.
TUBERCULOSIS: Night sweats, loss of appetite with weight loss.
HIV INFECTION: Multiple infections, diarrhea, severe weight loss.
HEART FAILURE: Short of breath with exertion.
WHOOPING COUGH: Coughing in spells with choking, vomiting.
AMEBIC LIVER DISEASE: Pain in upper right abdomen.
VISCERAL LEISHMANIASIS[4]: Huge spleen, large liver.
CANCER: Smoke exposure or other symptoms.

Continued on next page.

[1] Sickle Cell Disease: This affects Blacks of African genetic origin, mainly in Africa and the Americas. Some Indians and Arabs are also affected.

[2] This is dangerous for children under 2 y.o.

[3] A non-drying cough syrup is one that does not contain any antihistamine. Read the label. The names of antihistamines usually end with –amine.

[4] Visceral Leishmaniasis: Found in scattered areas of Central and South America, Africa north of the equator, the Mediterranean area, the Indian subcontinent, eastern Europe, central Asia, and mainland China.

(37 A. Dry Cough or with White Sputum, continued.)

Is there a high fever?

NO

YES

Probably PNEUMONIA, MEASLES; ENTERIC FEVER, AMEBIC LIVER DISEASE; rarely LASSA FEVER,[1] COCCIDIOMYCOSIS,[2] PLAGUE.

Consider alternatives	Fever	Other Characteristics
PNEUMONIA	Usual	Sudden onset, usually after a cold; fast respiration.
RESPIRATORY INFECTION	Low if any	Not very ill unless chronic or the patient is an infant.
ASTHMA	No	Prolonged expiration, tight cough, maybe wheezing.
==================		
AMEBIC LIVER DISEASE	Usual	Pain on right side; holds his side to minimize pain.
HEART FAILURE	No	Shortness of breath worse lying than sitting.
ALTITUDE SICKNESS	No	Severe headache, shortness of breath, worse lying.
WHOOPING COUGH	Mild	Much white mucus, coughing spells with gasps.
HYDATID DISEASE	No	Sudden coughing up of salty, watery stuff.
PLANT POISONING	No	Due to Muscarine; much saliva, sweat, and urination.
INSECTICIDE POISONING	No	Like Muscarine entry above; exposed to insecticide.
SMOKE INHALATION	Maybe	Within 72 hours of inhaling smoke, sudden onset.
LIVER FLUKE[3]	No	Large, tender liver, indigestion, general aching.

37 B. Cough With Green or Yellow Sputum:

***If the sputum has a foul odor, you must get the patient to a surgeon promptly!!

Symptomatic treatment: Try having the patient breathe near a cool mist vaporizer or steam. Have the patient sleep sitting up; a bean bag chair[4] or lazy boy chair is best. A non-drying COUGH SYRUP[5] may be helpful.

Has the patient been ill more than a month and the sputum has a foul, rotten odor?

No to either

YES to both

Due to a lung abscess which requires surgical care.

Consider alternatives	Fever	Other Characteristics
RESPIRATORY INFECTION	Maybe	Quite short of breath if chronic.
PNEUMONIA	High	Sudden onset, usually after a cold.
TUBERCULOSIS	Usual	Gradual onset, weight loss, night sweats.
AMEBIC LIVER DISEASE	Usual	Sudden onset after right-sided pains for a period of time.

[1] Lassa Fever: Occurs in epidemics in west Africa.

[2] Coccidiomycosis: Arid parts of the Americas only.

[3] This kind of liver fluke is fascioliasis, present in most areas other than Asia.

[4] A bean bag chair is dangerous for children under 2 y.o.

[5] A non-drying cough syrup is one that does not contain any antihistamine. Read the label. The names of antihistamines almost always end in "-amine".

37 C. Cough With Blood, Bloody, or Brownish Sputum:

Symptomatic treatment: Try having the patient breathe near a cool mist vaporizer or steam. Have the patient sleep sitting up; a bean bag chair or lazy boy chair is best. A non-drying COUGH SYRUP[2] may be helpful.

Has the patient been ill more than a month and the sputum has a foul, rotten odor?

NO to either | **YES to both**
Due to a lung abscess: requires surgical care.

Is the patient coughing up clots of pure red blood?

NO | **YES**
RESPIRATORY INFECTION (bronchitis), TUBERCULOSIS, HEART FAILURE, or CANCER. If it is part of a general bleeding problem, consult Protocol C-7.

Did the patient have bleeding from nose or mouth recently?

NO | **YES**
Do not worry about a small amount; the blood ran down and came up again. It may be part of a general bleeding problem in which case you should consult Protocol C-7.

Consider alternatives	Fever	Other Characteristics
ASCARIASIS	Usual	Ate soil-contaminated food in non-arid tropics.
RESPIRATORY INFECTION	Maybe	Chronic cough, not very sick otherwise.
PNEUMONIA	High	Short of breath, chest pain, or both.
TUBERCULOSIS	Usual	Slow onset, night sweats, weight loss.
PULMONARY EMBOLISM	Low if any	Foamy, pinkish sputum, sudden onset.
====================		
AMEBIC LIVER DISEASE	Usual	Sudden coughing spell, thick sputum; right side pain.
PARAGONIMIASIS[1]	Unusual	Coughing for a long time, little or no weight loss.
PLAGUE (rare)	High	Very rapid onset; highly contagious; almost universally fatal.

PROTOCOL 38. BREAST AND OTHER CHEST PROBLEMS

38 A. Breast Problems
38 B. Additional Chest Problems

38 A. Breast Problems:

Breast pain: See Protocol 35 E.

Breast lump: If there is a definite lump so you can feel definite borders, like a marble, and it becomes sore right before menstruation and less sore after, that is probably a cyst. A potentially cancerous lump will probably be a non-tender swollen area, irregular in shape, with no definite border. However, only a biopsy can determine if a particular lump is cancerous. Also consider TUBERCULOSIS of the breast. Breast TB is usually painful from the beginning, whereas CANCER is initially painless.

Breast development: In a newborn, due to mother's hormones; no problem. In an adolescent male, due to hormones during puberty; no problem. This is very common and nothing to worry about; it will go away in 18 months or less. Also may be due to LEPROSY, MUMPS, HEMOCHROMATOSIS[2], LIVER FAILURE, CIRRHOSIS, KIDNEY FAILURE, THYROID TROUBLE (high thyroid), MALNUTRITION and some drugs, notably CIMETIDINE, DIGITALIS, GRISEOFULVIN. Premature puberty is potentially serious; send the patient out.

Itchy rash under breast: CANDIDIASIS.

[1] Paragonimiasis: Mainly in Asia and Southeast Asia; occasionally India and western Africa; rarely the Americas and Pacific.

[2] Hemochromatosis: Mainly confined to certain ethnic groups who take in excessive iron in the form of blood or beer brewed in iron containers.

Discharge from the nipple: If the person has not just given birth to a baby, this is potentially serious. Contact a physician for advice or send out within a week.

Breast swelling: Normal with pregnancy and right before menstruation. May be due to CANCER or TUBERCULOSIS causing large nodes in the arm pit and this may cause swelling of the breast with swollen skin that looks like orange peel. Similar swelling and orange-peel skin may be due to IMPETIGO of the nipple area, MASTITIS, FILARIASIS.

Sores on breasts: IMPETIGO is most common; Also consider TREPONARID[1] in the infant, MASTITIS, CANCER. See Protocols 15 and 17.

38 B. Additional Chest Problems:

Wheezing:

Definition: Listening through your stethoscope, expiration sounds are the same length or longer than inspiration sounds with a high-pitched whining or squeaking quality to them. Frequently the patient will tell you that he has more trouble breathing out than breathing in.

Common causative diseases: ALLERGY, TUBERCULOSIS, MANSONELLOSIS PERSTANS,[2] ASTHMA, ANAPHYLAXIS, HEART FAILURE, ALTITUDE SICKNESS, RESPIRATORY INFECTION.

Symptomatic treatment for wheezing: No matter what the cause of the wheezing, THEOPHYLLINE is an appropriate medication if the patient is not already on it and there are no contraindications.

Other:

Hiccups: See HICCUPS in the *Disease Index*.

Congestion: ASTHMA, ALLERGY, PNEUMONIA, RESPIRATORY INFECTION, INSECITICIDE POISONING, PLANT POISONING due to Muscarine.

Chest pressure: See Protocol 35 A, chest pain, even if the patient denies that it is really pain.

Skipped beats/palpitations: See Protocol 3 D.

Vibration felt on the chest wall, synchronous with the pulse or heart beat: This is equivalent to a heart murmur. Check for signs of HEART FAILURE. If there are none, it can safely be ignored until it is convenient to have it checked out at a major medical center. However you should be careful to treat all infections in this patient.

Barrel-shaped chest: Usually due to RESPIRATORY INFECTION which has become chronic; otherwise SICKLE CELL DISEASE, SCURVY.

Bumps on either side of the breastbone: RICKETS, SCURVY, COSTAL CHONDRITIS.

Lump on the left, in the depression above the collar bone: Likely CANCER; send out for diagnosis.

Soft swellings on the chest, like abscesses but cool to touch: TUBERCULOSIS.

Sides of lower ribs pulled in: RICKETS.

---

[1] Treponarid: Found in arid areas only. The sores are on the breast of the mother who acquires the problem from her breast-feeding, infected infant.

[2] Mansonellosis Perstans: Found only in Africa (central and west) and in South America (northern Argentina and north of there).

VIII. ABDOMINAL PROBLEMS

Abdominal Protocols: Outline

Guide to Abdominal Protocols

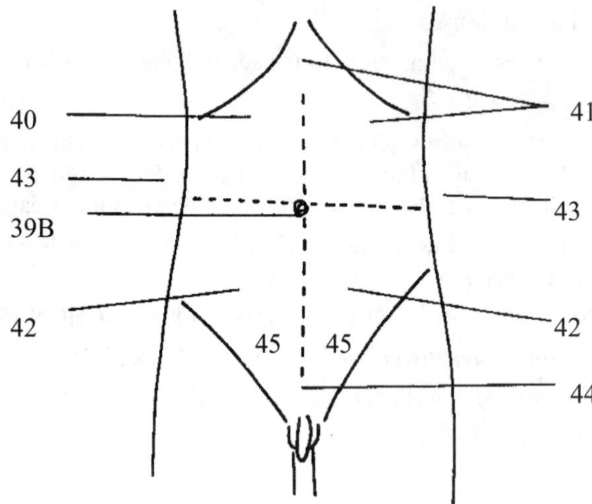

PROTOCOL 39. ABDOMINAL PAIN and/or SWELLING

If the patient has a high fever plus abdominal pain, see Protocol C-9.

39 A. Abdominal Pain. General Guide to Diagnosing Abdominal Problems
39 B. Non-Localized or Middle Abdominal Pain
39 C. Acute Abdomen - Three Different Types

39 A. Abdominal Pain. General Guide to Diagnosing Abdominal Problems:

Symptomatic treatment: A warm water bottle is appropriate for abdominal pain. Use no pain medication by mouth until the protocol suggests it, a physician orders it, or you have at least a tentative diagnosis.

Does the patient have definite signs of an ACUTE ABDOMEN (See Protocol 39 C)?

NO or not sure | **YES**: Treat as instructed in the *Disease Index*. Contact a physician.

(1) If the pain is in the middle of the abdomen, or if it is all over (generalized), or if it seems to be moving around to different locations, go to Protocol 39 B: Non-localized or Middle Abdominal Pain.

(2) If the pain appears to be on the abdominal wall, not deep inside, then ask the person about a possible injury; also consider SHINGLES, TRENCH FEVER, SPINAL NEUROPATHY, and similar diseases.

(3) If the pain is predominantly localized right or left, upper or lower, go to the Protocols 40 to 45, as follows (see also the accompanying diagram). The A protocols deal solely with pain; the B protocols deal with swelling, with or without pain and with or without tenderness.

(4) If the patient has general abdominal swelling, see Protocol 46.

39 B. Non-Localized Or Middle Abdominal Pain:

Definition: The patient points to his navel as the location of the pain or else he tells you that the pain moves around by sweeping his hand over his entire abdomen.

First check for ACUTE ABDOMEN (Protocol 39 C), if you have not done so already. If there is no ACUTE ABDOMEN and the patient is not very ill and the pain has lasted less than 48 hours, first consider HEAT ILLNESS and IRRITABLE BOWEL. Then pursue a diagnosis.

Does the patient have a high fever, 102°F or 39°C or more?

NO | **YES**: See Protocol C-9: General Abdominal Pain plus Fever.

Is the patient constipated off and on or continually?

NO | **YES**: **Consider** IRRITABLE BOWEL, IMPACTION, ENTERIC FEVER, ASCARIASIS, DYSENTERY,[1] TUBERCULOSIS, rarely LEAD POISONING.

Has the patient eaten inadequately cooked meat or fish?

NO | **YES**: **Consider** TAPEWORM, TRICHINOSIS, INTESTINAL FLUKE.[2]

Continued on next page.

[1] Due to amebae. Amebae may cause constipation before diarrhea begins.

[2] Intestinal Fluke: Not present in Africa south of the Sahara or in the Pacific. In the Americas it is present only in Guyana.

(39 B. Non-Localized Or Middle Abdominal Pain, continued.)

Has the patient had diarrhea?

NO **YES**

Consider GASTROENTERITIS, DYSENTERY, FOOD POISONING,[1] /// STRONGYLOIDIASIS, TUBERCULOSIS, PIG-BEL,[2] PLANT POISONING, ARSENIC POISONING.

Is there blood in the stool: either visible blood or the stool tests positive for blood[3]?

NO **YES**

HOOKWORM: Areas with sandy soil; ANEMIA is common.
DYSENTERY: Either red blood or black, foul, sticky stools.
TRICHURIASIS: Tiny worms, look like whips or coil springs.
PEPTIC ULCER: Burning pain with hunger, relieved by food.
STRONGYLOIDIASIS: Itchy rash by rectum off and on.
PIG-BEL: Meat meal in a child with prior MALNUTRITION.
SCHISTOSOMIASIS MANSONI[4]: Bloody diarrhea; liver problems.
SCHISTOSOMIASIS JAPONICUM[5]: Distended abdomen.

Consider alternatives	Fever	Other Characteristics
STRESS	No	Pain is usually mild and intermittent.
COLIC	No	Otherwise-healthy baby; passing gas relieves pain.
COSTAL CHONDRITIS	No	Young adult; tenderness along side(s) of breast bone.
MUSCLE STRAIN	No	After unusual exercise; aching abdominal muscles.
PEPTIC ULCER	No	Burning or aching, aggravated or relieved by food.
HERNIA	Unusual	Bulge in groin(s) or by navel, tender to touch.
===============		
TUBERCULOSIS	Usual	Weight loss, swelling (fluid) or lumps in the belly.
TUBERCULOSIS	Usual	Whole-abdomen burning pains.
SICKLE CELL DISEASE[6]	Common	Recurrent pains since a young age.
SHINGLES	Maybe	Abdominal wall tender to touch; rash by day three.
PLANT POISONING	No	Many different kinds[7]; vomiting, diarrhea common.
ARSENIC POISONING	No	Cramping pains; numbness and tingling of limbs.
PANCREATITIS	Maybe	Vomiting; pain goes to back.
INTESTINAL FLUKE[8]	No	Patient may have a swollen face.

[1] Eggs, milk, and chicken are common causes; pain is severe.
[2] Pig-bel: Developing countries near the equator.
[3] Do at least three tests for blood. Any one positive means there is blood in the stool. See Appendix 2 in Volume I.
[4] Schistosomiasis Mansoni: Scattered areas throughout Africa, some in the Middle East and the Americas.
[5] Schistosomiasis Japonicum: In parts of mainland China, the Philippines, parts of the Celebes, the upper Mekong, and the Thai-Malaysian border.
[6] Sickle Cell Disease: This affects Blacks of African genetic origin, mainly in Africa and the Americas. Some Indians and Arabs are also affected.
[7] Ackee, Botulism, Coral plant, Lolism, Manicheel, Nicotine.
[8] Intestinal Fluke: Not present in Africa south of the Sahara or in the Pacific area. In the Americas, present only in Guyana.

39 C. Acute Abdomen - Three Different Types:

Includes appendicitis, intestinal obstruction, and perforated ulcer.

If the patient has a high fever plus abdominal pain, see Protocol C-9.

Type 1. Acute Abdomen with Shock. The patient has an ashen color, is cool and moist, has a fast pulse or low blood pressure or both. Most often he is lying still, not writhing around. His pain may go to his back and he may be vomiting. If you lift the patient to a standing or sitting position, he will pass out. He may already be unconscious. If he is a male, usually the pain will have come on suddenly. With females, most often the pain will have come on gradually. Sometimes this kind of acute abdomen is due to injury. Frequently the patient complains of shoulder or back pain or both.

Type 2. Acute Abdomen with Infection. (Appendicitis type): The patient has had pain for 6 hours or more. It may have started out like ordinary cramps. The patient has lost his appetite. Usually he is vomiting. He frequently is constipated; diarrhea is unusual. Eventually he develops rebound tenderness with at least 2 of the first 3 signs below or (rarely) sign 4 alone being positive. His pain response must be spontaneous. If you must ask him to know if it hurts or not, his response is not spontaneous. (This is assuming your patient is from a Western culture. The criterion of spontaneity may be culturally modified.)

Signs:

1. If you ask him to take a deep breath and cough hard twice, he will either refuse or complain of pain the first time; he will definitely not cough hard the second time. He may just clear his throat.
2. If you jar him or the bed on which he is lying, he will wince or verbally complain of pain.
3. If you tap on his abdomen with one finger as if you were hitting a key on a big, old manual typewriter, this also will produce enough pain to make him wince. This pain is not as bad if the patient raises his head up off the bed as it is if his head is down.
4. With the patient lying flat on his back on a table, drop his leg off the side of the table so it hangs down toward the floor from the hip. This markedly aggravates the pain. If you listen to his abdomen with a stethoscope, usually you will hear no bowel sounds.
5. In a child with an umbilical hernia (a bulging, soft navel) you can test for Type 2 by tapping on the top of the hernia. If the child howls with pain, he has Acute Abdomen Type 2.

Acute Abdomen With Infection may be caused by injury, appendicitis, perforated ULCER, ASCARIASIS, amebic DYSENTERY, TUBERCULOSIS, or ENTERIC FEVER, as well as other diseases. PELVIC INFECTION, PANCREATITIS, and amebic DYSENTERY[1] can be indistinguishable.

Type 3. Acute Abdomen with Obstruction. The patient has had pain for 6 hours or more, and the pain comes in waves, anywhere from 3 minutes to 25 minutes apart. If the pains are quite frequent, the patient is vomiting and may be constipated also. In this case his abdomen might not be distended. If the pains are less frequent, the patient is constipated; he may be vomiting also. In the latter case, the vomit may look and smell like stool. (It is stool.) His abdomen is distended and if you tap it, it sounds hollow. Usually the patient is writhing rather than holding perfectly still. Listening with your stethoscope, as the patient has a pain, you will hear silence followed by rushing sounds, possibly followed by tinkles like water dripping into water from a height. The patient may have ASCARIASIS which will cause him to pass roundworms (visible earthworm size) or he may have a hernia that is tender and will not go back inside or he may have an old surgical scar on his abdomen. Occasionally small children have irregular pains and bloody diarrhea with this kind of acute abdomen. This may be caused by ASCARIASIS or TUBERCULOSIS, as well as some other diseases.

---

[1] Amebic DYSENTERY implies that the person has diarrhea, but frequently there is constipation before the diarrhea. If the intestines perforate (break open into the body cavity), the diarrhea will stop and the person again will be constipated.

PROTOCOL 40. UPPER-RIGHT ABDOMINAL PROBLEMS

40 A. Upper Right Abdominal Pain
40 B. Upper Right Abdominal Swelling

40 A. Upper Right Abdominal Pain:

If the patient has a high fever[1] plus abdominal pain, see Protocol C-9.

Does the patient have definite signs of ACUTE ABDOMEN (see Protocol 39 C)?

NO — continue below.
YES — Treat as outlined in the *Disease Index*.

Try DICYCLOMINE or CHAMOMILE TEA. Does this relieve pain?

NO, or little[2] — continue below.
YES, much — Pain is from a minor cause; continue with DICYCLOMINE or CHAMOMILE TEA.

Is the patient 6 months or more pregnant?

NO — continue below.
YES — **Consider** TOXEMIA.

Does eating change the pain, making it better or worse?

NO — continue below.
YES — **Consider** GALLBLADDER DISEASE, PEPTIC ULCER.

Consider alternatives	Fever	Other Characteristics
HEPATITIS	Maybe	Fatigue, nausea, maybe JAUNDICE.
AMEBIC LIVER DISEASE	Usual	The patient holds his right side to relieve pain.
ASCARIASIS	Maybe	Crampy, episodic pains, especially children.
GALLBLADDER DISEASE	Maybe	Pain in right shoulder; may be provoked by food.
==================		
HEART FAILURE	Unusual	Large, tender liver; swollen ankles; fatigue.
LIVER FLUKE[3]	No	Ate raw or rare fish or water plants; liver large and tender.
PELVIC INFECTION	Maybe	Adult female, pain with intercourse, pus in vagina.
MANSONELLOSIS PERSTANS[4]	No	Also joint pains, maybe a rash or short of breath.
PLANT POISONING	No	Crotalaria; used to make bush teas; large liver.
CANCER	Seldom	Lump(s) and/or weight loss.

[1] This implies equal to or more than 102°F or 39°C.
[2] Modify one's understanding of the answer according to the culture. Some cultures encourage an affirmative answer for politeness; others encourage a negative answer in order to elicit additional medication which is deemed desirable.
[3] Liver Fluke: Worldwide, especially in the Far East and Southeast Asia.
[4] Mansonellosis Perstans: Only in west and central Africa and in South America, northern Argentina and north of there.

40 B. Upper Right Abdominal Swelling:

See Protocol 14 if the swelling appears to be entirely within the abdominal wall, not originating or extending to deep within the abdomen.

Can you feel an edge of the swelling; and, if so, what is its direction?

Horizontal, or nearly horizontal, or diagonal.

The direction is left to right on the patient; if diagonal it is higher on the left than on the right.
The mass is probably the liver. See Protocol 46 B2.

Vertical, or nearly vertical.

The direction is head to foot on the patient—possibly with a notch in the middle of the swelling.
The mass is probably a kidney. See protocol 46 B3.

No edge felt, or rounded.

Send the patient out for diagnosis. This may be his gallbladder or a tumor. In any case, there is nothing you can do in a village situation.

PROTOCOL 41. UPPER-MID AND UPPER-LEFT ABDOMINAL PROBLEMS

41 A. Upper-Mid And Upper Left Abdominal Pain
41 B. Upper-Mid And Upper Left Abdominal Swelling

41 A. Upper-Mid And Upper Left Abdominal Pain:

Includes spleen pain.
If the patient has a high fever plus abdominal pain, see Protocol C-9.

Does the patient have definite signs of ACUTE ABDOMEN (See Protocol 39 C)?

NO or not sure	YES
	Treat according to directions in *Disease Index*.

Try treating with ANTACID and DICYCLOMINE or CHAMOMILLE TEA. If the treatment fails, go to next question:

Is the pain mid-upper abdomen with the right-upper side also hurting?

NO	YES
	Use Protocol 40 A; the problem is probably with the liver or the gallbladder.

Has the patient been ill for more than a week and does he have ANEMIA?

NO to either or both	YES to both
	Consider MALARIA, TROPICAL SPLENOMEGALY, VISCERAL LEISHMANIASIS,[1] THALLASEMIA, SCHISTOSOMIASIS MANSONI,[2] SICKLE CELL DISEASE.[3]

Continued on next page.

---

[1] Visceral Leishmaniasis: Found in scattered areas of Central and South America, Africa north of the equator, the Mediterranean area, the Indian subcontinent, eastern Europe, central Asia, and mainland China.
[2] Schistosomiasis Mansoni: Scattered areas within Africa, the Arabian peninsula, the Caribbean, and parts of eastern South America.
[3] Sickle Cell Disease: This affects Blacks of African genetic origin, mainly in Africa and the Americas. Some Indians and Arabs are also affected.

(41 A. Upper-Mid And Upper Left Abdominal Pain, continued.)

Consider alternatives	Fever	Other Characteristics
GASTRITIS	No	Burning pain, upper abdomen, like PEPTIC ULCER.
PEPTIC ULCER	No	Pain aggravated or relieved by food.
GALLBLADDER DISEASE	Maybe	Pain is also felt in right shoulder blade.
================		
HEART ATTACK	No	Western diet or SYPHILIS; probably sweaty, nauseous; commonly a sense of doom.
AMEBIC LIVER DISEASE	Usual	Center pain, worse with walking; night sweats.
PANCREATITIS	Maybe	Vomiting; severe pain goes to the back.
SCHISTOSOMIASIS MANSONI[1]	Unusual	Large liver, large spleen, constipation, or diarrhea.
LIVER FLUKE[2]	No	Ate rare or raw fish or water plants; liver large and tender.
CANCER	Seldom	Lump(s) and/or weight loss.

41 B. Upper-Mid Or Upper-Left Abdominal Swelling:

See Protocol 14 if the swelling appears to be entirely within the abdominal wall, not originating in or extending deep into the abdomen.

If you can feel a definite edge to the swelling:

Upper edge only: Probably spleen (46 B1).
Lower edge only: Spleen (46 B1) or left lobe of the liver (46 B2).
Vertical edge only: Probably kidney (46 B3), maybe spleen (46 B1).
U-shaped edge: Spleen if it goes up under the ribs on the left side; may be kidney (46 B3).

No edge felt, or a spherical swelling:

It may be a tumor or the gallbladder. Send the patient out.

If you can feel two edges, both upper and lower, or either plus vertical, it is likely spleen. See subprotocols under Protocol 46 B.

PROTOCOL 42. LOWER ABDOMINAL PROBLEMS, RIGHT OR LEFT

42 A. Lower Abdominal Pain, Right or Left
42 B. Lower Abdominal Swelling, Right or Left

42 A. Lower Abdominal Pain, Right Or Left:

If the patient has a high fever plus abdominal pain, see Protocol C-9.

This protocol is only to be used if the pain is definitely right lower or left lower. If it is not localized to either the right or left, see Protocol 44. For groin pain (pain in leg crease) see Protocol 45.

Does the patient have symptoms of ACUTE ABDOMEN (See Protocol 39 C)?

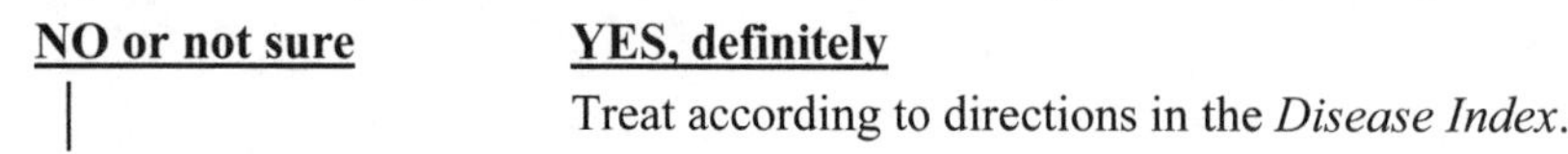

<u>NO or not sure</u> — <u>YES, definitely</u>: Treat according to directions in the *Disease Index*.

Is the patient a young woman who is not a virgin?

<u>NO</u> — <u>YES</u>: **Consider** TUBAL PREGNANCY, PELVIC INFECTION. If in doubt, send the patient out to a hospital.

Continued on next page.

[1] Schistosomiasis Mansoni: Scattered areas within Africa, the Arabian peninsula, the Caribbean, and parts of eastern South America.
[2] Liver Fluke: Present worldwide, especially in the Far East and Southeast Asia.

(42 A. Lower Abdominal Pain, Right Or Left, continued.)

Does the patient have a fever?

NO → (continue below)

YES → **Consider** ENTERIC FEVER, KIDNEY INFECTION, DYSENTERY, abdominal TUBERCULOSIS, BRUCELLOSIS.

Consider alternatives	Fever	Other Characteristics
Ovulatory pains	No	Female, 2 weeks before period. Use IBUPROFEN.
TURISTA	Unusual	Lower-left crampy pain before episodes of diarrhea.
DYSENTERY	Maybe	Tenderness over the large bowels, right or left.
TUBERCULOSIS	Usual	Slow onset; tender lump in the lower right abdomen.
EPIDIDYMITIS	Maybe	Male with tenderness behind his testicle(s).
STD[1]	Unusual	Also some abnormality of genitals.
KIDNEY STONE	Rare	Back or side pain also; one (either) side only.
================		
SHINGLES	Low if any	Rash in a band after skin pain for 3-4 days.
BRUCELLOSIS	Off & On	Slow onset; comes and goes; fatigue, joint pains.
SCHISTOSOMIASIS JAPONICUM[2]	Maybe	Skin exposed to water with infected snails.
CANCER	Seldom	Lump(s) and/or weight loss.

42 B. Lower Abdominal Swelling, Right Or Left:

See Protocol 45 B if the swelling is in the groin(s), not within the abdomen. See Protocol 14 if it appears to be entirely within the abdominal wall, not originating deep inside or extending to deep inside.

Is the swelling also in the central lower abdomen?

NO → (continue below)

YES, definitely → See Protocol 44B.

Does the mass extend into the upper abdomen?

NO → (continue below)

YES → Consult Protocols 40 and 41; it is probably kidney or spleen.

Is it in the lower right?

NO → (continue below)

YES → **Consider** TUBERCULOSIS or send out for diagnosis.

If there is a history of DYSENTERY, treat as AMEBIC LIVER DISEASE.
Otherwise send out for diagnosis.

PROTOCOL 43. FLANK/WAIST/SIDE ABDOMINAL PROBLEMS

43 A. Flank/Waist/Side Pain
40 B. Flank/Waist/Side Swelling

43 A. Flank/Waist/Side Pain:

Pain on either or both sides at the waist, possibly also around to the back or front or both, never down into the legs. See Protocols 60B and/or 63B if the pain goes to the legs. Also see large spleen (left) or liver (right), Protocol 46B.

(Continued on next page.)

---

[1] This is an abbreviation for SEXUALLY TRANSMITTED DISEASE; see Protocol C-1.

[2] Schistosomiasis Japonicum: In areas of mainland China, the Philippines, parts of the Celebes, the upper Mekong, and the Thai-Malaysian border.

(43 A. Flank/Waist/Side Pain, continued.)

Does the patient have bloody or cloudy urine?

NO

YES

Consider KIDNEY INFECTION, KIDNEY STONE, TUBERCULOSIS, CANCER, FILARIASIS, SCHISTOSOMIASIS HEMATOBIUM,[1] PLANT POISONING: Djenkol bean[2]; MALARIA.

Does or did the patient have a high fever?

NO to both

YES to either

Consider MALARIA,[3] AMEBIC LIVER DISEASE,[4] SICKLE CELL DISEASE.[5]

Consider Alternatives	Fever	Other Characteristics
Running pains	No	Onset while running, relieved by rest: No problem.
MUSCLE STRAIN	No	History of unusual exercise or injury; tight, aching pain.
KIDNEY STONE	No	Sudden onset, severe pain, usually vomiting also.
=================		
AMEBIC LIVER DISEASE	Usual	Right side only; patient holds his side with his arm.
KIDNEY FAILURE	Maybe	Urine abnormal in amount or urinalysis; maybe high BP.
CANCER	Seldom	Lump(s) and/or weight loss.

43 B. Flank/Waist/Side Swelling:

Is the swelling entirely within the abdominal wall, not extending deep inside?

No, it's deep inside

See Protocol 46 B3; it is probably kidney.
Also consider 46 B2, liver, if it is on the right.
Also consider 46 B1, spleen, if it is on the left.

Yes, abdominal wall only

See Protocol 14: Skin Lumps

PROTOCOL 44. LOW MIDDLE ABDOMINAL PROBLEMS

44 A. Low Middle Abdominal Pain
44 B. Low Middle Abdominal Swelling

44 A. Low Middle Abdominal Pain:

If the patient has a high fever plus abdominal pain, see Protocol C-9.

Does the patient have definite signs of an ACUTE ABDOMEN (See Protocol 39 C)?

No or not sure

YES, definitely

Treat according to directions in the *Disease Index*.

Does the patient have a high fever (over 39°C or 102°F), or is he/she very ill?

No to both

YES to either

Consider SEPSIS, ENTERIC FEVER, PELVIC INFECTION, a complication of pregnancy or abortion.

Continued on next page.

---

[1] Schistosomiasis Hematobium: Present in some areas of Africa and the Middle East.
[2] Present in Malaysia and Indonesia.
[3] The pain with MALARIA is either symmetrical or mainly on the left.
[4] Right side only.
[5] Sickle Cell Disease: This affects Blacks of African genetic origin, mainly in Africa and the Americas. Some Indians and Arabs are also affected.

(44 A. Low Middle Abdominal Pain, continued.)

Is the patient a male, a new mother, or someone with a genital injury?

NO | **YES**

Consider URINARY OBSTRUCTION, URINARY INFECTION, PELVIC INFECTION, PROSTATITIS.

(In a reproductive female, see Protocol C-1 for a possible sexually transmitted disease.)

Consider Alternatives	Fever	Other Characteristics
Labor	No	Cramping pain at regular intervals.
Menstrual cramps	No	Tight, crampy pain while menstruating.
URINARY INFECTION	Unusual	Cloudy urine, frequent urination with burning.
PELVIC INFECTION	Maybe	Females; pain with intercourse or tampon insertion.
PROSTATITIS (males)	Maybe	Heavy pain, center pelvis, between penis and rectum.
================		
SCHISTOSOMIASIS HEMATOBIUM[1]	Unusual	Blood in urine especially at end of urination.
SCHISTOSOMIASIS MANSONI[2]	Unusual	Pain in the bladder and rectal areas.
CANCER	Maybe	Recurrent, increasing frequency and severity.

44 B. Low Middle Abdominal Swelling:

See Protocol 14 if the swelling appears to be entirely within the abdominal wall, not originating or extending to deep inside the abdomen.

Is the patient an older man, a recently delivered woman, or someone with genital injury?

No | **Yes**

Consider URINARY OBSTRUCTION

Is the patient a reproductive female?

NO | **YES**

Consider pregnancy; URINARY OBSTRUCTION, otherwise send out for diagnosis.

Send out for diagnosis:

Consider: CANCER
URINARY OBSTRUCTION

[1] Schistosomiasis Hematobium: Present in some areas of Africa and the Middle East.

[2] Schistosomiasis Mansoni: Scattered areas within Africa, the Arabian peninsula, the Caribbean, and parts of eastern South America.

PROTOCOL 45. PROBLEMS IN GROIN(S)

45 A. Pain In Groin(s)
45 B. Swelling In Groin(s)

45 A. Pain In Groin(s):

Are there lumps in the groin—the leg creases or right below them—larger than a pencil eraser?

NO

YES or not sure

Medium consistency or not sure: See Protocol 52B.
Very soft like a water balloon: **Consider** ABSCESS, HERNIA.
Very hard like a rock: **Consider** CANCER.

Consider Alternatives	Fever	Other Characteristics
MUSCLE STRAIN	No	Had unusual exercise, aching pain. No swelling in groin.
KIDNEY STONES	Rare	Sudden onset, pain shoots down from flank area.
DENGUE FEVER[1]	High	Sudden onset, severe body pains in bones and joints.
HERNIA	Unusual	Patient had a soft, painless bulge, now it is painful.
BRUCELLOSIS	Off & on	Gradual onset of feeling generally very wretched.

45 B. Swelling In Groin(s):

Also see Protocol 52 if the swelling appears to be related to the legs or genitals.

Is, or was previously, the swelling soft like a water balloon?

No to both

Yes to either

Consider:
HERNIA: initially soft, may become hard.
SEXUALLY TRANSMITTED DISEASE: hard initially, becomes soft.
ABSCESS: hard initially, becomes soft.

Is the swelling firm like a ripe cherry?

NO

YES

Swollen lymph nodes due to an infection on the legs or feet, or due to a genital infection (See SEXUALLY TRANSMITTED DISEASE; see Protocol C-1). If there is a cauliflower-like surface, consider DONOVANOSIS..

Is the swelling rock-hard?

NO

YES

Consider CANCER.

Consider SEXUALLY TRANSMITTED DISEASE Protocol C-1.

[1] Dengue Fever: In the Americas only near or north of the equator. In Africa only Nigeria and southern Africa. Prevalent in India, Southeast Asia, and the Pacific. Occasionally found in the Mediterranean area.

PROTOCOL 46. GENERALIZED ABDOMINAL SWELLING

See Protocols 40B, 41B, 42B, 43B, 44B for guidance in using Protocol 46B. If the patient also has severe abdominal pain, first check for ACUTE ABDOMEN (Protocol 39 C). Use the chart below only if this is not the problem.

Groin Swelling: See Protocol 52.

46 A. General Or Central Abdominal Swelling:

Definition: The patient's abdomen sticks out in front more than one would expect from his general physical appearance with particular reference to the fat (or lack thereof) of his upper arm. Women who have previously given birth, even at a remote time, normally and commonly have protuberant abdomens.

Are the patient's ankles also swollen?

NO | **YES**: **Consider** LIVER DISEASE, LIVER FAILURE, CIRRHOSIS, MALNUTRITION, HEART FAILURE, KIDNEY FAILURE, MALABSORPTION, any chronic diarrhea.

Does the patient feel like he has to urinate but cannot?

NO | **YES**: **Consider** URINARY OBSTRUCTION, URETHRAL STRICTURE.

Does the patient complain of a heavy, dragging pain in his upper left abdomen?

NO | **YES**: **Consider** causes of a large spleen: See Protocol 46 B1.

Does the patient have free fluid in his or her abdomen (see Volume I, Chapter 1)?

NO: **See 46 A1 (below)**
YES: **See 46 A2 (below)**

46 A1. Abdominal Swelling Without Free Fluid:

Consider Alternatives	Other Characteristics
UMBILICAL HERNIA	Very soft bulge with the naval as a center, no general swelling.
ENTERIC FEVER	High fever, abdominal pain, lost appetite or vomiting, lethargic.
PANCREATITIS	Severe abdominal pains that go through to the back; vomiting.
ASCARIASIS	Passage of "earthworms", crampy pains, constipated.
TUBERCULOSIS	Night sweats or cough or weight loss or all three.
TUBERCULOSIS	Abdomen feels like a bean bag with many small nodes.

Continued on next page.

(46 A1. Abdominal Swelling Without Free Fluid, continued.)

Pregnancy	Lower abdomen, firm mass; Ruler test[1] positive after 6 months.
===============	
LIVER FLUKE[2]	Also constipation, indigestion, and nausea.
Tumor[3]	Lower abdomen, firm mass, Ruler test[1] positive.
BURKITT LYMPHOMA	Tumor in the abdomen, Ruler test[1] positive.
SPRUE	Severe, foul, watery diarrhea; sore mouth.
HYDATID DISEASE[4]	Tropical/arid areas with dogs. Ruler test[1] maybe positive.
AFRICAN SLEEPING SICKNESS[5]	Also swollen eyelids, maybe swollen neck or penis; headaches, slow onset.
INTESTINAL FLUKE[6]	Also abdominal pains; swollen face if severe.
PIG-BEL[7]	Poorly nourished children, recent high-protein foods.
TRICHURIASIS	Commonly much gas, abdominal pains, diarrhea, and ANEMIA.
SEPSIS	Patient is very ill with a high fever.

46 A2. Abdominal Swelling Due to Free Fluid:

(See also Protocol C-7)

Definition: The patient has a protuberant abdomen; his flanks bulge when he lies on his back and you can detect free fluid by the procedures outlined in Volume I, Chapter 1.

Does the patient also have **two or more** of the following?

- A large liver.
- Prominent veins on the front of his abdomen.[8]
- Spots on his skin that resemble little spiders.
- A large spleen.
- Yellow eyes.
- Personality changes.
- Trembling or lethargy.
- Easy bleeding.

Continued on next page.

---

[1] <u>Ruler test</u> distinguishes the 4 conditions so marked from everything else. Have the patient lie flat on his/her back. Take an ordinary ruler and lay it parallel to the floor crossways on the top of the swollen abdomen. Put it across the navel or a little lower. Hold it down firmly with one finger on each end of the ruler. If the swelling is due to pregnancy, tumor, HYDATID DISEASE, BURKITT LYMPHOMA, or URINARY OBSTRUCTION you may feel the patient's pulse in the ruler. This is because there is a solid mass between the large blood vessel by the back bone and the ruler. With any other condition, you will not be able to feel the pulse. Practice with a woman you know to be at least 6 months pregnant to be sure you are doing it correctly.

[2] Liver fluke (Fascioliasis): This is present worldwide except for Southeast Asia. See *Regional Notes*.

[3] This could be due to CANCER or something benign. In any case, you cannot deal with it.

[4] Hydatid Disease: This may also, rarely, be found in northern temperate or arctic areas, in people who eat food that may be contaminated by the stool of wild animals.

[5] African Sleeping Sickness: Scattered areas of Africa, south of Bamako, Mali and Lake Chad and north of Lusaka, Zambia.

[6] Intestinal Fluke: Not present in Africa south of the Sahara and in the Pacific. In the Americas only present in Guyana.

[7] Pig-bel: Developing countries near the equator.

[8] These are wiggly, blue lines, one half to one millimeter wide, visible below the skin. They may be hard to see on very dark skin but are easily seen in white or brown skin.

(46 A2. Abdominal Swelling Due to Free Fluid, continued.)

One or none of above symptoms

Two or more of above symptoms

Consider CIRRHOSIS, LIVER FAILURE; determine the cause(s).

Are the patient's feet and ankles also swollen?

NO

YES

Consider: KIDNEY FAILURE, HEART FAILURE, TUBERCULOSIS, PERICARDITIS, MALNUTRITION, MALABSORPTION, any chronic diarrhea such as SPRUE, CAPILLARIASIS.

Does or did the patient have severe abdominal pains going through to his back?

NO

YES

Consider PANCREATITIS

Consider: Abdominal TUBERCULOSIS, CANCER (rarely).

46 B. Swelling Of Abdominal Organs:

See also *Protocol C-7: Liver and Spleen Problems*, if applicable.

Lower Abdominal Lump[1]: URINARY OBSTRUCTION, pregnancy, TUBERCULOSIS,[2] old, ruptured appendicitis-turned-to-abscess[3], CANCER, HYDATID DISEASE, a tumor of the ovary (usually benign).

An Abdominal Lump may be an emergency in the presence of one or more of the following conditions:

1. Signs of Acute Abdomen Type 3 (See Protocol 39 B).
2. Significant weight loss (over 5 kg) in an adult; consider TUBERCULOSIS.
3. Fever.
4. The mass is quite tender; touching it causes a significant increase in pain.
5. There has been a recent injury after which the mass appeared or after which the mass became larger or became tender.

Note that lumps in the abdomen are particularly difficult to assess. If there are any symptoms other than a lump, then see additionally *Index* C or other protocols in *Index* A. With rare exceptions you should not trust any diagnosis based on only one protocol:

Identifying an enlarged, solid organ in the abdomen:

Divide the abdomen into four parts by drawing with an indelible marking pen, vertical and horizontal lines through the navel, at right angles to each other. The vertical line is the same as the midline of the body. The two lines divide the abdomen into four quadrants: right upper quadrant (RUQ); left upper quadrant (LUQ); right lower quadrant (RLQ); and left lower quadrant (LLQ). Now feel the edges of the enlarged organ and draw them on the abdominal surface. How many quadrants are involved?

One quadrant only: unlikely to be kidney.

Lower, either side: Requires higher-level care. *Upper:* Liver on the right, spleen on the left..

Two quadrants vertical:

Either side: Kidney if the axis is vertical, or it is not wider on top (toward the chest), and urine urobilinogen and bilirubin are normal.

Left: Spleen if it is wider upper (toward the chest) than lower; if you can feel a rounded tip, the tip points toward either the navel or toward the right pelvis.

Right: Liver but this is extremely rare.

(Continued on next page.)

[1] Rapid growth of any mass always causes pain because of stretching of nerve fibers.

[2] Usually a lump in the right lower abdomen.

[3] In this case the patient will have a history of ACUTE ABDOMEN Type 2 (see Protocol 39 C). He must be sent to a hospital.

Two quadrants horizontal:

RUQ and LUQ: Liver if it is mainly right and spills over to the left. Left lobe of the liver if it is centered and on both sides of the midline in the upper abdomen.

RLQ and LLQ: Probably a bladder or a pregnancy or a tumor.

Three quadrants: Determine which quadrant contains most of the mass.

Mainly left upper: Spleen mainly LUQ spills over to the lower right and lower left.

Mainly right upper: Liver mainly RUQ spills over to the upper left and lower right

Mainly lower: is a tumor; send the patient out.

Four quadrants:

Either liver or spleen depending on if it is predominantly right or left.

46 B1. Large Spleen:

It may be difficult to tell the difference between a large spleen and a large left kidney. Always check the urine with a dipstick. If the urobilinogen is normal on the dipstick,[1] the mass is more likely a kidney than spleen, especially if some of the other tests such as blood or protein or leukocytes are positive. If it is a kidney, then see Protocol 46 B3, Large Kidney, below. If most of the mass is toward the middle of the body from the nipple line (a plumb line dropped from the location of a male nipple), then it is likely an enlarged left lobe of the liver.

Note that, to save space, the disease entities in this chart are not upper case as in the rest of the Manual.

Disease	**Others**[2]	**Risk factors**	**Essential**	**Likely**	**Treatment**
Bartonellosis[3]	Yes, few, area	Residence in Peru or adjacent border areas; bitten by sand flies.	Either joint and bone pains or else skin bumps.	Fever, fatigue, anemia, easy bleeding.	Antibiotics
Brucellosis	Maybe, few, area	Contact with cattle or unpasteurized milk/ cheese.	Slow onset of back and joint pains, feels awful.	Fevers come and go.	Antibiotics
Cancer	Unlikely	Radiation exposure, other unknown factors, maybe liver cancer.	Slow onset, anemia, maybe large lymph nodes.	Fevers, frequent infections, abnormal bleeding.	Difficult
Cat-scratch Disease	Unlikely	Cat scratch or cat flea bite.	Large lymph nodes between scratch and trunk.	Fevers, rash, fatigue.	Antibiotics
Chaga's Disease	Maybe, few, area	C and S America but not much in the Amazon River valley; from parallel 41° south, north to the Texas border; low-class housing.	Heart trouble or swallowing problems or constipation.	History of a swollen eye, lasted more than a day.	Dangerous, special meds
Cirrhosis	Maybe, few, area	Alcoholics, those with schistosomiasis, exposure to various drugs and toxins, poor sanitation.	Distended abdomen; bilirubin in the urine.	Skin "spiders," easy bleeding.	Difficult

Continued on next page.

[1] It is normal for there to be some urobilinogen; abnormal is a color that is 2+ or more.

[2] "Others" tells whether the patient is likely to know others who have the same condition; whether these others are few or many; and whether they are from the same family or from the general community (area) where he lives.

[3] Bartonellosis: Scattered areas in Peru and adjacent border areas.

(46 B1. Large Spleen, continued.)

Disease	Others[1]	Risk factors	Essential	Likely	Treatment
Hydatid Disease	Maybe, few, area	Adults in arid tropics with dogs, or temperate forests with eating food gathered & raw.	Slow-onset; not children; soft tumors usually on the liver.	May be able to feel soft lumps on liver or spleen.	Surgery
Malaria	Yes, many, area	Mainly tropics and subtropics; no prophylaxis; mosquito bites.	Fever and chills or headaches.	Large spleen, fatigue, waist pain, shoulder pain.	Antimalarials Antibiotics
Mononucleosis	No	Young age, exposed to the disease.	Large tonsils and/or large neck lymph nodes; fever.	Extreme fatigue that lasts over a week.	Bedrest only
Ovalocytosis[2]	Yes, family	Asia/Pacific genetic heritage.	Anemia and family history of the same.	Occasional crises; early deaths in family.	Transfusion
Schistosomiasis Japonicum[3]	Maybe, area	Residence in some parts of Asia; exposed to water with snails.	Very distended abdomen; exposure in an affected area.	History of bloody diarrhea.	Praziquantel
Schistosomiasis Mansoni[4]	Maybe, area	Parts of Africa, the Middle East, and the Americas; exposed to fresh water with snails.	Present or previous bloody diarrhea.	Large liver, free fluid in the abdomen.	Praziquantel
Scrub Typhus[5]	Maybe, area	Rural SE Asia; bitten by chigger mites.	Fever, constipated, light avoidance, red eyes, fever.	Small scab from bite, large lymph nodes, rash.	Antibiotics
Sickle Cell Disease[6]	Yes, family	African, Arab, Greek or Indian heritages; African form is worst.	Children only; family history of ANEMIA and ill health.	Recurrent crises, early deaths in family.	Transfusions, IV fluids, oxygen
Syphilis	Unlikely	Mother or mother's partner was or is promiscuous.	Infant born with ill health.	Peeling hands, runny nose, rash in mouth.	Penicillin
Thallasemia	Yes, family	Mediterranean, African, or Asian heritage.	Ill health since birth or sudden onset of anemia with another illness.	Strange facial appearance, family history of ill health.	Transfusions

Continued on next page.

[1] "Others" tells whether the patient is likely to know others who have the same condition; whether these others are few or many; and whether they are from the same family or from the general community (area) where he lives.

[2] Ovalocytosis: Mainly the island of New Guinea; some in Malaysia. ELLIPTOCYTOSIS in a swathe in Africa between Algeria and Nigeria is virtually the same.

[3] Schistosomiasis Japonicum: In areas of mainland China, the Philippines, parts of the Celebes, the upper Mekong, and the Thai-Malaysian border.

[4] Schistosomiasis Mansoni: Scattered areas within Africa, the Arabian Peninsula, the Caribbean, and parts of eastern South America.

[5] Scrub Typhus: Present in the Indian subcontinent, central and southeast Asia, and the Pacific area.

[6] Sickle Cell Disease: This affects Blacks of African genetic origin, mainly in Africa and the Americas. Some Indians and Arabs are also affected.

(46 B1. Large Spleen, continued.)

Disease	Others[1]	Risk factors	Essential	Likely	Treatment
Trench Fever	Maybe, few; area	Poor sanitation, refugee camps, urban homeless, body lice.	Fevers and severe joint pains, lasts a long time.	Headache, shins painful.	Antibiotics
Typhus	Probably	Mainly tropical, body lice, rodent fleas, poor sanitation.	First ill, then fever, back and limb pain, constipated.	Musty odor, headache, red face, apathetic.	Antibiotics
Tropical Splenomegaly	Yes, many, area	Tropics, malarious areas.	Slow-onset; headaches, fatigue, anemia.	Enormous spleen that feels heavy.	Antimalarials Antibiotics
Visceral Leishmaniasis[2]	Likely; area	Residence in an affected area; bitten by sandflies.	Slow-onset; fevers off and on; liver also enlarges.	Fatigue, night sweats, poor appetite.	Special drugs

46 B2. Large Liver:

Upper right abdomen, long axis of the mass is horizontal or diagonal rather than vertical. If it is vertical, then it is probably a kidney: see 46 B3, below.

Disease	Others[1]	Risk factors	Essential	Likely	Tender?[3]	Urine[4]	Treatment
Alcoholism	Maybe; area	Daily alcohol usage or binge drinking.	Daily or binge drinking.	Distended abdomen.	N	B(U)	Counseling
Amebic Liver Disease	Maybe; area	Poor sanitation, history of dysentery.	Pain in right upper abdomen.	Hurts to jump, liver is tender to touch.	T	B	Metronidazole
Ascariasis	Likely; area	Poor sanitation, raw vegetables, clay soil, childhood.	Abdominal pain or seeing worms.	White "earthworms" visible in the stool.	T	B	Dewormers
Brucellosis	Likely; area	Pastoral areas; raw milk and meat, slaughter houses.	Joint pains and feeling awful, slow onset.	Fevers off and on, back and lower limbs only.	T	B	Antibiotic combinations
Cancer	Unlikely	Western diet, hepatitis, older age.	Varies according to kind.	Weight loss, lumpy liver edge, jaundice.	N→T	Varies	Difficult at best

Continued on next page.

[1] "Others" tells whether the patient is likely to know others who have the same condition; whether these others are few or many; and whether they are from the same family or from the general community (area) where he lives.

[2] Visceral Leishmaniasis: Found in scattered areas of Central and South America, Africa north of the equator, the Mediterranean area, the Indian subcontinent, eastern Europe, central Asia, and mainland China. Not present south of the equator.

[3] "Tender?" tells if the mass is tender—if pushing on it causes pain. N = not tender; T = tender; T→ N = tender changes to not-tender.

[4] "Urine" refers to the dipstick tests for bilirubin and urobilinogen. B = bilirubin positive; U = urobilinogen positive; letter in parentheses (U) or (B) - means maybe positive.

(46 B2. Large Liver, continued.)

Disease	Others[1]	Risk factors	Essential	Likely	Tender?[2]	Urine[3]	Treatment
Chaga's Disease[4]	Likely; area	Residence in affected area; poor housing with cracked walls.	Heart failure or constipated or trouble swallowing.	Had a swollen eye for more than a week.	T→ N	Neither	Difficult and dangerous
Gallbladder Disease	Unlikely	Western diet, ascariasis, some flukes, malaria.	Pain upper central or right abdomen.	Light-colored stools, itching.	T	B	Usually surgery
Heart Failure	Unlikely	Western diet, prior rheumatic fever or sepsis.	Short of breath or fatigued or both.	Swollen legs and feet.	T→ N	Neither	Special medicines
Hepatitis	Maybe area	Poor sanitation, blood exposure.	Jaundice or bilirubin in urine.	Joint pains, loss of appetite.	T	B(U)	Supportive, maybe antiviral
Hydatid Disease[5]	Likely, area	Residence in an affected area; adults only.	Slow onset of a soft tumor.	Nothing else.	??	B	Dewormers first, then surgery
Indian Childhood Cirrhosis[6]	Likely; ethnic	Indian cultural heritage, bronze drinking vessels.	Jaundice and/or fluid in the abdomen.	Slow onset.	probably N	B (U)	Very difficult
Liver Fluke[7]	Likely; area	Eating raw fish (Asia) or raw water vegetables .	No symptoms or else nausea, diarrhea, body pains.	Loss of appetite, upper abdominal pains.	T	B (U)	Special medicines
Pericarditis	Not likely	Tuberculosis, viral illnesses, occasionally bacterial infection.	Chest pain; fatigue, low pulse pressure.	Scraping heart sound per stethoscope or enlarged heart.	T→N	Neither	Difficult
Plant Poisoning (Various)	Likely; area	Using ethnic remedies or some drugs.	Symptoms vary by kind of poisoning.	Symptoms vary by kind of poisoning.	Varies	Probably B(U)	Variable

Continued on next page.

[1] "Others" tells whether the patient is likely to know others who have the same condition; whether these others are few or many; and whether they are from the same family or from the general community (area) where he lives.

[2] "Tender?" tells if the mass is tender—if pushing on it causes pain. N = not tender; T = tender; T→ N = tender changes to not-tender.

[3] "Urine" refers to the dipstick tests for bilirubin and urobilinogen. B = bilirubin positive; U = urobilinogen positive; letter in parentheses (U) or (B) - means maybe positive.

[4] Chaga's disease: Found in scattered areas in the Americas.

[5] Hydatid disease: There are two kinds; one is in cattle-raising areas of the tropics where there are dogs that live close to the people. The other kind is in temperate, rural areas where there are wild animals and people eat gathered, wild plant life that might be contaminated with the stool of the animals.

[6] Indian childhood cirrhosis: This is a form of liver failure that occurs in Indian children.

[7] Liver fluke: This may be either kind of liver fluke; one or the other kind is present in all general areas of the world.

(46 B2. Large Liver, continued.)

Disease	Others[1]	Risk factors	Essential	Likely	Tender?[2]	Urine[3]	Treatment
Relapsing Fever[4]	Likely: area	Exposure to ticks or lice in an affected area.	Sudden onset of headache, fevers, chills sweats.	Fatigue, bone, joint muscle pains.	Unknown	U(B)	Antibiotics
Rickets	Likely; area	Non-exposure to sunlight on the bare skin.	Bone pain and/or deformity.	Failure to grow in children.	N	Neither	Vitamin D
Schistosomiasis Japonicum[5]	Likely; area	Exposure to water with snails in an affected area.	Liver failure, large spleen, weight loss, big abdomen.	Diarrhea, brain damage, cough.	N	B(U)	Praziquantel
Schistosomiasis Mansoni[6]	Likely; area	Exposure to water with snails in an affected area.	Liver failure or chronic diarrhea, large spleen.	Urinary or reproductive symptoms.	N	B(U)	Praziquantel
Syphilis	Maybe; siblings	Mother had syphilis.	Baby under age 2.	Rash, runny nose, ill health.	Unknown	Unknown	Penicillin
Sickle Cell Disease[7]	Likely; family	African, Arab, Indian, or Greek genetic heritage.	Large spleen or history of one; anemia; family history.	Recurrent crises with pain.	N	U(B)	Transfusions, IV fluids, oxygen
Thallasemia	Likely; family	African, Asian, or Mediterranean genetic heritage.	Family history; recurrent crises, large spleen.	Strange facial appearance.	N	U	Transfusions
Visceral Leishmaniasis[8]	Likely; area	Exposed to sandflies in an affected area.	Large spleen; slow onset unless HIV+.	Night sweats, bleeding, loss of appetite.	N	U(B)	Special meds

[1] "Others" tells whether the patient is likely to know others who have the same condition; whether these others are few or many; and whether they are from the same family or from the general community (area) where he lives.

[2] "Tender?" tells if the mass is tender—if pushing on it causes pain. N = not tender; T = tender; T→ N = tender changes to not-tender.

[3] "Urine" refers to the dipstick tests for bilirubin and urobilinogen. B = bilirubin positive; U = urobilinogen positive; letter in parentheses (U) or (B) - means maybe positive.

[4] Relapsing Fever: Not in the islands of Southeast Asia or the Pacific.

[5] Schistosomiasis Japonicum: In areas of mainland China, the Philippines, parts of the Celebes, the upper Mekong, and the Thai-Malaysia border.

[6] Schistosomiasis Mansoni: Scattered areas within Africa, the Arabian Peninsula, the Caribbean, and parts of eastern South America.

[7] Sickle Cell Disease: This affects Blacks of African genetic origin, mainly in Africa and the Americas. Some Indians and Arabs are also affected.

[8] Visceral Leishmaniasis: Found in scattered areas of Central and South America, Africa north of the equator, the Mediterranean area, the Indian subcontinent, eastern Europe, central Asia, and mainland China. Not present south of the equator.

46 B3. Large Kidney:

Is the mass (presumably enlarged kidney) tender to touch?

NO

This may be cyst(s) on the kidney or it may be CANCER. Consider BURKITT LYMPHOMA; also consider TUBERCULOSIS of the kidney. If it is not TB, the patient must go to a higher-level facility.

YES

Consider: URINARY OBSTRUCTION; ABSCESS of the kidney; also consider TUBERCULOSIS of the kidney if the patient has TB elsewhere.

PROTOCOL 47. NAUSEA, VOMITING, or BOTH

This protocol deals only with usual vomiting. See Protocol 48 if the patient has vomited blood: red liquid or clots or brown stuff that looks like coffee grounds. For regular vomiting that only has streaks of blood, use this Protocol; ignore the blood.

Since this symptom is very common, it is better to focus on other, less common symptoms.

First check for DEHYDRATION. If your patient is dehydrated, treat him for that while working on the diagnosis. Severe dehydration with loss of consciousness is an emergency; use rectal or intraperitoneal fluids. See Volume I, Appendix 1.

Prompt vomiting of all food right after eating mandates sending the patient for surgery promptly, regardless of age, and treating for DEHYDRATION in the meantime using intraperitoneal fluids (Volume I, Appendix 1).

Symptomatic treatment: If the problem is not too severe and the patient is not too ill, try the following: Give nothing by mouth for 6 hours and have the patient lie as still as possible. At the beginning of this time, pour a bottle or can of Coca-Cola into a large-diameter container, and let it become warm. After 6 hours, all of the fizz will be gone. Give the patient a teaspoon at a time, every 2-5 minutes. If he keeps this down, advance the amount to a tablespoon at a time. In older children and adults it is acceptable to use PROMETHAZINE or HYDROXYZINE additionally, to settle the stomach.

Is the patient an infant, less than 4 months old?

NO

YES

Send him to the hospital if he is losing weight or if he vomits his entire feeding or if the whites of his eyes look yellow. If you cannot send him, consider SEPSIS, KIDNEY INFECTION. Treat for DEHYDRATION.

Does or did the patient have significant abdominal or chest pain, or is he unconscious?

Both NO

YES to either

Consider HEART ATTACK, ACUTE ABDOMEN, AMEBIC LIVER DISEASE, FOOD POISONING, new DIABETES, KIDNEY STONE, GALLBLADDER DISEASE, /// PIG-BEL,[1] INTESTINAL FLUKE.[2]

Continued on next page.

[1] Pig-bel: Developing countries, near the equator.

[2] Intestinal Fluke: Not present in Africa south of the Sahara or in the Pacific area. In the Americas it is only present in Guyana.

(47. Nausea, Vomiting, Or Both, continued.)

Does the patient have a high fever, or has he had one recently with this illness?

NO | **YES**

Extremely ill:
LASSA FEVER[1]: Weakness, aching; chest pain common.
MENINGITIS: Unconscious, a stiff neck or both, except in infants.
HEAT ILLNESS: Infant or elderly or exertion in heat.

No rash:
MALARIA: Chills, sweats, headaches.
EAR INFECTION: Ear pain. Fussiness in small children.
AMEBIC LIVER DISEASE: Pain in right upper abdomen.
RELAPSING FEVER[2]: Sudden chills, headache, body pain.
YELLOW FEVER[3]: General aching, headache, eye pain.
FAMILIAL MEDITERRANEAN FEVER: Recurrent abdominal/joint pains.

Maybe rash:
ENTERIC FEVER: Cough or abdominal pain; not alert.
ROSEOLA: Either rash or fever, not both.
TYPHUS: Whole body pains; intoxicated-like mental state.
LEPTOSPIROSIS: Sudden red eyes and whole body pains.
ARBOVIRAL FEVER: Variable symptoms; seek local lore.
RAT BITE FEVER: Inflamed bite wound or rash.
TULAREMIA[4]: Exposure to small animals and/or ticks.

Rash present:
MEASLES: Red-spotted or sandpapery rash.
SPOTTED FEVER[5]: Chills, headache, body pains.
KATAYAMA DISEASE: Episodes of fever and hives.

Does the patient also have diarrhea?

NO | **YES**

Consider CHOLERA if he is like an open faucet.
Otherwise: TURISTA, GIARDIASIS, DYSENTERY, GASTROENTERITIS, /// PLANT POISONING,[6] FOOD POISONING, SCHISTOSOMIASIS MANSONI,[7] RADIATION ILLNESS, INSECTICIDE POISONING, ARSENIC POISONING.

Does the patient also have a severe headache or eye pain?

NO or do not know | **YES**

Consider ALTITUDE SICKNESS, MIGRAINE, HEAT ILLNESS, CARBON MONOXIDE POISONING, GLAUCOMA.

Continued on next page.

---

[1] Lassa Fever: Only in the humid, rural areas of Africa.
[2] Relapsing Fever: Not in the islands of Southeast Asia or the Pacific.
[3] Yellow Fever: South America north of Sao Paolo, central and western Africa and the Sudan.
[4] Tularemia: North America, central Asia, Europe, Far East, the north coast of Africa; exposure to small animals..
[5] Spotted Fever: Not in the islands of Southeast Asia.
[6] Many kinds of plant poisoning cause vomiting.
[7] Schistosomiasis Mansoni: Scattered areas within Africa, the Arabian Peninsula, the Caribbean, and parts of eastern South America.

(47. Nausea, Vomiting, Or Both, continued.)

Does the patient have JAUNDICE, a swollen abdomen, or a large liver?

NO | YES

Consider LIVER DISEASE, LIVER FAILURE from any cause. Also consider HEPATITIS, LIVER FLUKE,[1] SCHISTOSOMIASIS MANSONI.[2]

Consider Alternatives	Fever	Other Characteristics
Pregnancy	No	Missed periods, daily nausea; early pregnancy only.
Overfeeding	No	Baby fed too much, vomits some; use smaller feedings.
ASCARIASIS	No	Crampy pain, constipated, common in children.
PEPTIC ULCER	No	Prompt vomiting of everything, right after eating.
==========		
ANGINA	No	Chest pain, sweaty, sense of doom.
GASTRITIS	No	Burning upper abdominal pains.
PLANT POISONING[3]	Unusual	Many types; check history of eating plant.
KIDNEY STONE	Unusual	Pain in back, side, groin, or genitals.
DIABETES	No	Sugar in urine, dehydrated, breathing fast.
============		
ARSENIC POISONING	No	Numbness, burning in hands; abdominal pains.
TRICHINOSIS	Usual	Ate rare meat within the last week.
WHOOPING COUGH	Low if any	Vomiting triggered by severe coughing spells.
KIDNEY FAILURE	Unusual	Eyes swollen in the morning, little or abnormal urine.

PROTOCOL 48. VOMITING BLOOD

Definition: The patient vomits either red blood or else a black substance that resembles coffee grounds (this is digested blood).

If this is part of a general bleeding problem: bloody nose, easy bruising, excessive menstruation, bloody stools, bleeding from minor wounds, then see the Protocol C-7.

Is the patient vomiting ordinary vomit with some streaks or small clots of blood in it?

NO | YES

Ignore the blood; use the previous Protocol.

Check for evidence of SHOCK: cool, moist skin, rapid pulse, low blood pressure.

SHOCK absent | SHOCK present

Treat for SHOCK and send out as soon as possible. **Consider** PEPTIC ULCER if there is a delay.

Continued on next page.

[1] Liver fluke: This might be caused by either kind of liver fluke. In Asia it is caused by eating raw or pickled fish; in other areas it is caused by eating water plants or drinking contaminated water from areas of sheep herding.

[2] Schistosomiasis mansoni: Scattered areas within Africa, the Arabian Peninsula, the Caribbean, and parts of eastern South America.

[3] Ackee, Argemone oil, Botulism, Claviceps, Coral plant, Lolism, Manicheel, Margosa oil, Mushrooms, Nicotine.

(48. Vomiting Blood, continued.)

Check the patient's nose and mouth for bleeding.

Bleeding absent

Bleeding present

Patient bled, swallowed the blood, then vomited it.
Consider HEMORRHAGIC FEVER if the patient is very ill.

Does the patient have a high fever or is he generally ill?

NO to both

YES to either

HEMORRHAGIC FEVER: Bleeding from multiple sites.
LIVER FAILURE: Distended abdomen, yellow eyes, or both.
LIVER DISEASE: Distended abdomen, yellow eyes, or both.
MALARIA: Chills, sweats, headaches.
ENTERIC FEVER: Cough or abdominal pain; not alert.
TROPICAL SPLENOMEGALY: ANEMIA, huge spleen.
VISCERAL LEISHMANIASIS[1]: Huge, spleen, large liver.
INDIAN CHILDHOOD CIRRHOSIS[2]: Bronze drinking vessels.
SCURVY: Diet lacking in fresh fruits and vegetables.
THALLASEMIA: Hereditary ANEMIA; spleen is large.
TYPHUS: Headache, aching all over, intoxicated mental state.
WHOOPING COUGH: Coughing, choking and vomiting.
YELLOW FEVER[3]: Headache, eye pain, aching all over.

A good general rule is to send anyone with an enlarged spleen to a hospital. Those with normal vital signs and without an enlarged spleen may be given symptomatic treatment.

Symptomatic treatment: Discontinue any ALCOHOL or ASPIRIN that the patient may be taking. Encourage intake of ORS (see *Drug Index*) initially and other liquids later, but allow no solid food intake for several days. Continue to check for SHOCK every few hours. An increase in the pulse rate, even without a drop in blood pressure, should prompt immediate evacuation. Consider a PEPTIC ULCER that has bled.

PROTOCOL 49. OTHER ABDOMINAL PROBLEMS

Appetite problems: see Protocol 9.

Abdominal wall stiff and hard like a board: Normal in an athletic person. If ill, consider ACUTE ABDOMEN, TETANUS.

Bleeding stump of umbilical cord in a newborn: treat with VITAMIN K by injection; put firm pressure on it meanwhile.

Infected stump of umbilical cord in a newborn: SEPSIS if the baby acts sick, otherwise CELLULITIS which may turn into SEPSIS.

Excessive gas: This is usually due to diet. Otherwise consider GALLBLADDER DISEASE, GIARDIASIS, GASTRITIS, PEPTIC ULCER, DYSENTERY (AMEBIC), CAPILLARIASIS,[4] SPRUE,[5] MILK INTOLERANCE, TRICHURIASIS, MALABSORPTION.

Loud, rumbling bowel sounds: Usually due to diet and of absolutely no consequence. Otherwise consider: GIARDIASIS, GASTROENTERITIS, TUBERCULOSIS, CAPILLARIASIS, SPRUE' MALABSORPTION.

Large veins on the abdominal wall: Normal in old age; LIVER FAILURE, CIRRHOSIS, TROPICAL SPLENOMEGALY.

---

[1] Visceral Leishmaniasis: Found in scattered areas of Central and South America, Africa north of the equator, the Mediterranean area, the Indian subcontinent, eastern Europe, central Asia, and mainland China.

[2] Indian Childhood Cirrhosis: Affects Indian children in India and elsewhere in the world.

[3] Yellow Fever: South America north of Sao Paolo, central and western Africa, and the Sudan.

[4] Capillariasis: Mainly in the Philippines; rarely in Thailand; found in Egypt with potential of spreading.

[5] Sprue: In the Americas only near or north of the equator. In Africa only Nigeria and southern Africa. Prevalent in India and Southeast Asia. Occasionally found in the Mediterranean area.

Indigestion: Usually this is from a dietary indiscretion. Occasionally it is from PEPTIC ULCER, HEARTBURN, ANGINA or a HEART ATTACK in those who have eaten a Western diet. PELLAGRA, INTESTINAL FLUKE,[1] SCHISTOSOMIASIS MANSONI,[2] CANCER, and LIVER FLUKE[3] may also cause chronic indigestion. ***Skin ulcer on the abdominal wall:*** AMEBIC SKIN ULCER, possibly SEXUALLY TRANSMITTED DISEASE if it is at or near the groin area.

IX. PELVIC AND RECTAL PROBLEMS

PROTOCOL 50. PELVIC AND RECTAL PAIN

In any sexually active patient, consider also the Sexually Transmitted Diseases which can seldom, if ever, be diagnosed separately without sophisticated lab. See the treatment protocol in *Index* C-1. The protocols below focus on non-reproductive problems and diseases.

50 A. Very Ill With a Fever
50 B. Rectal and/or Anal Pain
50 C. Pain With Urination
50 D. Genital Pain in Males
50 E. Vaginal and Pelvic Pain In Females
50 F Deep Bone Pain in Pelvis
50 G. Muscle Pains in Pelvis and Buttocks

50 A. Very Ill With a Fever:

Conditions	Characteristics
SEPSIS	Recent delivery, ABORTION, or miscarriage; infection, injury, or both.
ACUTE ABDOMEN	Pain with coughing, SHOCK, or both.
ABSCESS	Localized red, swollen, tender area which may feel soft.
STD[4]	Swelling or abnormal holes in the genital area; like an infected injury.
URINARY INFECTION	Burning and pain with urination, possibly with back pains also.
DENGUE FEVER[5]	Severe bone and joint pains, sudden onset, headache.
===============	
PLAGUE	Large, extremely tender lymph nodes with blackened skin on them.
LASSA FEVER[6]	Weakness, chest and general body pains.

[1] Intestinal Fluke: Found in Asia and the Middle East.
[2] Schistosomiasis Mansoni: Scattered areas within Africa, the Arabian peninsula, the Caribbean, and parts of eastern South America.
[3] Liver fluke: This kind of liver fluke (Fascioliasis) is found worldwide except for Southeast Asia. It is different than the kind of fluke found in Southeast Asia and East Asia.
[4] This is an abbreviation for SEXUALLY TRANSMITTED DISEASE; see Protocol C-1.
[5] Dengue Fever: In the Americas only near or north of the equator. In Africa only Nigeria and southern Africa. Prevalent in India, Southeast Asia, and the Pacific. Occasionally found in the Mediterranean area.
[6] Lassa fever occurs in epidemics in west and central Africa.

50 B. Rectal and/or Anal Pain:

Symptomatic treatment: Sitting in a tub of water frequently relieves pain.

Conditions	Fever	Other Characteristics
HEMORRHOIDS	No	Bluish bulge by rectum or blood on the outside of stool.
STD[1]	Maybe	Large groin nodes or visible sores or both; maybe pus.
PROSTATITIS (males)	Maybe	Heavy, aching pain between the rectum and the penis.
ABSCESS	Maybe	Red, warm bulge, tender to touch, near the rectum.
================		
PROCTITIS	Maybe	Pain inside with bowel movements.
FISSURE	No	Split in the skin, severe pain with bowel movements.
SCHISTOSOMIASIS HEMATOBIUM[2]	Unusual	Like PROCTITIS; maybe bloody urine also.
SCHISTOSOMIASIS MANSONI[3]	Unusual	Like PROCTITIS; maybe bloody urine also.

50 C. Pain With Urination:

Definition: The patient has pain either at the beginning of urination or at the end of urination or throughout. Usually there is also urgency (have to go RIGHT NOW) and frequency (frequent urination of small amounts).

First consider SEXUALLY TRANSMITTED DISEASES, Protocol C-1; this and URINARY INFECTION are most common.

Conditions	Fever	Other Characteristics
URINARY INFECTION	Usual	Urine cloudy; pain is usually burning or aching.
URETHRITIS	No	Pus from penis, males; like URINARY INFECTION.
==============		
TUBERCULOSIS	Usual	Gradual onset, no response to usual antibiotics.
SCHISTOSOMIASIS HEMATOBIUM	Maybe	Urine bloody, especially at the end of urination.
PROSTATITIS	Maybe	Pain between penis and rectum; tender prostate.
MYIASIS	Maybe	Maggots (little fat "worms") on genitals or in urine.
DENGUE FEVER[4]	High	Severe bone and joint pains, sudden onset, headache.
LASSA FEVER[5]	High	Weakness, chest and general body pains.
PLANT POISONING	No	Djenkol bean (Malaysia and Indonesia); bloody urine.

[1] This is an abbreviation for SEXUALLY TRANSMITTED DISEASE; see *Index C*, Protocol C-1.

[2] Schistosomiasis Hematobium: Present in some areas of Africa and the Middle East.

[3] Schistosomiasis Mansoni: Scattered areas within Africa, the Arabian Peninsula, the Caribbean, and parts of eastern South America.

[4] Dengue Fever: In the Americas only near or north of the equator. In Africa only Nigeria and southern Africa. Prevalent in India, Southeast Asia, and the Pacific. Occasionally found in the Mediterranean area.

[5] Lassa fever occurs in epidemics in west and central Africa.

50 D. Genital Pain in Males:

Symptomatic treatment: Have the patient wear a jock strap, or a homemade or cultural equivalent. Have him stay on bedrest and use IBUPROFEN for pain.

Visually examine the genital area. The skin of the scrotum and penis can be affected just like the skin elsewhere. Check Skin Protocols 14 - 17 in this *Index*, if nothing fits from this protocol. Try the symptomatic treatment first.

Two major alternatives to consider:

1. Sudden onset of pain.
2. Slow onset of pain.

If there was sudden onset of pain in a previously healthy person who has no fever now, and if the pain is not relieved by the Symptomatic Treatment, then send the patient to a hospital immediately. He may have a twisted testicle which he will lose if he does not have emergency surgery.

If the onset of pain was slow, or there is a fever, or pain was somewhat relieved with the symptomatic treatment, proceed as follows:

Does the patient have a high fever?

NO

YES
Consider: DENGUE FEVER,[1] FILARIASIS, BRUCELLOSIS, SPOTTED FEVER (in the Americas).

Does the patient have a swollen scrotum?

NO

YES
Consider: SEXUALLY TRANSMITTED DISEASEs; EPIDIDYMITIS,[2] FILARIASIS, MUMPS, HERNIA, BRUCELLOSIS, TUBERCULOSIS, AFRICAN SLEEPING SICKNESS.[3] See also Protocol 52A.

Conditions	Fever	Other Characteristics
Injury	No	Should see bruising or obtain a history of injury.
STD[4]	Maybe	Blister or ulcer or enlarged groin nodes.
EPIDIDYMITIS	Maybe	Back side of testicle very tender.
================		
PARAPHIMOSIS	No	Foreskin pulled back from penis tip and swollen there.
PHIMOSIS	No	Foreskin stuck to the (uncircumcised) tip of the penis.
SICKLE CELL DISEASE[5]	Maybe	Painful erection that won't go away.
PROSTATITIS	Maybe	Heavy aching between the penis and rectum.

Continued on next page.

[1] Dengue Fever: In the Americas only near or north of the equator. In Africa only Nigeria and southern Africa. Prevalent in India, Southeast Asia, and the Pacific. Occasionally found in the Mediterranean area.

[2] If you elevate and support the testicles for an hour, the pain is relieved. This distinguishes epididymitis from a twisted testicle.

[3] African Sleeping Sickness: Scattered areas of Africa, south of Bamako, Mali and Lake Chad and north of Lusaka, Zambia.

[4] This is an abbreviation for SEXUALLY TRANSMITTED DISEASE; see *Index C*, Protocol C-1.

[5] Sickle Cell Disease: This affects Blacks of African genetic origin, mainly in Africa and the Americas. Some Indians and Arabs are also affected.

(50 D. Genital Pain in Males, continued.)

Conditions	Fever	Other Characteristics
SCHISTOSOMIASIS HEMATOBIUM[1]	Rare	Dull aching in area behind scrotum.
SCHISTOSOMIASIS MANSONI[2]	Rare	Dull aching in area behind scrotum.
KIDNEY STONE	Rare	Pain in genitals, no tenderness[3]; sudden onset.

50 E. Vaginal and Pelvic Pain in Females:

If the problem is itching, see VAGINITIS. The skin of the genital area can develop skin problems just like skin anywhere else. Check skin protocols if applicable. See SEXUALLY TRANSMITTED DISEASE, Protocol C-1, if the patient is a sexually-active adult or sexually abused minor.

Conditions	Fever	Other Characteristics
PELVIC INFECTION	Usual	Pain with intercourse, tampon insertion, or jumping.
TUBERCULOSIS	Usual	Like PELVIC INFECTION; onset over months; usually cough also.
TUBAL PREGNANCY	No	Pain less than a month; more to right or left than center.
STD[4]	Maybe	A visible blister or sore or large groin lymph nodes.
CHANCROID	No	Large, tender groin nodes without a visible sore.
MENOPAUSE	No	Irritation with intercourse because of dry vagina.
=================		
DYSENTERY, amebic	Maybe	Painful and tender bowels, right, left, or both.
Injury	Rare	Visible or evident from history.
KIDNEY STONE	No	Severe pains, one side; usually vomiting.
MYIASIS	Maybe	Visible maggots in genital area.
SCHISTOSOMIASIS HEMATOBIUM[5]	No	Bloody urine, pain with urination.
CANCER	Rare	Abnormal pelvic exam; see Vol. I, Chapter 6.

50 F. Deep Bone Pain in Pelvis:

Definition: Deep bone pain is an aching pain, worse at night, with high humidity, and with weight bearing. It is invariably severe.

Symptomatic treatment: ACETAMINOPHEN or IBUPROFEN is always appropriate. ASPIRIN is usually appropriate in adults but should not be used until you have reached a diagnosis.

Conditions	Fever	Other Characteristics
TUBERCULOSIS	Maybe	Slow-onset, one joint only, limp; thin thigh muscles.
RICKETS	No	Inadequate sun, patient or baby's mother.
DENGUE FEVER[6]	High	Sudden onset, also limb pains and rash.
==============		

Continued on next page.

[1] Schistosomiasis Hematobium: Present in some areas of Africa and the Middle East.

[2] Schistosomiasis Mansoni: Scattered areas within Africa, the Arabian Peninsula, the Caribbean, and parts of eastern South America.

[3] No tenderness means that the pain is no worse when you push on the painful area than when you do not.

[4] This is an abbreviation for SEXUALLY TRANSMITTED DISEASE; see *Index C*, Protocol C-1.

[5] Schistosomiasis Hematobium: Present in some areas of Africa and the Middle East.

[6] Dengue Fever: In the Americas only near or north of the equator. In Africa only Nigeria and southern Africa. Prevalent in India, Southeast Asia, and the Pacific. Occasionally found in the Mediterranean area.

(50 F. Deep Bone Pain in Pelvis, continued.)

Conditions	Fever	Other Characteristics
OSTEOMYELITIS	High	Increased pain with tapping anywhere on the pelvis.
SICKLE CELL DISEASE[1]	Common	Recurrent abdominal pain, ANEMIA; hereditary.
BRUCELLOSIS	Erratic	Joint pains or shooting pains; slow onset.
BARTONELLOSIS[2]	Yes	General aching, bumps on backs of legs.
YAWS	Maybe	Skin over painful area is inflamed or broken open.

50 G. Muscle Pains in Pelvis and Buttocks:

Symptomatic treatment: ACETAMINOPHEN or IBUPROFEN is always appropriate. ASPIRIN is usually appropriate in adults but should not be used until you have reached a diagnosis.

Is this part of a general illness with a high fever and general whole body pains?

NO to either

YES to both
See Protocol 10 in this *Index* and also Protocol C-2.

Conditions	Characteristics
MUSCLE STRAIN	Patient fell or nearly fell or did unaccustomed exercise.
PYOMYOSITIS	Warmth and swelling; site of old injection or minor injury.
==========	
POLIO	Some weakness which is worse in pelvis than in feet and toes.
RICKETS	Inadequate sun, patient or baby's mother.
CYSTICERCOSIS	History of eating inadequately cooked pork.
TRICHINOSIS	Ate rare or raw meat within the past month.

PROTOCOL 51. RECTAL AND GENITAL ITCHING

Symptomatic treatment: Washing with cool water and soap, drying well, and using baby powder will frequently relieve itching. If this helps, the problem is mucous irritation only. Continue this treatment. Otherwise consider the following:

First consider SEXUALLY TRANSMITTED DISEASES, particularly in females; see Protocol C-1.

Conditions	Characteristics
VAGINITIS	Itching around or in vagina, maybe discharge or odor.
CANDIDIASIS	Bright, red rash with some red spots around it.
ENTEROBIASIS	Tiny worms visible by the rectum, about 1/2 hour after going to bed.
STRONGYLOIDIASIS	Pricking, itching sensation by rectum and/or buttocks.
LICE	Very small moving creatures and/or bumps (louse eggs) on pubic hairs.
SCABIES	Fine little spots or holes that are extremely itchy.
============	

Continued on next page.

[1] Sickle Cell Disease: This affects Blacks of African genetic origin, mainly in Africa and the Americas. Some Indians and Arabs are also affected.

[2] Bartonellosis: Scattered areas in Peru and adjacent border areas.

(Protocol 51. Rectal and Genital Itching, continued.)

Rat TAPEWORM	Try a treatment if rats are common.
Beef TAPEWORM	White rectangles visible by anus or in stool.
DIABETES	Known diabetic or sugar in urine and thirst and vomiting.
Food allergy	Itching 3 or 4 days after eating the offending food; keep a diet diary and eliminate the offending food[1].

If nothing else is evident, sometimes ERYTHROMYCIN, taken in usual doses for five days, will eliminate the itching. (See the *Drug Index.*)

PROTOCOL 52. ABNORMAL APPEARANCE OF PELVIS AND RECTUM

52 A. Groin Swelling and Genital Swelling
52 B. Enlarged Groin Lymph Nodes
52 C. Other Abnormal Appearance of Pelvis and Rectum

52 A. Groin and Genital Swelling:

Symptomatic treatment: Cold packs or cool, wet cloths on the swollen area may decrease swelling and help the patient's distress.

Abdominal swelling can go down into the scrotum in males or the genital lips in females. See Protocol 46 A if the abdomen is swollen. HERNIA is most common.

Note: In the following table, an asterisk (*) indicates conditions that affect males only.

Is the patient sexually active (or possibly an abused child)?

NO (continue below)

YES: **Consider** SEXUALLY TRANSMITTED DISEASE, *Index C*, Protocol C-1. Otherwise continue down the "No" arm of this question.

Is the swelling in the scrotum or vaginal area only with no swelling in the groin(s)?

NO (continue below)

YES: In a dark room, shine a bright flashlight behind the swelling; does the light shine through?

- NO: **Consider**: EPIDIDYMITIS*, FILARIASIS, MUMPS*, ABSCESS, LEPROSY*, LYMPHOGRANULOMA VENEREUM, DONOVANOSIS, rarely CANCER in men under 40 y.o.
- YES: **Consider** HYDROCELE*.

Is the swelling in the groin only, with the genital area not swollen?

NO (continue below)

YES: **Consider** enlarged groin lymph nodes (see Protocol 52 B), DONOVANOSIS, HERNIA, ONCHOCERCIASIS,[2] TUBERCULOSIS.

Undescended testicle (empty scrotum on that side).

Continued on next page.

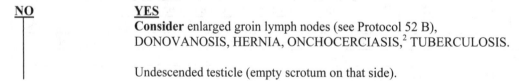

[1] Dairy products, fish, peanuts are the most common offenders.
[2] Onchocerciasis: Scattered areas in Africa, the Middle East, Central America, and northern South America.

(52 A. Groin and Genital Swelling, contnued.)

Is the patient a male with a swollen penis?

NO

YES

Consider: LYMPHOGRANULOMA VENEREUM, SCHISTOSOMIASIS HEMATOBIUM,[1] AFRICAN SLEEPING SICKNESS,[2] PARAPHIMOSIS, PHIMOSIS, CANCER, SICKLE CELL DISEASE[3] can cause a painful erection that will not go away.

Consider alternatives; both groin and genitals swollen:

Conditions	Characteristics
LYMPHOGRANULOMA VENEREUM	Genital swelling which may be massive, usually with swollen groin lymph nodes.
FILARIASIS	Both large nodes in groin and swollen genitals and/or leg.
HERNIA	Swelling is from the leg creases down into the scrotum or genital lips.
CELLULITIS	Skin red and swollen, warm, maybe tender.
ONCHOCERCIASIS[4]	Firm bulge, or lumps within "bags" of groin skin.
BRUCELLOSIS	Gradual onset of general pains, fevers, and weakness.
AFRICAN SLEEPING SICKNESS[5]	Gradual onset of fevers, headaches, and abnormal sleep-wake cycles.

52 B. Enlarged Groin Lymph Nodes:

Definition: There are lumps on or right above (touching) or right below (touching) the crease line, where the thigh comes up toward the trunk, just to the side of where one can feel the pulse in that area. Enlarged nodes the size of cherries or smaller are normal in anyone who walks barefoot.

First consider SEXUALLY TRANSMITTED DISEASES, *Index C*, Protocol C-1. If not, then proceed:

Does the patient have any sores on his or her legs or genitals

NO

YES

Injury: History of an injury or a scar or infection of legs/groin.
ABSCESS: There is a warm, swollen area on the legs/feet.
CELLULITIS: There is a warm, swollen area on the legs/feet.
TROPICAL ULCER: Crater-like wound on the legs/feet.
YAWS[6]: Some raised areas, some craters, both off-white.
SCRUB TYPHUS[7]: Fever, headache, muscle pains, small scab.
SPOTTED FEVER[8]: Fever, headache, muscle pains, rash.
TULAREMIA[9]: Fever, chills, headache, muscle pains.
PLAGUE: Black skin over tender lymph nodes; maybe black scab(s).
RAT BITE FEVER: Inflamed wound from animal bite.
ANTHRAX: Black wound with swelling around it.

(Continued on next page)

[1] Schistosomiasis Hematobium: Scattered areas of Africa and the Middle East only.

[2] African Sleeping Sickness: Scattered areas of Africa, south of Bamako, Mali and Lake Chad and north of Lusaka, Zambia.

[3] Sickle Cell Disease: This affects Blacks of African genetic origin, mainly in Africa and the Americas. Some Indians and Arabs are also affected.

[4] Onchocerciasis: Scattered areas in Africa, the Middle East, Central America, and northern South America.

[5] African Sleeping Sickness: Scattered areas of Africa, south of Bamako, Mali and Lake Chad and north of Lusaka, Zambia.

[6] Yaws: Only the humid tropics.

[7] Scrub Typhus: Present in the India area, central and southeast Asia, the Far East, and the Pacific.

[8] Spotted Fever: Not in the islands of Southeast Asia.

[9] Tularemia: North America, central Asia, Europe, Far East, the north coast of Africa; exposure to small animals.

(52 B. Enlarged Groin Lymph Nodes, Continued.)

Is the patient an adult female?

NO

YES

Question her as to whether she or her partner may be promiscuous. If yes or evasive, then treat her for whatever SEXUALLY TRANSMITTED DISEASE she is likely to have; see Protocol C-1. Many such diseases have no or minor symptoms in females for an extended time. If an STD is unlikely, follow the "No" arm for this question. Consider also HIV INFECTION, seroconversion illness.

Does the patient have a skin condition affecting much or most of his body?

NO

YES

Consider: LEPROSY reaction,[1] ONCHOCERCIASIS,[2] HIV INFECTION, maybe SPOTTED FEVER,[3] MONKEYPOX,[4] FILARIASIS, SYPHILIS.

Does the patient have a very large spleen?

NO

YES

Consider: VISCERAL LEISHMANIASIS,[5] AFRICAN SLEEPING SICKNESS,[6] BARTONELLOSIS, SYPHILIS.[7]

Conditions	Characteristics
CHANCROID	Groin nodes are tender to touch; genital sore may not be present.
FILARIASIS	Episodes of pain and swelling of legs/feet/genitals.
HIV INFECTION seroconversion illness	Flu-type illness, maybe with a measles rash, under 4 weeks post-exposure.
HIV INFECTION	Fevers, weight loss, diarrhea, cough; any one or more of these.
STD[8]	Sexually active adult or sexually abused child; See *Index C*, Protocol C-1.
================	
SCURVY	Bleeding gums, easy bruising, eats no fresh fruit or vegetables.
AFRICAN SLEEPING SICKNESS[9]	Erratic fevers, abnormal sleep pattern, maybe uncoordinated.
SCRUB TYPHUS[10]	Fevers, very ill, rural areas, bitten by a mite.
PLAGUE	Exquisitely tender, swollen lymph nodes; high fevers; very ill.

[1] A leprosy reaction is a sudden change in leprosy, usually in response to drug treatment. It is not an ALLERGY to the medication being used to treat the disease.

[2] Onchocerciasis: Scattered areas in Africa, the Middle East, Central America, and northern South America.

[3] Spotted Fever: Not in the islands of Southeast Asia.

[4] Monkeypox: In northern D R Congo and adjacent Central African Republic; rarely in western Africa.

[5] Visceral Leishmaniasis: Found in scattered areas of Central and South America, Africa north of the equator, the Mediterranean area, the Indian subcontinent, southern Europe, central Asia, and mainland China.

[6] African Sleeping Sickness: Scattered areas of Africa, south of Bamako, Mali and Lake Chad and north of Lusaka, Zambia.

[7] Bartonellosis: Scattered areas within Peru and adjacent border areas.

[8] This is an abbreviation for SEXUALLY TRANSMITTED DISEASE; see Protocol C-1.

[9] African Sleeping Sickness: Scattered areas of Africa, south of Bamako, Mali and Lake Chad; north of Lusaka, Zambia.

[10] Scrub Typhus: Present in the Indian area, central and southeast Asia, the Far East, and the Pacific area.

52 C. Other Abnormal Appearance of Pelvis and Rectum:

Pink, moist bulge hanging out of rectum: RECTAL PROLAPSE.

Cannot tell sex of a newborn: Send to a major medical center; do not guess.

No testicle in scrotum. Usually with bulge(s) in groin area(s): Check again after warming the genital area. If still not there, send out when convenient.

Painless ulcers, cracks, or bumps in genital or groin areas: DONOVANOSIS; SYPHILIS; REITER SYNDROME; possibly other SEXUALLY TRANSMITTED DISEASES.

Painful ulcers, blisters, cracks, or bumps in genital or groin area: AMEBIC SKIN ULCER, CHANCROID, LYMPHOGRANULOMA VENEREUM, HERPES, FISSURE, MONKEYPOX,[1] SEXUALLY TRANSMITTED DISEASE.

Extra holes in genital area: GONORRHEA (males), LYMPHOGRANULOMA VENEREUM, DONOVANOSIS, AMEBIC SKIN ULCER.

Large groin lymph nodes that hang down in loose bags of skin: ONCHOCERCIASIS.[2]

Swollen scrotum: See Protocol 52 A.

Foreskin stuck on end of penis: PHIMOSIS.

Foreskin stuck behind end of penis: PARAPHIMOSIS.

Visible worms: ASCARIASIS (earthworm-size), ENTEROBIASIS (short/skinny), MYIASIS (short/fat), STRONGYLOIDIASIS (under the skin, near rectum), TRICHURIASIS (coiled), TAPEWORM (flat, rectangular segments), MYIASIS (under the skin of buttocks)

Scars in groin area: an old injury, prior hernia surgery, maybe SEXUALLY TRANSMITTED DISEASE.

Erection that will not go away: SICKLE CELL DISEASE,[3] RABIES, BRAIN DAMAGE, any spinal cord injury. This is an emergency. It must be dealt with quickly or it will cause impotence.

Black, discolored dead genital skin: TYPHUS, SPOTTED FEVER,[4] other causes of GANGRENE.

PROTOCOL 53. ABNORMAL VAGINAL BLEEDING

53 A. Probably Not Pregnant
53 B. First Three Months of Pregnancy
53 C. Second Three Months of Pregnancy
53 D. Last Three Months Of Pregnancy

First check patient's vital signs, check her for SHOCK, and treat if necessary.

53 A. Probably Not Pregnant: (As far as the patient can tell)

Definiton: Vaginal bleeding with no prior missed periods or no sexual activity or used reliable birth control. (Condoms are not reliable birth control.)

If this is part of a general bleeding problem: easy bruising, bloody nose, vomiting blood, bloody stool, etc, see Protocol C-7 additionally.

Is bleeding a heavy menstruation in someone who usually menstruates?

NO

Continued on next page.

YES

Try to wait it out, checking frequently for SHOCK and ANEMIA. If either occurs, send her out. You may try BIRTH CONTROL PILLS.
Consider: THALLASEMIA, SCURVY, TYPHUS, HEMORRHAGIC FEVER, PELVIC INFECTION due to TUBERCULOSIS.

---

[1] Monkeypox: Northern D.R. Congo and adjacent border area in Central African Republic; rarely West Africa.

[2] Onchocerciasis: Scattered areas in Africa, the Middle East, Central America, and northern South America.

[3] Sickle Cell Disease: This affects Blacks of African genetic origin, mainly in Africa and the Americas. Some Indians and Arabs are also affected.

[4] Spotted Fever: Not in the islands of Southeast Asia.

(53 A. Probably Not Pregnant, continued.)

Consider alternatives:

If the patient *just had a baby*, see Chapter 7 of Vol. I.

If the patient is *going through MENOPAUSE* (40's or 50's), send out for higher level care.

Irregular periods: ignore for the time being unless they are very heavy and the patient is developing ANEMIA. Treat ANEMIA if it develops. Have the patient seen by a physician when it is convenient. Otherwise try a few months of BIRTH CONTROL PILLS.

Very heavy menses during menopause or in a girl who is just starting to menstruate: have her take BIRTH CONTROL PILLS for a few months.

Vaginal bleeding in a woman past menopause: Possibly CANCER; needs to be sent out to a medical facility within a few weeks.

Bleeding (slight) after intercourse: usually no problem, but send the patient to a physician to be checked for SEXUALLY TRANSMITTED DISEASE and CANCER. Make an effort to distinguish between bleeding in the woman and bloody semen in her husband. Blood in semen is potentially quite serious.

Some light bleeding in the middle of the month at the time of ovulation is common and normal.

53 B. First Three Months of Pregnancy:

(See also Chapter 6 of Volume I.)

Definition: Vaginal bleeding after one or two missed periods in a woman who is sexually active; the upper rim of the uterus is no higher than half-way between the pubic bone and the navel..

If this is part of a general bleeding problem: easy bruising, bloody nose, vomiting blood, bloody stool, etc, see Protocol C-7 additionally.

If there is a fever or patient is very ill, see SEPSIS. If the patient is having pain, or had pain, consider TUBAL PREGNANCY. Otherwise:

Is bleeding as much as a regular period?

NO, not as much	**YES, as much or more**
Threatened miscarriage: bed rest, no tampons, no intercourse until bleeding stops. If it becomes as much as a regular period, send her out.	Send the patient out or call for advice. Treat SHOCK if it occurs.

53 C. Second Three Months of Pregnancy:

(See also Chapter 6 of Volume I.)

If this is part of a general bleeding problem: easy bruising, bloody nose, vomiting blood, bloody stool, etc, see Protocol C-7 additionally.

If bleeding is more than slight, it probably means a spontaneous ABORTION (miscarriage) which may be due to any one of a large number of diseases and/or drugs. Wait it out as these miscarriages usually complete themselves. If there is heavy bleeding (enough to soak 3 pads or more), then send the patient to a hospital right away. If it goes on for more than a day or two or the patient develops a fever or is very sick see SEPSIS.

53 D. Last Three Months Of Pregnancy:

(See also Chapter 6 of Volume I.)

If this is part of a general bleeding problem: easy bruising, bloody nose, vomiting blood, bloody stool, etc, see Protocol C-7 additionally.

The patient may be in labor. If so, bleeding enough to soak one pad is normal. If the patient is not (or should not be) in labor or the bleeding is heavier, send her out immediately. If you do not, she and the baby both are likely to die.

PROTOCOL 54. ABNORMAL VAGINAL DISCHARGE

Definition: The patient has an unusually large amount of watery or creamy liquid flowing out from her vagina, either with or without an odor, either blood-tinged or not, with either pain or itching or both or neither.

In the following, "sore" means a visible break in the skin or vaginal surface with raw flesh, something like a skin ulcer, laceration, or wound; it may or may not be painful or tender.

First see SEXUALLY TRANSMITTED DISEASES: Protocol C-1; it is best to treat according to that protocol unless there is some reason not to do so.

Condition	Sore	Odor	Other Characteristics
PELVIC INFECTION	No	Unlikely	Pus present, usually abdominal pain also.
VAGINITIS, bacterial	No	Fishy	No itching, moderate discharge; bad odor.
VAGINITIS, candida	No	Little	Usually much itching; white thick discharge.
VAGINITIS, trichomonas	No	Little	Moderate itching; foamy, yellow-green.
ENTEROBIASIS	No	None	Little worms visible at night.
Tampon, forgotten	No	Foul, rotten	Remove tampon, rinse vagina.
SEPSIS	Maybe	Maybe	High fever, very ill, severe pain.
MYIASIS[1]	Maybe	Maybe, foul	Maggots visible (short, fat "worms").
DONOVANOSIS	Yes	Maybe foul	Sore relatively painless; ragged edges.
CHANCROID	Maybe	Foul	Sore, if there is one, is painful; large nodes.
Infection after childbirth	Usual	Foul (usually)	Recent childbirth with tearing; see SEPSIS.

Also see Chapter 7, Volume I.

PROTOCOL 55. CONSTIPATION

Definition: The patient has bowel movements much less frequently than his usual pattern, and when he does move his bowels, it is difficult to pass the stool. The stool is usually dry and comes out in small rather than large pieces. What constitutes constipation varies greatly between cultures and between individuals within a culture.

Note: DEHYDRATION is the most common cause of constipation. Any rectal pain will cause constipation because the patient will try to avoid pain by holding his stool; see Protocol 50 B if this appears to be the reason for the constipation. The most common pain-mediated causes of constipation are HEMORRHOIDS, genital HERPES, and FISSUREs.

Symptomatic treatment: Do not do this if there is a fever or signs of ACUTE ABDOMEN. If there is neither of these and if the bowel sounds are not very active, then you may give the patient prunes or Ex-lax, or any culturally equivalent medication obtained from a pharmacy. In tropical areas papaya seeds work well. Enemas may also work.

Does the patient have definite signs of ACUTE ABDOMEN (see Protocol 39 C)?

NO or not sure	**YES, definitely**
↓	Send out immediately, treating meanwhile.

Continued on next page.

[1] This only occurs if the patient sometimes lies naked and uncovered in a place where flies can access her genital area. This is generally amongst the poor, disabled and/or socially disadvantaged.

(Protocol 55. Constipation, continued.)

Does the patient have a high fever?

NO

YES

Consider ENTERIC FEVER /// DENGUE FEVER,[1] TYPHUS, BRUCELLOSIS, SCRUB TYPHUS,[2] LEPTOSPIROSIS, FAMILIAL MEDITERRANEAN FEVER. See Protocol C-9.

Did the patient previously have severe diarrhea for a day or more?

NO

YES

It is normal not to move bowels for a week after. If this is alternating constipation and diarrhea, consider IRRITABLE BOWEL, DYSENTERY, IMPACTION, SPRUE.[3]

Is the patient taking strong pain medications?

NO

YES

Usual side-effect; use any laxative to relieve it.

Does the patient have a dry mouth?

NO

YES

Constipation is due to DEHYDRATION or else one of the drugs such as DIPHENHYDRAMINE; treat the dehydration or stop the drug.

Does the patient have numbness, tingling, weakness, or paralysis of his lower limbs or pelvic area?

NO

YES

Consider: SPINAL NEUROPATHY, SYPHILIS, TROPICAL SPASTIC PARAPARESIS, STROKE, BRAIN DAMAGE.

Consider alternatives:

Conditions	Characteristics
Old age	Most common cause of constipation; use a high-fiber diet.
DIABETES	Definite diagnosis or else excessive thirst and urination.
DEPRESSION	Possibly appetite change; sleep disturbance.
MALNUTRITION	If adequate food doesn't go down, stool won't come out the bottom.
HEMORRHOIDS	Pain with moving bowels, sometimes blood on stool.
ASCARIASIS	Crampy pains also, especially in children; areas with clay soils with poor sanitation.
IMPACTION	Common with old and disabled persons. Frequently DEHYDRATION also.
===============	
DYSENTERY (amebic)	Crampy pains in lower left abdomen; diarrhea later.
TUBERCULOSIS	Abdominal TB, usually due to swallowed sputum in a coughing patient.
HERPES (genital)	Also back pain, history of painful genital blisters.
FISSURE	Extreme rectal pain; small split in skin by the opening.

Continued on next page.

[1] Dengue Fever: In the Americas only near or north of the equator. In Africa only Nigeria and southern Africa. Prevalent in India, Southeast Asia, and the Pacific. Occasionally found in the Mediterranean area.

[2] Scrub Typhus: Parts of the Indian subcontinent, central and southeast Asia, East Asia, and the Pacific; mainly rural.

[3] Sprue: In the Americas only near or north of the equator. In Africa only Nigeria and southern Africa. Prevalent in India and Southeast Asia. It is occasionally found in the Mediterranean area.

(Protocol 55. Constipation, continued.)

===============	
BRUCELLOSIS	Joint pains or sharp, shooting pains or both; severe fatigue, slow onset.
INTESTINAL FLUKE[1]	Comes from eating raw water plants, e.g. lotus and watercress.
CANCER	Progressive constipation, maybe lumpy liver or weight loss.
HYDATID DISEASE[2]	Tropical/arid areas with dogs; progressive constipation.
THYROID TROUBLE	Always tired, weight gain, slow pulse, brittle hair.
CHAGA'S DISEASE[3]	Also trouble swallowing, maybe HEART FAILURE.
LEAD POISONING	Also ANEMIA, crampy pains, maybe a metallic taste in the mouth.

PROTOCOL 56. DIARRHEA

56 A. Non-Bloody Diarrhea
- *56 A1. Watery Diarrhea, Sudden, Recent Onset, Not Grossly Bloody*
- *56 A2. Recurrent Diarrhea*
- *56 A3. Persistent Diarrhea*
- *56 A4. Chronic Diarrhea*

56 B. Bloody Diarrhea

56 A. Non-Bloody Diarrhea:

Definition: Diarrhea is an increased frequency and volume of stool relative to the patient's usual habits.

Symptomatic treatment: Check for DEHYDRATION first and treat for that. If the patient is not vomiting and does not have DIABETES[4], give him ORS to drink. If he is vomiting, consider rectal fluids if the diarrhea is not so bad. If the patient is having both severe vomiting and diarrhea, he is very dehydrated, and you cannot send him to a hospital, consider intraperitoneal fluids. See Volume I, Appendix 1. Diarrhea that follows antibiotic usage is best treated with yogurt, brewer's yeast, or giving an enema of normal stool dissolved in water. In any case, stop the antibiotic if at all feasible. Yogurt or powdered yogurt culture may be used to treat any kind of diarrhea.

Diarrhea in Children: Persistent diarrhea[5] in children is frequently associated with another underlying bacterial infection: PNEUMONIA, EAR INFECTION, and URINARY INFECTION being the most common. Children with CANDIDIASIS in their mouths, those with MALNUTRITION, and those with PNEUMONIA are the most likely to die. It is important to examine children with persistent diarrhea for these other conditions, and to treat for them. Treatment for the other conditions may also take care of the diarrhea.

Terminology

Kind:
- Watery diarrhea - is 90% or more liquid.
- Mushy diarrhea - is the consistency of runny mashed potatoes.
- Mucous diarrhea- contains white, stringy material; it may be mushy or watery.

Amount: (assuming patient is an adult).
- Small - less than a cup at a time.
- Moderate - more than a cup, but less than a liter, at a time.
- Large or huge - more than a liter at a time.

Smell:
- Usual - ordinary stool odor.
- Foul - indicates a particularly offensive and strong odor.

---

[1] The kind of intestinal fluke that can cause constipation early in the course of the disease occurs throughout Asia.

[2] Hydatid Disease: This may also rarely be found in northern temperate/arctic areas where people eat food that may be contaminated with wild animal stool. In this case the disease may be very aggressive.

[3] Chaga's Disease: Present in scattered areas of the Americas.

[4] If he does have DIABETES, give him plain water with 1 teaspoon of salt per liter.

[5] Sudden onset, lasted more than 14 days, less than 2 consecutive days without diarrhea.

56 A1. Watery Diarrhea, Sudden, Recent Onset, Not Grossly Bloody:

Is the patient's mouth very dry, his skin very loose, and his eyes sunken?

NO | **YES**

YES: Rehydrate and arrange transport while you work through the rest of this protocol, following the "No" arm.

Is the diarrhea of recent onset: (Has the patient had normal bowels for the past two months?)

Yes, recent onset | **No, this has been happening for a while:**

No, this has been happening for a while:
Go to one of these Protocols:
56 A2. Recurrent Diarrhea.[1]
56 A3. Persistent Diarrhea.[2]
56 A4. Chronic Diarrhea.[3]
Or see MALABSORPTION.[4]

Is the diarrhea watery — it fills the container to the edges with a flat or almost flat surface and there is no visible blood?

No, mushy, bloody, or both | **YES, watery and no blood**

YES, watery and no blood
For patient under 2 years, consider ROTAVIRUS.
Otherwise consider CHOLERA, GIARDIASIS, CYCLOSPORIASIS, or CRYPTOSPORIDIOSIS.

Try the following treatments, in this order:
1. Give ORS.
2. Eliminate milk and milk products from the diet.
3. Treat with DOXYCYCLINE.
4. Treat with COTRIMOXAZOLE.

Is there either visible blood or a very foul odor or both in the diarrhea?

NO | **YES**

YES: **Consider**: GIARDIASIS.[5]
Also see Bloody Diarrhea, Protocol 57A.

Did the patient eat anything unusual or tainted?

NO | **YES**

YES: **Consider**:
PLANT POISONING.
FOOD POISONING.

Is the diarrhea small amounts in a patient who is otherwise constipated?

NO | **YES**

YES: **Consider** IMPACTION.

Continued on next page.

[1] Recurrent Diarrhea: Sudden onset, lasted more than 14 days, more than 2 consecutive days without diarrhea.
[2] Persistent Diarrhea: Sudden onset, lasted more than 14 days, less than 2 consecutive days without diarrhea.
[3] Chronic Diarrhea: Gradual onset, lasted more than a month.
[4] Whatever is eaten comes out the bottom quickly, almost unchanged; see MALABSORPTION in the *Disease Index*.
[5] In Nepal and Latin America also consider CYCLOSPORIASIS which is indistinguishable.

(56 A1. Watery Diarrhea, Sudden, Recent Onset, Not Grossly Bloody, continued.)

Does the patient have a fever of 102°F/39°C or more?

NO fever, or low fever	YES
	Consider: MALARIA, MEASLES, ENTERIC FEVER, KATAYAMA DISEASE, VISCERAL LEISHMANIASIS.[1]

Is there blood in the stool? Test the stool and consider the alternatives:

Stool probably negative for blood:	Stool probably positive for blood:
MALARIA	HOOKWORM
INFLUENZA	SCHISTOSOMIASIS MANSONI[3]
TRICHURIASIS	SCHISTOSOMIASIS JAPONICUM[4]
THALLASEMIA	INTESTINAL FLUKE[5]
ZINC DEFICIENCY	STRONGYLOIDIASIS
LIVER FLUKE[2]	ARSENIC POISONING
DEPRESSION	**Also see Bloody Stool, Protocol 57A!**

56 A2. Recurrent Diarrhea:

This is sudden onset, lasted more than 14 days, some diarrhea-free intervals lasting more than 2 days, either watery or mushy, either bloody or not bloody.

Treatment: To be treated the same as acute, watery diarrhea, looking for changes in lifestyle that might decrease the numbers of episodes. In particular, look at the availability of clean water, sanitation in food preparation, and hand-washing after bathroom duties.

56 A3. Persistent Diarrhea:

This is sudden onset, lasted more than 14 days, no more than 2 consecutive days without diarrhea, either watery or mushy, either bloody or not-bloody.

- Frequently associated with another underlying bacterial infection: PNEUMONIA, EAR INFECTION, and URINARY INFECTION being the most common. Children with CANDIDIASIS in their mouths, those with MALNUTRITION, and those with PNEUMONIA are the most likely to die. It is important to examine children with persistent diarrhea for these other conditions, and to treat them. Treatment for the other conditions may also take care of the diarrhea.
- Tends to occur in malnourished children and increases malnutrition because of wastage of food substances in the stool as well as loss of appetite.
- Is common in children less than 6 months old who are not exclusively breast-fed and who consume cow's milk during an episode of acute diarrhea.
- Persistent diarrhea in returning travelers from Nepal or the environs in spring or summer is probably due to CYCLOSPORIASIS.

Continued on next page.

---

[1] Visceral Leishmaniasis: Found in scattered areas of Central and South America, Africa north of the equator, the Mediterranean area, the Indian subcontinent, eastern Europe, central Asia, and mainland China. Not present south of the equator.

[2] This kind of Liver Fluke (Fascioliasis) is not present in Southeast Asia or eastern Asia or the Pacific.

[3] Schistosomiasis Mansoni: Scattered areas within Africa, the Arabian peninsula, the Caribbean, and parts of eastern South America.

[4] Schistosomiasis Japonicum: In areas of mainland China, the Philippines, parts of ethe Celebes, the upper Mekong, and the Thai-Malaysia border area.

[5] Intestinal Fluke: Not present in sub-Saharan Africa or the Pacific. In the Americas it occurs only in Guyana.

(56 A3. Persistent Diarrhea, continued.)

Treatment: Try the following treatments in order. If there is one treatment that works in several cases in your area, then elevate that treatment to the #1 position. In any case, provide clean drinking water, preferably as ORS, and nutritious food throughout the episode.

1. Give a general deworming treatment with MEBENDAZOLE, LEVAMISOLE, or both in succession.
2. Give METRONIDAZOLE for 5 days to eliminate GIARDIASIS and amebic DYSENTERY.
3. Try at least two different antibiotics in succession: DOXYCYCLINE, CO-TRIMOXAZOLE, CIPROFLOXACIN, AMOXICILLIN, CHLORAMPHENICOL are possibilities.
4. NITAZOXANIDE is a new drug that works for some parasites associated with HIV INFECTION.

56 A4. Chronic Diarrhea:

This is diarrhea of gradual onset that has lasted more than 30 days which may or may not be bloody.

This is most often due to coeliac disease, inflammatory bowel disease, hereditary problems, SPRUE, all of which require high-tech diagnosis and/or treatment. Thus these patients should be sent out.

56 B. Grossly Bloody Diarrhea; Sudden, Recent Onset:

Definition: The patient passes either bright red blood on or mixed into his stool, or he passes coal-black stool that is mushy and extremely foul-smelling. (This is digested blood).

Is the patient's skin cool and moist and his pulse rapid, OR is he very lethargic or unconscious or both?

NO — continue below.

YES — Arrange transport immediately. Meanwhile treat SHOCK.

Does he have severe abdominal pains?

NO — continue below.

YES — **Consider**: ACUTE ABDOMEN, PIG-BEL. If neither of these, follow the "No" arm.

Is there evidence of a general bleeding problem with bloody urine, heavy menstruation, bloody nose, minor cuts that won't stop bleeding?

NO — continue below.

YES — **Consider**: Conditions listed in Protocol C-7. Also: THALLASEMIA, SCURVY, TYPHUS. ARBOVIRAL FEVER,[1] ONYALAI.[2]

Does the patient have a high fever, over 102°F / 39°C?

NO — continue below.

YES — **Consider**: DYSENTERY, ENTERIC FEVER, TYPHUS, MEASLES, RELAPSING FEVER,[3] LASSA FEVER,[4] HEMORRHAGIC FEVER (early), YELLOW FEVER,[5] KATAYAMA DISEASE.

Continued on next page.

[1] Arboviral Fever can turn into HEMORRHAGIC FEVER; bloody diarrhea might be the first manifestation.
[2] Onyalai: This is a hereditary tendency to bleed abnormally, found in southern Africa only.
[3] Relapsing Fever: Not in the islands of Southeast Asia or the Pacific.
[4] Lassa Fever: Found in scattered areas in Africa only, mostly West Africa.
[5] Yellow Fever: South America north of Sao Paolo, central and western Africa, and the Sudan area.

(56 B. Grossly Bloody Diarrhea; Sudden, Recent Onset, continued.)

Was the patient in an area with SCHISTOSOMIASIS?

NO

YES

Consider: SCHISTOSOMIASIS MANSONI,[1] SCHISTOSOMIASIS JAPONICUM,[2] rarely SCHISTOSOMIASIS HEMATOBIUM.[3]

Conditions	Characteristics
HOOKWORM	Sandy, moist, shaded areas where people walk barefoot.
DYSENTERY	Blood dark or bright red, with obvious white, stringy mucus.
TUBERCULOSIS	Diarrhea off and on with blood and mucus. Blood mixed with stool.
PROCTITIS	Rectal pain, red blood on outside of the stool.
HEMORRHOIDS	Blood is on outside of the stool or toilet paper; there may be pain.
PEPTIC ULCER	Usually stool is black. If red, the patient may go into SHOCK.
============	
CANCER	Recent significant weight loss.
TRICHURIASIS	Similar to HOOKWORM, similar treatment; ANEMIA uncommon.
PIG-BEL[4]	Malnourished children who suddenly eat a heavy protein meal.
FISSURE[5]	Exquisite rectal pain, minimal bright red blood.

PROTOCOL 57. ABNORMAL STOOL

57 A. Bloody Stool
57 B: Other Abnormal Stool

57 A. Bloody Stool, Not Diarrhea:

Either blood-red or black, tarry stool, or a positive test of the stool for blood. (Hematest is positive in at least one of three tests.) If the stool is foul, shiny and sticky, the blood came from swallowed blood or PEPTIC ULCER.

First check for ACUTE ABDOMEN Type 3 (Symptom Protocol 39 C).
If the patient has SHOCK, send out immediately!

If he does not have ACUTE ABDOMEN and is not in SHOCK, proceed:

Did the patient recently eat rare meat or blood?

NO

YES

Ignore the problem for now; recheck in four days.

Is there bleeding elsewhere: bloody urine, heavy menstruation, minor cuts, bloody nose?

NO

YES

Consider: THALLASEMIA, SCURVY, TYPHUS, YELLOW FEVER,[6] HEMORRHAGIC FEVER, LIVER DISEASE, LIVER FAILURE, ONYALAI.[7] Also see *Index C*, Protocol C-7.

Continued on next page.

[1] Schistosomiasis Mansoni: Scattered areas within Africa, the Arabian peninsula, the Caribbean, and parts of eastern South America.

[2] Schistosomiasis Japonicum: In areas of mainland China, the Philippines, parts of the Celebes, the upper Mekong, and the Thai-Malaysian border.

[3] Schistosomiasis Hematobium: Present in some areas of Africa and the Middle East.

[4] Pig-bel: Found in developing countries near the equator, mainly New Guinea..

[5] Fissure may be due to damage to the rectum caused by anal intercourse or by masturbation using sharp objects.

[6] Yellow Fever: South America north of Sao Paolo, central and western Africa, and the Sudan.

[7] Onyalai: This is a hereditary tendency to bleed abnormally, found in southern Africa only.

(57 A. Bloody Stool, Not Diarrhea, continued.)

Does the patient have a high fever?

NO | **YES**

Consider: DYSENTERY, ENTERIC FEVER, TYPHUS, MEASLES /// RELAPSING FEVER,[1] LASSA FEVER,[2] HEMORRHAGIC FEVER, YELLOW FEVER.

Was the patient in an area with SCHISTOSOMIASIS (see the *Regional Index* for your area)?

NO | **YES**

Consider: SCHISTOSOMIASIS MANSONI,[3] SCHISTOSOMIASIS JAPONICUM,[4] rarely SCHISTOSOMIASIS HEMATOBIUM.[5]

Conditions	**Characteristics**
HOOKWORM	Sandy, moist, shaded areas where people walk barefoot.
DYSENTERY	Blood dark or bright red, with obvious white, stringy mucus.
TUBERCULOSIS	Diarrhea off and on with blood and mucus. Blood mixed with stool.
PROCTITIS	Rectal pain, red blood on outside of the stool.
HEMORRHOIDS	Blood is on outside of the stool or toilet paper; there may be pain.
PEPTIC ULCER	Usually stool is black. If red, the patient may go into SHOCK.
============	
CANCER	Possibly weight loss, probably over 40 y.o.
TRICHURIASIS	Similar to HOOKWORM, similar treatment; ANEMIA uncommon.
PIG-BEL[6]	Malnourished children who suddenly eat a heavy protein meal.
FISSURE[7]	Exquisite rectal pain, minimal bright red blood.

57 B. Other Abnormal Stool

White or light stool: HEPATITIS, JAUNDICE from many causes, LIVER FAILURE, GALLBLADDER DISEASE.

Green stool: Due to diet (can also be other colors); also common in newborns.

Wormy stool: ASCARIASIS, TRICHURIASIS, STRONGYLOIDIASIS, ENTEROBIASIS, MYIASIS, TAPEWORM.

Flat worm segments: TAPEWORM.

Black, sticky stool: See bloody stool, Protocol 57 A. Black, sticky stool with a foul odor is due to blood in the stool.

---

[1] Relapsing Fever: Not in the islands of Southeast Asia or the Pacific.

[2] Lassa Fever: Found in scattered areas in Africa only.

[3] Schistosomiasis Mansoni: Scattered areas within Africa, the Arabian peninsula, the Caribbean, and parts of eastern South America.

[4] Schistosomiasis Japonicum: In areas of mainland China, the Philippines, parts of the Celebes, the upper Mekong, and the Thai-Malaysian border.

[5] Schistosomiasis Hematobium: Present in some areas of Africa and the Middle East.

[6] Pig-bel: Found in developing countries near the equator, mainly New Guinea..

[7] Fissure may be due to damage to the rectum caused by anal intercourse or by masturbation using sharp objects.

PROTOCOL 58. ABNORMAL URINE

58 A. Various problems
58 B. Bloody Stool, Not Diarrhea
58 C. True bloody urine without a fever

58 A. Various problems:

Full bladder but can't urinate: See Protocol 59.

Too little urine[1]: DEHYDRATION, TOXEMIA, KIDNEY FAILURE, SHOCK, HYPERTENSION, URETHRAL STRICTURE, CANCER, POLIO.

Too much urine: MALARIA, drinking too much, DIABETES, some kinds of KIDNEY FAILURE, side-effect of some drugs used to treat HEART FAILURE.

Frequent urination of small amounts: Pregnancy, STRESS (bathroom is an escape), possibly KIDNEY INFECTION, TUBERCULOSIS, URINARY INFECTION, SCHISTOSOMIASIS HEMATOBIUM,[2] URETHRITIS, PROSTATITIS.

Bed-wetting: Usually due to STRESS; also consider ENTEROBIASIS, ATTENTION DEFICIT DISORDER.

Milky or pink milky: FILARIASIS.

Cloudy but not milky: may be normal, or URINARY INFECTION, KIDNEY INFECTION.

Pain with urination: See Protocol 50 C.

Foul-smelling urine: KIDNEY INFECTION, URINARY INFECTION, TYPHUS, sometimes due to drugs or food, possibly VAGINITIS or SEXUALLY TRANSMITTED DISEASE.

Dark urine but not black or coke colored: DEHYDRATION, HEPATITIS or other LIVER DISEASE, LIVER FAILURE, some medications such as METRONIDAZOLE and TINIDAZOLE.

Other colored urine: Usually due to foods or drugs; ignore the problem.

Bloody urine with a few drops of blood at the end of urination, not all mixed through is from the bladder or the urethra (the tube between the bladder and the genital area): SEXUALLY TRANSMITTED DISEASE, URINATRY INFECTION, SCHISTOSOMIASIS HEMATOBIUM, CANCER of the bladder or urethra, TUBERCULOSIS of the bladder, BLADDER STONE.

Bloody urine: red, black, or coke colored, or positive test for blood. Consider vaginal origin of the blood. Ask the person if he/she ate red beets or took the drug RIFAMPIN recently. All red urine is not necessarily bloody. For some people, beets will color the urine. For everyone, RIFAMPIN will color urine red. A urine dipstick (Volume I, Appendix 2) test for blood is the only way to distinguish blood from other red color.

If the urine is truly bloody and this is part of a general bleeding problem — nosebleeds and easy bruising — then see the Protocol C-7.

58 B. True bloody urine with a fever:

Brownish urine, not red, color the same throughout, no clots:

KIDNEY INFECTION: Severe mid-back pain, one or both sides; burning with urination.
TUBERCULOSIS: Initially at least, the bloody urine is off and on, not continual; also weight loss.
MALARIA (severe): Mostly in patients of Mediterranean ethnic origin; coke-colored urine; very ill.
TYPHUS: Mental state appears intoxicated; headache, general body pains occur before the fever.
HEMORRHAGIC FEVER: Headache and/or general body pains first, then severe bleeding.
RELAPSING FEVER[3]: Sudden onset of severe fever and chills with headache and general aching.
BARTONELLOSIS[4]: First fatigue, then fever, then general pains, especially chest and back.
YELLOW FEVER[5]: Headache, eye pain, general aching, nausea; patient unimmunized.
SEPSIS: Very sick, unconscious or almost so.

Reddish urine, maybe clots, color not the same throughout:

URINARY INFECTION: Similar to KIDNEY INFECTION but the pain is low central abdomen.

---

[1] Minimum urine output: Infants 5 ml/hr.; 1 y.o. 10 ml/hr.; 5 y.o. 15 ml/hr.; 10 y.o. 20 ml/hr.; adults 25 ml/hr.
[2] Schistosomiasis Hematobium: Present in some areas of Africa and the Middle East.
[3] Relapsing Fever: Not in the islands of Southeast Asia or the Pacific.
[4] Bartonellosis: Scattered areas within Peru and adjacent border areas.
[5] Yellow Fever: South America north of Sao Paolo, central and western Africa, and the Sudan.

58 C. True bloody urine without a fever:

Brownish urine, not red, color the same throughout, no clots:

THALLASEMIA: Hereditary ANEMIA; large spleen; maybe a retarded facial appearance.
PLANT POISONING: Djenkol bean[1]: History of eating this bean; also mid-back pain.
KIDNEY FAILURE: Due to nephritis. Commonly there is history of a recent skin infection. BP is high.
CANCER: Probably from the kidney area.

Either brownish or reddish urine; color the same throughout or variable:

CANCER: Frequently painless initially with no other symptoms.
Injury: History of injury to the middle of the back or to the lower abdomen.
KIDNEY STONES: Sudden onset of severe pain flank(s) and/or groin(s), with nausea and vomiting.
URETHRITIS: Males with a history of pus or another abnormal discharge from the penis tip.
Poisonous snake bite: History of a snake bite; see Volume I, Chapter 9.
SCURVY: Diet devoid of fresh fruits and vegetables; bleeding gums, loose teeth present.
SCHISTOSOMIASIS HEMATOBIUM[2]: From a culture where bloody urine is common in boys.
SCHISTOSOMIASIS MANSONI[3]: Either DYSENTERY or LIVER DISEASE or LIVER FAILURE.
ONYALAI[4]: History of bleeding episodes from other parts of the body.

PROTOCOL 59. OTHER PELVIC AND RECTAL PROBLEMS

Pus from penis: URETHRITIS, GONORRHEA. See *Index C*, Protocol C-1.

Bladder full, cannot urinate or only dribbles: URETHRAL STRICTURE, URINARY OBSTRUCTION, genital HERPES, SYPHILIS, POLIO, PROSTATITIS, any other disease or injury that causes weakness or paralysis of the lower limbs (e.g. SLIPPED DISC).

Interrupted urine stream: PROSTATITIS, URETHRITIS, URETHRAL STRICTURE. If he needs to jump up and down to urinate, probably a BLADDER STONE. Send out if possible.

Bloody semen: SCHISTOSOMIASIS HEMATOBIUM, injury, TUBERCULOSIS, CANCER.

Groin scar: Any SEXUALLY TRANSMITTED DISEASE; SCRUB TYPHUS[5] in rural Asia, prior surgery.

Impotence: May be emotional[6] (see STRESS) or else due to SYPHILIS, SPINAL NEUROPATHY, TROPICAL SPASTIC PARAPARESIS, DIABETES, LEPROSY, ZINC DEFICIENCY, AFRICAN SLEEPING SICKNESS,[7] PLANT POISONING (Lathyrism[8]), (previous) MUMPS; could be a side effect of METHYLDOPA or other drugs; HOOKWORM, and any paralysis could cause it. Regional and rare: HEMOCHROMATOSIS.[9]

Redness and itching in vaginal area: VAGINITIS, ENTEROBIASIS, STRONGYLOIDIASIS.

Erection that will not go away: See Protocol 52 C.

Worm-like creatures: ASCARIASIS, STRONGYLOIDIASIS, ENTEROBIASIS, MYIASIS, TRICHURIASIS, TAPEWORM.

Swelling in pelvic/genital area: See Protocol 52.

---

[1] Djenkol bean poisoning occurs in Malaysia and Indonesia.

[2] Schistosomiasis Hematobium: Found in areas of Africa and the Middle East.

[3] Schistosomiasis Mansoni: Scattered areas within Africa, the Arabian Peninsula, the Caribbean, and parts of eastern South America.

[4] Onyalai: This is a hereditary tendency to bleed, found in southern Africa only.

[5] Scrub Typhus: Present in the Indian area, East Asia, central and southeast Asia, and the Pacific area.

[6] One can distinguish emotional from other causes with a simple test. For several consecutive nights, before retiring, place a row of connected small postage stamps snugly around the penis. Moisten the last one to secure the stamps. If there is a night-time erection, in the morning some of the stamps will be separated. This indicates physical ability to achieve an erection and therefore an emotional cause of impotence.

[7] African Sleeping Sickness: Scattered areas of Africa, south of Bamako, Mali and Lake Chad and north of Lusaka, Zambia.

[8] Lathyrism poisoning occurs in the Indian area, in eastern Africa, and in the Mediterranean area where "Khasari" is eaten.

[9] Hemochromatosis: Mainly confined to certain ethnic groups who take in excessive iron in the form of blood or beer brewed in iron.

Small-sized testicles: LEPROSY, previous MUMPS, LASSA FEVER.[1]

Numbness and tingling in the saddle area between the legs: SPINAL NEUROPATHY

Very small bladder capacity: Pregnancy, BLADDER STONE, SCHISTOSOMIASIS HEMATOBIUM,[2] CANCER.

Incontinent of urine: SEIZURE, SEXUALLY TRANSMITTED DISEASE,[3] STROKE, URINARY INFECTION, KIDNEY INFECTION, sometimes after hard childbirth or multiple childbirths, after injury to the neck or back, SYPHILIS (tertiary), SCHISTOSOMIASIS HEMATOBIUM, PLANT POISONING due to Lathyrism, TROPICAL SPASTIC PARAPARESIS, SPINAL NEUROPATHY, BRAIN DAMAGE, TYPHUS.

Incontinent of stool: Same causes as above except not KIDNEY INFECTION, or URINARY INFECTION. Consider SYPHILIS. Additionally, any severe diarrhea, especially GIARDIASIS, can cause incontinence of stool. Disabled people are frequently constipated; liquid stool forms behind the constipated stool, flows around it, and comes out. If this is the case, see IMPACTION. If generally ill, consider TYPHUS. This may be due to damage to the rectum caused by anal intercourse or by masturbation with objects that tear the rectal muscles. It may also be caused by injuries during childbirth, a fractured pelvis, RECTAL PROLAPSE, STROKE, BRAIN DAMAGE and various SEXUALLY TRANSMITTED DISEASEs, especially LYMPHOGRANULOMA VENEREUM.

Large amounts of very foul gas: See Protocol 49.

Foreskin stuck behind the pink part of penis: PARAPHIMOSIS.

Foreskin stuck onto the pink part of the penis: PHIMOSIS.

Passing gas or stool through the penis or vagina or female urinary tract: This indicates a fistula, which is an abnormal hole between pelvic organs. It requires surgical treatment.

No menstruation in a female: Not old enough, pregnant, MALNUTRITION, MENOPAUSE, AFRICAN SLEEPING SICKNESS,[4] SCHISTOSOMIASIS HEMATOBIUM, SCHISTOSOMIASIS MANSONI,[5] sometimes a hormone problem.

---

[1] Lassa Fever: Found in scattered areas in Africa only, mainly West Africa.

[2] Schistosomiasis Hematobium: Found in scattered areas of Africa and the Middle East

[3] In this case the person is incontinent because there are abnormal holes in the genital areas out of which urine runs. Men may have a watering-can-type area between their legs. Females may have a hole or holes between bladder and vagina. In some cases these problems can be fixed surgically and in other cases they cannot be fixed.

[4] African Sleeping Sickness: Scattered areas of Africa, south of Bamako, Mali and Lake Chad and north of Lusaka, Zambia.

[5] Schistosomiasis Mansoni: Scattered areas within Africa, the Arabian peninsula, the Caribbean, and parts of eastern South America.

X. LOWER LIMB PROBLEMS

PROTOCOL 60. PAIN IN HIPS, LEGS, AND FEET

If there is severe pain in (usually) one or (sometimes) both legs along with at least two of the following: paleness, weakness or paralysis, numbness and tingling, no pulses, and the limb(s) feel(s) cold, that is an emergency which requires prompt surgical care or the patient will lose the limb and possibly his life also.

60 A. Skin Pain, Lower Limbs
60 B. Neuritis, Legs and Feet
60 C. Muscle Pain, Legs
60 D. Bone and Joint Pain

60 A. Skin Pain, Lower Limbs:

Symptomatic treatment: ACETAMINOPHEN or IBUPROFEN is always appropriate. ASPIRIN is usually appropriate in adults but should not be used until you have reached a diagnosis.

Also see Protocols 14 - 18 on Skin Problems. Conditions which especially affect the legs and feet are listed.

Conditions	Characteristics
CELLULITIS	Area red, warm, tender; large groin nodes.
TROPICAL ULCER	Crater in skin of leg; pus or raw flesh in center; sharp edges.
TINEA	Cracks between toes with itching and burning, peeling skin.
FILARIASIS	Swelling and warmth initially, big groin nodes.
MALNUTRITION	Severe pain in feet, unable to tolerate anything touching feet.
HIV INFECTION	Pain in the area normally covered by stockings.
TUNGIASIS[1]	Tiny, black spots where sand fleas burrowed in; area touched soil.
YAWS	Skin of soles of feet thick and cracked; humid tropics only.
PELLAGRA	Burning in soles; rough, flaky rash; maize (corn) diet.
GUINEA WORM[2]	Very painful blister that breaks open.
TROPICAL SPASTIC PARAPARESIS	Also stiffness of the legs; maybe back pain, incontinent of urine.
VISCERAL LEISHMANIASIS[3]	Burning foot pain, particularly in Sudan, Africa.
ELEPHANTIASIS, endemic	Red clay soil areas, near old volcanoes; burning foot pain.

[1] See *Regional Notes* for Africa, the Americas, and South Asia.
[2] Guinea Worm: Scattered areas in Africa and the Middle East only.
[3] Visceral Leishmaniasis: Found in scattered areas of Central and South America, Africa north of the equator, the Mediterranean area, the Indian subcontinent, eastern Europe, central Asia, and mainland China. Not present south of the equator.

60 B. Neuritis, Legs and Feet:

Definition: Neuritis is nerve inflammation, it causes pain that is sharp and shooting though occasionally it is burning or aching. The pain goes up and down the legs, maybe from the back; frequently there is numbness and tingling, muscle cramps, or muscle weakness.

Symptomatic treatment: ACETAMINOPHEN or IBUPROFEN is always appropriate. ASPIRIN is usually appropriate in adults but should not be used until you have reached a diagnosis.

Is the patient very ill or does he have a fever or both?

NO | **YES**

Consider: DENGUE FEVER,[1] BRUCELLOSIS, DYSENTERY (bacterial), TUBERCULOSIS.

Does the patient have severe back pain that shoots down the legs?

NO | **YES**

Consider: BRUCELLOSIS, MUSCLE STRAIN, SCIATICA, SLIPPED DISC, genital HERPES, TUBERCULOSIS, rarely HYDATID DISEASE.[2]

Does the patient eat a very poor diet?

NO | **YES**

Consider: MALNUTRITION, PELLAGRA, BERIBERI, PLANT POISONING due to Cassava.

Conditions	**Characteristics**
LEPROSY	Skin changes are evident; there may be numbness or lack of pain sense.
SYPHILIS (tertiary)	Severe pains; maybe uncoordination; 10+ years incubation.
ISONIAZID (drug)	Side-effect of this TB drug; treatable with vitamins.
DIABETES	Known DIABETES or sugar present in urine.
LOIASIS[3]	Swellings come for a few days and then go.
ARSENIC POISONING	Numbness, tingling, and burning in feet, skin changes.
TROPICAL SPASTIC PARAPARESIS	Also stiffness of the legs; maybe back pain, incontinent of urine.

60 C. Muscle Pain, Legs:

Definition: The calves, thighs, or both are tender when squeezed. Pain is increased when the patient moves his own limbs, but when he relaxes (if he can) and you move his limbs, the pain is not much worse than it is at rest. If this is part of generalized muscle pains, see also Protocol 10 C.

If this is part of a generalized illness with fever, headache, and body pains, then see *Index C*, Protocol C-2.

Symptomatic treatment: ACETAMINOPHEN or IBUPROFEN is always appropriate. ASPIRIN is usually appropriate in adults but should not be used until you have reached a diagnosis. Night cramps may sometimes be treated with QUININE.

(Continued on next page.)

[1] Dengue Fever: In the Americas only near or north of the equator. In Africa only Nigeria and southern Africa. Prevalent in India, Southeast Asia, and the Pacific. Occasionally found in the Mediterranean area.

[2] Hydatid Disease: There are two kinds: one is in cattle-raising areas of the tropics where there are dogs that live close to people. The other kind is in temperate, rural areas where there are wild animals and people eat gathered, wild plant life that might be contaminated with the stool of anomals.

[3] Loiasis: Present in humid, rural areas of western and central Africa.

(60 C. Muscle Pain, Legs, continued.)

Does the patient have a fever or did he have one recently?

NO — YES

YES: Is the illness of gradual onset, over 3 days or more?

- NO, rapid onset: **Consider**: INFLUENZA, ARBOVIRAL FEVER, DENGUE FEVER,[2] LEPTOSPIROSIS, TYPHUS (louse), SPOTTED FEVER, RELAPSING FEVER,[3] POLIO, RAT BITE FEVER.
- YES, gradual onset: **Consider**: TYPHUS (murine), POLIO, PYOMYOSITIS BRUCELLOSIS, TRICHINOSIS, CYSTICERCOSIS, SPOTTED FEVER,[1] TETANUS

NO: Does the pain occur after unusual exercise, heat exposure, or standing all day?

NO — YES

YES: **Consider**: MUSCLE STRAIN, VARICOSE VEINS, HEAT ILLNESS.

NO:

Conditions	Characteristics
Night cramps	Older people or pregnant. Use QUININE if not pregnant.
BERIBERI	Weakness also, broad-based gait; poor diet or alcoholic.
ANEMIA	Pale fingernails; leg cramps with walking.
============	
PYOMYOSITIS	Swelling and warmth also, usually thigh or buttock.
POLIO	History of cold or flu followed by muscle cramps and weakness.
CHOLERA	History of severe watery diarrhea; muscle cramps.
PLANT POISONING	Claviceps or Ergot; aching pain with numbness, feet cool to the touch.
GANGRENE	Similar to Claviceps above; skin discolored.
PELLAGRA	Also rash, diarrhea, mental changes, or a combination.

60 D. Bone and Joint Pain:

Definition: A deep, boring, frequently throbbing pain, worse with movement and weight bearing. The pain usually increases as much if someone else moves the limbs as if the patient moves them. Firm pressure over the painful areas aggravates the pain.

Symptomatic treatment: ACETAMINOPHEN or IBUPROFEN is always appropriate. ASPIRIN is usually appropriate in adults but should not be used until you have reached a diagnosis.

Does the patient have brittle bones that fracture easily?

NO — YES

YES: **Consider**: old age, paralysis, SYPHILIS,[4] CANCER, THALLASEMIA, HYDATID DISEASE.[5]

NO:

Continued on next page.

[1] Spotted Fever: Not in the islands of Southeast Asia; the pain is mainly in the calves rather than the shins.

[2] Dengue Fever: In the Americas only near or north of the equator. In Africa only Nigeria and southern Africa. Prevalent in India, Southeast Asia, and the Pacific. Occasionally found in the Mediterranean area.

[3] Relapsing Fever: Not in the islands of Southeast Asia or the Pacific.

[4] In infants born with the disease.

[5] Hydatid Disease: There are two kinds: one is in cattle-raising areas of the tropics where there are dogs that live close to people. The other kind is in temperate, rural areas where there are wild animals and people eat gathered, wild plant life that might be contaminated with the stool of animals.

(60 D. Bone and Joint Pain, continued.)

Does the patient have a high fever or did he have one recently?

NO

YES

With a severe headache: see *Index C*, Protocol C-2.

With a visible inflammation over the painful area: see *Index C,* Protocol C-6.

With neither severe headache nor visible inflammation, **consider**:

FAMILIAL MEDITERRANEAN FEVER (Also gives episodic abdominal/chest pain).

TUBERCULOSIS: Slow-onset pain and swelling in one joint.

FILARIASIS: Recurrent initially, then permanent; geographic.

BRUCELLOSIS: Fevers come and go; back and joint pains.

SICKLE CELL DISEASE[1]: Episodes of pain since childhood.

RUBELLA: Patient not extremely ill; red spotted rash after "flu".

RHEUMATIC FEVER: Joint pains migrate; small and large joints.

Conditions:	Fever	Other Characteristics
HEPATITIS	Low if any	Recent onset; nausea or itching; knees or ankles.
ARTHRITIS	Maybe	Redness and swelling over joint(s).
TUBERCULOSIS	Usual	Hip or knee, one side only, thin thigh muscles, that side.
============		
GOUT	Maybe	Affluent patient, single joint, usually big toe or ankle.[2]
SYPHILIS	Maybe	Swollen joints, worse with heat; infant of syphilic mother.
SICKLE CELL DISEASE	Maybe	Recurrent episodes of pain, beginning before 2 y.o.
RICKETS	No	Legs have an abnormal shape; deficient sun exposure.
AFRICAN SLEEPING SICKNESS[3]	Maybe	A tap on the shin causes severe pain after a delay.
AINHUM[4]	No	Pain and narrowing at the base of a toe.
YAWS[5]	Maybe	Skin over the affected area is inflamed or broken open.
MANSONELLOSIS PERSTANS[6]	No	Also upper limb pains, maybe itching or short of breath.
ONCHOCERCIASIS[7]	No	In expatriates; back pain, large lymph nodes, itchy rash.

PROTOCOL 61. SWELLING OF LEGS AND FEET

61 A. Swelling; Pitting, Slow Filling
61 B. Swelling; Non-Pitting or Rapidly Filling
61 C. Joint Swelling
61 D. Swelling of Soles of Feet

61 A. Swelling; Pitting, Slow Filling:

Definition: Press a swollen area to the bone with your thumb and then lift your thumb; there is a dent where you pushed. This dent gradually fills over more than 40 seconds. The most common cause for this is standing or sitting in one place for a prolonged period. If this is not the case, check below. See also Protocol 61 B.

[1] Sickle Cell Disease: This affects Blacks of African genetic origin, mainly in Africa and the Americas. Some Indians and Arabs are also affected.
[2] This is the way it starts but it may involve multiple joints, including small ones, later on.
[3] African Sleeping Sickness: Scattered areas of Africa, south of Bamako, Mali and Lake Chad and north of Lusaka, Zambia.
[4] Ainhum: Parts of Africa and the Americas only. Affects small toe first; never affects big toe.
[5] Yaws: Only found in the humid tropics.
[6] Mansonellosis Perstans: West and central Africa; South America, northern Argentina and north of there.
[7] Onchocerciasis: Scattered areas in Africa, the Middle East, Central America, and northern South America.

The protocol below assumes that the swelling is symmetrical or nearly symmetrical left and right. If it is asymmetrical, it is likely to be due to injury (see Volume I), infection, localized heat or cold injury, ALLERGY, blood clots, or CANCER.

See *Index C*, Protocol C-6: Limb Swelling.

Symptomatic treatment: Have the patient sit or lie with his legs and feet elevated above the level of his heart, as much as possible.

Is the patient six months or more pregnant?

NO

YES
Consider TOXEMIA, VARICOSE VEINS.

Does the patient have a skin condition affecting a large part of his body?

NO

YES
Consider LEPROSY reaction, KIDNEY FAILURE, MALNUTRITION, FILARIASIS.

Conditions	Characteristics
VARICOSE VEINS	Soft, bluish bulges on legs; swelling worse at the end of the day.
HEART FAILURE	Also fatigued or short of breath; swelling worse PM's.
MALNUTRITION	Also brittle hair or hair color change; thin upper arms.
============	
FILARIASIS	Initially swelling is episodic; swollen legs common in the community.
KIDNEY FAILURE	Face swollen in the morning; little urine or abnormal urinalysis.
PLANT POISONING	From Argemone oil or anything causing KIDNEY FAILURE.
LIVER DISEASE	Yellow eyes, distended abdomen, or both.
LIVER FAILURE	Yellow eyes, distended abdomen, or both.
CAPILLARIASIS[1]	Patient ate raw fish; persistent, severe diarrhea and loud bowel sounds.
CHAGA'S DISEASE[2]	Large liver which may be tender; fatigued or short of breath.
VISCERAL LEISHMANIASIS[3]	Enormous spleen; usually children or parents of children with the disease.
HEMOCHROMATOSIS	Black males in southern Africa who drink beer brewed in steel containers.
SICKLE CELL DISEASE[4]	Hereditary; episodes of pain since early childhood.
HOOKWORM	ANEMIA, with dizziness, fatigue, pale inside lower eyelids.
RAT BITE FEVER	Inflamed bite wound or rash; fever; headache; large lymph nodes.

[1] Capillariasis: Mainly in the Philippines, rarely in Thailand; found in Egypt with potential of spreading.

[2] Chaga's Disease: Scattered areas in Central and South America.

[3] Visceral Leishmaniasis: Found in scattered areas of Central and South America, Africa north of the equator, the Mediterranean area, the Indian subcontinent, southern Europe, central Asia, and mainland China.

[4] Sickle Cell Disease: This affects Blacks of African genetic origin, mainly in Africa and the Americas. Some Indians and Arabs are also affected.

61 B. Swelling; Non-Pitting or Rapidly Filling:

Definition: If you press into the swelling with a finger tip and then let go, the swelling pops right out to where it has been; either there is no dent or the dent fills in less than 40 seconds.

Symptomatic treatment: Have the patient sit or lie with his legs and feet elevated above the level of his heart, as much as possible.

Does the patient have a high fever?

NO

YES
Consider PYOMYOSITIS, TRICHINOSIS, CELLULITIS, GANGRENE, OSTEOMYELITIS.

Was the onset of the problem over less than 2 weeks?

NO

YES
Consider PYOMYOSITIS, CYSTICERCOSIS, GANGRENE, LOIASIS.[1]

Is there a skin condition affecting the swollen limb?

NO

YES
Consider LEPROSY, YAWS, FILARIASIS, ONCHOCERCIASIS,[2] GANGRENE, HEMOCHROMATOSIS,[3] ELEPHANTIASIS (endemic), MYCETOMA.

Conditions	Characteristics
PYOMYOSITIS	Swelling with tenderness at site any break in skin.
FILARIASIS	Swelling comes and goes by itself early in disease.
============	
TUBERCULOSIS	Large, non-tender lymph nodes; upper, inner thighs.
Repeated infections	CELLULITIS, ABSCESS, or TROPICAL ULCER on the leg.
ELEPHANTIASIS, endemic	Red clay soil area; see *Regional Notes*.

61 C. Joint Swelling, Lower Limbs:

If there is pain with the swelling, see Protocol 60 also.

Symptomatic treatment: An elastic bandage, wrapped with using about 50% of the stretch, may be helpful. Use a 6-inch (15 cm) bandage for knees and 3-inch (8.5 cm) for ankles and feet.

Do the joints look very abnormal in shape but they are relatively painless?

NO

YES
Consider: SYPHILIS, LEPROSY, DIABETES

Are the joints red (or warm)?

NO

YES
Consider: RHEUMATIC FEVER, ARTHRITIS, GOUT

Continued on next page.

[1] Loiasis: Humid, rural west and central Africa only.
[2] Onchocerciasis: Scattered areas in Africa, the Middle East, Central America, and northern South America.
[3] Mainly confined to certain ethnic groups who take in excessive iron in the form of blood or beer brewed in iron. There are also some hereditary cases. The skin is generally darkened.

(61 C. Joint Swelling, Lower Limbs, continued.)

Conditions	Characteristics
SYPHILIS	8-15 y.o.; painless, symmetrical knees swollen.
TUBERCULOSIS	Knee swelling before pain; thigh muscles thinner than the other side.
RICKETS	Inadequate sunlight exposure; leg bones curved in or out.
ONCHOCERCIASIS[1]	Expatriates only; also back pains and an itchy rash.
SCURVY	Swollen ankles; also bleeding gums and spontaneous bruising.

61 D. Swelling of Soles of Feet:

Conditions	Characteristics
YAWS	Skin thick, cracks, very painful.
LEPROSY	Also parts of fingers or toes missing, poor pain sensation.
ARSENIC POISONING	Thick skin of palms and soles; belly pains and diarrhea are common.
TUNGIASIS	Black spots with swelling; from sand fleas.

PROTOCOL 62. OTHER LEG AND FOOT PROBLEMS

Groin pain: See Protocols 45 and 52 B.

Groin swelling: See Protocols 52 A and B.

Appearance: size/ shape

Shins bowed forward: SYPHILIS, congenital.

Strangely shaped legs: long-standing ARTHRITIS, RICKETS, TUBERCULOSIS, SYPHILIS, YAWS, CRETINISM, any weakness or paralysis.

Feet or foot becomes shorter: LEPROSY or MYCETOMA.

One leg shorter than the other: Old POLIO, TUBERCULOSIS of the hip, prior injury.

One toe narrow at the base and then falling off: AINHUM.

Appearance: skin

Abnormal color: GANGRENE, PLANT POISONING: Claviceps or Ergot; FROSTBITE. See Protocol 16.

Leg ulcers: THALLASEMIA, SICKLE CELL DISEASE,[2] TROPICAL ULCER, BURULI ULCER, GUINEA WORM,[3] any old, infected wound, rarely TUBERCULOSIS, MYCETOMA.

Slow growth of hard, painless swellings on the feet: TUBERCULOSIS, ELEPHANTIASIS, MYCETOMA, FILARIASIS, BURULI ULCER.

Big, blue, soft veins on the legs: VARICOSE VEINS.

Function: movement

Abnormal gait: see Protocol 7 C.

Spasms: If cramps, see Protocol 7 B; if seizures, Protocol 7 A.

Paralysis or weakness: See Protocol 8.

Stiff leg muscles: SCURVY, ARTHRITIS, TETANUS, TROPICAL SPASTIC PARAPARESIS, PLANT POISONING due to Lathyrism,[4] also see Protocol 8 C.

Joints bend abnormally: RICKETS, SYPHILIS, LEPROSY, DIABETES, some hereditary problems.

Function: feeling

Numbness: See Protocol 10 A.

Cold feet: Exposure to cold, prior injury, GANGRENE if very ill.

Itching and peeling skin between toes: TINEA, SCABIES.

Itching soles: ALLERGY; maybe FOOD POISONING due to fish in the Pacific area.

---

[1] Onchocerciasis: Scattered areas in Africa, the Middle East, Central America, and northern South America.

[2] Sickle Cell Disease: This affects Blacks of African genetic origin, mainly in Africa and the Americas. Some Indians and Arabs are also affected.

[3] Guinea Worm: Scattered areas in Africa and the Middle East only.

[4] Lathyrism: Found in eastern African, Indian area, and the Mediterranean area.

XI. BACK PROBLEMS

PROTOCOL 63. BACK PAIN

63 A. Back Pain Due to Kidney or Liver Problems
63 B. Back Pain Due to a Spine or Muscle Problem
63 B1. Back Pain With No Fever
63 B2. Back Pain With High Fever
63 C. Back Pain Due to Neuritis (Nerve irritation)

***If the back pain does not increase with touching or pushing on the back but it does increase with pushing on the abdomen, then the origin of the problem is probably not the back but is the abdomen. The back pain is referred pain. See Protocol 39 rather than a protocol below.

See also:
Severe back pain with SHOCK: Protocol 39 C (ACUTE ABDOMEN).
Pain in the back above the waist: Protocol 35.
Back pain with abdominal pain: Protocol 39.

63 A. Back Pain Due to Kidney or Liver Problems:

Definition: The pain is not dead center back but is more to the right, left, or both. The pain may travel down to the groin or genitals; it may be felt in the shoulder or shoulder blade. Also see Protocol 43: Flank Pain, or Protocol 10 C: Aching All Over, if applicable. This kind of pain may be due to enlarged lymph nodes in the back. These nodes drain the pelvic/genital areas as well as the legs. Check for SEXUALLY TRANSMITTED DISEASEs as well as various causes of enlarged lymph nodes in the groin. If the times of onset correlate, any large, tender lymph nodes in the groin may well be the cause of back pain as well.

Conditions	Characteristics
MALARIA	Fevers, headache, sudden onset; back pain both sides.
KIDNEY INFECTION	Cloudy urine; fever and pain with urination are common; back pain one side.
AMEBIC LIVER DISEASE	Fever; tender liver; pain right lower chest or upper abdomen.
GALLBLADDER DISEASE	Also pain in upper abdomen, center or right; vomiting common.
============	
FILARIASIS	Swollen limbs common in the community; may have swelling.
KIDNEY STONE	Sudden onset of severe pain; urine test positive for blood.
HYDATID DISEASE[1]	Tropical/arid areas with dogs; may feel a big bulge in the kidney area.
SCHISTOSOMIASIS HEMATOBIUM[2]	Blood in urine, at first just at end of urination.
LIVER FLUKE	The patient ate raw fish or water plants.
PLANT POISONING	Djenkol bean with bloody urine; Malaysia and Indonesia.
BARTONELLOSIS[3]	Episodic fevers, headaches, and ANEMIA.
URINARY OBSTRUCTION	The patient is not urinating at all, or he just dribbles.
CANCER	Swelling, blood in urine, weight loss.

[1] This may also rarely be found in northern temperate/arctic areas where people eat food that may be contaminated with wild animal stool.
[2] Schistosomiasis Hematobium: Present in some areas of Africa and the Middle East.
[3] Bartonellosis: Scattered areas in Peru and adjacent border areas.

63 B. Back Pain Due to a Spine or Muscle Problem:

Definition: Back pain may be dead center back or slightly off to one side; if it is off to both sides, almost invariably one side will hurt much worse than the other. The pain is always aggravated by movement. Urinalysis is normal unless the patient also has a kidney problem. If this is part of general body pains, see Protocol 10 C.

If this problem is part of a general illness with fever, headache, and general body pain, then see Protocol C-2.

Symptomatic treatment: ACETAMINOPHEN or IBUPROFEN is always appropriate. ASPIRIN is usually appropriate for adults but should not be used until you have reached a diagnosis.

63 B1. Back Pain With No Fever:

Conditions	Characteristics
MUSCLE STRAIN	Had some unusual exercise; sudden or gradual onset.
TUBERCULOSIS	There is a bulge in the spinal column or pain or tenderness.
ARTHRITIS	Painful area of the spine is also warm and tender.
POLIO	Weakness or paralysis after a "cold" or diarrhea; back pains.
============	
SICKLE CELL DISEASE[1]	Recurrent bone and abdominal pain, problem began before 2 y.o.
SLIPPED DISC	Very severe pain, usually sudden with some movement; no fever.
BRUCELLOSIS	Joint pains; fevers and illness comes and goes; fatigue.
RICKETS	Also curved leg bones; inadequate sun exposure.
ONCHOCERCIASIS[2]	In expatriates; also itchy skin, joint pains, large lymph nodes.
TROPICAL SPASTIC PARAPARESIS	Also stiffness in legs and some urinary difficulty.
RABIES	Also throat spasms with swallowing or a breeze.
HYDATID DISEASE[3]	Tropical/arid areas with dogs or northern temperate/arctic areas.
TETANUS	Whole body spasms; can't open mouth.

63 B2. Back Pain With High Fever:

a. Problem is either recurrent or slowly developing (over a week or more):

Consider:

BRUCELLOSIS: Fever off and on, slow onset.
RHEUMATIC FEVER: Recurrent, sudden onset.
ARTHRITIS: Recurrent; painful area warm
TUBERCULOSIS: Slow onset, tender to touch.
RELAPSING FEVER[4]: Each relapse less.
SICKLE CELL DISEASE: Also belly pain.
OSTEOMYELITIS: Maybe pus drainage hole.
PYOMYOSITIS: Very swollen muscles.

---

[1] Sickle Cell Disease: This affects Blacks of African genetic origin, mainly in Africa and the Americas. Some Indians and Arabs are also affected.

[2] Onchocerciasis: Scattered areas in Africa, the Middle East, Central America, and northern South America.

[3] Hydatid Disease: There are two kinds: one is in cattle-raising areas of the tropics where there are dogs that live close to people. The other kind is in temperate, rural areas where there are wild animals and people eat gathered, wild plant life that might be contaminated with the stool of animals.

[4] Relapsing Fever: Not in the islands of Southeast Asia or the Pacific.

b. Problem is not recurrent and is not slowly developing; it developed over less than a week:

(If this is the first episode and is rapid onset over less than a week, it may still be due to condition listed above as being recurrent.)

Also consider non-recurrent illnesses:

LEPTOSPIROSIS: Red eyes, whole body pains.
TYPHUS: Intoxicated mental state; fatigue before fever.
RELAPSING FEVER[1]: Severe pains in the calves.
PYOMYOSITIS: One area of swollen, painful muscle.
MENINGITIS: Stiff neck or unconscious; severe headache.
POLIO: Muscle spasms and weakness after a cold or "flu".
LASSA FEVER[2]: Epidemics; headache and chest pains.
ARBOVIRAL FEVER: Variable symptoms.
SPOTTED FEVER[3]: Severe headache, aching, rash.
DENGUE FEVER[4]: Excruciating bone pains; rash.
TRICHINOSIS: Muscle swelling; ate rare meat.
RABIES: Muscle spasms with paralysis; maybe bat bite.
ENCEPHALITIS: Stiff neck or unconscious or both.
MONKEYPOX[5]: Fever first; blistery skin rash later.
TETANUS: Can't open mouth; stiff neck.

63 C. Back Pain Due to Neuritis (Nerve irritation):

Definition: The back pain is in a band around the back or goes down one or the other leg or both. Urinalysis is normal unless the patient also has a kidney problem. If this is part of General Body Pains, see Protocol 10 C.

Symptomatic treatment: ACETAMINOPHEN or IBUPROFEN is always appropriate. ASPIRIN is usually appropriate for adults but should not be used until you have reached a diagnosis.

Consider the problems listed above under spine. Also consider SPINAL NEUROPATHY, LEPROSY, SHINGLES, TRENCH FEVER.

---

[1] Relapsing Fever: Not in the islands of Southeast Asia or the Pacific.

[2] Lassa Fever: Present in West Africa, usually as epidemics.

[3] Spotted Fever: Not in the islands of Southeast Asia.

[4] Dengue Fever: In the Americas only near or north of the equator. In Africa only Nigeria and southern Africa. Prevalent in India, Southeast Asia, and the Pacific. Occasionally found in the Mediterranean area.

[5] Monkeypox: Occurs in northern D. R. Congo and adjacent parts of Central African Republic. Rarely in western Africa.

PROTOCOL 64. OTHER BACK PROBLEMS

Pain in a band from the back around to the front: SHINGLES, TRENCH FEVER.

Sideways curved backbone with one shoulder blade sticking out: SCOLIOSIS.

Pit or lump along center line in back: old injury; TB; birth defect. If it is a birth defect, ignore it if it is on the tail-bone. Send out if further up. (Requires a major medical center for treatment.)

Stiff back, arched back: cerebral MALARIA, SEIZURES (see Protocol 7A), POLIO, TETANUS, MENINGITIS, TUBERCULOSIS, ENCEPHALITIS, (rarely) HEAT ILLNESS, RABIES.

Lump on back flank area: HYDATID DISEASE,[1] maybe ABSCESS, CANCER.

Hunched back: may be due to weak muscles, SCOLIOSIS, RICKETS, TUBERCULOSIS, BRUCELLOSIS, or an old injury. A very similar condition may be the side-effect of the drug PREDNISONE or a similar drug.

Pimples on the back: ACNE.

Back pains with abdominal pains: ACUTE ABDOMEN, PANCREATITIS.

[1] Hydatid Disease: There are two kinds: one is in cattle-raising areas of the tropics where there are dogs that live close to people. The other kind is in temperate, rural areas where there are wild animals and people eat gathered, wild plant life that might be contaminated with the stool of animals.

Index B. Disease Index

ALPHABETICAL LISTING OF DISEASES

DISEASE CLASSIFICATIONS

Class 1: You can treat safely, assuming a correct diagnosis.

Class 2: You will have an occasional death or disability that a medical professional would not.

Class 3: You will mistreat 20-80% of patients resulting in deaths and disabilities.

Class 4: You will lose 80% or more patients, or they will have permanent disabilities. (A medically trained person may do much better in these cases.)

TERMINOLOGY

Who = who tends to get the disease; what habits, foods, ethnic origins or other factors are associated with this disease.

Send out = arrange transportation to a hospital.

Results = time after the beginning of treatment until you should expect to see some improvement.

Entry Category:

- **Disease** – a single ailment.
- **Disease cluster** – a group of diseases with related causes but possibly different treatments.
- **Syndrome** – a group of symptoms which tend to occur together but may be caused by different diseases.

Words in UPPER CASE refer to other entries in the *Disease* or *Drug Indices*.

REGIONAL INDEX Code Letters.

E = Eastern Europe and Central Asia.
F = Africa; the Sahara and south.
I = Indian Subcontinent (South Asia from Afghanistan to Burma).
M = The Americas (Central and South plus the Caribbean).
O = East Asia including China and nearby countries.
R = The Mediterranean area and the Middle East, including North Africa.
S = Southeast Asia (Indochina, Malaysia, Indonesia and the Philippines).
U = The South Pacific (New Guinea, Australia, and the other Pacific islands).

Areas near the boundaries of these regions may be covered in either or both of the applicable Indices.

See the maps on the following page.

MAPS SHOWING AREAS OF THE WORLD COVERED BY THE REGIONAL INDICES

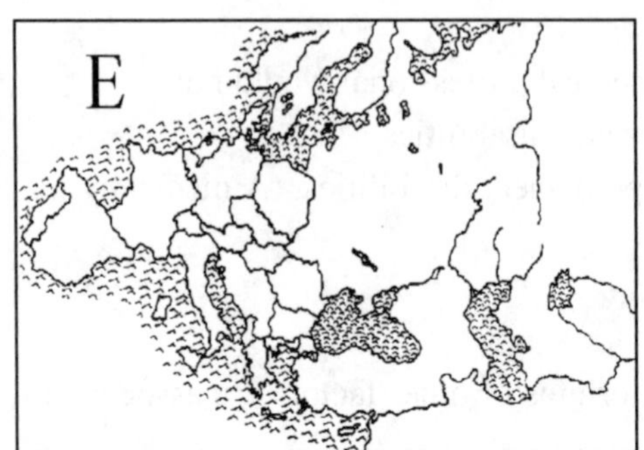

Region E: Eastern Europe and Central Asia

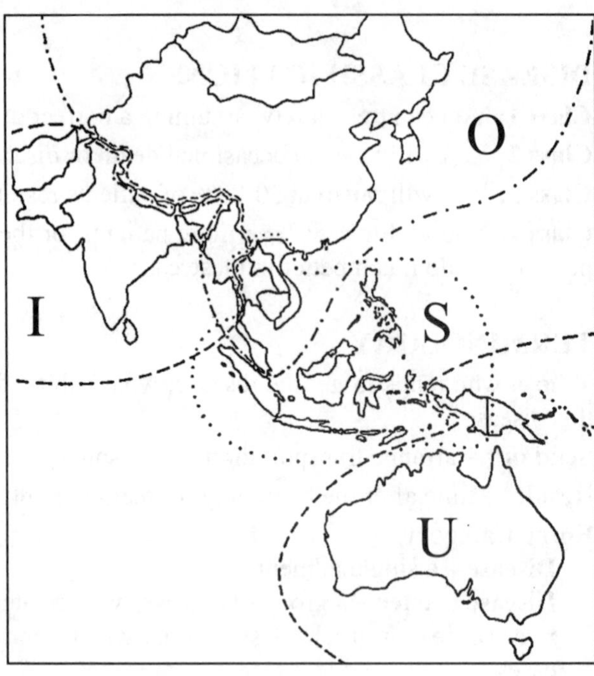

Region I: India Subcontinent (– – –)
Region O: East Asia (– · – · –)
Region S: Southeast Asia (· · · ·)
Region U: Australia and the South Pacific (– – –)

Region M: Central and South America

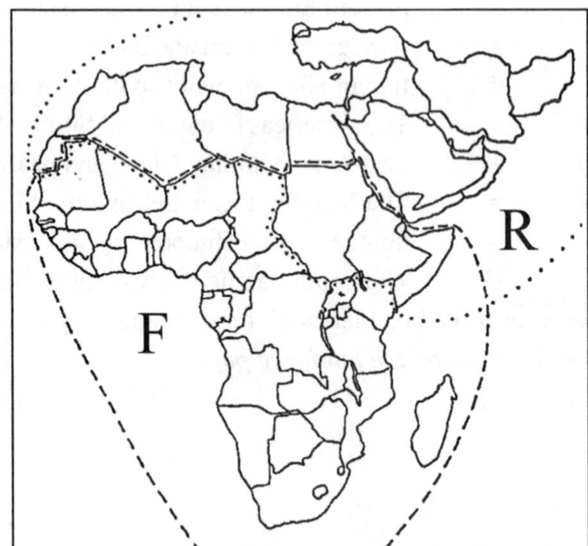

Region F: Africa (– – –)
Region R: Mediterranean and Middle East (· · · ·)

Index B: Disease Index

ABORTION

Regional Notes: F.

Definition: Abortion refers to either the spontaneous process (in which case this is synonymous with miscarriage), or else to the deliberate act of interrupting a pregnancy.

Clinical:

Symptoms: The initial symptoms are usually cramping pains, like labor, and vaginal bleeding.

Causes: Most abortions occur for no discernable reason. The most common causative diseases in the tropics are probably MALARIA and HIV INFECTION. If the patient has eaten moldy rye, it may be due to PLANT POISONING from Ergot. If the patient had a fever, see MALARIA, SEPSIS, HEPATITIS E, MEASLES, ENTERIC FEVER, and TYPHUS. If she has swelling on her lower, front neck, see GOITER. If she has no fever, see Chapters 6 and 7 in Volume I.

Complications: SEPSIS, ANEMIA, subsequent infertility.

Higher-Level Care. Send the patient to a hospital, preferably Level 3 or 4 but Level 2 is better than nothing. She should be seen, ideally, by an obstetrician/gynecologist or at least by a surgeon or midwife.

***Treatment*:**

Prevention: Good nutrition, malaria prophylaxis, boil the drinking water of the pregnant woman.

Patient Care: None in the village situation unless there is SEPSIS or ANEMIA.

ABSCESS

Cause: Bacteria.

Includes: Perirectal abscess, Boil

Definition: An abscess is a localized infection that causes the accumulation of a pocket of pus.

Mildly to moderately ill; Class 1-2, class 3 if the patient has any of the contraindications listed in Appendix 1 Procedure 17; Worldwide, common in developing areas.

Age: Any. **Who:** Anyone, especially diabetics, weakened, malnourished, old injuries, nursing mothers (breast abscesses). **Onset:** 1-7 days.

Clinical:

Necessary: Warm or red, painful, tender,[1] swollen area on the body, like a pimple or a water balloon if it is near the surface. In the mouth an abscess may cause swelling of the gums or the outside of the face. In the breast it causes local pain and swelling as well as a fever. If it is deep in the muscle, it appears to be a generally swollen muscle, usually the thigh, the buttock, or anywhere the skin was broken. Rectal abscesses are usually to the right or left of the anus and the onset of pain is gradual. Near the rectum it causes severe pain with bowel movements and refusal to walk.

Probably: At first the skin over the abscess will look normal. If the abscess is near the surface, as it ripens (becomes ready to drain) the surface skin first becomes shiny and then thin and scaly. Its texture changes from hard to soft; the abscess is then said to be fluctuant; one can feel that there is fluid inside. Probably the lymph nodes adjacent to the abscess will be swollen.

Maybe: Fever, pus draining out of the swollen area, a center spot or hole in the swelling.

Complications: If the abscess is not cared for properly, it will come back and the patient may develop SEPSIS and die.

Similar Conditions: See Protocol C-6.

Black scab on the swelling: ANTHRAX, TUBERCULOSIS.

Abscess in the genital area: SEXUALLY TRANSMITTED DISEASE, PELVIC INFECTION (females).

No center spot: CELLULITIS (near surface), PYOMYOSITIS, OSTEOMYELITIS (deep in).

Hands and feet swollen in a child: SICKLE CELL DISEASE

Higher-Level Care. Send out if possible. *Laboratory:* Possibly helpful if level 2 or 3. Essential capability is doing gram and AFB stains and having a microscope. *Practitioner*: Generalist or surgeon, level 2 or more; some competent nurses might do this.

***Treatment*:**

Prevention: Cleanliness in caring for injuries. Use only sterile needles for injections.

Patient Care[2]:

- To check if an abscess is ready to drain, (or to drain it in the case of the diseases listed above), pierce it with a sterile 18 gauge needle attached to a disposable syringe (since it is very hard to clean pus out of a glass or nylon syringe); if you can withdraw pus, it is ready.

[1] Tender means that pushing on the area causes the pain or aggravates it.

[2] **Cautions:** Sometimes an abscess is over an artery. In this case you will feel a pulse in the abscess. **Do not drain this kind of abscess!** If the abscess is due to CHANCROID or LYMPHOGRANULOMA VENEREUM, or PLAGUE, drain the abscess with a large-bore needle and syringe rather than cutting it open.

- If it is not ready, lay warm, wet towels on it. Cover them with thin plastic. Do this until it is ready. Then drain the abscess according to Appendix 1 in Volume I. Rinse the abscess cavity daily after draining; squirt clean water into it with a syringe. A capsule of PHENYTOIN sprinkled into the cavity daily will hasten healing.
- Antibiotics are not helpful unless the patient has a fever. In any case, they are no substitute for draining the pus. If there is fever treat with ERYTHROMYCIN plus SULFADIAZINE. CIPROFLOXACIN and RIFAMPIN are also good choices but expensive. RIFAMPIN is particularly good if there is a foreign body (e.g. bullet or splinter) in the abscess cavity. Switch to CHLORAMPHENICOL or COTRIMOXAZOLE if the fever does not drop in 48 hours. Some more expensive antibiotics that work more reliably are AUGMENTIN, CLOXACILLIN, or one of the CEPHALOSPORIN antibiotics. Be sure the patient eats a diet adequate in protein; otherwise he will not heal.

Results: Improved in 3 days, healed in 3 weeks. If the patient still has pain or is not healed, continue antibiotics, supplement his diet with protein, and send him out to further medical care.

ACNE

Cause: Bacteria or mites.
Definition: Small, localized infections of the hair follicles, mainly in teenagers.
Not ill; Class 1; Worldwide, worse in humid, tropical climates.
Age: Teenagers, sometimes middle aged. **Who:** Those with oily skin. **Onset:** Over days.

Clinical:

Pimples on the face or back.

Similar Conditions: *With a fever*: ENTERIC FEVER, SPOTTED FEVER (Rickettsial pox), CHICKEN POX (in the early phase).

Treatment:

Have the patient wash with soap and warm water four times a day. Some surface washing agents like BENZOYL PEROXIDE may be helpful. Use oral ERYTHROMYCIN. DOXYCYCLINE works but it may be dangerous to use; it masks the signs of appendicitis in those who still have an appendix.

ACROMEGALY

Cause: Tumor or hormone problem.
Definition: Acromegaly is an excess of growth hormone, causing a child to grow to excessive height or causing growth of only the face, hands, and feet in adults. In either case the facial features are heavy and coarse. Send the patient to a major medical center.
Entry category: Syndrome, worldwide, rare.
Higher-Level Care. Level 4 or 5, endocrinologist.

ACUTE ABDOMEN

Cause: Variable.
Synonyms: Surgical abdomen. *Includes:* PANCREATITIS Perforated ulcer, TUBAL PREGNANCY, Appendicitis, Obstructed bowel and other problems too numerous to mention, Volvulus (Type 3).
Regional Notes: F, I, M, S, U.
Definition: A serious abdominal condition that requires the services of a surgeon for treatment.
Entry category: Disease cluster, worldwide, occasional
Moderately to very ill; Class 4; Worldwide, type is regional, generally not common, not rare.
Age: Any. **Who:** Anyone. **Onset:** Sudden to 4 days or more.

Clinical:

Necessary: The patient has abdominal pain. He is sick enough not to be walking around and doing his usual work or play. The pain is either of sudden onset or else it has lasted for 6 hours or more. The symptoms match one of the types listed below.

➢ **Type 1. With Shock:**

The patient has an ashen color, his skin is cool and moist, he has a rapid pulse rate and possibly a low blood pressure. Generally he is lying still, not writhing about. He is unconscious, or he becomes unconscious if you lift him to an upright position. Usually the onset is sudden in males and slow in females. This kind of acute abdomen may be due to injury to the abdomen or a complication of TUBAL PREGNANCY, amebic DYSENTERY, or PEPTIC ULCER. Sometimes the patient has shoulder or back pain.

➢ **Type 2. Due to Infection:**

Appendicitis is the most common form. The patient has pain for six hours or more. There is a loss of appetite and frequently vomiting or constipation. (But the pain usually comes before the other symptoms.) Pushing on the abdomen makes the pain worse; with simple abdominal cramps, pushing relieves the pain. There is rebound tenderness - the patient will not cough hard twice because it hurts too much after coughing the first time. Jarring the bed or tapping on the abdomen with one finger causes pain. Frequently bowel sounds are absent. The pain is constant. If there is fever, it probably is not high. Usually, the abdominal wall is stiff so that the patient is unable to relax it. The pain may be felt in the pelvis or rectum. Acute abdomen due to infection may be caused by appendicitis, injury, ENTERIC FEVER, abdominal TUBERCULOSIS, and quite a number of other conditions. (Also see Protocol 39, Abdominal Pain, in the *Symptom Index*; it is more complete than the preceding description.)

➢ **Type 3. Due to Bowel Obstruction:**

The patient has had pain for six hours or more, coming in waves, anywhere from 3 to 25 minutes apart. If the pains are closer together, the patient is vomiting and may be constipated also. If they are farther apart, he will be constipated, may vomit also, and the vomitus may look and smell like stool. (It is stool.) Usually the patient is writhing about. Bowel sounds may be absent or they may be rushing, followed by tinkles like dripping water. The most frequent causes are ASCARIASIS, previous surgery, a HERNIA that will not go back, intestinal TUBERCULOSIS, and HYDATID DISEASE. Small children sometimes have lethargy, irregular pains, a soft lump in the abdomen, and bloody diarrhea. There is a more complete description in Symptom Protocol 39C.

Similar Conditions:

Type 1: SEPSIS may be indistinguishable; both require hspitalization.

Type 2: If the respiratory rate is twice normal or more, the patient may have PNEUMONIA, which can closely mimic this. PELVIC INFECTION and TUBAL PREGNANCY may be indistinguishable; in any case the patient must be sent to a hospital. ENTERIC FEVER involves a sustained, high fever which acute abdomen seldom has. Consider FAMILIAL MEDITERRANEAN FEVER for patients with a Mediterranean genetic heritage. AMEBIC LIVER DISEASE and GALLBLADDER DISEASE causes local tenderness in the mid or right upper abdomen.

Type 3: Check for IMPACTION before evacuating a patient for this.

Bush Laboratory: Check hemoglobin, stool hematest and urinalysis. (See Appendix 2.) These are usually normal in acute abdomen. Hospital labs can do blood counts and x-rays to determine diagnosis. If you have the kind of thermometer that is a strip of plastic, check the temperature of the right lower abdomen if you suspect Type 2. If it is higher than the skin temperature of the rest of the abdomen, appendicitis is likely. You can try to relieve the pain with DICYCLOMINE or CHAMOMILE TEA. This will relieve many other abdominal pains but not the pain of an acute abdomen.

Higher-Level Care. Speedy send out is essential; see Volume I, Appendix 13 for referral guidelines. *Laboratory:* Possibly helpful if level 3 or more; essential capability is doing blood counts, urinalysis, blood chemistries. *Facilities:* On occasion x-ray, ultrasound, or CT scan may be helpful. A surgical theatre is essential. *Practitioner:* Level 3-4, surgeon and anesthesiologist. Some generalists can cope.

Treatment:

If it is Type 3 in a disabled patient, first check for IMPACTION; pulling stool out with your fingers might be curative. Otherwise send the patient to a surgeon as soon as possible. *Meanwhile do as follows:*

- Absolute bed rest, partially sitting up for Type 2.
- Give the patient nothing to eat or drink, only a wet cloth to moisten his mouth. The patient will become dehydrated but this is unavoidable if you do not have IV fluids. If you do have IV fluids, start an IV and give the usual maintenance fluid.
- Put a stomach tube in, preferably large diameter, but small diameter is better than nothing. (See Appendix 1 of Vol. I.)
- Empty the patient's stomach frequently with a syringe.
- During a delay in transport, try the following: For Type 2, give the following antibiotics: (TINIDAZOLE or METRONIDAZOLE), plus AMPICILLIN plus GENTAMYCIN. CHLORAMPHENICOL can substitute for GENTAMYCIN. CIPROFLOXACIN is also a good choice.
- For all types, in malarious areas, also treat for MALARIA.
- Consult a medical doctor; he may have additional advice by radio if at all possible. He may want you to give antibiotics.
- Do not give pain medication unless either the receiving physician orders it, or you are sure it will be worn off before reaching the hospital. (Medication is worn off if it is an hour or more past the time for the next dose.)

ADDICTION

Synonyms: Drug abuse, Drug dependency.

Regional Notes: F, O, R, S, U.

Definition: The continued use of a drug in spite of its having an adverse effect on social and economic functioning. The routine use of a drug per se does not constitute addiction or abuse.

Entry category: Syndromes.

Worldwide: Which drug or drugs are used or abused varies with place and ethnic group. Some areas and cultures have major problems, others have minor or no problems.

Age: Any, but mostly preteen to adult. Infants of addicted mothers will be addicted at birth and have withdrawal problems. **Who:** Anyone, with individual variations. Some people become addicted readily, while others do not. **Onset:** Variable. Addiction seldom occurs with less than a week of drug use and it usually requires several weeks to several months.

Clinical:

Necessary: The patient takes a drug regularly and seeks it in spite of its having a negative effect on his social and economic status. There are three main types of abused drugs: If a patient takes a drug, it will give a drug effect. If he has taken a drug regularly over a week or more and then suddenly stops, he may have withdrawal effects.

Sometimes: People who are hyperactive,[1] or were as children, may have reverse effects with uppers and downers; they will become calm with uppers and stimulated with downers. Some of them lack a brain hormone; they use "uppers" to be calm enough to function socially.

➢ **Uppers:**

Uppers speed up bodily and mental processes.

Drug effect: Loss of appetite, trembling, rapid pulse and respiration, fast speech, hyperactivity, confusion, nervousness. Some uppers can cause fevers and high blood pressure. There may be weight loss with a good appetite. Betel nut causes a red/black discoloration of the tongue and mouth.

Withdrawal effect: excessive sleep, depression, uncoordination, low blood pressure, panicky drug-seeking behavior.

Examples: Caffeine, amphetamines, cocaine, khat, betel nut.

➢ **Downers:**

Downers slow down bodily and mental processes.

Drug effect: Slurred speech, sleep, slow pulse and respiration, uncoordination, lowered blood pressure.

Withdrawal effect: nervousness, rapid pulse, anxiety, seizures. Withdrawal from narcotics causes excessive saliva.

Examples: ALCOHOL, tranquilizers, barbiturates, KETAMINE, and narcotics; sometimes cannabis (marijuana).

➢ **Outers:**

Outers cause crazy behavior.

Drug effect: Dangerous, violent, or crazy behavior; nonsense speech; hallucinations.

Withdrawal effect: None, but flashbacks[2] are common.

Examples: LSD, KETAMINE, some mushrooms, sometimes cannabis (marijuana). Drugs taken in connection with animistic rituals are frequently in this class.

Similar Conditions:

Uppers addiction or downers withdrawal: ATTENTION DEFICIT DISORDER may appear similar but has been present since childhood. THYROID TROUBLE with high thyroid or MALARIA (cerebral) involves a fever also. Consider DEMONIZATION. Withdrawal of downers may cause trembling similar to PARKINSON'S DISEASE or HYPOGLYCEMIA or LIVER FAILURE.

Downers addiction or uppers withdrawal: Consider HYPOGLYCEMIA (also sweaty), THYROID TROUBLE, low thyroid (also low body temperature). In Africa consider AFRICAN SLEEPING SICKNESS. See Protocol C-10.

Outers effect: If there is a fever, consider MALARIA, (cerebral) and similar conditions. DEMONIZATION does not cause a fever. LIVER FAILURE may also cause bizarre behavior. Consider TOXEMIA in a pregnant woman, BERIBERI or PELLAGRA in a malnourished patient, SYPHILIS (tertiary) in a middle aged or older person, HIV INFECTION which has progressed to full-blown AIDS.

Higher-Level Care. Send out if possible. *Laboratory:* Level 4 only, capability of blood and/or urine tests to determine kind of drug and amount. *Practitioner:* Level 3-4; generalist or internal medicine. Competent nursing is essential. A psychiatrist, counselor, or clergy might be helpful.

Treatment:

Uppers: Excessive drug effect may be treated with downers if there is no history of ATTENTION DEFICIT DISORDER. Withdrawal from uppers must be done slowly.

Downers: Excessive drug effect must be treated with assisting the patient's breathing until the drug wears off. Withdrawal from downers must be done slowly.

Outers: Excessive drug effect should be treated with a quiet, semi-dark, calm environment with someone to talk quietly to the patient and reassure him. It frequently takes two or three days for these effects to wear off. Withdrawal is not a problem. Flashbacks should be treated like excessive effects.

AFRICAN SLEEPING SICKNESS.

See *Regional Notes* F.

AFRICAN TICK TYPHUS

See SPOTTED FEVER. African Tick Typhus is one form of Boutonneuse Fever, listed under SPOTTED FEVER. The other form of Boutonneuse Fever is Mediterranean Tick Typhus, a similar disease but not so severe.

AIDS

See HIV INFECTION.

AIDS refers to HIV INFECTION that has progressed enough to cause severe symptoms: repeated infections; weight loss; diarrhea; failure to thrive in children.

AINHUM

Cause: Unknown.

Regional: present in South Africa, African Americans, Pacific islanders, and South Asians.

Clinical:

A painful narrowing develops around the base of the little toe and gradually tightens until the toe falls off. This may subsequently happen to adjacent toes.

[1] See ATTENTION DEFICIT DISORDER.

[2] A flashback is a drug effect which occurs again without the patient's taking the drug again. Flashbacks can occur months or years after the last dose of drug.

Higher-Level Care. Send out if possible. *Practitioner:* Level 2-4, generalist or surgeon.

Treatment:

If the little toe is amputated surgically when this starts, the process will not spread to the other toes.

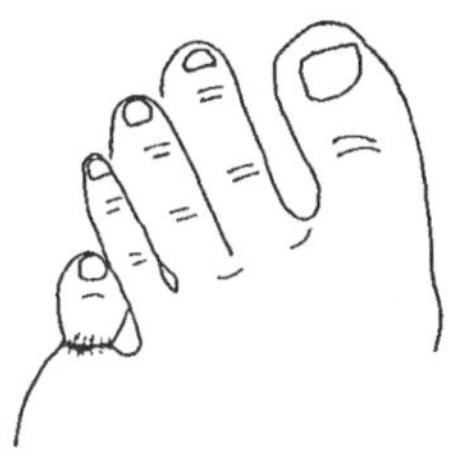

Ainhum of the little toe; note the narrowing.

ALBINISM

Cause: Birth defect.

This is a condition characterized by a complete lack of brown skin pigment. The skin is very fair, the hair is a very light blond, and there are eye problems connected with it. You can do nothing about it except to advise avoiding sunburn. Albino skin is very vulnerable to skin CANCERs. It is important to assure the family that the condition was not caused by marital unfaithfulness.

ALCOHOLISM

Cause: ADDICTION.

Definition: The continued use of alcohol, either as regular drinking or as occasional binges, in spite of its causing adverse physical and/or social consequences.

Not ill to very ill; Class 1-4; Worldwide, common

Age: Adults. **Who:** Anyone, but especially those who are impulsive or who have a family history of alcoholism. **Onset:** Over weeks to years.

Clinical:

Necessary: The person cannot control his drinking and it interferes with his social functioning at least some of the time.

Usually: He has been drinking excessively for months to years. This can be either regular intake or binges. He usually denies that his drinking is a problem.

Occasionally: He has a sore tongue. Chronic alcoholics may have a red face with a red, bumpy nose. They may have swollen cheeks, especially right in front of their ears. DEPRESSION is a common cause as well as a common effect of alcoholism.

➢ **Withdrawal:**

Usually: Symptoms include sweating, nervousness, and desperate alcohol-seeking behavior.

Commonly: Patients have SEIZURES with alcohol withdrawal.

Sometimes: Withdrawal also involves "DT's": vivid, long-lasting hallucinations (usually terrifying but sometimes pleasant), associated with severe shaking. This may cause bizarre behavior. There is a 15% death rate from DT's in the States.

Complications: BERIBERI, HEART FAILURE, and CIRRHOSIS. CIRRHOSIS typically causes a large, distended abdomen full of fluid, and swelling of the lower limbs, especially at the end of the day. The patient's blood might not clot properly, causing abnormal bleeding.

Similar Conditions:

See Protocol C-10 for confusion and lethargy. See Protocol C-7 for liver disease which is a consequence of alcoholism

Indistinguishable from alcohol withdrawal: ADDICTION to other downers,. HYPOGLYCEMIA.

Mental symptoms: ATTENTION DEFICIT DISORDER, LIVER FAILURE, DEMONIZATION.

Swollen cheeks MUMPS, MALNUTRITION, or HIV INFECTION.

Higher-Level Care. Send out for treatment if possible, having a responsible adult watch the patient during withdrawal. *Laboratory:* Level 2 or more, basic capabilities. *Practitioner:* Generalist or internal medicine; psychiatrist, counselor, or clergy might be helpful.

Treatment:

Usually alcoholics are malnourished; treat them with MULTIVITAMINS. Minor tranquilizers such as DIAZEPAM may be useful for withdrawal. Large hospitals with psychiatric units have treatment programs which may be successful. For nationals in remote areas, pastoral counseling once the initial withdrawal stage is past is probably most appropriate.

ALLERGY

Synonym: Mango fever.

Includes: Hives, Hay fever, ASTHMA, Vernal conjunctivitis.

Definition: Allergy is an illness caused by the body's reaction against some substance, inhaled, eaten, or encountered through skin contact.

Entry category: Syndromes, worldwide, common.

Mildly to moderately ill; Class 1-4; Worldwide, generally common.

Age: Any. **Who:** Anyone, but especially those with prior episodes of allergy or a family history of allergy. PENICILLIN or IRON shots, and bee stings frequently cause severe reactions. **Onset:** 5 minutes to one day; onsets tend to be rapid with lung symptoms.

Clinical:

This commonly occurs in three forms (Lungs, Head, and Skin). Any one, two, or all three may be present in any patient. In severe cases the patient may faint or develop ANAPHYLAXIS. Other forms of allergy are SERUM SICKNESS and DRUG ERUPTION.

THREE FORMS OF ALLERGY

LUNGS	HEAD	SKIN
Short of breath	Red eyes	Itchy palms
Long expiration	Tearing eyes	Itchy soles
Wheezing	Swollen eyes	HIVES
Turning blue	Swollen face	ECZEMA
Raspy inspiration	Swollen throat	CONTACT DERMATITIS
Congestion	Itchy eyes	
	Itchy throat	
	Itchy ears	
	Sneezing	
	Stuffy nose	
	Runny nose	
	Loss of smell	

Hives: Hives are very itchy, raised, flat-topped bumps on the skin.

Complications: Allergy that affects the lungs may make a person susceptible to RESPIRATORY INFECTION. Sometimes patients die from severe allergic reactions.

Causative Diseases: Allergy plus fever or ASTHMA plus fever may indicate TUBERCULOSIS (mainly adults), SWIMMER'S ITCH, KATAYAMA DISEASE or possibly KIDNEY INFECTION. See also SERUM SICKNESS and DRUG ERUPTION.

HYDATID DISEASE, GUINEA WORM, and MANSONELLOSIS PERSTANS and some other infections may also cause allergic symptoms.

Similar Conditions: ANAPHYLAXIS is a form of severe allergy with a sudden onset. ANTHRAX swelling may look similar but there is a sore and fever.

Bush Laboratory: Check the urine dipstick. Occasionally liver problems (bilirubin in the urine) and URINARY INFECTION (leukocytes or nitrites in the urine) may cause hives. Blood tests are not helpful.

Higher-Level Care. Send out if possible. *Laboratory:* Generally not helpful. *Practitioner:* Level 2-4, Generalist or internal medicine.

Treatment:

Prevention: Clean the person's environment. One of the common causes of allergy is the presence of insects. When insects die their parts contaminate dust, causing allergy.

Patient Care:

For a *bee sting or an injection*, see ANAPHYLAXIS. If the patient is short of breath, but this is not due to bee sting or a shot, see ASTHMA. IPRATROPIUM may be helpful.

Treat *skin allergies*: SERUM SICKNESS, DRUG ERUPTION, ECZEMA, and CONTACT DERMATITIS according to their own descriptions.

Allergy without trouble breathing: Treat with DIPHENHYDRAMINE or CHLORPHENIRAMINE or DEXCHLORPHENIRAMINE. If you have some HYDROCORTISONE or PREDNISONE and the problem is either severe or recurrent, use it for 1 to 5 days, but not longer unless a physician so orders. There are better drugs than those listed here, available in Western facilities.

Allergy with trouble breathing: See ANAPHYLAXIS.

Vernal conjunctivitis:

A common form of allergy that affects the eyes in dry climates.

Not ill; Class 1-2; Regional, in hot areas.

Age: Any but especially 3-16 y.o. **Who:** Anyone. **Onset:** Usually gradual.

Clinical: The patient has itching of the eyes, with a white, mucous discharge. With time there is thickening of the clear membrane that covers the white part of the eye, with a dark ring forming around the cornea. The lining of the eyelids may also thicken.

Similar Conditions: TRACHOMA, EYE INFECTION, XEROPHTHALMIA, ONCHOCERCIASIS. See Protocol C-8: Red, painful eyes.

Higher-Level Care. Send out if possible. *Laboratory*: Level 3-4, Culture capabilities. *Practitioner*: Generalist or Ophthalmologist.

Treatment of vernal conjunctivitis:

Send out if possible for a firm, definitive diagnoses. PREDNISOLONE EYE DROPS are very helpful; they clear the condition in a few days. However, they are dangerous. They must not be used for more than 2 weeks at a time. Once the condition is cleared, CROMOGLYCATE eye drops will keep the eyes clear.

ALTITUDE SICKNESS

Cause: High altitude.

Synonym: Acute mountain sickness; Mountain sickness, High altitude illness.

Includes: High altitude cerebral edema (HACE), and High altitude pulmonary edema (HAPE).

Definition: Altitude sickness is an illness caused by problems in the body's adaptation to high altitudes.

Moderately to very ill; Class 4; High altitudes only.

Entry category: Disease, regional, occasional

Age: Any. **Who:** Those at an altitude of 2000 meters (6000 feet) or more for mild illness. It is more likely if the patient has previously been at high altitudes and/or previously had altitude sickness. In a large party of people, usually only one or two will have the problem. **Onset:** Usually 12-24 hours after arriving at high altitude; sooner with rapid ascent and exertion.

Clinical:

Necessary: There are three types; the second and third types are life-threatening. Usually it begins with the first type and then progresses to the second or third type. Altitude sickness does not cause fever.

- **Mild Altitude Sickness**

This consists of fatigue and mild shortness of breath and/or headache, worse with exertion. The headache is similar to a hangover.

- **HAPE (High Altitude Pulmonary Edema):**

The patient is very short of breath and he has abnormal lung sounds. He may faint. The shortness of breath is worse lying than sitting. His respiration is rapid, irregular, or both, and he may turn blue. You may hear fine crackles or wheezing in his chest with your stethoscope. The patient may have a pressure-type chest pain or a cough which is either dry or productive of white or foamy sputum. This starts 2-4 days after ascent; it is worse at night.

- **HACE (High Altitude Cerebral Edema):**

The patient has a severe headache and mental changes with slurred speech or crazy behavior. He may be uncoordinated. This starts within 48 hours of ascent.

Complications: HEART FAILURE, RESPIRATORY FAILURE, STROKE.

Similar Conditions: HYPERVENTILATION is similar but the patient's hands are cramped; they are never cramped with altitude sickness. ASTHMA may be indistinguishable. CARBON MONOXIDE POISONING involves exposure to a fire or an engine. See Protocol C-4 for other causes of shortness of breath. See Protocol C-10 for other causes of confusion and lethargy.

Higher-Level Care. *Laboratory:* Generally not helpful. *Practitioner:* Level 2-4; generalist or internal medicine; a competent nurse might be adequate.

Treatment:

Prevention: Ascend gradually, spending a day or two at intermediate altitudes. Altitude gain above 9000 feet should be only 1000 feet per day for those prone to altitude sickness. Consider using ACETAZOLAMIDE.

Patient care: For mild illness and to hasten acclimatization, give ACETAZOLAMIDE daily for 3 days. Do not use any diuretic. In more serious illness:

- Have someone arrange to take the patient to a lower altitude. This is essential.
- Keep the patient at bed rest, sitting up.
- Give DEXAMETHASONE if possible but only with the third (mental) type of illness.
- Keep track of vital signs, and make repeated efforts to get the patient to a lower altitude.
- Give the patient oxygen if possible.

AMEBIC LIVER DISEASE

Cause: Protozoa.
Synonym: Amoebic liver disease (British spelling).
Includes: Amebic liver abscess.
Regional Notes: All regions.
Definition: Amebic liver disease is an inflammation of the liver, (either a formed abscess or an abscess in the process of forming) caused by the protozoa *Entameba histolytica.*

Entry category: Disease, mainly tropical, worldwide, common.

Moderately to very ill; Class 3-4; Worldwide, mostly in areas where there is poor hygiene. The disease is frequently carried by cockroaches and flies, which contaminate food and water.

Age: Rare in children. **Who:** Anyone, especially prior exposure to DYSENTERY without actually having gotten the disease, and those who are malnourished. Males are much more susceptible than females. **Onset:** Slowly usually; if it appears abruptly the patient will admit to having had prior symptoms if he is asked. Incubation is 1-2 weeks if the exposure is minor; it is days for major exposures.

Clinical:

Usually: Fevers or chills or night sweats; loss of appetite or nausea; pain or burning in the upper abdomen, or (usually) the right shoulder, side, or back which is worse with walking, with a gentle punch, or with pushing between the ribs in the painful area.

Sometimes: The patient may have only weight loss without pains or fever.

Maybe: Vomiting, tender, soft lump in upper right abdomen, large, tender liver, mild JAUNDICE, cough (5-7%), pain with breathing, diarrhea, insomnia, general lethargy and fatigue. If it is advanced, then jumping up and down causes severe pain in the liver.

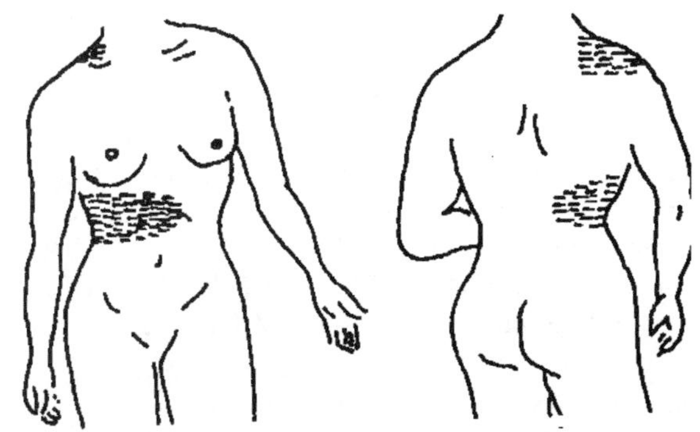

Amebic Liver Disease: The pain is most often felt in the shaded areas.

Complications: ANEMIA, HICCUPS, spread to the brain causing STROKE or SEIZURES. In Blacks and Asians especially, the amebae may eat through the diaphragm and the pus in the liver pour into the chest. (PREDNISONE and related drugs may provoke this.) The patient then suddenly develops a cough with lavender or brown (occasionally yellow or green) sputum, severe PLEURISY-type chest pains, and sometimes a scraping sound that can be heard with each breath. If the pus breaks out into the abdomen, he will develop an ACUTE ABDOMEN. In both cases the patient must be sent to the hospital quickly.

Similar Conditions: PEPTIC ULCER also involves burning pain, but the pain varies with hunger or a full stomach. HEART FAILURE is a common cause of a tender, enlarged liver. KIDNEY INFECTION on the right may look similar, but the urine is cloudy. PNEUMONIA, HEPATITIS, and GALLBLADDER DISEASE are of more sudden onset. With HEPATITIS the JAUNDICE is apt to be intense, not slight. SYPHILIS and CANCER may look similar, but the lower border of the liver is lumpy. MALARIA and SEPSIS can have a similar fever pattern, but the liver is not so tender. HYDATID DISEASE shows an enlarged liver; check the geography for your area. See Protocol C-5 for other causes of fever and jaundice.

Bush Laboratory: The urine may contain bilirubin and possibly urobilinogen and protein. You may find positive ketones also. Blood, leukocytes, or nitrites in the urine indicate a kidney problem.

Higher-Level Care. Send out if possible. See Volume I, Appendix 13. *Laboratory:* Level 3-4, capable of blood chemistries. Hospital labs may check stool for amebae. A stool test must be done and found to be negative seven times on seven different, very fresh specimens before you can be sure the patient does not have the disease. The test is not at all sensitive (there are many false negatives) but it is specific (rare false positives). Usually it is easier to just treat without a positive lab report. *Facilities:* X-ray, ultrasound, CT scan: Level 3-4. *Practitioner:* Tropical/travel generalist, may need a surgeon.

Treatment:

Prevention: Filter or boil drinking water; do not eat food from street vendors.

Patient Care: Severe cases frequently need surgery. However, you can try METRONIDAZOLE or TINIDAZOLE. The patient will improve within 72 hours if the treatment will ultimately be successful. If he is not improved within this time, he must be sent to a hospital for surgery. ORNIDAZOLE and SECNIDAZOLE are new, related drugs. PROMETHAZINE might be helpful for nausea.

Results: Some improvement before one week.

AMEBIC SKIN ULCER

Definition: A skin ulcer, found on the genitals or on the trunk, due to the protozoa Entameba histolytica.

Entry category: Disease, regional, tropical.

Clinical:

The appearance is a skin ulcer on the trunk or genitals. It is sometimes due to amebae which have infected the bowel and now are eating a hole through the abdominal wall. It might be due to a direct skin infection with amebae. The ulcer is very painful and there is usually a lot of discharge from the wound. It is essential to start treatment soon since these ulcers can progress rapidly and the bowel contents can spill out through them. They can destroy the genitals within a few days to a week.

Similar Conditions: See Sexually Transmitted Diseases, Protocol C-1, which may be indistinguishable from this although they do not usually have a discharge from the ulcer. See Protocol C-11 for skin ulcer plus general illness.

Higher-Level Care. Send out if possible, see Volume I, appendix 13. *Laboratory:* Level 3-4, capable of culturing bacteria, doing stained smears for amebae. *Practitioners:* Level 3-4, internist, possibly a surgeon.

Treatment:

The treatment is the same as for AMEBIC LIVER DISEASE above. The ulcers usually respond rapidly to treatment.

ANAPHYLAXIS

Cause: Allergy.

Synonyms: Anaphylactic shock.

Regional Notes: M.

Definition: An overwhelming allergic reaction to some substance, usually inhaled or injected.

***Life-threatening, treat immediately!!

Very ill; Class 1-4; Worldwide but relatively rare.

Age: Any. **Who:** Anyone, especially after injection of PENICILLIN or IRON or an insect sting. May occasionally come from food, particularly nuts, milk, and eggs. **Onset:** Sudden, over seconds to minutes.

Clinical:

The patient has one or more of the following: sudden swelling of the face or throat, shortness of breath, blue skin color, loud wheezing, loss of consciousness, sudden death. The blood pressure may drop. The patient may vomit or develop hives. He may have abdominal pain. After a severe episode, he may develop KIDNEY FAILURE or SHOCK (which must be treated).

Causative Diseases: HYDATID DISEASE as well as PLANT POISONING due to Claviceps or Cassava can cause anaphylaxis.

Similar Conditions: Anaphylaxis is a severe form of ALLERGY.

With cramped hands: HYPERVENTILATION

With a sore and fever: ANTHRAX

Higher-Level Care. Sending out is not possible since the problem progresses rapidly, over minutes. The exception is if you live across the street from a level 3-4 hospital in which case you should not be using this manual.

Treatment:

EPINEPHRINE 1:1000 injection. Repeat this every 5-10 minutes as long as the patient is either unconscious or blue, and then every 30 minutes as long as he is having severe symptoms but conscious and not blue.

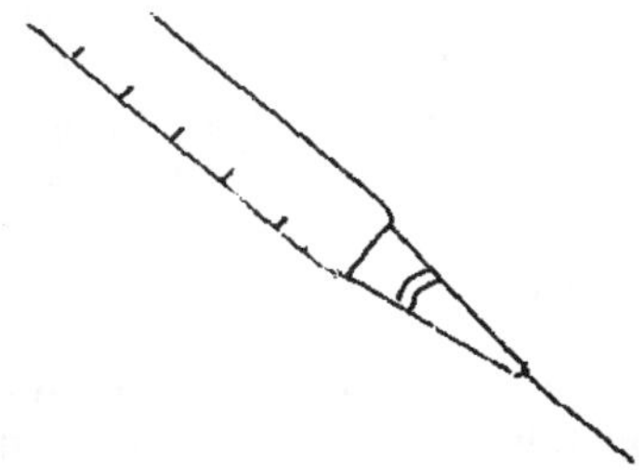

Epinephrine dosage in ml, according to size of patient

Start CIMETIDINE, DIPHENHYDRAMINE, and PREDNISONE as soon as the patient can swallow. Continue the DIPHENHYDRAMINE for 2-3 days but give only 1-2 doses of PREDNISONE.

Result: A few minutes after the epinephrine injection.

ANEMIA

Cause: Variable.

Regional Notes: F, I, M, O, R, S, U.

Definition: Hemoglobin of less than 10 (11-18 is normal at sea-level; normals are higher at high altitude). Hemoglobin is the red stuff in the blood that combines with oxygen in the lungs and releases oxygen in the organs of the body. When there is a lack, it puts a stress on all the organs of the body, particularly on the heart which must pump much more blood to deliver the same amount of oxygen.

Entry category: Syndrome.

Not ill to very ill; Class 3-4 in a pregnant woman with paleness. Class 2-3 in non-pregnant people who are pale or have a hemoglobin of 7 or less; Class 1 in non-pregnant people who are not pale. Worldwide, extremely common.

Age: Any. **Who:** Anyone, especially children, pregnant women, those with a poor diet or suffering from various diseases. In agricultural areas it is frequently due to HOOKWORM. A diet of goat's milk causes folic acid deficiency anemia. A diet deficient in animal products causes vitamin B-12 anemia. In women, anemia increases with the number of children, the use of IUD's, and an early age of first pregnancy. In most cultures, more than 50% of pregnant women have anemia. **Onset:** Usually over weeks to months unless there is obvious blood loss.

Clinical:

Necessary: The patient feels weak, lethargic, and tired. He will have pale skin, fingernails, inner lower eyelids, and tongue or inner mouth; the fingernails usually turn pale before the inner eyelids or mouth. He will have a rapid pulse and respiration and a high pulse pressure[1] if the anemia is severe. He may feel short of breath.

Maybe: He will be dizzy and faint easily. Some patients have scooped-out fingernails or bluish whites of the eyes. The tongue may be sore. There may be leg cramps with climbing stairs. The skin may turn a darker color if the problem is a lack of vitamin B_{12}. With anemia due to lack of iron, there may be difficulty swallowing, splits at the angles of the mouth, long ridges on the fingernails, and intolerance of cold. There may also be numbness and tingling. His heart size may be large (see Volume I, Chapter 1) and he may develop HEART FAILURE. At high altitudes other symptoms (especially shortness of breath) appear before paleness

There are five main types of anemia:

- Due to red cell destruction.
- Due to vitamin deficiency.
- Due to iron deficiency.
- Due to chronic disease.
- Due to bone marrow problems.

➢ Anemia Due To Red Cell Destruction

This occurs in THALLASEMIA, MALARIA, SICKLE CELL DISEASE, OVALOCYTOSIS, BARTONELLOSIS, and TROPICAL SPLENOMEGALY. It may also occur as a complication of bacterial DYSENTERY. There is usually urobilinogen in the urine. The patient may have JAUNDICE. Usually his spleen is enlarged. See Protocol C-7.

➢ Anemia Due To Vitamin Deficiency

This occurs with other diseases: Fish TAPEWORM, PELLAGRA, any MALNUTRITION, MALABSORPTION, or THALLASEMIA. It occurs after 3 years on a strict vegan[2] diet. In those on vegan diets, the problem is lack of VITAMIN B_{12}. In those who eat no vegetables, the problem is lack of FOLATE.

In persons of northern European or African genetic heritage over 60 years old, a condition called pernicious anemia occurs which requires Vitamin B_{12} injections.

Frequently the patient has darkening of the creases on the palm side of his hands and dark discoloration of his tongue. He may have trouble walking (he cannot tell where is feet are without looking) or have numbness or tingling in his feet. He might not feel light touch or be able to sense vibrations. These symptoms are symmetrical (or nearly so), right and left. There may be easy bruising, excessive bleeding, premature graying, burning of the tongue, and susceptibility to infection. Some-

[1] The pulse pressure is the difference between the two numbers of the blood pressure. It should not be more than 50 or so. If someone has a blood pressure of 100/10, then his pulse pressure is 90 which is abnormally high.

[2] A vegan diet is one that does not include any animal products whatsoever, including no milk and no eggs.

times there are mental changes—emotional upset—and this may predate the obvious anemia. In any case you should treat with both B_{12} and folate. Don't treat with folate if the person eats no animal products and you have no B_{12}.

➢ **Anemia Due To Iron Deficiency**

This is usually due to MALNUTRITION (not eating enough iron), blood loss, or pregnancy (using iron to make the baby). It may be due to rapid growth with a poor diet. The most common cause of blood loss is HOOKWORM. The patient should be able to tell you of any visible blood loss. If he has not had any visible loss, ask about black and tar-like stools and check his stools for blood. Also ask about diet to see if he takes in enough IRON in the form of red meats, blood, sorghum, or IRON-containing medicines. With iron deficiency there may be crampy pains in the legs when walking up stairs.

➢ **Anemia Due To Chronic Disease**

This may be indistinguishable from that due to IRON deficiency. Check the patient for TB and other chronic diseases.

➢ **Anemia Due To Bone Marrow Problems**

This comes from RADIATION ILLNESS or from a side-effect of CHLORAMPHENICOL or some other drug. This type of anemia is not treatable in a remote setting.

➢ **Childhood Anemia:**

In a child, the cause of anemia can be guessed from his age in many cases:

0-3 months: Some hereditary problem, bacterial infection (RESPIRATORY INFECTION, KIDNEY INFECTION, SEPSIS most common), congenital SYPHILIS.

3-24 months: Bacterial infections as above, MALARIA, THALLASEMIA, nutritional anemia from a malnourished mother; (SICKLE CELL DISEASE).

2-5 years: Anemia from IRON deficiency; vitamin deficiency (responds to FOLATE) occurs occasionally. (In vegan[1] families, this responds to VITAMIN B_{12}.)

5-15 years: Almost all anemia is due to iron deficiency, usually from HOOKWORM or beginning menstruation in females.

Complications: HEART FAILURE, RESPIRATORY FAILURE, other complications depending on the cause.

Similar Conditions: Also see Protocol C-4 if the patient is short of breath, Protocol C-10 for other causes of lethargy.

Pale skin: TUBERCULOSIS, MALNUTRITION

Bush Laboratory: The patient's hemoglobin must be 8 or less before you will notice paleness inside the lower lids. The SKALA or Talquist paper test will give you a rough idea; do not trust other tests that compare the color of a drop of blood to a standard. Most hospital labs can determine hemoglobin. There are inexpensive devices that are useful in villages. .If the anemia is due to red blood cell destruction, there will be excess urobilinogen in the urine, as seen on a urine dipstick. (Note: 1+ urobilinogen is normal; 2+ or more is excess.) The following table gives the kinds of symptoms to be expected with low hemoglobin.

Hemoglobin mg/dl[1]	Hemoglobin mg/liter	% on the paper test	Low altitude symptoms
12	120	80%	none
10	110	70%	fatigue
8	80	52%	short of breath on exertion
6	60	38%	short of breath at rest
4	40	25%	short of breath, maybe heart failure
2	20	13%	heart failure, may die

The normal hemoglobin range is 11-17 mg/dl, or 110-170 mg/liter. A hemoglobin of 5 mg/dl is considered severe anemia at low altitidue, while 7 mg/liter is severe at high altitude or in pregnant women. Papers to measure anemia are indexed as % of the normal.

Higher-Level Care. Send out if possible, see Volume I, Appendix 13. *Laboratory:* Level 3-4. Capability of blood smears, a microscope, and sometimes blood chemistries. Should be able to do stool tests for various kinds of worms. With severe anemia a blood bank might be helpful. Large labs can also do specific tests for the various kinds of anemia. A good technician or physician can guess the cause from examining the blood smear. It is important that hospitals can and do check transfused blood for HIV and don't use blood that tests positive. If there is a delay in finding blood and/or transfusing it and if the patient is somewhat improved in the meantime, then it is good to refuse transfusion. Patients who truly need blood need it quickly. If they survive an initial delay of 3 days, they will survive longer without transfusion. Even blood that tested negative can transmit HIV INFECTION. People who will die from anemia usually do so within 24-48 hours or with childbirth, surgery, or some other physical stress. *Facilities:* Blood bank, IV fluids and associated equipment. *Practitioner:* Level 3-4. pathologist is ideal; internist or generalist might suffice. Since some final diagnoses are peculiarly tropical/travel, tropical/travel expertise is desirable.

Treatment:

Prevention: All pregnant women should take IRON and folate. Those in malarious areas should also take MALARIA-preventive medication throughout pregnancy. They should eat some animal products in order to get Vitamin B_{12}. Educate people on the best diet to eat using local foods. Treat all HOOKWORM and other worms.

---

[1] dl = deciliter, i.e., one tenth of a liter.

➢ **Patient Care: Hemoglobin 4 or less:**

Send to a hospital for transfusion. In patients who are elderly or have prior heart problems, HEART FAILURE is common; these patients need transfusion. Anyone with severe anemia plus pregnancy or any major illness is likely to die without transfusion.

➢ **Patient Care: Hemoglobin above 4:**

Treat both the anemia and the cause.

If you are not sure of the cause of the anemia, treat the patient with IRON, FOLATE, and MULTIVITAMINS. Also give a treatment for HOOKWORM and a treatment for MALARIA if you are in a malarious area. If the patient has evidence of HEART FAILURE or PNEUMONIA, treat that also. In malnourished mothers and their infants, injections of Vitamin B_{12} might be helpful.

If you are fairly certain of the cause of the anemia:

- *Anemia due to red cell destruction* is treated with FOLATE alone if the patient eats meat, with FOLATE plus IRON if he eats no meat. If he eats meat, then do not add IRON.
- *Anemia due to vitamin deficiency* is treated with FOLATE and either VITAMIN B_{12} or ground raw beef liver. Usually these patients require IRON also.
- *Anemia due to iron deficiency or chronic disease* is treated with both IRON and FOLATE, together with B_{12} if the diet does not include animal products.

Results: Some improvement in 2 weeks. Recheck the patient every 2 weeks until he is normal.

ANGINA

Definition: Angina is chest pain caused by a heart problem.

Entry category: Syndrome.

Age: Usually middle-aged or older. **Who:** Usually Westerners. **Onset:** Usually rapid, over seconds; sometimes gradually, over hours.

Clinical:

It is heavy, aching, or burning; center front, going to the neck, left shoulder, left jaw, or left arm. Frequently there is nausea and/or vomiting, shortness of breath, severe sweating, poor (possibly bluish) skin color, and an irregular pulse. It goes away in less than 20 minutes. A longer duration may indicate a HEART ATTACK.

Higher-Level Care. Send out if possible. *Laboratory:* Level 3-4: EKG machine, blood chemistries. *Facilities:* Oxygen, heart monitors. *Practitioners:* Level 3-4: Cardiologist is ideal; internist or generalist might suffice.

Treatment:

Have the patient rest quietly in a sitting position and give him his usual angina medication if he has any. Oxygen may be helpful.

ANTHRAX

Cause: Bacteria (Bacillus anthracus).

Synonyms: Charbon, Malignant edema, Malignant pustule, Ragpickers' disease, Woolsorters' disease.

Regional Notes: E, F, M, R, U.

Definition: Anthrax is a bacterial infection causing a localized infection where it enters the body, as well as consequent surrounding swelling.

Entry category: Disease, mainly tropical, worldwide, maybe terrorist-related.

Moderately to very ill; Class 2-4; the material from a skin sore is infectious but the respiratory form is not contagious; Occurs in areas of animal husbandry. Most prevalent in the early and late rainy seasons, in areas where the soil is neutral or alkaline.

Age: Any. **Who:** Anyone who has not already had the disease, especially those who process skins and bone meal, handle sick animals, or eat their meat. Lab technicians who handle material from the patient are also vulnerable. **Onset:** Incubation less than a week. The initial bump becomes a big sore in 3-4 days; a black scab forms within a week. The respiratory incubation is 1-3 days.

Clinical:

➢ **Skin:**

90% of all infections are the skin form, usually on exposed part(s). A tiny pimple appears, which then enlarges over 1 day to become a sore with a black scab. It is painless but it may itch initially. There is no pus. It is regular and round, with raised edges but there may be little satellite sores. The patient develops a fever and severe swelling which may involve half his body; the swelling is the kind that fills rapidly when it is pressed to make a dent. The swelling is general and always involves the lymph nodes; the nodes may be painful. This may disappear very slowly or the patient may develop SEPSIS and die. It takes 6 weeks to heal; the delayed healing does not necessarily imply antibiotic failure. Antibiotic treatment does not hasten the healing but it does prevent serious complications.

➢ **Respiratory:**

The respiratory form is the same, except that the pimple and swelling are within the throat and windpipe and death is almost inevitable since the swelling cuts off air flow. The disease might dominate on left or right. The patient may have pain with swallowing and shortness of breath. It is caused by inhaling contaminated body fluids or dust. This can, at times progress to MENINGITIS.

➢ **Intestinal:**

This form is indistinguishable from bacterial DYSENTERY. It can also be similar to intestinal TULAREMIA and ENTERIC FEVER. SEPSIS and death are common. It is found almost exclusively in Africa and comes from eating contaminated, poorly-cooked meat.

Similar Conditions: See Protocol C-4 for shortness of breath, C-6 for limb swelling, C-11 for a skin ulcer plus general illness, C-12 for large lymph nodes.

Sore(s) with black scab(s): PLAGUE, SPOTTED FEVER, SCRUB TYPHUS, TULAREMIA, CANCRUM ORIS, TUBERCULOSIS.

Severe swelling: DIPHTHERIA, MUMPS, ABSCESS, CELLULITIS.

Two Anthrax sores on the cheek

Higher-Level Care. Send out if possible. See Volume I, Appendix 13. *Laboratory:* Level 4; Capable of gram stain with very high-tech laboratory safety precautions. An excellent hospital lab can do cultures and gram stain, but handling the material is dangerous. There is a new skin test for this that is better and safer than bacterial culture for diagnosis. *Practitioner:* Level 3-4; infectious disease specialist is ideal; internist or generalist might suffice, tropical/travel expertise is very desirable.

Treatment:

Prevention: Human immunization is available. Immunize animals against the disease. Be extremely careful when handling body fluids from the patient. If you inadvertently inhale some of the material from the anthrax wound, immediately seek immunization plus take DOXYCYCLINE for 60 days.

Patient Care: Do send the patient out if possible. Because this disease is so dreadful, ignore contraindications as regards pregnant women and children.

- Use (CIPROFLOXACIN or LEVOFLOXACIN or DOXYCYCLINE) plus (CLINDAMYCIN or RIFAMPIN). Otherwise use PENICILLIN or AMPICILLIN. COTRIMOXAZOLE is good also. Don't use any CEPHALOSPORIN except for Cefoperazone.
- If the patient is very ill, initially give antibiotics IV until he is much improved; then change to oral medication. It is essential to treat for an entire 60 days.
- In case of swelling involving the head or neck, use high doses of PREDNISONE by mouth or HYDROCORTISONE IV, as for severe ENTERIC FEVER, just until the swelling subsides.

APHTHOUS STOMATITIS

Cause: Virus.

Definition: Aphthous stomatitis is a viral infection of the inner surface of the mouth.

Not ill to mildly ill; Class 1; Worldwide.

Age: Any. **Who**: Anyone. **Onset**: Variable.

Clinical:

The patient has grayish ulcers in his mouth, anywhere. They are 1-1.5 cm in diameter. The normally pink surface is red around the ulcers and the ulcers are painful. They may be associated with REITER SYNDROME, which is an after-effect of some infectious diseases.

Similar Conditions: HERPES occurs mainly at the junction of the pink and the skin, and where the pink, moist surface is right over bone.

Treatment:

None. These go away by themselves.

ARBOVIRAL FEVER

Cause: Viruses.

Includes: Numerous diseases; most contain the name of a location. See *Regional Notes* as follows: Rift Valley Fever (F); Ross River Fever (S, U); West Nile Fever (F); Igbo Ora Virus (F); Crimean-Congo hemorrhagic fever (E, F, R); Sand Fly Fever (E, F, I, R). Some of these are also discussed under HEMORRHAGIC FEVER.

Regional Notes: E, F, I, M, O, R, S, U.

Definition: Arboviral fever is a large class of viral diseases that are transmitted to humans by various insects. These diseases are all infectious; some are also contagious.

Entry category: Disease cluster, regional, mainly tropical, occasional outbreaks.

Mildly to very ill; Class 1-4; Some Contagious; Worldwide; Caused by many different viruses.

Age: Any. **Who:** Anyone, especially mosquito-bitten anywhere. It may be transmitted by hard ticks occasionally. Sometimes it comes from direct contact with a sick patient or from milk. **Onset:** Sudden, usually.

Clinical:

Symptoms are quite variable depending on the local virus. Seek local lore. Many times local place names followed by the word "fever" are used to identify the various forms of this.

There are seven groups of symptoms in arboviral diseases; any one disease will have more than one group of symptoms. See the table below to determine what disease you are dealing with. There generally are not good treatments for any of them in remote areas, but it is important to know if you are dealing with something highly contagious and life-threatening.

➢ **Undifferentiated:**

This form causes a general flu-like illness with fever, headache, and aching all over. All arboviral fevers start out with this symptom group.

➢ **Encephalitic or meningitic:**

This form causes, in addition to the undifferentiated symptoms, a very severe headache with a stiff neck and possibly seizures, mental symptoms (personality changes lasting over 24 hours), or lethargy or coma. There may also be asymmetrical limb weakness. See ENCEPHALITIS for a specific description. West Nile Virus is occasionally in this category, particularly in the elderly. It occurs worldwide.

➢ **Arthritic or Arthralgic:**

This form, in addition to the undifferentiated symptoms, causes pains and possibly swelling and redness of the joints. See ARTHRITIS.

➢ **Skin:**

There are prominent rashes in addition to the undifferentiated symptoms.

➢ **Eyes:**

There are fevers affecting the eyes, making them red and possibly sore also.

➢ **Hemorrhagic:**

This causes abnormal bleeding, usually after several days of the undifferentiated symptoms. See HEMORRHAGIC FEVER.

➢ **Respiratory:**

There are prominent respiratory complaints in addition to the undifferentiated symptoms.

Complications: Long-term consequences of the encephalitic form are common: floppy weakness of the limbs, depression, personality changes, blindness, deafness, trembling. This may be permanent or last for a long time and it may occur with mild as well as severe disease.

Similar Conditions: See Protocol C-2 for fever/headache/body pains; C-6 for limb swelling; C-8 for red, painful eyes; C-9 for fever plus abdominal pains; C-10A for fever plus lethargy, C-13 for fever plus back pain. The most common similar condition is INFLUENZA; pursue one of the diagnoses listed on the chart only if the condition is obviously more serious than simple flu: temperature over 102° F (39° C) and the patient is totally bedridden. Also, if it is a malarious area treat MALARIA first.

With a rash and fever: RAT BITE FEVER, SCRUB TYPHUS.

With prominent joint pains: HEPATITIS, ERYTHEMA INFECTIOSUM, RUBELLA.

With prominent mental symptoms: AFRICAN SLEEPING SICKNESS in Africa only.

Bush Laboratory: None and it's best not to handle blood, urine, or stool.

How to use the Table of Arboviral Fevers (following page):

- Determine the characteristics of your patient's illness. What are the most distressing symptoms? If you are not sure, for example eyes just slightly red, then don't list that.
- Find which diseases have the "yes" answers that match your patient. Disregard the discrepency if your patient does NOT have something marked "yes". However, if he definitely has something marked "no", that eliminates the diagnosis.
- Now from the list of possible diagnoses, eliminate those diseases that do not occur in your geographic area. Consider where the patient may have traveled.
- From the possibilities, determine if any is/are contagious. If so, notify the local health authorities, be very careful about hand-washing, gowns, gloves, masks and the like. Keep children away from the patient and his family. Be sure your will is up to date. Don't send the patient out on public transport.

Higher-Level Care. See Volume I, Appendix 13. Send out if possible unless the patient might be contagious. See the chart in Protocol C-2. Also consult the *Regional Notes* for your area. *Laboratory:* Level 4-5 only; a level 3-4 lab might be helpful to exclude alternatives. The definite diagnosis of the various arboviral fevers requires a large lab in a Western university. The other possibilities can be excluded by small to middle-sized hospital labs. *Practitioner:* Level 4-5; an infectious disease specialist is ideal; a hematologist might be helpful; internist or generalist can cope in some cases. Hospitals may be able to use RIBAVIRIN or serum from patients who have recovered. Tropical/travel medicine expertise is desirable.

Treatment:

Prevention: Keep patients under mosquito nets to avoid infecting local mosquitoes and thus transmitting the disease. It is essential to consider one of the contagious hemorrhagic fevers, especially if you are in Africa! Your own health is at risk and you can cause a major, worldwide epidemic by indiscreetly transporting a contagious patient on public transportation. See Protocol C-2: Fever, Headache, body pain, which contains a description of contagious HEMORRHAGIC FEVERS.

In general, there are no helpful drugs for these diseases. However, there are some exceptions to this rule; seek advice locally or by phone or e-mail.

Patient Care: Treat the patient with ACETAMINOPHEN. Have him stay in bed. Sore joints may linger for months. Deaths are not common unless HEMORRHAGIC FEVER develops. However, disabilities are common with ENCEPHALITIS.

Table of Arboviral Fevers

"Index" gives relevant Regional Indexes. y = yes; n = no;

Disease	Index	Geography	Flu-like	Encephalitis[1]	Arthritis	Skin rash	Eyes red	Bleeding[2]	Lungs[3]	Contagious[4]
Chikungunya	B	Africa/Asia Pacific/Europe	y	n	y	y	y	rare	n	n
Crimean-Congo H. F.	B	Asia/Africa	y	y	n	n	y	y	y	y
Dengue Fever	B	Tropics	y	n[5]	y	y	pains	rarely	n	n
Ebola H.F.	F	Africa	y	n	n	y	n	y	y	y
Japanese B Encephalitis	B, Encephalitis	Asia	y	y	n	n	n	n	n	n
Kyasanur Forest disease[6]	I under Arboviral Fever	India and Saudi Arabia	y	y	n	y	y	y	y	maybe
Lassa Fever	F	Africa	y	y	n	n	y	y	n	y
Monkeypox	F	Africa	y	n	n	y	n	n	n	slight
Murray Valley Encephalitis.		S Pacific	y	y	n	n	y	n	n	n
Rift Valley Fever	F	Africa	y	y	n	n	y	y	n	maybe
Ross River Fever	U under Arboviral Fever	S Pacific	y	n	y	y	n	n	n	n
South American Hemorrhagic Fever[7]	B; Hemorrhagic Fever	South America	y	y	n	y	y	y	y	some
Sand Fly Fever[8]	F, R	Africa and Mediteranean	y	n	n	n	y	n	n	n?
Tick-borne Encephalitis	B, Encephalitis	Europe/Asia	y	y	n	n	n	n	n	n
West Nile Fever	B	Worldwide	y	y	y	y	y	n	n	n
Yellow Fever	F, M	Africa and S. America	y	n	n	n	y	y	n	n

Notes:

[1] This refers to unusual lethargy or crazy behavior, inability to move body parts or abnormal, involuntary movements, along with a severe headache and possibly changes in sensation: numbness and tingling are most common. See the entry ENCEPHALITIS in the *Disease Index.*

[2] This refers to abnormal blood clotting. It may manifest as nosebleed, bleeding gums, vomiting blood, bloody or black stools, excessive menstruation, bleeding frominor wounds, spontaneous black and blue marks from little or no injury.

[3] This refers to a prominent cough or shortness of breath.

[4] This means you can get it directly from a patient, without an intervening bug bite.

[5] There may be severe depression.

[6] An alternative name is Monkey Fever.

[7] This is a group of diseases with the names of various South American countries: Argentina, Bolivia, Brazil, Venezuela. For our purposes we lump them together because they are similar.

[8] This refers to the kind of Sand Fly Fever of the Eastern Hemisphere. The fever of the Western Hemisphere called Sand Fly Fever is entirely different.

ARSENIC POISONING

Cause: Pesticides, herbicides, ethnic herbs and medicines, some old medicines.

Definition: Arsenic poisoning is a type of poisoning due to the heavy metal, arsenic, found in some old medicines, in some pesticides, and in some herbal products. Some of these products are: Croccidile bile, Crude red pills, Crude Tan Pills.

Entry category: Disease, toxic.

Age: Any. **Who:** Suicide or homicide victims; work-related exposures, those using some herbal products. This is especially common in Taiwan, Mexico, Chile, India, and Bangladesh. It can come from drinking water, mines, glass work, metal work, burning plywood, or the manufacture of semiconductor computer chips. Arsenic is found in wine, glues, and pigments. It can be absorbed through the skin from pressure-treated wood. **Onset:** Variable. With small amounts frequently there is a latency period (like the incubation for infections) between exposure and symptoms. With large amounts there will be immediate symptoms.

Clinical:

- **Taken in a large dose**

Arsenic causes nausea, vomiting, bloody diarrhea, a burning pain in the hands, feet, mouth and throat, bleeding gums, and abdominal pains with diarrhea. It causes death by KIDNEY FAILURE, LIVER FAILURE, or bleeding into the bowel.

- **Taken in small amounts over a long period**

The patient develops numbness, tingling, burning, and a weakness of the hands and feet which then moves toward the trunk. His eyes, throat, and windpipe become red and irritated. His skin becomes dry, scaly, and flaky, his face and limbs swell, and a horizontal white line forms on his fingernails.

Similar Conditions: See Protocols C-7: Liver/Spleen problems and C-6: Limb Swelling. Check other causes of KIDNEY FAILURE and LIVER FAILURE.

Skin changes and burning, tingling: PELLAGRA, BERIBERI, other nutritional diseases.

Diarrhea: CHOLERA, DYSENTERY or FOOD POISONING.

Higher-Level Care. Requires a level 4 or 5 laboratory and sophisticated drugs and monitoring. A large laboratory can analyze hair and fingernails for arsenic. See Volume I, Appendix 13.

Treatment:

Aside from stopping the exposure, treatment involves a physician and hospital facilities.

ARTHRITIS

Section Outline:

- I. Introduction
- II.Clinical In General
    - a. Determining which joints are affected
    - b. Determining symmetry
    - c. General clinical description
- III. Determining Causative Diseases
    - a. Complex diseases
    - b. Simple arthritis
- IV. Symmetrical Arthritis With General Illness
- V. Symmetrical Arthritis Without General Illness
- VI. Asymmetrical Arthritis, Multiple Joints, Usually With A Fever
- VII. Asymmetrical Arthritis, One Or Two Joints
- VIII. Similar Conditions To Arthritis
- IX. Treatment Of Arthritis In General

I. INTRODUCTION

Cause: Variable.

Includes: Arthralgia, Rheumatoid arthritis, Osteoarthritis; Septic arthritis, which includes that caused by GONORRHEA.

Entry Category: Syndrome.

Regional Notes: F, I, M, O, R, U.

Definition: Arthritis is a syndrome consisting of pain, redness or warmth, and swelling of a joint or joints.

Well to moderately ill; Class 2-4; Worldwide, prevalence varies, no predictable pattern.

Age: Any, even children. **Who:** Anyone; see causative dieseases below. **Onset:** Over months, usually; occasionally rapid.

II. CLINICAL IN GENERAL

a. Determining which joints are affected:

In the small joints of the hands and feet, pain is accurately localized but large joint pain may be referred to other locations, especially hip pain which may be in the groin, buttocks, front of the thigh or the knee. *The arthritis is located in whatever joint is tender: the pain (wherever it is located) increases with pressure on that joint.* For example, the pain of a diseased hip might cause mostly knee pain. Moving or pressing the knee does not increase the knee pain but pressing on or moving the hip does increase the knee pain. In this case the arthritis is in the hip, not the knee.

b. Determining symmetry:

Symmetry is usually obvious but sometimes is questionable. In general, if there is any symmetry at all, the arthritis is considered to be symmetrical. For example, if both wrists, the right shoulder, and the left knee are affected, that may be symmetrical. If there is symmetrical involvement of two joints, (e.g. both wrists and both thumbs), that is symmetrical for sure. If only a mid-body joint is involved (for example one portion of the spine), then symmetry is meaningless.

c. General clinical description:

Necessary: The patient has swollen, red, warm, and/or painful joints.

Frequently: The problem is symmetrical; the same joints are involved on the right and left. However, if it affects the spine in back, (neck, back of the chest, or lower back) then symmetry is meaningless—one ordinarily cannot distinguish right and left spinal arthritis. Fevers are common.

Sometimes: There had been soreness and stiffness before the pain began. Sometimes the patient is generally ill. Many times arthritis is one symptom of an illness with many other symptoms.

III. DETERMINING CAUSATIVE DISEASES

Once you know which joints are affected and whether to consider the arthritis to be symmetrical or not, you should consider what disease caused the problem. Most commonly, there is no specific identifiable cause for arthritis, but when a cause can be identified it should be treated. See the table on the following page for some common causative diseases. There are two categories:

a. Complex diseases:

Diseases with arthritis as one prominent aspect, described in separate entries:

- ARBOVIRAL FEVER
- BRUCELLOSIS
- FAMILIAL MEDITERRANEAN FEVER
- FILARIASIS
- GONORRHEA
- GOUT
- HIV INFECTION
- LYME DISEASE
- RAT BITE FEVER
- REITER SYNDROME
- RHEUMATIC FEVER
- SICKLE CELL DISEASE
- TUBERCULOSIS

b. Simple arthritis:

Diseases that present as simple arthritis, described here as subcategories of arthritis:

- Osteoarthritis
- Rheumatoid Arthritis
- Septic Arthritis

Characteristics of these subcategories of simple arthritis are described in the following table.

Subcategories of Simple Arthritis:

	Osteoarthritis	**Rheumatoid Arthritis**	**Septic Arthritis**
Age/Who/Onset	Older people, slow onset, involving joints with wear and tear.	Usually 35-50 y.o. but sometimes children, family history, usually slow onset, recurrent.	Any age, variable onset, usually single joint, commonly related to injury or another infection.
Clinical	Not much if any redness or swelling; variable symmetry.	At first morning stiffness; arthritis is usually symmetrical and migratory.	Redness, swelling, pus in the joint which must be removed; may develop rapidly.

IV. SYMMETRICAL ARTHRITIS WITH A GENERAL ILLNESS

Usually one of these:

RHEUMATIC FEVER	Sudden onset, related to STREP INFECTION.
LYME DISEASE	Acquired in temperate areas from a tick bite; knees, ? small joints.
SICKLE CELL DISEASE	Family history of anemia and early deaths.
HIV INFECTION	Africa; large joints, sym metrical.
RAT BITE FEVER	Asia, inflamed open wound; history of a rat bite.
ARBOVIRAL FEVER	Africa or the Pacific area; seek local lore.

Occasionally: RUBELLA, HEPATITIS, ERYTHEMA INFECTIOSUM, MENINGITIS (during treatment), ENTERIC FEVER, RUBELLA, BRUCELLOSIS

Some Causative Diseases of Arthritis:

Type of Arthritis[1]	Inflammatory?[2]	Risk Factors	Onset[3]	How Many or Which	Symmetry[4]	Fever	Swelling	Recurrent[5], Continual[6]	Migration[7]	Distinctives
BRUCELLOSIS	Yes	Cattle or milk	Slow	Hip Pelvis, <1 joint	Usual	Maybe	No or minimal	Continual, relapses	No	Feels horrid, complains
GOUT	Yes	Adult Affluent	Sudden	Lower limb, one[8]	Not usual	No	Yes!	Recurrent	No[9]	Pain is extreme.
HIV INFECTION[10]	Yes	Adults, Africa	Sudden	Large Multiple	Usual	Yes	Yes!!	Recurrent	Maybe	Promiscuity[11]
Injury	No	Injured	Sudden	Injured and adjacent[12]	Unusual	No	Yes	Continual	No	History of injury
LYME DISEASE	Yes	Tick-exposed history[13]	Slow	Knees usually maybe small	Maybe	Maybe	Yes	Recurrent	Unusual	History of rash[14]
Osteo-ARTHRITIS	No	Older	Slow	Large, usually[15]	Usual	No	Minimal[16]	Continual but varies	No	Stiffness less than 15 min.
REITER SYNDROME (Reactive Arthritis)	Yes	Young Adults[17]	Unknown	>1, usually lower limb[18]	No	Usual	Yes	Continual	Additive	Commonly also sores[19]
Rheumatoid ARTHRITIS	Yes	Adults usually	Varies	Any, fingers>1 usually	Usual	Common	Yes	Recurrent	Yes	Stiffness over 30 minutes.
TUBERCULOSIS	??	Usually adults	Slow	Usually single large leg/hip	No	Low if any	Yes but gradual	Continual	No	Joint may feel spongy
Septic ARTHRITIS	Yes	Any[20]	Sudden	Any, 1 or 2 asymmetrical	No	Half of patients	Yes	Continual	No	Generally ill

Notes on Arthritis Table:

1. Some of the arthritis is described in this entry. In other cases the descriptions and treatments are listed separately. The use of upper case in this column indicates conditions listed alphabetically in this (B) index.
2. Inflammatory arthritis hurts both at rest and with movement. When moving, the pain is worse when starting the movement. Non-inflammatory arthritis does not cause a lot of pain at rest unless it has been present in a large joint for a long time. There is pain with movement which then gets better quickly when the joint is rested.
3. Sudden onset is minutes to hours. Slow onset is days to weeks to months.
4. Symmetry does not have to be absolute; any symmetry indicates symmetrical. If both knees are painful, plus one elbow, that is considered symmetrical.
5. That is, the arthritis gets better and worse by itself but keeps coming back.
6. That is, the arthritis does not get better by itself but after treatment will likely stay away
7. This refers to the arthritis moving from one joint or set of joints to another as the first gets better. If the migration is additive, that means other joints become painful but the first set don't improve as other joints are added.

Notes on Arthritis Table, continued.

8. This is the initial manifestation. Later on it may be symmetrical and involve the small joints.
9. The pain does not migrate during one episode but which joint is affected may vary from one episode to the other
10. Reportedly this is a kind of reactive arthritis: sudden onset, short duration, no recurrance, no joint destruction, occuring late in the course of the disease.
11. It may be a promiscuous spouse; if it is a child, it might be an ill parent.
12. For example, if a knee is injured, that knee will get arthritis causing the patient to walk abnormally on that side so the hip or ankle may also become arthritic.
13. There is usually a history of ill health with a variety of symptoms including some skin rashes. The disease is transmitted by ticks and is usually a temperate climate problem.
14. The skin lesions are ERYTHEMA MULTIFORME—see the disease entry for this.
15. The joints involved are those that have had prior rough use.
16. When there is swelling it does not vary much over time.
17. In particular, those who have had CHLAMYDIA or DYSENTERY or some other whole-body disease.
18. The arthritis is additive, with additional joints affected while the first ones are still involved.
19. Reactive arthritis may also cause plantar fascitis—pain just in front of the heel on the sole of the foot, worst the first few steps in the morning. It also might cause sharp, shooting pains in the limbs.
20. This is commonly associated with sexually transmitted diseases or with some whole-body infection or some injury to the joint. In adults it commonly involves the knee; in children it commonly involves the hip. In this case the child will have the knee and hip flexed with the thigh tilted toward the side of his body. He may complain of knee pain rather than hip pain although the problem is really in the hip.

V. SYMMETRICAL ARTHRITIS WITHOUT A GENERAL ILLNESS

Rheumatoid ARTHRITIS	Migrating arthritis with morning stiffness; large and small joints.
GONORRHEA	History of sexual misconduct; no obvious redness or swelling.
RHEUMATIC FEVER	Sudden onset, related to STREP INFECTION.
Osteoarthritis	Older people, joints with wear and tear or an injury, mostly large joints.
GOUT (late)	After ankles and feet, small joints may be symmetrical.
LYME DISEASE	Usually knees, maybe small joints.
FAMILIAL MEDITERRANEAN FEVER	Hereditary; large joints.

VI. ASYMMETRICAL ARTHRITIS, MULTIPLE JOINTS, USUALLY WITH A FEVER

REITER SYNDROME (Reactive Arthritis)	From STD or DYSENTERY.
HIV INFECTION	Large joints, symmetrical or asymmetrical.

VII. ASYMMETRICAL ARTHRITIS, ONE OR TWO JOINTS

GONORRHEA	Sometimes single joint like septic arthritis.
Septic ARTHRITIS	Single joint, develops rapidly; needs immediate care.
GOUT (early)	Sudden onset single large toe or ankle.
BRUCELLOSIS	Below the waist, general illness, slow onset.
TUBERCULOSIS	Night sweats, slow onset.
FILARIASIS	Usually lower limb; swollen limbs in the community.

Complications: This largely depends on the causative disease. Patients will limp because of leg pain and any limb that has been affected for long will eventually become misshapen. Some kinds of arthritis destroy the bone or joint structures.

VIII. SIMILAR CONDITIONS TO ARTHRITIS

See Protocol C-6: Limb Swelling; C-12: Large Lymph Nodes; C-13: Fever and Back Pain.

With a fever: RUBELLA, ERYTHEMA INFECTIOSUM, and HEPATITIS cause multiple joint pains without warmth or swelling. ARBOVIRAL FEVER may be indistinguishable. If the pain is due to SYPHILIS, it will be made worse with heat applied to the joints. CELLULITIS and similar conditions, if they happen to be near a joint, may be indistinguishable. Consider FAMILIAL MEDITERRANEAN FEVER for persons of Mediterranean genetic origin.

Without a fever: MANSONELLOSIS PERSTANS, HEPATITIS and RICKETS are quite similar but the painful joints are neither red nor warm. SYPHILIS (see note above) may also be without a fever.

Higher-Level Care. *Laboratory:* Level 3 might be helpful; generally Level 4 or 5 is necessary. *Facilities:* X-ray may be helpful. Surgical theatre might be helpful; also there are some sophisticated drugs available at Level 4. *Practitioner:* Initially internal medicine at a Level 3 or higher facility. A surgeon with level 4 or higher capabilities might be necessary at some point.

IX. TREATMENT OF ARTHRITIS IN GENERAL

Prevention: Treat all DYSENTERY, GONORRHEA and STREP THROAT. Treating arthritis earlier rather than later prevents permanent damage to the joints.

Patient Care - General Rules:

- Treat with an anti-inflammatory drug: aspirin or ibuprofen are best; don't use aspirin if you are considering the diagnosis of GOUT. In that case use COLCHICINE and give non-aspirin pain relief.
- If it is a single joint, send the patient out since it may be septic arthritis. Meanwhile treat with antibiotic; see the chart below:
  - Treat it as GONORRHEA or REITER SYNDROME if it may be sexually transmitted.
  - Use DEC (DIETHYLCARBAMAZINE) in areas with FILARIASIS.
  - Treat it as GOUT if it is the big toe (possibly also an ankle) and the diagnosis fits
- Any rapid-onset arthritis with a fever: use PENICILLIN to cover RHEUMATIC FEVER.
- Look up and follow the treatment for whatever fits best as the cause of the arthritis.

Treatments of Some Causes of ARTHRITIS:

Cause:	**Treatment:**
BRUCELLOSIS	Use antibiotics and give IBURPOFEN.
GOUT	Use COLCHICINE; do not give aspirin.
HIV INFECTION	Use IBUPROFEN
LYME DISEASE	Treat the disease with antibiotics; IBUPROFEN may help additionally.
REITER SYNDROME	Treat DYSENTERY or CHLAMYDIA; use IBUPROFEN or a similar drug
Osteoarthritis	Pain medication only; rest the joint.
Rheumatoid arthritis	Use ASPIRIN in high doses.
Septic arthritis	Make every effort to have the pus drained from the joint. High-dose antibiotics for 28 days. Use only gram-positive antibiotics except in the elderly, in drug abusers, and those with poor immunity. In that case use gram-negative antibiotics also. Give the antibiotics by injection for 14 days followed by oral antibiotics for another 14 days. Drugs of choice are ceftriaxone and cefazolin (CEPHALOSPORIN).
TUBERCULOSIS	Treat the disease and use IBUPROFEN.

Results: 48-72 hours improvement.

ASCARIASIS

Cause: Roundworm.
Synonyms: Ascaridiasis, Roundworm.
Regional Notes: F, I, O, R, S, U.
Definition: Ascariasis is a disease caused by the infestation of the bowels with the worm Ascaris lumbricoides.

Not ill to very ill; Class 1-3; Worldwide, tropical mainly, most common where soil is clay or loam and humidity is high. It is not likely to be a big health problem in areas with less than 1200 mm rainfall per year. If it is a problem in your area, people will report occasionally passing light-colored "earthworms" by rectum or by mouth.

Age: Any, but especially children. **Who:** Those eating raw foods which have not been soaked in bleach- or iodine-water. (Washing does not eliminate the worm eggs.) **Onset:** Usually gradual, but may be without symptoms and then have sudden onset. The initial cough, if it occurs, comes 4-16 days after eating the contaminated food.

Clinical:

Necessary: Cramping abdominal pains or the patient reports seeing earthworm-sized worms in his stool or in his mouth or nose. Ascaris worms are the size and shape of earthworms or larger; they are the only worms that are in this size range.

Maybe: There is an initial cough and fever for 2-3 months after eating the offending food. The sputum coughed up may be bloody. If the case is severe there will be vomiting. The abdomen may be distended and the patient may be constipated. There may be pain in the right upper abdomen. Diarrhea is unusual. MALNUTRITION occurs even with mild cases; there may be refusal to eat or a good appetite, in both cases with weight loss. (Children will have a growth spurt after deworming.) Strange cravings may occur. With heavy infections or with fasting, worms migrate into the mouth and nose and may be vomited.

Complications: ACUTE ABDOMEN, MALNUTRITION, RESPIRATORY FAILURE, HEART FAILURE. It may occasionally cause liver problems similar to AMEBIC LIVER ABSCESS. The worms may cause GALLBLADDER DISEASE; children have pains every 15-30 minutes, lasting 5-10 minutes, and their upper-right abdomens are tender. The gallbladder is enlarged so it is possible to feel it; there is greenish-yellow discoloration of the whites of the eyes; the patient has general, whole-body itching without a skin rash; the patient's bowel movements are light-colored.

Similar Conditions: IMPACTION is likely in disabled or bed-ridden patients. TUBERCULOSIS of the abdomen may be indistinguishable. Treat for ascariasis and see what happens. In areas where TUBERCULOSIS is common, treat for that if two treatments for ASCARIASIS don't help. HYDATID DISEASE is found in very few areas. The early stage of ascariasis (cough and fever) is indistinguishable from ordinary PNEUMONIA.

Higher-Level Care. *Laboratory:* Stool examination for worms, Level 2 or higher. Almost any hospital lab with a microscope can find the ascaris eggs in one stool specimen. The test is both sensitive and specific so both a positive test and a negative test are significant. During the initial 2-3 months' migration through the lungs, the blood count will show many eosinophils but the stool will be negative for eggs. Once the eggs appear in the stool, then the eosinophils disappear from the blood. *Facilities:* Abdominal x-ray with contrast material, Level 3 or higher. *Practitioner:* Generalist, pediatrician, or internist for diagnosis; for complications, a surgeon.

Treatment:

Prevention: Encourage the use of outhouses. Wash hands well and clean fingernails. Soak food in bleach or iodine water between market and use; see Chapter 2. Mass treatment should be repeated every 6 months.

Patient Care:

With ACUTE ABDOMEN or GALLBLADDER DISEASE, do not kill the worms! If there is GALLBLADDER DISEASE, initially use LOPERAMIDE rather than one of the worm medicines listed below. Kill the worms only after the symptoms have abated.

Without complications, to kill the worms, use ALBENDAZOLE, LEVAMISOLE, MEBENDAZOLE, IVERMECTIN, or PYRANTEL PAMOATE are the best drugs. FLUBENDAZOLE, THIABENDAZOLE, BEPHENIUM HYDROXYNAPHTHOATE, and PIPERAZINE are also effective. If symptoms are severe, give repeated small doses before giving full doses.

ASTHMA

Cause: Allergy.
Synonyms: Asthmatic bronchitis, Bronchospasm.
Regional Notes: F, M, O, U.
Definition: Asthma is a disease, an allergic reaction to some inhaled substance, causing narrowing of the airways with subsequent shortness of breath.

Mildly to very ill; Class 2-4; Worldwide, common.

Age: 1-10 usually, for first attack. **Who:** Anyone, especially those with allergies or family allergies. **Onset:** Minutes to hours for each attack. Asthma tends to recur.

Clinical:

Necessary: The patient is short of breath; it is always harder for him to breathe out than in. He is either wheezing or he has a tight, dry cough without wheezing.

Sometimes: He is blue around the lips. He may have any other symptoms of ALLERGY. He is probably congested. With your stethoscope you may hear long expiration with wheezing. The patient usually has a fast respiratory rate and a fast pulse. In severe cases, his respiratory rate may be normal or slow, but then he is obviously struggling to breathe. In long-lasting cases the patient may have an irregular pulse.

Complications: Asthma may result in RESPIRATORY FAILURE, HEART FAILURE, RESPIRATORY INFECTION.

Causative Diseases: Adult-onset asthma is frequently due to TUBERCULOSIS or ALLERGY to ASPIRIN. MANSONELLOSIS PERSTANS is possible in Africa or South America. HYDATID DISEASE and SMOKE INHALATION may cause asthma. If there is a fever, consider KATAYAMA DISEASE and the underlying infections that cause it. In areas where FILARIASIS is common, asthma may be due to that; try treating for it. Asthma due to FILARIASIS is called tropical pulmonary eosinophilia; treat the FILARIASIS.

Similar Conditions: See Protocol C-4: Shortness of Breath. HEART FAILURE may be indistinguishable; treat with THEOPHYLLINE if you are concerned about this. GOITER can also cause wheezing. ALTITUDE SICKNESS should be obvious if you know your location.

Higher-Level Care. See Volume I, Appendix 13. *Laboratory:* Level 3 or higher; a respiratory care team, ability to determine blood gases. *Facilities:* Chest x-ray, Level 3; occasionally more sophisticated tests at Level 4 or 5. Monitored bed, anesthesia equipment, ventilator, oxygen if there is severe distress. *Practitioner:* Generalist or internist or pediatrician.

Treatment:

Prevention: Discourage people from smoking within the patient's home, whether the patient is there at the time or not. Dust, sweep, or otherwise raise dust only when the patient will be absent for several hours. Sometimes asthma is caused by a tiny insect in which case regular spraying of the house with an insecticide may be very helpful.

Patient care: At Level 3 or above referral hospitals, In the West there are likely to be excellent inhaled medications for asthma that work much better than the medications listed below. These older medicines are listed because they are more commonly available and much less expensive.

Mild attack: THEOPHYLLINE or ALBUTEROL.

Severe attack: THEOPHYLLINE and EPINEPHRINE both. You may also add either HYDROCORTISONE or PREDNISONE for severe or recurrent asthma. IPRATROPIUM or METAPROTERENOL may be used if they are available.

Results: 15 minutes improvement with EPINEPHRINE, 60 minutes with the other drugs except for PREDNISONE which takes 6 hours. Entirely well in 7-10 days, unless the patient has a second attack or is a chronic asthmatic.

ATTENTION DEFICIT DISORDER

Cause: Heredity; lack of a brain hormone.
Synonyms: ADD, ADHD, MBD, Hyperactivity.
Not ill; Class 1-3, depending on severity.

Definition: Attention deficit disorder is a hereditary condition causing a "sticky valve" effect as regards attention. The person has trouble either paying attention or else switching attention from one thing to another in a calm, controlled manner. It may or may not be associated with hyperactivity.

Age: Any, but the problem is more common and obvious in children than adults. **Who:** Members of affected families; boys more than girls; common in adopted children. Some ethnic groups are more affected than others. **Onset:** Chronic and recurrent problems dating from birth or early childhood; adult onset is rare.

Clinical:

Necessary: The person has either trouble paying attention or trouble switching attention in a calm, controlled manner. Some people are physically hyperactive; others sit immobile for long periods while their minds race.

Common: Consequences of this are as follows, but not every patient has every symptom: Nervousness; impulsive behavior; inner rage; addictions; learning disabilities;[1] sleep disorders;[2] inconsistent performance in school;[3] lack of depth perception;[4] uncoordination;[5] lack of social skills and conscience; emotional immaturity; irritability (for example, from labels in clothing); bed wetting; reverse response to sedative or stimulant medications.[6]

Similar Conditions: If there is a crisis, consider the conditions in Protocol C-10: Confusion/lethargy. Consider various forms of malnutrition, e.g. PELLAGRA and BERIBERI which can cause mental symptoms. ADDICTION may be indistinguishable except for age of onset. Also consider DEMONIZATION. If the pa-

---

[1] Reading disability, left/right and north/south/east/west disorientation are common manifestations of this.

[2] This may take the form of insomnia, abnormally deep sleep, or bed-wetting.

[3] The student will get an A without trying in one subject and struggle for a D in a closely related subject.

[4] This will manifest as inability to judge speed and distance with consequent uncoordination and poor judgment when driving.

[5] This may be either fine (handwriting) or gross (sports) or both.

[6] The person may be calmed by stimulants such as caffeine, theophyllin, and Ritalin, but become agitated with sedatives.

tient has a fever, consider MALARIA, TYPHUS and similar conditions.

Higher-Level Care. *Laboratory, Facilities*: Nothing is helpful. *Practitioner:* Pediatrician, psychiatrist, counselers, Level 4 or above.

Treatment:

Remove artificial colors and preservatives from the diet. Avoid large-group situations. Avoid fluorescent lights. Since conscience development is deficient, parents should stress consequences of actions. At times, medication may be helpful. Adults should seek counseling with someone who is familiar with the phenomenon.

BARTONELLOSIS

See *Regional Notes* M. The term also recently refers to CAT-SCRATCH DISEASE and sometimes TRENCH FEVER. These are all caused by related organisms although the diseases differ greatly from each other.

BEDSORE

Definition: This is an open sore that spontaneously arises due to the person putting pressure on the same part of his body for an extended period of time.

Clinical:

Looks the same and is treated the same whether or not the patient is in the tropics. Bedsores tend to occur on the body parts on which a patient lies or sits without moving. See Protocol C-11 for similar conditions.

Higher-Level Care. *Laboratory and Facilities:* Level 3 or above might be helpful in stubborn cases. *Practitioner:* Physicians or nurses with experience in long-term care facilities might be most helpful. The treatment is labor-intensive and takes a long time but is not difficult. Even an e-mail contact—send close-up pictures of the wound and get advice—can be very helpful. You might be able to train a national to do the hands-on work. Detailed instructions are beyond the scope of this book.

Treatment:

Prevention is easier than treatment; turn any patient who does not turn himself, at least every two hours during the day and every four hours at night to avoid constant pressure on one part of his body.

Patient Care: See TROPICAL ULCER.

Results: Slow improvement over weeks and months.

BELL'S PALSY

Cause: Variable.
Synonym: Seventh cranial nerve paralysis.
Regional Notes: F, I, M, R.
Definition: This is a paralysis of the muscles on one side of the face.

Entry category: Syndrome.

Not ill to mildly ill; Class 2-3; Worldwide, not common, not rare.

Age: Any, especially adults. **Who:** Anyone; **Onset:** Suddenly.

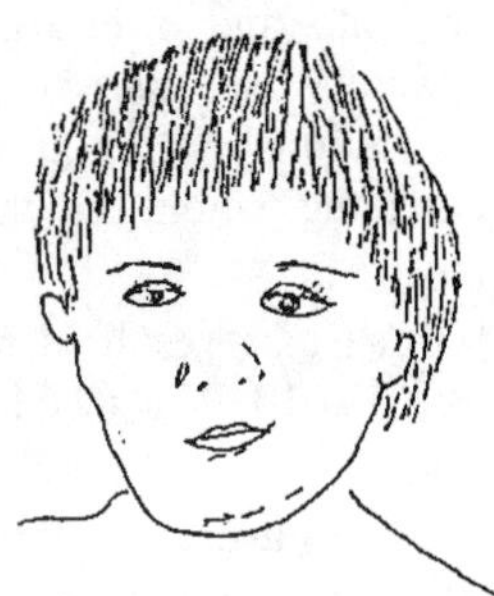

Bell's palsy: note the drooping right face. The patient cannot close that eye completely.

Clinical:

Sudden drooping of one side of the face with inability to close the eye on that side, usually with no pain, no warning, and no other symptoms. This is easily confused with STROKE. The problem may occur for no known reason, or may be due to RELAPSING FEVER (never with the first fever, always with a relapse), POLIO, LEPROSY, LYME DISEASE (may be on both sides with this), DIPHTHERIA, or EAR INFECTION, MIDDLE (which may be due to ordinary bacteria or TUBERCULOSIS). A child with a draining ear plus Bell's palsy most likely has TUBERCULOSIS. If the problem is both right and left it is likely due to LYME DISEASE.

Higher-Level Care. *Practitioner:* Generalist, internist, pediatrician. A neurologist is most helpful.

Treatment:

It usually goes away by itself in a matter of weeks or months, and is treated only by keeping the eye moist. ARTIFICIAL TEARS are best. Sterile saline will do. See Volume I, Appendix 1, Procedure 1. Put drops or ointment in the eye and patch the eye at night.

BERIBERI

Cause: Poor nutrition (Thiamine deficiency).
Synonyms: Thiamine deficiency.
Includes: Dry and wet Beriberi, Wernike-Korsakoff syndrome.
Regional Notes: F, I, O, R, S.
Definition: Beriberi is an illness caused by a deficiency of the vitamin thiamine.

Mildly to severely ill; Class 1-2; Worldwide, areas with white rice and/or alcohol consumption.

Age: Any. **Who:** Those eating a diet deficient in THIAMINE, especially those who also consume ALCOHOL. (See ALCOHOLISM.) It is most common in cultures consuming polished white rice that is milled by machinery. (Rice milled by hand retains enough THIAMINE.) THIAMINE is found in yeast, brown rice, peanuts, wheat, barley, millet, pork, liver, and to a small extent in legumes. The disease may also occur in infants of affected, breast-feeding women. It may be associated with pregnancy, nursing, or MALARIA. **Onset:** Usually slow in dry beriberi. May be rapid in wet beriberi.

Clinical:

Necessary: The patient eats a diet without whole grains or meats. His legs and feet do not work normally. There may be cramping of leg muscles. Additionally, he has symptoms of one or more of the 4 types: infant, paraplegic, wet, or mental. There is no fever due to this.

- **Infant Beriberi**

These are the offspring of malnourished women. They have a hoarse or silent cry or else SEIZURES, abnormal eye movements, and vomiting. They might have large livers.

- **Paraplegic (Dry) Beriberi**

This causes general weakness of the limbs, with numbness, tingling, burning pains, and loss of muscle. Squeezing the calves causes pain. The patient is unable to squat or get up from the squatting position with his hands on his head. The skin is shiny. Because of the weakness, the patient is uncoordinated. He walks with his feet wide apart and may lift his legs high with each step. The legs are affected first and mainly; he may also have arm symptoms later if the problem is severe. He may have trouble looking left with his left eye and right with his right eye. He has no trembling, however, and the muscles of his face and those of bladder and bowel function are not affected unless he is near death.

- **Wet Beriberi**

This causes HEART FAILURE in addition to the symptoms of dry beriberi. The patient, however, has little or no protein in his urine. His blood pressure will have a very low second number, so his pulse pressure will be high. His ankles are always swollen. His body and face may swell also. He may have a heart murmur.

- **Mental Beriberi**

This usually involves one of the other types also. The patient has severe and persistent loss of appetite. In addition, the patient is confused and makes up fantastic stories. This is especially common in alcoholics. It may be precipitated by diarrhea, SEPSIS, or MALARIA.

Similar Conditions: Most similar conditions also cause fever, which beriberi does not. Non-feverish similar conditions: see Protocol 10B and the conditions outlined below.

Paraplegic and mental: Tertiary SYPHILIS is different in that it causes sharp, shooting rather than burning pains. Mental symptoms can be similar. Also consider DEMONIZATION. STROKE usually involves weakness on one side only; beriberi weakness is roughly symmetrical. PLANT POISONING onset is rapid. ARSENIC POISON may be similar; look for the rough rash.

Wet beriberi: HOOKWORM can also cause HEART FAILURE, but burning pains and specific leg weakness are not present. Consider other causes of HEART FAILURE also.

Higher-Level Care. *Laboratory,* Facilities are generally not helpful. Diagnosis is by trying the treatment and seeing what happens. The symptoms improve spectacularly over a couple of hours or less with THIAMINE. *Practitioner:* Generalist, internist, pediatrician. A dietician familiar might also be helpful.

Treatment:

Send out for wet or mental beriberi, treating in the meantime. Give THIAMINE, preferably by injection, but by mouth is acceptable. If you don't have the vitamin, try giving thiamin-containing foods. It is good to add multivitamins since multiple deficiencies are common.

Results: Some symptoms resolve rapidly, some slowly. If the diagnosis is correct, you should see some improvement within a day. Severe HEART FAILURE, however, may not improve.

BLADDER STONE

Regional Notes: F, I, O, R.

Clinical:

A stone forms in the bladder, usually in school-aged boys. They pull on their penises to begin urinating and their stream may be interrupted at times as the stone blocks the urine. If it is not taken care of, when they get older they may have to jump up and down or lie down to urinate. If the stone becomes large, it can decrease the capacity of the bladder.

Treatment:

Surgery which is simple and effective; at a Level 3 or above, possibly some Level 2 facilities.

BOUTONNEUSE FEVER

African tick typhus or Mediterranean tick typhus, both listed under SPOTTED FEVER.

BRAIN DAMAGE

Cause: Variable.
Synonym: Encephalopathy.
Regional Notes: F, I, M, O, R, S, U.
Definition: Brain damage is a malfunction of the brain due to some injury or illness.

Entry category: Syndrome.

Clinical:

Symptoms of brain damage are any combination of the following: Lack of muscle control with abnormal gait; trembling, jerking, or seizures; weakness or paralysis (initially floppy but later stiff); retention or incontinence of urine or stool; inability to concentrate; confusion or mental retardation; dizziness, blindness, deafness, loss of smell; difficulty understanding or speaking; trouble swallowing; abnormal pupil size and/or eye movements; irregular respirations; drooping of one side of the face.

Causative Diseases: HIV INFECTION, LIVER FAILURE (see Protocol C-7), PELLAGRA, BERIBERI, ADDICTION, TRICHINOSIS, SICKLE CELL DISEASE, CYSTICERCOSIS, ENCEPHALITIS, EPILEPSY, head injury, HEAT ILLNESS, MALARIA (cerebral), MEASLES, MENINGITIS, RADIATION ILLNESS, SCHISTOSOMIASIS JAPONICUM, SCHISTOSOMIASIS MANSONI, STROKE, SYPHILIS. See CEREBRAL PALSY also. Any symptoms that have been present over six months probably will be permanent. LIVER FAILURE might cause this—mild involves just confusion, more severe a tremor in addition, and very severe SEIZURES or coma. In this case the damage may be reversible with treatment.

Similar Conditions: SPINAL NEUROPATHY and the conditions listed in Protocol C-10.

Higher-Level Care. Sending out is mandatory to a Level 4 or above facility with a neurologist and/or a neurosurgeon.

Treatment:

Until sending out, attend to SEIZURES, DEHYDRATION, MALNUTRITION and be sure that the patient is breathing adequately and does not choke on his secretions. See the appendix in Volume I that deals with the care of a very sick patient.

BRAIN TUMOR

This refers to any lump in the brain. It may be an ordinary tumor (benign or malignant) or else something like HYDATID DISEASE or CYSTICERCOSIS. There may be no symptoms at all, or it may cause symptoms of BRAIN DAMAGE listed above. It may also cause headache, the most common pattern being an intermittent, localized headache, with increasing frequency and severity of pain. Sending the patient to a Level 4 or above facility is mandatory.

BRUCELLOSIS

Cause: Bacteria.

Synonyms: Bang's disease, Malta fever, Mediterranean fever, Undulant fever.

Regional Notes: All regions.

Definition: Brucellosis is a slow-onset bacterial infection of animals and secondarily of humans, caused by the bacteria Brucella abortus or Brucella melitensis.

Mildly to very ill; Class 2-4: Contagious; Worldwide, mainly tropical, pastoral, mainly in the Mediterranean and Middle east, the northern part of Mexico, Mongolia, and Central Asia.

Age: Any. **Who:** Anyone handling meats or domestic animals: goats, sheep, cattle, pigs, rarely horses and dogs; and those drinking unpasteurized milk. It can come from breathing dust in pastoral areas or being with patients who have the disease. **Onset:** Over weeks. Incubation time 2-4 weeks

Clinical:

Necessary: Insidious onset, fevers off and on, general body pains, symptoms have lasted for more than two weeks. The person might be without a fever for 3-4 days at the most. There are cycles of illness lasting 2-4 weeks at a time. The patient complains bitterly of feeling terrible; his complaints appear to be exaggerated.

Usually: There is an ARTHRITIS caused by this in the lower body: lower back, hip(s) or knee(s). A recurring SCIATICA is most common. Joints are usually not visibly red or swollen.

Maybe: Night sweats; lethargy, insomnia; an irregular pulse; loss of appetite; weight loss; headache; pain in the neck, back, and abdomen, especially the lower-right abdomen. The patient may have sharp, shooting pains down one or more arms or legs. Joint pains are very frequent and severe so the patient may limp. The liver, spleen, or both, may be enlarged early in the disease; they are usually not tender. The eyes may be yellow.

Occasionally: Brucellosis causes skin rashes: usually little lumps under the skin with purplish discoloration over top; occasionally bumps under the skin with redness over top; sometimes a general measles-like rash.

Some distinctive symptoms which may or may not be present are pain in the eyes with looking sideways, and pains in the gums and just in front of the ears when trying to chew. Thirst, constipation, enlarged lymph nodes, and migrating ARTHRITIS are common. There may be emotional changes, most commonly depression; rarely this and the fever may be the only symptoms. Male genitals may be swollen and painful. When the disease becomes chronic, there may be chronic depression, fatigue, and headache.

When brucellosis affects the brain (usually in children) there may be MENINGITIS, paralysis, or uncoordination. There may be chronic headache, changes in mood and behavior, or SEIZURES.

There are 3 common clinical pictures:

- An *ENTERIC FEVER-type illness*, but not as severe as typhoid, at any age, chronic.
- A *fever and ARTHRITIS* of a single hip or knee in a young child.
- *General misery, fever, and low back or hip pain.* This is usually in an older man. In the Middle East, this disease tends to be so common that it is the most likely diagnosis in any older man with fever and difficulty walking due to pain.

If in doubt about the diagnosis, try the treatment. Sometimes the first dose of medicine makes the patient sicker. This is due to dying germs. **Do not stop treatment for this. It is evidence that the diagnosis is correct**. If the patient does not get either better or worse within 4 or 5 days, the diagnosis probably is not correct. If the patient has a relapse, give a full second treatment.

Complications: LIVER DISEASE, HEART FAILURE, BRAIN DAMAGE, and infection in bones resembling TUBERCULOSIS. Neurobrucellosis affects the brain in which case it looks like MENINGITIS with a slow onset. When this happens, blindness, deafness, and paralysis are common.

Similar Conditions: See Protocols C-10 and C-12. Take the patient's temperature several times a day for a week. If he never has a fever, he probably does not have brucellosis. Also see Protocol 12: Large Lymph Nodes if applicable.

Bones and joint pains: RUBELLA can involve similar joint pains and rash, but the onset is faster. RHEUMATIC FEVER joints are always red or warm as well as painful and swollen; the joints of brucellosis are not red or warm. Bone TB pain does not migrate like brucellosis pain initially does. In the spine the two conditions may be indistinguishable. The joint pains of PELLAGRA may be similar. See Protocol C-6: Limb Swelling or Protocol C-13: Fever plus Back Pain.

Inflammation of the testicles may resemble MUMPS, TYPHUS, EPIDIDYMITIS, or TB.

Flu-like symptoms: Brucellosis is distinguishable from ENTERIC FEVER and SEPSIS in that the highest daily fever occurs at noon or early afternoon. In these other conditions, the peak fever occurs toward night time.

JAUNDICE: See Protocols C-5 and C-7.

Mental symptoms: Rarely it can look like MENINGITIS due to TUBERCULOSIS or LEAD POISONING. See Protocol 10.

Bush Laboratory: Maybe a high sedimentation rate, maybe not. There may be protein in the urine but this also occurs in some other diseases.

Higher-Level Care. Sending out to a Level 4 facility is very desirable. See Volume I, Appendix 13. *Laboratory:* Blood cultures can be done in Level 3 or above hospitals. They must be held for 6 weeks before they are thrown out as being negative. An antibody test is available. Level 2 and some Level 3 laboratories are probably useless. *Facilities:* Level 4 or above, x-ray might be helpful. *Practitioner:* Generalist, internist, pediatrician; infectious disease specialist with tropical/travel expertise is most desirable. The diagnosis is elusive and the treatment is complex.

Treatment:

Prevention: Destroy affected animals, pasteurize milk.

Patient Care: Send the patient to a Level 3 or more hospital. Treatment is with at least 3 drugs, for 6 weeks if the symptoms have been present for less than a month, for over 3 months if the symptoms have been present for more than a month. One or two drugs are inadequate. Choose three of the following for the entire time. It is better to not treat at all than to treat inadequately. (STREPTOMYCIN or GENTAMYCIN), DOXYCYCLINE, CO-TRIMOXAZOLE, CIPROFLOXACIN (or a related medication), RIFAMPIN, CEPHALOSPORIN (Ceftriaxone). Recent evidence indicates that adding LEVAMISOLE to the antibiotics hastens recovery.

Results: Gradual, over weeks and months.

BURKITT LYMPHOMA

Causes: Variable.

Regional Notes: F, R, U.

Definition: A childhood cancer of the lymph nodes.

Entry category: Disease, a type of CANCER.

Moderately to very ill; Class 4; Regional, occurring in highly malarious areas, mostly in Africa and New Guinea, but also elsewhere in the tropics. It exists only with rainfall over 500 mm (20 inches) per year, a mean temperature over 16°C (60°F), and an altitude less than 160 meters (500 feet) and only between 10° North and 10° South of the equator.

Age: Children, mainly 5-7 years old. **Who:** Those with chronic MALARIA, possibly interacting with some viruses. **Onset:** Over hours to days.

Clinical:

This is a CANCER which begins with swelling of the face (usually the middle of the face) or abdomen; it progresses very rapidly. It is surprisingly painless, which distinguishes this from tooth ABSCESS.

Complications: Damage to the spinal cord with paralysis or tumor in the brain with BRAIN DAMAGE.

Similar Diseases: MUMPS, DIPHTHERIA, ANTHRAX, TUBERCULOSIS (abdominal).

Higher-Level Care. See Volume I Appendix 13. *Laboratory:* A Level 3 or above hospital can do a biopsy which is both sensitive and specific so you can believe both a negative or positive result. *Practitioner:* Hematologist/oncologist is ideal. A pediatrician or internist with tropical/travel medicine expertise may be adequate.

Treatment:

This must be treated at a hospital. It is treatable and frequently curable if it is treated early. Do not give any immunizations to patients who have this disease.

BURSITIS

Cause: Unknown.

Definition: Pain and swelling of the bursa which are like small, slippery water balloon-type structures that help muscles to slide smoothly over bones.

Clinical:

This is similar to ARTHRITIS, except that the patient can identify one particular spot, near but not right over the joint, that is very painful and tender. The shoulder is the most common site. Treat bursitis like ARTHRITIS without a fever.

Higher-Level Care. *Facilities:* X-ray might be helpful to exclude alternative diagnoses. *Practitioner:* Generalist, internist, pediatrician.

BURULI ULCER

Regional notes: F, I, M, O, S, U; this does not occur in Europe or the Middle East. It is found mostly in east and west Africa and in the Pacific region.

Synonym: Bairnsdale Ulcer (in Australia)

Definition: Buruli Ulcer is a skin ulcer cause by Mycobacterium ulcerans.

Mildly to moderately ill; Class 2; Worldwide, south of 10° north of the equator, regional, tropical, swampy areas, rare to common. Particularly common in Benin and in Amansie West, Ghana.

Age: Any but most common in older children; **Who:** Those with minor skin injuries, especially near swamps or flooding; the water might be stagnant or slow-flowing. **Onset:** Slowly, over weeks, not hours and not days.

Clinical:

It usually occurs on areas of the body not covered by clothing, the arms and the legs. There is no preference for right or left, for upper or lower limbs. Occasionally it might occur on the trunk, head, or neck. About half the time it is over joints.

At first: This starts out with a firm, spontaneous lump under the skin; the bump is attached to the skin so one cannot move the skin back and forth over top the lump. It may look like a piece of crust sitting on the skin or like simple swelling. It may or may not itch, but it is not painful. The swelling may be severe but the area is not hot or red. The patient has no fever.

Later: The bump then breaks open to form an round or oval, open skin ulcer. The edges of the ulcer are somewhat raised, slightly ragged, discolored, firm rather than soft, and swollen. There is a large overhang of skin over the ulcer base; one can put half a toothpick under the skin edge along an ulcer radius. Joints near the ulcer might be painful. The ulcer itself is not painful unless there is secondary infection with other bacteria.

Still later: Usually it enlarges slowly over months but may enlarge rapidly over weeks. Satellite ulcers may form around the main ulcer. The ulcer is likely to last for 3 years or so and then spontaneously heal. It commonly recurs or relapses.

Complications: This may become secondarily infected, resulting in SEPSIS. The patient may develop TETANUS. The infection may enter the bones and become OSTEOMYELITIS.

Similar conditions: See Protocol C-11: Skin Ulcer plus "Flu" if applicable.

Higher-Level Care. *Laboratory:* There is none that you can do but a Level 3 or above, possible a Level 2 hospital can do a smear and stain of a scraping from the base of the ulcer. The bacteria that cause this are close relatives to the bacteria that cause TUBERCULOSIS. *Practitioner:* Tropical/travel medicine expertise for diagnosis, surgeon for treatment.

Treatment:

Prevention: BCG vaccine for TUBERCULOSIS does no good for this. One should simply advise avoiding exposure.

Patient Care: If possible, send out for a surgical consult; drugs do no good if the disease is advanced. Otherwise:

- Daily cleaning and dressings.
- Sprinkle PHENYTOIN in the ulcer.
- If diagnosed early, STREPTOMYCIN, ISONIAZID or RIFAMPIN as they are used for TUBERCULOSIS or LEPROSY might be helpful, given for 8 weeks.

CANCER

Cause: Variable.

Synonyms: Neoplasia, Neoplasm, Neoplastic disease, Carcinoma, Sarcoma.

Regional Notes: All regions.

Definition: Abnormal growth of some cells of the body some of which then break off and go to other parts of the body and grow abnormally there.

Entry category: Disease cluster.

Not ill to very ill; Class 4; Worldwide with widely varying manifestations.

This is not taken up specifically, as these problems cannot be treated by non-medical people in remote areas. Any medical problem that does not respond to ordinary medicines in a reasonable length of time needs to be sent to a medical facility whether it is cancer or something else.

Clinical:

Symptoms of cancers anywhere in the body:

An abnormal lump or swelling, usually initially painless, usually slow-growing. If it is on the right or the left, that side is different from the opposite side. (Cancers never grow symmetrically right and left.) If it is in the midline, it usually will usually not be exactly symmetrical, i.e. the same right and left. These are general rules, but any lump needs to be biopsied to determine if it is cancer.

An abnormally-colored spot or an open sore or lump on the skin or the moist, pink parts of the body. It does not heal and it changes color or appearance slowly. It does not respond to repeated washing and dressing changes.

Any persistent evidence of obstruction or inflammation of one of the tubes or hollow parts of the body: constipation, indigestion, stuffy nose, hoarseness or trouble breathing, trouble swallowing, cough, difficulty urinating, a lump in the vagina or by the rectum. Suspect cancer when these symptoms do not respond to treatment for infection that might cause them.

Any persistent enlargement of an organ, particularly when the organ in question feels lumpy (rather than just large but normal shape) and, at least initially, is not tender to touch.

Cancers may cause fevers.

Loss of appetite with weight loss.

Enlarged lymph nodes which are typically painless, and rocky hard to the touch. There may be multiple nodes matted together.

Cancer Symptoms

Body part	Usual first symptom(s)	Associated factors (sometimes)
Esophagus	Trouble swallowing	Unknown
Mouth	Sore or lump	Tobacco
Nose	Swelling or obstruction	Family origin southern China
Liver	Weight loss, JAUNDICE	HEPATITIS B, moldy peanuts or grains
Abdomen	Increased girth	Pain, free fluid in abdomen
Penis	Sore or bump	Poverty, poor hygiene, uncircumcised
Thyroid	Lump in neck	Radiation
Blood	Bleeding, Large lymph nodes	Virus, radiation
Breast	Lump	Westerner; women from areas with GOITER

In the tropics, lung, colon, and rectal cancer are common only amongst the affluent. Cancer of the cervix in women is common throughout the tropics, especially with poor hygiene, early marriage, promiscuity, and uncircumcised male partner(s). For other cancers that are common in your area, see the *Regional Indices*.

Similar Conditions: Too many to list. See applicable protocols in C. Any patient that does not respond to treatment needs hospitalization for evaluation. A particular problem is distinguishing TB of the breast from breast cancer. TB of the breast tends to cause an aching pain initially whereas breast cancer is usually initially painless. If the lump is removed and cut in two, the inside of the lump will be like cheese if it is due to TB and most likely not if it is cancer. HYDATID DISEASE can look similar; if exposed, seek laboratory tests for hydatid disease before consenting to surgery for cancer. Surgery can be disastrous if the diagnosis is in error.

Higher-Level Care. See Volume I, Appendix 13. *Laboratory:* A Level 3 or above hospital can do a biopsy for diagnosis. *Practitioner:* At a minimum a generalist or internist or pediatrician. An Oncologist and a Surgeon will probably be necessary, as well as the facilities of at least a Level 3 hospital. If HYDATID DISEASE is a possibility, seek tropical/travel medical expertise.

Treatment:

This must be done in a hospital. In remote areas, you might be obliged to provide terminal care for very ill patients. See Appendix 8 in Volume I. It is important to provide pain relief, even if this shortens the patient's life. CHLORPROMAZINE does not relieve pain but it relieves suffering by making the patient not care if he has pain or not. DIPYRONE is an excellent non-narcotic pain reliever that is frequently available in developing areas and is useful for pain relief.

CANCRUM ORIS

Cause: Spirochete.

Synonyms: Noma, Gangrenous Stomatitis.

Regional Notes: F, I, M, O, R.

Definition: An infection of the lower face in malnourished children, causing extensive destruction of the lower face and mouth.

Very ill; Class 3-4; requires surgery. Worldwide, tropical, found mainly in Africa, the Indian subcontinent, and South America south of the equator.

Age: Mostly children. **Who:** Malnourished only, mostly with a recent illness such as MALARIA or MEASLES. **Onset:** Over days, mostly during the dry season.

Clinical:

Necessary: There is a spontaneous wound which eats a big hole in the child's cheek. It develops from first symptoms to a huge hole within 2 weeks. It may also destroy an eyelid or a thumb or finger (especially one that is sucked). The patient may have a foul/rotten odor.

Similar Conditions: See Protocol C-11. In the Americas consider CUTANEOUS LEISHMANIASIS that has become mucocutaneous. Also consider TUBERCULOSIS of the skin and GANGRENE; cancrum oris is a kind of GANGRENE.

Higher-Level Care. Speedy referral to a Level 3 or above hospital is mandatory if the child is to live.

Treatment:

Send the child out to a major hospital immediately if at all possible. Meanwhile:

- Use PENICILLIN and METRONIDAZOLE to stop the infectious process. DOXYCYCLINE[1] might be helpful if you lack PENICILLIN.
- Treat other diseases the child may have (WORMS, MALARIA, etc.).
- Treat the cancrum oris like a TROPICAL ULCER.
- Treat for MALNUTRITION.

[1] Don't worry about discolored teeth.

Results: These children generally do poorly and frequently die in spite of best efforts.

CANDIDIASIS

Cause: Fungus.
Synonyms: Candidosis, Monilia.
Includes: Thrush, Crotch Itch, Diaper Rash.
Definition: An infection with a fungus. In people with good immunity, it is usually annoying but not serious; in those with poor immunity it can be life-threatening.

Mildly ill; Class 1-4; Worldwide, especially humid tropics.

Age: Any. **Who:** Anyone, especially those with white skin, HIV patients, those who have taken antibiotics, and the poorly nourished. **Onset:** Over days.

Clinical:

The patient has a very itchy, very red rash. It is either entirely spotted or solid red in the center with satellite red spots around. It develops first and possibly only on the warmer parts of the skin: the groins, the armpits, under large breasts, between rolls of fat, sometimes in the ear canals. It commonly includes the scrotum and the rectal area. In patients with good immunity when it involves the skin only, it does not cause fever.

In the mouth it is painful and it looks like white scum on the pink surface. If the patient also has pain with swallowing, the candida has invaded his esophagus. It may cause cracks at the sides of the lips. In some areas when this problem recurs or will not respond to treatment it is likely that the patient has HIV. In these patients it may cause diarrhea and fevers.

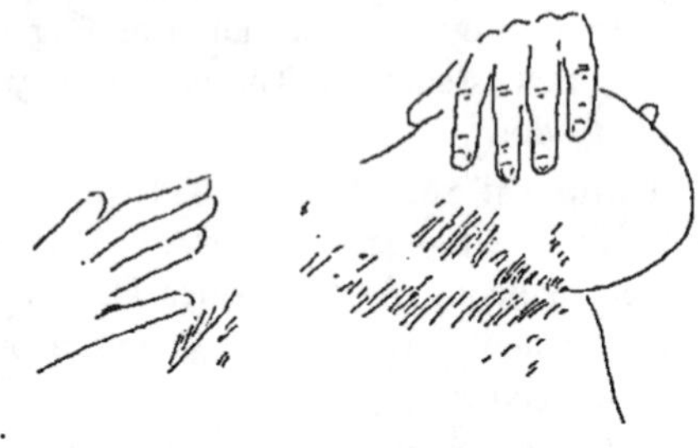

Candidiasis: Note that it is in a warm, moist area of the body.

Similar Conditions: ECZEMA occurs in people with a family history of allergies; in the developing world this is usually the more affluent. CONTACT DERMATITIS is found in an area of contact with a particular substance. In the rectal area, ENTEROBIASIS may seem similar; check for the worms.

Higher-Level Care. *Laboratory:* Level 3, possibly Level 2 can do a skin scraping. HIV testing might be helpful in severe cases. *Practitioner:* Generalist, internist, pediatrician.

Treatment:

Prevention is by frequent showering.

Patient care: Send the patient out if he is ill. Otherwise:

- Treat with NYSTATIN, CLOTRIMAZOLE, MICONAZOLE, or KETOCONAZOLE.
- Frequent washing, drying, and use of baby powder is also helpful. GENTIAN VIOLET or tincture of IODINE may help.
- Exposing the affected area to direct sunlight (not filtered through glass) for a half-hour daily usually will clear it promptly.
- In the mouth GENTIAN VIOLET or NYSTATIN are best.

CAPILLARIASIS

Cause: Worm.
Synonym: Intestinal capillariasis.
Regional: It is found in tropical coastal regions of northern Luzon, the Philippines; occasionally in south and northeast Thailand; in northern Java; in Egypt. A related parasite is found in Iran but it is rare and causes entirely different symptoms. The disease is listed here rather than in the *Regional Notes* because of its potential for spreading to other areas in addition to those mentioned.

Mildly to severely ill; Class 2.

Age: Usually adults. **Who:** Those eating raw fish. **Onset:** Slowly.

Clinical:

The patient has diarrhea with loud, rumbling bowel sounds and much gas for a long time. He loses his appetite, gradually loses weight, and develops various vitamin deficiencies and swelling of the ankles and feet. He will die of MALNUTRITION eventually if he is not treated.

Similar Conditions: MALABSORPTION and the causes thereof are indistinguishable. See Protocol C-14.

Higher-Level Care. *Laboratory:* Stool specimen for diagnosis of this and other worms.

Treatment:

Prevention: Discourage the consumption of raw or poorly cooked fresh-water fish.

Patient Care: MEBENDAZOLE, ALBENDAZOLE, THIABENDAZOLE.

CARBON MONOXIDE POISONING

Cause: Toxic gas.
Definition: Poisoning by carbon monoxide which is a toxic gas that is generated by internal combustion engines and fires.

Clinical:

Exposure to fumes from an internal combustion engine, furnace, or a fire in an enclosed space leads to carbon monoxide poisoning. Symptoms are nausea, vomiting, shortness of breath, and headache initially; lethargy progressing to loss of consciousness if severe. The face (in Whites) and the inside of the mouth may be redder than normal. There is no fever due to this.

Similar Conditions: See Protocol C-4 if the patient is short of breath. ALTITUDE SICKNESS looks similar but the inside of the mouth is never bright red. SMOKE INHALATION is similar and may be present along with this. There is sooty sputum.

Higher-Level Care. *Laboratory:* At least Level 3: Blood gases, respiratory care team. *Facilities:* At Level 3 oxygen may be helpful. At least Level 4: A hyperbaric oxygen chamber. *Practitioner:* Pulmonologist is ideal; internist or pediatrician or generalist might be helpful.

Treatment:

Remove the patient to fresh air. Giving oxygen hastens the clearing of the carbon monoxide from the body.

CARPAL TUNNEL SYNDROME

Cause: Pressure on one of the nerves that travels from the spine to the hand as it goes through the wrist area.

Entry category: Syndrome.

Age: Mostly over 30 y.o.; **Who**: Urban more than rural, females more than males, short more than tall, fat more than thin, mostly those doing work requiring repetitive hand motion such as factory workers. It may be the result of a one-time injury. It is very uncommon in rural, developing areas. **Onset:** Days to months.

Clinical:

Pain and numbness and tingling, maybe weakness on the palm-thumb side of the hand, the thumb, index, and middle fingers. It may involve both hands. Usually it starts in the dominant hand and is worse at night. It is initially relieved with awakening and shaking the hand or hanging the hand down over the side of the bed.

Treatment:

There are both surgical and non-surgical treatments. Medication such as IBUPROFEN may be helpful. Splinting the wrist in a neutral position might help. Sometimes local steroid injections are helpful but usually surgery is required eventually.

CAT SCRATCH DISEASE

Definition: Cat-scratch disease is an infection with the gram-negative bacillus Bartonella henselae. The bacterium is related to the causative organism of BARTONELLOSIS but the disease is entirely different. It should not be called Bartonellosis and is not so called in this book.

Synonym: Subacute regional lymphadenitis.

Not ill to mildly ill in patients with good immunity; moderately to very ill without good immunity. Class 2; Probably worldwide.

Age: Any, especially children; adults may experience more serious symptoms. **Who**: Those who have been scratched by cats or bitten by cat fleas. Infected cats are not generally ill. **Onset:** Unknown; incubation 3-30 days.

Clinical:

The patient has large, tender lymph nodes closer to the trunk than where the cat scratched or the flea bit. Initially the wound might look like a small bump or blister, reddish brown in color. The large lymph nodes persist for 3 weeks and then go away. They may be soft and resemble ABSCESSes. There may be fever, weight loss, large spleen, a (non-itchy) rash, or fatigue connected with this.

Complications: Sometimes this causes SEPSIS, ENCEPHALITIS, ERYTHEMA NODOSUM, PNEUMONIA, and abnormal bleeding.

Similar Conditions: See Protocol C-12 for other causes of large, tender lymph nodes.

Treatment:

RIFAMPIN, CIPROFLOXACIN, AZITHROMYCIN and GENTAMYCIN work fine for treatment, given in standard doses for 10 days. COTRIMOXAZOLE works about half of the time. Other antibiotics are not usually helpful.

CATARACT

Cause: Variable.

Regional Notes: F.

Definition: Opacities in the lens of the eye.

Entry category: Symptom.

Not ill; Class 2-4, depending on hospital facilities; Worldwide, more common in arid and high-altitude tropics, especially in the Indian subcontinent.

Age: Any, more common in older people but occurs in babies. **Who:** Anyone; MALNUTRITION, DEHYDRATION, RADIATION ILLNESS, and bright sunlight contribute to it. When it is present from birth, it may be hereditary or else due to prenatal infection such as RUBELLA, HERPES, or SHINGLES. **Onset:** Slowly in older children and adults.

Clinical:

Necessary: The pupil of the eye looks cloudy (white or gray rather than the normal black) or the patient gradually loses vision with blurring being worse in bright than in dim light. He may see halos around lights. Early cataract is hard to see; there are streaks of gray or white on the pupil.

Higher-Level Care. Surgical referral is mandatory; An ophthalmologist is ideal.

Treatment:

Prevention: Bright sunlight as well as DEHYDRATION seem to increase the rate of development of cataract. Issue plain sun glasses to those with early cataract. There is some evidence that ASPIRIN will retard the development of cataract.

Patient Care: Some hospitals can do surgery for cataract but the person usually must wear glasses thereafter. If he refuses to wear glasses or is likely to break or lose them, the surgery will do no good. An alternative is having a lens implant put into the eye; in that case glasses are necessary just for reading. Babies born with cataract must have surgery within 6 months. There is some evidence that daily, small doses of ASPIRIN might slow the development of cataract.

CELLULITIS

Cause: Bacteria.
Includes: Erysipelas.
Definition: An infection of the skin and the tissues under the skin, usually caused by gram-positive bacteria.

Mildly ill; Class 1-2 if previously healthy; Class 3-4 if previously ill; Probably not in most cases but use good hygiene; Worldwide, Erysipelas is common.

Age: Any. **Who:** Anyone, especially those with poor hygiene, chronic illness, or both. **Onset:** Few days to a week or two; faster with bites, embedded foreign bodies, and in hot, humid climates.

Clinical:

Necessary: An area of skin is reddened or warm. There is one of the clinical pictures described in the following Table.

Frequently: It is painful and tender to the touch. There may be swelling. The lymph nodes closer to the trunk may be enlarged and tender. If the area is on an arm or a leg, there may be red streaks from the reddened area going towards the trunk.

Commonly this involves the breast or the eyelids. If it involves the stump of the umbilical cord in a newborn, check for SEPSIS.

Occasionally: There is fever.

Bacteria Causing Cellulitis.

Kind of bacteria	History	Appearance	Symptoms	Treatment
Erysipelas (most common)	Varioius	Red or warm swollen skin	Usually on the face or by a wound	Gram positive antibiotic(s)[1]
Aeronomas	Exposed to fresh or salt water.	Watery pus, gas bubbles	Pain excessive, high fever, foul smell	Emergency surgery
Clostridium	Major wound or fracture; dead tissue	Watery pus, gas bubbles	Pain excessive, high fever, foul smell	Emergency surgery
Fasciitis	Various	Large area, large blisters.	Pain excessive, some numbness, high fever	Emergency surgery
Pasteurella	Dog or cat bite or contaminated wound	Ordinary wound infection—swollen and red.	Few, if any	Various[2]
Vibrio vulnificus	Sickly patient and salt water exposure	Red rash → big blisters → ulcers, dead centers	Low blood pressure Many deaths	Doxycycline plus a third generation CEPHALOSPORIN

Warning: Ordinary cellulitis involves obvious redness and/or warmth and some but not extreme pain and tenderness. There is a type of gangrene called NECROTIZING FASCIITIS, which can look similar. However, the pain and tenderness are extreme, all out of proportion to the redness and warmth. Ordinary cellulitis looks worse than what it feels. NECROTIZING FASCIITIS feels much worse than what it looks.

[1] You must treat both strep and staph.
[2] Amoxicillin with calvulanate, doxycycline, ciprofloxacin, a second or third generation CEPHALOSPORIN.

Similar Conditions: See Protocol C-6 for Limb Swelling and/or C-11 for Skin Ulcer plus "Flu", C-12 for large lymph nodes; C-8 if the problem involves the eye(s), C-13 if it involves the back. If the area involved is the genital area, then see Protocol C-1.

If there is a raised area with a center, see ABSCESS.

Redness and swelling over a joint: see ARTHRITIS.

With deep bone pain: OSTEOMYELITIS.

Mediterranean genetic heritage: FAMILIAL MEDITERRANEAN FEVER

FILARIASIS can look similar, but with this the red streak moves away from the heart; with cellulitis it moves toward the heart. (You can decide which way it is moving by marking the end of the streak with a pen and then checking it again the next day.)

Higher-Level Care. *Laboratory:* At Level 3 or more, culture and blood count might be helpful. In stubborn cases there may be other appropriate tests. *Practitioner:* Generalist, internist, pediatrician, maybe a nurse; infectious disease expertise is helpful.

Treatment:

Prevention: Frequent use of soap and water. Care of wounds.

Patient Care: If the cellulitis is in the leg or groin, check the genitals and foot for an infected wound. Likewise, check the hand for a wound or wounds if the cellulitis is between the wrist and the shoulder. See Chapter 10 in Volume I for treatment of an infected wound. Send the patient out to a hospital if at all possible. Sending out is essential if there is excessive pain, large blisters, a foul smell, or gas bubbles. Otherwise treat as follows:

- Bedrest with elevation of the body part is helpful for severe cases.
- Treat with PENICILLIN or another gram-positive antibiotic for 10 days. Use ERYTHROMYCIN in PENICILLIN allergy; use AMPICILLIN in children under 5. A CEPHALOSPORIN is also helpful.
- If there was an animal bite then use both gram positive and gram negative antibiotics.
- If it is due to exposure to contaminated water, then use gram-negative antibiotics: DOXYCYCLINE, CHLORAMPHENICOL, or GENTAMYCIN.
- Other drugs that might help but are expensive are AZITHROMYCIN, CLARITHROMYCIN, OFLOXACIN.
- If there is a relapse after a partial treatment, give a full treatment. If there is a relapse after a full treatment, then use CEPHALOSPORIN or CLOXACILLIN.

Results: 4 days.

CEREBRAL PALSY

Entry category: Syndrome

Regional Notes: F, I, S.

Definition: This is a type of BRAIN DAMAGE, a permanent problem of movement and coordination, possibly due to lack of oxygen at birth, being born prematurely, ENCEPHALITIS, cerebral MALARIA, poisoning, head injury, untreated JAUNDICE after birth, and sometimes other diseases.

Clinical:

The patient has uncoordinated movements and garbled speech. Most often these people are mentally normal, though their inability to speak clearly and their uncoordination gives the impression of retardation.

Treatment:

Obtain professional advice from a physical therapist or another appropriate professional. Higher-Level Care must be Level 3 or above.

CHAGA'S DISEASE

See *Regional Notes* M.

CHANCROID

Cause: Bacteria.

Synonyms: Soft chancre, Soft sore, Ulcus molle.

Regional Notes: O, S, U.

Definition: A sexually transmitted (venereal) disease caused by the bacterium Hemophilis ducreyi.

Not ill to mildly ill; Class 1-2; Contagious; Worldwide more in tropical areas, especially sub-Saharan Africa, and South Asia.

Age: Sexually mature, usually, but sexually abused children can get it. **Who:** Sexually active; symptoms are more common in males than females, more common in uncircumcised than in circumcised males. Females are likely to have no symptoms whatsoever if the genital ulcers are inside the vagina. **Onset:** Incubation from infection to a bump is 1-3 days; infection to an ulcer is 3-60 days. Large lymph nodes develop within a week.

Clinical:

Necessary: The patient has or had small red pimple(s) which became ulcer(s) with irregular (not smooth) edges on the genitals. When there is more than one, they tend to form on skin surfaces that normally touch each other. They may be painful and may be tender to touch but there is no swelling around them. They bleed easily if they are disturbed.

Usually: There is a red halo around the inside rim of the ulcer(s). The inside part of the ulcer has a yellowish appearance. It may have a foul odor. The groin lymph nodes on one side are large and tender, possibly rupturing and spilling pus. They subsequently heal with scarring. In females, the pimples and ulcers may be inside so only the enlarged lymph nodes are visible. The internal ulcers may not be painful.

Maybe: Females may have pain with intercourse, pain with urination, or a visible ulcer on the outside genitals. Ulcers may simply disappear.

Occasionally:

Ulcers coalesce. The initial bump stays as a bump and does not develop into a full ulcer.

The ulcer, rather than being depressed below the skin surface, may be raised up above the skin surface.

There may just be pain with urination and/or pus coming from the hole in the penis rather than a visible ulcer.

The large, swollen lymph nodes in the groin develop without there being a visible ulcer or pus in the genital area.

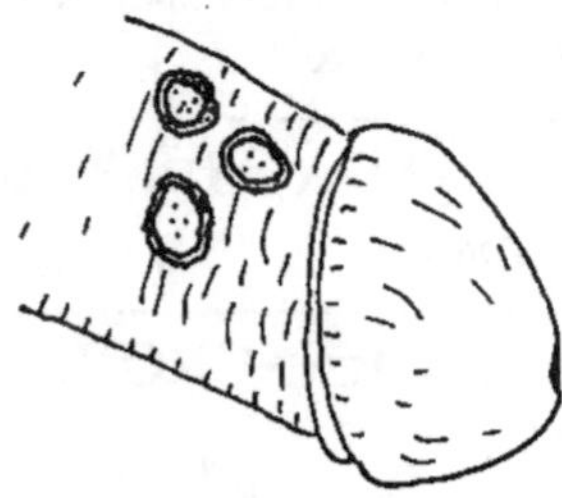

Chancroid: Note the lack of swelling and the bloody halo.

Complications: If there is secondary infection, there may be a stinky discharge from the ulcer and there may be rapid destruction of the genitals. Chancroid can cause PHIMOSIS.

Similar Diseases:

See Protocol C-1. Common diseases that cause genital ulcers like this are impossible to distinguish from each other except for HERPES which is usually distinctive. However, chancroid ulcers may, at times, resemble HERPES. Hence you should consult the C-1 protocol for genital ulcers (if appropriate), pus from the penis (if appropriate), or pelvic pain (if appropriate) rather than trying to distinguish. The swollen nodes in the groin might be due to any infection on the legs or the feet.

Bush Laboratory - is useless.

Higher-Level Care. *Laboratory:* A middle-sized to large hospital laboratory can do a stained smear and culture. The laboratory procedures for this are either fairly high-tech or else neither sensitive nor specific--you can believe neither a positive nor a negative result. It is not worth the trouble unless it's very high-tech. *Practitioner:* A sexually-transmitted disease clinic is ideal. A generalist or internist can provide decent care. A surgeon can drain the pus from the groin nodes.

Treatment:

Prevention: Discourage promiscuity. Prostitutes spread the disease. In some large, tropical cities, the majority of the prostitutes are infected.

Patient care: Send out to confirm the diagnosis and provide professional treatment. If this is not possible: Patients should be treated according to Protocol C-1: SEXUALLY TRANSMITTED DISEASES. The following drugs work for chancroid: AZITHROMYCIN, cephtriaxone (CEPHALOSPORIN), CIPROFLOXACIN, ERYTHROMYCIN, RIFAMPIN. Withdraw the pus from the lymph node with a syringe: **do not cut it to drain it**. It is important to treat all sexual partners.

Results: Few days. Uncircumcised males do not respond as well as circumcised.

CHICKEN POX

Cause: Virus.

Synonym: Varicella zoster.

Regional Notes: F, I, O, S.

Definition: A viral infection that usually causes a mild disease in children.

Mildly to moderately ill; Class 1-4; Contagious; Worldwide, common, usually in small epidemics.

Age: Any, especially young children. **Who:** Anyone who has not yet had the disease. **Onset:** Over days; 10-23 days incubation.

Clinical:

Necessary: A fever and a rash which consists of red spots initially. The spots become tiny, soft blisters on red bases, appearing in crops, first here and then there. It is on the trunk first and heaviest, then the head, neck, upper arms, and legs. The blisters break, crust over, and heal.

Maybe: There are blisters on the white of the eye and inside the mouth.

Sometimes: In older children, there is a low fever and fatigue first; the rash comes later. In young children, the fever and rash occur together. The disease may be fatal with MALNUTRITION.

Complications: HYPOGLYCEMIA, IMPETIGO. Adults - ENCEPHALITIS. Reye's Syndrome is a rare complication characterized by severe vomiting. It is a major emergency requiring immediate evacuation.

Similar Conditions: See Protocol C-8 for other causes of red, painful eyes.

Blisters break out at one time: MONKEYPOX

Skin bumps firm like warts with center holes: MOLLUSCUM CONTAGIOSUM

Blisters in one area of skin or a band: SHINGLES

Few, countable blisters: SPOTTED FEVER (Rickettsial pox), GONORRHEA

Clinical:

There are two kinds of cretinism,

- **First Kind:**

With the first kind, the main symptoms are hearing and speech defects and deformed, uncoordinated, stiff limbs; the patient cannot walk normally. Stature is normal.

- **Second Kind:**

The second kind of cretinism causes short stature, badly formed teeth, and symptoms of THYROID TROUBLE of the low-thyroid type.

- **Both Kinds:**

There is severe mental retardation, mongoloid appearance, and possibly crossed eyes. An infant is likely to have decreased activity with poor feeding and weight gain, floppy muscles, and a hoarse cry. He may have a large tongue, large fontanelles, and cool, dry skin.

Similar Conditions: MONGOLISM, THALLASEMIA.

Higher-Level Care. *Laboratory:* A Level 3 or above lab might be helpful. *Practitioner:* pediatrician, internist, physical therapist.

Treatment:

Prevention: If there are any cretins in your area or more than one or two cases of GOITER, treat all young women with low doses of IODINE.

Patient Care: Symptoms of THYROID TROUBLE can be treated with medicines. Mental retardation and deafness will not change.

CRIMEAN-CONGO HEMORRHAGIC FEVER

Also see HEMORRHAGIC FEVER and Protocol C-2. **This disease is contagious!** This is found in the Middle East; the western portion of the Indian subcontinent; Asia west of China; the Crimean, Caspian, and Ural Sea areas; eastern, central, and southern Africa; Nigeria, and Mali. It is common in NE Turkey and in SE Iran. It is most common during the spring and summer, in males, and at time of civil unrest, when there is less agriculture and more wild animals. The virus does not make the animals sick, but almost all human cases have had contact with animals or else they are healthcare workers. It is frequently associated with domestic animals being moved in herds and/or slaughtered.

Age: Most patients are teens or older. **Who:** The disease is directly contagious but usually is transmitted by the bite of a tick—Hyalomma—or from crushing a tick. **Onset:** Incubation is 1-9 days, longer in patients exposed to blood contamination rather than a tick bite. Onset is sudden.

Clinical:

There is a severe headache first. There is also dizziness; a painful, stiff neck; eyes that are sore, red, and sensitive to light; fever, chills, vomiting, and general body pains. The fever tends to come and go. The patient's emotional state may be sleepy, confused, depressed, or aggressive. There may be a sore throat, red eyes or hair loss. The liver and spleen and lymph nodes may be enlarged. A rash of tiny black-and-blue marks may appear, which may become large bruises. There may be abnormal bleeding from nose, mouth, genital, or rectal areas. Patients typically seek care about the fourth day. About 30% of patients die, usually between the fifth and fourteenth day of illness. Recovery takes months.

Bush Laboratory: The sedimentation rate will be elevated—the test is sensitive but not specific.

Treatment:

Prevention: Use gowns and masks when caring for a patient. Avoid tick bites. You should be aware that the virus has bioterrorist potential.

Patient Care: The drug RIBAVIRIN may be helpful. Avoid using ASPIRIN, IBUPROFEN, or similar drugs. PARACETAMOL is acceptable. Avoid injections. Avoid sending the patient out by public transport because of the possibility of thereby starting an epidemic.

CRYPTOSPORIDIOSIS

Cause: Protozoa.

Definition: Cryptosporidiosis is a bowel infection with Cryptosporidium parvum.

Mildly to very ill; Class 1-3; Contagious; Worldwide, especially in developing areas, rare to common.

Age: Any, especially 1-5 years old; also in adults, especially those with poor immunity, as in HIV infection. **Who**: Those drinking contaminated water, eating contaminated food, those in contact with manure from domestic animals. **Onset**: Sudden; incubation 1-14 days.

Clinical:

Necessary: Watery diarrhea, resembling GIARDIASIS, it may be severe. The disease tends to hang on for months unless treated.

Maybe: Cramping and vomiting. With normal immunity the diarrhea persists from 2-26 days.

Complications: DEHYDRATION is common. The patient may develop REITER SYNDROME, described under reactive ARTHRITIS.

Similar Conditions: See Protocol C-14.

Higher-Level Care. *Laboratory:* Level 3 or above, stool for parasites; not detected in normal tests; a test for this must be specifically ordered. The test is not very sensitive so you should submit at least 2 specimens before believing a negative report. The parasites are small but stain well with the stains usually used for TUBERCULOSIS. *Facilities:* IV's and fluids. Some of the drugs may only be available at Level 4 or above facilities.

Practitioner: Level 3 or above, pediatrician, internist, generalist.

Treatment:

Prevention: The protozoa are resistant to chlorine so soaking vegetables in bleach-water does not help. They can be killed by heating water to 65° Celcius for 30 minutes; this may be accomplished with a hot water heater.

Patient Care: Treat DEHYDRATION. Also give PAROMOMYCIN, AZITHROMYCIN, CLARITHROMYCIN or NITAZOXANIDE.

CUTANEOUS LEISHMANIASIS

Cause: Protozoa.

Synonyms: Aleppo boil, Baghdad boil, Delhi boil, Oriental sore.

Definition: A skin infection caused by protozoa transmitted by the bites of sand flies.

Includes: Localized cutaneous leishmaniasis (LCL); Mucocutaneous leishmaniasis (MCL); diffuse cutaneous leishmaniasis (DCL).

Excludes: VISCERAL LEISHMANIASIS (VL) and a complication of it called post-kala-azar dermal leishmaniasis, (PKDL).

Regional notes: E, F, I, M, R.

Entry category: Disease, Tropical.

Not ill to mildly ill; Class 2-3; Regional, does not occur in the Pacific area.

Age: Any, but mostly children and teenagers. **Who:** Bitten by sand flies, males more than females, rainy season more than dry season. These sand flies (see Volume I, Appendix 10) bite especially at dusk but they feed throughout the night. **Onset:** variable according to geography and different types of organisms; see the chart below and the notes in the *Regional Indices*.

A leishmania complex is a group of leishmania species that need not be distinguished. You should first determine the species or complex to which your patient might have been exposed. The Web site, www.who.int/leishmaniasis, shows distribution maps. Local lore usually is more reliable than published maps.

Present in Europe, Africa, the Middle East, and Asia:

- Leishmania Donovani and Leishmania infantum[1] usually manifest as VISCERAL LEISHMANIASIS.
- Leishmania Major.
- Leishmania Tropica.
- Leishmania Aethiopica (Ethiopia only).

Present in the Americas: There are two main complexes:

- Leishmania Mexicana (mexicana, amazonensis, venezuelensis).
- Leishmania Viannia (braziliensis, guyanensis, panamensis, peruviana).
- (There is also a third leishmaniasis complex, which causes VISCERAL LEISHMANIASIS)

CUTANEOUS LEISHMANIASIS and VISCERAL LEISHMANIASIS are caused by similar organisms but the diseases are entirely different. If you are living in an area where an unusual manifestation is VL, then consult the description of VISCERAL LEISHMANIASIS. Two unusual manifestations of CUTANEOUS LEISHMANIASIS are listed below: mucocutaneous (MCL) and diffuse (DL). Unusual manifestations occur in people with decreased immunity, due to HIV INFECTION, MALNUTRITION, CANCER, or old age.

Clinical, General Picture:

Necessary: The patient has been in an area where CUTANEOUS LEISHMANIASIS occurs **and** the skin problem develops slowly **and** it does not hurt much **and** it has some of the following characteristics:

- It starts as tiny, painless, maybe-itching pimples which enlarge to ulcers with raised edges.
- One can feel that part of the sore lies underneath the skin; it does not have the appearance or feel of being right on the surface. It may be saucer-shape, with raised edges and a depressed center.
- It occurs on parts of the body not ordinarily protected with clothes.

Commonly there are satellites—new, small sores that form around the larger, major sores.

Clinical, Specific Forms:

➢ **Localized Cutaneous Leishmaniasis: LCL**

LCL is the most common form of cutaneous leishmaniasis. It causes spontaneous lumps or sores which may become ulcers, shaped like craters or flattened volcanos with raised edges. They are almost always on exposed parts of the body, not on parts commonly covered with clothing. The face is a very common location. The color is reddish or purplish on white skin but dark-colored on dark skin. Sometimes they are nodules: lumps under the skin or bumps on top of the skin; they are usually painless and may be slightly itchy; in any case the pain or itchiness is not severe unless there is secondary infection from bacteria. There may or may not be satellite sores—tiny sores that form around the outside of the main sore. Healing is always with scarring: usually pink or white scars on light skin and dark scars on dark skin though the scars may be normal skin color but have a wrinkled appearance (especially with Aethiopica).

---

[1] This is reportedly also now found in the Americas. It is, for the most part, present only along the Mediterranean rim, in the Balkan Peninsula and west of there. As the name indicates, it affects mostly small children. Aside from its preferred host being young rather than adult, it is nearly indistinguishable from L. Donovani and hence is listed together with that.

➢ **Diffuse Cutaneous Leishmaniasis: DCL**

DCL is a form of the disease where the skin lesions, rather than staying as well-defined bumps, ulcers, or sores, spread over a wide area of skin. The color is reddish or purplish on white skin but either purplish or lighter or darker than the normal skin color on dark skin. There are not usually ulcers. They spread slowly over months to years and never heal spontaneously. The scarring causes deformity of the body part. The appearance of DCL can be like cobblestones on the face, very similar to lepromatous LEPROSY. It also may resemble post-kala-azar dermal leishmaniasis, a complication of VISCERAL LEISHMANIASIS. DCL is a rare complication of cutaneous leishmaniasis, due to a decreased immunity.

➢ **Mucocutaneous Leishmaniasis: MCL**

MCL is a highly destructive disease which affects the mucous membranes: the pink, moist parts of the body—in the mouth, the nose, and possibly the genital area. The most common cause is Leishmania Viannia braziliensis; the second most common cause is Leishmania Mexicana. It causes big, disfiguring holes and wounds that ulcerate, may become secondarily infected, and cause difficulty in breathing and eating. It can be fatal. Mucocutaneous leishmaniasis usually occurs after a skin form. The history of the previous skin sore distinguishes it from CANCRUM ORIS which it otherwise resembles.

Similar Conditions:

See Protocol C-11.

On the mouth or nose: CANCRUM ORIS, SEXUALLY TRANSMITTED DISEASE.

Very tender with rounded edges: DIPHTHERIA.

Painless, black center: TUBERCULOSIS.

Limb exposed to tropical swamp: BURULI ULCER.

Old wound site: TROPICAL ULCER, RAT BITE FEVER.

Cutaneous Leishmaniasis: Summary

Abbreviations: LCL = localized cutaneous leishmaniasis—one or more sores in one area. DCL = diffuse cutaneous leishmaniasis—a rash that spreads out from its original location MCL = mucocutaneous leishmaniasis, involving the pink, moist surfaces of the body: mouth, nose, genital areas. VL = visceral leishmaniasis—see the separate entry.

Area	Species or Complex	Appearance of the cutaneous (skin) form of the disease	Incubation	Healing	Usual Form	Unusual Forms
Europe Americas NW Africa	Donovani and Infantum	Face, many small bumps, ulcers unusual	Days to years	1-3 years	VL	LCL, DCL
Africa Mideast India Asia	Major	Moist sores, no satellites, 2-6 cm round, oval, or irregular; inflamed, maybe multiple, lymphatic spread[1]	1-10 weeks	2-8 months	LCL	DCL
Africa Mideast India	Tropica	Dry, reddish, satellites, ulcers are crusted; 1-4 cm, usually single, usually on face, may be chronic	2-4 months	2 years	LCL	VL
Ethiopia only	Aethiopica	Bumpy, usually single, satellites common, wet or dry; no crusting or ulceration	??	2-5 years	LCL	DCL
Americas	Mexicana	Single, bump or ulcer, face and ears commonly	less than 6 months	6-8 months	LCL	DCL VL
Americas	Viannia[2]	Various; may spread by lymph nodes	??	??	LCL, MCL	MCL, DCL, VL

[1] In this case one will feel rows of lumps underneath the skin in a line, usually along the long axis of a limb.

[2] In this case one will feel rows of lumps underneath the skin in a line near the sore. See the chart in *Regional Notes* M.

Higher-Level Care. See Volume I, Appendix 13; this requires tropical/travel expertise. *Laboratory:* The following may be done in a clinic or hospital, probably Level 4 or above.

Leishmanin Skin Test: Montenegro Test: This is positive in any kind of cutaneous leishmaniasis except for diffuse cutaneous leishmaniasis, in which case it is negative. It does not show that the current problem is due to CL but merely that the patient has been exposed to some leishmanial organisms at some time in his or her life.

Obtaining materials for microscopic examination: Several areas should have samples taken; the edges of open sores are best but with intact bumps, samples should be taken from the center. The material can be taken by scraping with the edge of a knife blade, by pulling material into a syringe with a needle, or by cutting out a chunk of tissue, a biopsy. The parasites are very small and difficult to find. They can only be seen with a 100x lense, using immersion oil.

Serological tests: These are blood tests that show whether there are proteins in a person's body to fight the disease. These tests are very sensitive for VL and reasonably sensitive for MCL (you can usually believe a negative result) but they are generally negative in simple, localized CL. They may remain positive after the disease has been treated and cured. *Facilities:* IV's and fluids; some of the drugs are hard to obtain and require technology to administer. *Practitioner:* Experience with this disease is most desirable. An infectious disease specialist is ideal. Otherwise an internist or generalist might be helpful. A surgeon can get tissue for microscopic examination.

Treatment:

Prevention: The sand flies that cause this are weak fliers; they have trouble biting in a breeze. A fan is protective. Use insecticide on dogs and in rodent burrows. Use insect repellent or insecticide on clothing. A fine-mesh mosquito net is helpful, especially if it is treated with insecticide or insect repellent.

Patient care (if sending out is not possible):

❖ **Injectible drugs:**

STILBOGLUCONATE; PENTAMIDINE; AMPHOTERICIN B given daily or every other day, for 20 – 40 days. Whole body medicine is essential in cases where mucocutaneous disease might develop. Additional forms which require whole body drugs are cases which involve lymph nodes, body joints, the outer ear, or extensive areas of skin. In addition to whole body medicines, you can try the following topical treatments. Some work in some areas and others in other areas; none works really well. Local lore is particularly valuable.

❖ **Oral drugs:**

KETOCONAZOLE, ITRACONAZOLE, ALLOPURINOL though they work slowly. MILTEFOSINE might work. Reportedly FLUCONAZOLE works for the Major type; it is quite expensive but will be cheaper when it is available as generic or you may be able to obtain free samples. A new drug under investigation is Sitamaquine; there is no other information available. An article from Baghdad states that oral zinc sulfate, 5-10 mg/kg daily cures the problem—this should be confirmed from another source. If it works, that would be great because the stuff can be purchased by the kilogram from chemical companies.

❖ **Topical drugs:**

For Major and Tropica-type CL in the Old World and for New World CL in Mexico, injecting STIBOGLUCONATE-type drugs into and under the sore may work well, about 1 ml of the undiluted drug, every other day or twice a week for 2-3 weeks. This avoids the toxicity of whole-body drug injections.

AMINOSIDINE in 15% methylbenzethonium chloride can be used as a skin cream.

PAROMOMYCIN ointment; apply locally twice a day for 10-20 days.

Results: The sore first becomes flat and then heals. It may only heal partially during the treatment but the healing will likely be completed after treatment. It will heal as much as it is going to heal by 6 weeks after treatment so if it is still open then, it needs retreatment. If and when the problem relapses, it usually does so around the outer edges of the scar. DCL, leishmaniasis on the nose or ear, and chronic leishmaniasis are particularly difficult to treat.

CYCLOSPORIASIS

Cause: Protozoa.

Not ill to moderately ill; Class 2; Nearly worldwide in pockets; especially in Nepal and Latin America.

Age: Any; more common in children than adults. **Who:** Those who travel and those who consume contaminated food or water or have contact with contaminated soil; it is not transmitted person to person. Chlorination does not kill the cysts. It is seasonal. **Onset:** Sudden after an incubation of 1-11 days.

Clinical:

There is a sudden onset of diarrhea which may be explosive, with fatigue, loss of appetite, nausea, much gas, and abdominal cramps. There may be a low fever. The problem lasts for weeks to months. In patients with normal immunity, it cures itself; in people with poor immunity it may be exceedingly serious or fatal.

Similar Condition: This is indistinguishable from GIARDIASIS which is much more common in general. Also see Protocol C-14.

Treatment:

COTRIMOXAZOLE is the only thing that works consistently. CIPROFLOXACIN is an alternative that works sometimes. NITAZOXANIDE might also work.

Use standard doses for 7 days in the absence of HIV INFECTION; for 10 days in the presence of HIV INFECTION.

CYSTICERCOSIS

Cause: Worm larva.

Definition: An infection of the larval form of pork tapeworm.

Regional Notes: F, I, M, O, S, U.

Moderately to very ill; Class 3; Regional.

Age: Generally only older children and adults. **Who:** Those who live in areas where pigs are raised in such a way that they can come into contact with human waste. **Onset:** Unknown.

Clinical:

This is a form of pork TAPEWORM that forms lumps the size of dry green peas. The lumps go to the skin, the muscles, and the brain. In the skin, they are underneath the surface but one can feel them easily; the skin will move back and forth over them and they are not tender. There usually are many. In the muscles they cause soreness and frequently tremendous swelling. In the brain they usually cause no symptoms at all for 3-5 years. Then they cause headache, SEIZURES and BRAIN DAMAGE. SEIZURES most often involve only one part of the body; they are not generalized.

Similar Diseases: Check the causes of SEIZURES and BRAIN DAMAGE if the patient has either. The skin lumps along with muscle pains are distinctive. In some areas consider HYDATID DISEASE or SCHISTOSOMIASIS.

Higher-Level Care. *Laboratory:* A skin or muscle biopsy is needed to confirm the diagnosis. *Practitioner:* A surgeon to obtain a specimen from muscle and a pathologist to examine the biopsy specimen. A generalist, pediatrician, or internist is helpful for treatment. If there are signs of BRAIN DAMAGE, a neurologist or neurosurgeon is desirable.

Treatment:

Prevention: Don't consume pork that was raised in areas without sanitation. Overcook all pork before eating it. Wash your hands carefully after using a toilet.

Patient Care: Send the patient to a hospital. Otherwise:

- In the absence of SEIZURES, use (PRAZIQUANTEL or ALBENDAZOLE) plus DEXCHLORPHENIRAMINE. It is good to treat with PREDNISONE or DEXAMETHASONE from 2 days before the deworming drug until 2 days after. If you have a choice, ALBENDAZOLE is safer.
- FLUBENDAZOLE is a veterinary drug which may work without significant side effects.
- Treat SEIZURES with ordinary seizure medicines. Hospitals use high doses of PRAZIQUANTEL plus (PREDNISONE or DEXAMETHASONE) plus CIMETIDINE. It is safer for you to use the lower dose unless you are sure your patient does not have STRONGYLOIDIASIS or AMEBIC LIVER DISEASE.
- HYDROCORTISONE or PREDNISONE should be given before the deworming (anthelmintic) medicines.

DEHYDRATION

Cause: Body fluid loss.

Definition: Lack of an adequate amount of body water.

Entry category: Syndrome

Not ill to very ill; Class 1-3; Worldwide, very common everywhere. **Not a diagnosis!** Look for the cause of dehydration. Frequently the patient, if a child, also suffers from MALNUTRITION.

Age: Any, especially children. **Who:** Those with vomiting or diarrhea or not drinking or DIABETES. **Onset:** 1/2 hour to 2 days.

Clinical:

Necessary: The patient is thirsty if he has any dehydration at all. He may be constipated. His pulse will increase and his blood pressure decrease as he moves from a lying-down to a standing position. He may have a rapid respiratory rate. He will be making very little urine, if any, unless the dehydration is caused by DIABETES.

Severity of Dehydration:

➢ **Mild Dehydration:**

The patient is thirsty. The top of his tongue is dry but it is moist beneath his tongue.[1] He may have a rapid pulse and respiration.

➢ **Moderate Dehydration:**

The patient is thirsty. It is dry beneath his tongue. The top of his tongue has lengthwise grooves. His eyes are somewhat sunken, and his skin a bit loose on his upper, inner thighs.[2] He is not unconscious from the dehydration. He has a rapid pulse and respiration. His blood pressure is lower than usual and he faints easily.

➢ **Severe Dehydration:**

The patient is unconscious or lethargic. He has a fever from the dehydration alone. His skin is very loose, his eyes are sunken, and his entire mouth is dry. His pulse is fast and his respirations are both fast and deep. Complications: KIDNEY FAILURE, CATARACT.

Bush Laboratory: The patient's urine will be an intense yellow color and the specific gravity or urea nitrogen content will be elevated, unless the cause of dehydration

---

[1] If the patient is mouth-breathing, his tongue will normally be dry. In this case, check the inside of his lower lip; if that is dry, he is dehydrated.

[2] In elderly people whose skin is naturally loose, check the skin on the forehead. That remains tight longer than other skin.

is DIABETES. In that case the urine will be a light color but it will test positive for sugar with a urine dipstick.

Higher-Level Care. Level 3 or above. A hospital blood test will show an elevated blood urea nitrogen. *Facilities:* IV's and fluids. *Practitoner*: generalist, internist, pediatrician, senior nurse.

Treatment:

Patient care: Send the patient out for professional help, if possible. If this is not possible:

- **Look for a cause and correct it.**

If the patient refuses to drink, check his mouth for sores. If he is very lethargic or unconscious, you cannot give fluids by mouth but must start an IV or else give intraperitoneal fluid. (See Procedure 17 in App. 1, Vol. I, and *Symptom Protocols* 29, 47, and 56.)

Someone with DIABETES, either previously undiagnosed or out of control, can also become dehydrated. This patient must be sent out immediately. Dehydration resulting from uncontrolled diabetes must be treated differently than other kinds of dehydration. *Do not* use ORS to rehydrate, as that contains sugar. Instead, use *half-strength saline* (3/4 teaspoon or 4.5 gm salt in a liter of water; see Procedure 1 in App. 1, Vol. I.)

- **Determine the daily amount of fluids:**

The amount to be given in the first 24 hours is the sum of the *Dehydration Correction* and *Maintenance Fluid.* For subsequent days, only the maintenance fluids and correction for abnormal losses will be given.

Dehydration Correction Table

Cause	Mild	Moderate	Severe
Not drinking	30 ml/kg, ORS:water 50:50	70 ml/kg, ORS:water 50:50	100 ml/kg, ORS:water 50:50
Vomiting	30 ml/kg, ORS:water 50:50	70 ml/kg, ORS:water 50:50	100 ml/kg, ORS:water 50:50
Diarrhea	30 ml/kg, full strength ORS	70 ml/kg, full strength ORS	100 ml/kg, full strength ORS
Diabetes	30`ml/kg, 3/4 tsp (4.5 gm) salt per liter water	70 ml/kg, 3/4 tsp (4.5 gm) salt per liter water	100 ml/kg, 3/4 tsp (4.5 gm) salt per liter water

Dehydration Correction: Dehydration should be corrected the first day that you are caring for the patient. Determine the composition and amount to be given from the Dehydration Correction Table (above), based on the patient's weight and the severity of the dehydration.[1]

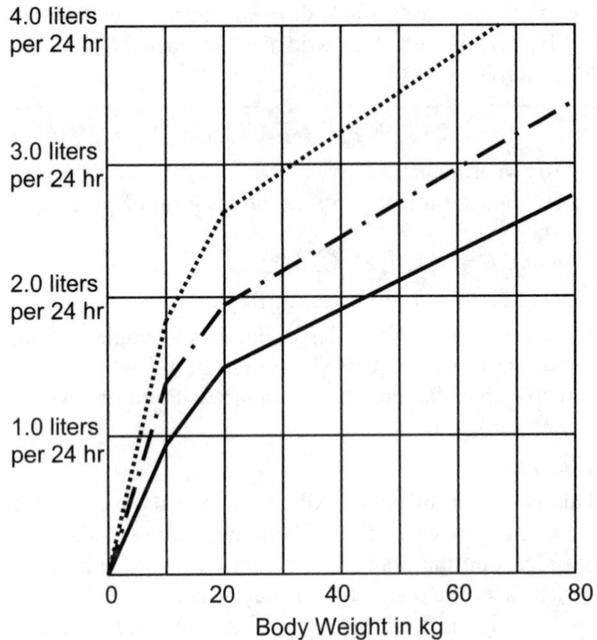

Maintenance Fluid Graph. Volumes per 24 hours, based on body weight.

A. Basic maintenance.
B. Either fever or hot environment.
C. Both fever and a hot environment.

Maintenance Fluids. In addition to correcting the dehydration, it is necessary to provide fluid to maintain his fluid balance, i.e., the fluids which would normally be needed for that period of time. Use ORS:water 50:50 for the maintenance fluids. But if the patient is diabetic, use *half strength saline.* Determine the volume per 24 hours from the curves on the Maintenance Fluid Graph (above).

First locate the patient's approximate weight on the horizontal axis of the graph, and then read off his daily maintenance fluid requirement from the vertical axis, using the appropriate curve. Use Curve A if there is no fever and it is not too warm. Use Curve B if it is hot weather (above 90°F or 32°C), *or* if the patient has a fever over 100°F (38°C.) Use Curve C if it is both hot and there is a fever.

Abnormal losses are the amounts of vomit or diarrhea that the person has lost in the previous 24-hours. It is added on Day 2 and subsequent days. Replace diarrhea by full strength ORS, and vomit by ORS:water, 50:50. Measure or estimate the amount of vomitus or diarrhea and replace it with an equal volume of fluid. If this is not done, your patient will remain dehydrated. In very dry climates, it may be necessary to provide additional fluid, at times up to four times the usual amount. Check

[1] The water from the inside of coconuts may be used instead of ORS. Add 1 teaspoon (5 ml) of baking soda to each liter of coconut water. But do not use the coconut water with KIDNEY FAILURE.

the inside of the patient's mouth daily. If it is moist he is getting enough; if it is dry he needs additional fluid.[1]

- **Fluid administration.**

Give 20 ml/kg quickly; give the remainder slowly over 24 hours. Give the fluid by mouth if the patient can swallow, or by stomach tube if he cannot swallow and is not vomiting.

If he is vomiting, try to settle his stomach with PROMETHAZINE. A *severely dehydrated, vomiting patient* who does not have diarrhea may be given plain, half-strength non-sterile saline by enema. He should be sent to a hospital but this will hydrate him meanwhile.

In case of vomiting plus diarrhea in a severely dehydrated patient, use intraperitoneal fluid. See Procedure 17 in App. 1, Vol I. Intraperitoneal fluids are acceptable to use with DIABETES.

- **Protect the eyes.**

With severe dehydration, the eyes are sunken so the lids do not properly cover them. The cornea is exposed, resulting in damage to the eyes and consequent blindness. You can prevent this by putting antibiotic eye ointment in the eyes and then covering them. The patient will pull the eye covers off when he wakes up.

- **Consider your patient's nutrition.**

If the patient is unable to eat or drink over more than a few days, he should be given calories, protein, and vitamins as well. Give the refeeding mixture used for malnourished children, as described in Chapter 5. For an adult, give about 1/4 to 1/3 of his daily fluid requirement as refeeding mixture. Once a day crush a multivitamin tablet and give this also.

DEMONIZATION

Definition: This refers to diseases, usually not following recognized patterns, brought on by animistic or occult powers.

Entry category: Syndrome.

Age: Usually older children or adults; **Who**: It can affect anyone, Christian or not, and those most susceptible are those who believe it does not exist or it cannot happen to them. **Onset**: Highly variable; if it is sudden it is commonly after an occult or emotionally traumatic experience.

Clinical:

Violent, emotional, upset, speaking in other voices, lethargy, weakness, seizures, jerking, day-night reversal, fatigue, paralysis, panic attacks, and unusual susceptibility to disease are common patterns. There may be depression, decreased appetite, and difficulty walking. Commonly the symptoms vary widely both qualitatively and in severity over hours and days; they are not constant. The following are common characteristics:

- An illness that does not make sense medically.
- A medical crisis right before a critical ministry obligation.
- An irrational hatred of a godly person.
- A seizure, panic attack, or other disruptive behavior in the context of Christian worship.

Similar problems: See Protocol C-10B. Demonization does not generally cause fevers; if there is a fever, consider cerebral MALARIA BRUCELLOSIS, and similar diseases. Other similar problems are ADDICTION, ALCOHOLISM, ATTENTION DEFICIT DISORDER, BERIBERI, PELLAGRA, RADIATION ILLNESS. PLANT POISONING due to mushrooms can both mimic and be a causative factor in this. Demonization can coexist with any of these.

Higher-Level Care. This is essential to rule out other causes of the problem. Referral should be to Level 3 or 4 at least. If the problem is due to demons, a Western-trained practitioner will probably tell you that it is psychiatric or psychogenic.

Treatment:

This is problematic since anyone with a Western education is likely to think you are crazy for suggesting the diagnosis. The effects are readily reversed by audible prayer in the name of Jesus, by Christian exorcism, or by both. National pastors are frequently helpful with treatment. It is essential to avoid treatment by traditional healers who are not mature Christians; they may use occult means which will make the final problem worse.

DENGUE FEVER

Cause: Virus.

Synonym: Breakbone fever.

Regional Notes: F, I, M, O, R, S, U.

Definition: A general whole-body viral infection, a type of ARBOVIRAL FEVER, caused by a virus transmitted by *Aedes* mosquitoes, mainly tropical. The mosquito that transmits the disease in urban and semi-urban areas is black with white spots on the joints of its limbs and also white spots along the sides of its body.

Includes: Dengue Hemorrhagic Fever (DHF), Dengue Shock Syndrome (DSS).

Mildly to severely ill; Class 1-3; Not Contagious; Regional; See the *Regional Notes*.

Age: Mostly children in Asia and the Pacific; both children and adults in the Americas. **Who**: Mosquito-bitten, especially urban dwellers, some rural people, mostly during the rainy season. There are major epidemics every 3-5 years in Asia and the Americas. The epidemics are every 5-6 years in the Pacific area. In the Americas there are additional small outbreaks every year. Dengue Hemorrhagic Fever is most likely to arise in areas that normally have many dengue cases. There are

[1] If the patient is mouth-breathing, the top of his tongue might be dry even when he is well-hydrated. In this case, check between his lower lip and his lower, front gums. If this is moist, he is probably doing well.

4 kinds of Dengue Fever; 1, 2, 3, 4; each person can get each kind only once. **Onset:** Suddenly, 2-15 days after the bite. The patient becomes very ill within less than 12 hours.

Clinical:

Necessary: Sudden onset of high fever and severe general body pain. The length of time from the first symptom to when the patient is in bed is less than 12 hours.

Usually: The patient has a fever which drops to normal about day 4 and then rises again after 1/2 to 3 days. With this second fever rise, the pains and depression are worse than before. He has aching or shooting pains all over, especially in the front of his head, in his back, and his eyes; the pains are particularly severe in his muscles, joints, and bones. His eyes hurt worse when he moves them to look sideways.

Commonly: Patients believe they will die. There is insomnia, nightmares, and depression. Constipation is usual. The patient may have a slow pulse relative to the fever. Local lore is helpful as the disease varies from place to place.

Frequently: An intensely itchy rash that fades with pressure develops with the first fever. It looks like a sunburn or like measles or like scarlet fever on white skin. It starts on the chest and the trunk and moves from there to the limbs and the face. It may involve the palms and the soles. Sometimes the skin flakes off. With the second fever, a rash develops in which, in Whites, the skin is red with white dots. Lymph nodes may be large and the abdomen, tender, causing confusion with ACUTE ABDOMEN. Watch for the rash and bone pain which are not present with ACUTE ABDOMEN.

Sometimes: He has chills, loss of appetite, fatigue, stiffness, and possibly a strange sense of taste. The liver may be large.

Occasionally: Symptoms include weakness, dizziness, light avoidance, red eyes, drenching sweats, sore throat, cough, nosebleed, pain with urination, pain in the groin and testicles, and crazy behavior. There may be neurological signs with dengue: lethargy, irritability, drowsiness, coma, seizures, a stiff neck, sharp, shooting pains down limbs, or paralysis. This might occur in either Dengue Fever or Dengue Hemorrhagic Fever, and in both adults and children, and may result in paralysis or recurring seizures (EPILEPSY). About 10% of patients with neurological symptoms die from the disease. Strange symptoms also might occur with this; do not discount the diagnosis just because your patient has some other symptom not listed here.

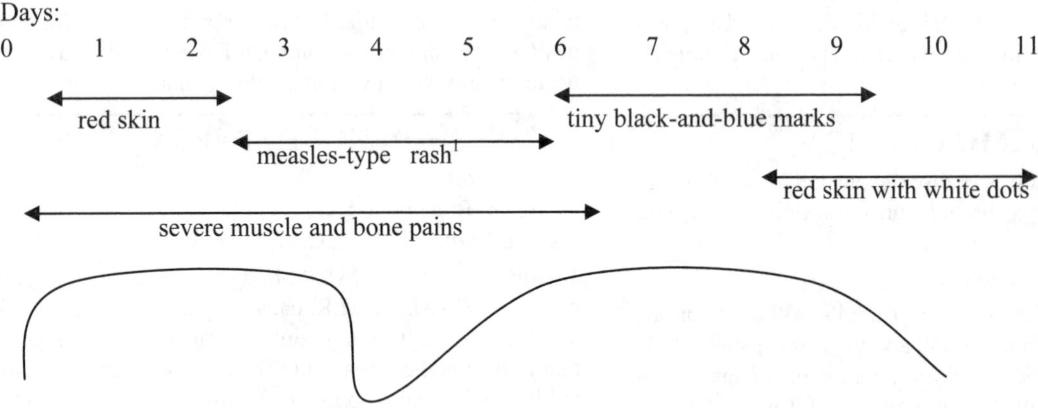

Dengue Fever. The general pattern of the fever; this may vary.

[1] This starts on the chest and trunk and moves from there to the limbs and the face.

Dengue Fever Complication: Dengue Hemorrhagic Fever (DHF

Entry category: Disease complication.

This is a major problem in Asia, the Pacific region, and Latin America. There have been major epidemics since WW 2 in Thailand, the Philippines, Indonesia, the South Pacific, Cuba, Nicaragua, and Brazil. It can occur almost anywhere.

Age: Any in the Americas; usually children and teens only in other areas. **Who**: Those for whom this is a second infection. **Onset**: Sudden

Clinical:

There may or may not be the ordinary signs and symptoms of dengue fever. With DHF the pulse will become rapid and the blood pressure will drop because plasma (watery part of blood) leaks from the small blood vessels. There may be abnormal hemorrhage and the liver will be enlarged. There may be rapid respiration and decreased urine. There may also be DENGUE SHOCK SYNDROME which is severe DHF that has progressed until it is life-threatening. It is treated like ordinary SHOCK.

Treatment of Dengue Hemorrhagic Fever*:*

See HEMORRHAGIC FEVER; the disease is not directly contagious so there is no risk with sending out on public transport

Complications of Dengue Fever: DEPRESSION may last for years. In some cases Reye syndrome, a type of LIVER FAILURE, develops during recovery. Its manifestation is severe vomiting. It requires immediate evacuation. When a pregnant woman gets dengue fever during pregnancy, near term, the infant may become very ill and die shortly after birth.

Similar Diseases: See Protocols C-2, C-8, C-9, C-13.

Bush Laboratory: Check hemoglobin, urine, and stool. Lab should show only ketones in urine unless HEMORRHAGIC FEVER has developed. In that cases there will also be blood in the urine. Do a torniquet test. The torniquet test might be negative and the patient has the disease but if it is positive he certainly has the disease or a similar HEMORRHAGIC FEVER: Inflate a BP cuff on an upper arm and leave it inflated for 5 minutes at a pressure half-way between the lower number and the higher number; then deflate it. The test is positive if there are more than 3 red spots per square centimeter on the skin below where the cuff had been. These might not be visible on very black skin. However, you might see the spots on the fingernails in that case.

Higher-Level Care. See Volume I, Appendix 13. *Laboratory:* A very sophisticated lab, Level 4 or above, can definitely diagnose the disease. In a Level 2 or above laboratory, there will be an increased hematocrit with development of DHF. *Facilities:* At Level 3 or above, IV equipment and fluids; monitoring equipment is desirable. *Practitioner:* An infectious disease specialist is ideal. A generalist or internist or pediatrician is acceptable.

Treatment of Dengue Fever:

Prevention: Mosquito control: don't keep house plants. Prevent mosquito contact with patients for 5 days after the onset of the illness. The kind of mosquito that carries dengue fever is the kind that bites during the day. The disease is not contagious; you will not get it by caring for a patient that has it, unless a mosquito transmits it from him to you. In rural areas, discourage monkeys from being around your house since they may act as a reservoir for the disease, keeping the local mosquitoes infected. Keep fish in containers that collect drinking water; they eat mosquito larvae. Lids or screens on water collection surfaces help. Clean water collection containers often. Temphos kills the mosquito larvae.

Patient Care: Prevent DEHYDRATION and keep the patient in bed. **Antibiotics are not helpful.** However, you may give ACETAMINOPHEN for fever, MILK OF MAGNESIA for constipation, pain medicines, etc. Do not use ASPIRIN since it may trigger bleeding or Reye's syndrome (a form of rapid-onset LIVER FAILURE).

Results: The disease lasts 1-2 weeks. Except for occasional LIVER FAILURE, it is not dangerous in an otherwise healthy person. Case-fatality rate is 1-15%.

DEPRESSION

Cause: Variable.

Regional Notes: F, O.

Definition: Either a feeling of sadness or a group of physical symptoms commonly associated with emotional sadness.

Entry category: Syndrome

Mildly to very ill; Class 1-4; Worldwide.

Age: Mid-childhood and older. **Who:** Those dealing with guilt or anger, especially if they find it hard to express the anger; religious people who are angry with God; anyone who has experienced a significant loss. (The loss is not always obvious. A job promotion may involve the loss of significant relationships.) **Onset:** May be sudden or gradual.

Clinical:

If the person cries or acts sad, depression is obvious. Many times, however, the patient is not consciously sad. Loss of appetite or eating binges (depending on whether the person is genetically slim or overweight), and change in bowel habits (either constipation or diarrhea) are usual. The patient may have a pressure-type chest pain. He may sigh or breathe irregularly. The most frequent symptom is alteration of the sleep cycle; the person has no trouble falling asleep, but wakes up very early and cannot get back to sleep. He may complain only of chronic fatigue. Also see STRESS as this is invariably associated.

Causative Diseases: DEMONIZATION may be causative. Depression may also be physiological. Childbirth, DENGUE FEVER, BRUCELLOSIS, DIABETES, TUBERCULOSIS, HEAT ILLNESS, and chronic pain from any cause, are some of the possible causes. Some families are prone to depression, so any stress will provoke it. Some women become depressed each month during the menstrual cycle.

Similar Diseases:

Malnourished patients: BERIBERI, PELLAGRA, ALCOHOLISM.

History of occult activity: DEMONIZATION

History of drug abuse: ADDICTION

Patient has an enemy: ARSENIC POISONING, DEMONIZATION, RADIATION ILLNESS.

History of a recent illness with a fever: DENGUE FEVER, ENTERIC FEVER, ARBOVIRAL FEVER.

Higher-Level Care. *Laboratory, Facilities:* Generally not useful except to exclude alternative diagnoses. *Practitioner:* generalist or internist is adequate; a psychiatrist is ideal.

Treatment:

Send the patient out if at all possible. Otherwise:

- Do not try to cheer the person up by telling him how good his life is! This only adds guilt to his depression.
- Teach him to mistrust his feelings by pointing out other cases where feelings do not reflect reality.
- Point out some aspect of his work that was helpful to you or someone else.
- Listen to him, encourage him to talk, and do not be critical of what he says.
- Urge him to exercise in spite of his depression; go for walks or go swimming together.
- Ask him about suicidal thoughts, and if he admits having them, ask if he has thought of how he would do it. Someone who has a specific suicide plan requires more help than you can give. Suicidal people are relieved to have someone ask; others do not take offense at this question. Take away the gun, rope, medication, or whatever he intended to use to kill himself.
- Beware of the person who was depressed and now is cheerful. One can attain peace by deciding on a suicide plan.
- If a depressed person gives away valuable possessions, he intends suicide even if he denies it. His gifts are a cry for help. In these cases, keep the person in view of a responsible adult until he can be sent out for professional care.
- Be aware that ALL antidepressant medicines (with few exceptions) are potent suicide agents. Giving a bottle of these to a depressed patient is asking for trouble.

DERMATITIS

See CONTACT DERMATITIS, TINEA, and CANDIDIASIS.

DIABETES

Cause: Hormone deficiency (Insulin)

Regional Notes: F, I, S, U.

Definition: Lack of the hormone insulin which helps sugars to enter into the cells of the body. This results in the starvation of the cells for lack of sugar, and excess sugar in the blood.

Mildly to very ill; Mild is class 2 and severe, class 4; Worldwide, variably common.

Age: Any. **Who:** Anyone, especially older folks and relatives of diabetics; this may be a consequence of severe MALNUTRITION, PANCREATITIS, or PLANT POISONING: Cassava. **Onset:** Usually over weeks.

Clinical:

In mild diabetes, the patient has thirst, excessive urination, increased appetite, and weight loss.

With severe diabetes he will have rapid respiration, rapid pulse, low blood pressure, vomiting, DEHYDRATION, SHOCK and loss of consciousness in addition. His breath may smell like glue (acetone). He may lose his sense of smell. He is apt to be lethargic before he becomes unconscious.

Complications: Blindness, heart problems, and bad circulation which may result in STROKE or KIDNEY FAILURE or GANGRENE. There may be impotence or sharp, shooting pains in the legs and feet. Females who are diabetic during pregnancy may have very large babies. Diabetics are prone to CANDIDIASIS. Because of lack of feeling, they may have deformed joints which move abnormally and look awful but are not painful.

Similar Diseases: If the patient is lethargic, see Protocol C-10. TAPEWORM can cause the increased appetite with weight loss. The subsequent abdominal pain, vomiting, etc. can look like INFLUENZA. There is no fever with diabetes and the respiratory rate is always fast. The leg pains might resemble BERIBERI, SYPHILIS, or rarely ARSENIC POISONING. The symptoms of low blood sugar with treatment may resemble alcohol intoxication.

Bush Laboratory*:* Urine has sugar and possibly ketones in it.

Higher-Level Care. See Volume I, Appendix 13. *Laboratory:* A Level 2 or above laboratory blood test shows a high blood sugar, positive serum ketones, and possibly abnormal blood electrolytes. *Facilities:* IV's and fluids, monitoring equipment if the patient is very ill. *Practitioner:* An internist is ideal, a generalist or pediatrician might be helpful. A Western-educated diabetic with experience managing his own diabetes might be helpful if other care is unavailable.

Treatment:

Prevention: Prevent MALNUTRITION or treat it early. Urge people to properly process cassava. Avoid a high-sugar diet and obesity.

Patient care: Varies according to the severity of the disease. Check the urine and then seek advice. Send out if at all possible; there is not much you can do otherwise.

Complications of treatment: Too much insulin, too much exercise, insufficient food, or another illness may drop the blood sugar too far; the patient becomes sweaty, shaky, and hungry. He may have SEIZURES, lose consciousness, and have permanent BRAIN DAMAGE. He needs sugar by mouth or stomach tube or rectum.[1]

Results: 2 hours to 1 day.

DIARRHEA

See TURISTA. This refers to ordinary diarrhea, caused by ordinary bacteria or viruses that do not cause disease in local residents who are used to them.

DIPHTHERIA

Cause: Virus-infected bacteria

Includes: Veld sore (Skin diphtheria).

Regional Notes: E, F, I, M, O, S, U.

Definition: This is an infection of the combination of a virus and a bacterium, causing a severe illness in unimmunized people, usually children.

Usually very ill; Class 2-4; Contagious, very; Worldwide, related to crowding and lack of immunization, more common in cooler areas. Frequently occurs in epidemics. The skin ulcer form is most common in hot, dry environments and during conditions of war.

Age: Any, but mostly children over 1 year old. Deaths occur mostly in those under 5 y.o. or over 40. **Who:** Not immunized; the D of DPT stands for diphtheria, as does the D in DT and dT. Occasionally an immunized person may get it. **Onset:** Incubation 1-10 days, variable onset, usually gradual; patients seek help within several days.

Clinical:

Necessary: Unimmunized patient, pain and a white, black, or gray leathery scum on the normally moist, pink parts inside the nose or in the throat. Nasal diphtheria starts out as a simple head cold with congestion and a slightly bloody, runny nose.

Usually: Usually if it affects the throat, the patient is very ill and the lymph nodes in the neck are enlarged, possibly causing the neck to swell. There is a low fever; with more severe and more rapid onsets there may be a high fever with a pulse more rapid than one would expect from the fever. There may be HEART FAILURE after one or more weeks. After 3-7 weeks there may be facial numbness, blurred vision; a nasal voice; difficulty speaking, swallowing or chewing; or shortness of breath. Usually after the head/neck symptoms, there is weakness of limbs (like polio), uncoordination especially in the dark, inability to feel limbs. There may be swings in blood pressure, pulse, and respiration. If the patient survives, these nerve symptoms usually resolve completely.

Maybe: The patient has foul breath. With nasal diphtheria there may be significant blood loss from the nose. He may not be able to open his mouth wide enough for you to see his throat. He may not be able to swallow or talk or move his eyes normally. If it affects the throat, he may be hoarse, short of breath or unable to speak at all.

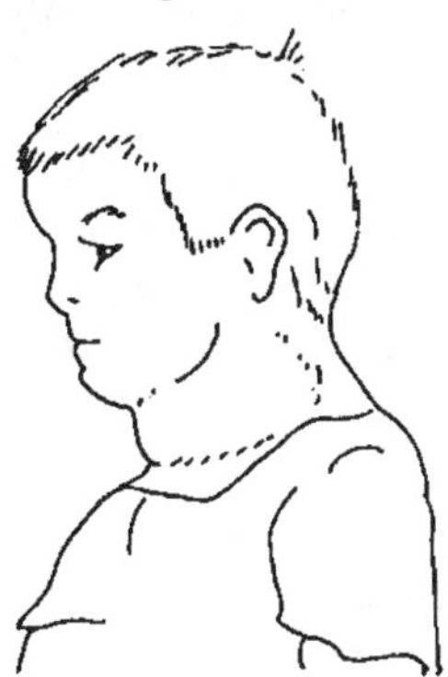

Diphtheria: The child is not fat; his neck is swollen.

Sometimes: If it infects just the nose, the patient has low fever, congestion, and a clear, white, or slightly bloody runny nose. It is a mild disease with no heart problems but it makes a rash on the upper lip resembling IMPETIGO.

Skin Diphtheria (Veld Sore):

This usually affects exposed parts of the body.

Occasionally: Diphtheria also infects the eyes, the ears, wounds, and the genital area, causing pain.

Sometimes: The organism causes a very painful blister which then bursts after 2-3 weeks, leaving a hole resembling a TROPICAL ULCER, 3-10 cm in diameter. There is a gray scum in the ulcer, a scum that sticks tightly to the surface below. This is extremely painful and tender to the touch. There may be multiple blisters and/or ulcers. The edges of the hole are distinct; they become swollen so the sore resembles a donut under the skin. The rim of the ulcer is turned inward. The edges may be undermined, hanging over the crater, but the overhang is never very much. These sores tend not to heal and they can cause the same symptoms as diphtheria of the throat: blurred vision; numb, cold limbs; trouble

[1] An Indian and Chinese vegetable, karela, lowers the blood sugar and can cause problems with diabetes control.

swallowing; uncoordination; weakness, especially in or near the involved limb.

Complications: Sudden death is possible up to eight weeks after the original illness. Heart failure may start early in the disease or during convalescence.

Similar Diseases:

If the patient is short of breath, see Protocol C-4.

Nasal diphtheria early on: Consider RESPIRATORY INFECTION, a common cold.

Neck swelling: See Protocol C-12.

Skin diphtheria: If the sore is on the genitals, hands, or face, see Protocol C-1: Sexually Transmitted Diseases. IMPETIGO may look similar but it does not make the person ill.

Bush Laboratory: There is almost always protein in the urine.

Higher-Level Care. See Volume I, Appendix 13. *Laboratory:* Hospitals, Level 3 or above, can do a culture and a stain. *Facilities:* There is a wide variety of equipment, Level 4 or above, that might be helpful. Antitoxin is extremely important; that is unlikely to be available below a Level 4 facility. *Practitioner:* Anesthesiologist for airway management; infectious disease specialist, neurologist, generalist, pediatrician, internist, surgeon.

Treatment:

Prevention: Immunize. Do not allow unimmunized people near the patient. If you have been exposed, take ERYTHROMYCIN or else benzathine PENICILLIN as for STREP INFECTION.

Patient Care: Send the patient out; this is essential. He will probably die without antitoxin. If this is out of the question, treat as follows:

If the skin is infected, treat it with antibiotic ointment. PENICILLIN, ERYTHROMYCIN, or CLINDAMYCIN must also be used. The patient must stay in bed for 3 weeks to decrease the chances of HEART FAILURE. Immunize the patient against diphtheria.

DONOVANOSIS

Cause: Bacteria.

Synonyms: Granuloma inguinale, granuloma venereum

Regional Notes: F, I, M, O, S, U.

Definition: A sexually-transmitted disease caused by a bacterium, Klebsiella granulomatis.

Not ill to very ill; Class 1-3; Contagious by direct contact between warm, moist body parts; Worldwide but just in restricted areas, mainly large urban areas and/or ports, particularly in South Africa, Brazil, India (southeast coast), New Guinea, New Britain, and aboriginal Australia. It is also found in Vietnam, the Caribbean, Zambia, and Zimbabwe. It is associated with poverty, prostitution, and poor personal hygiene.

Age: Usually sexually mature but sexually abused children can get it. **Who:** Sexually active, males more than females, Blacks more than Whites; poverty and poor hygiene promote transmission. **Onset:** Incubation 3 days to 3 months, occasionally up to 1 year.

Clinical:

Everybody who has the disease has symptoms, in contrast to other venereal diseases which may be without symptoms. However, in females where the sore is deep inside the vagina, the disease might not be obvious on the outside and there may be a delay before she knows she has it. There is no fever or fatigue unless there are complications with secondary infection. When this happens the prognosis is poor.

Necessary: The disease begins with a little painless pimple or crust on the skin; it may be dry or wet. It may resemble genital warts. The surface rubs off and it exudes a discharge. It bleeds readily. The surface of the ulcer may be below or above the skin surface. The disease spreads from the penis to the groins in males. Ulcers may develop on adjacent skin. There are no enlarged lymph nodes unless another infection starts on top of this but there may be a raw, pink or red, cauliflower-type bump(s) in the groin(s) that may be mistaken for large lymph nodes. The disease extends slowly on skin surfaces which then heal with scarring. It extends rapidly on the pink, moist areas which then do not heal. In females the ulcers are usually on the inner genital lips but sometimes inside. They become much worse during pregnancy. As in males, in the groins the lymph nodes are not enlarged but there may be pink or red cauliflower-like lumps. The disease may infect the inside of the mouth, causing swelling, bleeding, and loose teeth. If the sores develop internally (in women especially) they may become rapidly fatal due to severe tissue destruction. If there is secondary infection in addition to the donovanosis, there may be a very foul-smelling discharge.

Donovanosis: Primary ulcer. Edges are irregular.

Commonly: There is shiny, deep tissue showing in the middle of the ulcer. The edges are usually irregular, not smoothly circular or oval; they may be swollen. The ulcer looks more painful than it is. Pain, if any, is minimal.

Sometimes: Instead of an ulcer there may be a round area without any skin, with a raised-up, beefy-red, cauliflower-like raw surface. Sometimes this raised-up area has a split down the middle, like the split on the top of homemade bread. The appearance of these raised areas is rather distinctive, in appearance like the meat of a half-walnut lying flat-side down, but red instead of tan and sometimes lacking the split-center line.

Uncommonly: There may be some spontaneous healing in which case there is bumpy scar tissue, similar to KELOIDS. A primary sore might be in the mouth after oral sex. A primary sore might be on the skin other than the genital area, usually the head or neck.

Complications in females: In the vagina the ulcer may cause widespread destruction, forming holes into the bladder or rectum. Urine or stool then passes from the bladder or rectum into the vagina, causing incontinence and bacterial infection. These holes need surgery. After antibiotics, the scarring may interfere with urination, bowel movements, sexual activity, and childbirth. Untreated women may have massive, fatal bleeding at the time of childbirth.

Complications in males are PHIMOSIS or PARAPHIMOSIS.

Complications in either sex: the genitals may be swollen and eventually roughened like ELEPHANTIASIS. There may be bony lesions—a kind of OSTEOMYELITIS—and are associated with weight loss, fevers, night sweats, and fatigue. It can affect the spine or pelvis with dastardly consequences. See SPINAL NEUROPATHY.

Similar Diseases:

On the face: CUTANEOUS LEISHMANIASIS, CHANCROID, SYPHILIS, TUBERCULOSIS.

In the mouth: Like on the face and also SCURVY.

Wart/cauliflower surface: Secondary SYPHILIS, WARTS

With SYPHILIS the warty lesions are white or pale; with donovanosis they are red. SYPHILIS clears within 1 week of PENICILLIN treatment; donovanosis lesions do not clear with penicillin and they heal slowly over about 2 weeks or more.

Higher-Level Care. *Laboratory:* A stained smear can be done by a hospital lab, Level 3 or above. The name of the stain is Giemsa (GEEMsuh), if you have opportunity to ask before sending the patient. *Practitioner:* A sexually-transmitted disease clinic is ideal. Previous experience in dealing with this is essential. A surgeon might be necessary in advanced cases.

Treatment:

Send the patient out if at all possible. Follow Protocol C-1 if you are not sure of the diagnosis. If you are sure of the diagnosis, then treat as follows:

- Clean the area four times a day.
- Treat with an antibiotic: AZITHROMYCIN, DOXYCYCLINE, ERYTHROMYCIN, CO-TRIMOXAZOLE, CHLORAMPHENICOL, or STREPTOMYCIN, CIPROFLOXACIN, and CEFTRIAXONE are alternatives. If there is no response at all in a few days, add a second antibiotic; patients who are HIV infected should get two drugs in the first place. If the patient has intolerable side-effects from the antibiotic or if there is no improvement in a week, then the antibiotic needs to be changed. Generally a minimum of 14-21 days of antibiotic is recommended.
- Be sure to treat the sexual partner or partners for the disease.
- If you are not totally sure of the diagnosis or if the disease is not known to be common in your area, also treat for other genital ulcers according to the protocols under SEXUALLY TRANSMITTED DISEASEs.
- If an infected woman delivers a baby, it is important to treat the newborn.

Results: There is usually severe scarring. Healing is slow, over 2 weeks or more.

DOWN SYNDROME

This is the most common birth defect, also known as Trisomy 21 or Mongolism. Down Syndrome is the better term but MONGOLISM is used in this book because of space considerations in the *Symptom Index*. Look for details under MONGOLISM.

DRUG ERUPTION

Clinical:

This is a reaction to a drug which can be seen with PENICILLIN therapy for SYPHILIS, GRISEOFULVIN or KETOCONAZOLE for TINEA, and DIETHYLCARBAMAZINE for ONCHOCERCIASIS. It involves older more than younger patients and frequently causes swelling of lymph nodes. There are two types:

➢ **An Immediate Reaction:**

This is from the **first dose**, due to bacterial debris liberated by the death of microorganisms. The reaction is characterized by fever; tender, large lymph nodes; sore joints; transient bumps or HIVES on the skin; and worsening of the skin rash with the original disease. You should not stop treatment because symptoms resolve with continued therapy.

➢ **A Delayed Reaction:**

This occurs **7 to 20 days after starting** a new drug. (This can occur within hours after restarting a drug that was used previously.) Serious reactions are of five types and for these the drug must be stopped:

- Any reaction that involves blistering and/or peeling (EXFOLIATIVE DERMATITIS)
- Red/raised/target-like round skin swellings (ERYTHEMA MULTIFORME),
- Significant swelling, abnormal bruising, and areas of skin or flesh that appear to be dead.
- A reaction that affects the pink, moist parts of the body.

- Anything that looks like a sunburn but isn't sunburn by history.

Similar Conditions: See Protocol C-12 if the patient has large lymph nodes. Also see SERUM SICKNESS and KATAYAMA DISEASE.

DYSENTERY

Cause: Variable.
Synonyms: Bacillary dysentery (bacterial), Amebic dysentery (amebae).
Includes: Bacterial and amebic dysentery
Regional Notes: All regions, largely but not exclusively tropical.
Definition: An infection with bacteria or ameba which affects the lining of the bowel, usually causing diarrhea with blood, mucus, or both; plus fever, abdominal pain, or both.
Entry category: Disease cluster.

Mildly to very ill; Class 1-4 depending on severity; Contagious; Worldwide, relatively common, causes vary by region.

Age: Any. **Who:** Anyone, especially where sanitation is poor. For amebae the disease tends to be worse in children under 1 year old, in the malnourished, in pregnant women, and in persons taking PREDNISONE or related drugs. **Onset:** Variable. Sometimes there is a long history (weeks) of vague abdominal discomfort. Shigella (a type of bacterial dysentery) has an abrupt onset after a 2-4 day incubation. For amebae, the incubation is 1-2 weeks for small exposures but only days for major exposures.

Clinical:

Necessary: The patient has either constipation with lower abdominal pain (right or left) or else he has diarrhea with mucus, blood, and sometimes pus.

Sometimes: He may have cramps, headache, nausea and vomiting, or fever. His abdomen may be tender. DEHYDRATION will develop if the diarrhea is severe. Dysentery can be caused by either amebae or bacteria. Listed below are some of the characteristics of each. If the diarrhea is small amounts, very frequent, accompanied by fever, and 90% or more bright, red blood, it is due to bacteria, generally Shigella.

➢ **Bacterial Dysentery:**

Most common in children, the incubation is less than a week. It has a sudden onset and usually a group of cases occurs. The diarrhea stools are small in amount, frequent, (perhaps 100 times a day) gelatinous, and almost odorless or with an odor resembling rancid fat. The patient becomes ill rapidly; he usually **seeks help within 5 days**; the blood is bright red rather than reddish brown or black. Severe cramping pains are common. If the abdomen is tender, it is tender all over. The patient may have a high fever.

Complications: REITER SYNDROME; red lumps under the skin, sharp, shooting pains in limbs; SEPSIS; and death. There may be new ANEMIA and KIDNEY FAILURE.

➢ **Amebic Dysentery:**

More common in adults and in malnourished children. Its incubation is 20-90 days and it has a gradual onset; patients usually have the disease **more than a week** before seeking help. Bowel movements are infrequent (1-4 daily), large, and incredibly foul, their odor resembling that of very rotten meat. (A piece the size of the head of a pin will smell up a whole house.) There may be alternating constipation and diarrhea. The stool color is usually dark brown or black, rarely red. Mucus is usually more visible than blood. The cramping abdominal pains are usually localized to the right or left lower abdomen. The patient may have localized tenderness in his lower right abdomen, mimicking ACUTE ABDOMEN Type 2. Women may have vaginal or pelvic pain. With time the patient will lose weight and develop ANEMIA. *Complications*: DYSENTERY due to amebae may result in ACUTE ABDOMEN and in AMEBIC SKIN ULCERS.

Similar Diseases:

See Protocols C-1, C-3, C-9, C-11, C-14.

With anal pain: Consider CHLAMYDIA, LYMPHOGRANULOMA VENEREUM.

With heavy blood loss: If the bloody stool is part of a general bleeding problem (also with easy bruising and nosebleeds), see the protocol C-7. HEMORRHAGIC FEVER can be very contagious and almost always fatal.

Fever and/or very sick: ACUTE ABDOMEN—watch carefully for this; falciparum MALARIA, ENTERIC FEVER, MEASLES, abdominal TUBERCULOSIS, KIDNEY FAILURE, SEPSIS.

No fever, not real sick: TRICHURIASIS, STRONGYLOIDIASIS, HOOKWORM, or ARSENIC POISONING may also look similar. Consider SCHISTOSOMIASIS in some regions.

Bush Laboratory: Stool tests positive for blood in both kinds and positive for leukocytes with bacterial dysentery. Urine and hemoglobin are normal except possibly ketones in urine.

Higher-Level Care. See Volume I, Appendix 13. *Laboratory:* Hospital laboratories, Level 3 or more, can examine stools for white cells which indicate bacteria as a cause; they can culture the stool and can examine it for amebae. A lab report that reports bacteria in stool means nothing; stool **is** bacteria. The microscope test for amebae is specific but not sensitive. You need to have 7 negative tests done by experienced technicians on very fresh stool before you can conclude that there are no amebae. Usually it is easier to just treat rather than to go through that. *Practitioner:* Level 3 or more, internist, generalist, pediatrician; tropical/travel expertise is helpful.

Treatment:

Prevention: Eliminate flies, roaches, contamination of water supply. Avoid food from street vendors. Boil, filter, or treat all water. Soak food in iodine water or cook it. Wash hands after moving bowels; teach people to use leaves or toilet paper rather than rags to wipe themselves.

Patient Care:

If there is severe abdominal pain plus fever or if the diarrhea is associated with ground beef ingestion, then send the patient out for sure. He may develop new ANEMIA and KIDNEY FAILURE. Best not to use CO-TRIMOXAZOLE as this may increase the likelihood of this complication.

Send out if at all possible. Otherwise treat as follows:

- Rehydrate just as you would for plain diarrhea. (See TURISTA.)
- Use antibiotics: **If the patient has a fever**, treat with DOXYCYCLINE, COTRIMOXAZOLE, AMPICILLIN or CIPROFLOXACIN, assuming that it is bacterial. Also ceftriaxone or another 2nd or 3rd generation CEPHALOSPORIN is ideal. If it appears that the problem is due to shigella, avoid using AMPICILLIN. With a very sick patient, use CIPROFLOXACIN first; treat until a week after the diarrhea stops. NORFLOXACIN is a new, expensive, unproven drug that might work where others fail.
- If the patient is both very sick and either a child or pregnant or taking PREDNISONE (or a related medication), then treat for dysentery due to amebae also.
- **If there is no fever**, treat with METRONIDAZOLE, SECNIDAZOLE, TINIDAZOLE, or with [DOXYCYCLINE plus CHLOROQUINE] on the assumption that it is amebic. ERYTHROMYCIN may be used if the symptoms are not severe. The patient should respond within 2 days. If he does not, he may need surgery. After the treatment clear the remaining amebic cysts from the bowel with DILOXANIDE FUROATE or IODOQUINOL or PAROMOMYCIN. NIRIDAZOLE is an old/dangerous drug that might be available in some areas.
- PAROMOMYCIN is a new drug that works for both bacterial and amebic dysentery.
- If the dysentery responds to neither treatment for amebic nor treatment for bacterial dysentery, treat for HOOKWORM, STRONGYLOIDIASIS, or TRICHURIASIS. Since the cause of dysentery varies so much from one area to the other, seek local lore.
- If the patient is a baby, encourage continued breast feeding. Give ORS as well.

Results: 2-3 days.

EAR INFECTION, EXTERNAL

Cause: Variable.

Synonyms: Otitis externa, Swimmer's ear.

Definition: Infection of the ear canal.

Mildly to moderately ill; Class 1; Worldwide; common everywhere.

Age: Any. **Who:** Anyone, especially swimmers and those who have had foreign objects in their ears. **Onset:** Usually over minutes to hours.

Clinical:

Necessary: The patient has excruciating ear pain, made worse with moving the external ear.

Usually: He has no fever. If you have an otoscope, you will see red, possibly swollen, ear canals. The eardrums will be normal, but you probably will not be able to see that far in.

Higher-Level Care. *Laboratory:* Level 3 or more: If there is visible pus, a hospital can do a smear or culture. *Practitioner:* Ear-nose-throat specialist, generalist, internist, pediatrician.

Treatment:

If there is a fever or swelling of the ear canal, treat patient as for CELLULITIS. Otherwise mix CORTISONE CREAM or OINTMENT, and ANTIBIOTIC CREAM or OINTMENT, 50:50. Use the kinds labeled “ophthalmic” rather than the kinds intended for outer skin. Thin creams with water; thin ointments with oil. Put a few drops of this into the canal(s) four times a day until it is better plus two more days; you may use it more often. You may also use otic medication, drops intended for this problem. Put a cotton wick in the ear canal to absorb the drops and keep them against the inflamed walls. Use pain medicines. See Volume I, Appendix 1 for directions for the ear wick. *Results:* One day.

EAR INFECTION, MIDDLE

Cause: Variable.

Synonym: Otitis media.

Regional Notes: U.

Definition: Infection of the middle ear, the part between the ear drum and the brain.

Mildly to moderately ill; Class 1. Worldwide, generally common where colds are common.

Age: Any. **Who:** Anyone, especially children after a cold. **Onset:** Hours to a day or two.

Clinical:

Necessary: Moderate or severe ear pain. A child pulls on his ear or is fussy.

Maybe: He may have a fever and vomiting. Moving the external ears does not worsen the pain. The patient may feel dizzy-off balance, tilting, spinning, or being in a spinning room. Through the otoscope you will see red or opaque-white eardrums. There may be visible pus or enlarged lymph nodes in the neck.

Complications: MENINGITIS, hearing loss if not properly treated, FEBRILE SEIZURE.

Similar Conditions: The disease is easy to diagnose in older children and adults. A chronic, painless, draining ear that does not get better with antibiotics is probably due to TUBERCULOSIS. In children too young to localize pain, ear infection may resemble GASTROENTERITIS, MALARIA, URINARY INFECTION, or RESPIRATORY INFECTION. In all these conditions, there may be fever, vomiting, and diarrhea.

Higher-Level Care. *Laboratory:* Level 3 or above: If there is visible pus, a hospital can do a smear or culture. *Practitioner:* Most physicians unless the problem is recurrent.

Treatment:

Prevention: HIB immunization.

Patient Care: Send the patient out if at all possible. Otherwise treat as follows:

- Treat with PENICILLIN in adults, in children over 7 y.o., and in those under 7 y.o. who have had HIB VACCINE.
- Use AMPICILLIN in children under 7 y.o. who have not had the vaccine.
- In PENICILLIN-allergic patients, use either ERYTHROMYCIN with SULFADIAZINE or else COTRIMOXAZOLE alone as a substitute for AMPICILLIN. Use ERYTHROMYCIN alone as a substitute for PENICILLIN.
- CHLORAMPHENICOL can be used if other drugs are not available. Some recent drugs are AZITHROMYCIN and CLARITHROMYCIN but they are expensive.

Results: 3-5 days for ordinary infection.

Ebola Fever

See *Regional Notes* F.

ECZEMA

Cause: Allergy.

Definition: An allergic skin disease causing roughness and peeling of the skin.

Not ill to mildly ill; Class 1-2; Worldwide, common, runs in families.

Age: Any. **Who:** Anyone, family history of ALLERGY, affluent more than poor. **Onset:** Begins over a day or two; changes over that period.

Clinical:

Necessary: The patient's skin has a roughened rash, in circular patches or large areas. The skin may peel.

Commonly: It affects hands frequently immersed in soapy water. It may be itchy; may be on any part of the body.

Similar Conditions: CANDIDIASIS may be indistinguishable. Treat for ECZEMA first if the patient is from an allergic family; treat for CANDIDIASIS first if the area is hot and humid. Also consider SCABIES (much more itchy), TINEA (may be indistinguishable), PELLAGRA (malnourished patient), ARSENIC POISONING.

Higher-Level Care. *Practitioner*: Dermatologist.

Treatment:

Send the patient out to confirm the diagnosis. If this is not possible, treat as follows:

Find the cause and remove it. Use local ice packs 15 minutes three times a day. HYDROCORTISONE OINTMENT may be helpful. Some stronger steroid ointments may be available. In severe cases, PREDNISONE for a few days may help.

ELEPHANTIASIS, ENDEMIC

Cause: Variable.

Synonyms: Mossy Foot, Podoconiosis.

Regional Notes: F, I, M, R, S, U. Endemic elephantiasis is found only in tropical Africa, Central America, and northern India; there may be one location in Java.

Definition: Elephantiasis is massive swelling of a body part. The skin resembles that of an elephant. It is a tropical condition. Endemic elephantiasis only occurs in the legs and feet, not in the upper limbs, breasts, or scrotum.

There are two kinds of Elephantiasis: (1) Non endemic, caused by FILARISIS infection (*see* FILARASIS*),* and (2), Endemic, also called Mossy Foot, described below.

Age: Usually older teen-agers and adults. School-aged children, 8-10 years old, may show early symptoms. **Who:** Those who walk barefoot in certain geographical areas. These places are all at more than 1000 meters (3000 feet) in elevation with rainfall over 1000 mm (40 inches) per year; near old volcanoes with red, clay soil. **Onset:** Slowly over years.

Clinical:

Endemic Elephantiasis is swelling and thickening of the skin in the absence of FILARIASIS. Elephantiasis in this case always affects the lower limbs only. It is apparently caused by fine particles of clay from particular kinds of soil, which penetrate the feet of people who walk barefoot. This causes a blockage of the lymphatic ducts in the feet and legs, resulting in fluid accumulation and swelling. It usually starts on one side first and then spreads to the other side. The first symptom, usually in children, is burning pain in the feet and up the inside of the lower leg. Then there is itchy swelling, starting on the feet and progressing to the trunk. As it progresses, the foot swells and the skin becomes grossly wrinkled and rough, like an elephant's skin. Breaks in the skin develop which become infected.

Similar Conditions: See Protocol C-6B.

Higher-Level Care. In severe cases, surgical removal of the roughened skin and tissue is possible, but the results of the surgery are often poor. Much can be accomplished by the procedures described below under "Treatment," without surgery.

Treatment:

Prevention: Wearing shoes from childhood prevents the problem; in those already affected, shoes keep it from getting worse.

Patient Care:

- Wash three times a day with soap and water.
- Soak the feet, up to the ankles, in a bleach solution for 20 minutes once a day. This helps kill infections and will help stop the oozing out of fluids, which often occurs. The bleach solution is made by adding one teaspoon of ordinary bleach to 3 liters of clean water. (This should not be used if the patient has open wounds on the feet, however.) The use of topical antibiotic salves is also helpful.
- After soaking and drying the feet, apply WHITFIELD'S OINTMENT, once a day. This will help soften the rough, hardened skin. (Whitfield's Ointment is commonly available in pharmacies).
- Wrap the leg during the daytime with bandaging in order to minimize the swelling. At night, the leg should be elevated above the level of the heart.
- Shoes, or at least flip-flops, should be worn at all times, to prevent further irritation and infection of the feet. For patients with fully developed mossy foot, custom made shoes are necessary since no ordinary shoe will fit over the grossly enlarged feet.
- In children who are just beginning to experience the mossy foot symptoms (i.e., burning sensation), washing and soaking of the feet as described above, together with wearing shoes, will probably result in a complete cure.

ENCEPHALITIS

Cause: Usually virus.
Definition: An inflammation of the brain, usually due to a viral infection.
Includes: Many specific types which usually carry geographic names, e.g., Japanese B Encephalitis (for which see ENCEPHALITIS, *Regional Index* S). Many are listed under ARBOVIRAL FEVER. HERPES and HIV INFECTION can also cause encephalitis.
Entry category: Disease cluster or Syndrome
Regional Notes: All regions.
Very ill; Class 3; Usually not contagious; Worldwide, not common except during epidemics.

Age: Any. **Who:** Usually those insect-bitten or tick-bitten; see Vol. I, Appendix 10. Sometimes a complication of childhood diseases. **Onset:** Sudden; incubation about a week.

Clinical:

At least one symptom from Set 1 (below) and at least one from Set 2, all lasting for over 24 hours. In addition, there may or may not be a stiff neck.

- Set 1. One or more of the following:
  - A decreased level of consciousness
  - A personality change; new-onset crazy behavior.
  - Impaired judgment or inexplicable emotions
- Set 2. One or more of the following:
  - Fever.
  - Seizure, new-onset.
  - Abnormal feeling: asymmetrical new-onset numbness, tingling, unaware of body position, hot/cold insensitivity, loss of pain sensation.
  - Abnormal movement: new-onset, asymmetrical weakness or paralysis, trembling, uncoordination.

Complications: BRAIN DAMAGE, death.

Causative Diseases:
This may be caused by HERPES, MUMPS, MEASLES, CYSTICERCOSIS, TOXOPLASMOSIS, LARVA MIGRANS, ARBOVIRAL FEVERs, AFRICAN SLEEPING SICKNESS, MONKEYPOX, or LOIASIS. HERPES encephalitis presents with a 1-7 day history of a "cold" and then headache, fever, and bizarre psychiatric symptoms. If you see this pattern, sending for further care is very worthwhile because there are good medications to treat this whereas most of the other causes are not very treatable.

Similar Conditions: See Protocol C-10 and/or Protocol C-13. FEBRILE SEIZURE may look similar but the patient is totally normal once the fever is treated. It may be indistinguishable from TYPHUS, cerebral MALARIA, HEAT STROKE, or MENINGITIS. If in doubt, use antibiotics. RELAPSING FEVER may also be indistinguishable. The brain damage effects of LIVER FAILURE might be similar to encephalitis; sometimes a simple change of diet can make a big difference.

Higher-Level Care. Speedy referral is necessary. See Volume I, Appendix 13. *Laboratory:* A very sophisticated laboratory, Level 4 or above, can test the blood to determine the cause of the encephalitis. This can provide a prognosis regarding probable degree of recovery. *Facilities:* A well-equipped Level 4 or above intensive care unit. *Practitioner:* Infectious disease specialist, internist, pediatrician, neurologist, anesthesiologist, expert nursing care.

Treatment:

Prevention: Keep an ill patient under a mosquito net to avoid infecting local mosquitoes and transmitting the disease.

Patient Care: Sending out is mandatory. Until this is possible: Treat for SEIZURES if they occur. In malarious areas treat for MALARIA. For some types of encephalitis some viral drugs work well. If you cannot send out, place a stomach tube to provide food and water through the tube. See Appendix 1, Vol. 1. See Volume I, Appendix 8: for instruction in long-term care.

ENTERIC FEVER

Cause: Bacteria.
Synonyms: Salmonellosis typhi, Typhus abdominalis.
Includes: Typhoid fever, Paratyphoid fever.
Regional Notes: All regions.
Definition: An infection, primarily of the bowel, but extending to the body as a whole, caused by the bacterium *Salmonella typhi* or related organisms. It is largely but not exclusively tropical.

Entry category: Two diseases, nearly indistinguishable

Mildly to severely ill; Class 1-3; Contagious through body secretions; Typhoid is present worldwide and common in areas of unsanitary food and water supply; paratyphoid is mainly from unsanitary food. Both are most common in the Indian subcontinent, in Southeast Asia, and in the Caribbean.

Age: In nationals, it is most common in children and young adults; in travelers there is no age selection. **Who:** Anyone not immunized, particularly those eating foods from street vendors or prepared in an unsanitary environment. Those eating shellfish taken from water with sewage pollution; those who are taking treatment for GASTRITIS or PEPTIC ULCER are more susceptible. Patients who also have SCHISTOSOMIASIS are prone to relapse because the bacteria can hide in the parasites, away from the body's defenses. **Onset:** Usually incubation 1-3 weeks and gradual onset in typhoid which is more severe; may be sudden with a short incubation period in paratyphoid which is milder. A longer incubation time implies a more serious illness.

Clinical:

➢ **Classical Typhoid Fever:**

The diagnosis is difficult because of many symptoms in common with other diseases. The clinical diagnosis is defensible if any three of these five are present:

- Fever that has lasted over 7 days.
- Some abdominal symptoms: vomiting, diarrhea, constipation, pain, or any combination of these
- The patient is not alert and talkative; he appears withdrawn and inattentive. This is common in typhoid but uncommon in paratyphoid.
- His tongue has a yellow-gray coating.
- The patient cannot name the day and hour of the onset because it was gradual.

Necessary: The patient has a fever (unless he is a malnourished child). Either the fever is sustained (it goes up and down but is never less than 100°F [38°C]), and/or the patient has at least one of the following symptoms: headache, apathetic or crazy behavior, abdominal pain with constipation (early in the disease) or diarrhea (more common later in the disease), a cough, aching all over.

Usually: Other symptoms are extremely variable by region and by patient. Children over 2 y.o. are likely to have abdominal pain and a large, soft spleen, possibly also a large liver; those under 2 y.o. are more likely to have vomiting and diarrhea. The pulse may be slow relative to the fever, a phenomenon that develops during the second or third week. Bowel sounds are decreased or absent and the abdomen is swollen. The patient will not eat normally; he has loss of appetite and weight loss. His tongue has a gray-yellow coating.

Commonly: The patient is bedridden by the third day with typhoid, each day sicker than the previous day. Diarrhea, when it occurs, is usually in the third week, sometimes earlier; it looks like pea soup and smells foul. Late in the disease there are nervous changes: SEIZURES, mania or extreme apathy, depression, confusion, dizziness, crazy behavior, trembling, incoherent speech, uncoordination (see ENCEPHALITIS). The spleen or liver is sometimes enlarged and tender. When the spleen is enlarged, it is not greatly enlarged and it is soft rather than firm. Lymph nodes may also be enlarged.

Sometimes: There may be a red, sore throat or nosebleed. There are symptoms of PNEUMONIA (cough, chest pain), KIDNEY INFECTION (pain with urination, back pain), or MENINGITIS (severe headache, stiff neck). There may be a peculiar body odor similar to that of freshly-baked bread. If there is a rash, it is mainly or completely on the trunk, occurs in White people only, and looks like very slightly raised rose-colored freckles, 2-4 mm in diameter. If you push on them, they disappear but they reappear quickly when the pressure is released. They first occur on the seventh to the tenth day of illness. As each one disappears it leaves a brown stain in the skin.

Complications: Deafness, ANEMIA, PNEUMONIA, ACUTE ABDOMEN Type 2, BRAIN DAMAGE, MENINGITIS, HEART FAILURE, HEPATITIS, SEPSIS, BRONCHITIS. The disease may become chronic and relapsing, especially with SCHISTOSOMIASIS. The patient may bleed into his bowel and have bloody bowel movements, particularly after the first week of illness; he may be incontinent of urine and stool. This signifies a bad prognosis.

➢ **Mild Paratyhoid:**

This is just like ordinary INFLUENZA or GASTROENTERITIS; it resolves without treatment.

Similar Conditions: See the chart in Protocol C-2 for general fever, headache and aching; see Protocol C-4 if the patient is short of breath, C-7 for liver/spleen involvement, C-9 for abdominal pain, C-10 for lethargy, and C-12 for large lymph nodes.

Diarrhea: DYSENTERY and similar conditions.

With mental symptoms consider MENINGITIS, ENCEPHALITIS, MALARIA, HEAT STROKE, and similar conditions. TYPHUS may be indistinguishable. *Mediterranean genetic origin*, consider FAMILIAL MEDITERRANEAN FEVER.

Bush Laboratory: There may be protein in the urine. Stool may be positive for blood. Enteric fever does not cause urobilinogen in the urine but MALARIA does cause this.

Higher-Level Care. See Volume I, Appendix 13; speedy referral is necessary. *Laboratory:* The Widal test is useless. Latex agglutination is not reliable until after 9 days of illness. Culture of blood, stool, and urine is difficult; many must be done for one to be positive and results are never available before 48 hours. There are some new, better tests available at large hospitals and at smaller ones that have special kits. A MALARIA smear will be negative, and a white count will be normal. *Facilities:* At Level 3 or above, IV fluids and IV antibiotics. *Practitioner:* Infectious disease, internist, generalist; a surgeon is helpful for complications.

Treatment:

Prevention: Immunize. Both oral and injectable immunizations are available. Neither of these gives absolute protection; one must still be careful of sanitation in water, food, and personal hygiene. The immunizations only protect against typhoid, not paratyphoid.

- From Merieux, a single injection with minimal side-effects, only for those over 18 months old; immunity lasts for 3 years.
- Oral vaccine, Ty21a, one capsule every other day for 3 or 4 doses, also gives protection for 3 years. The oral immunization capsules must be swallowed whole and they must be kept cold until they are taken. The patient must not take PROGUANIL at the same time as the oral immunization; if he does, the immunization is likely to not work.

Patient Care: Send out if at all possible. If not possible treat as follows:

- Antibiotics of choice: For mild to moderate illness only, use AZITHROMYCIN. For severe disease Ceftriaxone (see CEPHALOSPORIN) is best.
- Alternatives: CHLORAMPHENICOL, COTRIMOXAZOLE, AMPICILLIN in areas where there has not been much prior medical care. In areas where there has been prior care (especially India) one must use a CEPHALOSPORIN, CIPROFLOXACIN,[1] OFLOXACIN, or GENTAMYCIN.
- Supplementary treatment: In very sick patients, use additionally (METRONIDAZOLE or TINIDAZOLE) plus (DEXAMETHASONE or PREDNISONE, or HYDROCORTISONE) for the first 3 days of treatment. This considerably reduces the death rate. Do not use ASPIRIN for fever.

[1] In India there is much resistance to CIPROFLOXACIN so if the patient is very ill, it is best to start with another antibiotic.

ENTEROBIASIS

Cause: Worm.
Synonyms: Oxyuriasis, Pinworm (American[2] term).
Regional Notes: E, F, U.
Definition: A bowel infestation caused by the worm *Enterobius vermicularis*.

Not ill; Class 1; Contagious; Common worldwide, especially crowded areas.

Age: Any, but especially children. **Who:** Anyone. **Onset:** Over a day or two.

Clinical:

Necessary: The patient has no symptoms at all or else rectal and genital itching, mainly at night; small children may just be restless and fussy at night.

Commonly: The child loses his appetite or starts to wet his bed after being dry for some time. Vaginal discharge is common in little girls. If you look at the rectal area with a flashlight a half-hour after bedtime, you will see little, white, wiggly worms that look like pieces of thread. They are mainly around the rectal opening and are less than a half centimeter long. They may be seen in the stool. They may cause vaginal itching.

Pinworm shown actual size, above a 1 cm marker.

Similar Conditions: TAPEWORM, Dwarf TAPEWORM, CANDIDIASIS, and food ALLERGY may produce similar rectal itching. There are no other kinds of worms that look the same.

Higher-Level Care. *Laboratory:* The eggs, deposited by the rectum, can be picked up on a piece of scotch tape which is then checked with a microscope.

Treatment:

Prevention: Treat all family members at the same time as well as children's friends. Recommend daily washing of bedding and pajamas for 2 weeks, very meticulous hand-washing after toilet or diaper change. Reinfection is common.

Patient Care: It is usually necessary to treat the whole family and to repeat the treatment weekly for 4 weeks. Use MEBENDAZOLE, ALBENDAZOLE, PYRANTEL PAMOATE, or THIABENDAZOLE. IVERMEC-

[2] That is, originating in the USA rather than in the UK. In the UK, "pinworm" refers to STRONGYLOIDIASIS.

TIN is 85% effective. PIPERAZINE works but must be given for 6 days.

EPIDIDYMITIS

Definition: Epididymitis is an infection of the collecting tubules of the testes, found on the back side of the testes within the scrotum.

Mildly ill; Class 1; Worldwide, common.

Age: Teens and older. **Who:** Males only; sexually active, physically strained. Any male can get it. **Onset:** Minutes to hours, sometimes a day or two.

Clinical:

➤ **Ordinary Epididymitis:**

Necessary: The patient has pain, swelling, or both in his scrotum. His testicle is tender, swollen, or both on its back side.

Maybe: Fever may be present.

Sometimes: The patient is tender into his groin and lower abdomen.

Occasionally: Both testicles are involved.

Complications: Rarely ABSCESS formation—check for a localized, red, tender area.

Causative Diseases: This may be due to a SEXUALLY TRANSMITTED DISEASE. If you suspect this, then you should treat the patient's sexual partner(s) as well.

➤ **Tuberculous Epididymitis:**

There is slow, maybe painless swelling of the testicle. There may be holes through to the outside of the scrotum. The epididymis (the back side of the testicle) will be hard and large, with an irregular surface. It will be only slightly tender. This is easily misdiagnosed as CANCER.

Similar Conditions:

Indistinguishable: MUMPS, FILARIASIS (early)

Pain but no tenderness, consider KIDNEY STONE.

Generalized illness: BRUCELLOSIS, TUBERCULOSIS, CANCER.

Mediterranean genetic origin, consider FAMILIAL MEDITERRANEAN FEVER.

Higher-Level Care. *Laboratory:* Evaluation for various SEXUALLY TRANSMITTED DISEASEs, Level 3 or above. *Practitioner:* Urologist is ideal; an internist or generalist is o.k.

Treatment:

If elevation and support of the testicle does not relieve the pain within an hour, send the patient out since he may have torsion (twisting) of his testicle, which needs surgery within 6 hours of the onset of pain.

Ordinary epididymitis: Keep the patient in bed, support his scrotum with towels between his legs, apply warmth to his scrotum, and use AMPICILLIN or SULFADIAZINE or COTRIMOXAZOLE. Follow Protocol C-1: Sexually Transmitted Diseases, if there was a possible exposure.

Tuberculous epididymitis: Treat for TUBERCULOSIS if it appears that that is the problem.

Consider FILARIASIS or CANCER if the problem does not respond to treatment.

Results: 2-3 days usually; 3-4 weeks for TUBERCULOSIS.

EPILEPSY

(*See also* SEIZURES.)

Regional Notes: F, M, R.

Definition: A chronic condition characterized by recurrent seizures as a result of head injury, heredity, some diseases affecting the brain, various drugs and/or poisons, lack of oxygen, or for an unknown cause.

Entry category: Syndromes

Age: Any; **Who:** Those with prior head injuries, with reactions to various drugs, or with hereditary seizures. Some children who have had a FEBRILE SEIZURE develop epilepsy. It may be a consequence of various illnesses; see ENCEPHALITIS and similar conditions. Those who begin to have SEIZURES as adults without any prior illness or head injury, probably have CYSTICERCOSIS if they eat pork. MEFLOQUINE, CHLOROQUINE, CIPROFLOXACIN occasionally cause this. **Onset:** Each seizure onset is sudden but the pattern of frequent seizures develops slowly over days to weeks.

Clinical:

See the description of seizures under FEBRILE SEIZURE. Not all seizures are like that; they vary greatly. Seek further information from other sources. Petit mal epilepsy manifests as staring, fluttering eyelids, lasting only a few seconds. Sometimes this occurs on awakening in infants and in teens.

Similar Conditions: See Protocol C-10. DEMONIZATION can cause seizure-like activity which usually happens in the context of Christian worship or prayer.

Higher-Level Care. See Volume I, Appendix 1.

Laboratory: Level 4 and above—EEG, many different blood tests. *Facilities:* Level 4 and above; many things can be helpful. *Practitioner*: Neurologist is ideal; a neurosurgeon or internist or pediatrician may be appropriate. The receiving facility should be a Level 3.

Treatment:

Send out if at all possible. The greater the frequency of seizures, the more urgent this is. Patients should be started on medicine to control the SEIZURES. This should be done under a physician's supervision but, lacking that, see PHENYTOIN SODIUM or PHENOBARBITAL in the *Drug Index*. Those who have been on medication and have either gained weight or have had a period of STRESS may again have seizures. They need to have their seizure medication dosage increased.

ERYTHEMA INFECTIOSUM

Synonyms: Fifth Disease, Parovirus B-19.
Cause: Virus; Parovirus B-19
Definition: Erythema Infectiosum is an infection with Parovirus B-19.
Not ill to moderately ill; Class 1; Contagious; Probably worldwide.
Age: Mostly children. **Who:** Those who have not yet had the disease. **Onset:** Sudden after an incubation period of about one week.

Clinical:

In children, initially there is a fever which responds poorly to fever medications, but there are no other symptoms. Then the fever suddenly drops as the patient develops a rash, first on the cheeks and then mainly on the trunk. In adults, there may additionally be sore joints, possibly with redness and swelling. In patients with SICKLE CELL ANEMIA or THALLASEMIA or OVALOCYTOSIS, there may be a crisis in which their anemia suddenly worsens.

Higher-Level Care. This is usually not helpful unless it is necessary for ANEMIA.

Treatment:

None, since the disease will run its course and cure itself. Transport to a hospital for transfusion might be necessary for patients with ANEMIA.

ERYTHEMA MULTIFORME

Clinical:

Necessry: This is a skin condition characterized by red (warm in Blacks), irregular areas on or under the skin, shaped like targets or donuts.

Maybe: These are symmetrical on knees, elbows, palms, soles, sometimes all over, sometimes on pink, moist surfaces. With time the skin may become crusted.

Commonly: There is a lighter red ring around a darker, inner reddened area. The problem usually starts on the limbs, usually the hairy surfaces. The center of the targets might be pale or violet. The individual areas last at least 7 days.

Causative Diseases: HERPES, a type of PNEUMONIA, AFRICAN SLEEPING SICKNESS, LYME DISEASE, TUBERCULOSIS, LEPROSY, RHEUMATIC FEVER, or some drugs,[1] vaccinations, or environmental toxins.

Treatment:

This is symptomatic. If it is caused by a drug (see DRUG ERUPTION), then you must stop the drug. If there are spontaneous blisters or sores on the moist, pink parts, or if this involves more than 10% of the body surface, this is very serious and the patient must be sent out. Do not use STEROIDs for treatment.

[1] *Commonly:* antibiotics (especially sulfa-type), IBUPROFEN and related pain medications, and medicines for SEIZURES.

ERYTHEMA NODOSUM

Definition: a skin condition characterized by red (warm in Blacks) lumps under the skin.

Age: It usually does not affect the elderly. **Who:** Mostly young females are affected. **Onset:** Unknown.

Clinical:

Necessary: The lumps are larger than a normal pimple, about 0.4 to 4 cm in diameter, with ill-defined edges. Initially red lumps become purplish, very tender, usually on the lower legs but may be on the arms. They change from hard to soft, change color, and possibly cause the skin to peel.

Sometimes there are also sore joints, fever, and fatigue. The joint pains last longer than the skin problem but eventually they disappear.

Causative Diseases: STREP THROAT, FUNGAL INFECTIONS, LEPTOSPIROSIS, TUBERCULOSIS, RESPIRATORY INFECTION, TULAREMIA, TYPHUS, CAT SCRATCH DISEASE, CHLAMYDIA, LEPROSY (being treated), or drugs such as PENICILLIN, BIRTH CONTROL PILLS, SULFA DRUGS; sometimes pregnancy or there may be no discernable cause.

Treatment:

This is symptomatic. They do not become ulcers; they heal in weeks without scarring.

EXFOLIATIVE DERMATITIS

Cause: Variable.
Includes: Toxic epidermal necrolysis, Scalded skin syndrome, Stevens-Johnson syndrome.
Definition: Exfoliative dermatitis is a skin condition in which the outer layer of skin peels off.

Entry category: Syndrome.

Moderately to very ill; Class 2-4; Worldwide.

Age: Any, but especially children and the elderly. **Who:** Malnourished, poor immunity, taking antibiotics. **Onset:** Usually sudden, over hours to a day.

Clinical:

Necessary: The skin blisters and then peels off in sheets, leaving red, raw surface beneath. There may also be spontaneous inflammation of the moist, pink parts of the body.

Maybe: There is a high pulse pressure. (See Symptom Protocol 2C.)

Similar Conditions: Burns, which you can distinguish by history. Also with certain kinds of MENINGITIS, some MALNUTRITION, and SEPSIS a similar condition may occur. Onyalai in South Africa may appear similar but the blisters are bloody.

Higher-Level Care. See Volume I, Appendix 13; speedy referral is necessary. *Laboratory:* Level 3 or above, blood chemistries to monitor the patient's fluid balance; possibly blood counts and cultures. *Facilities:* If severe, a Level 4 monitored bed and intensive care unit; in a hot, dry climate this is essential for all cases. *Practitioner:* Dermatologist, infectious disease specialist, internist, pediatrician, generalist.

Treatment:

Send the patient out for higher-level care.

- If the patient is a malnourished child who is not taking medicine, treat him with AUGMENTIN, one of the CEPHALOSPORINs, or CLOXACILLIN.
- If this developed in a patient who was taking an antibiotic, stop the antibiotic. Treat him with HYDROCORTISONE IV if you have it, or PREDNISONE, using high doses initially.
- In either case, treat the patient with large amounts of fluid as if he had a 50% burn. (See Volume I, Chapter 9.)

Results: Some improvement within 48 hours.

EYE INFECTION

Cause: Bacteria, virus.

Synonyms: Conjunctivitis, Pink eye. See also TRACHOMA.

Includes: Sty.

Regional Notes: M.

Definition: Eye infection (in this context) is an infection, usually bacterial, of the surface structures of the eye.

Entry category: Disease cluster.

Mildly ill; Class 1-3; Contagious, very; Worldwide, common.

Age: Any. **Who:** Anyone, especially those with poor hygiene. **Onset:** Hours to 1-2 days.

Clinical:

Necessary: Any one of the following: an irritated eye with pus; a red, painful bump on the upper or lower lid or the inside corner of the eye; a red, (burning) painful eye with tears; an eye that is swollen, with red lids and red around the eye, or with visible pus within the eye. The clear membrane over the white of the eye may be swollen. The patient may have an enlarged lymph node on his cheek in front of his ear. An infection caused by a virus causes a burning pain in the eye with a watery discharge. This continues for several days and then the white of the eye may turn partly or completely blood red. This cures itself. ANTIBIOTIC EYE OINTMENT prevents additional bacterial infection but it does not cure the viral eye infection. Sometimes patients with this problem develop an illness resembling POLIO: they are paralyzed for a period of time but the paralysis eventually disappears.

Causative Diseases: GONORRHEA, TULAREMIA, (in Europe, Asia, and the north coast of Africa), CHLAMYDIA.

Similar Conditions: REITER SYNDROME, ARSENIC POISONING, TRACHOMA, KERATITIS. See Protocol C-8 if the eyes are both red and painful. XEROPHTHALMIA can mimic and also may be associated with eye infection. You will see small amounts of white, foamy stuff in the corner of the eye, sometimes with wrinkles in the thin membrane next to the cornea. Check carefully! It is an important preventable cause of blindness and it can be subtle.

If eye infection occurs right after birth or if it is due to GONORRHEA or CHLAMYDIA, it is very severe. It may cause loss of vision very quickly. Treat for GONORRHEA and CHLAMYDIA both, also.

ALLERGY (vernal conjunctivitis) causes discharge that is white, thick, and sticky but does not look like pus.

See Protocol C-1 if this may be due to a SEXUALLY TRANSMITTED DISEASE.

Higher-Level Care. *Laboratory:* A Level 3 or above hospital lab can do a smear or culture or both. This will help to predict which antibiotic will work best. *Practitioner:* Ophthalmologist is ideal; internist or pediatrician might be helpful.

Treatment:

Prevention: Keep flies away from the patient's eyes. Wash the faces of children who come near the patient. Wash your hands after touching his face. If the patient is a newborn who developed the infection at less than a week of age, you should also treat both parents for GONORRHEA and CHLAMYDIA, whether or not they appear to have it. See Protocol C-1: Sexually Transmitted Diseases.

Patient Care:

- A pussy discharge indicates a bacterial infection which requires ANTIBIOTIC EYE OINTMENT plus (oral or injectable antibiotics). In newborns, treat for both CHLAMYDIA and GONORRHEA since it is hard to tell the difference without laboratory support. Newborns must be treated with antibiotic by mouth or injection in addition to ointment.
- In all cases, treat both eyes even if only one is infected. Be sure to use drops or ointment intended for eyes; the product must be labeled "ophthalmic".
- Use ANTIBIOTIC EYE DROPS every hour while awake, every 2 hours during the night until the problem improves. Then decrease the frequency to half that until it is entirely better plus 2 more days. Once the problem is improved ANTIBIOTIC EYE OINTMENT may be used every 4-6 hours instead. Ointment will blur vision for about 10 minutes.
- If there is a fever or red, swollen eyelids or a bulging eyeball, send the patient to a hospital. If you

cannot, treat with PENICILLIN plus CHLORAMPHENICOL also; this is potentially very serious.

- Infection with a small, localized bump on the eye requires only drops or ointment. Gently massaging the bump may be helpful. Never patch an infected eye.

Results: Should be evident in 2 days.

FAMILIAL MEDITERRANEAN FEVER

Cause: Heredity.
Synonym: Recurrent hereditary polyserositis.

Mildly to moderately ill; Class 2; Mostly in the Mediterranean area and the Middle East. Since it is a hereditary condition, it will affect those of this genetic background wherever they are located. The ethnic groups mainly affected are Jews (Sephardic, not Ashkanazi), Arabs, Armenians, and Turks. The carrier state affects between 1/3 and 1/5 of the population. It is autosomal recessive.

Age: Usually the first symptoms occur before age 20. **Who:** Those of Mediterranean genetic heritage; males more than females. **Onset:** Sudden; the pain peaks at 12-24 hours and then gradually gets better over about 4 days. The presence of the problem in family members and the recurrent nature of the illness in the patient are most distinctive.

Clinical:

Any one or more of the following symptom groups:

- *Most Commonly:* there is abdominal pain with vomiting and fever, a fast pulse rate, and possibly constipation. Diarrhea is unusual. This may resemble ENTERIC FEVER.
- *Sometimes:* Chest pain, worse with deep breathing, possibly with fever and shortness of breath, resembling PNEUMONIA.
- *Sometimes:* There may be ARTHRITIS, affecting the large joints symmetrically. This is particularly common and severe in Sephardic Jews.
- *Occasionally:* Red, swollen, painful skin, mostly affecting the legs below the knees, resembling CELLULITIS.
- *Other associated symptoms:* Headaches; sore throat; eye problems; swollen, painful testes; failure to grow in children.

Complications: PERICARDITIS, ARTHRITIS.

Similar Conditions: Many, including those listed above. If the patient is short of breath, see Protocol C-4; see C-9 for fever and abdominal pain. The recurrent nature of the disease and the family history should help distinguish this. The pattern of ARTHRITIS is similar to that in HIV INFECTION in Africa.

Higher-Level Care. *Laboratory:* None is useful in a rural setting but some large hospitals might have confirmatory lab tests. *Practitioner:* Someone with experience in dealing with this.

Treatment:

A diet low in fat and/or a diet avoiding chocolate, aged cheeses, and wine might be helpful. COLCHICINE taken daily will prevent attacks.

Favus.

See *Regional Notes* R.

FEBRILE SEIZURE

Cause: Fever (in children).
Definition: A seizure due to the rapid onset of a fever, occurring in a child less than 6 years old.

Entry category: Syndrome.

Moderately ill; Class 1; Worldwide, common.

Age: 3 months to 6 y.o. only, never older; patients younger than 3 months probably have MENINGITIS. **Who:** Any child who has a fever, especially one of sudden onset and rapid rate of rise, especially with MALARIA and EAR INFECTION. **Onset:** Sudden.

Clinical:

Necessary: Age under 6 y.o; fever started suddenly. A generalized seizure is a rhythmic jerking of the muscles of the body, usually including all 4 limbs plus the face, in a patient who is unconscious. A febrile seizure lasts less than 15 minutes and is always associated with a fever over 38 C. After the seizure stops, the child may sleep for up to an hour. The patient is alert an hour after the seizure. Physical exam is normal except for evidence of whatever illness originally caused the fever.

Caution: If the seizure involves just a part of the body or if it lasts more than 15 minutes or if there is more than one seizure, then there is something else wrong with the child and he should be sent out for further care.

Febrile seizure in a child

Complications: Rare if the seizure lasted less than 15 minutes. Occasionally EPILEPSY complicates febrile seizures for children who seize at age less than 1 y.o.

Similar Conditions: Watch carefully for MENINGITIS and cerebral MALARIA. If the fever responds to cooling and ASPIRIN or ACETAMINOPHEN and the child is alert an hour after the seizure stopped, it is unlikely that he has cerebral MALARIA or MENINGITIS. If he is still lethargic or has a second seizure in spite of being cooled, consider these options as well as HEAT ILLNESS and ENCEPHALITIS.

Higher-Level Care. This might be helpful but usually there is no time to get the patient there. However, this is mandatory, Level 3 or above, if the seizure recurs because then it is not an ordinary febrile seizure.

Treatment:

Prevention: Train mothers to cool children with fevers.

Patient Care:

Institute immediate cooling. Treat FEVER *per se*. Diagnose and treat whatever illness prompted the fever.

FELON

Cause: Bacteria.

This is a painful, tightly swollen, red or warm tip of a finger. See Chapter 10 in Vol. I whether or not there is a history of a wound.

FEVER per se.

Cause: Variable.

***Not a diagnosis; pursue a diagnosis.

Entry category: Symptom.

***Treat for this when fever is more than 39°C or 102°F unless the patient has VISCERAL LEISHMANIASIS. There are no other contraindications except those associated with the specific medications; look these up in the *Drug Index*.

Treatment:

Bathe the patient in cool water. Give ACETAMINOPHEN (Tylenol) and ASPIRIN, so the patient will get either ASPIRIN or ACETAMINOPHEN every 2 hours. Use IBUPROFEN instead of ASPIRIN if you are giving QUININE or if the patient is a child who has CHICKEN POX, ENTERIC FEVER, DENGUE FEVER, INFLUENZA, SEPSIS, or HEMORRHAGIC FEVER. Keep the patient uncovered and in as cool a place as possible, within reason.

FIFTH DISEASE

See ERYTHEMA INFECTIOSUM

FILARIASIS

Cause: Worm larvae.

Includes: Bancroftian filaraisis (Wuchereriasis) and Brugian filariasis.

Synonym: Elephantiasis, non-endemic.

Excludes: MANSONELLOSIS PERSTANS (see F and M *Regional Notes*).

Regional Notes: F, I, M, O, R, S, U.

Definition: An infection of the body with one of two particular kinds of worms and their larvae, *Wuchereria bancrofti* or *Brugia malayi*. It is a tropical disease. Bancroftian filariasis is the common kind and is most widespread. Brugian filariasis mainly occurs in Southeast Asia (see *Regional Notes* I, O, and S).

Not ill to very ill; Class 2; Regional; Mostly below 1200 meters (4000 feet), mostly rainy season, mostly heavily populated areas. See the *Regional Indexes*.

Age: Usually adults, both sexes. **Who:** Mosquito bitten. See Volume I, Appendix 10. In infected areas, almost everyone has the parasites. However, only expatriates and those with large numbers of parasites are apt to have symptoms. **Onset:** Variable; incubation is usually 8-12 months, never less than 4 or more than 18 months. In expatriates, symptoms may first occur after the person has left the tropics. Full-blown filariasis occurs within 1-2 years of the initial symptoms, except in children under 5 years old in whom it may take longer.

Clinical:

➢ **Initial Symptoms:**

Usually: The patient has or had episodes of sudden onset of fever with headache, chills, and sweats, resembling MALARIA. Expatriates tend to have a more sudden onset and a more rapid progression of the disease than nationals. Initially they may have just cough and wheezing, resembling ASTHMA.

Sometimes: There are no obvious symptoms like those listed above, but the patient just has enlarged lymph nodes.

Thereafter: The patient has one or more of the following numbered symptoms. With Symptoms 1 to 6, there are frequently multiple attacks which go away spontaneously, until the problem finally persists. In Wuchererian filariasis, the upper and lower legs and genitals may all be affected; in Brugian filariasis, the genitals are rarely affected and the legs are affected only below the knees. However, the arms and breasts are commonly affected.

➢ **Full-blown Filariasis:**

- A body part is painful, red, swollen, and stiff, with large, tender lymph nodes in the armpit, groin, neck, or elbow areas, maybe with a mild fever and a general flu-like illness. The swelling is slow-filling at first; it may become rapid-filling later.
- The patient's scrotum is painful and swollen.
- An arm or leg or breast is painful, with red streaks, large lymph nodes, and high fever.
- The patient's scrotum is painful, red, and swollen and he has a high fever. This was of sudden onset.
- The lymph nodes in the patient's groin are swollen and painful.
- The patient's groin nodes are very large but not painful.
- The patient's urine is milky, and it may be pinkish also. He had flank or belly pain before his urine turned milky. He may have a fever. (But generally not in Brugian filariasis.)
- In advanced filariasis, the patient may have ELEPHANTIASIS: darkened, thickened skin and a huge limb, breast, or scrotum. The swelling usually progresses from the trunk to the feet.

- The patient may have a painful, swollen joint, usually a knee or ankle, which promptly gets better with DEC. It may be hard to distinguish this from a joint infection due to TUBERCULOSIS.

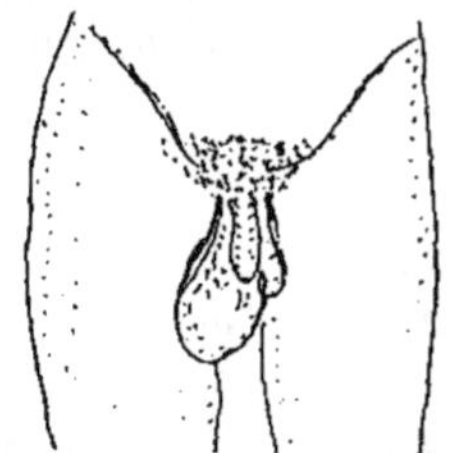
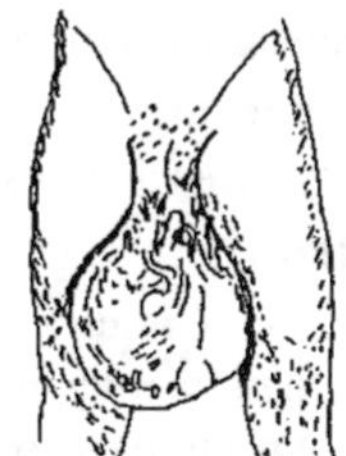

One testicle on the left is mildly swollen; the ones on the right are very swollen.

Complications: ARTHRITIS, KERATITIS, GLAUCOMA Another complication is tropical pulmonary eosinophilia: TPE. Patients have a severe, dry cough and wheezing that is worse at night, and many eosinophils (a kind of white blood cell) in their blood. It responds to DEC. TPE is neither common nor rare.

Similar Conditions: *Limb swelling*: See Protocol C-6B.

Breast swollen: MASTITIS is indistinguishable and far more common in most areas.

Scrotum swollen or painful: HYDROCELE, EPIDIDYMITIS, KIDNEY INFECTION, HERNIA (skin thin or normal, not thick), FAMILIAL MEDITERRANEAN FEVER

Bush Laboratory: Urine may test positive for blood. Urine may be milky. Milky urine due to filariasis, if it is left to settle in a glass jar, will divide into three layers: creamy on top; milky in the middle; and red, muddy urine on the bottom.

Higher-Level Care. *Laboratory*: Hospitals can do a blood test for the disease but usually the test will be negative until the disease has been present for a very long time. They either draw blood at night or give a dose of medicine before drawing it. If a hospital lab accidentally finds the parasites in someone who does not have any symptoms, this does not need to be treated. Usually an ordinary blood count shows many eosinophils; this abnormality does not go away with time. However, there are many other diseases that can also cause eosinophilia. If the number of eosinophils is normal, then the patient does not have this disease. *Practitioner*: Someone with experience in this disease; tropical/travel expertise is helpful.

Treatment:

Prevention: Eliminate mosquitoes and treat infected persons. The mosquitoes that cause this in most places are night-biters. Mosquito nets are helpful in disease prevention. To prevent the disease, use DIETHYLCARBAMAZINE (DEC) once a month. An alternative is DEC-medicated salt, using 4 parts DEC to 1000 parts salt, and keeping the community on it for at least 6 months out of the year. If you put a whole community on preventive medicine, the problem in the mosquitoes will disappear; then even those who do not take DEC can not become infected. Check the precautions in the Drug Index. IVERMECTIN may also be used for mass treatment or mass prevention.

Patient Care: Send out if possible. If this is not possible treat as follows:

- Medications: (DIETHYLCARBAMAZINE plus ALBENDAZOLE) (the best of the options), or (ALBENDAZOLE + IVERMECTIN), or (DIETHYLCARBAMAZINE + IVERMECTIN).
- Patients with milky urine should stay in bed with the foot of the bed raised up on cinder blocks.
- For swollen legs, wrap the entire foot and leg in an elastic bandage, from the foot up, not too tightly.
- DIPHENHYDRAMINE is helpful for both red streaks on the legs and reactions to DIETHYLCARBAMAZINE; HYDROCORTISONE or PREDNISONE may be used in severe cases. Reactions can be severe. You must have DIPHENHYDRAMINE and EPINEPHRINE available. Keep the patient near you for about an hour after the first dose.

Additional information: There are bacteria called Wolbachia connected with filariasis. Wolbachia are essential for female filarial fertility. Killing them with DOXYCYCLINE helps cure the disease. If possible, the DOXYCYCLINE should be given for 6-8 weeks before other drugs; at least 3 weeks is necessary.

Results: Advanced elephantiasis of the lower limbs usually does not improve much with drug therapy; swelling of the upper body will decrease over 2-4 years with treatment.

FISSURE

Cause: Unknown.

Synonyms: Rectal fissure.

Definition: An abnormal crack in the perimeter of the anus.

Mildly ill; Class 1; Worldwide, neither rare nor common.

Age: Any, infants and children as well as adults. **Who:** Anybody. **Onset:** Days to weeks.

Clinical:

Necessary: Severe pain with bowel movements.

Maybe: Pain between bowel movements, small amounts of blood on the stool or on the toilet paper, a visible crack by the rectum. There is so much pain that the patient holds his bowel movements and thus becomes constipated.

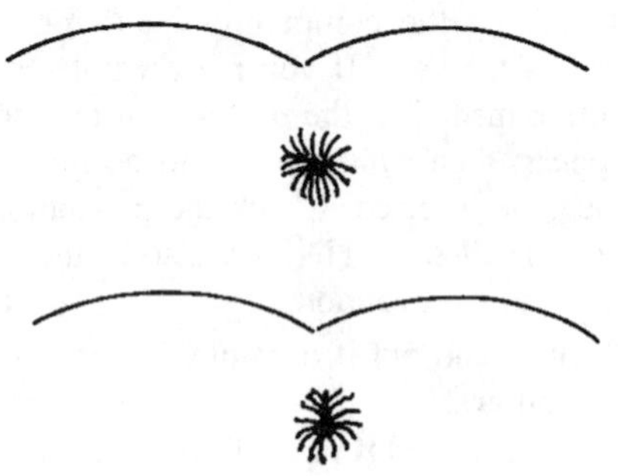

Similar Conditions: The pain of HEMORRHOIDS and some SEXUALLY TRANSMITTED DISEASE's are similar but the appearance of the rectum is different. Also consider Protocol C-1: SEXUALLY TRANSMITTED DISEASES.

Higher-Level Care. *Laboratory,* level 3 or above can eliminate alternative diagnoses. *Practitioner*: A surgeon is most appropriate; a generalist might be helpful.

Treatment:

Use warm sitz baths for 10-15 minutes after each bowel movement. See the directions in Appendix 1 of Vol. I. Use laxatives or enemas if needed and suppositories with LIDOCAINE OINTMENT smeared on the outside. The suppositories must be held half-way in with the fingers; if they go all the way in, they do no good. *Results:* Slow healing over 1-2 weeks.

FISTULA

This is an abnormal hole that forms between the rectum and the vagina or the bladder. It may be due to DYSENTERY due to amebae, or to DONOVANOSIS or some other infection, or it may be due to injury from abnormal sexual activity or from childbirth. The end result is that gas and stool from the rectum passes out through the vagina (in females) or from the penis in males. This might be corrected surgically.

FLEAS

Cause: Insect. (*See also* Appendix 10 in Volume I.)
Entry category: Infestation.

Aggravated but not ill; Class 1; Contagious; Worldwide.

Age: Any, but especially children. **Who:** Those near animals or other humans who have fleas. **Onset:** Almost immediately after exposure.

Clinical:

Necessary: Little, itchy, red spots are visible where the fleas bit the patient.

Sometimes: There are visible fleas—little jumping creatures, usually black.

Complications: Rodent fleas[1] can transmit some TAPEWORMS, PLAGUE, and TYPHUS.

Similar Conditions: LICE, ticks, MYIASIS, very tiny flies. Bedbug bites look similar but the creatures are nocturnal and they look like tiny, black dots. They do not jump and they are very seldom seen. The red bite marks appear each morning frequently in straight lines.

Bush Laboratory: A strong magnifying glass will help to identify these as fleas.

Treatment:

Prevention: It is unwise to kill rats and other rodents without first treating their holes with insecticide; fleas leave dying animals to bite humans. When fleas are a nuisance, they are controlled by cleaning floors thoroughly with soap and very hot water, by using repellents, sprinkling detergents or powdered insecticides in corners and rodent holes, and by using flea collars on pets. Wash floors weekly with 5-10 ml of 50% MALATHION in a bucket of water.

Patient Care: Bathe. Remove and wash all clothing, towels, and sheets. 0.5% MALATHION and pyrethrin flea powder work well for humans.

FLUOROSIS

Cause: Excessive fluoride.
Regional Notes: F.
Definition: Fluorosis is a toxic condition caused by chronic consumption of excess fluoride, usually in water.

Not ill to very ill; Class 1-4; Regional in very few places.

Age: Mostly children. **Who:** Anyone drinking from a particular contaminated water source; nursing infants of affected mothers. **Onset:** Variable.

Clinical:

Necessary: The patient has dark, irregular discoloration of the teeth and bone deterioration in the neck.

Sometimes: The neck bones deteriorate, putting pressure on the spinal cord, causing symptoms resembling SLIPPED DISC: sharp shooting pains in the shoulders, arm, and hands, plus floppy weakness of some part(s) of the upper limb(s). See SPINAL NEUROPATHY.

Similar Conditions: Bone TUBERCULOSIS or BRUCELLOSIS, in which case there is always a fever, at least off and on. Otherwise SLIPPED DISC which may occur because of some injury or for no good reason

[1] There are many kinds of fleas. Each kind prefers one kind of host. Hence there are rodent fleas, human fleas, chicken fleas, cat fleas, and dog fleas. However, if the preferred host is not available, fleas will bite whatever warm-blooded creature they can find. Hence humans might be bitten by rodent fleas.

at all. The dark teeth discoloration can resemble a side-effect of TETRACYCYLINE taken during childhood.

Higher-Level Care. Probably only Level 5; a toxicologist should manage the patient.

Treatment:

Prevention: The fluoride cannot be removed by boiling or filtering. An entirely different water source must be found.

Patient Care: None in the village situation and possibly none in regional hospitals either. The advice of a toxicologist by e-mail or telephone might be most helpful.

FOOD POISONING

Cause: Bacteria.
Regional Notes: O, S, U.
Entry category: Disease cluster

Mildly to very ill; Class 2-4, depending on severity; Worldwide, generally common.

This description refers mainly to meats and cooked foods with meat in them. Poisoning from plants, traditional medicines, and oils is listed under PLANT POISONING. ARSENIC POISONING is listed separately, as is LEAD POISONING. For botulism, see PLANT POISONING for a description though sausage is a common offender since it usually contains some plant products.

Age: Any except exclusively nursing infants. **Who:** Anyone eating tainted food. **Onset:** Sudden; from a few hours to 2 days after the meal.

Clinical – Three Kinds:

➢ **Ordinary Food Poisoning:**

Necessary: The patient has severe abdominal cramps with vomiting, diarrhea, or both. Pain is usually extreme, but tenderness to touch is minimal. Pushing on the abdomen does not greatly aggravate the pain.

Usually: Everyone eating together becomes ill within a few hours of each other.

➢ **Botulism**

This is caused by homemade sausages mostly; it can be from beans. At first there is vomiting and diarrhea followed by weakness, especially as regards the head and neck—double or blurred vision, difficulty swallowing, dry mouth, then weakness of the rest of the body, possibly urinary and stool retention. See also the entry under PLANT POISONING.

➢ **Aflatoxin**

This is a poison that comes from a kind of mold. It causes liver CANCER, with a slow onset. It is worst in animal products: dairy, seafood, and poultry but may also occur in plant products such as peanuts and grains.

Similar Conditions: Many. The pattern of disease with all those eating together getting sick within a few hours is distinctive. With infectious diseases, the incubation period varies by days. GASTROENTERITIS and PLANT POISONING may otherwise be indistinguishable. ACUTE ABDOMEN, types 1 and 2, have tenderness which food poisoning does not. Type 3 may be similar. ARSENIC POISONING usually causes bloody diarrhea and may be associated with food. On the island of New Guinea and possibly elsewhere, PIG-BEL may be indistinguishable. Botulism resembles POLIO and DIPHTHERIA.

Higher-Level Care. *Laboratory and Practitioner:* Level 3 or more might be helpful. If the patient has botulism, higher-level care is critical—there is an antitoxin which is most useful. Antibiotics are not useful.

Treatment:

Try to send the patient for professional care. If this is not possible the treat as follows:

- Use PROMETHAZINE for vomiting. Give ORS for diarrhea. Use pain medication if you have any. DICYCLOMINE or CHAMOMILE TEA often helps with abdominal cramping. It will not eliminate the pains but may make them tolerable.
- If the incubation period was less than 6 hours, do not use antibiotics. If the incubation period was more than 6 hours plus there is fever, use DOXYCYCLINE if the abdominal pain is mild to moderate. Use ERYTHROMYCIN if the abdominal pain is severe or if DOXYCYCLINE doesn't work.
- Check for DEHYDRATION and treat it if necessary.

FROSTBITE

Definition: Cold injury of the skin.

Clinical:

The skin surface is white and it may be frozen hard. Depending on the severity, the patient may or may not have pain.

Higher-Level Care. This is mandatory for severe cases.

Treatment: Initially, gently warm the body part. Then treat it like a burn. See Chapter 9 in Vol. I.

FUNGAL INFECTION

Fungal infection of the skin: *See* TINEA and CANDIDIASIS.

Fungal infection of the vagina: *See* VAGINITIS.

G6PD DEFICIENCY

This is a genetic defect in persons of Mediterranean heritage: Jews, Arabs, Turks, Spaniards, Greeks, Slavs, Italians, and some ethnic groups in Southeast Asia. It also occurs in the Irish and in Hispanics in the Amercas, because of migrations. It is more common in males than females since it is inherited recessively on the x chromosome. Generally there are no symptoms except if the person takes certain medications. The most common problematic medications are those used for MALARIA, particularly PRIMAQUINE.

GALLBLADDER DISEASE

Cause: Variable.
Synonyms: Gallstones, Biliary colic.
Includes: Cholecystitis, Cholangitis.
Regional Notes: F, I, M, O, R, S, U.
Definition: Gallbladder disease is a malfunction of the gallbladder. This inhibits the bile made by the liver from being properly stored and released.
Entry category: Disease cluster.

Moderately to very ill; Class 2, class 3 with fever; Worldwide.

Age: 20's to 50's, occasionally younger; children with ASCARIASIS. **Who:** Anyone, especially females who have had children, those overweight, and those who have THALLASEMIA or ASCARIASIS. **Onset:** Suddenly for a given attack, usually within a few hours of eating. Recurs unpredictably.

Clinical:

Necessary: The patient has severe upper-right or upper-middle abdominal pain which goes to the shoulder blade (usually the right side) or back.

Usually: The pain lasts 2-5 hours and goes away by itself. The patient passes excessive gas.

Sometimes: The patient vomits. Pressing on the patient's abdomen, just to the right of center, and below the ribs as you have him inhale deeply reproduces or aggravates the pain.

Occasionally: Patients may have fever or JAUNDICE. Children with ASCARIASIS causing this have pains every 15-30 minutes, lasting 5-10 minutes, and they vomit.

Complications: PANCREATITIS and ACUTE ABDOMEN.

Causative Diseases: LIVER FLUKE in regions E, S, and O only; any disease causing ANEMIA with a large spleen. It also occurs in those eating a high-fat diet.

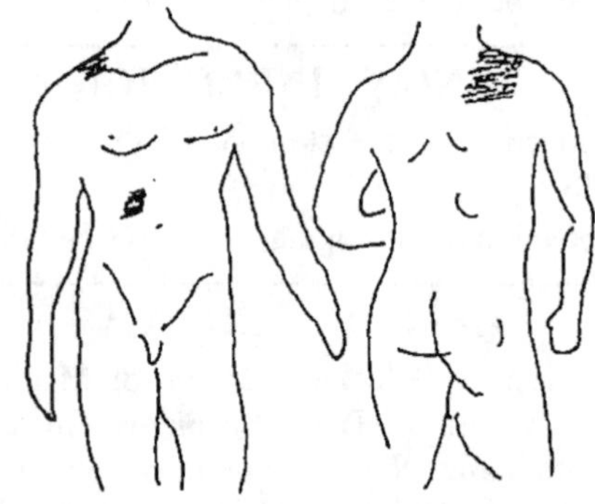

Gallbladder disease: The shaded areas are where the pain is usually felt.

Similar Conditions: See Protocol C-7 since liver and spleen problems are frequently indistinguishable. Also see Protocol C-9 for fever plus abdominal pain.

With JAUNDICE: See Protocol C-5.

With a fever: Consider ENTERIC FEVER, HEPATITIS, AMEBIC LIVER DISEASE, PNEUMONIA involving the right lower front of the lung (check respiratory rate).

With no fever: Consider HYDATID DISEASE (check geography), ACUTE ABDOMEN, GASTROENTERITIS (pain all over, not so localized). MANSONELLOSIS PERSTANS may be similar but there are usually joint pains also.

Higher-Level Care. See Volume I Appendix 13. *Laboratory Facilities:* A Level 4 hospital can do blood tests, x-ray, and ultrasound. *Practitioners:* A surgeon is most likely to be helpful.

Treatment::

Send the patient out if possible. If not possible, treat as follows:

- Try DICYCLOMINE and a low-fat diet. Send out for surgery when it is convenient if there is no fever; send immediately if there is a high fever, meanwhile treating with GENTAMYCIN or an injectable CEPHALOSPORIN.
- With ASCARIASIS, give pain medication and LOPERAMIDE and wait for worms to emerge, up to 6 weeks if there is no acute abdomen. Do not give any medication to kill the worms until after the symptoms are gone; then kill them.
- If the patient has a complication, send out quickly, treating for ACUTE ABDOMEN in the meantime. There are occasional deaths.

Gallbladder of Raw Fish

See Regional Indexes O, S. This is used as an ethnic remedy.

GANGRENE

Definition: Gangrene is the death of tissue.

Age: Mostly older. **Who:** Mostly poor health, obese, or both. **Onset:** Variable.

Clincial:

The problem is usually in a limb, resulting in coldness, color change, swelling, pain, maybe a high fever and lethargy, and frequently a watery discharge or pus with a bad smell. There may be dark blisters that break and peel or the limb may become pale. The skin might be chalk white or coal black and crusty. The patient may have a fast pulse out of proportion to the fever, pain out of proportion to the appearance. There may be gas bubbles coming out of the skin.

Causative conditions: This can be caused by poisonous snake bite, injury, TROPICAL ULCER, DIABETES, PLANT POISONING with Claviceps or Ergot, and occasionally SPOTTED FEVER, TYPHUS, BARTONELLOSIS, or FROSTBITE. It may be caused by the plant toxin, ricin (see PLANT POISONING: Ricin).

Similar Condition: See Protocol C-11. CANCRUM ORIS is a type of gangrene.

Higher-Level Care. This is mandatory; a surgeon at a Level 4 or above facility. See Volume I, Appendix 13. Speedy referral is necessary.

Treatment:

Sending the patient out or amputating the limb (*see* Chapter 11 in Vol. I) are the only ways to save his life. There is no sense in wasting antibiotic if surgery is out of the question. In the meanwhile, antibiotics should treat all possible germs: Use CEPHALOSPORIN, plus CIPROFLOXACIN plus METRONIDAZOLE.

GASTRITIS

Cause: Bacteria, sometimes drug side-effects, dietary indiscretion.

Definition: Gastritis is an inflammation of the stomach.

Clinical:

See PEPTIC ULCER. Gastritis is similar except it is an inflammation, not an ulcer. The person is likely to have burning upper abdominal pain that is worse with hunger and partially relieved by food. At times the pain may be aggravated by food, especially by hot-spicy foods and by coffee. The patient may also have nausea, vomiting, and a lot of gas passed by rectum.

Higher-Level Care. Laboratory and a gastroenterologist might be helpful to exclude alternative diagnoses.

Treatment:

If sending the patient out is impossible, treatment is the same as PEPTIC ULCER. Usually diet change and ANTACIDS suffice. Sometimes antibiotics are necessary.

GASTROENTERITIS

Cause: Virus, dietary indiscretion, other.

Synonyms: Gastroenteropathy, Stomach flu

Regional Notes: F, R, S.

Definition: Gastroenteritis is (usually) a viral infection of the stomach and intestines.

Entry category: Syndrome

Mildly to moderately ill; Class 1; Contagious; Worldwide, very common.

Age: Any, especially infants. **Who:** Anyone, especially travelers and recently weaned children. **Onset:** Variable.

Clinical:

The patient does not have a significant fever with this (not over 100°F or 38°C).

Necessary: The patient has any one or more of the following: abdominal pain, nausea, vomiting, diarrhea. The diarrhea contains no blood or mucus.

Frequently: He has very active bowel sounds and some abdominal tenderness.

Similar Conditions:

With a fever: Many; check carefully for other alternatives, especially if the patient is quite ill! If the patient has a fever over 100°F, he probably has something other than gastroenteritis.

With no fever: Consider ACUTE ABDOMEN, HEAT ILLNESS, GIARDIASIS, GALLBLADDER DISEASE, FOOD POISONING, KIDNEY FAILURE, PLANT POISONING: Castor beans, Mushrooms, RADIATION ILLNESS.

Higher-Level Care. This excludes other diagnoses.

Treatment:

- Treat diarrhea with ORS.
- Treat vomiting as VOMITING per se.
- Use DICYCLOMINE or CHAMOMILE TEA for abdominal pain.
- Check for DEHYDRATION, sending the patient out if it develops and you cannot keep up with fluids.
- If the problem is persistent or severe or both, try ERYTHROMYCIN, as this helps for one particular type of gastroenteritis; stop the drug if it makes the problem worse.
- In infants it is essential to give high-calorie food supplements for at least 1-2 weeks after the problem resolves. *See* MALNUTRITION.

GIARDIASIS

Cause: Protozoa.

Synonyms: Beaver fever, Giardia enteritis, Lambliasis.

Regional Notes: E, F, I, O, R, S, U.

Definition: Giardiasis is an infection by *Giardia lambia.* It is not only in the tropics, but tropical/travel expertise is helpful.

Not ill to very ill; Class 1; Contagious (fecal-oral transmission). Worldwide; it occurs in dry as well as humid areas, and cold as well as warm. It is common throughout the United States.

Age: Any except exclusively breast-fed infants. **Who:** Those drinking contaminated water, children more than adults, expatriates more than nationals, particularly those who had no prior exposure to the disease. It does not occur in exclusively breast-fed infants. It can also spread by person-to-person contact, both sexual and otherwise, or through contaminated food. Animals get the disease and pass it on to humans via their droppings into water supplies. People can develop immunity to giardiasis but only after multiple exposures. **Onset:** Incubation 1-45 days, usually 1-2 weeks; onset is then sudden.

Clinical:

Note: Giardiasis does not cause fever! Also, it is no worse in HIV-infected persons than in others.

Necessary: In nationals, the disease is without symptoms or else causes a mild, chronic diarrhea. Babies have a persistent, odorless, watery diarrhea, possibly with nausea, vomiting, or both. Expatriate adults have watery diarrhea, frequently explosive, with much gas. It may come so fast that the patient is incontinent. It is foamy, floating, and very foul smelling. In mild cases foul gas alone may be present.

Usually: There are loud, rumbling bowel sounds.

Maybe: There is mild to moderate abdominal pain. Nausea and vomiting are common in any severe case.

Occasionally: Children fail to thrive and gain weight, but they have neither diarrhea nor vomiting.

Complications: In severe cases, there may also be loss of appetite and vomiting with consequent DEHYDRATION from both the diarrhea and vomiting. Patients may develop MILK INTOLERANCE from having giardiasis. The problem may cure itself or become MALABSORPTION. See Protocol C-14.

Similar Conditions: GASTROENTERITIS, TURISTA, FOOD POISONING, KIDNEY FAILURE, CHOLERA (spectacular diarrhea and painful muscle spasms), MALABSORPTION from any other cause. See Protocol C-14.

Higher-Level Care. *Laboratory:* Stool or fluid withdrawn from the duodenum may be checked with a microscope. Many specimens may be required before one is positive; the test is not sensitive but it is specific. It will almost always be negative early in the disease. ELISA is a test to detect giardia in stool—both sensitive and specific but unlikely to be available in developing areas. Blood tests are not helpful since they remain positive for a long time after the infection is gone. *Facilities:* IV fluids and associated equipment. *Practitioner:* Level 3 or above, generalist, pediatrician, or internist.

Treatment:

Prevention: Filter or boil all drinking water or treat it with IODINE in an emergency. Bleach does not work for giardia; heating water to almost boiling works for giardia but not for ENTERIC FEVER. Use outhouses and keep animals away from wells.

Patient Care: Try to send the patient out. If this is impossible treat as follows:

- TINIDAZOLE single dose is best. Otherwise: METRONIDAZOLE, ALBENDAZOLE, SECNIDAZOLE. NITAZOXANIDE is a new drug that reportedly works.
- YOGURT is helpful if the patient has MILK INTOLERANCE (a common complication).
- Give rehydration fluid if the patient is dehydrated. (See DEHYDRATION.)
- If the patient has ANEMIA, Vitamin B_{12} might be helpful.
- Oral PAROMOMYCIN may work in pregnant women; it is not absorbed into the blood stream and therefore does not affect the baby. Use the same dose as if you would for amebic DYSENTERY.

GINGIVITIS

This refers to infected gums; treat like CELLULITIS.

GLAUCOMA

Cause: Unknown.
Regional Notes: F.
Definition: Glaucoma is an abnormally increased pressure of the fluid within the eyeball.

Not ill to very ill; Class 3-4 depending on type and drugs you have; Worldwide, not common.

Age: Usually adults. **Who:** Anyone; susceptibility varies with race. **Onset:** Suddenly for acute, slowly for chronic.

Clinical:

In both kinds, if the patient closes his eyes and you gently push on his eyeball through the lid, the eyeball feels hard in comparison to a normal eyeball. In acute glaucoma pushing makes the pain worse.

➢ **Acute glaucoma**

This causes a sudden onset of sharp, aching eye pain, frequently with nausea. The patient is almost always over age 60. The eye is red, the cornea is hazy, and vision is poor. The patient may see rainbows or halos around lights. This may happen and then go away and then happen again several times before one final severe attack. It is usually on one side only, and usually happens when the patient is in dim light. The white of the eye may have a bluish cast. The pupils may be irregular or oval rather than round, with a vertical long axis.

➢ **Chronic glaucoma**

This causes gradually decreased vision with peripheral vision decreasing first and most. The patient develops very narrow tunnel vision. This may occur on both sides. The patient may see halos around lights. It is painless.

Similar Conditions: See Protocol C-8.

Higher-Level Care. *Facilities:* Hospitals may have a special instrument to measure eye pressure. *Practitioner*: Optometrist, ophthalmologist, some generalists, internists, or surgeons.

Treatment:

Send the patient out if possible. Speed is of utmost importance in acute glaucoma. Put drops in the eye to make the pupil small. (This is the opposite of the kind used for a scratched cornea.) PILOCARPINE is most frequently used. ACETAZOLAMIDE, a water pill used to hasten acclimatization to high altitude is useful also. PILOCARPINE drops alone are used in chronic glaucoma. They must be used for the rest of the patient's life.

GOITER

Cause: Iodine deficiency or excess.
Regional Notes: F, I, O, R, S, U.
Definition: Goiter is a swelling of the thyroid gland on the lower front of the neck.

Entry category: Symptom

Usually not very ill; Class 2; Regional, especially inland and high altitude areas.

Age: Any. **Who:** Those living in affected areas; those eating a diet high in cassava, cabbage, soy beans, bamboo shoots, or food originating in the salt water seas. **Onset:** Months to years, usually during childhood and adolescence.

Clinical:

Necessary: Swelling of the center-front of the lower neck, just above the breastbone, maybe extending to the sides. It is generally not tender. The patient may complain of difficulty swallowing and a choking sensation. The patient may wheeze or be short of breath when lying down or raising his arms.

Occasionally: Symptoms of THYROID TROUBLE, usually low-thyroid but occasionally high-thyroid. Babies born to mothers with goiter may have CRETINISM. Iodine deficiency may cause frequent spontaneous ABORTIONs.

Similar Conditions: None.

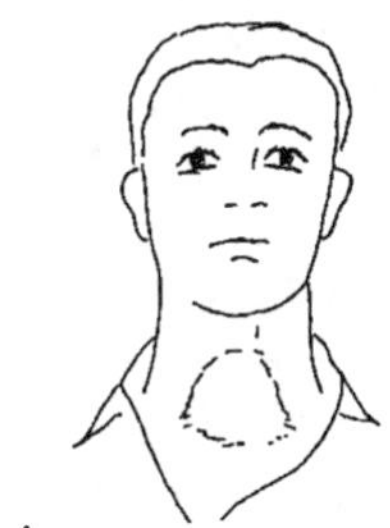

Goiter - medium sized.

Higher-Level Care. *Laboratory:* Blood tests may be helpful to determine what medication, if any, is most useful. This will require a Level 4 or more facility. *Practitioner*: Internist for initial evaluation; a surgical referral might be necessary. The surgery is one that can easily go wrong so it is important to get a surgeon who has extensive experience with this.

Treatment:

Prevention: In areas where most of the diet is derived from the sea, the problem is too much iodine. In these areas, supplement the diet with food grown inland. In areas remote from the sea, or where people do not eat sea foods, use iodized salt, treat drinking water with iodine occasionally, or use any kind of sea food in moderate amounts. If the cause is cassava, the water in which the cassava is boiled should not be used and the cassava should be properly processed before being eaten. In some areas public health officials inject young teens with iodinated oil.

Patient Care: It is best to send the patient out for professional care. If this is not possible:

- Don't treat older patients having lumpy goiters with iodine. It will not reduce the size of the goiter and it may cause major problems.
- If there is no CRETINISM in the area or if there is only one patient with goiter, do not use the following treatment! Send the patient to a Level 4 or more hospital; he may have CANCER.
- Give IODINE made up as straight LUGOL'S SOLUTION or else tincture of IODINE diluted 1:3 with water; use this in the same dose as LUGOL'S SOLUTION. (See the Drug Index for details.) You can put small amounts of iodine solution in a plastic bag and have the patient put her finger in once a week and lick it. This will be sufficient iodine to make the goiter become smaller slowly, over a long period of time. Caution the patient against becoming impatient and overdosing.

Complication of treatment: THYROID TROUBLE of the high-thyroid type. Watch for this and discontinue iodine treatment at the first sign.

GONORRHEA

Cause: Bacteria.
Synonyms: Clap, Dose, Gleet, Strain, Drip.
Regional Notes: F.
Definition: Gonorrhea is a sexually transmitted bacterial infection of the genital tract, caused by the bacterium Neisseria gonorrhea.

Not ill to very ill; Class 1-3; Contagious; Worldwide and very common everywhere.

Age: Usually adults or newborns, sometimes children. **Who:** Sexually active, sexually abused, and infants born to infected mothers. **Onset:** Symptoms begin in males within two weeks of exposure; in infants within the first 10 days of life; in women usually only many months after exposure.

Clinical:

There are almost always symptoms in men but most women have no symptoms. However, even without symptoms they have the disease, pass it on, and develop complications.

➢ **Ordinary gonorrhea:**

Necessary: Pain with urination (either sex) or a discharge (at first scant mucous, later much pus) coming from the penis or eyes or (in females) pain with intercourse. There may be a history of these symptoms without their being present when the patient is seen.

Sometimes: The affected part may be red. Eyes always are. Shortly after exposure, the disease may cause mild URINARY INFECTION symptoms in females, similar to URETHRITIS in males. Female patients commonly have a vaginal discharge and abdominal pain. There may be a tender, red, swollen gland on the genital lips.

➢ **Rectal gonorrhea:**

This may occur in females with contamination from the vagina or from anal intercourse. In men it is most often from homosexual acts. Many times there are no symptoms. If there are symptoms, there will be a pus discharge, rectal pain or itching, burning with passing stool, bleeding, or constipation.

➢ **Throat gonorrhea:**

This is most often from oral sex. Many times there are no symptoms. If there are symptoms they are likely to be fever, sore throat, visible redness or sores in the throat, and large lymph nodes in the neck.

➢ **Disseminated gonorrhea:**

This can cause ARTHRITIS. Initially there are pains in multiple joints on both sides of the body, usually less than 4 joints, without obvious redness and swelling. There may be inflamed tendons over the hairy surfaces of the wrist, hand, knees or ankles. Along with this there may be (in either sex) a rash consisting of small bumps or blisters with red halos around them, mostly on the hands and feet. These are painless but tender to touch and there is a countable number. Fever, if there is any, is low. Then there develops an intense inflammation of one joint only, with obvious redness and swelling.

Complications: Gonorrhea may cause KIDNEY FAILURE, ARTHRITIS, HEART FAILURE, PELVIC INFECTION, and MENINGITIS. Males may have holes through the skin in the crotch through which urine leaks out. The hole at the end of the penis may swell shut, then heal and scar so urine does not pass easily. There may be swollen lymph nodes in the groin (either sex), a red, tender, swollen testicle, and infection of the prostate (PROSTATITIS) or bladder or both. It may cause male infertility but that is rare. It is the most frequent cause of female infertility.

Similar Conditions:

Penis: URINARY TRACT INFECTION, URETHRITIS of other causes, CHLAMYDIA.

Female genitals: CHLAMYDIA.

Eyes: EYE INFECTION.

Throat: STREP THROAT, MONONUCLEOSIS, DIPHTHERIA.

Skin: CHICKEN POX, insect bites, pimples, SHINGLES.

Joint swelling: Protocol C-6.

Higher-Level Care. *Laboratory:* A smear of pus is stained, or a culture may be done. *Practitioners:* generalist or internist or pediatrician; a referral to a surgeon might be necessary.

Treatment:

Prevention: Anyone who is exposed to a known case of gonorrhea must be treated. After the treatment, the person is still contagious for 48 hours; he should abstain from sexual activity during that time.

Patient Care: See Protocol C-1 for sexually transmitted diseases. Most gonorrhea now is resistant to PENICILLIN and DOXYCYCLINE.

Gonorrhea in homosexuals or acquired in urban areas: do not use CIPROFLOXACIN, OFLOXACIN, or similar drugs. One of the CEPHALOSPORINs is best in this case.

Gonorrhea acquired in rural areas: AZITHROMYCIN or DOXYCYCLINE are best because they also treat CHLAMYDIA. DOXYCYCLINE given for 2 weeks (but not AZITHROMYCIN) also works for SYPHILIS which frequently coexists. CIPROFLOXACIN, ceftriaxone (see CEPHALOSPORIN) cefixime (see CEPHALOSPORIN) or SPECTINOMYCIN all work for gonorrhea. CIPROFLOXACIN and OFLOXACIN work fine for this but do not affect SYPHILIS which frequently coexists.

Throat infections: Use CEFTRIAXONE or CIPROFLOXACIN; SPECTINOMYCIN does not work well.

Disseminated infections: Use CEFTRIAXONE or SPECTINOMYCIN at increased dosages; see the *Drug Index*. Ciprofloxacin is no longer appropriate in the western USA or in infections that originated in Asia or the Pacific regions. Give antibiotics for at least 1 week.

Eye infections: Treat patients with eye infections with oral antibiotic as well as ANTIBIOTIC EYE OINTMENT

GOUT

Cause: Heredity, diet, some drugs.

Definition: Gout is a form of ARTHRITIS that usually affects the big toe, sometimes the ankles or wrists.

Age: Usually adults; in men over age 30, in women almost all postmenopausal. **Who:** More men than women; usually affluent Whites; it is rare in Blacks; it is especially common amongst the Maori of New Zealand.

Onset: Usually sudden; maximally painful in 8-12 hours.

Clinical:

Necessary: ARTHRITIS causing such extreme pain that the patient will scream at the vibration caused by someone's walking by.

Usually: It affects a single joint, particularly the base of the big toe or ankle, possibly the knee. There may be a fever. When and if the disease becomes recurrent, it can involve upper limbs and/or small joints, resembling rheumatoid ARTHRITIS. Frequently there are hard lumps under the skin of the outer ear.

Complications: Gout may cause KIDNEY STONES, especially during DEHYDRATION.

Similar Conditions: See Protocol C-6. GONORRHEA and ARTHRITIS, septic are two important considerations. One important characteristic of gout is that the joint initially returns to normal between attacks. Skin bumps on the ear may resemble LEPROSY.

Higher-Level Care. Level 3 or above hospital laboratories can do blood tests for this. Some advanced drugs may be useful. Fluid may be taken from the joint and tested.

Treatment:

Weight reduction, low-fat diet, no alcohol, no organ meats, minimal other meats, no shellfish. There are some special medicines that are more helpful than the usual ARTHRITIS medicines, but these should be obtained from and supervised by a physician. ASPIRIN should not be used. ALLOPURINOL is useful to prevent attacks, but it will increase the pain when used during an attack. COLCHICINE works well for treating an acute attack.

Guinea Worm

See *Regional Notes* F, I, R.

HALITOSIS

Entry category: Symptom.

This is bad breath. It may be caused by STREP THROAT, GINGIVITIS, TYPHUS, RESPIRATORY INFECTION (sinusitis) or poor dental hygiene.

HANGOVER

Entry category: Syndrome.

This is a headache and general aching without a fever the morning after ALCOHOL excess. It does not cause a fever. It should not be treated.

HEART ATTACK

Cause: Heredity; Western diet; SYPHILIS.
Synonyms: Myocardial infarction, Coronary occlusion.
Regional Notes: O.
Definition: A heart attack is the death of a portion of heart muscle, usually from blockage of one of the heart's arteries.

Mildly to severely ill; Class 3-4; Regional; Consider this diagnosis only in those who have eaten Western diets or had SYPHILIS.

Age: Generally over 30 y.o. **Who:** Affluent nationals and Westerners; achiever types, smokers, those with HYPERTENSION, DIABETES, obesity, or SYPHILIS.
Onset: Usually sudden.

Clinical:

Usually: The patient has one or more of the following:

- Chest pain, usually pressure-like, which lasts 20 minutes or more and is not aggravated by deep breathing; the painful area is not tender to touch.
- Pale, ashen, sweaty skin.
- A feeling of weakness along with an abnormal pulse (slow, rapid, or irregular) and a drop in blood pressure.
- Shortness of breath which is worse lying down than sitting up. The patient might turn blue with this.

Sometimes: Nausea, vomiting, indigestion, a sense of doom, coughing up frothy sputum, loss of consciousness, HEART FAILURE. This may be painless in some, especially in DIABETES.

Similar Conditions: ANGINA is the pain of a threatened heart attack that doesn't progress to actual heart damage; the pain lasts less than 20 minutes. If it lasts more than 20 minutes, then damage is likely and the patient should be sent to a hospital. If the frequency and severity of the pain is increasing over time, this likewise warrants evacuation to a hospital. HEART BURN is more of a burning than a pressure pain. PERICARDITIS pain is relieved somewhat by leaning forward; it is aggravated by lying on one's back. PLEURISY is aggravated by deep breathing. DEPRESSION can cause a general chest heaviness that does not vary much with time. GALLBLADDER DISEASE can cause pain identical with heart attack, but the pain is usually more on the right whereas the pain of a heart attack is more on the left.

Higher-Level Care. *Laboratory:* A level 3 or more hospital can do an electrocardiogram and some blood tests. A level 4 or 5 hospital may have life-saving surgical facilities. *Facilities:* Oxygen, intensive care unit, monitored bed, specialized imaging and facilities to dissolve clots in the heart. *Practitioners:* A cardiologist is ideal; a generalist or internist can usually manage fine. A referral to a level 4 or above hospital in a Western nation might be appropriate.

Treatment:

Send out immediately, having the patient sit up meanwhile. Oxygen is helpful. Relieve pain if you can.

HEART FAILURE

Cause: Variable.
Synonyms: Congestive heart failure, CHF.
Includes: Right and left heart failure.
Regional Notes: F, I, M, O, R, S, U.
Definition: Heart failure is the inability of the heart to perform up to the body's demands.

Entry category: Syndrome cluster.

Moderately to very ill; Class 2-4 depending on severity; Worldwide, highly variable frequency. Dilated (floppy) heart failure in the context of childbirth occurs in tropical Latin America, Africa south of the Sahara, India, China, and Korea.

Age: Any, including children. **Who:** Anyone. It may occur with no obvious cause; in infants it is commonly due to a birth defect. **Onset:** Gradual over weeks to months unless the patient is quite sick with a fever or has a HEART ATTACK. It can also be sudden in an infant with a heart murmur (see Volume I, Chapter 1).

Clinical:

Necessary: The patient is either short of breath, worse lying than sitting, or he becomes lethargic or fatigued very easily or he has swollen ankles or a combination of these symptoms.

Maybe: His skin color may be bluish. In severe cases the patient may have loss of appetite, dizziness, and swelling of the abdomen with a large, tender liver and spleen. His pulse may be slow, fast, or irregular. His blood pressure may be high or low. His respiration may be fast, irregular, or labored. He may have a low body temperature. He may have a cough or wheezing. He may have JAUNDICE. Children might have delayed sexual development.

There are 4 types of HEART FAILURE:

- dilated (floppy)
- restrictive (tight)
- hypertrophic (muscular)
- valvular (bad valves)

In any particular geographic area, one or another type of heart disease will be most common. At times an individual might have a combination of two types of heart failure.

➢ **Dilated Heart Failure**

The heart is large and floppy. The patient is usually very short of breath while lying down, preferring to sit up to rest. The blood pressure is not high. Frequently the pulse is irregular and there are extra heart sounds or heart murmurs. The beat is not easily felt on the chest wall. The liver may be large, and the ankles swollen. This occurs in BERIBERI, DIPHTHERIA, many viral diseases, and sometimes in connection with childbirth. When it is due to childbirth, it occurs 2-20 weeks after delivery. Sometimes the patient dies and sometimes she recovers. This problem in children is frequently caused by severe ANEMIA.

➢ **Restrictive Heart Failure**

In restrictive heart disease, the heart size is usually small or normal. The veins in the neck are distended, and the heart beat can be seen in them. Fatigue with exercise bothers the patient more than shortness of breath with lying down. The two numbers of the blood pressure are not far apart, and the pressure is never high, e.g., 110/96. The liver may be enlarged and tender. This occurs with PERICARDITIS and TUBERCULOSIS and sometimes for unknown reasons.

➢ **Hypertrophic Heart Failure**

The heart is large and muscular. The patient may be short of breath with lying down. He will have either HYPERTENSION or chest pain, or both, when he attempts to exercise. The heartbeat is easily felt on the chest wall unless the patient is fat. The veins in the neck may be distended and the pulse easily seen there.

➢ **Valvular Heart Failure**

There is a murmur. It might be possible to feel the murmur as a vibration on the chest wall. In addition, there are signs of either hypertrophic disease or dilated disease or a mixture of these, depending on which valve is involved. There may be an abnormally large or small difference between the two blood pressure numbers (e.g., 130/20 or 120/110), or the patient may faint immediately after exercise or at unpredictable times. It may cause clubbing of the fingernails (see Illustration below). The patient may have blue lips.

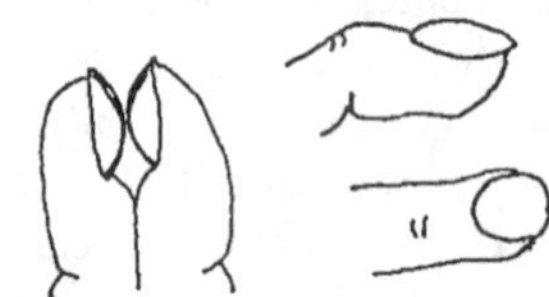

Valvular disease may cause clubbed finger nails. The nails are wide and shaped like saucers. When placed together, there is a big gap between them. (see also RESPIRATORY INFECTION, which may give a similar effect.)

This type is most common; it is seen in SYPHILIS, RHEUMATIC FEVER, in children with birth defects, and sometimes SPOTTED FEVER.

Causative Diseases:

In a patient with a high fever and sudden heart failure, who was perfectly healthy previously, consider RHEUMATIC FEVER. RHEUMATIC FEVER may also cause slow-onset heart failure.

Heart failure may be associated with AFRICAN SLEEPING SICKNESS, ALCOHOLISM, ALTITUDE SICKNESS, ANEMIA, BERIBERI, BRUCELLOSIS, CHAGA'S DISEASE, childbirth, DIPHTHERIA, HEART ATTACK, HOOKWORM, HYPERTENSION, LOIASIS, MALARIA, MONGOLISM, PERICARDITIS, Q FEVER, RELAPSING FEVER, SCHISTOSOMIASIS JAPONICUM, SEPSIS, SICKLE CELL DISEASE, SYPHILIS, TOXEMIA, TRENCH FEVER, TRICHINOSIS, TUBERCULOSIS, TYPHUS, and viral infections.

Similar Conditions:

Body swelling: See Protocols C-6 and C-7. LIVER FAILURE also causes body swelling, but the patient is not short of breath with lying down and the veins on the surface of his abdomen may be very visible. KIDNEY FAILURE also can cause swelling. Either the blood pressure will be high or else the urine dipstick will be abnormal.

Shortness of breath See Protocol C-4; this can be similar to RESPIRATORY INFECTION and diseases similar to that; both are worse lying down and better sitting up.

Finger clubbing: TRICHURIASIS can also cause finger clubbing and growth retardation.

Confusion/lethargy: See Protocol C-10.

Higher-Level Care. See Volume I, Appendix 13. *Laboratory:* A level 3 or above hospital may offer blood tests, electrocardiogram. *Facilities:* A level 3 or above intensive care unit, monitoring equipment, oxygen, and imaging technology might be helpful. *Practitioners:* A cardiologist is ideal; a generalist or internist might be helpful. Consider that the cause may be a tropical/travel disease. A surgical referral might be appropriate but this must be to a Western level 4 or above.

Treatment:

- Keep the patient in bed, sitting up. Use THEOPHYLLINE if he is wheezing.
- Treat for MALARIA if it is prevalent in your area.
- Consider what diseases in your area might cause heart failure, question the patient as to other present or prior symptoms, and treat whatever you think might have caused it.
- Treat children who have severe ANEMIA with DIGOXIN and HYDROCHLOROTHIAZIDE and IRON and FOLIC ACID.
- Heart medications:

  In dilated disease, use DIGOXIN and HYDROCHLOROTHIAZIDE, and give the patient an ASPIRIN each day if his pulse is irregular.

  In restrictive disease, use HYDROCHLOROTHIAZIDE and HYDROCORTISONE.

  In hypertrophic disease, HYDROCHLOROTHIAZIDE is helpful, as well as PROPRANOLOL. DIGOXIN might be helpful. Treat HYPERTENSION until the blood pressure is near-normal.

  In valvular disease, HYDROCHLOROTHIAZIDE is safe if the patient is short of breath. DIGOXIN may be used additionally, if necessary, but PROPRANOLOL must not be used unless a physician directs you to do so. Use AMPICILLIN for one day when the patient requires any surgical or dental procedure or delivers a baby.

  FUROSEMIDE may substitute for HYDROCHLOROTHIAZIDE.

Results: 1-24 hours with drugs.

HEARTBURN

Entry category: Syndrome.

Definition: Heartburn refers to a burning chest pain caused by stomach acid. The symptoms are similar to HEART ATTACK. The patient has a burning sensation underneath his breastbone and an acid taste in his mouth. He may also have indigestion. Treat with ANTACID and have the patient sit upright for 2 hours after eating.

HEAT ILLNESS

Cause: Hot environment.

Includes: Heat exhaustion, Heat stroke. The difference between these is the severity.

Definition: Heat illness is an illness caused by failure of the body to adapt to a hot environment.

Mildly to very ill; Class 1-3; Worldwide in hot climates, especially humid; mild is common; heat stroke is uncommon.

Age: Any, especially very young and very old.

Who: There are two classes of people who are particularly susceptible to heat illness: (1) Those who are very old or very young or in poor health; and (2) Those in good health, especially expatriates doing physical work in a hot climate, and/or having a sleep deficit.

Drugs for diarrhea and/or nausea tend to aggravate or precipitate the problem. **Onset:** Minutes to hours.

Clinical:

Necessary: The patient is exposed to a very hot environment. If it is dry heat, he is thirsty; if it is humid heat he is or was sweating profusely and may also be thirsty.

➢ **Heat exhaustion (mild heat illness):**

This causes fatigue; headache; nausea; vomiting; muscle cramps in the arms, legs, and abdomen. The skin is warm and moist. There is sometimes a rash with tiny bumps. The blood pressure may drop, causing fainting. Initially there is no or a low fever. Sometimes there are mental changes; the person may be very emotionally irritable and irrational. He may lose his appetite and complain of dizziness. If he is not treated, it may progress to heat stroke.

➢ **Heat stroke (severe heat illness):**

Initially there are symptoms of heat exhaustion, as given above. Thereafter:

- *In babies and the elderly*, there is little sweating but very rapid respiration.
- *In previously healthy patients* who are exercising, they tend to be very sweaty and may have a low blood sugar.

In all cases there is likely to be loss of consciousness; wild, combative behavior; SEIZURES. Body temperature will be high, at least 40°C (104°F) and possibly up to 44°C (111°F). If the patient is not cooled immediately he will die.

Complications: BRAIN DAMAGE, death.

Similar Conditions: Heat exhaustion may coexist with and be similar to ZINC DEFICIENCY; treat both. It is also similar to GASTROENTERITIS, INFLUENZA, and early HEPATITIS.

Heat stroke is indistinguishable from cerebral MALARIA, ENCEPHALITIS, and sometimes MENINGI-

TIS. If you suspect any of these, you should treat for all of them. Also see Protocol C-10A.

Bush Laboratory: With heat stroke, the patient's urine might look like machine oil and test strongly positive for both protein and blood.

Higher-Level Care. See Volume I, Appendix 13. Speedy referral is essential with heat stroke. *Laboratory:* A level 3 or above hospital will probably have a variety of blood tests which will help manage the complications of heat stroke. *Facilities:* In countries that are usually very hot, there might be special cooling units at level 2 or above. In areas with a moderate climate, such cooling units are only found at level 4 and above. *Practitioners:* An internist is ideal; a generalist can manage.

Treatment:

Prevention: Prevent the problem with salt in the diet and drinking water on hot days. Patients who are taking diuretic medicines should decrease the dose. Low salt diets should be modified when salt is being lost in the sweat. Frequent cooling is helpful. Restrict exercise and avoid sleep deficits.

Patient Care:

Heat exhaustion: Have a conscious patient take two salt tablets or eat 1/2 teaspoon of salt and drink a liter of water. Pretzels and popcorn are convenient forms of salt. If this diagnosis is at all possible, try the treatment. Check for DEHYDRATION and treat that also. If the patient is not acclimatized to the hot environment, ZINC might also be helpful. *Results:* 1-2 hours.

Heat stroke: Cool the patient as rapidly as you can. Packing him in ice is best, but immediate care is more important than ideal care. CHLORPROMAZINE will lessen shivering. If he has SEIZURES, keep him from hurting himself. Try to give sugar water if he is able to swallow, or put down a stomach tube. Be aware that patients are usually combative when they awaken. **Send him to a hospital even after he has regained consciousness; complications are numerous and unpredictable.** If this is impossible, give the patient plenty of fluids. Give him baking soda in sufficient quantity to keep his urine pH between 8 and 9. (Measure pH with urine dipsticks.)

If there is falciparum MALARIA in your area, treat that; it may be indistinguishable. PARALDEHYDE is best for SEIZURES and it may also prevent combative behavior. DIAZEPAM is an alternative.

HEMOCHROMATOSIS

Cause: Iron overload.

Definition: This is a cause of failure of multiple organs and functions, due to too much iron. The common causes thereof are blood transfusions, some hereditary problems, and an abnormally high dietary iron intake.

Clinical:

LIVER DISEASE, LIVER FAILURE, DIABETES, reproductive dysfunction, ARTHRITIS, JAUNDICE, free fluid in the abdomen (increased abdominal girth), HEART FAILURE, increased skin pigmentation.

Send to a hospital, level 2 or above.

HEMORRHAGIC FEVER

Cause: Virus.

Includes: Kyasanur Forest Disease, CRIMEAN-CONGO HEMORRHAGIC FEVER, and many others, most of which contain names of places. There are separate entries for EBOLA FEVER, MARBURG FEVER, LASSA FEVER, and DENGUE HEMORRHAGIC FEVER.

Regional Notes: All regions.

Definition: Hemorrhagic fever is a group of viral illnesses which cause the blood to fail to clot properly. Because of this there is abnormal bleeding.

Entry category: Disease cluster.

Very ill; Class 3-4; Some kinds contagious; Regional, mostly tropical, Africa, Middle East, and southern Asia.

Age: Any. **Who:** Anyone, but especially bug-bitten. **Onset:** Variable; incubation period varies by type.

Clinical:

The patient has a fever and general illness. He then begins to bleed. Nosebleed; bleeding gums; bloody urine, vomitus, and stool; very heavy menstruation and heavy wound bleeding are common. The patient may have bleeding into the whites of his eyes (does not need treatment) or into his skin, causing a bruised appearance. If the bleeding is severe, the patient becomes dizzy with a rapid pulse and low blood pressure. He develops SHOCK and dies.

Similar Conditions: MALARIA, TYPHUS, LEPTOSPIROSIS, SEPSIS, and any disease that causes a very large spleen (see Protocol 46 B in the *Symptom Protocols Index*) can cause abnormal bleeding.

Bush Laboratory: Do a tourniquet test:

- Determine the patient's blood pressure.
- Choose a number about half-way between the two numbers of the blood pressure.
- Inflate the blood pressure cuff on the arm to that half-way number and leave it inflated for 5 minutes. (This will cause some pain.)
- Look at the arm below the cuff. If there are multiple bruise marks, then the patient may have hemorrhagic fever.

Higher-Level Care. See Volume I, Appendix 13 paying special attention to the caution. *Laboratory:* Hospitals at level 3 or above can do blood tests and may be able to transfuse blood. *Facilities:* Blood bank, IV fluids and means to give them, an intensive care unit with isolation; a monitored bed. Level 4 or above is desirable. *Practitioners:* A hematologist and an infectious disease specialist with tropical/travel expertise. An internist or generalist might be helpful.

Treatment:

Prevention: Talk to local or government medical personnel to find out what is the source of the problem locally. Then institute public health measures to prevent the underlying disease. See Protocol C-2.

Patient Care: VITAMIN K injections may help if there is JAUNDICE. Treat SHOCK with fluids until you can get the patient to a hospital. Transfusions are frequently necessary. RIBAVIRIN may be available at a hospital. Reportedly it works for all kinds of viral hemorrhagic fevers except EBOLA FEVER. Do not use ASPIRIN or IBUPROFEN. ACETAMINOPHEN is o.k.

HEMORRHOIDS

Cause: Variable.
Synonym: Piles.
Definition: Hemorrhoids are veins by the anus or rectum, that become abnormally large and bulge out, causing pain and bleeding.

Mildly ill; Class 1-2 depending on severity; Worldwide, variable frequency.

Age: Adult, usually middle-aged and older. **Who:** Anyone, related to constipation, eating low fiber diets, sitting on the toilet reading, pregnancy, LIVER DISEASE, CIRRHOSIS, LIVER FAILURE, and old age. **Onset:** Days to weeks.

Clinical:

Necessary: The patient passes bright red blood by rectum, coating the outside of his stool. Pain is negligible to severe, sometimes crampy; it is worse with bowel movements.

Sometimes: The pain may be so severe that the patient becomes very constipated. You may see big, blue veins protrude from the rectum; sometimes you can feel veins with rectal exam, but frequently examination is normal. There may be rectal itching and mucus. If external hemorrhoids clot, they become suddenly painful. The pain lasts 1-2 weeks and then disappears.

Bush Laboratory: Check for ANEMIA.

Higher-Level Care: A surgeon may be helpful.

Treatment:

Use sitz baths; see Appendix 1 in Vol. I for directions. Recommend a high-fiber diet. Correct constipation with MILK OF MAGNESIA or another laxative. Hemorrhoids are not serious unless the patient has a large blood loss. However, they usually require the services of a hospital and a surgeon.

HEPATITIS

Cause: Virus or toxin.
Includes: Hepatitis A, B, C, D (Delta), E, G.[1] It also includes toxic hepatitis from industrial or waste substances, INH (a TB medicine), some other Western drugs, and many ethnic medicines.
Regional Notes: All regions. Hepatitis E is common in all of Asia and in northern Africa.

Definition: Hepatitis is an inflammation of the liver.

Entry category: Disease cluster.

Mildly to very ill; Class 1-3, depending on severity; Contagious through body secretions; Worldwide, generally common.

Age: Any. **Who:** Anyone, usually from unsanitary water, food, personal contact, or blood exposure; may be due to drugs, chemicals, excessive ALCOHOL, or poisonous fumes. Expatriates are vulnerable to viral hepatitis, especially the unimmunized. Some common liver-toxic herbs are listed under PLANT POISONING. Many drugs are liver-toxic, especially those used to treat TUBERCULOSIS. **Onset:** This varies with toxic exposures, depending on the amount of poison and the duration of exposure. For viral hepatitis the onset is over a few days to a week or two. Incubation is 2-8 weeks for water-borne and 2-6 months for blood-borne.

---

[1] *Hepatitis A* is water-borne. It is the mildest type of hepatitis, seldom fatal. There are no severe long-lasting consequences. An immunization is available.
Hepatitis B is blood-borne and sexually transmitted. There is some evidence that it is also transmitted within families in areas of poor hygiene. It is long-lasting. Sometimes patients recover and sometimes they develop a very severe form and die. Hepatitis B is also a cause of liver CANCER. There is a good immunization for hepatitis B.
Hepatitis C is also blood-borne, but it is rarely or never sexually transmitted. It is usually mild initially, but many patients develop severe, chronic hepatitis over the longer term. No immunization is available but some anti-viral drugs may work.
Hepatitis D is a blood-borne virus which does not infect people by itself, but is associated with hepatitis B. It causes severe illness. The hepatitis B immunization also protects against hepatitis D.
Hepatitis E is a water-borne, non-A/non-B hepatitis, which occurs in southern Asia, the Middle East, Latin America, and Africa. It causes mild illness in most people. There is no immunization.
Hepatitis G is a blood-borne virus, and most common in the India area. It is thought to be sexually transmitted as well as to be transmitted mother to baby. It is a common cause of chronic hepatitis.

Clinical:

For all kinds of hepatitis, the general symptoms are similar. The length of the illnesses and the prognoses vary according to the type of hepatitis.

Necessary: Nausea, loss of appetite, and fatigue at first. A large, painful, tender liver and either JAUNDICE or bilirubin in the urine or both after the first week or two.

Maybe: Fever which is never over 101°F (38.3°C), very dark urine, light-colored stool, itching all over. Usually there are joint pains along with general itching, nausea, and fatigue for 2 days to 6 weeks before the jaundice starts. When the patient develops jaundice, the other symptoms improve. The joint pains are mostly in the hands, sometimes the knees and ankles.

Complications: HEMORRHAGIC FEVER, liver CANCER, LIVER FAILURE, ABORTION, death. A common terminal event is a condition resembling ENCEPHALITIS: mild involves confusion, hallucinations, or apathy; severe involves seizures and coma.

Similar Conditions: *The initial illness with joint pains* can easily be confused with RUBELLA in adults, with other forms of ARTHRITIS, and with early BRUCELLOSIS. KIDNEY FAILURE might also appear similar.

Once JAUNDICE *develops*: See Protocols C-5 and C-7. Falciparum MALARIA may easily be confused with hepatitis with disastrous results. If in doubt, treat MALARIA. LEPTOSPIROSIS causes severe muscle aching, red eyes, or both; the fever is higher than in hepatitis. Also consider GALLBLADDER DISEASE (usually episodic very localized pains), AMEBIC LIVER DISEASE (also localized pains), HEART FAILURE (swollen ankles), THALLASEMIA (anemia), RELAPSING FEVER (higher fever), SPOTTED FEVER (higher fever), SYPHILIS (secondary with a rash), LIVER FLUKE (check geography), MONONUCLEOSIS (also large, tender spleen), SEPSIS in a newborn. PELVIC INFECTION in females can cause liver tenderness mimicking hepatitis. If the patient had contact with newborn animals, the hepatitis might be due to Q FEVER, in which case it might respond to DOXYCYCLINE or RIFAMPIN. Seek local professional medical advice.

Bush Laboratory: Urine shows bilirubin, maybe ketones and urobilinogen. If you put the urine in a closed glass container and shake it, there will be foam on top similar to soapy water, and the foam will be yellowish. Compare this to a sample of normal urine, the same amount of urine in the same kind of container. Stool may be positive for blood.

Higher-Level Care. See Volume I, Appendix 13. *Laboratory*: Level 4 and above can do specific blood tests to determine the type of hepatitis and how severe it is. *Facilities:* Level 4 and above may have drugs that are helpful. *Practitioners:* An infectious disease specialist is ideal; an internist or generalist may be adequate.

Treatment:

Prevention: During an epidemic, boil all drinking water. Filtering and chemical treatment are not adequate. Dispose of sewage away from water supply. Wash hands and foods before eating. Avoid illicit sexual contacts.

Pressure cooker treatment of needles and syringes is mandatory. **No amount of boiling will kill Hepatitis B.** Use gloves when handling wounds. Take extreme care to avoid any blood or sewage contamination.

Injection with GAMMA GLOBULIN gives short term protection against hepatitis. (This is not the same as immunization.) The American product prevents hepatitis A only; the French product prevents both hepatitis A and hepatitis E. It must be refrigerated.

Immunizations are available for hepatitis A and hepatitis B. Hepatitis B immunization also prevents hepatitis D. Infants of affected mothers who carry Hepatitis B should be immunized right after birth. Note that Hepatitis B immunizations must not be given in the buttock. The intradermal Hepatitis B immunization does not give as good long-term immunity as the IM does.

Patient Care: Send the patient to a hospital for treatment. There are now good drugs (although they are high-tech) to treat hepatitis B and C.

- If the disease was caused by drugs, chemicals, or fumes, remove the offending substance.
- Advise bed rest and good food, avoiding ALCOHOL, chocolate, and fatty food.
- Watch vital signs carefully, checking for DEHYDRATION and weight loss. Send out if vital signs become very abnormal.
- VITAMIN K injections may help for bleeding.
- RIBAVIRIN, a new anti-viral drug, may work for some kinds of hepatitis, and may be tried in severe cases.

Results: Gradual recovery over 1-12 months for water-borne hepatitis (A and E). Hepatitis B and C can cause LIVER FAILURE and result in death. Hepatitis A might be fatal in patients over 50 years old. Hepatitis E might be fatal to pregnant women or their new-born infants.

HERNIA

Cause: Usually birth defect.

Synonym: Rupture

Regional Notes: F, M.

Definition: A hernia is a weak spot on the abdominal wall, where a piece of bowel can (and usually does) pass through the deeper layers of the wall until it lies right underneath the skin.

Not ill to very ill; Class 1-4; Worldwide, common.

Age: Any. **Who:** Anyone, especially males. **Onset:** Sudden or may be there since birth.

Clinical:

Necessary: The patient has a soft bulge in his groin, at his navel, or by an old surgical scar. A groin hernia may extend part or all the way into the scrotum on that side, causing the scrotum to hang down as far as the knees. The swelling is soft like a water balloon, unless it has become painful and tender.

Maybe: If it is not tender and no one has pushed on it within the last 20 minutes, you can hear bowel sounds in it with your stethoscope.

Complications: Navel hernias that have been present since birth and scar hernias seldom cause problems. A tender naval hernia is an emergency. Groin hernias and acquired navel hernias can cause ACUTE ABDOMEN. In this case there is general abdominal pain as well as pain and tenderness in the hernia.

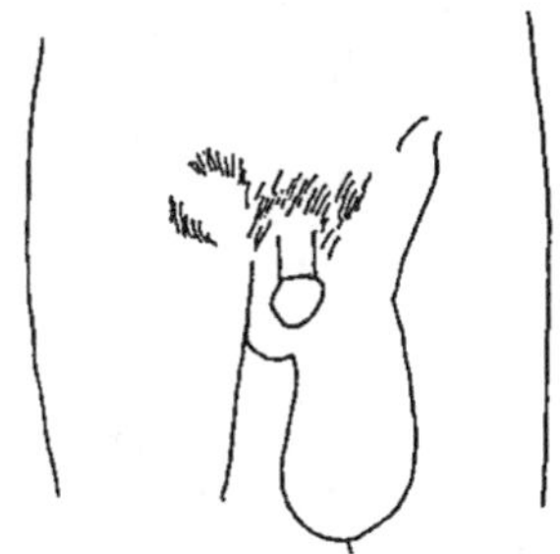

Hernias: Note that the bulge starts in the groin; it is a small hernia on the patient's right and a large one on the patient's left.

Similar Conditions: An ordinary hernia is not tender.

Non-painful, non-tender scrotal swelling: HYDROCELE (light shines through), HYDATID DISEASE (check geography), TUBERCULOSIS, and CANCER (light doesn't shine through).

Painful, tender scrotal swelling: FILARIASIS (probably common in the community), ABSCESS, EPIDIDYMITIS.

Groin swelling only; scrotum appears normal: Swollen lymph nodes or an abscess from any infection on the legs or feet, or from SEXUALLY TRANSMITTED DISEASE. If the swelling is black and extremely tender, in a very sick patient, consider PLAGUE.

Higher-Level Care. A level 2 or above hospital with anesthesia, a surgical theatre, and a surgeon are most helpful.

Treatment:

A patient with a tender hernia or signs of ACUTE ABDOMEN must be sent to a hospital immediately; otherwise send him when convenient if a physician agrees to repair the hernia. A hernia that can be ignored goes back into the abdomen easily. Most large ones do so with gentle pushing. To encourage a stubborn groin hernia to go back into place, put the foot end of the patient's bed on concrete blocks and give him a sedative. If it still will not go back in, send him out for repair within 48 hours. Do not try to close a hole in a hernia that drains stool.

HERPES

Cause: Virus.

Synonyms: Herpes simplex, Cold sore, Fever blister, Genital herpes.

Regional Notes: I.

Definition: Herpes is a viral infection of the skin or of pink, moist surfaces, e.g., in the mouth or genital areas.

Mildly to very ill; Class 1-3; Contagious; Worldwide; it is the most common genital ulcer disease in both developed and developing countries.

Age: Any. **Who:** Anyone, especially those who have had the problem before. Patients with HIV are especially prone to this. **Onset:** Over a day or two. In the tropics, the incubation is 2-14 days if the problem is in the genital area.

Clinical:

➢ **Ordinary Herpes**

Necessary: First there is a reddened area of skin. Then that red area becomes swollen. Then painful blisters form on the red base—in or near the mouth or the genital areas, occasionally on the skin or in the eyes. They are multiple, small, close together, and tender to touch. The blisters may break and then blend into each other to make ulcers. Episodes of blisters and ulcers come and go multiple times. The first episode is the worst, with a larger area involved, and it is most likely to be symmetrical, i.e. the same or nearly the same right and left. The symptoms are usually at their worst about a week after the infection started.

Maybe: The skin or blisters might itch, burn, or tingle. There may be pain with urination. The patient might have fever and chills or enlarged lymph nodes. The enlarged nodes are tender to touch. He may have fatigue and loss of appetite. His neck might be stiff. The surfaces might peel. The disease can cause blindness if the eye is affected. With an eye infection, light will hurt the eye(s). Herpes may cause pain so severe that a child refuses to eat or drink. He may require a stomach tube for nourishment and fluids. Babies born to mothers with herpes may have CATARACT at birth.

Complications of Genital Herpes: Secondary infection, MENINGITIS, constipation; urinary retention (can't release urine); pains down legs.

➢ **Herpes and HIV:**

Herpes increases the likelihood of acquiring HIV INFECTION. HIV INFECTION makes the symptoms of herpes worse. With HIV INFECTION, herpes is harder to treat because it frequently is resistant to ACYCLOVIR.

➢ **Infants born to women with herpes infection:** These babies have multiple problems that you will not be able to handle. They should be sent out for care. ACYCLOVIR is not an approved drug during pregnancy but a physician might justify its use to prevent a disastrous outcome for the newborn.

Similar Conditions: See Protocols C-1 (genital) and C-8 (eyes). In the mouth, consider APHTHOUS STOMATITIS. For herpes that affects the eye, see KERATITIS. SHINGLES is a closely related disease that also causes painful blisters. Burns may appear similar.

Higher-Level Care. *Laboratory:* Large hospital laboratories and those with special kits can do tests for this.

Treatment:

- Pain medication may be helpful.
- Cool wet-to-dry compresses and sitz baths may be helpful. See Appendix 1 in Volume I.
- ACYCLOVIR is available in both cream and pill form. Famciclovir is a similar, related drug. Since the disease is recurrent, you should try to give your patient medication to start taking as soon as he feels another episode starting. When started early, even just one day of medication can prevent a full-blown episode.
- You can try using a paste made of crushed BISMUTH SUBSALICYLATE tablets to treat sores on the mouth.
- Eye doctors can treat infected eyes; the patient must be sent out promptly.

Results: Herpes in the absence of HIV INFECTION will usually go away in two weeks without treatment. However, it is likely to recur and the patient may still be contagious during the time when he has no symptoms.

HICCUPS

Entry category: Symptom.

See *Symptom Index* 7B and 38. After trying the usual home remedies, CHLORPROMAZINE (in the dose usually used for sedative effects) usually works. Treat the underlying disease, if possible.

HIV INFECTION

Cause: Virus.

Synonyms: Retroviral Infection, AIDS.

Includes: ARC (AIDS-Related Complex) and full-blown AIDS.

Definition: Infection with the human immunodeficiency virus, type 1 or type 2.

Regional Notes: All regions.

Not ill to very ill; Class 1-4; contagious; those infected with both HIV and TUBERCULOSIS usually die within 2 months and are particularly contagious; HIV is present worldwide.

Age: Any, also including the 5-16-year age range. **Who:** Babies born of infected mothers; sexually active adults; sexually abused children; those who receive contaminated blood transfusions or needle sticks. **Onset:** Incubation between the infecting event and the development of a positive antibody blood test (seroconversion illness) is 2-12 weeks. At the time of the blood test becoming positive, the patient has a flu-like illness that lasts 1-2 weeks. After that the disease is dormant for 5-15 years before it manifests as AIDS. The incubation to AIDS is shorter in older people and in those with severe or long-lasting symptoms of the seroconversion illness. It is also shorter in those whose infection was caused by blood transfusion.

Clinical:

The disease occurs in three stages:

➢ **Seroconversion illness:**
This is a mild, flu-like illness 2-4 weeks after infection, lasting 1-2 weeks but occasionally longer. At times this may cause ENCEPHALITIS.

The symptoms are as follows: fever; fatigue; a sore throat; a measles-like rash, not painful or itchy; general aching; night sweats; enlarged lymph nodes. Occasionally there is general body itching, hair loss, and sores in the mouth. During this time there is an abnormally high sedimentation rate: [see Volume I, appendix 2, lab procedures]. This becomes normal again during the second incubation period of years. The infection is highly contagious during this illness.

➢ **Early AIDS:**
This occurs 5-15 years after the seroconversion illness. The symptoms are as follows: weight loss, diarrhea, fever, enlarged lymph nodes at 2 or more sites, especially on the face near the ears (chipmunk look); tiredness, night sweats, sores in the mouth, reddish face, rash, SHINGLES, increased symptoms from some SEXUALLY TRANSMITTED DISEASES.

➢ **Advanced, full-blown AIDS:**
This develops gradually from early AIDS and causes more and more infections which become increasingly difficult to treat. In about 20% of the patients, the virus affects the brain causing poor concentration and memory, poor coordination, abnormal emotions and behavior, pains in the hands and feet in the areas normally covered by stockings and gloves, weakness in the hips and shoulders with muscle pains, uncoordination, and stiff weakness of the limbs.

The spleen may be enlarged.

There is a kind of reactive ARTHRITIS associated with this: the sudden onset of symmetrical joint pains and swelling. The ARTHRITIS lasts a short time, does not come back, and there is no destruction of the joints. The presence of full-blown AIDS encourages the development of some malignancies, the most common being Kaposi's sarcoma which is a skin CANCER, appearing as black bumps on the skin surfaces, with some surrounding red halos.

➢ **Women with AIDS:**

Kaposi's sarcoma (a kind of CANCER) is less common than in men. With female circumcision, there is an increase in HIV transmission. The following genital conditions are worse in women with AIDS than those without: CANCER, HERPES, PELVIC INFECTION. Babies born to these women are more likely to die before or shortly after birth; they are more likely to have low birth weight. Malaria in pregnancy is both more common and worse in HIV positive women.

➢ **Newborns and HIV:**

Those born by C section are less likely to acquire HIV than those born vaginally. Some HIV is acquired through breast milk, but survival is still better, in most developing areas, by having the children exclusively breast fed than by using bottle feeds.

➢ **Children with HIV:**

There is slower growth and developmental delays; there may be a stiff weakness and a very small head. PNEUMONIA is common. There may be swelling of the parotid glands in front of the ears, giving a chipmunk-type appearance. There will be a poor response to immunizations so you might see clinical diseases against which the child has been immunized. Also there will be delayed closure of the soft spot on the heads of infants; and delayed teething.

Similar Conditions: See Protocols C-6 (limb swelling); C-12 (large lymph nodes); C-10A (fever and lethargy) TUBERCULOSIS may be indistinguishable. VISCERAL LEISHMANIASIS may also appear similar as may the weight loss that follows MEASLES. RADIATION ILLNESS may also appear similar. MALNUTRITION as well as MUMPS and ALCOHOLISM can cause similar swellings by the ears. Rickets causes similar developmental delays.

Diseases Interacting With HIV Infection:

Most diseases make HIV infections worse, and the presence of HIV infection makes other diseases worse.

Diseases Not Interacting With HIV Infection:

LEPROSY, AFRICAN SLEEPING SICKNESS, CHAGA'S DISEASE, SCHISTOSOMIASIS, FILARIASIS.

Higher-Level Care.

See Volume I, Appendix 13. *Laboratory:* There are varying tests of varying accuracy. Almost all the tests in developing countries are antibody tests which means that they measure the proteins in the body that fight the virus rather than the virus itself. This means that if the person just got infected recently, his test might be falsely negative. It might also be falsely negative if he has such advanced disease that his body ceases to fight the infection anymore. Two simple, rapid tests especially for developing countries are the particle agglutination assay and the dot immunobinding assay.

Hospital tests:

p24 becomes positive at less than one month.
IgM becomes positive at less than 6 months.
IgG becomes positive at less than 1 year.

The standard diagnostic test is ELISA which, however, may fail to detect some infections and it may be falsely positive. The Western Blot test can differentiate the two kinds of HIV (1 and 2) and it is needed to confirm a positive ELISA. Beware of a positive test that does not make sense; it might be due to laboratory glassware not having been washed well. Have the test repeated at a different, preferably a more elite facility.

Following the course of the disease: In developed countries laboratories CD4 lymphocyte counts are determined. CD4 lymphocytes are a kind of lymphocyte, which is in turn a type of white blood cell. If the CD4 count is 500 or more, then the patient still has decent immunity. If the CD4 count falls below 200, then immunity is poor and the patient is at risk of infection. A substitute for CD4 count is the total lymphocyte count. If the total lymphocyte count falls below 1000, this indicates a probable CD4 count of less than 200, since CD4 lymphocytes constitute 20% or less of the total lymphocytes.

If a person has a CBC (Complete Blood Count) that includes a total white cell count and also gives the percent of the different types of white cells, one can calculate the total lymphocyte count. Multiply the total white cell count by the percent of lymphocytes (converted to a decimal); this gives the total lymphocyte count. For example, if the total white count is 8,000 and the percent of lymphocytes is 25%, then the lymphocyte count is 8,000 x 0.25 = 2,000. Then the CD4 count may be estimated to be not greater than 20% of this number (2000 x 0.20 = 400, indicating a borderline immunity). But if the total white cell count is 2,000 and the percent of lymphocytes is 40%, then the lymphocyte count is 800, and the CD4 count is probably below 200. *Facilities:* IV's and advanced drugs at level 3, 4 or 5 might be helpful. *Practitioners:* An infectious disease specialist is ideal; a generalist or internist or pediatrician might be helpful.

Treatment:

Prevention: Dispose of used syringes and needles and/or pressure cook them or else use bleach water to wash and then boil them. Use gloves when suturing or handling blood or other body fluids. Wash your hands. Avoid promiscuity. Avoid injections of any sort. Avoid dental care in heavily infected areas. Even if your dentist is conscientious, it's likely that he hires a low-paid employee to do his cleaning and sterilizing.

In case of an inadvertent exposure (blood or rape), there are preventive medications that might be helpful. An appropriate protocol and a reserve supply of medicines should be kept by each family residing in a remote area. The best protocol changes from time to time and there are coexisting conditions that contraindicate the use of these medicines.

Patient Care: Generally none in developing areas unless you can get your hands on some anti-retroviral drugs: ABACAVIR; INDINAVIR; LAMIVUDINE; LOPINAVIR; NEVIRAPINE, RITONAVIR; ZIDOVUDINE. The treatment of HIV infection is beyond the scope of this book and thus only those drugs used in prevention after an HIV exposure are listed. See Volume I Chapter 2 for body fluid exposures; Volume I Appendix 14 for evaluation post sexual assault.

- The program of anti-retroviral drugs is called HAART. HAART must be used under professional medical supervision. Do not give HAART at the same time as RIFAMPIN because the HAART drugs are expensive and the RIFAMPIN will make them ineffective. Either delay the HAART until after the patient has finished RIFAMPIN, or else choose drug(s) other than RIFAMPIN (and related drugs). When using HAART avoid St John's Wort, Garlic, and Vitamin C. Fish oil is good to take with HAART drugs.
- If the patient has persistent diarrhea that is not responsive to the usual treatments, it may respond well to ALBENDAZOLE or else a change in diet. Avoid wheat and rye, substituting corn and rice for other grains.
- PNEUMONIA might respond to PENTAMIDINE if other antibiotics fail.
- There are some unsubstantiated reports that the animalarial herb, ARTEMISININ, made up as a tea (dose is a liter a day for a month) will reverse some of the symptoms of advanced AIDS when it is given together with a high-protein diet, multivitamins, and minerals.

HIVES

See ALLERGY and/or DRUG ERUPTION. Hives are very itchy, raised, flat-topped bumps on the skin.

HOOKWORM

Cause: Worm.

Includes: Ancylostomiasis, Necatoriasis, Uncinariasis.

Regional Notes: F, I, M, O, S, U.

Definition: Hookworm is a bowel infestation with either one of two similar species of worms: *Necator americanus* or *Ancylostoma duodenale*. The worms are so small they are barely visible to the naked eye.

Not ill to very ill; Class 1-2; Worldwide, mostly with sandy, moist, shaded soil. Unusual with clay soil. Occurs almost exclusively in tropical areas, below 2000 meters (6000 feet) in areas with loam or sandy soil.

Age: Any. **Who:** Those whose skin touches contaminated soil; those eating contaminated food. **Onset:** Rash develops rapidly; other symptoms develop over weeks.

Clinical:

May be without symptoms but diagnosed by a medical laboratory; without lab, one should suspect it in a patient with ANEMIA in the arable tropics.

Initially: A rash might appear on skin exposed to soil, usually on soft skin (e.g., between toes).

Days to weeks later: Symptoms of PNEUMONIA or ASTHMA occur as the worms travel through the lungs.

Then: Abdominal pain and ANEMIA develop. With severe infections, the patient may have black, tarry, obviously bloody, or mucous diarrhea stool like DYSENTERY.

Later still: He may have shortness of breath, leg swelling, loss of appetite, leg cramps with walking. Men may become impotent.

Occasionally: In severe cases there may be general body swelling and HEART FAILURE. Children may have strong food cravings.

Similar Conditions:

The initial rash might resemble SCABIES.

The lung migration phase is indistinguishable from PNEUMONIA or ASTHMA.

The bowel phase: the disease resembles other types of WORMS, DYSENTERY, or other causes of ANEMIA. *Severe ANEMIA from hookworm* may cause HEART FAILURE. In this case it may be difficult to distinguish from wet BERIBERI; the use of MULTIVITAMINS during treatment will cover this possibility.

Bush Laboratory: Check stool for blood three times; it should be positive at least once. Check for ANEMIA.

Higher-Level Care. *Laboratory:* Those that have microscopes, possibly level 2, certainly level 3, can check stool for hookworm eggs; it is an easy and reliable test. It is moderately sensitive but very specific; three negative samples from 3 days, collected and processed fast, would eliminate the diagnosis. There are commonly false-negatives if any time elapses—as much as 3 hours—between the patient passing the stool and the lab examining it. Before the stool is positive for the eggs (for a couple weeks to a couple months) there will be an increase in the number of eosinophils in the blood. However, other diseases can also cause this. *Facilities:* With severe ANEMIA, a blood bank for transfusion might be helpful. *Practioner:* Generalist, internist, pediatrician.

Treatment:

Prevention: Wear shoes, encourage use of outhouses.

Patient Care: Treat ANEMIA using IRON. For deworming, use MEBENDAZOLE, PYRANTEL PAMOATE, TETRACHLOROETHYLENE,[1] or AL-

[1] This drug does not work against ASCARIASIS. Therefore, if you use it, you should treat for ASCARIASIS first if it occurs in your area. You will know that

BENDAZOLE. FLUBENDAZOLE, BEPHENIUM HYDROXYNAPHTHOATE, or LEVAMISOLE may work also. Treat a second time a week later if possible, but one treatment is better than none.

HYDATID DISEASE

Cause: Tumor, caused by dog hookworm.
Synonyms: Echinococcosis, Unilocular echinococcosis.
Regional Notes: All regions.
Definition: Hydatid Disease is an infestation with a larval form of animal hookworm.

Entry category: Two indistinguishable diseases.

Not ill to very ill; Class 2-4; Regional, mainly tropical. Areas are Greece, Argentina, Xinjiang China, Australia, and Kenya's Turkana region. It is also common in the rural, semi-rural, and suburban areas of western Europe, related there to the fox population.

Age: Any above 5 y.o. **Who:** Common amongst pastoral groups that keep dogs, where the dogs live close to the people; it also occurs in temperate, forested areas. **Onset:** Slowly; the incubation period is measured in years.

Clinical:

This depends on the organ(s) affected. The following are from the most to the least common.

- **Liver:** The liver enlarges. There may be a lump on the liver's edge. The tumor may burst causing sudden ANAPHYLAXIS, ACUTE ABDOMEN, or both.
- **Lung:** Cough, shortness of breath, fever, and PLEURISY. He may have symptoms of ALLERGY. If the tumor ruptures, the patient will cough up a mouthful of salty fluid.
- **Bowel:** Abdominal swelling with progressive constipation leads to ACUTE ABDOMEN, Type 3.
- **Skin:** A lump is under the skin; it feels like a water balloon.
- **Breast:** A lump which feels like a water balloon.
- **Bone:** Pain, possibly with spontaneous fracture.
- **Spleen:** Similar to liver, but on the left side. The liver is usually larger than the spleen.
- **Brain:** STROKE, BRAIN TUMOR.
- **Kidney:** A big bulge develops in the back waist area, possibly with pain. KIDNEY FAILURE may occur after a time.

Complications: ANAPHYLAXIS, ALLERGY, ASTHMA, all common with dog-transmitted disease. Also consider LIVER FAILURE, RESPIRATORY FAILURE, ACUTE ABDOMEN, KIDNEY FAILURE, STROKE, BRAIN DAMAGE.

ASCARIASIS occurs if anyone says he has passed worms by rectum or by mouth. ASCARIASIS worms are the size of earthworms or larger.

Similar Conditions: See Protocol C-7 for other causes of a large liver and/or spleen.
Liver: AMEBIC LIVER DISEASE, GALLBLADDER DISEASE, liver CANCER.
Lung: PNEUMONIA, TUBERCULOSIS.
Bowel: ASCARIASIS, abdominal TUBERCULOSIS.
Skin: SYPHILIS (tertiary), CYSTICERCOSIS.
Breast: MASTITIS, CANCER, TUBERCULOSIS.
Bone: TUBERCULOSIS, CANCER
Spleen: TROPICAL SPLENOMEGALY.
Brain: CYSTICERCOSIS and similar diseases.
Kidney: CANCER.

Higher-Level Care. See Volume I Appendix 13. *Laboratory:* Hospitals can do blood tests, x-rays, or ultrasound. The blood tests are more reliable in the wild animal-transmitted than in the dog-transmitted forms of the disease. *Facilities:* X-ray and ultrasound might be helpful; in some cases a surgical theatre is necessary. *Practitioners*: Infectious disease specialist with tropical/travel expertise is ideal; a generalist or internist might be helpful. A surgeon may be necessary.

Treatment:

Traditionally this has always been surgical. However, recently it has been shown that MEBENDAZOLE in enormous doses works quite well; a 70 kg man would take 140 tablets a day! Given this amount, patients near death have made full recoveries within 6 months.

The drug must be given the entire 6 months. The drug is not toxic at this dose, but for some people side effects are intolerable. ALBENDAZOLE also works, reportedly better than MEBENDAZOLE, and FLUBENDAZOLE may work well. Reportedly PRAZIQUANTEL might be helpful.

HYDROCELE

Cause: Unknown.

Clinical:

Hydrocele is a swelling next to one or both testicles in males of any age, due to a pocket of watery fluid.

Similar Conditions: It differs from a hernia in that the swelling is confined to the testicles, not extending up to the groin. It differs from tumor in that a small light placed behind the swelling in a dark room shows it to be translucent; only the testicle is opaque. It generally is not at all painful or tender. The testicle is totally surrounded by water so it cannot be felt within the scrotum.

Treatment:

Hydrocele can be treated whenever it is convenient to do so. Send the patient to a hospital.

HYPERIMMUNE MALARIAL SPLENOMEGALY

See TROPICAL SPLENOMEGALY.

HYPERTENSION

Cause: Variable.
Synonym: High blood pressure.
Regional Notes: E, F, U.
Definition: Adult BP over 140/90 for Westerners and 130/80 for nationals, both at rest.

Entry category: Syndrome.

Not ill to moderately ill; Class 1-4, depending on severity; Somewhat related to salt consumption.

Age: Any, but mainly adults. **Who:** Anyone, but especially Westerners and those with KIDNEY FAILURE. Many of the medicines used for ASTHMA can cause this, as well as licorice (a kind of black or red candy). **Onset:** Over months; more rapidly in pregnancy and KIDNEY DISEASE.

Clinical:

Necessary: Blood pressure is higher than normal, even at rest.

Maybe: The patient may have no symptoms or he may have headaches.

Complications: If the pressure goes very high, he will have HEART FAILURE, KIDNEY FAILURE, or STROKE. He may become blind. Hypertension can both cause KIDNEY FAILURE and be caused by it. It may cause nosebleed which can be severe and will not stop until the blood pressure can be lowered.

Similar Conditions: TOXEMIA, STROKE, KIDNEY FAILURE and HEART FAILURE are or can be associated with hypertension. Check for these but do not fail to treat the hypertension in the meantime.

Bush Laboratory: Urinalysis might show protein.

Higher-Level Care. See Volume I, Appendix 13. *Laboratory:* Level 3 and above hospital labs can do blood tests and electrocardiograms to check for possible causes and for complications. *Facilities:* A monitored bed is desirable in critical cases. *Practitioner:* Internist, obstetrician/gynecologist, possibly other specialists if there is a specific cause.

Treatment:

Prevention: Frequent blood pressure checks; avoid eating salt.

Patient Care: Higher-level care is very desirable as you are incapable of determining the specific cause. In every case, tell the patient to avoid salt and baking powder in his diet; to lose weight if he is overweight; and to exercise regularly.

(Subtract 10 points off the following blood pressures for non-Westerners in developing areas.)

- ❖ **140/90 to 160/100:** HYDROCHLOROTHIAZIDE, 50 mg by mouth daily, and a low salt diet. If KIDNEY FAILURE is not a problem, then also increase dietary potassium intake (e.g., eat apricots, avocados, bananas, coconut water, dates, papaya, potatoes, pumpkin, spinach, tomatoes, or citrus fruits).
- ❖ **160/100 to 190/110:** drug and diet as above plus METHYLDOPA 250 mg by mouth every 6 hours.
- ❖ Anyone with blood pressure over this should be sent out, treating as above in the meantime.

HYDRALAZINE may substitute for METHYLDOPA. PROPRANOLOL or VERAPAMIL may be added.

FUROSEMIDE may substitute for HYDROCHLOROTHIAZIDE. If you substitute another drug, use the dose for that drug rather than for the original drug. In the presence of KIDNEY FAILURE, use that diet rather than the one listed above. Do not stop or reduce treatment when the pressure comes down to normal levels, but do reduce doses if the pressure goes below the normal range.

Results: 2 weeks for HYDROCHLOROTHIAZIDE alone; 6 hours for both drugs.

HYPERVENTILATION

Cause: Anxiety.
Regional Notes: O.
Definition: Hyperventilation is the state in which a patient is breathing deeper and faster than necessary for the amount of air exchange he requires.

Entry category: Syndrome.

Very ill during an episode; Class 1; Worldwide, related to culture.

Age: Usually only adults. **Who:** More females than males, more emotional than stoical. **Onset:** Suddenly over minutes.

Clinical:

Necessary: The patient breathes rapidly, feeling very short of breath. He is dizzy and very anxious or panicked. He is not blue and his breathing is not noisy with wheezing or raspy inspiration.

Maybe: He might feel numb around the lips, have numbness, tingling, and cramping of the hands, lose consciousness, and have a SEIZURE.

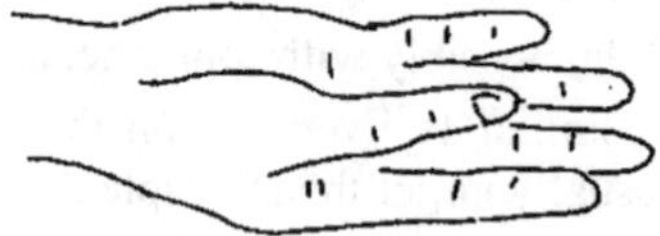

Cramped hand: Symptom of Hyperventilation.

Similar Conditions: With ANAPHYLAXIS the patient's hands are never cramped. Persistent vomiting, CHOLERA, RICKETS, and some hormonal problems can cause similar hand cramping without shortness of breath.

Treatment:

Put your cupped hands or a paper bag over the mouth and nose of the patient so he rebreathes some of the air he breathes out. (Never use a plastic bag.) This should solve the problem within 5 to 10 minutes. Deal with emotional causes if necessary.

HYPOGLYCEMIA

Synonyms: Low blood sugar, Insulin reaction
Regional Notes: F, M.
Definition: Hypoglycemia is the state of too little sugar in the blood.

Entry category: Syndrome.

Mildly to very ill; Class 1-3; Worldwide with varying causes.

Age: Any. **Who:** Anyone, especially those with MALARIA or MALNUTRITION. May also be caused by some PLANT POISONs or certain drugs, especially insulin. **Onset:** Slow onset and recurrent usually. Rapid onset when caused by various diseases, drugs, or poisons.

Clinical:

Necessary: The patient is either weak and sweaty and shaky or he is sweaty and unconscious.[1] Sugar abolishes the symptoms.

Maybe: The patient may be quite emotional, laughing or crying with the slightest provocation. He may appear to be drunk. He may have SEIZURES. His pulse will be rapid and he is likely to be lethargic or fatigued.

Causative Diseases: Treated DIABETES; MALARIA and/or the QUININE used to treat it; MALNUTRITION; PLANT POISONING due to Akee; poisoning with drugs used to treat DIABETES (especially INSULIN).

Similar Conditions: Alcohol withdrawal, see ALCOHOLISM; RELAPSING FEVER treatment; SHOCK from any cause.

Bush Laboratory: There are blood dipsticks, similar to urine dipsticks, that can indicate if the blood sugar is low, normal, or high. If you do much medical care, they are worthwhile to obtain.

Higher-Level Care. *Laboratory:* Level 3 or above. *Facilities:* In severe cases, IV's with fluids are helpful. *Practitioners:* Generalist, internist, pediatrician.

Treatment:

If the patient is not alert, prompt treatment is essential. Use IV fluids with sugar or use a stomach tube with sugar water.

For the spontaneous type in an alert patient, recommend six small, sugar-free meals a day. Sugar helps the problem immediately but tends to provoke more episodes. Provide nourishment in MALNUTRITION.

[1] Some people who are on beta-blocker drugs such as PROPRANOLOL may fail to be sweaty or shaky and will just be unconscious or lethargic. This kind of drug is generally only available in developed areas and it is usually prescribed for people who have HYPERTENSION or who have had ANGINA or a HEART ATTACK.

HYPOTHERMIA

Cause: Cold exposure.
Synonyms: Exposure.
Regional Notes: F.
Definition: Hypothermia is an abnormally low body temperature.

Entry category: Syndrome, environmental.

Moderately to very ill; Class 1-3 depending on how cold the patient is.

Age: Any. **Who:** Inadequately clothed and exposed to cold, especially infants, old people, and those wet or hungry. **Onset:** Variable.

Clinical:

Necessary: The patient has been exposed to cold, maybe lost and wet and cold overnight. He has a low body temperature, 35.5°C (96°F) or less.

Maybe: He is either very lethargic or unconscious and may have a low or no blood pressure and a slow or no pulse.

Complication: GANGRENE.

Similar Conditions: See Protocol C-10B.

Treatment:

Even if you do not find a blood pressure or pulse, the patient may be alive. The patient is not certainly dead until he is warm and dead!

- Remove cold, wet clothing. Warm him gently with heated blankets. As soon as one blanket cools, replace it with another dry, warm one. If he is conscious, give him hot tea to drink.
- Breathe for the patient if he is unconscious and does not appear to be breathing adequately.
- Watch closely for signs of life. Give up after a few hours or after the body is warm and dead.
- If you are successful (and he was unconscious), send him out. This is not necessary if he never lost consciousness.
- Check for FROSTBITE and treat this if it occurs.

IMPACTION

Cause: Constipation in bedridden people.
Definition: An impaction is hard-packed stool in the rectum, which the patient is unable to pass.

Mildly to moderately ill; Class 1 usually; Worldwide.

Age: Any. **Who:** Anyone, especially chronically ill and old, paralyzed. **Onset:** Days.

Clinical:

Necessary: The patient is constipated. If you put a gloved finger in the rectum, you will feel it packed with hard stool.

Sometimes: He has small amounts of watery diarrhea that flows past the hard stool. Abdominal pain is frequent.

Similar Conditions: ACUTE ABDOMEN, Type 3; always check first for impaction and remove the stool before sending out the patient. It may make the hospital trip unnecessary. ASCARIASIS, abdominal TUBERCULOSIS, CANCER, and HYDATID DISEASE can cause bowel obstruction but in these cases there is no hard stool in the rectum.

Higher-Level Care. For severe or recurrent problems, a level 3 or above hospital with a surgeon might be helpful.

Treatment:

Remove hard stool by pulling it out with your gloved fingers. Then try an oil enema. Do not use laxatives or enemas until some stool is out. *Results:* Within a day.

IMPETIGO

Cause: Bacteria.

Regional Notes: I, U.

Definition: Impetigo is a bacterial infection of the outer layers of the skin, almost always gram positive.

Not ill; Class 1; Contagious; Worldwide and very common everywhere.

Age: Any, especially babies and children. **Who:** Anyone; usually a history of some minor injury. **Onset:** Hours to a day or two.

Clinical:

Necessary: An area of skin is rough, with irregular bumps like pimples or blisters which are broken open and weeping. These break open, forming an off-white to gray to honey-colored crust with a rough, variously-colored surface. In some cases the skin resembles sandpaper. The area might be painful or itch, but not intensely.

Usually: There is yellow, crusted, dried pus on the affected area.

Maybe: Fever occurs if the problem is severe.

Complications: KIDNEY FAILURE, nephritic type; TETANUS, other bacterial infections.

Similar Conditions: DIPHTHERIA which affects the nose, causing a similar skin condition on the upper lip. YAWS has discreet circles whereas impetigo is over irregularly-shaped areas. SEXUALLY TRANSMITTED DISEASEs cause spontaneous wounds on the genital area or near the mouth. Lupus vulgaris, a form of skin TUBERCULOSIS may be indistinguishable but the patient usually has symptoms of lung TUBERCULOSIS.

Treatment:

Prevention: Cleanliness; encourage the use of soap and water.

Patient Care: Washing with warm water and soap and drying well 4 times a day will usually suffice if there is no fever. Cover the area with IODINE ointment or ANTIBIOTIC CREAM or ANTIBIOTIC OINTMENT between washings. Use an oral antibiotic such as PENICILLIN, ERYTHROMYCIN, CEPHALOSPORIN, or AZITHROMYCIN if the problem is severe.

Results: It should improve within a week.

INDIAN CHILDHOOD CIRRHOSIS

Cause: Probably toxin.

Definition: ICC is a severe, progressive type of LIVER FAILURE which affects Indian children both in India and in other parts of the world.

Cause: It is thought to be caused by feeding milk from bronze drinking vessels. It occurs less often where bronze drinking vessels are not used.

Entry category: Disease, probably toxic.

Age: Children. **Who:** It affects boys more than girls, middle class more than upper class or poor, and Hindus more than non-Hindus. It tends to run in families, mostly in families originating in southern India, Calcutta, and Punjab.

Onset: The disease begins gradually, but once it begins, death is inevitable.

Clinical:

There may be a low-grade fever. The child is irritable and has a tender, swollen abdomen full of fluid (See Volume I Chapter 1). The liver is first enlarged and then it shrinks. The spleen is enlarged and hard. There is JAUNDICE and fluid in the abdomen. There may be abnormal bleeding: nosebleeds; bloody urine, stool, or vomit; bleeding gums; excessive bleeding from minor wounds. Sometimes HYPERTENSION develops.

Higher-Level Care. A level 3 or above hospital is essential to confirm the diagnosis and eliminate treatable causes of liver failure. Find someone familiar with this disease. Most physicians don't know about it.

Treatment:

It is difficult but there are some newer treatments that permit survival. Higher-level care is mandatory.

INFLUENZA

Regional Notes: E.

Synonym: Flu.

Definition: Influenza is a general viral infection of the body, causing muscle aching amongst other symptoms.

Mildly to moderately ill; Class 1; Contagious; Worldwide and common everywhere.

Age: Any. **Who:** Anyone. **Onset:** Over a day or two.

Clinical:

Necessary: The patient feels tired and his muscles ache all over.

Usually: He may have nausea, vomiting, abdominal pain, diarrhea, fever under 39°C (102°F), and headache. If he has a rash or the problem lasts over 3 days, or an adult has mental changes, it is likely to be something else. A rare complication in children, Reye's Syndrome, causes mental changes and severe, persistent vomiting. This requires hospital treatment; give sugar in the meantime

Similar Conditions: See Protocol C-2. In malarious areas treat for MALARIA if there is a fever.

Treatment:

Keep the patient in bed and treat FEVER *per se* but do not use ASPIRIN or antibiotics.

INSECTICIDE POISONING

Cause: Toxin.

Clinical:

Insecticides vary one from another, but generally they cause an outpouring of body fluids and they activate involuntary muscles. As a result the patient has tearing, much saliva, sweating, coughing due to secretions in the respiratory tract, much urine, and diarrhea. See PLANT POISONING, Muscarine also; the effects are similar.

Treatment:

ATROPINE, giving repeated, small doses frequently, as much as necessary to counteract the symptoms. This may involve giving much more than the usual dose.

INTESTINAL FLUKE

Cause: Worm.
Includes: Fasciolopsiasis, Heterophyiasis, Metagonimiasis, Echinostomiasis, Gastrodisciasis.
Regional Notes: E, I, M, O, R, S.
Definition: Intestinal fluke is a bowel infestation of any one of the flukes (flat worms) named above.

Not ill to very ill; Class 1.

The problem occurs in all major regions of the world except Africa south of the Sahara and the Pacific area. It is a tropical disease. The different varieties of intestinal flukes are found in different areas:

- *Fasciolopsiasis* is found throughout Asia (Regions I, O, S); it is the most serious.
- *Heterophysiasis* is found throughout Asia also (Regions I, O, S), plus in Tunisia and Egypt (Region R). It is second in seriousness.
- The other kinds, *Metagonimiasis, Echinostomiasis, Gastrodisciasis,* are found in Regions E, I, O, S, and in Guyana.

Age: Any except nursing infants. **Who:** Those eating raw or rare fish. *Fasciolopsiasis* may also be acquired by eating raw water plants or by peeling them with the teeth. **Onset:** Incubation 2-3 months; slow, insidious onset.

Clinical:

This varies by type and geographic area:

➢ **Fasciolopsiasis:**

Most patients have no symptoms at all. In heavy infections, they may have diarrhea alternating with constipation and abdominal pain when hungry, relieved by food. With very severe disease, the patient will have loss of appetite, nausea, vomiting, continuous abdominal pain, and swelling of the face and body. He may develop MALABSORPTION: a prompt, watery diarrhea whenever the person eats anything. He may accumulate fluid in his abdomen making him look pregnant.

➢ **Heterophysiasis:**

This causes indigestion, abdominal pain, diarrhea like dysentery, and occasionally HEART FAILURE or sudden death.

➢ **Echinostomiasis, Gastrodisciasis, Metagonimiasis:**

These each cause only diarrhea with no long-term consequences.

Similar Conditions: *Abdominal pain* relieved by food: PEPTIC ULCER. Alternating *constipation and diarrhea*: IRRITABLE BOWEL. *Severe diarrhea*: MALABSORPTION. See Protocol C-14

Higher-Level Care. *Laboratory:* Level 3 or above. When the disease is fully developed, worm eggs might be found in the stool. Earlier in the disease, there will be a large number of eosinophils in a blood smear. However, other diseases can also cause that.

Treatment:

Prevention: Cook fish and water plants well before eating. Do not use teeth to peel plants when they are raw.

Patient Care: PRAZIQUANTEL is the drug of choice for most kinds; seek local lore. TETRACHLOROETHYLENE might be more available and/or cheaper. Give a low-fat meal in the evening. Give PROMETHAZINE in the morning; then give TETRACHLOROETHYLENE and 4-5 hours later give MILK OF MAGNESIA or something else to cause diarrhea. NICLOSAMIDE also works but it is not safe.

IRITIS

Cause: Variable.
Synonyms: Uveitis.
Regional Notes: F, M, R.
Definition: Iritis is inflammation of the iris and the surrounding structures of the eye, behind the cornea but in front of the eye's lens.

Mildly ill; Class 2-3; Worldwide.

Age: Any. **Who:** Anyone, especially those with LEPROSY, TUBERCULOSIS, SYPHILIS, LARVA MIGRANS, REITER SYNDROME, LEPTOSPIROSIS during the recovery phase, or eye injury. **Onset:** Usually sudden, may be gradual.

Clinical:

Necessary: The patient has pain in the eye(s) and his vision is blurred. His pupil is small and irregular, not round; the shape is like a key-hole or oval or scalloped. This is more obvious if you use drops to dilate the eye (HOMATROPINE OPHTHALMIC). If the problem has been for a long time, he may have little or no pain but only blurry vision.

Usually: The white of the eye is red but the redness is more around the cornea than further out (in contrast to other problems in which the redness is either worse further out or the same all over). The patient avoids light since it aggravates the pain; he has increased tears. The pain may be aggravated when a light is shone into the opposite (good) eye, or when the patient shifts between near and far vision.

Occasionally: The patient has a fever.

If you have an ophthalmoscope, move the magnification to +20-30. If you look at the eye, you will see black dots on the shiny red pupil.

Similar Conditions: See Protocol C-8. SYPHILIS (tertiary) might cause iritis. Also consider TB of the eye and XEROPHTHALMIA (poor vision in dim light).

Higher-Level Care. A level 3 or above facility with an ophthalmologist (an optometrist at a minimum) is most helpful.

Treatment:

Do not treat for this unless you are sure of the diagnosis! If the pupil has an irregular shape and this is not the way it was before, and there is no facial rash, then treatment might be safe. But you should still seek outside advice. Use steroid eye drops, such as PREDNISOLONE EYE DROPS (labeled ophthalmic), using one or two drops every hour until the inflammation has subsided, then use them 4 times a day for 4 days, but no longer.

IRRITABLE BOWEL

Cause: Stress.

Synonyms: Spastic bowel, Spastic colitis.

Regional Notes: F, I, M, R.

Definition: Irritable bowel is bowel spasms caused by stress.

Mildly ill; Class 1; Worldwide, related to culture.

Age: Any. **Who:** Anyone, especially those who have had this before. **Onset:** Variable.

Clinical:

Necessary: The patient has crampy abdominal pain with either diarrhea or constipation or both, alternating. The location of the pain is around the navel or all over, or the location moves. (However, if it just moves from upper or center abdomen to the lower-right and then stays there, it may be ACUTE ABDOMEN.) There is no fever.

Maybe: The abdomen may be tender all over, but the patient does not howl if someone jars the bed. (DEPRESSION is a common cause of irritable bowel, as are unfamiliar foods and STRESS.)

Similar Conditions: STRONGYLOIDIASIS may be similar but it causes an itchy rectum. Check for a blue line on the gums; if you find it, the patient may have LEAD POISONING. GASTROENTERITIS and FOOD POISONING (if the patient eats alone) might be indistinguishable. Early DYSENTERY due to amebae might be similar. Various WORMS might cause similar symptoms.

Higher-Level Care. *Laboratory*: Level 3 or above might be useful to eliminate other possible diagnoses. *Practitioner:* Generalist, internist, pediatrician.

Treatment:

Use DICYCLOMINE or CHAMOMILE TEA to relieve the pain. Suggest a vacation or counseling if appropriate.

JAUNDICE

Cause: Variable.

Regional Notes: F, I, M, O, R, S, U.

Definition: Jaundice means yellow skin, yellow whites of the eyes, or both.

Entry category: Syndrome cluster; See Protocol C-7.

Note: Jaundice is a syndrome cluster, not a diagnosis; proper treatment depends on establishing a diagnosis.

Clinical:

- **Ordinary Jaundice, Not Newborn:**

When mild, the yellow color is first visible underneath the tongue, in the tab of tissue that holds the tongue to the floor of the mouth. It is easiest to see in sunlight and hardest to see under fluorescent lights. With true jaundice, the whites of the eyes are always yellow. With excess consumption of yellow/orange foods such as carrots, the skin will turn yellow but the whites of the eyes are still white. This is not true jaundice; it will pass with a dietary change.

- **Jaundice in Newborns:**

Jaundice: in newborns becomes visible the first or second day. If it is after the second day, then it is probably due to some illness, not the normal transient jaundice that many babies have. It is seen first on the face and forehead. Firm pressure on the skin makes it more visible. After that it is seen on the trunk and limbs. The infant is apt to be drowsy. If there are stiff or floppy muscles, SEIZURES, or a change in voice, this mandates immediate transfer to a hospital. Neonatal jaundice occurs more in east Asians and at high altitudes, less in Black children.

There are 3 kinds of jaundice:

➢ **Due to Destruction of Red Blood Cells:**

In this case the jaundice is a pure yellow. There is urobilinogen in the urine, but no bilirubin. It is normal to have 1+ urobilinogen in the urine. Only 2+ and more are abnormal. This is the usual kind that newborns have.

➢ **Due to Liver Damage:**

In this case the jaundice is orangish-yellow and there is bilirubin in the urine. There is more bilirubin than urobilinogen. If you don't have the urine dipsticks to check for bilirubin, put some of the patient's urine in a clear glass container. Put some normal urine in a similar container. Shake them both together. If there is bilirubin in the patient's urine, it will get a larger head of foam on the top than the normal urine, and the foam will be yellowish.

➢ **Due to Bile Blockage:**
The bile cannot pass from the liver to the intestines. In this case the jaundice is greenish-yellow. There is bilirubin in the urine. Frequently jaundice from this cause will result in severe, whole-body itching. The patient will say that he itches deep inside his body, where he can't scratch. If the jaundice is intense, the stool is likely to be white or very light-colored.

Causative and Similar Conditions: See Protocols C-5 (Fever + Jaundice) and C-7 (Liver/Spleen Problems).

Diseases that cause jaundice by destroying red cells (result in more urobilinogen than bilirubin in the urine): MALARIA, SICKLE CELL DISEASE, TROPICAL SPLENOMEGALY, THALLASEMIA, BARTONELLOSIS, OVALOCYTOSIS, VISCERAL LEISHMANIASIS.

Diseases that cause jaundice by liver damage (result in more bilirubin than urobilinogen in the urine): HEPATITIS, PNEUMONIA, SCHISTOSOMIASIS JAPONICUM, SCHISTOSOMIASIS MANSONI, YELLOW FEVER, INDIAN CHILDHOOD CIRRHOSIS, LIVER FLUKE.

Diseases that cause jaundice by blocking bile flow (give light colored stools): ASCARIASIS, GALLBLADDER DISEASE, LIVER FLUKE, CANCER.

Help with Diagnosis and Treatment:
Jaundice with Fever: Protocol C-5. Other causes are: THALLASEMIA, RELAPSING FEVER, SPOTTED FEVER, YELLOW FEVER, SEPSIS, SICKLE CELL DISEASE, PNEUMONIA (only in Blacks and those of Mediterranean origin), BARTONELLOSIS (small areas of NW South America), PYOMYOSITIS.

Jaundice without Fever: Painless in middle age: check CANCER. Also consider MALARIA if the patient is seen when the temperature happens to be down but he had either fever or chills previously.

Newborn: See Volume I, Chapter 6.

Infant: See MALARIA, HEPATITIS, TUBERCULOSIS SYPHILIS; check similar diseases listed under these.

Higher-Level Care. *Laboratory:* A level 3 hospital can do a blood test to determine the seriousness of the jaundice and sometimes the cause also. *Facilities:* Many imaging and other facilities at a level 4 or 5 might be helpful. *Practitioner:* A gastroenterologist is ideal. A generalist or internist is appropriate initially. In some cases a referral to a surgeon should be made.

Treatment:

Newborns: Put the infant under a special intense light, no more than 50 cm (20 inches) away. Sunlight also works but not as well as the specially-made artificial lights. Newborns who have jaundice may have green teeth later in life.

Other patients: One can only treat symptoms. For itching due to jaundice: try CHOLESTYRAMINE; RIFAMPIN; sun exposure 1-2 hours daily.

JET LAG

Definition: Jet lag is a problem of a change in day and night cycles, frequently with profound emotional changes (irritability, DEPRESSION) which lasts for up to 2 weeks after travel over 6 or more time zones. It is worse with traveling east than traveling west. It is treatable with MELATONIN (see *Drug Index.*)

KATAYAMA DISEASE

Cause: Allergy/worm.
Regional Notes: F, I, M, O, R, S.
Definition: Katayama disease is an allergic reaction to a worm infestation. It is the initial stage of a number of diseases, especially HYDATID DISEASE, GUINEA WORM, and SCHISTOSOMIASIS (any kind but especially JAPONICUM); how common it is and which diseases it is related to in a particular area, vary greatly. It is one particular type of SERUM SICKNESS. Also see SERUM SICKNESS.

Mildly to severely ill; Class 2-3; Worldwide.

Entry category: Syndrome.

Age: Any **Who:** Those exposed to these diseases, almost always expatriates. **Onset:** Usually rapid, 3-8 weeks after exposure.

Clinical:

Katayama disease causes fever, hives, nausea, diarrhea, headache, fatigue, loss of appetite, or any combination of these symptoms. It may resemble ASTHMA. It may be severe and life-threatening. At least initially the symptoms tend to come and go. Usually the respiratory complaints are first and the abdominal complaints follow thereafter. The patient may give a history of having had SWIMMER'S ITCH 3-6 weeks before.

Similar Conditions: KIDNEY INFECTION may appear identical but in this case fresh urine will smell like stale urine and the urinalysis will be abnormal. Also consider ASTHMA and ALLERGY though in these cases there usually is no fever. TRICHINOSIS can be similar but it is rare except in outbreaks with a number of patients. HEPATITIS, ENTERIC FEVER, MALARIA, and other diseases can also cause headache and fever but in these cases there usually are no allergic symptoms.

Bush Laboratory: When the cause is SCHISTOSOMIASIS, the stool might (or might not) be positive for the eggs. (See Appendix 2 of Volume I: Egg Hatching Lab Test). Eventually it will become positive, in a matter of days or weeks. You might be able to check this yourself with the lab procedure for hatching the eggs.

Higher-Level Care. *Laboratory:* A blood count may show an abnormally large percentage of eosinophils (over 5%). However, there are a number of other diseases that will also cause this. There is no definitive test. *Facilities:* It is safest to treat this in a Level 3 or higher facility with IV's and a monitored bed. *Practitioners:* Generalist, internist, pediatrician.

Treatment:

Prevention: Reportedly, ARTEMISININ, taken shortly after exposure, prevents Katayama Disease. It is uncertain if it prevents the infection or only the symptoms.

Patient Care: ASPIRIN and, if absolutely necessary, HYDROCORTISONE or PREDNISONE. Also treat for whatever seems to be the most likely cause. Be sure to use PREDNISONE together with PRAZIQUANTEL.

KELOID

Cause: Hereditary.

Clinical:

Keloid is a skin condition, found mostly in Blacks, causing huge scars in response to any injury, however minor. Something as trivial as a pimple or an insect bite can result in a bumpy lumpy scar the size of a small egg. Once formed, the scars remain.

Treatment:

You can do nothing about it, nor can most physicians. Some plastic surgeons can remove the scars.

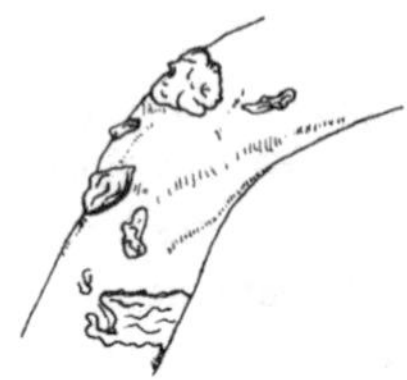

Keloids

KERATITIS

Cause: Variable.

Includes: Corneal abrasion, Corneal burn, Corneal ulcer, Herpes keratitis.

Definition: Keratitis is an inflamed (painful) cornea caused by some irritation of the corneal surface.

Entry category: Syndrome.

Age: More often adults than children. **Who:** Those who have a scratched cornea, a foreign body in the eye, exposure to UV light (such as in welding), or a variety of diseases such as TRACHOMA, HERPES, SYPHILIS, ONCHOCERCIASIS, or LEPROSY. It may occur because of the eyes being dry. In hot, humid areas corneal ulcers due to fungi form around corneal foreign bodies of vegetable origin. At high altitudes or sea shores keratitis may be caused by sunlight which reflects off white rocks or snow or white sand. This causes burned corneas, similar to those of welders who do not wear special glasses. **Onset:** Sometimes immediately after the injury, but many times after a delay of 2-12 hours.

Clinical:

Unless the eye is numb, there is severe pain and watering. Usually the whites of the eyes are somewhat red. The patient complains that light hurts his eyes. With SYPHILIS, ONCHOCERCIASIS and LEPROSY, the patient may see halos or rainbows around lights. His vision is distorted. Keratitis due to congenital SYPHILIS starts in the middle of the cornea; that due to TRACHOMA starts in a ring around the outside of the cornea.

If the problem is due to HERPES and you stain the cornea(s) with fluorescein, you will see a stained branching or a puddle-of-water shape.

Keratitis: Patterns of corneal staining with Herpes.

Complications: IRITIS, blindness.

Similar Conditions: See Protocol C-8. TB of the eye causes a little white blister right at the border between the cornea and the white of the eye. Also check for XEROPHTHALMIA.

Higher-Level Care. *Facilities:* A level 3 or above hospital with a slit lamp. If the problem is due to HERPES, there are expensive, antiviral eye drops available in major medical centers. *Practitioner*: An optometrist or ophthalmologist is most helpful.

Treatment:

- Check for GLAUCOMA before treating for keratitis.
- If the problem is due to ONCHOCERCIASIS, LEPROSY, or SYPHILIS, PREDNISOLONE EYE DROPS may be helpful but their use requires accurate diagnosis which is best done in a hospital.
- Treat the causative disease(s).
- If the problem is due to a fungus, try ANTIBIOTIC EYE OINTMENT made with sulfadiazine, or else oral THIABENDAZOLE.
- See Chapter 9 in Vol. I for removing any foreign body; this must be done before the keratitis will heal. Thereafter, use ATROPINE, HOMATROPINE, or TROPICAMIDE EYE DROPS to make the pupil big and then put in some ANTIBIOTIC EYE OINTMENT and patch the eyes for 72 hours. Renew the ointment every 6 hours. If you use ANTIBIOTIC EYE DROPS the drops must be renewed every 2-4 hours. The patient may require oral pain medication, repeated HOMATROPINE, or both.

Keshan Disease.

See *Regional Notes* O.

KIDNEY DISEASE

This is the same as KIDNEY FAILURE—see entry below—except that it is not as severe. The patient may have an abnormal urinalysis (see Volume I, Appendix 2) and may have a somewhat high blood pressure. Many times kidney disease is without symptoms until full-blown KIDNEY FAILURE occurs.

KIDNEY FAILURE

Cause: Variable.
Synonyms: Renal failure.
Includes: Glomerulonephritis, Nephrotic syndrome, Hydronephrosis.
Regional Notes: F, I, M, O, R, S, U.
Definition: Kidney failure is the inability of the kidney to properly handle the wastes that the body presents to it, causing an accumulation of these wastes in the body.

Entry category: Syndrome cluster.

Moderately to very ill; Class 3-4; Worldwide, related to MALARIA, crowding, and level of medical care. Commonly: due to tropical diseases.

Age: Any. **Who:** Anyone, mainly children and aged; mostly a complication of other diseases but it may happen for no obvious reason. In the developing world, untreated KIDNEY INFECTION is the most common cause. LIVER FAILURE may cause kidney failure also. **Onset:** Over days, usually; may be over weeks or months.

Clinical:

There are six types of kidney failure, according to causation, with some symptoms peculiar to each. These are listed in the table, *Types of Kidney Failure.*

The following symptoms are common to all:

Necessary: Fatigue, ANEMIA, dry and flaky skin, urine which is abnormal either in amount or in dipstick test, rapid respiration,

Commonly: High blood pressure. There is nausea, vomiting, and a decrease in appetite. The patient's eyes are swollen in the morning; his ankles and feet are swollen later in the day. In severe cases his whole body, including his abdomen, may swell. He may have pain over his kidneys. There may be an abnormal skin color—a yellow/bronze.

Occasionally: He has a headache. His respiration may be very irregular. He may have a body odor resembling ammonia or urine. In some cases he has involuntary trembling, similar to LIVER FAILURE. He is likely to have muscle cramps. He may have abnormal bruising of the skin or bloody diarrhea. Males may develop breast tissue like females.

Types Of Kidney Failure

Type	Most Common Causes	Usual Symptoms	Urinalysis	Treatment
Nephrotic (leaky)	Variable.[1]	Swollen eyes mornings; swollen legs and feet evenings.	Always much protein.[2]	Diet.[3] Bed rest. PREDNISONE or HYDROCORTISONE.
Nephritic (inflamed)	Any skin infection, other.[4]	High blood pressure.[5] HEART FAILURE.	Positive for blood. Maybe positive for protein.	Diet.[6] Bed rest, sitting. HYDROCHLOROTHIAZIDE.[7]
Obstructive (blocked)	FILARIASIS. KIDNEY STONE. HYDATID DISEASE. PROSTATITIS. TUBERCULOSIS Urethral stricture.	Side pain or low abdominal pain.	Maybe no urine. Urinalysis variable.	Treat cause. Surgical removal of a single diseased kidney may help.
Infective or toxic (poisoned)	MALARIA. SEPSIS. TRICHINOSIS. LEPTOSPIROSIS. Drugs and poisons. ARSENIC POISONING. ENTERIC FEVER. PLANT POISONING.	Decreasing quantity of urine, otherwise like nephritic type.	Varies, always abnormal, commonly bloody.	Treat cause. Send out. Diet.[6] Bed rest, sitting. HYDROCHLOROTHIAZIDE.[7] Surgical removal of a single diseased kidney may help.
Prerenal (dehydrated)	SEPSIS, Burns, Injuries DEHYDRATION.	Decreasing quantity of urine, followed by huge quantities.	Urinalysis probably normal.	Fluid balance.[8] Treat cause.
Hemolytic (bloody)	MALARIA, THALASEMIA, DYSENTERY, SICKLE CELL DISEASE, Some drugs.	Similar to prerenal.	Urobilinogen probable. Maybe bilirubin. Maybe blood.	Lots of fluids. Give baking soda to raise urine pH to 8-9.

Notes to Kidney Failure Table:

1.The most common cause of *nephrotic* kidney failure is MALARIA. Other causes are TUBERCULOSIS, STREP THROAT, SYPHILIS, HEPATITIS, SICKLE CELL DISEASE, SCHISTOSOMIASIS MANSONI, and ENTERIC FEVER. It has a poor prognosis.

2. See laboratory procedures, Appendix 2, Volume I.

3. Diet: High protein, high carbohydrate, low salt, low potassium. (There is much potassium in avocados, bananas, coconut, citrus fruits, dates, papayas, potatoes, pumpkin, spinach.).

4. Other causes of *nephritic* kidney failure are STREP THROAT, FILARIASIS, some WORMS, LEPROSY, HYPERTENSION, SICKLE CELL DISEASE, and DIABETES.

5. Use HYDRALAZINE to bring the pressure down to near normal.

6. Diet: Low protein, low carbohydrate, low salt, low potassium, high fat and calorie. (There is much potassium in avocados, bananas, coconut, citrus fruits, dates, papayas, potatoes, pumpkin, spinach.).

7. FUROSEMIDE may substitute.

8. Fluid balance: Treat DEHYDRATION. If he has signs of HEART FAILURE, give him FUROSEMIDE and restrict his fluid intake to just the amount of urine that he puts out. If he shows signs of neither HEART FAILURE or DEHYDRATION his total daily fluid intake is restricted to his urine output plus (600 ml per day for adults), or plus (12 ml per kg per day for children). **Do this whether the urine produced is too much or too little.** This might require very small or enormous amounts of fluid! In arid areas the patient will lose a lot of water through evaporation. In this case these directions must be modified; seek professional advice. *Results:* If the patient does not start urinating in a week, he will probably die. None of these problems is properly treated in the village; send the patient to a hospital.

Similar Conditions: See Protocols C-6, C-7, C-10, and C-13. *All types or most types*: GASTROENTERITIS, HEPATITIS, GIARDIASIS, PARKINSON'S DISEASE, DYSENTERY, SCURVY. HEART FAILURE, LIVER DISEASE, LIVER FAILURE, CIRRHOSIS, abdominal TUBERCULOSIS, HEMORRHAGIC FEVER.

Bush Laboratory: Blood tests can demonstrate kidney failure, the extent, and sometimes the cause. Urinalysis might be helpful.

Treatment:

Seek higher level care within a few days; See Volume I, Appendix 13. Only treat if sending is impossible. Treat any causative disease(s)

KIDNEY INFECTION

Cause: Bacteria.
Synonym: Pyelonephritis.
Regional Notes: F, M, R.
Definition: Kidney infection is a bacterial infection (usually gram-negative) of the upper urinary tract.

Mildly to moderately ill; Class 1 first episode; Class 2 subsequently; Worldwide, common.

Age: Any. **Who:** Anyone, especially females and babies; may be caused by ENTERIC FEVER. **Onset:** Hours to days or weeks.

Clinical:

Necessary: The patient has pain in his back, at the level of his waist, on one or both sides of the spine. These areas are tender. His urine looks cloudy.

Maybe: The patient may feel pain in his abdomen, in any portion or in his entire abdomen. The urine may have a foul odor. He may be quite sick with fevers, have pain with urination, nausea, and vomiting. He may be incontinent of urine. Children may have only abdominal pain. Newborns, especially low-birth-weight males, may have fever, JAUNDICE, and failure to gain weight.

Occasionally: Fever plus ALLERGY symptoms which may come and go.

Complication of repeated infection: SEPSIS, KIDNEY FAILURE.

Similar Conditions: See Protocols C-9 and C-13.

Bush laboratory: Urine will test positive for leukocytes and/or nitrites. Sometimes there is just a very high pH but these other tests are negative. The urine might or might not test positive for blood additionally.

Higher-Level Care. *Laboratory:* A hospital laboratory can do a complete urinalysis and possibly a culture. *Facilities:* IV fluids with special antibiotics might be helpful. *Practitioners:* Most generalists, internists, and pediatricians can manage this.

Treatment:

Use SULFADIAZINE, or COTRIMOXAZOLE if possible. AMPICILLIN also usually works. DOXYCYCLINE will work occasionally. CHLORAMPHENICOL will work but it is not safe. PENICILLIN will not work. CIPROFLOXACIN and OFLOXACIN are expensive drugs good for adults. Some CEPHALOSPORINS may work. If treatment with two different drugs fail, then consider TUBERCULOSIS as a cause of the kidney infection.

Results: 1-2 days. Continue treatment for 3-5 days for a first episode, for 10 days for subsequent episodes.

KIDNEY STONE

Cause: Variable.
Synonym: Ureteral colic.
Regional Notes: F, R.
Definition: A kidney stone is a small piece of hard crystal formed by the salts in urine.

Moderately ill, usually severe pain; Class 2-3; Worldwide.

Age: Any, but not usually children. **Who:** Anyone, but especially males; those with DEHYDRATION; sometimes it runs in families. Common in Muslims during Ramadan. **Onset:** Sudden, recurrent.

Clinical:

Necessary: The patient has pain in the side, back, groin(s), testicle(s) or vagina.

Sometimes: The pain shoots from the back (the right or left flank) or side to the lower abdomen or groin.

Frequently: The patient vomits. If there is an infection also, the patient will have fever or chills and feel ill. KIDNEY INFECTION with a stone can be exceedingly serious.

Complications: KIDNEY FAILURE, obstructive type.

Similar Conditions: ACUTE ABDOMEN is tender; kidney stones cause no tenderness unless there is a tear in the urinary tract. KIDNEY INFECTION and FILARIASIS onsets are slower.

Bush Laboratory: Blood in the urine. It is usually too little to be seen; it should be detected with a urine dipstick or a microscope.

Higher-Level Care. *Facilities:* There is some special equipment that can locate, snag, and remove kidney stones; Level 3 or above. *Practitioners:* A urologist is ideal; a surgeon might be helpful.

Treatment:

Have the patient drink large amounts of water, using PROMETHAZINE to keep him from vomiting. Treat KIDNEY INFECTION, if present. Use strong pain medications if you have them. Strain all urine through a cloth; save the stone if one passes, and send it to a hospital. (A stone looks like a grain of sand.)

Results: The patient will feel better when the stone passes into the bladder. When this happens is totally unpredictable; it can happen in 10 minutes or the problem can last weeks.

LACTOSE INTOLERANCE

See Milk intolerance.

LARVA MIGRANS

Synonym: Creeping eruption (skin type).
Includes: Cutaneous larva migrans, Gnathostomiasis, Toxocariasis, Visceral larva migrans.
Regional Notes: E, F, I, O, R, S, U.
Definition: Larva migrans is a human infestation of the larvae of worms which ordinarily affect animals.

Not ill to severely ill; Class 1-4; Worldwide, type varies, mostly tropical.

Age: Any, frequently children. **Who:** *Skin type*: skin-soil contact, like HOOKWORM *Deep type* may be caused by eating something contaminated with dog or cat stool. In Asia it is acquired by handling raw meat. **Onset:** Usually rapid.

Larva migrans on the buttocks.

Clinical:

➢ **Skin type Larva Migrans:**

There is a red outline of a worm is visible, moving beneath the skin. Sometimes the patient can feel the movement and there is swelling in the area.

➢ **Deep Larva Migrans:**

Symptoms vary with the organ of the body that is affected. In the eye there may be itching, pain, or loss of vision. In the liver it may mimic HEPATITIS or LIVER DISEASE or LIVER FAILURE. In the brain it will cause ENCEPHALITIS, SEIZURES, STROKE, and frequently death.

Similar Conditions: *Skin LM* is similar to STRONGYLOIDIASIS and MYIASIS. In larva migrans the lines are more definite and they last for weeks rather than for hours. With STRONGYLOIDIASIS there is more red, and a definite track is hard to see.

Deep LM may mimic almost any other disease as the worm in migrating might damage any internal organ. In Africa, consider LOIASIS.

Complications: Deep LM can damage any organ, depending where it is. In Southeast Asia, a kind of deep LM can cause SERUM SICKNESS.

Higher-Level Care. For deep larva migrans, speedy referral is essential; see Volume I, Appendix 13. *Laboratory:* A white blood count shows a large number of eosinophils; however, this is also found in some other diseases. *Facilities:* Level 4 or above imaging might be helpful. *Practitioners:* At times an infectious disease specialist or a surgeon is appropriate.

Treatment:

Prevention: Treat pets for worms; keep them indoors. In Southeast Asia, use rubber gloves to handle raw meat and fish to prevent a form of deep larva migrans.

Patient Care:

Skin LM near the buttocks should be treated as STRONGYLOIDIASIS. Other skin LM can be treated with ALBENDAZOLE or THIABENDAZOLE. Reportedly 10% THIABENDAZOLE is effective when rubbed on the surface of the skin.

Deep LM should be sent to a hospital for care. IVERMECTIN or ALBENDAZOLE might be helpful.

Results: The symptoms resolve in weeks to months after the larvae die. The patient will have itching until then.

Lassa Fever

See *Regional Notes* F.

LEAD POISONING

Cause: Lead ingestion.
Slightly ill to very ill; Class 3-4; Worldwide, more urban than rural, related to cottage industries involving batteries, ceramics, fishing weights, paints. There is frequently lead in illegal alcoholic drinks. Lead poisoning may result from a retained bullet or shrapnel fragments. Parent occupations associated with poisoning include lead mining, scrap metal work, glass-making, printing, welding.

Age: Any. **Who:** Lead poisoning occurs when people, especially children, breathe fumes or ingest chemicals containing lead. It is also seen in gold and silver workers who extract precious metals by heating them to high temperatures with lead. Some native eye ointments e.g. Kohl contain lead. Children get the ointment on their hands which then enter their mouths. Paints and fuels may contain lead. Many herbal supplements contain lead, including the following: Alarcon, Alkohl, Ayurvedic tonic, Azarcon, Bali goli, Clamshell powder, Coral calcium, Crocodile Bile, Crude Pills, Deshi Dewa, Gilasard, Greta, Liga, Paylooah, Rueda, Surma.

Onset: Usually slow.

Clinical:

The symptoms of lead poisoning are ANEMIA that does not respond to treatment, and sometimes symptoms of a slow-onset MENINGITIS. Adults get crampy abdominal pains, a sweet metallic taste in the mouth, constipation, and loss of appetite. A blue line may be seen on the gums above the teeth. The gums in the mouth may bleed. There may be a fever but it is usually low.

Similar Conditions: TB MENINGITIS, IRRITABLE BOWEL, IMPACTION. The blue line on the gums is distinctive; it occurs in no other disease.

Higher-Level Care. See Volume I, Appendix 13. *Laboratory:* Large hospital laboratories can sometimes test for lead poisoning. Lead causes a peculiar appearance on an ordinary blood smear which some technicians can detect. *Facilities:* There are some special medications to bind and remove lead from the body; at level 4 Western hospitals. *Practitioners:* A toxicologist is ideal.

Treatment: *Prevention:* Have parents change their clothes at work. Keep children away from dangerous cottage industry work.

Patient Care: Not feasible in the bush.

LEISHMANIASIS

See CUTANEOUS LEISHMANIASIS if the condition involves mainly skin; see VISCERAL LEISHMANIASIS if the condition mainly involves the abdomen.

LEPROSY

Cause: Bacteria - *Mycobacterium leprae.*
Synonym: Hansen's disease.
Regional Notes: All regions.
Definition: Leprosy is a slow-onset bacterial disease of the nerves, which secondarily affects the skin and other structures of the body.

Not ill to moderately ill; Class 2-3; Contagious, mildly;[1] Worldwide with variable frequency; most common in India, Brazil, Congo, Nepal, Mozambique, Tanzania.

Age: Any, but rare under 2 y.o. School-aged and older children tend to get tuberculoid leprosy. **Who:** Living or having lived in a community where the disease is common. Africans tend to get tuberculoid. Whites and Chinese tend to get lepromatous. The presence of HIV in a patient does not seem to have any effect on the development of leprosy. **Onset:** Slowly over weeks to months. The incubation period averages 5 years (range - from a few weeks to 30 years); minimum incubation is 6 months.

Clinical:

Types of Leprosy*:*
There used to be four kinds, as described in the following table but these are now considered under two headings because the treatment varies according to two classes, not four. Usually the disease starts out as indeterminate and then becomes one of the other kinds. It is unlikely that you will see much indeterminate; patients usually ignore this stage. Which kind a person gets depends on his body's resistance; it does not depend on the kind he was exposed to. All kinds of leprosy are more common and worse on the cooler parts of the body, not in the armpits, groin, or below large breasts.

➤ **Paucibacillary:**
The kinds of leprosy previously called Indeterminate and Tuberculoid are now called *Paucibacillary.* Only one or few nerve trunk(s) are affected: each nerve trunk involves only one side, right or left, on the face or trunk. If it is a limb, only the thumb/big toe side or only the little finger/little toe side is affected. There is an area of the skin where the patient cannot tell the difference between hot and cold. There may be fine, dry scales so it looks like TINEA. There are less than 5 abnormal areas on the skin.

➤ **Multibacillary:**
The old classification of Borderline and Lepromatous is now called *Multibacillary* leprosy. Multiple nerve trunks are involved so there are multiple areas of skin affected, generally more than five. There are symptoms on more than one limb or on a limb and the face and/or more than one side of a limb and/or both right and left sides of a limb or face.

There may be thickening and tenderness of one or more nerves: Thick nerves feel like strings of irregular diameter right underneath the skin. There may be pains along the thickened nerves.

It is important to test the patient for nerve function.

Check for temperature sense by asking the patient to tell the difference between test tubes with hot and cold water.

Check for light touch by having the patient close his eyes and tell you when you touch him with a wisp of cotton.

Check for pain by having the patient distinguish the sharp and dull ends of a new hypodermic needle.

Other manifestations of leprosy may be as follows:

Hands: The muscles of the thumb side of the palm are wasted, so there is no bulge on the palm below the thumb. Compare the two hands. The fingers may be stiff and bent, so the hand appears like a claw. There may be painless injuries on the fingers. The patient may have a weak wrist so that his hand drops to the palm side and he is unable to bend his hand back. Fingers may be shortened.

Face: There is likely to be a lack of eyebrows or eyelashes. One or both side(s) of the face may droop. There may be bumps on the face, especially the earlobes. The eyes may not close all the way. The corneas may be scarred or even totally opaque. The eyes may be excessively wet or dry. Vision is apt to be poorest in bright light. There may be pus coming from the nose. There may be hoarseness or decreased smell and taste.

[1] The only contagious leprosy patients are those with lepromatous (bumpy) leprosy. These are contagious through their respiratory secretions: mainly sneezing and coughing. No leprosy is contagious by touching intact skin. Some lepromatous leprosy might be transmitted by inoculation, e.g. sitting with a bare bottom on a rough surface that a leprous patient with buttock involvement had just vacated.

Types of Leprosy

Type	Appearance	Bodily Distribution	Disability
Indeterminate, Paucibacillary	Light or reddish coloration.[1] Flat. Margins indistinct.	One or few areas only, not symmetrical left/right.	Cannot feel hot or cold. No pains, hair loss, or paralysis.
Tuberculoid, Paucibacillary	Light or red. Dry, pebbly. Flat or edges slightly raised.	Less than 5 spots, may be symmetrical but usually not.	Decreased light touch.[2] Pains, hair loss, paralysis common.
Borderline, Multibacillary	Mostly red. Raised or punched out or rings.[3] Not shiny.	Over 5 spots, symmetrical.	Poor pain sense.[4] Maybe shooting pains or hair loss or paralysis.
Lepromatous, Multibacillary	Cobblestones of many sizes. Red. Smooth, shiny.	Innumerable bumps, especially ear lobes. Symmetrical.	Sensation. o.k. Eyes, hands, feet, testes affected.

Notes:

1. Light means that the skin looks like the normal skin of someone from a fairer ethnic group. In light-skinned patients, the skin may appear reddish rather than lighter than normal. Indistinct margins implies that the transition from darker to lighter skin is gradual; it is not at a definite, sharp line.

2. Decreased light touch means that the patient cannot consistently say "now" correctly whenever he is touched by a wisp of cotton. Pains means sharp, shooting pains along the course of the nerve(s). Hair loss (that is head hair) occurs in Europeans and Japanese. Anyone may have loss of eyebrows.

3. Punched out means that the edges are raised up with the center lower, like a little saucer.

4. Poor pain sense means that the patient cannot tell the difference between the sharp and the dull ends of a needle. This may lead to loss of fingers or toes since rats can eat them without the person knowing it, while he is sleeping.

Eye leprosy may cause inability to close the eye, eyelid rolled in or out, KERATITIS, or IRITIS; blindness is common. Hand and foot leprosy causes short feet, skin ulcers, and deformities. Testicular involvement causes shrinking of the testicles, impotence, and breast development. Teens have delayed sexual development.

Legs and Feet: There may be painless ulcers on the soles, loss of toes, or shortening of the feet. The foot may hang down and turn inward so the patient must lift his leg high at the hip and knee to avoid injuring his foot. There may be grossly deformed, abnormally-moving joints which are relatively painless.

Leprosy Appearance

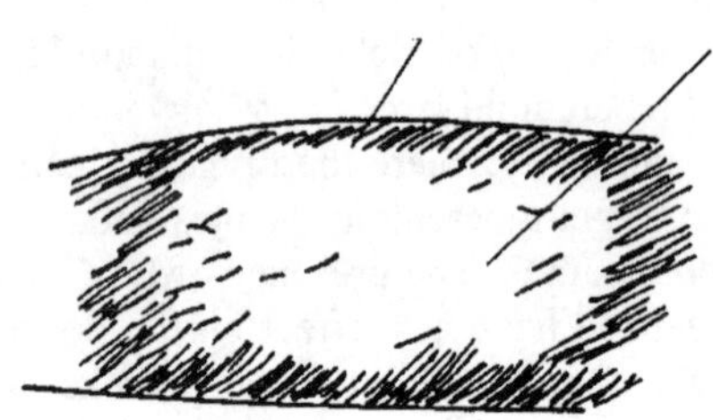

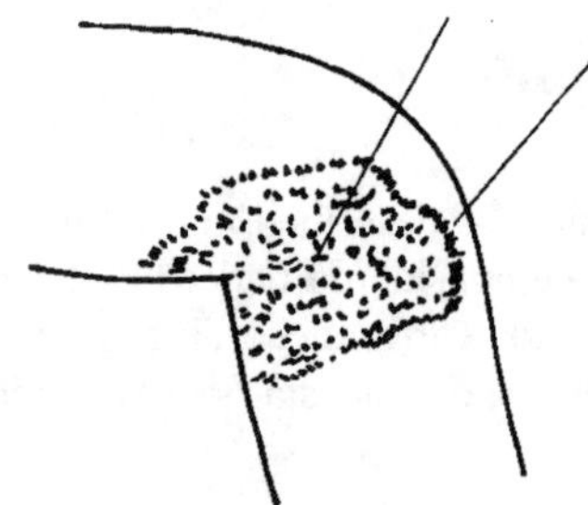

Leprosy: Swollen nerves

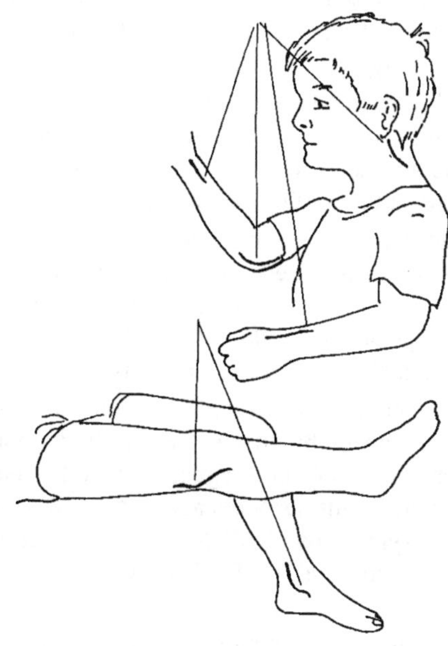

Leprosy Reactions to Treatment:

These reactions are most common in patients who are more than 20 years old.

➢ ***Type 1***

This reaction occurs in borderline leprosy only. It occurs within the first 6 months of multi-drug therapy and in women near the time of childbirth. This reaction .causes sudden fever, possibly lasting for months, redness and swelling of the skin, rash, and possibly the formation of skin ulcers. The hands and feet may be swollen. There are severe pains along nerves, perhaps with weakness or paralysis.

➢ ***Type 2***

This reaction occurs in lepromatous leprosy during treatment. It can be associated with pregnancy, birth, breast feeding, trauma, or some other infection. It causes fever, red bumps that last just a few days, sometimes swollen areas with sores forming, large lymph nodes, large liver and spleen, swollen and tender nerves, swollen testicles, and IRITIS. It is a kind of ERYTHEMA NODOSUM. It is most common in young females during pregnancy.

Other Complications: Loss of limbs, blindness, vulnerability to injury, decreased immunity to other diseases.

Similar Conditions: *Paucibacillary (tuberculoid) type*: The most common in Blacks is light skin color in an area of skin that had an inflammation or injury (such as diaper rash) and then healed. Also check VITILIGO (always flat and roughly symmetrical, except on the face), TINEA (itchy)..

Multibacillary (lepromatous) type: Tertiary SYPHILIS and tertiary YAWS may cause bumps under the skin, but never any numbness. MYCETOMA may look similar but one can see dry grains and it is almost never symmetrical. Consider also CUTANEOUS LEISHMANIASIS, BARTONELLOSIS. In THYROID TROUBLE of the low thyroid type, the eyebrows may disappear.

Nerve damage: PARKINSON'S DISEASE or BELL'S PALSY can cause a droopy face also, as also can STROKE. SCHISTOSOMIASIS can cause nerve damage.

If there is ulceration: TUBERCULOSIS of the skin (lupus vulgaris) CUTANEOUS LEISHMANIASIS can cause ulceration (spontaneous, open skin wounds) but there is never nerve damage.

Leprosy reaction: See Protocols C-6 for limb swelling and C-8 for eye symptoms.

Higher-Level Care. See Volume I, Appendix 13. *Laboratory:* Most hospitals can make skin scrapings on *lepromatous* leprosy; the bacteria show up under the microscope but the test is difficult to do correctly; there are many false negatives and some false positives. Level 3 and above hospitals can biopsy any leprosy to diagnose it. *Facilities:* A specialty hospital that treats large numbers of leprosy patients is most helpful. *Practitioners*: Nurses, generalists, and surgeons with experience in treating this disease.

Treatment:

Prevention: BCG immunization (used for TB) also gives partial protection against leprosy.

Patient Care: The most important part of treatment is the education of the patient in how to care for his body. It is entirely beyond the scope of this book to outline this, let alone describe it in detail. If there is an established leprosy program in your country, see if you can visit it and learn. Figure on spending at least two weeks. Books and other learning materials may be obtained from Teaching Aids at Low Cost: TALC; PO Box 49; St. Albans Herts; AL1 4AX; UK; info@talcuk.org. It is possible to visit their location which is accessible by British Rail from London. There is very much to learn about the management of this disease with all its social and psychological implications.

Surgery can be helpful for leprosy patients. Make contact with your closest receiving hospital to find out what sorts of patients they can care for, particularly if there are eyes which do not close properly. In general, surgeons can care for eyes that will not close and for feet that hang down so that they easily become injured. They can also care for injuries and fit patients with orthopedic appliances to help them manage their lives better.

Drug therapy is not difficult but it is time consuming; it requires that you be with the patient for 6 months to 2 years. Do not begin a treatment that you cannot complete! Check the *Drug Index* before beginning treatment.

- *Single skin spot only:* Give a single dose of RIFAMPIN plus OFLOXACIN plus MINOCYCLINE.
- *Paucibacillary: Indeterminate* and *tuberculoid* and mild *borderline* leprosy: RIFAMPIN once a month, plus DAPSONE daily, for 6 months.
- *Multibacillary:* Definite *borderline* and *lepromatous* types: RIFAMPIN once a month plus DAPSONE daily, plus CLOFAZIMINE daily with a monthly larger dose. This is continued for at least 2 years.

Treat skin ulcers due to leprosy like any other TROPICAL ULCER. PHENYTOIN, removed from capsules and sprinkled into the ulcers, hastens the healing. Give the patient ZINC also to hasten healing.

At night use ARTIFICIAL TEARS to keep eyes that don't close adequately from drying out.

Pregnancy: RIFAMPIN, DAPSONE and CLOFAZIMINE are considered to be reasonably safe.

There are five antibiotics that are still experimental but seem to work for leprosy. They are expensive unless you can get free samples: MINOCYCLINE, CLARITHROMYCIN, OFLOXACIN, and PEFLOXACIN. Only change from the old schedule on good authority; don't use hearsay drugs or dosages.

- **Treatment of leprosy reactions:**

ASPIRIN alone for ordinary *Type 1* that is not too severe. Add PREDNISONE (for 3-4 days only) if it is severe. For *Type 2*, use CHLOROQUINE and either HYDROCORTISONE. or PREDNISONE. In both cases **do not stop the usual leprosy drugs!** They **must** be continued. PREDNISOLONE EYE DROPS might be helpful for IRITIS.

LEPTOSPIROSIS

Cause: Spirochete (related to bacteria).

Synonyms: Canicola fever, Hemorrhagic jaundice, Mud fever, Swineherd's disease Weil's disease.

Regional Notes: All regions.

Definition: Leptospirosis is a whole-body infection caused by one of the spirochetes, a type of bacterium.

Moderately ill; Class 2; Contagious; Worldwide temperate as well as tropical areas, especially common in China, Brazil, and Southeast Asia., In temperate climates, it is most common in summer and fall; in tropical climates it's most common during the rainy season. It is carried by animals, especially rodents, near stagnant and flood waters. Occurs in epidemics.

Age: Any. **Who:** Water, plant, soil, animal, or patient contact. Usually from wading through flood or stagnant waters contaminated by rodent urine. The disease can be acquired by blood transfusion. **Onset:** Sudden; incubation from a few days to 3 weeks.

Clinical:

Necessary: Fever and either red, sore, eyes (without pus) or severe muscle pains or both. Muscle pains are especially in the calves, back, and abdomen.

Maybe: Other symptoms are variable. Sometimes a patient will have the germ without being sick at all. Usually a high fever rises and falls unpredictably, and there is headache. There is frequently a rash on the back part of the roof of the mouth.

Sometimes: The patient loses his appetite and vomits. He is usually constipated. He may have JAUNDICE beginning the second or third day. He might have red lumps under the skin on his shins. He may have a swollen abdomen and a tender liver.

If there is no JAUNDICE, the initial symptoms last 4-7 days and then go away by themselves, even without treatment. Then the fever starts again after a 1-3 day period without fever. This second stage lasts 4-30 days. During this time symptoms of MENINGITIS are common, as are eye symptoms (IRITIS as well as visual loss).

If there is JAUNDICE, the symptoms are more constant, without the relapsing quality.

Complications: PNEUMONIA, LIVER FAILURE, KIDNEY FAILURE, MENINGITIS, HEART FAILURE, STROKE, HEMORRHAGIC FEVER, ANEMIA due to destruction of red cells, SHOCK, and death. Older patients are more likely to die than younger ones. Relapses are common. Convalescence is long, 8-10 weeks in severe cases. The patient may be lethargic during this time, and he may develop IRITIS.

Similar Conditions: See Protocols C-2, C-5, C-7, C-8, C-10, C-13.

Bush Laboratory: Protein may be in the urine with the second temperature rise and bilirubin or blood or urobilinogen at any time.

Higher-Level Care. See Volume I, Appendix 13. *Laboratory:* Hospitals can do darkfield examination of the blood for leptospires. Tests that measure antibodies will be negative until the patient has been ill for 5 days at which time treatment is not very effective. It is necessary to treat without a positive antibody test. *Facilities:* IV's and IV antibiotics might be helpful. *Practitioner*: An infectious disease specialist with tropical/travel medicine expertise is ideal.

Treatment:

Prevention: Wear a gown and mask and gloves while caring for the patient. Be very careful to dispose of body secretions properly in an area free of rodents.

Patient Care: PENICILLIN, DOXYCYCLINE, CHLORAMPHENICOL, ERYTHROMYCIN, AMPICILLIN, AMOXICILLIN, all work. The patient may become much sicker with his first dose, but do not stop the antibiotic. The patient may die.

LICE

Cause: Insect.
Synonyms: Pediculosis, Body lice, Crab lice.
Includes: Body lice, Head lice, Pubic lice.
Regional Notes: I.

Entry category: Infestation.

Not ill to mildly ill; Class 1; Contagious; Worldwide, related to crowding, common all over.

Age: Any, especially children. **Who:** Anyone, especially poor hygiene. **Onset:** Soon after exposure.

Clinical:

Necessary: There are little moving creatures on hairy areas of the body: head, genitals, eyebrows. In addition, there are little bumps present on hairs, the lice eggs. Pubic and head lice lay eggs on hairs; body lice lay eggs on seams in clothing. With head lice, the heaviest infestation is behind the ears. After a person has had body lice he may feel ill for several days with general fatigue and aching all over. (the origin of the term "feeling lousy").

Lice: Actual size louse, and eggs on a hair.

Similar Conditions: Fleas also live on humans and bite, but they are black and they jump, which body lice do not. (Some lice change color to blend with the color of the skin or hair which makes them very hard to see.) Bedbugs don't live on skin; they just bite at night and then leave. They are rarely seen.

Treatment:

- MALATHION, 0.5% is best but it kills only the lice, not the eggs. The eggs can be washed off the body with showering but they do not wash out of hair. The eggs must be eliminated from cloth by immersing the cloth in boiling water or by ironing it. Repeatedly comb the hair with a fine comb to get the eggs off. MALATHION must be repeated weekly until the eggs are all hatched or combed out. The nightly use of mosquito nets impregnated with insecticide is another effective treatment for head lice.
- One can kill lice and eggs by sealing clothing/stuffed toys/bedding in a plastic bag for 12 days. IVERMECTIN in a single dose cures both scabies and lice.
- Alternatives are BENZYL BENZOATE, PERMETHRIN, or 1% LINDANE. Phenothrin and Carbaryl are available in England.
- Total shaving works for head lice. Reportedly shampooing with kerosene also works for head lice but it must be repeated because it also fails to kill the louse eggs.
- Custard apple (Annoa squamosa) seeds, ground, and soaked in coconut oil, kills head lice in less than an hour.

LIVER DISEASE

See LIVER FAILURE. This is a milder form. It is a disease cluster, not a diagnosis. There is bilirubin in the urine. There may be yellowing of the whites of the eyes. In dark-skinned people, liver disease may make the facial skin darker. Over time, liver disease will cause scarring of the liver, described under CIRRHOSIS, or else it may quickly deteriorate into LIVER FAILURE—see the next entry.

Effects of Liver disease

Organ	Mild	Moderate	Severe
Kidneys	----	----	Decreased urine
Blood	----	Anemia	Won't clot
Food	Poor appetite	same	same
Mental	----	Personality change, Trembling	Unconscious Seizures
Lung	----	----	Short of breath
Liver	? large ? tender	Large, usually	Small, usually
Yellow eyes	None	Some	Severe

This chart reflects general rules but the symptoms may, nevertheless, vary with the nature of the liver disease.

LIVER FAILURE

Cause: Variable.
Synonym: Hepatic failure.
Regional Notes: F, M, O, R, S, U.
Definition: Liver failure is the malfunction of the liver so that it is unable to remove toxins and/or unable to make bile.

Causes: Various infections, herbs, and drugs. TOXEMIA of pregnancy might also cause this. The most common are PLANT POISONING, BRUCELLOSIS, SCHISTOSOMIASIS, HEPATITIS, HEMOCHROMATOSIS, GALLBLADDER DISEASE, TOXOPLASMOSIS ARSENIC poisoning, BIRTH CONTROL PILLS, and occasionally other drugs.

Entry category: Syndrome or disease cluster.

Moderately to severely ill; Class 3-4; Rarely a contagious cause; Worldwide; many causative diseases are tropical.

Age: Any, adults more often than children. **Who:** Those who have underlying disease or who take certain drugs or herbal supplements.[1] **Onset:** Variable—over months

[1] Herbal supplements associated with liver failure are as follows: Camphor, Cascara sagrada, Chaparral, Com-

to years for CIRRHOSIS, over days to weeks for acute (sudden) LIVER FAILURE.

Clinical:

For a diagrammatic picture see the protocol in C-7. Liver failure is a diminution or cessation of liver function. There are two types:

➢ **Cirrhosis:**

This is scarring of the liver which develops over months to years, causing gradual symptoms though some event may make worsen the problem rapidly. See the separate entry for this.

➢ **Acute (Fulminant) Liver Failure:**

This develops over days to weeks. This is most often due to drug and herbal toxins (in anyone); or HEPATITIS E in pregnant women.

The liver is either tender or large or both if the disease just started. Later on the liver might shrink and no longer be tender.

JAUNDICE: the whites of the eyes are yellow.

Bleeding problems because the blood won't clot normally: nosebleeds, easy bruising, excessive menstruation, excessive bleeding from minor wounds, vomiting blood, bloody stool or urine. Sometimes, with some causes, there may be intolerable whole-body itching.

BRAIN DAMAGE which at first responds to treatment and later does not:

- Stage 1: apathy, restlessness, confusion, poor handwriting, day/night reversal.
- Stage 2: drowsiness, disorientation, trembling, mood and behavior changes.
- Stage 3: Sleeps all the time but can be awakened. Very active reflexes, episodes of craziness.
- Stage 4: Seizures and Coma.

Complications: SHOCK, KIDNEY FAILURE, SEIZURES, coma and death.

Similar Conditions: The symptoms 1-4 may also develop with rapid-onset liver failure. For other causes of free fluid in the abomen, see Symptom Protocol 46 A. For other causes of a large spleen, see Symptom Protocol 46 B. Also see Protocols C-6, C-7, and C-10.

Bush Laboratory: Normally there is some urobilinogen in the urine. With most causes of liver failure there will be somewhat larger than normal urobilinogen and excessive bilirubin. With some causes of liver failure that may respond to surgery (i.e. it is worthwhile to send the patient out), the urobilinogen in the urine will be zero, the bilirubin in the urine will be very high, the stools will have a light color, and the patient will have intolerable itching.

Higher-Level Care. It is useful to send a patient out to a higher-level facility, both for diagnosis (some types of cirrhosis can be treated successfully) and relief of symptoms. It is sometimes desirable to remove fluid from the abdomen in order to help the patient to breathe better. However, that should not be done in remote areas because it is easy to introduce bacteria with disastrous consequences. Facilities that can transfuse the patient can probably also deal with bleeding tendencies. A gastroenterologist is the most appropriate specialist; also consider tropical/travel expertise for treating causative diseases.

Treatment:

It may be futile by the time full-blown liver failure has developed, but try the following:

- Low sodium diet; no salt or baking powder.
- A nutritious diet; some authorities recommend low-protein and others recommend high-protein.
- Multiple vitamins and minerals, including ZINC.
- Medications for itching: DIPHENHYDRAMINE or CHOLESTYRAMINE.
- Avoid the following drugs which may harm the patient: IBUPROFEN and related medications; AMOXICILLIN/CLAVULANIC ACID; KETOCONAZOLE, ISONIAZID, GENTAMYCIN and related antibiotics; ERYTHROMYCIN and related drugs; CHLORPROMAZINE and similar drugs; all herbal teas and ethnic medicines.

LIVER FLUKE

Cause: Worm.

Includes: Fascioliasis, Clonorchiasis. Opisthorciasis.

Regional Notes: All regions.

Definition: Liver fluke is the infestation of the human body with one of the following creatures: Fasciola hepatica, Opisthorcis viverni, or Clonorchis sinensis.

Entry category: Disease cluster.

Mildly to moderately ill; Class 2; Regional:

- *Fascioliasis*: Worldwide wherever there are sheep-raising areas with low, wet pastureland harboring snails. It is not necessarily tropical, since it occurs in Siberia and Tibet. It is very common in the Altiplano region of Bolivia, in Egypt, and Wisconsin.
- *Opisthorciasis* occurs in central and eastern Europe, and throughout Southeast Asia and the Far East. It is decreasing in Thailand due to government efforts but is common in Laos and China. The type of Opisthorcis that affects cats mainly and secondarily humans occurs in Poland, Kazakhstan, Russia, Ukraine, Siberia: Tyumen and Khanty regions.
- *Clonorchiasis* occurs throughout Southeast Asia and the Far East; it is similar to Opisthorciasis.

Age: Any except nursing infants. **Who:** *Fascioliasis*: Those who eat raw watercress or drink contaminated water. Larvae of the worm develop in snails. *Opisthor-*

---

frey, Ephedra, Germander, Jin Bu Huan, Kava kava, Kombucha, Margosa oil, Pennyroyal oil, Heliotropium, Crotalaria, Sassafras, Valerian.

ciasis and *Clonorchiasis*: Those who eat raw or pickled fish. **Onset:** Slow for Fascioliasis; may be sudden for Opisthorciasis and Clonorchiasis.

Clinical:

➢ **Fascioliasis:**

The disease may be entirely without symptoms. If there are symptoms, they will be indigestion, a large tender liver, nausea, diarrhea, general aching all over, loss of appetite, cough, itchiness, JAUNDICE, or any combination of these. There may be a high fever and chills. Usually the problem resolves by itself, but it may become chronic.

➢ **Opisthorciasis and Clonorchiasis:**

Most patients are without symptoms but there may be fever, muscle aches, diarrhea, loss of appetite, upper abdominal pains, and sometimes a large, tender liver. It may lead to serious GALLBLADDER DISEASE. *Clonorchiasis* may cause SERUM SICKNESS in the initial stages.

Similar Conditions: HEPATITIS and AMEBIC LIVER DISEASE may be indistinguishable. For SCHISTOSOMIASIS MANSONI and SCHISTOSOMIASIS JAPONICUM, check the geography.

Higher-Level Care. *Laboratory:* Early in the disease, a blood count will probably show increased eosinophils; this is sensitive but not specific; a negative result eliminates the diagnosis. Later on a laboratory with a microscope can check stool for the eggs of these flukes. Sometimes it takes many specimens before an egg is found. The eggs do not appear until the patient has been ill about 4 months in fascioliasis. Therefore an early negative test means nothing. Antibody tests remain positive long after the infection is gone. New stool antigen tests should be helpful. *Practitioner:* Tropical/travel expertise is most helpful.

Treatment:

Fascioliasis: A veterinary drug, TRICLABENDAZOLE, (brand name Fasinex) is recommended by the WHO. There is resistance to this in disease acquired in developed countries (because of vet usage) but not in disease acquired in the developing world.

Opisthorciasis/Chlonorchiasis: PRAZIQUANTEL (which may not work), BITHIONOL, EMETINE (very toxic), possibly ALBENDAZOLE given at twice the usual dosage. Hexachloroparaxylol is used for Opisthorciasis but it is not as good as PRAZIQUANTEL.

Loiasis

See *Regional Notes* F.

LYME DISEASE

Cause: Spirochete.
Synonym: Lyme borreliosis.
Regional Notes: E, O, R, U.
Definition: Lyme disease is an infection with a spirochete.

Moderately to severely ill; Class 3; Not contagious; Regional; found in Europe west of the Ural mountains, along the north coast of Africa, some locations in East Asia, in coastal Australia, and in North America, particularly east of the Mississippi and along the west coast.

Age: Any. **Who:** Bitten by a tick. **Onset:** Variable, probably gradual in most cases. Incubation to first symptoms is 3-32 days.

Clinical:

➢ **Stage 1:**

There is a fever, fatigue, and aching all over, along with a rash consisting of red circles or ovals with clearing centers.

➢ **Stage 2:**

There is either MENINGITIS (the usual treatment for this is appropriate), or BELL'S PALSY, or ARTHRITIS[1] or HEART FAILURE with an abnormally slow pulse. The lymph nodes may be large. There may be numbness and tingling in the hands and feet, the areas normally covered by gloves or stockings. The symptoms tend to come and go. The disease may cure itself without treatment, or become chronic.

➢ **Stage 3:**

Stage 2 symptoms may become chronic.

Complications: There may be BELL'S PALSY which may affect both sides of the face rather than just one side. The patient may have abnormal eye movements. He may have difficulty in thinking and remembering. There may be transverse myelitis, a condition that affects the spinal cord with loss of sensation, weakness, paralysis, and/or disturbances in bowel and bladder function, depending on where the spinal cord is affected.

Similar Conditions: See Protocols C-2: Fever/Headache/General pains; C-6: Limb Swelling; C-10: Confusion/Lethargy; C-12: Large Lymph Nodes.

Initial stage: Similar to diseases listed under ARBOVIRAL FEVER, but the rash is distinctive.

Subsequent stages are similar to MENINGITIS, BELL'S PALSY, ARTHRITIS, or HEART FAILURE of other causes. RELAPSING FEVER can appear quite similar, but it is of more rapid onset.

Higher-Level Care. See Volume I, Appendix 13.

Laboratory: A level 4 or above laboratory will probably show a positive blood test result after 2 weeks of illness. *Practitioner:* An infectious disease specialist.

Treatment:

Prevention: Try to avoid tick bites by using DEET repellant. After a tick bite, give antibiotics only if the tick is engorged with a lot of blood or if the patient gets any kind of rash at the site of the bite. Look for a rash daily

[1] The arthritis involves one or few joints, usually at least one knee. Swelling is out of proportion to the pain. The arthritis comes and goes itself over weeks to months.

for 30 days after a bite.[1] A tick is engorged if the dark-colored head part is less than 1/3 of the whole body area, looking down at the tick from above.

Patient Care: DOXYCYCLINE (first stage only), PENICILLIN, AMOXICILLIN, CHLORAMPHENICOL, CEPHALOSPORIN. In the first stage treatment is for 14 days; treatment during stage 2 is initially 30 days oral; change to 30 days IV if there is no cure. Treatment during stage 3 must be continued for 6 weeks. CEPHALOSPORIN (ceftriaxone) given intravenously is usually used in advanced stages. Use injected antibiotics if the patient has a severe headache and/or symptoms of HEART FAILURE.

LYMPHOGRANULOMA VENEREUM

Cause: Bacteria (*Chlamydia trachomatis).*

Synonyms: Climatic bubo, Esthiomene, Lymphogranuloma inguinale, Tropical bubo.

Regional Notes: R, U.

Definition: Lymphogranuloma venereum is a sexually transmitted bacterial infection of the genital area, caused by Chlamydia trachomatis.

Not ill to mildly ill; Class 1-4; Contagious; Worldwide, especially ports and urban areas. It is particularly common in sub-Saharan Africa, India, South America, the Caribbean, and Southeast Asia.

Age: Any; usually sexually mature but sexually abused children may get it. **Who:** Promiscuous partner or more than one partner, especially sailors, prostitutes in port cities. Accounts for about 3% of all SEXUALLY TRANSMITTED DISEASES in these areas. **Onset:** Incubation period 4-21 days from exposure to primary; 3-16 weeks to secondary.

Clinical:

This usually affects the genitals but may affect other areas of the body which have had sexual contact: hands, mouth, and breasts.

➢ **Primary:**

Only 45% of all cases have this. A small bump forms on the genitals, less than 6 mm in diameter. This becomes a painless ulcer or a little blister; urine touching it causes burning pain. It disappears in 2-5 days.

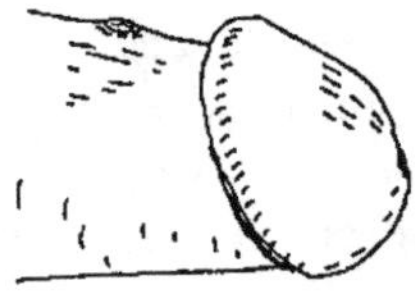

Lymphogranuloma venereum: Stage 1 sore.

➢ **Secondary:**

The lymph nodes on one side of the groin enlarge, both above and below the leg crease, creating a firm bulge with a groove down the middle. They are slightly painful at first and the pain increases with time. The patient may have fevers, chills, headaches, loss of appetite, nausea, and vomiting. The large nodes may become an ABSCESS which will rupture, releasing pus; it heals with scarring.

Lymphogranuloma venereum: Enlarged lymph nodes in left groin.

➢ **Tertiary:**

The genital area develops firm swelling, possibly with PROCTITIS. Ulcers, ABSCESSes, and abnormal holes form between rectum, bladder, and vagina or penis. Urine, stool, and semen come out of abnormal places. In females it can cause PELVIC INFECTION and infertility. In either sex it may cause gross swelling of the genitals, narrowing of the rectum, and rectal CANCER.

Similar Conditions: *Primary:* See Protocol C-1. Rarely, in the Americas only, CUTANEOUS LEISHMANIASIS (MCL type) might be similar, especially if it involves the genitals (very unusual).

Secondary: CELLULITIS or OSTEOMYELITIS of the legs can cause large nodes and general symptoms. Generally the leg problem is obvious. TYPHUS is similar but has a peculiar body odor. PLAGUE has black discoloration over the enlarged nodes.

Tertiary: is similar to advanced DONOVANOSIS.

Higher-Level Care. *Laboratory:* Large hospitals may be able to do a culture or a blood test. *Facilities and Practitioners:* A specialty clinic for sexually transmitted diseases is most helpful.

Treatment:

Use Protocol C-1 for treatment in most cases.

Primary: DOXYCYCLINE is the drug of choice; use ERYTHROMYCIN or AZITHROMYCIN in pregnancy. CIPROFLOXACIN might work. The minimum duration is for 3 weeks but longer is good, especially in the presence of HIV INFECTION.

Secondary: Same drugs plus pierce the swelling with a syringe and large needle to draw off the pus. Do not drain the pus by cutting with a knife.

Tertiary: can be managed only by surgery.

---

[1] This is a reddening of the skin in an irregular, oval area around the site of the bite, with some measles-like spots around the red area, possibly a small black ulcer in the middle of the red. There may be a lighter-colored, central area inside the darker red around the outside, giving a target-like appearance.

MALABSORPTION

Cause: Variable. See Protocol C-14.

Regional Notes: F, I, M, O, R, S, U.

Definition: Malabsorption is the failure of the bowel to absorb the food and water taken in by mouth; the result is that the food and water pass directly from mouth to anus.

Entry category: Syndrome.

Moderately to severely ill; Class 2; Worldwide, but the cause varies from one region to another.

Age: Any. **Who:** Anyone, but especially expatriates and those with MALNUTRITION. **Onset:** Usually slow, over weeks; may be sudden.

Clinical:

The patient has a large quantity of light-colored diarrhea, sometimes with abdominal pain. Whenever the patient eats, he loses it promptly with foul-smelling diarrhea which has fat in it, floats on top of the toilet water, is hard to flush, and leaves residual oil droplets on the water. There is usually much rectal gas. Usually he has loss of appetite, weakness, lethargy, weight loss (or failure to gain weight in children), general abdominal swelling, and possibly a sore tongue and mouth. The problem lasts a week or more.

Complications: These are associated with MALNUTRITION: fluid in the abdomen and symptoms of ANEMIA, PELLAGRA, BERIBERI, XEROPHTHALMIA, SCURVY. There may be abnormal bleeding because of lack of vitamin K. The patient may have SEIZURES.

Similar Conditions: For diarrhea that is somewhat milder than that described above, see TURISTA in the *Disease Index*.

Higher-Level Care. See Volume I, Appendix 13. *Laboratory:* Large hospital labs, level 4 or above, may be able to determine stool fat content to diagnose this; other tests on stool or blood may be done to diagnose the cause. *Practitioner:* Tropical/travel disease expertise is important since many of the causes are tropical; otherwise a gastroenterologist.

Treatment:

Since this is a syndrome, not a disease, the treatment depends on the cause which should be discovered by working through Protocol C-14. Treat the possible causes for your patient, one at a time; try first whatever is common in your area. Give rehydration fluid also. FOLATE and other vitamins should be given whatever the cause is. Other helpful medications might be DOXYCYCLINE, PYRANTEL PAMOATE, or TINIDAZOLE.

MALARIA

Section Outline:

I. Introduction
II. Clinical
- A brief history
- Kinds of malaria
  - Ordinary malaria (mostly non-falciparum)
  - Severe malaria (mostly falciparum)
  - Subcategories of severe malaria
- Malaria and pregnancy
- Malaria in children
- Table: Diagnosing malaria in children
- Complications for both adults and children
- Similar conditions
- Bush laboratory

III. Prevention
- Table: Methods of malaria prevention

IV. Treatment of Malaria: Principles
- Treatment of ordinary malaria, not severe
- Treatment of severe malaria
- Treatment of complications
- Table: Classes of antimalarial drugs

V. Higher-Level Care in Developing Countries
VI. Higher Level Care in Western Countries

I. INTRODUCTION

Cause: Protozoa. (Plasmodium vivax, Plasmodium falciparum, and a few other Plasmodium species.)

Regional Notes: All regions.

Includes: Blackwater fever; Bilious Remittent Malaria, Algid Malaria, Cerebral Malaria.

Definition: Malaria is an infection with one of the plasmodia protozoa. "Falciparum malaria" is caused by Plasmodia falciparum and is the most serious kind; "non-falciparum malaria" is caused by any other Plasmodia (P. vivax, P. malariae, and P. ovale).

Not ill at all to very ill; mild is Class 1; severe falciparum malaria is Class 3. Widespread in the tropics, more common at low altitudes. In large tropical cities with substantial air pollution, the adult anopheles mosquito cannot survive and thus there is no malaria transmission. Chloroquine-sensitive malaria is found mostly in areas where mosquito reproduction does not occur during some part of the year.

Age: Usually over 6 weeks old, more common in well-nourished children and in expatriate adults. **Who:** Bitten by anopheles mosquitoes. In many areas of the world, these mosquitoes bite without being noticed. See Volume I, Appendix 10. Expatriates, pregnant women, and HIV patients are especially vulnerable. HIV infection makes malaria worse and malaria makes HIV infection worse but the effects both ways are not spectacular. Malaria is more severe in patients who have had their spleens removed. **Incubation**: Usually about 2 weeks; it may be as short as 3 days. If the patient is a national from a malarious area or if he has taken preventive medicines or has been partly treated, then the incubation can be much longer. Sometimes the incubation period of non-falciparum malaria from temperate climates is very long—measured in months. **Onset:** Variable; it might be sudden or gradual. If the fever and chill cycle is of sudden onset and has typical every-other-day timing right from the beginning, the malaria is likely to be sensitive to CHLOROQUINE.

II. CLINICAL

A Brief History

There is a difference between the following clinical descriptions of malaria and those found in some medical texts. In the early 20th century, tertiary syphilis patients were treated with transfusions of malarious blood. The descriptions of malaria in Western texts were based largely on these cases. Transfusion-induced malaria resulted in highly regular cycles of chills and fevers, and the textbook writers assumed that all malaria would present in this manner. But in fact naturally acquired malaria fevers are erratic at first, and only become periodic after a considerable time.

Another problem was that blood smears of transfusion-induced malaria were positive for all donors and recipients. But when the disease becomes severe, particularly with falciparum malaria, smears may be *negative* even though the infection is overwhelming. This is also at odds with medical orthodoxy, but it has been well substantiated.

The end result of these misunderstandings has been that in the USA, malaria patients commonly die. Since the disease is rare, physicians don't consider the diagnosis. Those who do expect periodic fevers and insist on seeing a positive malaria smear before treating, but neither of these conditions will necessarily be found.

Kinds of Malaria

There are four kinds of malaria; for convenience we will consider them under two categories.

Usually a patient will be infected by only one of the two categories; if that is falciparum he will be much sicker than if it is non-falciparum. However, if there is infection with both forms, he will not be as ill; his risk of dying will be less than infection with falciparum alone.

Falciparum can kill quickly but it is also totally curable. Most falciparum causes *severe malaria*; it occasionally causes *ordinary malaria.*

Non-falciparum tends to last long and relapse, but usually does not kill. Almost all non-falciparum causes *ordinary malaria*; occasionally it causes *severe malaria.* Two of the three species of non-falciparum have forms that hide in the liver and erupt at unpredictable times, perhaps years after the last exposure.

➢ **Ordinary malaria (mostly non-falciparum):**

Non-falciparum malaria in expatriates (and national children) may cause erratic fever or regular up and down fevers, every day, every other day, or every third day. The longer the illness has lasted, the more likely it is that the fevers and sweats have regular timing. Shaking chills alternate with episodes of sweating; the patient's temperature goes up when he feels cold and comes down when he feels feverish and sweaty. There are usually at least 12 hours between chills and sweats. He may have previously felt somewhat ill. Other symptoms are general aching, shoulder pain, dizziness, lethargy, headache, eye pain, left upper abdominal or waist pain, appetite loss. There is likely to be a large urine production, nausea, and vomiting. The spleen may be large and tender. Children commonly have rapid respirations, cough, and SEIZURES with simple malaria but these symptoms are uncommon in adults.

Pregnancy: Non-falciparum malaria is generally more severe in pregnant than in non-pregnant women. It may be fatal.

Newborns: Occasionally babies are born with malaria. They have ANEMIA, JAUNDICE, and a large spleen.

Ethnic considerations: Occasionally non-falciparum malaria may become severe malaria in persons of Mediterranean genetic heritage. See *severe malaria* below.

Relapses of ordinary, non-falciparum malaria that has been acquired in tropical areas tend to occur at 3-6 weeks after the first illness; those acquired in subtropical or temperate areas tend to relapse after much longer intervals—months or years. In both cases taking preventive medication will make those intervals longer. In either case, the relapse is more likely than the original illness to have a sudden onset and regular cycles of fever and chills.

➢ **Severe malaria (mostly falciparum):**

Definition: Severe malaria is malaria with one or more of the following complications:

- Coma
- KIDNEY FAILURE
- Shortness of breath worse lying than sitting
- HYPOGLYCEMIA
- Severe ANEMIA
- Low blood pressure
- Rapid respirations
- Spontaneous bleeding
- Unable to sit up
- JAUNDICE.

It is usually caused by falciparum malaria. In persons with G6PD DEFICIENCY, it may be caused by non-falciparum. The onset is frequently gradual in adults, and sudden in children. Malnourished patients seldom develop severe malaria; it is almost always those who were healthy beforehand.

Fever may be continuous or may go up and down, cycling every 24 or 48 hours. As in non-falciparum malaria, there are at least 12 hours between chills and sweats. Expatriates usually have continuous fevers. In mild cases this may look like non-falciarum malaria. JAUNDICE in adults and ANEMIA are common when the patient has been ill for some time. Adults frequently develop KIDNEY FAILURE with little or no urine output;, the urine appearing bloody. This may happen initially or it may happen as the patient is recovering. Severe shortness of breath likewise may happen initially or during recovery. Restlessnes is worrisome.

➢ **Subcategories of severe malaria:**

Cerebral malaria causes a severe headache and fever. The patient may appear drunk or crazy, may be unconscious, and may have SEIZURES. His respirations may be irregular or rapid. MENINGITIS may be indistinguishable without laboratory facilities. ENCEPHALITIS and HEAT STROKE might also be indistinguishable. The eyes may become crossed. There may be abnormal lip movements. The legs are likely to be stretched out straight and stiff with the arms also stiff or else flexed at the elbows with the hands on the chest. Patients with cerebral malaria are never completely alert and able to identify the date. About 1/3 have JAUNDICE. *Negative blood tests are common because all the infected red cells are stuck onto the walls of the blood vessels. Anyone who has been exposed to malaria and has both a fever and mental symptoms must be treated for falciparum malaria. Awaiting laboratory confirmation is likely to prove fatal.*

Blackwater fever: There are fever, chills, back pain, and vomiting. The patient's urine is dark red or black. He probably has JAUNDICE. He is very sick and may be unconscious; death is likely. Blackwater fever occurs under three conditions:

- Severe falciparum malaria treated with QUININE, MEFLOQUINE, or ARTEMISININ, regardless of the patient's genetic heritage. It is especially common when malaria is undertreated with QUININE.
- Any malaria treated with QUININE if the patient has a Mediterranean genetic heritage with G6PD deficiency (this can be tested in Western countries).
- Patients with G6PD DEFICIENCY who take PRIMAQUINE, FANSIDAR or related drugs, regardless of the type of malaria.

Algid malaria causes vomiting, diarrhea, SHOCK, low temperature, JAUNDICE, and severe ANEMIA. The blood pressure is low and the pulse is rapid. It is difficult to distinguish from CHOLERA and DYSENTERY, so it is good to use DOXYCYCLINE for treatment. It is rare.

Bilious Remittent malaria causes LIVER FAILURE, KIDNEY FAILURE, hiccups, vomiting (possibly bloody), diarrhea, and possibly JAUNDICE.

Choleraic malaria causes a watery diarrhea, very similar to CHOLERA.

Pulmonary malaria causes lung damage and death through shortness of breath. It is hard to distinguish from shortness of breath due to HEART FAILURE. Lung damage and RESPIRATORY FAILURE might occur even after all the malaria parasites have been cleared out of the blood.

❖ **Malaria and Pregnancy**

In areas with very much malaria (most symptomatic patients are children), pregnant women are more anemic and babies weigh less when they are born. In areas with some but not a lot of malaria (most symptomatic patients being adults), women tend to give birth early if they become ill late in pregnancy. Pregnant women are also at increased risk of developing severe malaria and when they do, the maternal (and fetal) death rate is high. Post-partem maternal death from malaria is also common in rural areas. ARTEMISININ-type medications should not be used in early pregnancy unless the patient acquired the malaria in Southeast Asia where there is much resistance to QUININE. There is some question as to its safety in early pregnancy when other alternatives are available.

❖ **Malaria in Children**

In areas with very much malaria (most symptomatic patients are children), babies under 2 years old do not commonly get severe falciparum malaria but they do commonly develop ANEMIA. Older children, however, do get severe malaria which tends to progress rapidly; there is a high mortality rate and death may occur in less than 24 hours. KIDNEY FAILURE is not a common complication in children. Common symptoms right before death are rapid respirations and deep coma (the patient does not respond to pain such as rubbing one's knuckles on his breastbone). A clinical scoring system using the following table may be helpful:

Diagnosing malaria in children.

A score of 7 or more makes malaria very likely.

Patient feels hot to the touch.	3 if yes; 0 if no
Patient has loss of appetite.	1 if yes; 0 if no
Patient has no rash.	1 if no rash 0 if there is rash
Patient has no cough.	1 if no cough 0 if there is cough
Mother reports shivering.	1 if yes; 0 if no
Tongue or fingernails pale.	1 if yes; 0 if no
Patient acts sleepy.	1 if yes; 0 if no
Patient breathes rapidly.	1 if yes; 0 if no

Complications for both adults and children:

- *Bacterial infection*: PNEUMONIA, URINARY TRACT INFECTION, ENTERIC FEVER is common, especially in children.
- *SEPSIS*, will cause a sudden drop in blood pressure with loss of consciousness during recovery.
- *KIDNEY FAILURE* is a common complication in adults but not in children.
- *HYPOGLYCEMIA* may develop either as a result of the malaria or as a result of QUININE treatment, especially in young children and pregnant women.
- *BRAIN DAMAGE* and STROKE.

- Malarial *SHOCK* may develop the second or third day of treatment, especially in pregnant women and those recently delivered.
- *Cough* and HEART FAILURE.
- *ANEMIA* due to destruction of red blood cells and, over the longer term, lack of FOLATE.

Similar Conditions:

See Protocols C-2, C-3, C-5, C-7, C-9, C-10, C-13, C-14.

Similar to both kinds of malaria: RELAPSING FEVER is very similar except that the interval between chills and sweats is considerably less than 24 hours; it is frequently an hour or two.

Similar to simple, recent-onset malaria: See Protocol C-2: Fever, Headache and Pains.

Similar to chronic malaria: HEPATITIS is the most common misdiagnosis. Also consider MALNUTRITION, EAR INFECTION, TUBERCULOSIS, KIDNEY INFECTION, MONONUCLEOSIS, VISCERAL LEISHMANIASIS. See the protocols in *Index C.*

With yellow eyes, similar to sudden onset falciparum malaria: see Protocol C-5.

Cerebral: May be indistinguishable from MENINGITIS, ENCEPHALITIS, and HEAT STROKE. Treat for all of the above. Consider HYPOGLYCEMIA which may coexist or be caused by MALARIA or the treatment thereof.

Algid: May be indistinguishable from bacterial DYSENTERY. Use DOXYCYCLINE for treatment.

Blackwater fever: Very similar to HEPATITIS. Also see Protocol C-5 and C-7.

Billious remittent: See Protocol C-7. Consider also other causes of KIDNEY FAILURE and LIVER DISEASE, LIVER FAILURE from other causes.

Choleraic: Similar to CHOLERA and may be indistinguishable. Treat for both.

Bush Laboratory:

Urinalysis shows positive urobilinogen when the patient has fever. Ketones are positive if the patient is not eating. Blood and protein are positive in blackwater fever; protein alone may be positive in chronic malaria. The patient may have ANEMIA. Some of the antibody blood tests listed below under higher level care might be obtainable and usable in bush situations. They are expensive.

III. PREVENTION

- Treat known cases of malaria.
- Learn the breeding habits of malaria mosquitoes in your area and eliminate breeding sites.
- Malaria mosquitoes bite between dusk and dawn. Use repellents, mosquito netting, or both at night. (Mosquito nets impregnated with insecticide also help to eliminate head LICE and bedbugs.)
- Put screens on houses.
- Drugs for prevention are useful in some areas, especially for pregnant women and young children. See the table on Malaria Prevention and Prophylaxis, below. Unfortunately, no option is either ideal or a sure guarantee against getting malaria. Which option is followed depends in part upon the degree of drug resistance of the prevalent malaria, and also on what kinds of drug side effects cause trouble for the individual in question.
- HIV positive pregnant women and their babies are particularly susceptible to malaria and preventive treatment is essential. In locations where small shopkeepers stock and dispense chloroquine for "headache plus fever", the incidence of malaria will decrease. Immunization for malaria is not currently available, but may become so in the future.

Methods of Malaria Prevention

Method	Malaria Type	Adult Dose	Advantages	Disadvantages and Notes.
Avoid bites[1]	All	N/A	No drugs	Daily hassle.
Chloroquine[2]	Non-falciparum.	300 mg base weekly.	Old, safe	Bitter taste. May damage vision after many years.
Mefloquine	Falciparum mainly.	250 mg weekly.	Weekly	Expensive; Seizures in Whites[3]; Night-mares common.
Proguanil mainly	Falciparum	200 mg daily.	Old, safe; O.K. in pregnancy	Daily dose. Also take chloroquine.
Chlorpro-guanil	Falciparum	20 mg twice weekly.	Old, safe	Twice weekly dose. Also take chloroquine.
Fansidar	All	1 tablet weekly.	Weekly	Sulfa drug; Rare fatalities; not recom-mended.
Pyrimethamine (Daraprim)	Falciparum mainly.	50 mg weekly.	Weekly	Also take chloroquine; unreliable; Danger-ous if used alone[4].
Maloprim (Pyrimethamine plus Dapsone)	Falciparum mainly.	(12.5 mg Py + 100 mg Dap-sone), weekly.	Weekly	Must also take chloroquine. Dangerous with G6PD deficiency.
Primaquine	Non-falciparum.	15 mg daily for 14 days.	Old, safe	Only prevents recurrence from. liver stor-age. Dangerous with G6PD deficiency.
Doxycycline	All[5]	100 mg daily.	Safe	Not in pregnancy. Not in children under 7 y.o. Promotes sun sensitivity[6].
Malarone (Atovaquone + Proguanil)	Falciparum mainly.	1 tablet daily.	No resis-tance.	New, unproven. Daily dose.

Notes:

1. This is done the following way: Malaria mosquitoes only bite for 2 hours in the evening and early night, plus sometimes for 2 hours shortly before dawn. When you first arrive in your community, put pads of paper around your house. Show your family how to identify anopheles mosquitoes. See Volume I, Appendix 10. Whenever someone sees an anopheles mosquito, he jots the time down on a pad of paper. After a week or so, you will know when you need to be careful. Then shower each day and apply repellent during the hour before the biting time. Sleep under a mosquito net. Sometimes repellent soaps are available. They are a bad idea, since they are expensive and do not work well. Since people normally rinse soap off, only a small amount of the repellent remains, and the effects do not last long.

2. The safe upper limit for long-term use is 2.5 mg/kg chloroquine base per day, or 4 mg/kg chloroquine phosphate tablets. It is acceptable to use larger amounts for a few days now and then, as long as the average over a month is no more than the amounts stated above.

3. This occurs rarely in Whites that take the drug. It does not generally cause brain damage, but the stigma of having had a seizure may haunt a person when he applies for employment or a driver's license.

4. There have been reports of deaths in children who used pyrimethamine alone for prophylaxis and then came down with falciparum malaria. It is thought that the drug delays the manifestations of the disease and therefore delays the diagnosis until it is too late.

5. In theory it works for all. In the author's experience, there commonly are break-throughs of non-falciparum malaria.

6. For people with fair skin, it makes their skin more prone to sunburn. This is a distinct disadvantage for Whites whose job is largely outdoors.

IV. TREATMENT OF MALARIA: PRINCIPLES

There should be malaria medicines in the blood for at least 7 days. Since most malaria medicines are eliminated from the body quickly, this usually means the patient must take the medicine for at least 7 days. This is especially important in expatriate adults and in all children. The only malaria medicine eliminated slowly is MEFLOQUINE and, to a lesser extent, CHLOROQUINE.

It is important to prevent the development of resistant malaria in the community. Therefore, it is good to use at least two anti-malaria drugs at the same time, drugs that work in different ways.

Drugs are categorized in four groups below, based on their structure and mechanism of action. Try to choose drugs from at least two lists. ATOVAQUONE is a fifth kind of drug, different than the other four classes. It is relatively new and very expensive. It is sold in combination with proguanil.

FANSIDAR is a combination of two drugs, from the second and fourth lists, but it should count as if it were a drug from only one list rather than from two lists.

Artemisia-derived products act faster than any other kind of anti-malarial; this is important in very sick patients. The drug can be made as a tea from a garden plant (see Appendix 12 in Volume I), or it can be purchased in pill form as a combination drug. Some of the very old aminoalcohols which were developed in the 1920's are again becoming available, combined with various of the artemisinin-related drugs. These fixed-combination drugs are particularly useful as they provide rapid improvement together with sustained levels of drug in the body, to prevent relapses.

a. Treatment of ordinary malaria, not severe.

Ordinary Malaria – Requirements:

- The patient is not a pregnant woman during her last trimester. He has neither had his spleen removed nor does he have SICKLE CELL DISEASE.
- The patient is arousable and able to speak rationally. (A baby should do some things appropriate to his age.) His mouth is moist in front, underneath his tongue. Vomiting, if it occurs, is not excessive. His urine is not brown or black and the amounts are reasonable. The whites of his eyes are not yellow. He is not short of breath at rest. His body is not swollen.

Option #1: CHLOROQUINE if this has worked in your area in the past.

Option #2: CHLOROQUINE plus CHLORPHENIRAMINE. CHLORPHENIRAMINE appears to reverse resistance to CHLOROQUINE. This works fine in some areas. One can also add FANSIDAR.

Option #3: Day 1: Oral medication of the ARTEMISININ variety. Days 2 and 3: MEFLOQUINE plus ARTEMISININ-type medication. This is particularly good in patients who are from Southeast Asia where there is much malaria resistant to QUININE.

Option #4: In non-pregnant females and in children over seven years old, use QUININE for three to five days along with DOXYCYCYLINE for at least seven days. The patient must have sugar with quinine.

Option #5: QUININE alone which must be used for seven days since it is eliminated rapidly from the body. The patient must have sugar with quinine.

Option #6: An ARTEMISININ-type medication for 7 days.

Option #7: ATOVAQUONE-PROGUANIL which is very expensive.

Option #8: PIPERAQUINE or PYRONARIDINE or MEFLOQUINE in a fixed combination with one of the ARTEMISININ-type drugs.

Option #9: ARTEMISININ for 3 days followed by a curative dose of MEFLOQUINE.

Option #10: New combinations. Independent information is necessary:

ARTEMISININ as Artesunate 4 mg/kg plus DAPSONE 2.5 mg/kg plus PROGUANIL 8 mg/kg, all daily for 3 days.

ARTEMISININ plus LUMEFANTRINE in fixed combination. The brand name is Coartem and it is safe to use in children.

Artesunate ½ mg/kg plus Fosmidomycin 30 mg/kg both every 12 hours for 3 days.

Tafenoquine 200 mg base per day for 3 days, then 200 mg base weekly for 8 weeks.

Fosmidomycin 30 mg/kg plus CLINDAMYCIN 10 mg/kg both every 12 hours for 3 days.

b. Treatment of severe malaria:

- *Keep the patient in bed.* Check vital signs every two hours. MULTIVITAMINS and FOLATE are helpful for nutritional support.
- *Give malaria medication,* using PROMETHAZINE or HYDROXYZINE to prevent vomiting. Choose an option from the malaria medications listed above, but not options # 1 or #2.
- Use sugar for all patients (except diabetics) and DIAZEPAM additionally if the patient has SEIZURES.
- Cool the patient according to FEVER PER SE. Do not use DEXAMETHASONE, HYDROCORTISONE, PREDNISONE, or any other similar drug.
- Monitor fluid balance: If the patient is not drinking, manage his fluids to prevent DEHYDRATION; see Volume I, Appendix 1 and DEHYDRATION in the

Disease Index. Also, in adults watch for KIDNEY FAILURE and treat that appropriately. If the patient is a nursing baby, empty his mother's breasts and put the milk down a stomach tube if you can do that without making him vomit.

- Monitor ventilation: If breathing is deep and rapid, give fluids with sugar as long as there is no KIDNEY FAILURE. Another option, instead or in addition, is to raise the patient to a sitting position. If the respirations are slow with some foaming at the mouth and abnormal eye movements, the problem is probably SEIZURES; treat him accordingly. If the respirations are grossly irregular, most likely the patient is dying.
- *Transfer the patient to a hospital* as soon as possible. There are many more options at a hospital than what you will have in a village situation. For severe malaria , *transfusion* might be helpful provided that the hospital can and does check the blood for HIV and doesn't use blood that tests positive. If there is a delay in finding blood and/or transfusing it and if the patient is somewhat improved in the meantime, then it is good to refuse transfusion. Even blood that is tested can transmit HIV. *General transfusion guidelines are as follows*:
    - If the patient is pregnant, near delivery, and her hemoglobin is 7 or below, she should be transfused.
    - For a non-pregnant patient, a hemoglobin of over 5 should be treated with just IV fluids, no transfusion.
    - For a non-pregnant patient, a hemoglobin of 4-5 should be treated with transfusion if and only if the patient is very short of breath.
    - For a non-pregnant patient, a hemoglobin of 4 or under should be treated with transfusion regardless of symptoms.

Results: Some improvement in 6-8 hours; children with cerebral malaria may not gain consciousness for a week. This does not necessarily imply treatment failure. The patient may still become more anemic for the next 1-3 weeks; this also does not imply treatment failure.

c. Treatment of complications:

Bacterial infections: Children with PNEUMONIA or URINARY TRACT INFECTION should be treated with CIPROFLOXACIN or CEPHALOSPORIN; in areas without previous medical care, AMPICILLIN, CHLORAMPHENICOL, and CO-TRIMOXAZOLE might work well. If there is a sudden drop in blood pressure due to SEPSIS, treat that like ordinary SEPSIS.

KIDNEY FAILURE: Sending the patient for kidney dialysis is worthwhile because usually kidney function will resume in a week or two; you are not committing to life-long dialysis.

HEART FAILURE: It must be treated like ordinary HEART FAILURE as well as continuing the malaria treatment. If the patient is short of breath due to HEART FAILURE, you can try using HYDROCHLOROTHIAZIDE or a related diuretic. However, if he is also in KIDNEY FAILURE, this won't work.

ANEMIA: If ANEMIA is severe enough to cause shortness of breath, then transfer to a hospital that can do blood transfusions is essential.

SEIZURES: Use medication for seizures only if the patient is actually having seizures, not otherwise.

Classes of Antimalarial Drugs

Aminoalcohols	Anti-fols	Artemisia-derived	Antibiotics[1]
Chloroquine Quinine Quinidine Mefloquine Lumefantrine Primaquine Piperaquine Pyronaridine Isoquine (new)[2]	Pyrimethamine Proguanil Chlorproguanil Trimethoprim	Artemisinin Artesunate Artemether Dihydroartemisinin	Doxycycline Tetracycline Rifampin Sulfa drugs Ciprofloxacin Chloramphenicol Azithromycin

Notes:

1. Except for doxycycline, these are generally weak antimalarials and should not be purposely used for malaria prevention. However, if the patient is on one or more of these anyway, additional malaria preventive should not be necessary.

2. This is such a new drug that there is not much information. It is similar to amodiaquine but has less side-effects and is safer. Before using it you should get independent information.

V. HIGHER-LEVEL CARE IN DEVELOPING COUNTRIES

If the patient is too sick to carry on a conversation, then speedy referral is necessary. See Volume I, Appendix 13.

Laboratory:

Blood smears are commonly available. Usually, if the technician is experienced, the smears will read positive by the time of the first fever. However, with severe falciparum malaria, even when properly and repeatedly done, smears may be negative. They will usually be negative in blackwater fever. On the other hand, an adult national might not be ill at all and yet have a positive blood smear because he has developed immunity. Expatriates, however, often have to be extremely ill before a malaria blood smear will turn positive.

> There are two kinds of blood smears: thick and thin. A **thick smear** examines more blood so it will be positive in a fairly mild case, while the thin smear might still be negative. However, it is difficult or impossible to tell the kind of malaria on a thick smear. A **thin smear** will reveal the kind of malaria, but the person has to be much sicker before it is positive because it involves looking at less blood. Sometimes the percentage of infected cells in the blood is determined. In an expatriate adult or any child, 5% infected cells is life-threatening. But an adult national might tolerate as many as 20% infected cells and still survive.

Antibody tests are new tests that involve putting a drop of blood on a small stick or card or in a tiny plastic well, washing it off, and then looking at the color. These must be used carefully according to directions. The dipstick and card tests for falciparum malaria become positive with the first high fever; they will be negative for non-falciparum malaria. PfLDH turns negative quickly after the malaria is treated; PfHRP2 remains positive, possibly as much as a month. Patients with some kinds of severe ARTHRITIS may have false positive tests and there may be false negatives in some geographic areas. Some new antibody tests are being developed which detect all kinds of malaria.

Facilities: Expert nursing care, IV fluids, a blood bank and transfusion facilities, a monitored bed, level 3 or above. However with few exceptions Western-staffed hospitals in temperate climates are not desirable.

Practitioner: An infectious disease specialist is best; however, a generalist or internist with tropical/travel medical experience is preferable to an infectious disease specialist without tropical/travel experience.

VI. HIGHER-LEVEL CARE IN WESTERN COUNTRIES[1]

The bad news

Most American doctors will not treat malaria unless they have a lab report stating that there is malaria on the blood smear. If you can find a doctor trained in India, or a former missionary doctor, he might treat you without a positive smear.

Most lab techs and pathologists don't know how to do malaria smears properly. Most of them would not recognize malaria on a properly-done smear unless it was an overwhelmingly severe infection.

The United States has the highest case fatality rate in the world for malaria. There are not many cases so doctors don't know about it. Treatment is delayed or inadequate or both, and proper drugs are hard to find.

Severe falciparum malaria may be present even with a properly-done negative malaria smear. In Bangkok, Thailand, 30% of autopsy-proven cases of cerebral malaria had repeatedly negative malaria smears done by experienced technicians. (Technicians in the USA are generally not experienced and there are but few in Europe that are.) All the malaria parasites get stuck in the tiny blood vessels so the blood that is examined appears to be free of malaria. With blackwater fever, the malaria smear is almost always negative; with cerebral malaria it is commonly negative.

The most common mis-diagnosis in severe malaria is HEPATITIS. The second most common mis-diagnosis is MENINGITIS.

American doctors, once they diagnose malaria, may want to use injectable QUININE, but it is not available in the States.

A reasonable response

If you have been exposed to malaria, seek tropical/travel medical expertise per Volume I, Appendix 13. The clinic in London is particularly good.

When returning to the West on furlough, take your own medicines with you; include some oral and intravenous QUININE which can be bought over the counter in most developing countries, but is hard to find in the States. If you come down with malaria and it is not too bad, treat yourself with oral medicines. Take a course of PRIMAQUINE after you are done with your preventive. Hopefully this will prevent your becoming ill again.

Try to choose a doctor of tropical ethnic origin. In most places an Indian is best but it must be one who took most of his training in India.

---

[1] This section concerns typical care in the USA, Canada, and most locations in Europe. Competent tropical medical expertise is available in London, Liverpool, and Tubingen (Germany). See Appendix 13 of Volume I for recommended treatment locations.

If you do end up in a hospital, ask your doctor to have the lab tech do a hematocrit. This is a little tube of blood that is spun to separate the red cells from the watery part. If the lab tech breaks the hematocrit tube by the buffy coat and smears out the red cells from right underneath the buffy coat, making and staining it like an ordinary thin blood smear, the malaria parasites will be concentrated there and they are more likely to be seen.

If a family member has a spinal tap for meningitis but he actually has cerebral malaria, the spinal tap will either be normal or it might indicate a viral meningitis. Sometimes the lactate content of the spinal fluid is elevated but this is not a routine determination.

Severe malaria should be treated on suspicion of the diagnosis, without waiting for confirmation. Anyone who has been in a malarious area and is seriously ill should be treated for malaria plus whatever else he has. The heart drug, QUINIDINE, is a very close relative (stereoisomer) of the anti-malarial QUININE. It works just fine for severe malaria, but the person must be on a monitor in an intensive care unit to watch his heart rhythm. Eli Lily Company (800-821-0538) and/or Center for Disease Control malaria hotline (770-488-7788) in the USA might help with procurement. Oral medication may be substituted when the patient improves. Since oral quinine is absorbed rapidly, if vomiting can be prevented, a feeding tube can be used even in unconscious patients to give quinine although IV is better.

The blood sugar might drop precipitously during an episode of severe malaria, from the malaria or from the QUININE or QUINIDINE. Pregnant women and children are particularly prone to this complication. The patient should have a glucose solution running intravenously and his blood sugar should be monitored. This is particularly problematic for diabetics.

If you are truly desperate, go to a liquor store and buy quinine water over the counter. Drinking a liter or two may buy you some time to get yourself to an appropriate place. However, it may also make your blood test false-negative so you will be refused treatment.

MALNUTRITION

Cause: Lack of a balanced diet.

Includes: Kwashiorkor, Marasmus, Vitamin deficiencies.

Regional Notes: F, I, M, O, R, S, U.

Definition: Malnutrition is the failure to take in, process, or absorb enough food stuffs to sustain life or development.

Entry category: Syndrome cluster.

Mildly to very ill; Class 1-2; Worldwide, frequency variable and related to the culture. Use of alcoholic beverages aggravates malnutrition.

Kwashiorkor (malnutrition with swelling) occurs mainly in cool, humid areas. These are generally cultures with diets of manioc-tuber, millet-sorghum, or wheat. Marasmus (skinny malnutrition) is common in other areas, particularly those that are hot and dry.

Age: Any; children are most susceptible. Ordinary malnutrition is most common under 1 year of age; kwashiorkor, after 1 y.o. Either type can occur in adults. **Who:** Babies, especially bottle-fed; an older baby when a younger one has taken his place at the breast. Any poor diet. More likely with severe diarrhea. Malnutrition with kwashiorkor is very common after MEASLES or diarrhea. **Onset:** Usually slow unless an illness tips the balance in a marginally-nourished child.

Clinical:

(For more details, see Volume I, Chapter 5.)

➤ **General malnutrition:**

Necessary: Children fail to grow normally. The upper arms are thin; at least the roots of the hair and possibly all of the hair is a lighter-than-normal color in Blacks but darker-than-normal in blond persons. Some ethnic groups develop straight and brittle hair rather than a color change. Black skin becomes paler than normal. Whites may have darkening of skin. Measure the circumference of the upper arm, half way between the shoulder and the elbow. (See the illustrations and standard measurements in Volume I, Chapter 5.) The smaller the arm measurement, the greater the child's risk of dying. Malnourished children never smile. If you can get a child to smile, he is probably not malnourished.

Frequently: Malnourished children are lethargic, with big bellies so that they look pregnant. They have swollen feet which can be dented with pressure from a finger. They may have a sore tongue. Their sexual and mental development is delayed. Menstruating females may stop menstruating.

Sometimes: They are just skinny without any swelling. The skin of their lower legs may peel. They may have open sores. Their eyes may be affected by XEROPHTHALMIA. Vertical cracks in lips are common. They may have a glue-like body odor. Their appetites may also decrease so that they refuse food when it is offered. A sore tongue is common so that eating is painful. They may have sharp, shooting, or chewing pains in their lower legs. Some children have swellings by their ears, similar to MUMPS and/or HIV INFECTION.

Complications: ANEMIA, BRAIN DAMAGE, chronic diarrhea or MALABSORPTION (See Protocol C-14), HYPOGLYCEMIA, DIABETES, MILK INTOLERANCE, susceptibility to infections. PNEUMONIA is a common cause of death.

➤ **Vitamin deficiencies:**

Deficiency in FOLATE and VITAMIN B_{12} can cause a disease very similar to tertiary SYPHILIS. The symptoms develop slowly over months. They begin with severe aching in the feet. Then sharp pains develop in the foot followed by shooting pains up and down the leg.

Pressure on the legs or feet aggravates the pain. Problems with vision and hearing may follow. The patient becomes uncoordinated and he cannot tell where an arm or leg is without looking. The tongue is sore.

A deficiency of niacin causes PELLAGRA: rough, scaly skin, diarrhea, and irrational behavior.

A deficiency of B Vitamins occurs in adults, characterized by burning and aching feet, and later severe pains shooting up and down the feet and lower legs. Pressure on the feet or legs aggravates the pain so patients sleep with their feet outside the blankets. This is caused by a deficiency of one or more of the B Vitamins and responds readily to MULTIVITAMINS.

Deficiency in Vitamin E can cause uncoordination.

Causative Diseases: ASCARIASIS, GIARDIASIS, TUBERCULOSIS, MALABSORPTION (Protocol C-14) and all the causative diseases of that, MEASLES, BRUCELLOSIS.

Similar Conditions: See Protocols C-6: Limb Swelling and C-7: Liver/Spleen Problems. In any arable area, first treat for GIARDIASIS and ASCARIASIS. If the patient consents to eat thereafter, just feed him and don't worry about similar diseases. If he refuses to eat or if he has general body swelling, see the appropriate protocols in Index A.

Bush Laboratory: Usually ANEMIA. Urine usually shows ketones. Blood tests show low serum albumin.

Higher-Level Care. There are two options: a refeeding program run by an NGO, if locally available, is ideal. A general level 2 or level 3 hospital is useless. A level 4 or 5 hospital might be useful but anyone who can afford that can also afford food so he does not become malnourished in the first place.

Treatment:

Prevention: Agricultural development; nutrition education. Provide supplementary feeding for children after any diarrhea (especially watery) and after any serious illness. See Volume I, Chapter 5 to ascertain what deficiency diseases are likely to be prevalent in your area, and what locally-available foods are needed. Then routinely educate parents to both eat and give their children these foods.

Patient Care: See the detailed instructions in Volume I, Chapter 5. It is essential to distinguish between *marasmus* (skinny malnutrition) and *kwashiorkor* (swollen malnutrition) since the initial treatments of the two conditions differ.

The child's weight in kg x 30 is the number of ml of milk a child should consume in 24 hours.

When giving antibiotics initially, be sure not to use any for which LIVER DISEASE is listed as changing the dosage. A malnourished liver doesn't handle these antibiotics well.

Results: There should be significant weight gain within 7 days. Length and/or height should increase over 2 months.

Mansonellosis Perstans

See *Regional Notes* F, M.

MASTITIS

Cause: Bacteria.

Clinical:

Mastitis is CELLULITIS or ABSCESS of the breast, most common in nursing women. It occurs after 2 weeks following deliver and is usually caused by missed feedings which stagnates the milk. Usually there is a moderate to high fever, pain, redness or warmth, and swelling. There may be a pus discharge from the nipple or the mass and the nipple may be inverted.

Similar Conditions: FILARIASIS and TUBERCULOSIS are similar, as well as some types of breast CANCER.

Treatment:

Treat for CELLULITIS or ABSCESS first; consider alternatives if no better in 3-4 days. Keep the breasts empty after draining pus. Milk will normally leak for a while through the drainage incision.

MASTOIDITIS

Cause: Bacteria.

Definition: Mastoiditis is an infection of the bony bump behind the ear.

Age: Usually children. **Who:** Those with ear infections.
Onset: Usually gradual.

Clinical:

This is an infection of the bone behind the ear. It is a complication of an untreated EAR INFECTION. The swelling pushes the ear forward. There may be local redness and drainage. Invariably there is a fever. If left untreated, it may cause MENINGITIS.

Treatment:

The same as for EAR INFECTION, MIDDLE, but continue for at least 2 weeks. Surgery may be necessary; Level 4 or higher.

MEASLES

Cause: Virus.

Synonyms: Hard measles, Morbilli, Red measles, Rubeola, Ten-day measles.

Regional Notes: E, F, I, S, U.

Definition: Measles is a viral infection of the body, most common in children.

Moderately to very ill; Class 2; Contagious, highly; Worldwide, common except where there are immunizations. Occurs in epidemics.

Age: Over 4-5 months, mostly before 4 y.o., occasionally adults. **Who:** Unimmunized; far worse in malnourished children; both worse and more common with overcrowding. **Onset:** 9-14 days after exposure; then over a day or two.

Clinical:

Necessary: The patient has a high fever, a cough, runny nose, and red eyes. His eyes are painful and light makes the pain worse. A rash breaks out about the third day of illness. It is red spots in Whites, sandpapery in Blacks. It starts on the head, then spreads to the rest of the body. By the third day of the rash, it is heavy all over. HIV patients may have no rash with measles.

Sometimes: There may be sneezing before the other symptoms. The patient may have white, raised spots on a red base in his mouth early in the disease. These spots may be painful. Babies may stop nursing because of sores in the mouth. In severe measles, the rash darkens and the skin peels after 4-11 days.

Commonly: The patient develops diarrhea (which may be bloody), vomiting, and DEHYDRATION. A couple of days after the rash breaks out, the patient may develop PNEUMONIA or EAR INFECTION, MIDDLE. He may become short of breath. In patients who develop PNEUMONIA, there is a 50% death rate.

Complications: KERATITIS (sometimes due to HERPES), BRAIN DAMAGE, MALNUTRITION, EYE INFECTION, XEROPHTHALMIA, GANGRENE of the limbs, blindness, deafness, SEIZURES, aggravation of TUBERCULOSIS, and death. Death is particularly likely in children under 1 y.o. After measles is done, the patient may develop POST-MEASLES CACHEXIA, a condition of lethargy, refusal to eat, MALABSORPTION, and weight loss, resulting in death. In immunized patients, measles is mild if it occurs at all.

Similar Conditions: See Protocols C-8, C-10, and C-12. If the patient had a very sudden onset and he has severe bone pain, as if his bones are broken, he has DENGUE FEVER. If the rash broke out right after he took AMPICILLIN, consider MONONUCLEOSIS which causes a drug reaction. Check on immunizations and eliminate those diseases for which the patient has been immunized.

Higher-Level Care. *Facilities and Practitioners:* IV fluids, antibiotics, nutritional support, a generalist or a pediatrician might be helpful, at level 2 or more.

Treatment:

Prevention: Immunize all children six months old or older, except those with BURKITT LYMPHOMA, TUBERCULOSIS or severe MALNUTRITION. Check with a local M.D. to find out at what age to give it in your area. There is a heat-stable vaccine available. It can be held at room temperature (70's °F) for 2 days and at body temperature for 7 hours.

Patient Care:

- Right at first, before anything else, give VITAMIN A to prevent blindness. ZINC is also helpful.
- Check vital signs every 4 hours.
- *Diet*: Milk as much as tolerated. Pass a stomach tube if necessary. Use soy milk if diarrhea is severe. Empty the mother's breasts during the illness; and insist on nursing for 2 months after, or use a high-protein diet. The refeeding mixture used in MALNUTRITION is excellent. Encourage fluid intake.
- Treat FEVER *per se*.
- Watch the respiratory rate, listen to the lungs, and watch for signs of EAR INFECTION daily. If EAR INFECTION, or PNEUMONIA develops, treat with PENICILLIN. If that does not seem to work, use CLOXACILLIN or a CEPHALOSPORIN.
- Use BISMUTH SUBSALICYLATE for diarrhea, PROMETHAZINE for vomiting.
- Treat DEHYDRATION with fluids. See Volume I, Appendix 1.
- Treat POST-MEASLES CACHEXIA just like MALNUTRITION from any other cause.

Results: 90% death rate in malnourished Blacks; rare deaths in previously healthy Whites.

MEDITERRANEAN TICK TYPHUS

See SPOTTED FEVER. Mediterranean tick typhus and African tick typhus are two forms of Boutonneuse Fever, both listed under SPOTTED FEVER. Mediterranean tick typhus tends to be less severe than African tick typhus.

MELIOIDOSIS

See SEPSIS and your *Regional Notes*. This is a kind of sepsis that is common in Southeast Asia and aboriginal Australia but it may occur elsewhere. It most commonly starts with PNEUMONIA or URINARY INFECTION. Patients frequently have had previous poor health and the death rate is high.

MENINGITIS

Cause: Usually bacteria or virus.

Synonym: Cerebrospinal meningitis.

Regional Notes: E, F, I, O, R.

Definition: Meningitis is an infection of the meninges which is the covering over the brain.

Entry category: Disease cluster.

Always very ill; Class 3; Contagious usually; Worldwide, quite uncommon, easily confused with cerebral MALARIA which is more common. TB meningitis occurs wherever TUBERCULOSIS is common; it is not contagious.

Age: Any. **Who:** Anyone, especially those with previous EAR INFECTION (ear pain) and SINUSITIS (headaches), also those with previous head injury or PNEUMONIA or active TB. **Onset:** Hours to days. If the onset is over a week or more, it is probably due to TUBERCULOSIS or BRUCELLOSIS.

Clinical:

➢ **Ordinary Meningitis:**

Necessary: Patients are always very ill; adults stay in bed and children are never alert and playful. Adults have a high fever and a severe headache, frequently going down the neck to the back. *Exceptions*: Elderly patients, diabetics, newborns, and HIV-infected patients may not have the usual signs; they may not have fevers. Meningitis caused by TUBERCULOSIS may not cause a fever.

Usually: A conscious patient over 2 y.o. has a stiff neck; he cannot put his chin on his chest and trying causes pain, but he can turn his head from side to side without pain. The stiffness may be subtle; look for it. Shaking the head increases pain. A baby will cry harder rather than being comforted when held by his mother. The patient prefers to lie on his side, back arched.

Sometimes: Vomiting occurs in adults; it is almost invariable in children. Babies under 2 y.o. and those who are unconscious may not have the stiff neck. Those under 7 months may have a bulging soft spot on the top front scalp but this occurs late in the disease. Failure to find this is no argument against the diagnosis. Confusion, lethargy, or loss of consciousness is common if the problem has persisted for some time; initially babies and children may be irritable. There may be irregular respirations. There are sometimes abnormal pupils (do not get smaller in the presence of light) or SEIZURES. Sometimes the patient has a rash which may be red spotted. The covering over the white of the eye may be swollen. The patient may have eye pain in the presence of light. There may be diarrhea.

The first symptom is sometimes crazy behavior. ARTHRITIS may develop during treatment, as may dark blisters on the skin. (These blisters resemble second-degree burns and are treated similarly.)

➢ **Tuberculous Meningitis:**

There is always a slow onset, an abnormal mental state, and some abnormality of the movement of the face, the eyes, or the pupil response to light, e.g. a new-onset "lazy eye" or unequal pupils. The patient may be dizzy.

Complications: STROKE (especially when due to TUBERCULOSIS). Stroke causes floppy weakness of the limbs, usually just on one side, which later becomes stiff. Other complications: deafness, BRAIN DAMAGE, SEPSIS, and death. With SEPSIS the skin might turn black, blistered, or both; there may be abnormal bleeding; loss of consciousness; GANGRENE; ARTHRITIS; BRAIN DAMAGE.

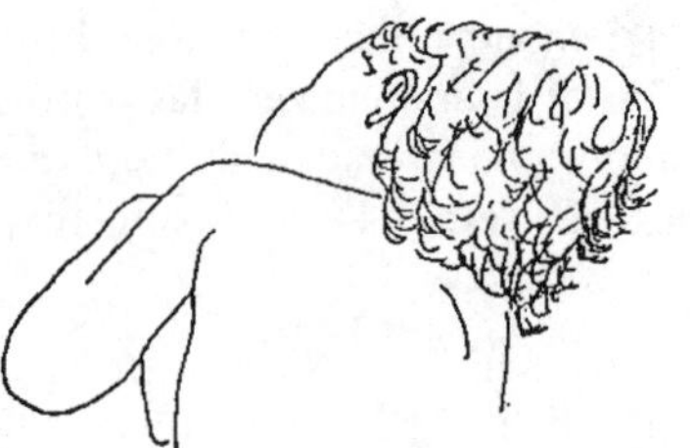

Meningitis: Note the child's head position.

Causative Diseases: Meningitis may be caused by SYPHILIS or TUBERCULOSIS, rarely by ENTERIC FEVER, BRUCELLOSIS, or PLAGUE.

Similar Conditions: See Protocols C-8, C-10, and C-13

<u>*Indistinguishable*</u>: Cerebral MALARIA, HEAT STROKE, ENCEPHALITIS, RELAPSING FEVER. Patients with secondary SYPHILIS who harbor the HIV virus might appear to have meningitis when they, in fact, have SYPHILIS.

<u>*Slow-onset*</u>: TUBERCULOSIS meningitis, BRUCELLOSIS, or else LEAD POISONING.

Also consider TRICHINOSIS (swollen muscles), POLIO (limb paralysis), TETANUS (general muscle spasms), RABIES (spasms with swallowing water or a breeze on the face), SPOTTED FEVER (rash beginning on limbs).

Higher-Level Care. Speedy referral to at least a level 2 facility is mandatory. See Volume I, Appendix 13. Consider that public transport may be inadvisable because of contagion. *Laboratory:* A blood count and examination of the spinal fluid obtained with a spinal tap might be useful. For a spinal tap, sterile equipment, good technique, and a very clean environment are essential. This might be available at a level 2 facility. At a level 3 or 4 facility, there might be cultures available as well as other more sophisticated tests. *Facilities:* IV equipment and fluids, injectable antibiotics, at least level 2. *Practitioner:* pediatrician, internist, generalist. an infectious disease specialist is ideal.

Treatment:

Prevention: The kind of meningitis that is very contagious and occurs in epidemics has sudden onset; a healthy person becomes extremely ill within hours. You can prevent the disease in those who are exposed with RIFAMPIN or vaccine. Vaccines are available for the epidemic types: meningococcal vaccine for types A, C, Y, and W135; there is no immunization for type B.

Patient Care: Begin immediately! Arrange transport. Until the patient departs:

- Record vital signs every 2 hours.
- Give fluids orally or down a stomach tube to prevent DEHYDRATION. (See Appendix 1 for using a stomach tube.) MULTIVITAMINS are helpful for nutritional support.
- Use antibiotics: Use them IV if you are able. IM is second-best and oral is third-best. If the onset was

slow, use drugs appropriate for TUBERCULOSIS and/or BRUCELLOSIS rather than the antibiotics listed below. In an area where there is much HIV INFECTION, try to use medication that is also appropriate for SYPHILIS.

- o AMPICILLIN for 14 days. Do not substitute ERYTHROMYCIN.
- o Give CHLORAMPHENICOL for 14 days in addition; use CHLORAMPHENICOL alone, if the patient has PENICILLIN allergy, adding an appropriate[1] CEPHALOSPORIN if possible. If you will not be able to treat for 14 days, a single large dose of IM long-acting CHLORAMPHENICOL is about 95% effective.
- o Better than AMPICILLIN plus CHLORAMPHENICOL but expensive: a CEPHALOSPORIN, a kind that is listed for meningitis.

- Add DEXAMETHASONE, if you have it. This reduces the long-term bad consequences in many cases. PREDNISONE or PREDNISOLONE may substitute, if necessary.
- Treat for cerebral MALARIA in malarious areas.
- Expect improvement in 2-3 days; stiff neck persists for 2 weeks.
- Give food and MULTIVITAMINS as soon as possible.
- In breast-fed babies, empty mother's breasts at least four times a day. Give the milk down the stomach tube if you can do so without making the child vomit.
- For vomiting, use PROMETHAZINE.
- For SEIZURES, use PARALDEHYDE, PHENYLTOIN, or PHENOBARBITAL. If you use anti-seizure medications, increase the dosage of CHLORAMPHENICOL by 10 to 15%.

Results: Improvement should be evident within 72 hours; the stiff neck may take weeks to resolve.

MENOPAUSE

Regional Notes: F.
Definition: Menopause is the cessation of a woman's monthly periods anywhere from age 40 to 55.

There may be episodes of sweating, heavy menstruation, personality changes, and drying of the vagina making intercourse uncomfortable. Hormonal therapy is available under a physician's supervision. CALCIUM plus estrogen and exercise can help prevent the bone thinning that occurs with menopause. Contraceptive cream helps with vaginal dryness.

[1] Appropriate in this case means one that is listed as suitable for meningitis.

MENSTRUAL CRAMPS

Definition: Menstrual cramps are low abdominal pains during menstruation. The problem is responsive to IBUPROFEN. If severe, try BIRTH CONTROL PILLS for three months.

MENTAL ILLNESS

Definition: Mental illness is illness caused by emotional problems.

Clinical:

Symptoms may be depressed, hyperactive, or bizarre behavior. Diagnose this only when other causes of the problem have been excluded. This is easily confused with ATTENTION DEFICIT DISORDER, DEMONIZATION, and some physical illnesses such as cerebral MALARIA and BRUCELLOSIS. Also see STRESS and DEPRESSION. It may be confused with, cause, or be caused by drug ADDICTION. It may be associated with increased or decreased appetite and weight gain or loss.

Similar Conditions: It is important to distinguish mental/spiritual causes from physical causes. The following factors indicate a physical (infectious or toxic, usually) cause for the illness.

- Either the problem started suddenly or it changes markedly over hours or days.
- The patient cannot pay attention.
- Either the patient talks nonsense or he is lethargic or hyperactive.

Treatment:

Some medications that are useful to control behavior over the short term are: DIAZEPAM, PHENOBARBITAL, CHLORPROMAZINE.

MIGRAINE HEADACHE

Cause: Heredity.
Synonym: Vasospastic headache.
Regional Notes: F.
Definition: A recurrent throbbing headache, usually one-sided, due to spasm of the blood vessels in the brain.

Mildly to moderately ill; Class 1; Worldwide, culturally variable, common in Westerners.

Age: 15-50 y.o. for the first episode. **Who:** Anyone, especially relatives of those with migraines, recurrent. **Onset:** Minutes to hours.

Clinical:

Necessary: Severe eye pain or headache, aggravated by light, sound, or shaking of the head. It is always throbbing initially, but it may be constant later. It may last 1 hour to 4 days. It never causes a fever.

Usually: One-sided headache, or one side worse than the other; vomiting is common.

Occasionally: The patient complains of numbness and tingling or weakness of one side of the body, and there may be temporary paralysis or double vision.

Similar Conditions: ALTITUDE SICKNESS (altitude over 8000 feet), HEAT ILLNESS (hot environment), MALARIA.

Treatment:

Prevention: At times PROPRANOLOL or VERAPAMIL might be helpful. A diet avoiding chocolate, cheese, and wine sometimes decreases the incidence and severity.

Patient Care: Dark and quiet and pain medicines, injectable if necessary; NALBUPHINE works fine. DIPYRONE works o.k. but there are occasional deaths from using it; do not use it unless you are truly desperate and the family agrees to the risk. Try to get the patient to sleep. Use PROMETHAZINE or HYDROXYZINE for vomiting and sedation.

MILK INTOLERANCE

Cause: Heredity.

Synonyms: Lactase deficiency; Lactose intolerance, Milk allergy.

Definition: Milk intolerance is abdominal distress (diarrhea, gas pains, vomiting) due to one of the sugars in milk which the body is unable to digest.

Not ill to mildly ill; Class 1; Worldwide.

Age: Any, after weaning. It most often happens in weaned children. It may occur for the first time in an adult who had diarrhea from some other cause. **Who:** Anyone, especially Asians, South Americans, Blacks, and those who have had MALNUTRITION or any intestinal disease. Many women with milk intolerance before pregnancy again become tolerant during pregnancy. **Onset:** Over hours to weeks.

Clinical:

The patient has watery diarrhea, possibly with abdominal cramps, and gas whenever he drinks milk. He may vomit.

Bush Laboratory: Collect some of the diarrhea and let it sit for an hour or two. Test the watery part with a urine dipstick. It will show an acid pH (5 or 6) and a negative dipstick test for sugar. The sugar test, however, will be positive with Clinatest tablets.

Similar Conditions: See Protocol C-14. The treatment for milk intolerance will not help any other diarrhea.

Treatment:

LACTAID replaces the missing enzyme for digesting milk. Otherwise a milk-free diet is helpful. Diluting milk 50:50 with clean water may help. Fermented milk products such as YOGURT can usually be used. Soy milk is always tolerated. Sometimes the problem lasts only a week or two but usually it is lifelong. See Chapter 5 for recipes for milk-free granola and grape-nuts, both high-protein foods.

MISCARRIAGE

See ABORTION. Miscarriage is a spontaneous (unintentional) abortion.

MOLLUSCUM CONTAGIOSUM

Cause: Virus.

Definition: A viral skin infection causing skin bumps.

Not ill; Class 1; Contagious; Worldwide.

Age: Any. **Who:** Anyone, but most common in the developing world in people with HIV. It can be transmitted sexually and also by non-sexual direct contact. **Onset:** Over days to weeks.

Clinical:

The patient develops little, fleshy skin bumps of nearly uniform size, usually 2-200 of them but sometimes huge numbers, about 2-4 mm diameter with flat or slightly rounded tops with center holes. In children they are mostly on the face, trunk and limbs. In adults they are mainly in the genital area. They neither itch nor hurt. Their color is somewhat lighter than dark brown or black skin. The patient is not ill because of them. The insides are cheesy, not watery.

Treatment:

It sometimes works to disrupt the bumps with a sharp blade or sterile needle. Reassure an otherwise-healthy patient that they will go away by themselves in 8 weeks or sooner. In a patient with HIV, the number of bumps is inversely related to his level of immunity. If the numbers increase, he is likely to die soon.

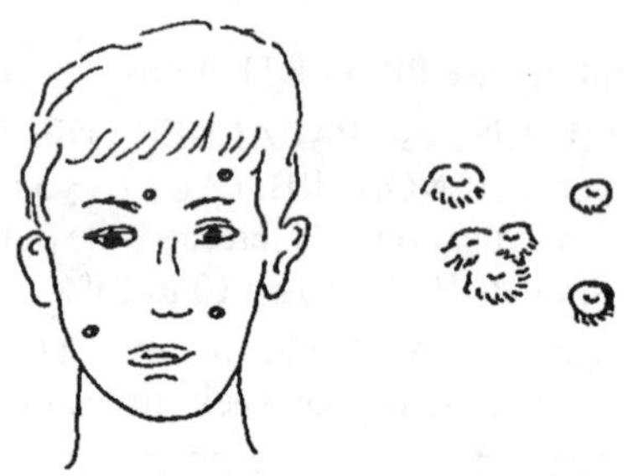

Molluscum contagiosum

MONGOLIAN SPOT

Definition: Mongolian spot is a darker colored area of skin on the lower back or buttocks of a baby.

Not ill; Class 1; Worldwide.

Entry category: Normal variant

Age: Children. **Who:** Mainly those with intermediate skin color, neither white nor dark black. **Onset:** Usually present since birth.

Clinical:

Necessary: The patient has what looks like a black and blue spot over the back or buttocks. It is roughly symmetrical. The skin is never broken and it never itches or hurts. It does not change color over several days like a bruise does. This rather than the symmetry is the most important differentiation.

Treatment:

None. This is a normal skin color variation. It is included with the diseases so it will not be mistaken for abuse or an illness.

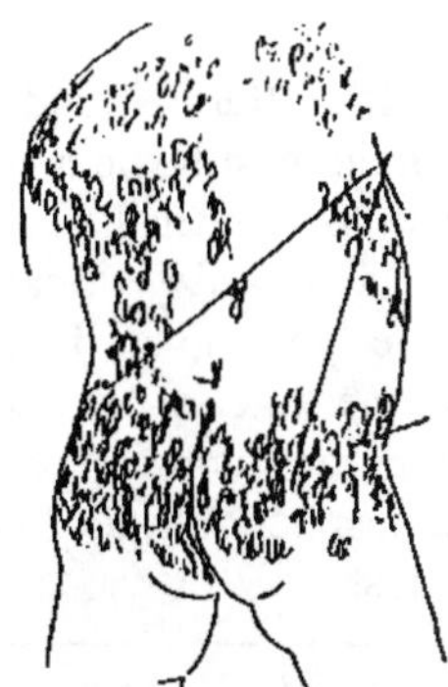

Mongolian spot

MONGOLISM

Cause: Birth defect.

Synonyms: Down Syndrome, Trisomy 21.

Definition: Mongolism is a birth defect, caused by an extra chromosome.

Age: The problem is evident from birth, though the parents might not initially recognize or admit it. **Who:** Anyone can give birth to a mongoloid child; nothing can prevent it aside from prenatal diagnosis and abortion. **Onset:** From conception, evident from birth.

Clinical:

This is a common kind of mental retardation; the degree of retardation varies greatly. The child's eyes are widely set and slant downward from the temples to the nose. The bridge of his nose is low. The tops of the outer ears may be folded down. His mouth usually hangs open, showing a large tongue. The crease on his palm, closest to his fingers, goes across his hand without interruption. His fingers are shorter than normal. Heart problems are common. CRETINISM and THALLASEMIA may look similar. There is no good treatment for mongolism.

Complications: HEART FAILURE, CANCER of the blood (leukemia), frequent infections, Alzheimer's disease, premature graying of the hair.

Monkeypox

See *Regional Notes* F.

Monkey Fever

See Kyasanur Forest Disease in *Regional Index* I, entered under ARBOVIRAL FEVER.

MONONUCLEOSIS

Cause: Virus.

Synonyms: Epstein-Barr virus infection, Glandular fever, Mono, Kissing disease.

Regional Notes: F, R.

Definition: Mononucleosis is a viral infection of the lymphatic system.

Mildly to moderately ill; Class 1-2 depending on severity; Contagious; Worldwide, neither common nor rare.

Age: Teenagers in Western cultures, children in tropics. **Who:** Anyone; a person cannot get it twice but relapses are common. **Onset:** 1-2 days.

Clinical:

Necessary: The patient has a fever and complains of extreme fatigue. The lymph nodes in the front of his neck are swollen and possibly those in back also. The swollen nodes are tender to touch.

Sometimes: He may have a sore throat but the pain is not severe. He has large, red tonsils (provided they were not previously removed) with white blotches. His spleen and liver may enlarge, causing some upper abdominal pain. He mat have a measles-type red rash, especially if he takes AMPICILLIN.

Similar Conditions: See Protocols C-7, C-9, and C-12.

Higher-Level Care. *Laboratory:* There is a reasonably simple blood test for this; it is likely to be found in a level 3 hospital.

Treatment:

Bed rest only. Antibiotics do no good. Allow no contact sports or rough-housing. If the spleen is bruised, it may rupture and kill the patient.

Results: 2 weeks to 12 months with frequent relapses.

MUMPS

Cause: Virus.

Synonyms: Infectious parotitis, Parotitis.

Definition: Mumps is a viral infection of the salivary glands and sometimes the testicles and pancreas.

Mildly to moderately ill; Class 1; Contagious; Worldwide, common, frequently epidemics among those not immunized.

Age: Any, especially children. **Who:** Usually those not immunized. **Onset:** 12-25 days incubation.

Clinical:

Necessary: First the patient has general achiness, loss of appetite, and fever. Then he develops swelling of the glands in front of and below his ears. The swelling is neither red nor warm. It may be painful with eating certain foods but it is not tender to the touch.

Sometimes: He may have abdominal or ear pain. The gums by the molars may swell. Adults may have painful swelling of the testicles. Symptoms of ENCEPHALITIS or eye problems are rare.

Complications: Infertility is rare in sexually mature males. Patients with mumps ENCEPHALITIS usually recover fully.

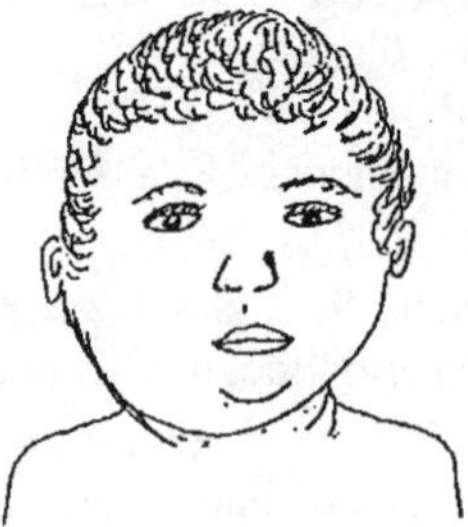

Mumps - right sided. Note the swelling by the ear.

Similar Conditions: See Protocol C-8 if the eyes are red and painful. ABSCESS of a tooth (decayed tooth visible). If very ill, consider TYPHUS. BURKITT LYMPHOMA may be similar in children. ALCOHOLISM (generally only adults), LIVER DISEASE or LIVER FAILURE (yellow whites of the eyes or distended abdomen), PELLAGRA (rash on sun-exposed skin). A similar kind of swelling is present in young children with MALNUTRITION and/or HIV INFECTION.

Treatment:

Prevention: Immunization is 70% effective.

Patient Care. Treat FEVER PER SE. Place ice packs on swollen areas. Antibiotics do no good.

MUSCLE STRAIN

Cause: Injury.

Synonyms: Pulled muscles, Myositis.

Definition: Muscle strain is muscle damage caused by unaccustomed exercise, making small tears in the muscles.

Not ill to mildly ill; Class 1; Worldwide, very common everywhere.

Age: Mostly older children and adults. **Who:** Those engaging in unaccustomed physical activity. Those whose bodies have been jolted. **Onset:** Sometimes immediately, worse 1-2 days after the activity or accident.

Clinical:

Necessary: The patient has aching, sore muscles. He may have chest or abdominal pain if he exercised those muscles. Neck strain tends to produce shoulder pain and maybe arm pain as well as neck pain. Low back strain is similar to SLIPPED DISC. It may cause painful pelvic muscles. The two are frequently indistinguishable at first, both causing sudden onset of pain and both causing shooting pains in the legs. Muscle strain never causes fever.

Similar Conditions: The pain of a fractured bone is maximum immediately after the accident. It does not get worse over a couple of days. Also consider BRUCELLOSIS (fevers off and on), TUBERCULOSIS of the bone (specific bone tenderness), SCIATICA (may be indistinguishable), POLIO (limb weakness or paralysis). PYOMYOSITIS may appear similar but the tenderness and swelling are in one local place only and there is usually a fever.

Higher-Level Care. *Facilities:* X-ray may be helpful to exclude other diagnoses. *Practitioner:* Generalist, internist, surgeon.

Treatment:

Rest, heating pads, IBUPROFEN, and pain medicines. Patients with back strain must lie on a very firm surface, on the back (with a pillow under the knees) or on either side, for 4 days, 24 hours a day. Meals and bathroom duties should be done lying down. If there is still pain after 4 days, extend the time to 2 weeks. If the patient has difficulty urinating or numb feet, or persistent pain, he must be sent to a hospital. *Results:* 1-7 days, longer if the patient does not rest.

MYCETOMA

Cause: Fungus.

Synonyms: Madura foot, Maduromycosis, Deep mycosis, Mycosis.

Regional Notes: F, I, M, R.; Present worldwide in tropical and subtropical areas, more arid than humid, from 15° South to 30° North.

Definition: Mycetoma is a fungal or bacterial infection of the soft tissues of the body, usually the feet or the lungs. The bacterial kind predominates in India and Mexico; the fungal kind predominates elsewhere.

Entry category: Disease cluster.

Not ill to moderately ill; Class 2-4; Worldwide.

Age: Any; mainly older children and young adults. **Who:** Anyone, poor hygiene, minor wounds in hands and feet especially from acacia trees and cacti; males more than females, mainly farmers and herders. **Onset:** Slow, over weeks to years; incubation also over years. There are two kinds: fungal and bactrial. The fungal progresses slowly whereas the bacterial progresses more rapidly.

Clinical:

This may affect either the lungs or the skin.

- **Lung form:**

This is a slowly progressive disease, mimicking TUBERCULOSIS and indistinguishable without lab facilities.

- **Skin form:**

This commonly starts on the foot with painless swelling. Then a bump, ABSCESS, ulcer, or IMPETIGO-like sore, about 1 cm in diameter, begins. There are small amounts of an oily substance with some dry grains like chalk, yeast, or coal dust coming out. The grains are off-white, yellow or black; rarely red, orange, or brownish. They may be hard or soft. Pain, if any, is usually minimal but there may be deep itching. The patient may develop pain after some time if there is secondary infection of the wound with bacteria. Then there may be ordinary pus in larger amounts. There may be destruction of the underlying bones and muscles, but the pain is surprisingly little, considering how bad the swelling and open sores look. There may be multiple holes connecting the various wounds so that the whole area looks like a sponge. The foot may become shorter. The patient is likely to complain of awkwardness in walking rather than pain. In some areas this may cause ulcers which destroy the nose.

Similar Conditions: *Skin form*: CANCRUM ORIS (on the face); tertiary SYPHILIS; tertiary YAWS; IMPETIGO (which is seldom on the feet); ABSCESS (tender to touch); TROPICAL ULCER. Also consider CUTANEOUS LEISHMANIASIS and BURULI ULCER. The dry grains are distinctive for mycetoma.

Higher-Level Care. *Laboratory:* A hospital lab may be able to examine the grains or culture the wounds to determine the type of mycetoma and suggest a likely treatment. It is not difficult to distinguish fungal and bacterial types and thus to predict a helpful treatment.

Treatment:

It varies with the form. Local medical lore may help. The kind with black grains requires surgery; those with white, yellow, or red grains, those caused by bacteria, can sometimes be cured with medicines: DAPSONE plus STREPTOMYCIN for a month, or COTRIMOXAZOLE plus RIFAMPIN for 3-4 months (more expensive). GRISEOFULVIN, ITRACONAZOLE, KETOCONAZOLE, DAPSONE may work for some types. The types caused by fungus require surgery. IODINE, locally applied, might be helpful in the early stages.

MYIASIS

Cause: Fly larvae.
Synonyms: Maggot infestation, Maggots
Includes: Screw worm.
Regional Notes: F, M, R.
Definition: A skin or moist surface problem caused by fly larvae (maggots) that penetrate the body surface or invade an open wound or body cavity.
Entry category: Infestation.

Mildly ill; Class 1; Regional: Mostly tropical areas although temperate areas also have wound myiasis. It is present nearly worldwide. The type of myiasis varies from place to place. Local lore is helpful in this regard. Nasal and ear myiasis are found in Asia and Africa.

Age: Any. **Who:** Those who are exposed to certain kinds of flies; especially those with open wounds, sleeping unprotected, sick, crippled, or not motivated to chase flies away. **Onset:** Variable, usually soon after exposure.

Clinical:

The symptoms vary according to the body part affected:

- *Wound myiasis:* Open wounds get maggots in them; they look like little worms. They enlarge wounds and cause infection.
- *Eye myiasis:* Same kinds as wound myiasis, plus some others which are common where sheep and goats are raised. These may produce severe eye infections (pain, redness, swelling, pus) and blindness.
- *Ear, nose, throat myiasis:* Same kinds as eye and wound get into ears, nose, and throat, producing infection (pain, redness, swelling, inability to hear, inability to smell, inability to swallow).
- *Intestinal myiasis:* Many different kinds of flies deposit eggs on food. The larvae then are passed in the stool. They are harmless.
- *Genito-urinary myiasis:* Flies lay their eggs in the genital area. The maggots may cause urinary, vaginal, or rectal injury: pain with urination, sexual relations, or bowel movements. They may be seen during childbirth or sexual encounters.
- *Skin myiasis:* Some maggots can penetrate intact skin; see Regional Notes for the specific type(s), if any, for your area. Usually there are red, swollen spots on the skin.

Complications: Secondary infection (CELLULITIS, ABSCESS); TETANUS.

Similar Conditions: Nothing else has visible, short, fat creatures. The worms of GUINEA WORM are very long. LOIASIS (only rain forest Africa) worms are larger than myiasis larvae; they are the size and shape of small earthworms. STRONGYLOIDIASIS and LARVA MIGRANS cause itchy lines underneath the skin, which myiasis larvae do not.

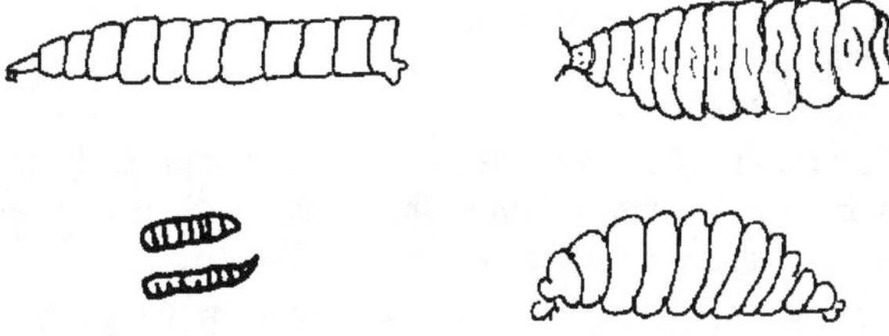

Typical maggots: Note the segmentation and the relative length and width.

Higher-Level Care. This condition may require surgery, at level 3 or higher.

Treatment:

Prevention: Insect repellent might be helpful. IVERMECTIN, a deworming medication, dissolved in skin cream and rubbed on the skin, works for animals and is harmless for humans.

Patient Care: Varies with the type of fly. Remove maggots if they can be removed easily. If you place petroleum jelly (Vaseline) over them they may be easy to remove as they come up for air. In the case of the Tumbu fly, the petroleum jelly makes the diagnosis. If you watch the little hole carefully, you will note little air bubbles rising through the petroleum jelly. The development of the larva is over 6 days; you must wait at least until day 4 before removing it. Use ANTIBIOTIC EYE DROPS rather than the eye ointment for eye myiasis. Maggots that are in eyes, ears, throat, and genital areas, if they cannot be removed easily, must be removed at a hospital. After removing the maggots, treat all skin myiasis wounds like TROPICAL ULCER.

Nairobi Eye

See *Regional* Notes F.

NECROTIZING FASCIITIS

This is a type of GANGRENE. It looks like CELLULITIS with minimal redness and swelling. However, pain and tenderness are extraordinarily severe. It starts rapidly, over a matter of hours. There is nothing you can do but send out to a surgical facility. However, do give antibiotics as for GANGRENE in the meantime.

NEURALGIA, NEURITIS, NEUROPATHY

These terms refer to a variety of problems causing pain, weakness, loss of sensation, and other symptoms of nerve dysfunction. Generally there are no viable options other than referral to higher-level facilities. *See* Symptom Protocols 8B, 10B, 33B, and 60B, Protocol C-13, and SPINAL NEUROPATHY.

ONCHOCERCIASIS

Cause: Worm larvae.
Synonym: River blindness.
Includes: Sowda.
Regional Notes: F, M, R.
Definition: Onchocerciasis is an infection with the worm *Onchocerca volvulus*, the larvae of which damage the eyes and the skin. It is a tropical disease.

Not ill to very ill; Class 2 or 3; Regional, only regions F, M, and R. **Age:** Any, but serious problems with eyes are generally seen only in adults. **Who:** Bitten by simulium (black) flies which breed in fast-flowing water. **Onset:** Several months after the bite, nodules develop and grow slowly over 3-4 years.

Clinical:

Necessary: A national complains of itchy skin but does not initially have a rash. For expatriates (Westerners) see below.

Sometimes: The patient describes a feeling of creatures moving around within his skin. He may have KERATITIS with eye pain, tearing, and light avoidance. IRITIS may develop. This disease causes blindness, sometimes by clouding the front of the eye and sometimes by destroying the inside or back of the eye. When it causes opaque scars on the cornea, the process starts at the outer rim at 4 and 8 o'clock, and moves inward. It always affects both eyes, though one may be worse than the other. The entire cornea(s) may be covered with "snowflakes". The eye may be painful. There may be decreased vision which is apt to be worse in bright light.

Usually: Nodules (rubbery cysts, like a bunch of small grapes), form right underneath the skin, mainly in areas where the skin normally lies right over bone such as scalp, breast bone, and shin. Nodules may range in size from a pea to a small egg. They feel bumpy inside, not smooth like LOIASIS. They are painless, not tender to touch, and not particularly itchy. When the nodules are on or near the head, it is important to have them surgically removed.

20% of affected patients have white spots or irregular areas on their skin, where the pigment is lost. This resembles VITILIGO or LEPROSY, but there is no numbness with onchocerciasis. A common location for this is the shins. The patient may have hanging folds of skin by his groin, sometimes with big lymph nodes in the folds.

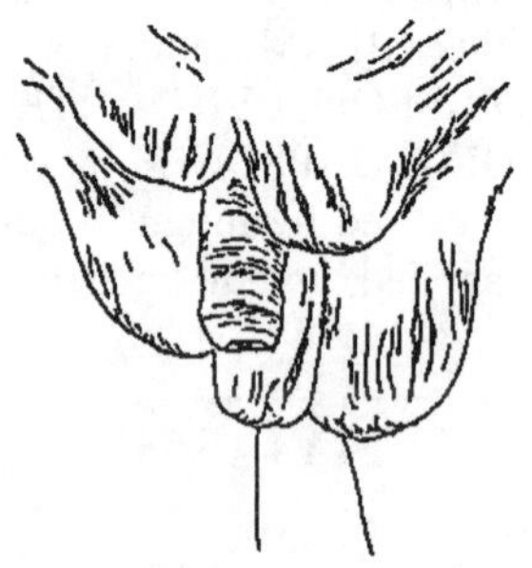

Onchocerciasis: Hanging Groin

Occasionally: Onchocerciasis may cause ELEPHANTIASIS of the limbs like FILARIASIS does. It may cause general darkening of the skin or may cause skin changes so that the skin surface resembles orange peel or becomes very wrinkled. There may be swelling of the skin with scaly bumps in patients living in the arid Sahel (Africa). *Complications:* EPILEPSY, IRITIS, blindness.

HIV INFECTION makes the symptoms worse.

In expatriates, symptoms which are common to a number of diseases may develop in the homeland; they are frequently ignored or treated with symptomatic medication which may help for a while. Common symptoms in expatriates are: back pain; enlarged lymph nodes; a generalized, red, spotted rash with itching; and joint pains with swelling.

Onchocerciasis: Wrinkled, thin skin in a young patient.

Similar Conditions: *Eye symptoms*: See Protocol C-8: Red, Painful Eyes.

Itching all over: Distinct from HEPATITIS and JAUNDICE in that the eyes are not yellow and onchocerciasis does not cause bilirubin in the urine.

Nodules: CYSTICERCOSIS nodules are smaller. HYDATID DISEASE nodules might look similar but they are soft; onchocerciasis nodules are firm. SYPHILIS and YAWS might cause similar firm nodules, but there will be other symptoms also, as well as a different history.

Skin changes: VITILIGO might look similar, but it is not itchy. LEPROSY also involves sharp, shooting pains and it is never itchy. FILARIASIS also causes skin changes and limb swelling.

Back and joint pains are similar to other causes of ARTHRITIS. Also consider BRUCELLOSIS and bone TB.

Higher-Level Care. *Laboratory:* Many hospitals can take a little piece of skin and examine it under the microscope to make a definite diagnosis. A blood count will probably, but not certainly, show increased eosinophils (other diseases do also). In the absence of eye symptoms, a definite diagnosis may be made by giving 25 mg of DIETHYLCARBAMAZINE (DEC). This will provoke a tremendous itching response with onchocerciasis. A cream made of ordinary hand lotion and crushed DEC, rubbed on the skin, will give an itching response within 48 hours. This is safer but more time-consuming.

Treatment:

Prevention: Control of fly population; wear trousers and hats, put screens on houses. Avoid building houses near fast-flowing streams. Find out what time of day the flies bite and avoid visits to the river during those hours. Inquire about the WHO control project.

Patient Care.

- Treatment of everyone in a village with IVERMECTIN is safe and results in a decreased incidence of eye problems. It should be done every 6 months to prevent recurrences. IVERMECTIN is better than DEC.
- DIETHYLCARBAMAZINE (DEC) is the older, traditional drug. Do not treat severe cases with it as you may cause fatal ANAPHYLAXIS. Use maximum doses of DIPHENHYDRAMINE along with the DEC and use PREDNISOLONE EYE DROPS for the first five days of therapy in the presence of eye symptoms. If there were no prior eye symptoms, eye drops, PREDNISONE, and DIPHENHYDRAMINE may be used only as needed. In either case, do not use the DIETHYLCARBAMAZINE unless you have EPINEPHRINE and DIPHENHYDRAMINE on hand. DIETHYLCARBAMAZINE does not kill adult worms in nodules. The patient needs repeated treatments over a long period of time or should be sent to a hospital for suramin treatment or nodule removal.
- MEBENDAZOLE plus LEVAMISOLE may destroy the adult worms safely.

An additional consideration: Wolbachia are bacteria that are essential for female worm fertility. Killing them with DOXYCYCLINE helps cure the disease. It should be given for 6 weeks; 3 weeks is the minimum to do any good. Give this before giving the other drugs.

Complication of treatment: DRUG ERUPTION may be seen with DIETHYLCARBAMAZINE given for ONCHOCERCIASIS. Before treating your patient, become familiar with this.

Onyalai

See *Regional Notes* F.

OSTEOMYELITIS

Cause: Bacteria.

Definition: Osteomyelitis is a bacterial infection of the bone.

Moderately to very ill; Class 2-3; Worldwide; more common in Africa and Saudi Arabia than elsewhere in patients with SICKLE CELL DISEASE.

Age: Any; most common in 7-25 age range for those with SICKLE CELL DISEASE. **Who:** Those with wounds or TROPICAL ULCERs, especially the malnourished. Patients with BURULI ULCER or DONOVANOSIS are prone. **Onset:** Over days to weeks.

Clinical:

This is a bone infection, causing fever, general fatigue, and deep bone pain. Lightly tapping or rolling a pencil along the bone aggravates the pain. When it affects the leg there is a limp. There may be muscle cramps or spasms. Usually it is mainly localized either above or below a large joint (e.g. elbow or knee), though it may be anywhere: back, pelvis, jaw, shoulder. There is always pain and swelling in the affected area. There may be holes in the skin which drain pus. In advanced cases the bones may be so weak that they fracture from very slight trauma as in turning over in bed. Except in SICKLE CELL DISEASE, or after multiple injuries, it almost always affects one location only on the body.

If it is a patient who has SICKLE CELL DISEASE, the site is usually the hands in those under 5 y.o.; it is anywhere on the limbs in those who are older. In this case it may be symmetrical rather than one-sided.

Similar Conditions: See Protocol C-6 for limb(s), C-13 for the back. If the onset is slow, consider bone TUBERCULOSIS, BRUCELLOSIS, and DONOVANOSIS.

Higher-Level Care. *Laboratory:* Level 3 or above might be able to do cultures to determine the correct antibiotic. *Facilities:* If the symptoms have been for only a short while (a matter of days) x-rays might not show anything; in any case, plain x-ray will not distinguish bone death (in SICKLE CELL DISEASE) from osteomyelitis. Osteomyelitis is more likely if the patient's fever is high and he has a whole-body illness. *Practitioners:* A generalist, internist, or pediatrician is essential; a surgeon might be helpful.

Treatment:

Treatment should be started on the basis of clinical assessment because the condition can advance very rapidly.

- If the illness is of recent onset (within less than a week), use antibiotics: 6 weeks minimum with CLOXACILLIN, AUGMENTIN, a CEPHALOSPORIN, CLINDAMYCIN or CIPROFLOXACIN. CHLORAMPHENICOL or GENTAMYCIN might work.
- If you cannot tell if it's due to TUBERCULOSIS or not, use RIFAMPIN, CIPROFLOXACIN, and two other TB drugs. RIFAMPIN is also the best drug if there is a foreign object (e.g. bullet) lodged in the area.
- If the patient has SICKLE CELL DISEASE, then first try a CEPHALOSPORIN or CIPROFLOXACIN. CIPROFLOXACIN is not supposed to be used in children, but this illness is so very serious and disabling that it is probably worth the risk. If the illness has been for more than a week or if he becomes worse while on treatment, the patient must be sent to a hospital immediately; his bone must be drilled open to release pus.
- Without surgery, the disease will not respond to antibiotics over the long term.

OVALOCYTOSIS

Cause: Heredity.

Includes: Elliptocytosis (a related hereditary defect), Spherocytosis.

Definition: Ovalocytosis is a hereditary defect in the structure of red blood cells.

Not ill to very ill; Class 2-4; Regional. Ovalocytosis mainly occurs in Malaysia and New Guinea, but it affects some families throughout the world. Elliptocytosis is common in North Africa and West Africa; for your purposes it is indistinguishable. Spherocytosis occurs in Europeans; this is also indistinguishable. These are mainly tropical diseases but don't require tropical/travel expertise for treatment.

Age: 3 months and older. **Who:** Those from affected families; the gene is dominant. **Onset:** Variable.

Clinical:

Ovalocytosis is similar to THALLASEMIA but not as serious. There may be ANEMIA and a large liver and spleen. Ovalocytosis protects against MALARIA and thus is a survival advantage.

Complications: It sometimes causes crises with viral illnesses, when the spleen suddenly destroys many red cells, causing large amounts of urobilinogen in the urine with sudden ANEMIA, JAUNDICE, and possibly KIDNEY FAILURE or SHOCK. Persons with this disease are prone to GALLBLADDER DISEASE.

Similar Conditions: See Protocols C-3 and C-7.

Higher-Level Care. See ANEMIA. If the anemia is severe, then speedy referral is important. See Volume I, Appendix 13. *Laboratory:* A blood smear and some other tests can help with diagnosis, level 3 facility or above. *Facilities:* A blood bank and transfusion facilities with HIV testing, level 3 facility. *Practitioner:* A hematologist is ideal; an internist or pediatrician might be helpful. Sometimes surgery (spleen removal) is necessary.

Treatment:

Mild cases are treatable with FOLATE.

Overdose

See Symptom Protocol 11.

Palpitations

See Symptom Protocol 3D.

PANCREATITIS

Cause: Variable.

Regional Notes: F, I.

Definition: Pancreatitis is an inflammation of the pancreas, a gland in the upper abdomen.

Very ill, usually; Class 4; Worldwide.

Age: Adults, usually. **Who:** Usually a complication of ALCOHOLISM, childhood MALNUTRITION, GALLBLADDER DISEASE or ASCARIASIS. Sometimes due to injury. **Onset:** Over minutes to hours.

Clinical:

There is intense central or upper-central abdominal pain going through to the back, and severe vomiting.

The abdomen may be swollen. It may cause MALABSORPTION, DIABETES, or both; it may result in death.

In Africa, Malaysia, and India, there is a type of pancreatitis that is not associated with the conditions listed. It affects mostly males, starting in their teens. It leads to DIABETES and/or MALABSORPTION.

Similar Conditions: See Protocol C-7: Liver/Spleen Problems if appropriate.

Abdominal pain: Consider ACUTE ABDOMEN, GALLBLADDER DISEASE (pain more right than central), PEPTIC ULCER (pain more burning), AMEBIC LIVER DISEASE (pain more burning and usually right-sided).

Diarrhea: See Protocol C-14.

Higher-Level Care. Speedy referral is important; see Volume I, Appendix 13. *Laboratory*: Various blood tests are helpful to confirm the diagnosis. *Facilities*: Level 3 or above: stomach tubes, suction, IV's, surgical theatre. *Practitioner:* At least an internist; a gastroenterologist is ideal. A surgeon may be required.

Treatment:

Treat like ACUTE ABDOMEN and send the patient to a hospital. There is nothing else you can do.

PARAGONIMIASIS

Cause: Worm.
Synonyms: Lung fluke disease, Pulmonary distomiasis.
Regional Notes: F, I, M, O, S, U.
Definition: Paragonimiasis is an infection of the lung with the lung fluke, *Paragonimus westermani*. It is a tropical disease.

Mildly to moderately ill; Class 1-2; Regional.

Age: Anyone. **Who:** Anyone living in an affected area who eats raw or poorly-cooked shellfish. It may also be acquired from eating wild animals that are infected or from contaminated hands or utensils used to prepare such foods. **Onset:** 6-8 weeks incubation; symptoms develop over days.

Clinical:

Necessary: The patient has a cough which is worse in the mornings and after exertion, producing brownish or reddish sputum.

Usually: This does not cause weakness as TB does; patients may have bloody sputum for 20 years without diminished capacity for work.

Sometimes: Patients have night sweats, shortness of breath or chest pain that is worse on inspiration. There is fever in 1/4 to 1/2 of patients.

Occasionally: Patients have diarrhea resembling DYSENTERY and abdominal pain. The patient may develop finger clubbing similar to that of HEART FAILURE.

Complications: Uncommonly STROKE, BRAIN DAMAGE, SEIZURES, blindness, paralysis, lumps under the skin, more common in children than in adults.

Similar Conditions: *Cough*: TUBERCULOSIS

Diarrhea: *See* DYSENTERY and similar diseases.

Higher-Level Care. *Laboratory:* A hospital laboratory can examine sputum for the eggs of the fluke. They are quite large and not hard to find but the test is not sensitive. You must have several negative tests before you believe it. In some places there are blood tests available. There are always a lot of eosinophils in the blood count.

Treatment:

Prevention: Do not eat raw shellfish.

Patient Care: PRAZIQUANTEL, BITHIONOL.

PARAPHIMOSIS

Cause: Poor hygiene.
Definition: Paraphimosis is a condition in an uncircumcised male in which the foreskin is pulled back and then swells so it cannot be replaced over the pink part of the penis. The condition may be painful.

The foreskin should be cut within a short time. See Appendix 1 in Vol. I for the procedure. Then the patient can be sent for circumcision when it is convenient.

PARKINSON'S DISEASE

Cause: Unknown.
Regional Notes: F, I.
Definition: Parkinson's disease is a type of brain damage that causes a particular type of trembling and uncoordination.

Mildly to very ill; Class 3; Worldwide, uncommon.

Age: Elderly; younger people on certain tranquilizing drugs. **Who:** Anyone, especially those on tranquilizers (CHLORPROMAZINE and similar drugs). Reportedly this can also be caused by repeated exposures to insecticides. **Onset:** Slow, over weeks to months.

Clinical:

Initially: There may be the loss of a sense of smell.

Thereafter: The patient's hand(s) tremble(s), especially when at rest. The trembling improves if he tries to do something and it usually starts on the dominant side before affecting the other side also. There are few or no spontaneous body movements. The face is expressionless (symmetrically droopy); the voice soft, slurred, and difficult to understand. Because of not swallowing, the patient may begin to drool. The gait, is peculiar. He looks as if he is falling forward and moving his legs to keep up with his body. His limbs appear to be stiff. He may "freeze" when turning or going through a doorway.

Sometimes: There is imbalance and difficulty in recovering from a stumble. Later there may also be problems with urine and bowel functions and loss of intelligence.

Similar Conditions: *With a fever or history of fevers*: consider RELAPSING FEVER, ENTERIC FEVER.

Trembling: Withdrawal (see ADDICTION), LIVER DISEASE and LIVER FAILURE (also yellow eyes or distended abdomen), KIDNEY FAILURE (also flaky skin and urine-like body odor), BRAIN DAMAGE from any cause, PELLAGRA (also rash).

Droopy face: LEPROSY that affects both sides of the face.

Higher-Level Care. There are good drugs available in the West, a level 3 or above hospital may help. There are no helpful labs or other facilities. A neurologist might be helpful also, to confirm the diagnosis.

Treatment:

If the problem has not been going on for long, stopping tranquilizer drugs may bring improvement. In the West there are drugs both to retard the development of the disease and to treat symptoms. Drugs for treatment are generally not available in developing countries. Consult a local physician.

PARONYCHIA

Definition: A paronychia is a small abscess that sometimes forms on the side of a fingernail. *See* the section on Wound Infection, Chapter 10 in Vol. I, for instructions on how to treat this.

PAROVIRUS

See ERYTHEMA INFECTIOSUM

PELLAGRA

Cause: Poor nutrition.

Synonyms: NIACIN deficiency.

Regional Notes: E, I, O, R.

Definition: Pellagra is a deficiency of the B vitamin niacin (niacinamide, nicotinamide).

Mildly to moderately ill; Class 1; Worldwide.

Age: Mostly middle-aged. In some areas, children and infants also. **Who:** Those eating a diet deficient in NIACIN; corn or sorghum diets. The TB drug ISONIAZID is sometimes associated with this. **Onset:** Symptoms get better and worse over weeks to months.

Clinical:

Necessary: At least two of the following: diarrhea, a roughened skin rash, difficulty swallowing and mental changes. Pellagra does not cause fevers.

Initially: Pellagra causes indigestion, mental changes, and diarrhea. The patient has little or no stomach acid so his vomit does not taste sour like it normally would. He has MALABSORPTION and ANEMIA. His urine has a pH of more than 7. He is pale, listless, has large pupils, headaches, and vague pains. The whites of his eyes look bluish. He is irritable and depressed. He is likely to become irritated with bright lights, colors and noises. The symptoms are seasonal, changing with diet.

Later: He is rambling and disoriented. Children stop growing and gaining weight; they are mentally slow at school.

Sometimes: The patient also has burning, tingling, and aching of the palms, soles, or both. He may develop trembling or stiff muscles, uncoordination or stiff weakness. There may be a sore tongue which looks beefy red, cracks by the sides of the mouth, and a poor appetite. This is due to the coexistence of a deficiency of other B vitamins.

A rash appears on the areas of the skin exposed to the sun or subject to clothing irritation. The skin in this area is swollen. First it is like a sunburn which burns, itches, and blisters. The burning and itching are worse with sun exposure. Then it flakes and peels. The color of the rash is purplish or dark black in Blacks and East Asians. Over time the skin thickens.

Maybe: The rash may affect the inside of his mouth, decreasing his sense of taste and making it difficult to swallow. There is excessive saliva.

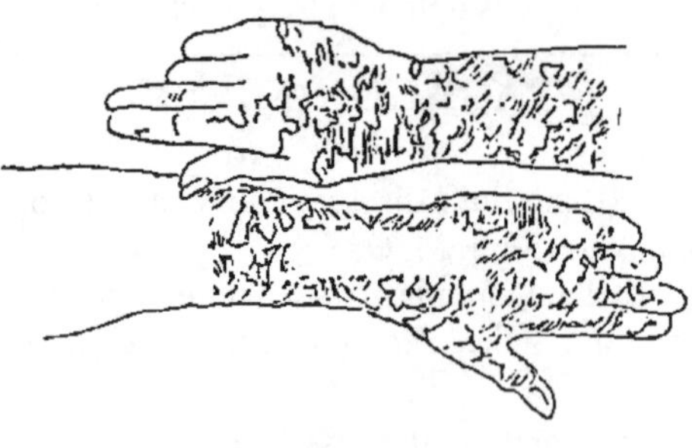

Pellagra

Similar Conditions: See Protocols C-10 and C-14.

Trouble swallowing: POLIO, RABIES, CHAGA'S DISEASE.

Diarrhea: There is excessive saliva in pellagra but not in SPRUE.

Skin changes: ONCHOCERCIASIS has more itching and it is similar all over the body; ECZEMA or TINEA might appear similar but they are not worse in sun-exposed skin.

Mental changes: ATTENTION DEFICIT DISORDER, Tertiary SYPHILIS, mental BERIBERI, ALCOHOLISM, LEAD POISONING, tuberculous MENINGITIS, TROPICAL SPASTIC PARAPARESIS. Try the treatment for pellagra and see if it works.

Pains in limbs: BERIBERI.

Treatment:

Prevention: Soaking corn in lime before using it prevents pellagra in corn-only diets.

Patient Care: NIACIN, NIACINAMIDE. Also MULTIVITAMINS containing these. An alternative is feeding the patient a diet including whole grains other than corn.

Results: Within 48 hours for NIACIN; more slowly with a change in diet.

PELVIC INFECTION

Cause: Bacteria.

Synonyms: Pelvic inflammatory disease, PID.

Includes: Tubo-ovarian abscess.

Regional Notes: E, F, R.

Definition: Pelvic infection is a bacterial infection of the female genital organs.

Entry category: Disease cluster.

Moderately to very ill; Class 2; Contagious; Worldwide, related to sexual activity and hygiene.

Age: Mostly sexually mature. **Who:** Any sexually active female, especially promiscuous. The cause is likely TB if the patient is postmenopausal. **Onset:** Variable; slow with TB, rapid with GONORRHEA or CHLAMYDIA although the incubation period is long. SCHISTOSOMIASIS HEMATOBIUM may cause an indistinguishable condition.

Clinical:

See Protocol C-2: Sexually Transmitted Diseases and also C-9: Fever and Abdominal Pain.

Necessary: After a long symptom-free interval, there is right-lower, left-lower, or lower-mid abdominal pain and pain with intercourse. If the patient pushes a tampon deep into her vagina she will aggravate the pain.

Usually: The pain is centered, not markedly worse right or left.

Maybe: There is fever and rectal pain. The patient may have pus flowing from her vagina. There may be ARTHRITIS, a rash, or both.

Complications: Infertility, HEPATITIS with pains in the upper-right abdomen.

Similar Conditions: Check carefully for TUBAL PREGNANCY. Consider SEPSIS if the patient just had a baby or a miscarriage. If the pain is on the right, appendicitis (ACUTE ABDOMEN Type 2) may be indistinguishable. Consider HEPATITIS (bilirubin in urine) and KIDNEY INFECTION (fresh urine smells like stale urine).

Higher-Level Care. *Laboratory*: A hospital lab can do a smear or culture for GONORRHEA, CHLAMYDIA, and TB; they can check urine for the eggs of SCHISTOSOMIASIS HEMATOBIUM. *Facilities* and *Practitioners*: An abstinence-based sexually transmitted disease clinic is ideal.

Treatment:

Prevention: Discourage promiscuity, treat partner(s), treat TUBERCULOSIS. All sexual contacts of the patient should be treated, whatever the cause.

Patient Care: If the pain is localized more right or left, if pain is severe, or if there is a high fever, send the patient to a hospital.

Sexually active patients and babies born to infected mothers may have EYE INFECTION; it must be treated to prevent blindness, using both injected or oral antibiotic plus ANTIBIOTIC EYE OINTMENT.

Drug options:[1]

Option #1: Ceftriaxone (see CEPHALOSPORIN), a single dose IM plus DOXYCYCLINE plus [either METRONIDAZOLE or CHLORAMPHENICOL], continuing the two oral medications for 14 days.

Option #2: COTRIMOXAZOLE plus DOXYCYCLINE plus METRONIDAZOLE, continuing all for 14 days.

Option #3: [Either OFLOXACIN or LEVOFLOXACIN] with METRONIDAZOLE.

Option #4: AZITHROMYCIN plus FLUCONAZOLE plus SECNIDAZOLE, single dose. AZITHROMYCIN otherwise must be used over 5 days and it is expensive. In the regimens above, one can substitute CLINDAMYCIN for 14 days of the other drugs once the patient's pain is gone.

Option #5: Drugs for TUBERCULOSIS - if the other options do not work and/or the patient has had a cough for over a month.

PEPTIC ULCER

Cause: Stress, heredity, bacteria.

Includes: Duodenal ulcer, Stomach ulcer.

Regional Notes: F, I, O, R, U.

Definition: Peptic ulcer is a spontaneous wound of the inside of the stomach or duodenum.

Mildly to very ill; Class 1 unless vomiting blood, "coffee grounds" or passing black, tarry stool; then class 2-3; Worldwide.

Age: Anyone, even children. It is especially common in Indian children who usually present with upper abdominal pains. **Who:** Those under stress; alcoholics especially prone. **Onset:** Usually gradual, occasionally sudden.

Clinical:

Peptic ulcer does not cause fever. It is possible that this may be entirely without symptoms.

Usually: The patient complains of central or upper-right abdominal pain 2-3 hours after meals, followed by relief after eating. It is bad enough to awaken him at night.

[1] The following options are recent, but recommendations are always changing due to the development of resistance to antibiotics. It is best to follow the advice of local health authorities. It is essential to keep records of dates, drugs given, duration of treatment, and results so you have an idea what works in your particular area.

Sometimes: There is indigestion or pain after meals. The patient may suddenly vomit blood or "coffee grounds" which is digested blood. He may pass blood by rectum as foul-smelling, black, tarry diarrhea. He may pass a lot of gas by rectum. There may be nausea and vomiting.

Complications: If the ulcer perforates, the patient has sudden onset of ACUTE ABDOMEN with pain going straight through to his back. If it suddenly bleeds vigorously, he may develop SHOCK. If he promptly vomits all his food right after he eats, then his upper intestine is blocked and he needs surgery.

Similar Conditions: GASTRITIS is a minor form of the same thing and is treated the same. GALLBLADDER DISEASE is usually worse rather than better with food. AMEBIC LIVER DISEASE may be very similar with burning upper abdominal pains, but there are usually night sweats and at least occasional fevers. IRRITABLE BOWEL usually involves more vague symptoms and an alternating constipation and diarrhea.

Higher-Level Care. *Laboratory*: A basic laboratory to check for anemia might be helpful. *Facilities*: X-ray with contrast material; endoscopy might be available at level 3 or above. A stomach tube and suction might be available at level 2. *Practitioner:* Gastroenterologist or generalist; a surgeon might be helpful.

Treatment:

In many areas this problem is caused by bacteria. Treatment with AMOXICILLIN plus [either CLARITHROMYCIN or METRONIDAZOLE] plus [BISMUTH SUBSALICYLATE or RANITIDINE or CIMETIDINE] may be curative. TINIDAZOLE can substitute for METRONIDAZOLE. The English drug Tripotassium dicitratobismuthate is basically the same as BISMUTH SUBSALICYLATE. Treat for 14 days. Do not allow him to use ASPIRIN or IBUPROFEN. Tell him to avoid spicy-hot foods, coffee, tea, and colas. If the patient has significant weight loss, the problem may be due to CANCER. Send him to a hospital.

If he is vomiting blood send him to a hospital, especially if he has a large spleen. (See Volume I, Appendix 13.) Meanwhile:

- Keep the patient in bed and check his vital signs frequently; watch for SHOCK.
- Place a large diameter stomach tube if you have one, larger than the one made from IV tubing. Put a vial or two of EPINEPHRINE in a liter or two of cold, clean water. Use a large syringe to empty the stomach through the tube. Then put your cold EPINEPHRINE and water solution into the syringe and squirt it down the tube. Immediately pull it back out into the syringe and empty it into a waste bucket. *Repeat* this process until the returning water is clear. Take the stomach tube out as soon as you are done emptying the stomach.
- Give the patient ANTACID hourly while awake, every 4 hours at night. Do this for a week and then treat like a regular ulcer.
- Keep the patient on a bland diet without milk or milk products for a week. (Milk relieves pain immediately but makes the ulcer worse over time.)
- In some areas, special medications may be used which decrease the production of stomach acid: CIMETIDINE and RANTIDINE are most common. They should not be used routinely in developing areas because they decrease resistance to various bacteria.

Results: Relief in a week; treat for a month.

PERICARDITIS

Cause: Variable.

Includes: Restrictive pericarditis, Pericardial effusion.

Regional Notes: F.

Definition: Pericarditis is inflammation of the pericardium, the sack that the heart lies in.

Moderately to severely ill; Class 3-4; Worldwide.

Age: Any. **Who:** Those with KIDNEY FAILURE, PNEUMONIA, or other RESPIRATORY INFECTIONS. Common with LASSA FEVER and some other viral infections. Not common but may occur with RHEUMATIC FEVER, FAMILIAL MEDITERRANEAN FEVER, and reactive ARTHRITIS. It is common with TB but if it is painless you may not recognize it. **Onset:** Variable.

Clinical:

Necessary: One or the other or both of the following symptom-groups:

HEART FAILURE (restrictive type) with nearly inaudible heart sounds. Usually there is a large, tender liver; fever; and a very small difference between the two blood-pressure numbers (e.g. 100/96).

The patient may have chest pain, either like PLEURISY, or else worse with leaning back, improved with leaning forward. There may be pain with swallowing, over the lower breastbone, and/or straight back from there. The pain may go to the ridge of muscles on top of his shoulder, near his neck on the right, left, or both sides.

Maybe: He may have a harsh, murmur-type sound audible with a stethoscope. There may be a fever but it is usually not high.

Similar Conditions: See Protocol C-7 if the liver is enlarged. The pains of ANGINA, HEART ATTACK, and PLEURISY do not change with swallowing or leaning forward. COSTAL CHONDRITIS might give similar pain but the chest wall is tender to touch; it is not tender with pericarditis. AMEBIC LIVER DISEASE, if it occurs on the left side of the liver, might cause similar pain and may, in fact, cause true pericarditis. Rarely, in specific geographical areas only, consider HYDATID DISEASE.

Higher-Level Care. See Volume I Appendix 13. *Laboratory*: A microscopic examination of fluid taken from the pericardium might be helpful, as well as examining sputum for evidence of TUBERCULOSIS. *Facilities*: Electrocardiogram or ultrasound, level 3. *Practitioner:* A cardiologist is ideal.

Treatment:

Check for the diseases that may cause this and treat accordingly. If TB is most likely, also give PREDNISONE along with the anti-TB drugs. **Do not** give PREDNISONE instead of or before the anti-TB drugs! Keep the patient in bed, sitting. Use IBUPROFEN for pain. Send the patient out if at all possible.

PHIMOSIS

Cause: Poor hygiene.
Regional Notes: F, R.
Definition: Phimosis is a condition in an uncircumcised male in which the foreskin is stuck to the pink tip of the penis.

Mildly ill; Class 2; Worldwide, related to hygiene.

Age: Any. **Who:** Uncircumcised males with poor hygiene. **Onset:** Gradual, over weeks.

Clinical:

The foreskin is stuck to the pink part of the end of the penis. The penis is usually painful and sometimes swollen. This may be caused by CHANCROID. Be sure to check the penis well for ulcers, including under the foreskin after you coax it back.

Similar Condition: PARAPHIMOSIS.

Treatment:

Soak the penis, gradually coaxing the foreskin back by hand. LIDOCAINE ointment may help. The patient needs circumcision. *See* Volume I, Appendix 1.

PIG-BEL

Cause: Bacterial toxin.
Synonyms: Enteritis necroticans, Necrotizing enteritis, Necrotizing jejunitis.
Regional Notes: F, O, S, U.
Definition: Pig-bel is a bowel malfunction due to a bacterial toxin in malnourished children.

Mildly to severely ill; Class 1-4 depending on how sick the patient is; Regional.

Age: Children and teens, not nursing infants. **Who:** Poorly nourished children who suddenly overindulge in protein, especially pork. Especially common where the staple food is sweet potatoes or yams. **Onset:** Fairly sudden, 24 hours to 1 week after the overindulgence.

Clinical:

Necessary: Crampy abdominal pain, bloating, and vomiting.

Frequently: Diarrhea with bloody stools. Fever. Symptoms may vary between a mild GASTROENTERITIS, a chronic MALABSORPTION (prompt diarrhea anytime the patient eats anything), and an overwhelming ACUTE ABDOMEN (type 2) that results in death.

Similar Conditions: Many. In most cases only the historical setting of a pig feast after chronic MALNUTRITION will cause you to consider this diagnosis.

In mild cases consider GASTROENTERITIS and/or FOOD POISONING.

With MALABSORPTION see Protocol C-14.

In severe cases consider FOOD POISONING and ACUTE ABDOMEN.

Higher-Level Care. Speedy referral is important. See Volume I, Appendix 13.

Surgery at level 2 or 3 might be helpful. It is important that the surgeon be familiar with the condition. Laboratory and imaging is not particularly helpful.

Treatment:

Prevention: Before a pig feast, restrict the use of sweet potatoes. Offer children an alternative carbohydrate with small protein supplements. Treating ASCARIASIS might also help.

Immunization is available but it is not safe; a small percentage of children die from the immunization. It should be used only in areas where this disease kills large numbers of children and people will not change their habits.

Patient Care. If possible, empty the person's stomach with a large-diameter stomach tube. Correct DEHYDRATION if possible. Give PENICILLIN, AMPICILLIN, or CHLORAMPHENICOL. Send very ill patients to a local hospital. Surgery is frequently helpful.

PINGUECULA

Definition: A pinguecula is a fleshy, white bump which grows on the white of the eye, close to the edge of the cornea. It is a common problem in the tropics. Since it sticks out a little, it may become irritated as the upper lid moves over it. It looks quite similar to CHICKEN POX or TB that has affected the eye. Treatment should be supervised by a physician. Treatment is not urgent.

Pinta

See *Regional Notes* M.

PLAGUE

Cause: Bacteria.
Synonyms: Black death, Peste, Yersinia pestis infection.
Includes: Bubonic plague.
Regional Notes: All regions.
Definition: Plague is an infection with the bacterium *Yersinia pestis*.

Moderately to severely ill; Class 3; Contagious, highly; Potentially worldwide, largely tropical, reported from the southwestern United States, Uganda, Kazakhstan (related to gerbils rather than rats), Madagascar; Central, East, and Southern Africa; India; mountainous South America; Southeast Asia (especially Burma); Mongolia and western China; and the former USSR.

Plague is spread by fleas of rodents (rats, mice, prairie dogs, and ground squirrels). At present it is mostly a rural disease but does, at times, become urban. If and when this is used as a biological weapon, it will most certainly be urban. Cats are often the link between the rodents and humans. Plague occurs sporadically and also in epidemics. It is likely to occur when people move into a rodent-infested area or when rodents move into populated areas as, for example, when an area is temporarily evacuated so that untended food is left in houses. If the rodent population spontaneously dies or is killed, an epidemic is likely.

Age: Any; those over 40 are particularly prone to the septicemic form of plague. **Who:** Those bitten by fleas or exposed to humans or animals with plague. **Onset:** Rapid, over hours. Incubation 2-15 days.

Clinical:

➢ **Pneumonic, Meningitic, Septicemic Plague:**

Death occurs within hours, too soon for treatment. PNEUMONIA due to plague is rapid in onset. There is cough and shortness of breath early, with rapid, shallow respiration and much watery sputum which then becomes blood-stained.

➢ **Bubonic (lymph node) plague**

Necessary: There is an irregular fever, and (beginning the first or second day) extremely painful, swollen, lymph nodes, most often in the groin in adults, sometimes in the armpit(s) or neck (especially in children). The skin over the nodes is darkened. The area around the nodes is very swollen. The patient is very ill.

Usually: He will have a headache. After some initial anxiety, the patient is apathetic. He may appear to be drunk. The size of the lymph nodes varies from the size of an almond to the size of a child's head. There is no relationship between the size of the nodes and how sick the patient is. There may be a tiny scab where the patient was bitten by the flea that infected him.

Frequently: The skin around the node(s) is inflamed. The skin may die, turn black, or peel. There may be spontaneous black and blue areas on the skin. The spleen and liver may be large and tender.

Occasionally: The disease may have minimal symptoms and recovery may be spontaneous. Don't discount a report of bubonic plague that presents that way.

Similar Conditions: See Protocol C-10 for lethargy, C-11 for a skin ulcer plus "flu", and C-12 for large lymph nodes.

Pneumonic and *meningitic* plague are indistinguishable from PNEUMONIA and MENINGITIS, respectively.

Septicemic plague is indistinguishable from SEPSIS from other causes except that death occurs much sooner.

Bubonic plague: The apathy is similar to ENTERIC FEVER but the black, discolored lymph nodes should distinguish the two diseases. TYPHUS usually has a rash associated with it. If in doubt, treat for both. If the large lymph nodes are in the groin, consider one of the SEXUALLY TRANSMITTED DISEASE's. However, with SEXUALLY TRANSMITTED DISEASE's there is usually normal skin color and the patient is not as ill. Also consider CAT-SCRATCH DISEASE and ANTHRAX.

Higher-Level Care. See Volume I, Appendix 13 but pay attention to the cautions for using public transport. Treatment should not be delayed to seek a hospital unless it is very nearby. *Laboratory*: Hospitals can do smears and cultures but the procedures are dangerous for the technicians and one should not wait for results before treatment in any case. *Facilities*: IV's with fluids and injectable antibiotics. *Practitioners*: Generalist or infectious disease specialist with **tropical/travel** expertise.

Treatment:

Prevention: Do not kill rats or other rodents in quantity without first spraying insecticide in their habitats. Do not handle a dead rodent without first spraying the body with insecticide. In areas with plague, an epidemic may begin with the spontaneous death of rodents. (Fleas leave the dying and dead rodents, bite humans, and thus transmit the disease.) Immunization is available but it only works for bubonic plague, not pneumonic or septicemic plague. It is better to take daily DOXYCYCLINE than to be immunized. Burn contaminated cloth; treat any other contaminated objects with Lysol or heat. **The dead must be buried immediately, with only one person handling the corpse, and then that person must be treated.**

Give DOXYCYCLINE for 10 days to anyone who had contact with a patient, even children and pregnant women because of the big risk in not treating.

Cats get sick with plague but dogs do not. One can contract pneumonic plague from an infected cat. To get plague from a dog, you need to be bitten by a flea from an infected, healthy-appearing dog; this will result in bubonic plague.

Patient Care: Wearing gloves and mask, and using a disposable 10 ml syringe, withdraw the pus from the abscessed node(s). Then thoroughly heat the syringe and contents in a covered container to destroy them. **Immediately** start high-dose antibiotics, preferably by injection. GENTAMYCIN or STREPTOMYCIN is best. (CHLORAMPHENICOL plus AMPICILLIN), or DOXYCYCLINE may work also. STREPTOMYCIN may make the person sicker at first. If there is a severe headache or signs of MENINGITIS, use (CHLORAMPHENICOL plus AMPICILLIN). CEPHALOSPORIN and RIFAMPIN are no good. CIPROFLOXACIN might work but is unproven.

Results: This usually responds well. If the patient is not treated, he will probably die in 3-6 days.

PLANT POISONING

Plants and Plant Products Listed in this Section:

Ackee	Gallbladder of Raw Fish	Mantakassa
Aflatoxin	Ginger Jake	Margosa Oil
Argemone Oil	Ginseng	Miraa
Atriplicism	Heliotropium	Miscara
Ava	Hypericum perforatum	Muiragi
Betel Nut	Impila	Muscarine
Botulism	Jequirity Beans	Mushrooms
Cassava	Jimson Weed	Nicotine
Castor Beans	Kava kava	Outers
Claviceps	Kawa	Panax
Comfrey	Khasari	Ricin
Coral Plant	Khat	Senecio
Crotalaria	Konzo	St. John's Wort
Datura	Lathyrism	Strychnine
Djenkol Bean	Lolism	Uppers
Downers	MaHuang	Valerian
Ephedra	Manicheel	
Ergot		
Ginkgo Biloba		

Cause: Plant Toxins.
Regional Notes: F, M, O, R, S, U.
Entry category: Syndrome cluster

Not ill to severely ill; Class 1-4; Worldwide: type varies.

(ARSENIC POISONING and LEAD POISONING are listed separately. If the patient has taken drugs, check the *Drug Index*. *See* FOOD POISONING if meats are involved. The division is sometimes arbitrary.)

Age: Any. **Who:** Those eating the offending substance, having skin contact, or inhaling fumes. **Onset:** Extremely variable, from within less than a minute to possibly after years of habitual consumption.

General Treatment for Plant Poisoning[1]:

If the patient is alert, if he has taken the poison within the past two hours, and if the specific type of poisoning does not prohibit it, give him several bottles of ACTIVATED CHARCOAL. This is best and it eliminates the need to induce vomiting. If you don't have enough charcoal, then make him vomit. IPECAC is ideal; it causes violent stomach spasms, thus emptying the stomach completely. When the patient has just dry heaves, settle his stomach with DICYCLOMINE, PROMETHAZINE, HYDROXYZINE, or similar medication. In either case, give him something to induce diarrhea; this will decrease the chance of his absorbing more poison. If the poison he took causes diarrhea, treat him with ORS instead.

Specific Plants, Toxins, and Treatments:

Ackee:
See PLANT POISONING in *Regional Notes* F, M.

Aflatoxin:
This is a mold found in peanuts and grains, purplish color. Sausages are also a source of the toxin since they usually contain moist grains. Exposure to small doses over a long time causes liver CANCER. Exposure to large doses rapidly causes immediate toxicity: LIVER FAILURE, swelling of the lower limbs, abdominal pain and vomiting.

Argemone Oil:
See also PLANT POISONING in *Regional Notes* F, U. Also known as epidemic dropsy, Argemone oil poisoning is due to cooking oil made from the seeds of Mexican poppy. The death rate is about 5%. The patient develops swelling of his lower limbs, his face, or his whole body for about two weeks. He has fever, diarrhea, vomiting. This lasts about 6 weeks. Usually there are patches of darker skin on the faces of Indians. Bumps appear on the skin. They are the size of small, thick coins and are full of blood vessels which bleed readily. Later, HEART FAILURE (dilated type) develops. ANEMIA, KIDNEY FAILURE (nephrotic type), severe weakness, and eye problems may occur. *Treatment:* DIPHENHYDRAMINE is helpful, as are MULTIVITAMINS, and a high-protein, high-fat diet.

Atriplicism:
See PLANT POISONING in *Regional Notes* O.

Ava:
See Kava kava below. This is another name for the same thing.

Betel Nut:
This is commonly chewed with lime and areca nut. It is a mild stimulant, producing flushing of the face. It stains the teeth black and the lips red. Used over a long time, it causes mouth CANCER. Treatment*:* Not necessary.

Botulism:
A kind of FOOD POISONING which occurs 6 hours to 6 days after eating the offending food, usually badly preserved, cooked beans or sausage. It is present worldwide. The sequence of symptoms is as follows: abdominal pain, nausea or vomiting, diarrhea, difficulty swallowing or speaking, difficulty opening the eyes, double vision, weakness in limbs, inability to urinate, and difficulty breathing. The pulse and blood pressure

[1] These directions contradict the current standard of care in the States which discourages the use of ipecac and activated charcoal. However, they are useful for remote rural areas in developing countries. If western medical care is available, it should be used, rather than these directions.

fluctuate. The mouth may be very dry. There is no numbness or tingling. Also see FOOD POISONING.

Treatment: Not feasible in a rural setting. Send the patient out. He may require help with breathing. Hospitals also can give antitoxin which is most helpful. Antibiotics don't work.

Cassava:

Also known as *manioc, tapioca,* or *mantakassa,* it is a common source of carbohydrate throughout the tropics. (There is *sweet cassava* and *ordinary cassava;* sweet cassava does not require special preparation but ordinary cassava does. Both the solid food and the cooking water contain the toxin.) Hungry people sometimes shorten the preparation, eating the plant material raw or insufficiently cooked or insufficiently fermented. This causes cyanide poisoning. High doses cause sudden onset of SEIZURES, loss of consciousness, cessation of breathing, and death. This occurs within a minute or two after drinking cooking water. Medium doses cause dizziness, increased respiration, flushed face, headache, big pupils, low blood pressure, and rapid pulse. This occurs within an hour or so. Patients who take in low doses over extended periods of time may develop pains in their limbs, stiff weakness of the limbs, slurred speech, fevers, headache, dizziness, GOITER, DIABETES, and MALABSORPTION. It may cause blindness or deafness.

Treatment: Unless you have access to a cyanide poison kit, you probably cannot treat the problem. There are some reports that high doses of VITAMIN B_{12} may help.

Castor Beans:

Castor Beans are the source of the toxin ricin. They are brown with black streaks, tear-drop-shaped, about 1 cm in length, with a slight nipple-type bulge on the sharp end. The plants have 6 lobes—they are about 30 cm high on the average, common along the roadside. The beans are used for making castor oil (used in brake and hydraulic fluid) cause ordinary diarrhea. As few as 8 beans, if chewed, are potentially fatal. Symptoms start 8-24 hours after swallowing, with nausea, vomiting, diarrhea, LIVER FAILURE, KIDNEY FAILURE and death. See the separate entry for ricin (also under plant poisoning), a poison that is derived from castor beans. The two poisonings overlap.

Claviceps:

Poisoning due to a fungus that grows on grains. It causes abdominal pain, diarrhea, and vomiting, sometimes hallucinations. The blood vessels shrink, cutting off circulation to the limbs, producing paleness, coolness, and pain in the fingers and toes, possibly the chest also. This may cause GANGRENE and HEART ATTACK. The patient may have a headache, a slow pulse, low blood pressure, SEIZURES, coma, and death.

Treatment: Nitroglycerin, used for heart trouble, may be helpful, but you probably will not have this.

Comfrey:

This is used for fractures, tendon injuries, internal ulcers, and lung congestion. There is a major problem with liver toxicity and subsequent LIVER FAILURE.

Coral Plant:

Present in Africa, the Americas, and the Mediterranean. It is a traditional medicine for constipation, made from the nuts. It causes abdominal cramps, thirst, vomiting, and diarrhea.

Treatment: Not necessary as the poison is eliminated with the vomiting that it causes.

Crotalaria:

Poisoning from a variety of plants present worldwide, used to make bush teas. It causes LIVER FAILURE by making the veins in the liver narrow so blood cannot pass as it should. Within 10 days the patient develops abdominal pain, a large liver, and fluid in his abdomen.

Treatment: Bed rest, and a low-salt, high-protein diet.

Datura:

This is a criminal poison used to make a victim unconscious or kill him; a similar poison is present in the leaves and in the green skin of potatoes that have been exposed to light. There is loss of consciousness with large pupils, possibly nausea, vomiting, uncoordination, and hallucinations.

Treatment: There are drugs available to treat this, but they are not feasible to keep or use in the village situation. Many insecticides, however, contain similar compounds to these drugs. In a desperate situation, you can try spraying some insecticide on a cloth and holding it near the patient's nose. If he improves in a few minutes, repeat this as needed until the poison wears off, using just enough to keep him conscious.

Djenkol Bean:

See PLANT POISONING in *Regional Notes* S.

Downers:

See ADDICTION.

Ephedra:

This is an "upper" or stimulant. It can cause sudden death, HEART ATTACK, HEART FAILURE, STROKE, and LIVER FAILURE. It is similar to the drug EPINEPHRINE and to caffeine.

Ergot:

This is a fungus that grows on rye. It makes the blood vessels contract, thus causing poor circulation to the limbs and heart. Symptoms may be similar to claviceps poisoning. It may result in blood clots that go to the lung (see PULMONARY EMBOLISM), ABORTION, and GANGRENE. Treatment: Like Claviceps (see above).

Ginkgo Biloba:

This is an herbal product that is used to reverse normal aging; reportedly it improves memory, helps ringing in the ears, impotence, and age-related visual problems. The usual symptoms associated with this are stomach upset, headache, and various rashes with stinging and burning sensations. It may also be associated with seizures, and abnormal bleeding.

Gallbladder of Raw Fish:
See GALLBLADDER OF RAW FISH, *Regional Notes* O, S.
Ginger Jake:
This is paralysis which occurs in outbreaks, caused by mixing a lubricating oil with cooking oil. It first causes floppy weakness of the lower legs and later of the hands. About two years later, the weak muscles become stiff rather than floppy. *Treatment*: None.
Ginseng:
This is supposed to increase one's sense of health. It is used to treat sexual problems, HEART FAILURE, low immunity, and CANCER. Adverse effects are irrational behavior, vaginal bleeding, and LIVER FAILURE.
Heliotropium:
See Crotalaria, above.
Hypericum perforatum:
See St. John's Wort, listed below. It is another name for the same thing.
Impila:
See PLANT POISONING in *Regional Notes* F.
Jequirity Beans:
These are red, oval, with a black cap on one end, length about 1 cm. The beans are used to make rosaries and also used in rattle-like noisemakers. The poison is the same as castor beans but symptoms are delayed for about 3 days; then there is LIVER FAILURE and death.
Jimson Weed:
This is a poisonous plant, present worldwide, with effects similar to the drug ATROPINE or the plant Datura. Crazy behavior is a prominent part of the picture.
Treatment: Send the patient out to a major medical facility if he is very ill. If he is not very ill, it is feasible to just let the effects wear off. This should happen within 24 hours.
Kava kava:
This is used for a variety of conditions, among them its being an "upper" and also sedative or "downer". Adverse effects include a whole-body, scaly skin rash (which subsequently peels), difficulty in coordination, and LIVER FAILURE.
Kawa:
See Kava kava.
Khasari:
See Lathyrism.
Khat:
See PLANT POISONING in *Regional Notes* F, R.
Konzo:
African term for poisoning due to cassava. Refers to the sudden onset of stiff weakness. Resembles TROPICAL SPASTIC PARAPARESIS.
Lathyrism:
This occurs in the Mediterranean, east Africa, and India where "khasari" is eaten. The problem is caused by a plant that grows wild, looks similar to the edible variety, and contaminates food when the plants are harvested together. The patient develops muscle spasms in his legs which pull his left leg to the right and his right, to the left. As a result, he walks cross-legged, as if he had a full bladder and was trying not to wet his pants. The arm and trunk muscles are not affected. Sexual impotence and incontinence of urine occur frequently. The condition is permanent. *Treatment*: None is good, though some claim that MULTIVITAMINS and a high-protein diet help.
Lolism:
See PLANT POISONING in *Regional Notes* F, R.
MaHuang:
See PLANT POISONING, Ephedra. This is another name for the same thing.
Manicheel:
See PLANT POISONING in *Regional Notes* M.
Mantakassa:
See Cassava, above.
Margosa Oil:
This is a traditional medicine, used in India and by Indians elsewhere. It is a deep yellow extract of the seeds of the *Neem Tree*; the darker the oil, the more poisonous it is. It has a bad smell and a bitter taste. Within hours it causes vomiting, either frantic behavior or loss of consciousness, and possibly SEIZURES and death.
Treatment: The only effective treatment is in a hospital. In the meantime, sugar may help. Give the patient sugar until he arrives at a hospital.
Miraa:
See PLANT POISONING, Khat, in *Regional Notes* F, R.
Miscara:
See PLANT POISONING, Lolism, in *Regional Notes* F, R.
Muiragi:
See PLANT POISONING, Khat, in *Regional Notes* F, R.
Muscarine:
This is a poison found in some mushrooms and insecticides. Symptoms begin in less than an hour. There is a general outpouring of body fluids: sweat, tears, diarrhea, saliva, and fluid in the lungs causing ASTHMA, choking, and coughing. Also there may be blurred vision, small pupils, cramps, and slow pulse.
Treatment: ATROPINE; this may require very large doses, as much as 5-10 times the usual dose. Give it a little at a time. DIPHENHYDRAMINE, DICYCLOMINE, and other medications that give the side-effect of a dry mouth may be helpful. Give just enough to keep the vital signs reasonably normal.
Mushrooms:
There are many kinds. *Muscarine mushroom* poisoning is described above. Most poisonous mushrooms cause GASTROENTERITIS. Some are used in animistic rituals to produce hallucinations. The deadly mushrooms have a long incubation period, more than 6-8 hours, and cause LIVER FAILURE, KIDNEY FAILURE, coma, and death. *Treatment*: Use the general treatment listed below, and send the patient to a hospital.

Nicotine:
Present in tobacco; children sometimes eat it. Poisoning causes nausea, excess saliva, abdominal pain, diarrhea, sweating, headache, temporary loss of hearing and eyesight, and mental changes. The patient then becomes dizzy, faint, and short of breath. He may die.
Treatment: Give ACTIVATED CHARCOAL.
Outers:
See ADDICTION.
Panax:
See Ginseng, listed above. It is another name for the same thing.
Ricin:
If ricin is inhaled, it causes fever, nausea, vomiting, cough, congestion, shortness of breath, and death within 72 hours. Ricin swallowed causes belly pain, vomiting, diarrhea, bleeding, death of liver, spleen and kidneys. Ricin injected causes local pain, swelling, later life threatening—pain at site of injection, followed by death of the tissues in that area and death of adjacent body organs. Ricin comes from castor beans, a common shrub that grows beside roads in tropical areas. See the separate entry under Plant Poisoning for Castor Beans.
Senecio:
Similar to Crotalaria (above); it affects children 2-5 years old. It occurs in southern Africa, India, the West Indies, and Ecuador. It causes painless enlargement of the liver. **Treatment:** Bed rest and a high-protein diet.
St. John's Wort:
This is an herbal supplement used as a sedative and to treat various kinds of pains. It causes sensitivity to sunlight, and sometimes irrational behavior. The herb interferes with some HIV medicines.
Strychnine:
Used as a criminal poison worldwide, it produces spasms of all muscles and small pupils. The patient dies because he cannot breathe due to the muscle spasms. He may have SEIZURES. **Treatment:** None. The patient will die.
Uppers:
See ADDICTION.
Valerian:
Used as a sedative. See the "downers" section of drug ADDICTION.

Similar Conditions: Too many to list; see the appropriate C protocols. In cases where multiple people take the same thing at the same time, the onset of symptoms is within hours of each other. With exposure to the same infection, the onsets are within days.

Higher-Level Care. This is generally helpful if the patient is quite ill. Familiarity with the particular ethnic situation is more important than paper credentials on the part of the practitioner. A level 3 or above facility is desirable. A consult with a toxicologist is most desirable, even if he has no tropical/travel experience. A consultant toxicologist can be accessed through the internet.

PLEURISY

Cause: Variable.
Synonyms: Devil's grippe, Pleurodynia.
Definition: Pleurisy is an inflammation of the covering over the lungs, between the lungs and the chest wall.
Entry category: Syndrome.

Not ill to severely ill, depending on cause; Class 1-3; Worldwide, causes vary with region.

Age: Mostly adults. **Who:** Anyone. **Onset:** Usually sudden.

Clinical:

Necessary: The patient has sharp chest pains, worse with deep breathing. The chest wall is not tender to touch.

Usually: In temperate climates, most pleurisy is caused by a virus and is not serious; it lasts about a week. If it lasts longer or if the patient has a fever, you should find the cause. In the tropics, most pleurisy is due to one of the diseases listed.

Causative diseases:
PNEUMONIA, TUBERCULOSIS, AMEBIC LIVER DISEASE (especially in nationals), PERICARDITIS, HYDATID DISEASE.

Similar Conditions: COSTAL CHONDRITIS (tenderness to touch over the joints next to the breast bone), chest injury, RHEUMATIC FEVER, FAMILIAL MEDITERRANEAN FEVER

Treatment:

For simple pleurisy, treat with pain medication such as CODEINE or NALBUPHINE. DIPYRONE is frequently available, but there are occasional deaths from it; it should not be used under these circumstances. If the problem persists, use ASPIRIN or IBUPROFEN in the doses for ARTHRITIS. ACETAMINOPHEN is not helpful. Identify and treat the underlying disease.

PNEUMONIA

Cause: Bacteria, viruses, fungi.
Synonyms: Pneumonitis.
Regional Notes: E, F, M, S, U.
Definition: Pneumonia is a lung infection.

Entry category: Disease cluster.

Moderately to very ill; Class 1-3 depending on severity; Contagious; Worldwide, very common.

Age: Any. **Who:** Anyone, especially those with poor immunity. **Onset:** Usually rapid, over 12-24 hours. Occasionally slow.

Clinical:

Necessary: Cough, and at least one of the following: shaking chills, chest, shoulder, or upper abdominal pain, shortness of breath, rapid respiration, fine crackly sounds heard through a stethoscope.

Usually: Fever in patients over 6 months old.

➢ **Simple pneumonia:**

This occurs in previously healthy children or adults or ones who have had, at most, a prior cold or EAR INFECTION. Initially the patient has a shaking chill and then develops a fever. His chest is congested. He has a cough with sputum which may be white, yellow, green, bloody, or rusty. His respiration is rapid and he may feel short of breath, especially when lying down. Chest pain is common. As the patient improves, he may have drenching sweats. Blacks may have some JAUNDICE. Children may have diarrhea. This kind of pneumonia responds to PENICILLIN in older children and adults; use AMPICILLIN in children under 6 y.o.

➢ **Complicated pneumonia:**

This does not respond to PENICILLIN. It occurs in infants, in children under 5 y.o., in those with prior illnesses that have left them weak, and after SEIZURES, head injuries, or alcoholic binges. Symptoms are similar, but chills and fever may be absent. In infants who are short of breath, the fronts of their abdomens, just below the ribs, pull in with every breath. They will not nurse or eat well because they are too short of breath.

➢ **Any pneumonia:**

You may be able to hear rales: fine, high-pitched, crackly sounds like newly-washed hair rubbed between two fingers by the ear. (See also Chapter 1 in Vol. I.) Rales usually occur first at the end of inspiration. Sometimes rather than rales you will hear a longer expiration than inspiration; this indicates a particularly severe pneumonia. In severe cases, there is grunting with each breath and Whites look blue around the mouth. In Black children, the bluish coloration may be seen by comparing the tongue color to that of a sibling. The patient will have a fast respiratory rate or he will be lethargic or both.

Normal Respiratory Rates (breaths per minute):	
Newborn	30-60
1 y.o.	20-40
2-3 y.o.	20-30
5 y.o.	20-25
10 y.o.	17-22
Adults	12-20

Complications: If the patient is not getting better with treatment, he may have pus in his chest which will require drainage at the hands of a surgeon. In this case the patient will have continuing chest pain, chills or fever, and night sweats. Send the patient to the nearest hospital, treating for complicated pneumonia meanwhile.

Causative and Associated Diseases:
RESPIRATORY INFECTION, ASCARIASIS, HOOKWORM, TUBERCULOSIS, ENTERIC FEVER, rarely PLAGUE.

Similar Conditions: This is one type of RESPIRATORY INFECTION; see that entry for a description of related diseases. Also see Protocols C-4, C-5, C-9, and C-13 if applicable.

Recent-onset pneumonia is indistinguishable from early HOOKWORM, STRONGYLOIDIASIS or ASCARIASIS as these worms migrate through the lungs. PULMONARY EMBOLISM may also involve a fever and be indistinguishable.

If the patient is *apathetic and very ill*, consider ENTERIC FEVER, TYPHUS, RELAPSING FEVER, rarely PLAGUE.

In the presence of *abdominal pain* consider ACUTE ABDOMEN, AMEBIC LIVER DISEASE.

In areas *where dogs live* close to people and lick children's faces: consider HYDATID DISEASE.

If the patient has recently *handled newborn animals*, he may have Q FEVER, a form of pneumonia that responds to DOXYCYCLINE or RIFAMPIN.

Higher-Level Care. Speedy referral is important if the patient is short of breath. See Volume I, Appendix 13. *Laboratory*: A blood count and sputum for gram stain and culture might be available at a level 3 or above. Most hospital labs can do smears and stains of sputum to determine which antibiotic will be best. *Facilities*: Chest x-ray, IV's with fluids and injectable antibiotics, oxygen, expert nursing care and respiratory therapists. *Practitioners*: Pediatricians, generalists, internists.

Treatment:

General suggestions: If the patient cannot tolerate oral medicines, you should use injectable medicines. High humidity is also helpful. Prop the patient in the sitting position and have him drink large amounts of water.[1] If an infant will not nurse, empty the mother's breasts at least every 4 hours and give the milk to the child, using a stomach tube if you can do so without making him more short of breath. Be careful for MALNUTRITION and for DEHYDRATION.

Initial Choice of Anitbiotics:

<u>Patients under two months old, those malnourished or HIV-infected</u>: Use a CEPHALOSPORIN initially, second or third generation.

<u>Patients over two months but less than 6 months old and previously healthy</u>: Use ERYTHROMYCIN or AZITHROMYCIN if possible, otherwise AMOXICILLIN; do not use CEPHALOSPORIN.

<u>Preschool patients, previously healthy, without HIV INFECTION</u>: AMOXICILLIN initially; if that doesn't work go to CEPHALOSPORIN.

---

[1] The high humidity and hydration help to make the secretions moist and therefore easier to bring up. If the patient becomes dehydrated, his secretions are thick and sticky and they tend to stay in the lungs for a longer time, thus delaying recovery.

School-aged children: initially use ERYTHROMYCIN, AZITHROMYCIN, or CLARITHROMYCIN and if that doesn't work, try CHLORAMPHENICOL.

Sputum with a putrid odor: Send the patient out or, failing that, use PENICILLIN plus (METRONIDAZOLE or TINIDAZOLE).

Simple pneumonia: Give PENICILLIN by mouth for 10 days. Under 6 y.o. but previously healthy, use AMOXICILLIN. You may substitute ERYTHROMYCIN.

Previously healthy with sudden-onset pneumonia, high fever, bloody or rusty sputum: Use PENICILLIN, AZITHROMYCIN, CLARITHROMYCIN, or ERYTHROMYCIN, **not** CIPROFLOXACIN.

With initial sore throat, achiness or chest pain: try ERYTHROMYCIN first.

Pneumonia after a chest wall injury: Use CLOXACILLIN. Send the patient out soon if he is not rapidly improving.

Complicated pneumonia: Use CHLORAMPHENICOL alone or AMPICILLIN plus CHLORAMPHENICOL.

Pneumonia in HIV patients: When a patient with HIV acquires ordinary PNEUMONIA, he must be treated with CHLORAMPHENICOL plus AMPICILLIN. CIPROFLOXACIN, OFLOXACIN, or COTRIMOXAZOLE may work. Standard treatment with PENICILLIN or AMOXICILLIN is inadequate for someone HIV positive, even if he does not have full-blown AIDS. There is a peculiar type of pneumonia that tends to affect AIDS patients. PENTAMIDINE, COTRIMOXAZOLE, or ATOVAQUONE might be useful.

Results: Improvement in 12-24 hours. If not, switch to CHLORAMPHENICOL in a previously healthy person. In patients with HIV INFECTION, switch to PENTAMIDINE, COTRIMOXAZOLE, or ATOVAQUONE. In other previously ill patients add METRONIDAZOLE. Consider TUBERCULOSIS if the patient does not improve after two or three different antibiotics.

PNEUMOTHORAX

Cause: Variable.
Regional Notes: F, M, O, S.
Definition: Pneumothorax is a collapse of a lung, a condition in which there is air between the chest wall and the lung surface.

Moderately to very ill; Class 2-3; Worldwide.

Age: Mostly teens and young adults. **Who:** Anyone, especially Asians. **Onset:** Usually instantaneous.

Clinical:

The patient will have sharp chest pain and shortness of breath. This is the collapse of a lung in a previously healthy young person, or as a result of TB or some other lung problem. You will not be able to hear breath sounds on the side of the collapsed lung.

Similar Conditions: See Protocol C-4.

Higher-Level Care. Speedy referral is important. See Volume I, Appendix 13. A level 3 facility is important; the patient will need a chest tube with suction. A surgeon is most appropriate but many generalists can manage this condition. X-ray is most important.

Treatment:

If the patient is short of breath, arrange to have him sent out but be sure he is not exposed to lower air pressure in an unpressurized aircraft. If he appears to be dying, passing a long hypodermic needle into his chest on the side where you hear no breath sounds may be lifesaving. Put it in below the armpit. Feel where there is a rib and try to put the needle in **over top** of the rib. (Nerves and blood vessels run along the lower edge of each rib and it is best to avoid these.) You will hear a rush of air as the needle enters. Leave the needle in until the patient arrives at a hospital.

POISONING

See Symptom Protocol 11: POISONING; *See also* ARSENIC POISONING, LEAD POISONING, PLANT POISONING and FOOD POISONING, in this Index.

POLIO

Cause: Virus.
Synonyms: Infantile paralysis, Poliomyelitis.
Regional Notes: F, I, M, O, R, S, U.
Definition: Polio is a viral infection affecting mainly the nerves that control movement; it does not usually affect the nerves that control feeling.

Mildly to very ill; Class 2-4 depending on how well the patient is breathing; Contagious; Worldwide, related to immunization, most common in the tropics.

Age: Anyone; usually less than 6 y.o.; commonly under 2 y.o. **Who:** Not immunized. Fatigue, pregnancy, tonsillectomy, and injections of any sort predispose to paralysis in someone who is developing polio. **Onset:** 6-48 hours. The onset of paralysis is sudden.

Clinical:

Necessary: After a "cold" or diarrhea or burning eye pain (see EYE INFECTION) the patient develops a fever, stiff neck, sharp and crampy muscle pains in his limbs, severe back pain or headache, and weakness. The muscles closer to the body are affected more than those further out; it is easier to move fingers and toes than hips and shoulders. There is no loss of feeling. The paralyzed limbs are floppy, or else the muscles of the face, head, and neck are affected. The pain is not aggravated but may be relieved by someone else moving the patient's limbs.

Usually: The weakness is in the lower limbs only; upper limb weakness is unusual in developing countries. The paralysis is not generally symmetrical, i.e., the right or left is affected more than the other. The patient has trouble walking. He becomes as paralyzed as he will be in 3-5 days.

Sometimes: The patient is not able to urinate on his own. He may stop breathing. His face may droop and he may have trouble swallowing.

Complications: RESPIRATORY FAILURE, PNEUMONIA, URINARY INFECTION, URINARY OBSTRUCTION, IMPACTION.

Similar Conditions:

Pains may be similar to those of DIPHTHERIA (sore throat) PELLAGRA (rash or mental symptoms), ARSENIC POISON (horizontal white line on fingernails), BERIBERI (poor diet), and tertiary SYPHILIS (stiff weakness). See Protocol C-13 if there is back pain.

Spasms may be similar to TETANUS (face and arm spastic also), RICKETS (no sunlight exposure), and PLANT POISON due to strychnine (more sudden onset).

Floppy weakness may be similar to PLANT POISON due to botulism (starts upper body), BERIBERI (poor diet), and DIPHTHERIA (sore throat). Polio is a kind of SPINAL NEUROPATHY; other causes of that condition may be indistinguishable. RABIES can be similar but the patient is always dead within a week. He will have muscle spasms by feeling a breeze or by attempting to drink water. There may be a history of an animal bite (most often a bat) or some kind of bat exposure.

Higher-Level Care. Speedy referral is important; see Volume I, Appendix 13. *Facilities* at least level 3 or 4 are required, preferably Western-run. Laboratory and X-ray are occasionally very helpful but oxygen and professional respiratory therapy are essential. A high-tech facility might have a new antiviral drug that reportedly works for this. Tropical/travel expertise is not necessary.

Treatment:

Prevention: Immunize. The most recent immunizations are single, not triple, because one of the three original kinds of polio has been eliminated. (Immunization does not protect against the kind that begins with burning eye pain.) If there is any possibility of RABIES, see the entry for that disease.

Patient Care:

First entirely undress the patient and check him for ticks. TICK PARALYSIS can mimic this and is easily remedied by removing the tick.

Avoid all IM injections in a patient for whom you suspect this diagnosis; IV's are o.k..

The patient may require assistance to breathe. Watch for PNEUMONIA, and URINARY INFECTION. If you cannot send the patient to a hospital:

- Keep the patient near you and at bed rest for a week. Keep him lying on either side, head down, so he will not choke on his tongue or his saliva. Watch his airway.
- Diet: give whatever he will take. Be sure to check to see if the patient can swallow water before giving each meal. Give a liquid diet by stomach tube if the patient cannot swallow.
- Check twice daily to make sure the patient urinated; if not, put in a urinary catheter. *See* Volume I, Appendix 1.
- Check vital signs every 4 hours.
- If the respiratory rate falls well below normal, he will die unless you send him out. Seek advice.
- Check daily for shortness of breath along with a fever. Treat for PNEUMONIA if this develops.
- Give no sedatives and no CODEINE or other narcotics for pain. Use ACETAMINOPHEN or IBUPROFEN instead. Moist heat is useful for muscle pains.
- Move each limb daily as far as it can be moved in every direction; you will not injure the patient with this. Do not allow him to do the exercises himself until a week after paralysis begins.

Results: Recovery is very slow. If eye pain was the initial illness, recovery will be complete. With ordinary polio, recovery varies from slight to complete. It may result in RESPIRATORY FAILURE. As long as the patient can speak or cry loudly, his respiration is adequate. If he can speak or cry only very softly, he is breathing inadequately. A paralyzed limb will not grow normally.

PORPHYRIA

Clinical:

This is an inherited disease which runs in families and presents variably with skin manifestations (especially sensitivity to light) or else recurrent abdominal pains together with mental illness and/or weakness. The abdominal/mental symptoms seldom start before puberty. The weakness affects the muscle groups closest to the trunk, i.e. the shoulders and hips. Attacks may occur spontaneously or as a result of taking some drug. The drugs listed in the drug index have notes if/when they should not be used in the presence of porphyria. Discontinue any of the drugs that might have caused the crisis. Send out for further treatment; there is not much else you can do beside offering pain relief.

POST-MEASLES CACHEXIA

Definition: Post-measles cachexia is the refusal to eat that often occurs when a malnourished child is recovering from MEASLES. Also see the chart under MALNUTRITION in this index for similar diseases. It may result in kwashiorkor (malnutrition with general body swelling) or in MALABSORPTION (prompt, watery diarrhea whenever the patient eats). See Protocol C-14 for similar conditions.

POSTPARTUM SEPSIS

Definition: Postpartum sepsis is SEPSIS after an ABORTION, miscarriage, or childbirth. *See* Chapter 7 in Vol. I.

PREMENSTRUAL TENSION

Synonym: PMS.
Definition: Premenstrual tension is emotional distress, frequently DEPRESSION, occurring a few days to a week before menstruation. It can be mild or severe. Use sedation or IBUPROFEN if necessary.

PROCTITIS

Cause: Variable.
Regional Notes: F, R.
Definition: Proctitis is inflammation of the rectum.
Entry category: Syndrome.

Proctitis is rectal pain along with the symptoms of DYSENTERY. Bleeding is bright red but not large amounts. The patient passes much mucus and has little warning before defecating. There may also be crampy abdominal pain. It may be due to SCHISTOSOMIASIS MANSONI, DYSENTERY due to amebae, LYMPHOGRANULOMA VENEREUM (mainly in females and homosexual males), or GONORRHEA. It is particularly common in homosexuals but may occur in anyone. Treat the underlying disease as well as DYSENTERY.

PROSTATITIS

Cause: Bacteria, usually.
Synonyms: Enlarged prostate, Prostate trouble.
Regional Notes: F, R.
Definition: Prostatitis is an inflammation of the prostate, a gland that lies between the rectum and the base of the penis.

Age: Adults; **Who:** Males only, sexually active usually. **Onset:** Minutes to hours.

Clinical:

This is a type of URINARY INFECTION in males which causes rectal pain or a heavy feeling or aching between the base of the penis and the rectum. It is a common complication of TUBERCULOSIS, SCHISTOSOMIASIS MANSONI, and/or SEXUALLY TRANSMITTED DISEASE, in particular GONORRHEA and CHLAMYDIA.

Commonly: There is fever, chills, fatigue, joint and muscle pain, and genital pain. The patient may have a discharge from his penis.

Maybe: The patient has to bear down to urinate. He might urinate small amounts frequently and have pain in doing so. If the condition is severe, he may develop URINARY OBSTRUCTION.

Treatment:

Treat it like any other URINARY INFECTION. CO-TRIMOXAZOLE is particularly good for this. OFLOXACIN is also o.k. If you use CEPHALOSPORIN it should be second or third generation since the problem is usually gram negative.

PTERYGIUM

Cause: Bright sunlight.
Definition: A pterygium is an opaque, white area on the cornea, prevalent in those living outdoors in sunny areas.

Clinical:

The white area grows from the edge of the cornea of the eye to the center, like a slice of pie, at the 3 or 9 o'clock position.

Treatment:

It can be prevented by wearing dark glasses. Eye drops may be useful, but they should not be used without a physician's guidance. Surgery may also be helpful.

PULMONARY EMBOLISM

Includes: Pulmonary infarct.
Definition: Pulmonary embolism is a crisis caused by a blood clot which formed somewhere in the body and then broke loose and went to the lungs.

Age: Mostly adults; **Who:** It usually happens in ill or sedentary people, or it is related to PLANT POISONING: Ergot. **Onset:** Usually sudden.

Clinical:

It causes sudden shortness of breath, chest pain, and maybe HEART FAILURE and death. There may be fever and the patient is likely to cough up pink, frothy sputum.

Treatment:

Not feasible in developing areas.

PYOMYOSITIS

Cause: Bacteria.
Synonym: Deep muscle ABSCESS
Regional Notes: F, M, U.
Definition: Pyomyositis is a deep muscle abscess.

Mildly to moderately ill; Class 2-3; Worldwide, related to level of medical care, may be due to injections or arise spontaneously.

Age: Any, mostly 5-25 y.o. **Who:** Anyone, especially those with poor immunity. **Onset:** Over days, maybe longer

Clinical:

Necessary: There is a tender, warm swelling of the muscles in the patient's back, buttock(s), or one of his limbs. It is due to a muscle ABSCESS. The tenderness and swelling are always the worst over muscle rather than over a joint. The swelling is always firm, never soft.

Usually: Fever, chills. It most often affects the hip, thigh, or lower leg. It is difficult to tell the difference between this and a bone infection. If the muscles involved are essential for walking, the patient will limp or refuse to walk.

Similar Conditions: See Protocol C-6 [limb(s)]or C-13 [back]. If the warmth and swelling are worst over a joint, consider various causes of ARTHRITIS.

Higher-Level Care. Speedy referral is necessary; See Volume I, Appendix 13. *Laboratory*: Hospital labs can do a smear and culture of the pus to determine which antibiotic to use. *Facilities*: IV's and injectable antibiotics are helpful, as is x-ray and/or ultrasound. *Practitioner:* An orthopedic surgeon is ideal.

Treatment:

Early stage: Symptoms less than a week and you cannot withdraw pus with an 18-gauge needle: First try antibiotics only: AUGMENTIN, RIFAMPIN, CIPROFLOXACIN, or one of the CEPHALOSPORINs. GENTAMYCIN might also work. *Results:* 1 week.

Middle stage: You can withdraw pus but the patient has no fever: Send the patient out if you do not know where the nerves and arteries are so you can avoid them. If you do know the anatomy: Make a deep cut through the skin and fat into the pocket of pus to drain it. *See* Volume I Appendix 1. Rinse the ABSCESS cavity with sterile saline and place a long strip of clean or sterile cloth in the cavity, which you will change daily. *Results:* Improved 1 week, healed 1-2 months, depending on the size.

Late stage: Symptoms more than a week and there is a fever: Send out or drain the abscess cavity as for the middle stage. Then start the patient on antibiotic. If you cannot drain it, antibiotics will do no good. If it drains but then does not heal well, it may need to be drained again. The patient may require surgery.

Results: Improvement in a matter of weeks with proper nursing care.

Q FEVER

Cause: Bacteria.

Synonyms: Balkan grippe, Red River FEVER, Nine Mile fever.

Regional Notes: E, F, R.

Definition: Q fever is a mild bacterial illness, caused by the bacterium Coxiella burnetti, that resembles INFLUENZA.

Not ill to very ill; Class 1; Contagious from infected animals; it is particularly common in the southern Europe/Mediterranean area, especially Iraq. It does not occur in Southeast Asia or in the central part of South America. It falls in the category of tropical/travel medicine. **Age:** Any **Who**: Those exposed to infected domestic animals or the dust thereof, especially newborn animals. The sex ratio is 1 before puberty; after puberty there are many more females than males affected. It may be sexually transmitted. **Onset:** Probably gradual, possibly sudden; incubation 2-4 weeks.

Clinical:

Headache, chills, fever, fatigue, muscle pains, loss of appetite, lasting a few days to a few weeks if there are no complications. There is rarely a rash. The liver is large and tender.

Complications: PNEUMONIA, HEPATITIS (commonly), HEART FAILURE (uncommonly) due to the infection entering the heart valves.

Similar Conditions: This most closely resembles TYPHUS which can be treated with some of the same drugs. See Protocol C-2 (for fever and body pains) and C-4 (if the patient is short of breath).

Higher-Level Care. *Laboratory* diagnosis is useless unless a person is at a high-tech laboratory and specimens are taken within a couple days of onset of illness and before any antibiotics have been taken. *Facilities:* With very sick patients IV's and injectable antibiotics might be useful.

Treatment:

It responds well to ERYTHROMYCIN, CIPROFLOXACIN, DOXYCYCLINE, or RIFAMPIN. A vaccine is available.

RABIES

Cause: Virus.

Synonyms: Hydrophobia, Lyssa.

Regional Notes: F, I, O, S, U.

Definition: Rabies is a kind of viral encephalitis.

Very ill; Class 1: Nearly 100% death rate in anyone's care; maybe contagious; virus is present in saliva, urine, and tears[1]; Present in all regions, mostly tropical, although some islands are free of it.

Age: Any. **Who:** Those bitten by a rabid animal and not immunized. Occasionally exposure to the droppings of rabid bats will cause rabies. A rabid animal will die. Any animal that survives and looks healthy for 10 days is not rabid. **Onset:** Usually sudden, frequently after a 2-3 day period of just not feeling good. Incubation period is 4 days to years, usually weeks to months, shorter with head, neck, and hand wounds, shorter with severe bites or bites from wild animals.

[1] However, no case of human-to-human transmission has ever been reported. This is probably because people are afraid enough of the disease to take precautions.

Clinical:

➢ **Ordinary (Furious) Rabies:**

Initially the patient has pain or tingling or itching at the site of the bite, which then spreads. He becomes very sensitive to light and sound. The onset of symptoms may include episodes of excitability, crazy behavior, and incoherent speech.

➢ **Paralytic Rabies:**

Initially this begins like POLIO with simple paralysis which progressively becomes worse; this is usually from bites of bats. There is no loss of sensation with this—the patient can still feel touch and pain. It may also resemble MENINGITIS with SEIZURES and a stiff neck. Paralysis moves from limb toward trunk.

➢ **Both Kinds:**

When fully developed, the most constant symptom is painful spasm of the throat with attempts to swallow liquids, and sometimes with a breeze blowing over the skin.

Usually: The patient has a fever and a general influenza-like illness.

Sometimes: He has back pain, arching of the back, and an erection that will not go away. The patient develops muscle spasms of his throat, paralysis of his limbs, or both. When the disease causes paralysis, the paralysis starts at the bite and moves toward the head. Vital signs may change rapidly; thus one might see either a rapid or slow pulse and respiratory rate, a high or low temperature and blood pressure.

Similar Conditions: POLIO must be differentiated from paralytic rabies. Polio usually involves lower limbs only and the patient does not have spasms from a breeze blowing over his skin or by drinking water (as is true for rabies). Rabies may also resemble other forms of ENCEPHALITIS, of which this is one kind. DEMONIZATION may also be similar as may TETANUS and occasionally ALCOHOLISM. See Protocol C-13 if there is back pain.

Higher-Level Care. Only a level 5 facility has any hope of saving the patient. However, a lower level facility might be helpful in terms of keeping him comfortable until he dies. *Facilities:* IV fluids to prevent dehydration; major sedative and pain medication; an air conditioned room free of breezes, spiritual counsel.

Treatment/Prevention:

Pre-exposure prevention:

If you are in an area of high rabies incidence, you should be immunized. Human Diploid Cell Vaccine is very safe. To immunize before exposure, give 0.5 ml IM on each of days 0, 7, and 21 or 28. Alternatively, give 0.1 ml intradermal, (ID) like a TB skin test, on each of these days. The intradermal is not as reliable as the IM but it is far cheaper. It does not work reliably in the presence of CHLOROQUINE. In Western countries, a blood test is available to determine if the immunization was effective. Antiserum and vaccine are still needed after a bite, though in fewer doses. A previously unimmunized person should have the vaccine within 48 hours of a bite, but later immunization is better than none.

Post-exposure ID immunization is as follows:

On day zero, inject 0.1 ml ID in each of these 8 places: the right and left upper arms; below the right and left shoulder blades in back, the right and left thighs, and on the right and left lower abdomen. On day 7 do the same at 4 sites: the upper arms and the thighs. On days 28 and 90, do the same at one site, on one upper arm.

Treatment of an animal bite when the animal is possibly rabid:

- Thoroughly cleanse and rinse out wounds with alcohol or iodine or both. Open puncture wounds with a scalpel blade. Provide a tetanus shot if necessary.
- If the bites were provoked[1] and made by a domestic animal that had rabies shots, no further prevention is necessary. If bites were unprovoked or made by an unimunized or wild animal, the patient should have one dose of hyperimmune antiserum or hyperimmune globulin IM. Give this shot in the upper arm, not in the buttocks. Follow the directions with the product. If using animal serum, you must check for sensitivity first. You should have EPINEPHRINE on hand and review the treatment of ANAPHYLAXIS. Draw 0.1 ml of serum into a syringe. Then draw 0.9 ml of saline into the same syringe so you have a total of 1 ml. Mix this by tipping the syringe back and forth. Drop 0.1 ml of this diluted solution inside the lower eyelid. A little bit of redness is normal. A strong allergic reaction within 15 minutes indicates you should not proceed with the serum or globulin injection. Only vaccinate. If you can send the patient to a doctor or nurse for desensitization, then he might be able to take the serum or globulin.
- 24 hours after the globulin or antiserum, or immediately if the patient had an allergic reaction, vaccinate the patient. Follow the directions with the product. Two older, cheaper types of vaccine are available in developing countries: Semple and Duck Embryo. ALLERGY can be a problem. Read the package inserts carefully. The Semple type may cause redness, swelling, itching, and pain at the injection site after the first or subsequent doses. Stop the vaccination if this happens. You may continue with a different type and use PREDNISONE. Human Diploid Cell Vaccine (HDCV) as well as yet

[1] Provoked means that one can understand that the animal's attack was defensive. Examples would be a child trying to pull a bone out of the mouth of a dog, or coming between a mother animal and her young one.

newer RVA and PCEC are more expensive, safer (as regards allergy) and not as available. Read the package inserts carefully.

Treatment of a patient with rabies:
There have been occasional reports of survivals with long-term intensive care in a major university hospital setting. Send the patient out for this care promptly if possible. Otherwise use high doses of sedatives and pain medicines until death. Inform the family that the patient will die. Be careful of contact with saliva, urine, and tears. Rabies is not thought to be contagious but the virus is present in saliva and tears.

Results: The patient is not unconscious until late in the illness. Death occurs within a week in furious rabies, within 3 weeks in paralytic rabies.

RADIATION ILLNESS

Cause: Radiation.
Regional Notes: E.
Definition: Radiation illness is an illness due to the damaging effects of ionizing radiation.

Not ill to very ill; Class 1-4; Worldwide, but rare in nations that have no nuclear history. Some developing areas may have a problem if they are used as nuclear waste dumps, or if there are natural deposits of radioactive minerals, e.g., uranium.

Age: Any. **Who:** Those exposed to a source of radiation; those who drink contaminated water, eat contaminated food, or ingest radioactive materials. **Onset:** Within hours for major exposures; after years or possibly in the next generation for small-dose, chronic exposures.

Clinical:

There are two classes of effects: the acute effects occur with sudden exposure to large doses; and the chronic effects occur with continual or frequent exposures to small doses.

➢ **Acute Effects:**
Within a couple of hours there is loss of appetite. Thereafter there is nausea, vomiting, and diarrhea; anemia and susceptibility to infection; weight loss; loss of hair; sterility; apathy alternating with agitation; loss of coordination; seizures; coma and death. Death, if it occurs, almost always is within 30 days.

➢ **Chronic Effects:**
With exposures during very early pregnancy (from conception until 2 weeks after the second missed period), either the baby will die or he will grow normally. Exposures after that time are likely to cause retarded growth, mental retardation, or significant disabilities such as blindness or deafness. Exposures later in life may cause CANCER: leukemia and bone tumors appear after 2-4 years and other CANCERS (especially thyroid, lung, skin, and breast) after 10-40 years. Radiation may also cause CATARACT.

Similar Conditions: Acute effects may be similar to GASTROENTERITIS, ANEMIA from other causes, HIV, TUBERCULOSIS, BRAIN DAMAGE from other causes. Prenatal effects may be similar to the prenatal effects from RUBELLA, TOXOPLASMOSIS or HERPES.

Higher-Level Care. Speedy referral is necessary for major exposures, with caution in using public transport if the patient consumed radioactivity, in contrast to merely being near a source. Symptomatic care only is generally available: IV's, transfusions and the like at a level 3 or above.

Treatment:

Prevention: If you live in an area where this is likely to be a problem, obtain a radiation counter to check your water and food. There is no way to reliably purify contaminated water although some systems may work under some circumstances. Contaminated food must be discarded. If someone has ingested contaminated food others should be protected from his body secretions.

Patient Care: There is no effective treatment for the problem. Persons who have been exposed to radiation should be watched so that early treatment of CANCERS can be initiated.

RAT BITE FEVER

Cause: Bacteria or spirochete.
Includes: Haverhill fever, Sodoku.
Regional Notes: I.
Definition: Rat bite fever is either one of two similar relapsing fevers caused by a bacterium (Actinobacillus muris) or a spirochete (Spirillum minor) transmitted by the bite of a rat.

Entry category: Two nearly indistinguishable diseases.

Mildly to very ill; Class 1-3; Worldwide, but rare in the Americas and common in Asia. It is tropical.

Age: Any but mostly children. **Who:** Those bitten by rats or rat-eating animals or who consumed food contaminated by rat urine. **Onset:** Over about 3 days, after an incubation of 3-30 days.

Clinical:

Necessary: There are chills and fevers, headache, nausea, and weakness. With one type, the wound heals and then breaks open; with the other type it stays healed but there is a rash. Without treatment, the fever falls on its own at about 4-6 days, stays down for a few days, and then comes back.

Sometimes there are joint pains, general muscle aching, and a rash. The rash consists of purplish spots or lumps, mostly on the chest and arms. The pulse is not slow relative to the fever. If left untreated, the fever and other symptoms come back repeatedly over months. There may be a large liver.

Complications: HEART FAILURE.

Similar Conditions: See Protocols C-2, C-6, and C-11. RELAPSING FEVER is the main one; the treatments are similar.

Higher-Level Care. See Volume I, Appendix 13. *Laboratory:* Only Level 4 and above in a specialty center for tropical/travel medicine. *Facilities:* IV's and injectable antibiotics, level 3 or above.

Treatment:

Use PENICILLIN as for STREP THROAT. DOXYCYCLINE and STREPTOMYCIN are alternatives.

RECTAL PROLAPSE

Cause: Variable.

Regional Notes: F, M, R.

Definition: Rectal prolapse is the rectum falling out of the anus, so the pink, moist part that should be inside sticks out.

Clinical:

The rectum turns inside out so it is hanging out with some of the pink, moist surface visible on the outside. It may be a tiny bit or a large amount. The problem mostly affects women and children. There may be incontinence.

Rectal Prolapse. The bulge is pink and moist; note the lines around it.

Causative conditions: This is a problem with the rectum, usually due to chronic diarrhea, WHOOPING COUGH, KIDNEY FAILURE (Nephrotic), or TRICHURIASIS. It can also be related to constipation, malnutrition, or GIARDIASIS.

Similar Conditions: HEMORRHOIDS usually affects adults and the bulge is never larger than the patient's little toe; it has a smooth surface whereas a prolapse has a wrinkled surface and an obvious center hole.

Higher-Level Care. A hospital that has experience in treating this might be helpful, level 2 or above.

Treatment:

Gently push the rectum back in with your gloved hands **if and only if** the rectal surface is still pink. (A little dark color right around the rectal opening itself is normal in dark-skinned people.) If a significant portion of the part that should be pink is black instead, the patient must be sent to a hospital. If you have trouble pushing it back in, then sprinkle table sugar on the pink, moist part, covering the entire surface with sugar. This will reduce the swelling which will allow you to successfully push it in.

After the rectum is all the way back in, the buttocks must be taped together. Take the tape off for bowel movements only, and then replace it after pushing the prolapse back in again. Treat the patient for TRICHURIASIS. Treat for MALNUTRITION and for diarrhea if this is appropriate. He will not heal if his nutrition is poor.

REITER SYNDROME [Reactive arthritis]

Definition: Reiter syndrome[1] is an autoimmune disease that follows after venereal CHLAMYDIA infection or bacterial DYSENTERY.

Entry category: Disease.

Moderately to very ill; Class 2-3; Worldwide, related to sexually transmitted diseases and sometimes other diseases.

Age: Usually young adults. **Who:** Those who have had bacterial DYSENTERY or else CHLAMYDIA INFECTION, males more commonly than females. There may also be a predisposing genetic factor. This kind of arthritis may be caused by HIV INFECTION. **Onset:** Unknown, after a 1-3 week interval after the infection that caused the problem.

Clinical:

Pain with urinating and/or pus in the urine.

- EYE INFECTION or IRITIS symptoms.
- Chest pain due to PERICARDITIS.
- Pain and swelling in:

One joint, mainly the large joints of the spine, pelvis, or the lower limbs, made worse with rest, not symmetrical—OR—

One tendon, most commonly by the back of the heel or in front of the heel or by an elbow; or one digit—usually a toe rather than a finger.—OR—

One finger or toe so the digit looks like a sausage.

- Spontaneous wounds:

The wounds must be searched for; they are relatively painless.

Mouth ulcers which are painless or APHTHOUS STOMATITIS which is painful.

[1] Reactive arthritis or Reiter syndrome is almost the only cause of asymmetrical multiple joint arthritis with a fever. Reiter syndrome is the older name. The disease was described by a Dr. Reiter who participated in the Holocaust. The scientific community therefore boycotts using his name. I use it here because of the confusion of "arthritis" causing eye symptoms, mouth sores, and other non-joint manifestations.

Red, raw areas around the base of the penis tip in uncircumcised males. The same problem in a circumcised male causes crusts rather than red, raw areas.

Rough, scaly changes in the skin of the soles, palms, and nail beds.

Higher-Level Care. Referral to a sexually-transmitted disease clinic is highly desirable. A level 3 or above hospital might have some alternative treatments.

Treatment:

Retreat the underlying infection. Then use IBUPROFEN or a similar medication.

Results: About half these patients have a total cure and the other half develop a chronic arthritis.

RELAPSING FEVER

Cause: Spirochete.
Synonym: Borreliosis.
Includes: Tick-borne relapsing fever, Louse-borne relapsing fever.
Regional Notes: E, F, M, O, R.
Definition: Relapsing fever is an illness caused by a spirochete.

Mildly to severely ill; Class 2; Louse-borne: Andes, Africa north of the equator, Asia south of the 35th parallel. Tick-borne: Mountainous areas of Asia and the Middle East; Horn of Africa and Africa south of the equator; scattered areas in the western half of South America; northern Mexico. This is not known to occur in the islands of Southeast Asia or in the Pacific area; yet it is mainly tropical.

Age: Any. **Who:** Infection is by crushing head or body lice, or by being bitten by ticks. In the tick-borne fever, the ticks are soft ticks (See Volume I, Appendix 10) These ticks feed only for minutes, do so at night, and the bite is painless. Then they drop off of the host so more than likely the person is not aware of having been bitten. **Onset:** Sudden; incubation 2-14 days.

Clinical:

➢ **Both Kinds:**

Necessary: The patient has chills; sweats; fevers; headache (forehead or back of the head); fatigue; and general bone, joint, and muscle pains. It involves both large and small joints. The shaking chills last about 30 minutes as the temperature rises. The fever is sustained until the crisis. Then there is an additional chill followed by severe sweating within minutes to hours, weakness, and low blood pressure during which time death is common.

Usually: He has a dry cough and abdominal pain. In tick-borne relapsing fever, there are joint pains which involve large and small joints both. The pain may be severe but the joints are not red or swollen. The patient commonly acts "spacy" as in ENTERIC FEVER. The liver may also be large and tender, as well as the spleen.

Sometimes: There is JAUNDICE (especially with louse-borne disease) and a rash over the upper body with tiny black and blue marks (also more common with louse-borne). The patient may vomit. He may be dizzy or have trouble swallowing. He is likely to have a dry mouth and seek darkness. Louse-borne fever commonly causes vomiting. Tick-borne fever may cause lethargy and weight loss.

Occasionally: There is abnormal bleeding with a drop in blood pressure which may result in coma or death.

➢ **Tick-Borne:**

The episodes last less than 7 days, each episode similar to the previous ones.

➢ **Louse-Borne:**

The episodes last less than 10 days, each episode shorter and milder than the previous ones. Convalescence is prolonged; see Volume I, Appendix 8 on the care of the seriously ill patient.

Complications: Nosebleed and visual problems, loss of consciousness, BELL'S PALSY, SEIZURES, STROKE, MENINGITIS, HEMORRHAGIC FEVER (louse-borne), PNEUMONIA, trembling like PARKINSON'S DISEASE, paralysis like POLIO, mental symptoms like cerebral MALARIA, SEPSIS, ARTHRITIS, IRITIS, LIVER DISEASE or LIVER FAILURE, HEART FAILURE, ABORTION, death.

Similar Conditions: See Protocols C-2, C-7, C-8, C-9, C-10. RAT-BITE FEVER may be similar but there is a history of the bite. In no other disease do chills and sweating follow this closely. In other diseases the episodes of sweating are separated from the chills-and-fever by at least 12 hours.

LEPTOSPIROSIS may be quite similar but the fever-free interval is 1-3 days rather than 3-10 days. YELLOW FEVER shows protein in the urine and causes a peculiar body odor. DENGUE FEVER causes excruciating bone pain. LYME DISEASE may be similar but it has a slower onset and slower progression. Also, fevers above 101° F are common in relapsing fever, but uncommon in LYME DISEASE.

Bush Laboratory: There is usually protein in the urine with louse-borne fever.

Higher-Level Care. See Volume I, Appendix 13. *Laboratory:* A thick blood smear done during a fever (the same as is done for malaria) may show the spirochetes; they are easier to find in louse-borne than in tick-borne relapsing fever. They look like skinny cork-screws. Failure to find them does not exclude the diagnosis; the test is specific but not sensitive. *Practitioner:* Tropical/travel medicine expertise is desirable but speed is more important.

Treatment:

Prevention: Avoid ticks and body LICE. Try not to sit closely—clothes touching—to someone who is ill with this, lest you be bitten by his lice. Remove ticks and treat the bites with IODINE.

Patient Care: PENICILLIN, DOXYCYCLINE, or ERYTHROMYCIN. Sometimes the treatment makes the patient sicker or causes a mild SHOCK for a few hours; have him lie down for 6 hours after he takes his antibiotic. Give the patient fluids but do not stop treatment for this. It will not recur with subsequent doses after the first one or two.

RESPIRATORY FAILURE

Synonym: Ventilatory failure.

Definition: Respiratory failure is a patient's breathing inadequately.

Entry category: Syndrome.

Age, Who, Onset: Anyone, fast or slow onset.

Clinical:

Symptoms are blueness around the mouth (check the color of the tongue in Blacks), an abnormally slow respiratory rate, and finally progressive lethargy leading to loss of consciousness and death. There may be grunting or nodding of the head with each breath.

Causative conditions: It may be due to muscle weakness as in POLIO; to fatigue when breathing requires excess work as in ASTHMA, HEART FAILURE and ANTHRAX; or to diseased lungs as in TUBERCULOSIS or PNEUMONIA.

Higher-Level Care. Almost any level 2 or above facility can be helpful—send the patient to the highest level possible. Oxygen, a chest-ray, IV fluids and injectable antibiotics might all be helpful.

Treatment:

When this occurs in a previously-healthy adult who has PNEUMONIA, treat with large doses of ERYTHROMYCIN. Decrease his fluids to 75% of what you calculate that he needs as long as he is making the minimum amount of urine (Symptom Protocol 58); he will recover better if he is slightly dehydrated. Have him rest in a sitting position.

RESPIRATORY INFECTION

Cause: Viruses or bacteria.

Includes: Bronchitis, Cold, Croup, Emphysema, Obstructive lung disease, Sinusitis, Chronic obstructive lung disease.

Regional Notes: I, M.

Definition: Respiratory infection is a viral or bacterial infection of the airway, from the nose and lips down to the lungs.

Entry category: Disease cluster.

Mildly to severely ill; Class 1-4; Some contagious; Worldwide, related to crowding and nutrition.

Age: Any, especially children. **Who:** Anyone, especially malnourished, crowded conditions, smoke and/or dust exposure, and some genetic factors. **Onset:** Usually over days; occasionally minutes.

Clinical:

Necessary: Any two or more of the following: Nasal congestion; plugged ears with hearing loss; runny nose; tiredness; cough; fever; chest pain; shortness of breath; fast respiratory rate; face pain, swelling, or headache; sore throat; red eyes; large lymph nodes in the neck; loss of smell; foul breath; loss of taste. In severe cases, Whites may look bluish around the lips. (The bluishness may be seen on the tongue in Blacks.) There may be appetite and weight loss.

Types of respiratory infection

Kind	Symptoms
Cold	Congestion, plugged ears, runny nose, cough, white sputum.
Bronchitis	Lingering cough after a respiratory infection; green or yellow or bloody sputum; maybe chest pain.
Sinusitis	Congestion, face pain or headache, sometimes pus in nose or throat, maybe upper teeth pain.
Croup	Barking, dry cough in a child less than 6 y.o., sudden onset, low or no fever, short of breath, hoarse.

Chronic Respiratory Infection:

This is also known as *emphysema* or *chronic obstructive lung disease*, consists of cough, shortness of breath, and wheezing which is present most if not all the time. The patient may sleep sitting up and have a severe cough when awakening each morning. He will be short of breath when exercising. He may have a barrel-shaped chest. His fingernails may have a peculiar rounded appearance, as with HEART FAILURE. The patient may have an irregular pulse.

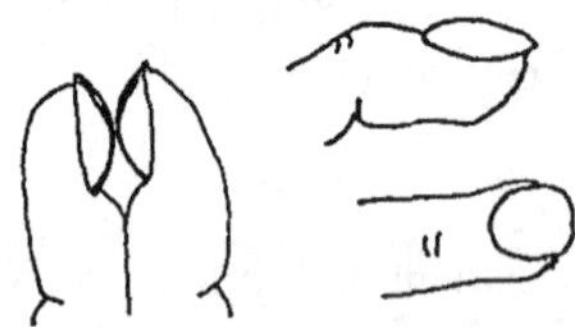

Chronic respiratory infection: The nails may become wide and shaped like saucers. When placed together, there is a big gap between them. (A similar abnormality may occur with Valvular Disease: see HEART FAILURE.)

Similar Conditions: PNEUMONIA, WHOOPING COUGH, DIPHTHERIA, TUBERCULOSIS, FILARIASIS which may cause something resembling ASTHMA. See Protocols C-4 for shortness of breath and C-10 for lethargy. Another cause of bloody sputum is migrating ASCARIASIS. TUBERCULOSIS is a frequent cause of adult-onset wheezing. If and when a cough has gone on for over 3 months, consider the diseases listed for chronic cough.

Higher-Level Care. *Laboratory:* A smear and culture of the sputum, done in a hospital lab, might be helpful, level 3 or more. *Facilities:* X-ray and/or ultrasound might be helpful. Surgery may be helpful on occasion; seek a level 3 or higher facility.

Treatment:

With croup (a tight or barking cough), use steam or high humidity, but **not** decongestants or antihistamines.

With any other cough, use COUGH SYRUP.

With adults: First check the description of PNEUMONIA; if it fits well, follow those directions rather than the ones below.

With wheezing, use THEOPHYLLINE or ALBUTEROL or METAPROTERENOL. Do **not** use antihistamines. Do not use antibiotics unless there is a fever.

With nasal congestion or a runny nose give VITAMIN C and fluids. You may also use PSEUDOEPHEDRINE tablets or EPHEDRINE NOSE DROPS provided there is no tight or barking cough or wheezing. **Do not use antibiotics unless there is a high fever or visible pus.**

Cough with a fever of more than 38°C (101°F) or if there is pus coming from the nose or back of the throat or yellow-green sputum, treat with antibiotic. PENICILLIN, AZITHROMYCIN, CLARITHROMYCIN, or ERYTHROMYCIN are best; DOXYCYCLINE, SULFA, AMPICILLIN, or COTRIMOXAZOLE are acceptable. If wheezing is present, use THEOPHYLLINE or METAPROTERENOL additionally.

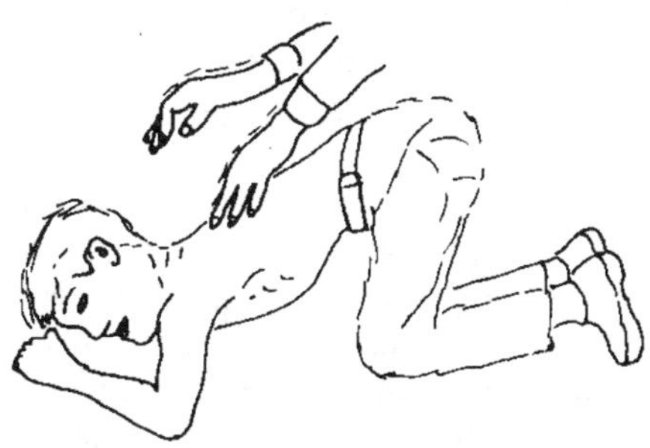

Chronic cough: Knee-chest position.

Treatment Of Coughs In Children

A simple but reliable system is as follows:

Severity of illness	Rapid Breathing[1]	Chest Suction[2]	Treatment
Mild	No	No	No antibiotic
Moderate	Yes	No	Antibiotic
Severe	Maybe	Yes	Hospitalize

[1] Rapid breathing means over 50 if less than 12 months old; over 40 if 1-3 years; over 30 if over 3 years.

[2] Chest suction means that the child's lower chest and abdomen pull way in with each breath.

With a chronic cough, first check for TUBERCULOSIS. If he has no TB, he may need to be on THEOPHYLLINE continually. You may add PREDNISONE for short periods. He should sleep sitting up. Once a day put him in the head down, knee-chest position (see figure above) and beat on his back with your open hand while he breathes in steam. This loosens stuck mucus and enables the patient to cough it up.

RHEUMATIC FEVER

Cause: STREP THROAT.

Regional Notes: All regions.

Definition: Rheumatic fever is a disease caused by a misguided immune reaction against strep throat, which ends up damaging the heart and the joints.

Mildly to severely ill; Class 1-4; Worldwide, especially in developing countries where it accounts for 1/2 of all heart disease. It is related to the level of available health care.

Age: Usually children for a first episode; HEART FAILURE is most common at 10-15 y.o., sometimes younger. The disease is more severe in older children and adults than in younger children. **Who:** Those who have had inadequately treated STREP THROAT or prior rheumatic fever. Malnourished children are particularly vulnerable. Polynesians and Maoris are particularly prone. **Onset:** Hours to a day or two. The problem tends to recur. The HEART FAILURE usually develops slowly, over weeks to months, but it may develop rapidly, causing death within days to weeks.

Clinical:

Necessary: The patient is tired, loses his appetite, has fever, and has at least one pair of swollen joints. To diagnose the disease, the patient must have had a sore throat 1-6 weeks earlier, or have current evidence of a STREP THROAT. In addition, he must have at least one of the following:[3]

- Previous rheumatic fever.
- A fever with no other obvious cause.
- Pain and swelling in 2 or more joints, usually large joints and the lower limbs before the upper limbs. The pain is maximal at 12-24 hours and lasts about a week, never more than 3 weeks.
- Either a heart murmur, HEART FAILURE, or an enlarged heart.[4]

Usually: The fever is sustained and high; it never returns to normal. The pulse is rapid. The sore, swol-

[3] Criteria for the diagnosis of rheumatic fever are more stringent in the States, but some of the symptoms and findings seen there just do not occur in the tropics. Hence, only one additional criterion is needed to make a diagnosis.

[4] See Volume I Chapter 1 to learn how to determine heart size.

len joints are the same joints on the two sides (e.g., both ankles) unless the joints are in the midline (e.g. the spine). The pain moves from one set of joints to another. There is, however, no morning stiffness which improves with exercise.

Occasionally: The fingernails have a scooped-out appearance and the patient has heavy chest pains which may go to the shoulder, arm, or jaw. He may have large lymph nodes in the front of his neck. He may have a skin rash which consists of either raised, donut-type rings on the skin or else tender, red bumps over the hairy surface of the arms, the front of the legs, and the spine in back.

Complications: STROKE, HEART FAILURE, PERICARDITIS, PLEURISY.

Similar Conditions: See Protocol C-6: Limb Swelling or C-13: Back Pain.

Joint pains: BRUCELLOSIS involves fever and joint pains also, but the joints are never red or warm as they are in rheumatic fever, and the onset is slower. RUBELLA has joint pains and fevers but there is also a red spotted rash. GONORRHEA can cause a red, swollen joint. If the patient is sexually active, give enough antibiotic to take care of that possibility.

Heart problems: HEART FAILURE from other causes are also similar.

Skin rash may be similar to AFRICAN SLEEPING SICKNESS (parts of Africa only).

Bumps under the skin may be similar to those caused by TUBERCULOSIS.

Higher-Level Care. Speedy referral; see Volume I, Appendix 13. *Laboratory:* An electrocardiogram and some blood tests and throat culture may be helpful. Seek a level 4 facility, preferably with a cardiologist. *Facilities*: In severe cases a level 4 or 5 facility with advanced injectable drugs, a monitored bed, and advanced surgical capabilities might be appropriate.

Treatment:

Prevention: Treat all patients with STREP THROAT for a full 10 days, preferably using long-acting, injectable PENICILLIN.

Patient Care:

- Absolute bed rest until the patient has recovered from this episode.
- Treat HEART FAILURE if necessary.
- Use ASPIRIN (high dose) initially, and PENICILLIN. With an allergy to PENICILLIN, try to find independent advice and, failing that, use CEPHALOSPORIN, preferably a first generation.
- After the patient is done with PENICILLIN, it is good to give CLINDAMYCIN, which eliminates any strep from the throat.
- The patient must have PENICILLIN monthly for the rest of his life if he has any evidence at all of heart trouble.
- Females with loud heart murmurs or HEART FAILURE should be cautioned against becoming pregnant. Contraceptives must be offered. Pregnancy may be fatal.

RHEUMATOID ARTHRITIS

Definition: Rheumatoid arthritis is a largely hereditary chronic joint inflammation, wherein the body's immune system attacks the joints, both large and small. See ARTHRITIS. It is a type of ARTHRITIS, usually with low or no fever, and with morning stiffness that improves during the day.

Age: It may affect children as well as adults.

Treatment:

It is treatable with high doses of ASPIRIN. Advanced, level 4 Western facilities have more helpful medications. Sometimes surgery is helpful.

RHINITIS

In areas other than Africa this refers to a runny nose caused by a cold. For Africa, see *Regional Notes*: F which describes another kind of disease altogether.

RICKETS

Cause: Vitamin D deficiency, resulting from inadequate exposure to sunlight.

Synonym: Vitamin D deficiency.

Regional Notes: E, F, I, M, O, R, U.

Mildly to moderately ill; Class 1; Worldwide, related to clothing and housing which eliminate exposure to sun; especially common in Muslim and Arctic areas.

Age: Any, 6 months and older; children are usually 1-2 y.o. **Who:** Those whose skin is not exposed to sun. It tends to occur in adults where there are high-rise buildings and/or air pollution, in women with a first pregnancy, and in Muslim women. Dark skin requires more sun exposure than light skin. Rickets may also be caused by lack of calcium in the diet. Good sources of calcium are: fish, green, leafy vegetables, milk and milk products. This may also be due to KIDNEY FAILURE or cereal diets. There is very little vitamin D in unprocessed milk. **Onset:** Slowly.

Clinical:

➢ Infants and Children*:*

In *infants*, the forehead is very prominent. The soft spot on the head stays open for a long time. (Normally it closes between 6 months and a year.) The child's head sweats excessively. In *babies*, the joints beside the breast bone are swollen. The lower ribs may be pulled in, like a second waist above the normal one; this lasts into adulthood. They have a delay in teething. They are likely to be floppy and irritable, have stiff muscle weakness and spasms, and they may have SEIZURES. There is loss of appetite, and failure to gain weight.

Children refuse to use their legs.

Frequently: The bones at the ankles and wrists look swollen; the increased size is bony, not soft. They develop a hunchback appearance along with either knock knees or bowed legs. They may be able to bend their joints abnormally.

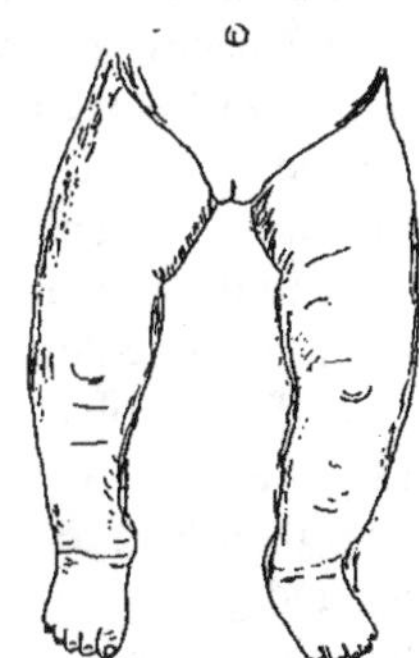

Rickets: Note the bowed legs and swollen ankles.

➢ **Adults:**

Adults with rickets develop thin bones, resulting in deep bone pain. The spine, pelvis, legs, and ribs are particularly affected, causing back, pelvic, or chest pain. The pain is worse with movement, weight bearing, and any pressure on the affected area. Bowed legs may develop later. In patients with thin bones, minor injuries may result in fractures. The gait becomes waddling as the muscles weaken.

Similar Conditions:

See Protocol C-6: Limb Swelling.

Small children: SCURVY in infants is almost identical; if you suspect either, treat for both. However, in rickets the swellings beside the breast bone are rounded rather than angular. The breast bone itself is normal or sticks out, it is not depressed as it is in SCURVY. Consider MENINGITIS due to TUBERCULOSIS, LEAD POISONING, and SYPHILIS acquired before birth. TETANUS can appear similar but the spasms become obvious quite soon. Many of the symptoms are similar to SCURVY and to HIV INFECTION, including the teething delay and delay in the closure of the soft spot on the head.

In older children and adults: also consider ARTHRITIS, TB of the spine, BRUCELLOSIS, BERIBERI.

Higher-Level Care. A large hospital lab might be able to do some helpful blood tests.

Treatment:

VITAMIN D, either in capsule form or by injection, or (preferably and more cheaply) exposure of the skin to sun **without** intervening glass. This may be difficult for females in Muslim cultures. Milk to which vitamin D has been added may be helpful. Milk naturally does not contain much vitamin D. MULTIVITAMINS which contain Vitamin D might also be useful. (Most MULTIVITAMINS include Vitamin D.) Results: 2-3 months.

ROSEOLA

Cause: Virus.

Synonym: Exanthem subitum.

Definition: Roseola is a general viral infection that affects mostly children.

Mildly to moderately ill; Class 1; Contagious; Worldwide.

Age: 6 months to 3 years. **Who:** Any child. **Onset:** 10-15 days incubation

Clinical:

Necessary: There is a sudden fever of 39.5°-41°C (103°-106°F) which lasts 3-5 days, then leaves, as a fine, red rash appears over the neck and trunk for 1-2 days and the child feels better.

Sometimes: With the fever there are cold symptoms (nasal congestion and cough), fussiness, and vomiting.

Complications: FEBRILE SEIZURE.

Similar Conditions: *Fever:* MALARIA. *Rash:* SCARLET FEVER in which case there is always a fever as long as there is a rash.

Treatment:

Follow the treatment for FEVER per se, but the fever responds poorly to the usual medications. Use no antibiotics.

ROTAVIRUS INFECTION

Cause: Virus.

Mildly to very ill; Class 1-3; Contagious; Worldwide.

Age: Mostly 3 months to 2 years; nearly every child in the world has had an episode before age 5. It also occurs in adults. **Who:** Those who consume infected water, especially the immune deficient. **Onset:** Sudden after an incubation of 1-3 days.

Clinical:

Necessary: There is a milky-smelling, watery, severe diarrhea in infants. If the disease is untreated, it lasts 5-7 days.

Sometimes there is a mild fever, abdominal pain, and/or symptoms of a common cold

Higher-Level Care. *Facilities:* A level 3 or above hospital may be helpful. There are some specific laboratory determinations for this as well as IV fluids to prevent dehydration.

Treatment:

Prevention: Rotavirus is the cause of at least half the watery diarrhea in infants worldwide. A vaccine is being developed.

Patient Care: Treat DEHYDRATION. Lactobacillus casei GG might also be helpful. Reportedly the drug NITAZOXANIDE is helpful.

RUBELLA

Cause: Virus.

Synonyms: German measles or Three-day measles.
Regional Notes: F.
Definition: Rubella is a general viral infection that affects mostly children.

Mildly to moderately ill; Class 1; Contagious; Worldwide, epidemics are common.

Age: Any. **Who:** Anyone not immunized. **Onset:** Incubation 12-23 days.

Clinical:

In older persons there is a prodrome of fever, fatigue, and cold symptoms for 4-10 days before the rash. Young children develop the rash and fever together.

For children, after the prodrome as described for adults, the patient has a red, spotty rash for 3 days with enlarged lymph nodes in front and back of his neck. On the first day the rash is heaviest on the face and trunk. By the third day it has cleared on the face and trunk and is heaviest on the limbs. There may be aching all over and a peculiar body odor, like fresh feathers. Adults may have joint pains, starting with the rash or within 3 days thereafter. The pains last for up to 4 weeks. When pregnant women have the disease, their babies may be born with CATARACT, HEART FAILURE, deafness, mental retardation, or any combination of these.

Similar Conditions: *Fever and rash:* MEASLES (does not clear as the rash progresses), LEPTOSPIROSIS, SPOTTED FEVER, DENGUE FEVER, and diseases similar to these.

Joint pains: RHEUMATIC FEVER and check similar diseases under that. Also consider BRUCELLOSIS (slower onset) and other causes of ARTHRITIS.

Treatment:

Prevention: Immunize with MMR or rubella alone. Do not immunize pregnant women!

Patient Care: Follow the directions for FEVER *per se* only. Antibiotics are not helpful; do not use them.

Sand Fly Fever

See Arboviral Fever in *Regional Notes* E, F, I, R.

SCABIES

Cause: Mite.
Synonyms: Sarcoptic itch, Acariasis.
Regional Notes: F, I, M, U.
Definition: Scabies is a skin infestation with a type of mite.

Entry category: Infestation.

Miserable but not ill; Class 1; very contagious. Worldwide, common everywhere.

Age: Any, especially children. **Who:** Those in contact with someone who has the disease, by touch, sexual contact, or shared clothing or bedding. See Volume I Appendix 10 for a picture of the scabies mite. **Onset:** Over hours to days, after an incubation of 6-8 weeks.

Clinical:

Itching red spots like MEASLES spots, but it may be possible to see little lines between the spots. With a magnifying glass you might see the causative mites although the mites are not necessarily where the rash is present. Just a few mites will make a whole-body rash. It frequently starts in the web spaces of the fingers or toes, or on the wrists, waist, or ankles. For diagnosis, apply a little watery ink to the skin and then wash it off. SCABIES will show little ink-colored lines remaining between the red spots. If it involves the face, it looks like whitish dry crusts, not red spots. Facial scabies is always in children less than 5 years old. In infants 0-1 year old, the buttocks and genital area may be most severely affected. After the disease has progressed, the spots may turn into a generally rough, scaly skin area. In HIV patients, scabies may not itch.

Complications: IMPETIGO or CELLULITIS which may, in turn, cause KIDNEY FAILURE. If there is secondary infection, it should be treated with antibiotics.

Scabies: Rash on foot (left); close-up of rash (right).

Similar Conditions: IMPETIGO which may also be a complication. Ordinary IMPETIGO doesn't itch, but if it is due to scabies it will itch. Also consider TINEA, ECZEMA, CONTACT DERMATITIS none of which itch as badly as scabies. With early STRONGYLOIDIASIS and LARVA MIGRANS a red, wormy-type line is visible under the skin. The lines of scabies are very short.

Treatment:

Wash all clothing, towels, and bedding while being treated and treat all members of a family at once, regardless of whether they have symptoms. Use 0.5% MALATHION, applied to the whole body (skipping the face if that is not affected) and repeated a week later. Itching may persist for 1-2 weeks; this does not imply treatment failure.

Alternatives are PERMETHRIN, 1% LINDANE, 10% CROTAMITON (Eurax)[1] and 25% BENZYL BENZO-

[1] Apply nightly for 2 nights, bathing 24 hours after the second application.

ATE (Ascabiol).[1] 6% SULFUR in petroleum jelly for two days may also be used. LINDANE and SULFUR have been taken off the market in England. Oral IVERMECTIN reportedly also works well. IVERMECTIN is effective for both scabies and LICE but it should not be used in areas with LOIASIS (generally central and west Africa).

SCARLET FEVER

STREP THROAT with a rash. See STREP THROAT.

SCHISTOSOMIASIS

SCHISTOSOMIASIS HEMATOBIUM. *See Regional Notes* F, R.

SCHISTOSOMIASIS INTERCALATUM. *See Regional Notes* F.

SCHISTOSOMIASIS JAPONICUM. *See Regional Notes* O, S.

SCHISTOSOMIASIS MEKONGI. *See Regional Notes* O, S.

SCHISTOSOMIASIS MANSONI

Cause: Worm

Synonyms: Intestinal bilharziasis, Snail fever, Bilharzia.

Regional Notes: F, M. R

Not ill to very ill; Class 3; Regional, only in scattered areas of Africa, the Middle East, and the Americas. It is a tropical disease.

Age: Any, especially boys 5-15 y.o. who like to swim. **Who:** Skin exposed to water with infected snails. **Onset:** Immediate itching; other symptoms in 4-13 weeks.

Snails that carry Schistomiasis mansoni are flat-shaped. The center swirls on both sides are indented. Diameters are 1-2 cm.

Clinical:

Initially: There is itching where the organisms entered the body. Expatriates especially may begin with KATAYAMA DISEASE. Nationals frequently skip this stage.

30-90 Days After Exposure: (Development stage): Regardless of whether or not there was itching or KATAYAMA DISEASE, the patient develops fever, fatigue, abdominal discomfort, nausea, and cough. Expatriates are particularly likely to develop fatigue and indigestion. There may be refusal to eat with weight loss. This stage can resemble ENTERIC FEVER, BRUCELLOSIS, or VISCERAL LEISHMANIASIS.

Later: When the disease is fully developed, there is either chronic DYSENTERY with MALABSORPTION or else symptoms of LIVER FAILURE with a large liver and spleen. The liver enlarges before the spleen, in contrast to MALARIA, which happens the other way. Many times it is the left lobe of the liver that is primarily enlarged; this may, to the inexperienced, appear to be spleen rather than liver. There might be sharp, shooting pains, weakness of the limbs, and numbness or tingling. This might also cause the same symptoms as SCHISTOSOMIASIS HEMATOBIUM.

Much Later: LIVER FAILURE occurs. The patient has thin limbs and an abdomen full of fluid so he looks pregnant. He may have JAUNDICE. He may bleed very easily, coughing up blood or developing major bruises from very minor injuries. At this stage his liver may be very small.

Complications: A common consequence is ANEMIA due to either blood loss or destruction of blood cells by the spleen. The growth of children is slowed. Adolescents may have delayed sexual maturity. It may cause RECTAL PROLAPSE, HEART FAILURE, vomiting blood. Rarely this may cause STROKE, BRAIN DAMAGE, MALABSORPTION, SHOCK, death.

Similar Conditions:

See Protocol C-7: Liver/Spleen Problems.

Initially: consider other causes of KATAYAMA DISEASE.

Development stage: consider ENTERIC FEVER, and the initial stages of other worms: TRICHURIASIS, STRONGYLOIDIASIS, HOOKWORM.

Late-stage disease: MALABSORPTION: see Protocol C-14. If there is LIVER FAILURE, check other causes in the *Disease Index*. There may be *VAGINITIS-type symptoms*. Males may have symptoms similar to SCHISTOSOMIASIS HEMATOBIUM with irritation of the bladder, bloody urine, or PROCTITIS. KIDNEY INFECTION may appear similar.

***Bush Laboratory**:* Maybe protein, urobilinogen, blood, or bilirubin in urine. It is possible to hatch the worm eggs and see the larvae with simple equipment. See Volume I, Appendix 2.

Higher-Level Care. *Laboratory:* Hospital laboratories can examine stool for the worm eggs, but they may be hard to find. It requires a good technician and many samples to conclude that a person does not have the problem. There will be increased eosinophils on a blood count during the initial stages in about half of the infected expatriates. *Practitioners:* Tropical/travel expertise is desirable. A surgeon may be necessary.

[1] Apply daily for 2 days while wearing the same clothing. On the third day, bathe, change clothes and bedding, and launder them.

Treatment:

Prevention: Use latrines. Avoid exposure to water with infected snails. Let a bucket of water without snails stand overnight before washing with it. During the initial skin stage (SWIMMER'S ITCH) PRAZIQUANTEL does not work as a preventive; it must be given again 2 months later.

Patient Care:

- Treat with PRAZIQUANTEL. OXAMNIQUINE works also and MEBENDAZOLE may work. NIRIDAZOLE is an old, dangerous drug that should no longer be used.
- In acute schistosomiasis (see KATAYAMA DISEASE) the symptoms can become worse with the first dose of PRAZIQUANTEL. One should use PREDNISONE or another STEROID for two days before giving PRAZIQUANTEL plus 3 days afterward.
- In advanced liver disease PROPRANOLOL might be helpful. In either case seek professional medical advice.
- Reportedly ARTEMISININ, a drug usually used for MALARIA, suppresses the disease without curing it. There is not yet any dosage schedule.

Results: Good in an otherwise-healthy person. You should evaluate whether the patient is cured by doing lab determinations at 1, 3, and 6 months after treatment. Where schistosomiasis coexists with HEPATITIS the prognosis is very poor.

SCIATICA

Cause: Variable.
Synonyms: Sciatic nerve irritation.
Definition: Sciatica is an inflammation of the right or left sciatic nerve, the nerve that runs from the lower back, across the buttock, and down the back side of the leg.
Entry category: Syndrome.

Mildly ill; Class 1-4; Worldwide.

Age: Usually adults. **Who:** Anyone, especially those with prior back trouble. **Onset:** Hours to days.

Clinical:

There is no fever with this in and of itself. Only when it is caused by another illness can you expect to see fever.

Necessary: The patient has pain in the low back, buttocks, down the back of one or both legs, or any combination of the above. Pushing the center of the buttock aggravates the pain in that leg. With the patient lying flat on his back, raising his leg at the ankle with the knee held straight, aggravates the pain in the back of the thigh. The pain may be sharp-shooting and there may also be pains of muscle cramps. The pain is worse on movement, with coughing, and with straining to have a bowel movement.

Causative Diseases: If BRUCELLOSIS causes this the episodes of pain are accompanied by fevers and general fatigue and joint pains. TUBERCULOSIS affecting the bones of the spine and also BURKITT LYMPHOMA may cause it.

Similar Conditions: If it lasts a long time, consider SLIPPED DISC.

Higher-Level Care. *Facilities* at level 3 or above may be most helpful. X-ray, MRI and lab can help with the diagnosis of the specific cause.

Treatment:

Like MUSCLE STRAIN.

SCOLIOSIS

Cause: Unknown, usually.
Synonym: Curvature of the spine.
Definition: Scoliosis is sideways curvature of the spine so that, instead of being dead center in the back, it curves toward the right or the left.

Mildly to moderately ill; Class 2-4; Worldwide.

Age: Usually teens and older. **Who:** Anyone. **Onset:** Gradual, over weeks to months.

Clinical:

This is curvature of the spine which usually begins in the teen years unless it is due to TUBERCULOSIS or BRUCELLOSIS or POLIO. One shoulder or hip is higher than the other, and the bone on the back of the higher shoulder or hip is more prominent than the other, giving a hunch-back appearance.

Treatment:

If the curvature is due to TUBERCULOSIS or BRUCELLOSIS, then medication is essential. If it is due to unknown causes but it is diagnosed early, it may be correctable by exercises alone. If it is allowed to continue, it may be correctable only with surgery, or not at all. Seek professional advice at level 4 or 5.

SCRUB TYPHUS

Cause: Rickettsia.
Synonym: Tsutsugamushi disease.
Excludes: Tick typhus which is listed under SPOTTED FEVER; murine typhus and louse-borne typhus which are described under TYPHUS in this Index and in the Regional Indexes.
Regional Notes: I, O, S, U.
Definition: Scrub typhus is a rickettsial disease that affects the entire body.

Mildly to very ill; Class 2-3; Regional; occurs in tropical rural Asia and Pacific areas. It is not present in the Americas, Africa, or the Mediterranean area.

Age: Any. **Who:** Bitten by a mite carrying the disease. These mites live in grasses and bite those walking by. **Onset:** Variable; incubation about a week.

Clinical:

Necessary: There is a gradual onset of fever which begins on the first day and rises each day thereafter until the fifth day. When the fever falls, it does so abruptly. There is always headache, light avoidance, red eyes, enlarged spleen, and constipation.

Sometimes: There is a tiny, black scab with a red halo where the mite bit (commonly on or near the genital area) and large, mildly tender lymph nodes nearby or further toward the trunk. Other nodes may also be enlarged but less so. The pulse may be slow relative to the fever. About the seventh day, the patient develops a measles-like rash which starts on the face and then spreads to the trunk and legs. Cough is common.

Complications: In 98% of the patients blind spots develop as a result of the disease. Deafness is also common. Death may occur during the first two weeks. Untreated pregnant women and older patients frequently die. The disease will make AIDS worse.

Similar Conditions: See Protocols C-8, C-9, C-11, and C-12. TYPHUS is similar but other symptoms precede the fever. Also see similar diseases listed under ARBOVIRAL FEVER. PLAGUE can appear similar but then the enlarged lymph nodes are extremely painful and tender. LEPTOSPIROSIS may be indistinguishable.

Bush Laboratory: Protein is in the urine.

Higher-Level Care. See Volume I, Appendix 13. *Laboratory:* Ordinary labs are useless. Very advanced laboratories with specific tropical/travel medical capabilities may be helpful. A test called PCR is specific but not sensitive; don't believe a negative result. *Facilities* with IV's and injectable antibiotics might also be helpful—level 2 or above. *Practitioners:* Tropical/travel medical expertise is most helpful.

Treatment:

Prevention: One dose of DOXYCYCLINE or CHLORAMPHENICOL can prevent the disease. However, it is better to use bug repellants.

Patient Care: Follow the general treatment for TYPHUS. DOXYCYCLINE and CHLORAMPHENICOL work fine for this. In northern Thailand and possibly some other areas, it is resistant to these drugs so you should use RIFAMPIN or AZITHROMYCIN. In pregnancy the treatment is a single dose of AZITHROMYCIN. Do not use CIPROFLOXACIN or any CEPHALOSPORIN.

SCURVY

Cause: Vitamin C deficiency.

Regional Notes: F, I, R..

Definition: Scurvy is a disease caused by a deficiency of Vitamin C (Ascorbic acid).

Mildly to moderately ill; Class 1; Worldwide, related to diet, common in tropical areas, especially refugee camps.

Age: Any; infants develop symptoms from 6-12 months of age. **Who:** Diet low in Vitamin C. Most common in hot/dry areas. **Onset:** Usually gradual, over days.

Clinical:

Scurvy does not cause a fever.

Necessary: A history of a diet lacking fresh fruits and vegetables.

Usually: There is weight loss; weakness; stiff leg muscles; swollen, bleeding gums resulting in loosened teeth which fall out easily; large tongue; enlarged lymph nodes; and dry, rough skin with tiny black and blue spots, like halos, around the bases of the hairs on the legs. There is swelling of the ankles and excessive bleeding: Nosebleeds, blood-red spots on the whites of the eyes, heavy menses, bloody urine, bloody stool, bloody vomitus, bleeding from minor wounds. There may be a putrid-sweet body odor. There may be swelling of the joints in the front of the chest, between the ribs and the breastbone, resembling rosary beads under the skin. This is similar to RICKETS but the bumps beside the breastbone are angular rather than round and the breast bone sticks out rather than being depressed.

Infants refuse to use their legs; they lie with their legs bent at the knees and hips, their feet turned inward. The legs are stiff. Their gums bleed with teething.

Complications: Occasionally sudden death or severe pain in the long leg bones.

Similar Conditions: *Weakness, stiffness, and weight loss*: MENINGITIS due to TUBERCULOSIS, HIV, and LEAD POISONING might be similar in children.

Swollen joints: See Protocol C-6. RICKETS is almost identical; if you suspect either, treat for both. In infants consider congenital SYPHILIS. Other types of MALNUTRITION (PELLAGRA, BERIBERI) may be similar and may coexist. Usually the bleeding gums are distinctive.

Bruising might also be caused by LIVER FAILURE.

Bush Laboratory: Diagnosis can be made with a blood pressure cuff. Inflate the cuff above the upper number of the patient's blood pressure, leave it there for 30 seconds, and then let it down. In scurvy this will result in a fine blue-red rash on the skin beyond the cuff. (The other diseases in which this test will be positive are HEMORRHAGIC FEVER, some MENINGITIS, and SEPSIS.) Urine and stool may be positive for blood.

Treatment:

Vitamin C is present in citrus fruits, papaya, and most fresh, green vegetables, as well as in most ordinary vitamin tablets.

Results: With treatment, improved in hours, completely better in a week.

SEABATHER'S ERUPTION

Definition: Seabather's eruption is an infestation with jellyfish larvae.

Age: Any; **Who:** Those who swim in the sea, particularly in the Caribbean area. **Onset:** Rapidly right after bathing.

Clinical:

This is a very itchy, spotted rash after swimming in the ocean, mainly under clothing pressure points, e.g. waistbands. With severe infestations, the patient may develop a fever. The spots may become inflamed; blisters and secondary infection are common. It is especially common in the Caribbean.

Treatment:

Frequent washing with soap and water, and DIPHENHYDRAMINE for the itching. Gentle electrical zapping as for snakebite might also help the itching. See Volume I, Chapter 9.

SEIZURES

Cause: Variable.

Synonyms: Convulsions, Fits.

Regional Notes: F, I, O, R, S, U.

Definition: Seizures are involuntary movements caused by abnormal spontaneous electrical activity in the brain.

Entry category: Syndrome.

Very ill during seizure, variable thereafter; Class 1-3; Worldwide, common, related to local illnesses.

***This is not a diagnosis; it gives a general approach to the problem. You still must figure out the cause of the seizures. See Symptom Protocol 7 A if you have not done so already.

Age: Any. **Who:** Anyone, especially with FEBRILE SEIZURE (children), DIABETES, after severe head injury, ALCOHOLISM, TOXEMIA (pregnant), MALARIA, MENINGITIS, ENCEPHALITIS, KIDNEY FAILURE, RESPIRATORY FAILURE, CYSTICERCOSIS, or HEAT ILLNESS, side-effect or overdose of certain medications or withdrawal from some drugs, STROKE. Some people have seizures from time to time for no apparent reason. Either they are just prone to them or seizures may result from a previous severe illness or injury. This is called EPILEPSY. There are good medicines to prevent the seizures. **Onset:** Suddenly, within seconds.

Clinical:

Necessary: If both right and left are affected, the patient is unconscious. Some or all muscles jerk or twitch rhythmically. Trembling or fluttering motions are not seizures.

Frequently: The patient is arched back. He is incontinent of urine, stool, or both. His eyes are rolled back. He may slow or stop his breathing and turn blue. He will be lethargic for a few minutes to an hour after such an episode.

Complications: Sometimes BRAIN DAMAGE.

Causative Diseases: Many diseases can cause seizures; almost anything that can cause unconsciousness can also cause seizures.

With no fever: consider HYPOGLYCEMIA, HYPERVENTILATION, TOXEMIA, EPILEPSY, ALCOHOLISM (withdrawal), SYPHILIS, STROKE, CYSTICERCOSIS, PLANT POISONING, DEMONIZATION (seizures tend to occur selectively during worship services), ADDICTION (withdrawal from downers). Injuries, especially head injuries, can also cause seizures.

With a fever: HEAT ILLNESS, FEBRILE SEIZURE, MENINGITIS, ENCEPHALITIS, MALARIA, TRICHINOSIS, SCHISTOSOMIASIS JAPONICUM, SEPSIS, RELAPSING FEVER.

Similar Conditions: TETANUS (almost continual spasms, not as much movement); PLANT POISONING (strychnine), SCURVY, POLIO, RHEUMATIC FEVER, RABIES, and RICKETS (general muscle spasms without loss of consciousness). See Protocol C-10 if the patient is merely unconscious.

Higher-Level Care. *Laboratory:* A large hospital lab may be able to do an electroencephalogram, and blood tests which may determine the cause of the problem. *Facilities:* Level 4 or 5. *Practitioners:* A neurologist is most helpful. For simple seizures a pediatrician or internist might suffice.

Treatment:

- Cool patients with fevers.
- Time the seizure with a clock or watch. If it lasts over five minutes **by the clock,** or if the patient has a second one before becoming conscious, he must be treated. If the patient has or might have MALARIA or DIABETES, give him something sugary to drink when he awakens or put a stomach tube in to give sugar water. Be sure to position him on his side, head down. Sugar may also be given by rectum.
- Use PHENYTOIN, PARALDEHYDE, DIAZEPAM, or PHENOBARBITAL to prevent more seizures.
- If a patient with a fever has a second seizure or if his seizure will not stop, he probably has cerebral MALARIA, MENINGITIS, or HEAT ILLNESS. Give PHENYTOIN SODIUM for EPILEPSY.

SEPSIS

Cause: Bacteria.

Synonyms: Septicemia, Septic shock.

Regional Notes: F, I, O, R, S, U.

Definition: Sepsis is an overwhelming whole-body bacterial infection where parts of the body which should be sterile are infected. It usually results from an inadequately treated local infection.

Entry category: Disease cluster.

Very ill; Class 4; Some forms may be contagious; Worldwide, related to level of medical care. Melioidosis is a particular type of sepsis that is prevalent in SE Asia and aboriginal Australia—it is tropical.

Age: Any; especially newborns and reproductive women. **Who:** Prior or current infection; injury or childbirth under unclean conditions; rupture of the bag of waters 18 hours or more before birth; HIV; LEPROSY; MALARIA; CANCER; pregnancy, those who have had their spleens removed for any reason; other diseases that decrease immunity. **Onset:** Few hours to a day or two; this frequently starts out as a localized infection such as PNEUMONIA or URINARY INFECTION, which then becomes a whole-body infection.

Clinical:

Necessary: The patient is unconscious or nearly so. His pulse and respiration are fast or irregular. He has an infection of some sort or had one recently. Either he has a high fever or he is cold and clammy. If it is an infant within 48 hours of birth, he may be irritable and have feeding difficulties but no fever.

Maybe: The source of the original infection may or may not be obvious. He may have abdominal pain with evidence of ACUTE ABDOMEN. He may have a musty body odor. His blood pressure may be low. He may have a red, spotted rash. If the original infection was PNEUMONIA, he will be short of breath. Vomiting is usual. The patient may have a low pulse pressure along with a change in his alertness.

Occasionally: There are little bits of blood beneath his fingernails, resembling splinters.

Women: Those who have just delivered or miscarried may have pus coming from the vagina, and pain in the genital area. See Chapter 7 in Vol. I regarding treatment.

Newborns: These will be lethargic and suck poorly; they may or may not have a fever. They vomit. They may have a low body temperature; diarrhea, a swollen abdomen, an infected umbilical cord and SEIZURES are common. They will have a weak cry and JAUNDICE. There may be signs of PNEUMONIA or MENINGITIS which will resemble or precede sepsis. There is no need to distinguish between these.

Complications: SEIZURES, SHOCK, death, which may occur rapidly.

Causative Diseases: Any disease for which an antibiotic is ordinarily prescribed.

Similar Conditions: See Protocols C-2, C-4, C-9, and C-10.

Bush Laboratory: An easy way to diagnose the problem is to draw some of the patient's blood into a glass (not plastic) syringe or test tube. Draw some normal blood into a similar syringe or test tube. Let both blood specimens clot with the syringes or tubes in an upright position (about an hour). With sepsis, the blood clot will form mostly on the bottom of the tube or syringe; a normal blood clot will form mostly along the side of the tube.

Higher-Level Care. *Laboratory:* A level 4 hospital lab can do blood cultures to determine which antibiotic is best. *Facilities:* IV's and injectable antibiotics are very important. The patient may require a monitored bed at level 4 or 5. *Practitioners:* Infectious disease with tropical/ travel expertise is most helpful.

Treatment:

Prevention: Treat minor infections promptly and adequately. Drain all ABSCESSes. A patient who has a heart murmur (see Volume I Chapter 1) should have antibiotics before any dental or surgical procedure and after any dirty injury or animal bite.

Patient Care: Send the patient to a hospital. Until then:

- Keep the patient in bed on his side, head down if unconscious. Check his airway.
- Use PROMETHAZINE or HYDROXYZINE to prevent vomiting. Place a stomach tube and give as much rehydration fluid as the patient will tolerate until his blood pressure and pulse are reasonably normal. See Volume I Appendix 1 for directions on how to make and use stomach tubes. See the first page of Volume 2 *Symptom Index* for a list of normal pulse and blood pressure numbers.
- Give a liquid diet by stomach tube as soon as possible.
- Check vital signs every 2 to 4 hours.
- Use IBUPROFEN and ACETAMINOPHEN alternately every 2 hours, plus cool bathing for fever.
- Try to find the source of infection and treat that. Drain any ABSCESS. See Volume I Appendix 1.
- Antibiotics:

➢ Ordinary Sepsis: Use (PENICILLIN plus CHLORAMPHENICOL) or an appropriate CEPHALOSPORIN. Intravenous OFLOXACIN is also good. You may substitute AMPICILLIN for PENICILLIN or COTRIMOXAZOLE for CHLORAMPHENICOL. Add METRONIDAZOLE or TINIDAZOLE if the patient is a woman who just had a baby, if this is due to PNEUMONIA, if the bowel is involved, or if it occurs after an injury. In infants use ACYCLOVIR plus high-dose AMPICILLIN & GENTAMYCIN or else ACYCYLOVIR plus CHLORAMPHENICOL or a third-generation CEPHALOSPORIN.

➢ Melioidosis: In Southeast Asia and aboriginal tropical Australia, in sepsis that started with PNEU-

MONIA or KIDNEY INFECTION, use Ceftazidine or one of the carbapenems (both under CEPHALOSPORIN) for 3 months followed by at least 3 months of COTRIMOXAZOLE.

- *Results:* 48 hours.

Septic Abortion

See SEPSIS and ABORTION.

SERUM SICKNESS

Entry category: Syndrome.

This is a complex type of ALLERGY, originally found to occur when an animal or human was injected with the serum of a dissimilar creature. It can also be caused by certain drugs, particularly ASPIRIN, ALLOPURINOL, IBUPROFEN, FUROSEMIDE, PENICILLIN, DILANTIN, STREPTOMYCIN, and SULFA drugs. It can also be caused directly by some diseases: LARVA MIGRANS, MENINGITIS, STREP THROAT (causing RHEUMATIC FEVER), DENGUE FEVER, MALARIA, HEPATITIS, for example. KATAYAMA DISEASE is one form of serum sickness. **Onset** is usually about 10 days after starting the drug or the introduction of the germ into the body.

Clinical:

Initially there may be nausea, vomiting, shortness of breath with wheezing, fever, chills, HIVES, prostration. After 2-16 days there may be protein in the urine and, in about half of the patients, a large-joint ARTHRITIS. In the skin there is first redness (warmth in Blacks), then a rash like MEASLES or HIVES. The lymph nodes may be enlarged.

Complications: KIDNEY FAILURE, HEART FAILURE, ARTHRITIS.

Similar Conditions: See Protocol C-12.

Treatment:

This should be medically determined and supervised.

SEXUALLY TRANSMITTED DISEASE

(Also see *Disease Index* entries for the individual diseases.)

Synonyms: STD, Venereal Disease.

Entry category: Disease cluster.

Regional Notes: F, I, M

Definition: Sexually transmitted diseases are bacterial diseases acquired through direct contact of the warm, moist surfaces of the body.

Clinical:

These diseases are GONORRHEA, CHANCROID, SYPHILIS, CHLAMYDIA, LYMPHOGRANULOMA VENEREUM, HERPES, DONOVANOSIS, which are all described separately. If you suspect any one of these, you should not try to diagnose, but to treat according to Protocol C-1, unless the particular diagnosis is obvious from the history. An example would be a spouse diagnosed in a laboratory as having one of these.

The symptoms of sexually transmitted diseases are as follows: For these purposes, the rectum is considered to be part of the genital area.

- Spontaneous sores in either sex, on the skin of the genital region, hands, breasts, or face. These are skin ulcers.
- Large lymph nodes in the groin in either sex.
- Burning with urinating or pus from the penis in a male.
- Vaginal pain or itching or discharge in a female, possibly with some bleeding.
- Swollen scrotum in a male.
- Low abdominal pain in a female; pain with intercourse.

Similar Conditions: See Protocols C-1, C-11 and C-12.

Skin bumps and ulcers: See the chart in C-1. Consider AMEBIC SKIN ULCER and DIPHTHERIA. Consider WARTS and VISCERAL LEISHMANIASIS (PKDL) if there are bumps.

Treatment:

Prevention: In the case of sexual assault or body fluid exposure, see Volume I, Chapters 9 and 2 respectively for prophylactic medications.

Patient Care: See Protocol C-1.

SHINGLES

Cause: Virus.

Synonym: Herpes zoster.

Definition: Shingles is a nerve infection with Herpes zoster, the causative virus of chicken pox. It secondarily affects the skin.

Mildly to moderately ill; Class 2; Contagious in that children can get CHICKEN POX from an adult with shingles. Worldwide.

Age: Mostly older adults; adults and children with DIABETES or HIV. **Who:** Almost anyone, but especially those with poor immunity. **Onset:** Over several days.

Clinical:

This is a painful (sometimes also itchy) rash[1] in a band, usually on one side of the trunk, sloping down from the back and around to the front. The rash breaks out after several days of pain in that area of skin. The rash never crosses the center line more than an inch. It may be on the face or the shoulder in which case it is in an area rather than a band. It may also affect the inside of the mouth and the white of the eye. Usually there are blisters at first, which then break and crust.

[1] Children do not commonly get shingles, and when they do get it, it may be painless.

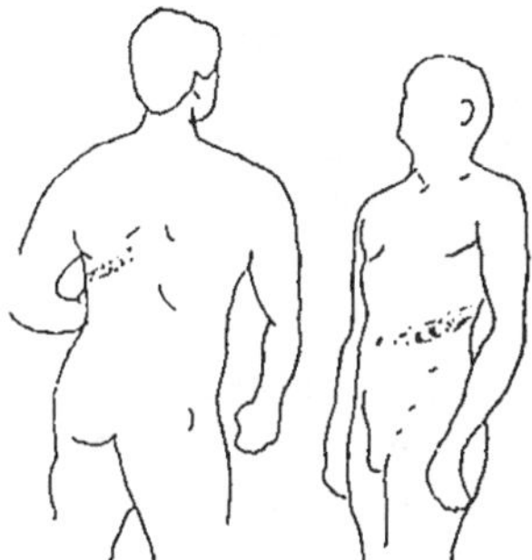

Shingles rash: It is higher on the back than on the front.

Similar Conditions: See Protocol C-8 if the eyes are involved. CHICKEN POX (whole body affected, itchy rather than painful), HERPES (usually just the face or genital area), TRENCH FEVER (similar pain, also general fever, body pains, fatigue; SPINAL NEUROPATHY (similar pains, usually also numbness, tingling, weakness, or bladder/bowel problems).

Treatment:

Prevention: Children exposed to adults who have shingles may get CHICKEN POX, but shingles is not directly contagious.

Patient Care: Cool wet-to-dry compresses (see Vol. I, Appendix 1) and pain medicines may be helpful. The rash lasts 2-3 weeks and the pain at least 6 weeks. ACYCLOVIR may work for treatment.

SHOCK

Cause: Variable.

Definition: Shock is a crisis in which the circulation of blood is inadequate to sustain life. (This refers to physiological shock, not to someone's being emotionally upset. Emotional upset is not shock even if the patient faints.)

Entry category: Syndrome.

***Life-threatening emergency!!!

Very ill; Class 4; Worldwide.

If this is from an insect sting or an injection, treat for ANAPHYLAXIS with EPINEPHRINE.

Age: Any. **Who:** Severe DEHYDRATION, blood loss, SEPSIS, some injuries, ACUTE ABDOMEN, THALLASEMIA, HEMORRHAGIC FEVER, treatment of RELAPSING FEVER. **Onset:** Within minutes with bleeding and ANAPHYLAXIS. Variable otherwise.

Clinical:

Necessary: The patient's skin is ashen, cool, and moist. If he is conscious, his pulse is fast. His blood pressure is low. He is not urinating much if at all, unless he had a full bladder beforehand. He is weak and lethargic. If you try to raise him to a sitting or standing position, he will lose consciousness. Anyone who can stand upright and remain conscious is not in shock.

Usually: Respiration is rapid.

Similar Conditions: Someone who is upset or excited will pass out and look as if he is in shock, but it lasts only a minute and it does not need treatment. Other similar diseases: SEPSIS; HYPOGLYCEMIA; sudden drop in blood pressure or temperature during MALARIA; RELAPSING FEVER; reaction to medication for RELAPSING FEVER (can both mimic and cause shock).

Higher-Level Care. Treatment in a facility that has IV's with fluids and injectable drugs is essential. Send the patient to whatever such facility is closest. Send him out as quickly as possible. He will probably die in your hands.

Treatment:

- If you can start an IV, do so. Give a salt solution (normal saline, Darrow's solution, or Lactated Ringer's) as quickly as possible until the patient's vital signs are reasonably normal or he has had 20 ml/kg.
- If you do not have IV's, position the patient on a slanted board, head down, and legs up. If you have elastic bandages, put them on the legs, rolling them snugly from the ankles up to the thighs. Be sure to start at the ankles. This squeezes the blood out of the leg veins so it goes into the body.
- Give fluids by stomach tube or rectum. Position the patient on his side and watch his airway continually.
- If the shock is due to infection or ACUTE ABDOMEN, treat that also.

SIBERIAN TICK TYPHUS

See SPOTTED FEVER. This is one type of spotted fever that occurs in eastern Europe, and throughout Asia. Although it is mostly a temperate and arctic problem, it falls in the category of tropical/travel medicine.

SICKLE CELL DISEASE

Cause: Heredity.

Synonyms: Sickle cell anemia, SS Hemoglobinopathy.

Regional Notes: E, F, I, M, R.

Definition: Sickle cell disease is an inherited problem, caused by the patient's having an abnormal hemoglobin. Hemoglobin is the red stuff in the blood that captures oxygen in the lungs and releases it in the rest of the body. The abnormal hemoglobin causes the red blood cells to assume abnormal shapes and break apart easily. This, in turn, causes the blood vessels to become plugged up; the usual symptoms of this disease follow from this.

Mildly to extremely ill; Class 2-3; Found worldwide mainly in persons of African genetic heritage; it rarely occurs in Arabs and Indians.

Age: Begins 3-6 months old, occasionally older. **Who:** Offspring of two parents, both of whom carry the gene for the condition. Both parents must be of one of these genetic heritages: African, Arab, Indian (i.e. South Asian), Greek. Consider the condition in places like Australia, Malaysia, and Indonesia, where there are ethnic communities that might be affected. It affects both sexes equally. **Onset:** Individual episodes over a few hours; recurrent crises.

Clinical: General

History:

There is almost always a family history of an illness consistent with sickle cell disease: large spleen; anemia; abnormal blood film; jaundice; severe infection. The spleen and liver swelling causes a continual ANEMIA and makes the patient prone to having overwhelming infections. (African spleens stay large until age 3-5 y.o.; then they shrink.)

There are two other problems with spleens swelling:

- If it suddenly enlarges, then the patient develops sudden ANEMIA. This tends to happen between ages 4 months and 5 years. The patient needs a blood transfusion the first time this happens. If it happens repeatedly, then the spleen should be removed.
- If it is very large after age 5 (most common in eastern Saudi Arabia and in India), then children stop growing. The spleen may be removed.

Growth and development: short height before puberty with a growth spurt afterwards and normal height. Puberty is delayed. There are very long limbs and narrow pelvis and shoulders. Weight is usually low throughout life.

➢ **Acute Chest Syndrome:**

In children over 2 years old, this is the most common cause of death: shortness of breath, chest pain that is worse with deep breathing, fever, turning bluish from lack of oxygen. Infection affecting the upper lungs is common. This may cause permanent lung damage. Permanent damage causes the chest to become more round in cross-section. The lung changes can lead to HEART FAILURE, causing swelling of the liver and of the legs and feet.

Patients over 20 years old tend to have more pain and shortness of breath but less fever with the acute chest syndrome. There is less often infection. The pain is usually in the lower chest rather than the upper chest. There may be sudden death associated with blood clots traveling to the chest.

During the last trimester of pregnancy and immediately after childbirth there is risk of this for the mother. (However, in developing areas many patients don't live long enough to become pregnant.) It is due to a combination of infection, chest pain (due to bone marrow emboli), which decreases the depth of breathing, and abnormal blood cells getting stuck in the lung's blood vessels.

➢ **Bone Crises:**

When blood clots travel to bones, there is severe bone pain—deep pains that never let up but are worse at night. There may be permanent bone damage. Children less than 5 y.o. commonly have swollen hands, feet, fingers, and toes; older children and adults (especially pregnant women) have bone crises in their long limb bones, backs, and pelvises. If there is infection in the bone(s), then there will be a high fever; see the entry OSTEOMYELITIS.

➢ **Kidney Crises:**

When clots travel to the kidneys there may be blood, protein, or urobilinogen in the urine, maybe large quantities of urine. With nephrotic KIDNEY FAILURE there is much protein in the urine and the patient has swelling of his/her legs and feet; prognosis is poor. With nephritic KIDNEY FAILURE there will be blood in the urine and shortness of breath; prognosis is good.

➢ **Skin Rash:**

When clots lodge in the skin, they may cause little bruise marks, the size of the heads of pins.

➢ **Neurological Crises:**

When clots go to the brain there may be symptoms of BRAIN DAMAGE or STROKE. The patient may have SEIZURES, coma, vomiting, and headache. He/she may become blind.

➢ **Aplastic Crises :**

This causes sudden ANEMIA. Usually this is due to infection with ERYTHEMA INFECTIOSUM which makes the bone marrow stop making blood for a little while. In normal people, this is no problem but with SCD it may be fatal. Epidemics occur every 3-7 years. Blood transfusion in this case is life-saving.

➢ **Leg Ulcers :**

These are most common in the Americas and between 10-30 y.o. First there is pain, then lightening or darkening, and hardening of the skin. The ulcers are deep and painful. They heal very slowly and frequently break open again and then heal again, lasting a long time (a matter of years). They heal by forming a ring of healing around the edges and then filling in to the center. The skin around the ulcers is darker than normal whereas the skin of the healed area is lighter than normal.

➢ **Gallstones:**

Gallstones develop in older patients.

➢ **Abnormal Erections:**

These are persistent and painful, may occur in children over 4 y.o. and in adults. There are two kinds: 1. Come-and-go: recurrent at night, lasting 3-6 hours, with normal function otherwise; 2. Major: lasting 24 hours or more, mostly in adults, frequently resulting in impotence. Usually people with major attacks have had episodic attacks before. Dehydration can contribute to the problem.

Complications: SCD may cause ANEMIA, HEART FAILURE, KIDNEY FAILURE, OSTEOMYELITIS, GALLBLADDER DISEASE, SEPSIS, STROKE even in children.

Similar Conditions:

See Protocols C-3, C-4, C-5, C-6, C-7, C-9, and C-13. The most common are listed below:

Hot, swollen body parts: CELLULITIS, ARTHRITIS.

Shortness of breath: See Protocol C-4.

Failure to grow well may look like ordinary MALNUTRITION, or HIV.

ANEMIA with large spleen and fatigue: Protocols C-3 and C-5.

Frequent fevers and infections—may resemble HIV INFECTION, MALARIA, ACUTE ABDOMEN, HEPATITIS, and RHEUMATIC FEVER.

Swelling of the hands: LOIASIS (Africa only) can cause similar swelling.

Bush Laboratory: If you measure hemoglobin, you will find ANEMIA. Urine during a crisis will probably contain excessive urobilinogen.

Higher-Level Care. See Volume I, Appendix 13.

Laboratory: Level 3 or more hospitals can do blood tests to show the sickle-shaped red cells under a microscope but these tests are unreliable if the patient has had a recent transfusion. They are also unreliable on babies under 3 months of age. A sophisticated lab can test normal people to see if they carry the gene and thus advise them concerning a marriage partner. Sometimes the problem is found on an ordinary blood smear. *Facilities:* There are many facilities at a level 3 or more that are useful: IV fluids, oxygen, transfusion capabilities, respiratory therapy. These facilities are so essential to survival that patients, once diagnosed, should make every effort to live near such a place. *Practitioners:* A hematologist is most helpful, or a generalist, pediatrician, or internist with experience.

Treatment:

❖ **Routine Patient Care:**

All patients should take FOLATE, ZINC, and medication to prevent MALARIA. The diet should contain animal products or else the patient should receive injections of VITAMIN B_{12}. MULTIVITAMINS might also be helpful.

❖ **Crisis Patient Care:**

Send the patient to a hospital. Otherwise and until:

- Give a large amount of fluid by mouth or stomach tube. Even slight DEHYDRATION can cause major problems. Use HYDROXYZINE or PROMETHAZINE to prevent vomiting.
- Keep the patient warm; cold tends to aggravate the problem.
- Give extra FOLATE or feed the patient fresh, raw, or only slightly-cooked leafy vegetables. Daily folate is critical in pregnancy.
- Children with this problem should be checked for blood in their stools and should be questioned as to diet. If there is blood in the stool or the patient eats a diet low in IRON or VITAMIN C, you should give IRON supplements but not if he has had multiple transfusions. Daily oral PENICILLIN from time of initial diagnosis until age 5 improves chances for survival. Pregnant women should all get IRON, VITAMIN C, and FOLATE.
- If you have pain medications, use these freely.
- Treat leg ulcers with packing and ointments (see TROPICAL ULCER). Sprinkling PHENYTOIN in the ulcers helps healing. If there is not a prompt response to local treatment, use oral antibiotics: PENICILLIN plus CHLORAMPHENICOL.
- When the spleen is very large, it is helpful to give daily PROGUANIL as a MALARIA preventive; this may decrease the spleen size within 6 months.
- Persistent bone pain with fever should be treated as OSTEOMYELITIS with CHLORAMPHENICOL plus CLOXACILLIN.
- For respiratory symptoms use PENICILLIN plus (ERYTHROMYCIN or AZITHROMYCIN).

❖ **Treatment of Abnormal Erections:**

There are some hormone treatments. One can try sedatives such as valium, exercise, pain relievers, cold showers, or cold compresses to the penis. In-hospital: hydration with drinking or IV fluids; some blood-pressure-lowering medicines (but NOT diuretics); oxygen inhalation; blood transfusion. Surgery may be helpful.

Results: Pain should improve within 24 hours. If it does not, the patient should be sent to a hospital.

SLIPPED DISC

Cause: Unknown or injury or overweight condition.
Synonyms: Herniated disc.
Definition: Slipped disc is a nerve irritation caused by the spinal cartilage pushing on the nerves where they come out between the bones.

Moderately ill; Class 2-3; Worldwide, frequency depends on heredity and culture. Not generally common; MUSCLE STRAIN and SCIATICA are similar and much more common.

Age: Adults, usually. **Who:** Anyone, sometimes hereditary or may be due to FLUOROSIS, BRUCELLOSIS, or TUBERCULOSIS. **Onset:** Usually sudden, possibly gradual.

Clinical:

Necessary: The patient has excruciating neck or back pain.

Usually: The pain is sharp and it shoots down the legs or arms. In the case of back and leg pain, holding the leg straight at the knee and raising it by bending at the hip, causes severe pain in the back of the thigh. The patient cannot walk well if at all.

Sometimes: He may be weak or numb or tingling in one or both legs, and may not be able to walk or urinate or both. If the slipped disc is in the neck, then the pain goes down one or both arms with weakness or numbness in the arm or hand.

Causative Diseases: BRUCELLOSIS, BURKITT LYMPHOMA, FLUOROSIS (neck only), TUBERCULOSIS. It might happen for no good reason at all.

Similar Conditions: Many. The most common similar disease is ARTHRITIS that affects the lower spine. Also consider SCIATICA and MUSCLE STRAIN. With a very gradual onset and stiff weakness, consider TROPICAL SPASTIC PARAPARESIS. With slipped disc, straight leg raising (see Vol. I, Chapter 11) of the leg on the good side may worsen the pain on the bad side.

Higher-Level Care. See Volume I, Appendix 13. This is essential, at a level 3 or higher facility with an orthopedic surgeon or a neurosurgeon.

Treatment:

If unable to send out: Six weeks of **absolute** bed rest except that the patient may get up to go to the bathroom to move his bowels. Urination should be into a urinal. Use pain medication. If he lies on his back, he should have a pillow under his knees. He may lie on either side, but not belly down. If the problem is in the neck rather than the lower back, the patient should wear a collar as for a broken neck. Seek outside advice how long to continue this. Other treatment is not feasible in remote areas. Check for numbness and weakness of the limbs. If the patient has either, send him within a day. If he has trouble urinating use a urinary catheter until you can send him. See Appendix 1 in Volume I. Treat BRUCELLOSIS or TUBERCULOSIS if necessary.

SMOKE INHALATION

Definition: Smoke inhalation is a malfunction of the airways due to the irritant effect of smoke. Symptoms range from a slight cough to moderate shortness of breath to sudden RESPIRATORY FAILURE. This can develop suddenly up to 72 hours after exposure. High humidity and THEOPHYLLINE may be helpful. Use no CODEINE for the cough unless a physician approves. A similar disease is ASTHMA. Also see Protocol C-4.

SPINAL NEUROPATHY

Entry category: Syndrome.

This term refers to problems that develop in the spinal cord, sometimes from injury, other times from diseases.

Causative diseases are: SCHISTOSOMIASIS (mostly MANSONI but may be one of the others), TUBERCULOSIS, HERPES, MENINGITIS, SYPHILIS, ENTERIC FEVER, CANCER, LYME DISEASE, some viral infections, some immunizations, any tumor or injury of the spine. The onset can be sudden or gradual. It may be symmetrical or asymmetrical, frequently with back pain which wraps around the trunk like a band, somewhat higher in the back and lower in the front. (This is similar to SHINGLES.) There is numbness and/or tingling and/or weakness of one or both limbs or the genital area. The patient may have trouble with starting to urinate or with passing stool or he may be incontinent or impotent. If the underlying disease is diagnosed and treated promptly, there may be recovery. Otherwise the prognosis is poor. In any case, if you consider this diagnosis, seek care at a level 4 or 5.

SPOTTED FEVER

Cause: Rickettsiae.

Synonyms: Rickettsiosis, Boutonneuse fever.

Includes: Tick typhus and *Rickettsial pox.* In many places there are place names attached to the term "Tick Typhus". Includes Mediterranean tick typhus and African tick typhus.

Excludes: Rocky Mountain Spotted Fever, also known as American Tick Typhus, a disease of the Americas. This disease looks quite different and is more serious than the Tick Typhus and Rickettsial pox described below. For Rocky Mountain Spotted Fever, See the SPOTTED FEVER entry in the M (Americas) *Regional Notes*.

Regional Notes: All regions.

Moderately to very ill; Class 2-3.

Age: Any. **Who:** Tick-bitten for tick typhus. Rickettsial pox is transmitted by mites, or by consuming contaminated food and drink. It is mainly urban, in South Africa and northeastern Asia. **Onset:** Rapid; incubation less than 12 days.

Clinical:

➢ **Tick Typhus:**

There is sudden onset of a high fever, with headache, stiff neck, and red eyes. A rash breaks out by day 4 or 5. It begins on the limbs and may involve the palms and soles. The rash is heaviest on the wrists and ankles. It is not itchy. There may be a scar from a tick bite. There may be severe muscle pains and vomiting. The patient may become delirious and may develop GANGRENE. Lymph nodes are likely to be large.

➢ **Rickettsial Pox:**

There is sudden onset of fever. The rash, consisting of tiny blisters, which resemble CHICKEN POX, starts on day 2 of the fever; it does not involve the palms or soles. There may be a scar from the tick bite - black spot(s) with red halos. Headache is common. There are muscle pains and large lymph nodes. There may be vomiting, a stiff neck, dizziness, and an enlarged spleen.

Complications: KIDNEY FAILURE, STROKE, internal bleeding.

Similar Conditions: Rickettsial pox may be similar to CHICKEN POX. For tick typhus consider ARBOVIRAL FEVER and the similar diseases. See Protocols C-2, C-8, C-10, C-11, and C-13. The distinctions between many of these diseases can be subtle. If tick typhus is a possibility, treat for it. In some areas it can be rapidly fatal if not treated.

Higher-Level Care. *Laboratory*: A blood test, the Felix-Weil, is available. It is not very reliable. *Practitioners*: Tropical/travel medical expertise is essential.

Treatment:

Prevention: Avoid tick bites: exclude dogs from houses, protect arms and legs when pushing through brush; do not sleep on the ground.

Patient Care: For Rickettsial pox, use only DOXYCYCLINE or RIFAMPIN. For other types of spotted fever: DOXYCYCLINE, CHLORAMPHENICOL, CIPROFLOXACIN, RIFAMPIN plus ERYTHROMYCIN, possibly CLARITHROMYCIN. You should treat until 3 days after the fever is gone.

Results: Fever will drop within 4 days, usually.

SPRUE

Cause: Unknown.

Synonyms: Tropical enteropathy, Tropical sprue, Post Infectious Malabsorption.

Regional Notes: F, I, O, R, S, U. It may occur anywhere but it is mainly in Asia, south of the 40th parallel; in the Pacific islands and northern Australia; in West Africa and Africa, south of the DRC; in South America, north of the Amazon; throughout Central America and the Caribbean.

Definition: Sprue is a malfunction of the bowel, due to some unknown factor associated with residence in certain tropical areas.

Moderately ill; Class 1-2; Nearly worldwide, especially India, Southeast Asia, and the Caribbean. It is rare in Africa except in Nigeria and South Africa.

Age: Usually adults. **Who:** Anyone, especially expatriates but natives can get it also. **Onset:** Usually slow, within 6 months of arriving in an area; the onset might also be rapid on occasion and the diarrhea always lasts at least 3-4 months.

Clinical:

Necessary: Continual or recurrent severe diarrhea which is foul, greasy, and floating. There is no fever from this. The patient has much gas; loud, rumbling bowel sounds; and a bloated abdomen (gas, not fluid).

Usually: There is an initial sensitivity in the mouth; ALCOHOL or acidic or spicy foods cause pain. Then the patient complains of fullness in the upper central abdomen. The diarrhea starts in the morning and it may at first alternate with constipation.

Later: The tongue becomes red and shiny and blisters or ulcers form within the mouth. There may be vertical cracks in the lips. The patient develops ANEMIA (in the Americas only), has loss of appetite, weight loss, weakness, and is likely to become apathetic and irritable, with DEPRESSION and inability to concentrate. Physical exam shows a large, non-tender liver; there may be mild JAUNDICE.

Similar Conditions: MALNUTRITION or ANEMIA from other causes. PELLAGRA can look very similar, but it also causes excessive saliva production which sprue does not. See Protocol C-14.

Bush Laboratory: Urine dipsticks used on the stool show a stool pH of 6 or less.

Higher-Level Care. See Volume I, Appendix 13. A level 4 or 5 facility with a gastroenterologist experienced in tropical/travel medicine is most appropriate.

Treatment:

DOXYCYCLINE, COTRIMOXAZOLE, or AMPICILLIN. FOLATE is essential, as well as a low-fat, high-protein diet. Give a shot of VITAMIN B_{12} if you can. If you are not able to and the patient does not improve within a week, minced, raw beef liver taken orally is a substitute for the B_{12} injection. B_{12} by mouth is not adequate for treatment nor is cooked liver.

STD: See SEXUALLY TRANSMITTED DISEASE

Also see Protocol C-1.

STREP INFECTION; STREP THROAT

Cause: Bacteria.

Synonyms: Tonsillitis, Bacterial pharyngitis.

Includes: Scarlet Fever.

Excludes: RHEUMATIC FEVER

Regional Notes: F, I.

Definition: Strep infection is a throat infection with Group A beta-hemolytic streptococci. Scarlet Fever is Strep infection with a rash.

Mildly ill; Class 1 usually, occasionally Class 4; Contagious; Worldwide, common everywhere.

Age: Any. **Who:** Anyone. **Onset:** Sudden. Incubation for scarlet fever is 1-4 days.

Clinical:

Necessary: Adults have a sore throat and pain with swallowing; children have either abdominal pain or a sore throat or both.

Usually: The patient has a fever. His breath may have a foul odor. He has no cough and no stuffy nose. The patient's tonsils are red and swollen, with white pus spots on them. His tongue is spotted like a strawberry. Neck lymph nodes in front are swollen and tender.

Sometimes: If the patient has a fine, red rash except for a pale circle around his mouth, he has SCARLET FEVER. The rash appears smooth and lobster-color at first, being worse in the skin folds. Then it appears like a sunburn. Finally it has a sandpapery texture. It may eventually peel. It begins on the lower body and moves up. This is simply a STREP THROAT with a rash and sometimes vomiting, fatigue, and whole body pains. The rash lasts 5-7 days without treatment.

Complications: RHEUMATIC FEVER and KIDNEY FAILURE, usually nephritic type. An ABSCESS may form on a tonsil which must be treated in a hospital facility. It can be fatal.

Similar Conditions: The most common confusion is between strep throat and a viral infection. With a viral infection the onset is gradual; pain is not severe; nodes in the neck are not enlarged; there are watery eyes and a runny nose; the throat is red with tiny blisters and ulcers. With a strep throat, the onset is sudden; pain is severe; the nodes in the neck are large and tender; the eyes and nose are normal; the throat is red with white pus on the tonsils.

Large Lymph Nodes: See Protocol C-12.

Abnormal tonsils: MONONUCLEOSIS and DIPHTHERIA can look identical; the only reliable distinction in most areas is that with MONONUCLEOSIS the patient still has a fever and fatigue after 3 days of antibiotic.

Fever and abdominal pains: ENTERIC FEVER (apathetic), PNEUMONIA (rapid respiration), MALARIA (more than one chill). Protocol C-9.

Fever and rash: See Protocol C-2.

Higher-Level Care. *Laboratory:* A hospital, level 3, can culture the bacteria or do a rapid test for strep. *Facilities:* If the patient is very ill, then IV fluids, injectable antibiotics may be appropriate.

Treatment:

PENICILLIN or ERYTHROMYCIN for a full 10 days. Taken for less time, it does not prevent the development of RHEUMATIC FEVER. AZITHROMYCIN is a very good alternative since it is eliminated from the body very slowly. Use this treatment for ANY sore throat in a patient with prior RHEUMATIC FEVER, with RHEUMATIC FEVER in the family, or with a heart murmur.

Results: 2-3 days. The patient is no longer infectious 48 hours after beginning antibiotics.

STRESS

Definition: Stress is physical illness with emotional causes.

Entry category: Syndrome.

Each person has his own peculiar pattern of response to stress. Some have increased or decreased appetite with weight gain or loss. Some people develop abdominal pain with vomiting or diarrhea. Some get headaches, neck pain, or heavy chest pain. The patient may urinate frequently. Children may start bedwetting after having been dry. They may be very nervous with insomnia or day-night reversal and may sigh frequently. Adults and older children may be short of breath. See DEPRESSION also as these are frequently associated.

If a person under stress has physical symptoms which he has had before and if, in addition, his vital signs are reasonably normal, he probably has another stress reaction. Therapy is directed toward the symptoms (for example, ASPIRIN for the headache) and relieving the stress. It may be difficult for achievers to withdraw from a situation when they think this is giving up. An authority should encourage or order them to withdraw, thus removing moral responsibility. See Protocol 10-B for other, similar conditions.

STROKE

Cause: Variable.

Synonyms: Apoplexy, Cerebrovascular accident, CVA.

Regional Notes: F, M, O, R, S.

Definition: Stroke is brain damage caused by interruption of the circulation to the brain.

Very ill; Class 3; Worldwide.

Age: Any; mostly adults but sometimes children, particularly those with SICKLE CELL DISEASE. **Who:** Varies with the cause. In tropical areas, usually due to some infectious disease; in Blacks, frequently HYPERTENSION, prior HEART FAILURE (valvular), RHEUMATIC FEVER. May be due to head injury. **Onset:** Variable but usually sudden.

Clinical:

Necessary: The patient has one or more of the following: Slurred speech, drooping of half of his face, weakness or paralysis on one side of his body, lethargy or loss of consciousness, or SEIZURE.

Usually: The weakness or paralysis is initially floppy and becomes stiff later. Because of the weakness the patient may appear uncoordinated and have trouble walking.

Sometimes: The patient understands speech and knows what he wants to say, but cannot say it. Confusion and trouble swallowing are common.

Occasionally: There may be dizziness, numbness and tingling, fainting, irregular or slow respiration, incontinence of urine. If there is a severe headache at onset, the patient may have a stiff neck like MENINGITIS.

Causative Diseases: *Without fevers*: TOXEMIA (if pregnant), head injury, HYPERTENSION, CYSTICERCOSIS, SICKLE CELL DISEASE, SYPHILIS, HYDATID DISEASE, SCHISTOSOMIASIS JAPONICUM, ALTITUDE SICKNESS, CHAGA'S DISEASE.

With fevers: RELAPSING FEVER, DIPHTHERIA, TYPHUS, RHEUMATIC FEVER, LARVA MIGRANS, AMEBIC LIVER DISEASE, ENCEPHALITIS, MENINGITIS.

Similar Conditions: POLIO (onset slower, usually lower limbs only), RABIES, SYPHILIS, BERIBERI. See Protocol 10-B.

Higher-Level Care. See Volume I, Appendix 13. A level 4 or 5 hospital with a neurologist and rehabilitation facilities is most appropriate. If the patient is having trouble swallowing, a level 2 or 3 hospital might help with IV's to prevent dehydration.

Treatment:

Send the patient to a hospital if possible. If you cannot, then treat whatever disease (if any) caused this. The patient may not be able to swallow; he may need a stomach tube, a liquid diet, and fluids to prevent MALNUTRITION and DEHYDRATION. See Volume I, Appendix 1. Be sure to position him head down so he will not choke if he vomits. Check his airway. Have a family member daily move each of his limbs as far as it will go in all directions. This will prevent stiffening. The patient should be turned at least every 2 hours during the day and every 4 hours during the night to prevent BEDSORES. No other treatment is possible in a remote location.

Results: Recovery is unpredictable; it ranges from none to complete.

STRONGYLOIDIASIS

Cause: Worm.

Synonyms: Pinworm (British), Threadworm (American). Swollen Baby Syndrome: *see* STRONGYLOIDIASIS in Index U.

Regional Notes: All regions. It is especially common in Southeast Asia and the western hemisphere.

Definition: Strongyloidiasis is a bowel infestation or a whole-body infection with the worm Strongyloides stercoralis.

Not ill to very ill; Class 1 (usual) or 4 (with SEPSIS); Widespread in tropical climates, especially those with sandy soil.

Age: Any. **Who:** Anyone with skin touching infected soil or anyone eating soil-contaminated foods. Once a person has it, he will reinfect himself. **Onset:** Variable.

Clinical:

➢ **Bowel Infection:**

Either there are no symptoms at all or abdominal pain plus ANEMIA, or an itchy rectal-genital area. There may be an itchy, red rash (raised spots or lines) where the worm larvae penetrated the skin. The lines may be on the buttocks or lower back, radiating up from the rectum; otherwise they are on parts of the body that contacted soil. These lines last for a few hours to a few days and then diasppear. These lines or spots are less definite than for LARVA MIGRANS. They recur multiple times. The larvae migrate through the lungs causing a temporary fever and a cough similar to ASCARIASIS, but it is usually not as severe.

Maybe: After the worm enters the bowel, the patient may develop diarrhea, possibly with MALABSORPTION and weight loss. If you look carefully, you may see the worms. They are the size and shape of a comma in small print. This disease may cause constipation, cravings, DYSENTERY, MALABSORPTION, MALNUTRITION, ANEMIA.

➢ **Whole-Body Infection:**

There are always some abdominal complaints: nausea, vomiting, diarrhea, pain, bleeding. There are also respiratory complaints: cough or shortness of breath.

Complications: This may cause SEPSIS in the presence of PREDNISONE and related drugs, or in the presence of the following conditions which decrease natural immunity: HIV INFECTION, LEPROSY, pregnancy, chronic MALARIA, TUBERCULOSIS.

Similar Conditions: *Abdominal pain plus ANEMIA*: HOOKWORM, TRICHURIASIS, DYSENTERY, SICKLE CELL DISEASE.

Itchy rectum: LARVA MIGRANS, TAPEWORM, ENTEROBIASIS, ALLERGY, CANDIDIASIS.

Severe diarrhea: See Protocol C-14.

Bush Laboratory: Do the strongyloides hatching test, Volume I, Appendix 2.

Higher-Level Care. Speedy referral is necessary if the patient is very ill. See Volume I, Appendix 13. *Laboratory:* Hospitals can do stool tests, but the best tests done by good technicians still detect only 1/4 to 1/2 of all cases. There will be increased eosinophils in the blood, but this occurs in other diseases also. *Facilities:* If there is SEPSIS, IV fluids and injectable antibiotics at a level 3 or above facility are essential. *Practitioner:* Someone experienced in tropical/travel diseases.

Treatment:

THIABENDAZOLE, IVERMECTIN, and ALBENDAZOLE are the only drugs that have a high cure rate. IVERMECTIN is now the drug of choice and the only drug you should use if the patient has a whole-body infection. MEBENDAZOLE, and PYRANTEL PAMOATE have a much lower cure rate. LEVAMISOLE kills only the larval stage of the worm. The patient will reinfect himself if there are any worms left at all. If the first treatment fails, give a second treatment for double the time. CAMBENDAZOLE is a veterinary drug which reportedly works well with no side-effects.

SWIMMER'S ITCH

Cause: larval form of human or animal schistosomes; see SCHISTOSOMIASIS.

Synonyms: Cercarial dermatitis.

Definition: Swimmer's itch is an allergic reaction to penetration of the skin by larval schistosomes.

Age: Any; **Who:** Those swimming or bathing in water inhabited by human or animal schistosomes. **Onset:** Suddenly, within minutes of exposure.

Clinical:

Sudden onset of severe itching, redness, and swelling of the skin. The symptoms are much worse with animal (usually water bird) schistosomes than with human schistosomes. In areas with human SCHISTOSOMIASIS, see KATAYAMA DISEASE to know what to look for a 3-6 weeks hence. The problem will last 2-3 days without treatment and resolve itself.

Treatment:

Prevention: Immediate rubbing alcohol on the skin, as soon as the problem is first noticed. Take along a bottle of alcohol whenever swimming in a lake where there are water birds.

Patient Care: DIPHENHYDRAMINE, steroid creams. Using PRAZIQUANTEL at this stage will not prevent the development of human SCHISTOSOMIASIS. With water bird schistosomes, the parasites cannot develop anyway.

SYPHILIS (venereal)

Cause: Spirochete.

Synonyms: Lues, Treponematosis.

Regional Notes: All regions.

Definition: Syphilis is an infection with the spirochete Treponema pallidum.

Includes: Venereal syphilis only, in this entry.

Not ill to very ill; Class 1-3; Contagious; Worldwide and very common in the tropics.

Note: Venereal syphilis is sexually transmitted; endemic syphilis is transmitted non-sexually. There are three kinds of endemic syphilis: PINTA (Americas only; see M Index), TREPONARID (arid areas only; see this Index and *Regional Indices*), and YAWS (humid areas only; see this *Index* and *Regional Indices*). Venereal syphilis, PINTA, TREPONARID, and YAWS are all closely related diseases; each gives partial immunity to the others. SYPHILIS (i.e., venereal syphilis) is described here; see the separate listings for the three kinds of endemic syphilis.

Age: Any; usually adults but sexually abused children may also get it; babies of infected mothers. **Who:** Those who are promiscuous or have a promiscuous partner; children born to infected mothers. **Onset in adults:** Incubation time 9-90 days, from infecting contact until appearance of primary ulcer. Incubation 2 weeks to 6 months until symptoms of secondary syphilis. Usually there are no symptoms at all for the next two years; Incubation 1-20 years until symptomatic tertiary syphilis. **Onset in newborns:** Incubation to primary and secondary, up to 2 years. Incubation to tertiary, a few months to 20 years. **Onset with HIV INFECTION:** the symptoms of primary and secondary syphilis may occur at the same time, and progression of the disease to tertiary may be much faster.

Clinical (Usually):

➢ **Primary Syphilis:**

This starts with a painless, round ulcer on the genital area, usually only one, usually swollen at the base, usually without pus. Non-genital primary ulcers (face, hands, buttocks) may be painful and not swollen. Painless enlargement of the groin (or the neck) lymph nodes starts a week later, usually on both sides. The enlarged nodes are hard and are not stuck to the flesh around them. The skin over top has a normal appearance.

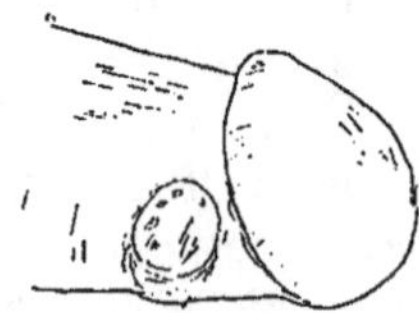

Primary Syphilis of the penis; note the swelling.

➢ **Secondary Syphilis:**

This develops about 6 weeks after primary syphilis but it may develop at the same time in patients who are HIV infected. Secondary syphilis may occur without the ulcer of primary syphilis, or primary syphilis without the symptoms of secondary. In the latter case, primary syphilis may advance directly to tertiary. The secondary stage happens but the patient is not aware of it.

These are the most common scenarios:

- A symmetrical, red- or brown-spotted rash (which may be subtle) develops mainly on the trunk and face; it may also include the limbs, palms, and soles.
- The patient may have fever, headache, enlarged and tender lymph nodes, weight loss, loss of appetite, and fatigue.
- The patient may have round, painless, white patches on moist, pink surfaces, silver-gray in color, with red halos. He may have splits in the skin by the side of his mouth, long grooves or an ulcer

on his tongue. He may have bleeding gums so the condition resembles SCURVY.

- He may have flat-topped, pale, moist "warts" near the site of the primary ulcer[1], sometimes elsewhere.
- Patches of hair on his head or his eyebrows may fall out. The head has a moth-eaten appearance.
- Secondary syphilis may cause spontaneous ABORTION. Rarely there is HEPATITIS, IRITIS, MENINGITIS.

➢ **Tertiary Syphilis:**
This may be totally without symptoms. When there are symptoms, they occur 10-30 years later in about 2/3 of those who have had primary or secondary syphilis. This may affect many different parts of the body, as follows:

Skin/face: A patient may have lumps under his skin. The lumps that form may break open to become ulcers resembling TROPICAL ULCERS which heal very slowly if at all. If this affects the face, it can eat a big hole in the roof of the mouth or destroy the nose.

Head/Brain: It may cause STROKE, SEIZURES; paralysis (usually stiff); leaking stool or urine; sharp, shooting pains in limbs; insanity; impotence; double vision; blindness; unequal pupils; or uncoordination. His gait will be abnormal. Uncoordination is always worse with closed eyes; the patient cannot tell where his limbs are without looking at them. He will probably have trembling, poor handwriting, slurred speech, and pupils which change size with focusing but not with light shone in them. He finally becomes bedridden and dies with BRAIN DAMAGE.

Mental symptoms: If the patient becomes insane, this usually begins at age 35-50. It starts with headache and insomnia, trouble concentrating, and easy fatigue. Then his personality changes, becoming either stupid or grandiose. He may have day-night reversal. Usually he is unaware of his poor functioning.

Eyes: He may have KERATITIS or IRITIS, see flashes of light, and have distorted vision. This is particularly common in the presence of HIV INFECTION.

Mouth: There may be longitudinal cracks in the tongue.

Heart: There may be an irregular pulse, especially with lying down, and ANGINA (chest pain) or HEART FAILURE. His pulse pressure may be high. He may be dizzy because of this.

Testicles: Painless lumps may form.

Limbs: Slow-growing, painful lumps may form in the bones. The joints may be swollen and move abnormally. Sometimes a joint may be grossly swollen and deformed but relatively painless.

[1] Not all genital warts are due to syphilis. Some are viral. Warts due to syphilis are usually moist and they have a broad rather than narrow base.

➢ **Syphilis During Pregnancy:**
Syphilis during pregnancy causes miscarriages during the last 6 months as well as stillbirths.

➢ **Congenital Syphilis:**
Onset before birth or before age 2 (most after 4months): Abnormally large placenta, large liver, spleen, and/or lymph nodes; skin rash; runny nose (as if born with allergies); white patches in his mouth, hoarseness, skin bumps that look like warts, will not use limbs (not true paralysis but refuses to use limbs because of pain); JAUNDICE, ANEMIA, poor growth. He may have brittle bones that fracture with slight movement.

Age 2-25 onset: Skull bone bossing (bones bulge out on the forehead, and above ears), depressed bridge of the nose, shins bow forward, KERATITIS, hearing loss, notched permanent two front teeth; painless swelling of both knees, any symptom of tertiary syphilis such as paralysis, uncoordination, and insanity.

Similar Conditions: Very many, too many to list all. See the relevant C protocols.

Primary syphilis is similar to other SEXUALLY TRANSMITTED DISEASEs. Its distinguishing characteristics are that there is usually only one ulcer, there is swelling beneath the ulcer, and it is both round or oval and painless.

Secondary syphilis See Protocol C-2. Syphilis can be confused with INFLUENZA or MEASLES or any other mild illness with a fever, but the rash of syphilis develops slowly, over weeks. Syphilic warts do not resemble ordinary dry WARTS since they have moist, flat, light-colored surfaces. They differ from the wart-like skin bumps of DONOVANOSIS in that they are skin color or pale whereas those caused by DONOVANOSIS are red. The warts of syphilis clear within a week with PENICILLIN but those of DONOVANOSIS take more than two weeks with any antibiotic.

Tertiary syphilis affecting the heart may be similar to HEART FAILURE due to bad valves. BERIBERI causes leg weakness also, but the trouble walking is no worse in the dark and the pains of BERIBERI are more burning. The bone problems can be similar to the other diseases listed in Protocol C-6. Some MALNUTRITION can be nearly identical but it is reversed with MULTIVITAMINS. Tertiary syphilis is one of many causes of BRAIN DAMAGE. See Protocol C-10 B: Confusion and/or Lethargy.

Congenital syphilis: RICKETS, SCURVY, HIV INFECTION, THALLASEMIA.

Higher-Level Care. Speedy referral for syphilis in a newborn and tertiary syphilis is very desirable. See Volume I, Appendix 13.

Laboratory: Fairly simple blood tests are available which may give false positives (the test indicates the patient has the disease when he does not) or false negatives (the test indicates he does not have the disease when he, in fact has it). More reliable tests are more expensive and less available. The blood tests for syphilis should become negative a year after treatment for primary syphilis, two years after treatment for secondary syphilis, and five years after treatment for tertiary syphilis.

Since venereal syphilis and the various forms of endemic syphilis (PINTA, YAWS, TREPONARID) are all closely related, all laboratory tests will be positive regardless of which form (venereal or endemic) of the disease the patient has. This should be kept in mind when missionary parents are confronted with a question of childhood sexual abuse. **A positive blood test for syphilis can readily be acquired non-sexually in the Third World.**

Practitioner: An abstinence-based, sexually transmitted disease clinic is ideal for primary and secondary. A pediatrician should treat a newborn. An infectious disease specialist should manage tertiary syphilis.

Treatment:

Prevention: Find and treat sexual contacts. Wash your hands well. Wear gloves while doing physical exams on high-risk patients.

Patient Care: Unless you are very sure of the diagnosis, treat according to Protocol C-1 rather than for syphilis alone. PENICILLIN is still the drug of choice for this.

Caution: With the first dose of PENICILLIN the patient might have a DRUG ERUPTION. Do not stop the medication for that.

Before starting antibiotic, give one dose of DIPHENHYDRAMINE, if you have it, an hour before the first dose. Then give PENICILLIN. Syphilis requires continual treatment without missing doses. Many of the effects of *tertiary* SYPHILIS will not change in spite of treatment, but treatment may prevent their worsening. DOXYCYCLINE, ERYTHROMYCIN,[1] AZITHROMYCIN,[2] CEPHALOSPORIN or CHLORAMPHENICOL in usual doses are also effective. Because of problems with keeping people on medicine, WHO recommends benzathine PENICILLIN; one injection replaces ten days of drug by mouth. Infants born with the disease should have PENICILLIN for 4 weeks.

TAPEWORM

Cause: Flat worm.
Includes: Diphyllobothriasis (fish), Hymenolepiasis (rat), Taeniasis (beef and pork).
Regional Notes: E, F, I, M, O, R, U.
Definition: Tapeworm is a bowel infestation with one of the flat worms listed above.

Not ill to mildly ill; Class 2; Some contagious; Worldwide, related to diet. *Beef and/or pork tapeworm* is found almost worldwide. *Fish tapeworm* is found in temperate climates and in fish from fresh or slightly brackish water, 4°-25°C (39°-77°F), having vegetation and not fast flowing. There must be some (but not gross) contamination by raw sewage. Currently it is found almost exclusively across northern Russia and in parts of South America. It used to be prevalent in Scandinavia and eastern Europe. *Rat tapeworm* is common in Sicily, Argentina, Southeast Asia, and the southern areas of the former Soviet Union. It is contagious from stool contamination.

Age: Any except breast-fed infants. **Who:** Anyone eating insufficiently cooked pork or beef or fish. Rat tapeworm is from direct contact with human or rat stool or from eating grain with insects in it. **Onset:** 2-3 months after eating the offending food.

Clinical:

Either no symptoms, or worm segments seen in the stool, or rectal itching, or else increased appetite plus weight loss. Children fail to grow properly. Rat tapeworms cause itching of the rectum.

Sometimes: There is abdominal pain. Segments of pork or beef tapeworm are flat and quadrangular, measuring about 0.2-0.5 x 0.5-1 cm.; thus they can be seen and identified with a magnifying glass.

Tapeworm, pork or beef, showing one segment. The marker indicates 1 cm.

Complications: CYSTICERCOSIS is caused by *pork* tapeworm eggs from stool getting back into the mouth. It is essential, therefore, to be very careful in handling contaminated stool. Give medication to cause diarrhea after a worm treatment; be sure this stool is properly disposed of and the patient well washed afterward. *Fish* tapeworm can cause severe ANEMIA, nutritional type, but reportedly only in Scandinavia.

Similar Conditions: *Abdominal pain*: IRRITABLE BOWEL may be similar.

Itchy rectum: STRONGYLOIDIASIS, LARVA MIGRANS, ENTEROBIASIS, food allergies.

Weight loss with increased appetite: DIABETES may have weight loss with increased appetite, but also thirst and increased urination, which are not found with tapeworm. Also consider THYROID TROUBLE, high thyroid.

Higher-Level Care. *Laboratory:* A hospital lab can check stool for tapeworm eggs or pieces of the worms.
Practitioner: Tropical/travel medicine is helpful.

[1] Don't use the ERYTHROMYCIN estolate; any other type of erythromycin is fine.

[2] Reportedly this works most of the time but there is some resistance to it.

Treatment:

Treat ASCARIASIS first, if it occurs in your area (most parts of the arable tropics). For tapeworm: PAROMOMYCIN, PRAZIQUANTEL, BITHIONOL, NICLOSAMIDE. PRAZIQUANTEL is best if you have it, but it requires special precautions with pork tapeworm. MEBENDAZOLE is useful for pork tapeworm only. NICLOSAMIDE is unsafe with pork tapeworm. ALBENDAZOLE reportedly works fine for both beef and pork tapeworm.

TETANUS

Cause: Bacterial toxin.
Synonyms: Lockjaw.
Regional Notes: E, F, I, R, S.
Definition: Tetanus is a spastic muscle disease caused by the toxin produced by the bacterium Clostridium tetani.

Very ill; Class 3; Worldwide, related to immunization.

Age: Any. **Who:** Non-immunized and injured. The injury may be so minor that the patient does not remember it. In newborns, the mother was not immunized and the cord was cut with a dirty knife. The disease is particularly common in areas where there are livestock and where hygiene is poor. **Onset:** 4-20 days after injury. The disease may start rapidly, over 1-2 days, or slowly, over a week. In newborns it occurs within 10 days of birth.

Clinical:

Initially:
The patient is irritable and restless, feverish, aching in all his muscles, and complaining of a headache.

Later:
He has muscle spasms and cannot open his mouth. He has excessive secretions such as saliva. He has a stiff back, neck, limbs, and abdomen with spells of muscle spasms all over-painful and exhausting. He remains conscious. Spasms are triggered by any disturbance. Spasm of the face muscles produces a peculiar grimacing expression. Spasm of the respiratory muscles may slow respiration and eventually entirely prevent breathing and lead to death. The patient may have drenching sweats. His blood pressure is apt to rise and fall unpredictably.

Newborns:
They first stop sucking. Then they develop spasms similar to adults.

Similar Conditions: See Protocol C-13.

Initial fever and headache may resemble INFLUENZA or diseases similar to that If the muscle spasms start in the neck, it may, for a short time, resemble early MENINGITIS.

Muscle spasms: PLANT POISONING due to strychnine (in which case the symptoms begin within 30 minutes), RABIES, POLIO. MENINGITIS can look similar but with this the abdomen is not rigid whereas it is rigid with tetanus. Do not confuse the side-effects of CHLORPROMAZINE and similar drugs (causing spasm of facial muscles) with this disease. If this may be the cause, try to treat the jaw spasms with DIPHENHYDRAMINE. If the treatment works, the problem is not tetanus.

Bush Laboratory: With the handle of a spoon, touch the back of the patient's throat. Normally the patient will gag and try to eject the blade. If he has tetanus, he will bite down on the blade.

Higher-Level Care. Advanced lab is useless for diagnosis; it might be helpful for management. IV fluids and advanced drugs are helpful. An advanced level 3 hospital or any level 4 or 5 will be helpful. *Practitioners:* Anesthesiologists, emergency doctors, pediatricians.

Treatment:

Prevention: Immunize everyone you can, especially pregnant women. Five doses gives 99% protection. Give wrapped, clean or sterile razor blades to each midwife to cut umbilical cords. Replace each used blade with a clean one when it is returned. For immunization, children should get DPT and adults (including pregnant) dT or plain tetanus toxoid. Give an initial injection, a booster 6 weeks later, and another at one year. Immunizations last for 5-10 years. Clean wounds well and bandage them.

Patient Care: Send to a hospital. Until then:

- Keep the patient in bed in dark and quiet, positioned on his side. Turn him every 2 hours during the day and every 4 hours during the night.
- Put a stomach tube in place.
- For babies, empty the mother's breasts every 4 hours and put the milk down the tube. (See the instructions below for others.)
- Keep a bulb syringe handy and suck out saliva when the patient cannot swallow. There will be excessive secretions; the patient may develop DEHYDRATION and KIDNEY FAILURE.
- Medication is given as adult doses; reduce dose according to weight for children. First give MAGNESIUM SULFATE. This will minimize the need for other sedatives and will make it easier to keep the patient stable.
- Then give: DIAZEPAM 20 mg by stomach tube; 2 hours later, CHLORPROMAZINE 50 mg. Continue alternating DIAZEPAM and CHLORPROMAZINE, giving one or the other every 2 hours. With the DIAZEPAM, give 150 ml of water. With the CHLORPROMAZINE give 250 ml of refeeding mixture. Additionally, give PARALDEHYDE by rectum, as often as spasms occur. PROMETHAZINE may substitute for CHLORPROMAZINE; PHENOBARBITAL may substitute for DIAZEPAM. Check doses and precautions in the *Drug Index*.

- Initially, also give TETANUS IMMUNE GLOBULIN: 3,000 units adult dose-give in 3 injections in 3 sites-one time dose only, IM, never IV. Try to obtain this, but it may not be available.
- There is increased need for fluids—patients tend to become dehydrated. Put down an NG tube if the patient cannot swallow. Magnesium sulfate may be helpful for constipation.
- If there is a wound, however minor, open it, clean it out, and give METRONIDAZOLE or TINIDAZOLE (preferably), or PENICILLIN for infection even if the wound looks good.
- Check daily for PNEUMONIA; use PENICILLIN if this develops.
- When the patient has had no spasms for the past 2 days, then every other day lower the dose of DIAZEPAM by 5 mg at a time, and lower the dose of CHLORPROMAZINE by 10 mg at a time. If spasms recur, return to the previous doses. If they do not recur, continue to lower the doses every 2 days.
- Start the patient on food through a straw when he is able to swallow.

Results: 1-3 weeks; 75% death rate at least. If the wound was a quinine injection, or if the incubation was 4 days or less, or if the time from first symptom to spasms is less than 48 hours, the prognosis is bad.

THALLASEMIA

Cause: Hereditary hemoglobin abnormality.
Includes: Alpha Thallasemia, Beta Thallasemia, and a variety of other abnormal hemoglobins.
Regional Notes: F, I, M, O, R, S, U.
Definition: Thallasemia is an inherited abnormality of the hemoglobin (red pigment) in the blood. Thallasemia is labeled alpha or beta; alpha thallasemia is not very severe; this entry focuses on beta thallasemia.

Not ill to severely ill; Class 3; Worldwide, it affects those of Mediterranean, Asian, and African genetic heritages. Consider migrations in previous centuries; Hispanics in the western hemisphere, Irish (because of migration from Spain) and Jews worldwide are at risk.

Age: Symptoms start at age 6-12 months in severe cases; occaionally they are delayed until 5 years. In minor cases first symptoms might be a crisis in later childhood or in adulthood. **Who:** Certain families and ethnic groups. **Onset:** Gradual.

Clinical:

Necessary: ANEMIA and family history of a similar problem. There are three kinds of beta thallasemia corresponding to three levels of severity:

➢ **Beta Thallasemia Minor:**
This is without symptoms and can be ignored.

➢ **Beta Thallasemia Intermedia:**
This causes occasional problems requiring transfusion but the patient is healthy most of the time.

With beta thallasemia intermedia, patients usually have no symptoms at all until adult life when eating some food or taking some medicine causes sudden ANEMIA due to destruction of red cells. The patient develops JAUNDICE. With this episode, KIDNEY FAILURE, HEART FAILURE, SHOCK, and death may occur.

➢ **Beta Thallasemia Major:**
This causes severe anemia and requires frequent blood transfusion. With transfusion, there is a danger of getting too much iron in the body which can cause other problems. Western-type medical facilities can deal with the excess iron.

With beta thallasemia major, the patient may be born healthy but during the first year develops feeding problems, fevers, diarrhea, and failure to grow properly. He has a prominent forehead similar to RICKETS, wide set eyes, and a low bridge of the nose. He might look similar to a child with MONGOLISM but he is not retarded. He has a large liver and spleen. If the spleen enlarges rapidly during a crisis, there will be left upper abdominal pain. The patient may have ANEMIA of the *nutritional type*, frequent infections, dental problems, and brittle bones, with bone and joint pains.

Complications: There may be a tendency to bleed easily: nosebleeds, bloody urine, bloody stool, bloody vomitus, heavy menstruation, and excessive bleeding from minor wounds. Patients may develop TROPICAL ULCERS. Most will die between 6 and 12 years old, from HEART FAILURE or infection. Those who reach their teens may have delayed sexual maturity, MALABSORPTION, or DIABETES. Thallasemia may cause GALLBLADDER DISEASE, or KIDNEY FAILURE.

Similar Conditions: *ANEMIA* and large spleen: See Protocols C-3 and C-7.

Failure to thrive in an infant: See the chart under MALNUTRITION in this *Index*; also consider RICKETS, CRETINISM, MONGOLISM if the facial appearance is peculiar. Congenital SYPHILIS may be very similar as it also causes brittle bones.

Yellow whites of the eyes in a crisis in an adult: See JAUNDICE.

Higher-Level Care. *Laboratory:* A well-equipped, level 3 or above hospital laboratory can do a blood test (hemoglobin electrophoresis) for this. The diagnosis can be surmised from an ordinary blood smear, if a competent pathologist or technician reviews it. *Facilities*: A hospital can also prolong life with blood transfusions and expensive medicines. *Practitioner:* If the patient has a very large spleen, it might be appropriate for a surgeon to remove it. Otherwise a hematologist is most appropriate.

Treatment:

In the village, use FOLATE, VITAMIN C, and ZINC regularly. Make sure the patient eats animal products or else give VITAMIN B_{12}. Treat infections and HEART FAILURE. If they have not been transfused, pregnant women from affected families should take FOLATE and IRON throughout pregnancy. Do not treat ANEMIA with IRON in patients that have had transfusions; females who have not had transfusions and who eat a low-iron diet may receive IRON for a month.

THYROID TROUBLE

Cause: Variable.

Includes: Hypothyroidism, Thyrotoxicosis.

Definition: Thyroid trouble is malfunction of the thyroid gland of the lower front of the neck. The gland regulates the rate at which the body uses food stores to produce energy.

Entry category: Disease cluster.

Mildly to severely ill; Class 2-4; Worldwide, varying frequency; generally uncommon.

Age: Usually adults. **Who:** Anyone; some ethnic groups are more susceptible than others. **Onset**: Usually gradually over weeks or months.

Clinical:

There are two types: low thyroid and high thyroid.

➤ **Both types:**

There may be hoarseness, GOITER, or eyes that appear to pop out at you because you can see the whites above the corneas when the patient looks at you. Beyond that the two types differ.

➤ **Low thyroid:**

The patient is always tired, gains weight, has thin brittle hair, low body temperature, slow pulse, and constipation. He will not tolerate being cold. He may have loss of the outer 2/3 of the eyebrows. He may have a floppy weakness of his limbs, particularly the upper legs and arms. He may sleep excessively and be depressed. His heart size may be enlarged (see Volume I, Chapter 1). This is very common with GOITER and with CRETINISM.

Low thyroid – sleepy appearance

High Thyroid – prominenet eyes

➤ **High thyroid:**

The patient is nervous, has insomnia, and loses weight. He may have a sustained, high fever, fast pulse, high blood pressure, and may have swollen skin on the front of the shins. He complains of weakness in his hip and shoulder muscles. He has trouble walking up stairs. Males may develop breasts. This may be a complication of GOITER, of treatment for GOITER or of treatment for low thyroid.

Similar Conditions: *High thyroid* may be similar to ATTENTION DEFICIT DISORDER (present since childhood), ADDICTION to uppers or withdrawal from downers (drug usage history), TOXEMIA of pregnancy, BERIBERI (poor diet), some kinds of MENTAL ILLNESS and occasionally DEMONIZATION.

With a fever: consider cerebral MALARIA and TYPHUS.

Low thyroid may resemble DEPRESSION, ADDICTION to downers or withdrawal from uppers, PELLAGRA, rarely RADIATION ILLNESS. There is never a fever associated with low thyroid; the temperature tends to be subnormal. See Protocol C-10B: Confusion/Lethargy.

Higher-Level Care. See Volume I, Appendix 13. *Laboratory:* A well-equipped hospital lab can do blood tests to confirm the diagnosis and determine the appropriate dose of medicine. *Facilities:* At least a level 3 hospital, probably level 4 is necessary to treat this. There are good treatments for both. An endocrinologist is essential.

Treatment:

Do not try to treat high thyroid. If your patient has symptoms of low thyroid and GOITER and you are in an area where both GOITER and CRETINISM are common, then treat with IODINE. Check the patient twice a week for the first two months. If he develops thyroid trouble of the high thyroid type, stop the IODINE treatment and send him to a hospital.

TICK PARALYSIS

With certain types of tick bites (worldwide distribution) a poison is injected which makes the patient weak and paralyzed. Any unexplained weakness or paralysis should prompt you to totally undress the patient and check his entire body surface for ticks. If you find one and remove it, the weakness or paralysis should resolve quickly, over a matter of minutes or hours.

TICK TYPHUS

See SPOTTED FEVER.

TINEA

Cause: Fungus.
Includes: Ringworm, Athlete's Foot, Mycosis, Dermatomycosis, Dermatophytosis, Epidermophytosis, Trichophytosis.
Regional Notes: F, I, M, O, R, S, U.
Definition: Tinea is a class of fungus infections of the skin.

Entry category: Disease cluster.

Not ill; Class 1; Contagious; Worldwide, especially humid and poor hygiene; common.

Age: Any, especially children. **Who:** Anyone. Tinea versicolor is most common in warm, humid areas where it may affect most of the population. **Onset:** Slowly, usually.

Clinical:

- **Scalp tinea:**

This is otherwise known as ringworm, causes circular or oval bald spots.

- **Athlete's foot:**

On the feet this is manifests with itching, burning, cracking and peeling of the skin between the toes.

- **Tinea versicolor:**

Otherwise known as body tinea this causes a rash consisting of red, raised rings with clear centers, or little scattered patches of skin that are lighter or darker or redder than the surrounding skin. Wiping the area results in scales of dirty skin coming off on a damp washcloth.

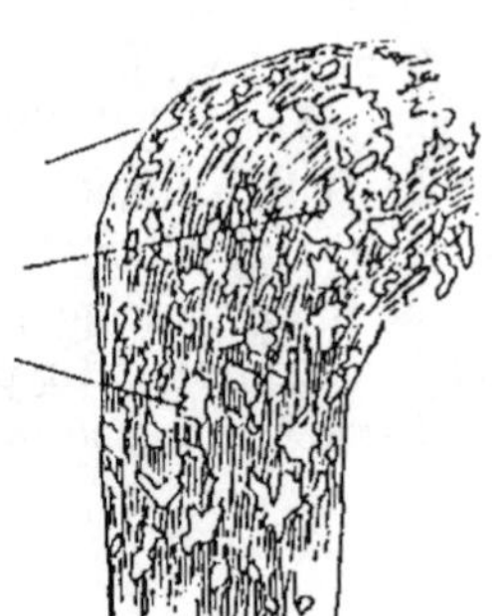

Tinea versicolor (Body tinea)

- **Tinea imbricata:**

This consists of concentric rings and swirls of silvery flakes on the surface of the skin. It itches. It is found only in humid tropical areas.

Swirls of Tinea imbricata

Similar Conditions: LEPROSY is never itchy which this usually is. Tinea never causes sharp, shooting pains or numbness which LEPROSY usually does. PELLAGRA also causes mental symptoms or diarrhea. The rash of secondary SYPHILIS can look similar, as also (rarely) ARSENIC POISONING.

Higher-Level Care. *Laboratory:* A hospital laboratory can examine skin scrapings, probably level 3, or the office of a dermatoligst. *Facilities:* Most dermatologists can treat this successfully.

Treatment:

Try local treatment first: NYSTATIN, TOLNAFATE, MICONAZOLE, WHITFIELD'S OINTMENT, CLOTRIMAZOLE, GENTIAN VIOLET. Sometimes painting the skin with tincture of IODINE is helpful. Stubborn cases can usually be cured with GRISEOFULVIN or KETOCONAZOLE. If you use KETOCONAZOLE, have the patient swallow it with citrus juice or a cola soft drink. After that have him exercise until he sweats but not shower until several hours later. However, with these drugs the patient may have a DRUG ERUPTION with the first dose. Do not stop the medication for this. (But do stop medication in the case of a true drug ALLERGY or SERUM SICKNESS.)

TORTICOLLIS

Cause: Unknown.
Synonym: Wry neck.
Definition: Torticollis is spontaneous spasm of the muscles of the neck, usually on one side only.

Not ill; Class 1; Worldwide, very common.

Age: Usually teens and adults. **Who:** Anyone. **Onset:** Usually sudden but may be gradual.

Clinical:

Necessary: After sleeping or relaxing, the patient finds that his neck is extremely painful. He holds his head tipped to one side and will not straighten it because of pain. There is no fever and the patient is not ill otherwise. His arms, legs, and back are not affected.

Similar Conditions: TRICHINOSIS (also swollen muscles and fever), TETANUS (also other pains and spasms), side-effect of CHLORPROMAZINE or similar medications. Slow onset torticollis may be due to TUBERCULOSIS or CANCER.

Torticollis: Note the stiffly tilted head.

Treatment:

Pain medicines, a neck collar, bedrest, and local heat for 3-4 days. Results: 3 days with a neck collar, longer without one.

TOXEMIA

Cause: Unknown.
Synonyms: Pregnancy-induced hypertension, PIH.
Includes: Eclampsia, Pre-eclampsia.
Regional Notes: F, I, O.
Definition: Toxemia is a disorder of late pregnancy, of unknown origin, that causes failure of the regulation of body water.

Mildly to very ill; Class 2, mild; Class 3-4, severe; Worldwide, more frequent amongst poor, at high altitudes, and young women.

Age: Young first pregnancy, middle-aged multiple pregnancies, relatives had the problem. **Who:** Pregnant, during last 3 months of pregnancy. Previous toxemia increases the chance the problem will recur during another pregnancy. Toxemia may also occur up to 7 days after delivery. **Onset:** Days to weeks.

Clinical:

Note that there is no fever connected with this.

Necessary: High blood pressure (a rise of 30 points or more or a pressure over 130/80 in non-Westerners, 140/90 in Westerners); either swollen feet or protein in urine or both.

Usually: Initially there is headache and swelling of legs and feet, particularly at the end of the day. There is usually a decrease in the amount of urine produced. A crisis may occur at the time of delivery; she may have SEIZURES, become unconscious, or have a STROKE. Crazy or panic-type behavior is common at this stage. She may die. Some warning signs that this crisis is coming are abdominal pains (especially upper-right), itching of the face, decreased vision, seeing flashing lights, headache, and increased blood pressure.

Complications: STROKE, KIDNEY FAILURE, HEART FAILURE, LIVER FAILURE,[1] BRAIN DAMAGE. In spite of a decrease in blood pressure after delivery, the patient may develop HYPERTENSION as a life-long problem.

Similar Conditions: *High blood pressure*: HYPERTENSION of other causes.

Swelling of legs and feet: HEART FAILURE, KIDNEY FAILURE, LIVER DISEASE, LIVER FAILURE, VARICOSE VEINS, FILARIASIS, endemic ELEPHANTIASIS. See Protocol C-6B.

Mental symptoms: BERIBERI (poor diet), DEMONIZATION.

Bush Laboratory: Protein in the urine, 1+ or more. A bedside test is helpful. Have the patient lie on her left side for 15 minutes. Then take her blood pressure. Have her roll onto her back. In 5 minutes, take her pressure again. If the second pressure is 20 points or more higher, she is very likely to develop toxemia.

Higher-Level Care. *Laboratory:* At a level 3 or more it is helpful in management though there are no nifty diagnositic tests. *Facilities:* IV's and fluids; facilities for rapid delivery or surgery; oxygen; injectable medications, at least level 3. This is essential if the problem develops before 5 months. *Practitioner:* Generalist or obstetrician.

Treatment:

Prevention: Good diet. Watch every pregnancy you can in order to diagnose and treat this early and prevent complications.

Patient Care: If the problem is mild or just threatening, treat the patient with CALCIUM and ASPIRIN. If a crisis is occurring, send the patient to a hospital if possible. If this is not possible:

- Keep the patient in bed, lying on her left side.
- Use PHENOBARBITAL for sedation and to prevent SEIZURES.
- Use HYDRALAZINE or METHYLDOPA to lower blood pressure.
- Use FUROSEMIDE or HYDROCHLOROTHIAZIDE to make the patient urinate and get rid of fluid.
- Check the patient at least twice weekly. Send out for delivery, for SEIZURES, and if symptoms do not improve. If you cannot possibly send out, try to contact a physician or midwife for instructions on how to use MAGNESIUM SULFATE IM. If no instructions are available and the situation is critical, use the directions in the *Drug Index*.

TOXOPLASMOSIS

Cause: Protozoa.
Regional Notes: F, I, M, O, R, S, U.
Definition: Toxoplasmosis is an infection with the protozoa Toxoplasma gondii.

Not ill to severely ill; Class 2-3; Worldwide, related to cats and the eating of rare meat, especially lamb. It is

[1] There will be pain and tenderness in the right upper abdomen; the patient may have abnormal bleeding and bruising.

generally less prevalent than average in arid, cold, and hot regions and at high elevation. Slaughterhouse workers are particularly prone to infection.

Age: Any. **Who:** Anyone, especially those with decreased immunity due to HIV, TB, MALARIA, CANCER. **Onset:** Variable. Incubation 1-3 weeks.

Clinical:

Sometimes: No symptoms at all; or a fever plus enlarged lymph nodes in the neck; or severe fatigue, a large spleen, and a fever. The symptoms are like MONONUCLEOSIS, except the tonsils usually appear normal. The patient sleeps almost all day every day for 2-10 weeks if untreated, and usually recovers. In those with poor immunity, it may cause ENCEPHALITIS which usually results in death. A woman who has the disease during pregnancy may have a baby who is mentally retarded, who has other severe abnormalities, or who dies. Sometimes the baby looks normal but later becomes blind.

Similar Conditions: See Protocols C-10 and C-12.

Higher-Level Care. Speedy referral in the presence of pregnancy or HIV. See Volume I, Appendix 13. *Laboratory:* Sometimes a hospital lab can do a smear for diagnosis. Sophisticated labs can do blood tests. *Practitioners:* Infectious disease specialist is best; a pediatrician, internist, or generalist is o.k.

Treatment:

Prevention: Cook all meat well. Pregnant women must avoid cats and anything that may be cat-contaminated.

Patient Care: Be sure the patient eats and drinks enough. Use PYRIMETHAMINE and SULFAMETHOXAZOLE in combination. FANSIDAR or CLINDAMYCIN work well. Pregnant women need daily treatment with spiramycin until delivery.

TRACHOMA

Cause: Bacteria.
Regional Notes: E, F, I, R, U.
Definition: Trachoma is an eye infection with the bacterium Chlamydia trachomatis.

Not ill to mildly ill; Class 1-2; Contagious; Worldwide, especially common in hot, dry, low-income areas with dirt, flies, and overcrowding; less common amongst nomads and in sparsely populated areas.

Age: Any. **Who:** Anyone, especially close personal contacts of infected persons. Females are more susceptible than males. **Onset:** Over days initially; it takes years from first symptoms to blindness.

Clinical:

Initially: No symptoms at all or else a mild, irritated-type eye discomfort. (If there are no symptoms initially, you probably will not recognize the problem until the advanced stage when the eyelid scars and droops.)

Sometimes: Bubbles underneath the upper eyelid, with or without symptoms of an EYE INFECTION (red, scratchy, weeping eyes). Turn the eyelid inside out. (See Appendix 1in Vol. I.) Underneath the lid you will find whitish, bubbly, pimple-like spots, sometimes few and hard to see, sometimes like cobblestones.

Later: As these spots heal, they scar; the scarring contracts the under side of the upper lid, which makes the lashes turn inward. The lashes scratch the cornea whenever the patient blinks. These scratches heal with scarring, causing the cornea to become opaque starting from the top and always worse on top than on the bottom. The eyelid may droop. There may be little gray pits around the edge of the cornea.

Complications: Blindness. In areas where this is common, 10% of the older population may be blind from this.

Similar Conditions: See Protocol C-8. ALLERGY (vernal conjunctivitis) can cause similar bubbles underneath the upper eyelid. The opacities in the cornea always start on the top with trachoma; they start on the bottom, middle, or sides with other diseases.

Higher-Level Care. *Laboratory*: Ordinary smears are useful only in 50% of the most severe cases. Cultures may be helpful. *Practitioners*: An ophthalmologist with tropical/travel medicine exposure is best.

Treatment:

Prevention: For mass treatment of a village, treat all children twice daily with eye ointment for five consecutive days, once a month for 6 months. In those with obvious disease, also give DOXYCYCLINE by mouth daily for 5 consecutive days, each month for 6 months. If you can teach mothers to wash children's faces frequently, this will do much to decrease the incidence of blindness in the community.

Patient Care: ANTIBIOTIC EYE DROPS or OINTMENT as in EYE INFECTION; sulfa or tetracycline or chloramphenicol ointment is the best, used together with oral medicines: SULFADIAZINE or COTRIMOXAZOLE as in URINARY INFECTION, continued for 10 days. DOXYCYCLINE and ERYTHROMYCIN also work; ERYTHROMYCIN is better.

Some people prevent the corneas' being scratched by plucking eyelashes. This practice should be encouraged. In advanced cases surgery may be helpful if the patient can perceive light and tell what direction it is coming from. It is quite feasible for a non-medical person to learn to do this surgery, but he must be personally tutored.

There is an antibiotic that will cure trachoma infection with one dose. It will not, however, heal a damaged cornea. Free samples may be available. The drug is AZITHROMYCIN. It can be used for mass treatment of whole communities; one should treat at least 80% of the persons for it to have a good effect. It is similar to ERYTHROMYCIN.

Results: Improvement 3-6 weeks; continue drops or ointment for 2 months total.

TRENCH FEVER

Cause: Bacterium: Bartonella quintana

Definition: Trench Fever is a whole-body infection with the bacterium Bartonella quintana.

Moderately to very ill; Class 1-4; Worldwide in times of war, refugee situations, and in the context of urban homelessness, mainly in temperate climates.

Age: Any; **Who:** Those who live with body lice: usually soldiers in trenches and the urban homeless; **Onset:** Usually sudden; there is a 4-36 day incubation.

Clinical:

This varies from a very mild, flu-like illness to a single fever to a slow-onset, long-lasting fever, to multiple episodes of relapsing fever.

Usually: There is sudden onset of a severe, flu-like illness with a high fever; a headache mostly behind the eyes; and severe back and leg pain, especially the shins. Symptoms increase over 2-3 days, then decrease over 2-3 days. The patient usually stays in bed.

Maybe: There may be sensitivity to touch in bands around the chest or back and abdomen, similar to SHINGLES. There may or may not be a red rash or an enlarged spleen. The fever may be up and down many times. Recovery takes a long time, frequently 2 months.

Complications: Blindness, HEART FAILURE, very prolonged invalid status.

Similar Conditions: INFLUENZA, RELAPSING FEVER (which causes calf, not shin pain), SHINGLES, DENGUE FEVER, perhaps conditions listed under SPINAL NEUROPATHY. See Protocols C-2 and C-13.

Higher-Level Care. See Volume I, Appendix 13. *Laboratory:* A specialty lab for tropical/travel diseases is necessary; there are blood cultures and various antibody tests but they are not simple and routine. *Facilities:* IV fluids and injectable antibiotics might be helpful. *Practitioners:* Tropical/travel exptertise is best for initial treatment, a cardiologist and/or expert nursing for complications.

Treatment:

Prevention: Discourage body lice by frequent washing and delousing. Insecticides will kill living lice but many of them do not kill the eggs. Boiling clothing or ironing might be necessary.

Patient Care: Antibiotics should be given for 4-6 weeks; there are many relapses with shorter courses. DOXYCYCLINE, CHLORAMPENICOL, ERYTHROMYCIN, AZITHROMYCIN. If the patient has HEART FAILURE, that should be treated with ceftriaxone (a type of CEPHALOSPORIN) plus GENTAMYCIN.

TREPONARID

Cause: Spirochete.

Synonyms: Endemic syphilis, Dichuwa, Njovera (Zimbabwe).

Regional Notes: F, O, R, U.

Definition: This is a non-sexually-transmitted disease found in arid areas, caused by Treponema pallidum, the same organism that causes SYPHILIS (which is sexually transmitted).

Not ill to very ill; Class 1-3; Contagious; Common in arid areas, especially during the (relatively) rainy season. TREPONARID, PINTA, YAWS, and SYPHILIS are all related diseases; each gives partial immunity for the others.

Age: Any age, but especially children. **Who:** This is spread by direct contact, flies, and shared drinking vessels. It is found mainly in poor, rural areas with overcrowded housing. **Onset:** Days to weeks.

Clinical:

➢ **Primary:**

The disease begins with white patches on the pink inside of the mouth, splits on the corners of the mouth, or sores on the breasts of a mother who nurses an affected child.

➢ **Secondary:**

Moist warts appear on the warm areas of the body: the armpits and in folds of skin. These may be itchy. The lymph nodes may be enlarged. There may be "split peas" under the skin of the fingers. There may be pains in the limb bones, especially at night, with misshapen bones. There may be thick, possibly peeling skin of the palms and the soles, with ulcers.

➢ **Tertiary:**

The patient may develop big holes where the disease has eaten away the nose, the roof of the mouth, or the skin elsewhere.

Similar Conditions:

Initial skin problem: The disease is quite similar to YAWS and the treatment for either will cure the other.

Moist warts may be indistinguishable from secondary SYPHILIS; the treatments are the same.

Skin bumps may be similar to those with RHEUMATIC FEVER.

Facial skin ulceration: CANCRUM ORIS, CUTANEOUS LEISHMANIASIS.

Higher-Level Care. *Laboratory:* Any blood test for SYPHILIS will be positive in this as the organisms that cause the two are indistinguishable. See the laboratory paragraph under SYPHILLIS. *Practitioners:* Tropical/travel expertise is best.

Treatment:

Prevention: Wash your hands well. Discourage flies and the sharing of drinking cups. Treat existing cases.

Patient care: Same as described for SYPHILIS.

TRICHINOSIS

Cause: Worm.

Synonyms: Trichinellosis, Trichiniasis.

Regional Notes: E, F, I, O, R, S, U.

Definition: Trichinosis is a whole-body infection with the larval worm Trichinella spiralis.

Mildly to very ill; Class 1-3; Usually occurs in small epidemics; it is rare worldwide. It is considered a tropical disease.

Age: Any but nursing babies. **Who:** Eating poorly-cooked pork or wild carnivore meat. Usually there are groups of cases. **Onset:** Begins 1-7 days after eating infected meat.

Clinical:

Initially (Necessary): The patient has nausea, vomiting, abdominal pain, and headache.

Later: Muscle stiffness, swelling, and an aching pain (especially of the chest wall), fever, and facial (including eye) swelling develop 9-28 days after eating the infected meat. The fever is high and it always develops after the muscle swelling.

Maybe: The patient has trouble chewing, breathing, and swallowing. A thin man may look muscular because of the muscle swelling.

Sometimes: There are mental problems. There may be little spots of blood in the fingernails. Finally the patient may become very lethargic and lapse into a coma.

Complications: HEART FAILURE, blindness, deafness, PNEUMONIA. Occasionally symptoms resemble MENINGITIS.

Similar Conditions: *Initial symptoms:* INFLUENZA, FOOD POISONING, ENTERIC FEVER, ENCEPHALITIS, STRONGYLOIDES, or multiple other minor illnesses.

Fever and muscle stiffness resemble TETANUS, RABIES (faster progression) and TROPICAL SPASTIC PARAPARESIS (much slower progression). Also see Protocols C-2 and C-13. The distinctive characteristic of trichinosis is that there is usually prominent muscle swelling. It is generally a rare disease in all areas.

Body swelling: MALNUTRITION, HEART FAILURE, KIDNEY FAILURE. See Protocol C-6.

Mental problems, lethargy and coma: check BRAIN DAMAGE of other causes. See Protocol C-10.

Higher-Level Care. *Laboratory:* Blood test or biopsy at a hospital. The blood count shows many eosinophils, but this is also present with other diseases; the test is sensitive but not specific—a negative result means the person does not have the disease. *Facility:* A tropical/travel medical specialty facility is most appropriate.

Treatment:

Use THIABENDAZOLE or ALBENDAZOLE initially. MEBENDAZOLE might be helpful. These drugs are useful for the abdominal symptoms, not for muscle pains or heart problems, though it may keep them from becoming worse. PREDNISONE may be helpful when the disease is advanced.

TRICHURIASIS

Cause: Worm.

Synonyms: Whipworm, Trichocephaliasis.

Regional Notes: All regions.

Definition: Trichuriasis is a bowel infestation with the worm Trichuris trichuris.

Not ill to mildly ill; Class 1; Worldwide, related to hygiene and clay soil in warm, humid areas. It is generally extremely common, with 10-70% of the population's being infected in all but the most arid areas of the world. It is tropical.

Age: Any, especially children. **Who:** Consumers of contaminated food, water, or soil. **Onset:** Slowly, usually.

Clinical:

Usually: The patient has one or more of the following: General abdominal pains, diarrhea, ANEMIA, blood in his stool, and slow growth. Trichuriasis does not cause a fever. It might cause MALABSORPTION: prompt diarrhea that occurs whenever the patient eats anything.

Sometimes: This causes RECTAL PROLAPSE; little worms will be visible on the pink, moist surface that sticks out. The worms may also be visible in the stool. The patient passes large amounts of gas by rectum. Children who have this develop a craving for eating dirt and they stop growing. (The craving will disappear after treatment and the child will have a growth spurt.)

If there are many worms, the patient may have swollen feet, the ends of his fingers may grow wider than normal (giving them a clubbed appearance), and his abdomen may be distended with fluid so that he waddles when he walks.

Complications: RECTAL PROLAPSE, ACUTE ABDOMEN, Type 2.

Trichuriasis (Whipworm) Worm shown actual size. Note that one end is thicker than the other. The worms may curl up and resemble coil springs. The marker is 1 cm.

Similar Conditions: *RECTAL PROLAPSE* may also be caused by WHOOPING COUGH or KIDNEY FAILURE, nephrotic type or, at times, it may happen for no good reason at all.

Bloody diarrhea with no fever may also be caused by DYSENTERY, STRONGYLOIDIASIS, HOOKWORM, rarely ARSENIC POISONING.

MALABSORPTION: See Protocol C-14

Swollen feet and abdomen may resemble MALNUTRITION (kwashiorkor) or abdominal TUBERCULOSIS.

Swollen finger tips resemble those due to HEART FAILURE or chronic RESPIRATORY INFECTION.

Higher-Level Care. *Laboratory:* With a microscope, worm eggs may be found in stool. It is a reasonably simple and reliable test. Two negative results eliminate the diagnosis.

Treatment:

Prevention: Encourage the use of outhouses. Discourage the use of human waste as fertilizer. Keep barnyard animals from eating human waste. Keep flies off food. In mass treatment campaigns it is most important to treat the 2-10 y.o. children.

Patient Care: See RECTAL PROLAPSE if that is a problem. Use MEBENDAZOLE, ALBENDAZOLE, IVERMECTIN, or FLUBENDAZOLE to kill the worms. In severe cases with rectal prolapse, enemas containing MEBENDAZOLE may be necessary in addition to oral medicine.

TROPICAL SPASTIC PARAPARESIS

Cause: Virus, usually.
Regional Notes: F, I, M, O, U.
Definition: Tropical spastic paraparesis is probably a manifestation of a viral infection, causing stiff weakness of the lower body.

Mildly to moderately ill; Class 2-3; Widespread, probably worldwide; most common where HIV INFECTION is common, mainly tropical.

Age: Over 30 y.o. **Who:** Females more than males, mainly those who are promiscuous or have a promiscuous partner. **Onset:** Very gradual.

Clinical:

Necessary: The patient initially has back pain and over time develops stiffness and inability to use his lower limb(s).

Usually: This affects right and left similarly. Incontinence of urine in anyone and impotence in males occur early in the course of the disease.

Maybe: There is burning pain in the legs and numb feet. The upper limbs may also be similarly affected. There may be loss of temperature sense and inability to tell where a limb is in space. The patient may be constipated.

Similar Conditions: *Stiff weakness* might also be caused by BRAIN DAMAGE of any sort. Back pain and stiff weakness of lower limbs may resemble tertiary SYPHILIS. Also consider PLANT POISONING due to Konzo or Cassava.

Inability to tell where a limb is in space may resemble either SYPHILIS or ANEMIA due to Vitamin B_{12} deficiency. Most other causes of lower limb weakness result in floppy weakness rather than stiff weakness.

Burning pain may be similar to BERIBERI but in this case the weakness is floppy and bowel/bladder function is not affected.

Higher-Level Care. A physical therapist might be helpful. Other than that, there is nothing to do.

Treatment:

Prevention: Discourage promiscuity.

Patient Care: You can try treating the patient for HIV INFECTION with ARTEMISININ. It might or might not help. There is nothing else to do.

TROPICAL SPLENOMEGALY

Cause: Chronic MALARIA.
Synonyms: TSS, Hyperreactive malarial splenomegaly.
Regional Notes: F, I, M, O, R, S, U.
Definition: Tropical splenomegaly is an abnormally large spleen, the enlargement being caused by chronic malaria plus some other unknown factor.

Entry category: Syndrome.

Not ill to severely ill; Class 1-2.

Age: Older children and adults. **Who:** Those who have had MALARIA repeatedly. Pregnant women are especially vulnerable to sudden crises from this. It occurs in some geographical areas and not in others. See the *Regional Notes*. **Onset:** Very slow, over months. Those who have the illness may have a sudden crisis.

Clinical:

Necessary: The patient has a very large spleen. (Normally the spleen is the size of the fist, cannot be felt, and is tucked under the lower ribs on the left side.) As it enlarges, the patient has a heavy achiness in his upper-left abdomen. The spleen may become the size of a full-term pregnancy, filling the entire abdomen and extending down into the pelvis. The swelling in the abdomen is more left and upper than right or lower, thus differing from pregnancy and LIVER DISEASE.

Maybe: This may cause ANEMIA, susceptibility to infection, and easy bleeding (nosebleed; bloody urine, stool, and vomitus; heavy menstruation; excessive wound bleeding). Other symptoms are cough, loss of energy, a large liver, nosebleeds, difficulty swallowing, and JAUNDICE.

Occasionally: Heart murmurs, HERNIA, and TROPICAL ULCERS may result.

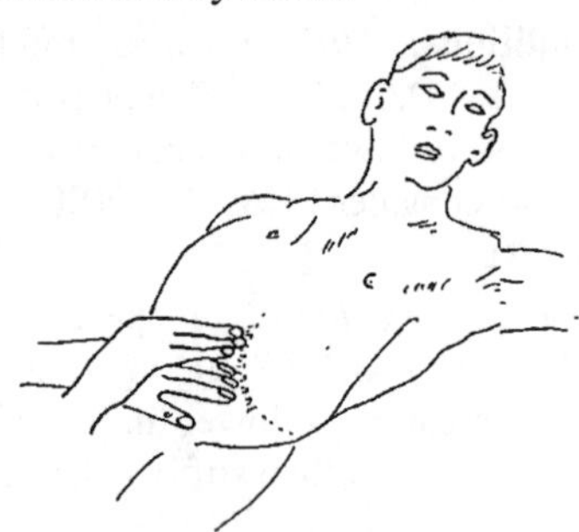

Tropical Splenomegaly: The dotted line outlines the large spleen which the examiner is feeling.

Complications: A crisis with sudden ANEMIA, SEPSIS, KIDNEY FAILURE, death. Sometimes the spleen becomes infected and an ABSCESS develops in it. If this happens it becomes very tender and probably needs to be removed to save the patient's life. The patient will have a fever and it may cause ACUTE ABDOMEN.

Similar Conditions: See Protocol C-3.

Bush Laboratory: The patient has ANEMIA and he will probably have urobilinogen in his urine.

Higher-Level Care. *Laboratory:* At level 3 or above, blood tests might be helpful in order to exclude primary liver disease that is making the spleen swollen as a result. *Facilities:* X-ray, CT scan, Ultrasound might all be helpful. The patient might need surgery to remove the spleen, especially if he has a spleen ABSCESS. *Practitioners:* Tropical/travel expertise is most appropriate. A hematologist will be helpful.

Treatment:

MALARIA-preventive medicines are most important. PROGUANIL is probably the best. These medicines must be given over at least 6 months before a reduction in spleen size occurs and treatment must be continued for a year in all. (See MALARIA in the *Disease Index*.) Some surgeons may remove such spleens. If they are removed, however, the patient must have access to MALARIA medicines and antibiotics without fail for the rest of his life. Otherwise simple infections will become life-threatening.

TROPICAL ULCER

Cause: Variable.

Regional Notes: F, I, M, R, S, U.

Definition: Tropical ulcer is a spontaneous wound of the skin that grows into a crater; it occurs in warm climates. Mildly to moderately ill; Class 1-2; Contagious; Widespread in the tropics, related to poor hygiene. It is mostly a rural problem.

Age: Any. **Who:** Anyone, especially the malnourished and dirty; common when flies land on open sores. **Onset:** Over days, occasionally slowly.

Clinical:

Necessary: The patient has an open sore on his leg with a scooped-out center, like a crater.

Usually: There is visible pus and large groin lymph nodes. The ulcer is painful.

Sometimes: He has a fever or he is very ill. Tropical ulcers may have red (hot in Blacks) raised edges and may be very large; part or all of a toe or finger or calf may be eaten away. There may be maggots in the ulcer, in which case the patient should be treated for MYIASIS also.

Complications: SEPSIS, GANGRENE, loss of limb, death.

Similar Conditions: See Protocol C-11.

Indistinguishable: SYPHILIS, YAWS, BARTONELLOSIS, CUTANEOUS LEISHMANIASIS, and LEPROSY.

Abdominal or genital ulcers: AMEBIC SKIN ULCERS, SEXUALLY TRANSMITTED DISEASEs.

Ulcerated part raised up with a cauliflower surface: DONOVANOSIS, CANCER or YAWS.

Painless ulcer with a black center: TB, ANTHRAX, DIABETES, and SYPHILIS.

Painless ulcer with a fleshy center: BURULI ULCER: the edges of the ulcer are flat rather than raised, and the edge overhangs the ulcer.

Excessive swelling around the ulcer: ANTHRAX.

Donut-edged, very painful ulcer: DIPHTHERIA; there is frequently a general whole-body illness.

Higher-Level Care. *Laboratory:* A smear or culture in a hospital laboratory may be helpful. *Facilities:* With very large ulcers, plastic surgery might be helpful.

Treatment:

Prevention: Frequent bathing. Clean and cover all cuts and scrapes, no matter how minor they are. Eating fish or using bag balm may prevent the formation of ulcers.

Patient Care: Any ulcer more than 5 cm in diameter probably will not heal in your care unless you can do skin grafting. Send the patient to a hospital. For ulcers less than 5 cm:

- Check the patient for DIABETES.
- Clean the ulcer daily with a dilute antiseptic in water, rinsing it out well. Soap and strong antiseptics kill the healing cells. Then pack it with either sugar, papaya fruit, or papaya leaves; cover it with a bandage. Change the bandage daily, checking for fly larvae and picking out those you find. Keep the area covered continually. Cool wet-to-dry com-

presses are an alternative for removing the debris. See Volume I, Appendix 1. Once the worst of the debris has been removed, sprinkle the ulcer daily with the contents of a capsule of PHENYTOIN. This will aid healing. ANTIBIOTIC OINTMENT is also helpful.

- Give MULTIVITAMINS and extra dietary protein.[1] ZINC is also helpful as a nutritional supplement.
- Antibiotics: Give the patient METRONIDAZOLE or TINIDAZOLE if the ulcer is on the trunk or the genitals. PENICILLIN or DOXYCYCLINE might be helpful for other ulcers. If you do not see improvement within a week, use a CEPHALOSPORIN instead. CIPROFLOXACIN or CHLORAMPHENICOL might work. If the pus is bluish, the patient must be sent to a hospital.
- As soon as the pus and dead tissue are gone so you can see healthy, pink flesh, stop the antibiotic and packing treatment. Wash the ulcer daily with normal saline (see Volume I, Appendix 1) and keep it covered with a clean bandage, preferably with ANTIBIOTIC OINTMENT on it. Continue this until it is totally healed. ZINC by mouth or a zinc paste or tape over the ulcer may also help.

Results: Begin 1 week, complete 2 months.

TUBAL PREGNANCY

Cause: Variable.
Synonyms: Ectopic pregnancy.
Regional Notes: F, R.
Definition: Tubal pregnancy is a pregnancy that implants and grows in the tube that leads from an ovary to the uterus. This is one kind of ectopic pregnancy, 'ectopic' referring to its not being in the right place.

Mildly to very ill; Class 4: Nearly 100% deaths unless sent out. Worldwide, common with PELVIC INFECTION and TUBERCULOSIS.

Age: Any reproductive female. **Who:** Anyone, especially someone with prior PELVIC INFECTION. **Onset:** Hours to a few days.

Clinical:

Necessary: The patient complains of lower abdominal pain.

Usually: The pain is localized to the right or left. She has a history of an irregular, late, or light period. She may have had some bleeding since, and may be bleeding when you see her. There is pain either with intercourse, or with pushing a tampon deep inside. There may be shoulder pain.

Maybe: The patient had previous symptoms of pregnancy: nausea, fatigue, sore breasts.

The pain worsens over hours or days until the tube ruptures. The rupture causes SHOCK: fast pulse; low blood pressure; cool, clammy skin; and fainting. It is usually less than one week from the first pains until rupture.

Causative Diseases: This may be caused by TUBERCULOSIS, FILARIASIS, CHLAMYDIA, GONORRHEA or other PELVIC INFECTION. It may occur by itself.

Similar Conditions: An ABSCESS due to PELVIC INFECTION may be indistinguishable, as may a twisted ovarian cyst or a twisted fibroid. Surgery is necessary regardless. ENTERIC FEVER and DYSENTERY due to amebae may have similar localized pain, as may ACUTE ABDOMEN due to appendicitis. If in doubt, send the patient out.

Higher-Level Care. *Laboratory:* A blood test for pregnancy may be helpful; urine tests are not reliable. *Facilities:* A surgeon, anesthesia, and operating theatre are essential, as are IV fluids. A blood bank and facilities for transfusion are highly desirable.

Treatment:

Prevention: Treat PELVIC INFECTION and TUBERCULOSIS.

Patient Care: Send the patient to a hospital for surgery. She will certainly die otherwise and a surgeon can save most patients. Treat for SHOCK meanwhile. Check the patient's blood pressure every half hour, at least; never leave her unattended.

[1] An egg a day or a glass of milk daily is appropriate.

TUBERCULOSIS

Section Outline:

I. INTRODUCTION [1]

Cause: Bacteria.
Synonyms: TB, Consumption, Phthisis.
Includes: Pott's disease (spine), Mesenteric lymphadenitis (abdomen); Skin TB (Lupus Vulgaris).
Regional Notes: All regions.
Definition: Tuberculosis is an infection with mycobacteria.

Not ill to very ill; Class 2-3; Some lung TB is contagious; Worldwide but reportedly not common in the Caribbean.

Age: Any but uncommon 5-10 years old. **Who:** Household of infected persons, especially those who are malnourished or have poor immunity. Those who drink unpasteurized milk from infected cattle. Nursing babies of untreated mothers. Children are especially vulnerable in the year following an episode of MEASLES. Children under 5 y.o. get the childhood form, while those over 10 y.o. get the adult form of lung TB. Children between 5 and 10 usually do not get TB, but if/when they do, it may be either form. Persons with HIV INFECTION are most susceptible and often get non-lung forms of TB. People of Indian ethnic origin are more susceptible than other ethnic groups. Elderly people commonly get TB but they may not have typical symptoms. **Onset:** Slowly, over weeks or months; more rapidly in the presence of HIV INFECTION.

II. CLINICAL: CHILDHOOD FORM

TB in children is hard to detect. Frequently in infants there is merely failure to thrive. It is rare for babies to be born with TB. When they are, they have large livers, fevers, and failure to gain weight. They may have yellow whites of the eyes and difficulty breathing.

The table below will enable you to rationally make a decision to treat or not to treat: A total of 7 points requires immediate treatment; with less than 7 points, treat other diseases first, wait, reevaluate in 2-4 weeks.

[1] The descriptions given here are only a general summary. If tuberculosis is common in your area, it is essential that you obtain more complete information. The best book available is *Clinical Tuberculosis* by Crofton, Horne, and Miller, ISBN 0-333-56690; published by TALC; PO Box 49; St Albans; Herts; AL1 4AX; UK. This book is understandable by non-medical as well as medical people.

Symptoms of TB in Young Children	Points
Cough lasting over 1 month and unresponsive to routine antibiotics and dewormers	2 points
Length of illness 2-4 weeks	1 point
Illness over 4 weeks	3 points
Body weight 60-80% of normal	1 point
Weight under 60% of normal	3 points
Family history of TB probable	1 point
Family history of TB definite	3 points
Large lymph nodes in neck	3 points
Night sweats or unexplained fever	2 points
Abnormal sounds all over the chest[1]	3 points
Deformed spine: new, slow onset	4 points
Malnutrition not improved in 4 weeks of treatment	3 points
Firm, unexplained, non-tender joint swelling	3 points
Unexplained abdominal swelling[2]	3 points
Slow-onset loss of consciousness for over 48 hours	3 points

III. CLINICAL: ADULT FORMS

The manifestations of TB vary with what organ or organs are involved. Frequently lung TB coexists with other forms, though any single organ or any combination of organ involvement may occur. With all forms of TB there may be fevers, night sweats, loss of appetite, weight loss, failure to gain weight in children and delayed sexual development. Patients may feel feverish without having an objective, measurable fever.

➢ ***Lung TB:***

Lung TB is by far the most common in developed areas and in most areas it accounts for at least half the cases.

In adults there may be no symptoms whatsoever or the patient may have general weakness and fatigue, with loss of appetite, a cough (which may be mild), and weight loss. In some areas, lung TB may present with wheezing like ASTHMA; this is especially common amongst elderly patients.

Commonly: there are very abnormal lung sounds but the patient does not appear to be very short of breath. The chest x-ray looks worse than what one would expect from the few symptoms observed. (This being the case, it is important to refer patients for chest x-ray readily, including ones with few symptoms. Tuberculous patients with obvious symptoms plus very abnormal sounds can be treated without a chest x-ray.)

Sometimes: The patient may have fever in the late afternoon, or perhaps all day, and be unaware of this. The fever comes and goes gradually; it is not obvious as in MALARIA and lack of fever is no argument against the diagnosis. The patient may have night sweats, HICCUPS, hoarseness, or chest pains. In advanced lung disease the patient has a chronic cough and white, yellow, green, or bloody sputum. He loses weight and may become short of breath.

Occasionally crackles or noisy breath sounds can be heard over the upper lungs (adults) or any part of the chest (children). Young children are apt to have abnormal sounds throughout their chests. His windpipe in his lower neck may be pulled to one side rather than being dead center. Blacks may have a skin color lighter than normal (common with malnutrition of any cause, including TB).

Lung TB in the presence of HIV: In areas of high prevalence of HIV infection and TB, the presence of cough for longer than 3 weeks with chest pain, enlarged neck lymph nodes, a dry cough, and shortness of breath, suggests tuberculosis rather than pneumonia. HIV makes the chest x-ray abnormalities different than the usual tuberculous appearance One may use a single course of antibiotic to exclude ordinary pneumonia or bronchitis.

Similar Conditions to lung TB: See Protocol C-4.

Mild cough is also found in many diseases, including ALLERGY, RESPIRATORY INFECTION, and SMOKE INHALATION; it may occur for no good reason at all.

Loss of appetite and weight loss are prominent features of HIV INFECTION which may be indistinguishable and commonly coexists with TB. See Protocol C-10.

Wheezing: Consider FILARIASIS and ASTHMA.

Chronic cough: In adults with night sweats and/or weight loss, the presence of abnormal breath sounds in the upper lungs but not the lower makes TB the most likely diagnosis. Failure to respond to a course of antibiotic and failure to gain weight in spite of adequate food supply makes the diagnosis of TB likely. Also see the chart in Index C-4 if the patient is short of breath.

Bloody sputum is also found in the initial stage of ASCARIASIS as well as in PARAGONIMIASIS and in RESPIRATORY INFECTION.

Fever alone: See the paragraph at the end of the clinical descriptions.

➢ ***Non-lung TB:***

This either coexists with lung TB or occurs alone. In children and young adults ordinary lung TB progresses to involve other parts of the body. In older adults it is

[1] Front, back, top, bottom, left, right.

[2] Commonly this takes the form of a 'beanbag belly", an abdomen that has multitudinous tiny split-pea-sized lymph nodes in it. This finding in the abdomen plus failure to grow properly is enough to make a diagnosis of TB in a child.

usually due to previous lung TB which has healed or gone dormant and then started up again. Most patients with non-lung TB have no feverishness, fatigue, or loss of appetite. Most of them also have no active lung TB at the time.

➢ *Chest Wall TB:*

Sometimes TB breaks out on the chest wall so the patient has soft, painless, cool swellings on the chest wall. These swellings may break open and crust over, resembling IMPETIGO. A tuberculous breast may have swollen skin resembling an orange peel. This may resemble breast CANCER but there is ususally an aching pain whereas breast CANCER is initially painless. Chest wall TB might cause a lung to collapse or it might cause a pool of pus to accumulate in the chest, or both. High fevers, severe chest pains with deep breathing, and shortness of breath are common. It can look very similar to PNEUMONIA that does not respond to the usual antibiotics.

➢ *Disseminated TB:*

This refers to many organs being affected at the same time. It used to be called miliary TB. It is most common in children, in patients 65 or older, and in Blacks. Most of the patients have whole-body symptoms such as fatigue, feverishness, weight loss, and night sweats, along with cough in 2/3 of the patients. Usually there is objective fever though it might not be high. Chest x-ray might be negative, or it may show white dots all over. Usually other symptoms reflect the involvement of one or more other organ systems, the most common being the lungs, liver, spleen, kidney, and bone marrow. See Protocol C-3: Fever with Anemia.

Treatment should begin on the suspicion of the diagnosis since delay in treatment can be disastrous.

➢ *Lymph Node TB (Scrofula):*

TB of the lymph nodes is most common in females and in those of Asian/Pacific genetic heritage. It causes the nodes in the sides and the back of the neck (by far the most common), armpit (rare), or groin (rare) to be painlessly and gradually (over weeks to months) enlarged. At first they are not tender to touch and they are separate from each other and movable. Later they may become tender and stick together. They are not warm or hot to the touch. They may drain through a spontaneous hole in the overlying skin. If there is fluid drainage, the area of skin will have a faint odor similar to the odor of a bar—like stale beer. You must put your nose close to perceive this. There may be at least one large, firm node or there may be many soft nodes that are all stuck together and feel either firm or mushy, like cold ABSCESSes. There may be swelling of the breast or limb near the nodes. The large nodes may push against the windpipe, causing a dry cough similar to WHOOPING COUGH. This is especially common in children.

Similar Conditions to Lymph Node TB:

See Protocol C-12: Large lymph nodes.

➢ *Eye TB:*

TB of the eye causes white or yellow, painful, 1-2 mm diameter bumps on the border between the white and the cornea with some redness nearby. This may start rapidly. There may be itching or pain; there is tearing and light avoidance. The condition is most common in girls 5-10 years old. There may be ulcers on the cornea. Sometimes the back of the eye is affected, decreasing vision.

➢ *Head/Neck TB:*

Patients may have chronically draining ears that do not clear with treatment for ordinary EAR INFECTION. They may have ear pain; ringing or roaring in their ears; dizziness (spinning or off-balance sensation); hoarseness with or without pain; a moist whispering voice; difficulty swallowing; or tiny, painful crater-like ulcers on their tongues. The patient may develop BELL'S PALSY. The symptoms are always of gradual onset except for the BELL'S PALSY. In these cases there is almost always lung TB also.

➢ *Bone TB:*

TB of the bone is of two types. It may be *in the bone itself*, especially the spine (most common). This is a kind of slow-onset OSTEOMYELITIS. Alternatively it may be *in a joint*, usually a large, weight-bearing joint such as a hip, knee, spine, or foot. Occasionally the elbows are affected. Children but not adults might develop TB of the fingers with whole-finger swelling.

The patient has mild to moderate pain, stiffness, or both in the affected area but usually no tenderness. The symptoms start slowly, over months. Any single-joint, slow-onset arthritis in a weight-bearing joint or in the spine should be treated as if it were TB. Most often there are NOT accompanying symptoms of night sweats, weight loss, and chronic cough. On examination, the joint may feel a bit spongy, different from other joints. Sometimes holes develop in the skin and release watery pus. Bone TB preferentially affects women and patients that are older rather than younger.

TB of the spine

- *Spinal TB:* In the chest area, pain comes first, then back stiffness, then abnormal shape. The area may be tender to touch. In the neck area, the patient refuses to turn his head from side to side. His neck may be stiff with his head tilted to one side; see TORTICOLLIS. His shoulders or arms may hurt. The patient may have floppy weakness with walking or with using his arms. The affected area of the spine usually sticks out if the disease is advanced. The patient may become hunch-backed. Spinal TB may benefit from surgery. Rapid diagnosis and treatment are essential—treat on the mere suspicion—becuase any delay might cause paraplegia or quadriplegia.

- *Hip TB:* The patient limps and has thin, wasted thigh muscles compared to his other side. He may have pain and the affected leg may be shorter than the other. The patient has trouble swinging his leg out to the side.
- *Knee TB:* There is swelling followed by pain and thin thigh muscles.

Similar Conditions to Bone TB:

ARTHRITIS of other causes, LYME DISEASE, HEPATITIS, RUBELLA, ordinary TORTICOLLIS. In these cases the symptoms usually start over hours to weeks at the most. With BRUCELLOSIS the onset may be gradual like TB, i.e., over weeks to months or years. FLUOROSIS may also appear similar but it gives a dark discoloration of the teeth. See Protocol C-13 if the problem is in the back. Consider also DONOVANOSIS and OSTEOMYELITIS.

➢ *Abdominal TB:*

TB of the abdomen has several forms: about 1/3 of the patients with abdominal TB have loss of appetite, lethargy, and weight loss in addition. The others will have one of the symptom groups listed below, without loss of appetite or lethargy.

- *Big Belly or TB Peritonitis*: a distended abdomen full of fluid. When the person lies down, he bulges out on both sides, just below his ribs. In the author's experience, this is a common presentation in children with failure to thrive. On physical exam, multitudinous tiny nodes can be felt within the abdomen, a "bean-bag belly". Response to anti-tuberculous drugs is rapid—within a week an observant parent will notice improvement.
- *Cramps:* The patient has crampy, central abdominal pains off and on with loud bowel sounds, and he is sometimes constipated. He might vomit. This problem has not responded to treatment for ASCARIASIS. It may turn into ACUTE ABDOMEN type 3.
- *Lump and/or diarrhea:* There is a painful, slowly-developing lump in the lower right abdomen, either not tender or mildly tender. In addition or instead the patient may have off-and-on diarrhea with lower central abdominal cramping and fevers. The diarrhea may be bloody or have mucus in it. It may become MALABSORPTION—see below.
- *MALABSORPTION:* severe, immediate diarrhea whenever the person eats anything. In extreme cases this may resemble KWASHIORKOR in children, even though it is usually in adults.
- ACUTE ABDOMEN Type 2.
- *Upper right abdominal pain* with distension and a large, tender liver, similar to HEPATITIS. There may be a large spleen, fluid in the abdomen, and occasionally JAUNDICE.

Similar Conditions to Abdominal TB:

See Protocol C-7: Liver/Spleen Problems.

A distended abdomen with fluid may also be due to HEART FAILURE, LIVER DISEASE, LIVER FAILURE or TRICHURIASIS. Try to distinguish this from other causes of abdominal distension due to gas or an enlarged abdominal organ.

Crampy central abdominal pain is most likely due to WORMS; treat for that first. IRRITABLE BOWEL might also appear similar, but then there is usually diarrhea also, at least off and on.

A lower right abdominal lump plus diarrhea might also be due to amebic DYSENTERY. The lump might be due to an ovarian cyst and the diarrhea might be due to DYSENTERY.

A large, tender liver might be due to HEPATITIS, ASCARIASIS, AMEBIC LIVER DISEASE, and HEART FAILURE. In most cases the onset will be much faster than in TB. In some areas of the world, consider the various forms of SCHISTOSOMIASIS which may also be of slow onset. In this case it will take a hospital to sort out the possibilities or you can try the hatching test for schistosomes—see Volume I, Appendix 2.

MALABSORPTION: See Protocol C-14.

➢ *Male Genital TB:*

Tuberculosis causes swelling of the testicles which might be painful. Sometimes a hole forms in the skin and drains. In advanced cases there may be bloody semen. This may cause PROSTATITIS.

Similar Conditions to Male Genital TB:

CANCER of the testicle (mainly in young men) might be similar. Other causes of EPIDIDYMITIS and PROSTATITIS have a more rapid onset.

➢ *Female Genital/Pelvic TB:*

Pelvic infection in females may be due to TB. (It is treated like TB rather than like ordinary PELVIC INFECTION.) It causes pain with intercourse and it is a common cause of infertility. There may be either no menstruation or excessive menstruation. It may be a cause of slow-onset ACUTE ABDOMEN. In areas where there is much TB, it should be treated when the ordinary PELVIC INFECTION treatment does not work.

➢ *Urinary TB:*

As in other forms of non-lung TB, the patients usually do not have fever, fatigue, night sweats, and loss of appetite. Urinary TB is most common in native Americans and older people; there is an average of over 20 years between the primary TB and the development of urinary symptoms. Initially there is frequent urination without pain or urgency. In the more advanced disease there is pus and/or blood in the urine and severe (frequently burning) back pain (usually just one side), or lower center-front abdominal pain. When this happens there is likely to be urgency (the need to go RIGHT NOW!!) and pain with urination. Abnormal holes may form between the bladder and the rectum or vagina. In this case, the patient may be incontinent, with gas, urine and stool coming out of abnormal places.

Similar Conditions to Urinary TB:

Ordinary KIDNEY INFECTION and SCHISTOSOMIASIS HEMATOBIUM (Africa and Middle East only); also consider the various SEXUALLY TRANSMITTED DISEASEs.

➢ *Pericardial TB:*

TB pericarditis may result in HEART FAILURE with a low pulse pressure.[1] It is indistinguishable from PERICARDITIS of other causes, but the patient usually has some other form of TB also. It is more common in Blacks than in others. Symptoms include cough, chest pain (relieved by sitting up and leaning forward), shortness of breath with lying down, and night sweats, as well as the other symptoms of right-sided HEART FAILURE.

➢ *Adrenal TB:*

TB infection of the adrenal glands causes hormone problems. The patient may have a low blood pressure and may develop a craving for salt.

➢ *Meningeal TB:*

Meningitis due to TB occurs much more commonly in children than in adults. It may be one manifestation of disseminated TB. It requires Western subspecialty diagnosis and treatment which must be initiated early in the course of the illness. There are three stages:

- *First,* a non-specific illness of fever, fatigue, loss of appetite, headache, and backache, frequently with vomiting.
- *Second,* a severe headache, changes in personality, decrease in mental functioning, along with fever. It's not uncommon for patients to present to psychiatrists at this stage.
- *Third,* seizures, abnormal eye movements, stiff neck, and markedly decreased mental functioning to the point of coma.

Similar Conditions to Meningeal TB:

See Protocol C-14. LEAD POISONING; BRUCELLOSIS that affects the central nervous system, CYSTICERCOSIS, some slow-onset ARBOVIRAL FEVERs which have a component of ENCEPHALITIS.

➢ *Skin TB:*

- *Ulcers:* Skin TB that presents as a skin ulcer is described under BURULI ULCER.
- *Sores:* Skin TB can also present as redness (warmth in black skin); lumps; flat, raised areas; or cracks in the skin. It may destroy cartilage. This is known as lupus vulgaris. It usually, but not always, occurs in patients with lung TB
- *Lumps:* Another form, known as ERYTHEMA NODOSUM, consists of tender red lumps along the shins.
- *Abscesses:* This can also cause various ABSCESSes.

Similar Conditions to Skin TB:

See Protocol C-11: Consider LEPROSY, CUTANEOUS LEISHMANIASIS, tertiary SYPHILIS, CANCER for lupus vulgaris. ERYTHEMA NODOSUM can be caused by STREP THROAT, MONONUCLEOSIS, LEPROSY, CHLAMYDIA, and various kinds of CANCER.

IV. DISEASES SIMILAR TO TB IN GENERAL

An unexplained fever lasting a week or more is probably TB, MALARIA, BRUCELLOSIS, or ENTERIC FEVER. If the fever varies by more than 2°F on most days, it is probably not ENTERIC FEVER; if it is continually high, it is probably ENTERIC FEVER in a national or MALARIA in an expatriate. If the patient became ill over 2-5 days, it is most likely ENTERIC FEVER. With severe joint pains in multiple joints and a slower onset, BRUCELLOSIS is most likely. With a more rapid onset, MALARIA is more likely.

V. PREVENTION

Germs are carried by water droplets exhaled by the adult patient with lung TB. Children under 5 years old and patients with only non-lung TB are generally not contagious. Usually the only contagious ones are older children and adults with lung TB. Hoarse patients are very contagious.

Examine all patients from behind as much as possible. Treat all children who have had contact with an active case. As long as they do not have HIV INFECTION, contagious patients become non-contagious after about 2 weeks on medication. Patients with both HIV INFECTION and TB remain contagious for a very long time. They should be housed separately.

BCG is an immunization for tuberculosis. It is anywhere between 5% and 80% effective in preventing the disease, according to different studies.

VI. HIGHER-LEVEL CARE

See Volume I, Appendix 13, remembering that lung TB is contagious and other forms usually are not.

Tests for tuberculosis:

- *Skin testing* is useless in developing countries. There are so many sources of false negatives and false positives that it really doesn't give any information at all.
- *Sputum smear:* positive in 50% to 70% of proven TB; occasional false-positives, particularly if there is dust or dirt mixed in with the sputum or contaminating the slide.

[1] See Vol. I, Chapter 1 for description of pulse pressure.

Some governments provide testing of sputum for TB. (But an HIV-infected patient with TB will likely have a negative sputum test.) A hospital laboratory can do a sputum smear or culture for lung TB. The sputum specimen must be fresh; by the time it is 24 hours old it is useless. Find out if the lab uses the cold method or the hot method. If they use the cold method, the only positives they will report have overwhelming infections; the cold method is insensitive. The hot method is much more sensitive.

- *Sputum culture:* positive in 85% to 90% of lung TB; occasional false-negatives; no false-positives.
- *Chest x-ray* becomes positive later in the disease; after a year or more, it is rarely negative.
- *Blood tests:* The sedimentation rate is useless. In Western facilities a new antibody test is available, called quantiferon. It is reportedly both sensitive and specific.
- In TB other than lung, a biopsy is necessary; if this is not possible, try treating the patient for a month. If the patient improves, this is evidence that the problem was indeed TB rather than something else. An exception is lymph node TB; this gets worse at first and then improves very slowly.

Facilities: Facilities for injections may be helpful. Also a surgical theatre for biopsy, or removal of diseased organs.

Practitioner: An infectious disease specialist is most appropriate.

VII. TREATMENT: GENERAL PRINCIPLES

❖ *Who to Treat:*

In some developing countries TB smears are done by a staining method (the cold method) that is not at all sensitive. This means that a patient may have active TB, even fairly severe, but still have a negative result from his sputum smear. Find out how the sputum smears are done in your area—ask the technician if he or she heats the slide or if the slide remains room temperature. If it remains room temperature, then don't believe negative results if the patient looks as if he has TB.

Do not start the treatment unless you believe the patient will continue it as instructed. Otherwise you will cause drug resistance in the community. The patient will die anyway, and many others will die also because their disease will not respond to the drugs. Recent evidence has shown that it is best to start with 4 drugs and then reduce to 3 drugs after 2 months. Giving two drugs or less causes resistance in the community. The patient will die anyway if you give less than the prescribed number of drugs.

Don't treat any patient who is dying. It is a waste of precious medication and it fosters distrust of TB treatment in the community. If the patient can either walk (with help) or sit up on his own, he has potential to recover.

MDR: Multi-drug resistant TB. If the patient has been treated before unsuccessfully or if he caught his TB from someone who was treated unsuccessfully, he may have resistant TB. TB bacteria that are resistant to RIFAMPIN and ISONIAZID are called MDR or multi-drug resistant. These are very difficult to treat. You cannot treat such patients but you might refer them to a major TB treatment center in a large city. If you cannot do that, at least keep them isolated from other people so they cannot spread the germs. Everybody who becomes infected with such germs will die unless he can be treated in a specialty location. Involve community leaders so everyone understands how dangerous these people are. Institute programs to teach people to cover their mouths when they cough and not to share eating or drinking utensils with those who are ill.[1]

❖ *Compliance:*

Getting patients to comply with treatment programs is difficult. Many will stop treatment when they feel better. It is a good idea to have patients leave a deposit at the start of treatment, and get their deposit back if they finish. This increases compliance. If the patient has large lymph nodes, they may enlarge further at the beginning of treatment; do not allow the patient to stop treatment for this. The problem will resolve.

❖ *Nutrition:*

Nutrition is extremely important. It is throwing money away to treat for TB when the patient has a low-protein diet that is devoid of vitamins. Give protein supplements and MULTIVITAMINS if this is the case.

❖ *Drugs:*

There are some antibiotics that seem to work fine for TB. They are expensive when bought commercially, but if you can get them free or cheap, you may substitute one or more of these for one or more of the usual TB medications listed below. It is essential to independently confirm the appropriate dosage.

Do not give RIFAMPIN or RIFABUTIN together with HAART (the medicines for HIV INFECTION). The RIFAMPIN decreases the effect of the HAART and thus the precious HAART medicines are wasted. Either delay the HAART drugs until after the TB is treated or treat the TB with drugs other than RIFAMPIN (and related drugs).

RIFABUTIN is a new drug that is useful for TB. It is related to RIFAMPIN, but is used at half the RIFAMPIN dosage. Do not use RIFABUTIN and RIFAMPIN together.

---

[1] The author has found that in developing areas few people really believe the germ theory of disease and there is no innate sense of sanitation.

CIPROFLOXACIN, CLARITHROMYCIN, OFLOXACIN and PEFLOXACIN are also antibiotics that seem to be active against TB. Do not use more than one of the "-oxacin" drugs at the same time.

PAS (Para-aminosalicylate) is an old drug that is very cheap and is sometimes used for TB. The problem is that it requires the patient to swallow huge numbers of pills (10-20) each day so that compliance is a problem.

Choosing Drugs To Use For TB

N.B.: The following chart is only a summary. It is important to look up each intended drug in the *Drug Index* in order to be sure that the drug is used correctly.

Drug	Advantages	Side-effects/ Disadvantages	Patients to avoid using
Isoniazid	Cheap. Works well. Oral.	Requires using pyridoxine.	Liver disease.Allergic reactions to this are rare.
Rifampin	Works well. Low dose. Oral.	Expensive. Stomach upset.	Liver disease.
Thiacetazone	Cheap. Oral.	Weak. Belly pain.	HIV positive patients. Caucasians and Asians. Liver disease.
Streptomycin	Cheap.	Injectable only. Dizziness. Cost of syringes.	Pregnant women. Hard of hearing[1]. Fluid in abdomen.[2] Bone TB.
Ethambutol	Works well. Oral.	Expensive. Decreased vision.	Kidney patients. Visual problems.[3] Very young children.
Pyrazinamide	Works well. Oral.	Expensive. Requires high dose.	Liver disease.
Ciprofloxacin	Oral.	Expensive. Should take 2-3x daily.	Not for children or pregnant women. Should be taken in the morning. Sometimes abdominal distress.

Notes:

1. Streptomycin can cause irreversible hearing loss if it is given in excessive dosage. If a person is already hard of hearing, even a slight hearing loss can cause a major disability.
2. Fluid in the abdomen causes the abdomen to be distended. When the patient lies flat on his back, his waist bulges out on both sides. If you measure from the bottom tip of his breast bone to the top of his pubic bone in the midline while he is in the standing position, his navel is below the half-way point. See Volume I, Chapter 1.
3. Ethambutol can cause irreversible blindness if it is used for more than 2 months. If the patient reports visual difficulties as soon as they occur and the drug is stopped right away, then usually vision will be recovered. If the drug is given to children too young to report visual problems, they might be permanently blinded.

❖ ***Corruption:***

There is frequently much corruption in association with national TB treatment programs. For example:

"All TB treatment is free" is equivalent to "Only the rich are treated." The government program will unload multiple boxes of TB drugs at a dispensing station and the place will have none a half-hour later because they were sold out the back door. Even with donated medicines, if NGO's cannot recover part of their costs, they just will not offer treatment. If the government says, "It has to be free," NGO's will say, "Then it won't be given." Even when treatment is absolutely free, it might be necessary for patients to bribe the NGO employees to do the job they are already salaried to do, to dispense the medicine.

Patients will take some of their meds and then sell the rest on the black market when they start to feel better. A solution to this problem is to grind all TB meds since the ground medicines are not easily salable; only intact pills can be sold. Find some readily available, small, uniform measuring devices (such as the caps off the backside of plastic syringe holders) to measure. If necessary, dilute the ground medicines with powdered granola (Volume I Chapter 5), protein powder, or multivitamins.

You can tell if patients are selling their medicines on the black market: patients who swallow pills are glad to finish the course of treatment. Those who sell their pills will ask for more when told they are finished.

Healthy people will bribe a lab tech to issue a false positive sputum smear in order to obtain the TB meds to sell on the black market. Such people usually report a chronic cough. Have the patient sit and wait for an hour before you listen to his chest. While he waits, observe if he actually coughs or not. If he reports coughing up bloody sputum, ask him to do so while you watch (from a distance). It is possible to tell a real cough from a fake cough by the sound. Check the sputum for blood with your urine dipstick if (and only if) he has no evidence of sores or bleeding in his mouth. Genuine sputum from the lungs is gooey, not frothy. Saliva from the mouth is frothy, not gooey.

❖ *Clinical Factors:*

- *Children without symptoms*, living with a TB patient: use ISONIAZID as a single daily dose for 6 months.
- *For a child with symptoms*, if his diagnostic score is 1-6 and there is no chest x-ray, then give antibiotic 4 times daily for 7 days. If there is no response, try another antibiotic 4 times daily for 7 days. If there is still no response, then start treatment for TB. Choose a protocol for non-lung TB according to the list below, if necessary .
- *Pregnant women* who have TB should be treated, even in very early pregnancy, but do not use STREPTOMYCIN before delivery since it might cause the baby to be deaf. After delivery STREPTOMYCIN is okay since the little that appears in the breast milk will not be absorbed into the baby's blood stream.
- *Lymph node TB:* Treat for an extended period of time, at least 9 months and preferably a whole year.
- *Meningitis TB and Pericardial TB*: Initially use DEXAMETHASONE, PREDNISONE, or PREDNISOLONE in addition to the other medications, to decrease the long-term disability.
- *Bone TB*: Follow the directions below for general TB treatment but treat the patient with at least 4 drugs for 1.5 to 2 times the recommended duration, depending on how severe the initial problem is/was.

❖ *Logistical Factors:*

First decide which drugs you cannot use. This might be due to unavailability, due to inability to sterilize syringes (STREPTOMYCIN), or due to a high prevalence of HIV INFECTION (THIACETAZONE), or due to high cost (PYRAZINAMIDE). Check his urine with a dipstick. If there is protein or blood, avoid drugs that are toxic for kidneys. If there is bilirubin, avoid drugs that are toxic for liver.

Then decide which medications you can use. See the above table, "Choosing Drugs To Use For TB". List alternatives that you might be able to use if the primary medications fail. If you use isoniazid, you must also use pyridoxine to counteract the side-effects. The protocols below do not include CIPROFLOXACIN, but you can substitute that for another medication. You can even convert a partly-injectable protocol to an all-oral protocol by substituting CIPROFLOXACIN for STREPTOMYCIN.

Then consider what personal, logistical, geographical, and cultural factors will influence how you will give the TB medications:

- How responsible or irresponsible, motivated or unmotivated is your patient? The more motivated/responsible he is, the more likely you will succeed in using the cheaper options that require treatment over a year or more. You can increase motivation by bonding with the patient socially—having tea with him and affirming his worth.
- What is the financial condition of your patient? Patients who are extremely poor may not even be able to afford the cheaper treatment options. For most patients, however, cost is an important factor. But if you choose an option solely on the basis of finances, you may end up with defaulters and consequent deaths or retreatments. It can be false economy.
- How feasible is it to have a community worker supervise the treatment of your TB patient? If your patient can have good supervision, you are more likely to be able to use twice-weekly and thrice-weekly options. Evangelists and church planters are particularly good for this since it gets them into the local homes. You must pay them if you expect them to be honest. However, even with paying, it is unwise to trust the ethics of such a person unless you have independent evidence. At least once or twice you need to make a surprise visit to determine if a patient has been given his medication that day. If rifampin was given, the person's urine must be orange an hour or two later. If it is not orange, the rifampin was not swallowed. Try to talk to your patients privately and ask them if the supervisor requires additional payment from them.
- How far away from your clinic does your patient live? Does he live near a road that you travel regularly? If he lives far away, you will need a local temporary residence for starting treatment or else your treatment options will be very limited. If he lives near a road that you travel regularly, it might be possible for him to meet you at the roadside to obtain his medicines.

***Approximate Cost Of Treatment Using Various Drugs*[1]**

Drug	Unit Size	Bulk Price[2] (£)	Typical Cost for a Month Treatment (£)		
			Taken Daily	Thrice Weekly	Twice Weekly
Rifampin *plus* Isoniazid	300 mg rifampin + 150 mg isoniazid	17.65£ per 1000	0.99£	0.42£	0.28£
Rifampin[3]	300 mg	2.75£ per 100	15.40	6.60	4.40
Isoniazid	300 mg	2.80£ per 1000	0.08	0.10	0.07
Ethambutol	400 mg	8.45£ per 1000	0.47	0.36	4.08
Pyrazinamide	500 mg	12.35£ per 1000	0.87	0.56	6.20
Streptomycin	1 gram	4.15£ per 50 doses	2.32	1.00	0.26
Ciprofloxacin	500 mg	1.95£ per 100	1.65	---	---
Syringes, disposable	---	3.30£ per 100	0.92	0.40	0.26

Notes:

1. This table gives the cost for treating a 50 kg adult for four weeks with the various drugs.
2. The bulk prices are from the 2002 Durbin catalog. 2009 prices are more than double.
3. Plain rifampin truly is more expensive than rifampin combined with isoniazid.

❖ *Estimation of Treatment Cost:*

In some situations the cost of the treatment may be an important factor in determining which medicines to employ. The table below gives the relative costs of using different drugs schedules. But when estimating the total treatment cost, remember that several of these drugs must be used simultaneously.

Once a treatment schedule has been worked out, you can estimate its total cost as follows, using the cost data given in the table. Note that the daily dosage of some drugs is the same as the intermittent dosages whereas others require an increase when used intermittently.

First two months (Initial Phase):
Drug #1 _____ per month x 2 months = ________
Drug #2 _____ per month x 2 months = ________
Drug #3 _____ per month x 2 months = ________
Drug #4 _____ per month x 2 months = ________
Syringes _____ per month x 2 months = ________

Subsequent months (Continuing Phase):
Drug #1 _____ per month x __ months = _______
Drug #2 _____ per month x __ months = _______
Drug #3 _____ per month x __ months = _______

Total cost for treatment = Sum of above.

VIII. TREATMENT PROGRAMS

❖ *Choice of Initial Schedule:*

Is it better to (A) treat daily for a long time; (B) treat intermittently (2 or 3 times weekly); or (C) treat with a combination of daily and intermittent schedules? First read the paragraphs below. Then consult the section below entitled "Treatment Schedule Options." It gives a list of optional schedules along with prices.

Daily dosages of only oral medications are good to use with reliable patients. The patient can take his own medication daily, without supervision. However, if he forgets, it is harder to ascertain that he has, in fact, forgotten and his forgetting leads to wasted medication, relapses, and drug resistance. It is best to give a patient only one weekly packet of medication at a time at first, to get him in the habit of taking it responsibly. Require him to return the empty envelopes or other containers as evidence that he took the medication. As you form a relationship with him and he learns to take it each morning, you can start giving medication for 2-4 weeks at a time. Daily dosages including injectable medication are only feasible if the patient is staying at or very near a clinic facility. This is an advantage with very sick patients if you have a place for them to stay. It keeps their contagious sputum out of their home and it gives a time of bonding between them and you during the initial phase of their treatment.

Intermittent dosages of only oral medications may be used with semi-reliable patients, preferably with supervision. Even illiterate supervisors are fine; ethics are more important than smarts. You can put a picture of each patient on his bag of medication and have the volunteer make a check mark whenever the patient gets his medication. It is easy to find out quickly if a patient has defaulted and this eliminates some medication wastage. The patient receives encouragement several times a week and he feels accountable to his supervisor and to you.

Intermittent dosages including injectable medications can be used for patients living within less than a 30-

minute walk of a health professional who is qualified to give injections. Provision must be made for the patient to receive his oral medications anyway, even if the health professional is out sick, on holiday, or has just not shown up.

❖ *Getting Started:*

Weigh the patient and decide on the dosage of each medication. See the *Drug Index*. Consider contraindications and precautions. Be sure to write down the correct dosage on the basis of the patient's weight and the best schedule. Children's dosages are different than adult dosages; daily dosages are different than intermittent dosages.

Give the medication for a month and reexamine the patient. Ask him if he has taken his medication. If he says "no", find out why not. If he has had intolerable side-effects offer to change the medication. If he chokes and gags, coach him on a better technique for swallowing.[1] If he has no good excuse, discharge him from treatment so as not to waste precious medication or develop drug resistance in the community. To confirm an affirmative answer, ask him about how many he takes, when he takes them, and what their colors and sizes are. If he says he took the medicine but doesn't know what it looks like, he's lying (assuming he is not blind). If he claims to have taken RIFAMPIN within the last 12 hours, his urine should be an orange color.

Evaluate improvement. Weigh him and see if he has gained weight. Ask him if he feels any better. If he is a child, ask the parent or sibling if he runs and plays now or if he helps with chores. If he says he is not improved, try to evaluate if this is an honest answer or if there is some cultural reason why he is denying improvement. (In some cultures, people think that they will get their money back or that they will get injections which they desire.) If he has gained weight, he is probably improved.

❖ *Continuation:*

Decide whether and how to continue. If he has taken his medication and feels better, then continue the same medication. If he truly does not feel any better, then you have two options: either send him to a center for drug-resistant TB (if he has drug-resistant TB) or else stop treatment (if he has the HIV virus).

Consider the possibility of drug resistance. Suspect drug resistance if either the patient or if others in the community have had inadequately treated TB. This commonly happens when a TB treatment program runs out of drugs for a time. If the patient has to buy his own medication each month, he will stop buying the medication as soon as he feels better.

Consider the possibility of HIV INFECTION. Since TB treatment is expensive, it is a judgment call whether or not to treat patients with both TB and evidence of HIV. The argument for treatment is compassion alone. Arguments against treatment are the risk of developing resistant TB in the community; the expense; and the poor chance for long-term survival of the patient. If donors are supplying the funds for the drugs, they should have a voice in this decision. If the patient or his family can pay the cost of the drugs, then it is feasible to treat, provided they can pay up front for the entire treatment.

❖ *Treatment Schedule Options:*

Note that these recommendations are simplified from standard sources because the typical reader is not medically trained. They are also modified for developing areas where the only patients diagnosed are those with advanced disease. The assumption is that there are no reliable sputum or blood tests to confirm or deny the patient's response to treatment. There are second-line drugs which may substitute for these; seek independent information: amikacin, kanamycin, PAS, or capreomycin. It is essential to look up each drug in the *Drug Index* for contraindications, precautions, and side-effects.

Option #1: Ordinary Patients

For patients with -

- No LIVER DISEASE.
- No bone TB.
- No signs of MENINGITIS (headache, stiff neck, weakness or paralysis).
- No HIV INFECTION.
- No previous treatment; this is the first time he is being treated for TB.

Choose four of the following six drugs to use for the first two months. Your choice should include either isoniazid or rifampin or both:

1. RIFAMPIN, 2. ISONIAZID, 3. ETHAMBUTOL, 4. PYRAZINAMIDE, 5. CIPROFLOXACIN 6. OFLOXACIN, 7. STREPTOMYCIN.

- Avoid any —OXACIN in children, pregnancy, and breast-feeding.
- Don't use two —OXACIN drugs.
- Avoid STREPTOMYCIN during pregnancy; there is no problem with breast-feeding. Avoid this or reduce the dose in the elderly.
- Avoid ETHAMBUTOL and STREPTOMYCIN in the presence of KIDNEY DISEASE or KIDNEY FAILURE.
- Avoid ETHAMBUTOL in children who are too young to report loss of vision; if this is difficult, use it for 2 months only.

[1] For capsules, take a glass or cup that is full to the brim. Put one capsule in your mouth and, looking down at the floor, take a generous mouthful of liquid. The capsules, being lighter than water, will float to the back of the throat For tablets, start out the same way but then throw the head back, looking at the ceiling or sky as you swallow. Tablets being heavier than water will sink toward the back of the throat.

Choose three of the same four drugs to use for the next 7 months, making a total of 9 months of treatment. (Under some circumstances the total treatment duration must be increased to 12, 18, or 24 months, mainly for non-lung TB or in the presence of HIV INFECTION.)

Choose how to give them: the options are:

- Intermittent: three times weekly for an entire 9 months.
- Two months of daily treatment, followed by twice-weekly for the next 7 months.

Option #2: Drug or Liver Problems

The patient has LIVER DISEASE or is resistant to both isoniazid and rifampin or has severe side-effects to both and thus cannot take them. Seek independent advice. But if this is not possible:

- Use the other four drugs for an entire 18 months, watching the patient carefully to see if his liver disease worsens.
- If the liver disease worsens, stop PYRAZINAMIDE and continue with the other three for 24 months in all.

Option #3: Bone or Meningeal TB

The patient has evidence of TB in his bones or he has TB meningitis: Treat as above for 18 months, using four drugs for two months followed by three drugs for 16 months.

Option #4: HIV INFECTION present:

With AIDS, you must isolate the patient since whether you treat him or not, he is contagious and will remain so, even with optimal treatment. It may be best not to treat him since the drugs are precious, you will prolong his suffering, and he will infect more people during the added time. If you do treat, follow the recommendations below.

With no AIDS but an HIV-positive blood test, treat as above for a minimum of 12 months. The books say to treat until the sputum is free of TB bacteria for 6 months; at the very least the patient should be free of a cough productive of sputum with blood for a minimum of 6 months. If the patient is taking HAART (the anti-AIDS drugs), then do not use RIFAMPIN since that makes HAART ineffective. A new drug, related to rifampin, called RIFABUTIN might substitute. It is probably expensive.

Option #5: Second Time Around

Relapse or recurrence of previously treated tuberculosis:

If the patient defaulted after a matter of months, ascertain why this happened. If he is likely to default again, then **do not treat him**. Arrange for him to live in isolation until he dies, using the legal system to enforce this. He is dangerous.

If he did not default the first time or if he is unlikely to default again, then use five of these drugs initially for 3 months followed by four drugs for the next 5 months to make a total of 8 months of treatment.

IX. RESULTS

Sometimes the patient feels better within 2 weeks. Observable improvement is seen within 2-3 months usually. Lymph nodes may swell more with treatment, before they begin to decrease in size. TB in the presence of either VISCERAL LEISHMANIASIS or HIV is usually fatal. TB in HIV patients remains contagious, even after the patient has taken medication for a year, but the skin test is almost always negative.

TULAREMIA

Cause: Bacteria, gram negative.

Definition: Tularemia is a whole-body infection by the bacterium Pasteurella tularensis.

Moderately ill; Class 3; Regional: N America (especially Missouri/Arkansas), Europe, central Asia, China, Japan, north coast of Africa.

Age: Any. **Who:** Those exposed to small wild animals: rabbits, squirrels, and field mice, or to the arthropods that feed on them or to water, grain, or dust that is affected by them, to pus or to a coughing patient. There is bioterrorist potential. **Onset:** Suddenly, after an incubation of 1-14 days.

Clinical:

Necessary: A high fever, chills, headache, fatigue, and generalized muscle pains. The fever may be constant or up and down. Vomiting is common. The person becomes bed-ridden early. The fever may leave for 1-3 days and then return.

Maybe: A rash which changes to a small skin ulcer may appear at the site of the animal or tick bite, usually about 3 days after the onset of the fever. If this happens, the lymph nodes closer to the trunk will be enlarged and painful. In adults it is usually the groin lymph nodes that are enlarged; in children it is usually the armpit, elbow, or neck lymph nodes. The enlarged nodes persist for months. There may be little lumps underneath the skin between the skin ulcer and the enlarged lymph nodes. They are tender to touch.

Rarely: The disease may cause symptoms that resemble PNEUMONIA, EYE INFECTION (pus and painful, yellow bumps on the white of the eye), or STREP THROAT. There may be ERYTHEMA NODOSUM.

Similar Conditions: ANTHRAX. See also Protocols C-2, C-11, and C-12.

Higher-Level Care. This is probably not worthwhile unless it is at a location like London or Tubingen. See Volume I, Appendex 13. *Laboratory:* Cultures can be done, bacteria can be injected into animals which are then sacrificed, and there are various antibody tests. There is no test which is simple and reliable. Blood tests don't turn positive until almost 2 weeks after the onset of the disease. *Facilities:* IV fluids and injectable antibiotics may be helpful.

Treatment:

Prevention: Avoid small wild animals in affected areas. If you are caring for a patient, be careful about hand-washing, eye protection, wearing gloves and masks, disposing of pus and body secretions carefully. There is an immunization available for those at high risk.

Patient Care: CIPROFLOXACIN, STREPTOMYCIN or GENTAMYCIN. DOXYCYCLINE, RIFAMPIN, or CHLORAMPHENICOL may work. Reportedly relapses are common with CIPROFLOXACIN. Do not use CEPHALOSPORINs or PENICILLIN or ERYTHROMYCIN or related drugs. Treat for at least 10 days. Do not drain abscessed lymph nodes until the patient has been on antibiotic for at least a few days.

TUNGIASIS

Cause: Sand flea.
Synonyms: Sand flea, Jigger, Chigoe, Chica, Pico, Pique, Suthi.
Regional Notes: I, M.
Definition: Tungiasis is a skin infestation of the sand flea Tunga penetrans.

Entry category: Infestation.

Not ill; Class 1; Widespread in Africa, India, and the Americas.

Age: Any. **Who:** Exposed to a particular kind of sand flea. **Onset:** Soon after exposure.

Clinical:

The flea penetrates the skin causing swelling and a black bump the size of a split pea on or beneath the skin. These are usually beneath toenails, between toes, or where skin touched bare ground. The swellings are painful, at times possibly itchy, and there may be many of them. This may possibly contribute to endemic ELEPHANTIASIS.

Similar Conditions: MYCETOMA might look similar.

Treatment:

Prevention: Wear enclosed shoes. Sweep floors regularly. Avoid exposure of skin to dirt.

Patient Care. Remove the surface of the skin with a sterile needle (hypodermic or sewing needle) or a sharp, pointed scalpel blade and take the flea out with forceps. Then treat these holes like any other open wound. For fleas under the toenails, shave off the nail. Use the directions in Volume I, Chapter 9, for removing a splinter embedded underneath the nail. Prevent further problems by wearing enclosed shoes at all time, not flip-flops or sandals.

TURISTA; TRAVELER'S DIARRHEA

Cause: Variable but usually gram-negative bacteria.
Synonym: Traveler's diarrhea.
Regional Notes: E, F, I, M, R, S, U.
Entry category: Syndrome

Mildly ill; Class 1-2; Contagious; Worldwide, very common everywhere, cause is regional. See also Protocol 56: Diarrhea, in the *Symptom Index*, this Volume.

Age: Any. **Who:** Anyone, especially travelers. These are the risk factors:

- A developing environment.
- An adventuresome spirit.
- Using ice in soft or alcoholic drinks; alcohol does not kill germs.
- Moist or wet food worse than dry.
- Undercooked hamburger is very risky.
- History of HIV INFECTION, CANCER, or taking medicine for GASTRITIS or PEPTIC ULCER.
- Swimming in untreated water.
- Arrival within the past two weeks.

Onset: Few hours to a day or two after an incubation of 1-2 days.

Clinical:

Necessary: The patient has watery diarrhea, more frequently than usual. He may have lower-right or lower-left abdominal pain or both. He may also have loss of appetite, vomiting, and cramps. To distinguish this ordinary diarrhea from other problems, see the chart in Symptom Protocol 56; a summary is given in the following:

Diarrhea due to antibiotic usage:
Try YOGURT, brewer's yeast, or (perish the thought) an enema with stool from a normal person, mixed in water.

Diarrhea due to feeding in malnutriton:
Use LOPERAMIDE and dilute the refeeding mixture 50:50 with plain, clean water. YOGURT might also be helpful.

Diarrhea with fever or blood or mucus:
See DYSENTERY, STRONGYLOIDIASIS, TRICHURIASIS, abdominal TUBERCULOSIS.

Diarrhea lasting over 2 weeks:
MALABSORPTION (see Protocol C-14), GIARDIASIS, STRONGYLOIDIASIS, HIV INFECTION, TUBERCULOSIS, MILK INTOLERANCE.

Huge amounts of rice-water diarrhea:
CHOLERA.

Diarrhea with vomiting:
GASTROENTERITIS, GIARDIASIS, MILK INTOLERANCE. Otherwise check out the conditions in the paragraph below—there frequently is vomiting along with diarrhea in feverish children.

Persistent diarrhea with fever in children:
This is frequently associated with another underlying bacterial infection: PNEUMONIA, EAR INFECTION, and URINARY INFECTION being the most common. Children with CANDIDA in their mouths, those with MALNUTRITION, and those with PNEUMONIA are

the most likely to die. It is important to examine children with persistent diarrhea for these other conditions, and to treat for them. It is possible that treatment for the other conditions will also take care of the diarrhea.

Complications: muscle cramps, DEHYDRATION, MALABSORPTION, CATARACT, reactive ARTHRITIS, new ANEMIA due to destruction of red blood cells; KIDNEY FAILURE. Severe diarrhea can negate the effects of birth control pills, blood thinners, and SEIZURE medications.

Ordinary diarrhea:
Use the treatment outlined below.

Higher-Level Care. It is important to send out the following patients: Those dehydrated, obviously bloody or black stool, severe vomiting, severe abdominal pain, high fever, diarrhea still severe after 1-2 days. See Volume I, Appendix 13. *Laboratory:* Any hospital lab with a microscope can check the stool for white cells which indicate whether or not the problem is due to bacteria. A report of bacteria in the stools is meaningless since this is the case with all stool, both normal and abnormal. A check for parasites and cultures for bacteria can also be done. *Facilities*: IV fluids and injectable antibiotics might be helpful.

Treatment:

Prevention: Boil water before drinking, or filter with a good filter (e.g., Katadyne). All foods (e.g. salads) that will not be cooked should be soaked in bleach- or iodine-water; see Vol. I, Chapter 2. Avoid consuming food or drink from street vendors. At restaurants, buy hot foods; don't eat their salads. Order hot tea or coffee, bottled soft drinks or carbonated water, or pre-packaged bottled water. Don't accept non-carbonated water served in a glass. Long-term residents (e.g. missionaries) should avoid treating diarrhea with antibiotics as much as possible, in order to develop immunity to the local germs.

Patient care. Begin with ORS and move to the other stages of treatment if and when the first options fail. For very sick patients move down the treatment options quickly. For those not so sick, have them spend a few days at each stage. For infants, move directly to Item #6 if they are very ill. If the diarrhea is severe and the patient is on medicine for high blood pressure, or on diuretics (water pills) or both, reduce the dosages of these, watching the blood pressure in the meantime.

- *Fluids*: ORS (Oral Rehydration Fluid) is the best initial treatment. Check for dehydration. Give rehydration fluid (ORS or the recipe in Volume I, Appendix 1) alone for three days, provided the patient is not desperately ill. If the diarrhea is severe, it is helpful to use more than the recommended amount of water. (The three days is to allow the person's immune system to build its defenses against that particular germ. If you give antibiotics too soon, the person will have diarrhea more often.) If the patient is vomiting also, use DICYCLOMINE or PROMETHAZINE or HYDROXYZINE so you don't lose the fluids that you put down. Encourage mothers to continue breast-feeding. If coconuts are readily available and the patient has no KIDNEY FAILURE, an alternative to ORS is to use coconut water with 1 teaspoon (5 ml) of baking soda added to each liter of the water.
- *General anti-diarrhea agents:* KAOPECTATE and/or BISMUTH SUBSALICYLATE might help.
- *Nutritional support:* Use MULTIVITAMINS or else VITAMIN A plus ZINC. Potassium might make a person recover faster. Salt substitute is one form; foods high in potassium are potatoes, citrus fruits, bananas, and avocados.
- *Antibiotics:* Don't use antibiotics for mild diarrhea without a fever unless the problem developed with ground meat consumption; then use them. If there is fever, abdominal pain, or vomiting (any two of these), then consider antibiotics. Use ERYTHROMYCIN for travelers, DOXYCYCLINE or CIPROFLOXACIN for those over 7 y.o. and not pregnant. RIFAMIXIN is a new antibiotic that is not absorbed into the blood stream. In India and Southeast Asia, use that or else AZITHROMYCIN. A second or third generation CEPHALOSPORIN is desirable for very sick patients. For younger patients and pregnant women, use SULFADIAZINE or COTRIMOXAZOLE. Reportedly COTRIMOXAZOLE works well for diarrhea originating in Nepal or inland Mexico during the summer. CIPROFLOXACIN is useful for those over 12 years old but there is some resistance, especially in the Indian subcontinent.
- *If first-stage antibiotics fail,* use METRONIDAZOLE or TINIDAZOLE for GIARDIASIS or else MEBENDAZOLE or PYRANTEL PAMOATE for WORMS, depending on what is prevalent in your area. If this also fails, treat for amebic DYSENTERY and perhaps consider MALABSORPTION.
- *Dietary alteration:* Persistent diarrhea that is neither MALABSORPTION nor DYSENTERY should be treated with an ordinary good diet, but eliminating milk and milk products except for fermented products such as YOGURT.
- *Infants:* If diarrhea is severe, measure or weigh it. Infants who lose more than 30 ml or 30 grams per kg of body weight per day cannot maintain body weight or grow; they should be sent to a hospital. If you are forced to treat them, add FOLATE to the diet.

  Diarrhea in infants which is persistent but does not qualify as MALABSORPTION can be treated with colostrum, the fluid from the breast of a mother who has just given birth but who does not yet have milk. Alternatively, give GENTAMYCIN (ordinarily an injectable drug) and CHOLESTYRAMINE; give each of these by mouth or stomach tube 4 times a day but NOT at the same time. Do this until the diarrhea stops plus a few extra doses.

Results: 2-3 days.

TYPHUS

Cause: Rickettsiae.

Synonyms: Louse-borne (Endemic) typhus, Murine (Flea-borne) typhus, Shop typhus (Murine), Typhus Fever.

Includes: Murine Typhus, Louse-borne Typhus, Brill-Zinser Disease.

Excludes: Tick typhus, Rocky Mountain Spotted Fever, and Rickettsial pox which are all included under SPOTTED FEVER. Also excludes SCRUB TYPHUS and Q FEVER, which are listed separately.

Regional Notes: All regions.

Definition: Typhus is a whole-body infection caused by certain rickettsiae.

Entry category: Disease cluster.

Mildly to very ill; Class 1-3; Regional; Louse-borne typhus is found in higher and cooler areas with crowding and body LICE: Central America, South America, Africa (especially East African highlands), Russia, and the Himilayan area. It also occurs in epidemics following social, economic, or political instability. Murine typhus occurs near ports, commercial areas, and areas of grain storage where there are rats, more during the summer than the winter.

Age: Any. **Who:** Bitten by a louse or flea, depending on the type of typhus. **Onset:** Variable. Louse-borne typhus incubation is about 12 days and the onset is rapid. Murine typhus incubation is 6-14 days, and onset is slow.

Clinical:

➢ ***Louse-borne (endemic) typhus:***

The symptoms of louse-borne typhus develop over 2 days. Initially the patient has chills, headache, pains in his back and limbs (especially the shins), vomiting, and giddiness. On the third day there is a sudden fever. The face and eyes are red and there is increasing headache. The spleen is usually large. The patient is apathetic but has insomnia with day-night reversal. His body odor is musty, like wet, leather boots forgotten in a plastic bag for a month. His urine also has a musty odor and may test positive for blood.

Louse-borne typhus may relapse years after the primary episode. This is called Brill-Zinsser Disease. It is usually mild and responds well to antibiotics.

➢ ***Murine (flea-borne) typhus:***

Symptoms are generally similar to those for louse borne typhus but are less severe, and death is rare. The main murine typhus symptoms are headache and muscle pains. Painful eye movements and painful muscles are prominent. Some patients have a rash on the trunk on the fifth or sixth day which then moves to the limbs, possibly the palms and soles. There is usually a history of exposure to rats.

➢ ***Both Kinds:***

Necessary: A severe flu-like illness, with the headache and general pains coming before the fever. The patient is somewhat giddy initially then becoming stuporous, delerious, trembling, awake but unresponsive. He might appear intoxicated.

Frequently: The patient is constipated and has sores in his mouth with a dry, black tongue. A red rash appears between the third and seventh days in 90% of cases. It starts in the armpits and at the waist and spreads from there to the trunk and limbs. It does not affect the face. At first the rash spots disappear temporarily if they are rubbed. Later they remain when rubbed and still later they itch. The patient is unable to stick his tongue out because of swelling below it.

Maybe: The patient has painful swelling of his face in front of his ear(s), similar to MUMPS. He may have large lymph nodes. There may be a slow pulse relative to the fever,[1] and low blood pressure. The disease may be very mild in children. With murine typhus, there may be agitation, a cough, nausea, and vomiting.

Without treatment, the temperature remains elevated for 12-14 days. When it finally falls it does so very rapidly. Fingers may be painful, pale, and cold; the palms may peel. The patient may become short of breath or have a STROKE, deafness, loss of hair, or GANGRENE. He may become unconscious or exhibit crazy behavior. He may be incontinent of urine or stool and have abnormal bleeding: nosebleed; bloody urine, stool or vomit; excessive menstruation; excessive bleeding from minor wounds.

In untreated cases, death occurs at the end of the second week. The death rate is high for older people (about 50% at age 50) and exceedingly high in pregnancy. Survivors have a long convalescence, frequently complicated by BEDSOREs.

Complications: BRONCHITIS, PNEUMONIA, HEPATITIS, HEART FAILURE, MENINGITIS, ABORTION.

Similar Conditions: See Protocols C-2, C-8, C-9, C-10, and C-13. MEASLES can be very similar, but it may cause spots in the mouth, which typhus does not. TRENCH FEVER may be very similar but then there is fever from the beginning. Also the rash of MEASLES is severe on the face whereas with typhus it is not. In LEPTOSPIROSIS and RELAPSING FEVER, the muscles are tender to touch. SCRUB TYPHUS is

[1] See Volume I, Chapter 1.

treated similarly. ENCEPHALITIS and ARBOVIRAL FEVER(s) may be indistinguishable. Treat for both.

Higher-Level Care. *Laboratory:* A Weil-Felix blood test is not very useful. *Facilities:* IV fluids, injectable antibiotics, and expert nursing care are most helpful, level 3 or above. *Practitioners:* Tropical/travel medical expertise is most helpful.

Treatment:

- Keep the patient near you.
- Give food and water as tolerated; supplement his diet with MULTIVITAMINS.
- Give ACETAMINOPHEN for the fevers.
- Bathe him and change sheets at least daily to prevent BEDSOREs. Turn him at least every 2 hours during the day and every 4 hours at night.
- For antibiotics, DOXYCYCLINE is best. Use CHLORAMPHENICOL or CIPROFLOXACIN if it is uncertain whether you are dealing with TYPHUS or ENTERIC FEVER. PREDNISONE, may be helpful in very seriously ill patients; use it as recommended for ENTERIC FEVER.

Results: 3-4 days a little improved; long convalescence, over 2-3 months for murine typhus, possibly faster in louse-borne. Mortality rate may be as high as 60% for louse-borne but it is less than 5% for murine typhus. Adequate nursing during this time is very important. See Volume I, Appendix 8.

ULCERATIVE COLITIS

This is an inflammation of the bowel, indistinguishable from DYSENTERY with your facilities and expertise. Treat it like DYSENTERY; send the patient to a hospital if his problem persists or recurs.

ULCERS

Definition: An ulcer is a structural defect of a body surface, either external or internal.

See KERATITIS (corneal [eye] ulcer), PEPTIC ULCER (stomach pain), TROPICAL ULCER (skin ulcer, usually on the leg), TUBERCULOSIS of the skin (Buruli ulcer which may be anywhere), SEXUALLY TRANSMITTED DISEASE (genital ulcers), AMEBIC SKIN ULCERS (on the trunk or genital area).

UMBILICAL HERNIA

Cause: Unknown.

Definition: Umbilical hernia is a weak spot in the abdominal wall at the navel, allowing the bowel to pass through the deeper layers of the wall until it lies right under the skin.

Entry category: Structural defect.

Not ill; Class 1; Worldwide.

Age: Mainly children. **Who:** Anyone, especially Blacks. **Onset:** Over days to weeks.

Clinical:

This is a large, soft, bulging navel common amongst some children. It is only rarely of consequence, and then only when it is small. Large ones look funny but they usually cause no trouble. A paraumbilical hernia (identical appearance) in adults might cause ACUTE ABDOMEN Type 3.

Treatment:

None or surgery, the difference being if there is significant abdominal pain and/or tenderness of the hernia.

URETHRAL STRICTURE

Cause: Variable.

Regional Notes: F, R.

Definition: A urethral stricture is a narrowing of the tube that passes urine from the bladder to the outside of the body.

Entry category: Syndrome.

Mildly to very ill; Class 3-4; Worldwide, caused by GONORRHEA, CHLAMYDIA, MYIASIS, URETHRITIS, TUBERCULOSIS, SCHISTOSOMIASIS MANSONI, and injuries.

Age: Usually adults. **Who:** Anyone, especially promiscuous males; rarely, females. Usually due to illness in those over 30 y.o.; injury, under 30 y.o. **Onset:** Usually slowly.

Clinical:

Necessary: The patient is unable to urinate normally. At first he bears down to urinate; subsequently he may not be able to urinate at all. His bladder becomes distended. This is called URINARY OBSTRUCTION.

Sometimes: He will dribble a little with a very full bladder, but he is unable to empty it himself.

Complications: If left untreated, KIDNEY FAILURE will result.

Causative Diseases: GONORRHEA, CHLAMYDIA, URETHRITIS, BLADDER STONE.

Similar Conditions: PROSTATITIS may be indistinguishable but usually occurs in those over 50 years old. URINARY INFECTION is more common in females.

Higher-Level Care. At a level 3-4 hospital, it is possible with an instrument to enlarge the urethra under anesthesia. This may need to be done multiple times.

Treatment:

Attempt to pass a urinary catheter twice only. If you are unable to pass it in two attempts, empty the bladder with a needle. See Volume I, Appendix 1. This may be repeated. Send the patient out for further care; you can do nothing more.

URETHRITIS, MALES

Cause: Bacteria.
Definition: Urethritis is an inflammation of the tube that passes urine from the bladder to the outside of the body.
Entry category: Syndrome

Mildly ill; Class 1-2; Worldwide, common.

Age: Teens and older. **Who:** Anyone; usually sexually active and promiscuous. (It usually occurs with SEXUALLY TRANSMITTED DISEASE but may occur in the absence of SEXUALLY TRANSMITTED DISEASE.) **Onset:** Frequently sudden, but may be gradual.

Clinical:

Necessary: There is burning pain with urination, erection, or both.

Usually: Pus drips from the penis. Groin lymph nodes are large and tender. There may be frequent urination of small amounts of urine. The urine may be bloody and the stream may be poor.

Complications: PROSTATITIS, EPIDIDYMITIS, KIDNEY INFECTION, KIDNEY FAILURE.

Higher-Level Care. *Laboratory*: Hospital and clinic labs can examine a smear of the pus with a microscope to determine the cause. *Facilities*: A sexually transmitted disease clinic is ideal.

Treatment:

Prevention: Treat all sexual contacts.

Patient Care: If the patient or his partner has been unfaithful, see Protocol C-1. If unfaithfulness is unlikely, treat with SULFADIAZINE or COTRIMOXAZOLE as for a KIDNEY INFECTION. OFLOXACIN is a new drug that may be useful. If this fails, follow Protocol C-1.

URINARY INFECTION

Cause: Bacteria.
Synonyms: Urinary tract infection, Bladder infection, Cystitis.
Definition: Urinary infection is a bacterial infection of the bladder and urethra.
Entry category: Disease cluster.

Mildly ill; Class 1-2; Worldwide, very common in females of all ages and in infant boys.

See KIDNEY INFECTION. A urinary infection is the same except the patient has abdominal instead of back pain. It is treated the same way. Symptoms may be fever; frequent, painful urination of foul, cloudy urine; incontinence; and low abdominal pain. There may be pain with urination and occasionally incontinence. Urine will be cloudy. The urine test will be positive for leukocytes and/or nitrates. If you suspect it, treat it; treatment is safe and inexpensive. If the problem has been of slow onset, has been going on for more than a month, and does not respond to two drugs, it is probably due to TUBERCULOSIS. If the treatment does not work, see Protocol C-9 for similar diseases.

URINARY OBSTRUCTION

Synonyms: Urinary retention, Obstructive Uropathy.
Regional Notes: F, R.
Definition: Urinary obstruction is blockage of the outflow of urine.
Entry category: Syndrome.

It may be due to STD (see Protocol C-1) URETHRAL STRICTURE, SYPHILIS, FILARIASIS, SCHISTOSOMIASIS MANSONI, KIDNEY STONE, or CANCER. Sometimes it is associated with paralysis of the legs. If it develops rapidly, there is severe pain like that of KIDNEY STONE. It may be painless if it develops slowly. If the blockage is below the bladder, the bladder becomes big and hard, like a pregnancy; it can be drained by a needle or a catheter. (See URETHRAL STRICTURE.) If the blockage is further up, the pain will be only or mainly on one side. The patient will probably be able to urinate normally when his bladder fills with urine from the healthy side. See Volume I, Appendix 1 for draining a full bladder. Refer to a urologist if possible.

VAGINITIS and VAGINOSIS

Cause: Variable.
Regional Notes: F, R.
Definition: Vaginitis is an inflammation of the birth canal. Vaginosis is infection without inflammation.
Entry category: Syndrome.

Mildly ill; Class 1; Contagious; Worldwide, very common.

Age: Puberty and older. **Who:** Any female, especially those with poor hygiene, sexually active, or on antibiotics, but anyone can get it. **Onset:** Hours to weeks.

Clinical:

See the chart below, "Kinds of Vaginitis". Vaginitis may also be caused by MYIASIS, ENTEROBIASIS, or SEXUALLY TRANSMITTED DISEASE. Check SCHISTOSOMIASIS HEMATOBIUM also. See HERPES also, especially if the pain is burning or there are blisters.

Higher-Level Care. *Laboratory:* Hospital labs can examine the vaginal discharge to determine the cause. You can check the pH with a urine dipstick. *Facilities:* Referral to a sexually transmitted disease clinic is ideal.

Kinds Of Vaginitis

Cause	Itch/Pain	Odor	Discharge	Treatment
Bacteria (Gardnerella)	Neither or minimal	Strong Fishy Foul	White or gray. Runny/creamy. pH = 5 or more.	SULFA, oral or vaginal. METRONIDAZOLE or TINIDAZOLE oral. METRONIDAZOLE vaginal gel. No need to treat partner.
Trichomonas	Some itching	Some	Much. Foamy, greenish. pH = 5 or more.	METRONIDAZOLE or TINIDAZOLE or CLOTRIMAZOLE. Treat partner also.[1]
CANDIDIASIS (Yeast)[2]	Severe itching is usual	No	White. Variable thick, sticky. pH under 4.5.	NYSTATIN. Treat partner also. YOGURT as a douche may help.
PELVIC INFECTION	Pain	Maybe putrid	Pus.	See PELVIC INFECTION.

Notes:

1. Trichomonas increases the transmission of HIV. It can cause PROSTATITIS in men and male infertility as well as cervical CANCER in females. Use metronidazole, not tinidazole in pregnancy.
2. The external genital area looks reddened with both Trichomonas and Candidiasis.

Treatment:

Use the drug(s) listed in the chart. Also, it is important to use ERYTHROMYCIN in addition, for 7 days, to eliminate mycoplasma, a kind of bacteria that causes premature labor.

VARICOSE VEINS

Cause: Unknown.

Definition: Varicose veins are swollen veins on the surface(s) of the lower limb(s).

Entry category: Structural defect

Mildly ill; Class 1; Widespread, culturally related.

Age: Adults. **Who:** Those who stand in one place, women who have had babies or are currently pregnant. **Onset:** Usually gradual.

Clinical:

Big, soft, lumpy, bluish veins are visible beneath the skin of the patient's legs. Frequently the patient complains of an aching pain in his legs and swelling in his feet while standing. The big veins collapse and become invisible if the patient lies down with his feet up, above the level of his heart.

Similar Conditions: *Large veins* occur on the abdominal wall with LIVER FAILURE.

Swollen legs may occur with HEART FAILURE, LIVER FAILURE, KIDNEY FAILURE, ELEPHANTIASIS, and FILARIASIS.

Treatment:

Elastic bandages or stockings help, but are not practical in the tropics. Have the patient sit with his legs up for 30 minutes several times a day. Surgery may help.

VISCERAL LEISHMANIASIS

Cause: Protozoa.

Synonyms: Kala-azar, Black sickness, Dum-dum fever.

Includes: Post Kala-azar Dermal Leishmaniasis, PKDL.

Regional Notes: E, F, I, M, O, R.

Definition: Visceral leishmaniasis is an infection with protozoa of the leishmania family, usually Leishmania Donovani. It affects mostly the lymphatic system (spleen, liver, lymph nodes).

Mildly to severely ill; Class 2-3. Not directly contagious. Regional, not found in Southeast Asia or in the Pacific areas.

Age: Usually children; affected ages vary by region.

Who: Those living in affected areas and bitten by sand flies. Sand flies bite particularly at dusk but they feed throughout the night. In South Asia and in Africa the disease is transmitted from other humans by means of sand flies. In the Mediterranean, Middle East and Brazil, dogs get the disease and humans get it from dogs. Patients do not get the disease a second time but relapses are common. People with poor immunity are particularly vulnerable.

Onset: Incubation 10 days to 2-3 years; may be sudden but usually slow onset over weeks to months.

Clinical:

➢ **Ordinary Visceral Leishmaniasis:**

Necessary: Patients have fevers off and on (possibly with chills), weight loss, and very large spleens. Initially, the patient is likely to feel reasonably healthy, walking around and eating normally. The spleen is always down to the navel by the third month and the liver is obviously large by the sixth month. The spleen and liver are soft and smooth and the spleen is the larger of the two. (See the illustration of a large spleen under TROPICAL SPLENOMEGALY.) There is always ANEMIA and usually it is severe.

Usually: Night sweats, fatigue, loss of appetite, cough, nosebleeds, bleeding gums, and ANEMIA occur.

Sometimes: The lymph nodes in the groin are enlarged. The appetite is good but the patient loses weight, anyway. Children do not grow normally. Teenagers have delayed sexual development. There is some JAUNDICE and the fever rises and falls 2 to 4 times in each 24 hours. Newborn babies of pregnant women with VL might have large livers and spleens. In severe cases the patient may lose his hair or have swollen ankles. If the spleen enlarges rapidly, the patient may complain of aching in his upper-left abdomen.

Complications: CANCRUM ORIS, PNEUMONIA, ANEMIA, SEPSIS, PKDL, death. Patients are vulnerable to other infections.

➢ **With HIV Infection:**

There may be symptoms which are not at all typical such as lack of fever and *lack* of an enlarged spleen. Commonly there is watery diarrhea, sore throat, difficulty swallowing, abdominal pains, and rectal pains. These patients usually do not respond well to drugs; the prognosis is poor.

➢ **Post-Kala-azar Dermal Leishmaniasis:**

Uncommonly, after the original illness has passed, the patient develops lighter patches of skin and bumps, mainly on his face. He may have a fever. Bumps range in size from peas to grapes, may be red and neither itch nor hurt. The appearance is similar to ACNE but it's harder to tell where one bump stops and another one starts. There is no loss of feeling, and they never occur below the knees. It may be indistinguishable from lepromatous LEPROSY.

Similar Conditions: See Protocols C-3, C-5, C-7, and C-12.

The *fever pattern* is distinctive: it rises 2-4 times a day rather than once a day as in ENTERIC FEVER and most other fever-causing illnesses. The fever pattern is similar to BRUCELLOSIS, with the fever going away for as much as 2-4 days at a time. However, VL does not cause the joint pains, and sharp, shooting pains of BRUCELLOSIS. Likewise, the pulse is rapid all the time; it does not become slower as the fever decreases.

Chills may cause confusion with MALARIA.

Large groin lymph nodes may cause confusion with SEXUALLY TRANSMITTED DISEASE's.

The *very large spleen* might resemble TROPICAL SPLENOMEGALY.

The *weight loss and liver swelling* might resemble abdominal TB, some CANCER, or LIVER FAILURE of other causes.

The *loss of hair and general fatigue* and loss of appetite resembles secondary SYPHILIS.

If the whites of the eyes are yellow, see JAUNDICE.

Bush Laboratory: There is sometimes protein or urobilinogen or both in the urine. Hospitals with fairly good facilities can definitely diagnose the disease by doing a smear and stain of bone marrow or a spleen biopsy. Western-trained physicians generally abhor the idea of spleen biopsies, but many physicians in the tropics do them quite safely. The formol gel test is accurate and easy to do but it does not turn positive until the patient has been ill for 3 months. One drop of 37% formalin added to serum turns the serum milky white within a few minutes. The only other diseases for which this is positive is HIV INFECTION and a certain rare CANCER (multiple myeloma).

Higher-Level Care. *Laboratory:* In the India area (South Asia), the parasites can sometimes be found in blood, stained for malaria parasites. High-tech labs: There are two serological (blood) tests: DAT is harder to perform and requires frozen chemicals. K39 is easier to perform and does not require refrigeration. They may be falsely negative in people with AIDS so it is probably useless to spend the money to have them done. The tests will be positive in people without full-blown AIDS who have the HIV virus but are not yet sick. They will also be positive in those who have been treated and have recovered, staying positive for a couple of years. Another test, the latex agglutination, uses urine rather than blood and turns negative after successful treatment.

Facilities: There are a number of different injectable drugs that *must* be given under physician supervision. It is essential to find a facility in a large city of a developing country where the disease is common, even if this involves international travel. Tropical/travel medicine expertise is critical. The tropical/travel medicine hospitals in London or Tubingen will be helpful. See Volume I, Appendix 13.

Treatment:

Prevention: The sand flies that cause this are weak fliers; they have trouble biting in a breeze. A fan is protective. Use insecticide on dogs and in rodent burrows. Use insect repellent or insecticide on clothing. Fine-mesh mosquito net is helpful, especially if it is sprayed with insecticide or insect repellent.

Patient Care:

- Anti-VL drugs: STIBOGLUCONATE, PENTAMIDINE, ALLOPURINOL, maybe PAROMOMYCIN or AMPHOTERIIN B. VERAPAMIL, KETOCONAZOLE, ITRACONAZOLE might be useful. Give IRON with the other drug(s)

  but do not give it alone if you are not able to treat the disease.

- MILTEFOSINE is a new drug which can be given by mouth for both VL and PKDL. It is safer than STIBOGLUCONATE in the presence of HIV INFECTION but relapses are more likely. Sitamaquine is a new anti-leishman drug; there is little information available since it is still experimental.
- ASPIRIN should never be used in someone with this disease. Do not treat the fevers at all since they are beneficial.
- Treat PKDL the same as ordinary visceral leishmaniasis.
- Check for and treat TUBERCULOSIS; patients with both this and TUBERCULOSIS commonly die.

Results: The patient usually feels somewhat better within the first week after commencing treatment. The spleen size will decrease within several weeks. You can tell if a patient is responding by measuring his spleen size. If his spleen size is decreasing, he is getting better.

VITAMIN A DEFICIENCY

See XEROPHTHALMIA.

VITILIGO

Cause: Unknown.

Regional Notes: F, M, R.

Definition: Vitiligo is a defect in pigmentation of skin, of unknown cause.

Entry category: Structural anomaly.

Not ill; Class 1; Worldwide, more common in the tropics.

Age: Any. **Who**: Any but the fairest skin. **Onset:** Gradual.

Clinical:

Areas of normally dark skin become light, usually on the hands, feet, or face first. It usually starts out with a few small areas which then enlarge and blend into each other. The areas involved are symmetrical[1] except for the face. There is no fever, no rash, no scaly texture, and no numbness. The color and texture of the skin in the affected areas resemble the skin of a normal white person.

Similar Conditions: Normal scaring in black skin; LEPROSY (light skin color is never both flat and symmetrical); maybe TINEA (which usually itches).

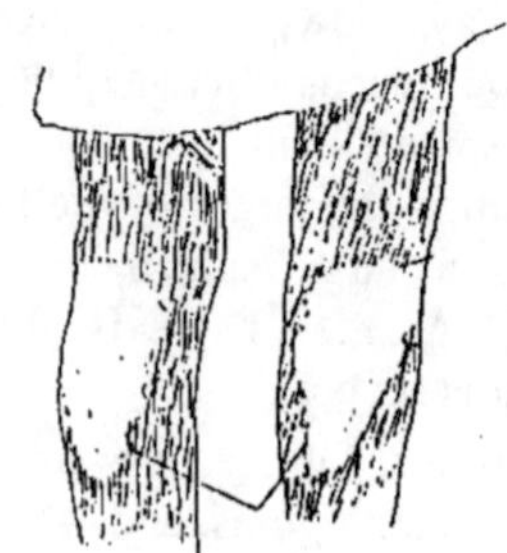

Vitiligo—typical. Note the distinct edges.

Treatment:

Dark cosmetic cream. The condition is of no consequence except for the social stigma connected with its similarity to LEPROSY.

VOMITING per se

Cause: Variable.

Includes: Motion Sickness, Air Sickness.

Entry category: Syndrome.

**Not a diagnosis. This gives an approach to symptomatic treatment. You still must pursue a diagnosis. (See Symptom Protocol 47.)

Bush Laboratory: Significant vomiting is always accompanied by ketones in urine. Do a complete urinalysis to check for the cause of vomiting. Consider pregnancy in females.

Higher-Level Care. *Laboratory:* A number of blood tests at level 2 or more might be helpful. *Facilities:* IV fluids are most helpful.

Treatment:

Check for DEHYDRATION. With severe DEHYDRATION and inability to drink, give fluids by rectum if the patient does not have diarrhea. If he has diarrhea, is severely dehydrated, and PROMETHAZINE will not settle his stomach enough to allow him to drink, use intraperitoneal fluids. See Vol. I, Appendix 1.

For vomiting of pregnancy, give the patient PYRIDOXINE, 25 mg every 8 hours. In the absence of pregnancy, give the patient PROMETHAZINE or CHLORPROMAZINE by mouth, injection, or suppository. Then have him eat or drink nothing at all for 2 hours. After that start with a teaspoon or two of plain water every 15-30 minutes, until you are sure it will stay down. If he vomits again, wait another 2 hours with nothing by mouth; then try again. Gradually increase the amount of water and clear liquids (liquids you can see through). Give nothing except clear liquids for 24 hours. Then add dry crackers for another 12 hours, then thin soups. Use no milk or milk products until the stomach has been settled for 24-48 hours on an otherwise-full diet.

[1] Symmetrical means that the pattern of affected skin is roughly (though not exactly) the same on the right and left halves of the body.

WARTS

Cause: Virus.
Includes: Condyloma acuminata, Papilloma venereum, Verruca vulgaris.
Excludes: Condyloma lata (the "warts" of secondary syphilis)
Regional Notes: F, M.
Definition: Warts are bumpy swellings on the skin caused by microorganisms.
Not ill; Class 1-4; Worldwide, common.
Age: Any. **Who:** Anyone. **Onset:** Variable.

Clinical:

➢ **All kinds:**

The patient has roughened, dry bumps on the skin, less than 1 cm in diameter, painless and not itchy. There is no fever with this. They may be flat-topped or rounded.

➢ **Genital warts:**

There are three distinct appearances; in all cases the warts are multiple, painless, and not itchy. They have a dry appearance.

- *Dome-shaped with smooth tops,* skin-colored or slightly pinkish, a few millimeters in diameter. These usually form on the drier areas of the genital skin.
- *Irregular, grainy or cauliflower-like surfaces*, either with or without a narrow stem between the wart and the skin surface. These may grow in either dry or moist areas. The color is skin-colored or whitish or grayish.
- *Giant warts* may be irregular and grainy, multiplying and blending together. This usually happens when immunity wanes such as in HIV INFECTION, pregnancy, or diabetes. The color may change from skin-colored to bright red or dark-colored (brown or black).

Complications: There may be secondary infection or ulceration. Giant warts may obstruct the birth canal. There may be bleeding. Wart viruses can cause CANCER. With HIV infection, warts tend to multiply, becoming both larger and more numerous. They are harder to treat and get rid of.

Similar Conditions: MYCETOMA (check geography); ELEPHANTIASIS; TREPONARID, YAWS, and SYPHILIS (all have moist warts). MOLLUSCUM CONTAGIOSUM looks like warts but there is a tiny center hole in each bump; true warts do not have center holes.

Treatment:

On the outer skin, not in the genital area, do nothing. A surgeon can remove them. They may disappear by themselves. In the genital area there are various local treatments that can help with symptoms and improve appearance. These treatments do not get rid of the virus and they do not prevent malignancies. You should send the patient for a firm diagnosis because of the possibility of malignancy.

WHOOPING COUGH

Cause: Bacteria.
Synonyms: Pertussis.
Includes: Parapertussis.
Regional Notes: E, F, S, U.
Definition: Whooping cough is a specific bacterial infection of the airways causing prolonged cough.
Very ill but may not appear ill; Class 2; Contagious; Worldwide, epidemics among unimmunized.

Age: Children, usually before 2 y.o. Most serious in infants. It might occasionally occur in people over 60 years old. **Who:** Children having any contact with another child who had a cough. Only unimmunized ("P" of *DPT*) are susceptible. In older people, frequently their immunity has waned because of their age. **Onset:** 6-12 days after exposure; initially a 1-2 week period of "cold" symptoms, before the cough develops.

Clinical:

Necessary: The patient has severe coughing spells, frequently turning blue, choking, and vomiting. At the end of each coughing spell, the patient takes a deep, fast breath, giving a "whoop" sound. The cough sounds dry but he produces thick, sticky, white sputum.

Sometimes: He may cough or vomit blood. The whites of his eyes may become blood-red. The eyes and face may swell and he may be short of breath. This will resolve in time. The younger the patient, the more severe the disease.

Occasionally: He may have SEIZURES and become unconscious. The severe coughing may cause RECTAL PROLAPSE, or HERNIA. When you see the child between spells, he may be sleeping comfortably and look like the picture of health. If he has teeth, check below his tongue. Children who cough hard with their tongues out frequently cut the little tab of tissue that secures the underside of the tongue to the bottom of the mouth, in the midline. (This does not need treatment.)

Babies less than 6 months old and those who are malnourished are most likely to die. They may have coughing spells without the "whoop" and they may die.

Complications: PNEUMONIA, HERNIA, SEIZURES, BRAIN DAMAGE, RESPIRATORY FAILURE, death.

Similar Conditions: Usually the type of cough is distinctive in babies. In older children it may resemble any other chronic cough. Consider TUBERCULOSIS. See Protocol C-4 if the patient is short of breath.

Higher-Level Care. *Laboratory:* A sophisticated hospital lab can do a culture. *Facilities:* IV's and nutritional support are very important, a level 3 or 4 facility. *Practitioners:* Pediatrician or internist.

Treatment:

Prevention: Immunize children as soon as possible, preferably before 2 months old. A new, safer immunization is now available. Treat "cold" symptoms in an older susceptible child who has been in contact with a known case as if he has active whooping cough (he probably has). If you are exposed and not immune, take ERYTHROMYCIN.

Patient Care:

- Keep the patient near you, lying on his side, head down.
- Place a stomach tube if the patient will not take food on his own.
- Empty the mother's breasts every 3-4 hours. Put the milk (or a refeeding mixture) down the tube: 20 ml/kg every 3 hours or 150 ml/kg daily.
- If the patient vomits, put the milk or food right back down. *Do not use PROMETHAZINE for vomiting. It will not help.*
- Keep the humidity high; use steam in an enclosed space, or hang wet sheets around the bed.
- Use ERYTHROMYCIN or CHLORAMPHENICOL for 14 days, ONLY if you can begin the drug during early "cold" symptoms. ERYTHROMYCIN is by far the better. COTRIMOXAZOLE may work also. Otherwise PREDNISONE may be helpful.
- Use PARALDEHYDE for repeated SEIZURES but observe precautions carefully.
- Watch the patient's weight closely. Give MULTIVITAMINS; MALNUTRITION is a common consequence of whooping cough.

Results: 10 weeks with mild relapses up to a year. 50% of infants will die. Deaths are rare in older children and in older adults.

WORMS

This a general term covering HOOKWORM, STRONGYLOIDIASIS, ASCARIASIS, TRICHURIASIS, ENTEROBIASIS. (TAPEWORM, GUINEA WORM, FILARIASIS, LARVA MIGRANS, and TRICHINOSIS are in different categories.) It is useful to give a worm treatment twice a year to all children; use PYRANTEL PAMOATE, ALBENDAZOLE, or MEBENDAZOLE. This probably will not cure STRONGYLOIDIASIS; if the patient has evidence of worms after the treatment, give a specific treatment for this.

XEROPHTHALMIA

Cause: Nutritional.

Regional Notes: F, I, M, O, R, S.

Definition: Xerophthalmia is a defect in the outer surface of the eye, caused by a deficiency of VITAMIN A. Mildly ill to very ill; Class 1; Occurs worldwide; Widespread and many times seasonal—when fruits are not available. It is most common in southern India, Bangladesh, and Indonesia.

Age: Any. **Who**: Those eating a diet deficient in Vitamin A, fat, or both;. Nursing babies of mothers with marginal Vitamin A consumption are also susceptible, especially those with WORMS, diarrhea, MEASLES, and general MALNUTRITION. Refeeding malnourished children may cause blindness if Vitamin A is not provided simultaneously. **Onset***:* Usually gradual but may be very rapid, especially in the presence of other diseases or when refeeding a malnourished child.

Clinical:

Necessary: Night blindness occurs initially. This is frequently called "chicken eyes" in the local language. The inner part of the lower lids and the whites of the eyes look dry and dull, not normally moist. They may have a wrinkled appearance. Then small, roughened, whitish, foam blobs form beside the outer edge of the cornea or on the lid margins. These areas look like bits of meringue or soapsuds. Then the same thing happens along the edge closest to the nose, and finally along the lower part of the cornea. There is frequently tearing and light avoidance.

In more advanced disease, there is dryness and haziness of the cornea. Areas of the whites of the eyes may look wrinkled and brownish, like white nylon ironed with a too-hot iron. Finally the cornea is totally destroyed. During all this, the eye is surprisingly pain-free but there is tearing. The dry eyes are not from lack of tears but rather the change in the surface of the eye so tears don't stick to the surface.

ZINC, IRON, protein, and fats are necessary for the body to use Vitamin A. If these are missing from the diet the disease will advance more rapidly.

Sometimes: The final stage is associated with EYE INFECTION. A dry rash may appear over the outer parts of the upper arms and forearms. At times a small hole develops in the cornea. The iris moves forward and a little piece gets caught in the hole, giving the pupil an irregular shape. The skin and the bowel are also affected. The skin is rough and dry; there may be diarrhea.

Complications: In all cases of xerophthalmia and in some cases of marginal Vitamin A intake, there is a profound immune deficiency; these children may die from any infectious disease.

Similar Conditions: See Protocol C-8. With TRACHOMA, the destruction of the cornea starts at the top and works down. In xerophthalmia it starts in the central and lower cornea first. IRITIS can look similar but it is painful. RUBELLA in a newborn can cause similar eye changes. Many diseases cause immune deficiency as also does pregnancy. ZINC DEFICIENCY will also cause night blindness. Zinc is necessary to process Vitamin A. Hence night blindness or xerophthalmia that does not respond to Vitamin A should be treated as ZINC DEFICIENCY.

Treatment:

Prevention: Urge the consumption of foods containing Vitamin A (see below). Cooking, especially frying in oil, aids the absorption of the vitamin. Try to give the vitamin to breast-feeding mothers and women of child-bearing age. However, during pregnancy high doses might be toxic to the fetus.

Patient Care: In areas where this is common, it is reasonable to treat all sick children. In the presence of eye symptoms it is vital to start treatment immediately. Even a few hours may save vision. Give the patient VITAMIN A by mouth, or by injection. Use water-based VITAMIN A, not oil-based initially; the water-based form is absorbed more rapidly. Then give a diet rich in the vitamin. Vitamin A is found in liver, eggs, dairy products, and green and yellow fruits and vegetables. Red palm oil contains large amounts of the vitamin.

Results: Start in 1-3 days; complete in 2 weeks.

Yanonga

See *Regional Notes* U.

YAWS

Cause: Spirochete.

Synonyms: Endemic treponematosis, Endemic Syphilis, Bouba, Frambesia, Parangi, Pian.

Regional Notes: F, I, M, O, R, S, U.

Definition: Yaws is a specific spirochete infection, closely related to SYPHILIS but not sexually transmitted. It is caused by the spirochete Treponema pertenue.

Includes: Gangosa—which refers to the nose deformity caused by yaws, and Gondou—which refers to the enlargement of the bones of the face caused by yaws.

Not ill to very ill; Class 1; Contagious; Widespread in undeveloped humid areas. YAWS, PINTA, SYPHILIS, and TREPONARID are all related; each gives partial immunity to the others.

Age: Primary yaws is mostly in children and mothers. In areas where the disease had been eradicated and then came back, it may be epidemic in adults. Tertiary yaws occurs mostly in people in their 20's and 30's, males more than females. **Who:** Anyone living in an affected area, especially those with exposed minor wounds. It is commonest in rural areas where there is poverty and overcrowded housing. Tertiary is more common during the rainy season. **Onset:** Over weeks.

Clinical:

The disease occurs in 3 consecutive stages: Primary, Secondary, and Tertiary.

➢ **Primary yaws:**

This causes an ulcer or a lump at the site of a previous minor injury. This starts small and enlarges to 3-5 centimeters. It usually itches. If it is a lump it looks like a blob of dried pus on the skin; the surface is similar to that of cauliflower or an irregular wart. Frequently the patient also complains of aching limbs, fever, and enlarged lymph nodes. He may have splits by the corners of his mouth or general swelling of his fingers.

➢ **Secondary yaws:**

This begins 2-16 weeks after the primary. Similar ulcers or lumps form around the primary site or spread out over the body. Ulcers may be round or crescent-shaped. They are most common on the face, armpits, and the pelvic area. They may be itchy, but they are painful if they are on the palms or soles. As some heal, others form. Sometimes there are bone changes: painful swellings along the lower legs, fingers (especially the parts closest to the palms), and nose, not affecting joints specifically as ARTHRITIS does. The painful swellings may be tender to touch.

Secondary yaws: Note the varying sizes and the distribution.

➢ **Tertiary yaws:**

You should be able to find scarring from old primary or secondary yaws. This may take any one of 5 forms:

- Bumps under the skin which break open, causing ulcers. These are identical to those caused by SYPHILIS.
- Extremely dry, thick skin on palms and soles which develops painful cracks and ulcers.
- Bone pain with inflammation on the top; when on the nose or in the mouth this may form an ulcer that eats away like CANCER. This is called GANGOSA. Bone pain is a deep, aching pain, worse at night, in high humidity, and with weight bearing.
- Painless little hard bumps next to joints.
- Swelling of the facial bones, called GONDOU.

Tertiary yaws: Part of the face is eaten away.

Complications: There has been evidence that yaws can also cause the same complications as tertiary SYPHILIS: HEART FAILURE, STROKE, uncoordination, and blindness.

Similar Conditions: Primary and secondary yaws resemble CUTANEOUS LEISHMANIASIS (check geography) or WARTS (dry surface) or TREPONARID (arid areas) or LEPROSY. Also check other causes of skin ulcers. Swollen fingers are like TUBERCULOSIS and SICKLE CELL DISEASE.

Bone changes resemble other bone diseases: TUBERCULOSIS, OSTEOMYELITIS, BRUCELLOSIS, SICKLE CELL DISEASE, CANCER.

Tertiary yaws resembles tertiary SYPHILIS. The distinction is unimportant since the diseases are related and the treatments are the same.

The painless little hard bumps might resemble those of RHEUMATIC FEVER or TUBERCULOSIS, diseases which are in other ways quite different. Gangosa resembles CANCER, CANCRUM ORIS and some forms of CUTANEOUS LEISHMANIASIS and skin TUBERCULOSIS.

Higher-Level Care. *Laboratory:* Some level 3 hospital labs can do darkfield microscopic examination of scrapings from the wounds. See the laboratory note under SYPHILIS also.

Treatment:

Prevention: Teach parents to use the cultural equivalent of band-aids and ANTIBIOTIC OINTMENT for minor cuts and scrapes. Treat existing cases.

Patient Care: Use PENICILLIN, DOXYCYCLINE, or ERYTHROMYCIN. Long-acting, injectable PENICILLIN is helpful.

Results: Some results in 48 hours; complete in one week in primary and secondary; healing may take weeks with tertiary and it may never be complete. Sometimes surgery is necessary.

Yellow Fever

See *Regional Notes* F, M.

ZINC DEFICIENCY

Cause: Nutritional and environmental.

Regional Notes: F.

Mildly to moderately ill; Class 1; Worldwide, tropics.

Age: Any. **Who**: Anyone, especially expatriates not acclimatized to the tropics, those with diarrhea, and those exercising. **Onset**: Days to 2 weeks.

Clinical:

Necessary: Night blindness, lethargy, apathy, and general weakness.

Usually: There is a decreased sense of taste and smell, behavioral problems, diarrhea, skin rashes, loss of hair, decrease in growth in children, delayed sexual development in teenagers, impotence, abnormal menstrual cycles, delayed wound healing, and susceptibility to infections.

Similar Conditions: Night blindness is just like XEROPHTHALMIA. The failure to grow in children resembles other causes listed in the chart under MALNUTRITION in this *Index*.

Susceptibility to infection is also seen in HIV INFECTION, TUBERCULOSIS, VISCERAL LEISHMANIASIS, XEROPTHALMIA and DIABETES.

Treatment:

ZINC may be taken as tablets. Zinc is eliminated mostly in sweat and stool, so the hotter the weather and the more diarrhea the patient has, the more zinc he needs. The average adult needs a minimum of 10 mg of zinc for each liter of fluid he drinks during the day to a maximum of 50 mg. Someone zinc-deficient to begin with should have more for about a week. High-zinc foods are whole grains, meats other than fish and sausage, eggs, low-fat milk products, shellfish, leafy and root vegetables.

Index C. Differential Diagnosis Protocols

TABLE OF CONTENTS

INDEX C: INTRODUCTION

How To Use The C Protocols.

The objective of these protocols is to enable a health worker to make an educated guess at a probable diagnosis, when working under circumstances where little or no laboratory or other diagnostic facilities are available. If such facilities are available, they should be used. This *Index* is not to be used as a "cookbook;" rather, is intended to be an aid for making an intelligent choice between possible diagnoses.

In each protocol, a few major presenting symptoms are named in its title. Choose the protocol that covers the main symptoms your patient is experiencing. If the patient has symptoms named in more than one protocol, then study each applicable protocol. First go through the list of diseases, eliminating those which are not found in your area. (Geographical information is provided.) Secondly, check the incubation and onset time, as they may give an indication whether that disease is a possible candidate. Then look at the other columns that give further information on the characteristics of each disease, in order to determine which one (or a few) is/are the most probable diagnosis. Also pay attention to the column labeled "Contagious," included in some of the protocols, as in some diseases (e.g., hemorrhagic fever) extreme care must be exercised in dealing with the patient. Look up the most probable diagnoses in the *Disease Index* to make a final determination.

Assumptions.

The following assumptions apply:

1. The reader is in a developing area where the vast majority of diseases are infectious.
2. There is no Western-type facility available.
3. The reader has a Western education at a minimum through 2 years of college.
4. The reader can both read and understand English fluently.
5. The reader and patient have a common language and good rapport.
6. The reader has mastered the contents of the first volume of this book and has had supervised practice in using the logic of the second volume.

To the extent that these assumptions are valid, the protocols below will be helpful. To the extent that they are not valid, other medical care must be obtained.

Notes on Column Headings and Abbreviations (applies to several Protocols).

Incubation (I): The time from exposure to first symptom. (N/A – not applicable.)

Onset (O): The time from first symptom to the person being sick enough to seek help.

Secs – seconds; Mi – minutes; H – hours; D – days; W – weeks; Mo – Months; Y – years.

Groups?: Would one expect to find others in the same community having this disease?

"Yes": definitely expect groups; "No": definitely do not expect groups. Other terms also used: Rare; Maybe; Usual; ?? (indeterminate or unknown); Family (genetically linked diseases); N/A, Not applicable.

For some (not all) diseases which are transmissible, and for conditions resulting from certain environmental factors, one is likely to find multiple individuals having the same symptoms. Information about this tendency is useful for diagnostic purposes. If, for example, there is only one person in the community known to have the particular symptoms, it is unlikely to be a disease that occurs in groups. But if there are other similar cases, then one should focus on group diseases. Genetically inherited diseases also tend to occur in family or kinship groups; these are labeled as "Family" in the protocols.

Risk factors: Factors in a patient's life that make him at risk of getting the disease. "Residence" means he lives in an affected geographical area. Absence of risk factors does not eliminate the diagnosis.

Essential symptoms: Symptoms *in addition to* the defining symptoms listed in the title of the chart.

Likely Symptoms: Other symptoms which are frequently also present but may be absent.

Treatment: See the *Disease Index* for more details on the treatment.

Contagious?: Whether the disease can be transmitted directly from one person to another.

PROTOCOL C-1. STD - SEXUALLY TRANSMITTED DISEASES (And Similar Diseases)

C1-A. Abstinence or Faithfulness Counseling.

These protocols are fashioned similarly to those put out by WHO, substituting abstinence outside of marriage and faithfulness within marriage (rather than the use of condoms) as the only feasible way of preventing infection or reinfection with sexually transmitted diseases. Other sexually transmitted diseases promote the transmission of HIV and the presence of HIV makes the symptoms of some STD's worse. Condoms fail as contraceptives 10% of the time, which means that sperm pass through or around them. HIV viruses are vastly smaller than sperm. Even when condoms don't break or leak, they do not cover all skin that sheds STD organisms. Recommending condoms is like recommending Russian roulette; the odds are similar.

The problem with abstinence/faithfulness is that the only abstinence/faithfulness one can be sure of is his or her own. A crisis arises within a marriage relationship when one suspects his or her partner of unfaithfulness. In this case it might be feasible to practice abstinence for 4 months at which time negative HIV and STD tests can again permit a normal marital sexual relationship. This necessarily involves confronting one's partner which is easier said than done. However, the alternative of continued marital relationships is suicidal. With twice-weekly sexual activity with consistent usage of condoms, within 4 months one would still have 3 exposures to STD's including deadly HIV.

Partner treatment:

Traditionally this was mere notification—having the patient tell his or her partner to show up at the clinic and then treating him or her as a separate patient. There are obvious problems with that approach. The current thinking is to give the patient the medicine to take back home for the partner, in addition to urging a separate examination. The partner must be treated at the same time as the patient; otherwise the disease just passes back and forth.

C1-B. Genital Skin Ulcers: Summary.

Disease	Initial	Ulcer	Pain	Big nodes	Long term
Syphilis	Bump.	Usually single, oval,[1] swollen.	Rare	Usual; non-tender.	Insanity, ANGINA, blindness.
Chancroid	Bumps.	Multiple, ragged edges.	Yes	Big/tender. One side.	Groin scar.
Lympho-granuloma Venereum	Bump or blister. Single.	50% of patients.	Yes	20% of patients. One side. Tender.	Swelling, pain, destruction of genitals causing incontinence.
Donovanosis	Bump.	Yes, shape irregular.	Minimal	No.	Destruction. of genitals causing incontinence.
Herpes	Blister.	Shallow if any.	Usual	Maybe.	Recurrent.

[1] There commonly are multiple ulcers in the presence of HIV INFECTION.

STD appearance in males.

(In females, the ulcers may be difficult to detect.) There are many exceptions to the typical appearance; do not diagnose from appearance alone!

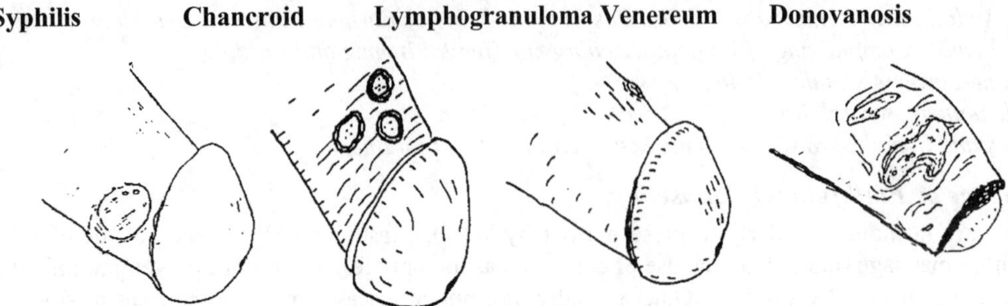

C1-B1. Genital Ulcers, Male or Female.

Is the ulcer

a. on or very near the abdominal wall?
b. discharging some sort of fluid?
c. painful?

<u>NO - only one or none of these apply:</u>

<u>YES – two or three of these apply:</u>

Consider AMEBIC SKIN ULCER and treat it aggressively.

Find out the history and examine him or her: Is there a visible genital ulcer (penis in men, vagina in women)?

<u>YES</u>

<u>NO</u>

Find out if there was one that healed. If so have the patient describe it and treat accordingly. If not, counsel abstinence and/or faithfulness.

Are or were there many small blisters tender to touch?

<u>NO</u>

<u>YES</u>

Treat for HERPES; treat partner(s) also and counsel. Consider REITER SYNDROME in males which may cause sores on the penis indistinguishable from HERPES; it is also likely to cause mouth sores.

Treat for SYPHILIS and CHANCROID (also consider DONOVANOSIS and LYMPHOGRANULOMA VENEREUM)
Treat partner(s) also and counsel.

C1-B2. Male Complaining of Pus from his Penis or Burning with Urinating.

Find out the history and examine him. Have him try to push pus out of the tip of the penis. Can you see pus?

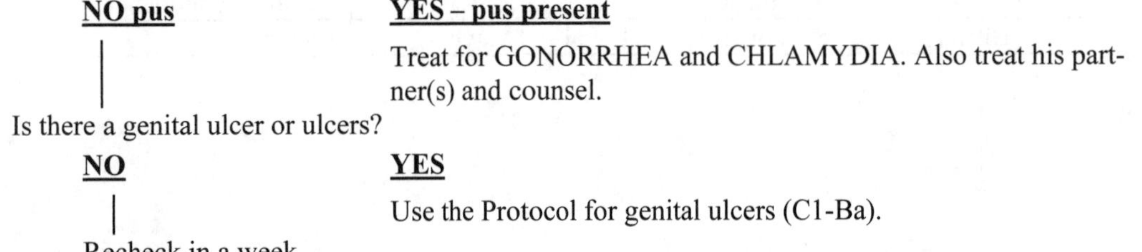

<u>NO pus</u>

<u>YES – pus present</u>

Treat for GONORRHEA and CHLAMYDIA. Also treat his partner(s) and counsel.

Is there a genital ulcer or ulcers?

<u>NO</u>

<u>YES</u>

Use the Protocol for genital ulcers (C1-Ba).

Recheck in a week.
Counsel.

C1-B3. Male Patient Returned with More Pus from his Penis or Burning Pain with Urinating.

Check, as before, if there truly is pus.

YES | **NO**

Check for a genital ulcer. Is there one?

YES — Use the Genital Ulcer Protocol (C1-Ba)

NO — Counsel

Did the person fail to take all his medicine or did he get reinfected?

NO, neither | **YES, either**

YES, either: Repeat the treatment for CHLAMYDIA and GONORRHEA; treat partner(s) also; counsel.

NO, neither: Treat as you would for VAGINITIS due to trichomonas. Treat partner(s) also at the same time and counsel. If no improvement, then refer to a hospital.

C1-B4. Female Complaining of Vaginal Discharge or Genital Itching and Burning.

History and examination: Is there an abnormal discharge?

YES | **NO**

NO: Find out if the patient is worried and if so, why; counsel abstinence and/or faithfulness. (See the Genital Ulcer Protocol C1-Ba) if applicable.

YES: Does the patient have abdominal tenderness and/or pain with pushing a tampon applicator deep into her vagina, and/or pain with intercourse?

NO | **YES**

YES: See Protocol C1-C, "Female Lower Abdominal Pain."

NO: Has she or her husband possibly had illicit sexual contact ? [1]

NO | **YES**

YES: Treat for GONORRHEA and CHLAMYIDIA. Treat the partner(s) also; counsel.

NO: Is there severe itching and a white, cheesy discharge?

NO — Treat for bacterial VAGINITIS and trichomonas VAGINITIS only. Treat partner at the same time; counsel.

YES — Treat for candida VAGINITIS. Treat her partner(s) at the same time; counsel.

[1] First ask about any rape. If the answer is negative, then you must have a great deal of suspicion. If the patient and her husband have no strong religious scruples, you should assume risky behavior. If the woman denies risky behavior but appears nervous or about to cry, then assume risky behavior, regardless of religious scruples or status as missionaries, pastors, or church leaders. If they have strong religious scruples and she denies it with the palms of her hands outstretched and looking you in the eye, there probably is no risky behavior. Look at the hands and arms to determine truthfulness; palms out indicates truth; crossed arms or touching one's face indicates lying.

C1-C. Female Lower Abdominal Pain.

Take a history and examine the patient. Does she have any one or more of the following:?

1. Missed or late period?
2. Recent abortion, miscarriage, or delivery?
3. Is her pain increased with her coughing or your jarring her bed?
4. Does she have bleeding more than an ordinary period?
5. Fever over 38° C/100° F?
6. Abnormal mental state?

No to all — **YES to any or all**: Send her to a hospital for treatment immediately.

Is there any one of the following:

1. Increased pain with a tampon or fingers being pushed deep inside, to touch the cervix?
2. Lower abdomen tender to gentle pushing?
3. Vaginal discharge looks like pus?
4. Pain with intercourse?

YES to any: Treat for PELVIC INFECTION.

NO to all: Check for genital ulcers; see Protocol C1-A.

Is the patient improved in a few days?

YES: Complete the treatment. Be sure to treat her partner(s) and counsel.

NO, not improved: Send her to a hospital with partner(s).

C1-D. Male Patient, Scrotal Swelling.

Take a medical history and do a physical examination.

If the person has not had illicit sexual contact, consider non-contagious causes of scrotal swelling:

Non-contagious causes of scrotal swelling:

Hydrocele: The swollen area is a little bag of water through which light shines.

TUBERCULOSIS: Very slow onset, patient or family member has TB, light won't shine through.

HERNIA: Swelling is soft and goes all the way up to the leg creases; it is not confined to just the scrotum. Light won't shine through but you can hear bowel sounds if you haven't pushed on it.

FILARIASIS: Either the patient himself or many others in his community have massively swollen legs and feet; some have swollen scrotums.

CANCER: Almost always less than age 30; testicle cancer is one of the few cancers that affects younger people and one of the few that is curable. Light won't shine through. Very similar to tuberculosis.

If the diagnosis is not one of the above, then proceed:

Is the testis on that side higher than the other, or turned around, or does the patient give a history of some testicular injury, pain, or tenderness?

No to all: Treat for Chlamydia and Gonorrhea. Keep the patient on bedrest and support his scrotum. Is he improved in a week?

YES to any: Send to a hospital immediately.

YES: Continue the treatment. Treat his partner(s) and counsel.

NO: Send to a hospital.

C1- E. Males and Females: Swellings in the Leg Crease(s); Inguinal Bubo(s).

Before starting this protocol, you should know that a swollen lymph node in a very sick patient, the node being extremely painful and tender and the skin on top abnormally black, may be due to PLAGUE, a disease that is both deadly and contagious. The health authorities must be notified. Also consider ANTHRAX if there is a black scab and excessive swelling.

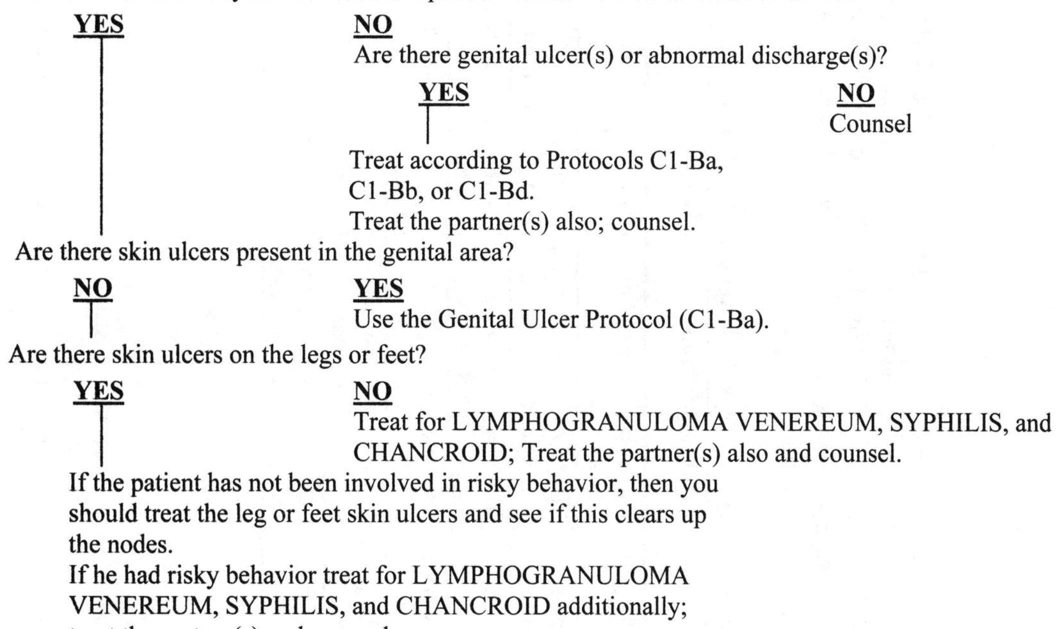
Take a medical history and examine the patient: Is there a swollen node or nodes?
YES
NO
Are there genital ulcer(s) or abnormal discharge(s)?
YES
NO
Counsel
Treat according to Protocols C1-Ba, C1-Bb, or C1-Bd.
Treat the partner(s) also; counsel.
Are there skin ulcers present in the genital area?
NO
YES
Use the Genital Ulcer Protocol (C1-Ba).
Are there skin ulcers on the legs or feet?
YES
NO
Treat for LYMPHOGRANULOMA VENEREUM, SYPHILIS, and CHANCROID; Treat the partner(s) also and counsel.
If the patient has not been involved in risky behavior, then you should treat the leg or feet skin ulcers and see if this clears up the nodes.
If he had risky behavior treat for LYMPHOGRANULOMA VENEREUM, SYPHILIS, and CHANCROID additionally; treat the partner(s) and counsel.

PROTOCOL C-2. FEVER, HEADACHE, AND GENERAL BODY PAINS

C2 A. Fevers, Headache, and General Body Pains
C2 B. Viral Hemorrhagic Fevers (VHF's): Arboviral Fevers which Become Epidemic-Type
C2 C. Tourniquet Test for Hemorrhagic Fever

C2 A. Fevers, Headache, and General Body Pains.

In a malarious area, first treat MALARIA and then see what, if any, symptoms are left. Be sure to use some form of ARTEMISININ so that the treatment works rapidly. If the patient is not improved within 12 hours, then proceed to use the chart below. If the patient is improved but still quite ill, consider ENTERIC FEVER, which frequently coexists with malaria. Also consider the possibility of HEMORRHAGIC FEVER: see Chart C2 B, below. For the first week, use strict precautions in nursing your patient: Gown, gloves, mask, sterilizing eating utensils, care in disposing of waste—until you are sure this is NOT Hemorrhagic Fever. These are also good precautions as regards other contagious conditions.

See Introduction to *Index C*: Notes on Column Headings and Abbreviations.
Abbreviations for Incubation (I) and Onset (O) times: Secs – seconds; Mi – minutes; H – hours; D – days; W – weeks; Mo – Months; Y – years.

Disease	Incubation; Onset	Groups?	Risk factors	Essential symptoms	Likely symptoms	Treatment	Contagious?
African Sleeping Sickness[1]	I: varies O: W-Y[2]	Rare	Residence; bitten by a fly that dives	Swollen bite area or large lymph node(s)	Large spleen, heart failure, weight loss	Difficult, dangerous; fatal if untreated	No
Arboviral Fever[3]	I: varies O: D-W	Some kinds	Residence; insect bite	Varies with the geography and the kind	Mental changes, red eyes, joint pains, bleeding	Supportive or antivirals; some fatal or disabling	Some kinds
Bartonellosis[4] Oroya	I: 4-16 W O: W-Mo	??	Residence; sandfly bite	Joint pains, bone pain, chest pain	Irrational, large spleen, large lymph nodes	Antibiotics; fatal if untreated	No
Dengue Fever	I: 2-15 D O: H	Usual	Tropics, urban, house plants	Severe bone pains, eyes red and painful	Rash, very ill, depression	Supportive only; rarely fatal if untreated	No
Enteric Fever	I: 1-3 W O: D-W	??	Poor sanitation, food or water	Acts "spacy" and belly pain; fever is high by day 4	Constipation, diarrhea, vomiting, body odor	Antibiotics; some fatal if untreated	Yes
Leptospirosis	I: 2-21 D O: H	??	Exposure to rat urine; flood water; food	Sore eyes or muscle pains or both	Fever goes up and down unpredictably	Antibiotics; must be started soon; may be fatal	No

Continued on next page.

[1] Scattered, small areas throughout Africa, from 15° North to 20° South. The great lakes area of East Africa has both kinds; east and south of there it is all Rhodesian; west and north of there it is all Gambian. However, the boundaries do move; there may be exceptions.
[2] West Africa: initial incubation period is a month; mental symptoms start after months to years with slow onset. East Africa: Incubation to the first fever is under 3 weeks; mental symptoms start within a month or two, onset over weeks.
[3] Arboviral fevers which are contagious and may cause hemorrhage and death are listed in a chart following this one, called Hemorrhagic Fever. They start out as ordinary arboviral fevers and then the patient develops abnormal bleeding. All arboviral fevers with abnormal bleeding are not, however, necessarily contagious.
[4] Only present in Peru and adjacent border areas.

(C2 A. Fevers, Headache, and General Body Pains, continued.)

Disease	Incubation; Onset	Groups?	Risk factors	Essential symptoms	Likely symptoms	Treatment	Conta-gious?
Lyme Disease	I: 3-32 D O: Varies	Rare	Temperate and sub-tropics; tick bite, rural	Rash or history of one	Joints red and swollen	Antibiotics; rarely fatal	No
Malaria	I: 3-21 D O: Varies[1]	Usual	Humid tropics and sub-tropics	Shaking chills; sweats[2]	Waist and shoulder pains; tired	Antimalarials; may be fatal	No
Q Fever	I: 2-4 W O: Varies	Rare	Exposed-newborn ani-mals, Middle East	Nothing additional; mildly ill	Like hepatitis or pneu-monia	Antibiotics; not generally fatal	??
Rat bite Fev	I: 3-30 D O: D	Rare	Rodent bite; residence Asia	Wound healed initially or there is a rash	Wound broke open, nau-sea, weakness	Antibiotics to prevent recur-rences	No
Relapsing Fever, louse	I: 2-14 D O: Mi	Usual	Crowding, cool, refu-gee camps; crushing head or body lice	Fevers are high, over 101F or 38C	Short of breath, cough, chest pains, large spleen	Antibiotics; may be fatal	Yes[3]
Relapsing fever, tick[4]	I: 2-14 D O: Mi	??	Caves, abandoned houses, camps	Fever drops in less than 7 days	Cough, belly pain, quite ill	Antibiotics	No
Spotted Fever, various	O: H-D I: < 12 D	??	Tick/mite exposure, eastern hemisphere	Rash on limb(s), moderately or very ill	Tiny scab(s) from insect bite(s)	Antibiotics; may be fatal	Pox type only
Spotted Fever, Rocky Mtn	O: H-D I: 6-10 D	Rare	Americas; tick expo-sure	Spleen tender, big; nausea; joint and muscle pains	Rash on wrists and an-kles; black scab	Antibiotics; may be fatal if untreated	No
Syphilis secondary	I: 2-24 W O: D	Usual	Sexual contact or infant of syphilic mother	Skin or mouth problems.	Spotted rash, hair loss, history of a genital ulcer	Antibiotics prevent tertiary syphilis	Yes very
Trench Fever	I: 4-36 D O: H-D	Usual	Temperate; urban, homeless	Poor hygiene, body lice	Shin pains, bone pains	Antibiotics; may be fatal	Yes[5]
Trichinosis	I: < 30 D O: D-W	Usual	Ate pork or wild game	Muscles swollen and sore	Other eaters also are sick	Steroids, no antibiotics	No

Continued on next page.

[1] Onset is likely to be rapid if the person is not taking prophylactic medicines but slow if he/she was taking them.
[2] The shaking chills and sweats are essential only if the patient has not taken prophylactic medicines. The medicines might negate these symptoms.
[3] Anyone who cares for the patient is likely to acquire a louse or two. It is not otherwise contagious.
[4] It is unlikely that the patient will report a tick bite because these ticks are nocturnal, their bites are painless, and they drop off quickly. They are soft ticks.
[5] It is not contagious by direct contact but anyone who touches a person with lice is likely to get a louse bite or two.

(C2-A. Fevers, Headache, and General Body Pains, continued.)

Disease	Incubation; Onset	Groups?	Risk factors	Essential symptoms	Likely symptoms	Treatment	Conta-gious?
Tularemia[1]	I: 1-14 D O: D	Rare	Contact, small mam-mal(s) or their insects	Insect bite with a red ring around	Red lumps or streaks from the bite to the trunk	Antibiotics	No
Typhus, Louse	I: 12 D +/- O: H-D	Usual	Poverty, crowding, body lice	Had body lice; other symp-toms before fever	Mental changes, musty body odor, shin pain	Antibiotics; may be fatal	Yes[2]
Typhus, murine	I: 6-14 D O: D-W	??	Rodent contact, fleas or urine	Muscle pains	Red eyes, rash, musty body odor	Antibiotics; may be fatal	No
Yellow Fever[3]	I: 3-6 D O: D	??	Unimmunized; mos-quito bitten, residence	Jaundice or bilirubin in the urine	Slow pulse relative to fever; protein in urine	Only supportive; may be fatal	No

[1] Northern hemisphere, temperate and sub-tropical, as far south as the northern coast of Africa.
[2] It is not contagious by direct contact but anyone who touches a person with lice is likely to get a louse bite or two.
[3] South America north of Sao Paolo, central and western Africa and the Sudan.

C2-B. Viral Hemorrhagic Fevers (VHF's). Arboviral Fevers Which Become Epidemic-Type.

(Warning: You can catch VHF's by caring for patients, and you can start an epidemic by transporting affected patients.)

See Introduction to *Index C*: Notes on Column Headings and Abbreviations.
Abbreviations for Incubation (I) and Onset (O) times: Secs – seconds; Mi – minutes; H – hours; D – days; W – weeks; Mo – Months; Y – years.

Disease	Incubation; Onset	Exposure	Distinctives[1]	Other symptoms[2]	Geography
Lassa Fever	I: 5-35 D. O: gradual.	Rodents	Chest pain, sore throat, swollen face	Fatigue, red eyes, belly pain, vomiting, diarrhea	D R Congo and West Africa, north and west of there, south of the Sahara
Ebola Fever	I: 4-16 D. O: sudden.	Monkeys or bats	Blisters in mouth and throat, very red eyes, bleeding gums, maybe a measles-type rash	Belly pain, diarrhea. Bleeding starts from Day 5 to Day 7	Eastern D R Congo, southern Sudan, adjacent Kenya, Uganda, CAR, Gabon maybe elsewhere
Marburg Fever	I: 3-13 D. O: sudden.	Monkeys. bats, prairie dogs	Like Ebola	Like Ebola	Eastern D R Congo, Uganda, western Kenya, ? west and south Africa
Crimean-Congo Hemorrhagic Fever	I: 1-3 D with tick bite; 5-6 D direct. O: sudden.	Farm animals	Neck pain, large, tender liver, large lymph nodes, red face	Bleeding from all over	Much of Africa, southeastern Europe, entire Middle East, Asia.
South American VH Fevers (3 types)	1. I: 7-16 D. O: gradual onset. 2. I: 5-19 D; O: ? 3. O: gradual onset	Rodents, farm animals	1.Low back pain; brain damage, bleeding, 2.Maybe brain damage. 3. Sore throat	1. Red eyes. 2. Fatigue 3. Red eyes	1.Argentine pampas 2.Beni area of Bolivia 3.Plains of Venezuela
Rift Valley Fever[3]	I: 2-7 D. O: sudden.	Sick or aborting farm animals	Back pains, eye symptoms	Jaundice, rash, may cause blindness	Kenya and across sub-Saharan Africa and the middle east

C2-C. Tourniquet Test for Hemorrhagic Fever.

A. Determine the patient's blood pressure.
B. Find the number half-way between the higher and lower blood pressure numbers.
C. Inflate the blood pressure cuff to that number and keep it inflated there for five minutes; the patient will have pain.
D. Deflate the blood pressure cuff and look at the arm below the cuff to see if there is a rash. If you can see a rash—little spots like measles or pin-head bruises—then the test is positive. Your patient has hemorrhagic fever. The spots may be hard to see in very dark skin; look at the fingernails.

[1] Distinctives are symptoms that are not present with most arboviral diseases but ones that should alert you to the fact that this patient may be contagious. It is important, if you note a distinctive symptom, to do the tourniquet test which will tell you if this person is likely to have a hemorrhagic fever.
[2] That is, in addition to fever, headache, general body pains and distinctives.
[3] It is unknown if this is transmissible from patient to patient but it is treated as if it is because it can be transmitted from animal blood to humans.

PROTOCOL C-3. FEVER,[1] FATIGUE, and ANEMIA (Large Spleen, Jaundice)

See Introduction to *Index C*: Notes on Column Headings and Abbreviations
Abbreviations for Incubation (I) and Onset (O) times: Secs – seconds; Mi – minutes; H – hours; D – days; W – weeks; Mo – Months; Y – years.

Disease	Incubation; Onset	Groups?	Risk factors	Essential Symptoms	Likely Symptoms	Treatment	Contagious?
African Sleeping Sickness[2]	I: Varies O: W-Y[3]	Rare	Residence; bitten by a fly that dive-bombs	Headache, body pains, swollen bite area, big lymph nodes	Mental symptoms, loss of weight, sleepiness, large spleen	Special drugs, dangerous, may be fatal	No
Bartonellosis[4] Oroya	I: 4-16 W O: W-Mo	??	Residence; bitten by sandflies	Joint pain, anemia came on rapidly	Chest pain; lymph nodes and liver are big	Antibiotics, may be fatal	No
Cancer	I: N/A O: Mo-Y	No	Many; old age; radiation, hepatitis	Pale tongue and fingernails	Lump(s) somewhere, weight loss, bleeding	Difficult Expensive	No
Dysentery	I: 2-14 D O: H-D	Usual	Poor sanitation for water or food	Bloody diarrhea, maybe with mucus	Pain, left lower abdomen	Antibiotics Metronidazole	Yes
Hemorrhagic Fever	I: Varies O: Varies	Usual	Residence; bitten by insects	Fever, body pains, headache, bleeding	Varies by the kind; bleeding	None or difficult	Some kinds yes
Malaria	I: 3-21 D O: H-W[5]	Usual	Humid tropics and sub-tropics mostly	Chills,[6] headache, sweating	Waist, shoulder, joint pains	Antimalarials (antibiotics[7])	No
Ovalocytosis	I: N/A O: Mo-Y	Family	Family affected; Malaysia and Papua	Large spleen; urobilinogen in urine	Jaundice, sometimes recurrent crises	Transfusion	No
Sickle Cell Disease	I: N/A O: Mo-Y	Family	Family affected; early deaths[8]	Child—big spleen, but not adult(s)	Bone pain, chest pain, jaundice	IV's, oxygen, transfusion	No

Continued on next page.

[1] The patient may not have a fever at the moment but he should have a history of fevers (chills, sweats, elevated temperature).

[2] Present in Africa between 15° North and 20° South. Both kinds are present in the great lakes area of east Africa; west and north of there it is all Gambian whereas east and south of there it is all Rhodesian. The boundaries might move and there may be exceptions.

[3] The West African form comes on slowly over years after an initial incubation of a month, followed by a brief illness. The East African form comes on rapidly over weeks after an incubation of less than 3 weeks.

[4] Only in Peru and adjacent border areas.

[5] The onset is likely to be rapid if the person was not taking preventive medication; it is likely to be gradual otherwise.

[6] Usually only if the patient has not been taking malaria prophylaxis.

[7] Some ordinary antibiotics also are active against malaria but they are generally weak antimalarials.

[8] This affects mainly those with an African genetic heritage; some Arabs, Indians, and Greeks are also affected but rarely and not severely.

(Protocol C-3: Fever, Fatigue, and Anemia, continued.)

Disease	Incubation; Onset	Groups?	Risk factors	Essential Symptoms	Likely Symptoms	Treatment	Contagious?
Thallasemia	I: N/A O: Mo-Y	Family	Genetic heritage	Family history; urobilinogen in the urine	Bone pain, growth problems, strange facial appearance	Transfusion	No
Tropical Splenomegaly	I: Y O: Mo-Y	Usual	Malarious area; humid tropics	Heaviness, left upper abdomen; large spleen	Urobilinogen in the urine; frequent infections	Antimalarials, long-term	No
Tuberculosis any kind	I: W-M O: Mo-Y	Usual	Contact with a coughing adult; unimmunized	Varies with the organs infected with the TB.	Cough, large neck lymph nodes, weight loss	Special antibiotics	Some kinds
Visceral Leishmaniasis[1]	I: 10 D-3 Y O: Mo-Y	??	Residence; bitten by sandflies	Large liver, weight loss, large spleen	Night sweats, no appetite, bleeding	Special drugs Difficult	No

[1] Present in scattered areas of Africa, the tropical Americas, the Mediterranean, and Asia; may be locally common

PROTOCOL C-4. SHORTNESS OF BREATH (Fever, Chest Pain, Cough)

Be aware that respiratory distress with noisy inhalations is an emergency: send out!!

See Introduction to *Index C*: Notes on Column Headings and Abbreviations.
Abbreviations for Incubation (I) and Onset (O) times: Secs – seconds; Mi – minutes; H – hours; D – days; W – weeks; Mo – Months; Y – years.

Disease	Incubation; Onset	Groups?	Risks	Essential Symptoms	Likely Symptoms	Treatment	Contagious?
Altitude Sickness	I: N/A O: Mi-H	??	Recent ascent to 2000 meters or more	Rapid respiration, rales in lungs, cough	Headache, confused, no fever	Descent, oxygen, rest in a sitting position	No
Anemia from any cause	I: Varies O: Varies	??	Blood loss, poor diet, some illnesses, or hereditary	Pale tongue or fingernails, fatigue	Dizzy, jaundice, no cough, large spleen	Various, depends on the cause; transfusion	Some kinds
Anthrax	I: <7d O: H-D	Likely	Animal meat or hides; mostly arid areas	Scab with massive swelling or windpipe closing	Fever; sore is not painful; may itch;	Antibiotics	Skin form only; pus is infective
Asthma	I: N/A O: Mi-H	No	Expatriates; Western culture, rare in nationals	Wheezing or struggling to breathe or both	Recurrent, wheezing, no fever, breathing fast or slow	Special drugs	No
Cancer	I: N/A O: H-Y	No	Old age, Western culture, some toxins, smoking, tumor	Cough or abnormal breath sounds	Weight loss, chest pain, fever, coughing blood	Difficult and high-tech	No
Carbon Monoxide Poisoning	I: Mi-D O: Mi-D	??	Fire or engine exhaust exposure	Nausea, headache	Red inside the mouth, no fever	Oxygen	No
Diphtheria	I: 1-6 D O: Varies	Rare	Exposure to someone similarly ill; unimmunized	Swollen neck or painful wound; low fever if any	Muscles weak; scum on tonsils; sweet body odor	Anti-toxin; antibiotics	Yes
Enteric Fever	I: 1-3 W O: D	??	Poor sanitation, food and water contaminated	Acts "spacy", abdominal pain, cough	Nausea, constipation, diarrhea, fever high	Antibiotics	Yes
Familial Mediterranean Fever	I: N/A O: Varies	Family	Mediterranean genetic heritage; family history	Skin or mental or abdominal symptoms	Varies, fever; recurrent problems	Diet, special drugs	No

Continued on next page.

(Protocol C-4: Shortness Of Breath, continued.)

Disease	Incubation; Onset	Groups?	Risk Factors	Essential Symptoms	Likely Symptoms	Treatment	Contagious?
Filariasis[1]	I: 4-18 Mo O: D-W	Usual	Rainy season, tropics, crowded area, expatriates; mosquitoes	Wheezing, fever, chills, swelling of a body part	Swollen, rough skin on body part--later	Special drugs	No
Goiter	I: N/A O: Mo-Y	Usual	Residence inland, mountainous or river delta by the sea	Swelling center front lower neck, fatigue	Difficulty swallowing,	Iodine if not lumpy	No
Heart Failure	I: Varies O: D-Mo	Rare	Western diet; prior infection(s)	Rales, fatigue, or swollen ankles	Heart murmur or chest pain	Special drugs	No
Pneumonia	I: Varies O: H-D	??	Previous cold or another illness	Fever, coughing, abnormal breath sounds	Chest pain worse with breathing	Antibiotics	Yes
Pneumothorax	I: Mi-H[2] O: Secs-Mi	No	Chest wound or spontaneous	No breath sounds one side	Chest pain one side; no fever	Emergency surgery	No
Q Fever	I: 2-4 W O: Varies	??	Newborn animal contact, esp. the Middle East	Fever, headache, chills, fatigue	Jaundice, joint pains; large tender liver	Antibiotics	Unknown
Respiratory Infection	I: Recurs O: Varies	??	Smoking, heredity, childhood	Breathing labored, fast, or slow	Chest pain, cough, fever, phlegm	Antibiotics, other medicines	Maybe
Sepsis	I: Varies O: H-W	Rare	Previous infection not totally cured	High fever unless malnourished; very ill	Lethargic; abnormal vital signs	Antibiotics, IV's high-tech meds	Maybe
Sickle Cell Disease	I: Recurs O: Mi-Y[3]	Family	African, Arab, Indian, or Greek heritage	Chest pain, anemia, growth delays	Bone pain, kidney trouble, leg ulcers	High-tech, oxygen, IV's	No
Smoke Inhalation	I: Sec-3 D O: Mi -3 D	??	Exposure to a smoky fire	Smoke exposure, cough	Sputum has black flecks	Oxygen, high-tech	No
Tuberculosis	I: Mo-Y O: Mo-Y	Usual	Exposed to a coughing adult; not immunized	Slow onset, productive cough, night sweats	Chest pain, weight loss, pale skin, phlegm	Special drugs, antibiotics	Yes
Whooping Cough	I: 1-2 W O: D-W	??	Unimmunized; infants and elderly mostly	Violent coughing followed by noisy breathing in.	Vomiting from coughing hard; bloody eyes	Supportive, oxygen, maybe antibiotics	Yes

[1] Coastal South America, the Caribbean, and scattered areas throughout the tropics of the Eastern Hemisphere; especially common in the Pacific.
[2] That is, the length of time from the causative injury until the first symptoms. This is irrelevant if the pneumothorax is spontaneous.
[3] The individual episodes start rapidly; the problem is recurrent over years.

PROTOCOL C-5. FEVER, JAUNDICE (Large Liver, Tender Liver)

See Introduction to *Index C*: Notes on Column Headings and Abbreviations.
Abbreviations for Incubation (I) and Onset (O) times: Secs – seconds; Mi – minutes; H – hours; D – days; W – weeks; Mo – Months; Y – years.

Disease	Incubation; Onset	Groups?	Risk Factors	Essential Symptoms	Likely Symptoms	Urine[1]	Treatment	Contagious?
Amebic Liver Disease	I: 2-14 D O: Varies	??	Poor sanitation, usually from food	Pain, right upper abdomen	Hurts to jump and cough; liver tender	?B	Metronidazole	No
Bartonellosis[2] Oroyo	I: 2-16 W O: D-W	??	Residence; bitten by sand flies	Fatigue, headache, joint pains	Big spleen & liver; craziness	?U ?B	Antibiotics	No
Brucellosis	I: 2-4 W O: Mo	Rare	Pastoral areas; hides, meat, milk, cheese	Back pain, joint pains, no swelling	Feels awful; fevers come and go	??	Three antibiotics for 6 weeks	No
Cancer	I: Unknown O: Mo-Y	Rare	Old age; smoking; refined diet; hepatitis; toxins	Symptoms vary; initially painless	Weight loss; lumpy liver; light-colored stool	?B; ?U	Surgery; otherwise difficult	No
Gallbladder Disease	I: Varies O: Varies	Some kinds	Obesity, malaria, fatty diet; some worms	Pain, upper right or mid abdomen	Shoulder pain, pains come and go	B	Surgery	No
Hepatitis	I: Varies O: H-D	??	Poor sanitation, blood exposure	Jaundice or urine bilirubin	Joint pains, vomiting, weight loss	B ?U	Supportive; high-tech medicines	Some kinds contagious
Leptospirosis	I: 2-21 D O: H-D	??	Flood water, rodent urine, poor sanitation	Red eyes or muscle pains	Fever up and down, headache	?B	Antibiotics	No
Malaria	I: 3-21 D O: H-D	Usual	Humid tropics and subtropics	Chills, headache sweats	Pain left upper abdomen	U	Antimalarials Some antibiotics	No
Pneumonia	I: Varies O: H-D	Rare	Prior cold; Black genetic heritage	Productive cough, high fever	Short of breath, abnormal breath sounds	U	Antibiotics	Yes
Sickle Cell Disease	I: Recurs O: Varies	Family	African genetic heritage; stress	Episodic bone pain, fatigue, anemia	Chest, bone pain, poor growth	U	Complex; high-tech, transfusions	No
Visceral Leishmaniasis[3]	I: 3D-3Y O: W-Mo	Rare	Residence; sandflies	Large spleen, weight loss	Large liver; fever episodes	U	Special medicines	No
Yellow Fever[4]	I: < 7 D O: H-D	??	Residence; unimmunized; mosquitoes	"Flu-like" illness before jaundice	Butcher body odor; protein in urine	B	Supportive	Not directly

[1] Urine: whether bilirubin (B) or urobilinogen (U) is found in the urine. A question mark (?) before the letter means Maybe. But any time there is bilirubin, there may also be excess urobilingen. If only U appears, it implies that bilirubin is absent. These are general rules; there are exceptions.
[2] Only found in Peru and adjacent border areas.
[3] Present in scattered areas of Africa, the tropical Americas, the Mediterranean, and Asia. May be locally common.
[4] Present in parts of Africa and the Americas; see the regional indices.

PROTOCOL C-6. LIMB SWELLING, PAIN, (Fever, Stiffness)

C 6 A. Limb Swelling and Pain, Initially and Only, or Mainly Over Joints
*C 6 B. Limb Swelling and Pain, **Not** Initially and Only or Mainly Over Joints*

C6-A. Limb Swelling and Pain, Initially and Only or Mainly over Joints

If the pain and swelling started out somewhere on the limb other than right in or on a joint, then it moved to a joint, see Protocol C-6B below.

See Introduction to *Index C*: Notes on Column Headings and Abbreviations.
Abbreviations for Incubation (I) and Onset (O) times: Secs – seconds; Mi – minutes; H – hours; D – days; W – weeks; Mo – Months; Y – years.

Disease	Incubation; Onset	Groups?	Risk Factors	Essential Symptoms	Likely Symptoms	Treatment
Arboviral Fever	I: D -W usual O: H-D	Usual	Bitten by insects or ticks; maybe contagious	Headache, fever, joint pain, general body pains	Bleeding, red eyes, muscle pains	Supportive only
Arthritis, Osteoarthritis	I: N/A O: Y; comes and stays	No	Rough sports or excessive stress on the joint(s)	Slow onset; adult patient or prior injury; no fever	Not red, minimally swollen	Anti-inflammatory medicines
Arthritis, Rheumatoid	I: recurs O: H-D	No	Western culture; family history, rare in poor nationals	Multiple joints, symmetrical, migrates; morning stiffness	Joints red and swollen; fever, hands affected	Anti-inflammatory medicines
Reiter Syndrome	I: 1-3 W O: Unknown	??	Sexual exposure or dysentery	Single large joint or one digit; fever	Skin, mouth, penis sores, little pain	Antibiotics, special medicines
Arthritis, Septic	I: Varies O: H-D	No	Injury; infection, poor immunity	Single joint usually, not symmetrical	Joint is red and hot, fever	Surgery, antibiotics
Arthritis, Tuberculous	I: Mo-Y O: W-Y	Rare	Much TB in the community	Pain, stiff/swollen, abnormal shape	Joint not tender; thin muscles, gait problems	Anti-TB medicines, surgery
Bartonellosis[1] Verugga	I: 4-16 W O: D-W?	??	Residence; sandfly bitten	Fever drops with bumpy swellings appearing	Skin bumps; face affected also	Antibiotics
Brucellosis	I: 2-4 W O: Mo	??	Pastoral areas; hides, meat, milk, mostly arid	Complaining bitterly, back pain, fevers	Joints not red; tender; minimal swelling	3 antibiotics for six weeks

Continued on next page.

[1] Only in Peru and adjacent border areas.

(C6-A: Limb Swelling and Pain, Initially and Only or Mainly over Joints, continued.)

Disease	Incubation; Onset	Groups?	Risk Factors	Essential Symptoms	Likely Symptoms	Treatment
Gonorrhea	I: 2 W - Mo[1] O: H-D	Usual	Sexual exposure; body secretions	Sudden onset, single joint	Red/hot joint; swollen, fever	Antibiotics
Gout	I: N/A O: H	No	Affluent; from some medicines; rich diet	One toe or ankle; severe pain and tenderness	Red/hot joint; very swollen	Special medicines
HIV Infection	I: Y; recurs O: H-D	Usual	Sexual or blood exposure; Africa especially	Large joints; not small joints	Symmetrical; red/hot, comes and goes	Special medicines
Leprosy	I: 2-10 Y O: Mo-Y	??	Residence in an area with much leprosy	Skin condition or history of same; limb numbness	Painless deformed joints with abnormal motion	Special medicines Antibiotics
Lyme Disease[2]	I: 3-32 D Recurs O: Varies	Rare	Forested, rural areas; exposure to ticks	Initial rash; one or few joint pains recur; swelling	History of fever, and fatigue	Antibiotics for 2-6 weeks
Osteomyelitis	I: varies O: Varies	Rare	Prior injury or infection	Severe pain, fever, very tender over the area	Red/hot joint,[3] maybe pus drainage.	Antibiotics for 6 weeks
Rheumatic Fever	I: Recurs O: H-2 D	Rare	Strep infection, poorly treated	Symmetrical arthritis, fever	Red/hot joints; migrates, heart murmur	Anti-inflammatory; antibiotics
Rickets	I: varies O: W-Mo	Usual	Little or no sun exposure for weeks to months	History; deformity of bones	Not red/hot; chest deformity	Vitamin D, surgery
Scurvy	I: Mo O: W-Mo	Usual	No fresh produce in the diet	History; swelling, bleeding, stiffness	Loose teeth, putrid-sweet body odor	Vitamin C
Syphilis tertiary	I: Y adult I: ? child O: W-M	??	Middle aged or born to syphilic mother	Swelling worse than pain, very movable joints, gait problems	Skin bumps or ulcers, curved bones	Antibiotics to prevent worsening

[1] The incubation is on the order of 2 weeks for males but months for females.
[2] Present in the temperate northern hemisphere plus subtropical areas such as the north coast of Africa and coastal Australia.
[3] Osteomyelitis is a bone infection. If it happens to be near a joint, it is indistinguishable from septic arthritis.

C6-B. Limb Swelling and Pain, Not Only or Mainly Over Joints

See Introduction to *Index C*: Notes on Column Headings and Abbreviations.
Abbreviations for Incubation (I) and Onset (O) times: Secs – seconds; Mi – minutes; H – hours; D – days; W – weeks; Mo – Months; Y – years.

Disease	Incubation; Onset	Groups?	Risk Factors	Essential symptoms; most specific	Likely symptoms	Varies?[1]	Treatment
Abscess	I: varies O: D-W	No	Prior injury, even slight	Swollen, warm area, initially firm	Becomes soft; tender, large lymph nodes	No	Surgery
Anthrax	I: D O: H-D	??	Exposed to ill animals, meat, hides	Skin bump or ulcer, then fever and swelling	Severe swelling, little pain, maybe itching	No	Antibiotics
Arsenic Poisoning	I: Varies O: Varies	??	Ethnic remedies, occupational, homicidal	Numbness, tingling, weakness, burning	Skin is rough, dry, flaky, face swells	??	High-tech
Cancer	I: N/A O: W-Y	No	HIV positive, toxins, radiation, old age	Weight loss, big lymph nodes, not symmetrical	Painless at first	No	Difficult and high-tech
Cellulitis	I: H-D O: D	Rare	Prior injury, even slight	Swelling, warmth in a confined area of the skin	Red streaks from the area to the trunk	No	Antibiotics, maybe surgery
Cysticercosis	I: Unknown O: Unknown	Rare	Poor food sanitation	General muscle swelling and soreness	"Split peas" under the skin	No	Not much
Elephantiasis, Endemic	I: Y O: Mo-Y	Yes	Childhood spent barefoot on red, clay soil; locally common	1st burning/itching feet; then skin thickens, clumsy gait	Symmetrical or almost, moves from feet to trunk	Slightly at first only	Shoes, soaking, maybe surgery
Filariasis	I: < 18 Mo O: < 2 Y	Usual	Tropical, humid, crowded, esp Asia/Pacific	Comes and goes at first; skin rough	Maybe symmetrical, usually moves trunk to feet	At first only	Medicines early; surgery later
Heart Failure	I: N/A O: Varies	No	Western diet, rheumatic fever, infection	Fatigued or short of breath or both, symmetrical	Chest pain, heart murmur, fast respiration	Yes	Special medicines, surgery
Kidney Failure	I: Varies O: Varies	No	Many illnesses and poisonings can cause this	High BP or abnormal urinalysis, symmetrical	Little urine or much protein in urine	Yes	High-tech, and/or difficult
Leprosy Reaction	I: < 6 Mo[2] O: H-D	No	Leprous patients on medication	Symmetrical bumpy skin rash before starting meds	Missing toes and fingers; skin ulcers	Maybe	Special medicines
Liver Failure	I: Varies O: W-Y	No	Alcoholics, TB patients, various drugs and toxins	Jaundice or swollen abdomen, symmetrical leg swelling	Skin spiders, fatigued, waddling gait	Yes	Diet, maybe high-tech

Continued on next page.

[1] Varies?: How the swelling behaves. "Yes" means the swelling varies; it goes down at night or when the swollen area is elevated above the level of the heart.
[2] That is, the time from starting the leprosy medication until the reaction occurs. It is not the incubation period for the leprosy itself.

(C6-B: Limb Swelling and Pain, Not Only or Mainly Over Joints, continued.)

Disease	Incubation; Onset	Groups?	Risk Factors	Essential symptoms	Likely symptoms	Varies?	Treatment
Loiasis	I: 1 Y O: H-D; recurs	Rare	Residence in humid central or western Africa	Bumps that arise here and there, then disappear, size of small eggs	Patient reports a worm in his eye	Only at random times	Dewormers
Malabsorption	I: Varies O: Varies	??	Any one of a large number of conditions	Chronic diarrhea, weight loss, symmetrical swelling	Swollen legs, worse the end of the day	Yes	Variable
Malnutrition	I: Varies O: Varies	Usual	Famine, poverty; cancer, anorexics	Poor diet, symmetrical swelling	Swollen legs, worse the end of the day	Yes	Good food
Osteomyelitis	I: Varies O: Varies	No	Prior injury or illness	Severe bone pain, keeps awake at night, fever	Swellling feels hot, may see pus, one place	No	Antibiotics, maybe surgery
Pyomyositis	I: varies O: D-W	No	Prior injury or injection	Muscle pain, one place	Fever, swellling feels hot	No	Drain pus and give antibiotics
Rat bite Fever	I: < 30 D O: D	Rare	Rat bit the patient, mostly Asia	Fever; the bite healed or there is a skin rash	Chills, headache, nausea, weakness, wound broken open	??	Antibiotics
Sickle Cell Disease	I: N/A O: H-D	Family	African genetic heritage	Child, both hands swollen or recurrent crises	Anemia; delayed growth, pain episodes	Maybe	Oxygen, IV's, complicated
Toxemia of pregnancy	I: N/A O: D-W	No	Especially the last 3 months, first pregnancy	Last 6 months of pregnancy or just delivered	Protein in urine, headaches, high BP	Yes	Bedrest, special medicines
Trichinosis	I: < 30 D O: Unknown	Usual	Ate poorly cooked pork or wild game	All limbs swollen, trunk swollen also; fever after the swelling	General whole-body pains, symmetrical	No	Difficult or impossible

PROTOCOL C-7. LIVER and/or SPLEEN ENLARGED (Swollen Abdomen, Jaundice)

How To Use This Protocol.[1]

This protocol is for sorting out problems involving the liver and/or spleen. The table below, and the following diagram with the ovals, serve as guides to the tables in the remainder of this protocol. The first column in the table lists various conditions; some of these conditions are syndromes (groups of symptoms) and some are disease clusters. The second and third columns define what you and the patient will observe, if he has the stated condition—what he is likely to complain of and what you will see when examining him.

If the Symptoms and results of the physical exam fit *only one* of the conditions listed in Column 1, then go to the subsections of this protocol listed in Column 4. See also the other references given in Column 5.

If the patient shows symptoms and physical exam results that correspond to *more than one* of the conditions in Column 1, then he probably has *liver failure*.

There are two kinds of liver failure:

Cirrhosis, or slow-onset. Develops over 6 months or more.
Fulminant or fast onset. Develops over less than 3 months.
If the problem has been going on for well over 6 months, then it is slow-onset, but if it has been developing for a shorter time, then it may be either type.
You need to decide:
Which kind of liver failure your patient has.
Which disease(s) is/are the likely cause(s).
To do that, consult the diagram with the ovals on the following page. Not all patients will have all conditions. Most will lack at least one.
The causative disease(s) must also be treated. The urgency of referral is greater with fast-onset than with slow onset liver failure.

[1] It is important to note that this protocol is a gross generalization with many exceptions. In all cases advanced care must be sought ASAP.

Outline of Symptoms and Conditions.

Conditions	Symptoms[1]	Physical exam	Causative Disease Lists	Reference for Diagnosis and Diseases
Ascites: Free fluid in abdomen	Clothes fit tight, maybe ankle swelling.	**Abdomen distended** but you can feel no lump in the abdomen.	C7-D, 1 for only ascites, no other conditions	Vol. I, Chap. 1. *Symptom Protocol* A-46
Large spleen without big veins on the abdomen	**Heavy, dragging feeling in the left upper abdomen**.	Abdomen distended, you can feel a mass extending to the left ribs. Left upper abdominal mass.	C7-A; C7-D, 2 for only a large spleen, no big veins, no other conditions	Vol. I, Chap. 1. *Disease Index*, Tropical Splenomegaly *Symptom Protocol* A-46
Large spleen with big veins on the abdomen	**Heavy, dragging feeling in the left upper abdomen**.	As above, AND the abdominal wall has bluish, wiggly veins.	C7-A	Vol. I, Chap. 1. *Disease Index*, Tropical Splenomegaly *Symptom Protocol* A-46
Kidney Failure	Fatigue, **Little or no urine or abnormal urine.**	High blood pressure, maybe nosebleeds, urinary body odor.	C7-A; C7-D, 3 for only kidney failure, no other conditions	Vol. I,Chap. 1 *Disease Index*, Kidney Failure
Jaundic	**Yellow eyes, loss of appetite**, dark urine, fatigue.	**Yellow whites of the eyes**; yellow below the tongue, bilirubin in urine.	C7-A; C7-B; C7-D4 for only jaundice, no other conditions	Vol. I, Chap. 1 and Vol. I, App. 2. *Disease Index*, Jaundice
Bleeding	Nosebleeds, heavy periods, bloody urine, stool, vomits blood	Urine tests positive for blood. **Spontaneous bruising.**	C7-A; C7-B. C7-D, 5 for only bleeding, no other conditions.	Vol. I, App. 2.
Brain Damage	Difficulty understanding, moving; uncoordinated	**Abnormal mental state,** bizarre behavior or lethargy; trembling; uncoordinated.	C7-A; C7-B; C7-D, 6 for only brain damage, no other conditions	*Disease Index,* Brain Damage

[1] Not all patients will have all the findings, but they will all have the boldfaced ones.

Guide to Causative Diseases.

The boxes on the left give the various conditions associated with liver and spleen problems. The ovals in the middle state which disease lists apply to each. The arrows from the two vertical ovals show which conditions can result from the two types of Liver Failure: Cirrhosis and Fulminant. Not all patients will have all of these conditions. Most will lack at least one. C7-A and C7-B list the most common diseases or conditions which cause liver failure.

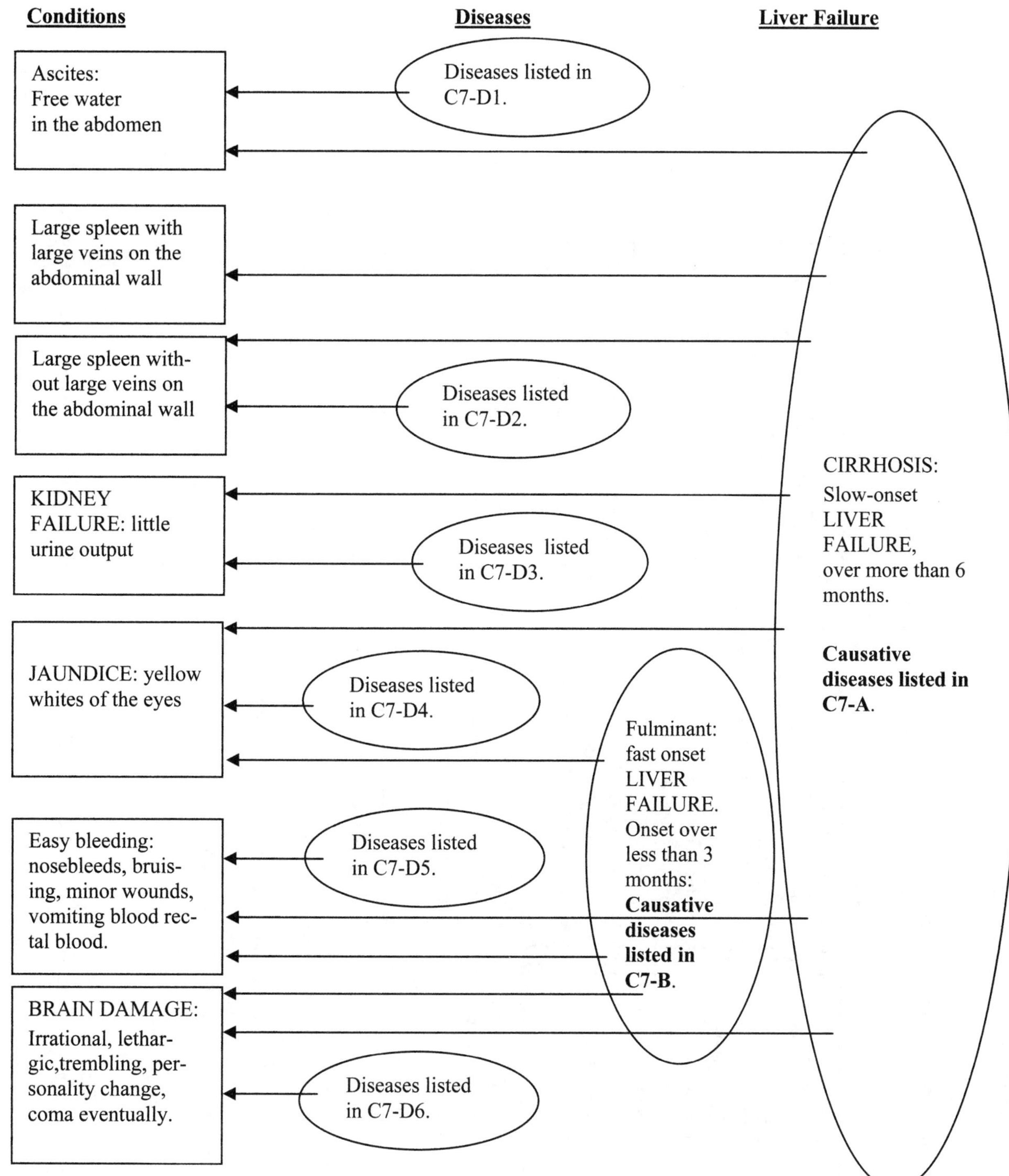

C7-A. Cirrhosis: Slow-onset Liver Failure.

Slow-onset, over more than 6 months. This is frequently due to ALCOHOLISM but may also be due to various drugs and poisonings as listed under B.

Condition	Usual Characteristics
Alcoholism[1]	Not a teetotaler; daily drinker or binge drinker.
Arsenic Poisoning	Slow-onset; due to occupational exposure, ethnic remedies, or homicidal intent.
Brucellosis	Pastoral area; exposed to cattle, hides, meat, or unpasteurized milk.
Cancer	Varied; usually weight loss; liver may feel lumpy without being tender.
Drugs And Herbs[2]	Ingests a liver-toxic substance.
Gallbladder Disease	Pain or lump in upper central abdomen; may be tender; shoulder pain is common; may be associated with liver flukes.
Hemochromatosis	History of blood transfusion or high iron diet or hereditary.
Hepatitis	Large, tender liver; frequently joint pains, nausea, jaundice.
Hydatid Disease	1. Arid tropics with dogs, or 2. Food from temperate forests; mostly adults.
Schistosomiasis	Exposure to fresh-water snails in an area with S. Mansoni or S. Japonicum.

C7-B. Fulminant (rapid-onset) Liver Failure.

Onset over less than 3 months: This is mostly due to drugs and poisons; PLANT POISONING from Crotalaria and other bush teas; overdose of ACETAMINOPHEN; sometime from ISONIAZID and other medicines for TUBERCULOSIS.

Does or did the patient have a fever or severe abdominal pain and/or a general body illness?

YES

Consider:
HEPATITIS: Obvious yellow whites of the eyes; poor sanitation or blood exposure.
PANCREATITIS: Severe pains go to the back.
LEPTOSPIROSIS: Exposure to flood waters or rat urine; erratic fevers.
MALARIA: Chills, headaches, regular or sustained fevers.
TOXEMIA: Related to pregnancy or delivery.

NO

The problem is probably due to drugs or herbs. See the chart C7-C (below) for the most common offending substances.

---

[1] Don't discount this diagnosis if the patient drinks but does not drink excessively. Some people have very sensitive livers which will fail with only a nightly glass of wine.

[2] Of the drugs listed in this manual, it is likely one in which liver failure is listed as a side-effect or a consequence of an overdose. Seek information on other drugs. Many natural herbs and ethnic remedies are toxic to the liver and might cause cirrhosis. See the drugs and herbs listed under B. Ingesting small amounts over a long period of time rather than a one-time overdose might result in cirrhosis rather than fulminent liver failure.

C7-C. Common Drugs And Plants That Can Cause Liver Failure.

Substance	Characteristics
Acetaminophen	Usually suicidal overdose.
Isoniazid	Tuberculosis drug, usually patients over 40 years old.
Chlorpromazine	Jaundice, light stool, dark urine, severe itching, rapid onset.
Gallbladder of Raw Fish	Chinese traditional medicine for poor eyesight.
Mushrooms	Those picked in the wild - usually more than 6 hours delay before symptoms occur.
Other Drugs[1]	Usually only when used in excess, but may be quickly problematic in sensitive patients. See the list of drugs in the footnote.
Plant Poisoning[2]	Most of these are used as "natural" herbal remedies. Some are used in herbal teas. Most people need to take large amounts before they get liver failure but some people are very sensitive. See the list of plants in the footnote.

C7-D1. Causes of Ascites (Free Fluid in the Abdomen).

Disease	Characteristics
Cirrhosis[3]	Usually due to alcohol or SCHISTOSOMIASIS.
Abdominal Tuberculosis	Children and others with only ascites, no other symptoms of liver failure; maybe numerous, pea-sized lumps in the abdomen.
Kidney Failure (Nephrotic)	Also urine contains much protein, swollen eyes in the morning, swollen ankles.
Heart Failure	Difficulty breathing lying down or fatigued; heart murmur, infection, or Western diet in an adult, swollen ankles the end of the day.
Malnutrition	Also swollen legs but no other symptoms of heart failure or kidney failure.
Malabsorption	Same as malnutrition; this is malnutrition due to losing foodstuff in the diarrhea.
Pericarditis	Swollen ankles, large liver, maybe abnormal heart sounds - very quiet or raspy.
Cancer (Rare)	May resemble abdominal TB.

---

[1] *Drugs known to cause liver failure*: Acetaminophen, Acetazolamide, Acyclovir, Albendazole, Atovaquone, Cephalosporin (some kinds), Chlorpromazine, Cloxacillin, Codeine, Cotrimoxazole, Dapsone, Dicyclomine, Diphenhydramine, Doxycycline, Furosemide, Gentamycin, Griseofulvin, Halofantrine, Hydralazine, Hydrocortisone, Ibuprofen, Isoniazid, Ketoconazole, Levamisole, Metronidazole, Pyrazinamide, Quinidine, Quinine, Rifampin, Suramin, Thiacetazone.

[2] *Plants known to cause liver failure*: Camphor. Cascara sagrada. *Castor beans. Chaparral. *Comfrey. *Crotalaria. *Ephedra. *Heliotropium. *Jequarity beans. *Kavakava. Kombucha. Ma-Huang. *Margosa oil, Pennyroyal oil, Ricin, Sassafras, *Senecio, *Valerian. Those herbs with * next to them have a more extensive description under PLANT POISONING in the B index. For the others, you need to find independent information.

[3] Initially there may not be big, easily visible veins on the abdominal wall, but eventually these will develop.

C7-D2. Causes of a Large Spleen. (See also Symptom Protocol 46 B1)

Disease	Characteristic	Onset[1]	Maybe Huge?
African Sleeping Sickness	Geographically confined, changed mental state, fevers and whole-body illness.	Slow	Yes
Bartonellosis	Peru area only, ANEMIA also, maybe JAUNDICE.	Slow	No
Brucellosis	Joint pains, feels awful, pastoral area or patient consumed unpasteurized milk products.	Slow	No
Cancer	Frequently ANEMIA, maybe easy bleeding.	Slow	Yes
Chaga's Disease	Americas only; HEART FAILURE also.	Slow	No
Cirrhosis	Slow-onset liver failure; see the page above with the large oval designating symptoms.	Slow	No
Enteric Fever	Unimmunized patient,[2] onset of abdominal symptoms over days, along with a high fever.	Rapid	No
Hydatid Isease	Arid rural areas with dogs or temperate,forested areas, from gathering plants.	Unknown	Yes
Malaria	Humid tropics; chills, fevers, headaches, general body aching.	Rapid	No
Malaria	See TROPICAL SPLENOMEGALY; the spleen may be enormous.	Slow	Yes
Mononucleosis	Tonsils look bad, extreme fatigue.	Rapid	No
Ovalocytosis	Hereditary ANEMIA, mostly Malaysian and Pacific islanders.	Unknown	Unknown
Relapsing Fever	Body lice associated with poor sanitation, rapid onset with severe prostration.	Very rapid	No
Sickle Cell Disease	Hereditary, mostly West African genetic heritage, some Greeks, Arabs, Indians.	Rapid or slow	Yes
Thallasemia	Hereditary ANEMIA, Mediterranean, Black, or Asian genetic heritage.	Slow	Yes
Tuberculosis	Children, weight loss, loss of appetite, history of exposure to tuberculosis.	Slow	Unknown
Visceral Leishmaniasis	Geographically confined; fevers, weight loss, night sweats, slow-onset illness.	Slow	Yes

[1] Onset is rapid if it is over a week or less and the spleen is tender; it is slow if it is over more than a week. These designations are not absolute. Also, they refer to the spleen enlargement, not the disease onset. Generally rapidly enlarging spleens are tender to touch and slowly enlarging spleens are not.

[2] That is, patients not immunized against typhoid fever.

C7-D3. Causes of KIDNEY FAILURE.

See the listing under this title in the *Disease Index*. In this case the kidney failure presents as very little urine.

C7-D4. Causes of JAUNDICE.

See the listing under this title in the *Disease Index*. If there is a fever, see Protocol C-5.

C7-D5. Causes Of Easy Bleeding.

There are four major categories of causes:

1. Liver problems, preventing the liver from making the chemicals necessary for normal clotting. In this case there will be other signs of liver failure: a large or tender liver, jaundice, ascites. The most common causes are alcoholism, certain drugs in sensitive people, various ethnic remedies, hepatitis, and malnutrition.
2. Bone marrow or blood problems, preventing the proper number and/or function of platelets which are the blood cell fragments necessary to initiate clotting. Aspirin and ibuprofen are the most common drugs causing this.
3. Even with a healthy bone marrow, a large spleen is apt to destroy the platelets, leaving a dearth of functional platelets.
4. Excessively fragile small blood vessels that burst at the slightest provocation. This is the least common cause.

C7-D6. Causes of BRAIN DAMAGE.

See the listing under this title in the *Disease Index*.

PROTOCOL C-8. EYES BOTH RED AND PAINFUL

See Introduction to *Index C*: Notes on Column Headings and Abbreviations.

Disease	Groups?	Risk Factors	Ill?[1]	Essential Symptoms	Likely Symptoms	Treatment
Arboviral Fever	Usual	Residence; insect bit-ten	Yes, severe	Fever, headache, aching all over	Varies with the type	Supportive, maybe high-tech
Cellulitis	Rare	Injury, usually minor	Unusual	Red or warm, tender skin	Swollen skin of eyelids	Antibotics
Chickenpox	Usual	Childhood; crowding	Yes, moderate	Whole-body blistery rash, breaks out over several days	Blisters are itchy	Supportive only
Dengue Fever	Usual	Child, urban, tropical Asia, Pacific; house plants	Yes, severe	Sudden onset, high fever, headache, severe bone pain	Rash, depression	Supportive only
Eye Infection	Usual	Poor sanitation; flies	No	More irritation than pain	Eyes stick shut, maybe pus	Antibiotics and antibiotic ointment
Glaucoma (acute)	Maybe	Genetic heritage, old age	Yes	Hard eyeballs	Sudden nausea with the pain	Ophthalmologist
Hemorrhagic Fever[2]	Maybe	Residence; insect-bitten	Yes, severe	Fever, headache, general body pain	Bleeding	High-tech, problematic
Herpes	Maybe	Other STD's	Unusual	Bistery rash, tender to touch	Comes and goes, genitals affected	Acyclovir
Iritis	Rare	Some illnesses, eye injury	??	Pupil(s) not round	Some other illness	Ophthalmologist
Keratitis	Rare	Prior injury or infection	Maybe	Cloudy corneas, severe pain, tearing[3]	White spot(s) on cornea(s)	Ophthalmologist

Continued on next page.

[1] Ill? - is the patient generally ill with a whole body illness (yes), or are only the eyes affected (no)?
[2] Hemorrhagic Fever - present in some scattered areas of Africa, southern Asia, and the Americas. See Protocol C-2.
[3] Keratitis caused by trachoma starts with opacity around the rim of the cornea; that caused by congenital syphilis starts with opacity in the central cornea.

(Protocol C-8. Eyes Both Red and Painful, continued.)

Disease	Groups?	Risk Factors	Ill?	Essential Symptoms	Likely Symptoms	Treatment
Leprosy Reaction	Rare	Lepromatous leprosy treatment	Yes	Symmetrical bumpy rash before starting meds	Pupil(s) not round	Special medicines
Leptospirosis	Usual	Exposed to flood water or rat urine.	Yes	Sudden onset, erratic fever, headache	Sore muscles, calves, back	Antibiotics
Loiasis[1]	Usual	Residence, fly bitten	Maybe	Worm in the eye, comes and goes; no fever	Worm causes swell-ings under the skin	Deworming medicines
Measles	Usual	Childhood, not immu-nized, crowding	Yes, severe	First a "cold"; rash starts day 2-4, spotted or sandpapery; high fever	Cough, vomiting, diarrhea	Vitamin A, supportive
Meningitis	Usual	Crowding, not immu-nized	Yes, severe	Sudden onset, headache or coma	Vomiting, not alert, fever, stiff neck	Antibiotics
Mumps	Usual	Childhood, not immu-nized, crowding	Yes	Swelling in front of the ears; chipmunk look, fever	Swollen, painful testicles in adult males	Supportive
Oncho-cerciasis[2]	Usual	Residence in an af-fected, hilly area, rural	Yes, mild	Skin thick, rough, itch-ing; eye symptoms vary	Peaked lumps under skin	Special medicines
Relapsing Fever	Usual	Residence, ticks or body lice	Yes, severe	Sudden onset, chills and sweats within 12 hours	Fever, headache, body pains; rash	Antibiotics
Scrub Typhus	Maybe	Tropical, rural Asia Pacific	Yes, severe	Rash, red spotted; fever	Small black scab, constipation	Antibiotics
Shingles	Rare	Adult; prior chicken-pox	Yes	Blisters in a patch (face) or band on the trunk	Painful; sharp shooting pains; skin irritation	Acyclovir Supportive
Spotted Fe-ver	Maybe	Residence, rural, ticks	Yes, severe	Fever, blistery or red spotted rash	Headache, general body pain	Antibiotics
Trachoma	Usually	Poor hygiene, flies	No	Bumps under the upper lid	Cloudy cornea starts on top	Antibiotics, maybe surgery
Typhus	Maybe	Exposed to body lice or rat fleas	Yes, severe	Other symptoms before the fever	Musty body odor, mental changes	Antibiotics

[1] Present in scattered areas throughout humid, central and western Africa.
[2] Present in scattered areas in Africa, the Americas, and the Middle East.

PROTOCOL C-9. ABDOMINAL PAIN AND HIGH FEVER[1]

See Introduction to *Index C*: Notes on Column Headings and Abbreviations.
Abbreviations for Incubation (I) and Onset (O) times: Secs – seconds; Mi – minutes; H – hours; D – days; W – weeks; Mo – Months; Y – years.

Disease	Incubation; Onset	Groups?	Risk Factors	Other symptoms[2]	Treatment
Arboviral Fever	I: Varies O: H-D	Usual	Residence, insect bitten	Headache, joint pains; rash; others vary according to kind	Supportive[3] high-tech meds
Dengue Fever	I: 2-15 D O: H	Usual	Residence urban tropical Asia Pacific	Severe bone pains, rash; headache; fever may drop and then recur; depression.	Supportive
Dysentery	I: D O: H-D	Usual	Poor sanitation, food and water	Bloody diarrhea, small amounts frequently; pain is lower abdomen	Antibiotics
Enteric Fever	I: 1-3 W O: D	??	Poor sanitation, not immunized	Mentally 'out of it'; constipation early, diarrhea later; fever is sustained; headache	Antibiotics
Familial Mediterranean Fever	I: N/A O: H	Family	Genetic heritage	Family history of recurrent pains, and/or mental illness and/or rash	Special meds
Gallbladder Disease	I: Varies O: Varies	??	Western diet, adult, malaria, some worms	Focus of pain upper central abdomen, maybe to shoulder; vomiting is common	Higher-level care; surgical
Kidney Infection	I: Varies O: H-W	Rare	Female, sexually active, poor	Cloudy urine, usually mid-back pain also; prior bladder infection	Antibiotics, maybe surgery
Malaria	I: Varies O: H-D	Usual	Tropics, mosquito bitten	Headache, waist pain, chills and sweats separated by day(s), shoulder pain, vomiting, diarrhea	Antimalarials
Mononucleosis	I: 1-2 M O: D	??	Age < 25 y.o.	Fatigue, large, tender spleen; fatigue; large lymph nodes; sore throat	Supportive only
Pelvic Infection	I: D-Mo O: H-D	Usual	Sexually active female	Pus from vagina or pain with intercourse; pain is lower abdomen	Antibiotics surgery
Pneumonia	I: Varies O: H-1 D	Rare	Prior "cold", infant or old age, poor health	Rapid respirations, cough with sputum, short of breath, pain is upper abdomen	Antibiotics

Continued on next page.

1 That is, 38°C or 100° F or above.
2 That is, symptoms in addition to fever and abdominal pain; not all patients will have all of those listed.
3 This means simply making the patient comfortable.

(Protocol C-9. Abdominal Pain and High Fever, continued.)

Disease	Incubation; Onset	Groups?	Risk Factors	Other symptoms	Treatment
Relapsing Fever	I: 2-14 D O: Mi-H	Usual	Crowding—lice Rural camp—ticks	Onset over minutes; whole body aching, chills and sweats separated by less than 12 hours; headache; rash	Antibiotics
Scrub Typhus	I: 4-11 D O: H-D	??	Rural Asia Pacific; chigger mite bites	Headache, red eyes, constipation, rash, a small scab where the patient was bit; eye pain, general body pain	Antibiotics
Sepsis	I: Varies O: Varies	No	Prior ill health, infants, elderly	Another infection, injury, or childbirth; very ill; mental changes;	Antibiotics surgery
Sickle Cell Disease	I: N/A O: H-D	Family	Genetic heritage[1]	Anemia, recurrent painful crises of bone, abdomen, chest pain	IV fluids, Special meds
Strep Infection	I: 1-4 D O: H-D	??	Contacted the disease	Sore throat or skin infection	Antibiotics
Typhus, louse or murine	I: 6-14 D O: H-louse O: D-murine	??	Tropics, crowding, poor sanitation, rodents	Other symptoms for days before the fever started; musty body odor; mental changes; headache; body pains; rash	Antibiotics
Urinary Infection	I: Varies O: Varies	No	Female, child or sexually active, poor hygiene	Cloudy urine, painful urinating or incontinent; pain is lower abdomen	Antibiotics
Yellow Fever[2]	I: 3-6 D O: 1-2 D	??	Residence, mosquitoes, unimmunized	Headache, general aching, eye pain, maybe JAUNDICE, protein in urine; pain is upper abdomen	Supportive

[1] Usually African genetic heritage; some Arabs, Indians, and Greeks are affected but usually not as severely as Africans

[2] Present in scattered areas throughout Africa and in the Americas from 22° North to 28° South latitude.

PROTOCOL C-10. LETHARGY OR CONFUSION

C10-A: Lethargy or Confusion plus a Fever
C10-B: Confusion or Lethargy, No Fever or Low Fever

C10-A. Lethargy or Confusion plus a Fever

The fever does not have to be present currently; a history of a fever during this illness suffices. See Protocol C-10B also, if the patient has no fever.

Lethargy or confusion plus a fever is most likely due to a physical cause, though mentally disturbed patients can also get fevers for other reasons. If the mental disturbance predated the fever by 5 days or more and was of gradual onset, it is likely a fever in a mental patient. If the mental disturbance was of sudden onset and/or the fever began at a proximate time, then the cause is most likely medical. See Protocol A-5 also. In elderly people, any simple infection such as urinary track infection or pneumonia will cause confusion.

See Introduction to *Index C*: Notes on Column Headings and Abbreviations.
Abbreviations for Incubation (I) and Onset (O) times: Secs – seconds; Mi – minutes; H – hours; D – days; W – weeks; Mo – Months; Y – years.

Condition	Incubation;[1] Onset	Groups?	Epidemics?	Risk Factors	Other symptoms[2]	Treatment
African Sleeping Sickness[3]	I: D-Mo O: W-Y	Rare	Unusual	Residence, fly bite	Increasing sleepiness; headache; weight loss	Difficult & dangerous
Arboviral Fever	I: Varies O: H-D	??	Maybe	Residence, insect bites	Fever, headache, body pains; See C-2; hot, swollen joints	Supportive
Bartonellosis[4]	I: 2-16 W O:D-W	??	Maybe	Residence; sand fly bites	Fatigue, headache, joint pains, up and down fevers, short of breath	Antibiotics
Brucellosis	I: 2-4 W O: W-Mo	Rare	Unusual	Pastoral area; meat, milk, cheese, hides.	Complaining, joint pains and/or back pain; headache; weight loss	3 antibiotics for 6 weeks
Encephalitis	I: Varies O: H-D	??	Maybe	Viral illnesses and/or insect bites	Headache, numbness, weakness, clumsy, mental changes	Supportive
Enteric Fever	I: 1-3 W O: D-W	??	Maybe	Poor sanitation; bad food or water	Abdominal symptoms; headache; body odor, sustained fever	Antibiotics

Continued on next page.

[1] "Incubation" is the time from first symptom to being lethargic or confused.
[2] Symptoms in addition to fever and lethargy or confusion; not all patients will have all of those listed.
[3] Present in scattered areas of Africa from 15° North to 20° South. Both kinds are present in the Great Lakes area of eastern Africa. North and west of there it is mostly Gambian; south and east of there it is Rhodesian.
[4] Found only in Peru and adjacent border areas.

(C10-A: Lethargy or Confusion plus a Fever, continued.)

Condition	Incubation; Onset	Groups?	Epidemics?	Risk Factors	Other symptoms	Treatment
Heat Illness	I: varies O: Varies	Usual	Maybe	Elderly, infants, exercising, hot environment	Sweaty or hot and dry; fever very high	Cooling and high-tech
HIV Infection[1]	I: Years O: Varies	Usual	Yes	Sexual or blood exposure; born to an infected mother	Recurrent infections; weight loss; diarrhea	Complicated Expensive
Leptospirosis[2]	I: 3D-3W O: H	??	Maybe	Flood water; rat urine contact	Red eyes, muscle pains, jaundice, liver pain	Antibiotics
Malaria, cerebral	I: N/A O: H-W	Rare	N/A	Prior malaria, tropical area	Vomiting, seizures, headache, jaundice	Anti-malarials Antibiotics
Measles	I: 9-14 D O: D	Usual	Yes	Childhood, unimmunized, black skin, malnourished	Initial 'cold'; rash starts on the forehead; peeling skin; vomiting, diarrhea	Supportive & antibiotics
Meningitis	I: Mi-D O: H-D	Some kinds	Yes	Crowding, Africa, residence, not immunized	Vomiting, severe headache, maybe stiff neck, peeling skin	Antibiotics
Plague	I: 2-15 D O: H	Usual	Yes	Exposure to dead or dying rodents or to animal fleas	Extreme pain, rapid onset; blackened, tender lymph nodes; scab	Antibiotics
Relapsing Fever, tick or louse	I: 2-14 D O: H	Usual	Yes	Body lice, crowding; or tick exposure rural area.	Headache, rapid onset, chills and sweats	Antibiotics
Sepsis	I: varies O: Varies	No	Yes	Previous illness; ill health; injury, childbirth, newborns	Headache, heart murmur, short of breath, cloudy urine	Antibiotics
Spotted Fever	I: 6-10 D O: H-D	??	Rare	Tick exposure; rural	Rash starts on limbs; headache	Antibiotics
Toxoplasmosis	I: 1-3 W O: W-Mo	Rare	Rare	Exposure to lamb meat or cat stool; HIV+	Big lymph nodes and/or spleen; weight loss, fatigue	Special meds
Typhus; louse or murine (fleas)	O: D-W I: 6-14 D	Usual	Maybe	Exposure to lice or to rodent fleas	Ill for days before the fever starts; musty body odor; headache; rash	Antibiotics

[1] This usually manifests as follows: trouble concentrating, mood changes, disorientation, withdrawal, lethargy, talking nonsense, being "hyper", having totally irrational ideas.

[2] Ordinary leptospirosis does not cause confusion or lethargy. However, it can cause sudden-onset liver failure and the liver failure causes confusion or lethargy. If your patient has no signs of liver failure, then his problem is not due to leptospirosis. Most causes of liver failure (aside from malaria and leptospirosis) are not associated with high fevers.

C10-B. Confusion Or Lethargy, no Fever or Low Fever

This protocol deals with decreased mental functioning—confusion or new-onset stupidity in the absence of a fever or in the presence of a low fever (under 38° C or 101° F).

—In newborns, the elderly, diabetics, and those malnourished, see also *Symptom Protocol* 10-A. These patients may not manifest a fever with diseases that ordinarily have high fevers.

—In elderly people, any simple infection such as urinary track infection or pneumonia will cause confusion.

—If a person cannot talk, he will appear to be confused; check his ability to speak by telling him what to say, having him repeat after you. If he cannot speak, ask him to look up or look down and see if he follows your command. There is a rare condition in which a patient cannot respond in any way except to look up or down, yet he is totally alert and needs to be treated as such—talked to, entertained, included in conversation, comforted.

This may also arise from Alzheimer Disease, which is decreased mental functioning without another reason.

See Introduction to *Index C*: Notes on Column Headings and Abbreviations.

Abbreviations for Incubation (I) and Onset (O) times: Secs – seconds; Mi – minutes; H – hours; D – days; W – weeks; Mo – Months; Y – years.

Disease or Condition	Incubation;[1] Onset	Groups?	Risks Factors	Other symptoms[2]	Treatment
Addiction	I: N/A O: W-Y	N/A	Recreational drug usage	Varies with the type of addiction; denial is common	Difficult
African Sleeping Sickness	I: W-Y O: W-Mo	Rare	Residence; fly-bitten	Headache, weight loss, gait problems, itching, trembling	Difficult and dangerous
Alcoholism	I: N/A O: W-Mo	N/A	Daily or binge drinking	Denial is common; distended abdomen, red nose	Counseling
Anemia	I: Varies O: Varies	N/A	Bleeding, poor nutrition, some illness	Pale tongue; pale fingernails; short of breath; fatigue	Varied
Attention Deficit Disorder (crisis)	I: N/A O: H	N/A	Western culture, male, heredity	Adjustment problems since childhood	Counseling, special meds
Beriberi	I: W-Mo O: W-Mo	Usual	Poor diet; alcohol consumption; white rice	Unaware; wide-based gait, heart failure, weight loss, weak	Thiamine, diet
Brucellosis	I: 2-4 W O: Mo	Rare	Pastoral area, hides, milk, meat, cheese	Back and/or joint pains, feels awful; complaining	3-antibiotics for 6 weeks

Continued on next page.

[1] Incubation is the time from the first symptom to being lethargic or confused.
[2] Symptoms in addition to the confusion or lethargy. Not all patients will have all the other symptoms.

(C10-B. Confusion Or Lethargy, no Fever or Low Fever, continued.)

Disease or Condition	Incubation; Onset	Groups?	Risks Factors	Other symptoms	Treatment
Cancer	I: N/A O: W-Y	No	Varied; possibly a history of cancer	Weight loss is common as are abnormal vital signs	Difficult
Dehydration[1]	I: N/A O: Varies	N/A	Vomiting, diarrhea, not drinking, diabetes	Very dry mouth, sunken eyes, loose skin, thirsty if conscious	Fluids; treat the causative disease
Demonization	I: N/A O: Varies	??	Occult activity or cursed	Symptoms that don't make medical sense; context[2]	Prayer and exorcism
Diabetes	I: N/A O: H-W	No	Diagnosed as such or weight loss	Thirsty, much urine, previously diagnosed or else gradual onset	Special meds
Drug side-effect	I: Varies O: Varies	No	Taking a new drug	Varies with the type	Stop the drug if possible
Head Injury	I: N/A O: Mi-D	N/A	Epilepsy, adventurous sorts, young males	Headache, vomiting, seizures, abnormal movements	Hospitalization, surgery
Heart Failure	I: Varies O: Varies	No	Western diet or prior rheumatic fever	Short of breath or swollen legs and feet or both; fatigue	Special meds
Hypothermia	I: Varies O: H	??	Cold exposure, very young and very old	Low body temperature	Warming
Kidney Failure	I: Varies O: D-Mo	No	Poisons, malaria, other diseases, drugs	High blood pressure or abnormal urine dipstick; swollen eyes	Special meds Dialysis
Liver Failure	I: Varies O: D-Mo	No	Poisons, alcohol, other diseases, drugs	Jaundice, distended abdomen, bleeding; swollen ankles	Varied, difficult
Lyme Disease[3]	I: 3-32 D O: Mo	Rare	Residence; tick bitten	Prior rash, arthritis, and ill health	Antibiotics

Continued on next page.

[1] This is a condition but not a diagnosis. You still must find out what caused the dehydration.

[2] "Context" refers to problems arising in the context of religious experience: either Christian worship, in which case it may be disruptive activity, or participation in some occult ritual.

[3] Present in temperate and subtropical, forested areas of the northern hemisphere and along the north coast of Australia.

(C10-B. Confusion Or Lethargy, no Fever or Low Fever, continued.)

Disease or Condition	Incubation; Onset	Groups?	Risks Factors	Other symptoms	Treatment
Meningitis[1]	I: Varies O: H-Mo	Rare	Newborns, elderly, previous TB, crowding	Headache, stiff neck, vomiting, cough, abnormal eye movements	Antibiotics
Pellagra	I: Varies O: D-Mo	Usual	Poor diet; much corn	Diarrhea; rough rash; may be unaware	Vitamins, diet
Plant Poisoning	I: Varies O: Varies	??	Ethnic remedies	Varies according to type	Varied
Respiratory Infection	I: Varies O: Varies	Rare	Smoking, prior cold, chest injury, prior pneumonia	Short of breath; fast, slow, or irregular breathing; patient is aware of the problem	Varies; maybe antibiotics
Seizure[2]	I: N/A O: Secs	Rare	Epilepsy, head injury; in a child sudden onset of fever	Rhythmic jerking of limbs, eyes, or facial muscles	Special medicines
Stress	I: N/A O: Varies	N/A	Emotional problems; personal disaster	Trembling, crying, insomnia; patient is aware of the problem	Emotional support and counseling
Stroke	I: N/A O: < 1 Mi	No	High blood pressure; elderly; sickle cell anemia	Sudden onset of weakness or paralysis, speech problem; patient is usually aware	Special medicines and/or procedures
Syphilis, (tertiary)	I: Y O: Mo-Y	Rare	Sexual exposure 10+ years ago or born to a syphilic mother	Patient does not perceive his problem; gradual deterioration of social behavior	Antibiotics (which may only prevent progression)
Thyroid Trouble	I: N/A O: Varies	??	Residence in mountainous area, not near the sea	Low body temperature, sleepy look, slow pulse	Thyroid replacement

[1] Meningitis usually causes a fever. However, in newborns (less than 4 weeks old) and in the elderly and in anyone who is malnourished, there may be little or no fever. It is rare to find these meningitis symptoms in a group of patients.

[2] "Seizure" is a condition but not a diagnosis. You still must find out why the patient has seizures. It is important to check for subtle seizure activity; blinking, twitching, lip-smacking, or any apparently automatic, repetitive movement (status epilepticus). If you find such repetitive motions, stopping them is an emergency. Seek higher-level care immediately.

PROTOCOL C-11. SKIN ULCER AND WHOLE-BODY ILLNESS

The conditions marked with * do not by themselves cause a general illness. However, any break in the skin is liable to become secondarily infected and result in such an illness.

See Introduction to *Index C*: Notes on Column Headings and Abbreviations.

Abbreviations for Incubation (I) and Onset (O) times: Secs – seconds; Mi – minutes; H – hours; D – days; W – weeks; Mo – Months; Y – years.

Condition or Disease	Incubation;[1] Onset	Groups?	Risk Factors	Usual location	Other characteristics	Treatment
Amebic Skin Ulcer	I: ?? O: D-Mo	No	Poor sanitation, prior dysentery	Lower trunk, genitals only	Painful; discharges pus or another liquid	Metronidazole, maybe surgery
Anthrax	I: 1-3 D O: D	??	Contact with sick animals, hides, meats, bioterrorism	Above the waist	Not painful but may itch; much swelling; black scab	Antibiotics
Bedsores	I: ?? O: D	No	Bedridden patient, not moving about	Body surface with constant pressure	First red and swollen; patient either very ill or paralyzed	Wound care; see Tropical Ulcer
Buruli Ulcer*	I: ?? O: W	??	Tropics, swamps	Limbs	Round or oval; ragged, overhanging edges	Surgery
Cancrum Oris	I: ?? O: H-D	No	Malnourished child	Face or a sucked finger	Dead-looking flesh; foul odor to the pus	Surgery, diet, antibiotics
Cutaneous Leishmaniasis*	I: W-Mo O: W-Mo	??	Residence; bitten by sandflies	Unclothed; face	May itch or hurt but neither is intense; variable appearance	Special medicines
Diphtheria	I: D O: D	Maybe	Unimmuinized; urban areas	Anywhere	Edges like a donut; painful, moist	Antitoxin; Antibiotics
Gangrene	I: ?? O: Varies	No	Severe injury or ill health, poor nutrition	Injured part or fingers or toes	Dead-looking flesh; pain, numbness	Surgery and antibiotics
Plague	I: 2-15 D O: H-D	Usual	Contact with other cases or with rodents or their fleas	Limbs but it can be anywhere	Big lymph nodes with blackened skin over top; tiny scab	Antibiotics
Rat bite Feve	I: 3-30 D O: D-W	??	Bitten by a rodent; mostly tropical Asia	Limbs but it can be anywhere	Healed and then broke open or a generalized rash	Antibiotics
Scrub typhus	I: D-W O: D-W	??	Rural tropical Asia Pacific, chigger mite bite	Commonly genital or lower limbs	Headache, red eyes, large spleen, constipation	Antibiotics

Continued on next page.

[1] Incubation: Many of these diseases are late complications so that the incubation cannot be known.

(Protocol C-11. Skin Ulcer and Whole-Body Illness, continued.)

Condition	Incubation;[1] Onset	Groups?	Risk Factors	Usual location	Other characteristics	Treatment
Spotted Fever Eastern hemisphere	I: < 12 D O: D	??	Mostly Africa and the Mediterranean; tick bites; rural areas.	Anywhere	Headache, stiff neck, red eyes, rash heaviest on the wrists and the ankles	Antibiotics
Spotted Fever, Rocky Mountain	I: 6-10 D O: D	??	North, Central, and South America; tick bites; rural areas	Anywhere	Headache, fatigue, joint and muscle pains, nausea, large spleen	Antibiotics
Sexually Transmitted Disease[2]	I: Varies O: D-W	Usual	Sexual or health care exposure	Exposed to secretions: genitals, hands, face	Varies by the type of disease; see protocol C-1	Antibiotics, antivirals, surgery
Tropical Ulcer*	I: ?? O: W	??	Tropics; poor hygiene, malnutrition	Usually legs, feet	Gradual onset, first red/swollen then breaks open & enlarges	Antibiotics
Tuberculosis	I: ?? O: W-Mo	Usual	Patient or family member has/had tuberculosis	Head and neck; may be elsewhere	Spontaneous wound with black scab	TB medicines
Tularemia[3]	I: 1-14 D O: H-D	Rare	Residence; child or hunter; rural	Upper or lower limbs; anywhere	Exposure small animal or insect	Antibiotics

[1] Incubation: Many of these diseases are late complications so that the incubation cannot be known.
[2] This includes Chancroid, Donovanosis, Herpes, Lymphogranuloma Venereum, Syphilis.
[3] Northern hemisphere, temperate and sub-tropical, as far south as the northern coast of Africa.

PROTOCOL C-12. LARGE LYMPH NODES

See Introduction to *Index C*: Notes on Column Headings and Abbreviations.

Abbreviations for Incubation (I) and Onset (O) times: Secs – seconds; Mi – minutes; H – hours; D – days; W – weeks; Mo – Months; Y – years.

Condition or Disease	Incubation; Onset	Groups?	Related Wound[1]	Risk Factors	Characteristics	Treatment
African Sleeping Sickness[2]	I: Varies O: D-Mo[3]	Rare	No	Residence; fly bite	Headache, fevers off & on; swelling of bite	Difficult and dangerous
Anthrax	I: <7 D O: H-D	??	Yes	Cattle, meat, hides, bioterrorism	Marked swelling; sore with black scab, not painful	Antibiotics
Arthritis, rheumatoid	I: N/A O: W	No	No	Western culture; old age, females, affluent	Symmetrical joint pains migrate; morning stiffness	Anti-inflammatory
Brucellosis	I: 2-4 W O: W-Mo	Rare	No	Pastoral areas or raw milk, cheese, meat, hides	Pains in back and/or lower limbs; complaints of feeling awful	3-antibiotic combination
Cancer	I: N/A O: W-Mo	No	Maybe	Old age; HIV infection, toxins	Weight loss; fatigue; easy bleeding; nodes hard or matted	High-tech
Cat-Scratch Disease	I: 3-30 D O: H-D	Rare	Yes	Cat contact, scratch or licking open wound	Lumps in a line between wound and trunk	Antibiotics
Cellulitis	I: Varies O: H-D	Rare	Maybe	Minor wound, HIV+, poor hygiene	Area of redness and swelling; maybe fever; maybe tender	Antibiotics
Chaga's Disease[4]	I: Varies O: D-W	??	No	Residence; poor housing	History of swollen eye; constipation or heart failure	Difficult
Coccidio-mycosis[5]	I: 10-14 D O: Varies	??	No	Residence; non-white ethnicity	Chronic cough	Special
Drug Eruption	I: N/A O: H-D	No	No	Western culture; drug usage[6]	Related in time to taking the drug	Stop drug

Continued on next page.

[1] Related wound: whether one is likely to see an open wound nearby or on a limb beyond the location of the large lymph nodes.

[2] Present in scattered areas of Africa, from 15° North to 20° South. Both kinds occur in the Great Lakes area of eastern Africa. North and west of there it is almost all Gambian whereas south and east of there it is almost all Rhodesian.

[3] In western Africa the large nodes develop within weeks to months; in eastern Africa they may develop rapidly, within days to weeks.

[4] Scattered areas in the Americas, between the 41° South and the northern border of Mexico. The Caribbean and the Amazon basin are largely spared.

[5] Arid areas in the Americas between 40° North and 40° South; low elevations; mostly late summer and early fall.

[6] These drugs in particular: Allopurinol; Cephalosporins; Hydralazine; Penicillin; Phenytoin; Pyrimethamine; Quinidine; Sulfa.

(Protocol C-12. Large Lymph Nodes, continued.)

Condition or Disease	Incubation; Onset	Groups?	Related Wound	Risk Factors	Characteristics	Treatment
HIV Infection	I: Y O: W-Mo	Usual	Maybe	Sexual or blood exposure	Repeated infections; weight loss, diarrhea, mental changes	Difficult Expensive
Lyme Disease[1]	I: 3-32 D O: W	Rare	No	Residence; rural; tick bite	Fevers and rash or history of such, joint pains	Antibiotics,
Measles	I: 9-14 D O: D	Usual	No	Unimmunized; crowding	Red eyes, cough, fever, vomiting, diarrhea, whole-body rash	Vitamin A, supportive
Mononucleosis	I: 1-2 Mo O: D	??	No	Child, teen-ager	Extremely tired; large tonsils with scum; fever, sore throat	Supportive
Plague	I: 2-15 D O: H-D	??	Yes	Rodent flea or patient contact;	Little scab(s), pain; skin blackened; fevers, mental changes	Antibiotics
Scrub Typhus	I: 3-10 D O: H-D	??	Yes	Rural Asia Pacific; bitten by mite	Moderately-very ill; fevers, rash, constipation, eye problems	Antibiotics
Serum Sickness	I: ? D-W O: H-D	No	No	Western culture; drug usage[2], some illnesses	Fever plus allergy symptoms; hives, joint pains	Special
Sexually Transmitted Diseases	I: Varies O: Varies	Usual	Yes	Sexual contact or contact with body secretions	Usually genital symptoms or history thereof; not very ill	Antibiotics
Strep Infection	I: 1-4 D O: H-D	??	No	Child, young adult, poor hygiene, crowding	Sore throat; rapid onset; no cold symptoms; red tonsils	Antibiotics
Toxoplasmosis	I: 1-3 W O: D-W	??	No	Contact—cat or rare lamb meat, HIV+	Fatigue, mental changes, large spleen	Special
Tuberculosis	I: M-Y O: W-Mo	Usual	No	Teen-ager or young adult contact with a coughing adult	Weight loss, cough, fever, night sweats; beer-like odor; neck nodes; may be matted	Special
Tularemia[3]	I: 1-14 D O: H-D	Rare	Yes	Contact-small mammal or insects, rural	Fever, general whole-body illness, red bumps by wound	Antibiotics
Visceral Leishmaniasis[4]	I: D-Y O: W-Mo	??	No	Residence; sandfly contact	Fevers, large spleen; initially not very ill	Special
Wound Infection	I: Varies O: H-D	No	Yes	Poor sanitation, dirty wound, poor nutrition	Maybe fever, visible pus, bad odor	Surgery, Antibiotics

[1] Found, at present, in temperate and subtropical areas of the northern hemisphere plus along the north coast of Australia.
[2] These drugs in particular: Allopurinol; Cephalosporins; Hydralazine; Penicillin; Phenytoin; Pyrimethamine; Quinidine; Sulfa.
[3] Present in temperate areas of the northern hemisphere plus along the north coast of Africa.
[4] Scattered areas worldwide but not in SEA or the Pacific.

PROTOCOL C-13. BACK PAIN WITH FEVER

See Introduction to *Index C*: Notes on Column Headings and Abbreviations.
Abbreviations for Incubation (I) and Onset (O) times: Secs – seconds; Mi – minutes; H – hours; D – days; W – weeks; Mo – Months; Y – years.
Abbreviations for Midline?: Is the pain in the midline (center line) of the back or is it off to one or both sides? M = midline; S = sides; B = both; ?? = unknown or variable.

Condition or Disease	Incubation; Onset	Groups?	Risk Factors	Type of pain	Midline?	Other Characteristics[1]	Treatment
Arboviral Fever	I: Varies O: H-D	Usual	Residence, insect bitten	Part of general whole-body pains	??	Headache, rash, red eyes, sore muscles	Supportive, maybe drugs
Arthritis	I: N/A O: H-Mo	Rare	Varies with the type; some STD's, some other diseases	Joints of the spine; maybe red and swollen	M, S[2]	Other joints may be affected; may come and go	Anti-inflammatory
Brucellosis	I: 2-4 W O: W-Mo	Rare	Pastoral residence; hides, meat, milk	Lower back, slow onset	M, S[3]	Feels generally awful	3 antibiotic combination
Dengue Fever	I: 2-15 D O: H	Usual	Tropical Asia-Pacific; urban; house plants	Severe general bone pains	B	Rash, depression, red eyes, fever may relapse	Pain meds only
Kidney Infection	I: ?? O: H-W	No	Female; sexually active; previous urine infections	One or both sides, mid-back	S	Tenderness to gentle punch; cloudy urine	Antibiotics
Leptospirosis	I: 3D-3W O: H-D	??	Exposure to flood waters, rodents, urine	General joint pains	U	Red eyes, jaundice, muscle pains, rash	Antibiotic
Malaria	I: 3D-3W O: H-W	Usual	Tropics; mosquito bitten, pregnant, no prophylaxis	Shoulder area, waist, other joints	B	Headache, chills, sweats; spleen pain	Anti-malarials
Meningitis	I: Varies O: H-W	??	Residence; epidemics; tuberculosis	Neck pain; lies arched back	M	Headache, vomiting; mental changes	Antibiotics
Osteomyelitis	I: ?? O: D-Mo	No	Prior injury or infection	One spot is hot, tender, swollen, over bone	??	Maybe wound and pus	Antibiotics
Pneumonia	I: Varies O: H-D	Rare	Poor immunity; children; prior cold;	Chest area; worse with breathing	S	Cough, rapid or slow breathing	Antibiotics

Continued on next page.

[1] Symptoms in addition to the back pain and fever. Not all patients will have all of these symptoms.
[2] In the upper back it is apt to be midline; in the lower back it is apt to be on either one or both sides.
[3] In the upper back the pain is likely to be midline; in the lower back/pelvis area it is likely to be on one side or the other or both sides.

(Protocol C-13. Back Pain with Fever, continued.)

Condition or Disease	Incubation; Onset	Groups?	Risk Factors	Type of pain	Midline?	Other Characteristics[1]	Treatment
Polio	I: ?? O: D	??	Unimmunized; child	Muscle spasms	S	Some weakness, not symmetrical	Supportive
Pyomyositis	I: Varies O: Varies	No	Prior injury or infection	One area; hot and red and swollen	S	Muscle pain and swelling	Surgery and antibiotics
Rabies	I: 4D-Y O: H-D	Rare	Bitten by mammal; not immunized; bats	Muscle spasms; stiff neck	M	Can't swallow water, headache	Supportive
Relapsing Fever	I: 2-14 D O: H	Usual	Lice or tick exposure; crowding; poor sanitation	Part of body pains, calf pain	B	Chills/sweats the same day	Antibiotics
Rheumatic Fever	I: W-Mo O: H-D	Rare	Prior strep infection	One or two spots red, swollen	M	Limb joint pains may be symmetrical	Aspirin Antibiotics
Sickle Cell Disease[2]	I: N/A O: H-D	Family	Genetic heritage; any stress	Variable	??	Anemia; bone pains, stress	Varies, mostly high-tech
Spotted Fever	I: <14 D O: Varies	??	Residence; tick exposure, food, drink	Part of general body pains	??	Red spotted or blistery rash	Antibiotics
Tetanus	I: 4-20 D O: H-D	No	Prior burn or wound; not immunized	General muscle spasms; stiff neck	B	Can't open mouth, grimacing	Mostly high-tech
Trench Fever	I: 4-36 D O: H-W	Usual	Temperate, urban homeless, body lice	Part of general body pains	M	Shin pains, headache	Antibiotics
Trichinosis	I: <30 D O: D-W	Usual	Ate rare pork or game	Muscles swollen and very sore	S	Patient looks muscular	Varies
Tuberculosis	I: W-Y O: Mo-Y	Usual	Exposed to a coughing adult or coughs	One part of spine painful and tender	M	Maybe cough, weight loss, night sweats	Special drugs
Typhus	I: 6-14 D O: D	??	Lice or rodent flea exposure	Part of body pains; rash	B	Lethargic; musty body odor, mental changes	Antibiotics

[1] Symptoms in addition to the back pain and fever. Not all patients will have all of these symptoms.
[2] This affects persons of African, Arab, Indian, and Greek genetic heritage.

PROTOCOL C-14. MALABSORPTION

Malabsorption is characterized by prompt fecal elimination of anything eaten, within an hour, the diarrhea being recognizably the food just eaten.

See Introduction to *Index C*: Notes on Column Headings and Abbreviations.

Abbreviations for Incubation (I) and Onset (O) times: Secs – seconds; Mi – minutes; H – hours; D – days; W – weeks; Mo – Months; Y – years.

Disease or Condition	Incubation; Onset	Groups?	Risk Factors	Other characteristics	Treatment
Capillariasis[1]	I: ?? O: W	??	Residence, ate raw fish	Loud bowel sounds, loss of appetite	Dewormers
Crypto-sporidiosis	I: 1-14 D O: Mi-H	Usual	Children; HIV+; poor sanitation	Cramping, vomiting, gas, diarrhea is explosive	Antibiotics
Cyclosporiasis[2]	I: 1-11 D O: Mi-H	Usual	Residence; spring and summer; poor sanitation	Vomiting, much gas, fatigue, maybe fever	Antibiotic
Giardiasis[3]	I: 1-45 D O: Mi-H	Usual	Water; poor sanitation	Vomiting, much gas, no fever	Metronidazole, Tinidazole
Intestinal Fluke[4]	I: 2-3 Mo O: W-Mo	??	Raw fish or water plants; poor sanitation	Abdominal pain, body swelling, abdominal fluid	Special meds
Milk Intolerance	I: N/A O: Mi-H	No	Genetic heritage; child; recently sick	Vomiting, gas, only with milk products	Diet or lactase
Pancreatitis	I: N/A O: H-D	No	Adults; alcohol, injury, gallstones	Severe pain goes to back; vomiting	Hospitalization

Continued on next page.

[1] Capillariasis: Currently known to be in parts of the Philippines, Thailand, Java, and Egypt. There is potential for its spreading to other areas.
[2] Cyclosporiasis may be locally common in scattered areas worldwide. At present it is mostly found in Nepal and Latin America.
[3] Giardiasis: Very common worldwide in arctic, temperate, and tropical areas. It is by far the most common cause of malabsorption in most areas.
[4] Most kinds of intestinal flukes don't cause malabsorption. The kind that does, fasciolopsiasis, is found only in Asia.

(Protocol C-14. Malabsorption, continued.)

Disease or Condition	Incubation; Onset	Groups?	Risk Factors	Other characteristics	Treatment
Pellagra	I: N/A O: D-W	Usual	Corn diet, malnutrition	Mental symptoms; skin rash, burning feet pain	Vitamins, Niacin
Pig-bel[1]	I: 1-7 D O: H-D	Usual	Near equator; meat meal after malnutrition	Severe pain; maybe bloody stool; maybe fever	Antibiotics Surgery
Plant Poisoning	I: Varies O: Mi-H	Rare	Herbal remedies	Varies; maybe severe pain; vomiting	Various
Schistosomiasis Japonicum[2]	I: Y O: D-W	??	Residence; fresh water with snails	Maybe bloody stool; fluid in abdomen; liver disease	Praziquantel
Schistosomiasis Mansoni[3]	I: Y O: D-W	??	Residence; fresh water with snails; adult	Maybe bloody stool; fluid in abdomen; liver disease	Praziquantel Artemisinin
Sprue[4]	I: < 6 Mo O: Varies	Rare	Residence; adult; expatriates	Much gas, mental symptoms, mouth pain	Antibiotics Vitamins
Strongyloidiasis	I: ?? O: Varies	??	Residence; poor sanitation, sandy soil	Itching by rectum, visible worms, maybe bloody stool	Dewormers
Trichuriasis	I: ?? O: D-W	??	Poor sanitation, clay soil, humid areas	Visible coiled worms; maybe bloody stool; cravings	Dewormers
Tuberculosis	I: Mo-Y O: W-Mo	Rare	Poverty; crowding; raw milk or cheese	Small lumps in abdomen, like a bean bag	Special meds Antibiotics

[1] Pig-bel: Present in tropical countries near the equator.
[2] Some scattered areas within Asia, including the SEA islands.
[3] Some scattered areas within Africa and the Americas.
[4] Sprue: Present mainly in Asia and the Caribbean.

Index D. Drug Index

ABACAVIR

Anti-HIV drug; nucleoside reverse transcriptase inhibitor.

Safety class unknown; Stability unknown; Pregnancy unknown; Breast-feeding unknown.

Brand names: This comes combined with LAMIVUDINE and ZIDOVUDINE. The combination brand name is Trizivir.

Indications: HIV INFECTION.

Contraindications: ALLERGY to this drug. Do not give to patients weighing less than 40 kg or to children under 12 years old.

Precautions: Patient must not drink alcohol while using this. Seek advice before using this together with CO-TRIMOXAZOLE. Observe the precautions for lamivudine and zidovudine also. Abacavir might cause fatal ALLERGY reactions after it is stopped and then started again. Seek independent advice for LIVER DISEASE and if contemplating prolonged usage. Also observe precautions for LAMIVUDINE and ZIDOVUDINE.

Side-effects: Unknown; See side-effects for LAMIVUDINE and ZIDOVUDINE.

Dosage: For older children and adults: 1 tablet two times a day.

ACETAMINOPHEN

Antipyretic, Analgesic
Safety class 1 Stability: A Pregnancy B
Brand names: Febrinol, Liquiprin, Panadol, Paracetamol, Tempra, Tylenol. Supplied, usually, as 325, 500, 650, or 1000 mg tablets. Sometimes available as liquid for children.

Indications: Fever, mild pain relief, pain relief after head injury.

Contraindications: ALLERGY to the drug, ENTERIC FEVER.

Precautions: If you use this at the same time as CHLORAMPHENICOL, see the precautions listed under that drug. Avoid prolonged use with ALCOHOLISM. May cause false blood glucose results in DIABETES.

Overdose and prolonged use: LIVER FAILURE (see Protocol C-7); KIDNEY FAILURE.

Dosage: 650-1000 mg every 4 hours as needed for adults; reduce dose for children. *Overdose*: See Protocol 11 in the *Symptom Index*.

Alternatives: ASPIRIN, IBUPROFEN.

ACETAZOLAMIDE

Diuretic, Water pill
Safety class 2 Stability: A Pregnancy C
Brand name: Diamox.

Indications: ALTITUDE SICKNESS, GLAUCOMA, adaptation to high altitudes.

Contraindications: ALLERGY to the drug, LIVER FAILURE, KIDNEY FAILURE, chronic RESPIRATORY INFECTION, pregnancy, SULFA allergy

Precautions: If the patient develops a skin rash, stop the drug. This may provoke KIDNEY STONES. In a patient on PHENYTOIN SODIUM, any heart medicine or other diuretics (water pills) use this only at a physician's direction. This drug interferes with many lab tests—don't believe lab results while the patient is taking this.

Side-effects: Sleepiness, numbness, tingling. This occurs with only a small percentage of patients. Sometimes there is nausea, vomiting, and weight loss. If used in a patient with LIVER FAILURE, it may cause confusion.

Overdose and prolonged use: KIDNEY FAILURE, LIVER FAILURE (see Protocol C-7).

Dosage: Reduce dose in the elderly.

ALTITUDE SICKNESS, altitude adaptation: 250 mg every 8 hours for 1-3 days.

GLAUCOMA: 125 mg by mouth every 8 hours which must be continued for the patient's whole life.

ACICLOVIR

See ACYCLOVIR; this is the British spelling for the same drug

ACT (Artemisinin Combination Therapy)

ACT stands for Artemisinin Combination Therapy. It is a new class of drugs—some of them having been developed in the 1920's, then abandoned because CHLOROQUINE was so good. Now that so much malaria is chloroquine-resistant, these are being resurrected and combined with artemisinin, giving the advantages of both immediate response and sustained repression of the disease. Some of the drugs thus combined are: ATOVAQUONE, PIPERAQUINE, MEFLOQUINE, PYRONARIDINE, and LUMEFANTRINE. Only LUMEFANTRINE has been approved for sale in the UK and Europe.

ACTIVATED CHARCOAL

General antidote for poisoning.
Safety class 1 Stability: A
Supplied as generic powder to mix with liquid.

Indications: To neutralize any swallowed drug or poison.

Precautions: If the patient is vomiting, give him something to settle his stomach first so he does not vomit the charcoal. Do not give this at the same time as IPECAC. It will neutralize the IPECAC. Charcoal does not taste bad, but it looks like black slime. Disguise it with Coca-Cola or have the person drink it through a straw out of a covered container.

Dosage: Not important as long as you give enough. Adult dose is 50 grams every 4 hours for serious overdoses; for children, the dose depends on the nature and amount of the overdose, not on the child's size.

ACYCLOVIR, ACICLOVIR (British)

Antiviral
Safety class 1 Stability: C Pregnancy B

Brand names: Zovirax. Supplied as cream and tablets.

Indications: HERPES, SHINGLES.

Contraindications: Pregnancy, prior ALLERGY to the drug, DEHYDRATION, other drugs that may cause KIDNEY FAILURE.

Precautions: If taken by mouth, avoid DEHYDRATION.

Side-effects: Headache, diarrhea, nausea, dizziness, joint pains, skin pain. These effects occur in only a small percentage of patients.

Overdose and prolonged use: Stomach upset, LIVER FAILURE (see Protocol C-7); KIDNEY FAILURE, dizziness, trembling, confusion agitation.

Dosage: Reduce the dose in the presence of KIDNEY FAILURE.

Initial episode of HERPES: 200 mg by mouth every 4 hours, five times a day for 7 days. For very severe cases, 800 mg every 4 hours, five times a day for 7-10 days.

Recurrent HERPES may also be treated with 800 mg twice daily for 5 days.

Initial episode of SHINGLES: 800 mg five times a day for 7-10 days.

Available in a 5% cream to be used every 4 hours for 5 days.

Alternatives: Valaciclovir and Famciclovir and Cidofovir are newer drugs that do about the same thing.

ALBENDAZOLE

Dewormer, Anthelmintic
Safety class 2 Stability: A Pregnancy: ?
Supplied as 200 mg and 400 mg tablets.

Brand names: Albazine, Alben, Valbazen, Zentel, Eskazol.

Indications: ASCARIASIS, CAPILLARIASIS, CYSTICERCOSIS, ENTEROBIASIS, FILARIASIS, GIARDIASIS, HOOKWORM, HYDATID DISEASE, LARVA MIGRANS, LOIASIS, MANSONELLOSIS PERSTANS, STRONGYLOIDIASIS, TAPEWORM, TRICHINOSIS, TRICHURIASIS, diarrhea due to HIV INFECTION.

Contraindications: Pregnancy, ALLERGY to the drug.

Precautions: If used in large doses for HYDATID DISEASE, it may cause HEPATITIS. Stop the drug if this occurs. Avoid pregnancy during treatment and for one month afterward. In the presence of carbamazepine or PHENYTOIN, the dose may need to be increased. If this drug is taken with CIMETIDINE, there will be a larger amount in the blood, so it might become toxic. If it is taken with a fatty meal or with grapefruit (or its juice), there will be a larger amount in the blood, so if you are giving a high dose, it might be toxic.

Overdose and prolonged use: LIVER FAILURE (see Protocol C-7).

Dosage: Unspecified doses are for adults. Reduce dose in the presence of LIVER DISEASE or LIVER FAILURE.

ASCARIASIS: Adults and children over 2 years old or 10 kg get a single dose of 400 mg. Those under 2 years old or 10 kg get 200 mg.

CAPILLARIASIS: 400 mg daily for 10 days.

CYSTICERCOSIS: 5 mg/kg every 8 hours for 21 days, followed by 1 week with no drug, followed by 7-10 mg/kg every 8 hours for 30 days. Use DEXCHLORPHENIRAMINE with this.

Diarrhea due to HIV INFECTION: 800 mg twice daily for 14 days.

ENTEROBIASIS: Same as ASCARIASIS.

FILARIASIS: 400-600 mg, single dose.

GIARDIASIS: 400 mg daily for 5 days.

HOOKWORM: 400 mg twice a day for 2 days.

HYDATID DISEASE: 400 mg twice a day for 28 days. Give this treatment 4 times, with 15 day rest periods between treatments. If the disease still recurs, the patient will need surgery.

LARVA MIGRANS - Cutaneous: 200 mg twice a day for 3 days. LARVA MIGRANS - Deep: 400 mg daily for 21 days.

LOIASIS: 200 mg twice daily for 21 days.

MANSONELLOSIS PERSTANS: 400 mg twice daily for 10 days.

STRONGYLOIDIASIS: 400 mg twice a day for 3 days. Give a second treatment after 3 weeks.

TAPEWORM, beef or pork: 400 mg daily for 3 days.

TRICHINOSIS: 5 mg/kg every 8 hours for 8 days.

TRICHURIASIS: Same as ASCARIASIS, daily for 4 days.

Alternatives: MEBENDAZOLE, THIABENDAZOLE, PYRANTEL PAMOATE.

ALBUTEROL

Antiasthmatic, Bronchodilator

Safety class 2 Stability: C

This is toxic in overdose in children; a small overdose can kill a child.

Supplied as tablets, as liquid, and as inhaler. The drug might be labeled in micrograms (mcg): 1000 mcg = 1 mg.

Synonym: Salbutamol.

Brand names: Proventil, Ventolin.

Indications: ASTHMA, chronic RESPIRATORY INFECTION, premature labor.

Contraindications: Heart problems, HEART FAILURE, pregnancy (except for use in premature labor).

Precautions: Not used in children under 12. It is very toxic in children; a small overdose can kill. Seek physician advice before using together with any heart medications or antidepressants.

Side-effects: If the patient develops a pressure-like chest pain (ANGINA), then stop the drug. Other side-effects: nervousness, trembling, rapid heart rate, headache, muscle cramps, insomnia, nausea, weakness, dizziness. These effects occur in only a small percentage of patients.

Dosage: Reduce the dose in the elderly. Adult dose: 2 mg to 4 mg tablet, every 6 to 8 hours, as needed. The inhaler may be used as 2 puffs inhalation every 4 hours. Do not use the inhaler in children under 12 except at physician's direction.

For premature labor, give 0.1-0.25 mg IM every 5-10 minutes until contractions have stopped; then give 4 mg by mouth every 6-8 hours. An alternative is terbutaline, similar dosage.

Alternatives: METAPROTERENOL, THEOPHYLLINE

ALCITABINE

This is an anti-AIDS drug.

ALCOHOL

Sedative, Muscle relaxant

Synonyms: Ethanol, Ethyl alcohol.

Safety class 2 Stability: A

Indications: Muscle relaxation to put a dislocated shoulder in place; antidote for PLANT POISONING: Ackee; antidote for poisons found in home-brewed alcohol and wood alcohol.

Contraindications: Loss of consciousness, inadequate breathing. Do not use this together with DIAZEPAM or with other sedatives. Do not give this to someone with a family history of PORPHYRIA.

Precautions: Try to avoid using this during pregnancy. An intoxicated patient may become combative; be prepared to deal with this. If the patient passes out, be sure he has an adequate airway and is lying belly down so vomit will run out of his mouth rather than down his throat. Always use alcoholic beverage for this; never use rubbing alcohol or wood alcohol.

Overdose and prolonged usage: LIVER FAILURE.

Dosage: 80 proof alcoholic beverage is 40% alcohol. The adult dose of 80 proof is 6 ml/kg, or 360 ml for a 60 kg person. It may be given by mouth or stomach tube. For 40 proof, double the number of ml given; or for 160 proof divide the dose in half. (For 160 proof, dilution may be desirable to prevent throat irritation.) Calculate the adult dose, then reduce it according to weight for children.

Table of alcohol dosages for muscle relaxation:

Weight

Proof	60 kg	40 kg	30 kg	20 kg	10 kg
160	180 ml	120 ml	90 ml	60 ml	30 ml
120	240 ml	160 ml	120 ml	80 ml	40 ml
80	360 ml	240 ml	180 ml	120 ml	60 ml
60	480 ml	320 ml	240 ml	160 ml	80 ml

(It is best not to use anything weaker than 60 proof.)

For alcohol abuse see ALCOHOLISM in the *Disease Index*.

ALLOPURINOL

Xanthine oxidase inhibitor.

Safety class 2 Stability: A

Pregnancy class C: don't use it.

Brand names: Lopurin, Zyloprim.

Indications: CHAGA'S DISEASE, CUTANEOUS LEISHMANIASIS (only the simple Mexicana type and must be used with another drug also), GOUT, VISCERAL LEISHMANIASIS.

Contraindications: ALLERGY to the drug, KIDNEY FAILURE, pregnancy, breast-feeding.

Precautions: This may bring on an episode of GOUT in those predisposed if the initial dose is too high for that person. Continue the drug at a reduced dosage. If it causes rash, stop the drug. Rashes occur more often if the person who has kidney disease than if his kidneys are normal. A rash may also appear if this is used with AMPICILLIN. If this is used at the same time as THEOPHYLLINE, it increases the amount of THEOPHYLLINE in the blood, possibly to toxic levels. Reduce the dose of THEOPHYLLINE.

Dosage:

CHAGA'S DISEASE: 7-10 mg/kg daily; consult a local physician as to how long to continue this and what other drugs to use additionally.

CUTANEOUS LEISHMANIASIS: 5 mg/kg four times daily for 28 days or 10 mg/kg twice daily for 18 days, combined with sodium STIBOGLUCONATE.

GOUT prevention: Begin at 100 mg daily for one week. The second week, increase it to 200 mg daily; if this dose is not adequate to prevent a recurrence, increase to 300 mg daily for the third and subsequent weeks.

VISCERAL LEISHMANIASIS: 5-10 mg/kg every 8 hours for 10 weeks. This must be combined with sodium STIBOGLUCONATE and it must be used in a hospital setting.

ALOE VERA

This is a common native plant with thick leaves. The gel, obtained by cutting a leaf and squeezing it, is useful for treating all kinds of skin problems, especially burns. Otherwise cut the leaf open and lay it on the wound.

AMIKACIN

Aminoglycoside, second-line anti-TUBERCULOSIS drug

Safety class 3; Stability: Unknown Pregnancy: D

Brand name: Amikin

Indication: TUBERCULOSIS

Contraindications: ALLERGY to this drug or any aminoglycoside (STREPTOMYCIN, GENTAMYCIN)

Precautions: Don't use with other aminoglycosides. Don't use with PENICILLIN, any CEPHALOSPORIN, or AMPHOTERICIN B or diuretics such as HYDROCHLOROTHIAZIDE or FUROSEMIDE. Watch for insufficient respiratory effort (stop the drug) hearing loss (stop the drug). Don't use in patients with any muscle weakness. Should not be given for a long time but temporarily is o.k.

Side-effects: Hearing loss, muscle weakness, KIDNEY FAILURE.

Dosage: 15 mg/kg IM 3-5 days per week. In obese patients, estimate the body weight if he were normal weight and use that weight in calculating the dosage.

AMODIAQUINE

Antimalarial

Safety class 3 Stability: C

Brand names: Basoquin, Camoquin, Flavoquin, Myaquin.

Same uses, same side effects, same doses as CHLOROQUINE for MALARIA; do not use it for amebic DYSENTERY. It may or may not be useful for CHLOROQUINE-resistant MALARIA, depending on the area. It can cause a severe skin reaction resembling a burn. Stop the drug immediately if this occurs. Rarely it kills the bone marrow and hence the patient. It can also cause HEPATITIS.

AMOXICILLIN

Synonym: Amoxycillin (British spelling)

Antibiotic

Safety class 2 Stability: B Pregnancy B

Brand names: Amoxil.

Caution: Do not use amoxicillin in patients with PENICILLIN ALLERGY.

Supplied as 250 and 500 mg tablets and in liquid. There is no injectable form.

Amoxicillin is a longer-acting AMPICILLIN, with less diarrhea as side-effect.

Dosage: The mg per dose amount is the same as AMPICILLIN, but it is given only every 8 hours rather than every 6. The dose for CHLAMYDIA is 500 mg orally, every 8 hours for 7 days. AMPICILLIN might also work but is not officially listed as an acceptable drug. To prevent LYME DISEASE the dose is 500 mg three times daily for 20 days.

AMOXICILLIN plus CLAVULANIC ACID

Antibiotic, gram positive and gram negative

Safety class 1-2 Stability: A

Brand names: Augmentin (USA), Co-amoxiclav (UK)

This is a combination of AMOXICILLIN plus CLAVULANIC ACID. It is supplied as chewable tablets of 125 mg amoxicillin with 31.25 mg of clavulanic acid, or 250 mg amoxicillin with 62.5 mg clavulanic acid. It is also available as adult film-coated tablets with 125 mg clavulanic acid for each 250 mg of amoxicillin.

Indications: ABSCESS, some CELLULITIS, CHANCROID, EXFOLIATIVE DERMATITIS, OSTEOMYELITIS, PYOMYOSITIS.

Contraindications: ALLERGY to any penicillin plus the same contraindications and precautions as AMPICILLIN and AMOXICILLIN. Do not use this in the presence of CIRRHOSIS or any significant LIVER DISEASE.

Side-effects: Upset stomach with higher doses.

Dosage: Reduce the dose in the elderly.

OSTEOMYELITIS: 500 mg (amoxicillin) every 8 hours for a minimum of 6 weeks.

Everything else: 250 mg (amoxicillin) every 8 hours until better plus three days.

AMPHOTERICIN B

Anti-fungal, anti-leishmania

Safety class 3 Stability C Pregnancy B

Brand names: Fungilin, Fungizone, Abelcet, AmBisome, Amphool

Indications: COCCIDIOMYCOSIS, MYCETOMA, VISCERAL LEISHMANIASIS, CUTANEOUS LEISHMANIASIS.

Contraindications: Pregnancy, breast feeding, allergy or previous bad reaction to the drug.

Precautions: This drug is dangerous and must only be used with physician supervision in a hospital context. If the blood pressure drops, the drug must be stopped. The drug is a kidney poison so it must not be given together with other drugs that affect the kidneys. Liposomal amphotericin B is expensive but safer to use.

Side-effects: Nausea, vomiting, diarrhea, abdominal pain, loss of appetite, headache.

Overdose and prolonged use: KIDNEY FAILURE.

Dosage: Per physician advice. Reduce the dose if there is KIDNEY FAILURE or any kidney disease. The usual dose is 0.5 to 1.0 mg/kg IV every day or every other day to a total dose of 15-21 mg/kg. For patients with HIV INFECTION, after a cure, you should give them 3 mg/kg every 2-4 weeks to prevent relapse.

AMPICILLIN

Antibiotic

Safety class 2 Stability: B

Brand names: Omnipen, Polycillin. Supplied as 250 and 500 mg tablets. Liquid supplied as 125 or 250 mg per 5 ml (1 tsp). Generic and injectable forms are available.

Caution: Do not use ampicillin in patients with PENICILLIN ALLERGY.

Indications: ACUTE ABDOMEN, ANTHRAX prevention, BARTONELLOSIS, CELLULITIS, CHLAMYDIA, DYSENTERY (except for Shigella), middle EAR INFECTION, ENTERIC FEVER, EPIDIDYMITIS, GONORRHEA, valvular HEART FAILURE, KIDNEY INFECTION, LEPTOSPIROSIS, LYME DISEASE, MENINGITIS, PELVIC INFECTION, PEPTIC ULCER, PIG-BEL, PLAGUE, PNEUMONIA, RESPIRATORY INFECTION, SEPSIS, SPRUE, URETHRITIS, URINARY INFECTION. It may be used as a substitute for PENICILLIN.

Contraindications: ALLERGY to PENICILLIN or any "cillin" drug. If the patient has MONONUCLEOSIS, ampicillin will cause a rash, necessitating stopping the drug.

Precautions: Diarrhea may occur. Treat the diarrhea but do not stop the drug unless the diarrhea is severe and you have an alternative drug with which to treat him or he is almost over his illness, so you can stop the drug. When given with ALLOPURINOL, a rash may develop. Oral contraceptives might not work well when taken along with this.

Dosage: Reduce dose in the elderly and for KIDNEY FAILURE or any significant kidney disease. Adult doses are given; reduce dose according to weight for children; see the chart at the beginning of this Index. The oral and injectable doses are the same. If the person will or might be sent out for surgery, the drug should be given by injection. When it is used as a substitute for PENICILLIN, it must be used in the same dose as PENICILLIN.

ACUTE ABDOMEN: 500 mg four times a day for 14 days.

ANTHRAX prevention—use only if the organism is sensitive to PENICILLIN: 500 mg every 6 hours for 60 days.

BARTONELLOSIS: Same as ACUTE ABDOMEN.

CELLULITIS: 250-500 mg, depending on severity, every 6 hours for 10 days.

CHLAMYDIA: 500 mg four times a day for 10 days.

DYSENTERY: 500 mg four times a day for 5 days.

EAR INFECTION: Same as CELLULITIS.

ENTERIC FEVER: Same as ACUTE ABDOMEN.

EPIDIDYMITIS: 250-500 mg every 6 hours for 3 days.

GONORRHEA exposure: 3500 mg by mouth in a single dose.

GONORRHEA disease: 3500 mg by mouth in a single initial dose, then 500 mg 4 times a day for 10 days.

HEART FAILURE: 3000 mg an hour before or during a medical or dental procedure; 1500 mg 6 hours later.

KIDNEY INFECTION: Same as CELLULITIS.

LEPTOSPIROSIS: 500 mg every 6 hours for 7 days.

LYME DISEASE: Same as CELLULITIS.

MENINGITIS: 50-60 mg/kg IM or IV every 6 hours for 14 days. The usual adult dose is 3000 mg every 4 hours. You may change to medication by mouth if and when the patient seems almost entirely well. Use this together with GENTAMYCIN if possible.

PELVIC INFECTION: Same as GONORRHEA (disease).

PEPTIC ULCER: 500 mg 4 times a day for 14 days, used together with CLARITHROMYCIN and CIMETIDINE or a similar drug.

PIG-BEL: Same as ACUTE ABDOMEN.

PLAGUE: Same as MENINGITIS.

PNEUMONIA: Same as CELLULITIS.

RESPIRATORY INFECTION: Same as CELLULITIS.

SEPSIS: Same as MENINGITIS, used together with GENTAMYCIN.

SPRUE: Same as DYSENTERY.

URETHRITIS: Same as GONORRHEA (disease).

URINARY INFECTION: Same as EPIDIDYMITIS.

Alternatives: In ALLERGY, it is best to use an alternative drug specific for the disease. Otherwise use CHLORAMPHENICOL or COTRIMOXAZOLE. In severe infections such as SEPSIS and MENINGITIS, an alternative is a third-generation CEPHALOSPORIN.

AMPICILLIN plus SULBACTAM

This is like AMOXICILLIN plus CLAVULANIC ACID, used the same way. The dosage refers to the AMPICILLIN component. If that is correct, the sulbactam dosage will also be correct.

AMPRENAVIR

This is an anti-AIDS drug.

ANESTHETIC EYE DROPS

Topical anesthetic
Safety class 2 Stability: C dark

Brand names: Ophthaine (0.5% proparacaine hydrochloride), Pontocaine (0.5% tetracaine), Dorsacaine (0.4% benoxinate hydrochloride). Many generic preparations are available. Use only drops labeled "ophthalmic".

Indications: Examination of an injured eye, and removal of a foreign body from the eye.

Contraindications: ALLERGY to any "-caine" drug.

Precautions: All of these drops burn as they go in the eye. Warn the patient not to squeeze his eye shut; blinking is o.k.

Dosage: 1 or 2 drops in the affected eye about 20 seconds before you begin examination or removal of the foreign body from the eye. You may use another drop or two if the first dose wears off during the examination.

Caution: **Do not send the patient out with a bottle of eye drops to keep comfortable.** Used more than once, these drops will cause blindess. Use HOMATROPINE ophthalmic drops to keep the patient comfortable longer.

ANTACID

Stomach acid neutralizer
Safety class 1; Stability A
Brand names: Maalox, and others.

Supplied as liquid or tablets, usually containing Magnesium Hydroxide or Aluminum Hydroxide. Some Calcium-containing compounds are also available but these should not be used as they, over the long term, aggravate the problems they are intended to treat.

Indications: GASTRITIS, PEPTIC ULCER, vomiting blood.

Contraindications: ACUTE ABDOMEN, KIDNEY FAILURE.

Precautions: Stomach acid protects against bacteria. When stomach acids are neutralized by antacids, bismuth preparations, or histamine antagonists (e.g. RANITIDINE) this protection is lost so that bacteria that are taken in by mouth are more likely to cause problems.

Maalox may give mild diarrhea. If the patient has HEART FAILURE, give him more DIURETIC if you use Maalox or any sodium-containing antacid.

Do not give this at the same time as DOXYCYCLINE, PHENYTOIN, or KETOCONAZOLE.

Dosage: Reduce the dose during pregnancy. Adults, severe symptoms: 30 ml by mouth every hour while awake, every 2 to 4 hours at night. Patient may keep a bottle with him and just take a swallow hourly. Reduce dose for children according to weight.

Alternatives: Amphojel, Gelusil, Mylanta; all are nearly equivalent, except some tend to give diarrhea and others tend to constipate.

ANTIBIOTIC CREAM

Topical antibiotic
Safety class 1; Stability A

Supplied as tubes of 15gm or 30gm, some varieties being Neosporin, Bacitracin, Polymixin.

Indications: IMPETIGO; various infected wounds. For EAR INFECTION, external use only preparations labeled "ophthalmic" or "otic".

Contraindications: ALLERGY to any of the components of the particular product.

Dosage: Wash the affected area and apply a small amount of the cream daily.

ANTIBIOTIC EYE DROPS / OINTMENT

Topical antibiotic
Safety class 1 Stability: A
Synonym: Ophthalmic Drops/Ointment

Brand names: Achromycin Ophthalmic (a tetracycline), Chloromycetin Ophthalmic (chloramphenicol), Erythromycin Ophthalmic, Garamycin ophthalmic, Sodium Sulamyd Ophthalmic (a sulfa drug). Many generic preparations are available.

Indications: Treatment of an eye injury; treatment after removal of a foreign body; treatment of EYE INFECTION, KERATITIS, TRACHOMA, and cuts near the eyes. For severe infections, eye drops are more reliable. Ointment is more convenient. 1% sulfadiazine ointment should be used for KERATITIS due to a fungus. These preparations may also be used for EAR INFECTION, external.

Contraindications: ALLERGY to the antibiotic in the drops or ointment. Do not use ointment if the patient may have a cut or hole in his eyeball. Drops may be used in this case. Do not use any old or contaminated drug; sterility is absolutely essential.

Dosage:

Drops: use 2 drops in affected eye(s) every hour until the condition improves, then every 2 hours.

Ointment: place about 1/4 inch of ointment anywhere inside the lower lid; repeat every 6 hours. Use for 2 weeks in TRACHOMA; until healed plus 2 days for other problems. You must use oral antibiotics also for TRACHOMA.

Caution: Ointment blurs vision for about 10 minutes. Use only products labeled "ophthalmic"—other antibiotic ointments should not be used. Avoid neosporin ophthalmic ointment if possible: there are frequent allergic reactions to it.

Alternatives: IODINE EYE DROPS; Using human milk as eye drops works fine in some places. It's harmless to try it.

ANTIBIOTIC OINTMENT

Topical antibiotic
Safety class 1 Stability: A
Includes: Neosporin ointment, Bacitracin ointment, Povidone Iodine Ointment.
Preparations labeled ophthalmic are expensive; they should be used only on eyelids and in eyes and ears. This listing refers to cheaper kinds which can be used anywhere else. A very cheap version may be made by stirring antibiotic into petroleum jelly (Vaseline), about 30 emptied TETRACYCLINE capsules (250 mg) in 225 ml (8 ounces) of jelly.

*****If needed for eyes or ears, see the previous entry!**

Povidone Iodine Ointment: See Procedures 9 and 10 in Appendix 1 of Volume I, for preparation of this.

Indications: External EAR INFECTION, IMPETIGO, TROPICAL ULCER; put on any wound-open or sewn-to prevent infection.

Contraindications: ALLERGY to ingredient(s) of specific preparation.

Dosage: Use sparingly for economic reasons. The amount used does not matter medically. Use until the wound or rash is healed.

ANTIBIOTICS

These are medicines that either kill bacteria or inhibit their growth. See AMOXICILLIN, AMPICILLIN, CEPHALOSPORIN, CHLORAMPHENICOL, CIPROFLOXACIN, DOXYCYCLINE, ERYTHROMYCIN, GENTAMYCIN, METRONIDAZOLE, NEOSPORIN, PENICILLIN, RIFAMPIN, SPECTINOMYCIN, STREPTOMYCIN, SULFA, TINIDAZOLE, COTRIMOXAZOLE.

ANTIVENIN SERUM

Safety class 3 Stability: D
See Snake Bite, Volume I, Chapter 9.

Artemisinin Combination Therapy (ACT)

See the explanation of this under ACT.

ARTEMISININ

Antimalarial
Includes: Artemether, Artesunate, Qinghasou.
Safety class 1
Stability: Varies; Artemether - Stability A. Pregnancy: Should be avoided in early pregnancy because in animals it is toxic to embryos. However, there is no firm evidence of its being problematic in humans. Also, malaria is very destructive in pregnancy so the risk may be very worthwhile.

Artemisia is the name of the plant from which the drug, artemisinin, is derived.

Artemisinin and *Qinghasou* are synonyms for the original natural product, a folk medicine from China. *Artemisinin* is available as oral, suppository, and IM injectable forms. The drug comes from a garden plant which can be grown in cool, moist climates, especially at high altitudes. The leaves are dried and made into a tea. Five grams of the dry leaves (one film canister-full, about 30 ml) is used to make a liter of tea. 250 ml of the tea every 8 hours is the usual adult dosage. The tea tastes terrible; sugar helps it go down.

Artemether and *artesunate* are related medicines that were manufactured from artemisinin. They are more expensive. *Artemether* is available in capsules for oral use and in a stable form for IM injection. *Artesunate* is available in oral tablets. It is also available in suppository form and for IM and IV use. The brand name of the suppositories is Plasmotrim Rectocaps; they come in 50 mg and 200 mg sizes. It is difficult to make up and use the injectable forms. A recent combination is AZITHROMYCIN 750 mg plus Artesunate 100 mg, AZITHROMYCIN is an antibiotic that is also active against malaria. It is expensive.

Artemether is sometimes combined with *benflumetol*, an anti-malarial that lasts for a long time in the blood stream. This seems to be safe and to work well against falciparum malaria. Usual adult tablets contain 20 mg of artemether and 120 mg of benflumetol. Half-sized tablets for children are available.

Artemether-lumefantrine is another drug combination. brand names are Coartemether, Co-artem, Riamet. There are no significant additional side-effects. Tablet size: 2.0 mg artemether plus 12.0 mg lumefantrine. It is safe and effective to use in children.

Dihydroartemisinin-piperaquine is another combination. The brand name is Artekin. One tablet contains 40 mg of DHA and 320 mg of piperaquine. There are minimal side-effects.

Artemison is a new derivative of artemisinin that seems to be less toxic. Not much is known about it.

Indications: MALARIA, especially that originating in Southeast Asia. The drug suppresses but does not cure SCHISTOSOMIASIS HEMATOBIUM and SCHISTOSOMIASIS MANSONI. If taken right after exposure to any SCHISTOSOMIASIS, it decreases the likelihood of KATAYAMA DISEASE. Reportedly the tea, in combination with a nutritious diet, reverses the symptoms of advanced HIV INFECTION, enabling bed-ridden patients to return to work. Reportedly it is active against some CANCERs.

Contraindications: Prior ALLERGY to this drug. Pregnancy is no longer a contraindication, though it should be avoided in early pregnancy. All the contraindications are not known since the drug has not been used for long in Western culture.

Precautions: Use it with another anti-malarial drug unless it can be used for a full 7 days without missing any doses. AZITHROMYCIN is a good drug to use with this.

Side-effects: Nausea and vomiting at higher doses, sometimes at ordinary doses when using the tea made from the dried leaves. The tea has a wretched taste, enough to aggravate the strongest stomachs. Reportedly there can be some adverse effects on hearing.

Dosages: If the patient is vomiting, Artesunate (and possibly also other forms) may be used rectally at twice the usual oral dose. The dose may have to be increased if used in pregnancy because pregnant women eliminate the drug faster than non-pregnant patients.

Artemisia-leaf tea: Measure out 5 grams (one film canister-full) of dried leaves. Make this up as a tea in a liter of water. Huge amounts of sugar masks the wretched taste.

MALARIA: Take 250 ml (one cup) of this tea every 8 hours for 4 doses.

HIV INFECTION: 1 liter of tea daily in divided doses (if it is drunk all at once the patient will vomit) for one month. In addition a high-protein diet and high-potency multivitamins should be given daily.

The doses below are for MALARIA only; probably the processed drug from the pharmaceutical companies does not work for HIV INFECTION.

Artemisinin: Use DOXYCYCLINE, MEFLOQUINE, or another antimalarial along with this. Oral dose of artemisinin is 10-20 mg/kg daily for 3 days; Adult dose by suppository is 600 mg at 0 and 4 hours, followed by 400 mg at 24, 36, 48, and 60 hours after the initial dose. Reduce dose according to weight for children.

Artemisone: This is a new derivative of artemisinin; there is no other information available.

Artesunate suppositories adult dosage is one 200mg suppository at 0, 4, 8, 12, 24, 36, 48, and 60 h; Oral artesunate dosage is 5-6 mg/kg single daily dose x 3 days. IV dosage is 2.4 mg/kg at 0, 12, and 24 hours, and then daily. IV artesunate is hard to obtain, even in Europe. You should not delay treatment in order to obtain it. All forms are effective; they should be used with MEFLOQUINE, FOSMIDOMYCIN, QUININE, or AZITHROMYCIN, possibly with other anti-malarials.

Artemether IM injectable dosage is 3.2 mg/kg initially, followed by 1.6 mg/kg daily, for two more days. It is probably less effective than IV Artesunate.

Combination: *artemether-benflumeto*: The usual adult dose is 4 tablets per dose at 0, 8, 24, and 48 hours.

Combination: *artemether-lumefantrine. 20 mg/120 mg.* Dose for adults: 4-6 tablets initially followed by 4-6 tablets at 8 hours and then 4-6 tablets twice daily for 2 days.

Combination: *Dihydroartemisinin-piperaquine.* Give one tablet for every 20 kg of patient daily for 3 days. Thus a 60 kg adult would get 3 tablets daily for 3 days. The dose is not fussy.

Combination: artesunate plus dapsone plus proguanil—brand name and correct dosage not available—reportedly works well in Thailand where there is much resistant malaria. Observe the contraindications for all three drugs.

For severe MALARIA:

Day 1 Artemether 3.2 mg/kg or else IV or IM Otherwise artesunate, 2.4 mg/kg IV at 0, 12, and 24 hours.

Subsequent days: 1.6 mg/kg daily artemether or artesunate 2.4 mg/kg daily until oral therapy is possible. Then use one of the other options to complete 10 days of treatment.

Another treatment regimen is as follows:

Ordinary malaria: Day 1: Oral artesunate 5 mg/kg or oral artemesinin 25 mg/kg
Days 2 &3: MEFLOQUINE 15-25 mg/kg + (either 2.5 mg/kg of artesunate or 12.5 mg/kg artemesinin)

Severe falciparum malaria: Day 1 Artemether 3.2 mg/kg IM or else IV or IM artesunate, 2 mg/kg
Subsequent days: 1.6 mg/kg daily artemether IM or artesunate 1 mg/kg daily until oral therapy is possible.

ARTIFICIAL TEARS

Wetting agent for ophthalmic use

Safety class 1 Stability: A

Brand names: Tears Naturale, many others

Indications: Dry eyes due to lack of tears, XEROPHTHALMIA, BELL'S PALSY, LEPROSY.

Contraindications: None

Precautions: Be sure not to contaminate the bottle by touching an infected eye with the tip and then touching another eye.

Dosage: Two drops as often as necessary to keep the eye moist. Patching may help at night.

ASPIRIN

Analgesic; Anti-inflammatory; Antipyretic

Synonym: Acetylsalicylic acid.

Safety class 2 Stability: A Pregnancy D

Brand names: Many. Supplied as 325 and 500 mg adult tablets and in 80 mg (USA) and 100 mg (Europe) children's tablets. There is no liquid form.

Indications: Fever, mild pain relief, blood clot prevention, ARBOVIRAL FEVER (Ross River Fever and Sandfly Fever only), ARTHRITIS, CATARACT, FEVER PER SE, HEART FAILURE, KATAYAMA DISEASE, LEPROSY reaction, PLEURISY, RHEUMATIC FEVER, TOXEMIA.

Contraindications: Previous ALLERGY to the drug, previous PEPTIC ULCER or vomiting of blood, any bleeding tendency. Should not be used along with QUININE. Should not be used with any viral illness in children or young adults. It should not be used in any ARBOVIRAL FEVER which potentially could become HEMORRHAGIC FEVER. It should not be used in AFRICAN SLEEPING SICKNESS, ENTERIC FEVER, GOUT, or VISCERAL LEISHMANIASIS. It should generally not be used in children or breast-feeding mothers or in the presence of G6PD DEFICIENCY.

Precautions: Patients with ASTHMA which began in adulthood frequently have aspirin ALLERGY.

Aspirin may provoke internal bleeding. BISMUTH SUBSALICYLATE (Pepto-Bismol) taken at the same time as aspirin may cause an overdose; the two drugs are related. Do not take these two drugs together.

Take aspirin with food or milk rather than on an empty stomach.

Aspirin may aggravate hyperactivity in some hyperactive people.

Aspirin interferes with many lab tests; don't believe lab results while the patient is taking this.

Watch the tablet size carefully. The usual tablet size in Western countries is 325 mg. Some countries have 500 mg tablets. 5 grains is 325 mg; 7.5 grains is 500 mg.

Side-effects: Ringing in the ears.

Overdose and prologed usage: See *Symptom Index,* Protocol 11 for overdose. In severe overdose there is a change in mental functioning: nervousness, hallucinations, confusion, and also shortness of breath.

Dosage: Adult doses are listed; reduce dose according to weight for children.

Pain and fever: 650-1000 mg every 4 hours as needed.

ARBOVIRAL FEVER: Like ARTHRITIS

ARTHRITIS: Begin with 750-850 mg every 6 hours. Give it faithfully on time, not only when symptoms are severe. Increase the dose every 4 days by 150-175 mg per dose until the patient starts to have ringing in his ears; then drop back to the previous dose. The idea is to give as high a dose as possible, without causing ringing in the ears. Give this amount until the problem is entirely cleared up and then for another week. Some people must take the drug for years.

CATARACT: One 325 or 500 mg tablet daily.

HEART FAILURE: One 100 or 325 mg tablet daily.

KATAYAMA DISEASE: Like ARTHRITIS.

LEPROSY reactions: Like ARTHRITIS.

PLEURISY: Like ARTHRITIS.

RHEUMATIC FEVER: Like ARTHRITIS.

TOXEMIA: 60 mg daily, adult dose.

Alternatives: ACETAMINOPHEN is not as good for ARTHRITIS. IBUPROFEN is an alternative for ARTHRITIS.

ATOVAQUONE

Antiprotozoal
Safety class 2 Stability A Pregnancy C
Supplied as 250 mg tablets
Brand name: Mepron
Brand name of Atovaquone + PROGUANIL is Malarone. It is very expensive. The usual adult tablets are 250 mg atovaquone plus 100 mg proguanil. Pediatric tablets are 62.5 and 25 mg respectively.

Indications: MALARIA, TOXOPLASMOSIS, occasionally PNEUMONIA in HIV INFECTION, when the patient cannot tolerate COTRIMOXAZOLE.

Contraindications: ALLERGY to the drug. If a patient has taken this drug for malaria prevention but he gets malaria anyway, he should not also take it for treatment.

Precautions: It is unknown if there are problems with this in children, during pregnancy, or in elderly people. Use cautiously, if at all, in breast-feeding women; in animal studies there was much drug in breast milk. Use only with physician supervision if the person has DIABETES. It may possibly make the diabetes worse. The drug should be taken with food since more drug gets into the blood stream that way. Do not use this together with ZIDOVUDINE, RIFAMPIN, or RIFABUTIN.

Side-effects: burning upper abdominal pain, nausea, vomiting, diarrhea, insomnia, headache, rash, itching.

Dosage: The drug should be taken with fatty foods for best effect. The dose may need to be decreased in the presence of LIVER DISEASE (see Protocol C-7), LIVER FAILURE or KIDNEY FAILURE.

PNEUMONIA: 750 mg three times a day for 21 days.

MALARIA prevention: 1 adult tablet daily for adults.
- Children 10-20 kg get 1 pediatric tablet daily.
- Children 21-30 kg get 2 pediatric tablets daily.
- Children 31-40 kg get 3 pediatric tablets daily.
- Children 41 kg or more get 1 adult tablet daily.

MALARIA treatment: 1000 mg daily for 3 days; this must be used with PROGUANIL. It does not work well alone.

TOXOPLASMOSIS: 750 mg with food for 21 days.

Alternatives: CHLOROQUINE plus CHLORPHENIRAMINE; MEFLOQUINE; FANSIDAR; QUININE; HALOFANTRINE.

ATROPINE

Anticholinergic
Safety class 3 Stability: A Pregnancy C
Supplied as generic drug in ampules and syringes for IM injection. There is no oral form.

Indications: Some scorpion bites, INSECTICIDE POISONING, PLANT POISONING: Muscarine. (These all cause much saliva, abdominal cramps, diarrhea, sweating, paralysis, slow pulse, small pupils, and vomiting.) Also used in eye drops to dilate the pupil and relieve the pain of KERATITIS.

Contraindications: Do not use this drug if the patient has less than three of the symptoms listed above. Infants are very sensitive to the drug—be particularly careful with dosages and stop if the child becomes excitable or any of his vital signs (pulse, respiratory rate, temperature) changes significantly. Do not give in the presence of GLAUCOMA. Should not be used in the presence of myasthenia gravis, a type of muscle weakness.

Side-effects of this class of drugs (anti-cholinergics):

Constipation, inability to pass urine (especially in older men), susceptibility to HEAT ILLNESS, dry mouth, decrease in sweating, rapid pulse, sensitivity to light, blurred vision.

Give ONLY enough to relieve the symptoms; how much will vary greatly from one patient to the next. Check the pulse. Unless the patient is very seriously ill do not allow the pulse to go above 1.5 times the upper limit of normal for his age. See the listing of normal vital signs in front of the *Symptom Index.*

Dosage: The following are the doses that you should start with. As long as the patient is very ill, give this amount IM repeatedly as needed: 2 mg in a large adult; 1.5 mg in a small adult; 1 mg in 10-15 y.o.; 0.75 mg for a 5-10 y.o.; 0.5 mg for a 1-5 y.o.; and 0.25 mg for less than 1 y.o.; all given by injection, subcutaneously. The drug should start taking effect in 5 minutes or less.

As eye drops, use 1 drop in the eye as often as necessary to keep the pupil dilated and the eye pain-free. The effects of one drop last up to a week. Assure the patient that it will wear off. Use HOMATROPINE EYE DROPS for shorter duration.

AUGMENTIN

See AMOXICILLIN + CLAVULANIC ACID

AZITHROMYCIN

Antibiotic, gram positive and some gram negative; macrolide-type

Safety class 1 Stability ? Pregnancy B

Brand name: Zithromax; generic drug is now available in the States. Comes in 250 mg capsules and 200 mg/5 ml liquid. There is also an injectable form.

Indications: May be used like ERYTHROMYCIN but it is more expensive. Also: BARTONELLOSIS (either type), CELLULITIS, CHANCROID, CHLAMYDIA, CRYPTOSPORIDIOSIS, DONOVANOSIS, mild to moderate ENTERIC FEVER, GONORRHEA, LYMPHOGRANULOMA VENEREUM, MALARIA, PNEUMONIA, Q FEVER, RESPIRATORY INFECTION, SCRUB TYPHUS, SPOTTED FEVER, STREP INFECTION, SYPHILIS (early); TRACHOMA, TOXOPLASMOSIS, TRENCH FEVER. Some sources say this can be used for PELVIC INFECTION and others say it should not be used. Seek independent advice.

Contraindications: Prior ALLERGY to this drug or to related drugs such as ERYTHROMYCIN or CLARITHROMYCIN; LIVER DISEASE.

Precautions: Makes the skin sensitive to the sun; might cause nausea and stomach pain; safety in pregnancy is uncertain. Do not take with antacids because it is then not well absorbed. Do not use this with THEOPHYLLINE or DIGOXIN or any blood thinners.

Side-effects: Nausea, vomiting, diarrhea, abdominal pain, loss of appetite, constipation, HEPATITIS, headache, dizziness, mental changes, joint pains, SEIZURES, skin sun sensitivity. Rarely it might cause LIVER FAILURE.

Dosage: Reduce dose with LIVER DISEASE. Otherwise the dosage is the same as ERYTHROMYCIN for similar indications. For most indications for most adults the usual dose is 500 mg once daily for 3 days unless listed otherwise. Reduce the dose according to weight for children.

CHANCROID and CHLAMYDIA: 1 gram single dose

CRYPTOSPORIDIOSIS: 600 mg daily for 28 days, used together with PAROMOMYCIN.

DONOVANOSIS: 1 gram weekly for 6 weeks or 5-10 mg/kg every 8 hours IV for 5-7 days.

ENTERIC FEVER (only mild to moderate, not severe): 500 mg once daily for 7 days.

GONORRHEA: 2 grams, single dose.[1]

LYMPHOGRANULOMA VENEREUM: The dose is uncertain. Seek local advice. In any case it is essential to withdraw pus from the buboe (large, soft lymph node) in addition to giving the antibiotic.

MALARIA: 750 mg twice daily or 1000 mg daily for 3 days, used with ARTEMISININ (artesunate) or with QUININE; don't use this alone. For malaria prevention the dose is 750 mg initially, then 250 mg daily.

PELVIC INFECTION: 1 gram single dose, given with FLUCONAZOLE and SECNIDAZOLE also in single doses. Some protocols call for using this daily for 5 days.

PNEUMONIA: 500 mg on day 1; 250 mg daily on days 2-5—for moderate pneumonia in patients under 60 years old. In those over 60 years old, also use CO-TRIMOXAZOLE for 10 days.

Q FEVER: 10 mg/kg initially, then 5 mg/kg every 6 hours for 4 days.

SCRUB TYPHUS: 500 mg single dose; this is the drug of choice in pregnancy.

[1] This large a dose may cause distressing side-effects but the alternative CIPROFLOXACIN, and related drugs, are no longer any good for GONORRHEA in homosexuals or that acquired in urban areas.

SPOTTED FEVER: 500 mg daily until 3 days after the fever drops.

STREP INFECTION: 500 mg daily x 10 days.

SYPHILIS: 500 mg daily for 10 days. (This does not work as well as PENICILLIN and there is resistance in some areas.)

TOXOPLASMOSIS: In the presence of AIDS, give 500 mg every 8 hours for 3-6 weeks. In the absence of AIDS, give 500 mg on the first day, then 250 mg daily for the next 4 days.

TRACHOMA: 20 mg/kg to a maximum of 1000 mg, single dose, for mass treatment.

TRENCH FEVER: 500 mg daily for 4-6 weeks.

BENFLUMETOL

This is a new antimalarial, frequently combined with ARTEMISININ (Artemether form). Originally it was thought to be the same as LUMEFANTRINE but now it is known to be different, though related and possibly more effective. It should be taken with fatty foods in order to increase absorption from the bowel. The usual adult dose is 480 mg at 0, 8, 24, and 48 hours. Seek physician input before using this. Sometimes new medications seem to work well but later are found to be useless or dangerous.

BENZNIDAZOLE

Anti-trypanosome
Safety class unknown Stability unknown
Brand name: Rochagan
Indications: CHAGA'S DISEASE
Contraindications: Unknown; pursue local information on this. It is a new drug and the information currently available is inadequate for you to use this for treatment.

Precautions/side effects: Skin rashes occur in half of the patients and nerve inflammations in many later during the course of treatment. Pursue further information before using the drug.

Dosage: 5-10 mg/kg by mouth daily for 2 months.

BENZOIC ACID OINTMENT

Topical antifungal ointment
Safety class 1 Stability: A
Supplied as Whitfield's ointment when the benzoic acid is combined with salicylic acid. It inhibits fungal growth and causes the surface layer of skin to shed. See WHITFIELD'S OINTMENT.

BENZOYL PEROXIDE

Anti-acne
Safety class 1 Stability: A
Brand names: Clearasil and others.
Indications: ACNE.
Contraindications: Previous ALLERGY to the drug.
Precautions: Discontinue if there is an allergic reaction.
Side-effects: Local irritation may occur; stop the drug temporarily. Resume using it in smaller amounts and less frequently.
Dosage: Apply 1-3 times daily.

BENZYL BENZOATE

Scabicide
Safety class 1 Stability: C
Brand names: Ascabiol, Benylate, Demodek, NBIN, Scabanca, Temedex, Tenutex, Vanzoate, Venzonate. Many veterinary forms. Supplied as 50% and 28% solutions, liquid, in bottles.

Indications: SCABIES. May also help for LICE, but this is questionable.

Contraindications: Previous ALLERGY to the drug. The American literature permits usage during pregnancy and infancy, but the British literature says that it is contraindicated. The manufacturer says it should not be used on the head and neck but other sources say it may be needed there. Some sources say it should not be used in children but these are the main ones that need it. In any case, it is much less toxic than the alternative, LINDANE.

Precautions: This may occasionally cause CONTACT DERMATITIS. Do not use the drug again if this occurs. The patient may still itch for 1-3 weeks after treatment; this does not imply that the treatment failed; it is normal. Do not apply this to the hands of babies and young children who will put their hands in their mouths; it is intended for external use only.

Dosage: Have the patient bathe first. Then apply the 28% lotion. If you have 50% lotion, first dilute it with water, 50:50. Apply it while the skin is damp, avoiding the pink, moist areas of genitals and mouth. Let the first application dry. Then apply a second layer and let that dry. Bathe 48 hours later. Repeat the treatment in 7-10 days if there are new scabies spots.

Alternatives: Crotamiton; LINDANE (which may not be used during pregnancy or infancy); Malathion 0.5%; SULFUR in petroleum jelly.

BEPHENIUM HYDROXYNAPHTHOATE

Dewormer, Anthelmintic
Safety class 1 Stability: A
Brand names: Alcopar, Frantin. Supplied in a small envelope with 5 grams of powdered drug. This has largely been replaced with better drugs, but you may still find it in developing countries.

Indications: ASCARIASIS, HOOKWORM. It is not useful for other worms.

Contraindications: ALLERGY to the drug, uncorrected DEHYDRATION.

Precautions: Correct DEHYDRATION before giving this drug. Reduce dose to 3 or 4 grams (1.5-2 gm base) in pregnancy. This drug has a bitter taste; disguise with sugar for children to avoid waste. Expensive.

Side-effects: Nausea, vomiting, diarrhea (usually mild).

Dosage: Bephenium alone is the base; this is the essential part of the drug. It is combined with hydroxynaphthoate, and the combined compound is the drug.

For children under 20 kg, use 1-2.5 gm of drug, (0.5-1.25 gm base.) For larger children and adults: 5 gm of drug (2.5 gm base) in 1/2 glass sugar water on an empty stomach. Allow no food for 2 hours afterward. Repeat daily for 1-5 days more, depending on how sick the patient is.

Alternatives: ALBENDAZOLE, FLUBENDAZOLE, MEBENDAZOLE, PIPERAZINE plus TETRACHLOROETHYLENE, PYRANTEL PAMOATE.

BIRTH CONTROL PILLS

Hormone

Safety class 2 Stability: C

Brand names: Demulen, Enovid, Loestrin, Modicon, Norinyl, Ortho-Novum, Ovulen, many others.

Indications: Abnormal menstruation, prevention of pregnancy.

Contraindications: Heavy cigarette smoking, HYPERTENSION, family history of blood clots or STROKE, artificial heart valve, age over 40, CANCER of the breast or genital or urinary area. The birth control pills with two drugs in them (progesterone and estrogen) are contraindicated in breast-feeding mothers since they dry breast milk. They should not be used in persons who have PORPHYRIA, a hereditary disease.

Precautions: The stronger kinds (those with higher numbers after the name), and to a lesser extent the others, are associated with an increased risk of STROKE and blood clots, especially for patients who eat a Western diet, are heavy cigarette smokers, or have HYPERTENSION. The pills may aggravate MIGRAINE headaches. Use no-estrogen tablets in breast-feeding women. Many different drugs interfere with the contraceptive function of BCP's. Use another form of contraception additionally while taking any other medication or seek independent information concerning the status of the particular drugs that you must take routinely.

Dosage: One tablet daily according to directions.

BISMUTH SUBCITRATE

This is another form of bismuth, used the same as BISMUTH SUBSALICYLATE. The usual adult dose is 120 mg four times a day. Sometimes the word "Colloidal" is attached to the name.

BISMUTH SUBSALICYLATE

Antidiarrheal; Antinauseant

Safety class 1 Stability: A

Brand names: Pepto-bismol, Pink bismuth.

The English drug Tripotassium dicitratobismuthate is basically the same as BISMUTH SUBSALICYLATE but it should not be used in KIDNEY FAILURE. Also see colloidal BISMUTH SUBCITRATE (previous entry).

Indications: TURISTA, nausea, PEPTIC ULCER. The crushed tablets may be made into a paste and used on HERPES as well as the rash of MEASLES.

Contraindications: Easy bleeding from any cause. Prior ALLERGY to the drug; do not use at the same time as ASPIRIN or IBUPROFEN or medication to lower the blood sugar in DIABETES. Do not use this along with medication for GOUT. If used along with DOXYCYCLINE or TETRACYCLINE, separate the times by at least 2 hours. Even then, the bismuth may bind to the doxycyclin or tetracycline so it does not work. Do not use it by mouth in the third trimester of pregnancy or in children or young adults with any viral illness. This drug may interfere with the test for urine glucose.

Side-effects: Temporary darkening of stool and tongue. (This is no problem but may be prevented by rinsing the mouth.) It may aggravate hyperactivity. The medication is visible on x-ray.

Dosage: Reduce the dose in the elderly.

PEPTIC ULCER: 1 tablet or 1 teaspoon (5 ml) of liquid every 6 hours for 14 days.

TURISTA (traveler's diarrhea) preventive: 2 tablets or 2 teaspoons of liquid 4 times a day. Tablets should be chewed.

Everything else: 2 tablets or 2 teaspoons of liquid every hour as needed to a maximum of 8 daily doses.

Alternatives: RANITIDINE for PEPTIC ULCER. Attapulgite is an aluminum silicate clay preparation that works similarly and is useful for mild diarrhea.

BITHIONOL

Anthelmintic, specifically for the flukes.

Safety class 2 Stability: Unknown

Brand names: Actamer, Bitin, Lorothidol.

Indications: LIVER FLUKE, PARAGONIMIASIS, TAPEWORM.

Contraindications: Prior ALLERGY to this drug.

Precautions: It may cause abdominal distress, hives, and some protein in the urine. It is essential to give a laxative after treatment for pork TAPEWORM. Dispose of the stool carefully since it is infectious—will cause CYSTICERCOSIS.

Dosage:

LIVER FLUKE: 30-50 mg/kg by mouth every other day for 14 days (7 doses).

PARAGONIMIASIS: Same as LIVER FLUKE.

TAPEWORM: 2 doses, 1 gram each, 30 minutes apart. Give MILK OF MAGNESIA or any other diarrhea-causing drug 2 hours later. One treatment is all that is necessary.

Alternative: PRAZIQUANTEL.

CALCIUM

Mineral

Safety class 1, oral Stability A

Brand names: Too numerous to mention

Indications: TOXEMIA, MENOPAUSE, some hormonal problems. IV Calcium Gluconate is useful for the spasms associated with CHOLERA.

Contraindications: Rarely some hormonal problems. Do not use along with any heart medicines as it may alter the functioning of these.

Precautions: In people who have PEPTIC ULCER, this may make the condition worse. It may lessen the absorption of other nutrients. Calcium lactate tablets should be chewed. If this is given IV, it will interfere with the lab test for magnesium.

Side-effects: Constipation.

Dosage: 500 mg four times a day.

CAMBENDAZOLE

Dewormer, Anthelmintic

Safety class 2 or 3 Stability: Unknown

Pregnancy: Unknown; however, other drugs in this class are contraindicated in pregnancy, especially the first trimester.

Brand names: Ascapilla, Bonlam, Camvet, Equiben, Novazole, Noviben, Porcam.

Indications: STRONGYLOIDIASIS. It is probably also effective for other worm problems.

Contraindications: ALLERGY to the drug, pregnancy.

Precautions: As of this writing, this is a veterinary drug which is not approved for human use. However, there are multiple reports of its being effective and safe for the use listed.

Dosage: A single dose of 5 mg/kg; 300 mg is the usual adult dose.

CARBAPENEMs

This is a class of antibiotics closely related to and described under CEPHALOSPORINs. Examples are imipenem with cilastatin, meropenem, ertapenem. Seek independent information before using these.

CEPHALOSPORINs

Safety class: 2 Stability: Variable

Includes: Cefalexin, Cefotaxime, Ceftazidine, Ceftriaxone, Cefuroxime (and others).

Note that this is a large <u>class</u> of drugs; as listed below. Closely related classes such as monobactams and carbapenems are listed herein also.

Cephalosporins are divided into three generations.

- First-generation cephalosporins are best for gram-positive infections;
- Second-generation are not as good for gram-positive but they work for some gram negative.
- Third-generation are good mainly for gram negative but they also work for some gram positive.
- The cephalosporin-related drugs cover most gram-positive and gram-negative infections.

Indications: ABSCESS, ACUTE ABDOMEN, CATSCRATCH DISEASE (third generation), CELLULITIS, CHANCROID, DONOVANOSIS, EAR INFECTIONS, ENTERIC FEVER, EXFOLIATIVE DERMATITIS, GALLBLADDER DISEASE, GONORRHEA,[1] KIDNEY INFECTION, LYME DISEASE, MEASLES complications, MENINGITIS, OSTEOMYELITIS, PELVIC INFECTION, PNEUMONIA, PYOMYOSITIS, SEPSIS, STREP THROAT, SYPHILIS, URINARY INFECTION, wound infections.

Contraindications: Prior ALLERGY to any cephalosporin is a contraindication to all cephalosporins and related drugs for the rest of the patient's life.

Precautions: Check the internet for additional and more recent precautions. Sometimes people who have an ALLERGY to PENICILLINs are also allergic to cephalosporins. Don't use these drugs in penicillin-allergic patients unless you have EPINEPHRINE on hand and you have reviewed what to do in an allergic emergency (see Volume I, Chapter 4).

Some of these drugs are toxic for those with KIDNEY DISEASE or KIDNEY FAILURE. (If your patient has a normal blood pressure [apart from pressure-lowering medications] and a normal urine dipstick, he does not have kidney failure.) In the presence of kidney problems, use these drugs only with expert medical advice.

Do not use these drugs with probenecid; the amounts in the blood might increase to the point of making the patient toxic.

Most of these drugs cause SEIZURES in large doses and/or in the presence of KIDNEY DISEASE or KIDNEY FAILURE. Stop the drug if this happens.

Stop the drug if the patient develops a new skin condition while taking it.

Most of them can cause pseudomembranous colitis, a devastating diarrhea that is only treatable with expensive drugs in Western facilities. If the patient develops diarrhea, stop the drug.

Most of these drugs also can cause KIDNEY FAILURE and a few may cause LIVER FAILURE (see Protocol C-7). Stop the drug if there is evidence of either.

Some cause SERUM SICKNESS: fever, sore joints and prostration; this is rare except for Cefachlor, in which it is common. Stop the drug for this.

[1] Although these drugs work for gonorrhea, they do not generally work for CHLAMYDIA which is frequently clinically indistinguishable and is very common in the developing world.

Some cause bleeding problems; this is relatively rare except for Cefoperazone and Cefotetan, in which it is common. Stop the drug for this.

Some of these can cause falsely positive tests for sugar in the urine.

Dosages and uses: (See the following tables).

The duration of therapy should be until the problem is completely gone plus another 2-3 days, unless specified otherwise. MENINGITIS must be treated for 2 weeks; OSTEOMYELITIS must be treated for 6 weeks. Generally any disease that makes the patient sick enough to be bedridden should be treated for a minimum of 10-14 days. If more current product information is available believe that rather than the dosages given here. In particular, lower doses might be useful for less serious infections. Nationals in developing countries frequently respond well to low doses. The doses given are for the more serious conditions.

Choosing a specific drug:

If you have one of these drugs, check if it is good for the disease you intend to treat with it. If you don't have any of these, make a list of which might be helpful and which generation each of these is. Then go to a pharmacy and ask for one of them. If the pharmacist doesn't have any of those listed, ask him for another cephalosporin of the same generation. Look at the package insert to check if it is useful for the purpose you have in mind.

If a drug that you have on hand is not listed, find out if it is called a *first, second,* or *third generation* cephalosporin. Most drugs of the same generation will be useful for the same sorts of things. Exceptions are: for MENINGITIS, LYME DISEASE, GONORRHEA, and CHANCROID, only use drugs listed for these diseases. Most cephalosporins are useful for OSTEOMYELITIS, skin and soft tissue infections, URINARY INFECTIONS, and PNEUMONIA, unless listed otherwise.

Tables of cephalosporin-type antibiotics:

Abbreviations used in the tables:

A = abdominal infections; Bj = bone/joint; Ch = chancroid; Ef = enteric fever; Ent = ear/nose/throat; G = gonorrhea; M = meningitis; O = other; P = pneumonia; Se = sepsis; Sk = skin/soft tissue[1]; U = urinary tract

First-generation Cephalosporins

Generic name; Brand names	Generation	Route of Admin.	Good for:[2]	Not good for:	Cautions[3]	Kinds of bacteria	Usual dosage in adults
cephalexin Keflex Panixine	1st	oral, empty stomach	Bj, Ent, Sk, P, U	G, Ef, M	usual	gram pos, some gram neg	250-500 mg every 6 hours
cephalothin Keflin	1st	IV	Ch, Ent, G, P, Sk	M	usual	gram pos, some gram neg	1-2 gm IV every 4 hours
cefadroxil Duracef, Ultracef, Baxan	1st	oral	P, Sk, U; ?A	Ent, M, G	usual	gram pos, some gram neg	0.5-1 gm every 12-24 hours
cephradine Anspor Velosef	1st	oral	Ent, Sk, P, U	M, Ef	usual	gram pos, some gram negative	0.25-1 gm every 6-12 hours
cefazolin Ancef Kefzol	1st	IM/IV	Bj, P, U, Sk, Se	M, Ef	usual	gram pos, some gram negative	0.25-1 gm every 6-12 hours

[1] This includes abscess, cellulitis, exfoliative dermatitis, pyomyositis, impetigo (severe), wound infections. Catscratch disease involves the skin and soft tissue but it reportedly should be treated only with third-generation cephalosporins.

[2] A drug still might not work for these conditions if the particular disease is caused by bacteria that are resistant to it.

[3] That is, in addition to the general cautions listed in the text under Cephalosporins in the *Drug Index*.

Second-generation Cephalosporins

Generic name; Brand names	Gener-ation	Route of Admin.	Good for:[1]	Not good for:	Cautions[2]	Kinds of bacteria	Usual dosage in adults
cefachlor Cechlor	2nd	oral, empty stomach	Ent, P, S, U, ? A	M	usual and SERUM SICKNESS side effect	gram pos gram neg	250-500 mg every 8 hours
cefamandole Mandole	2nd	IM/IV	A, Bj, Ent, Sk, U	Ef, M	usual and like antabuse[3]	gram neg some gram pos	1-2 gm every 4 hours
cefoxitin Mefoxin	2nd	IM/IV	A, Bj, C, G[4], P, Sk, Se, U,	M	usual and low blood pres-sure	gram neg anaerobes[5]	1000-2000 mg IM or IV every 6 hours
loracarbef Lorabid	2nd	Oral	Ent, Sk, P, U	M, Se, life-threatening	usual	gram pos some gram neg	
cefuroxime Ceftin [6] Zinacef	2nd	oral IM/IV	Bj, Ent, G, M, P, Sk, O[7]		usual plus take oral with food; occa-sional bleed-ing	gram neg, some gram pos	Bj, Sk: 0.75-1.5 gm every 8 hours inj. G: 1 gm single dose M: 60 mg/kg IV, 3 g max, every 8 hours Ent, P: 250 mg twice daily oral

Third-generation Cephalosporins

Generic name; Brand names	Gener-ation	Route of Admin.	Good for:[1]	Not good for:	Cautions[2]	Kinds of bacteria	Usual dosage in adults
cefixim Suprax	3rd	oral	Ent, P, G	Sk, Bj, Se, M, Ef, U	usual	gram neg mostly	G: 400 mg single dose Other: 400 mg, daily
ceftriaxone Rocephin	3rd	IM/IV	Bj, Ch, Ent,[8] Ef, G,[9] M, O,[10] Sk, U	Chlamydia	not in new-borns with jaundice; not with calcium solutions	gram pos gram neg	A, M, U, Sk: 1-2 gm, 1-2 x daily Ch, G: 250 mg single dose Ef: 2 gm daily x 10 days

---

[1] A drug still might not work for these conditions if the particular disease is caused by bacteria that are resistant to it.
[2] That is, in addition to the general cautions listed in the text under Cephalosporins in the *Drug Index*.
[3] The patient becomes very ill if he takes any alcohol or even gets alcohol on his skin.
[4] 2000 mg IM single dose with 1000 mg of probenecid.
[5] These are infections that occur in wounds, in the context of surgery, and/or those that have foul-smelling pus.
[6] This is cefuroxime axetil, the oral drug, which should be taken with food. Zinacef is the injectable form.
[7] Early Lyme Disease.
[8] Ear infections in children: 50 mg/kg single dose.
[9] Dosage for gonorrhea eye infections in newborns: 50 mg/kg single dose. Does not work for chlamydia.
[10] Lyme Disease (1-2 gm every 12-24 hours x 14 days), Syphilis (1 gm IM daily x 10 days for early disease, x 14 days for secondary and tertiary disease), Meningitis prevention (125 mg IM once).

Non-cephalosporins

Generic name; Brand names	Generation	Route of Admin.	Good for:[1]	Not good for:	Cautions	Kinds of bacteria	Usual dosage in adults
aztreonam Azactam	mono-bactam	IM/IV	Se, P, Sk, U, A	M, Bj	usual	gram neg	0.5-2 gm every 8 hours
Meropenem Merrem	carba-penem	IV	A, M, Sk, M[2]		usual	gram pos gram neg	0.5-1 gm every 8 hours
imipenem Primaxin	carba-penem	IM/IV	A, P, U, Se, Sk, Bj	M	usual, decrease dose if less than 70 kg	gram neg gram pos	0.25-1 gm every 6-8 hours
cefotetan Cefotan	cepha-mycin	IM/IV	A, G	M, Eye	bleeding with large doses	gram neg anaerobes	1-2 gm every 12 hours

[1] A drug still might not work for these conditions if the particular disease is caused by bacteria that are resistant to it.
[2] Only in patients more than three months old.

CHAMOMILE TEA

This is an herb tea, widely available, which is useful for COLIC in babies and for abdominal cramps due to dietary indiscretion in adults. It is a useful alternative to DICYCLOMINE to help distinguish between belly pain that needs a surgeon and belly pain that will run its course and go away. Reportedly it is toxic to the liver in large amounts.

CHLORAMPHENICOL

Antibiotic (mostly gram negative)
Safety class 2+ Stability: A
Pregnancy: Don't use near delivery time

Brand names: Chloromycetin, Mychel-S; generic veterinary drug available. Supplied as 250 and 500 mg capsules. There is a long-acting injectable form called Tifomycine. The nearly identical drug, thiamphenicol, which is good for GONORRHEA and some MENINGITIS, is included here.

Indications:

Usually: ABSCESS, ACUTE ABDOMEN, DONOVANOSIS, EAR INFECTION, ENTERIC FEVER, EYE INFECTION with fever, GONORRHEA, MENINGITIS, PLAGUE, SEPSIS, SPOTTED FEVER, TYPHUS.

Occasionally BARTONELLOSIS, BRUCELLOSIS, CHOLERA, DYSENTERY, LEPTOSPIROSIS, OSTEOMYELITIS, PIG-BEL, PNEUMONIA, TREPONARID, TROPICAL ULCER, TULAREMIA, wound infections.

Rarely KIDNEY INFECTION, LYME DISEASE, Skin ulcers due to SICKLE CELL DISEASE, SYPHILIS, URINARY INFECTION, WHOOPING COUGH.

Contraindications: Previous ALLERGY or other reaction to this drug, necessitating stopping it. Do not use during labor and delivery or the baby may die shortly after birth; see Volume I, Chapter 6. Do not use it in nursing mothers. Do not use this in diabetic patients who are taking oral medication to lower their blood sugar. Do not use it in non-Black persons who have G6PD DEFICIENCY. It is generally tolerated in Blacks.

Precautions: Many physicians are afraid of this drug because of rare fatal reactions due to bone marrow suppression. Such reactions are rarer than fatal reactions to PENICILLIN; they do occur in 1/30,000 patients. They are extremely rare in Blacks. If a patient develops a new infection or ANEMIA while on this drug, stop it immediately. Be sure the patient really needs it before giving it. Do not use it for INFLUENZA. If a newborn stops nursing, develops a swollen abdomen, and looks bluish, starting 2-9 days after beginning the drug, stop the drug immediately. ACETAMINOPHEN increases the amount of chloramphenicol in the blood stream and may cause toxicity.

Side-effects: Rashes and fevers due to the drug; nausea; vomiting; an unpleasant taste in the mouth; diarrhea; irritation in the private parts. These effects occur in only a small percentage of patients. Infants may have a decrease in appetite. When giving this drug for SYPHILIS, BRUCELLOSIS, or ENTERIC FEVER, the patient may get sicker before he begins to get better.

Dosage: Reduce doses for infants, and in LIVER DISEASE and in kidney disease or KIDNEY FAILURE.

The following doses are for adults except where stated otherwise. Reduce dose according to weight for children. For *ordinary* chloramphenicol, injectable IM dose equals oral.

The *long-acting*, injectable type is one dose IM for any and all diseases:

Adults and children over 40 kg: 3 grams IM

Children 25-39 kg: 2 grams IM

Children 10-24 kg: 1 gram IM

ABSCESS: 250 mg by mouth every 6 hours until healed plus 2 days, or for 10 days, whichever comes first.

ACUTE ABDOMEN: Adult dose is 25 mg/kg by mouth or IM every 6 hours for 14 days. Children get 17 mg/kg every 6 hours. Newborns over a week old (full term) get 8 mg/kg every 6 hours; those under a week old (full term) get 4 mg/kg every 6 hours. See precautions for newborns. For premature babies, use the dose for those under a week old until they weigh 4 kg or more.

BARTONELLOSIS: 500 mg by mouth every 6 hours for 14 days.

BRUCELLOSIS: 250 mg by mouth every 6 hours; use this with two other antibiotics.

CHOLERA: 500 mg by mouth every 6 hours until the diarrhea has decreased.

DONOVANOSIS: 500 mg three times daily until entirely healed plus another week.

DYSENTERY: Same as CHOLERA.

EAR INFECTION: 250-500 mg by mouth every 6 hours for 10 days. Begin at the higher dose and decrease the dose as the patient feels better.

ENTERIC FEVER: Same as BARTONELLOSIS.

EYE INFECTION (serious, with fever): Same as ACUTE ABDOMEN.

GONORRHEA: 500 mg of thiamphenicol 5 times a day for 2 days.

KIDNEY INFECTION: 500 mg by mouth every 6 hours for 5 days.

LEPTOSPIROSIS: 2000-3000 mg IM or by mouth initially, then 250-500 mg every 6 hours until the temperature is normal plus 3 more days.

LYME DISEASE: Same as EAR INFECTION.

MENINGITIS: Same as ACUTE ABDOMEN.

OSTEOMYELITIS: 500 mg by mouth every 6 hours for 6 weeks minimum.

PIG-BEL: Same as ACUTE ABDOMEN.

PLAGUE: 500 mg by mouth or IM or IV, every 6 hours for 5 days.

PNEUMONIA: Same as EAR INFECTION

SEPSIS: Same as ACUTE ABDOMEN.

SICKLE CELL DISEASE skin ulcers: Same as ABSCESS.

SPOTTED FEVER: Same as LEPTOSPIROSIS.

SYPHILIS: Same as BARTONELLOSIS.

TREPONARID: Same as BARTONELLOSIS.

TROPICAL ULCERS: Same as ABSCESS.

TULAREMIA: Same as BARTONELLOSIS.

TYPHUS: Same as LEPTOSPIROSIS; treat for 7 days.

URINARY INFECTION: Same as KIDNEY INFECTION.

WHOOPING COUGH: Same as BARTONELLOSIS.

Wound infection: Same as ABSCESS.

Alternatives: Nothing else cheap is as good, but use AMPICILLIN for MENINGITIS, TYPHUS, ENTERIC FEVER, PIG-BEL, KIDNEY INFECTION, or ACUTE ABDOMEN. CEPHALOSPORINs and CIPROFLOXACIN are more expensive alternatives.

CHLOROQUINE

Antimalarial

Safety class 2 Stability: C

This is very toxic in overdose for children; a small overdose can kill, especially on an empty stomach.

Brand names: Aralen, Avlochlor, Nivaquine, Resochin. Supplied as tablets with 125, 250, or 500 mg chloroquine phosphate of which 60% is chloroquine base. IM chloroquine usually comes as 40 or 50 mg base per ml.

Includes: Hydroxychloroquinesulfate (Plaquenil). Same actions, precautions and dosage as Chloroquine.

Indications: MALARIA prevention and treatment, amebic DYSENTERY if used with DOXYCYCLINE, LEPROSY reaction.

Contraindications: ALLERGY to this drug. If given at the same time as oral cholera vaccine, the vaccine will not work properly. It is better to delay giving one or the other. Do not give it in persons with severe G6PD DEFICIENCY or in those with PORPHYRIA (a hereditary problem). Do not use in patients who have EPILEPSY.

Side-effects: Headache, blurred vision, abdominal pain, temporary emotional problems (such as nightmares) with each dose (an effect that seems to be more prominent with old drug). Itching is common in Blacks; it may respond to Vitamin B Complex, or MULTIVITAMINS. Sometimes there is nausea, vomiting, diarrhea, and abdominal pain.

Cautions:

- Used over the long term, chloroquine sometimes damages vision. The safe upper limit for long-term use is 2.5 mg/kg chloroquine base per day, or 4 mg/kg chloroquine phosphate tablets. It is acceptable to use larger amounts for a few days now and then, as long as the average over a month is no more than the amounts stated above.
- An early sign of eye problems is seeing halos around lights. Check vision when using chloroquine at higher doses and discontinue if vision decreases.
- Neurological problems are apt to become worse with this drug.
- The drug is sometimes associated with altered electrical activity in the heart; this, in turn, may cause sudden death. Thus it should not be combined with other such drugs. The medical jargon is that it prolongs the QT interval.
- Falciparum MALARIA may be resistant to this drug.

Dosage: The dose is particularly fussy in children; be sure to weigh a child rather than estimating weight. A small overdose can kill.

Reduce the dose in those with LIVER DISEASE.

When determining dosage, keep in mind that the dose is usually given in terms of base. Base refers to chloroquine itself. Chloroquine is always attached to other substances. For example, chloroquine phosphate comes as 125 and 250 mg tablets, of which 60% is base. (The rest is phosphate.) Therefore these tablets contain 75 and 150 mg of base respectively.

Amebic DYSENTERY: Adults get 150 mg base by mouth, twice a day for 20 days. Reduce dose according to weight in children. The patient must get DOXYCYCLINE also, along with the CHLOROQUINE.

LEPROSY reaction: Adult dose is 200 mg base twice a day for 14 days.

MALARIA prevention: Adults take 300 mg base by mouth, once a week. Reduce dose according to weight for children. (See the chart at the beginning of this Index.) Begin 2 weeks before going and continue for 6 weeks after leaving.

MALARIA treatment: Mild attack: Expatriate adults get 600 mg of base by mouth initially, 300 mg base 6 hours later, then 300 mg base 12 hours after the second dose, 300 mg base 24 hours after the third dose.

Children get 10 mg/kg base by mouth initially, then 5 mg/kg at 6 hour, 12 hour, and 24 hour intervals, same schedule as for adults. The children's dose is not to exceed the adult dose.

If the patient is vomiting, first try to use PROMETHAZINE and oral chloroquine. If this does not work, give adults 200 mg base IM every 6 hours for 2 doses; children get chloroquine base: 5 mg/kg IM initially, 6 hours later, then daily for 2 days.

Alternatives: Adding CHLORPHENIRAMINE sometimes reverses chloroquine resistance. Alternatively, use FANSIDAR or QUININE or MEFLOQUINE.

CHLORPHENIRAMINE, CHLORPHENAMINE

Antihistamine

Safety class 1 Stability A Preganancy B

Brand names: Chlortrimeton, Piriton, Calimal

Indications: ALLERGY, MALARIA

Contraindications: Simultaneous treatment with a kind of antidepressant called MAOI, which stands for monoamine oxidate inhibitors.

Side-effects: Sleepiness, worsening of GLAUCOMA, constipation, inability to pass urine (especially in older men), susceptibility to HEAT ILLNESS, dry mouth, decrease in sweating, rapid pulse, sensitivity to light, blurred vision, seizures in children, agitation in elderly.

Dosage: Reduce dose in elderly and in patients with chronic RESPIRATORY INFECTION. Adult dose is 4 mg every 6 hours; reduce dose according to weight for children.

Alternatives: DEXCHLORPHENIRAMINE is a similar drug. The usual dose is half that listed above. It is unknown if this works for malaria or not.

CHLORPROGUANIL

Malaria preventive.

Safety class 1 Stability: Unknown

Brand name: Lapudrine

Indications: MALARIA prevention.

Contraindications: ALLERGY to the drug.

Side-effects: Occasional nausea and loss of appetite which decreases with continued usage.

Dosage: Adult dose is 20 mg by mouth twice weekly. Reduce dose according to weight for children.

CHLORPROMAZINE

Sedative, Anti-nausea.

Safety class 2 Stability: A Pregnancy C

This is very toxic in overdose in children; a small overdose can kill a child.

Brand names: Largactil, Thorazine. Comes in 10, 25, and 50 mg tablets and in IM injectable.

Indications: CHOLERA, emotional upset, MENTAL ILLNESS, HICCUPS, pain, VOMITING PER SE, in a cream for CUTANEOUS LEISHMANIASIS, used to decrease shivering when treating a person for HEAT ILLNESS, TETANUS, used to relieve suffering in terminal illness.

Contraindications: ALLERGY to this drug; KIDNEY FAILURE, CIRRHOSIS, LIVER FAILURE, EPILEPSY. Do not give to those with Parkinson's Disease, LIVER DISEASE or CONGESTIVE HEART FAILURE. Do not give this to patients who are already sedated for some other reason. Do not give to those on antidepressants. Do not give to nursing mothers.

Precautions: This can cause loss of muscle control, particularly of the jaws. It makes the skin sensitive to sunburn. It also makes patients sensitive to HEAT ILLNESS. Patients should not drink alcoholic beverages while taking this. ANTACIDs should not be taken within two hours.

Do not crush tablets. Wear gloves when using liquid forms so as not to get the medication on your hands.

This drug interferes with many laboratory tests, including pregnancy tests. Don't believe lab tests performed while the person is on this drug.

Warn the patient not to engage in any dangerous activity while taking this drug.

Side-effects: The most common one is a fall in blood pressure when the patient suddenly stands. Other effects are faintness, rapid heart rate, a stuffy nose, a dry mouth, blurred vision, and worsening of URINARY

RETENTION. These effects occur in only a small percentage of patients.

Overdose and prolonged usage: If given routinely for weeks or months, this can cause PARKINSON'S DISEASE with involuntary movements and trembling. It can also cause LIVER FAILURE; see Protocol C-7.

Dosage: Reduce the dose in the elderly and those with KIDNEY FAILURE, GLAUCOMA or URINARY RETENTION. It is very toxic in children; an overdose can kill.

The dose by IM injection is the same as that by mouth.

CHOLERA: 10 mg every 6 hours by mouth, adult dose; reduce dose by weight for children.

CUTANEOUS LEISHMANIASIS: Grind 1000 mg (twenty 50 mg tablets) and mix with 50 grams (a little less than 1/4 cup) of methylsalicylate cream. Use this three times a day for a month, applying it directly on the affected skin area.

Emotional upset, HICCUPS, pain, VOMITING *per se,* Shivering: 25-50 mg every 6 hours.

TETANUS: See TETANUS in the *Disease Index*.

Terminal care: Start with 25 mg every 6 hours and increase the dose as necessary. A probable maximum would be 200 mg every 6 hours. Don't be rigid. Use as much as necessary to relieve suffering.

CHOLESTYRAMINE

Absorbent

Safety class 1 Stability: A Pregnancy C

Brand names: Colestid, Questran.

Indications: A powder used in the West for high blood cholesterol, in the tropics it is used to treat persistent diarrhea in babies. It is also useful to treat the itching caused by JAUNDICE. May be used for TURISTA: traveler's diarrhea.

Contraindications: Constipation, LIVER FAILURE; ALLERGY to the drug.

Precautions: This will inactivate other drugs given at the same time. Stagger the times given by at least two hours and be aware that the other drugs may fail to work properly.

This interferes with many lab tests—do not believe lab results performed while the patient was taking this drug.

Side-effects: Nausea and excessive gas.

Dosage: For the itching of JAUNDICE: 4 grams 1-3 times daily as needed. For other problems adult dose is 1 gram by mouth every 6 hours. Reduce dose according to weight for children.

CIMETIDINE

Histamine receptor antagonist.

Safety class 1-3 Stability: A Pregnancy B

Brand name: Tagamet, Dyspamet

Indications: ANAPHYLAXIS, GASTRITIS, PEPTIC ULCER; used to counteract the negative effects of steroids such as PREDNISONE and DEXAMETHASONE.

Contraindications: If the patient has LIVER FAILURE or KIDNEY FAILURE, check with a physician about how much to lower the dosage.

Precautions: Stomach acid is a defense against bacteria that are taken in by mouth. With this medication as well as with ANTACIDs, this barrier is lowered or destroyed. Therefore sanitation in food preparation is more important.

Use this only under professional advisement in patients on any other medication. There are interactions with many other medications.

Do not believe lab tests performed while the patient is taking this drug. The drug interferes with many different tests.

Side-effects: This may cause breast development in males.

Dosage:

Reduce the dose in the elderly, in those with LIVER DISEASE or KIDNEY FAILURE.

ANAPHYLAXIS: adult dose is 300 mg IM/IV/PO every 6 hours for 5 days; reduce dose for children.

PEPTIC ULCER: 400 mg twice daily for 14 days, given along with antibiotics.

For other indications: Adult dose: 400 mg twice a day or 800 mg at night only. Reduce this to 400 mg at night once the symptoms are totally gone.

CIPROFLOXACIN

Quinolone-type antibiotic (gram negative and gram positive)

Safety class 2 Stability: C Pregnancy C

Brand names: Cipro, Ciproxin.

Indications: ABSCESS, ANTHRAX, BARTONELLOSIS, BRUCELLOSIS, ENTERIC FEVER, and SPOTTED FEVER (except not Rocky Mountain Spotted Fever). It can be used to prevent MENINGITIS after an exposure. It is sometimes used for the prevention of traveler's diarrhea: TURISTA. Stubborn infections, not responsive to other medications, especially CHANCROID, CHOLERA, CYCLOSPORIASIS, DONOVANOSIS, bacterial DYSENTERY, GONORRHEA, KIDNEY INFECTION, OSTEOMYELITIS, PNEUMONIA, PYOMYOSITIS, Q FEVER, TYPHUS, TUBERCULOSIS, TULAREMIA, TURISTA. Authorities differ as to whether this is useful for SCRUB TYPHUS. Do not try to use this for PELVIC INFECTION.

Contraindications: EPILEPSY. Pregnancy and breast-feeding. Possibly age less than 20 if the problem is not life-threatening. Do not use in the presence of psychiatric problems, KIDNEY FAILURE, LIVER FAILURE, with STEROIDS, or with blood thinners.

Precautions:

If the patient has SEIZURES while on this drug, stop it.

Avoid using the drug in the elderly and those on STEROIDS; they may develop tendonitis.

Do not give the drug with ANTACIDs or it will not work.

If given at the same time as THEOPHYLLINE, reduce the dose of the latter.

BRUCELLOSIS may relapse after being treated with this.

The drug damages the growth centers of bones in some animals and might do so in humans. However, it has never been shown to cause these problems in children in which it has been used. It is becoming more acceptable to use this in children.

If the patient has a blood test in a hospital laboratory, the test might falsely show liver or kidney abnormalities. Ciprofloxacin in the blood interferes with the blood test.

It is best to give the drug in the morning since it might cause insomnia

Side-effects: Children frequently have joint pains with using this, but the pains disappear when the drug is discontinued. There does not appear to be any long-term damage.

Dosage: Reduce the dose to 1/2 the usual dose in the presence of KIDNEY FAILURE.

For most diseases the dosage is 250-750 mg every 12 hours.

ANTHRAX: If the patient is very sick, give 400 mg IV every 12 hours until improved; then change to oral, 500 mg every 12 hours for 60 days. For prevention, 500 mg every 12 hours for 60 days.

BARTONELLOSIS (Oroya form): 500 mg three times daily for 14 days; This will also cure ENTERIC FEVER which frequently coexists.

BRUCELLOSIS: 250-750 mg by mouth every 12 hours for 6 weeks.

CHANCROID: 500 mg every 12 hours for 3 days.

CHOLERA: 250-500 mg every 12 hours until the problem is improved.

CYCLOSPORIASIS: 500 mg every 12 hours for 7-10 days.

DYSENTERY: A single dose of 750 mg is enough.

ENTERIC FEVER: 500 mg every 12 hours for 14 days.

GONORRHEA, genital or sore throat: 500 mg single dose.

GONORRHEA, disseminated (skin and/or joint) 500 mg twice daily for at least 3 days.

KIDNEY INFECTION: 500 mg every 12 hours for 5-7 days.

MENINGITIS prevention: 750 mg single dose.

OSTEOMYELITIS: 250-750 mg every 12 hours for 6 weeks.

PNEUMONIA: 500 mg every 12 hours for 10 days.

PYOMYOSITIS: 500 mg every 12 hours for 10 days—the pus must also be drained out.

Q FEVER: 500 mg every 12 hours for 14 days.

SPOTTED FEVER: Same as PNEUMONIA.

TUBERCULOSIS: Adult dose is 1500 mg daily.

TULAREMIA: 750 every 12 hours for 10 days; expect relapses in about half of the patients.

TURISTA prevention: 500 mg daily.

TYPHUS: 500 mg every 12 hours for 7-10 days.

Alternatives: Other fluoroquinolones such as NORFLOXACIN = Utinor; OFLOXACIN = Tarivid, Pefloxacin.

NORFLOXACIN 400 mg or OFLOXACIN 300 mg is roughly equivalent to CIPROFLOXACIN 500 mg.

For treatment of diarrhea, Bicozamycin, aztreonam, and rifaximin are non-absorbed (they do not enter the bloodstream but stay in the bowel) antibiotics that might work o.k., avoiding side-effects.

For TULAREMIA, alternatives are STREPTOMYCIN, GENTAMYCIN or DOXYCYCLINE.

For Mediterranean SPOTTED FEVER: DOXYCYCLINE, CHLORAMPHENICOL, RIFAMPIN plus ERYTHROMYCIN, Josamycin. Possibly NORFLOXACIN, OFLOXACIN or CLARITHROMYCIN might work.

CLARITHROMYCIN

Macrolide antibiotic, gram positives, some others.

Safety class 1-2 Stability ? Pregnancy C

Brand name: Klaricid, Clarosip, Klaricid XL.

Comes in 250 mg tablets.

Indications: CELLULITIS, EAR INFECTION, sometimes PEPTIC ULCER, PNEUMONIA, RESPIRATORY INFECTION, Mediterranean SPOTTED FEVER, TOXOPLASMOSIS, TUBERCULOSIS. Might be good for LEPROSY.

Contraindications: Prior ALLERGY to this or to related drugs such as AZITHROMYCIN or ERYTHROMYCIN. Do not use at the same time as astemizole or terfenadine, two antihistamines without the side-effect of sleepiness. Possibly contraindicated in KIDNEY DISEASE, LIVER DISEASE, pregnancy and breastfeeding.

Precautions: Consult a physician before using at the same time as warfarin, THEOPHYLLINE, drugs for HIV INFECTION, or carbamazepine (Tegretol).

The drug sometimes alters electrical activity in the heart which might cause sudden death. Thus it should not be combined with other such drugs. The medical jargon is that it prolongs the QT interval.

*Side-effects:*Nausea, vomiting, abdominal pain, problems with taste and smell, loss of appetite, HEPATITIS, headache, dizziness, mental changes, KIDNEY FAILURE, joint pains, SEIZURES, skin sun sensitivity. Rarely it might cause LIVER FAILURE.

Dosage: Do not give in patients with KIDNEY FAILURE unless you consult a physician about dose reduction.

For most uses, 250 mg every 12 hours for 7 days; in severe cases 500 mg every 12 hours for 14 days except as listed below.

PEPTIC ULCER: 250 mg every 12 hours for 7-14 days.

SPOTTED FEVER: 250-500 mg every 12 hours until 3 days after the fever has dropped.

TUBERCULOSIS: 250-500 mg every 12 hours.

LEPROSY: Dosage unknown. It is best not to use this unless you have information with good authority or there is no alternative.

TOXOPLASMOSIS: 2 grams (2000 mg) daily

Alternatives: For SPOTTED FEVER, CIPROFLOXACIN plus see the alternatives at the end of that entry.

CLINDAMYCIN

Antibiotic, gram-positive/anaerobic
Safety class 3 Stability: B Pregnancy B
Brand names: Dalacin C, Cleocin.
Indications: ANTHRAX, DIPHTHERIA, MALARIA, OSTEOMYELITIS, RHEUMATIC FEVER, TOXOPLASMOSIS. It is sometimes used with CIPROFLOXACIN or GENTAMYCIN for treating PELVIC INFECTION. It might be used for some other infections under physician direction.

Contraindications: Diarrhea of any sort. If diarrhea develops while the patient is on the drug, it must be discontinued immediately. It should not be used with any anti-diarrhea medications (aside from ORS which is o.k.) or with ERYTHROMYCIN. It is also contraindicated in CIRRHOSIS and LIVER FAILURE.

Precautions: It is better to use safer antibiotics. Be sure to inform the patient to discontinue the drug if he develops diarrhea while on it.

Side-effects: Nausea, vomiting, gas.

Dosage: Reduce dose in the presence of LIVER DISEASE.

ANTHRAX: 900 mg IV every 8 hours until improved; then change to oral medication. Treat for a total of 60 days.

DIPHTHERIA: Uncertain but other antibiotics are to be used for 14 days.

MALARIA: This should be used with a second drug. The adult dose is 900 mg by mouth two times a day for 5 days, used with another anti-malarial drug, usually FOSMIDOMYCIN.

OSTEOMYELITIS: 150-300 mg every 6 hours for 6 weeks.

PELVIC INFECTION: 450 mg four times a day for 14 days. If the patient is very ill and if you have IV facilities, you should start with 900 mg IV every 8 hours, (along with GENTAMYCIN) until she is improved, then switch to the oral.

RHEUMATIC FEVER: Used after PENICILLIN to thoroughly eliminate the strep: 7 mg/kg three times daily for 10 days.

TOXOPLASMOSIS: 600 mg every 6 hours for 6 weeks, taken along with PYRIMETHAMINE.

CLOFAZIMINE

Antileprosy
Safety class 2 Stability: ?? Pregnancy C
Brand names: B663, Lamprene.
Indications: BURULI ULCER (in the early stage); LEPROSY, lepromatous type.

Contraindications: Prior ALLERGY to the drug, breast-feeding.

Side-effects: It discolors light-colored skin, possibly permanently, and thus should not be used in fair-skinned Caucasians. It turns urine red. It causes nausea, vomiting, abdominal pain and/or diarrhea. It makes skin sensitive to sunburn.

Overdose and prolonged usage: LIVER DISEASE.

Dosage: You may need to reduce the dose in LIVER DISEASE or avoid using this.

BURULI ULCER: Dosage unknown; see alternative advice.

LEPROSY: 50 mg by mouth daily, plus 300 mg once a month. Some authorities recommend a higher dose at first. Do not give over 100 mg daily for more than three months. If the patient is having a LEPROSY reaction, Type 2, use a high dose while decreasing the dose of PREDNISONE. Then reduce the dose of clofazimine.

CLOTRIMAZOLE

Antifungal
Safety class 1 Stability: A
Brand names: Canesten, Empecid, Lotrimin, Mycelex, Mycosporin, Trimysten. Available in creams and lozenges.

Indications: CANDIDIASIS, TINEA, VAGINITIS due to trichomonas.

Contraindications: Prior ALLERGY to this drug.

Side-effects: May cause burning and itching.

Dosage:

Skin: Apply cream twice a day until the problem is gone plus 2 more days.

Vagina: Use the cream daily for 7 days.

Mouth: Suck on a lozenge 5 times a day for 14 days.

CLOXACILLIN

Synonym: Flucloxacillin.
Antibiotic, gram-positive, anti-staph.
Safety class 2 Stability ?? Pregnancy B
Brand names: Cloxapen, Tegopen. Available as capsules (250 and 500 mg) and as powder for liquid at 125 mg/5 ml.
Indications: ABSCESS with a fever; ARTHRITIS, especially if it develops suddenly in one joint only; PYOMYOSITIS; OSTEOMYELITIS; sometimes PNEUMONIA, especially after MEASLES in children.

Contraindications: ALLERGY to any PENICILLIN. Try not to use with DOXYCYCLINE, ERYTHROMYCIN or CHLORAMPENICOL. Don't give it to women who are breastfeeding.

Precautions: Observe the patient for ALLERGY: HIVES, swelling or redness of the skin, difficulty breathing, a feeling of faintness. This drug can cause ANAPHYLAXIS just like ordinary PENICILLIN and must be treated accordingly. The patient may never again take any PENICILLIN-type drug for the rest of his life.

Don't believe lab tests for protein or glucose, taken while the patient is on this drug. The drug interferes with the lab test.

Overdose and prolonged usage: LIVER FAILURE; see Protocol C-7.

Dosage: Reduce the dose with KIDNEY FAILURE, possibly also with LIVER FAILURE.

250-500 mg every 6 hours for adults; reduce dose according to weight for children. Give this until the problem is resolved plus for 2 more days. Give it for at least 3 weeks in ARTHRITIS.

Alternatives: Flucloxacillin which is better absorbed and thus preferable when and where it is available. A new alternative is NITAZOXANIDE.

CO-ARTEM

A combination antimalarial drug: LUMEFANTRINE plus ARTEMISININ (artemether): fixed combination of 120 mg of lumefantrine with 20 mg of artemether. See the entries for the individual component drugs. The dosage is under ARTEMISININ.

CODEINE

Narcotic; Pain medicine, Cough medicine.
Safety class 2 Stability: C, Dark. Pregnancy C
This is very toxic to children in overdose; a small overdose can kill.
Brand names: Comes combined with other drugs which are labeled with numbers such as Empirin #3, Tylenol #2, etc. Generally #1 contains 7.5 mg, #2 contains 15 mg, #3 contains 30 mg, and #4 contains 60 mg of codeine per tablet.

Indications: Pain, severe cough.

Contraindications: Head injury, shortness of breath (unless due to cough), POLIO, ALLERGY to codeine, diarrhea due to antibiotic usage, ASTHMA, chronic RESPIRATORY INFECTION, concurrent usage of other sedative drugs.

Precautions: Codeine decreases the urge to breathe; people who must struggle to breathe lose their incentive.

It also causes constipation; consider giving a laxative (MILK OF MAGNESIA). Patients may feel nauseated from codeine but the nausea usually is not severe enough to cause a problem.

Be very careful when traveling with this drug. It is a narcotic, and you may get a jail term if you are caught carrying it.

Addiction occurs after a week or more of use. There may be psychiatric effects similar to uppers or downers (see ADDICTION).

Overdose and prolonged usage: ADDICTION, LIVER FAILURE; see Protocol C-7.

Dosage: Reduce the dosage with LIVER DISEASE. Be very careful of the dosage in children; a small overdose can kill.

Children: 0.8-1.5 mg/kg/dose by mouth or IM injection, to maximum of the adult dose. Adults: 15, 30, or 60 mg by mouth or IM injection. This dose may be repeated every 3 hours as needed for pain. For cough, start with the lowest dose and increase it as necessary. Response: 20-30 minutes.

Alternatives: Dosage given comparable to 30 mg codeine (dosage range for adult given in parenthesis): Darvon 65 mg by mouth (50-100); Demerol 25 mg by mouth or IM (25-100); Nalbuphine 5 mg IM.

Withdrawal symptoms after addiction: Abdominal pain, diarrhea, tearing of eyes, agitation, desperation for drug.

COLCHICINE

Anti-gout
Safety class 3 Stability B Pregnancy D
Supplied as 0.5 mg tablets
This is very toxic to children; a small overdose can kill.
Indications: GOUT; FAMILIAL MEDITERRANEAN FEVER.
Contraindications: Pregnancy, breast-feeding, any disease of the stomach or bowels, any heart disease, KIDNEY FAILURE, LIVER FAILURE, any disease of the blood. Should not be taken at the same time as any drug that has psychiatric effects.

Precautions: The drug interferes with one lab test to measure a hormone. Other lab tests should be o.k.

Side-effects: Nausea, vomiting, abdominal pain, a decrease in immunity, ANEMIA.

Overdose and prolonged usage: KIDNEY FAILURE.

Dosage: Be very careful to keep this away from children; a small overdose can kill.

Reduce dose in LIVER DISEASE and/or KIDNEY DISEASE—seek professional advice.

GOUT: The final dose is 0.6 mg every 12 hours. If the patient has not taken it before, give 0.6 mg every hour for 4 doses, then every 2 hours for 2 doses, then twice a day.

GOUT: an alternative regimen: 1 mg initially followed by 0.5 mg every 2-3 hours until relief of pain or vomiting and diarrhea. Maximum: 10 mg.

FAMILIAL MEDITERRANEAN FEVER: 0.5-1.5 mg daily.

CORTISONE CREAM/OINTMENT

Topical steroid
Safety class 1 Stability: A

Synonyms: Similar products will be marked hydrocortisone, triamcinalone, or any of several other "-one" drugs, as cream or ointment. You should use cream on rashes that look moist, ointment on those that look dry.

Includes: Hydrocortisone Cream/Ointment

Indications: CONTACT DERMATITIS, external EAR INFECTION, any rash that itches, NAIROBI EYE.

Contraindications: None, but any products that contain the syllable "fluro" should not be used on the face.

Precautions: Not to be used on pink, moist areas such as lips, vagina, tip of penis, in or around eyes. Where this is applied leave the part unbandaged at least 8 hours a day.

Dosage: Use sparingly four times a day as needed.

COTRIMOXAZOLE

Antibiotic, Sulfa drug plus folate antagonist
Safety class 2 Stability: B

Synonyms: Trimethoprim/sulfamethoxazole, SMZ/TMP, Sulfatrim, TMP/SMZ, SMZ/TMP.

Brand names: Bactrim, Cotrim, Septra, others.

Indications: ABSCESS, ANTHRAX, BRUCELLOSIS, CHANCROID, CHLAMYDIA, CHOLERA, CYCLOSPORIASIS, DONOVANOSIS, DYSENTERY, EAR INFECTION (middle), ENTERIC FEVER, EPIDIDYMITIS, GIARDIASIS, GONORRHEA, KIDNEY INFECTION, LYMPHOGRANULOMA VENEREUM, MYCETOMA, PELVIC INFECTION, PNEUMONIA, PROSTATITIS, Q FEVER; RESPIRATORY INFECTION, SEPSIS, SPRUE, TOXOPLASMOSIS, TRACHOMA, TURISTA, URETHRITIS, URINARY INFECTION, occasionally for VAGINITIS, WHOOPING COUGH.

Contraindications: ALLERGY to this or any SULFA drug. Newborns, pregnancy (unless the patient takes FOLINIC ACID), maybe HIV INFECTION, ANEMIA, elderly. Do not give this in G6PD DEFICIENCY, with other drugs that are liver-toxic, with oral drugs for reducing blood sugar, or with the drug, methenamine (also used for URINARY INFECTION).

Side-effects: Nausea, vomiting, diarrhea, abdominal pain, dizziness, headache, fatigue.

Precautions:

Do not allow the patient to become or remain dehydrated (see DEHYDRATION) while on the drug.

If the patient develops HEPATITIS, stop the drug.

If a sunburn-like or a blistering or peeling rash develops, stop the drug immediately (see EXFOLIATIVE DERMATITIS).

The drug may cause sun sensitivity (easy burning) in Whites.

Because it kills normal vaginal bacteria, females may develop VAGINITIS due to CANDIDA.

Overdose and prolonged usage: LIVER FAILURE; see Protocol C-7.

Dosage: Reduce the dose with KIDNEY FAILURE.

The regular drug contains 80 mg of trimethoprim and 400 mg of sulfamethoxazole. This is known as single strength. The double strength drug, labeled DS or DF, contains twice these amounts. The given doses are for adults; reduce dose according to weight for children.

ABSCESS: 1 DS or 2 regular tablets every 12 hours until healed plus 2 more days.

BRUCELLOSIS: 1 DS or 2 regular tablets every 12 hours for 21 days.

CHOLERA: Same as ABSCESS.

CYCLOSPORIASIS: 1 DS or 2 regular tablets every 12 hours for 7 days with no HIV INFECTION or for 14 days in the presence of HIV INFECTION.

DONOVANOSIS: 1 DS or 2 regular tablets every 12 hours until entirely healed plus one more week. Repeat the entire treatment as soon as there is any evidence of relapse.

DYSENTERY: Same as ABSCESS.

EAR INFECTION: 1 DS or 2 regular tablets every 12 hours for 10 days.

ENTERIC FEVER: Same as BRUCELLOSIS.

EPIDIDYMITIS: 1 DS or 2 regular tablets every 12 hours for 3 days.

GIARDIASIS/cyclosporosis: 1 regular tablet every 12 hours for 7 days.

GONORRHEA: 2 DS or 4 regular strength tablets twice a day for 10 days.

KIDNEY INFECTION: Same as EAR INFECTION.

MYCETOMA: 2 regular or 1 DS tablet twice daily for 6-9 months.

Q FEVER: 1 DS or 2 regular tablets every 12 hours for 2 weeks.

PELVIC INFECTION: Same as GONORRHEA.

PNEUMONIA: Same as EAR INFECTION.

PROSTATITIS: Same as EPIDIDYMITIS.

RESPIRATORY INFECTION: Same as ABSCESS.

SEPSIS: Same as BRUCELLOSIS.

SPRUE: Same as ABSCESS.

TOXOPLASMOSIS: Dosage unknown.

TRACHOMA: Same as BRUCELLOSIS.

TURISTA: Same as ABSCESS. It should not be used for prevention since it is not much better than BISMUTH SUBSALICYLATE and has significant side-effects.

URETHRITIS: Same as GONORRHEA.

URINARY INFECTION: Same as EPIDIDYMITIS; extend the time to 7 days for children and elderly.

VAGINITIS: Same as ABSCESS.

WHOOPING COUGH: 1 DS or 2 regular tablets, twice daily for 5 days.

Alternatives: Other gram-negative antibiotics. For CHANCROID use ERYTHROMYCIN. For PNEUMONIA in a patient with HIV INFECTION, use ATOVAQUONE.

COUGH SYRUP

Used for RESPIRATORY INFECTION, this is usually a combination of two or more of the following classes of drugs:

Antihistamine, the most common being CHLORPHENIRAMINE. This type of drug dries secretions and is most helpful for runny noses and eyes. It should not be used if the patient is short of breath; it will aggravate croup, wheezing, and ASTHMA.

Decongestant, the most common being PSEUDOEPHEDRINE. This shrinks swollen membranes and so helps to open nasal passages. It may raise the patient's blood pressure.

Expectorant, the most common being guaifenesin, liquefies phlegm so it is easier to cough up. It is likely to make the patient cough more but it will help him recover sooner.

Cough suppressant, the most common being dextromethorphan hydrobromide, keeps the patient from coughing. If the patient does not cough up what he should, he may develop PNEUMONIA. It is best to use a cough suppressant only at night and let the patient cough during the day.

CROMOGLYCATE

Non-steroid ophthalmic anti-inflammatory

Brand name: Opticrom. Supplied as a 4% solution; expensive.

Indications: Prevention of eye irritation from ALLERGY (vernal conjunctivitis).

Contraindications: Do not use with soft contact lenses.

Dosage: 1-2 drops in each eye every 4-6 hours, without missing any doses.

CROTAMITON

Scabicide, Insecticide

Safety class 1 Stability: Unknown

Brand names: Crotamitex, Eurax, Euraxil, Veteusan. The human form of the drug is a 10% cream or lotion; if the product you buy is stronger, dilute it with hand lotion or hand cream before using it. For example, if it is 20%, dilute it 50:50 to make it 10%.

Indications: SCABIES.

Contraindications: Prior ALLERGY to the drug.

Precautions: This may cause irritation over inflamed skin or if it is applied for too long a period of time. Do not apply this to the hands of babies and young children who will put their hands in their mouths. If you splint their elbows, they will be able to play but they cannot put their hands in their mouths.

Dosage: Apply to the entire body from the chin down. Apply it while the skin is damp, avoiding the pink, moist areas of the genitals. Leave it on for 24 hours; then wash it off and apply it again. Change clothing and bed linen at that time. Wash off the second application after 24 hours and change clothing and bed linen again.

CYCLOSERINE

Anti-TUBERCULOSIS, second-line

Safety class: Unknown Stability: Unknown

Pregnancy: D

Brand name: Seromycin

Indication: TUBERCULOSIS

Contraindications: ALLERGY to this drug, mental illness, epilepsy, KIDNEY FAILURE, ALCOHOLISM, any neurological problems.

Precautions: Not to be taken with alcohol or with ISONIAZID. Discontinue the drug for ALLERGY, mental changes, new ANEMIA, new neurological symptoms

Side-effects: Unknown

Dosage: 250-500 mg by mouth twice daily; Children 10-20 mg/kg by mouth twice daily

DAPSONE

Sulfone, Antileprosy, MALARIA-preventive

Safety class 3 Stability: C, dark; Pregnancy C

Brand names: Avlosulfon, Croysulfone, DDS, Diphenasone, Diphone, Disulone, Dumitone, Eporal, Novophone, Sulfadione, Sulfona-mae, Udolac. Combination drug with PYRIMETHAMINE is MALOPRIM; it is used for MALARIA prevention.

Indications: CUTANEOUS LEISHMANIASIS, LEPROSY, MALARIA prevention, MALARIA treatment in combination with PROGUANIL and ARTEMISININ (artesunate); MYCETOMA, TOXOPLASMOSIS prophylaxis. Sometimes useful for recluse spider bites (see Appendix 10 in Vol.I).

Contraindications: ALLERGY to DAPSONE. People who are allergic to SULFA drugs can usually take dapsone but they should be watched for ALLERGY. Probably unwise to give with G6PD DEFICIENCY or in the presence of LIVER DISEASE. Do not give to patients with PORPHYRIA (a hereditary disease). Do not give this to women who are breastfeeding.

Precautions: There is a 0.1% chance of serious side-effects which may be fatal. Stop the drug if the patient develops a new fever, JAUNDICE, ANEMIA, blistering or peeling of the skin (see EXFOLIATIVE DERMATITIS), any new rash, or crazy behavior. (The peeling skin is quite common in the South Pacific and the drug should probably not be given to people native to that area.) Check the description of the complications of the treatment of LEPROSY before using the drug for that.

Serious side-effects may occur in persons with G6PD deficiency. Check the patient's urine just before the second dose. If it has turned quite dark or has more urobilinogen than previously, discontinue the drug. This is especially important in Irish, Arabs, Jews, Hispanics, others of Mediterranean origin, and some East Asians. It is best if such persons use this drug only at the recommendation of a physician and in as low a dose as possible.

Side-effects: Loss of appetite, nausea, and vomiting. These effects occur in only a small percentage of patients. Rarely, headache, nervousness, insomnia, blurry vision, numbness, weakness, and fever may occur. Very rarely and unpredictably this drug may destroy the bone marrow, causing ANEMIA and making the person susceptible to new infections.

Overdose and prolonged usage: LIVER FAILURE; see Protocol C-7.

Dosage:

CUTANEOUS LEISHMANIASIS: Consult an M.D. for dosage and directions.

LEPROSY: 100 mg daily for adults. This must be given for 6 months for tuberculoid and indeterminate leprosy, for 2 years minimum for other types. Reduce dose according to weight for children.

MALARIA prevention: two 100 mg tablets of Maloprim initially, then one weekly for adults.

MALARIA treatment: ARTEMISININ (artesunate) 4 mg/kg, dapsone 2.5 mg/kg, PROGUANIL 8 mg/kg, all daily for 3 days. Works well in Thailand.

MYCETOMA: 100 mg twice daily for six to nine months.

TOXOPLASMOSIS prophylaxis: 50 mg/day, used with PYRIMETHAMINE.

Spider bites: 100 mg twice daily.

DELAVIRDINE

This is a drug active against AIDS.

DEXAMETHASONE

A drug closely related to PREDNISONE but stronger, frequently used in CYSTICERCOSIS, severe ENTERIC FEVER and in MENINGITIS. See the description of PREDNISONE and use it similarly, noting that the comparable dosage is much lower (0.75 mg of dexamethasone is equivalent to 5 mg of PREDNISONE or PREDNISOLONE). It is good to use CIMETIDINE along with this to decrease side-effects.

Do not use this in the presence of PORPHYRIA, HIV INFECTION, at the same time as any vaccines, and during pregnancy and breastfeeding. It causes problems with many different drugs and diseases and thus should only be used at the recommendation of a physician.

The usual dose of dexamethasone for MENINGITIS due to TUBERCULOSIS is 12 mg/day for adults; for children use 0.1 mg/kg daily. Continue this dosage for 3 weeks and then stop it **gradually**, reducing the dose every other day until it is totally stopped.

ENTERIC FEVER dosage: 6 mg initially, followed by 3 mg every 6 hours for 2 additional doses. Physicians may prescribe higher doses.

ALTITUDE SICKNESS: 4 mg every 8 or 12 hours.

DEXCHLORPHENIRAMINE

Antihistamine
Safety class 2; Stability: C, dark;
Pregnancy B

Brand name: Polaramine.

Indications: Used with ALBENDAZOLE in the treatment of CYSTICERCOSIS. It may also be used as an ordinary antihistamine for ALLERGY.

Contraindications: Prior bad reaction to the medication. Must not be used in newborns. Do not use this during an acute ASTHMA attack. Do not use it with antidepressants.

Precautions: It should not be used with alcoholic beverages.

Side-effects: Drowsiness, worsening of GLAUCOMA, constipation, inability to pass urine (especially in older men), susceptibility to HEAT ILLNESS, dry mouth, decrease in sweating, rapid pulse, sensitivity to light, blurred vision.

Dosage: Reduce the dose in children and the elderly.

CYSTICERCOSIS: 2 mg by mouth every 4 hours around the clock when used with ALBENDAZOLE.

ALLERGY: Same as CYSTICERCOSIS but used alone.

Alternatives: CHLORPHENIRAMINE is a similar drug.

DIAZEPAM

Sedative, Muscle relaxant

Safety class 2-3 Stability: A, Dark Pregnancy D

Brand name: Valium. Supplied as tablets and injectable for IM or IV. IM = oral dose.

Indications: Emotional upset, SEIZURES, muscle relaxation for putting a dislocated shoulder back in place, TETANUS, sometimes to assist in withdrawing from ALCOHOL. (See ALCOHOLISM.)

Contraindications: Prior ALLERGY to the drug, any difficulty breathing, POLIO. It should not be used in the presence of KIDNEY FAILURE or in a person who is very lethargic or unconscious.

Precautions: Should not be used for more than a day or two because it is potentially addictive. When using higher doses, watch to be sure the person does not stop breathing. If the person has ALCOHOL in his blood stream, he will absorb more diazepam than he would otherwise. Therefore cut the dose by 1/3 to 1/2. If he frequently drinks alcohol but he has none in his blood stream right now, you may have to use higher-than-normal doses.

Used routinely, this drug causes DEPRESSION.

Warn the patient not to engage in any potentially hazardous activity while taking this. Do not give it to women who are breastfeeding.

This drug interferes with various lab tests; don't believe lab results drawn while the patient was taking this.

Side-effects: Sun sensitivity, drowsiness.

Dosage: Reduce the dose in patients who are elderly or sickly.

Adult dose: 2mg-20mg by mouth or IM injection, every 4 hours as needed. Reduce dose according to weight for children. Control of SEIZURES and fixing a dislocated shoulder requires the highest dose. Rectal dosage for control of seizures is 0.5 mg/kg (usual adult dose is 35 mg). Do not use tablets for this. Use the injectable form or else dissolve tablets in water and give as an enema. For TETANUS follow the dosage given under TETANUS treatment in the *Disease Index*.

DICYCLOMINE

Antispasmodic, Anticholinergic.

Safety class 1-2 Stability: C Pregnancy: ?

Brand name: Bentyl; generic drug is available. Supplied as 10 mg capsules and 20 mg tablets. Injectable drug also available. IM = oral dose.

Indications: Abdominal pain; TURISTA; FOOD POISONING; GALLBLADDER DISEASE; GASTROENTERITIS; IRRITABLE BOWEL; nausea and vomiting; PLANT POISONING, Muscarine.

Contraindications: Newborns, breastfeeding, prior ALLERGY to the drug; PROSTATITIS; difficulty urinating: a full bladder that will not empty, except with dribbling. (Usually this occurs in older men and in women who have just given birth.) Do not use this with bacterial DYSENTERY or poisonings. It will make the patient sicker.

Side-effects: Worsening of GLAUCOMA, constipation, inability to pass urine (especially in older men), susceptibility to HEAT ILLNESS, dry mouth, decrease in sweating, rapid pulse, sensitivity to light, blurred vision.

Overdose and prolonged use: LIVER FAILURE; see Protocol C-7.

Dosage: Reduce the dose for elderly patients. Adult dose is 20 mg by mouth or IM injection, every 6 hours as needed. Reduce dose according to weight for children.

Alternative: CHAMOMILE TEA.

DIDANOSINE

This is a drug that is used for HIV INFECTION.

DIETHYLCARBAMAZINE (CITRATE)

Anti-filarial

Synonym: DEC

Safety class 2+ Stability: A

Brand names: Banocide, Ethodryl, Filarizan, Hetrazan, Notezine, and many others; generic diethylcarbamazine is available as a veterinary drug. Supplied as 50 mg and 200 mg tablets.

Indications: FILARIASIS (wuchereria), LOIASIS, MANSONELLOSIS PERSTANS, ONCHOCERCIASIS, ASTHMA due to FILARIASIS.

Contraindications: Pregnancy, HEART FAILURE, KIDNEY FAILURE.

Precautions: An allergic reaction (see ALLERGY) when this drug is used probably is not a reaction to the drug itself, but to the dead worms. If this happens, decrease the initial dose of the drug. Give about 1/10 of the usual dose for a week, using PREDNISONE and DIPHENHYDRAMINE. Stop the PREDNISONE after the first five days, but continue with the DIPHENHYDRAMINE. Increase the dose weekly, using DIPHENHYDRAMINE as needed, until the patient can tolerate the recommended dose. Then follow the treatment schedule given below.

Side-effects: Headache, tiredness, joint pain, appetite loss, nausea, and vomiting. There may be enlargement of the lymph nodes with pain. Patients with recent MALARIA may relapse unless they are treated for that at the same time. DRUG ERUPTION sometimes occurs.

Dosage: All doses are oral. Reduce all doses according to weight for children.

In all cases, start the drug slowly and work up to the final dosage for the disease in question. If your patient may have a second condition that requires this drug, first treat the disease that requires the lower dosage, then treat the one requiring the higher dosage.

Use DIPHENHYDRAMINE and PREDNISONE for allergic reactions (see ALLERGY). It is essential to have both EPINEPHRINE and DIPHENHYDRAMINE or another antihistamine available when you start the drug. If you use PREDNISONE, give it six hours before the first daily dose for the first five days. Give DIPHENHYDRAMINE with each dose for the first week, then as needed thereafter.

Slow-start, 21-day schedule for adults:

This 21-day schedule *must* be used for ASTHMA due to Filariasis.

Day 1: 50 mg once.

Day 2: 50 mg every 8 hours.

Day 3: 100 mg every 8 hours

Days 4-21: 2 mg/kg, max 150 mg, every 8 hours.

Alternatives to slow-start, 21-day schedule:

6 mg/kg once a week for 12 weeks. Patient compliance and effectiveness is better with this schedule than with the other. Start slowly.

6 mg/kg in a single dose, given along with IVERMECTIN after a slow start as above.

FILARIASIS treatment final dosage schedule: 100-150 mg three times a day for 21 days is standard. It is good to use ALBENDAZOLE along with this to kill the adult worms.

FILARIASIS prevention: 300 mg in one dose once a month. If the patient had previous exposure to the disease, start out using small doses weekly along with DIPHENHYDRAMINE, building up to 300 mg. Beginning preventive therapy when entering the area avoids this problem.

LOIASIS treatment: Seek local advice before using DEC for this; it might be dangerous. Adult dose: 50 mg three times a day for 10 days. Then give no drug for 2 weeks. Follow this by 200 mg three times a day for 21 days.

LOIASIS prevention: Seek local advice before using DEC for this; it might be dangerous. Adult dose is 300 mg daily for 3 consecutive days once a month or 300 mg weekly.

MANSONELLOSIS PERSTANS: 200 mg daily for 21 days, used along with MEBENDAZOLE.

ONCHOCERCIASIS: 25 mg daily for 1 week, then 50 mg daily for l week, then 100 mg daily for 1 week, adult dose. Repeat the treatment after the patient has had a month off the drug and a third time after another month off the drug. If possible, use PREDNISONE 6 hours before the daily DEC for the first five days of treatment. In the presence of eye symptoms, it is mandatory to use PREDNISONE. If eye symptoms increase in spite of the PREDNISONE, reduce the dose of DEC and build up to the final dose while using the PREDNISONE. PREDNISOLONE eye drops may substitute for PREDNISONE taken by mouth.

Alternatives: IVERMECTIN is safer for FILARIASIS and ONCHOCERCIASIS.

DIGOXIN

Heart medicine, digitalis.
Safety class 3 Stability: A, Dark
Pregnancy C

Brand name: Lanoxin; generic drug is available, but it is best not to use generic or veterinary drug. Supplied as tablets of 0.125 and 0.25 mg.

Indications: HEART FAILURE, some kinds but not all kinds; seek higher-level advice.

Contraindications: Present or recent severe diarrhea or vomiting, MALNUTRITION with swelling of the abdomen or ankles, unreliable patient, inability to keep away from children, KIDNEY FAILURE, prior ALLERGY to the drug, pulse less than 60. This interacts badly with a variety of other drugs and conditions.

Precautions: Use only when and as an M.D. directs. Doses must be exact. **Never give extra.** Check the pulse before each dose and do not give it if the pulse is less than 60.

Side-effect: Breast development in males.

Overdose and prolonged usage: Extremely toxic. Twice the recommended dose may be fatal. Some of the early symptoms of too much drug are loss of appetite, nausea, and vomiting. Diarrhea and abdominal discomfort may also occur. Headache, fatigue, dizziness and sleepiness as well as mental symptoms or blurred vision also indicate too much drug. Stop the drug completely if any of these occur. Start it again after these symptoms are gone, using only half the prior dose.

Dosage: Reduce the dose in the elderly, in KIDNEY FAILURE, and in THYROID TROUBLE. The adult dose is 0.25 mg by mouth daily in one dose for adults of average size. Use 0.125 mg daily in small adults. Children get 0.005 mg/kg daily. This must be continued for a long time, perhaps for life.

DILOXANIDE FUROATE

Amebicide
Safety class 1 Stability: Unknown

Brand names: Ame-boots, Entamide, Furamide; combination with METRONIDAZOLE is called Entamizole. Supplied in 500 mg tablets.

Indications: DYSENTERY due to amebae; used to clear the bowel of amebae after the person has been treated for AMEBIC LIVER DISEASE.

Contraindications: Previous ALLERGY to this drug.

Precautions: The drug enters the blood poorly and thus has little or no whole body effect. It may cause hives, vomiting, itching, or excessive gas passage by rectum.

These effects occur in only a small percentage of patients.

Dosage: 500 mg by mouth every 8 hours for 10 days for adults. Reduce dose according to weight for children.

DIPHENHYDRAMINE

Antihistamine

Safety class 1 Stability: A Pregnancy B

Brand name: Benadryl; generic drug is available. Supplied as 25 and 50 mg capsules.

Indications: This is useful to counteract the side-effects of phenothiazines (PROCHLORPERAZINE, CHLORPROMAZINE); It is also used for ALLERGY, ANAPHYLAXIS, CHICKEN POX, FILARIASIS, insomnia, motion sickness, ONCHOCERCIASIS, PLANT POISONING: Argemone oil or Muscarine, SEABATHER'S ERUPTION, SWIMMER'S ITCH.

Precautions: Causes sleepiness and may make ASTHMA worse. The patient should not drink alcoholic beverages while taking this.

Side-effects: Worsening of GLAUCOMA, constipation, inability to pass urine (especially in older men), susceptibility to HEAT ILLNESS, dry mouth, decrease in sweating, rapid pulse, sensitivity to light, blurred vision. On occasion it may cause SEIZURES, dizziness, ringing in the ears, loss of appetite, nausea, abdominal pain. These effects occur in only a small percentage of patients.

Overdose and prolonged usage: LIVER FAILURE (see Protocol C-7); KIDNEY FAILURE.

Dosage: Adults: 25-50 mg by mouth or IM injection, every 4 hours as needed. Reduce dose according to weight for children. Reduce the dose for the elderly.

Alternatives: CHLORPHENIRAMINE, DEXCHLORPHENIRAMINE, Dramamine, histadyl, PROMETHAZINE, tripelennamine.

DIPYRONE

This is a pain medication, commonly available orally as well as by injection in developing countries. It has been taken off the market in the West, because of rare, fatal reactions. It works nearly as well as narcotics, but it is non-addicting and it is cheap. It should not be used for ordinary pain, but it is useful under emergency conditions and also for routine care of terminally-ill patients. It should not be used in patients with PORPHYRIA. The IM or oral dosage is 1000 mg.

DIURETICS

This refers to a class of drugs.

Synonym: "water pill".

The most common diuretics are HYDROCHLOROTHIAZIDE and FUROSEMIDE. ACETAZOLAMIDE is used less commonly.

DOXYCYCLINE

Antibiotic, similar to TETRACYCLINE. Gram negative.

Safety class 2 Stability: A, Dark Pregnancy D

Brand names: Tanamicin, Tecacin, Tetradox, Vibradox, Vibramycin, Vibra-Tabs, Vibravenos, and others. Generic drug is available.

This drug has nearly replaced TETRACYCLINE.

Indications: ACNE, ANTHRAX, BARTONELLOSIS, BRUCELLOSIS, CANCRUM ORIS, CAT-SCRATCH DISEASE, CHANCROID, CHLAMYDIA, CHOLERA, DONOVANOSIS, DYSENTERY, FILARIASIS, FOOD POISONING, GONORRHEA, LEPTOSPIROSIS, LYME DISEASE, LYMPHOGRANULOMA VENEREUM, MALABSORPTION, MALARIA prevention, ONCHOCERCIASIS, PELVIC INFECTION,[1] PEPTIC ULCER, PINTA, PLAGUE exposure, PLAGUE treatment, Q FEVER, RAT BITE FEVER, RELAPSING FEVER, RESPIRATORY INFECTION, SCRUB TYPHUS, SPOTTED FEVER (Rocky Mountain and Mediterranean, possibly other types), SPRUE, SYPHILIS, TRACHOMA, TRENCH FEVER, TREPONARID, TROPICAL ULCER, TULAREMIA, TURISTA, TYPHUS, URETHRITIS, YAWS. This will work for ACNE, but it is dangerous if the patient has not had his appendix removed. It is rarely used for KIDNEY INFECTION. It might possibly work for GIARDIASIS.

Contraindications: ALLERGY to any TETRACYCLINE-type drug; old drug, past expiration date. Pregnancy and breastfeeding are normally contraindications but when the drug is necessary for something potentially life-threatening (e.g. prevention of PLAGUE after a significant exposure) this may be violated since the benefit outweighs the risk. Do not use this in patients with PORPHYRIA (a hereditary disease)

Precautions: This drug stops the growth of bacteria but does not kill them; its effect depends on the body's own ability to kill the germs. Therefore it is not usually the best drug if the patient is very seriously ill or if his immunity is poor. It is also not the best drug to use if the disease progresses rapidly e.g. ANTHRAX, CANCRUM ORIS, CHOLERA, PLAGUE, some SPOTTED FEVER. These diseases are listed as indications only because, in developing areas, one's options are limited.

Doxycycline (like TETRACYCLINE) causes sun sensitivity so patients burn easily.

Oral contraceptives may fail with this.

[1] Recent information indicates that this is not useful for pelvic infection because of widespread resistance, especially in disease acquired in urban settings and/or amongst homosexuals. Seek local advice. Even if it locally effective, it should always be used with another drug, usually LEVOFLOXACIN.

It makes patients prone to CANDIDIASIS, masks the signs and symptoms of appendicitis, and causes dark staining of teeth in children under 7 and the offspring of pregnant women who take the drug. The latter effect, however, is not as common or as severe with this as with other forms of TETRACYCLINE.

Watch expiration dates; do not use expired drug.

If you use this together with milk, any ANTACIDs or BISMUTH SUBSALICYLATE; separate the times of taking the medications by at least 2 hours.

Side-effects: Abdominal pains, nausea, vomiting, diarrhea. Stop the medication for DYSENTERY that appears to be due to the medication.

Overdose and prolonged usage: LIVER FAILURE (see Protocol C-7); pregnant women are particularly prone to this.

Dosage: Reduce the dose with LIVER DISEASE.

ACNE: 50-100 mg daily until better

ANTHRAX exposure: 100 mg daily for 60 days plus immediate immunization.

ANTHRAX treatment: 100 mg IV every 12 hours for 10 days, then switch to oral medication for 60 days total.

BARTONELLOSIS: 100 mg twice daily for 6 weeks.

BRUCELLOSIS: 200 mg each evening; use this with other antibiotics.

CANCRUM ORIS: 100 mg twice daily until the problem is getting no worse, then for another 4 days.

CAT-SCRATCH DISEASE: 100 mg daily for 14 days.

CHLAMYDIA (without LGV): 100 mg twice daily for 2 weeks.

CHOLERA: 300 mg in a single dose.

DONOVANOSIS: 100 mg twice daily until entirely healed and then for another week; repeat this as necessary for relapses.

DYSENTERY: 100 mg daily for 10 days.

FILARIASIS: 200 mg daily for 6-8 weeks, before using other drugs such as DIETHYLCARBAMAZINE, ALBENDAZOLE, or IVERMECTIN; 3 weeks works but not as well.

FOOD POISONING: 100 mg daily until better, plus one more day.

GONORRHEA: 100 mg twice daily for 7 days.

LEPTOSPIROSIS: 100 mg twice daily for 7 days.

LYME DISEASE: 100 mg daily for 60 days Prevention after a tick bite is a single dose of 200 mg.

LYMPHOGRANULOMA VENEREUM: 100 mg twice daily for 21 days.

MALABSORPTION: 100 mg daily for 3 weeks.

MALARIA prevention: 100 mg daily.

MALARIA treatment: 100 mg twice daily for 10 days.

ONCHOCERCIASIS: 100 mg daily x 6-8 weeks

PELVIC INFECTION: 100 mg twice daily for 14 days; use this with LEFOFLOXACIN or another drug. There is much resistance to this so it may not work.

PEPTIC ULCER: 100 mg daily for 10-14 days, with other antibiotics.

PINTA: Same as SYPHILIS according to the stage of the disease.

PLAGUE exposure: 100 mg every 12 hours for two days.

PLAGUE treatment: 100 mg IV every 12 hours until improved, then switch to oral.

Q FEVER: 100 mg twice daily for 15 days.

RAT BITE FEVER: 100 mg twice daily for 7-10 days.

RELAPSING FEVER: 100 mg, single dose.

RESPIRATORY INFECTION: 100 mg daily until better, then for another 2-3 days.

SCRUB TYPHUS: 100 mg twice daily for 3 days.

SPOTTED FEVER: This is the drug of choice, even in children. 100 mg twice daily until fever is gone plus 3 more days. (Note that this does not work for all kinds of SPOTTED FEVER! It does work for Mediterranean SPOTTED FEVER and Rocky Mountain SPOTTED FEVER. Seek local lore.)

SPRUE: 100 mg single dose

SYPHILIS, primary and secondaary: 100 mg every 12 hours for 15 days.

SYPHILIS, tertiary: 100 mg twice daily for 28 days, being sure to not miss any doses. (Note that this does not work for tertiary syphilis that has gone to the brain.)

SYPHILIS, tertiary that has gone to the brain: Reportedly (not on good authority) 200 mg twice daily for 28 days works.

TRACHOMA: 100 mg daily for 3 weeks.

TRENCH FEVER: 200 mg daily x 28 days, used with GENTAMYCIN.

TREPONARID: Same as SYPHILIS, according to the stage of the disease.

TROPICAL ULCER: 100 mg daily until healed.

TULAREMIA: 100 mg twice daily for 2 weeks.

TURISTA: 100 mg, single dose.

TYPHUS: Same as SPOTTED FEVER.

URETHRITIS: Same as GONORRHEA.

YAWS: Same as SYPHILIS according to the stage.

EFAVIRENZ

This is an anti-AIDS drug.

EFLORNITHINE

Anti-trypanosome

Safety class 2 Stability: Unknown

Pregnancy safety unknown

Synonyms: DFMO, difluoromethylornithine

Brand name: Ornidyl

Supplied as oral and injectable drug.

Indications: AFRICAN SLEEPING SICKNESS, Gambian type. It does not work reliably for Rhodesian type but it might work in some patients.

Contraindications: ALLERGY to this drug, severe ANEMIA, uncorrected.

Side-effects: Diarrhea, abdominal pain, nausea and vomiting, loss of appetite, easy bleeding, occasionally hair loss. It may damage hearing, damage bone marrow (causing ANEMIA, abnormal bleeding, or susceptibility to infection) or cause SEIZURES. It may reduce the effectiveness of vaccines.

Precautions: The drug is hard to obtain but reportedly is available through the WHO. The loose chemical is a white powder resembling cocaine in appearance, so carrying it across borders could cause trouble. Severe diarrhea caused by the drug necessitates stopping the drug. Wait until the diarrhea goes away and then begin the drug again at the same dose. Injectable drug causes less diarrhea than drug given by mouth and relapse is less likely. The doses are the same both ways.

Dosage:

AFRICAN SLEEPING SICKNESS, early: 50 mg/kg every 6 hours (average adult dose is 3000 mg per dose, 12,000 mg daily) for 6 weeks.

AFRICAN SLEEPING SICKNESS with mental symptoms: 100 mg/kg every 6 hours (average adult dose is 6 grams [6000 mg] per dose, 24 grams [24,000 mg] daily) for 14 days, IV if possible. Follow this by 75 mg/kg by mouth every 6 hours for 21 to 28 days.

AFRICAN SLEEPING SICKNESS relapse: 100mg/kg every 6 hours for 7 days only.

Results should be evident in 1-2 weeks.

EMETINE

This, and its less-toxic cousin, dehydroemetine, are old drugs that previously were used for amebae, both DYSENTERY and AMEBIC LIVER DISEASE. Emetine is very toxic for heart and muscles. It is still used for LIVER FLUKE when safer alternatives are not available. It should be used only with a physician's supervision, unless circumstances force you to use it yourself. In that case, keep the patient at absolute bedrest until a week after the treatment. The dose for either emetine or dehydroemetine is 1 mg/kg IM daily to a maximum of 65 mg daily.

EPHEDRINE NOSE DROPS (1%)

Topical decongestant

Safety class 1 Stability: A, dark

Indications: RESPIRATORY INFECTION, stuffy nose.

Contraindications: HYPERTENSION not adequately treated.

Precautions: Using too many drops, or using them too frequently or for too long a time may cause congestion when the drug is stopped. Babies should have the drops diluted 1:7 or 1:15 as they are particularly sensitive to them.

Dosage: **One** drop in each nostril.

Alternatives: Croyban, Neo-Synephrine, Otrivin, Privine hydrochloride, Tyzine, all essentially the same as ephedrine.

EPINEPHRINE

ASTHMA and ALLERGY medicine

Safety class 2 Stability: C, Dark

Synonym: Adrenalin.

Supplied as glass vials with 1 mg in 1 ml; labeled 1:1000. Also 10 ml bottles, same strength. Preparations labeled 1:10,000 should not be used.

Indications: ALLERGY if severe; ANAPHYLAXIS; ASTHMA; FILARIASIS maybe; bleeding PEPTIC ULCER (class 1 used thus.)

Contraindications: None when used for ANAPHYLAXIS or severe ASTHMA. HEART FAILURE and HYPERTENSION when used for mild ASTHMA or ALLERGY. Do not use during pregnancy unless the situation is life-threatening.

Precautions: When given by injection, this drug aggravates HYPERTENSION and makes the pulse fast. Some patients become very shaky and agitated; reassure the patient and wait for it to wear off.

Dosages for ANAPHYLAXIS, assuming normal body size for age:

Adults	0.5 ml
8-12 y.o.	0.4 ml
5-7 y.o.	0.3 ml
2-5 y.o.	0.2 ml
6 mo.-2 y.o.	0.1 ml
Infant	0.05 ml

HIVES and other ALLERGY: Use half the doses listed above.

ASTHMA, *moderate to severe* and ANAPHYLAXIS: repeat the dose every 5-10 minutes until the patient shows some improvement. Then repeat every 30 minutes until the patient is very much improved.

ASTHMA, *mild to moderate*: repeat every 20 minutes from the beginning. Use a maximum of 3 doses.

ERGONOVINE MALEATE

Oxytocic

Safety class 3 Stability: D, dark

Alternative names: Ergometrine maleate, Methergine, Methylergonovine maleate, Methylergometrine maleate.

Brand name: Methergine. Supplied as 0.2 mg tablets and IM vials with 0.2 mg/ml. It may be unnecessary to refrigerate some forms. Check with your pharmacist or supplier.

Indications: Severe bleeding after childbirth or after a spontaneous miscarriage.

Contraindications: During delivery, do not use this if the patient has not yet delivered both baby and placenta. If she is miscarrying, do not use this if she has not yet passed the tissue (baby and placenta) and the bleeding is not severe. (If the bleeding is severe, more than a pint, in a miscarriage you may give the drug in spite of her not having passed the contents of her uterus.) Other contraindications in the States are HYPERTENSION and TOXEMIA. Do not use this in patients with PORPHYRIA, (a hereditary disease).

Precautions: Ordinarily you should use one dose only. It may, however, be used more often if the patient is developing signs of SHOCK. The drug causes severe cramping.

Side-effects: If a person is particularly sensitive to these drugs, it may cause her hands or feet to become cold, pale, and numb. Pulses will diminish. GANGRENE may occur if the dose is large enough. ANGINA may develop in people who have had prior heart trouble. Other symptoms are headache, nausea, diarrhea, dizziness, weakness, and inability to think right.

Dosage: 0.2 mg by mouth or IM injection.

Results: Bleeding should be decreased in half an hour.

ERYTHROMYCIN

Antibiotic (gram positive)
Safety Class 1 Stability: B Pregnancy o.k.

Brand names: E-Mycin, Ilosone, Wyamycin, Bristamycin. Supplied as 250 and 500 mg tablets.

Indications: ABSCESS, ACNE, BARTONELLOSIS (Verruga fever), CAT-SCRATCH DISEASE, CELLULITIS, CHANCROID, CHLAMYDIA, DIPHTHERIA, DONOVANOSIS, DYSENTERY due to amebae, middle EAR INFECTION (but not in young children), FOOD POISONING, GASTROENTERITIS, LEPTOSPIROSIS, LYMPHOGRANULOMA VENEREUM, PELVIC INFECTION **not** due to GONORRHEA, PINTA, PNEUMONIA, Q FEVER, RELAPSING FEVER, RESPIRATORY INFECTION, SPOTTED FEVER; STREP THROAT, SYPHILIS, TRACHOMA, TRENCH FEVER, TREPONARID, rarely TURISTA, VAGINITIS, WHOOPING COUGH, YAWS. It may be used for a tooth infection for any tooth except the third molar. It may substitute for PENICILLIN in someone who is allergic to PENICILLIN, but **not** with *MENINGITIS, **nor** tertiary SYPHILIS, **nor** SEPSIS, **nor** GONORRHEA!!*

Contraindications: Previous ALLERGY to the drug or any similar drug. Do not use with KETOCONAZOLE or with medication for SEIZURES. Do not use in the presence of LIVER DISEASE; see Protocol C-7.

Precautions: This drug frequently gives stomach pain and upset. Taking it with food minimizes this. Try only a single tablet as the first dose. Try to avoid using erythromycin estolate (use a form with another last name). Erythromycin can cause nausea, vomiting, and abdominal pain mimicking GALLBLADDER DISEASE.

When giving this drug along with THEOPHYLLINE, the dose of the latter should be decreased; toxicity may develop from ordinary doses.

Do not give this to patients with PORPHYRIA (a hereditary disease).

This alters the electrical activity of the heart which might cause sudden death. Thus it should not be combined with other such drugs. The medical jargon is that it prolongs the QT interval.

Dosage: The following doses are for adults; reduce the dose according to weight for children. Reduce the dose with LIVER DISEASE. Do not crush the tablets.

ABSCESS: 250 mg every 6 hours until better, plus 2 more days.

ACNE: 250 mg three times a day continuously.

BARTONELLOSIS: 250 mg four times daily for 14 days.

CAT-SCRATCH DISEASE: 250 mg four times daily for 14 days.

CELLULITIS: 250-500 mg every 6 hours for 10 days. Start at the higher dose and decrease the dose as the patient improves.

CHANCROID: 500 mg every 6 hours for 7 days

CHLAMYDIA: 500 mg every 6 hours for 14 days

DIPHTHERIA: Same as CELLULITIS.

DIPHTHERIA prevention: 500 mg every 6 hours for 7 days.

DONOVANOSIS: 500 mg 4 times daily until entirely healed, plus another week.

DYSENTERY: 250 mg 4 times daily for 10 days.

EAR INFECTION: Same as CELLULITIS.

FOOD POISONING: 250 mg every 6 hours until the symptoms are gone, plus another 1-2 days.

GASTROENTERITIS: Same as ABSCESS.

LEPTOSPIROSIS: Same as CELLULITIS.

LYMPHOGRANULOMA VENEREUM: 500 mg every 6 hours for 21 days.

PELVIC INFECTION: 250 mg every 6 hours for 21 days.

PINTA: 500 mg twice daily for 5 days.

PNEUMONIA: Same as CELLULITIS.

Q FEVER: 1000 mg every 6 hours for 14 days.

RELAPSING FEVER: 500 mg, one dose.

RESPIRATORY INFECTION: Same as CELLULITIS.

RESPIRATORY FAILURE: 1000 mg every 6 hours until much improved, then the same as for CELLULITIS.

SPOTTED FEVER: Used with RIFAMPIN; 500 mg every 6 hours until the fever is gone plus 3 more days.

STREP THROAT: Same as CELLULITIS.

SYPHILIS, primary and secondary: 500 mg every 6 hours for 14 days.

TRACHOMA: Same as PELVIC INFECTION.

TRENCH FEVER: 500 mg 4 times daily for 3 months.

TURISTA: Same as ABSCESS.

TREPONARID: Same as SYPHILIS.

VAGINITIS: 500 mg 4 times daily for 7 days.

WHOOPING COUGH: 250 mg every 6 hours for 14 days.

WHOOPING COUGH prevention: Same as DIPHTHERIA prevention.

YAWS: 500 mg every 6 hours for 14 days.

As a PENICILLIN substitute: same dose, same duration as PENICILLIN.

Tooth infection: 250-500 mg every 6 hours until the symptoms are gone plus another 2 days. The affected tooth should be pulled.

Alternatives: AZITHROMYCIN (Zithromax), CLARITHROMYCIN (Klaricid), SULFADIAZINE, CHLORAMPHENICOL. PENICILLIN is preferable in non-allergic patients. GENTAMYCIN (given by injection) is the best alternative in PYOMYOSITIS.

ETHAMBUTOL

Anti-tuberculosis

Safety class 1 Stability: C, Dark; Pregnancy: o.k.

Brand name: Myambutol; generic available.

Indications: TUBERCULOSIS.

Contraindications: Do not use with KIDNEY FAILURE. Do not use this with someone too young or otherwise disabled in a way that would prevent him from communicating concerning visual loss. Do not use it in someone with optic neuritis. Do not use this with any other neurotoxic drug: one that causes SEIZURES or problems with movement or numbness and tingling in side-effects or overdose.

Precautions: Patient may become color blind to green (rare); he may become totally blind with an overdose and occasionally with normal doses.

Side-effects: Decreased vision (stop the drug), decreased ability to distinguish red and green, rash, fever due to the drug. These effects occur in only a small percentage of patients. Check vision every 2 weeks in patients on the drug. This may make GOUT worse.

Overdose and prolonged usage: KIDNEY FAILURE.

Dosage: Reduce the dose with KIDNEY FAILURE or any kidney disease.

Daily dosage for first 8 weeks:

- 11-14 kg: 0.5 400-mg tablet daily
- 15-20 kg: 1 400-mg tablet daily
- 21-29 kg: 1.5 400-mg tablets daily
- 30-35 kg: 2 400-mg tablets daily
- 36-44 kg: 2.5 400-mg tablets daily
- 45-55 kg: 3 400-mg tablets daily

Subsequent daily dosage:

- Under 11 kg: Don't use this
- 12-19 kg: 0.5 400-mg tablet daily
- 20-34 kg: 1 400-mg tablet daily
- 35-44 kg: 1.5 400-mg tablets daily
- 45-55 kg: 2 400-mg tablets daily

Subsequent twice weekly dosage:

- Under 11 kg: Don't use this
- 12-19 kg: 1.5 400-mg tablets twice weekly
- 20-34 kg: 3 400-mg tablets twice weekly
- 35-44 kg: 4.5 400-mg tablets twice weekly
- 45-55 kg: 6 400-mg tablets twice weekly

Subsequent thrice weekly dosage:

- Under 11 kg: Don't use this.
- 12-19 kg: 1 400-mg tablet thrice weekly
- 20-34 kg: 2 400-mg tablets thrice weekly
- 35-44 kg: 3 400-mg tablets thrice weekly
- 45-55 kg: 4 400 mg tablets thrice weekly

If you want to calculate more accurately, the formula is 25 mg/kg daily for the first 8 weeks only; for an average adult this is 1400 mg. Then reduce to 15 mg/kg daily or 30 mg/kg thrice weekly or 45 mg/kg twice weekly. (See TUBERCULOSIS in the *Disease Index* for the duration of therapy.)

Alternatives: PAS, RIFAMPIN, STREPTOMYCIN (injectable only), PYRAZINAMIDE, CIPROFLOXACIN.

ETHIONAMIDE

Anti-TUBERCULOSIS, second-line drug

Brand name: Trecator-SC

Safety class: Unknown Stability: Unknown

Pregnancy: Unknown

Indication: TUBERCULOSIS

Contraindication: ALLERGY to this drug, LIVER DISEASE.

Precautions: Liver problems are likely when used with RIFAMPIN. Management of DIABETES may be more difficult. Stop the drug if HEPATITIS develops. Get frequent blood tests to check for liver damage.

Side-effects: Unknown

Dosage: 250-500 mg by mouth twice a day. Children get 15-20 mg/kg by mouth twice a day.

FAMCICLOVIR

Antiviral, similar to ACYCLOVIR. The usual dose is 250 mg every 8 hours for 7 days. Recently this has been used to prevent the development of HERPES: It is given as 1000 mg twice in one day when the patient first notices that a new episode is starting. It prevents the full-blown disease from developing.

FANSIDAR

Antimalarial
Safety class 1.5 Stability: B, dark Pregnancy C
Brand name: Fansidar; (Composition: PYRIMETHAMINE 25 mg + sulfadoxine 500 mg.)
Also supplied in ampules for IM use.

Indications: TOXOPLASMOSIS. Prevention and treatment of CHLOROQUINE-resistant MALARIA. In many areas MALARIA is resistant to this also. Fansidar does not work well in South America for malaria, due to resistance.

Contraindications: ALLERGY to this drug or any SULFA drug or PYRIMETHAMINE (Daraprim). Best not to use during pregnancy or breastfeeding if there are other alternatives but it is routinely used in later pregnancy. Do not give this to someone with ANEMIA due to a deficiency of FOLATE. Do not give this to patients with PORPHYRIA or to those with G6PD DEFICIENCY.

Side-effects: Nausea, vomiting, diarrhea, loss of appetite; these effects will pass. There is sometimes ANEMIA due to the bone marrow dying (this is commonly fatal), or SEIZURES. The drug must be stopped immediately for these. Some persons develop a skin reaction to this drug, resembling a burn (see EXFOLIATIVE DERMATITIS). If this happens, stop the drug immediately! There is a 0.1% chance of serious side-effects, some of them fatal.

Precautions: If the patient is pregnant, also give FOLINIC ACID, if you can.

This: interacts with zidovudine and with nevirapine, both anti-AIDS drugs.

Note that for MALARIA treatment, it takes 24-48 hours for Fansidar to start to work. Therefore for cerebral MALARIA or other severe forms, it is necessary to use QUININE also for at least the first few days.

Dosage: The dose may need to be increased in the presence of HIV INFECTION but these patients more often have serious side-effects also.

TOXOPLASMOSIS: 2 tablets daily for 6 weeks.

MALARIA prevention: Adult dose is 1 tablet weekly. Reduce dose according to weight for children. Begin when entering a malarious area, and continue for 6 weeks after leaving. (Not recommended.)

MALARIA treatment: 1 ampule IM or 3 tablets by mouth, one dose only, for adults. Children 9-14 y.o. get 2 tablets; 4-8 y.o. get 1 tablet, and less than 4 get 1/2 tablet. This assumes a normal (Western) weight for age.

FILICIN

An extract from a male fern plant, used to treat TAPEWORM. It works well, but is dangerous, causing blindness, HEART FAILURE, and occasionally death.

FLUBENDAZOLE

Dewormer, Anthelmintic
Safety class 2 Stability: Unknown
Brand names: Flubenol, Flumoxal, Flumoxane, Fluvermal.

Indications: ASCARIASIS, CYSTICERCOSIS, HOOKWORM, HYDATID DISEASE, TRICHURIASIS.

Contraindications: Pregnancy.

Precautions: This drug is mostly a veterinary drug; its use for humans is unproven and side-effects are largely unknown.

Dosage:

CYSTICERCOSIS: 20 mg/kg twice a day for 10 days. This is an average adult dose of 1200 mg per dose.

Everything else: 300 mg daily for 3 days. (But HYDATID DISEASE - dosage not known)

FLUCONAZOLE

This is a new drug. It alters the electrical rhythm of the heart and thus might cause sudden death. Thus it should not be used with other such drugs. The medical jargon is that it prolongs the QT interval.

It is used in a dosage of 150 mg once, for VAGINITIS due to yeast. You should seek further information elsewhere before using it. It has been also used for CUTANEOUS LEISHMANIASIS, 200 mg daily x 6 weeks but it is expensive and does not work well. It is sometimes used in a dose of 150 mg, together with AZITHROMYCIN and SECNIDAZOLE, to treat PELVIC INFECTION. It is worth trying if you can get it free or cheap. It needs dosage adjustment in KIDNEY DISEASE or KIDNEY FAILURE.

FLUROQUINOLONE

This refers to a class of drugs; see CIPROFLOXACIN. Other examples are OFLOXACIN and PEFLOXACIN. There is some recent evidence that the latter two drugs work well for LEPROSY. All of these drugs should be avoided in the elderly and those on STEROIDS.

FOLATE

Vitamin.
Synonyms: Folic acid. Folinic acid is a closely related compound.
Safety class 1 Pregnancy A (o.k.)
Stability: B; liquid preparations are very unstable.
Brand names: Many; usually available by generic name.
Folinic acid: Leucovorin. It is expensive.

Indications: ANEMIA due to folic acid deficiency; ANEMIA caused by MALABSORPTION, MALARIA, OVALOCYTOSIS, SPRUE, SICKLE CELL DISEASE, TURISTA, or THALLASEMIA.

Contraindications: A diet that contains only plant products (no milk or eggs or meat ever); MALABSORPTION. In both of these cases, it may be given if some VITAMIN B_{12} is given by injection first. Do not give to a patient with pernicious anemia or to someone on PHENYTOIN.

Precautions: Dose on bottles is frequently in mcg (microgram). 1 mcg is 1/1000 of a mg. Therefore 100 mcg is 1/10 mg and it will take 10 tablets of 100 mcg each to make 1 mg. Since VITAMIN A and VITAMIN D are harmful in large amounts, it is important not to take large amounts of MULTIVITAMINS containing these in order to obtain enough folate.

Dosage:

MALABSORPTION: 5 mg daily.

SPRUE: 5 mg three times daily for 30 days.

Pregnancy: 1 mg daily for 30 days.

Everything else: 1 mg by mouth daily, adults and children both; continue until the patient feels better and then for another week.

Alternatives: Diet with fresh vegetables, MULTIVITAMINS containing sufficient folate or folic acid (most do not).

FOLINIC ACID

See FOLATE. This is a form that is used by pregnant women who take PYRIMETHAMINE, FANSIDAR, PROGUANIL, or COTRIMOXAZOLE for a period of time. It provides FOLATE in a form that humans can use but bacteria cannot use. Folinic acid counteracts the negative effects of the other drugs on the baby.

FOSMIDOMYCIN

This is a new anti-malarial drug used in combination with CLINDAMYCIN or artesunate (ARTEMISININ). It should not be used alone. Seek independent information concerning contraindications, side-effects, and precautions. The usual dose is 900 mg every 12 hours for 7 days.

FURAZOLIDONE

This is a new medication that is used for some protozoal diseases: GIARDIASIS, amebic DYSENTERY. It has some nasty psychiatric side-effects; avoid using it!!

FUROSEMIDE

Water pill, Diuretic

Safety class 2 Stability: B, Dark Pregnancy C

Synonym: Frusemide (UK)

Brand name: Lasix; generic drug is available. Supplied as 40 mg tablets, sometimes other sizes.

Indications: Severe HEART FAILURE, HYPERTENSION; sometimes KIDNEY FAILURE, TOXEMIA.

Contraindications: ALTITUDE SICKNESS, DEHYDRATION, previous diarrhea or vomiting lasting a week or more, ALLERGY to any SULFA drug, CIRRHOSIS, LIVER FAILURE, KIDNEY FAILURE. Do not give this together with aminoglycoside-type antibiotics (e.g. GENTAMYCIN or STREPTOMYCIN) or with medication for HYPERTENSION unless it is prescribed for the particular patient.

Precautions: This drug wastes POTASSIUM from the body. If you give more than just a few doses, the patient should consume food high in potassium (apricots, avocados, bananas, citrus fruits, coconut water, dates, papaya, potatoes, pumpkin, spinach) unless he has KIDNEY FAILURE. If he does have KIDNEY FAILURE, he should not consume high-potassium foods.

This drug interferes with several lab tests; don't believe lab tests on blood drawn while the person was on this drug.

Side-effects: Nausea, abdominal pain, rashes, tingling. These effects occur in only a small percentage of patients. Deafness is a very rare side-effect; stop the drug if this occurs. The drug may make the skin sensitive to sunburn.

Overdose and prolonged use: LIVER FAILURE; see Protocol C-7.

Dosage: Reduce the dose in the elderly and in LIVER FAILURE and in KIDNEY FAILURE.

Adults: 40-80 mg by mouth; reduce dose for children. Repeat this every half hour until the patient has to urinate. (The drug increases urine production.) Then give the drug once or twice a day, forever with HYPERTENSION, only as long as there are symptoms for other conditions.

GAMMA GLOBULIN

This is a human blood product which is given by injection every 3-6 months to prevent HEPATITIS. The ordinary American product prevents HEPATITIS A only. The ordinary French product prevents HEPATITIS A and HEPATITIS E. A special product is available to prevent HEPATITIS B in those who are exposed but have not been immunized. The usual dose in all cases is 0.06 ml/kg, injected IM, one time only.

GANCICLOVIR

This is an anti-HIV INFECTION drug.

GATIFLOXACIN

Antibiotic: gram positive and gram negative

Safety class: unknown Stability: unknown

Pregnancy: unknown but related drugs are contraindicated.

Brand name: Tequin

Indication: ANTHRAX, possibly other indications similar to CIPROFLOXACIN.

Contraindication: Prior ALLERGY to this or to any "-oxacin" drug; age under 18 years old.

Precautions: Don't give this with ANTACID, IRON, ZINC, CIMETIDINE, PHENYTOIN, THEOPHYLLINE, DIGOXIN, or any blood thinners.

Dosage: Reduce the dose with KIDNEY DISEASE or KIDNEY FAILURE. Usual adult dose is 200-400 mg daily, by mouth or IV.

GENTAMYCIN

Antibiotic (gram negative)
Safety class 2-3 Stability: Unknown; Pregnancy C
Brand names: Garamycin, G-mycetin, Cidomycin, Genticin. Supplied as injectable, cream, ointment, and eye drops only; not available in an oral form.

Indications: Used by injection at the direction of a physician for a variety of bacterial infections, most commonly ACUTE ABDOMEN, BRUCELLOSIS, ENTERIC FEVER resistant to other drugs, GALLBLADDER DISEASE, MENINGITIS in a newborn, OSTEOMYELITIS, PLAGUE, PYOMYOSITIS, SEPSIS, TRENCH FEVER, TURISTA, or TULAREMIA. The injectable form of the drug (there is no oral form) may be given by mouth for severe, persistent diarrhea in infants. It counteracts the bacteria in the bowel but is not absorbed into the blood stream. (The eye drops or ointment may be used for EYE INFECTION, see ANTIBIOTIC EYE DROPS/OINTMENT.)

Contraindications: ALLERGY to the drug or to any other aminoglycoside such as STREPTOMYCIN. The injectable form is contraindicated in pregnancy and in KIDNEY FAILURE. Do not use this with other drugs that may cause KIDNEY FAILURE or in patients who have muscle weakness or trembling. Do not use in patients with CIRRHOSIS or LIVER FAILURE; see Protocol C-7.

Precaution: This drug is given with CHOLESTYRAMINE for diarrhea, but the two drugs must not be given at the same time of day; stagger the times they are given by two hours.

Side-effects: SEIZURES, BRAIN DAMAGE, or a drop in the blood pressure. With excessive IM doses, deafness and KIDNEY FAILURE may develop. This is not a problem with topical drug or when injectable forms are used orally.

Overdose and prolonged usage: KIDNEY FAILURE, deafness.

Dosage: Reduce the dose in the elderly and in the presence of KIDNEY FAILURE or hearing loss.

ACUTE ABDOMEN: Same as MENINGITIS.

BRUCELLOSIS: 1mg/kg IM every 8 hours for 6 weeks.

GALLBLADDER DISEASE: Same as MENINGITIS.

MENINGITIS: 1 mg/kg IM every 8 hours for 14 days.

OSTEOMYELITIS: 1 mg/kg IM every 8 hours for 6 weeks minimum.

PLAGUE: 2 mg/kg IV loading, then 1.7 mg/kg IV every 8 hours for 7 days.

PYOMYOSITIS: Same as MENINGITIS.

SEPSIS: Same as MENINGITIS.

TRENCH FEVER: 1 mg/kg every 8 hours IV x 14 days, used with DOXYCYCLINE.

TULAREMIA: Same as PLAGUE.

TURISTA: 8 mg/kg by mouth every 4 hours for 3 days.

Other uses: See ANTIBIOTIC EYE DROPS or ANTIBIOTIC OINTMENT.

Alternatives: In SEPSIS, use a third-generation CEPHALOSPORIN.

GENTIAN VIOLET

Topical disinfectant.
Safety Class 1 Stability: A
Synonym: Crystal Violet
Brand names: Aksuris, Oxiuran, Viocid.
Indications: Most commonly used for any and every skin problem. It gives a brilliant bluish-purple color to the skin which, with repeated use, may become permanent. May be used for CANDIDIASIS or TINEA when better treatments are not available.

Note that this is not very effective for preventing infections of the skin. Unsophisticated people love its brilliant color and prefer to use this to washing with soap and water. Soap and water are much more effective in preventing infection and in healing established infections.

GRISEOFULVIN

Antifungal
Safety class 3 Stability: A Pregnancy: X
Brand names: Fulvicin U/F, Grifulvin V, Grisactin. Supplied as 125, 250, and 500 mg tablets.

Indication: FAVUS, TINEA.

Contraindications: Pregnancy (causes fetal deformities). Avoid pregnancy while taking the drug and for one month afterward. A man should not father a child within 6 months of treatment. Also contraindicated while breast feeding and in any kind of liver disease (see LIVER FAILURE). Do not give with oral contraceptives, to patients who have PORPHYRIA, or with alcoholic drinks.

Precautions: Rarely the patient may develop a swollen face: STOP THE DRUG. Griseofulvin may cause ANAPHYLAXIS like PENICILLIN does. Be sure you can recognize this and can treat it before you give the drug. See Volume I, Chapter 4. Some people who are allergic to PENICILLIN are also allergic to this. (See ALLERGY.) Watch carefully.

Side-effects: Headache, which will disappear with continued use. There is sun sensitivity. Other side-effects include headache, pains in the limbs, lethargy, confusion, nausea, diarrhea, gas. The blood count may drop (causing ANEMIA and susceptibility to infection) as the drug damages the bone marrow. It may cause protein in the urine. It may cause breast development in males. There may be a DRUG ERUPTION.

Overdose and prolonged usage: LIVER FAILURE; see Protocol C-7.

Dosage: This should be given with a fatty meal.

Infants: 2.5 mg/kg every 6 hours; Children (30-50 lb): 30-62 mg every 6 hours; Children (over 50 lb.): 62-125 mg every 6 hours; Adults: 125-250 mg every 6 hours; Treat for 3 weeks if palms, soles and nails are not affected. Treat for 6-25 weeks if these are affected. Results: Begin in 2-3 days.

HAART

This is an acronym for "highly active anti-retroviral therapy"—a combination of drugs to treat HIV INFECTION. Detailing the treatment plan is beyond the scope of this book, but some individual drugs are listed.

HALOFANTRINE

Antimalarial, British only, not used much anymore
Safety class 3 Stability: ?? Pregnancy ??
Brand name: Halfan. Supplied as a liquid of 100 mg/ml and 250 mg tablets.
Indications: CHLOROQUINE-resistant and FANSIDAR-resistant MALARIA.
Contraindications: ALLERGY to the drug; pregnancy, nursing mothers, any personal or family history of heart disease involving abnormal heart rhythms, an abnormal EKG, usage of other drugs that cause LIVER FAILURE.

Precautions: **This is a dangerous drug. It should only be used on the advice of a physician**. Never give it at the same time or shortly after MEFLOQUINE, QUININE, or CHLOROQUINE, any psychiatric medications, any heart medications, or any ALLERGY medications. It can cause life-threatening heart problems even in otherwise-healthy children. CHLOROQUINE plus CHLORPHENIRAMINE works just as well as this for resistant MALARIA.

Side-effects: Transient nausea, vomiting, diarrhea, and stomach cramps. Itching may occur in Blacks. Try Vitamin B Complex to treat the itching. It is dangerous if taken with fatty foods. It can cause LIVER FAILURE; see Protocol C-7.

Dosage: **Take on an empty stomach.** 500 mg by mouth every 6-8 hours for 3 doses; repeat this after 7-14 days if this is the first time the person has ever had MALARIA. Children get 8-10 mg/kg per dose; give 3 doses, 6 hours apart.

HEXADECYLPHOSPHOCHOLINE

See MILTEFOSINE. This is an alternative generic name.

HIB

This is a new immunization which prevents some middle EAR INFECTIONs and one form of MENINGITIS in infants and young children.

HOMATROPINE EYE DROPS

Pupil dilator; Mydriatic
Safety class 1-2 Stability: C
Brand names: Isoptohomatropine; tropicamide is a generic equivalent.
Indications: KERATITIS, treatment of a scratched cornea, pain after removal of a foreign object.

Contraindications: GLAUCOMA; check for this!

Precautions: Unless the eye is numb, these drops burn as they go in; it is a normal effect which will pass after 10 minutes or so.

Dosage: One drop in the affected eye every 5 minutes for 2 doses. Then use ANTIBIOTIC EYE OINTMENT in it and patch it for at least 12 hours. You may repeat the drops whenever needed for pain. The patch may be removed after the pupil becomes small in response to light.

HYDRALAZINE

Blood pressure medicine, Antihypertensive
Safety class 2 Stability: A Pregnancy C
Brand name: Apresoline; generic drug is available. Supplied as 10, 25, 50, and 100 mg tablets.
Indications: HYPERTENSION, TOXEMIA, maybe KIDNEY FAILURE.

Contraindications: ALLERGY to the drug, prior severe HEART FAILURE or ANGINA or RHEUMATIC FEVER. Do not give this at the same time as IBUPROFEN or similar medications. Do not give to patients that have PORPHYRIA (a hereditary disease).

Precautions: Discontinue drug if any of the following occur: joint pains, fever, chest pains like ANGINA.

Side-effects: Common side-effects are headache, heart pounding, loss of appetite, nausea and vomiting, diarrhea, fast pulse. Less common are constipation, anxiety, sleep disturbances, and a stuffy nose. Sometimes there is fluid retention, with swelling of the feet and ankles toward the end of the day.

Overdose and prolonged usage: LIVER FAILURE; see Protocol C-7.

Dosage: 10 mg to 50 mg by mouth every 6 hours. Start at the lower dosage and work up, increasing every 3 or 4 days until the blood pressure is normal. Reduce the dose for the elderly and possibly also for LIVER FAILURE. Reduce the dose according to weight in children. Continue throughout life in HYPERTENSION, until after delivery in TOXEMIA. In a crisis in TOXEMIA, a physician or nurse can give 10 mg slowly IV every 30 minutes until the pressure comes down.

Alternatives: Aldomet, HYDROCHLOROTHIAZIDE.

HYDROCHLOROTHIAZIDE

Water pill, Diuretic
Safety class 2 Stability: A Pregnancy B

Brand names: Hydrodiuril; generic drug is available. Supplied as 25 and 50 mg tablets.

Indications: HEART FAILURE, HYPERTENSION, mild KIDNEY FAILURE, TOXEMIA.

Contraindications: DEHYDRATION; diet-controlled DIABETES, ALLERGY to any SULFA drug, total KIDNEY FAILURE in which the patient makes no urine. Do not give this to diabetics who take medication by mouth to lower their blood sugar. Do not give this to to women who are breastfeeding, to patients who have PORPHYRIA (a hereditary disease) or to those with G6PD DEFICIENCY, CIRRHOSIS or LIVER FAILURE.

Precautions: Unless this is used for KIDNEY FAILURE, the patient must take POTASSIUM or consume food high in POTASSIUM (apricots, avocados, bananas, citrus fruits, coconut water, dates, papayas, potatoes, pumpkins, spinach, tomatoes). If there is KIDNEY FAILURE, the patient should not consume extra potassium.

Side-effects: Weakness, sun sensitivity, low blood pressure, a feeling of faintness.

Overdose and prolonged use: KIDNEY FAILURE.

Dosage: Reduce the dose for the elderly and possibly with kidney disease. Adults get 25-50 mg by mouth once or twice daily. Reduce dose according to weight for children. Continue the drug throughout life in HYPERTENSION, just until problem is past in other conditions. It may be necessary to continue long-term in HEART FAILURE.

Alternatives: FUROSEMIDE, Aldactazide, Aldactone, and Hygroton. Do not use POTASSIUM with Aldactazide and Aldactone. With Hygroton the patient needs POTASSIUM as above.

HYDROCORTISONE

Steroid
Safety class 2-3 Stability: C Pregnancy ?

Brand names: Cortef, Hydrocortone, others. Supplied as tablets, and as short-acting and long-acting injection. Eye drops are usually made out of a similar, related drug, PREDNISOLONE.

Indications: ALLERGY; ANAPHYLAXIS; ANTHRAX; ASTHMA; CONTACT DERMATITIS; CYSTICERCOSIS; ECZEMA; ENTERIC FEVER; EXFOLIATIVE DERMATITIS; FILARIASIS; HEART FAILURE; KATAYAMA DISEASE; KIDNEY FAILURE; LEPROSY reactions; ONCHOCERCIASIS.

Contraindications: HIV INFECTION, ANGINA. some infections. Used in a patient with STRONGYLOIDIASIS it may cause SEPSIS and death. If this is a possibility, treat for STRONGYLOIDIASIS before using this drug. Probably should not be used in pregnancy because it may cause cleft palate in the baby. The drug may activate TUBERCULOSIS which is dormant. With a history of TB or in an area where TB is common, the drug should be used only with a physician's supervision. Do not use in the presence of CHAGA'S DISEASE. Don't use it if there is any history of MENTAL ILLNESS or HYPERTENSION.

Precautions: Unless directed otherwise by a physician for the particular illness, it is important not to use this drug for more than 5 days at a time before stopping it for at least a week. When using it for a longer time, one usually gives it only every other day. If the patient has already been on the drug for more than 5 days, stop it gradually, not abruptly. If the patient has an emotional breakdown, stop the drug gradually. The drug may activate a problem with amebae, causing AMEBIC LIVER DISEASE or DYSENTERY. Regard any diarrhea side-effect as amebic DYSENTERY.

Side-effects: MENTAL ILLNESS, increased appetite, failure to grow in children, with long-term usage, CATARACTS.

Overdose and prolonged usage: CATARACTS, KIDNEY FAILURE, LIVER FAILURE, (see Protocol C-7). There are bad long-term side effects of the drug: Muscle weakness, brittle bones, PEPTIC ULCER, DIABETES, SHOCK, death, to name a few. These never occur if the drug is used for 5 days or less. **The dose of the drug is not nearly as critical as the length of time it is used.**

Dosage:

Oral adult dose is 5-30 mg, 2-4 times daily for a maximum of 5 days unless ordered otherwise by a physician. Use the higher doses in very ill patients. Reduce dose according to weight for children.

IM adult dose is 100 mg in a single injection, which causes an anti-inflammatory action for 30-48 hours.

When this is used as an alternative to PREDNISONE, the usual dose is four times that of PREDNISONE; i.e., give 20 mg of HYDROCORTISONE in place of each 5 mg of PREDNISONE.

IBUPROFEN

Analgesic, Anti-inflammatory
Safety class 2 Stability: C Pregnancy B

Brand names: Pediaprofen, Motrin, Rufen, Advil. Comes as 200, 400, and 600 mg tablets and in liquid for children. The 200 mg size tablet is available without a prescription in the United States.

Indications: FEVER PER SE (reduction of any fever), ARTHRITIS, COSTAL CHONDRITIS, headaches, menstrual cramps, MUSCLE STRAIN, PERICARDITIS, PLEURISY, sprains.

Contraindications: ALLERGY to ASPIRIN or ibuprofen or any NSAID (non-steroidal, anti-inflammatory drug). Don't use this at the same time as ASPIRIN, ALCOHOL, HYDROCORTISONE, PREDNISONE, or related drugs. Do not use in the presence of CIRRHOSIS or LIVER FAILURE.

Precautions: May cause abdominal pain, nausea, and vomiting. Use carefully if at all if your patient has a PEPTIC ULCER or a history of one.

Side-effects: Dizziness, headache, nausea, vomiting, diarrhea.

Overdose and prolonged usage: KIDNEY FAILURE, LIVER FAILURE (see Protocol C-7).

Dosage: Give the drug with food. Adult dose is 200-600 mg by mouth every 6 hours as needed for adults. Reduce dose according to weight for children.

INDINAVIR SULFATE

Anti-HIV drug; Protease inhibitor
Safety class 3 Stability: Dry, room temperature
Pregnancy: Unknown
Indication: HIV INFECTION
Contraindications: Prior ALLERGY to this drug.
Precautions:

Don't use St John's Wort while taking this.
Indinavir interacts badly with many different drugs.
Don't consume grapefruit (or its juice) while taking this.
Seek independent advice before giving this in the presence of LIVER DISEASE or DIABETES.
Stop for worsening ANEMIA or abnormal bleeding.

Side-effects: KIDNEY STONES in children; nausea/vomiting/diarrhea/abdominal pains; mental changes; skin changes; JAUNDICE.

Dosage: Adult dose: 600-800 mg every 8 hours.

IODINE

Mineral; Antiseptic
Safety class 2-3; Stability: Varies; Pregnancy o.k.
Synonym: Lugol's Solution (an iodine solution).

Brand names: Lipoidol is iodine-oil to be taken by mouth. Ethiodol is iodine-oil for injection. Lugol's solution is 5% iodine and 10% potassium iodide; tincture of iodine is 2.5% iodine and 2.5% potassium iodide, made up in alcohol. Povidone iodine is iodine attached to an organic compound to stabilize it. It is available as a powder in 1 kg plastic tubs. It can be used to make iodine antiseptic or eye drops. See Volume I, Appendix 1, Procedures 9 and 10.

Indications: CANDIDIASIS, GOITER, IMPETIGO, MYCETOMA, THYROID TROUBLE (low thyroid), sometimes TINEA, CUTANEOUS LEISHMANIASIS. Also used to purify water for drinking and for soaking fruits and vegetables before eating.

Povidone iodine is dissolved in normal saline to make ANTIBIOTIC EYE DROPS which can be used for KERATITIS and EYE INFECTIONS. Mixing povidone iodine with petroleum jelly makes a good ANTIBIOTIC OINTMENT for wounds. (This is also available commercially.)

Contraindications: Older people with lumpy goiters—it will not help these and may harm them.

ALLERGY to iodine.

GOITER not due to iodine deficiency. (This will generally be in areas where most of the diet is from the sea and there is no CRETINISM.) Some sources list pregnancy as a contraindication but that is not true. It is only radioactive iodine that is contraindicated in pregnancy, not ordinary iodine. Goitrous pregnant women need iodine to prevent their babies being born with CRETINISM. On the other hand, large doses of iodine for prolonged times can cause fetal problems during pregnancy.

Precautions: Keep this out of reach of children. See the Symptom Index, Protocol 11 if it is taken in large doses. When treating patients for GOITER or THYROID TROUBLE (low thyroid), watch for symptoms of THYROID TROUBLE (high thyroid). If this occurs, stop the drug for the time being. Iodine preparations with 7% available iodine should not be used in wounds. First dilute them 1:3 with water.

Side-effects: Rash, discoloration of the skin and nails.

Dosage:

GOITER: one drop of tincture of iodine in a liter of drinking water weekly for 4 weeks, then monthly. Ethiodol: recommended dose is a single IM injection of 950 mg. Lipoidol dose is 2 ml in one dose yearly.

IMPETIGO, CUTANEOUS LEISHMANIASIS: Smear the tincture of iodine or iodine ointment over the affected area daily.

MYCETOMA: Use only on direction of an M.D.

THYROID TROUBLE: Same as GOITER.

TINEA: Apply the tincture of iodine to the skin (excluding the nipples in nursing women).

Drinking water purification: 5 drops of Tincture of Iodine per liter and wait for 15 minutes for everything but GIARDIASIS. If there is GIARDIASIS, use 12 drops and wait an hour.

Food purification: Put iodine of any sort in water, enough to make a solution the color of weak tea. Soak the food for 30 minutes and then rinse with clean drinking water.

IODOQUINOL

Amebicide
Safety class 3 Stability: Unknown
Brand Name: Yodoxin

This is a compound that is sometimes used to clear the bowel of amebae. DILOXANIDE FUROATE is safer than this. Excessive doses are associated with loss of vision. The maximum dose that may be used is 2 grams daily for 20 days for adults and 30-40 mg/kg for 20 days in children.

IPECAC, SYRUP OF

Emetic

Safety class 1 Stability: C, dark

Supplied as generic drug in 30 ml bottles.

Indications: To cause vomiting after poisoning.

Contraindications: Do not use this if the patient appears as if he may become unconscious or if he took anti-depressant medication. Do not use for acids, lye, or gasoline- or kerosene-type poisons. Check for mouth burns if you are not sure what the patient took; do not give ipecac in the presence of mouth burns. Instead, give PROMETHAZINE to prevent vomiting and give milk or water, ACTIVATED CHARCOAL, and MILK OF MAGNESIA.

Precautions: This description applies only to syrup of ipecac. **Do not use the fluid extract.**

Dosage: 15 ml (1 tablespoon) in children up to 2 y.o.; 30 ml (2 tablespoons) in children over 2 y.o. and adults, both followed by 2 glasses of warm liquid, any kind except milk.

Results: 15-30 minutes.

Alternatives: Put a large-diameter stomach tube down, empty the stomach, then rinse with large amounts of water (see Volume I, Appendix 1). If the patient is alert but refuses to swallow the ipecac, get enough people to help hold him down, put a stomach tube down, and put the ipecac and warm water down the tube. Then remove the tube and stand back.

IPRATROPIUM

Safety class 2 Stability: A Pregnancy B

Available as dry powder for inhalation and as an aerosol for inhalation. Available as 20 micrograms per inhalation or 40 micrograms per inhalation.

Indications: ASTHMA, ALLERGY

Contraindications: Previous bad reaction to this medication, currently a severe asthma attack. (The drug is used for asthma but it should not be given in the context of a severe attack going on—only for a mild attack or to prevent an attack.)

Precautions: Try not to use this in pregnancy or in older men who have difficulty urinating. Counsel patients not to exceed the recommended dosage. If the patient develops a rash with using this, then stop the drug.

Side-effects: Worsening of GLAUCOMA, constipation, inability to pass urine (especially in older men), susceptibility to HEAT ILLNESS, dry mouth, decrease in sweating, rapid pulse, sensitivity to light, blurred vision.

Dosage: Note that the dose is micrograms, not milligrams. One microgram is 0.001 milligram. Adults: 20-80 micrograms at a time, 3-4 times daily. Children 6-12 y.o. 20-40 micrograms 3 times daily. Children under 6 y.o. 20 micrograms 3 times daily.

Alternatives: ALBUTEROL, THEOPHYLLINE, EPINEPHRINE by injection.

IRON

Safety class 1 (oral) or 3 (shots).

Stability, oral: A; IM, unknown

Synonym: Ferrous sulfate.

Includes: Imferon and iron dextran are injectable iron. Ferrous fumarate, ferrous gluconate, and ferrous sulfate are generic names for oral iron. Ferrous sulfate is by far the best and cheapest. Some people tolerate one kind of iron better than another. It is essential to get enough in a person. Equivalent doses are as follows:

- Ferrous sulfate: 300 mg = 60 mg iron
- Ferrous sulfate anhydrous: 200 mg = 65 mg iron
- Ferrous fumarate: 200 mg = 65 mg iron
- Ferrous gluconate: 300 mg = 35 mg iron

Indications: ANEMIA, MALNUTRITION, pregnancy, occasionally VISCERAL LEISHMANIASIS.

Contraindications: THALLASEMIA or SICKLE CELL DISEASE or OVALOCYTOSIS that has been treated with transfusions. HEMOCHROMATOSIS. ALLERGY due to iron injection means you must not give another iron injection. Oral iron is still acceptable.

Precautions: Be sure to treat the patient for a minimum of 3 months in order to build up his/her iron stores. If you can buy iron combined with FOLIC ACID, that is always preferable to plain iron, especially in pregnancy. Iron may be constipating in older people. ANEMIA due to MALARIA or SICKLE CELL DISEASE should be treated mainly with FOLATE; iron may be useful in some cases (see the *Disease Index*). Detain the patient for 30 minutes after injection: watch for ANAPHYLAXIS. Use a long needle, and make sure the injection is into muscle; if it goes into the fatty layer it will permanently stain skin. Oral iron will turn stools black and may give a false-positive test for blood in the stool. Recheck after the patient has been off iron for a week.

Side-effects: Nausea, vomiting, abdominal pain.

Dosages:

Oral: Ferrous sulfate is better than ferrous with any other last name; it is absorbed the best. Children: 10 mg/kg ferrous sulfate three times a day to a maximum of 900 mg daily. Adults: 300 mg ferrous sulfate three times a day. Use this for a minimum of a three months. In case of overdose, see the *Symptom Index*, Protocol 11.

Injection: A single dose of 100 mg/ml Iron Dextran is used. Determine the volume to be used as follows: For a hemoglobin *above 6*, (or if the hemoglobin level is unknown), divide the child's weight (in kg) by 3 in order to get the dosage volume in ml (of 100 mg/ml solution) that you should give.

For a hemoglobin *below 6* (45%), divide the child's weight (in kg) by 2, to get the volume in ml (of 100 mg/ml solution) that you should give.

If your Iron Dextran solution is only 50 mg/ml, double the volume calculated above.

Weight	Dose: Hemoglobin more than 6	Dose: Hemoglobin less than 6
10 kg/22 lb	3.3 ml	5.0 ml
20 kg/44 lb	6.7 ml	10.0 ml
30 kg/66 lb	10.0 ml	15.0 ml
40 kg/88 lb	13.3 ml	20.0 ml
50 kg/110 lb	16.7 ml	25.0 ml

Each single injection should be a maximum of 5 ml. Larger patients will need multiple injections to reach the proper final dose. Give the injections in the buttocks only.

ISONIAZID

Antituberculous

Safety class 2 Stability: C, Dark Pregnancy C

Brand names: INH, Niconyl, Nicozide, Nydrazid, Rimifon, Tyvid.

Indications: Suspected or proven TUBERCULOSIS. All household contacts of patients with TB, especially spouse/children/parents; BURULI ULCER in an early stage of development.

Contraindications: Previous HEPATITIS which was the result of isoniazid therapy; current HEPATITIS or other liver disease, CIRRHOSIS, LIVER FAILURE; ALLERGY to the drug; current use of NIRIDAZOLE; unreliable patient who will not take the drug regularly. (If you give such a person the drug, it will not help him and it will cause resistant TUBERCULOSIS to develop in your community.) Do not give this at the same time as ALCOHOL or PHENYTOIN or CYCLOSERINE.

Precautions: Check patients monthly. Check the whites of eyes for yellow; stop the drug if this develops. (Normally there is slight yellow around the edges of the whites. This is not significant.) Check the urine for bilirubin (urine dipstick) and stop the drug if this is positive.

Give the patient a PYRIDOXINE tablet at least twice weekly while on isoniazid (1/4 or 1/2 tablet daily is o.k. also), more frequently if he develops numbness in his legs or feet.

Decrease the dose of isoniazid if a patient develops nausea, headache, loss of appetite, dry mouth, uncoordination, or drowsiness if this appears to be due to the drug.

Stop the drug immediately if the patient develops crazy behavior or JAUNDICE. Advise the patient not to drink alcoholic beverages.

The drug gets into breast milk but that is probably not a problem.

The drug interferes with a test for sugar in the urine.

Side-effects: Numbness and tingling of the limbs, nausea, vomiting, diarrhea, abdominal pain.

Overdose and prolonged usage: KIDNEY FAILURE, LIVER FAILURE (see Protocol C-7).

Dosages:

Daily dosage: Reduce the dose in those more than 35 years old and in the presence of KIDNEY FAILURE.

Under 6 kg: 1/2 of a 100-mg tablet daily
7-12 kg: 1 100-mg tablet daily
13-29 kg: 1/2 300-mg tablet daily
30-50 kg: 1 300-mg tablet daily

Twice- or thrice-weekly dosage:

3-4 kg: 1/2 of a 100-mg tablet
5-8 kg: 1 100-mg tablet
9-14 kg: 1/2 of a 300-mg tablet
15-25 kg: 1 300-mg tablet
26-34 kg: 1.5 300-mg tablet
35-45 kg: 2 300-mg tablets
46-52 kg: 2.5 300-mg tablets
Over 52 kg: 3 300-mg tablets

To calculate accurately for your patients, with a daily dose adults get 5 mg/kg to a maximum of 300 mg by mouth, single daily dose. Infants and children get 5-10 mg/kg to a maximum of 300 mg. For TB MENINGITIS all patients get 10 mg/kg daily and you must be sure to use two other anti-tuberculous drugs with it.

For any age, you may switch to 15 mg/kg (maximum of 900 mg) twice or thrice weekly after 2-8 weeks (preferably 8) on the above dosage. Results should be evident in 3-4 weeks.

Alternatives: ETHAMBUTOL, RIFAMPIN, STREPTOMYCIN, CYCLOSERINE, CIPROFLOXACIN, PYRAZINAMIDE, PAS.

ISOQUINE

This is a new antimalarial drug, related to AMINODIAQUINE and CHLOROQUINE. There is no further information available at this time.

ITRACONAZOLE

Anti-fungal, anti-leishmania

Brand name: Sporanox

Similar to KETOCONAZOLE; used in simple CUTANEOUS LEISHMANIASIS, Mexicana type, 200 mg twice daily for 28 days. It may also be useful in MYCETOMA and VISCERAL LEISHMANIASIS. Do not give the capsule form with medicines for PEPTIC ULCER. These must be taken with a full meal. Seek independent information elsewhere before using this.

IVERMECTIN

Dewormer, Anthelmintic

Safety class 1 Stability: ?? Pregnancy: D

Brand names: Cardomec, Heartguard 30, Ivomec, Mectizan, Oramec, Stromectol, Zymectin Supplied in 6 mg tablets, 1 mg capsules, and 1% liquid (10 mg/ml). It is also available as a 1.87% cream, veterinary form, brand name Equalan.

Indications: ASCARIASIS, ENTEROBIASIS, FILARIASIS treatment and prevention, LARVA MIGRANS prevention, LICE, MANSONELLA PERSTANS prevention, ONCHOCERCIASIS, SCABIES, STRONGYLOIDIASIS, TRICHURIASIS. It is **not** useful for *HOOKWORM.* Dangerous for LOIASIS; seek advice.

Contraindications: **Pregnancy**; Children under 5 y.o. or 15 kg; ALLERGY to the drug; any serious illness, especially MENINGITIS. Do not use this in areas with LOIASIS; it can cause BRAIN DAMAGE.

Precautions: The drug should not be used in pregnancy as it causes miscarriages as well as developmental problems in babies. The drug appears in breast milk and should not be used in nursing mothers with infants less than 7 days old. Keep the patient lying down for an hour or two after he takes the drug, or his blood pressure may drop, causing him to faint. Adverse effects are much more common in expatriates than in nationals.

Side-effects: Occasionally there is headache and general achiness, fever and chills, swelling and painful lymph nodes, and itching. Rarely a patient may develop severe low blood pressure and fainting. This should be treated by having him lie flat for a couple of days until he feels better. Patients with prior ASTHMA may get an attack; treat that like any other attack of ASTHMA. If the patient also has ASCARIASIS, he will pass the worms.

Dosage: Adults get 12 mg as one single dose for most purposes **except** STRONGYLOIDIASIS and FILARIASIS. Reduce the dose according to weight for children.

FILARIASIS treatment: 12-24 mg every 3 months until the problem has resolved. Alternatively, 0.4 mg/kg in a single dose, given with a single dose of DIETHYLCARBAMAZINE.

FILARIASIS prevention: 0.1 mg/kg (average adult dose would be 5-7 mg) in a single dose once or (preferably) twice a year. There is some evidence that even lower doses may work.

LARVA MIGRANS: Dissolve 500 mg of the drug in 100 ml (1/2 cup) of skin cream and apply this. Otherwise use 0.2mg/kg in a single oral dose.

LICE: 0.2 mg/kg in a single oral dose.

MANSONELLA PERSTANS prevention: 15 mg/kg every 3 months.

SCABIES: The veterinary cream is applied to affected areas weekly for 4 weeks or else 0.2 mg/kg in a single oral dose.

STRONGYLOIDIASIS: 0.2 mg/kg daily for 3 days has cured the problem, after repeated failures with THIABENDAZOLE.

KAOPECTATE

Antidiarrhea
Safety class 1 Stability: A

Indications: Mild to moderate diarrhea.

Contraindications: ACUTE ABDOMEN.

Precautions: Try not to give this at the same time as any antibiotics; it cancels the effect of antibiotics.

Dosage: Adults: 15-30 ml after each loose bowel movement. Children: 5-15 ml as above.

Alternatives: BISMUTH SUBSALICYLATE, Lomotil (diphenoxylate hydrochloride), Paregoric, Imodium.

KETAMINE

General anesthetic
Safety class 3 Stability: A Pregnancy: ?

Brand name: Ketalar, and generic veterinary drug. Supplied in a variety of strengths: 10 mg/ml, 50 mg/ml, 100 mg/ml. Be sure to check your supply.

Indications: Gives 30-45 minutes (IM) of unconsciousness needed for a painful procedure such as straightening a fractured limb or cleaning a dirty wound.

Contraindications: Do not use this if the patient has eaten within the past 6 hours. Do not use this if you have not had instruction on how to maintain an airway in an unconscious patient. Do not use this if your patient has had an allergic reaction to this drug. (See ALLERGY.) The drug raises blood pressure so do not give it to someone with uncontrolled HYPERTENSION. Do not use this in early pregnancy unless you are truly desperate.

Precautions: Possession of this drug can cause major legal problems in the States and the UK since it is abusable and thus tightly controlled. Awakening may take hours. Adults commonly have very bad dreams while awakening. They may become violent. Patients should be warned about this, and sedative medication such as PROMETHAZINE should be available, as well as a quiet, soothing environment and someone to calm the patient if he should become agitated. Be sure that fractures are well-splinted. Terrifying dreams may recur days or weeks later.

Side-effects: MENTAL ILLNESS, HYPERTENSION.

Dosage: Light sedation: 4 mg/kg IM. Anesthesia: 6-10 mg/kg IM, one dose. Be extremely careful with the dose. The following table gives ml at 100mg/ml. Give twice this ml volume if you have 50 mg/ml.

Weight	Sedation	Anesthesia
10 kg	0.4 ml	0.6-1.0 ml
20 kg	0.8 ml	1.2-2.0 ml
30 kg	1.2 ml	1.8-3.0 ml
40 kg	1.6 ml	2.4-4.0 ml
50 kg	2.0 ml	3.0-5.0 ml

You may repeat the full dose when the patient is fully awake or a half dose when he awakens enough to object to pain. It can be renewed repeatedly.

KETOCONAZOLE

Antifungal, and other uses.
Safety class 3 Stability A Pregnancy C
Brand name: Nizorol.

Indications: CANDIDIASIS; CHAGA'S DISEASE; CUTANEOUS LEISHMANIASIS, simple Mexicana type; MYCETOMA; TINEA; possibly VISCERAL LEISHMANIASIS.

Contraindications: ALLERGY to the drug or any other "–azole" drug, CIRRHOSIS, LIVER DISEASE, current use of ERYTHROMYCIN or astemizole or terfenadine (newer antihistamines). Contraindicated in pregnancy and breast-feeding.

Precautions: This drug will not work if taken by mouth with DICYCLOMINE, ANTACIDs, medicines for PEPTIC ULCER, or with RIFAMPIN. If it causes HEPATITIS, the drug must be stopped. Never use it for more than 2 weeks without physician approval. Warn the patient not to drink alcohol while on this; it may make him very ill. The drug causes falsely abnormal liver function blood tests. It also may damage the liver.

The drug is sometimes associated with altered electrical activity in the heart, which may cause sudden death. Thus this should not be combined with other such drugs. The medical jargon is that it prolongs the QT interval.

Side-effects: Nausea and vomiting are most frequent; taking the drug with food helps. Less common effects are headache, sensitivity to light, numbness and tingling in limbs, a rash, and a bleeding tendency. It can cause DRUG ERUPTION.

Overdose and prolonged usage: LIVER FAILURE; see Protocol C-7.

Dosage:

For adults, 200-400 mg by mouth daily. Children's daily dose is 3.3-6.6 mg/kg:

CANDIDIASIS 1-4 weeks.

TINEA of skin: 1-2 months.

TINEA of nails: 6-12 months.

For CUTANEOUS LEISHMANIASIS, it only is helpful in the type that rapidly cures itself. Given that the drug is expensive and dangerous, the wisdom of using it for this is questionable. The dosage for this is 600 mg daily for 4 weeks. Alternatively, use the commercial 2% cream, or else grind 1000 mg of the drug and mix it with 50 ml of dimethyl sulfoxide cream, obtained from your pharmacist. Other creams do not work as well. Apply this 3 times a day for a month.

MYCETOMA or CHAGA'S DISEASE: seek a physician's advice before using for either of these.

VISCERAL LEISHMANIASIS: Seek independent sources on dosages.

Alternatives: Itraconazole (Sporanox), Fluconazole (Diflucan)

LACTAID, LACTRASE

Lactase enzyme.
Safety class 1 Stability: C
Brand name: LACTAID
Indications: MILK INTOLERANCE
Contraindications: ALLERGY to this medication.
Dosage: 1 tablet before each glass of milk. The dosage is according to the amount of milk, not according to the patient's size. Do not reduce the dosage for children but do reduce it for lesser amounts of milk.

Alternatives For some people, using fermented milk products such as yogurt or cheese eliminates the need for this medication.

LACTOBACILLUS GG

This is a bacterium used to make YOGURT. It is available in powdered form in health food stores. It is helpful in treating diarrhea in infants. An alternative is to use yogurt itself.

LACTRASE

See LACTAID above.

LAMIVUDINE

Anti-HIV INFECTION; Nucleosidase analog
Safety class: Unknown, probably 2 Stability: Unknown
Pregnancy: Unknown
Brand name: Epivir
Indication: HIV INVECTION
Contraindication: ALLERGY to this drug
Precautions: COTRIMOXAZOLE increases the amount of this drug in the blood and therefore might cause toxicity. Don't use in children who have had PANCREATITIS

Side-effects: Unknown

Dosage: Decrease the dose with KIDNEY DISEASE or KIDNEY FAILURE.

LEVAMISOLE

Dewormer, Anthelmintic
Safety class 2 Stability: ?? Pregnancy C
Brand names: Anthelpor, Aviverm, Cevasol, Cyverm, Dilarvon, Ketrax, Levipor, Nemacide, and others. Supplied as 40 mg and 150 mg tablets.

Indications: ASCARIASIS, possibly HOOKWORM, STRONGYLOIDIASIS. Used with MEBENDAZOLE for MANSONELLOSIS PERSTANS and ONCHOCERCIASIS. Also useful in MALNUTRITION, to boost immunity.

Contraindications: Previous ALLERGY to this drug. Seek independent information before using this in anyone who has an autoimmune disorder or HIV INFECTION.

Precautions: Side-effects are headache, nausea, dizziness, and confusion. If the patient develops a flu-like illness, then stop the drug.

Overdose and prolonged usage: LIVER FAILURE (see Protocol C-7), KIDNEY FAILURE

Dosage:

MANSONELLOSIS PERSTANS: Adult dose is 300 mg daily for 1 week, used with MEBENDAZOLE.

ONCHOCERCIASIS: 2.5 mg/kg twice weekly the week before MEBENDAZOLE, plus the same dose continued for the 3 weeks the MEBENDAZOLE is given. Repeat every 6 months.

MALNUTRITION: 2.5 mg/kg daily for 2-5 days.

Everything else: 5 mg/kg, single dose.

LEVOFLOXACIN

Antibiotic, gram negative and gram positive, a second-generation quinolone related to CIPROFLOXACIN.

Safety class unknown Stability unknown

Pregnancy D

Brand name: Levaquin

Indications: Same as CIPROFLOXACIN and GATIFLOXACIN; also PELVIC INFECTION.

Contraindications: Prior ALLERGY to any drugs in this class; age under 18 years old.

Precautions and side-effects: The same as other drugs in this class; see CIPROFLOXACIN.

Dosage: Reduce the dosage in KIDNEY DISEASE.

Usual adult dose is 500 mg by mouth or IV daily. For PELVIC INFECTION, give this for 14 days. It was listed as to be used with DOXYCYCLINE. DOXYCYCLINE, however, is now no longer recommended for PELVIC INFECTION. Since OFLOXACIN (a related drug) is used with METRONIDAZOLE, it is reasonable to try to use this drug with METRONIDAZOLE also, albeit this is not standard treatment. Seek local advice. If DOXYCYCLINE seems to work in your setting, then use it.

LIDOCAINE

Local anesthetic

Safety class 1 Stability: C

Brand name: Xylocaine; generic drug is available. Supplied in 10 ml and 50 ml bottles of 0.5%, 1%, and 2%. See next entry for ointment.

Indications: Inject around a cut to numb the area for suturing. May be used intravenously for a regional block (see Chapter 8). Swab in the mouth for burns. Smear over scrapes to numb while cleaning, used for FISSURES and PHIMOSIS.

Contraindications: ALLERGY to any "-caine" drug except for procaine.[1] If the patient has had recent SEIZURES, or a history of frequent SEIZURES, use a maximum of 2 cc of 1%, or 4 cc of 0.5% at a time for adults, comparably less according to weight for children.

Precautions: Do not use lidocaine containing EPINEPHRINE on fingers, penis, nose, or toes. Do not give lidocaine with epinephrine IV. Have EPINEPHRINE handy for rare allergic reactions. If lidocaine goes down the throat, do not let the patient eat or drink until the numbness wears off (about 30-60 minutes).

Plain EPINEPHRINE should be used for allergic reactions to lidocaine (see ALLERGY), but it should be injected in the arm rather than at the site where the lidocaine was used.

Side-effects: SEIZURES, nervousness, irritability, insomnia, dizziness, double vision, sleepiness, irregular heart rates. These effects occur in only a small percentage of patients. If used excessively, it can destroy the bone marrow.

Dosage: Not specific, but use no more than 10 ml of 1% or 5 ml of 2% on an adult at any one time if the patient has never had a SEIZURE. (See *Contraindications* if he has.) Takes effect immediately when injected alongside a cut and it lasts for 20 minutes. You may reinject. It takes effect in 10-20 minutes for a nerve block. (See Volume I, Chapter 8 or Chapter 10 for directions on how to inject.)

Alternatives: Procaine 1% is like 1% lidocaine; it may be used in lidocaine ALLERGY. Marcaine 0.25% is used like 1% lidocaine except it should not be used IV. **It must not be used in lidocaine ALLERGY.** Its effects last longer than lidocaine.

LIDOCAINE OINTMENT 4% or 5%

Topical anesthetic

Safety class 1 Stability: C

Indications: Same as LIDOCAINE, but in semi-solid form and therefore more convenient for putting on cuts and scrapes and around rectum. Useful in FISSURES and PHIMOSIS as well as injuries.

LINDANE

Insecticide

Synonyms: Hexachlorocyclohexane, Gamma benzene hexachloride.

Safety class 2 Stability: A, Dark

Supplied as a 1% lotion, cream, or shampoo.

This is very toxic for children if it is swallowed; a small amount can kill a child.

Brand name: Gamene, Kwell, Lindatox, Scabene, Scabisan, many others. Veterinary lindane is called cattle dip.

[1] Procaine is unrelated chemically to lidocaine. Most other -caine drugs are related to lidocaine rather than procaine and therefore will cause similar allergy problems.

Indications: FLEAS, LICE, SCABIES, any other insect-type creature that inhabits the surface of the human body. Not useful for various kinds of worms or MYIASIS.

Contraindications: Infancy or pregnancy, raw skin or open cuts where the medication is to be applied. In pregnant women and small infants, use PERMETHRIN instead.

Precautions: This has been taken off the market in England because of toxicity but it is still on the market in the States. It is very toxic to cats. It is never to be taken internally. This is never to be applied to pink, moist areas of the body. Do not apply this right after a warm bath.

Side-effects: SEIZURES, nervousness, irritability, insomnia, dizziness, double vision, sleepiness, irregular heart rate. These effects occur in only a small percentage of patients. If used excessively, it can damage the bone marrow.

Dosage: Wash well. Then apply the lindane sparingly over all affected parts and adjacent areas. In SCABIES it must be applied over the whole body from the chin down. Leave on for 24 hours and then wash off. If you are treating more than just a few small areas, the treatment may not be repeated until a week after the first treatment and then only if fresh, new spots appear. Itching may continue for several weeks after a successful treatment. Wash all clothing and bedding while the drug is on the skin, before washing it off.

Alternatives: BENZYL BENZOATE, 10% crotamiton, SULFUR in petroleum jelly (off the market in Britain), 0.5% MALATHION, PERMETHRIN.

LOPERAMIDE

Antimotility agent
Safety class 2 Stability A Pregnancy B
Brand names: Imodium, Arret, Diasorb, Normaloe. Usually 2 mg tablets.

Indications: TURISTA, GALLBLADDER DISEASE due to ASCARIASIS.

Contraindications: Bacterial DYSENTERY, particularly that caused by Shigella. Any diarrhea with a fever. Diarrhea due to antibiotics. ACUTE ABDOMEN. Children under 4 y.o. (except by physician recommendation). Do not give to women who are breastfeeding.

Precautions: If the patient develops abdominal distension while on this medication, stop it immediately.

Side-effects: Worsening of GLAUCOMA, constipation, inability to pass urine (especially in older men), susceptibility to HEAT ILLNESS, dry mouth, decrease in sweating, rapid pulse, sensitivity to light, blurred vision.

Dosage: Adults: 4 mg initially, then 2 mg after each loose stool, maximum 16 mg daily. Reduce dose according to weight for children.

LOPINAVIR + RITONAVIR

Anti-HIV INFECTION; Protease inhibitor
Safety class: Unknown Stability: Unknown
Pregnancy: Unknown
Brand name: Kaletra
Indication: HIV INFECTION

Contraindication: ALLERGY to this drug; Current usage of any sedative such as DIAZEPAM.

Precautions: Try not to use together with QUININE, QUINIDINE, or RIFABUTIN.

CARBAMAZEPINE, PHENOBARBITAL, DEXAMETHASONE, PHENYTOIN, and RIFAMPIN will decrease the amount of this in the body.

Stop the drug for severe abdominal pain.

Don't use it with LIVER DISEASE.

The drug will worsen DIABETES.

Side-effects: Unknown

Dosage: For 15-40 kg: 10 mg/kg lopinavir twice a day (together with the ritonavir)

For 7-15 kg: 12 mg/kg lopinavir twice a day (together with the ritonavir)

LUMEFANTRINE

Anti-malarial, similar to BENFLUMETOL, related to CHLOROQUINE-type drugs.
Safety class unknown Stability unknown
Pregnancy unknown
Brand names: Riamet, Co-artem, Coartemether
Tablet size is 2.0 mg artemether plus 12 mg lumefantrine.

Indications: MALARIA, used in combination with some form of ARTEMISININ, usually artemether.

Contraindications: Previous ALLERGY to either component drug.

Precautions: Avoid using this in the presence of any heart disease, LIVER DISEASE, KIDNEY DISEASE, and pregnancy. Avoid using this with anti-HIV drugs, with antidepressants, antifungal medications, other antimalarial medications, CIMETIDINE, grapefruit or grapefruit juice, ERYTHROMYCIN-type drugs, heart medications, CIPROFLOXACIN and similar drugs.

Side-effects: Dizziness (warn the patient against hazardous activities) nausea, vomiting, diarrhea, abdominal pains, headache, insomnia, sore joints and muscles, itching, rash.

Dosage: Be sure to give the drug with a meal of fatty foods to increase its effect. Standard adult dose is 4-6 tablets initially, 8 hours later, then twice daily for 2 days.

MAGNESIUM SULFATE

Anti-toxemia, mineral, muscle relaxant
Safety Class 3 Stability: C Pregnancy o.k.
Supplied as generic drug.

Indications: TOXEMIA of pregnancy; SEIZURES or threatened SEIZURES during later pregnancy, labor, or within a week after delivery. It is also useful in TETANUS as it decreases the amount of sedative that must be given. This drug prevents SEIZUREs, but it lowers blood pressure little if any.

*Contraindications:*Some kinds of heart disease; KIDNEY FAILURE. Don't use this along with sedative drugs. It is contraindicated in severe HEPATITIS, CIRRHOSIS, LIVER FAILURE.

Precautions: Note that this listing is for the drug by injection. Oral magnesium sulfate is a laxative which is not useful for TOXEMIA or TETANUS. You should check the patient's respiratory rate and urine production continually. If respirations are less than 16 per minute or urine production is less than 100 ml for the last 4 hours, withhold the next dose until these become normal.

IM Injections are painful.

Watch the blood pressure; stop the drug and then resume at a reduced dose if the pressure becomes lower than normal or if the patient becomes weak.

Overdose: RESPIRATORY FAILURE, KIDNEY FAILURE. Antidote for overdose is calcium gluconate, 10%, 10-20 mg IV.

Dosage: The following are adult doses. Contact a physician or midwife for instructions. Use the following instructions only if this is not possible:

Readers with no experience with IV's should use a 50% solution, IM. For an average-sized woman, give 10 grams (20 ml) IM initially, 10 ml in each buttock. Then give 5 grams (10 ml) IM every 4 hours. Reduce the dose according to weight for small women. Stop the drug 2 hours before the anticipated time of delivery.

Readers with experience in IV medications: Give 4-6 grams (4000-6000 mg) IV over 20 min with maintenance of 1-2 g/h thereafter, being sure that the patient still has reflexes. Pediatric dose is 20-100 mg/kg/dose. If you can't test reflexes, then use the IM instructions.

MALATHION

Insecticide

Safety class 2 Stability: C dark

Brand names for dilute product: Derbac-M, Prioderm, Quellada M, Suleo-M. The concentrate (50%) is frequently available in markets that serve farmers. It is very toxic.

Indications: FLEAS, LICE, SCABIES, bedbugs.

Contraindications: ALLERGY to this substance; inability to accurately dilute and use it. Prior bad reaction to this product. Seek physician approval before using this on children under 6 months old or on anyone who is quite ill.

Precautions: Be sure that you buy malathion. There are products with similar names that a clerk will assure you can be used the same, but many of them are much more toxic. Make up small batches frequently since malathion decomposes in water.

DO NOT ALLOW THE CONCENTRATED (50%) PRODUCT TO TOUCH YOUR SKIN! If you accidently spill it on yourself, wash it off immediately. Malathion smells bad but the smell does not last for long. Be sure to keep this out of reach of children as it is very toxic if taken by mouth.

Toxic symptoms: A general outpouring of fluid from everywhere: salivation, urination, diarrhea, tears, shortness of breath because of respiratory secretions. Antidote is ATROPINE.

Dosage: Use the pre-diluted product according to the product directions. Dilute the concentrated (50%) malathion to 0.5%. This is a 100-fold dilution, e.g., 10 ml (2 teaspoons) per liter (1000 ml) of plain water. The diluted solution may be used on the skin or hair; it is also useful to add to rinse water to decontaminate louse-infected clothing.

If you dilute the concentrated malathion (10 ml per liter) with kerosene and use this to paint the legs of your bed (some morning, because of the smell), it will eliminate bedbugs within 1 or 2 nights.

Washing your floors once a week with just a teaspoon of the concentrate in a bucket of water will virtually eliminate most insect-type creatures from your house. The smell will leave in less than an hour.

MALOPRIM

Anti malarial; contains DAPSONE (100 mg) and PYRIMETHAMINE (12.5 mg).

Used for prevention of MALARIA especially in children.

Dosage: 2 tablets initially, then 1 tablet weekly for adults, reduced according to weight for children. Check precautions and contraindications of the individual drugs.

MEBENDAZOLE

Dewormer, Anthelmintic

Safety Class 1 Stability: A Pregnancy: C

Brand names: Equivurm, Fugacar, Mebenvet, Mebutar, Multispec, Nemasole, Ovitelmin, Pantelmin, Parmeben, Phardazone, Rumatel, Sirben, Telmin, Telmintic, Vermirax, Vermox. Supplied as 100 mg tablets.

Indications: ASCARIASIS, CAPILLARIASIS, ENTEROBIASIS, HOOKWORM, HYDATID DISEASE, LOIASIS, MANSONELLOSIS PERSTANS, ONCHOCERCIASIS, TRICHURIASIS.

Possibly: TURISTA, GUINEA WORM, MALABSORPTION, SCHISTOSOMIASIS HEMATOBIUM, STRONGYLOIDIASIS, and pork TAPEWORM.

Contraindications: ALLERGY to this, early pregnancy.

*Side-effects:*Nausea, vomiting, diarrhea, abdominal pain.

Dosage: Give the drug with a fatty meal. Reduce the dose in the presence of LIVER FAILURE.

ASCARIASIS: 100 mg twice a day for 3 days, regardless of age.

CAPILLARIASIS: 400 mg daily for 20 days; if the patient relapses, use the same dose for 30 days.

ENTEROBIASIS: 100 mg, single dose, same amount regardless of body weight. Give a dose now and one in 10 days; treat all family members.

GUINEA WORM: 200 mg three times a day for 6 days.

HOOKWORM: 600 mg, single dose (not so good), or 100 mg twice a day for 3 days.

HYDATID DISEASE: 200 mg/kg daily (120 tablets daily for a 60 kg person) for 6 months.

LOIASIS: 2000 mg (20 tablets) daily for 21-28 days.

MANSONELLOSIS PERSTANS: 100 mg twice a day for 1 week, used with LEVAMISOLE. 100 mg twice a day for 14-21 days used with DIETHYLCARBAMAZINE.

ONCHOCERCIASIS: 1000 mg (10 tablets) twice a day for 28 days, **plus** LEVAMISOLE.

SCHISTOSOMIASIS: 1000 mg (10 tablets) daily for 10 days. If no improvement, increase to 2000 mg daily for another 10 days.

STRONGYLOIDIASIS: 100 mg every 8 hours for 14-21 days.

Pork TAPEWORM: 300 mg twice a day for 3 days.

TRICHURIASIS: Like HOOKWORM.

All other worms, deworming, MALABSORPTION, TURISTA: 100 mg twice daily for 3 days. 500 mg in a single dose usually works, but not quite as well. Repeat this treatment every six months while living in a worm-infested area.

Alternatives: ALBENDAZOLE, CAMBENDAZOLE, FLUBENDAZOLE. These are better absorbed than mebendazole and thus require lower doses for diseases such as HYDATID DISEASE.

MEFLOQUINE

Antimalarial
Safety class 2 Stability: A Pregnancy C
Brand names: Lariam, Laricur. Combined with FANSIDAR in Fansimef and MSP.

Usually supplied in 250 mg tablets. In the States the drug has 250 mg total of which 228 mg is base. In many countries overseas one tablet has 274 mg of which 250 mg is base. The amount of drug and base is so close that one need not distinguish or calculate closely.

Indication: MALARIA, especially falciparum, both treatment and prevention. It may not work well for preventing non-falciparum MALARIA.

Contraindications: ALLERGY to this drug, simultaneous use of PROPRANOLOL or similar drugs. Mefloquine had been contraindicated in pregnancy. However, a large study in pregnant women who took it inadvertently has shown it to be safe. Do not use this in patients with a history of EPILEPSY, MENTAL ILLNESS, CIRRHOSIS, or LIVER FAILURE. It also should not be used in some kinds of heart disease. Do not use it at the same time as CHLOROQUINE, in anyone who is on medication for heart problems, or with valproic acid.

Precautions: When used with PHENYTOIN SODIUM or PHENOBARBITAL (SEIZURE medicines), it may lower the blood levels of those drugs, thus provoking SEIZURES.

Mefloquine ought to be combined with another drug, since resistance to it is developing in many areas. If ARTEMISININ is also given, then it is less likely that the malaria will recur or that resistance will develop in the community.

Warn the patient not to engage in hazardous activity while taking this medication.

The drug is sometimes associated with altered electrical activity in the heart; this, in turn, is sometimes associated with sudden death. Thus this should not be combined with other such drugs. The medical jargon is that it prolongs the QT interval.

Side-effects: Nausea, vomiting, and dizziness, especially in young children. These effects occur in only a small percentage of patients. Serious mental disturbances, hallucinations, or SEIZURES may occur. This is rare in males who take it for prophylaxis. It is more common in females and very common in anyone who takes the larger dose required for treatment. Nightmares are common, especially in Whites, even at the lower prophylactic doses. This may also cause burning, numbness, tingling, weakness, and uncoordination in fine movements.

Dosage:

MALARIA treatment: 750-1250 mg by mouth, one dose only. It is absorbed better if the tablets are crushed and dissolved in a liquid. The dosage for children is 15 mg/kg initially followed by 10 mg/kg 12 hours later. It is well tolerated and there are less adverse side-effects than in adults.

MALARIA prevention: 250 mg weekly, from one week before entering a malarious area until 4 weeks after leaving the area. Alternatively, 1 tablet daily for 3 days before travel, then 1 weekly. If you are short of medication, a tablet every other week might (or might not) be sufficient. This is poor for preventing non-falciparum MALARIA.

MELASOPROL

Trypanosomicide: Anti-African-Sleeping-Sickness
Safety class 3+ Stability unknown
Pregnancy: unknown, probably not safe.
Brand names: Melarsen Oxide-BAL, Mel-B, RP 3854.

This is an arsenic compound. See ARSENIC POISONING so you are acquainted with the problem.

Indication: AFRICAN SLEEPING SICKNESS except where there is resistance to the drug.

Contraindication: Previous ALLERGY or adverse response to this drug.

Precautions: The drug is fatal in 4-6% of the patients to whom it is given. It works for late-stage AFRICAN SLEEPING SICKNESS for which there are few if any options. It is given intravenously in a hospital setting only, used for advanced AFRICAN SLEEPING SICKNESS It is a dangerous drug, not to be used in a village setting.

Don't use this in the presence of KIDNEY DISEASE, HEART FAILURE, or LIVER DISEASE without independent physician recommendation.

Use PREDNISONE or PREDNISOLONE, 40 mg/day adult dose for several days before starting this drug.

Dosage: Adult dose is 1-3.6 mg/kg IV daily for 3 days. After 1 week without the drug, 3.6 mg/kg IV daily for 3 days. After 10-21 days, repeat this cycle. Although it is given IV, it must be given on an empty stomach.

Pediatric dose: 0.36 mg/kg IV initially, increased gradually to a maximum of 3.6 mg/kg IV at intervals of 1-5 days, for a total of 9-10 doses.

MELATONIN

Sleeping pill. Available without prescription at health foods stores in the States, not in the UK.

This is a natural sleep-producing substance that is marketed by natural food stores It is very useful for counteracting JET LAG. Some melatonin products are intended to be swallowed, but these do not work for everyone. Sublinguinal tablets which are dissolved under the tongue are more reliable and work better. Information on side-effects, precautions, and toxicities is not available.

Dosage: For Eastern travel, take 3-5 mg at 6-7 p.m. local time on the day of departure, even if that means during a flight. If this will interfere with an airline meal, eat your own bag lunch before so that you will be able to sleep as soon as you take it. After arrival, take 3-5 mg at bedtime for the first 3 nights.

For Western travel, take 3-5 mg at bedtime for the first 4 nights after arrival.

In both cases, you can take another dose before 4 A.M.

METAKELFIN

Antimalarial
Almost the same as FANSIDAR; used the same.

METAPROTERENOL

Bronchodilator
Safety class 1-2 Stability: C Pregnancy C
Brand names: Alupent, Metaprel. Supplied as tablets or inhaler.

Indications: ASTHMA, chronic RESPIRATORY INFECTION.

Contraindications: HYPERTENSION, excessively fast pulse, pregnancy, age under 6, some heart disease. Don't use it with drugs for depression or heart drugs.

Precautions: May cause trembling, nervousness, high blood pressure, and a fast pulse.

Dosage: Reduce the dose for the elderly. Adults get 20 mg three to four times a day, or 2 inhalations every 4 hours. Children get 10 mg (6-9 y.o.) or 20 mg (over 9) three to four times a day.

Alternatives: ALBUTEROL, THEOPHYLLINE, SALBUTAMOL.

METHYLDOPA

Blood pressure medicine, Antihypertensive
Safety class 2 Stability: A
Brand name: Aldomet, generic available.
Indications: HYPERTENSION, TOXEMIA.

Contraindications: Present or recent JAUNDICE, ALLERGY to methyldopa, LIVER DISEASE, some blood diseases, some tumors. Do not use this together with psychiatric drugs, LIVER DISEASE, KIDNEY DISEASE, or ANGINA. Do not give to a patient with PORPHYRIA (a hereditary disease).

Precautions: Be sure you treat your patient on the basis of a blood pressure taken when he is calm. Otherwise you will give him too much drug and lower his pressure too much. This drug may cause impotence in males. If so, switch to another drug. It may rarely cause LIVER DISEASE. If this happens, stop the drug. If the patient becomes drowsy, stop the drug. If he develops HEPATITIS, stop the drug. If he develops fever, joint pains, and diarrhea, stop the drug. Warn the patient not to engage in hazardous activity while taking this drug when he first starts it—until he has been stable on it for at least a week.

This drug interferes with many different lab tests; consider this if someone finds a strange lab result.

Side-effects: Sleepiness, feeling faint when standing up fast, dizziness, dry mouth, headache. Sometimes the patient cannot think well when he takes this. These effects occur in only a small percentage of patients. Rarer effects are mental disturbances, trembling, a dry mouth, and a stuffy nose.

Dosage: Reduce the dose in the elderly.

Blood pressure 160/100 to 190/110: 250 mg every 6 hours. Blood pressure 190/110 to 200/115: 500 mg every 8 hours. More than 200/115: 500 mg every 6 hours. Results: 6-8 hours.

Alternatives: HYDRALAZINE. HYDROCHLOROTHIAZIDE, which may also be used in combination with methyldopa for very high blood pressure. HYDROCHLOROTHIAZIDE is usually used as the first drug and methyldopa as the second if the first is insufficient to lower pressure adequately.

METRIFONATE

Antischistosome, Anthelmintic

Safety class 2 Stability: ?? Pregnancy ??

Brand names: Anthon, Bilarcil, Combor, Difrifon, Dipterex, Dylox, Dyrex, Mastotem, Neguvon, Tugon.

Indications: SCHISTOSOMIASIS HEMATOBIUM. (This is a cheap alternative to PRAZIQUANTEL which is very expensive.) This drug also helps for HOOKWORM although it is not intentionally used for it. It may work for FILARIASIS.

Contraindications: Recent (within the last few days) exposure to insecticides, or planned exposure within a day after taking the drug.

Side-effects: Mild spinning sensation, tiredness, nausea, and abdominal cramping. It may aggravate the symptoms of ONCHOCERCIASIS in patients who have that. The drug may interfere with anesthesia for 48 hours after it is taken. Inform the physician or anesthetist.

Dosage: SCHISTOSOMIASIS HEMATOBIUM: 500 mg (adults) or 7.5-10 mg/kg (children), one dose every 2 weeks for three doses. Give as many of these 3 doses as possible; 1 or 2 doses are also helpful, although not as good as three.

FILARIASIS: 10-15 mg/kg every 14 days for 5-16 doses.

METRONIDAZOLE

Antiprotozoal, Antibiotic

Includes: Benzyl Metronidazole

Safety Class 1 Stability: C, Dark Pregnancy B

Brand names: Arilin, Clont, Danizol, Flagyl, Gineflavir, Klion, Orvagil, Trichocide, Vagilen, and others.

Generic drug is available. Supplied as 250 mg tablets or capsules. *Entamizole* is the combination of this drug with DILOXANIDE FUROATE. A liquid form, benzoyl metronidazole, is available in some countries for children.

Indications: ACUTE ABDOMEN, AMEBIC LIVER DISEASE, CANCRUM ORIS, CHOLERA, amebic DYSENTERY, ENTERIC FEVER, severe cholera-like diarrhea, GIARDIASIS, LARVA MIGRANS (in Asia), PELVIC INFECTION, PEPTIC ULCER, PNEUMONIA, TETANUS, TROPICAL ULCER, VAGINITIS.

Sometimes TURISTA, gas, GUINEA WORM, MALABSORPTION.

Used with other drugs in SEPSIS, TETANUS, for wounds with foul-smelling pus, for tooth infections in third molars.

Contraindications: ALLERGY to this drug, some kinds of blood diseases, concurrent or anticipated use of alcohol. It should not be used in a patient who has SEIZURES or in one who has numbness and tingling. Do not give this to a patient who has PORPHYRIA (a hereditary disease).

Precautions: The patient must *not* drink ALCOHOL while on this drug or for 3 days after taking the last dose. If he does, he will get a severe reaction. There is alcohol in most cough syrups and even rubbing alcohol or hand cream on the skin can cause a reaction. Discontinue the drug if dizziness or uncoordination occur. If you use this medication in a child with ATTENTION DEFICIT DISORDER, he may temporarily become extremely hyperactive.

Side-effects: Nausea, vomiting, abdominal pain, sleepiness, headache, and dark urine occur in only a small percentage of patients. Avoid using this the first three months of pregnancy unless the situation is life-threatening.

Overdose and prolonged usage: LIVER FAILURE; see Protocol C-7.

Dosage: Reduce the dose with LIVER DISEASE. The following are adult doses; reduce dose according to weight for children. The drug is absorbed well rectally; give it this way if your patient is vomiting or he has an ACUTE ABDOMEN; the dose by rectum is 1000 mg every 8 hours.

ACUTE ABDOMEN: 1000 mg three times a day for 5 days by rectum.

AMEBIC LIVER DISEASE: 750 mg three times a day for 10 days.

DYSENTERY: 750 mg three times a day for 5 days or else 2000 mg, single dose, followed by another dose a week later.

ENTERIC FEVER: 500 mg 3 times daily for 10 days.

Gas: Same as TURISTA.

GIARDIASIS: Same as TURISTA. An alternative dose is 2000 mg daily for 3 days.

GUINEA WORM: 400-500 mg three times a day for 5 days.

LARVE MIGRANS in Asia: 400 mg 3 times daily for 3 weeks.

MALABSORPTION: Same as TURISTA.

PELVIC INFECTION: 500 mg twice daily for 14 days, to be used with OFLOXACIN.

PEPTIC ULCER: 500 mg every 8 hours for 14 days, with other medication listed.

PNEUMONIA: Same as ACUTE ABDOMEN.

SEPSIS: Same as ACUTE ABDOMEN.

TETANUS: 500 mg orally every 6 hours or 1000 mg by rectum every 8 hours, for 10 days.

TROPICAL ULCER: 250 mg three times a day until healed.

TURISTA: 250 mg three times a day for 5 days.

VAGINITIS: Bacterial or Trichomonas: 2000 mg, one dose; treat both partners in both cases.

Wound infections: Like TROPICAL ULCER.

Tooth infections: 250-500 mg three times a day until the swelling is down; then take the tooth out.

Alternatives: TINIDAZOLE. NITAZOXANIDE is a new antibiotic that has many of the same uses as Metronidazole. Seek recent information concerning it.

MICONAZOLE

Anti-fungal
Safety class 1 Stability: C Pregnancy: ??
Brand name: Monistat, Daktarin
Indications: CANDIDA, VAGINITIS, some MYCETOMA, TINEA.

Contraindications: ALLERGY to this drug or any "–azole" drug. Do not use in or around the eyes.

Side-effects: None when used in a cream form; do not use the injectable—it is dangerous.

Dosage: Use sparingly twice a day for 2-4 weeks.

MILK OF MAGNESIA

Laxative
Safety class 1 Stability: A
Synonym: Magnesium sulfate.
Indications: Constipation, used to cause diarrhea. Used for INTESTINAL FLUKE.

Contraindications: ACUTE ABDOMEN, ENTERIC FEVER, KIDNEY FAILURE.

Side-effects: Abdominal pain, cramping.

Dosage: 30 ml of 50% solution for adults, every four hours until bowel contents move. For children, 10-30 ml as above.

MILTEFOSINE

Anti-leishmanial drug
Safety class ?2; Stability unknown
Pregnancy: X: Confirm lack of pregnancy before starting and use reliable contraception while taking the drug and for 3 months thereafter.
Anti-Leishmania
Synonym: Hexadecylphosphocholine.
Brand name: Impavido
Indications: CUTANEOUS LEISHMANIASIS, VISCERAL LEISHMANIASIS, PKDL (a complication).

Contraindicaitons: Pregnancy, ALLERGY to this drug, KIDNEY DISEASE, KIDNEY FAILURE.

Precautions: Largely unknown but there are no problems with anti-HIV drugs.

Side-effects: Nausea, vomiting, diarrhea, KIDNEY FAILURE, possibly infertility, HEPATITIS.

Dosage: The usual adult dose in VISCERAL LEISHMANIASIS is 100 mg/day or 2 mg/kg/day for 4 weeks. Reduce the dose according to weight for children. It may be used down to 2 years of age. The dose may be increased up to 2.5 mg/kg/day for 4-6 weeks. For PKDL, the dose is 50 mg twice a day for 12 weeks.

MINOCYCLINE

Antibiotic, similar to DOXYCYCLINE.
Safety class 2 Stability: A, Dark Pregnancy D
Brand names: Minocin, Acnamino, Sebomin.
Indications: BRUCELLOSIS, and indications the same as DOXYCYCLINE. It might be useful for CHANCROID and LEPROSY.

Contraindications: ALLERGY to any DOXYCYCLINE-type drug. **Do not use after the expiration date.** Observe the contraindications under DOXYCYCLINE. Do not use this with oral anticoagulants (blood thinners) or with ANTACID.

Precautions: Like DOXYCYCLINE, this causes sun sensitivity so patients burn easily. It makes patients prone to CANDIDIASIS, masks the signs and symptoms of appendicitis, and causes dark staining of teeth in children under 7 and the offspring of pregnant women who take the drug. The latter effect, however, is not as common or as severe with this as with ordinary TETRACYCLINE. Watch expiration dates; do not use expired drug as it may cause KIDNEY FAILURE. Stop the drug if the patient develops HEPATITIS or a DYSENTERY-type diarrhea.

Side-effects: Abdominal pains, nausea, vomiting, diarrhea, sun-sensitivity.

Dosage: Reduce the dose in the presence of KIDNEY FAILURE.

ANTHRAX exposure: 100 mg twice daily for 60 days plus immediate immunization.

BRUCELLOSIS: 200 mg twice daily; used with other drugs.

CHOLERA: 300 mg, single dose.

LEPROSY: If there is one skin lesion only, it can be used as the sole drug: 100 mg every 12 hours for 6 months. Otherwise combine this with other drugs; the precise dosage is not available.

MALARIA prevention: 100 mg twice daily.

PLAGUE exposure: 100 mg every 12 hours for two days.

Other Diseases: 100 mg twice daily for the same duration as DOXYCYCLINE would be given.

MULTIVITAMINS

Safety class 1 Stability: Variable
Indications: Deficiency of a vitamin, inability to eat a balanced diet, ALCOHOLISM, MALNUTRITION, MENINGITIS, PLANT POISONING due to Argemone oil or Lathyrism, pregnancy, SICKLE CELL DISEASE, TROPICAL ULCER, TUBERCULOSIS, wounds that will not heal easily. It may be helpful in WHOOPING COUGH.

Contraindications: ALLERGY to the particular brand.

Dosage: 1 to 4 non-prescription tablets daily for adult; reduce maximum dose according to weight for children; follow the instructions for your particular preparation.

NALBUPHINE

Narcotic and narcotic antagonist
Safety class 1 Stability: A Pregnancy C
Brand name: Nubain. Generic product is available. Comes in vials of 10 mg.

Indications: Pain not due to head injury. It is particularly useful for HEART ATTACK, MIGRAINE, and PLEURISY.

Contraindications: Head injury, shortness of breath, ALLERGY to this drug, DYSENTERY due to antibiotic usage, any kind of PLANT POISONING or FOOD POISONING. Don't use in a patient who is short of breath or in one with ADDICTION to downers.

Side-effects: Nausea and vomiting; the patient may have a sensation of numbness from the neck down; this is normal and it will pass. The narcotic antagonist effect means that this will cause withdrawal symptoms in a narcotic addict. The patient may become agitated or sedated. He may become constipated.

Precautions: Warn the patient not to engage in hazardous activity while taking this drug.

Dosage: The usual adult dose for severe pain is 10 mg IM every 4 hours. Reduce the dose for less severe pain and according to weight for children.

NARCOTICS

This is a drug class. Examples: NALBUPHINE, CODEINE, meperidine, morphine. See specific drugs. CODEINE is the safest, medically and legally, and the medication which will least likely be stolen. NALBUPHINE and butorphanol are potent pain relievers, related to the narcotics. Do not use any of these drugs in POLIO or for someone short of breath. They decrease the urge to breathe and could kill. Warn patients not to engage in hazardous activities while taking any drug of this class.

NEMA WORM CAPSULE

Veterinary TETRACHLOROETHYLENE; may be used for humans. See TETRACHLOROETHYLENE.

NEOSPORIN, oral

Antibiotic
Safety class 1 Stability: A

Supplied in oral form and in ointments. (For the ointment form see ANTIBIOTIC OINTMENT.)

Indications: Persistent diarrhea; used in ANTIBIOTIC OINTMENTs.

Contraindications: KIDNEY FAILURE when used orally.

Dosage:

TURISTA: Adult dose is 1000 mg every 6 hours; reduce dose according to weight for children.

NELFINAVIR

This is an anti-HIV drug.

NEVIRAPINE

Anti-HIV; Nonnucleoside reverse transcriptase inhibitor
Safety class: Unknown Stability: Unknown
Pregnancy: Unknown
Brand name: Viramune; comes in 200 mg tablets
Indications: HIV INFECTION

Contraindications: ALLERGY to this drug.

Precautions: RIFAMPIN and RIFABUTIN decrease the effectiveness of this drug.

Side-effects: Unknown

Dosage: Pediatric dose is unknown. Adult dose is 1 tablet daily for the first 2 weeks, then 2 tablets daily, one every 12 hours.

NIACIN

B Vitamin
Synonyms: Niacinamide, Nicotinamide
Safety class 1 oral Stability: A Pregnancy C
Safety class 3 injectable

Indications: MALNUTRITION, PELLAGRA.

Contraindications: Prior ALLERGY to the particular form., GALLBLADDER DISEASE, LIVER DISEASE, PEPTIC ULCER, any bleeding problem. Don't use it in the presence of GLAUCOMA, DIABETES, or GOUT.

Precautions: This drug interferes with lab tests for glucose and one test for a hormone.

Side-effects: Flushing, nausea, vomiting, itching. The drug appears in breast milk but this should not be a problem.

Dosage: Initially 50 mg oral 10 times a day; reduce to once a day after the symptoms disappear.

The injectable form **must** be given IV, not IM, and it may cause ANAPHYLAXIS. The dose is 25 mg three times a day.

NICLOSAMIDE

Dewormer, Anthelmintic
Safety Class 2 Stability: ?? Pregnancy B
Brand names: Cestocide, Devermin, Fenasal, Lintex, Mansonil, Niclocide, Radeverm, Sagimid, Vermitin, Yomesan. Supplied as a chewable, 500 mg tablet.

Indications: INTESTINAL FLUKE, TAPEWORM.

Contraindications: This drug can be used in sick and pregnant patients (i.e. other illness and pregnanacy are not contraindications). If you intend to use this for pork TAPEWORM, it is essential that the person not vomit and that you give something to cause diarrhea after the treatment. Otherwise do not use it. It is not very safe for

INTESTINAL FLUKE. PRAZIQUANTEL is safer but more expensive.

Side-effects: Occasionally nausea, vomiting, diarrhea, abdominal pain.

Dosage: Give the drug in the morning on an empty stomach. Have the patient thoroughly chew and swallow the tablets with minimum water. Give something such as MILK OF MAGNESIA to cause diarrhea immediately after the drug, especially with pork TAPEWORM. Dispose of this stool very carefully in a septic system or by burying it deeply. Adults and children over 8 y.o.: 1000 mg hourly for 2 doses. Children 2-8 years old: 500 mg hourly for 2 doses. Children under 2: 250 mg hourly for 2 doses. For dwarf or rat TAPEWORM, use the two daily doses for 5-7 days. For everything else it is used one day only.

NICOTINIC ACID

This is another form of NIACIN except that patients experience flushing, dizziness, heart fluttering, and general itching as a side-effect of the drug. It is not as safe.

NIFURTIMOX

Antichagastic

Safety class 3 Stability: ?? Pregnancy ??

Brand names: Bayer 2502; Lampit. The drug is oral. It comes in tablets of 120 mg.

Indications: CHAGA'S DISEASE; might possibly work for AFRICAN SLEEPING SICKNESS under restricted circumstances.

Contraindications: Any severe previous reactions to the drug.

Precautions: Allergic reactions are common. (See ALLERGY.) Give the drug with ANTACID to avoid stomach upset. Numbness and tingling and weakness may occur. The patient may become very excited and have uncontrolled behavior. Do not use ALCOHOL while taking this drug. The drug is dangerous.

It is very important to treat for the entire duration. Do not undertreat; it is better not to treat at all!

Dosage:

Children: 6 mg/kg every 6 hours for 15 days, then 4 mg/kg every 6 hours for another 75 days; extend this to a total treatment of 120 days if there is chronic disease.

Adults: 5-7 mg/kg daily for 2 weeks; increase this by 2 mg/kg every 2 weeks to 15-17 mg/kg daily by week 10; continue treatment for 120 days total.

NIRIDAZOLE

Dewormer, Anthelmintic

Safety class 3 Stability: Unknown

Brand names: Ambilhar, Bulgarstan. Supplied as 100 mg and 500 mg tablets.

Caution: Ordinarily, this drug should not be used. It is included here because it still is available and used in some places.

Indications: SCHISTOSOMIASIS HEMATOBIUM, SCHISTOSOMIASIS MANSONI, occasionally GUINEA WORM and SCHISTOSOMIASIS JAPONICUM. Sometimes used for amebic DYSENTERY but does not work well for this. Formerly used for AFRICAN SLEEPING SICKNESS.

Contraindications: LIVER FAILURE, HEART FAILURE, severe MALNUTRITION, severe ANEMIA, current use of ISONIAZID. You should be extremely reluctant to use this if the patient has a history of MENTAL ILLNESS or SEIZURES.

Precautions: The drug usually causes nausea and vomiting; give PROMETHAZINE or another anti-nausea medication 1/2 hour before each dose.

Side-effects: Severe side-effects are more frequent in people who have LIVER DISEASE, whatever the cause. It may cause a crisis in those with G6PD DEFICIENCY: Irish, Arabs, Jews, and other persons of Mediterranean or Hispanic ancestry.

Check the urine just before the first dose and again just before the second dose. If the urobilinogen has definitely increased, do not give the second and subsequent doses. This drug turns urine dark and causes an unpleasant body odor. Be careful about the dose. Too much drug causes a change in mood, confusion, SEIZURES, and a rapid pulse. If this happens, decrease the dose. Other side-effects are abdominal cramps, diarrhea, headache, and loss of appetite.

Dosage:

GUINEA WORM: 25 mg/kg daily for 10 days.

SCHISTOSOMIASIS: 25 mg/kg to maximum of 1500 mg daily. May be given in one daily dose, but better to give half this dose twice each day.

S. HEMATOBIUM: 5 days.

S. MANSONI: 10 days.

S. JAPONICUM requires three treatments of 10 days each in three consecutive months. The treatment of S. JAPONICUM must be supervised by a physician.

Alternatives: PRAZIQUANTEL is a better drug for all diseases.

NITAZOXANIDE

Antibiotic

Brand name: Alinia. Available as a suspension of 20 mg/ml and in tablets of 500 mg.

Safety class 3 Stability unknown

Pregnancy unknown

Indications: Many of the same uses as METRONIDAZOLE (which is safer). It is also useful for LIVER FLUKE (in areas other than East Asia and Southeast Asia), in place of CLOXACILLIN for ABSCESS and related conditions, and when METRONIDAZOLE does not work well for PEPTIC ULCER, and/or GASTRITIS. It is used for CRYPTOSPORIDIOSIS and CYCLOSPORIASIS.

Contraindications: Prior ALLERGY to this or related drugs.

Precautions: This interacts badly with a variety of other drugs, causing toxicity.

Side-effects: Nausea, vomiting, diarrhea, abdominal pain.

Dosage: The drug should be given with food. Use higher doses for longer in patients with AIDS.

CRYPTOSPORIDIOSIS: 500 mg twice daily for 3 days in previously healthy patients. Double the dose and prolong the duration in patients with AIDS.

CYCLOSPORIASIS: 500 mg twice daily for 7-10 days.

LIVER FLUKE: 500 mg twice daily for 7 days.

It is best to seek recent advice before using this.

NORFLOXACIN

Brand name: Utinor

See CIPROFLOXACIN or OFLOXACIN and the package insert. This is used for bacterial DYSENTERY, the usual dose being 800 mg, single dose. It can also be used for ENTERIC FEVER in which case it need only be used for 7 days.

NYSTATIN

Antifungal
Safety class 1 usually Stability: C Pregnancy ?
Brand names: Mycostatin, Nystan, others.

Indications: CANDIDIASIS, TINEA, VAGINITIS.

Contraindications: Prior ALLERGY to this drug.

Side-effects: The taste is vile. Occasionally there is nausea, vomiting, and diarrhea. If the patient develops EXFOLITATIVE DERMATITIS, stop the drug immediately.

Dosage:

Vaginal tablets or suppositories: One twice a day for 7 days.

Cream or ointment: Smear sparingly on the affected skin after washing and drying well, twice a day until the rash is cleared plus 2 more days.

Mouth wash: Nystatin 100,000 units per ml; place 1 ml in the mouth and hold it there for as long as possible in the area of the white spots. Do this 4 times a day until the problem is resolved.

Alternatives: MICONAZOLE. Or, sun bathe the affected skin areas 15 minutes daily.

OFLOXACIN

Antibiotic, gram negative and anti-mycobacterial.
Safety class 2 Stability ? Pregnancy C
Brand name: Floxin, Tarivid

Indications: Gram negative infections; CELLULITIS, LEPROSY, TUBERCULOSIS, GONORRHEA, CHLAMYDIA, KIDNEY INFECTION, LYMPHOGRANULOMA VENEREUM, PELVIC INFECTION, PNEUMONIA, PROSTATITIS, SEPSIS, URETHRITIS, URINATRY INFECTION. It works pretty much the same as CIPROFLOXACIN.

Contraindications: ALLERGY to any "–oxacin" antibiotic; prepubertal children; pregnant women. Do not give this together with ANTACIDs. Do not give it to breastfeeding women. It should not be used in those with a history of MENTAL ILLNESS. Do not use this in the presence of LIVER DISEASE or KIDNEY DISEASE without independent professional confirmation.

Precautions: Warn the patient against engaging in hazardous activities when starting on this drug, until the side-effects are known for him. Diabetics may lose control of their blood sugar. Elderly may develop tendonitis.

Side-effects: Headaches, dizziness, insomnia, sun sensitivity, SEIZURES (stop the drug), EXFOLITATIVE DERMATITIS (stop the drug). There may be alterations in pulse and blood pressure, possibly leading to fainting. There may be psychiatric problems such as overt craziness or difficulty moving or feeling.

Dosage: Reduce the dose in the presence of KIDNEY FAILURE. Doses are all oral unless specified otherwise.

Most gram-negative infections: 200 mg twice a day until the patient is better, plus 2 more days.

CHLAMYDIA, 400 mg twice a day for 7 days.

ENTERIC FEVER, 15 mg/kg/day for 2 days or 10 mg/kg/day for 3 days

GONORRHEA: a single dose of 400mg

LEPROSY: 600 mg daily for 8 months.

PELVIC INFECTION: 400 mg twice a day for 14 days; use this with METRONIDAZOLE.

PROSTATITIS: 200 mg twice a day for 28 days.

SEPSIS: 200 mg IV twice daily.

TUBERCULOSIS: 800 mg daily.

URETHRITIS, URINARY INFECTION: 200-400 mg twice a day for 7 days.

OLTIPRAZ

An older worm medication, no longer in use because of bad side-effects.

ORAL CONTRACEPTIVES

See BIRTH CONTROL PILLS

ORNIDAZOLE

See TINIDAZOLE; the drug is similar. Check the package insert for dosage.

ORS

Safety class 1 Stability: A

Synonym: Oral Rehydration Solution.

Brand names: Pedialyte, Ricalyte, Diocalm Junior, Dioralyte, Electrolade, Rehidrat; usually generic product in developing areas.

Recipes to make ORS:

See also Appendix 1, Procedure 2, in Volume I.

(1) Coconut water, used just as it is, works well, or add 1 teaspoon of baking soda to each liter. Do not use this in the presence of KIDNEY FAILURE.

(2) Dissolve the following in 1.0 liter of drinking water:

Ingredient	Weight (grams)	Volume
Glucose	20.0 g	4 teaspoons
Salt (NaCl)	3.5 g	3/4 teaspoon
Baking Soda	2.5 g	1/2 teaspoon
KCl	1.5 g	1/4 teaspoon

Notes:

Glucose is also called dextrose. If unavailable, you may substitute 50 grams of ordinary sugar (1/4 cup), or 50 g uncooked rice powder (1/4 cup) (which should be cooked in some of the water before the other ingredients are added to make one liter of ORS).

Baking soda is sodium bicarbonate, $NaHCO_3$. It is not the same as baking powder. (Some commercial ORS preparations use sodium citrate.)

KCl is commonly available as "salt substitute". It is okay to omit this if it is unavailable. As the patient recovers, citrus fruits, bananas, and potatoes can supply this element.

Relationships: 3 teaspoons = 1 tablespoon; 4 tablespoons = 1/4 cup.

Use the cleanest water you can conveniently find; speed is more important than sterility. Do not heat or boil the solution once it is made up.

Indications: CHOLERA, DEHYDRATION, TURISTA, other diarrhea, DYSENTERY, GASTROENTERITIS, GIARDIASIS, HEAT ILLNESS.

Contraindications: DIABETES,[1] HEART FAILURE, KIDNEY FAILURE. There are no allergic reactions.

Precautions: This is frequently supplied as packets of powder that must be added to water. If too little water is used, the resulting strong salt solution will be deadly. If too much water is used, it will not work as well, but it will not be deadly.

Dosage: It is important to give enough; too much is never a problem. Dehydrated adults (see DEHYDRATION) get a minimum of 3 liters daily; school aged children, 2 liters; preschoolers 1 liter plus another 1/4 liter of plain water. After this minimum, continue giving it until the top of the patient's tongue is still moist 20 minutes after his last drink. Give POTASSIUM additionally unless the patient has KIDNEY FAILURE. In children under 6 months old, give an equal amount of clean, plain water in addition to the ORS and nourishment.

[1] In diabetes, any fluid with sugar in it will make the patient more dehydrated. It is best to rehydrate with a plain solution of 1.5 teaspoons (7 g) of salt per liter of water.

OXAMNIQUINE

Antischistosome, Anthelmintic

Safety class 2-3 Stability: ?? Pregnancy C

Brand names: Mansil, Vansil. Available in 250 mg tablets or 50 mg/ml liquid for children.

Indications: SCHISTOSOMIASIS MANSONI at any stage.

Contraindications: ALLERGY to the drug. Do not use this in patients who have SEIZURES.

Precautions: Warn the patient against engaging in hazardous activities until he knows what side-effects he will have from this drug.

Side-effects: Drowsiness, dizziness, maybe SEIZURES. These effects occur in only a small percentage of patients. The urine may turn orange-red because of the drug. If used excessively, the drug can destroy the bone marrow.

Dosage: Do not give this with food.

In the Americas and east Africa: 10 mg/kg twice a day for one day only.

In the rest of Africa: 15 mg/kg for 2 doses, given twice in one day or once a day for 2 days.

For treating a whole village or area: Treat everyone every 6 months.

PAIN MEDICINES

See Chapter 8 in Volume I, and NARCOTICS (this Index).

PARA-AMINOSALICYLIC ACID

Antituberculosis

Safety class 3 Stability: Unknown

Synonym: PAS

Brand name: Paser; also supplied as generic drug.

Indications TUBERCULOSIS

Contraindications: ALLERGY to this drug.

Side-effects: Nausea, vomiting, diarrhea, fever, rash, HEPATITIS, susceptibility to other infections, similar to CHLORAMPHENICOL fatal reactions. Children seem to have much less problem with side-effects than adults. At any rate, these severe side-effects are not common.

Dosage: 50 mg/kg three times a day. The usual adult dose is 10-12 grams daily.

PARALDEHYDE

Anti-seizure drug, Sedative, Muscle relaxant
Safety class 2 by rectum; 3 if IM
Stability: C Keep below 25°C / 68°F in dark.
Supplied as generic only; it is a liquid chemical.

Indications: Treatment of muscle spasms in TETANUS; treatment of SEIZURES that will not stop, as in HEAT ILLNESS, MALARIA, MENINGITIS, SEPSIS. Occasionally useful as a sedative and for WHOOPING COUGH.

Contraindications: **Do not use drug that is old or discolored or that comes from partially used containers!!!** Bad drug is a corrosive, strong acid. It is brownish or cloudy. It burns if a drop is placed on the skin. Good drug is clear and watery. It does not burn on the skin. Do not use this during pregnancy or breast-feeding unless the patient's situation is desperate and there are no alternatives.

Precautions: Be sure to observe requirements for safe storage. Give IM only in an emergency and then only in the buttocks, remembering to stay in the upper-outer quadrant. Put your needle in deeply. You should use a glass syringe; this drug will dissolve plastic syringes unless you draw up the drug and give it very quickly. Avoid letting the drug contact rubber or plastic.

Warn your patient against engaging in hazardous activities while he is taking it.

Side-effects: This drug has an awful smell, and so will your patient. This is expected. If you use this drug, your patient will be lethargic or unconscious for a longer time after his seizure than he would be otherwise. Pay special attention to his airway.

Dosage:

Sedative: Rectally, give 0.2 ml/kg, mixed in twice this amount of olive or cooking oil. The drug can also be given by mouth if your patient can swallow, same dose as rectally. The IM dose is 0.1 ml/kg, not mixed with oil.

SEIZURES from any cause: rectally, give 0.4 ml/kg, mixed in twice this amount of olive or cooking oil and given as an enema; by injection the dose is 0.2 ml/kg IM to maximum of 10 ml (not mixed with oil).

TETANUS: Same as SEIZURES.

WHOOPING COUGH: Same as the sedative dose.

Alternatives: DIAZEPAM, PHENOBARBITAL, PHENYTOIN SODIUM.

PAROMOMYCIN

Aminoglycoside antibiotic, Dewormer
Safety class 1 oral and cream; 3 injectable.
Stability: Unknown Oral drug probably safe in pregnancy; seek independent confirmation.
Synonym: Aminosidine

Brand names: Farmiglucin, Gabbromycin, Gabbroral, Humatin, Maramicina, Pargonyl, Tricardil. Supplied as 250 mg capsules.

Indications: CRYPTOSPORIDIOSIS, DYSENTERY, both bacterial and amebic; TAPEWORM. It might be useful for GIARDIASIS. By injection, used for VISCERAL LEISHMANIASIS; in a cream, for CUTANEOUS LEISHMANIASIS.

Contraindications: Prior ALLERGY to the drug, an obstructed bowel (abdominal pains and constipation), and KIDNEY DISEASE.

Precautions: The drug may cause abdominal pain and diarrhea. It is not absorbed from the bowel to any extent when given orally. The drug is dangerous when given by injection, but it may be used that way for VISCERAL LEISHMANIASIS; it may cause deafness and/or KIDNEY FAILURE. Do not use this with any other drugs that are toxic to the kidneys. Do not give this to anyone who has muscle weakness.

Dosage: The following are adult doses. Reduce the dose according to weight for children.

CRYPTOSPORIDIOSIS: 10 mg/kg three times daily for 28 days, then 500 mg twice a day maintenance.

DYSENTERY: 500 mg by mouth every 6 hours for 5-10 days.

TAPEWORM: Adults get 1000 mg (1 gram) by mouth every 15 minutes for 4 doses, a total of 4000 mg (4 grams). May be repeated daily for 5 days, but some authorities say that one day is enough.

CUTANEOUS LEISHMANIASIS: Follow local advice.

VISCERAL LEISHMANIASIS: 14-16 mg/kg IM daily for 20 days, **by physician order only**.

PEFLOXACIN

See OFLOXACIN. This drug is similar. The usual dose in LEPROSY is 400 mg daily for 8 months. It might be useful for TUBERCULOSIS; dosage unknown.

PENICILLIN

Antibiotic (gram positive)
Safety class 2 Pregnancy B
Stability: See below under forms of penicillin

Brand names: Too many to list. Generic human and veterinary drug is available.

Indications: ANTHRAX, ARTHRITIS, BARTONELLOSIS, CANCRUM ORIS, CELLULITIS, DIPHTHERIA, middle EAR INFECTION, EYE INFECTION, GONORRHEA, IMPETIGO, LEPTOSPIROSIS, LYME DISEASE, MEASLES, MENINGITIS, PELVIC INFECTION, PIG-BEL, PINTA, PNEUMONIA, RAT BITE FEVER, RELAPSING FEVER, RESPIRATORY INFECTION, RHEUMATIC FEVER, SEPSIS, STREP THROAT, SYPHILIS, TETANUS, TREPONARID, TROPICAL ULCER, URETHRITIS, YAWS. This may also be used for infected teeth other than third molars.

Contraindications: Symptoms of ALLERGY of **any** sort after having received penicillin or any "cillin" drug. There is some cross-allergy with CEPHALOSPORIN. It should not be used with certain diuretics (water pills) or with oral contraceptives (the contraceptives might not work). Some sources say it should not be used during breastfeeding.

Precautions: Keep your patient nearby for 30 minutes after the first dose. Do not use penicillin unless you have EPINEPHRINE available or the condition is life-threatening. Life-threatening conditions are those for which the adult dose is 1000 mg. Do not use this at the same time as DOXYCYCLINE or CHLORAMPHENICOL unless directed to do so. This may cause DRUG ERUPTION when used for SYPHILIS.

Forms of Penicillin:

- ***Penicillin V:***

(Pen VK, Penicillin potassium phenoxymethyl).

Stability: A.

This is the common penicillin *taken by mouth*. It is a form that is not destroyed by stomach acid. It is cheap. It must be taken every 6 hours. 62.5 mg = 100,000 units; 250 mg = 400,000 units.

- ***Penicillin G:***

(benzylpenicillin).

Stability: A dry. Liquid D; refrigerate.

Cheapest *injectable* penicillin. It does not work well by mouth. It must be injected every 2 to 4 hours. The IM injection is painful. It comes as Potassium Penicillin G and Sodium Penicillin G. The usual vial contains 5 million units. The relationship between mg and units is the same as ordinary penicillin and the two drugs are interchangeable. In a very sick patient or when a disease has progressed rapidly, it is best to use injected Penicillin G for the first few doses.

- ***Procaine Penicillin***:

Stability: A dry. Liquid D; refrigerate.

Longer-acting injectable penicillin. It is injected IM; one injection lasts 12-24 hours so it need be given only once or twice daily. It comes in units; use 2.4 million units daily instead of 500 mg of oral penicillin every 6 hours.

- ***Benzathine Penicillin:***

Stability: A dry. Liquid D; refrigerate.

Longest-acting injectable penicillin., it is used for IM injection. One shot lasts for 10 days, so it is ideal for someone who is traveling or who is unreliable. Dosage is one time only unless specified otherwise. Use 2.4 million units of this instead of 250 mg of oral penicillin every 6 hours for 10 days. Do not use this for very ill patients or those in whom the disease has progressed rapidly. Quite expensive.

- ***Triple penicillin:***

A mixture of the above three injectable penicillins.

Dosage:

The following are adult doses; reduce dose according to weight for children. Reduce the dose in KIDNEY FAILURE and in elderly patients. Double the dose in otherwise-healthy patients from Western cultures and in areas where there has been Western-type medical care.

ANTHRAX: 1-2 million units (625-1250 mg) every 2 hours for at least the first 5 days, preferably Penicillin G by injection. Reduce the dose to 500 mg every 4 hours after the patient is most of the way better. Continue the treatment for 14 days. If you have any alternative, do not use a long-acting form until the patient is almost entirely healthy.

ARTHRITIS: 250-500 mg of Penicillin V every 6 hours for 21 days. Long-acting forms may be used. A single injection of 2.4 million units of benzathine penicillin is equivalent to 10 days of oral penicillin for an adult. You should double the dose in a seriously-ill patient from a Western culture.

BARTONELLOSIS: 500 mg Penicillin V every 4 hours for 7 days. Long-acting forms may be used unless the patient is very ill.

CANCRUM ORIS: 500 mg Penicillin V every 6 hours until the hole is getting no worse, plus 4 more days. It is best to use injected Penicillin G for the first few doses.

CELLULITIS: 250-500 mg Penicillin V every 6 hours for 10 days.

DIPHTHERIA: Same as CELLULITIS.

Middle EAR INFECTION: Same as CELLULITIS.

EYE INFECTION with fever: Same as ANTHRAX.

GONORRHEA treatment: 3500 mg Penicillin V by mouth in a single initial dose; then 500 mg every 6 hours for 10 days. Do not use the long-acting forms.

GONORRHEA exposure: 3500 mg Penicillin V as a single dose.

IMPETIGO: Same dose as CELLULITIS until totally healed, minimum 10 days.

LEPTOSPIROSIS: Same as BARTONELLOSIS.

LYME DISEASE: Same as CELLULITIS.

MEASLES: Same as CELLULITIS.

MENINGITIS: Same as ANTHRAX.

PELVIC INFECTION: Same as GONORRHEA treatment.

PIG-BEL: Same as ANTHRAX.

PINTA: Same as TREPONARID.

PNEUMONIA: Same as CELLULITIS; double the dose for a patient from a Western culture.

PYOMYOSITIS: Same dose as CELLULITIS until totally healed; this also requires surgical drainage

RAT BITE FEVER: Same dose as CELLULITIS for 5 days.

RELAPSING FEVER: 500 mg Penicillin V, 4 times daily for 7 days.

RESPIRATORY INFECTION: Same as CELLULITIS.

RHEUMATIC FEVER: Same as CELLULITIS.

SEPSIS: Same as ANTHRAX.

SICKLE CELL DISEASE in children. 125 mg twice daily, from diagnosis until age 5.

STREP THROAT: Same as CELLULITIS.

SYPHILIS, *congenital (newborn):* 50,000 units/kg of Pen G or Procaine Penicillin IM daily for 10 days.

SYPHILIS, *congenital* (adult): 2.4 mu benzathine pen weekly x 3 weeks.

SYPHILIS, *Primary and Secondary*: 500 mg Penicillin V every 6 hours for 14 days, making sure not to miss any doses. Or 1.2 mu of procaine pen daily for 10 days. Or, a single IM injection of 2.4 million units of benzathine Penicillin for adults; 1.2 mu for children 6-15 y.o.; .6 mu for children under 6 y.o. Benzathine Penicillin is recommended by the World Health Organization because of the trouble getting patients to comply with the long treatment required with Penicillin V.

SYPHILIS, latent (between secondary and tertiary): Benzathine Penicillin 2.4 mu weekly for 3 doses.

SYPHILIS, *Tertiary*: Procaine Penicillin 1.2 mu daily for 20 days. or Penicillin G 12-24 mu IV in divided doses for 10-14 days.

TETANUS: Same as CELLULITIS.

TREPONARID: A single dose of Benzathine Penicillin, 600,000 units in children under 6 years old; 1.2 million units in 6-15 years old, and 2.4 million units in adults.

TROPICAL ULCER: Same dose as CELLULITIS until totally healed.

URETHRITIS: Same as GONORRHEA treatment.

YAWS: Same as TREPONARID.

Tooth infection: 250-500 mg every 6 hours until the problem is better, plus another two days. The tooth should also be pulled.

Alternatives: ERYTHROMYCIN in penicillin ALLERGY, but **not** in *MENINGITIS, nor SEPSIS, nor EYE INFECTION with fever;* in these cases use CHLORAMPHENICOL alone.

PENTAMIDINE

Antiprotozoal

Safety class 3 Stability: C Dark Pregnancy ??

Brand names: Lomidine, Pentacarinat, Pentam; Pentam 300, Nebupent. Supplied in vials of 300 mg. It is extremely expensive.

Indications: AFRICAN SLEEPING SICKNESS, Gambian type, prevention and treatment; CUTANEOUS LEISHMANIASIS; PNEUMONIA with HIV INFECTION; VISCERAL LEISHMANIASIS.

Contraindications: ALLERGY to the drug. If the patient has KIDNEY FAILURE or DIABETES, the drug must be given only in a hospital with a physician's supervision. Do not use it with any blood disease, with any heart disease, in the presence of DEHYDRATION, or together with any other drugs that are toxic for the kidney.

Precautions: If the patient becomes sweaty or shaky and panicky or loses consciousness, give him sugar.

Be sure to avoid giving the drug into a vein. It works that way but there are much more serious side-effects.

Warn the patient not to engage in hazardous activities while taking this drug.

This drug interacts badly with many other drugs. It is toxic for liver, kidney, heart, and bone marrow. It is likely to cause major problems in DIABETES.

Side-effects: A drop of blood pressure with fainting; a drop in blood sugar, muscle weakness, local irritation where the injection is given, occasionally PANCREATITIS.

Dosage: Reduce the dose with KIDNEY FAILURE.

AFRICAN SLEEPING SICKNESS prevention: adult dose is 300-400 mg IM every 6 months. Children get 4 mg/kg.

AFRICAN SLEEPING SICKNESS treatment: 4 mg/kg IM daily or every other day, for 10 doses. This does not work for advanced disease with mental symptoms. If it is going to work, you should see an improvement within 24 hours.

CUTANEOUS LEISHMANIASIS: 3 mg/kg every other day for 4 doses or 2 mg/kg every other day for 7 doses.

PNEUMONIA with HIV: 4 mg/kg IM daily for 12-14 days. Improvement should be evident in 4-6 days.

VISCERAL LEISHMANIASIS: 4 mg/kg per dose IM every other day or 3 times weekly for 15-30 doses

PERMETHRIN

Insecticide

Safety class 1-2 Stability unknown

Supplied as 5% cream and 1% lotion

Indications: SCABIES, LICE

Contraindications: ALLERGY to the drug. The drug is safe in pregnancy.

Side-effects: This may cause burning/stinging or an increase in itching.

Dosage:

SCABIES: use the cream; massage it into the skin from the neck on down (not just in the area where there is rash and itching). Leave it on for 12 hours before washing it off.

LICE: wash and dry the area. Put the lotion on for 10 minutes, then rinse it off. Treat clothing also by boiling or ironing.

PHENOBARBITAL

Barbiturate, Sedative, Antiseizure drug
Safety class 2-3 Stability: B
Pregnancy D
Supplied as generic drug.

Indications: Emotional upset, EPILEPSY, SEIZURES, TETANUS, TOXEMIA.

Contraindications: ALLERGY to the drug, breathing problem (such as ASTHMA) unrelated to the indication for the drug, MENTAL ILLNESS, PORPHYRIA. Don't use with other sedatives, in diabetic patients, with birth control pills, or with LIVER FAILURE or KIDNEY FAILURE.

Precautions: If someone has taken the drug regularly for more than 2 weeks and it should be stopped, stop the drug slowly, reducing the dosage over 3 weeks or more. It takes 2-3 days for the drug to start or stop acting. This drug is mildly addicting. Warn the patient not to engage in hazardous activities while taking this drug.

Side-effects: Sleepiness in some people, hyperactivity in some children, agitation and confusion in some elderly people. A rash is the most frequent manifestation of ALLERGY. Newborns of women who have taken the drug during pregnancy sometimes have a problem with bleeding. VITAMIN K is effective for this. The drug may make any pain worse.

More serious adverse reactions:

SERUM SICKNESS: an illness that begins after 10 days or so, with symptoms resembling ANAPHYLAXIS, plus, thereafter, protein in the urine and the development of KIDNEY FAILURE. Stop the drug.

EXFOLIATIVE DERMATITIS: Stop the drug.

Dosage:

Emotional upset: 15-30 mg every 6-12 hours for adults.

SEIZURES, treatment or prevention: 60 mg twice a day for adults. You may increase the dose if ordered by an M.D. Children get 2 mg/kg every 12 hours, by mouth. The dose may be increased to every 8 hours to prevent seizures.

TETANUS: 60 mg by IM injection every 6 hours. You may increase the dose as necessary for control of spasms. Give the lowest dose that will do the job. Reduce the dose according to weight for children.

TOXEMIA: Same as SEIZURES.

Alternatives: PHENYTOIN SODIUM, DIAZEPAM, PARALDEHYDE, others.

PHENYTOIN

Antiseizure drug
Synonym: Phenytoin sodium.
Safety class 3 Stability: A Pregnancy D

Brand name: Dilantin. Generic drug is available. Supplied in capsules of 100 mg and in liquid with 125 mg of drug per 5 ml (1 teaspoon).

Indications: EPILEPSY, LEPROSY, SEIZURES, sprinkled in ABSCESSes, TROPICAL ULCERs, and wounds to aid healing.

Contraindications: Prior ALLERGY to the drug. The other contraindications do not apply to the topical use of the drug for ulcer healing. Given orally: Do not give ACETAZOLAMIDE to a patient taking this drug, except at the direction of a physician. Do not give it to someone with any heart disease or any blood disease. The drug interacts badly with many others so it is best not to use it in patients taking any other drug regularly. Do not give this to patients who have PORPHYRIA, a hereditary disease.

Precautions: It is best to take this with or after a meal. Decrease the oral dose if the patient has evidence of LIVER FAILURE. After the patient has been on it for a while, withdraw the drug slowly over a few weeks or he will have SEIZURES again. Minimum length of time on the drug for seizures is a year.

Side-effects: The oral drug normally will make the gums of the mouth swollen; this is of no consequence. It may increase the growth of body hair. An overdose will cause uncoordination. It may cause a drop in blood pressure and the patient may appear to be intoxicated.

Dosage: There are long-acting forms available which can be taken as a single daily dose. Be sure not to take short-acting forms this way. Reduce the dose in LIVER FAILURE, KIDNEY FAILURE, DIABETES, and in the elderly.

SEIZURES, EPILEPSY: If the patient has not taken the drug for the last week, adults get 300 mg three times **on that first day only**. After that, the average adult gets 100 mg three times daily. Children get 2 mg/kg three times daily. Results: 2 days to 2 weeks.

LEPROSY ABSCESSes and wounds: Open a 100 mg capsule or two and sprinkle the contents into the skin ulcer, abscess, or wound daily before bandaging it.

PILOCARPINE

Eye drops which make the pupil of the eye very small; used in GLAUCOMA; use with the direction of a physician. Do not use this in a red eye (aside from GLAUCOMA) or in the presence of insecticides, anesthetics, ASTHMA, or EYE INFECTION. Side-effects are unusual.

PIPERAQUINE

*****Take care to distinguish this from PIPERAZINE, listed below. They are two entirely different drugs!!**

Anti-malarial, always combined with dihydroartemisinin (see ARTEMISININ)
Safety class: Probably 2 Stability unknown

Pregnancy: unknown

Brand names: Artekin, Duo-Cotecxin are piperaquine plus dihydroartemisinin. Artecom is the same plus TRIMETHOPRIM additionally. Some preparations add PRIMAQUINE as well: piperaquine 320 mg + DHA 32 mg + TRIMETHOPRIM 180 mg + PRIMAQUINE 10 mg.

Indication: MALARIA

Contraindications: Prior ALLERGY to any of the components. G6PD DEFICIENCY for preparations containing PRIMAQUINE.

Precautions: See the entries for each component drug.

Side-effects: Only a rash with piperaquine, and that rarely. Check the side-effects of the other components.

Dosage: Piperaquine 600-640 mg by mouth every 24 hours for 4 doses. If the piperaquine dosage is correct, the dosage of the other components will automatically be correct. Some authorities recommend giving a double dose at the beginning.

PIPERAZINE

*****Take care to distinguish this from PIPERAQUINE, listed above. They are two entirely different drugs.**

Dewormer, Anthelmintic

Safety class 2 Stability: A Pregnancy ??

Brand names: Antepar, Entacyl, Multifuge. Parazine, Perin, Piperate, Pipizan, Vermizine, Worm-expel. Generic veterinary drug is available. Different brand names have different last names for the drug. Adipate, Citrate, Hydrate, and Phosphate are all acceptable last names. Doses given are for piperazine hydrate. Drug labels will generally give equivalences of a particular dose to piperazine hydrate. Most tablets contain the equivalent of 250 or 500 mg piperazine hydrate. Liquids contain 100 mg/ml.

Indications: ASCARIASIS, ENTEROBIASIS.

Contraindications: ACUTE ABDOMEN; ALLERGY to the drug. Contraindicated also with current use of phenothiazines, (anti-nausea medicines) and in patients with a history of SEIZURES.

Precautions: The drug is not absorbed well. Do not use this with PYRANTEL PAMOATE. Piperazine merely paralyzes the worms. Because of this, if the patient is developing an ACUTE ABDOMEN type 3 because of a large wad of worms, it may make his situation worse. Hence it is best not to use it in severe cases. Warn the patient against engaging in hazardous activities while taking this drug.

Side-effects: Nausea, vomiting, diarrhea, abdominal pain, uncoordination. If the patient has a SEIZURE, stop the drug.

Dosage: Reduce the dose in KIDNEY FAILURE or LIVER FAILURE.

ASCARIASIS: Adults: 3500 mg daily for 2 days. Children: 75 mg/kg daily for 2 days to a maximum of 3500 mg daily. Repeat the treatment 2 weeks later, if possible.

ENTEROBIASIS: Same dose for 6 days.

Alternatives: BEPHENIUM HYDROXYNAPHTHOATE, MEBENDAZOLE, PYRANTEL PAMOATE. It is generally better to use the alternative drugs rather than piperazine, although piperazine may be more available.

POTASSIUM

Mineral

Synonyms: Potassium chloride, KCl

Safety class 2 Stability: A

Supplied as potassium chloride in packets of powder or large, dissolvable tablets. There are many forms and sizes.

Indications: To replace lost potassium due to taking FUROSEMIDE, or HYDROCHLOROTHIAZIDE; to replace lost potassium due to severe diarrhea, DYSENTERY, or VOMITING, thus supplementing ORS therapy.

Contraindications: KIDNEY FAILURE, patient taking triamterene or spironolactone.

Precautions: Some potassium preparations cause stomach pain or upset. Be sure to note that doses are given is in meq rather than mg. 75 mg of KCl = 1 meq potassium. Never use injectable potassium. If the patient is very dehydrated, be sure that he is urinating normally before starting this medication.

Dosage: Usual adult dose is 20-30 meq 1 to 3 times daily; reduce dose according to weight for children.

Alternatives: Any of the following foods (same contraindications): apricots, avocado, bananas, citrus fruits, coconut water, dates, papaya, potatoes, pumpkin, spinach, tomatoes. Salt substitute is usually potassium chloride.

PRAZIQUANTEL

Anthelmintic, Dewormer

Safety class 1 Stability: A

Pregnancy: B or C

Brand names: Biltricide, Cesol, Pyquiton. *Veterinary brand names*: Distocide, Droncit. Human drug is supplied as 600 mg tablets that are scored so as to break easily into fourths. The drug is very expensive.

Indications: CYSTICERCOSIS, HYDATID DISEASE; KATAYAMA DISEASE, LIVER FLUKE, PARAGONIMIASIS, SCHISTOSOMIASIS HEMATOBIUM, SCHISTOSOMIASIS INTERCALATUM, SCHISTOSOMIASIS JAPONICUM, SCHISTOSOMIASIS MANSONI, SCHISTOSOMIASIS MEKONGI, TAPEWORM.

Contraindications: ALLERGY to this drug, CYSTICERCOSIS involving the eyes.

Precautions: The drug appears in human milk. Mothers should not nurse for 72 hours after taking the drug. Safety in pregnancy is uncertain. No definite bad effects have been observed. The drug should be used under close physician supervision if it is used with steroids (DEXAMETHASONE, PREDNISONE, or PREDNISOLONE), or with anticonvulsants (DIAZEPAM, PHENYTOIN, or PHENOBARBITAL). Warn the patient not to engage in hazardous activities after taking this drug.

Side-effects: Occasional tiredness, abdominal pain, nausea, vomiting, loss of appetite, sweating, drowsiness, headache, and dizziness. In a patient with KATAYAMA DISEASE, the symptoms may worsen; either give PREDNISONE with the first dose or wait until the symptoms decrease by themselves before using this drug.

Dosage: Reduce the dose in LIVER DISEASE.

CYSTICERCOSIS: 30 mg/kg daily for 10 days; use PREDNISONE and CIMETIDINE also from the day before treatment through day 4 of treatment.

HYDATID DISEASE: 50 mg/kg daily x 2 weeks minimum, given along with ALBENDAZOLE until the cysts have disappeared.

LIVER FLUKE: 25 mg/kg 3 times in one day.

PARAGONIMIASIS: 25 mg/kg 3 times a day for 2 days.

SCHISTOSOMIASIS (all types): 20 mg/kg 3 times in one day. If the patient has SEIZURES because of the disease, repeat the treatment in 10 days and again in 3 weeks. In mass treatment programs for SCHISTOSOMIASIS HEMATOBIUM, a single dose of 20 mg/kg may be sufficient.

TAPEWORM: 10 mg/kg one dose only for fish TAPEWORM. Use 2.5 mg/kg (one dose) for beef TAPEWORM, and 3.4-7.5 mg/kg (one dose) for pork TAPEWORM; 25 mg/kg (one dose) for dwarf and rat TAPEWORM.

Alternatives: NIRIDAZOLE, but it has bad side effects and is not safe when used for SCHISTOSOMIASIS JAPONICUM or SCHISTOSOMIASIS MEKONGI. NICLOSAMIDE may be used for TAPEWORM.

PREDNISOLONE EYE DROPS

Steroid

Safety class 3 Stability: A

Brand name: Blephamide ophthalmic. Supplied as a 1% ophthalmic solution or suspension.

Indications: ALLERGY (vernal conjunctivitis); IRITIS; KERATITIS due to SYPHILIS or ONCHOCERCIASIS; TUBERCULOSIS that affects the eye; LEPROSY reaction.

Contraindications: Uncertainty of the diagnosis and GLAUCOMA. **When used in a patient who has KERATITIS due to HERPES, this drug as eye drops will cause blindness!** If you are not able to stain the eyes with fluorescein to check for HERPES, then do not use these drops. When used for longer than 2 weeks, it is likely to cause CATARACT or GLAUCOMA.

Dosage: One drop 2-4 times daily, depending on the severity of the condition. Do not use these drops for more than 2 weeks.

Result should be evident in less than 24 hours.

PREDNISOLONE

See PREDNISONE. The indications, contraindications, and doses are all the same. The two drugs can be used interchangeably.

PREDNISONE

Corticosteroid

Safety class 3 Stability: C Pregnancy ??

Brand names: Deltasone, Orasone. Supplied as 5 mg tablets, sometimes larger tablets with as much as 40 mg.

Indications: AFRICAN SLEEPING SICKNESS (Gambian type); ALLERGY; ANAPHYLAXIS; ASTHMA; CONTACT DERMATITIS; CYSTICERCOSIS; ECZEMA; ENTERIC FEVER; EXFOLIATIVE DERMATITIS; FILARIASIS; KATAYAMA DISEASE; KIDNEY FAILURE; LEPROSY reactions; some MENINGITIS; ONCHOCERCIASIS; PERICARDITIS; PLANT POISONING, Manicheel; RESPIRATORY INFECTION; spider bites; TRICHINOSIS; TUBERCULOSIS; TYPHUS; WHOOPING COUGH. Possibly useful for ANTHRAX. Used with DEC (drug). Used with PRAZIQUANTEL for SCHISTOSOMIASIS MANSONI or SCHISTOSOMIASIS JAPONICUM.

Contraindications: Used in a patient with STRONGYLOIDIASIS it may cause SEPSIS and death. If this is a possibility, treat for STRONGYLOIDIASIS before using this drug.

Probably should not be used in pregnancy because it may cause cleft palate in the baby.

The drug may activate dormant TUBERCULOSIS. With a history of TB or in an area where TB is common, the drug should be used only with a physician's supervision.

Do not use in the presence of CHAGA'S DISEASE or HEPATITIS B or C, or PORPHYRIA.

Do not use this with untreated fungal infections or with myasthenia gravis.

Do not give this in HIV INFECTION, heart disease, with any disease involving the bowel, with eye diseases or with medicines for ARTHRITIS.

Don't give it the same time as any vaccines (the vaccines won't work) or to someone on diuretics (water pills).

Precautions: It is very important not to use this drug for more than 5 days at a time before stopping it for at least a week, unless there are specific directions to the contrary. If used longer, it needs to be stopped gradually, over weeks, reducing the dose every other day. If the patient has an emotional breakdown, stop the drug, gradually if he has been taking it for more than 5 days. The drug may activate a problem with amebae, causing AMEBIC LIVER DISEASE or DYSENTERY. Regard any diarrhea side-effect as amebic DYSENTERY, in areas where amebae are common. Have the patient wear a medical ID bracelet if he travels while taking the drug.

Side-effects: The drug both decreases immunity (patients are likely to get something else) and it masks fever (the patient won't have a fever with a disease that ordinarily causes a fever) which makes diagnosis very difficult. Additionally, there are bad long-term side effects of the drug: muscle weakness, brittle bones, PEPTIC ULCER, DIABETES, SHOCK, death, to name a few. These never occur if the drug is used for 5 days or less. **The dose of the drug is not nearly as critical as the length of time it is used.**

Dosage: The adult doses are given. Reduce the dose according to weight for children.

AFRICAN SLEEPING SICKNESS: For Gambian type, give 1 mg/kg/day up to 40 mg, for the duration of the treatment, then gradually reduce the dose over about 3-4 weeks.

ALLERGY: 10 mg daily for 1-2 days, may extend to 5 days.

ANAPHYLAXIS: 40 mg, usually one dose but you may give this daily for 2 days.

ANTHRAX: 10 mg daily for 5 days.

ASTHMA: Same as ALLERGY.

CONTACT DERMATITIS: 10 mg daily for 2-3 days.

CYSTICERCOSIS: 40 mg daily for 5 days, beginning the day before treatment with PRAZIQUANTEL.

Given with DEC: Same as ANTHRAX.

ECZEMA: Same as ANTHRAX.

ENTERIC FEVER: 40 mg immediately, then 20 mg every 6 hours for 2 more doses.

EXFOLIATIVE DERMATITIS: Same as ENTERIC FEVER.

FILARIASIS: Same as ANTHRAX.

KATAYAMA DISEASE: Same as ANAPHYLAXIS.

KIDNEY FAILURE: Use 40 mg daily to begin with; this will have to be continued under a physician's supervision as it will probably need to be continued beyond 5 days.

LEPROSY reactions: 40 mg daily for 5 days.

ONCHOCERCIASIS: Same as ANTHRAX.

PERICARDITIS: Same as ANTHRAX.

PLANT POISONING, Manicheel: Same as ANAPHYLAXIS.

RESPIRATORY INFECTION: Same as ANTHRAX.

SCHISTOSOMIASIS: Same as ANTHRAX.

Spider bites: 20 mg daily for 2 days.

TRICHINOSIS: Same as ANTHRAX.

TUBERCULOSIS: 60 mg daily for 4 weeks, then decrease gradually over 3 months.

TYPHUS: Same as ENTERIC FEVER.

WHOOPING COUGH: Same as ANTHRAX.

Results: It takes about 6 hours for the drug to have any effect.

Alternatives: DEXAMETHASONE, HYDROCORTISONE. 0.75 mg of DEXAMETHASONE is equivalent to 5 mg of PREDNISONE or prednisolone and 20 mg of HYDROCORTISONE. In ASTHMA it is better to use inhaled corticosteroids rather than oral.

PRIMAQUINE

Malaria preventive.

Safety class 1 Stability: C Pregnancy ??

The drug is very toxic in overdose for children; a small overdose can kill.

Supplied as generic drug in 7.5 and 15 mg tablets.

Indications: Radical cure of MALARIA to be taken when leaving a malarious area for an extended period of time.

Contraindications: Pregnancy, ALLERGY to the drug, allergy to quinacrine, allergy to iodoquinol (a related drug).

G6PD DEFICIENCY which is most common in persons of Mediterranean descent. Do not give this to persons of Mediterranean (or Irish) descent unless they have been tested and have no or merely a mild G6PD DEFICIENCY.

Do not give it at the same time as the drug quinicrine.

It can be used in pregnancy if the infant has no G-6-PD DEFICIENCY.

Precautions: Watch for urobilinogen in the urine of people taking this drug and stop the drug if you find it.

Side-effects: Abdominal cramps, nausea, mild ANEMIA. These effects occur in only a small percentage of patients.

Dosage: 15 mg daily for 14 days; should be taken with food. For persons of Mediterranean heritage (with a mild G6PD DEFICIENCY), give 45 mg once each week for 6 weeks. In either case, the critical factor in preventing relapse is the total amount of drug taken. This should be 420 mg.

PROCHLORPERAZINE

Phenothiazine, Sedative, Antinausea

Safety class 2 Stability: B, Dark Pregnancy C

Brand name: Compazine. Generic drug is available. Supplied as 5 mg and 10 mg tablets, 10 mg and 25 mg suppositories.

Indications: Nausea, vomiting, emotional upset.

Contraindications: HEART FAILURE; LIVER DISEASE, some blood diseases, lethargic or unconscious patient, children less than 20 lb (10 kg), children who are quite ill or who have DEHYDRATION which is not yet corrected, or who have severe HEPATITIS. If you are desperate to get fluids or medicines down a small or ill child, you may use the drug, once or twice only. Do not use in breastfeeding women.

Precautions: Occasionally patients get muscle spasms as a side-effect. This is harmless but terrifying. Treat them with DIPHENHYDRAMINE IM; it is best not to give this unless you have DIPHENHYDRAMINE available.

Patients become sleepy. Warn the patient not to engage in hazardous activities while taking this drug.

The drug interferes with many different lab tests. Don't believe lab results on blood drawn while the person is taking this.

Side-effects: The most common one is a fall in blood pressure when the patient suddenly stands up. Other effects are worsening of GLAUCOMA, constipation, inability to pass urine (especially in older men), susceptibility to HEAT ILLNESS, dry mouth, decrease in sweating, rapid pulse, sensitivity to light, blurred vision. These effects occur in only a small percentage of patients. The drug causes sun sensitivity: burning with minimal exposure. Routine, long-term usage of this drug may cause PARKINSON'S DISEASE.

Dosage: Reduce the dose for the elderly. The dose by mouth and by IM injection is the same. By suppository more drug is given since less is absorbed.

Nausea: Adults: 5-10 mg orally every 3 hours as needed for nausea and vomiting. Rectal suppository dose is 25 mg every 6 hours.

Children 20-40 kg (44-88 lb): 2.5-5 mg oral every 6 hours.

Children 15-20 kg (33-44 lb): 2.5 mg oral every 6 hours.

Children 10-15 kg (22-33 lb): 2.5 mg oral every 8 hours.

Emotional upset: Adults get 10-20 mg orally once, then 5-10 mg every 6 hours. Children get the same dose as for nausea.

Alternatives: PROMETHAZINE is a cheaper and safer alternative. Other alternatives are CHLORPROMAZINE, Mellaril, Sparine, Stelazine. Dosages vary; indications, contraindications, precautions, etc. are similar. Check the package insert and follow instructions for your product. You may use PHENOBARBITAL as a sedative.

PROGUANIL

Malaria preventive
Safety class 1 Stability: A
Brand name: Paludrine.
Equivalent drug: Chloroguanide.

Indications: MALARIA prevention, enlarged spleen with SICKLE CELL DISEASE, TROPICAL SPLENOMEGALY, MALARIA prevention, MALARIA treatment, used with ATOVAQUONE.

Contraindications: ALLERGY to the drug.

Precautions: In some areas MALARIA is resistant to this. If the patient is in very early pregnancy, she should take FOLINIC ACID with this; it is not contraindicated in pregnancy. If this is taken at the same time as the oral typhoid immunization, the immunization might not take effect. Try to avoid this.

Side-effects: Occasionally nausea and loss of appetite occur. These decrease with continued usage.

Dosage:

200 mg daily, adult dose, for MALARIA prevention and for the large spleen of SICKLE CELL DISEASE.

MALARIA treatment: 400 mg daily for 3 days, together with ATOVAQUONE.

MALARIA treatment: There is a combination drug: ARTEMISININ (artesunate) 4 mg/kg plus DAPSONE 2.5 mg/kg plus proguanil 8 mg/kg all daily for 3 days.

PROMETHAZINE

Antinausea, Sedative
Safety class 1 Stability: A, Dark. Pregnancy C
Brand name: Phenergan; generic drug is available. Supplied as 25 and 50 mg tablets. Suppositories, 12.5, 25, and 50 mg available (same dosage). Injectable drug is available (same dosage).

Indications: Nausea, vomiting, emotional upset from any cause. It is used in many illnesses.

Contraindications: Prior ALLERGY to the drug; age under 1 year, possibly GLAUCOMA or ACUTE ABDOMEN. The drug should not be used with other sedatives or in a hot environment. It should not be used in women who are breastfeeding.

Precautions: Since the drug is sedative, do not give it to someone who has to drive or work machinery or stay awake. Do not use this drug for WHOOPING COUGH. The patient should not drink ALCOHOL while taking this. The drug causes sun sensitivity.

Side-effects: The most common one is a fall in blood pressure when the patient suddenly stands up. Other effects are worsening of GLAUCOMA, constipation, inability to pass urine (especially in older men), susceptibility to HEAT ILLNESS, dry mouth, decrease in sweating, rapid pulse, sensitivity to light, blurred vision. These effects occur in only a small percentage of patients. Long-term use can lead to PARKINSON'S DISEASE.

Dosage: Reduce the dose for the elderly.

Adults get 50 mg every 6 hours as needed. This may be increased to 75 or 100 mg if necessary. Children get 1 mg/kg every 6 hours as needed. The dose is the same by mouth, by suppository, or by IM injection.

Alternatives: CHLORPROMAZINE (Largactil), PROCHLORPERAZINE.

PROPRANOLOL

Beta blocker, Antihypertensive

Safety class 2 Stability: A, Dark Pregnancy C

Brand name: Inderal. Supplied as 10, 20, 40, 60, and 80 mg tablets. Long-acting forms are available which may be taken only twice daily. Do not use injectable.

Indications: HEART FAILURE, hypertrophic kind; HYPERTENSION; MIGRAINE HEADACHE; sometimes a rapid pulse; a physician might use it for ANGINA but you should not; advanced liver disease due to SCHISTOSOMIASIS MANSONI or SCHISTOSOMIASIS JAPONICUM.

Contraindications: ASTHMA; chronic RESPIRATORY INFECTION; other kinds of HEART FAILURE; pulse less than 60; DIABETES. Do not give this at the same time as anti-depressant medication. Do not use it with alcoholics.

Precautions: If HEART FAILURE develops, withdraw the drug. In a patient with heart trouble, the drug must be stopped gradually, not suddenly.

Blacks may be resistant to propranolol; it may not adequately lower their blood pressure.

Warn the patient against engaging in hazardous activities while taking this drug.

Side-effects: Nausea, vomiting, diarrhea, or constipation. These effects occur in only a small percentage of patients.

Rarely there is insomnia, bad dreams, or dizziness. Depression and fatigue are relatively common.

There may be decreased sexual functioning.

Dosage: 10-40 mg by mouth every 6-8 hours. Sometimes slow-release forms are available, which can be taken less frequently. In general this must be maintained indefinitely. Seek professional advice for the dosage in SCHISTOSOMIASIS.

PSEUDOEPHEDRINE

Decongestant

Safety class 1 Stability: A Pregnancy B

Brand names: Sudafed, Galpseud. Also comes under a variety of names as an ingredient in cold tablets. It is frequently combined with antihistamines. See DIPHENHYDRAMINE for a description of what antihistamines do. Comes as 30 mg and 60 mg tablets and 120 mg sustained release tablets.

Indications: Stuffy nose due to a RESPIRATORY INFECTION.

Contraindications: HYPERTENSION out of control, ANGINA, some kinds of HEART FAILURE. Do not give this at the same time as anti-depressant medicaion or blood pressure medications.

Precautions: May make the patient shaky; it is a mild stimulant. In rare cases it might cause SEIZURES and an irregular pulse.

Dosage: 30 or 60 mg by mouth every 4 hours as needed. Sustained release tablets are taken every 12 hours. Use this for a maximum of 5 days.

PYRANTEL PAMOATE

Dewormer; Anthelmintic

Safety Class 1 Stability: A Pregnancy ??

Brand names: Antiminth, Combantrin, Felex, Helmex, Imathal, Nemex, Piranver, Pyraminth, Strongit T. Supplied as 125 mg (base) tablets and as a liquid suspension for children, 250 mg base per 5 ml.

Indications: ASCARIASIS, ENTEROBIASIS, HOOKWORM, possibly STRONGYLOIDIASIS. Used for TURISTA, other diarrhea, or MALABSORPTION not responsive to other treatments. This is also a good drug for routine deworming.

Contraindications: ALLERGY to the drug. The drug is not absorbed to any extent and therefore is safe in pregnancy. Do not use this with PIPERAZINE. Do not use it in children less than 2 years old.

Precautions: Might cause some abdominal pain. Before using this, at least partially treat DEHYDRATION, ANEMIA, and/or MALNUTRITION if the patient has one or more of these. Do not use this medicine on an extremely ill, nearly-dying patient. The drug will increase blood levels of THEOPHYLLINE, possibly causing toxicity.

Side-effects: Nausea, vomiting, diarrhea, abdominal pains, headache, dizziness, or fever. These effects occur in only a small percentage of patients. If used excessively, it can destroy the bone marrow.

Dosage: You may need to decrease the dosage in LIVER DISEASE, ANEMIA, and/or MALNUTRITION. For everything: Start with small initial doses of 1 and 2 mg/kg; then give 11 mg/kg to a maximum of 1000 mg, single dose.

Alternatives: ALBENDAZOLE, BEPHENIUM HYDROXYNAPHTHOATE, MEBENDAZOLE, PIPERAZINE.

PYRAZINAMIDE

Antituberculous

Safety class 2 Stability: ?? Pregnancy C

Supplied as generic 500 mg tablets.

Indications: TUBERCULOSIS; particularly valuable if the patient has TB MENINGITIS or cavities in his lungs (very abnormal lung sounds).

Contraindications: LIVER FAILURE, HEPATITIS. Do not give in the presence of GOUT or DIABETES or PORPHYRIA. The drug appears in breast milk, but that is probably harmless since it is sometimes prescribed for babies.

Side-effects: Sore joints, nausea, vomiting, loss of appetite, fatigue, fevers, flushing. This may cause HEPATITIS, especially at higher doses; stop the drug for this. Also it may cause an attack of GOUT in someone predisposed. It tastes terrible.

Overdose and prolonged usage: LIVER FAILURE see Protocol C-7.

Dosage: Reduce the dose in KIDNEY FAILURE and in LIVER DISEASE.

Daily dosage:

- 3-5 kg: 1/4 of a 500 mg tablet daily
- 6-8 kg: 1/2 of a 500 mg tablet daily
- 9-15 kg: 1 500-mg tablet daily
- 16-21 kg: 1.5 500-mg tablets daily
- 22-28 kg: 2 500-mg tablets daily
- 29-34 kg: 2.5 500-mg tablets daily
- 35-44 kg: 3 500-mg tablets daily
- 45 kg or more: 4 500-mg tablets daily

Thrice-weekly dosage:

- 6-8 kg: 3/4 of a 500-mg tablet
- 9-15 kg: 1.25 500-mg tablets
- 16-21 kg: 2 500-mg tablets
- 22-28 kg: 2.5 500-mg tablets
- 29-34 kg: 3 500-mg tablets
- 35-44 kg: 4 500-mg tablets
- 45 kg or more: 5 500-mg tablets

Twice weekly dosage:

- 3-5 kg: 1/2 of a 500 mg tablet
- 6-8 kg: 1 500-mg tablet
- 9-15 kg: 2 500-mg tablets
- 16-21 kg: 3 500-mg tablets
- 22-28 kg: 4 500-mg tablets
- 29-34 kg: 5 500-mg tablets
- 35-44 kg: 6 500-mg tablets
- 45 kg or over: 7 500-mg tablets

PYRIDOXINE

B vitamin; Vitamin B_6

Safety class 1 Stability: A.

Indications: Prevention of side-effects of ISONIAZID, (used in the treatment of TUBERCULOSIS). May be used for the vomiting of pregnancy.

Contraindications: None

Dosage: 25 mg a couple times a week is probably more than enough for an adult. Reduce dose according to weight for children, but just to conserve drug. Pyridoxine is non-toxic. For the vomiting of pregnancy, use 25 mg three times daily.

Alternatives: Most multivitamins don't contain pyridoxine. Sweet bananas contain quite a bit of pyridoxine, as do peanuts and meat.

PYRIMETHAMINE

Antimalarial

Safety class 1 Stability: B, Dark Pregnancy C

Brand names: Daraprim, Malocide; combined with sulfadoxine in FANSIDAR. Supplied in tablet form as 25 mg of base per tablet and as a liquid with 7.8 mg per 5 ml (1 teaspoon).

Indications: Prevention of MALARIA; used with SULFADIAZINE in the treatment of TOXOPLASMOSIS; used with sulfadoxine (as in FANSIDAR) in the prevention and treatment of MALARIA. It should not be used in some people with ANEMIA.

Contraindications: Early pregnancy, ALLERGY to the drug. Do not use it with FANSIDAR. Do not give it to patients with PORPHYRIA.

Precautions: Best not to use during pregnancy for preventing MALARIA if there are other alternatives. Do not use this alone for MALARIA prevention in children; there have been reports of fatal MALARIA in children so treated. If used at all during very early pregnancy, give FOLINIC ACID. Not recommended for malaria prevention by some government agencies because of rare fatalities attributed to it. If there is new-onset ANEMIA, stop the drug.

Side-effects: Nausea, vomiting, diarrhea, loss of appetite.

Dosage:

MALARIA prevention **not recommended**: Expatriate adults get 50 mg weekly. Expatriate children get 50 mg on entering the area, then 25 mg per week. Nationals get the same dose once a month at first; if this is inadequate protection, increase to every 3 or 2 weeks. It is best to give CHLOROQUINE also with this.

TOXOPLASMOSIS: Adults with AIDS: 100-200 mg daily. Adults without AIDS: 25-50 mg three times a day for 2-5 days, then 25-50 mg daily for 3-4 weeks. The children's dose is 2 mg/kg, given according to the same schedule. This must always be given along with SULFADIAZINE or CLINDAMYCIN.

Alternative: CHLOROQUINE in areas where MALARIA is sensitive to that drug.

PYRONARIDINE

Antimalarial, always combined with ARTEMISININ

Safety class 2 Stability unknown

Pregnancy: Unknown Supplied as 100 mg tablets.

Brand name: Malaridine

Indications: MALARIA

Contraindications: ALLERGY to the drug, possibly pregnancy.

Side-effects: Abdominal pain and nausea, headache, diarrhea, not severe.

Dosage: For adults: Day 1: 8mg/kg every 12 hours for 2 doses; Days 2 and 3: 8mg/kg single dose daily.

QUINIDINE

Antimalarial; antiarrhythmic heart drug.
Safety class 3 Stability: C Pregnancy C[1]

Brand names: Cardioquin, Duraquin, Quinaglute, Quinalan, Quinidex. Generic drug is available. Supplied as injectable and as tablets of various sizes.

Indications: Falciparum MALARIA, when QUININE either is not available or does not work; occasionally for abnormal heart rhythms, when prescribed by a physician.

Contraindications: ALLERGY to this drug, some kinds of heart disease, an irregular pulse. Non-Blacks with severe G6PD DEFICIENCY should not take this drug.

Precautions: If this is taken at the same time as grapefruit or its juice, the drug may reach toxic levels, causing life-threatening side-effects.

This is ordinarily a heart medicine. It can cause sudden death when not used properly. It interacts badly with many other medications and thus should only be used on a physician's recommendation. In particular, avoid using it with MEFLOQUIN, QUININE, ACETAZOLAMIDE, any other heart medicines, with myasthenia gravis, and with any diuretics (water pills).

The drug is sometimes associated with altered electrical activity in the heart; this, in turn, is sometimes associated with sudden death. Thus this should not be combined with other such drugs. The medical jargon is that it prolongs the QT interval.

In Western countries it is more readily available than injectable QUININE. When given IV, it should be used in an intensive care unit, with heart monitoring. Where heart monitoring is not available, it must be used in life-threatening circumstances only, when there is no other alternative. If/when there are problems obtaining it, help may be obtained from the Eli Lilly Company: 800-821-0538 or from the CDC malaria hotline: 770-488-7788.

If given orally and "gluconate" is the last name, the drug is absorbed slowly. "Sulfate" is a better last name when rapid action is desirable. Other precautions are the same as for QUININE. with the additional provision that you should watch for a drop in blood pressure.

Side-effects: Headache, drop in blood pressure, ringing in the ears, nausea, vomiting, diarrhea, abdominal pains.

Dosage: Reduce the dose with KIDNEY FAILURE, LIVER FAILURE (see Protocol C-7), HEART FAILURE, and in the elderly.

MALARIA: 8 mg/kg of base orally every 8 hours for 7 days. The dose for Quinidine gluconate[2] IV is 10 mg salt/kg to a maximum of 600 mg, loading dose infused slowly over 1-2 hours, followed by 0.02 mg/kg/minute continuously until able to take oral therapy.

QUININE

Antimalarial

Synonym: Quinine sulfate.

Safety class 2 oral, 3 IV Stability: C

Pregnancy: rated as X (occasionally causes miscarriage or premature birth but malaria is more likely to do this)

Brand names: Aristochin, Dentojel, Quinate, Quinsan, Quiphile, others. Generic drug also available. Supplied as 100, 130, 195, 260, 300, and 325 mg tablets and capsules and as injectable. Sometimes quinine is combined with antibiotics. If you use these combinations, pay careful attention to the dose of quinine, since this is more toxic in overdose than the antibiotics with which it is combined.

Indications: Severe MALARIA; sometimes muscle cramps at night.

Contraindications: Pregnancy if used for muscle cramps; breastfeeding; pre-existing ringing in the ears; a recent, severe illness that resulted in loss of vision; a previous serious reaction to this drug, (ALLERGY or some other reaction). In patients with very irregular heart beats, it is best to use it with professional medical supervision.

Do not use this drug with ASPIRIN, nor with aluminum-containing ANTACIDs.

Do not use it with patients who have myasthenia gravis. (a type of muscle weakness) or in G6PD DEFICIENCY in non-Blacks.

Do not use the drug in diabetics except with physician supervision.

Precautions: **Never give quinine IM!** Quinine occasionally causes miscarriage but untreated MALARIA is much more likely to cause miscarriage.

The drug causes HYPOGLYCEMIA which can lead to SEIZURES, BRAIN DAMAGE, and death. Be sure to give sugar along with the drug. Pregnant women and children are particularly vulnerable to this problem.

Occasionally a patient will develop swelling around face and neck—**stop the drug.**

The drug is sometimes associated with altered electrical activity in the heart; this, in turn, is sometimes associated with sudden death. Thus this should not be combined with other such drugs. The medical jargon is that it prolongs the QT interval.

Side-effects: Occasionally a patient will experience flushing, itching, rash, fever, belly pain, ringing in the ears, decreased vision. Stop the drug if this occurs soon

[1] This rarely causes miscarriage but malaria is much more likely than the drug to cause miscarriage.

[2] That is, 10 mg/kg of the quinidine gluconate, the drug including both names as distinct from the base only.

after you start it. Reduce the dose if it happens after a couple of hours, then stop the drug if symptoms do not disappear within 6 hours or if it happens with the next (reduced) dose.

Stop the drug if the patient has a loss of vision that lasts more than an hour. Most vision loss is reversible when the drug is stopped, but this may occasionally cause permanent blindness.

Reduce the dose of the drug if the pulse becomes excessively fast, slow, or irregular.

Try to use another antimalarial drug along with this, to discourage the development of resistance.

Overdose: Permanent blindness (dilated pupils).

Prolonged usage: LIVER FAILURE (see Protocol C-7).

Dosage: Reduce the dose with KIDNEY FAILURE or with LIVER FAILURE.

Doses are given orally; use a stomach tube if the patient cannot swallow or is unconscious; see Volume I, Appendix 1. (It must not be injected IM, since it damages the muscle and it is dangerous used that way. It is absorbed into the blood stream erratically so the patient may get none at all at first and then get an overdose the next time it is given, killing him or making him blind.) The drug can be given rectally. The rectal dose is 2 times the oral dose if the liquid, injectable form is used.

MALARIA, severe: Initially 20 mg/kg for first dose only, given IV over 4 hours; thereafter 10 mg/kg IV or orally every 8 hours for 7-14 days for adults. Change from IV to oral medicines when the patient can swallow. Children's dose is 10 mg/kg every 8 hours. Quinimax is a liquid mixture of quinine-like drugs. It may be given IV at 8 mg/kg every 8 hours. It may also be given by rectum (enema) at 20 mg/kg initially followed by 15 mg/kg every 8 hours for a total of 3 days.

A good combination for MALARIA reportedly is AZITHROMYCIN 500 mg plus quinine 10 mg/kg, both every 8 hours for 3 days.

Leg cramps: 200-300 mg at night before retiring.

Alternatives: CHLOROQUINE used together with CHLORPHENIRAMINE. Totoquine is a cheap mixture of quinine and related compounds. It is used exactly the same as quinine, same doses, same precautions. QUINIDINE can likewise be used; see previous entry. It works better than quinine in some areas of the world.

QUINOLONES

This is a class of antibiotics; CIPROFLOXACIN, NORFLOXACIN, OFLOXACIN, and PEFLOXACIN are examples. These are fairly new drugs and therefore expensive. They are useful for infections that do not respond to other antibiotics, such as CHANCROID, KIDNEY INFECTION, PNEUMONIA, TYPHOID FEVER, bacterial DYSENTERY, BRUCELLOSIS, and SPOTTED FEVER. The last two drugs have been found to successfully treat LEPROSY. Other antibiotics in this class all end in "-oxacin". These drugs may (rarely) cause dizziness, confusion, hallucinations, seizures and sensory changes. Patients may develop tendonitis and/or tendon rupture due to these drugs. CIPROFLOXACIN 500 mg is roughly equivalent to NORFLOXACIN 400 mg or OFLOXACIN 300 mg.

RANITIDINE

Histamine receptor antagonist
Safety class 2 Stability A Pregnancy B
Brand name: Zantac

Indications: GASTRITIS, PEPTIC ULCER, ANAPHYLAXIS.

Contraindications: Prior ALLERGY to this drug.

Precautions: Stomach acid serves a useful function to kill bacteria taken in by mouth. When acid is neutralized or eliminated by antacids or drugs like this one, it leaves the patient vulnerable. Hence special attention should be paid to food sanitation.

This drug interacts badly with quite a number of other drugs, especially KETOCONAZOLE.

If the pulse increases or decreases, then stop the drug

Avoid using this in patients with PORPHYRIA.

Dosage: Reduce the dose to ½ of that prescribed in the presence of KIDNEY FAILURE. Reduce the dose somewhat with LIVER FAILURE. Reduce dose according to weight for children.

ANAPHYLAXIS: 500 mg IV, IM, or orally every 6 hours for 3 days.

Other indications: Adults: 150 mg twice daily or 300 mg at night only.

RIBAVIRIN

Antiviral
Safety class 2-3 Pregnancy: X[1]
Stability: C dry. Liquid, use within 24 hrs.
Brand names: Tibavirin, Virazole.

Indications: Some ARBOVIRAL FEVER, any HEMORRHAGIC FEVER caused by a virus except for EBOLA FEVER, some HEPATITIS, LASSA FEVER.

Contraindications: ALLERGY to the drug, patient taking DIGOXIN currently, possibly pregnancy. This drug causes harm to the fetus in all animals tested. However, if the mother and child will both die anyway if the drug is not given (for example, severe LASSA FEVER) it may be worthwhile to use it. Pregnant women should not be in a room where this is used and pregnant nurses should not handle it.

[1] Not only is it contraindicated for pregnant women but pregnant medical staff should not handle the drug nor should a pregnant woman be in the room where it is used.

Precautions: May cause ANEMIA, usually slight; may cause a headache or aggravate shortness of breath in someone with RESPIRATORY INFECTION.

Dosage: Adult dose is 30 mg/kg up to a maximum of 2000 mg by mouth initially followed by 16 mg/kg up to 1000 mg maximum every 6 hours for 4 days. Follow this with 8 mg/kg every 8 hours for 6 days. In very ill patients, use 2000 mg IV initially, then 1000 mg IV or orally every 8 hours for 4 days.

RIFABUTIN

Brand name: Mycobutin

This is a new antibiotic/antituberculous medication, related to RIFAMPIN, same indications, contraindications, and precautions. However, the usual dosage is about half that of RIFAMPIN and consequently the adverse side-effects are much less common and less severe. It will work in some cases even in TB that is resistant to RIFAMPIN. Being new, the drug is probably expensive.

RIFAMIXIN

Brand name Xifaxin

This is an antibiotic that is not absorbed from the bowel into the blood stream. It is used for bacterial infections of the bowel, in particular for TURISTA (traveller's diarrhea). The usual dose is 200 mg three times daily. Seek independent information before using this. It is new and thus very expensive.

RIFAMPIN

Antibiotic, Antituberculous

Safety class 1 Stability: C, dark

Synonym: Rifampicin

Brand names: Rifadin, Rifobac, Rimactane. Supplied as 150 and 300 mg tablets.

Indications: ABSCESS, ANTHRAX, BARTONELLOSIS, BRUCELLOSIS, BURULI ULCER, LEPROSY, MENINGITIS prevention, some MYCETOMA, OSTEOMYELITIS, PYOMYOSITIS, Q FEVER, some SPOTTED FEVER, TRENCH FEVER, TUBERCULOSIS, itching due to JAUNDICE.

Contraindications: ALLERGY to the drug; HEPATITIS, but an M.D. may overrule this, ALCOHOLISM. Current usage of some drugs for HIV INFECTION.

Precautions: Oral contraceptives may not work well when a patient is on this. You may need to increase the dose of some other drugs which the body eliminates more rapidly in patients taking rifampin. The drug appears in breast milk but this is probably harmless because it is, at times, prescribed for infants.

Side-effects: This turns urine, sweat, and tears bright orange. If the urine is not orange, the person has not taken the drug. It will turn soft contact lenses orange.

Other effects are abdominal pains, nausea, vomiting, diarrhea, fatigue, headache, itchiness, dizziness, and drunken behavior. ALLERGY may also occur. These effects occur in only a small percentage of patients. They can be managed by giving the medication last thing at night.

An unusual but not serious side-effect of intermittent treatment is a feeling of having the "flu": fever, chills, headache, aching bones.

Rare, serious side-effects are respiratory failure, abnormal bleeding, sudden-onset ANEMIA, HEPATITIS, LIVER FAILURE (see Protocol C-7), and/or KIDNEY FAILURE. The drug must be stopped for any of these and never used again.

Dosage: This drug should generally be given with a second drug because resistance develops rapidly.

All doses are oral. The drug should be taken on an empty stomach. Reduce the dose with any LIVER DISEASE.

ANTHRAX: 300 mg IV every 12 hours

BARTONELLOSIS: 600 mg daily for 14 days; used in the Verruga phase of the disease.

BRUCELLOSIS: 900 mg each morning for 21 days; used with DOXYCYCLINE.

BURULI ULCER: See TUBERCULOSIS.

Itching due to JAUNDICE: 10 mg/kg/day

LEPROSY: 600 mg once a month on an empty stomach, to be taken with other medicines. This may be given as the only drug if there is one skin lesion only.

MENINGITIS prevention: 600 mg daily for 3 days.

MYCETOMA: Seek advice from an M.D.

OSTEOMYELITIS: 600 mg daily for 6 weeks.

PYOMYOSITIS: 600-900 mg daily for 6 weeks.

Q FEVER: 600 mg daily for 15 days.

SPOTTED FEVER: 600 mg daily x 7-14 days, shorter if not so ill, 14 days if very ill.

TRENCH FEVER: 600 mg daily for 6 weeks.

TUBERCULOSIS:

Daily dosage:

4-7 kg: 1/4 300-mg tablet daily
7-15 kg: 1/2 300-mg tablet daily
16-30 kg: 1 300-mg tablet daily
31-44 kg: 1.5 300-mg tablet daily
Over 45 kg: 2 300-mg tablets daily

Twice or thrice weekly dosage:

4-7 kg: 1/4 300-mg tablet
7-15 kg: 3/4 300-mg tablet
16-30 kg: 1.25 300-mg tablet
31-44 kg: 2 300-mg tablet
45-55 kg: 2.5 300-mg tablet
Over 55 kg: 3 300-mg tablet

Alternatives: ISONIAZID, ETHAMBUTOL, STREPTOMYCIN, RIFABUTIN, PAS for TUBERCULOSIS.

RIFAPENTINE

This is a drug related to RIFAMPIN but longer-lasting. It should not be used in patients with lung cavities on chest x-ray. It is not approved for use in non-lung TB. It should not be used in children, in breastfeeding or in HIV-positive. It discolors body fluids and contact lenses and denture, just like RIFAMPIN.

The usual adult dose is 600 mg once or twice weekly. It is usually active against all the same organisms as RIFAMPIN. It should be taken with fatty food. It should not be taken with ANTACIDs. You may need to reduce the dose or stop the drug in the presence of LIVER DISEASE. The drug is pregnancy category C. Other precautions, side-effects, etc. are like RIFAMPIN.

RITONAVIR

This is an anti-HIV drug.

SAQUINAVIR

This is an anti-HIV drug.

SECNIDAZOLE

A drug similar to METRONIDAZOLE and TINIDAZOLE but not yet approved for humans. Reportedly 1500 mg daily for 5 days cures AMEBIC LIVER DISEASE. The dose for amebic DYSENTERY is a single dose of 2000 mg or two doses of 1000 mg each, 4 hours apart. The dose for GIARDIASIS is 30 mg/kg in one single dose. The dose for PELVIC INFECTION is 2 grams, single dose.

SILVER SULFADIAZINE

Antibacterial, burn ointment.
Brand names: Silvadene, Flamazine.

This is an antibacterial skin cream that is used especially for burns. It is contraindicated in LIVER FAILURE, KIDNEY FAILURE, pregnancy, breast feeding mothers, newborns, people with PORPHYRIA, and patients with ALLERGY to SULFA drugs. It interacts badly with many other drugs. EXFOLIATIVE DERMATITIS, HEPATITIS, or a newly developing ANEMIA are reasons to stop the drug. It should be applied sparingly, daily, after washing.

SITAMAQUINE

Anti-leishmania
This is a new drug for leishmaniasis, both CUTANEOUS LEISHMANIASIS and VISCERAL LEISHMANIASIS, currently being tested. It is presently uncertain whether it will be helpful, safe, both, or neither.

SPECTINOMYCIN

Antibiotic, Aminoglycoside
Safety class 2 Pregnancy ??
Stability: Dry C, Use liquid within 24 hours.
Brand names: Nebcin, Tobricin.

Indications: GONORRHEA; PELVIC INFECTION in those with an ALLERGY to PENICILLIN or when PENICILLIN-type drugs do not work; URETHRITIS. It is not a reliable treatment for CHANCROID but it may work.

Contraindications: ALLERGY to this drug or any related drug, such as GENTAMYCIN; KIDNEY FAILURE, probably pregnancy. Do not use this in the presence of CIRRHOSIS or LIVER FAILURE.

Precautions: Be careful not to exceed the recommended dosage or the drug may cause KIDNEY FAILURE, deafness, or both; it occasionally causes this even at recommended doses. Safety in pregnancy is unknown. If you use this, be sure to check the patient in a week or two.

Dosage: 2000 mg (2 grams) IM in a single dose except for GONORRHEA which has spread to become a whole-body infection. In that case the dose is 2 grams IM twice daily for 7 days.

SPIRAMYCIN

Anti-toxoplasmosis drug
Brand name: Rovamycine
Safety class: unknown Stability: unknown
Pregnancy: reportedly o.k., the drug of choice
Indication: TOXOPLASMOSIS
Contraindication: ALLERGY to this drug

Precautions: Unknown

Side-effects: nausea, vomiting, diarrhea, abdominal pain.

Dosage: 1000 mg three times daily for 3 weeks, then discontinue for 2 weeks, then give for another 3 weeks. Continue these 5-week cycles throughout pregnancy.

STEROID

A class of drugs, of which PREDNISONE, HYDROCORTISONE, and DEXAMETHASONE are the most common. These drugs reduce inflammation and decrease immunity. They are commonly abused because they make people feel better fast. However, they also make one more susceptible to infection, cause weight gain, brittle bones, and DIABETES. They will cause latent TB to become active (although they are useful for treating some types of TB). They tend to make CHAGA'S DISEASE worse. If someone takes them for more than a week and then stops abruptly, he can develop SHOCK and die. They should not be used in patients with PORPHYRIA.

Equivalent doses are 20 mg HYDROCORTISONE, 5 mg PREDNISONE or PREDNISOLONE, and 0.75 mg of DEXAMETHASONE.

STIBOGLUCONATE

Antimony compound
Safety class 3 Stability: Unknown
Synonym: Pentavalent Antimony

Equivalent drugs: Meglumine Antimoniate.
Brand names: Pentostam, Glucantime. Supplied as injectable drug; no oral form available. Two forms of the drugs are sodium stibogluconate and meglumine antimoniate—comparable to each other, different geographic availability; neither works well in India.
Indications: CUTANEOUS LEISHMANIASIS, PKDL, VISCERAL LEISHMANIASIS.

Contraindications: Breast-feeding mothers, ALLERGY to the drug, KIDNEY FAILURE, pregnancy.

Side-effects: Fever, fatigue, diarrhea, ACUTE ABDOMEN, PANCREATITIS, HEPATITIS, nausea, pains. If these occur, stop the drug and do not restart it. Pain may occur at the injection site and the patient may develop stiff joints.

Precautions: Do not give to obese pateints without independent advice. The drug prolongs the QT interval of the heart and thus should not be given along with other drugs which bear the same warning. IV drug should not be used by the inexperienced.

Dosage:

This varies from one region to another; following local advice is preferable to following the directions below.

CUTANEOUS LEISHMANIASIS: 20 mg/kg IM daily for 20-28 consecutive days. If this is used with PAROMOMYCIN cream, then just a week might be enough.[1]

PKDL: 20 mg/kg daily until healed; most are healed in 120 days but it may take up to 200 days.

VISCERAL LEISHMANIASIS: If you use Pentostam, give one injection of 10 mg/kg daily for 10 days; repeat this once or twice more, separating each course of treatment by 10 days without the drug. The dose for Glucantime is 6-10 mg/kg daily for 15 days; repeat for another 15 days after 15 days off the drug.

STREPTOMYCIN

Antibiotic (gram negative), Aminoglycoside, Antituberculous
Safety Class 2 Pregnancy: D
Stability: Dry: A. Wet: warm 2 days; cold: 4 weeks.
Supplied as generic drug. Veterinary drug is available. This drug is injectable only, never oral.

Indications: BARTONELLOSIS, BRUCELLOSIS, DONOVANOSIS, some MYCETOMA, PLAGUE, RAT BITE FEVER, TUBERCULOSIS, TULAREMIA, sometimes other infections.

Contraindications: ALLERGY to the drug, HEART FAILURE, protein in urine unless an M.D. overrules this, pregnancy unless the problem is life-threatening and there are no other options. KIDNEY FAILURE or kidney disease. Don't use this along with other drugs that are toxic to the kidneys. Don't use it with any muscle weakness or in patients who are hard of hearing. Don't use this in the presence of CIRRHOSIS or LIVER FAILURE.

Precautions: This drug may cause deafness or fever and rash. Be careful not to overdose. Check hearing every couple of days; stop the drug if hearing difficulty or fever and rash develop.

If the person begins to be off-balance or feel as if he is spinning, stop the drug immediately. Warn him not to engage in hazardous activities when he is taking this.

Do not give it to a patient suffering from DEHYDRATION.

It may on occasion cause SEIZURES or MENTAL ILLNESS.

Side-effects: The site of the IM injection may become excessively painful.

Overdose and prolonged use: KIDNEY FAILURE, deafness.

Dosage: Reduce the dose for the elderly.

The following doses for average to large adults must be reduced for the elderly and according to weight for small adults and children.

BARTONELLOSIS: 1000 mg (1 gm) IM daily for 5 days.

BRUCELLOSIS: 1000 mg (1 gm) IM daily, used with other medications, for at least the first 2 weeks of the 6-week treatment.

BURULI ULCER: 1000 mg IM daily, along with surgery or in ulcers that are just beginning.

DONOVANOSIS: 1000 mg (1 gm) IM daily until totally healed plus another week, used with TETRACYCLINE.

MYCETOMA: 1000 mg (1 gm) IM daily for 30 days, then on alternate days until healed. Use this with COTRIMOXAZOLE or DAPSONE.

PLAGUE: 1000 mg IV or IM twice daily for 7-10 days. Reduce the dose as the patient improves.

RAT BITE FEVER: 1000 mg (1 gm) IM daily for 14 days.

TUBERCULOSIS:

Daily dosage:
Under 50 kg: 750 mg IM
Under 50 years old/over 50 kg: 1000 mg IM
Over 50 years old: 750 mg IM
Children's dose: 20 mg/kg IM

TULAREMIA: Same dose as PLAGUE; continue this for 14 days.

[1] Don't cut the course short if your patient has one of the forms that might later develop MCL—the form that affects the pink, moist areas of the body, and/or the outer ear.

Other infections: 1000 mg (1 gm) IM daily until entirely better plus 2 more days.

Alternatives: Other antibiotics.

SULFA

Sulfa drugs, Antibiotic, gram negative.

Safety class 2 Stability: A, Dark.

Specific names included in this: Sulfadiazine, Sulfisoxazole, Sulfamethoxazole, Triple Sulfa. *Use this description for any of the sulfa drugs above. Do not use for Sulfapyridine and Sulfacytine.* Sulfatrim is the same as COTRIMOXAZOLE.

Brand names: Too many to list. Generic human and veterinary drug is available. Supplied as 500 mg tablets; also supplied as liquid.

Indications: ABSCESS, CHOLERA, ordinary diarrhea, middle EAR INFECTION, EPIDIDYMITIS, KIDNEY INFECTION, RESPIRATORY INFECTION, TOXOPLASMOSIS, TRACHOMA, TURISTA, URETHRITIS, URINARY INFECTION, VAGINITIS. Sulfadiazine ophthalmic ointment may be useful for KERATITIS due to a fungus. See ANTIBIOTIC EYE OINTMENT.

Contraindications: Do not give to pregnant women about to deliver (first 8 months are okay), to nursing mothers, or to babies under 2 months of age. Do not give any sulfa drug to anyone who has had a previous allergy to the sulfa drug in question or to any other sulfa drug. It is not to be used with G6PD DEFICIENCY or with PORPHYRIA (a hereditary disease). It interacts badly with quite a few other drugs and thus its usage should be supervised.

Precautions: The patient must drink much water, 2-3 liters a day; he must not become or remain dehydrated (see DEHYDRATION) while on this drug.

The drug may make Whites sensitive to sunburn. It occasionally causes nausea and vomiting. If a red rash resembling a burn or skin peeling develops while the patient is on the drug, stop the drug immediately (see EXFOLIATIVE DERMATITIS).

Stop the drug if the patient develops a new HEPATITIS or ANEMIA.

Side-effects: Loss of appetite, nausea, vomiting. These effects are less when the drug is taken with food.

Overdose or prolonged usage: HEPATITIS, LIVER FAILURE.

Dosage: The following are adult doses; reduce dose according to weight for children. Reduce the dose in the presence of KIDNEY FAILURE.

KIDNEY INFECTION: 1000 mg (1 gram) every 6 hours for 5 days

TRACHOMA: 1000 mg (1 gram) every 6 hours for 21 days.

TOXOPLASMOSIS: 1000 mg (1 gram) every 6 hours for 4 weeks; use sulfadiazine, not the other forms.

URINARY INFECTION: Same as KIDNEY INFECTION.

Everything else: 1000 mg (1 gm) every 6 hours until the patient is well and then for 2 more days.

Alternatives: AMPICILLIN, CHLORAMPHENICOL, TETRACYCLINE, STREPTOMYCIN, COTRIMOXAZOLE. For CHANCROID use ERYTHROMYCIN.

SULFUR

Elemental sulfur.

This is different from the drug SULFA. It is a yellowish powder that is one of the elements. It is useful as a body insecticide when mixed into petroleum jelly (Vaseline): 30 grams per 500 ml of petroleum jelly. It is particularly useful for SCABIES.

SURAMIN

Brand name: Metaret

Safety class 3 Stability unknown

Pregnancy unknown

Indications: AFRICAN SLEEPING SICKNESS in the early stages.

Contraindication: ALLERGY to this drug in response to the initial test dose or a history with prior administration.

Precautions: This does not work if the organism has already affected the brain.

Side-effects: Painful palms or soles, sharp-shooting pains, may cause KIDNEY FAILURE or LIVER FAILURE (see Protocol C-7) or loss of vision.

Dosage: First give a 100-200 mg test dose to check for ALLERGY. Then, if there is no allergic reaction, give 1000 mg IV on days 1,3,7,14,and 21 for adults. For children the schedule is the same, using 20 mg/kg.

TAFENOQUINE

This is a new antimalarial drug; not much is known about it. Seek independent information. The usual adult dose is 200 mg base per day for 3 days, then 200 mg base weekly for 8 weeks. It has been tested mostly for non-falciparum malaria but might also be useful for falciparum

TETANUS IMMUNE GLOBULIN

Synonym: TIG

An injectable blood product used to protect against TETANUS in an unimmunized patient with a wound, or to treat for the disease.

TETRACHLOROETHYLENE

Dewormer; Anthelmintic

Safety class 2 Stability: D Pregnancy: ??

Brand names: Didakene, Miranon, Nema, Terit, Tetracap. The drug is a liquid. It is supplied as 3 ml of drug in 45 ml of flavored water. Also supplied as 1 ml capsules.

Indications: HOOKWORM, INTESTINAL FLUKE.

Contraindications: ALLERGY to the drug, constipation, or JAUNDICE. Do not give in the presence of ASCARIASIS or if ASCARIASIS is present in your area, unless you give PIPERAZINE first; otherwise this drug might cause ACUTE ABDOMEN, Type 3. Do not give this to patients with severe MALNUTRITION, severe ANEMIA, or those who are very ill.

Do not use this in the presence of obvious LIVER DISEASE, LIVER FAILURE, or HEART FAILURE. Do not use this at the same time as or right after the patient has taken medication that causes a rapid pulse.

Precautions: This may cause burning pain, nausea, vomiting, and drunken behavior. There is no harm in this; you should anticipate it. Avoid ALCOHOL and fatty food for one day before and for 3 days after the treatment. The patient may eat 4 hours after the treatment.

Dosage: After a light meal the previous evening, in the morning give the drug 0.12 ml/kg by mouth to a maximum of 5 ml. or according to the following table:

Kg body weight	Form: 3ml in 45 ml	Form: 1 ml capsule
8 kg	no	1 capsule
16 kg	no	2 capsules
24 kg	1 unit	3 capsules
32 kg	1 unit plus 1 capsule	4 capsules
40 kg	1 2/3 units or 1 unit plus 2 capsules	5 capsules
48 kg	2 units	5 capsules
56 kg	2 units	5 capsules

Repeat every 4 hours for 3 or 4 doses. If treating for INTESTINAL FLUKE, it is essential to purge 4-5 hours later; give MILK OF MAGNESIA, castor oil, or anything else that causes diarrhea.

Alternatives: ALBENDAZOLE, BEPHENIUM HYDROXYNAPHTHOATE, MEBENDAZOLE, PYRANTEL PAMOATE

TETRACYCLINE

Antibiotic, gram negative
Safety class 1 Stability: B Pregnancy D

This is an old drug which has been almost entirely replaced with DOXYCYCLINE.

Related drugs: Oxytetracycline (Terramycin), Chlortetracycline (Aureomycin).

Brand names: Achromycin, Ambramycin, Partrex, Quartex, Sumycin, Tetracyn, Totomycin, Unimycin, Upcyclin, many others. Veterinary drug is available. Supplied as 250 and 500 mg capsules. The drug is a gold color. Brown drug is bad drug. Oxytetracycline is used interchangeably with plain tetracycline.

Indications: Same as DOXYCYCLINE.

Contraindications: ALLERGY to the drug, outdated or brown-colored drug, CHAGA'S DISEASE, PORPHYRIA (a hereditary disease). This drug, if used during pregnancy, may occasionally cause severe liver damage and death. It will cause bone and teeth problems in the fetus. These pregnancy problems are worse with this than with DOXYCYCLINE. It is contraindicated in KIDNEY FAILURE but then DOXYCYCLINE may be used.

Precautions: **Pay special attention to expiration dates; using outdated drug is dangerous.** This drug will stain teeth permanently when given to pregnant or nursing mothers or to children under 7 y.o. If the patient consumes milk, milk products, or ANTACID with the drug, the drug will not be absorbed. It will be just like not taking that dose. Occasionally this drug will cause abdominal distress. It may also cause a black, fuzzy tongue (no problem) and may give a false positive or false negative test for sugar in the urine. Tetracycline makes skin more susceptible to sunburn.

If the patient develops a DYSENTERY-type diarrhea while on the drug, stop it immediately.

With BRUCELLOSIS, RELAPSING FEVER, LEPTOSPIROSIS, and SYPHILIS the patient may become much sicker for a few hours after the first dose before starting to improve. Do not withdraw the drug for this.

Birth control pills might not work when taken with this drug.

Dosage: Reduce the dose in kidney disease. See DOXYCYCLINE and calculate comparable doses. Dosage equivalents with DOXYCYCLINE:

DOXYCYCLINE 100 mg daily = Tetracycline 250 mg four times a day.

DOXYCYCLINE 100 mg twice daily = Tetracycyline 500 mg four times a day.

THEOPHYLLINE

Bronchodilator
Safety class 2-3 Stability: A, dark
Pregnancy C
The drug is very toxic in overdose; a small overdose can kill.

Related drug: Aminophylline.

Brand names: Accurbron, Quibron, Theo-Dur, Theolair, Nuelin, Lasma. Supplied in many sizes, frequently 200 or 300 mg per tablet and 100 mg per 5 ml (1 teaspoon) liquid. Other sizes may be available. Generic drug is available.

Indications: Prolonged expiration with wheezing from any cause, usually ASTHMA, sometimes ALTITUDE SICKNESS, HEART FAILURE, RESPIRATORY INFECTION, SMOKE INHALATION, TUBERCULO-

SIS. Sometimes it is used for ATTENTION DEFICIT DISORDER but that is not an approved usage.

Contraindications: Previous bad experience with this medication, some kinds of heart disease, HYPERTENSION, prostrate problems. Do not give this with LIVER DISEASE, THYROID TROUBLE of the high thyroid sort. This drug interacts badly with many other drugs so you should seek confirmation of its use if the patient is on anything else.

Precautions: This drug has a narrow margin of safety; the minimally effective dose is not much less than the toxic dose. A mild overdose will cause nausea and vomiting. Reduce the dose if this happens, even if the patient is taking a low dose for his size.

The drug may cause an irregular heart rate causing the patient to complain of palpitations. Frequently patients become nervous when taking the drug. They are unable to sleep, and they may have to urinate a lot.

The drug makes many people sensitive to the stimulant effect of caffeine.

This should not be used in persons with a family history of PORPHYRIA.

The drug interferes with laboratory determinations of uric acid. Other drugs interfere with laboratory determinations of the theophylline level.

Overdose: This is very toxic in overdose; it is a potent agent for suicide.

Dosage: Decrease the dose for the elderly. Increase the dose in those taking PHENOBARBITAL and in smokers. Do not crush the long-acting forms or they will not be long-acting and the patient may overdose. The usual dose is 200-300 mg every 8 hours for adults. Children: 5 mg/kg every 8 hours. Long-acting theophylline is used in the same dose every 12 hours. Response: 45 minutes.

Alternatives: ALBUTEROL, METAPROTERENOL. For severe ASTHMA, use EPINEPHRINE; you may use both EPINEPHRINE and theophylline in full doses.

THIABENDAZOLE

Dewormer, Anthelmintic

Safety class 1 Stability: A Pregnancy C

Brand names: Bovizole, Coglazol, Equizole, Helmintazole, Hyozole, Mintezol, Nemapan, Omnizole, Polival, Soldrin, TBZ, Thibenzole. Veterinary generic drug available. Supplied as 500 mg chewable tablets and 100 mg/ml liquid.

Indications: ASCARIASIS, CAPILLARIASIS, ENTEROBIASIS, GUINEA WORM, KERATITIS due to a fungus, STRONGYLOIDIASIS. It may work for TRICHINOSIS, and some LARVA MIGRANS of the skin type. Not useful for TRICHURIASIS.

Contraindications: ALLERGY to the drug, LIVER FAILURE, KIDNEY FAILURE. Do not give this together with THEOPHYLLINE.

Precautions: If the patient develops a rash while on the drug, discontinue it.

Side-effects: Nausea, vomiting, diarrhea, loss of appetite, dizziness, headache, ringing in the ears, and stinky urine. Occasionally causes itching. These effects may occur in up to half of the patients. Less frequent side-effects are mental symptoms

Dosage: 25 mg/kg by mouth every 12 hours to a maximum of 1500 mg per dose.

ASCARIASIS: 2 days.

CAPILLARIASIS: Seek local advice.

ENTEROBIASIS: 1 day.

GUINEA WORM: 3 days.

KERATITIS due to fungus: Half the dose above, given until the problem is completely cleared plus another 3 days.

STRONGYLOIDIASIS: 3 days or same dose by rectum for 14 days.

TRICHINOSIS: 1000 mg every 12 hours for 2 days.

LARVA MIGRANS: Make a cream, mixing 1500 mg of the drug in 15 ml (1 tablespoon) of any skin cream. Apply to the area every 4 hours and leave on until the problem is resolved.

Alternatives: For STRONGYLOIDIASIS, try IVERMECTIN. For other worms, try MEBENDAZOLE or ALBENDAZOLE.

THIACETAZONE

Antituberculous

Note that this is not readily available as it has been taken off the market in many places, because of safety issues!!

Safety class 2 Stability: A

Brand name: Thiazina, or TB 450 when combined with ISONIAZID.

Indications: TUBERCULOSIS.

Contraindications: East Asian genetic heritage; possibly European genetic heritage; previous ALLERGY or any bad reaction to this drug; currently ill with HIV INFECTION, possibly HIV positive but not currently ill.

Side-effects: Nausea, vomiting, rash, fever, skin color changes, itching, skin peeling off (see EXFOLIATIVE DERMATITIS). Skin problems are common in patients of Chinese genetic heritage. **Stop the drug for skin redness or peeling!** This may also cause bone marrow problems like CHLORAMPHENICOL. The drug must be given daily, not less often. It may cause LIVER DISEASE (see Protocol C-7).

Dosage: Usually this is combined with ISONIAZID in the proper proportions (as in Thiazina and TB 450); in this case, just give the proper tablet dosage of ISONIAZID and the dosage of thiacetazone will automatically be correct. The table below is to be used if you buy thiacetazone separately.

Daily thiacetazone dosage:

Under 6 kg:	1/2 of a 50-mg tablet
7-12 kg:	1 50-mg tablet
13-29 kg:	1/2 150-mg tablet
30-50 kg:	1 150-mg tablet

THIAMINE

B Vitamin; Vitamin B_1
Safety class 1 Stability: A, Dark
Brand names: Albafort, Benerva; generic available.
Indications: BERIBERI.
Contraindications: ALLERGY to the drug.

Dosage: By mouth or IM injection: 200 mg initially, then 100 mg every 8 hours until all symptoms are gone; then give weekly.

THIAMPHENICOL

This is a form of CHLORAMPHENICOL which works particularly well for GONORRHEA and some MENINGITIS. It works, but not as well, for the other diseases that CHLORAMPHENICOL is used for. See CHLORAMPHENICOL for specifics.

TINIDAZOLE

Antibiotic, Antiprotozoal
Safety class 1 Stability: C Pregnancy: ??
Brand names: Fasigyn, Pletil, Simplotan, Sorquetan, Tricolam. Supplied as 500 mg tablets.

Indications: ACUTE ABDOMEN, AMEBIC LIVER DISEASE, amebic DYSENTERY, GIARDIASIS, PELVIC INFECTION, PEPTIC ULCER, PNEUMONIA, TROPICAL ULCER, VAGINITIS.

Sometimes TURISTA, gas, GUINEA WORM, MALABSORPTION, with other drugs in SEPSIS, TETANUS, for wounds with foul-smelling pus. It may be used for tooth infections in third molars.

Contraindications: ALLERGY to the drug.

Precautions: The patient must not drink alcohol nor allow any alcohol on his skin while taking the drug or for 3 days afterward. Almost all liquid and cream-type medicines have alcohol in them. They cause problems whether swallowed or rubbed on the skin. Also culinary products such as vanilla extract should be avoided.

Avoid using tinidazole during the first 3 months of pregnancy, except for life-threatening illness.

Side-effects: Nausea, vomiting, abdominal pain, sleepiness, headache, dark urine. These effects occur in only a small percentage of patients.

Dosage: The drug is absorbed well rectally; give it this way if your patient is vomiting or he has an ACUTE ABDOMEN; the adult dose by rectum is 1000 mg every 8 hours; reduce the dose according to weight for children.

The following are adult doses; reduce dose according to weight for children.

ACUTE ABDOMEN: 1000 mg three times a day for 5 days.

AMEBIC LIVER DISEASE: 750 mg three times a day for 10 days.

DYSENTERY: 750 mg three times a day for 3 days or else 2000 mg, single dose, followed by another (same) dose a week later.

ENTERIC FEVER: 500 mg twice daily for 10 days.

Gas: Same as TURISTA.

GIARDIASIS: 2000 mg, single dose.

GUINEA WORM: 400-500 mg three times a day for 5 days.

MALABSORPTION: Same as TURISTA.

PELVIC INFECTION: 400 mg every 8 hours for 10 days.

PEPTIC ULCER: 400 mg every 8 hours for 14 days, with other medication listed.

PNEUMONIA: Same as ACUTE ABDOMEN.

SEPSIS: Same as ACUTE ABDOMEN.

TETANUS: 500 mg orally every 6 hours or 1000 mg by rectum every 8 hours, for 10 days.

TROPICAL ULCER: 250 mg three times a day until healed.

TURISTA: 250 mg three times a day for 3 days.

VAGINITIS: Bacterial: 500 mg three times a day for 7 days; Trichomonas: 2000 mg, one dose; treat both partners in both cases.

Wounds with foul-smelling pus: 500 mg three times a day until healed plus another 2 days.

Tooth infections: 500 mg three times a day until the swelling is down; then pull the tooth.

TOLNAFTATE

Antifungal
Safety class 1 Stability: Unknown
Brand name: Aftate, Tinactin.
Usually supplied as a powder.
Indications: TINEA. Not useful for CANDIDIASIS.
Contraindications: ALLERGY to the drug. Do not use by the eyes.
Dosage: Apply every 12 hours for 2-4 weeks.

TRICLABENDAZOLE

Brand name: Fasinex

This is a new drug for LIVER FLUKE (fascioliasis) which occurs in areas other than East Asia and Southeast Asia, and also for PARAGONIMIASIS. The WHO trials in humans were done in Bolivia, Chile, Cuba, Peru, and Iran. The drug had been previously used in sheep by veterinarians. The usual dose is 10 mg/kg daily for 2-3 days. Repeat the treatment in 3 months. The drug should be taken with a fatty meal to increase the amount that is absorbed into the blood stream. Seek more local information, if possible. Do not use this for

LIVER FLUKE in Southeast Asia or East Asia. An alternative is a new antibiotic, NITAZOXANIDE.

TROPICAMIDE

Eye dilator
Safety class 2 Stability: C-D Pregnancy: C
Brand name: Mydriacyl. Supplied as a 1% solution for eyes (labeled ophthalmic).

Indications: KERATITIS, IRITIS, for pain relief after an eye injury.

Contraindications: GLAUCOMA. Do not use in patients with any kind of spastic weakness or in those with DOWN SYNDROME.

Precautions: This normally burns as it goes into the eye. Tell the patient to blink but not to squeeze his eye shut. It will make the eye very sensitive to light; he should wear sunglasses that eliminate UV light. The eye should be patched or the patient should stay in a dark room until the effects are worn off. Vision will be temporarily blurred after the drops are put in.

Dosage: One drop initially and one drop 5 minutes later. This will give an effect lasting for at least 6-12 hours. The medication can be renewed as it wears off.

VALACICLOVIR

Brand name: Valtrex

This is an anti-herpes drug, similar to ACYCLOVIR. You should seek independent information concerning it.

Dosage: 1 gram twice a day for 7 days.

VERAPAMIL

Calcium antagonist
Safety class 2 Stability: C Pregnancy C
Brand names: Berkatens, Calan, Cordilox, Isoptin, Securon.

Indications: HYPERTENSION, MIGRAINE HEADACHE. Possibly for VISCERAL LEISHMANIASIS. Possibly for CHAGA'S DISEASE which is resistant to usual drugs. It may be used for a rapid pulse that must be slowed; this must be supervised by a physician.

Contraindications: Previous ALLERGY to this drug; a slow pulse; current or recent use of PROPRANOLOL or a similar drug; HEART FAILURE; a low blood pressure; current or recent use of DIGOXIN or a similar medication, any muscle weakness.

Side-effects: Headache, dizziness, constipation, a red rash, swelling of the feet, a very slow pulse, a very low blood pressure with fainting. These effects occur in only a small percentage of patients.

Dosage: Begin with 120 mg once daily. The usual daily dose is 240 mg once daily, but it is better to start with the lower dose to minimize the chance of an adverse reaction. When stopping the drug it should be stopped slowly. For VISCERAL LEISHMANIASIS and CHAGA'S DISEASE, the dose should be determined by a physician.

VITAMIN A

Safety class 2 Stability: A.
Synonyms: Retinol, Retinaldehyde.
Brand name: Aquasol A. Generic drug is available. Supplied as a liquid with 5,000 units of vitamin A per drop (0.1 ml) and as capsules with 25,000, 50,000, or 200,000 units per capsule. Some capsules have nipples on the ends. The nipples must be cut off and the liquid inside the capsules squirted into the mouth.

Indications: A diet deficient in vitamin A. A high incidence of blindness in the community due to XEROPHTHALMIA indicates that all patients should have the vitamin. In particular, it should be used in all MALNUTRITION before beginning refeeding and in patients with MEASLES at the beginning of the treatment.

Precautions: Very high doses over long periods of time are toxic. A single overdose is probably harmless. ZINC is necessary in order to process Vitamin A. Hence it is good to give ZINC along with this or add ZINC if the patient does not respond promptly. Do not give large doses in pregnancy.

Dosage: In all cases reduce the dose according to weight for children.

Adults get 100,000 units daily for 3 days, then 50,000 units daily for 2 weeks.

In severe cases, children may not be able to absorb the oral form. In that case an initial injection of vitamin A as retinyl palmitate, 100,000 IU (International units), adult dose, is indicated. Give it IM.

Alternatives: A diet high in Vitamin A. (See XEROPHTHALMIA in the *Disease Index*.)

VITAMIN B_{12}

Safety class 1 Stability: Unknown
Synonyms: Hydroxocobalamin, Cyanocobalamin.
Brand name: Cobalin-H.

Indications: SPRUE, some ANEMIA, possibly PLANT POISONING due to cassava or tobacco-cow's urine.

Contraindications: ALLERGY to this drug.

Dosage: 1 mg IM every 2-3 days for 5 doses, then 1 mg every 3 months. Lesser doses may still be helpful.

VITAMIN C

Safety class 1 Stability: A
Synonym: Ascorbic acid.
Indications: RESPIRATORY INFECTION, SCURVY, HEMOCHROMATOSIS. Sometimes used to make urine more acid, in order to eliminate certain poisons.

Contraindications: ALLERGY to this drug.

Dosage: 250-500 mg daily; overdose is almost impossible.

VITAMIN D

Safety class 2 Stability: C
Synonym: Calciferol.
Indications: RICKETS.

Contraindications: ALLERGY to the drug.

Precautions: Overdose is possible with continued usage of very high doses. Give milk or milk products to provide calcium when giving this drug.

Dosage: The dose varies with the product. Follow the directions which come with your product..

VITAMIN K

Safety class 1 Stability: A, Dark
Brand name: Aquamephyton. Generic forms may be available.

Indications: Bleeding in a newborn, HEMORRHAGIC FEVER, HEPATITIS, YELLOW FEVER, LIVER FAILURE, CIRRHOSIS.

Contraindications: ALLERGY to this drug. This drug might not be tolerated by some people with G6PD DEFICIENCY.

Precautions: Be sure not to give this IV.

Dosage: By IM or SQ injection: Newborn: 0.5 to 1 mg; Adult: 10 mg.

WHITFIELD'S OINTMENT

Safety class: 1-2; Stability: A
Indications: TINEA.

Contraindications: ALLERGY to this.

Precautions: Do not use over more than 1/4 of the body surface at a time. Irritation will occur at the site of application; stop the drug and then, after clearing, resume using it in smaller amounts and less frequently.

Dosage: Wash the patient and dry him well twice a day. Then apply the ointment. Do this until the problem is resolved.

YOGURT

Food stuff.

This is made by bringing milk to a boil, then cooling it, then adding some active yogurt culture and letting the mixture stand in a slightly warm place for 12 hours. The ideal temperature is 110°F (or 43°C). At temperatures cooler than that, the brew cultivates yeast and becomes bubbly. Active yogurt culture can be found in some store-bought yogurt and also in powdered form in health-food stores in Western countries. Yogurt is a good form of milk to use in MILK INTOLERANCE. It works as a vaginal douche for VAGINITIS due to CANDIDIASIS. It may be helpful in GIARDIASIS. It may be helpful in treating ordinary diarrhea, TURISTA.

ZIDOVUDINE

Brand name: Retrovir

Safety class: 2-3; Stability: C; Pregnancy: B

Indications: HIV INFECTION, sometimes bleeding problems caused by HIV.

Contraindications: ALLERGY to this drug.

Preccautions: ACETAMINOPHEN decreases the amount in the blood. Do not give with AMPHOTERICIN, COTRIMOXAZOLE, CIMETIDINE, SULFADIAZINE, ASPIRIN, ACYCLOVIR, DAPSONE, RIBAVIRIN, GANCICLOVIR, ATOVAQUONE, or PENTAMIDINE except on physician advice. Seek advice before using this with LIVER DISEASE or KIDNEY DISEASE. Stop the drug if the patient develops abnormal bleeding or new or worsening ANEMIA.

Side-effects: Nausea, vomiting, abdominal pains, ANEMIA, muscle aching, fatigue, headache. Stop the drug if the patient develops new ANEMIA or has a low blood count. The drug may cause fat accumulation around the waist and in back of the shoulders.

Dosage: Decrease the dose in patients with LIVER DISEASE or KIDNEY DISEASE.

Adult dose: 100 mg by mouth every 4 hours while awake (500 mg daily) for HIV INFECTION without symptoms. For a bleeding problem due to HIV INFECTION, give 200-400 mg by mouth two or three times a day—only on physician recommendation after a blood test in a higher-level laboratory.

Child dose: Seek independent information; in case of child rape, the protocol is given in Volume I.

ZINC

Safety class 1 Stability: A
Supplied as generic drug; 125 mg zinc sulfate monohydrate contains 45 mg of zinc.

Brand names: Solvazinc, Zincomed, Z Span.

Indications: General fatigue in someone not accustomed to the tropics, skin ulcers of any sort, ordinary diarrhea, CUTANEOUS LEISHMANIASIS, HEAT ILLNESS, LEPROSY, SICKLE CELL DISEASE, THALLASEMIA, TROPICAL ULCER, TURISTA, ZINC DEFICIENCY. Given together with VITAMIN A for XEROPHTHALMIA, MALNUTRITION, and MEASLES.

Contraindications: ALLERGY to the drug.

Dosage: The following are adult doses; reduce dose according to weight for children. The doses are not precise.

Acclimatizing, HEAT ILLNESS, diarrhea: 45 mg zinc daily.

CUTANEOUS LEISHMANIASIS: 5-10 mg/kg zinc sulfate daily (might or might not work).

LEPROSY: 45 mg zinc daily.

SICKLE CELL DISEASE: 45 mg zinc three times a day initially; reduce dose to once daily as the patient improves.

THALLASEMIA: Same as SICKLE CELL DISEASE.

TROPICAL ULCER and skin ulcers: Zinc from crushed tablets combined with ANTIBIOTIC OINTMENT may help. Commercial zinc paste or tape may be available.

ZINC DEFICIENCY: Same as SICKLE CELL DISEASE.

Regional Notes

Index	*Region*
E	**Eastern Europe and Central Asia**
F	**Africa**
I	**India Subcontinent**
M	**Central and South America**
O	**East Asia**
R	**Mediterranean and Middle East**
S	**Southeast Asia**
U	**Australia and the South Pacific**

MAPS SHOWING AREAS OF THE WORLD COVERED BY THE REGIONAL INDICES

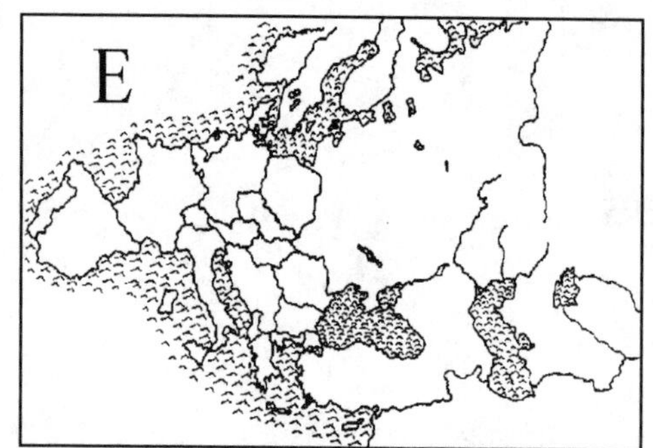

Region E: Eastern Europe and Central Asia

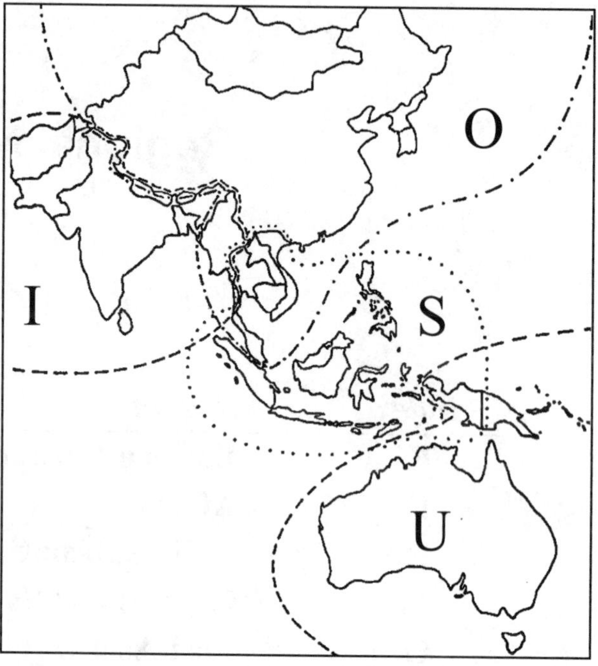

Region I: India Subcontinent (– – –)
Region O: East Asia (– • – • –)
Region S: Southeast Asia (• • • •)
Region U: Australia and the South Pacific (– – –)

Region M: Central and South America

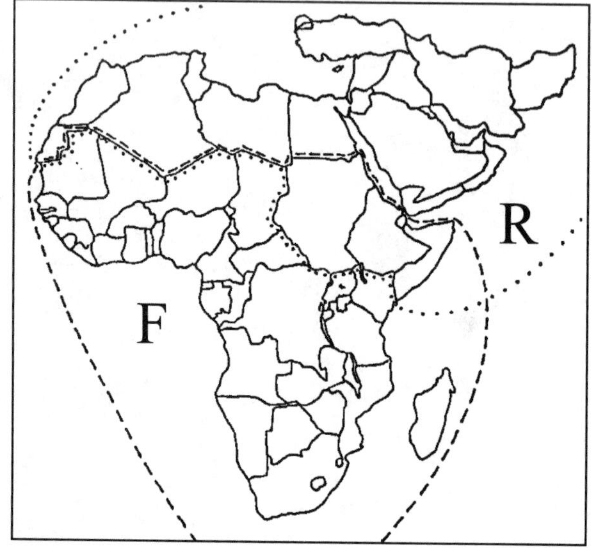

Regional Map F: Africa (– – –)
Regional Map R: Mediterranean and Middle East (• • •)

Regional Notes

Index E. Eastern Europe and Central Asia

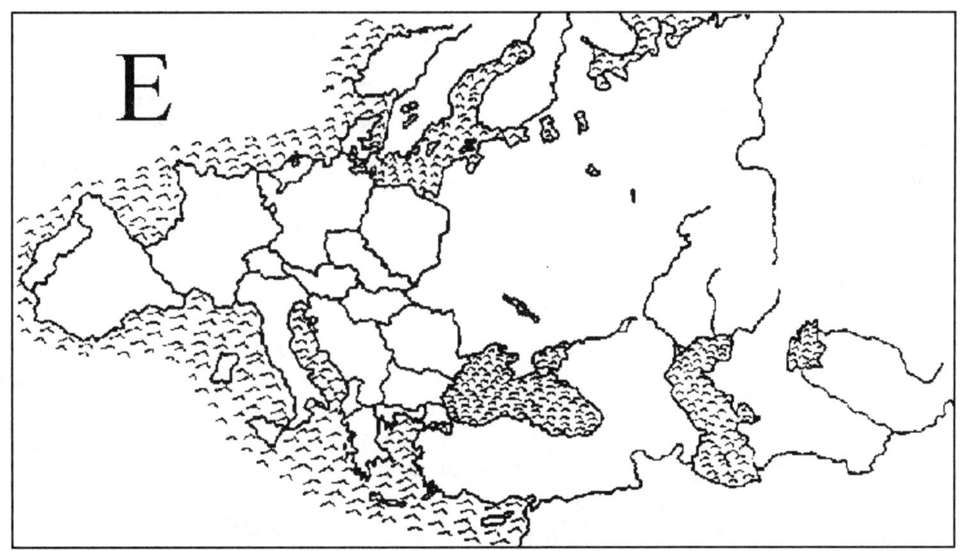

Index E: Eastern Europe and Central Asia

AMEBIC LIVER DISEASE

This occurs in the Caucasus region; it may also occur elsewhere.

ANTHRAX

This is especially common in the Slavic countries and in Russia.

ARBOVIRAL FEVER; Sand Fly Fever

In this area, there is Sand Fly Fever which is an undifferentiated arboviral fever; also CRIMEAN-CONGO HEMORRHAGIC FEVER occurs, and some ENCEPHALITIS.

Similar Conditions: See the diseases listed in the chart in the *Protocol Index,* C-2. Consider also HEMORRHAGIC FEVER (abnormal bleeding) and MENINGITIS.

Sand Fly Fever

Cause: Virus.

Moderately ill to very ill; Class 2; Regional; it occurs in the Balkan Penninsula and in a large area east of the Caspian Sea. It may occur in closely adjacent areas but not in the north because the flies that are carriers do not live there.

Age: Any. **Who**: Those bitten by sand flies. (This kind of sand fly feeds mostly on chickens, less on cows and horses, and only occasionally on humans. It bites at night and also 6:30-10:30 A.M.) **Onset**: Very sudden, over hours, with a short incubation of 3-6 days.

Clinical:

Necessary: An initial fever with headache, eye pain, and general muscle pains, lasting 2-4 days. The liver and spleen are normal size and non-tender. There is no rash.

Usually: The patient's eyes are red, the face is flushed, and the patient avoids light and eye movement because it causes more pain.

Commonly: The worst pain is in the low back. There may be nosebleed. There may be depression.

Sometimes: There is also nausea, vomiting, abdominal pains, and diarrhea. The neck may be stiff. The worst of the disease is over in a few days, but the patient does not feel healthy for weeks.

Treatment:

Prevention: Use insect repellants to avoid sand fly bites or wear clothing to cover all your skin.

Patient Care: Keep the patient hydrated and well fed. Use ASPIRIN, ACETAMINOPHEN, or IBUPROFEN for pain. RIBAVIRIN may be helpful. Do not use other antibiotics.

BRUCELLOSIS

Similar regional disease: TULAREMIA.

Brucellosis is common in a broad band across southern Europe and east Asia, including Spain, southern France, Italy, Turkey, the Balkans, and eastward to the Caspian and Aral Seas.

CANCER

Skin cancer, blood cancer (leukemia) and thyroid cancer are the result of radiation exposure in this area. Bone cancer may be from ingesting radioactive substances in food and water. See RADIATION ILLNESS in the *Disease Index*. Skin cancer occurs on the eyelids in fair-skinned people in the desert areas of the southern CIS republics.

CHOLERA

This occurs in the former USSR, Romania, and the Ukraine.

CUTANEOUS LEISHMANIASIS

In Europe, this occurs in the southern half of the Iberian Penninsula, throughout Italy and adjacent areas of southern France, throughout the Balkan Penninsula and throughout Turkey. It also occurs (Leishmania Major) across coastal North Africa. Farther east, it is present in Azerbaijan and the rest of the Caucasus area, in Turkmenistan, and in Uzbekistan. There has been a recent increase in the number of cases in southern Europe. In urban areas of central Asia the skin sores look dry and crusted over; the disease is carried by dogs as well as humans.

DIPHTHERIA

This occurs and is common in the former USSR. It is especially common in Kyrgyzstan, Tajikistan, Georgia, and the Caucasus.

DYSENTERY

The type due to amebae occurs in the Caucasus area.

ENCEPHALITIS

There is a tick-borne encephalitis in eastern Europe/ Russia. Immunization should be obtained in Europe for those who will be traveling in rural areas and who will be exposed to ticks. It is present in Europe proper east of the Rhine and west of the Black Sea. It is also present in Russia west of the Ural Mountains and north of Samara. Treatment at a hospital might help during the first week, but not after that.

ENTERIC FEVER

This occurs in Russia and southern Europe but is very rare in the rest of Eastern Europe.

ENTEROBIASIS

This occurs in Hungary and Armenia and probably the rest of eastern Europe and central Asia, since it tends to spread within temperate climates.

GIARDIASIS

This is common throughout this area. The city water in St. Petersburg is particularly notorious for transmitting giardiasis.

HEMORRHAGIC FEVER

In this area the most common form is CRIMEAN-CONGO HEMORRHAGIC FEVER which is a type of ARBOVIRAL FEVER. It is found in an area west of Vienna, Austria and south of Warsaw, Poland. It is transmitted by ticks and infects a variety of wild and domestic animals in addition to humans. However, it is not a common disease.

HEPATITIS

Hepatitis E is common in the former USSR, especially Turkmenia and Kirghiz. It is also common in Lithuania and in eastern Siberia. A kind of hepatitis that is due to Q FEVER is common in Spain and adjacent areas.

HIV INFECTION

This is common amongst the homosexuals of Moscow. It is common in France, Spain and Italy. In Spain intravenous drug users with AIDS commonly get VISCERAL LEISHMANIASIS.

HYDATID DISEASE

This is particularly common in Eastern Europe and throughout Russia. The kind that is found in this region is rare, and it is only transmitted when humans eat food contaminated with wild animal stool. (It is different than the tropical hydatid disease that is common wherever dogs and humans live very close together.) It affects mostly older adults, primarily the liver but it spreads from there to other organs and is very aggressive, like a cancer. It requires sophisticated facilities for laboratory diagnosis and surgical treatment.

HYPERTENSION

This is common in Bulgaria, Hungary, Romania, Russia, and Yugoslavia.

INFLUENZA

Similar regional diseases: ARBOVIRAL FEVER, LEPTOSPIROSIS, TULAREMIA, SPOTTED FEVER. See Protocol C-2.

INTESTINAL FLUKE

Metagonimiasis from fish occurs in Russia, Spain, and eastern Europe. The only symptom is a mild diarrhea.

Heterophyiasis from fish occurs in Turkey.

LARVA MIGRANS

The deep type (acquired from dogs and cats) occurs throughout the southern two thirds of the former USSR.

LEPROSY

This is relatively common in Romania and in the areas of the southern former USSR adjacent to Iran and Turkey.

LIVER FLUKE

Liver Fluke (Fascioliasis) is present in some areas only, mainly those that raise sheep or cattle. It occurs in Georgia and Poland and possibly elsewhere. Opisthorchiasis is found in Eastern Europe, parts of Asia, and in Siberia. It is specifically prevalent in Moscow and the Vladmir region.

LYME DISEASE

LYME DISEASE occurs east of Berlin, west of Samara, and north of the Black Sea, extending north into Finland. It also occurs in Croatia.

MALARIA

Falciparum malaria is reportedly not found in this area at all except rarely in areas adjacent to Afghanistan.

Non-falciparum malaria might be found in the southern areas, especially in areas adjacent to Afghanistan. It is found in Turkey.

Similar regional diseases: TULAREMIA, SPOTTED FEVER.

MEASLES

This is common in Poland, Russia, and Yugoslavia where few children are immunized.

MENINGITIS

This occurs throughout the area.

PELLAGRA

This used to be common in this area; it may still occur.

PELVIC INFECTION

CHLAMYDIA is a common cause.

PLAGUE

This occurs in the former USSR.

Similar regional diseases: TULAREMIA, SPOTTED FEVER.

PNEUMONIA

In this area, especially in Spain and adjacent areas of southwestern Europe, this may be due to Q FEVER, especially likely if the patient had recent contact with newborn animals.

Q FEVER

Q fever occurs across southern Europe and Asia, south of the 45th parallel west of the Balkans and south of the 50th parallel east of the Balkans.

RADIATION ILLNESS

This is common in this area because of contamination of the environment. CANCER is a complication of such exposure.

RELAPSING FEVER

This occurs throughout the former USSR. In most places it is a mild disease but a severe form occurs in the Caucasus area. In this area it is carried by ticks.

RHEUMATIC FEVER

This is common amongst the Yakut of eastern Siberia. It is especially common in Russia, Byelorussia, the Ukraine, and Bulgaria.

SAND FLY FEVER

See ARBOVIRAL FEVER

SPOTTED FEVER

In this area, this is Tick typhus only; it occurs commonly in Astrakhan, Russia in the summer time, transmitted by dog ticks in rural areas. A similar regional disease is TULAREMIA.

STRONGYLOIDIASIS

This is common in the eastern half of the former USSR, and in Bulgaria, Hungary, and Romania.

SYPHILIS

This is common in the former USSR; it is common in newborns. Congenital syphilis may manifest for the first time up to age 30, with symptoms of tertiary syphilis, particularly corneal opacities.

TAPEWORM

Fish tapeworm occurs in the indigenous people of the former USSR, in the Volga area, in the Baltic region, in the Danube area of Romania and in the Masurian lakes area of Poland. Reportedly it causes ANEMIA only in Scandinavia.

Beef tapeworm occurs in the southern republics of the former USSR from the Black Sea to China.

Pork tapeworm occurs in the southern republics of the former USSR and also in the western republics. It is particularly common in the Slavic areas of Europe.

Rat and dwarf tapeworm occur but they are rare.

TETANUS

This occurs in Poland, Romania, Hungary, Russia, the Ukraine, and Yugoslavia where few children are immunized. It can occur anywhere.

TRACHOMA

This is rare to unknown in Hungary.

TRENCH FEVER

This is common among the poor and homeless in urban areas.

TRICHINOSIS

This occurs throughout the area.

TRICHURIASIS

This occurs in the Caucasus area, Romania, Hungary, and Yugoslavia.

TUBERCULOSIS

This is common in Russia, Hungary, and the Ukraine. There are many cases of antibiotic-resistant TB in the newly independent states of the former Soviet Union: Georgia, Uzbekistan, Turkmenistan, and the Baltic States. One factor was crowded housing. Another factor was medication that was hard to take and lack of patient supervision so the patients could throw the detestable tablets rather than swallow them—or sell them on the black market. The government erratically supplied TB drugs so commonly treatment centers ran out. HIV entered the picture in the 1990's, making the situation worse. One needs a cure rate of at least 60% in order to interrupt the transmission of resistant TB.

TURISTA

A form that responds to ERYTHROMYCIN occurs around Moscow, in the Czech Republic, and in Slovakia. A viral form causing MALNUTRITION occurs in Tibilisi and surrounding areas.

TYPHUS

Flea-borne (murine) typhus occurs in Portugal and in Southeast Europe: Yugoslavia, Albania, and Rumania. It may occur elsewhere also. Louse-borne typhus occurs in Yugoslavia.

Similar regional conditions: TULAREMIA, SPOTTED FEVER, PLAGUE.

VISCERAL LEISHMANIASIS

This occurs south of the 45th parallel in this area. Reportedly it is absent from inland Turkey. In Spain it is commonly associated with AIDS, especially in intravenous drug users.

It tends to be of sudden onset and rapid progresssion in those who are HIV positive, whether or not they have full-blown AIDS. The prognosis is poor.

WHOOPING COUGH

This occurs in Hungary but is not common. It is common in the former USSR and the Ukraine where few children are immunized.

Regional Notes

Index F. Africa

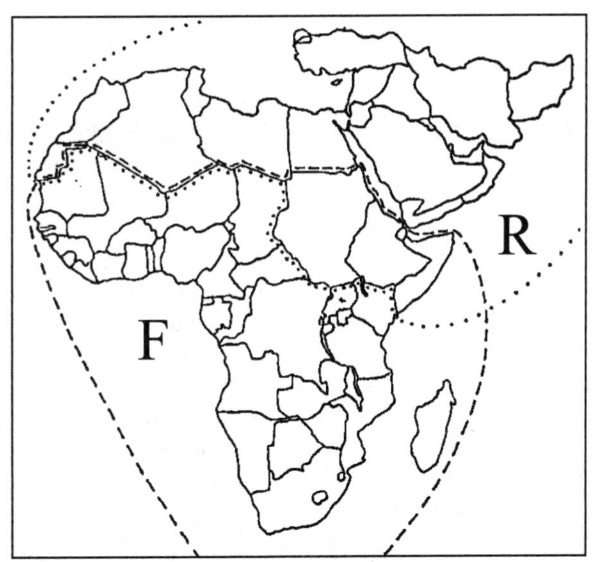

Index F: Africa

ABORTION

If there is a fever see AFRICAN SLEEPING SICKNESS and LASSA FEVER, as these may cause both fever and abortion. However, MALARIA is the most common cause of fever and abortion.

ACUTE ABDOMEN

Similar regional diseases: SICKLE CELL DISEASE may resemble acute abdomen but the whites of the eyes are yellow, the patient has ANEMIA, and a urine dipstick shows urobilinogen. If this is the case, do not send out if you can treat the SICKLE CELL DISEASE.

In Ethiopia and in South Africa there is a hereditary disease that can look very similar to acute abdomen. It is called PORPHYRIA. Ask your patient if other members of his family have had frequent abdominal pains. If he says "yes", then take some of his urine and set it in the sunlight. If he has porphyria, it will quickly turn a dark color. If that happens, just give pain medication. The patient does not need to be sent to a hospital unless he says "this time it is different".

ADDICTION

Examples of uppers in Africa are: khat in the Middle East and eastern Africa, and betel nut in Somalia and in Indian women.

AFRICAN SLEEPING SICKNESS

Cause: Protozoa
Synonym: African trypanosomiasis
Entry category: Two overlapping diseases
Mildly to very ill; Class 3-4.

Age: Any, but rare in children; may be transmitted from mother to fetus across the placenta. **Who**: Bitten by tsetse flies which tend to attack moving targets aggressively. There are two forms of the disease: Gambian or west African, and Rhodesian or east African.

In the Gambian form, (West Africa) the flies prefer human hosts; they live in places where people congregate, attacking them as they gather. They are aggressive biters, dive-bombing those walking or driving through their areas, especially at the end of the dry season. They may be plentiful in one area of several acres and totally absent in adjacent areas. Both sexes are affected equally. The Gambian form has been found in urban areas in the Democratic Republic of Congo.

In the Rhodesian form in East Africa, the flies prefer domestic or wild aimal blood; they live in trees in savanna. Males are affected most, especially hunters and fishermen, when they happen to go through tsetse-infested areas. Some of the eastern tsetse flies enter villages, causing severe epidemics but accidental encounters are more the norm.

Both forms: The disease is transmitted in scattered areas from 15° North to 20° South. The distribution is very spotty—it can be very common in one area and absent in adjacent areas. In general, the Gambian form is found north and west of the Great Lakes area, while the Rhodesian is found east and south of there. Both forms are found near Lake Victoria. The disease is an important problem in Tanzania, Malawi, Uganda, Guinea, Ivory Coast, Chad, and Central African Republic. Transmission seems to have stopped and no new cases have been reported for several decades in countries such as Benin, Botswana, Burundi, Ethiopia, Gambia, Ghana, Guinea Bissau, Liberia, Mali, Namibia, Niger, Senegal, Sierra Leone, Swaziland, and Togo.

Onset: *Gambian sleeping sickness* has a very gradual onset; after an incubation period measured in weeks symptoms come and go at first, then mostly disappear for a second incubation period measured in months to years before the mental symptoms begin. Expatriates may have an initial reaction to the bite, consisting of fevers and flu-like symptoms that come and go for a while, beginning 10-40 days after the fly bite. There may be swelling of the face, HIVES, and itching. Then they have no more symptoms for the long incubation period.

In Rhodesian illness, the onset is more sudden; death may occur within a few months. The initial skin swelling occurs in 5-15 days. Other symptoms begin with a fever in less than 3 weeks from the time of the bite.

In both forms, expatriates tend to have a more rapid onset and more severe disease.

Clinical:

➢ **Gambian:**

Necessary: Slow onset of symptoms which initially come and go; there are large lymph nodes (not tender but movable, not stuck to the skin or underlying muscle) in the back of the neck; fatugue; general muscle pains; after the disease has been present for some time there are mental changes such as sleep problems, uncoordination, dizziness, personality changes, or trouble thinking.

Usual: No or mild fever and fever is usually higher evenings than mornings; swelling of the eyelids, face, neck, abdomen or penis; headache; big spleen; fast pulse; impotence in males; no menstruation in females; a flat rash which looks like red rings on white skin (more visible when the skin is warm). There may be ANEMIA.

Maybe: Painful and swollen testicles in males; a sensation of insects crawling in the skin or general whole-body itching; irregular pulse; weight loss.

Symptoms during the early stage are more common in females than in males, and in Whites than nationals. Miscarriages, stillbirths, and newborn deaths are common. Children have delayed mental and sexual development.

➢ **Rhodesian:**

Necessary: History of the fly bite with subsequent swelling, history of high fevers that came and went, or both.

Usual: The area of the fly bite is discolored. The swelling goes away in about two weeks. One to three weeks later, the patient has headaches and fevers again.

Maybe: There may be swollen lymph nodes in the arm pit or in the groin. The patient's spleen and possibly his liver are enlarged. He may develop JAUNDICE, HEART FAILURE, KIDNEY FAILURE, or itching all over. The late stages described below occur within a few months unless the patient dies of HEART FAILURE first.

➢ **Both types:**

This disease is rapidly fatal in patients who are HIV infected and have poor immunity. Late sleeping sickness is best described by a quotation from Manson, the author of early editions of Manson's Tropical Diseases:

"There is a disinclination to exertion; slow, shuffling gait; morose mask-like vacant expression; relaxation of features; hanging of the lower lip; puffiness and drooping of the eyelids; tendency to lapse into sleep or a condition simulating sleep...during the daytime contrasting with restlessness at night; slowness in answering questions; shirking of the day's task. Dull headache is generally present. He will walk, if forced to do so, with unsteady and swaying gait. His speech is difficult to follow. He never spontaneously engages in conversation or even asks for food.... He forgets even to chew his food, falling asleep perhaps in the act of conveying it to his mouth, or with the half-masticated bolus still in his cheek.... The habits usually become bestial and he becomes a drooling, dribbling and drowsy idiot."

Intolerable itching is common, as are BEDSORES and severe weight loss. In Whites at least one of the following is always present in the final stages of this disease: Excessive sleep, trembling, crazy behavior, or abnormal eye movements.

Complications: HYPOGLYCEMIA, HEART FAILURE, ANEMIA, IRITIS, BRAIN DAMAGE, or abnormal bleeding. There is a deficiency in thyroid hormone in many patients in the Congo. This may apply elsewhere, also. It is something to check at a hospital and treat if necessary.

Similar diseases: See Protocols C-2, C-3, C-7, C-10, and C-12. MALARIA may be indistinguishable especially in the early Rhodesian form in expatriates. The disease's non-response to QUININE and the history of the fly bite are distinctive. ARBOVIRAL FEVER, RUBELLA, MONONUCLEOSIS, and scalp infections may also cause enlargement of lymph nodes on the back of the neck. It resembles STROKE and cerebral MALARIA in the later stages but the onset of coma in sleeping sickness is much slower, over days rather than over minutes to hours. It may be virtually indistinguishable from the late stages of SYPHILIS.

Bush Laboratory: A sedimentation rate under 90 is highly unlikely in a patient with sleeping sickness; the test is sensitive but not specific.[1]

Higher-Level Care.

Laboratory: In the early stage, before mental symptoms start, a thick blood smear stained with Field's stain may show the organisms. This is more sensitive in Rhodesian than Gambian illness. In Gambian illness if the patient has a large lymph node in the back of his neck because of this, a physician or technician might put a needle in it, pull some fluid out, and examine it under a microscope. It must be examined within 15 minutes to show the organisms.

When the mental symptoms begin, the organisms leave the blood and can be found only in spinal fluid obtained by a spinal tap.[2] Many times the parasites are hard to find. A well-equipped lab may be able to spin blood to concentrate the organisms and thus to detect them more readily.

There are various tests that show antibodies to the sleeping sickness germs, but they should not be the sole basis for treatment because the drugs are toxic. It is imperative to find the sleeping sickness organism in the patient's body. In any case, the antibody tests are totally useless for the Rhodesian type of the disease since the organisms change their proteins rapidly. Any antibody test is likely to be negative even with active infection.

Facilities: In the mental stage, imaging with CT or MRI might be helpful.

Practitioners: This being a tropical disease with a very restricted distribution, don't even think of getting care anywhere other than London. Since the British colonized most of the area where this occurred, and since the management of the condition is very complex, their expertise is the best. See Volume I, Appendix 13.

---

[1] Sensitive means that if a person has sleeping sickness, his sedimentation rate will certainly be abnormally high. However, there are many other diseases beside sleeping sickness that increase the sedimentation rate. Therefore a normal sedimentation rate is most significant since it tells you that the patient does not have the disease. An elevated rate tells you that the patient is sick, which you knew already before you did the test.

[2] The spinal fluid must be examined immediately after it is taken; the parasites will be destroyed in 20 minutes. If parasites are found in the blood, *any* abnormality of the spinal fluid indicates the disease is in the late stage.

Treatment:

Prevention: Eliminate tsetse flies. Blood tests and preventive medication are available for this disease. These must be obtained and used with the direction of a physician. In the Gambian form, dogs, pigs, and sheep may have the disease in their blood without becoming ill. They pass it on to flies which then transmit it to humans. These animals should not be housed near human dwellings. In western Africa and in Ethiopia, one of the flies that transmits this disease can be eliminated by feeding IVERMECTIN to pigs in the area (dosage unknown; seek other information). The flies feed on pig blood and take in the drug which kills the male flies and keeps the females from breeding. Since the flies that carry this breed in coffee, banana, and lantana trees, separating these from the houses might be helpful.

Patient Care: This is essential as, once the patient develops mental symptoms, the death rate is 100% without proper treatment. With appropriate treatment, the patient in coma should start to wake up within 72 hours. PENTAMIDINE is useful to prevent the Gambian form of the disease after a bite or in the early stages. Once mental symptoms start, treatment is complicated. Send the patient to London as soon as possible. Two drugs that might be used are SURAMIN and/or MELASOPROL. Both are toxic and require physician supervision. NIRIDAZOLE is a drug that was formerly used, but it is very toxic and should not be used anymore. Diminazene Aceturate (Berenil) is used for animals. It is still experimental in humans. Meanwhile:

- Be sure he takes in enough food and liquid to stay well-nourished and well-hydrated. Place a stomach tube if necessary, keeping the patient lying on one side once it is in. Use no ASPIRIN. Give plenty of starch and sugar; low blood sugar is a common complication.
- Turn the patient from one side to the other every two hours during the day. Move his arms and legs as far as they will go in each direction at least four times a day. See Appendix 8, Volume I.
- Treat the patient for SEIZURES if necessary.
- EFLORNITHINE is a drug that works well for Gambian but it only works for about 50% of Rhodesian cases. It is usually given IV at first and then orally later. If your patient is not very ill, you can try to give it orally from the beginning. In most cases of Rhodesian SS one of the older drugs must be used additionally. Below is a list of possibilities:
- If you are forced to use other toxic drugs, giving PREDNISONE initially might decrease the side-effects.
- The patient must have a spinal tap (lumbar puncture) after treatment is done and then every 6 months for two years thereafter, to be sure there are no more parasites.

Type	Gambian	Rhodesian
First stage	Pentamidine or Suramin or Eflornithine	Suramin or Eflornitihine
Late stage	Melasoprol or Eflornithine	Melasoprol or Eflornithine

AFRICAN TICK BITE FEVER AFRICAN TICK TYPHUS

See SPOTTED FEVER in the *Disease Index*. This is transmitted by cattle ticks. There are frequently multiple eschars (little black scabs) rather than only one.

AMEBIC LIVER DISEASE

Surveys show this to be particularly common in Central African Republic, Ethiopia, Gabon, Gambia, Niger, Rwanda, Somalia, D. R. Congo, in urban areas and the Jos Plateau of Nigeria rural South Africa, Tanzania, and Sudan. It is rare in the desert areas of SW Africa.

In Niger, and possibly in surrounding areas, those regions that are hot and damp tend to have amebic liver disease. Those hot and dry tend to have just the DYSENTERY without the liver's being infected.

This disease is a problem in Burundi; it can look just like HEPATITIS or ACUTE ABDOMEN.

ANEMIA

This is common all over Africa except in cultures that consume animal blood, use iron pots for brewing beer or cooking, or are pastoral at high altitudes.

In Chad, most anemia in pregnancy and half of all other anemias are due to IRON deficiency.

In The Gambia, much of the anemia is due to vitamin deficiency from lack of FOLIC ACID or VITAMIN B_{12}.

ANTHRAX

This is common in Zimbabwe, along the Rift Valley in Ethiopia, in southern Kenya amongst the Maasai, the northern and western parts of the continent, and around Lake Victoria. It may appear similar to CUTANEOUS LEISHMANIASIS or to TUBERCULOSIS of the skin but its onset is more rapid.

It occurs generally in western Africa and also in parts of Ethiopia, Zimbabwe, and Tanzania, frequently in epidemics, and many times with multiple cases within families. In about 90% of the cases, the person can trace the disease to some contact with a sick animal.

ARBOVIRAL FEVER

This is actually a group of diseases, not a single disease. In most areas these diseases are carried by mosquitoes. Two that are listed separately because of public health concerns are EBOLA FEVER and LASSA FEVER. See Protocol C-2.

Sand Fly Fever is a type of arboviral fever carried by sand flies in arid northern Africa. See the separate description with this entry below.

Rift Valley Fever occurs mainly in eastern Africa, south and east of a line between Alexandria, Egypt and Nouamrhar, Mauritania. Reportedly it is absent from the west African countries that border the Gulf of Guinea (the southern coast of West Africa). It occasionally results in loss of vision or ENCEPHALITIS, or HEMORRHAGIC FEVER. This is carried by mosquitoes. Incubation period is 2-7 days. It tends to occur in epidemics at the end of the rainy season in Zambia (Lusaka and Mazabuka), Burkina Faso, and Central African Republic (around Bangui). There have been outbreaks in NE and NW Kenya. In many areas of east Africa, RVF affects only cattle; however, in northern Kenya and southern Somalia, there are also human cases and significant numbers of deaths, particularly at times of flooding. This may be contagious. See Protocol C-2.

West Nile Fever is a kind of arboviral fever indistinguishable from HEPATITIS. It occurs occasionally in Central African Republic. It is considered a potential bioterrorist weapon. The incubation is 3-6 days.

Igbo Ora Virus is found in the rural areas of Ivory Coast. It produces joint pains, but no long-term disabilities and no deaths. It is carried by mosquito with an incubation period of 3-12 days.

Crimean-Congo Hemorrhagic Fever is most common in southern Africa. It may be present in scattered areas south and east of a line between Alexandria, Egypt and Nouamrhar, Mauritania. It is carried by ticks. The incubation is 1-14 days. Symptoms are fever, headache, muscle pains, and general bleeding. See Protocol C-2 and the *Disease Index*.

Similar regional diseases: AFRICAN SLEEPING SICKNESS with which the fever is either not high or is high only off and on, not continually. LASSA FEVER, also similar, has a sudden onset of fever; the patient has red eyes and chest pains. EBOLA FEVER commonly becomes HEMORRHAGIC FEVER.

Sand Fly Fever

Cause: Virus

Moderately ill to very ill; Class 2; Regional, especially in northern Africa and along the Nile; in June to August.

Age: Any. **Who**: Those bitten by sand flies. (This kind of sand fly feeds mostly on chickens, less on cows and horses, and only occasionally on humans. It bites at night and also 6:30-10:30 A.M.) **Onset**: Very sudden, over hours, with a short incubation of 3-6 days.

Clinical:

Necessary: An initial fever with headache, eye pain, and general muscle pains, lasting 2-4 days. The liver and spleen are normal size and non-tender. There is no rash.

Usually: The patient's eyes are red, the face is flushed, and the patient avoids light and eye movement because it causes more pain. There may be nosebleed. There may be depression.

Commonly: The worst pain is in the low back.

Sometimes: There is also nausea, vomiting, abdominal pains, and diarrhea. The neck may be stiff. The worst of the disease is over in a few days, but the patient does not feel healthy for weeks.

Complications: None.

Similar diseases: See Protocol C-2. Consider also HEMORRHAGIC FEVER (abnormal bleeding) and MENINGITIS.

Treatment: Keep the patient hydrated and well fed. Use ACETAMINOPHEN for pain. RIBAVIRIN may be helpful. Do not use antibiotics.

ARTHRITIS

Similar regional diseases: SICKLE CELL DISEASE also involves joint pains but there is either ANEMIA or episodic abdominal pain or both. In western and central Africa, consider MANSONELLOSIS PERSTANS. In expatriates consider ONCHOCERCIASIS. In East Africa consider HIV INFECTION which causes a symmetrical arthritis of large joints with sparing of the small joints. FILARIASIS can cause an arthritis of the knees which responds readily to DEC.

ASCARIASIS

This is extremely common in SW and central Cameroon; Bauchi, Oyo, and Ogun States in Nigeria; amongst the pygmies of D. R. Congo and Rwanda; around Kinshasa, D. R. Congo; and near Entebbe, Uganda.

ASTHMA

The association of asthma and allergies to tiny insects living in dust has been shown for the following areas: Zambia, Zimbabwe, and South Africa. It may also occur in other areas. In southern Ethiopia, "asthma" is most often due to TUBERCULOSIS.

BELL'S PALSY

Regional cause: SICKLE CELL DISEASE.

BERIBERI

Cause: Thiamine deficiency.

There have been outbreaks in western Africa where milled rice has replaced traditional grains and cereals. It occurs in the wet, dry, and mixed forms, most commonly in September and October. It seems to affect productive, working males first and most severely. This is also common amongst the Bushmen in the northern Kalahari.

Similar regional diseases: POLIO shows floppy weakness, but it starts with an illness with a fever. PLANT POISONING due to Lathyrism shows stiff rather than floppy weakness, as does TROPICAL SPASTIC PARAPARESIS.

BLADDER STONE

This is common in Niamey. Most (94%) of the patients are male.

BRAIN DAMAGE

This may be caused by AFRICAN SLEEPING SICKNESS and, less commonly, SCHISTOSOMIASIS (any type).

BRUCELLOSIS

This is especially common north of the equator and in Tanzania. In western Nigeria, about 1/2 of the adults have had this disease at some time. In Mali, about 1/4 of the adults have had this disease.

Brucellosis in Africa tends to invade bones, mainly the spine and the hip, but occasionally the knee(s) and rarely other bones. Mental changes from the disease are also common.

BURKITT LYMPHOMA

This is especially prevalent in the West Nile district of Uganda and in Nigeria. In western Cameroon it affects adults also and more often begins in the abdomen. In some areas it may be as common as TUBERCULOSIS.

BURULI ULCER

This is common in Benin and Ghana where it can cause significant disability, compromising the patient's prosperity. In Benin it occurs mostly in those under 15 y.o. and over 50 y.o. There is a significant association with swamp water.

CANCER

Stomach cancer is common near the southern Kenyan border, in Rwanda and Burundi, and in adjacent areas of D. R. Congo and Uganda.

Breast cancer in Nigeria tends to affect younger women than in the Western countries. When it is diagnosed during pregnancy or nursing, the prognosis is poor.

Bladder cancer is common wherever there is SCHISTOSOMIASIS HEMATOBIUM.

Cancer of the penis is particularly common in some areas of Uganda; it is more common in uncircumcised men. TUBERCULOSIS may look similar.

Cancer of the esophagus occurs mainly in eastern and southeastern Africa.

Liver cancer is common in Africans, more in humid than dry areas. In Nigeria, liver cancer is the most common kind of cancer. It may affect young people. It is also comon in Niger.

Cancer of the nose and throat is common in the Indian population of Africa.

Skin Cancers:

- Kaposi's sarcoma is a skin cancer that is associated with HIV INFECTION, occuring mainly in males. It looks like large, reddish or bluish WARTS. It is very common in Central African Republic and the Lake Victoria area.
- Melanoma is a very aggressive type of skin cancer. It is usually a dark color. It occurs in Whites (anywhere on the body), and on the soles and palms of Blacks.

CATARACT

This is very common in the Sahel and Ethiopia.

CEREBRAL PALSY

ARBOVIRAL FEVERs and AFRICAN SLEEPING SICKNESS are regional causes of this.

CHICKEN POX

Similar regional disease: MONKEYPOX is similar but is found almost exclusively in northern D. R. Congo and southern Central African Republic; occasional cases are seen in western Africa. With MONKEYPOX, the lymph nodes are large and the rash breaks out all at once rather than spreading from one part of the skin to another over several days. Also, with monkeypox the patient is moderately to very ill whereas in chicken pox the child is only mildly ill (although an adult with chicken pox may be very ill.)

CHOLERA

Cholera outbreaks occur in Cameroon, Sierra Leone, Uganda, Congo, Chad, Tanzania, Mozambique, Liberia, Kenya, Togo, D. R. Congo, Comoro Islands, Somalia. It may occur anywhere. There tends to be more cholera in NE Africa during years of heavy rainfall. In parts of east Africa, it may be resistant to DOXYCYCLINE and COTRIMOXAZOLE.

CIRRHOSIS

This may be due to HEMOCHROMATOSIS.

CRETINISM

The second kind is the one that affects most cretins in Africa. (See entry in main *Disease Index*.)

CUTANEOUS LEISHMANIASIS

Leishmania aethiopica occurs in 2/3 of Ethiopia, mainly the central, western, and northwestern areas and along the Rift Valley. It is not present in the Ogaden area and the Ethiopia/Kenya border area east of Turkana. It is common in Turkana. It spills over the border a bit into eastern Sudan and southwest Eritrea.

Leishmania Major occurs all along the north coast of Africa and in Niger, Senegal, northern Nigeria, and Mali. It is also present around Khartoum, Sudan. KETOCONAZOLE treatment reportedly works well in Sudan.

CYSTICERCOSIS

This is common in South Africa, Togo, Reunion Island, and Madagascar. It is found only in areas where pigs are raised in such a way that they come into contact with human waste.

DENGUE FEVER

This is present mostly in the western and eastern coastal areas. It occurs in the Comoro Islands. The mosquito that carries the disease is present inland also, so there is potential for the disease to spread inland. Recently it has been found in Djibouti, Sudan, Kenya, Ivory Coast, Egypt, and Burkina Faso.

DEPRESSION

Physiological causes in Africa include DENGUE FEVER, AFRICAN SLEEPING SICKNESS, EBOLA FEVER, and Marburg Fever (listed with EBOLA FEVER).

DIABETES

HEMOCHROMATOSIS is a regional cause, mainly in southern Africa. PANCREATITIS is a cause in eastern and western Africa.

DIPHTHERIA

This is known to be common in Algeria and Senegal; it may occur anywhere. Skin diphtheria is common in central Africa.

DONOVANOSIS

This occurs but is not common in Africa except for South Africa, Zambia, and Zimbabwe. The cases that occur are mostly in seaports and large urban areas.

DYSENTERY

Bacterial dysentery is especially common in the lakes region of D. R. Congo, western Uganda, Rwanda, and Burundi, especially where there is crowding. In this area outbreaks are apt to happen in times of drought. It is also extremely common in Ethiopia, Sudan, Chad, Mali, and Mauritania. It is usually sensitive to CHLORAMPHENICOL, COTRIMOXAZOLE, and GENTAMYCIN.

Amebic dysentery is common throughout Africa south of the Sahara, except for the desert area of the southwest. In Niger, hot and dry regions tend to have amebic dysentery.

EBOLA FEVER

Cause: Virus

This is a specific type of HEMORRHAGIC FEVER. The entry includes Marburg fever which is probably rare.

Very ill; Class 1 or 4; contagious; usually fatal but intensive care in a level 5 medical facility might be lifesaving. However, transporting a patient to that kind of facility can cause a public health disaster.[1]

This occurs in the tropical rainforests of Central Africa. There are two types: Sudan and Zaire strains. The Zaire strain is more severe. The Sudan strain occurs in southern Sudan (also adjacent border areas) and the Zaire strain in north central D. R. Congo (and adjacent border areas). Cases have been reported from near the Kenya-Uganda border, from Ivory Coast, and from NE Gabon.

Age: Any, more adults than children. **Who**: It affects pygmies, young adults, and farmers preferentially. First cases acquire the disease from unknown sources, possibly bats and/or dogs. Subsequent cases in an epidemic are usually relatives or medical care-givers of initial cases. It appears that those who handle bodies right after death are most susceptible. **Onset**: Sudden, over a day or so, after a 3-21-day incubation period.

Clinical:

Necessary: Sudden onset of fever, back pain, red eyes, weakness, loss of appetite, nausea, vomiting, diarrhea, and general aching.

Sometimes: Subsequently abdominal pain and jaundice may develop. The patient's eyes become red. He may develop a rash, beginning on the chest. He may have a sore throat, a cough, trouble swallowing, or hiccups.

Finally: The patient starts bleeding all over: nosebleeds, vomiting blood, bloody diarrhea, and bleeding from needle sticks. The patient at this point is either in a coma or appears "spacy" or "not there".

Similar diseases: See Protocol C-2. (This is one type of arboviral fever.) Also consider other types of HEMORRHAGIC FEVER. Marburg fever is similar but it causes a deep red coloring of the roof of the mouth, starting in the back and moving forward. It also destroys the testicles and can cause long-term emotional changes. It has been extremely rare.

Treatment:

Prevention: Recently-dead corpses are most likely to transmit disease to those who move, wash, or bury

[1] This is a tropical disease. If you seek higher-level care, it should either be in a facility of a country in which this disease is common, or else in a facility specializing in tropical medicine. See Volume I, Appendix 13.

them. Bleach kills the virus. Protective clothing is essential.

Patient Care: The usual anti-viral drugs do not work. It may be desirable to send a patient to a major Western university hospital with an intensive care unit, but any other referral is a waste and it will probably spread the epidemic because of in-transit exposures. Any transport must be by private vehicle with the patient in strict isolation; sending a patient on a commercial airline could cause a world-wide epidemic.

Results: Recovery takes months during which time the patient remains infective, particularly all his body secretions.

ELEPHANTIASIS, ENDEMIC

Synonym: Mossy foot.

See also FILARAISIS.

The following areas reportedly have endemic elephantiasis: Cameroon highlands; Morocco; the entire Rift Valley, and particularly the Wolaitta area of southern Ethiopia.

ENCEPHALITIS

Rift Valley fever, a type of ARBOVIRAL FEVER, is a regional cause of this, as is AFRICAN SLEEPING SICKNESS. See the epidemiology note under ARBOVIRAL FEVER in this index.

ENTERIC FEVER

Includes: Typhoid fever, Paratyphoid fever.

Typhoid fever is common all over. Paratyphoid fever is uncommon.

In The Gambia and Central African Republic this disease is peculiar in children. There is no progressive rise in fever and no relatively slow pulse. It causes mainly abdominal complaints in about 67% and mainly PNEUMONIA in most of the rest. Occasionally it presents like a KIDNEY INFECTION and occasionally there is no fever at all. It should be suspected in any seriously ill child who does not respond to other treatment. This is a common cause of death in patients with HIV INFECTION.

ENTEROBIASIS

This is common all over the world. It has been noted to be especially common near the northern Central African Republic/Cameroon border.

EPILEPSY

Additional causes in Africa are AFRICAN SLEEPING SICKNESS, and rarely ONCHOCERCIASIS.

FILARIASIS

Synonym: Elephantiasis, non-endemic.

The filariasis in Africa is all of the Bancroftian type. It occurs along the north coast of the continent and in scattered areas between 17° North and 25° South.

This is common in Madagascar, in the Igwum Basin of Nigeria, and the Logone Valley of northern Cameroon.

MANSONELLA PERSTANS is a form of filariasis listed separately.

FLUOROSIS

It is most common in Ethiopia in the Wonji-Shoa, Alem-Tena, Sami-Beta areas, and throughout the Rift Valley. It may occur in other areas.

GALLBLADDER DISEASE

This is not common in Africans except with SICKLE CELL DISEASE and THALLASEMIA.

GASTROENTERITIS

Similar regional disease: PLANT POISONING due to Lolism.

GIARDIASIS

It is found all over Africa, but is especially common around Kinshasa, D. R. Congo, and in central Uganda. It is uncommon amongst the pygmies of Rwanda and in Ogun State, Nigeria. It is common in Ethiopia.

GLAUCOMA

Acute glaucoma does not generally happen to Blacks. Chronic glaucoma is common in Blacks.

GOITER

This is common in the Wedya District of Zimbabwe, but CRETINISM occurs rarely. It is common in the Man Region of Ivory Coast, and around Bulape, D. R. Congo. In southern Africa it tends to be common at an altitude over 1000 meters (3300 ft.) and 15 km (9 mi.) or more from the sea. It is common in the central highlands of Ethiopia.

GONORRHEA

In some areas of Kenya, PENICILLIN, DOXYCYCLINE, and some CEPHALOSPORINs no longer work. SPECTINOMYCIN and CHLORAMPHENICOL are still useful. Seek local advice.

GUINEA WORM

Cause: Worm

Synonyms: Dracontiasis, Dracunculiasis

Mildly to moderately ill; Class 1; Regional, in rural agricultural areas where water is obtained from wells into which people step. There has been a big WHO effort to eliminate the disease. Therefore the maps are no longer reliable. The disease has been largely eliminated from Cameroon, Central African Republic, Chad, Kenya, and Senegal. On the other hand, it has spread to some areas that used to be free of it. It is most common in Ghana, Mali, Niger, Nigeria, Sudan, Togo, Uganda, Benin, and Burkina Faso. Among these, Sudan has by far the most cases, due to civil unrest and inability of the WHO to function within their borders.

Areas known to have had guinea worm

The following countries have had a major problem, though it is likely to be found only in some areas: Sudan, Togo, Benin, Burkina Faso, Central African Republic, Ethiopia, Ghana, Mali, Nigeria, Uganda. It is not found south of the equator. In Nigeria it is found mostly in the western half of the country. It is not common but it occurs in the Lake Chad area.

Age: Any. **Who**: Those who drink water contaminated with microscopic larvae. **Onset**: Variable; usually about 1 year after drinking infected water.

Clinical:

Necessary: A small bump forms on the skin, usually on the leg but it may be anywhere. This enlarges to become a blister. It is itchy and frequently burning; the pain is relieved by cold. When the blister breaks, one can see the end of the worm. There is only one worm per bump and each worm is 30-70 cm (12-28 in.) long. An incredibly painful sore forms in place of the blister.

Maybe: The worm will discharge a milky fluid.

Complications: Severe infections may develop because of the open wounds. When parents are infected, their children tend to suffer from MALNUTRITION because of loss of income and lack of care.

Bush Laboratory: There is no test for this, but the disease is so distinctive that no lab is required.

Similar diseases: MYIASIS is a skin ulcer with many short, fat "worms". The disease may initially cause KATAYAMA DISEASE. The very painful bump which becomes an ulcer may resemble skin DIPHTHERIA.

Treatment:

Prevention: Encourage the design of wells which eliminates the possibility of stepping into them. A simple sand filter works well to eliminate parasites from contaminated water, or you can use Temphos (Abate) to treat affected water.

Patient Care: The best treatment is for the worm to be surgically removed before the blister forms. This is a relatively easy procedure; it can be done at a level 2 or 3 facility. It reduces the period of disability from weeks to two days. If you already know how to suture wounds, it would be feasible for you to learn how to do the procedure.

Once the blister forms: Immerse the blister or sore in cold water. This makes the worm limp. IBUPROFEN helps to hasten this process. Wind the worm on a small clean stick, a few centimeters a day, not so tightly that the worm breaks. (If it breaks give the patient one of the drugs listed below.) This will gradually draw the worm out. If the patient is bedridden anyway, keeping the area continually wet will draw the worm out faster (in 2 weeks rather than 8-12 weeks). Otherwise keep the area clean and dressed with ANTIBIOTIC OINTMENT to prevent secondary infection. A number of different drugs are also useful, such as METRONIDAZOLE, TINIDAZOLE, MEBENDAZOLE, and THIABENDAZOLE. NIRIDAZOLE is an old, dangerous drug that should no longer be used.

HEART FAILURE

The *restrictive type* occurs with LASSA FEVER. It may also occur for no known reason in children with MALNUTRITION in eastern Africa. It is called endomyocardial fibrosis; it is treated like ordinary heart failure but the treatment is usually not successful.

The *dilated type* occurs with AFRICAN SLEEPING SICKNESS and with pregnancy.

The *hypertrophic type* occurs in patients with HYPERTENSION.

The *valvular type* is most common in Africa. It is usually because of RHEUMATIC FEVER.

Regional causative diseases are AFRICAN SLEEPING SICKNESS, LASSA FEVER, and HEMOCHROMATOSIS.

HEMOCHROMATOSIS

It occurs in areas of Botswana, Ghana, Kenya, Malawi, Mozambique, Swaziland, Tanzania, Zambia, and Zimbabwe. It is most common in males who drink beer brewed in iron or steel containers and females who consume the same but are neither menstruating nor pregnant. It is more common with a corn diet than with other diets. You should encourage patients to brew their beer in something non-metallic.

HEMORRHAGIC FEVER

Most Common Causative Diseases:

- LASSA FEVER: listed separately, this Index.
- YELLOW FEVER: listed separately, this Index.

Less Likely Causative Diseases:

- CRIMEAN-CONGO HEMORRHAGIC FEVER, described in the *Disease Index*.
- Rift Valley Fever is described under ARBOVIRAL FEVER, this Index.

Least Common Causative Diseases:

- EBOLA FEVER: listed separately, this Index.

- DENGUE FEVER: listed in the *Disease Index*.

Dengue has not yet caused hemorrhagic fever in Africa, but it does in Asia. Lassa, Ebola, Crimean-Congo, and Rift Valley Fevers can be directly transmitted from patients to bystanders. Hospital treatment is worthwhile as it can make a big difference in the chances for survival. However, transport to a higher-level facility can start an epidemic.

HEPATITIS

In Ivory Coast, about 1/3 is *Hepatitis B*, 1/3 is *Hepatitis E*, and 1/3 is Hepatitis A or other viruses.

Hepatitis B transmission from mother to child is not common in this area except in southern Africa where it is readily transmitted from person to person within households. There is some evidence that one means of this transmission is bedbugs. Elsewhere it tends to be transmitted mostly by blood.

In the Gezira Region of Sudan, Hepatitis B is more common in areas that are crowded and in people who have tattoos. 88% of those over 50 y.o. have had the disease.

In Niger, 100% of the people have had Hepatitis B before 40 y.o; 29% carry an associated virus (Hepatitis D) that causes liver CANCER.

In southern Africa, 5.5-14% of the people surveyed have had Hepatitis B; the percentage was larger near the coast than inland.

In Mali, 42% of the reproductive women have had Hepatitis B.

In Lagos, half the cases of hepatitis are Hepatitis B.

Hepatitis C is most common in Egypt, Libya, and D. R. Congo.

Hepatitis E is a common problem all over Africa, especially Algeria, Chad, Ethiopia, Gambia, Kenya, Nigeria, and Somalia. Hepatitis E epidemics occur in Somalia mid-May to Mid-June. The incubation is about 40 days. General whole-body itching is common.

Similar regional diseases: YELLOW FEVER, LASSA FEVER, and PNEUMONIA in Blacks. There is protein in the urine with YELLOW FEVER.

In Central African Republic, an ARBOVIRAL FEVER, West Nile Fever, may be indistinguishable.

In the Burundi area AMEBIC LIVER DISEASE can look very similar; a trial treatment with METRONIDAZOLE might be useful.

If the patient has had recent close contact with newborn animals, he may have Q FEVER.

HERNIA

This is common in the groins of African Blacks; In the Kauta, D. R. Congo area, about 1/4 of the population have groin hernias. UMBILICAL HERNIA is extremely common in Black children.

HIV INFECTION

African epidemiology:

The areas where HIV INFECTION is most prevalent in this region are: Botswana, Burundi, Central African Republic, Ivory Coast, Kenya, Mali, Mozambique, Namibia, Rwanda, South Africa, Zambia, and Zimbabwe. TUBERCULOSIS and HIV INFECTION overlap so much that the WHO definition is not very helpful where both are common. In Uganda (where it is a rural as much as an urban disease), it is spread mostly by sex rather than blood.

There is usually about a 3-4 month interval between becoming infected and converting the blood test from negative to positive. The disease is very contagious in this stage.

Clinical:

SHINGLES is commonly the first problem when a patient gets sick. Over 90% of patients with SHINGLES also have HIV.

In Central African Republic, the disease commonly presents with BELL'S PALSY; CANDIDIASIS and skin CANCER are common complications.

There is a peculiar rash that is common. It consists of little bumps, like soft warts, mainly on the hairy surfaces of the forearms, hands, and feet. These bumps itch and, when they are scratched, they break open and release a small drop of clear liquid. Then they heal with a dark scar. The disease progresses during pregnancy.

Africa-specific parameters: PNEUMONIA must be treated with both CHLORAMPHENICOL and AMPICILLIN, or else one of the CEPHALOSPORINs.

About 33% of patients with respiratory symptoms have TUBERCULOSIS. Their skin tests and their sputum smears are both likely to be negative in spite of their having active disease. Non-respiratory TB is more common in AIDS patients than the general population. Lung TB in the presence of AIDS frequently affects the lower rather than the upper lung. TB treatment is usually initially successful, but relapses are much more common in those HIV positive.

HOOKWORM

This is extremely common in central, NE, and SW Cameroon; in Chad, in the Bushmen of Namibia; in the pygmies of Rwanda and the Ituri region of D. R. Congo; on the Jos Plateau and in the Bauchi and Oyo States of Nigeria; and around Bangui, Central African Republic. It is common in central Burkina Faso; around Kinshasa, D. R. Congo; and in the Ogun State of Nigeria. In Ethiopia it is common only where there is agriculture and the altitude is less than 2000 meters (6600 ft.) though it occurs at higher altitudes.

HYDATID DISEASE

This is very common in arid northern Africa, especially along the Niger delta and Libya. It is also very prevalent amongst the people (especially Turkana) in NW and NE Kenya, amongst the Toposa of southern Sudan, the Dassenach, Nyangatom, Hamar, and Boran of SW Ethiopia and northern Kenya, and amongst the Maasai of Tanzania. It occurs in arable southern Africa also. Where it is common, it may be seen in children as well as adults though it affects mostly young to middle-aged adults.

HYPERTENSION

This is common in Africa, with complications being more common in Blacks than in Whites. Blacks may be resistant to PROPRANOLOL.

Treatment: Mainly salt restriction, no smoking, weight control, and no birth control pills for females, with available medications added as necessary.

HYPOGLYCEMIA

Other causes in Africa are AFRICAN SLEEPING SICKNESS and PLANT POISONING from unripe Ackee. With Ackee there is a rapid onset of symptoms. With AFRICAN SLEEPING SICKNESS the onset is gradual; nourishment should be provided with the treatment.

HYPOTHERMIA

This is a problem in the Sahara desert and at high elevations. (In the Sahara it gets very cold at night since the sand does not hold the heat well.)

INTESTINAL FLUKE

Heterophyiasis is a type of intestinal fluke that comes from eating raw fish in Egypt.

IRITIS

Regional causes are AFRICAN SLEEPING SICKNESS and LOIASIS.

IRRITABLE BOWEL

Similar regional disease: LIVER FLUKE.

JAUNDICE

Regional causes include YELLOW FEVER. The most common causes are HEPATITIS and MALARIA.

KATAYAMA DISEASE

In Africa, this refers to the initial stage of SCHISTOSOMIASIS (any kind), LOIASIS, GUINEA WORM, or HYDATID DISEASE. Sometimes LASSA FEVER can cause a similar problem. It is more common with SCHISTOSOMIASIS MANSONI than SCHISTOSOMIASIS HEMATOBIUM. It is more common in expatriates than nationals.

KIDNEY FAILURE

Nephrotic kidney failure can also be caused by SICKLE CELL DISEASE, SCHISTOSOMIASIS HEMATOBIUM, and PLANT POISONING due to Impila. The most common causes in Africa are HEPATITIS B, MALARIA, SYPHILIS, and SCHISTOSOMIASIS MANSONI. The prognosis is good if the cause is SCHISTOSOMIASIS and it is treated.

Regional causes:

Nephritic failure - SICKLE CELL DISEASE.

Obstructive failure - SCHISTOSOMIASIS HEMATOBIUM.

Infective failure - AFRICAN SLEEPING SICKNESS.

Hemolytic failure - SICKLE CELL DISEASE.

KIDNEY INFECTION

Similar regional diseases: SCHISTOSOMIASIS HEMATOBIUM.

KIDNEY STONE

Similar regional disease: SCHISTOSOMIASIS HEMATOBIUM.

LARVA MIGRANS

The skin type is common in the Niger delta. One deep type can be caused by the bite of a fly in humid areas of central Africa (see LOIASIS). LOIASIS causes itching, pain, and blindness. Other types of larva migrans may (in the absence of laboratory facilities) be indistinguishable from LOIASIS. One of these is caused by a worm whose larval form is present in giant snails in Madagascar and Mauritius. When people eat the raw snails, they can acquire the parasite.

LASSA FEVER

Cause: Virus

Synonym: African hemorrhagic fever (which may also refer to other diseases peculiar to Africa, such as EBOLA and Marburg).

Mildly to severely ill; Class 2-4; Contagious; Regional

The disease is present in West Africa, south and west of the Chad/Sudan/CAR border point. It is also present in SE Africa, the Lake Nyasa area and south of there to the SA border. The similar disease, EBOLA FEVER, occurs in D. R. Congo (especially NE) and southern Sudan.

Age: Any. **Who**: Anyone who has not had that kind of fever. Medical care-givers, especially midwives who have delivered an infected woman, are particularly susceptible. **Onset**: Usually slow, over days.

Clinical:

Necessary: A high fever with weakness and general body pains.

Usually: The patient has a headache, sore throat or chest pain. The chest pain is a kind of PERICARDITIS.

Occasionally: Other symptoms are cough, pain with urination, abdominal pain, vomiting, red eyes, abnormal bleeding, and a swollen face. Diarrhea occurs rarely.

The death rate is high, especially in pregnant women, those who have just delivered, in children under 12 y.o., and in babies born to infected mothers.

Complications: PERICARDITIS, HEMORRHAGIC FEVER, BRAIN DAMAGE, TONSILLITIS, HEART FAILURE, KIDNEY FAILURE, SHOCK. If HEMORRHAGIC FEVER develops, there is a sudden drop in blood pressure on the seventh day of illness. With Lassa fever, about 1/4 will become deaf on the average, but the probability varies from one community to the next. Convalescence takes 2-4 weeks. The patient may become bald but hair will grow back.

Similar diseases: See the list in ARBOVIRAL FEVERs; also YELLOW FEVER (also JAUNDICE), DENGUE FEVER (bone pain is worse), MALARIA (chest pain is unusual), SEPSIS.

There is a similar disease, O'nyong-nyong, in the Uganda/Rwanda/Tanzania area. It is carried by anopheles mosquitoes; see Volume I, Appendix 10. The difference is that O'nyong-nyong has a severe arthritis connected to it and it does not cause hemorrhage or death. Recovery is complete and spontaneous, but after a long time.

Bush Laboratory: There may be protein in the urine.

Higher-Level Care. *Laboratory*: Very sophisticated hospital laboratories can do blood tests for this. *Facilities*: Intensive care unit, at least level 3. *Practitioner*: Hematologist, infectious disease specialist, and/or someone with prior experience managing this disease.

Treatment:

Prevention: Wear gloves and mask when caring for patients. A vaccine is being developed.

Patient Care: It is desirable to send out any patient who is more than five months pregnant; these women have a very high death rate. However, transport is problematic due to contagion. Keep the patient sitting up as long as he is conscious.

Lassa fever responds well to RIBAVIRIN, and immune serum from recovered patients can also be used; therefore it is worthwhile to transport to a hospital. Neither the drug nor the serum should be used in the village situation.

LEPROSY

This is extremely common in the Sahel and less common, though not rare, in western and central Africa. Blacks tend to get the indeterminate and tuberculoid types; less than 10% of their leprosy is lepromatous except for in Ethiopia where lepromatous is more common. Whites get the borderline and lepromatous kinds. In Africa the distribution of leprosy is very patchy. If there is a tribal-language word for the disease, probably it was common in the past, and it probably still occurs. The countries where it is most common are, in order, Madagascar, Guinea, Niger, Ethiopia, Sudan, DR Congo, Nigeria. Other endemic countries: Benin, Burkina Faso, Chad, Ivory coast, Egypt, Mali, Mozambique, Senegal, Zambia.

Prevention: In Chad, a program of teaching patients about the disease and how to treat it and then letting them treat themselves, was extremely successful, resulting in good compliance.

LEPTOSPIROSIS

This is common in Ethiopia, the Comoros, Somalia, Reunion Island, Nigeria, and probably elsewhere. It is mostly a rural disease which occurs during the rainy season.

Similar regional disease: YELLOW FEVER. If in doubt, treat for both.

LIVER FAILURE

The most common causes in this area are HEPATITIS, ALCOHOLISM, SCHISTOSOMIASIS MANSONI, and SICKLE CELL DISEASE (mainly in West Africa).

Also consider the following diseases in Africa:

Disease	Liver	Jaundice	Other
HEMOCHROMATOSIS	Large, lumpy	Maybe	ALCOHOL brewed in iron or steel; mainly males.
YELLOW FEVER	Normal size, tender	After 3 days	Fever, aching, headache, eye pain.

LIVER FLUKE

Liver flukes are present only in some areas, mainly those that raise sheep or cattle. It occurs in Egypt, Madagascar, Uganda, Kenya, and Malawi, possibly elsewhere. Only Fascioliasis is present in this region.

Snails that carry the liver fluke. The heights of the snails are 1.4-2.5 cm

LOIASIS

Cause: Worm

Synonyms: Loa-loa, Eye worm, Calabar swellings.

Mildly to very ill; Class 2; Regional, humid areas, in and near rubber plantations and forested areas; never in urban areas.

In the Congo it is most common south and central, and more common amongst the Bantus than the Pygmies. About 50% of adults in some areas have or have had the problem, and it is one of the commonest medical complaints. Around Calabar, Nigeria, about 1.5% of the general population has this condition, and 11% around Kivu, D. R. Congo. In Uganda, the jungle has moved into previously arable areas and LOIASIS has come with it.

Age: Any. **Who**: Bitten by Chrysops flies. These usually bite below the knees. They prefer bare skin but can bite through socks. **Onset**: About 1 year after the bite.

Rain forest areas where Loiasis might occur.

Clinical:

Necessary: The patient has one or more of the following symptoms:

- Small egg-sized swellings, uncomfortable but not very painful, appear on the hands and forearms, sometimes elsewhere on the body. (They develop suddenly and last for 2-3 days only.)
- There is general swelling without a definite lump.
- Worms are seen or felt moving underneath the skin or crossing the whites of the eyes. They are 2.5-7.5 cm (1-3 inches) long.

Usually: When worms move under the skin, they cause numbness and tingling, or pricking, itching, creeping sensations; occasionally shooting pains or weakness may develop. Heat brings worms to the surface. They are seen and felt for minutes to hours, then disappear into the depths of the body. When they cross the eye, the patient complains first of itching, then of the sensation of having been punched in the eye. The eyes may swell, become red, and the patient may have loss of vision.

Sometimes: Expatriates have an immediate reaction to the bite. After the incubation period, in expatriates, symptoms of KATAYAMA DISEASE may occur first. In general, expatriates are more likely to have allergic reactions but negative blood tests (for the larvae) whereas nationals tend to have positive blood tests but few or no symptoms.

Complications: ENCEPHALITIS, blindness, STROKE, HEART FAILURE, KIDNEY FAILURE; PNEUMONIA when the worms first enter the body and migrate through the lungs. KIDNEY INFECTION occurs in about 1/3 of expatriates.

Swollen right arm

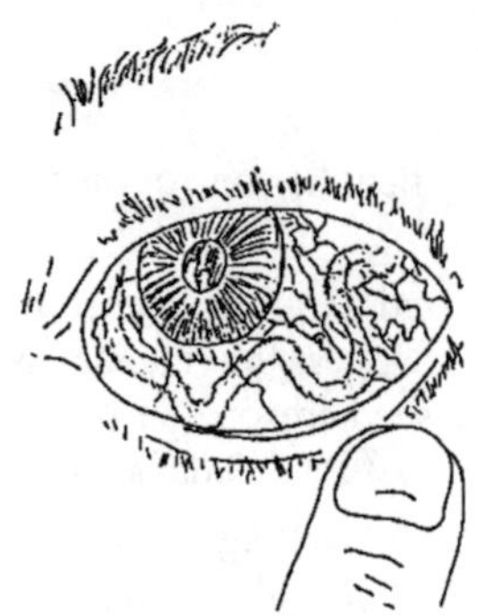

Worm crossing an eye

Similar diseases: See Protocols C-6 and C-8. SICKLE CELL DISEASE in children can appear similar, but in this case there is a history of the problem from an early age. Other types of LARVA MIGRANS (of which this is one kind) may be indistinguishable.

Bush Laboratory: The disease may cause protein, blood, or both in the urine.

Higher-Level Care. Hospital labs can do blood tests; blood for the tests must be taken between 10 A.M. & 4 P.M.; sometimes several samples must be taken before one is positive. This disease always causes increased eosinophils in the blood count (other diseases may also). You really should rely on history rather than lab for treatment because the history is so distinctive and the parasite larvae might not be found in the blood at all. The blood test is not sensitive.

Treatment:

Prevention: Control flies, wear long trousers, use screens on houses. Light-colored clothing helps since the flies are attracted to dark clothing.

Patient care. In the past, IVERMECTIN was used but there have been major problems with that; it is probably still safe in very mild cases. ALBENDAZOLE is probably safer. DIETHYLCARBAMAZINE might be useful. There can be major problems with any treatment. Check for ONCHOCERCIASIS with eye involvement. Check for FILARIASIS. In these cases, if you treat with DIETHYLCARBAMAZINE, the drug must be started slowly. Reactions to DEC or IVERMECTIN can be dangerous. Seek local and/or current advice. Normally DEC reactions are treated as ordinary ALLERGY, but they do not always respond to these medicines.

MALABSORPTION

The most common regional causes: SCHISTOSOMIASIS MANSONI, SPRUE (rarely). In eastern and western Africa it may be caused by PANCREATITIS.

MALARIA

Generally, in urban areas with major air pollution, there will be no disease transmission.

Areas without malaria transmission:

Zimbabwe: Harare

Mauritania: Parts of the north.

Ethiopia: Addis Ababa.

Kenya: Nairobi - transmission is rare.

Since the mid-1990's, malaria has been moving to progressively higher altitudes. In the past there was no transmission above 6000 feet, but now it is commonly transmitted up to 2500 meters or 8000 feet. Most of the malaria at the higher altitude is non-falciparum.

There have been recent outbreaks of malaria in the highlands of East Africa, mostly due to falciparum malaria. Because the people in these areas have not had long term exposure to P. falciparum, they have little or no natural immunity, and because of the often inadequate health care systems, there is a high mortality rate. Pregnant and postpartum women seem to be particularly vulnerable.

Cerebral malaria accounts for about 50% of all pediatric hospital admissions in some parts of Africa. It is a common cause of disability and death.

CHLOROQUINE resistance is present in Africa and is spreading rapidly. In most areas the disease responds well to CHLOROQUINE plus CHLORPHENIRAMINE or else to FANSIDAR plus five days of QUININE. In parts of eastern Sudan there is some QUININE resistance. ARTEMISININ eliminates the symptoms the soonest. The plant grows well in the highlands of central Ethiopia.

There is resistance to many drugs in Liberia; this is also a problem in Senegal and Guinea.

In Lekie, Cameroon, malaria is very common. Half of the serious cases are in children under age 4. Symptoms, in decreasing order of frequency, are: fever, vomiting and diarrhea, muscle pains, joint pains, weakness, SEIZURES, confusion or coma.

The percentage of malaria that is falciparum: Juba, Sudan: 84%; northern Cameroon: nearly 100%; Ituri region of D. R. Congo: 50%; over 50% in Rwanda. In parts of East Africa falciparum malaria is resistant to MEFLOQUINE.

A common complaint is pain in a band around the center back: "waist pain". In eastern Africa, there is frequently also pain in a band across the back of the shoulders. African children with malaria usually have vomiting and diarrhea. Chronic malaria causes TROPICAL SPLENOMEGALY, mainly in Uganda and Ethiopia.

Similar regional diseases: Severe SICKLE CELL DISEASE may be confusing. In expatriates in eastern Africa, AFRICAN SLEEPING SICKNESS may be very similar. Look for and ask about the initial skin swelling in response to the fly bite.

MALNUTRITION

This is common throughout Africa. ANEMIA and XEROPHTHALMIA are common consequences. African children may have swellings in front of their ears as a consequence of poor nutrition. Camel's milk has more vitamin C than milk from other sources.

Regional diseases associated with this are SICKLE CELL DISEASE, MEASLES, MONKEYPOX and (rarely) SPRUE.

MANSONELLOSIS PERSTANS

Cause: Worm larva.

Mildly ill; Class 1-2; Regional; it occurs between 20° North and 15° South, west of 35° longitude. It occurs, additionally in Tanzania and in northern Mozambique.

Age: Any, usually adults. **Who**: Bitten by culicoides (see the section on insects, Volume I). **Onset**: Gradual.

Clinical:

Necessary: General joint pains without fever.

Usual in expatriates, common in nationals: Shortness of breath, trouble breathing out, wheezing, itching. Other symptoms of ASTHMA or ALLERGY might also be present.

Sometimes: Abdominal pain, especially the right upper abdomen.

Similar Diseases:

Joint pains without high fevers: ARTHRITIS, BRUCELLOSIS

Wheezing: ALLERGY, HEART FAILURE

Abdominal pain: PEPTIC ULCER, AMEBIC LIVER DISEASE, GALLBLADDER DISEASE, IRRITABLE BOWEL.

Higher-Level Care. *Laboratory*: There is always an increased eosinophil count. The worm larvae might be seen in a blood smear. Unlike LOIASIS and FILARIASIS, they might be found any time of day or night.

Treatment:

Prevention: Culicoides are the same as "no-see-ems", tiny insects. See Volume I, Appendix 10 for instructions as to how to deal with them. One can prevent the disease by taking IVERMECTIN every 3 months.

Patient Care: (MEBENDAZOLE plus LEVAMISOLE) or else ALBENDAZOLE.

Results: within 1-2 weeks.

MEASLES

Most cases occur in children less than 5 y.o. in unimmunized areas, and in the 6-12 month-olds in immunized areas. MALNUTRITION in older children, and DEHYDRATION in babies, are common causes of death with measles. In all age groups, many deaths are caused by PNEUMONIA. A lack of VITAMIN A in the diet (yellow and orange produce) is associated with both blindness and a higher death rate in several areas. Measles is usually more severe in older children and adults than in babies.

MENINGITIS

Yearly epidemics occur in the Sahel meningitis belt, February to April. The meningitis belt is 10° North to 16° North from the Atlantic coast to western Sudan. The belt expands to cover the area from 5° South to 27° North latitude, as one proceeds east from the Chad/Sudan border. It extends from central Egypt down to central Tanzania and east almost to the Ethiopia/Somali border. The epidemics are caused by meningococcus group A. There have been major epidemics in Kenya and Uganda, including the southern parts of these countries, and also in Angola which is well outside the meningitis belt. Reportedly the meningitis belt is expanding because of deforestation; the disease tends to spread rapidly in hot, dry areas.

Similar regional disease: AFRICAN SLEEPING SICKNESS can also appear similar.

MENOPAUSE

African women seldom complain of these symptoms.

MIGRAINE HEADACHE

AFRICAN SLEEPING SICKNESS may appear similar.

MONKEYPOX

Cause: Virus

Moderately to severely ill; Class 1-3; Contagious, slightly; Regional The vast majority of monkeypox cases have been from D. R. Congo; other countries that sometimes have the disease are Cameroon, Ivory coast, Liberia, Nigeria, and Sierra Leone. In all cases this only occurs in tropical rain forest areas, not in dry savannah. Within the D. R. Congo the following areas are most affected: Bandundu, Equateur, Kasai Orientale. It is generally the most prevalent along the Congo River basin and near the DRC/Angola border.

Age: Any, mostly less than 15 y.o. **Who**: Mostly from towns with a population less than 5000. Most patients report contact with monkeys or small rodents; males more than females. **Onset**: Gradually after 7-17 days incubation, begins over 1-3 days, with illness before rash.

Clinical:

The clinical illness is less severe with merely touching or being near, more severe with a bite or scratch from an animal. It can and does infect prairie dogs.

Necessary: Fever, headache, backache, sick in bed. Lymph nodes are very large, differentiating this from CHICKEN POX. A fever occurs first. Thereafter, sometime during the first 4 days, a rash of tiny blisters begins on the face and rapidly spreads from there to the rest of the body.[1] The rash is

[1] Rarely the rash might begin on the limbs and spread to the center of the body.

heaviest on the face and limbs. There may be swelling of the skin with the blisters. It is very dense on the hands. It affects the palms and soles in 70% of cases and the mouth in more than half.

Sometimes: If it involves the eyes, the patient may develop KERATITIS. The fever may drop when the rash starts. The patient probably has swollen eye lids. About 1/2 have sore throats, and 1/4 have painful skin blisters in the genital area. In 1/3 there is a second fever, at which time the blister contents change from watery to milky. The rash is usually healed or healing by 4 weeks. The skin spots darken first, then lighten, then the color becomes normal.

Complications: Pitting scars, IMPETIGO, PNEUMONIA, DEHYDRATION, MALNUTRITION, EYE INFECTION, SEPSIS, ENCEPHALITIS, BRAIN DAMAGE, death. The death rate is 10% to 30% and occurs almost entirely in young children.

Similar diseases: See Protocol C-13: Fever and Back Pain. In only monkeypox and smallpox does a blistering rash break out over the whole body at once. Before the rash, the disease may resemble those listed in Protocol C-2. CHICKENPOX is similar and worldwide. With monkeypox, the lymph nodes are large and the rash breaks out within hours rather than spreading from one part of the skin to another over days. Also, with monkeypox the patient is moderately to very ill whereas in chicken pox a child is only mildly ill (although an adult with chicken pox may be very ill.)

Higher-Level Care. *Laboratory*: A very sophisticated hospital lab can do a blood test for this. This kind of facility is likely to be found only in Western countries and the results, in any case, will not likely influence the management of the disease.

Treatment:

Prevention: Immunization for smallpox also prevents monkeypox. This immunization is contraindicated in HIV-positive people.

Patient Care: Cidofovir is an antiviral medication that might be helpful but generally the treatment is merely supportive. Prevent DEHYDRATION and MALNUTRITION with water and food. PROMETHAZINE may be used for vomiting. Use ACETAMINOPHEN for fevers. Milk from a nursing woman who has had the disease (look for the pitting scars) may be helpful for children.

MONONUCLEOSIS

Children in Ethiopia develop the disease and immunity to it before 10 y.o.; therefore one would not likely see the illness in teens and adults.

Similar regional diseases: LASSA FEVER, BURKITT LYMPHOMA. AFRICAN SLEEPING SICKNESS (the kind found in West Africa) might cause large lymph nodes in the back of the neck.

MYCETOMA

This is especially common in Sudan and Niger. In Nigeria among the Igbos, it affects the nose. It is uncommon in Central African Republic and in the highlands of central Ethiopia. It is otherwise generally common in the area between a line drawn from Nouamrhar, Mauritania to the port of Bur Sudan on the Red Sea; and a line from Freetown, Sierra Leone to Mombassa, Kenya, on the Indian Ocean.

A related disease, chromoblastomycosis, is common in Madagascar, most common in barefoot males in rural areas. It gives the appearance of giant WARTS, covering whole areas of skin. It is treatable only with drugs that must be used by a physician in a hospital setting. Surgery can also help.

In Mali, the most common form in the south, (south of a line between Bamako and Gao) that which causes yellow grains, can be treated as follows: DAPSONE plus COTRIMOXAZOLE, both for 6-9 months. You may substitute STREPTOMYCIN for either one of these medicines, using the other oral medicine in addition. If this does not work, surgery may be necessary.

If the mycetoma has black grains, it most likely needs surgery, but MICONAZOLE may help.

MYIASIS

The Tumbu fly maggot and the Zaire floor maggot are common and peculiar to Africa. Other types of myiasis may also occur.

- **Tumbu fly maggot:**

This is also known as putsi fly or ver du cayor. It is found in scattered areas south of the Sahara. The fly lays its eggs early in the morning or late in the afternoon or in the shade; they are never laid under the noon sun. The egg is laid on wet clothing; when the clothing is worn, the larva burrows into the skin, causing swelling and a small ulcer. Treat by putting petroleum jelly on the holes, then squeeze or pick the larva out. This also helps with the diagnosis because the critter's attempts to breathe cause little bubbles to come up and out through the petroleum jelly. Prevent the problem by totally drying or ironing clothing before wearing.

Tumbu fly larva

- **Zaire floor maggot:**

This is found from northern Nigeria and southern Sudan south to Natal, from sea level to 2250 meters (7500 feet), in arid and humid areas both. The larva is off-white, resembling the tumbu fly larva. It becomes red after sucking the blood of a sleeping victim. When it is full, it drops off the person and hides in the floor near the sleeping mat. The bite is painless. Prevention lies in the use of sleeping surfaces up off the floor.

Similar regional diseases: LOIASIS only.

NAIROBI EYE

This is eye pain caused by a flying insect in East Africa. The insect is brown and orange, about 1 cm long and 3 mm wide. They are present in large numbers certain times of year. They tend to fly to the eyes. They cause severe, burning pain of the eyelids, possibly with swelling. The eyeballs seem to be unaffected. The pain responds well to CORTISONE CREAM or any other corticosteroid cream, rubbed on the lids. Do not get these creams into the eye!

ONCHOCERCIASIS

Synonym: Sowda.

This occurs throughout the countries of central and western Africa that border on the Atlantic ocean (not just their coastal areas). It also occurs around the border areas of eastern CAR and along the Blue Nile River basin of Sudan and northern Ethiopia. The geography of the disease is continually changing because of WHO interventions. New areas at risk are those adjacent to the areas where the disease has been eliminated.

It is more common in forested areas of Sierra Leone than in savanna. Most of the blindness there is due to problems in the back of the eye rather than the front.

In Kwara State, Nigeria, males are more affected than females, adults more than children, and farmers more than those of other occupations. The Volta River basin of West Africa is now largely free of the problem.

Persons with HIV INFECTION tend to have less oncho symptoms than those with good immunity.

Sowda is a form that is found in northern Sudan and northern Nigeria. The skin becomes swollen and covered with scaly bumps. There is marked swelling of the lymph nodes, usually in the groins.

In areas where there is much LOIASIS (and also onchocerciasis), IVERMECTIN should not be used for mass treatment: south-eastern Nigeria, southern and central Cameroon, southern Central African Republic, Equatorial Guinea, Gabon, the northern and western portions of D. R. Congo.

ONYALAI

Cause: Unknown

This is a bleeding problem, in some parts of Africa. It is a type of HEMORRHAGIC FEVER. The patient develops abnormal bleeding (nosebleed, heavy menses, bloody urine or stool, bleeding from minor wounds) that will not stop. It must be treated at a hospital. SCURVY may appear similar.

PANCREATITIS

A recurrent form of this that results in MALABSORPTION and DIABETES is common in eastern and western Africa.

PARAGONIMIASIS

This occurs in Cameroon, the Congo valley, and The Gambia. In Nigeria it is found in the areas surrounding Okigwi, southwest of Enugu. It is also in the Bong area of Liberia. It is not generally common.

PARKINSON'S DISEASE

Similar regional diseases: ENTERIC FEVER in Nigeria; Lathyrism (see PLANT POISONING). AFRICAN SLEEPING SICKNESS may also appear similar; it must be diagnosed by a spinal tap at a hospital; the parasites will rarely show in the blood at the stage of trembling.

PELVIC INFECTION

Common causes are CHLAMYDIA, TUBERCULOSIS, and GONORRHEA.

Similar regional disease: SCHISTOSOMIASIS HEMATOBIUM.

PEPTIC ULCER

This is particularly common in Northern Ethiopia, West African coastal countries, central D. R. Congo, great lakes area of east central Africa, Nairobi area. Frequently it is responsive to the combination of antibiotics and BISMUTH SUBSALICYLATE.

PERICARDITIS

This may occur with LASSA FEVER. Pericarditis is indistinguishable from a form of HEART FAILURE (restrictive type) found in east Africa, which affects malnourished children.

PHIMOSIS

Similar regional disease: SCHISTOSOMIASIS HEMATOBIUM.

PIG-BEL

Pig-bel occurs in Uganda.

PLAGUE

There is risk of plague in Madagascar, many areas; Malawi southern region; Mozambique, Tete Province; Tanzania, Tanga region; Uganda, Western Region; D. R. Congo, Haut Zaire Province; Zambia, Southern Province; and Zimbabwe, Matabeleland North. In Tanzania, it occurs mostly in outbreaks, especially in the Lushoto District, usually in January to March. In D. R. Congo, it occurs mostly January to March.

PLANT POISONING

See the *Disease Index* for types of plant poisoning that occur in multiple regions, and for the general treatment of plant poisoning. The types listed below occur in Africa somewhere, but not necessarily throughout Africa.

Ackee: This is present in West Africa. Also known as vomiting sickness, it is due to eating unripe ackee fruit, from the Irsin tree. (Only unripe fruit is toxic; the ripe fruit is good to eat.) There is a 90% death rate if it is not treated. The patient has abdominal pain, becomes sweaty and shaky and then falls unconscious from a low blood sugar. He later has persistent forceful vomiting and SEIZURES. His temperature will be low or normal. He may develop LIVER FAILURE. *Treatment:* Empty the stomach and give alcoholic beverage when the patient first becomes ill (see ALCOHOL in the Drug Index). If he is unconscious, give sugar whatever way you can, preferably IV. If you cannot give it IV, give ALCOHOL, ACTIVATED CHARCOAL, and sugar by stomach tube. Do not make the patient vomit any more than he already has.

Argemone oil is present in southern Africa.

Impila: A plant in southern Africa which causes KIDNEY FAILURE, nephrotic type.

Khasari: See Lathyrism under PLANT POISONING in the *Disease Index*.

Khat: A traditional drug used as a stimulant, it is widespread in the Middle East and eastern Africa. The leaves and twigs of a Miraa tree are chewed or smoked or used for teas. It is chemically and physiologically similar to amphetamines. It causes a rapid pulse. Some people become happy and gregarious; others become mellow. Repeated use may lead to ADDICTION. *Treatment:* Not required.

Konzo. See PLANT POISONING from Cassava in the *Disease Index*. Konzo refers to the sudden onset of stiff weakness. It looks similar to TROPICAL SPASTIC PARAPARESIS.

Lolism: Common in Africa; due to moldy wheat. Within 15 minutes the patient becomes dizzy, has a headache, slurred speech, trembling, and staggering. There may be diarrhea, vomiting, and abdominal pain. The patient may become unconscious or nearly so and remain that way about 10 hours. *Treatment:* Empty the stomach and give ACTIVATED CHARCOAL if possible.

Mantakassa: See Cassava under PLANT POISONING in the *Disease Index*.

Miraa: See Khat, above.

Miscara: See Lolism, above.

Muiragi: See Khat, above.

Tobacco-cow's urine: This is a folk medicine used in western Africa. It causes paralysis and blindness. See PLANT POISONING due to nicotine. The cow's urine doesn't do much; the main effect is the nicotine. *Treatment:* Send the patient to a major medical facility. If this is impossible, VITAMIN B_{12} may possibly help.

PNEUMONIA

In The Gambia, a single injection of triple PENICILLIN worked well for pneumonia in previously healthy people. In Zimbabwe, COTRIMOXAZOLE worked just as well as PENICILLIN.

PNEUMOTHORAX

This is rare in Blacks and common in Asians.

POLIO

In the following countries you may expect polio to be a major problem: Benin, Cameroon, Chad, Ethiopia, Ghana, Guinea, Liberia, Madagascar, Mali, Mozambique, Niger, Nigeria, Sierra Leone, Uganda, D. R. Congo. There has been a big immunization campaign, so the incidence may be decreasing.

PROCTITIS

The most likely causes are the SEXUALLY TRANSMITTED DISEASEs. This may be due to SCHISTOSOMIASIS MANSONI, SCHISTOSOMIASIS HEMATOBIUM, or SCHISTOSOMIASIS INTERCALATUM in areas where these are common.

PROSTATITIS

This may be caused by or mimic SCHISTOSOMIASIS MANSONI or SCHISTOSOMIASIS HEMATOBIUM as well as the worldwide similar diseases.

PYOMYOSITIS

This is more common in the rainy season in eastern Africa, but there is no change with seasons in Nigeria. It is almost always caused by staph; drugs that are specifically meant for staph are best, but they are expensive and may not be available. The best common treatment is a combination of CHLORAMPHENICOL plus ERYTHROMYCIN or else COTRIMOXAZOLE plus ERYTHROMYCIN. RIFAMPIN, a drug that is usually used for tuberculosis, is also active against staph. A similar condition in West Africa is SICKLE CELL DISEASE.

Q FEVER

This is found throughout Africa except for the Sahara and the Kalahari deserts.

RABIES

It is a major problem in Nigeria, Ethiopia, and probably in other parts of Africa as well. It does not occur on the Azores, Canary, and Madeira islands. It occurs in Mozambique but is not common. The form that begins with paralysis resembling POLIO is quite common in west Africa.

RELAPSING FEVER

Louse-borne usually occurs only in Ethiopia, Sudan, and Somalia though it may occur anywhere at times of civil unrest.

Tick-borne occurs southeast of a line between Djibouti and Kinshasa, DRC. It has also been reported the extreme northwest of the continent and in The Gambia, Ivory Coast, and Togo. The disease tends to be present for a while and generally devastating, then disappear. It is carried by a soft tick (about 8 mm long and roughly round) with habits similar to bedbugs (see Appendix 10, Volume I).

In eastern Africa, in addition to the other symptoms, there are also red eyes and red-orange urine. The initial fever lasts between 12 hours and 17 days, with the intervening fever-free period being between 1 day and 2 months. When the fever falls, it does so rapidly, with drenching sweats. When pregnant women get the disease they commonly die within the first 48 hours if they are not treated. Those who survive frequently give birth prematurely and commonly their infants die.

Similar regional diseases: YELLOW FEVER shows protein in the urine.

RHEUMATIC FEVER

This is more common in northern and southern Africa than in central and western. It tends to be severe and nearly always involves the heart. The most common age is 6-10 y.o. in central and eastern Africa, but teens and young adults in the Sudan. The rash is rare in any case and impossible to see on black skin.

RHINITIS

In Western countries this refers to the runny nose caused by ALLERGY or a RESPIRATORY INFECTION (a cold). In southern Africa there is a peculiar form in people with large noses who live in dry areas such as the highveld in Transvaal. Patient complains of an obstructed nose and a loss of smell; nose is full of fermenting, dried secretions. Relatives and friends complain of foul, rotten odor of the patient's breath.

Treatment: Clean out the nose with a pair of forceps. Then rinse it three times a day with 5 ml (1 teaspoon) of dry baking soda dissolved in a cup of water. Send the patient home with glycerin nose drops which will keep the nose moist and prevent the problem from recurring.

RUBELLA

This may resemble AFRICAN SLEEPING SICKNESS with large nodes in the back of the neck and the general aching and fever.

SCABIES

A common complication of scabies is IMPETIGO caused by strep; this may cause KIDNEY FAILURE of the nephritic type.

SCHISTOSOMIASIS HEMATOBIUM

Cause: Worm.

Synonyms: Urinary bilharziasis, Snail fever, Bilharziasis.

Not ill to very ill; Class 2; Regional. It is especially frequent where there are dams and irrigation canals. Over half the population may be affected. It is very common in the high veld area of Zimbabwe, mostly during the hot and dry season. It is common in Chad. In Natal, South Africa, 60-98% of the population is infected. It occurs near Ilakara, Tanzania where 21% of school children are infected. In Burkina Faso, it affects 33% of the population in the central, west-central, and north-central areas. It is found in scattered areas throughout the continent, except for the Kalahari Desert and the tropical rainforest of central DRC.

Age: Any but especially boys 5-15 y.o. who like to swim. **Who**: Skin exposed to water in which infected snails live. **Onset**: 10-12 weeks after exposure, then over days to weeks.

The kinds of snails that carry Schistosomiasis hematobium. The opening is more than half the height and there are only 3 or 4 swirls. Heights are 0.7-1.5 cm.

Clinical:

- **Initially:**

There may be itching of the skin for 2-3 days. Expatriates may begin with KATAYAMA DISEASE: fevers, low abdominal pain, fatigue, and symptoms of ALLERGY.

- **Later:**

Necessary: The patient develops bloody urine. Blood may be visible only or mainly at the end of urination. If it is not visible, a urine dipstick will demonstrate that it is present.

Usually: There is frequent urination and pain with urination. Nationals may just have bloody urine without other symptoms.

Maybe: There is kidney pain resembling KIDNEY STONE and leading to KIDNEY FAILURE. There may be swelling of the end of the penis and possibly bloody semen.

Occasionally: It can cause PROCTITIS, vaginal and pelvic pain in females, and menstrual cessation and/or irregularity. It might also cause the same symptoms as SCHISTOSOMIASIS MANSONI.

➢ **Still later:**

Maybe: The patient may have to urinate frequently and may dribble because the bladder becomes rigid; it cannot enlarge to hold its usual volume of urine.

Schistosomiasis in returning travelers is mostly without symptoms. However, spinal cord invasion, which is usually a late complication, may appear early.

Complications: ANEMIA and weight loss. The disease evidently contributes to MALNUTRITION, since children who are treated show a growth spurt after treatment. Bladder CANCER may occur, as may KIDNEY INFECTION, inability to urinate, sores and growths on the penis or in the vagina, sterility in females, KIDNEY FAILURE, URETHRAL STRICTURE, and occasionally RESPIRATORY INFECTION from migrating worms. It may cause bladder cancer.

This disease increases the transmission of HIV INFECTION because it, like SEXUALLY TRANSMITTED DISEASES disrupts the pink, moist surfaces.

Females may develop PELVIC INFECTION or CANCER and either sex may develop thinning and weakening of the bones, resulting in fractures from minor injuries. Sometimes, after years, the worms invade the lungs, causing RESPIRATORY FAILURE and HEART FAILURE. An occasional complication in males is a BLADDER STONE; men with stones cannot urinate unless they jump up and down. Their urine may be bloody during the day and normal at night.

In Sudan, one usually does not see the severe bladder problems in older people that are found in some other areas of Africa.

Rarely this may cause problems with the spinal cord: back pain, sharp, shooting limb pains, weakness, numbness and tingling and inability to initiate urination. Spinal cord schistosomiasis must be treated promptly with PRAZIQUANTEL and PREDNISONE, not waiting for lab results which may be falsely negative—do this with anyone who has had a prior exposure at any time in his/her life.

Similar diseases: SEXUALLY TRANSMITTED DISEASES; URETHRITIS (visible pus from penis or female urethra), KIDNEY INFECTION (also nitrites and/or leukocytes in urine), KIDNEY FAILURE of other causes, ALLERGY (Hives) from other causes, PROSTATITIS (usually men over 50 y.o. only), TB of the genitals, FILARIASIS. This disease may cause VAGINITIS-type symptoms.

Bush Laboratory: It is possible to hatch the worm eggs with simple equipment and see the larvae; see Appendix 2 in Volume I. Provided this is done carefully, it is more sensitive (but less specific) than looking for worm eggs under a microscope.

Higher-Level Care. *Laboratory*: Afternoon urine contains blood and protein when checked by dipstick. Laboratories can examine urine under a microscope to see worm eggs. There may be increased eosinophils on a blood count early in the infection, especially in expatriates, but they may be absent later on. *Facilities*: Advanced imaging such as CT and MRI might be helpful, as well as biopsies.

Treatment:

Prevention: Avoid physical contact with water in lakes and streams that may have schistosomiasis snails. Use latrines; eliminate snails. Let a bucket of water without snails stand overnight before using it for washing.

Patient Care: PRAZIQUANTEL; METRIFONATE is a cheaper alternative for widespread use. MEBENDAZOLE may work. PREDNISONE or PREDNISOLONE along with the PRAZIQUANTEL might be helpful. Seek medical advice. NIRIDAZOLE is an old, dangerous drug that should no longer be used. Recently some authorities have suggested adding ARTEMISININ (artesunate) to the treatment protocol; there are reports that it reduces egg counts by over 90%.

Results: Improvement starting one month from the PRAZIQUANTEL treatment, complete (if it ever will be) in 6 months. You should do lab determinations to evaluate the effect of the treatment 3 and 6 months after the drug is given.

SCHISTOSOMIASIS INTERCALATUM

Cause: Worm

Synonym: Bilharzia

Not ill to moderately ill; Class 2; Regional in western equatorial Africa.

In Port Harcourt, Nigeria, 6% of the children checked had the problem; there was no other kind of schistosomiasis in the area. It is common in equatorial Guinea, in a suburb of Bata. It occurs in Cameroon, Gabon, and in an area near Kinshasa, D. R. Congo. It also may occur in Chad, Central African Republic, and Congo. There is a very heavily-infected area in Cameroon, department of Mungo and town of Loum. Over half the children examined were infected. It does not cause human liver disease.

Age: Mostly children. **Who**: Those exposed to water containing infected snails. **Onset**: Slowly, over weeks to months.

Clinical:

This is cattle schistosomiasis that occasionally infects humans in central Africa. It causes pain in the left-lower abdomen which increases before each episode of diarrhea. The diarrhea may be bloody.

Similar diseases: DYSENTERY due to amebae; also see listing under SCHISTOSOMIASIS MANSONI in the *Disease Index*.

Treatment: PRAZIQUANTEL. PREDNISONE or PREDNISOLONE along with the PRAZIQUANTEL might be helpful. Seek medical advice.

SCHISTOSOMIASIS MANSONI

This is found in the lower Nile valley and otherwise in scattered areas between 18° North and 25° South. It is very common in Lama Kara, northern Togo, in Kpalime, SW Togo, in the Borkena River and the Rift Valley lakes of Ethiopia, and near the northern Central African Republic/Cameroon border.

It is common around Entebbe, Uganda; Bangui, Central African Republic; Bafia, Cameroon; and the Jos Plateau of Nigeria. It occurs, but not commonly, in Kavango Territory, Namibia and amongst the pygmies of the Ituri region of D. R. Congo. It occurs in the Rusizi Plain and the Lake Cohoha areas of Burundi and near Maniema, D. R. Congo.

In southern Sudan the disease has a more rapid onset than in the north and it tends to be more severe.

Treatment: PRAZIQUANTEL. In D. R. Congo sometimes this drug causes abdominal pain and bloody diarrhea within 30 minutes of the first dose. Do not to stop the drug for this.

SCURVY

Patients with HEMOCHROMATOSIS are also susceptible to this. It occurs in refugee camps since most relief foods are not fresh. It develops within a few weeks on relief foods. Older females are usually the first affected.

SEIZURES

Regional disease that may cause seizures is AFRICAN SLEEPING SICKNESS.

SEPSIS

Patients with TROPICAL SPLENOMEGALY are very susceptible.

SEXUALLY TRANSMITTED DISEASE

SYPHILIS and HIV INFECTION are most common in urban areas, except for Uganda and Central African Republic, where they are also common in the rural areas. Lower socio-economic prostitutes in Nairobi almost all have at least one SEXUALLY TRANSMITTED DISEASE; CHANCROID is by far the most common and SYPHILIS is second.

SICKLE CELL DISEASE

This generally occurs in persons whose genetic origins are from the countries of west and central Africa that border on the Atlantic.

This is quite rare in Burkina Faso and in east Africa. In Kenya most cases are along the eastern coast and along the southwest border with Uganda. It is neither very common nor very rare in Uganda.

SPOTTED FEVER; Tick Typhus

This occurs in three areas:

- Southeast of a line between Bur Sudan (on the Red Sea coast) and the westernmost Namibia/South Africa border.
- Along the Mediterranean coast.
- A few scattered areas of West Africa.

Synonyms in this area: African Tick Typhus, African Tick Bite Fever.

The African form of Spotted Fever, is especially common in Rwanda, in arid east Africa north of the equator, in arable and coastal southeast and southern Africa, and in the forested areas of coastal western Africa.

It is transmitted by cattle ticks. If you are considering this diagnosis, a valuable clue is finding a tiny black scab or scabs with red halo(s). There are frequently multiple scabs. The disease can be rapidly fatal.

SPRUE

This occurs rarely in Nigeria, Sudan, and Uganda. It is common in Blacks in southern Africa. It does not cause ANEMIA in this area.

STREP THROAT

This is the most frequent cause of sore throat; it must be treated adequately to avoid RHEUMATIC FEVER which is common.

STROKE

This is not uncommon in Uganda. It is most often due to HYPERTENSION. Next most common causes of stroke are SICKLE CELL DISEASE, SEPSIS, TOXEMIA, HEART FAILURE, RHEUMATIC FEVER, SYPHILIS, and ARBOVIRAL FEVER. In affected areas, it may be due to SCHISTOSOMIASIS (either S. mansoni or S. hematobium), but only rarely.

Similar regional diseases: AFRICAN SLEEPING SICKNESS (slower onset), SICKLE CELL DISEASE, LASSA FEVER (fever), and HYDATID DISEASE.

STRONGYLOIDIASIS

This is especially common in southwest Cameroon, in the area of Kinshasa, D. R. Congo, and in children of the Bushmen of Namibia. It is common in Ogum, Oyo, and Bauchi States, Nigeria; Congo; Guinea-Bissau; Central African Republic; and Somalia. It is also common amongst pygmies of D. R. Congo and Rwanda.

Other diseases that decrease natural immunity and thus cause the complication of SEPSIS with this are TROPICAL SPLENOMEGALY, and AFRICAN SLEEPING SICKNESS.

SYPHILIS

The rash of secondary syphilis may itch in Blacks. Uncoordination is a rare symptom in tertiary syphilis in

Blacks. In Uganda 33% of adults have positive blood tests for syphilis; in Rwanda, 2%-28%; in Tanzania, Congo, Gabon, Central African Republic, and Ethiopia about 17%; and in Burundi, 7.8%. Syphilis of newborns is very common in Mozambique.

Those with positive blood tests for syphilis are also more likely than others to be infected with HIV. In northern Mauritania and Burkina Faso, much of the syphilis is really TREPONARID, the kind that is not a venereal disease but is transmitted by flies and direct contact. This is probably also true in the rest of arid northern Africa.

TAPEWORM

Fish tapeworm occurs in Madagascar, Madeira Islands, and Central African Republic. Beef and/or pork tapeworms are common in Ethiopia, Kenya, and Bauchi State, Nigeria; they occur but are not common in Kavango Territory, Namibia. Rat and beef tapeworms are both common in central Burkina Faso and amongst the pygmies of Rwanda.

TETANUS

This is very common in newborns in Somalia, Nigeria, and Ivory Coast. In Ethiopia, it accounts for about 10% of all the deaths in newborns. Some newborns of immunized African mothers may have the disease. Hand washing by midwives has proved to be a very good preventive in Senegal.

THALLASEMIA

This is very common in Africa, but in Blacks it is usually a form that is not severe. Indians, Arabs, and persons from northern Africa may have a severe form of the disease. In southern Africa ONYALAI may appear similar.

TINEA

Similar regional diseases: AFRICAN SLEEPING SICKNESS rash in whites, YAWS, TREPONARID, ONCHOCERCIASIS, VITILIGO.

TOXEMIA

This is by far the most common cause of coma in pregnant women in most parts of Africa.

TOXOPLASMOSIS

This is common in Africa (especially in humid areas) but you may not recognize it because most cases have no symptoms at all. It is particularly important for pregnant women to avoid the infection.

TRACHOMA

This is not a major problem in Liberia or D. R. Congo, but it is in most of the rest of Africa. It used to be very common in northern Nigeria, but it is becoming rare there.

TREPONARID

This is mainly present in dry areas; it is found in the Sahara and Sahel, the Middle East, and in Botswana, Zimbabwe, and the Kalahari. Though it is found only in dry areas, it is more common during the wet season. In Burkina Faso, this is very common amongst the Touareg, Peul, and Deon peoples.

TRICHINOSIS

Similar regional diseases: AFRICAN SLEEPING SICKNESS, LASSA FEVER.

TRICHURIASIS

This is very common in Africa. In southwest and south central Cameroon, in the pygmies of Ituri region, D. R. Congo and Rwanda, and in Kinshasa, D. R. Congo, more than 50% of the population harbor this worm. It is also common in Bauchi State, Oyo State, and Ogun State, Nigeria, and amongst the adult bushmen of Namibia. It is uncommon in central Burkina Faso; in Calabar, Nigeria; and near the northern Central African Republic/Cameroon border.

TROPICAL SPASTIC PARAPARESIS

In Ivory Coast, 7.4% of the prostitutes are affected, as well as 13.7% of those with LEPROSY. It is a common cause of difficulty walking. It may occur in the absence of HIV INFECTION. A local similar disease is PLANT POISONING due to lathyrism.

TROPICAL SPLENOMEGALY

Found mainly and commonly in Nigeria, Sudan, Uganda, Zambia, Ethiopia, and D. R. Congo.

TROPICAL ULCER

This may be caused by SICKLE CELL DISEASE. CUTANEOUS LEISHMANIASIS and GUINEA WORM may be nearly indistinguishable. In Zimbabwe, it is most common in the rainy months, and in teens or younger children.

TUBAL PREGNANCY

The most likely cause is a SEXUALLY TRANSMITTED DISEASE such as CHLAMYDIA or GONORRHEA. SCHISTOSOMIASIS HEMATOBIUM or SCHISTOSOMIASIS MANSONI may also contribute to this.

TUBERCULOSIS

In most of Africa it is very common, especially in crowded, urban areas, and amongst the poor and malnourished. In almost all areas, at least 10% of the population has active TB. The following countries report many cases: Swaziland, Comoros, Lesotho, Somalia, D. R. Congo, Ethiopia, and Reunion Island. In Mauritania there is much drug-resistant tuberculosis.

A peculiar manifestation of TB is the slow growth of hard, painless swellings in the hands and feet. There is no effect on the skin in these cases and these areas do not become ABSCESSes.

Skin TB is particularly common in Ghana, Nigeria, Uganda, southern Sudan, and Mozambique. In Black children this may cause large, tender lumps on the shins and the hairy forearms. It is treated like ordinary TB. Surgery may be helpful.

Abdominal TB is common in Black Africans. It causes diarrhea, burning abdominal pain, lumps in the abdomen, fluid in the abdomen, and ACUTE ABDOMEN Type 3, in that order of frequency.

Bone TB affecting the spine is common in Africa; it accounts for about 6% of all TB cases in Burkina Faso, being particularly common there.

PERICARDITIS is commonly caused by TB in southern African Blacks.

Similar regional diseases: With TB in Blacks, facial skin will be lighter than the skin of others of the same ethnic group, and a little yellowish. HIV INFECTION is indistinguishable in most areas of Africa. PARAGONIMIASIS causes similar symptoms but the patient does not lose weight or feel ill.

About 1/3 of HIV INFECTION patients with respiratory symptoms have TUBERCULOSIS. They tend to respond well to treatment temporarily but are more likely than others to relapse. They remain contagious for a very long time.

In Malawi, 1/3 of the patients with TB have clubbed finger tips, similar to people with long-standing RESPIRATORY INFECTIONs.

TURISTA

Travelers' diarrhea is frequently responsive to ERYTHROMYCIN.

Diarrhea with blood may be caused by SCHISTOSOMIASIS (any kind).

Over 90% of Bantus have chronic diarrhea when they consume milk, due to LACTOSE INTOLERANCE.

In Zaria, northern Nigeria, severe diarrhea in children under 12 y.o. usually has a bacterial cause. The bacteria usually respond to ERYTHROMYCIN. Those over 12 y.o. more often have diarrhea caused by WORMS or GIARDIASIS or SCHISTOSOMIASIS MANSONI.

ROTAVIRUS is a common virus that causes diarrhea and vomiting; the problem lasts for long enough to cause or exacerbate MALNUTRITION. It occurs mostly in infants and mostly during the dry season all over Africa. Children should be fed extra when they recover enough to tolerate food.

Campylobacter, a bacterial cause of diarrhea, likewise occurs mostly in the dry season in Africa. Untreated, it lasts over 8 days, is associated with MALNUTRITION, and responds to ERYTHROMYCIN. Animals of all sorts may harbor the germ, and it is carried to humans by flies. It is common around Bangui, Central African Republic; and Kivu Province, D. R. Congo.

TYPHUS

Louse-borne typhus occurs primarily in the highlands of northeast Africa and also in Burundi, Kenya, Rwanda, Uganda, and Lesotho. It also occurs in scattered areas of West Africa. There have been major outbreaks during civil unrest.

Murine typhus occurs in Chad, Rwanda, Ethiopia, Kenya, Uganda, Tanzania, Sudan, and scattered areas of West Africa.

URETHRAL STRICTURE

This may also be caused by SCHISTOSOMIASIS HEMATOBIUM or SCHISTOSOMIASIS MANSONI.

URINARY OBSTRUCTION

This may also be caused by SCHISTOSOMIASIS HEMATOBIUM or SCHISTOSOMIASIS MANSONI.

VAGINITIS

This may also be caused by SCHISTOSOMIASIS HEMATOBIUM or SCHISTOSOMIASIS MANSONI.

VISCERAL LEISHMANIASIS

This occurs in a large area covering most of Ethiopia (north into NW Eritrea), southern Sudan, southwestern Somalia, northern Kenya, and northern Uganda. Additionally, it occurs in a wide swathe along the northern coast of the continent. Other foci are as follows:

- Near Donda, Angola
- East of Lake Bangweulu, Zambia
- North of Mongu, Zambia
- Near the border area of Malawi/ Zambia/ Mozambique
- Inland Algeria, 2 locations
- Southern Ivory Coast
- Central Nigeria
- South-central Gabon

In Ethiopia it is especially common in the far north and along the Omo River valley. In Ethiopia it is, at times, rapidly fatal. It is common in Sudan, especially in the Gadaref region. Sudan has a major proportion of the worldwide cases. In Kenya it occurs in arid and semiarid areas, all below 1500 meters (5000 ft.), especially near seasonal rivers, and in the southeast. It occurs in Chad and Burkina Faso but is not generally common. It occurs in Djibouti.

Clinical:

Sudanese patients frequently have generally enlarged lymph nodes. Africans tend to have large lymph nodes in their groins. Local lore is helpful since symptoms differ according to area. After the illness, Africans may have decreased black skin pigmentation and a dry, non-shiny skin texture.

In the Sudan area, there may be symptoms of burning feet or GALLBLADDER DISEASE. More than 50% of the patients get PKDL, the skin condition that resembles LEPROSY.

VITILIGO

Similar regional disease: ONCHOCERCIASIS may look quite similar but the history of itching and eye changes should make you suspect that.

WARTS

The rash of HIV INFECTION looks just like this but it is itchy and there is a drop of water in each bump which is released when it is scratched open.

WHOOPING COUGH

This is especially common in Ethiopia, D. R. Congo, Senegal, Benin, Chad, Congo, Guinea, Liberia, Mali, Mauritania, Togo, Uganda, and Burkina Faso.

XEROPHTHALMIA

Pygmies are particularly susceptible. In Tanzania, children who develop this have low-protein diets with mostly starches and few vegetables. It is neither common nor rare in Chad. It occurs in Ethiopia, in Burkina Faso, and elsewhere.

YAWS

Synonym: Siti (in the Gambia)

The following countries have significant numbers of cases: Benin, Cameroon, Central African Republic, Congo (especially pygmies), Ethiopia, Gabon, Gambia, Ghana, Guinea, Ivory Coast, Liberia, Nigeria, Nigeria, Senegal, Sudan (southeast), Togo, D. R. Congo. It is generally prevalent in humid areas between the equator and 10° North.

Similar regional diseases: CUTANEOUS LEISHMANIASIS can appear similar. Swollen fingers resemble SICKLE CELL DISEASE.

YELLOW FEVER

Cause: Virus

Moderately to very ill; Class 2-4; Regional

Epidemics occur during the rainy season. There are epidemics from time to time in west-central Kenya (Rift Valley), Nigeria, Ghana, Senegal, and probably elsewhere.

Age: Any but the majority of cases have been in children. **Who**: Unimmunized; frequently in epidemics, transmitted by mosquitoes that bite during the day. **Onset**: Over a day or two after an incubation of 3-6 days.

Areas where the mosquito lives which transmits yellow fever.

Clinical:

The WHO definition for yellow fever is as follows:

Fever *plus* JAUNDICE *plus* one or more of the following:

- a slow pulse relative to the fever
- abnormal bleeding
- upper abdominal pain
- protein in urine
- decreased amount of urine

Necessary: The patient has fever, nausea, and aching all over, especially in the back, the waist area and the limbs. JAUNDICE develops only after several days of illness. The spleen is not enlarged.

Usually: There is a severe headache and eye pain. The pulse is initially rapid, but by day 3 or 4, the pulse slows and may become slow relative to the fever. The mind is clear; the patient does not act intoxicated like he does with TYPHUS.

Frequently: There is a day of recovery before the disease starts a second time.

Sometimes: The yellow color of the whites of the eyes may be quite indistinct. It becomes worse gradually, if at all. The face may be swollen. There may be severe general bone and joint pains. Vomiting may occur early, as may insomnia and a tender but non-swollen liver. The vomit is probably mucous at first, turning to black or bloody later on. The patient may have a body odor resembling a butcher shop.

Complications: LIVER FAILURE, KIDNEY FAILURE. Mental symptoms start late and indicate a poor prognosis. An occasional complication is HEMORRHAGIC FEVER: nosebleeds; bleeding gums; bloody stool, urine, or vomitus; heavy menstruation; major bleeding from minor wounds. There is a high death rate during epidemics.

Similar diseases: See Protocols C-2, C-5, and C-9.

Bush Laboratory: Bilirubin in the urine is quite common. There is almost always protein in the urine by the second day of illness. There may be blood in the urine on the third or fourth day. Sophisticated hospital laboratories can do blood tests or liver biopsies.

Higher-Level Care.

Laboratory: This requires a level 4 lab at least.

Facilities: At least a level 4.

Treatment:

Prevention: Immunize. Excellent immunization is available. Immunity starts about 10 days after the injection. Persons should be reimmunized every 10 years.

Patient Care: Same as HEPATITIS and, if necessary, HEMORRHAGIC FEVER. VITAMIN K injections may be helpful.

Results: At least half the patients who develop severe symptoms die. Those who recover have a very long convalescence.

Regional Notes

Index I. India Subcontinent

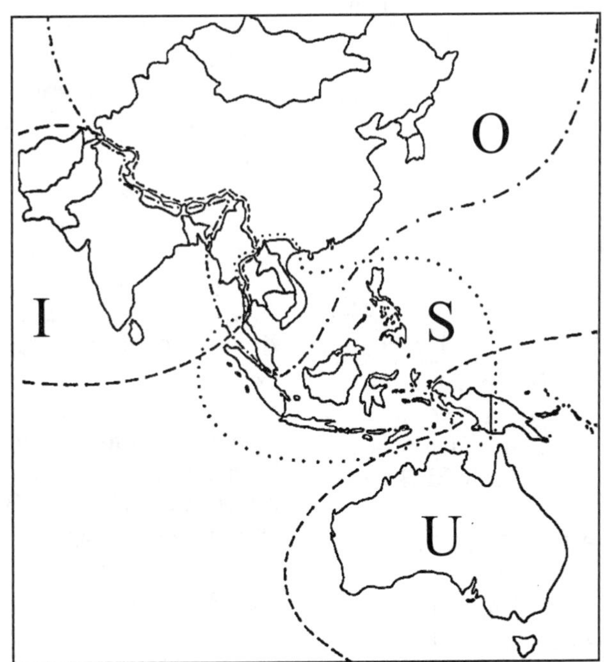

Index I: India Subcontinent

ACUTE ABDOMEN

Similar regional diseases: ASCARIASIS, being very common in this area, is a common cause of this as well as a common mimic. With SICKLE CELL DISEASE, the whites of the eyes are yellow, the patient has ANEMIA, and urobilinogen is in the urine.

AMEBIC LIVER DISEASE

This is extremely common in the Indian area.

ANEMIA

Anemia due to red cell destruction or due to vitamin deficiency can be caused by SICKLE CELL DISEASE which is relatively rare in India, occurring in certain ethnic groups only.

Anemia due to vitamin deficiency may occur in persons who are strict vegans, not eating animal products of any sort. (Vegetarians are those who eat milk and eggs as well as plant products. They are not prone to this.) Vegans develop anemia due to VITAMIN B_{12} deficiency after 3 years on a strict vegan diet. It is important not to treat these people with FOLATE or FOLIC ACID; give milk or eggs in the diet or a shot of VITAMIN B_{12}.

ANTHRAX

This is common in Afghanistan.

ARBOVIRAL FEVER; Sand Fly Fever; Kyasanur Forest Disease

The most common type in this area is DENGUE FEVER, listed separately in the *Disease Index*. Other types occur occasionally in the area. (See HEMORRHAGIC FEVER and ENCEPHALITIS).

CRIMEAN-CONGO HEMORRHAGIC FEVER is described in the *Disease Index*.

CHIKUNGUNYA is listed separately and also under ARBOVIRAL FEVER in the *Disease Index*. It is clinically indistinguishable from DENGUE FEVER. In Asia it is mostly an urban disease which occurs in epidemics. There are many outbreaks in India and the Reunion Islands.

The following types are described below:

- Sand Fly Fever
- Kyasanur Forest Disease

Sand Fly Fever

Cause: Virus

Moderately ill to very ill; Class 2; Regional.

It is present throughout Pakistan, Afghanistan, Iran, and north of these areas into the –stan countries by the Caspian and Ural seas. It is present in India north of the 20th parallel (Mumbai on the west coast). It reportedly does not occur in Bangladesh or Nepal.

Age: Any. **Who**: Those bitten by sand flies. (These sand flies feed mostly on chickens, less on cows and horses, and only occasionally on humans. They bite at night and also 6:30-10:30 A.M.) **Onset**: Very sudden, over hours, with a short incubation of 3-6 days.

Clinical:

Necessary: An initial fever with headache, eye pain, and general muscle pains, lasting 2-4 days. The liver and spleen are normal size and non-tender. There is no rash.

Usually: The patient's eyes are red, the face is flushed, and the patient avoids light and eye movement because it causes more pain.

Commonly: The worst pain is in the low back. Nosebleed is common. The patient may be depressed.

Sometimes: There are also nausea, vomiting, abdominal pains, and diarrhea. The neck may be stiff. The worst of the disease is over in a few days, but the patient does not feel healthy for weeks.

Complications: None.

Similar diseases: See Protocol C-2.

Treatment: Keep the patient hydrated and well fed. Use ASPIRIN, ACETAMINOPHEN, or IBUPROFEN for pain. RIBAVIRIN may be helpful.

Kyasanur Forest Disease

Cause: Virus

Synonym: Monkey Fever

Moderately ill to very ill; Class 2; Regional; mainly in India, rarely in Saudi Arabia. It occurs in India south of Ahmadabad and west of Bangalore. There is potential of its spreading throughout southern India since the ticks are present through this wider area.

Age: Any. **Who**: Those bitten by ticks. The disease occurs in monkeys, rats, lemurs, and other wild animals. Those living in areas where and when monkeys are dying are prone to get the disease. **Onset**: Very sudden, over hours, with an incubation of 4-12 days.

Clinical:

Necessary: An initial fever with headache, eye pain, vomiting, and general muscle pains. It is uncertain how long this initial phase lasts.

Usually: The patient's eyes are red, the face is flushed, and the patient avoids light and eye movement because it causes more pain.

Commonly: The liver and spleen and lymph nodes are large. HEMORRHAGIC FEVER, RESPIRATORY FAILURE and KIDNEY FAILURE may develop.

Sometimes: After apparent recovery lasting 1-3 weeks, the patient develops ENCEPHALITIS due to this virus.

Similar diseases*:* See Protocol C-2 and other relevant protocols.

Treatment: Keep the patient hydrated and well fed. Use ACETAMINOPHEN only for pain. The disease is possibly contagious so sending out for higher-level care is very problematic.

Results: Death rate 5-10%. KIDNEY FAILURE is a common complication.

ARTHRITIS

RHEUMATIC FEVER and REITER SYNDROME are local causes.

ASCARIASIS

This is very common in Kashmir, Bangladesh, central India, and southwest India. In many areas of India, especially the south, over 90% of the population harbor these worms. Ascariasis commonly mimics GALLBLADDER DISEASE and ACUTE ABDOMEN and it can cause both.

BELL'S PALSY

This may be caused by SICKLE CELL DISEASE.

BERIBERI

This is common in the area.

BLADDER STONE

Bladder stones are common in coastal Andhra Pradesh.

BRAIN DAMAGE

The most common local causes are HIV INFECTION and Japanese B ENCEPHALITIS.

BRUCELLOSIS

The problem occurs in the Rajasthan, Punjab, and Haryana areas and probably elsewhere. It is a disease of pastoralists. Those who consume unpasteurized dairy products are most at risk.

CANCER

In India, about 1/2 of all cancers are cancers of the mouth, in contrast to 1-3% in the rest of the world. It is found mostly in the poor and is related to chewing "pan", or to smoking "chutta" or "bidis". Look for a painless lump or thickening; a white or other abnormally-colored area of the pink, moist part; a sore that does not heal; trouble opening the mouth; or trouble swallowing. Hindus in India have a fairly high frequency of cancer of the penis. In women cancer of the cervix and cancer of the breast are most common.

CANCRUM ORIS

This is frequently a complication of VISCERAL LEISHMANIASIS.

CEREBRAL PALSY

An important cause in this area is Japanese B ENCEPHALITIS.

CHICKEN POX

In India much of the adult population is not immune to chicken pox. In teen-agers and young adults, there can be very serious complications, e.g. ENCEPHALITIS. Also chicken pox is very serious in pregnancy and amongst HIV-infected patients. When and if immunization is available, urge all acquaintances to be immunized.

CHOLERA

In this area it routinely accounts for a small percent of all diarrhea. Areas where the problem is common are those with stagnant or sluggish water, frequent flooding, and less than 100 meters elevation. This is mainly in coastal areas near the mouths of major rivers. It is also common in Nepal, mainly during the summer months. There have been outbreaks in Afghanistan. Cholera is becoming resistant to CIPROFLOXACIN in India.

CIRRHOSIS

INDIAN CHILDHOOD CIRRHOSIS is the most common regional cause of cirrhosis in children.

CRETINISM

In the Himalayan area, cretinism is common. About half have the first kind and half, the second. In the rest of south Asia, most cretins are of the first kind.

CUTANEOUS LEISHMANIASIS

Both Leishmania Major and Leishmania Tropica are present in this area, particularly north of the 20th parallel and west of Kanpur. It is particularly common in Afghanistan and Pakistan, extending northward to the Caspian and Ural sea areas and throughout the "–stan" nations.

CYSTICERCOSIS

This is found only in areas where pigs are raised in such a way that they come in contact with human waste. It is rare to unknown in Muslim and Hindu cultures where pork is rarely or never consumed. It is a common cause of EPILEPSY amongst the Gurkhas of Nepal.

DENGUE FEVER

This is quite common in urban and semi-urban areas. HEMORRHAGIC FEVER as a complication has not been common. It occurs in Sri Lanka, New Dehli, Vellore, Madras, Bangladesh, and in the Maldives.

DIABETES

This is commonly associated with PANCREATITIS in southern India.

DIPHTHERIA

This occurs mostly in the rainy season. In Bangladesh this is mostly a disease of the middle and upper classes

DONOVANOSIS

This is common along the southeast coast of India.

DYSENTERY

Bacterial dysentery occurs off and on all over this area. Usually there are blood and mucus in the stool from the beginning; sometimes there is watery diarrhea at first which changes to dysentery in 1-2 days. There is usually high fever and severe abdominal pain, but rarely DEHYDRATION. One complication is SEPSIS which is common in India and Bangladesh in children under 4 years old, and especially in those less than 1 year old. Up to 15% of the patients die. Another complication is REITER SYNDROME. In some areas bacterial DYSENTERY is resistant to COTRIMOXAZOLE.

Amebic dysentery is uncommon in urban areas of Bangladesh. It is common in children 0-2 y.o. in southern India.

ELEPHANTIASIS, ENDEMIC

Endemic elephantiasis (Mossy foot) occurs in parts of India and Sri Lanka.

ENCEPHALITIS

Japanese B encephalitis (JBE) occurs in Nepal and in nearby adjacent areas of India. There is potential of its occurring south of the 30th parallel and as far west as southern Pakistan. Reportedly it is absent from Afghanistan and from the Caspian/Ural sea area.

Thousands of cases of JBE have been recorded from west Bengal, with a 35% death rate and substantial long-term disabilities in survivors. There is less problem in Calcutta than in the surrounding rural areas. Pigs and water buffalo harbor the virus without becoming ill and mosquitoes pass it from them to human beings.

Patients are mostly well nourished; almost all had a depressed level of consciousness, paralysis, and seizures; following a 2-10-day prodrome of headache, fever, and vomiting.

An immunization for JBE is available; it involves 2 injections, 2 weeks apart. It works well but there are occasional bad reactions to it in adult Westerners.

Encephalitis may also result from CHICKEN POX. See the note above under CHICKEN POX.

Kyasanur Forest Disease, another form of encephalitis, is described under ARBOVIRAL FEVER in this Index.

ENTERIC FEVER

Synonyms: Typhoid fever, Paratyphoid fever

This is extremely common in Nepal. Paratyphoid occurs in the India area. It is mainly from unsanitary food.

Enteric fever is extremely variable by region and by patient. In India it frequently begins with a fever that rises and falls before it finally rises and stays there. In Nepal the chief complaint is usually a sustained, high fever. Other symptoms, if they occur, are similar to those in the rest of the world, but STROKE or paralysis is an occasional complication.

Similar regional diseases: See Protocol C-2

Treatment: Afghanistan, Pakistan and India report typhoid that is resistant to CHLORAMPHENICOL, AMPICILLIN, and COTRIMOXAZOLE. Use CIPROFLOXACIN or one of the CEPHALOSPORINs in these cases.

FILARIASIS

Synonym: Elephantiasis, non-endemic.

There are two types of filariasis: Brugian and Bancroftian.

Brugian filariasis causes attacks that come and go, usually lasting just 4 days at a time. It often affects arms and breasts as well as legs but only rarely the genitals. It occurs in the area around Bangalore and west of there to the coast.

Bancroftian filariasis often affects legs and the male genitals. It occurs all along the west coast of India and also east of Bangalore and south of the 28th parallel. It also occurs in the Maldives and Sri Lanka.

GALLBLADDER DISEASE

Persons with SICKLE CELL DISEASE or THALLASEMIA are particularly prone to this, and it is common in northern India.

GIARDIASIS

This is particularly common in urban Bangladesh. It also occurs commonly in southern India.

GOITER

This is especially common in inland and high-altitude areas. It may also occur in frequently-flooded river delta areas near the ocean, where iodine is continually washed out of the soil.

GUINEA WORM

Synonym: Dracunculiasis

This used to be reported from this area, from locations in eastern India, southeastern Pakistan, and north-central Pakistan. The World Health Organization states that it has been eradicated.

HEART FAILURE

In the Kerala area, restrictive failure develops for no known reason. It usually affects poor people with poor nutrition, mostly young males and older females. It develops over months to years. There is no known cure; it is inevitably fatal. Valvular heart failure is usually due to RHEUMATIC FEVER, which is very common, especially in northern India.

HEMORRHAGIC FEVER

In this area, this may (rarely) be associated with DENGUE FEVER as well as (more commonly) various ARBOVIRAL FEVERs. See Protocol C-2.

HEPATITIS

Hepatitis A, B, C, and E are all common in Afghanistan.

Hepatitis B is uncommon in mountainous Nepal. Most epidemics in the area occur during the rainy season and are due to hepatitis E, the kind that is dangerous during pregnancy. Non-pregnant patients do not become desperately ill from it, but it requires a very long convalescence. In India about 1/2 of all hepatitis is hepatitis A; 1/4 is hepatitis B and 1/4 is hepatitis E. Yearly epidemics are common. There is another, as yet unidentified waterborne hepatitis also. Hepatitis D is common in India.

If the patient had recent contact with newborn animals, he might have Q FEVER, a kind of bacterial hepatitis. This occurs in Afghanistan as well as elsewhere.

HERPES

This is very common in India.

HIV INFECTION

The spread of HIV INFECTION in India has been along the major transport routes. The most common symptoms are fever, weight loss, loss of appetite, large lymph nodes, and general body weakness. It is also very common in Burma.

Similar regional diseases: VISCERAL LEISHMANIASIS mainly affects the 2-15 y.o. population which is largely spared from HIV.

HOOKWORM

There is a very high frequency of hookworm in the south of India; it is a major cause of ANEMIA there.

HYDATID DISEASE

It occurs, but is not common, in this area. It occurs in central India, northern Pakistan, Afghanistan, and northward from there all the way to the Arctic. In these areas it is alveolar hydatid disease, and is caused by eating food contaminated by wild animal stool. It is a very aggressive disease that behaves like CANCER. It more often affects the abdomen than the lungs. In some areas ALBENDAZOLE works well and in other areas it does not.

INTESTINAL FLUKE

Fasciolopsiasis is found in India and Bangladesh. It is most common on the banks of large lakes with lotus plants and snails where there is sewage contamination of the water. In such areas, 15% to 22% of the population may be infected.

The type of snail that carries the larvae of the intestinal fluke. The diameter is about 1 cm.

Intestinal fluke is prevalent in Maharashtra State of India, in Northwest India, Bangladesh, and Burma.

IRRITABLE BOWEL

Similar regional diseases: LIVER FLUKE, INTESTINAL FLUKE.

KATAYAMA DISEASE

In this area, this is the initial stage of HYDATID DISEASE, usually in expatriates. It is rare.

KIDNEY FAILURE

In India 40% of the kidney failure is nephritic, mostly due to skin infections; 40%, nephrotic due to multiple causes including PLANT POISONING Argemone oil; 8% hemolytic failure due to bacterial DYSENTERY; and 12% slow failure due to unknown causes. SICKLE CELL DISEASE is a cause of hemolytic or nephritic or nephrotic kidney failure. KYASANUR FOREST DISEASE is a cause of this condition See ENCEPHALITIS and HEMORRHAGIC FEVER.

KYASANUR FOREST DISEASE

This is described under ARBOVIRAL FEVER in this index.

LARVA MIGRANS

A very severe deep type, gnathostomiasis, from handling raw meat with bare hands, occurs in Burma and in the Bengal area of India. Use rubber gloves when handling raw meat!

LEPROSY

This is very common in this area. India alone contains 76% of the world's leprosy patients. The disease is also very common in Bangladesh.

Similar regional diseases: PKDL, a complication of VISCERAL LEISHMANIASIS.

LEPTOSPIROSIS

This occurs mostly in Afghanistan, the eastern part of India and Nepal, most frequently during the yearly monsoons. It occurs but is not common in Madras. The death rate is 36%, usually from LIVER FAILURE.

LICE

Similar regional diseases: A similar disease is a fungal infection of the hair which causes white or black bumps on the hairs. This fungal infection is common in southern India. Wash the hair with commercial shampoo, and apply 1% CLOTRIMAZOLE lotion daily. Results in 4 weeks.

LIVER FLUKE

This is present in some areas only, mainly those that raise sheep or cattle. It reportedly occurs in some areas of Afghanistan and India. It is probably mostly fascioliasis.

One kind of snail that carries the liver fluke. Other carrier snails are similar in shape.

MALABSORPTION

The most common causes in this area are PANCREATITIS in southern India, SPRUE, and GIARDIASIS throughout the area.

MALARIA

The following areas reportedly have no malaria transmission, but you should seek locally current information. In many areas of the world, malaria has been moving to progressively higher elevations in recent years. It is reportedly present at least up to 2500 meters although the malaria at higher elevations is almost all non-falciparum. These are the areas reportedly free of transmission:

- Afghanistan: Kabul
- Bangladesh: Dhaka
- Burma: Urban areas
- Nepal: Urban areas and above 2500 meters

There has been an increase in the number of malaria cases in Afghanistan, particularly the north. The disease is most prevalent during the summer months, the peak being in August. It is about 98-99% non-falciparum malaria from April to September and mostly falciparum during September to November. It occurs mainly along the north and south borders of the country and in a north-south swathe near the eastern half of the country.

The malaria in Bangladesh, and Bhutan is at least 1/3 falciparum. In Bangladesh, falciparum is especially common in the Chittagong Division.

In Pakistan, malaria is 80% falciparum in Baluchistan, 50% in Sind, 26% in Punjab, and 21% falciparum in the northwest frontier provinces.

Sri Lanka, Nepal, and most of India have predominantly non-falciparum malaria. Recently there has been a rapid spread of CHLOROQUINE-resistant falciparum malaria in Pakistan. In Burma, 90% of the malaria is falciparum. In Maldivia, malaria is rare if it occurs at all.

MALNUTRITION

The northern half of India is a kwashiorkor area. All over India, general malnutrition, iron deficiency, xerophthalmia, and iodine deficiency are common.

MEASLES

In this area, it is the fourth most common cause of death in children. In urban areas, it occurs mainly in children between 1 and 2 y.o. and always under 5 y.o.; in rural areas it affects children in all age groups in a village at once, in epidemics which occur every couple of years. In small towns the pattern is something between urban and rural patterns. There are complications in about 50% of all cases. The most common is PNEUMONIA which may respond to PENICILLIN or alternatively CEPHALOSPORIN or CLOXACILLIN.

MENINGITIS

There have been epidemics of meningococcal meningitis in India and Nepal. This is the kind that has a very rapid onset and spreads rapidly in the community.

MONKEY FEVER

See Kyasanur Forest Disease described under ARBOVIRAL FEVER, this index.

MYCETOMA

In this area mycetoma is especially common in arid areas where there are thorny plants. It is almost all due to bacteria except in West Bengal, India where there are a variety of types.

PANCREATITIS

This is a cause of MALABSORPTION and DIABETES in southern and eastern India.

PARAGONIMIASIS

This occurs only in India and Sri Lanka for this region.

PARKINSON'S DISEASE

Similar regional diseases: PLANT POISONING: Lathyrism.

PELLAGRA

It occurs especially in northern India and Pakistan and with BERIBERI in Madras state.

PLAGUE

This occurs in the northern parts of this area, including Afghanistan, and in Burma. It occurs sporadically and also in epidemics.

POLIO

Polio is common in Bhutan, Burma, India, and Bangladesh; Afghanistan has the most polio in the world.

Q FEVER

This is present throughout this area except for the high-altitude Himilayas.

RABIES

This is a major problem in parts of India, especially west Bengal, and in Afghanistan.

RAT BITE FEVER

This is very common around Mombay.

RELAPSING FEVER

Tick-borne relapsing fever is present in this area north of the 30th parallel.

RESPIRATORY INFECTION

A regional cause is PARAGONIMIASIS. Croup is common in this area.

RHEUMATIC FEVER

This is more common in the Indian area than the rest of the developing world. Sri Lanka has the most in the world and it is very common in northern India. If you suspect this, give the patient monthly injections of benzathine PENICILLIN.

RICKETS

This is particularly common in Muslim cultures and around Mombay.

SCABIES

This is probably the most common skin problem in India. An ethnic cure is a Neem:Tumeric paste, 4:1 by weight, rubbed on the skin daily for 15 days or until the patient is cured, which ever is sooner.

SCHISTOSOMIASIS

Schistosomiasis reportedly is absent in South Asia.

SCRUB TYPHUS

This occurs mostly in rural areas; it is common in Nepal. It is present in most of Burma, all of Bangladesh, India east of longitude 85°. There are also some areas around the coastal area north of Mumbai, in the central Pakistan/Afghanistan border area, in the Kashmir area, and Himachal Pradesh. It also occurs in the Maldives and in the southern coastal area of Sri Lanka. It is mostly resistant to DOXYCYCLINE. Use AZITHROMYCIN or RIFAMPIN.

SCURVY

This occurs, but is not common, in the area.

SEIZURES

Common causes are FEBRILE SEIZURES, cerebral MALARIA, and Japanese B ENCEPHALITIS. PLANT POISONING due to Margosa oil may also cause seizures.

SEPSIS

In this area, this is most commonly related to TROPICAL SPLENOMEGALY, VISCERAL LEISHMANIASIS, or bacterial DYSENTERY. Melioidosis is a form of SEPSIS that occurs in rural areas in India and Sri Lanka.

SEXUALLY TRANSMITTED DISEASE

In general, the most common types of SEXUALLY TRANSMITTED DISEASEs are HERPES, SYPHILIS, and HIV INFECTION. In southern India the most common diseases are SYPHILIS in males and VAGINITIS due to trichomonas in females. GONORRHEA occurs commonly in both. CHANCROID, DONOVANOSIS, and LYMPHOGRANULOMA VENEREUM occur, but are not as common except DONOVANOSIS, in southeastern coastal India.

SICKLE CELL DISEASE

This occurs in the Tharu people of southern Nepal, in Orissa and Madhya Pradesh states of India amongst certain tribal groups, and in some tribal groups west, northwest, and southwest of Mysore, India.

SPOTTED FEVER

Synonym: Tick typhus

This occurs in various areas of India, Pakistan, and Nepal. It is the same kind as Mediterranean Tick Typhus. There is almost always an eschar—a tiny scab where the organism entered the body. Search for it. If you don't find it, the diagnosis is unlikely. The disease is generally milder than the African form, but there are occasional severe complications. Scrub Typhus also occurs in this area; see the separate entry.

SPRUE

This is more common in South Asia than in other areas of the developing world. It usually starts between March and September. It may affect children in southern India and these cases are quite unresponsive to treatment. In this region it does not usually cause ANEMIA.

In the Vellore, India area the problem tends to be sudden in onset. About half of the patients have fevers. It may occur in epidemics.

STREP INFECTION; STREP THROAT

This is common, as is RHEUMATIC FEVER, in northern India and in Sri Lanka. In these areas, treat any sore throat as strep throat. Be sure to treat for the entire 10 days.

STRONGYLOIDIASIS

This worm occurs commonly near Mysore, India. When this occurs along with TROPICAL SPLENOMEGALY, SEPSIS may result.

SYPHILIS

This is very common in southern India.

TAPEWORM

Rat tapeworm is common around Madras, India. Pork tapeworm occurs in India. Fish tapeworm occurs in Bangladesh.

TETANUS

Neonatal tetanus is very common in India and Bangladesh, affecting up to 7% of all live births.

THALLASEMIA

This is very common in Maldivia. In the Delhi area of India most families with this problem were originally Pakistani.

TINEA

This is very common in Maldivia and the Madras area of India.

TOXEMIA

In southern India, this is more common during the hot, dry season.

TOXOPLASMOSIS

Those with TROPICAL SPLENOMEGALY are especially vulnerable to becoming ill with this.

TRACHOMA

This is especially common in northern India, in Nepal, and in relatively arid central Burma.

TRICHINOSIS

This is rare in this area.

TRICHURIASIS

This is very common in southern India, with over 95% of children infected; it is less common in central India. It is common in urban Bangladesh, northeastern India, and in Sri Lanka.

TROPICAL SPASTIC PARAPARESIS

This is common in southern India.

TROPICAL SPLENOMEGALY

This is present in Bangladesh and in India.

TROPICAL ULCER

This is mostly a rural problem except in India where it is largely urban.

TUBERCULOSIS

Maldivia, Pakistan, Afghanistan, India, and Sri Lanka have very many cases. Skin tests in nationals are almost all positive by age 20. TB that affects the abdomen commonly causes ACUTE ABDOMEN, Type 3. Multiple drug-resistant TB is found in Nepal and in Gujarat, India. It will likely spread.

TUNGIASIS

This occurs especially in Pakistan and the west coast of India.

TURISTA

Watery diarrhea in the north of India is mostly due to virus in the winter months; antibiotics do no good. In Maldivia, diarrhea is usually due to TRICHURIASIS or GIARDIASIS. In Bangladesh, GIARDIASIS is common, as is a peculiar form of diarrhea that is curable with ERYTHROMYCIN. Diarrhea that responds to DOXYCYCLINE is common in both India and Bangladesh. In India, SEPSIS is a common complication of diarrhea; when this occurs, the patient may have urobilinogen in his urine so the disease resembles MALARIA. In Nepal consider CYCLOSPORIASIS.

TYPHUS

Louse-borne typhus is found in the northern highlands in this area, in the Himilayas.

Murine typhus is particularly common in Burma, especially coastal areas, especially summer and autumn.

VISCERAL LEISHMANIASIS

Visceral leishmaniasis occurs throughout Bangladesh and adjacent areas of India and Burma, as far west as Allahabad, and north into Nepal. It also occurs in large areas around Delhi and Madras. There is conflicting information about its presence in Afghanistan and Pakistan but it probably occurs in that area.

A large percentage of the worldwide VL is found in the Indian subcontinent. In India it is mostly in 5-15 year olds, more male than female, more rural and uneducated. The spleen is larger than the liver. Most but not all patients have a fever. There is a lot of resistance to STIBOGLUCONATE.

PKDL occurs in less than 20% of the patients in this area.

XEROPHTHALMIA

This is found especially in remote rural areas of the southern half of India, in Bangladesh, Nepal, and Bhutan. It occurs, but is less of a problem, in the far northern states of India. In most of Asia there is a very high mortality rate for blind children, up to 75% in the first 3 months of blindness. This is due to infection because the VITAMIN A deficiency that causes the xerophthalmia also decreases immunity. Small weekly doses of VITAMIN A will cut the death rate to half.

YAWS

This is found in humid rural areas of India, Burma (especially western), Sri Lanka, and possibly other areas. In India it is only in remote areas in the center of the country.

Regional Notes

Index M. Central and South America

Index M: Central and South America

AMEBIC LIVER DISEASE

This is especially common in Mexico, Columbia, and eastern South America.

ANAPHYLAXIS

Similar regional diseases: PLANT POISONING due to Atriplicism or Manicheel.

ANEMIA

Anemia due to red cell destruction occurs also with SCHISTOSOMIASIS MANSONI, VISCERAL LEISHMANIASIS, BARTONELLOSIS, and SICKLE CELL DISEASE.

ANTHRAX

It is especially in Haiti, Central America, and Chile.

ARTHRITIS

This occurs with COCCIDIOMYCOSIS.

Similar regional diseases: SICKLE CELL DISEASE (in Blacks) also involves joint pains but there is either ANEMIA or episodic abdominal pain or both. In expatriates consider ONCHOCERCIASIS.

ASTHMA

In Columbia, Brazil, Argentina, and Venezuela, this may be due to a small insect that lives in house dust. Where this occurs, occasional spraying with insecticide may be helpful.

BARTONELLOSIS

Cause: Bacteria

Synonyms: Oroya Fever, Verruga Fever, Guaitara Fever, Carrion's Disease.

Mildly to severely ill; Class 1-3; Regional in Peru and adjacent border areas.

Age: Any. **Who**: Bitten by sand flies which bite at night, especially January to April. **Onset**: Oroya fever incubation 2 weeks to 4 months, slow onset. Verruga fever occurs 2-3 months after the Oroya stage or possibly without Oroya.

Clinical:

There are two forms: Oroya fever, and Verruga fever.

➢ **Oroya fever:**

First there is marked fatigue, then an up and down fever and rapidly developing ANEMIA (shortness of breath, paleness, fatigue) and JAUNDICE. There is headache and severe joint, and bone pain. The pain over the center front of the chest is the worst. The patient may be irrational (hyperactive and/or bizarre). There may be a large spleen and large lymph nodes. The liver may also be enlarged and tender. In severe cases HEMORRHAGIC FEVER may develop. Death usually occurs in 2-3 weeks in untreated cases.

Bartonellosis distribution in Peru and vicinity.

➢ **Verruga fever:**

Initially there is a fever, usually low, plus severe joint pains. After that there are bumps on the skin; with the bumps, the fever drops. The bumps are most often small (2-4 mm) but sometimes large (up to 4 cm). The smaller bumps are most common on the face and on the hairy surfaces of the limbs. The larger bumps are mostly on the non-hairy surfaces of the limbs, near or on the larger joints. The larger bumps tend to kill the flesh, change into ulcers, or cause GANGRENE.

ENTERIC FEVER is frequently present along with Bartonellosis; this causes additional symptoms.

Similar Conditions: See Protocol C-2 for fever and headache; C-3 for fever and ANEMIA; C-6 for severe bone and joint pain; C-5 for fever and JAUNDICE. Oroya fever may be virtually indistinguishable from ordinary or cerebral MALARIA. Verruga fever may be quite similar to DENGUE FEVER but dengue does not cause skin bumps. The disease may resemble HEPATITIS.

Bush Laboratory: Urine tests positive for blood or urobilinogen or both.

Higher-Level Care. *Laboratory*: A medical laboratory can do a blood smear which is reliable. *Facilities*: A level 3 hospital will have IV antibiotics; surgery might be necessary.

Treatment:

Prevention: Eliminate sand flies; avoid bites. Sand flies are weak fliers; a fan is helpful. Spray clothing and fine-mesh mosquito nets with insect repellent or insecticide.

Patient Care:

<u>Current recommendations</u>: For Oroya phase, either CIPROFLOXACIN or else [CHLORAMPHENICOL plus PENICILLIN]. For the Verruga phase, RIFAMPIN or AZITHROMYCIN or ERYTHROMYCIN.

Previous recommendations: CHLORAMPHENICOL and AMPICILLIN are best as they are also useful for ENTERIC FEVER. PENICILLIN, STREPTOMYCIN, and DOXYCYCLINE work for BARTONELLOSIS, but do not touch ENTERIC FEVER. FOLATE is helpful for ANEMIA.

BRUCELLOSIS

This occurs in the western and northern portions of South America, in the Caribbean, and in Mexico. It is very common in Argentina, Peru, and the Minas Gerais area of Brazil.

CANCER

Cancer of the *cervix* is common in some countries of South America and in Costa Rica.

Stomach cancer is common in Costa Rica.

Cancer of the *penis* may be locally common.

Liver cancer is less common than in some parts of the tropics, but more common than in temperate western countries.

CHAGA'S DISEASE

Cause: Protozoa

Synonym: South American Trypanosomiasis Trypanosomiasis, American.

Mildly to very ill; Class 3-4; Regional; it does not occur in the Caribbean. The distribution is between the 41st parallel south and the northern border of Mexico. The Amazon basin is largely free of the disease. The intestinal and nerve problems are more common in the south than in the north.

Age: Any, especially children. **Who**: Bitten by reduviid or vinchuca bugs, usually near the eye. After the bug bites, it defecates and the organisms in the stool enter the small break in the skin. They also can enter pink, moist surfaces (like the eye and mouth) but they cannot enter intact skin. Once the feces are dry, they are not infective. Many people have the organism in their bodies but are perfectly healthy. They become ill when their immunity wanes because of old age, CANCER or HIV INFECTION. Infants of infected mothers may have the disease. There is also oral transmission, especially in the Amazon area, from eating food contaminated with the stool of the bug. **Onset**: Swelling develops around the site of the bug bite. In 14 days a rash develops and the generalized body problems follow up to 4-6 weeks later according to some authorities but years later according to others.

Clinical:

Symptoms may vary by geographic area and by altitude.

Usually: Initially there is swelling at the site of the bite, usually the eye. The swelling lasts for weeks, in contrast to a simple bug bite in which the swelling lasts for days. The swelling is painless. There may be a rough, discolored area on the skin.

Maybe: Swelling may appear elsewhere in the body also. The skin may look red or bruised. There may be fever, general aching all over, and evidence of an EYE INFECTION, a problem with which this is easily confused. The lymph nodes may be large. The cheeks may be swollen as in MUMPS.

Occasionally: Initially or else 4-6 weeks later the patient may develop the more advanced form of the disease: HEART FAILURE, a heart murmur, a very slow or fast or irregular pulse, but usually no shortness of breath. There may be sudden death. The person may have an enlarged liver and spleen; he may develop constipation and difficulty swallowing. These late changes may result in death.

Complications: About 5/8 of those infected have no long-term symptoms, 1/4 have heart problems, and 1/8 have swallowing or bowel or nerve problems. All patients with swallowing or bowel problems also have heart failure. The disease is rapidly fatal in those who have full-blown AIDS.

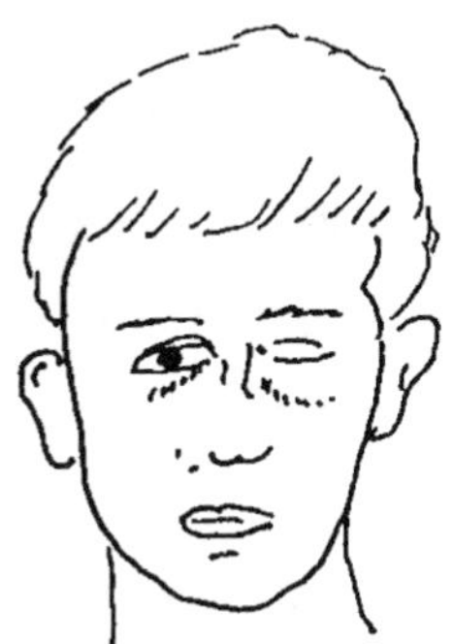

Early Chaga's disease

The history of the swelling around the eye, and the presence of any two of the following constitute sufficient grounds for diagnosis in an area where the disease is common:

- Large liver.
- Large spleen.
- Fever without any other obvious cause.
- Swelling of the feet.

In some areas, chest pains, abnormal pulse, and heart murmurs may be used instead of or in addition to the symptoms listed above.

Complications: MENINGITIS, ENCEPHALITIS.

Similar Conditions: In children, any bug bite on the eyelid results in a large swelling. Ordinarily this will go away in 48 hours. If it does not, then you should consider that it may be early Chaga's disease, in which case the swelling lasts for weeks. EYE INFECTION, and HEART FAILURE from other causes may have similar symptoms. INFLUENZA may look similar. See Protocols C-7 and C-12.

Higher-Level Care. *Laboratory*: There is no lab that you can do but hospitals can do serology. The serology is sensitive but not specific, however. The organisms are sometimes found in a blood smear, either an ordinary smear or one that has been spun, to make them all collect at one point. Another technique is to have bugs feed on the patient and then sacrifice the bugs to look for the organism. *Facilities:* The drugs to treat this are toxic and the complications are numerous so referral is highly desirable.

Treatment:

Prevention: All mammals are susceptible to the organism; one should avoid eating raw meat. Other infected mammals keep the bugs infected. Armadillos and opossums are the most important reservoirs—creatures that carry the organism and pass it on. The main way to discourage the disease is to make houses inhospitable to the bugs by plastering walls and spraying with residual insecticides. Systems have been developed for ridding whole communities of the bugs.

Patient Care: NIFURTAMOX and BENZNIDAZOLE are the two drugs that are most often used. They must be used in a hospital setting. Some new drugs which sometime work are ALLOPURINOL, VERAPAMIL, and KETOCONAZOLE. In the meantime, avoid using DOXYCYCLINE, PREDNISONE, and related drugs as they tend to make the disease worse.

CHOLERA

There have been epidemics in this area. The overwhelming majority of cases have been in Peru. Brazil, Columbia, Ecuador, Guatemala, Mexico, and Panama have also had quite a few cases. It appears to be absent at present from Uruguay and from the islands of the Caribbean.

COCCIDIOMYCOSIS

Cause: Fungus

Synonyms: Coccidioidal granuloma, Desert fever, Desert rheumatism, Valley fever

Mildly to severely ill; Class 3; Arid areas only, 40° North to 40° South, low elevation, mostly late summer and early fall.

Age: Any. **Who**: Those exposed to dust. The overwhelming, fatal form is most common in Blacks, Asians, native Americans, Mexicans, and pregnant women. **Onset**: Variable; incubation is 10-14 days.

Clinical:

Symptoms are variable, ranging from a mild, flu-like illness to an overwhelming, fatal PNEUMONIA. Typically, the patient has fever, cough, chest pain, and general fatigue, lasting from 3 days to 2 weeks. This may go away or it may become a chronic illness, resembling TUBERCULOSIS. There may be large lymph nodes which break open and drain. ERYTHEMA NODOSUM develops in 25% of the patients.

Similar Condition:

See Protocols C-4 and C-12.

Higher-Level Care. *Laboratory*: There are blood tests and sputum tests to confirm the diagnosis. This is really necessary because it looks just like TUBERCULOSIS but is treated entirely differently. *Facilities*: Imaging might be helpful. MRI is better than CT scan for this.

Treatment: The drug of choice is AMPHOTERICIN B. It is dangerous and should not be used by the medically untrained. Send the patient out for treatment. FLUCONAZOLE or ITRACONAZOLE might also be helpful.

CRETINISM

In the Americas, the first kind of Cretinism affects 90% of the cretins. (See listing in the main *Disease Index*)

CRYPTOSPORIDIOSIS

This is very common in northeast Brazil.

CUTANEOUS LEISHMANIASIS

Synonym: Chiclero Ulcer

This is very common in some areas of Costa Rica. In French Guiana this occurs only in those who have gone into the jungles; it never occurs in those who have remained in an urban area. It is common in northern Brazil. In Peru it is absent in the extreme south and extreme east of the country. The high-risk period for acquiring this disease is the end of the dry season.

In this area you should watch for the complication of mucocutaneous leishmaniasis and treat it aggressively.

Leishmania Mexicana extends from the 15th parallel south up to and past the Mexico/Texas border. It is also present in Hispaniola.

Leishmania Viannia occurs from the Tropic of Capricorn in the south up to and including the Yukatan Penninsula in the north.

CYSTICERCOSIS

This is the most common cause of adult-onset EPILEPSY in this area. It is found where pigs are raised in such a way that they come into contact with human waste. It is particularly common in Mexico.

DENGUE FEVER

In this region it is found in Central America, South America north of Argentina, and in the Caribbean. There have been epidemics with HEMORRHAGIC FEVER, resulting in deaths. Those who die do so on or about the sixth day of illness. Many of them had ASTHMA or SICKLE CELL DISEASE before becoming ill with this. About half have itching and about 1 in 7 have a visible rash. If a person lives past the seventh day of illness, he usually recovers.

DIPHTHERIA

This is found especially in Barbados and the Dominican Republic.

DONOVANOSIS

In this area it is found mostly in the Caribbean and along the northern coast of South America.

DYSENTERY

Amebic dysentery is particularly common in Mexico, Brazil (especially the Amazon), and Chile.

ELEPHANTIASIS, ENDEMIC

Endemic elephantiasis (Mossy Foot) has been reported from Ecuador, Guatemala, Mexico, and Peru.

ENCEPHALITIS

The most common kind is the Venezuelan Equine Encephalitis, found in Venezuela and adjacent countries. Other less common kinds occur in Central America and in the Caribbean. Rocio encephalitis occurs in a small area south of Santos, Sao Paulo State, Brazil. The disease may occur anywhere. A *Similar regional disease* is Rocky Mountain SPOTTED FEVER.

ENTERIC FEVER

This is common in the Caribbean, Mexico, Venezuela, Chile, and Peru. Paratyphoid occurs mainly on the north coast of South America.

EYE INFECTION

Similar regional disease: CHAGA'S DISEASE.

FILARIASIS

Synonym: Elephantiasis, non-endemic.

The filarasis in this area is all of the ordinary (Bancroftian) type. It only occurs in coastal areas of South America plus Haiti and some of the smaller Caribbean islands.

HEART FAILURE

Restrictive heart failure of unknown cause occurs in Mexico, Columbia, Venezuela, and possibly Brazil.

Regional causes of heart failure are SCHISTOSOMIASIS MANSONI, and CHAGA'S DISEASE.

HEMORRHAGIC FEVER

Hemorrhagic fever due to DENGUE FEVER occurs in the Dominican Republic, El Salvador, Nicaragua, St. Lucia, Columbia, and possibly elsewhere. A regional cause of hemorrhagic fever is YELLOW FEVER. Aside from YELLOW FEVER and DENGUE FEVER which are listed separately, the most common types are Argentine Hemorrhagic Fever with epidemics every January to August, and Bolivian Hemorrhagic Fever. These are both carried by rodents. Venezuelan HF is similar to LASSA FEVER (see F Index); it is probably contagious. There are yearly outbreaks in the states of Portuguesa and Barinas, especially during November to January, involving mostly agricultural workers. About one third of the patients die.

HEPATITIS

Hepatitis B is very common in the Amazon Basin, moderately common in the Caribbean, Central America, the Andes, and Brazil, and relatively uncommon in Mexico and in temperate South America.

Hepatitis E reportedly occurs in Mexico. If the patient had contact with newborn animals, the hepatitis may be due to Q FEVER which responds well to DOXYCYCLINE or RIFAMPIN.

Similar regional diseases: BARTONELLOSIS.

HERNIA

This is particularly common in Blacks.

HIV INFECTION

This is very common in the Caribbean. It is most common in Bermuda, the Bahamas, Barbados, Trinidad and Tobago. It is more heterosexually than homosexually transmitted, with about half the cases being in the 25-35 y.o. age range.

HOOKWORM

This is common in the Caribbean. In South America, give a second treatment a week after the first.

HYDATID DISEASE

This is particularly common in Argentina, Uruguay, southern Brazil, and Chile in sheep- and cattle-raising areas; it is transmitted by dogs.

HYPOGLYCEMIA

This may be caused by PLANT POISONING: Ackee, in which case it is of sudden onset and requires immediate treatment.

INTESTINAL FLUKE

Only one kind is found in this region, Gastrodisciasis. It is found only in Guyana and it causes diarrhea only.

IRRITABLE BOWEL

Similar regional diseases: CHAGA'S DISEASE.

JAUNDICE

Regional causes are YELLOW FEVER and BARTONELLOSIS.

KIDNEY FAILURE

Nephritic failure is common in Trinidad, West Indies. Preschoolers usually survive it well with treatment, but adolescents do not do as well. Regional causes of hemolytic failure are SICKLE CELL DISEASE (Blacks only), and BARTONELLOSIS (Peru and adjacent border areas only).

LEPROSY

The countries in this region where it is common, from the most common on down are: Brazil, Paraguay, Venezuela, Dominican Republic, Colombia, Guyana, Cuba, Trinidad and Tobago, Argentina, Ecuador, Mexico. Reportedly it is absent from Chile.

LEPTOSPIROSIS

This is common in Belize, Barbados, Nicaragua, and urban Brazil. It occurs all over Latin America.

LIVER FAILURE

Add the following regional causes:

Disease	Liver	Jaundice	Other
PLANT POISONING (Ackee)	Large, ? tender	Yes	Large spleen, sudden onset.
YELLOW FEVER	Normal size, tender	After 3 days	Fever, headache, aching, eye pain.

LIVER FLUKE

Fascioliasis is present in some areas only, mainly those that raise sheep or cattle. There is an area with much liver fluke in Asillo zone, Puno Region, Peru. It occurs in Argentina, Brazil, Central America, Chile, Columbia, Cuba, Mexico, Peru, Puerto Rico, Uruguay.

MALARIA

In some parts of the world malaria is spreading to previously malaria-free areas. Hence the information below might change over time. The following areas reportedly have no malaria transmission, but you should seek locally current information.

- Bolivia: Urban areas, and above 2500 m (8250 ft.)
- Brazil: Some urban areas
- Columbia: Urban areas and above 2500 m.
- Ecuador: Galapagos islands and above 1500 m (5000 ft.)
- Guyana: Central Georgetown
- Mexico: Urban areas; rural areas above 2500 m.
- Panama: Urban areas
- Peru: Urban areas
- Surinam: Paramaribo; interior over 2500 m
- Venezuela: Urban areas

In the Amazon area of Brazil, it is useless to try to eradicate malaria by treating those who are ill since many people have the disease without feeling sick at all.

There reportedly is much FANSIDAR resistance all over South America. There is reportedly no CHLOROQUINE resistance in Haiti, the Dominican Republic, in Central America north of the Panama Canal, or in the northern 1/5 of Argentina.

MANSONELLOSIS PERSTANS

Cause: Worm larva

Mildly ill; Class 1-2; Regional: Yucatan Penninsula; Venezuela; the Amazon Basin, coastal Brazil and Argentina, the southern half of Central America.

Age: Any, usually adults. **Who**: Bitten by culicoides (see the section on insects, Volume I, Appendix 10). **Onset**: Gradual.

Clinical:

Necessary: General joint pains without fever.

Usual in expatriates, common in nationals: Shortness of breath, trouble breathing out, wheezing, itching. Other symptoms of ASTHMA or ALLERGY might also be present.

Sometimes: Abdominal pain, especially the right upper abdomen.

Similar Conditions:

Joint pains without fevers: ARTHRITIS and similar diseases. See Protocol C-6.

Wheezing and itching resemble ALLERGY of other causes.

Abdominal pain is similar to PEPTIC ULCER, AMEBIC LIVER DISEASE, GALLBLADDER DISEASE, LIVER FLUKE, or IRRITABLE BOWEL.

Higher-Level Care. *Laboratory*: There is always an increased eosinophil count. The worm larvae might be seen in a blood smear. Unlike FILARIASIS, they might be found any time of day or night.

Treatment:

Prevention: Deal with culicoides—see Volume I, Appendix 10.

Patient Care: MEBENDAZOLE or else ALBENDAZOLE. One can prevent the disease by taking IVERMECTIN every 3 months.

Results: within 1-2 weeks.

MYCETOMA

A local form of this, Lobo's disease, occurs in the Amazon basin, Costa Rica, and Panama. Lumps the size of small bird eggs form on the skin. The skin on top is red and shiny. The disease progresses slowly. There is no treatment.

Similar Condition: Tertiary SYPHILIS.

MYIASIS

Forms that occur worldwide are particularly common in Paraguay.

A local form of skin myiasis is the macaw worm. The eggs are carried on other insects and deposited on the skin. The larvae are shaped like little gourds. They may be removed by stretching the hole and popping them out.

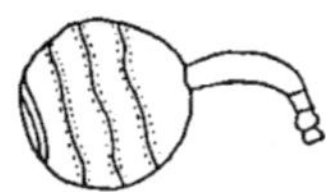

Macaw worm larva (magnified)

ONCHOCERCIASIS

This occurs in some scattered areas in Mexico, Guatamala, Venezuela, and the western Andes area of Columbia and Ecuador. It also occurs in the Brazil/Venezuela border area. The flies that carry Onchocerciasis have a much more extensive range than the disease. Hence there is much potential for the spread of the disease.

PARAGONIMIASIS

This occurs in Columbia, Costa Rica, Mexico, Peru.

PINTA

Cause: Spirochete

Synonyms: Endemic treponematosis, Endemic syphilis.

Mildly to moderately ill; Class 1-2; Regional: In Brazil it is found among the Indians in the Western Amazonas and along the Rio Negro tributaries; in Mexico it is found in the states of Guerrero, Michoacan, Chiapas, and Oaxaca; in Venezuela it is found close to the Columbia border and possibly a bit into Panama. In the past it has been in Cuba, Dominican Republic, Guadaloupe, and Haiti.

Age: Any, mainly in children and young adults. **Who**: Those living near others who have the disease. It is not extremely common anywhere but it is mostly in poor rural areas that are over-crowded. It is more common in arid than in humid areas. **Onset**: Incubation 7-20 days, then within hours to days.

Clinical:

➢ **Primary and Secondary:**

At first there are red, itchy bumps on parts of the skin not covered with clothing. These grow over months to flat, scaly, irregular areas. At first these areas are darker than normal skin but with time they become lighter than normal skin or they may be various abnormal colors. These areas persist for years and finally heal with significant scarring. The skin problem is mostly on the front of the lower leg and on the top of the foot. Lymph nodes near the skin areas may become enlarged but there is no other general body illness.

➢ **Tertiary:**

In tertiary disease, the skin is whitish and dry with much thickening and many folds. There does not appear to be whole-body symptoms like tertiary SYPHILIS or related diseases.

Similar Conditions: Flat, scaly, irregular areas might resemble LEPROSY (never itchy), TINEA (indistinguishable), CUTANEOUS LEISHMANIASIS (usually not flat), YAWS (no need to distinguish). The thick, swollen skin might resemble ELEPHANTIASIS as a result of FILARIASIS or else the mossy-foot kind.

Higher-Level Care. *Laboratory*: All blood tests for SYPHILIS will be positive.

Treatment:

Prevention: General sanitation; early treatment of known cases.

Patient Care: Use PENICILLIN, DOXYCYCLINE, or ERYTHROMYCIN.

Results: Some results in 48 hours; complete in one week in primary and secondary; healing may take weeks with tertiary and it may never be complete.

PLAGUE

Plague occurs in Bolivia, LaPaz Department; Brazil, Bahia and Paraiba States; Ecuador, Chimborazo Province; Peru, many areas. It may occur anywhere.

PLANT POISONING

Regional types are as follows:

Ackee. It is present in the West Indies. Also known as vomiting sickness, it is due to unripe ackee fruit, and some bush teas. (Ripe ackee is nonpoisonous.) There is a 90% death rate if it is not treated. The patient has abdominal pain, becomes sweaty and shaky and then falls unconscious from a low blood sugar. He later has persistent forceful vomiting and SEIZURES. His temperature will be low or normal. He may develop LIVER FAILURE. Treatment: Empty the stomach and give alcoholic beverage (see ALCOHOL in the *Drug Index*) when the patient first becomes ill. If he is unconscious, give sugar whatever way you can, preferably IV. If you cannot give it IV, give ALCOHOL, ACTIVATED CHARCOAL, and sugar by stomach tube. Do not make the patient vomit any more than he already has.

Manicheel: In the western hemisphere a kind of large tree produces a corrosive resin. All parts of the tree are poisonous; even sleeping under it or breathing its sawdust can cause problems. Eating its fruit may be fatal. Bumps resembling blisters form on the skin. They produce intense pain; the face swells. Eaten, the fruit burns the mouth and esophagus, and may cause abdominal pain, vomiting, diarrhea, paralysis, and death. *Treatment:* Treat skin problems like burns. Give ACTIVATED CHARCOAL if any part is eaten. PREDNISONE may be helpful also.

PNEUMONIA

This might be caused by Rocky Mountain SPOTTED FEVER.

Similar regional diseases: PARAGONIMIASIS, COCCIDIOMYCOSIS.

PNEUMOTHORAX

This is rare in Blacks and common in Asians.

POLIO

Similar regional disease: CHAGA'S DISEASE.

PYOMYOSITIS

This is common in the indigenous peoples of eastern tropical Ecuador.

RECTAL PROLAPSE

This may be due to SCHISTOSOMIASIS MANSONI.

RELAPSING FEVER

Louse-borne relapsing fever occurs at high elevations in the Andes, especially in Peru.

Tick-borne relapsing fever might occur anywhere within this region.

RESPIRATORY INFECTION

Similar regional diseases: COCCIDIOMYCOSIS, PARAGONIMIASIS.

RHEUMATIC FEVER

This is very common in Chile, affecting 5-20 y.o. people almost exclusively. The death rate is high. It is also very common in Mexico City.

SCABIES

This is very common in the Caribbean, with epidemics occurring.

SCHISTOSOMIASIS MANSONI

In the Caribbean it occurs in Haiti and in all the islands east of there. In South America it is confined to the coast and nearby inland areas of Brazil.

SEXUALLY TRANSMITTED DISEASE

GONORRHEA is very common all over, especially in Jamaica; CHANCROID is common and is increasing in El Salvador. DONOVANOSIS occurs in the Caribbean.

SICKLE CELL DISEASE

This occurs in Blacks of African descent. In the Americas the ancestors of almost all Blacks came from Africa with the slave trade.

SPOTTED FEVER

Cause: Rickettsiae

Synonyms: Rickettsiosis, Rocky Mountain Spotted Fever.[1]

Moderately to very ill; Class 2-3, depending on how ill.

Rocky Mountain Spotted Fever is found in scattered areas throughout Central America and the adjacent portions of Colombia. It is also in the Sao Paulo area of southern Brazil. It is also found in many areas of the States, especially the south-central and southeast, not just the Rocky Mountains. It is particularly common in the southeastern States.

Age: Any. **Who**: Tick-bitten. Susceptible patients are those who spend time outdoors or who have dogs that run freely outside and bring ticks home. People who have G-6-PD DEFICIENCY and the elderly are generally sicker. It affects Blacks more than Whites and males more than females. **Onset**: Sudden; incubation 6 to 10 days.

Clinical:

Necessary: Fever, chills, headache, fatigue, joint and muscle pains (especially in the larger joints), nausea, vomiting, and loss of appetite. The spleen is large and firm.

Usually: The rash appears between days 2 and 5, sometimes as early as day 1 and sometimes not at all. It occurs first on the ankles and forearms, and then on the trunk, palms, and soles. At first the spots are red and they blanch with pressure; later they become little black-and-blue spots. It can cause symptoms of PNEUMONIA or ENCEPHALITIS or KIDNEY FAILURE. If the patient dies, it is usually between days 8 and 15. Death is particularly common in males of African or Mediterranean (Hispanic, Italian, Greek, Jewish, Irish, Arab) genetic heritage. Sometimes there is a small scar from the tick bite.

Other symptoms: There is swelling around the eyes and possibly swelling of the hands and feet. The neck may be stiff. Muscles are very tender; gentle

[1] In this region, almost all spotted fever is Rocky Mountain Spotted Fever rather than the more mild Tick Typhus. Therefore it is important to use this description rather than the description in the main *Disease Index*.

squeezing will cause severe pain. The patient may have a big liver. His spleen will be large and tender. He may have genital pain and his genitals may be destroyed with GANGRENE.

Complications: Blindness, deafness, HEART FAILURE, BRAIN DAMAGE, death.

Similar Conditions: See Protocols C-2 and C-11.

Bush Laboratory: The patient may have bilirubin in his urine.

Higher-Level Care. *Laboratory*: A blood test, the Felix-Weil, is available but it is not very reliable. In larger hospitals, more advanced tests may be available. With the usual tests, the disease must be present for 6 days before they turn positive. It is important not to wait for a positive lab test before starting treatment.

Treatment:

Prevention: Avoid tick bites: Exclude dogs from houses; protect arms and legs when pushing through brush; do not sleep on the ground. Remove ticks immediately after they attach.

Patient Care: CHLORAMPHENICOL, DOXYCYCLINE. For this disease DOXYCYCLINE can be used at any age. The risk from it is less than the risk from CHLORAMPHENICOL and there are currently no other proven options. CIPROFLOXACIN works in the laboratory but it is not reliable for treating patients. The patient must be treated until he has been without a fever for a full two days. CO-TRIMOXAZOLE and other sulfa drugs tend to make the disease worse. RIFAMPIN might work; give it for 7-14 days, the shorter time if the patient is not so sick and for 14 days if he/she is very sick.

STRONGYLOIDIASIS

This is particularly common in Brazil, the Caribbean, Ecuador, Costa Rica, Panama, and Columbia. It is less common but still not rare in Venezuela and in Bolivia.

VISCERAL LEISHMANIASIS and HIV decrease natural immunity. Where either of these occur along with strongyloidiasis, SEPSIS may result.

SYPHILIS

This is very common in Trinidad and presumably in the rest of the Caribbean also.

TAPEWORM

Fish tapeworm is especially found in Argentina, southern Chile, and the coast of Peru.

Pork tapeworm is especially found in Mexico, Central America, and Peru.

THALLASEMIA

In the western hemisphere it is present to a significant extent only in ethnic groups from Europe, Africa, or Asia. In persons of Hispanic ancestry, this may cause severe problems similar to those of the Arabs, Jews, and others of Mediterranean genetic origin.

Similar regional diseases: SICKLE CELL DISEASE, BARTONELLOSIS, TROPICAL SPLENOMEGALY, VISCERAL LEISHMANIASIS.

TINEA

Tinea imbricata occurs in Central and South America.

TOXOPLASMOSIS

This is extremely common in Brazil, more so than anywhere else in the world. Try to protect pregnant women.

TRICHURIASIS

This is very common in the Caribbean.

TROPICAL SPASTIC PARAPARESIS

This is common in the Americas, particularly Jamaica; Columbia; and Martinique, French West Indies. In the Caribbean area 90% of the cases are females.

TROPICAL SPLENOMEGALY

This occurs in the Amazon area. In Venezuela, it is most common in the Amazonas Territory where it affects 44% of the inhabitants over 10 y.o.

TUBERCULOSIS

This is very common in the Caribbean and in Bolivia, Peru, Chile, and Panama. BURULI ULCER occurs in Mexico, especially in areas that are marshy or have frequent floods, as well as in Cuba, Dominican Republic, Bolivia, and French Guiana. Multiple drug-resistant TB is common in Bolivia.

TUNGIASIS

This occurs in all of Central America and Mexico, and the northern 3/4 of South America.

TURISTA

In Venezuela, about 60% of the diarrheas in children should respond to DOXYCYCLINE.

TYPHUS

Louse-borne typhus occurs in the higher and cooler areas of the Andes and in the mountains of Guatemala.

Murine typhus is especially common in Mexico, Central America, Argentina, and Chile. It is more common in the coastal areas than further inland.

VISCERAL LEISHMANIASIS

This occurs in dry or only moderately humid mountainous areas below 800 m (2500 ft.). It is mainly rural. There have been large outbreaks in urban Brazil, especially Teresina and Sao Luis. Epidemics are more likely after a drought. It occurs only rarely in the Amazon River Basin. In El Callejon, Columbia, visceral leishmaniasis is very common; it is harbored by dogs and possums. In addition to the areas shown, it occurs in the Caribbean in southwestern Guadaloupe and in central Martinique.

Age: In Brazil, most less than 5 y.o.; everywhere else most patients are under 20 y.o.

VITILIGO

Similar regional diseases: ONCHOCERCIASIS, PINTA.

WARTS

Similar regional disease: BARTONELLOSIS.

XEROPHTHALMIA

This is known to occur in Haiti and Brazil.

YAWS

Columbia (especially Pacific coast), Guyana, Haiti, Martinique, Suriname (especially Blacks in the interior).

YELLOW FEVER

Cause: Virus

Moderately to very ill; Class 2-4; Regional

Epidemics occur during the rainy season. Most cases are from Peru; some are from Bolivia, Brazil, and Ecuador. The disease is present from 22° North to 28° South latitude but is reportedly absent from the high Andes.

Age: Any. **Who**: Unimmunized; frequently in epidemics, transmitted by Aedes mosquitoes that bite during the day. (See Volume I, Appendix 10.) This affects mostly adult males exposed to forested environments. **Onset**: Over a day or two, incubation 3-6 days.

Clinical:

The WHO definition for yellow fever is as follows:
Fever *plus* JAUNDICE *plus* one or more of the following:

- a slow pulse relative to the fever
- abnormal bleeding
- upper abdominal pain
- protein in urine
- decreased amount of urine

Necessary: The patient has fever, nausea, and aching all over, especially in the back, sides, and limbs. JAUNDICE develops only after several days of illness. If it intensifies, it does so slowly, over days. The spleen is not enlarged.

Usually: There is a severe headache and eye pain. The mind is clear; the patient does not act intoxicated like he does with TYPHUS. The pulse is initially rapid, but by day 3 or 4, the pulse slows and may become slow relative to the fever.

Sometimes: The yellow color of the whites of the eyes may be quite indistinct. The face may be swollen. There may be general bone and joint pains. Vomiting may occur early, as may insomnia and a tender but non-swollen liver. Initially the vomit is mucous, but it may become black or bloody. The patient may have a body odor resembling a butcher shop.

Complications: An occasional complication is HEMORRHAGIC FEVER: nosebleeds; bleeding gums; bloody stool, urine, and vomitus; heavy menstruation, heavy bleeding from minor wounds. There is a high death rate during epidemics.

Similar Conditions: DENGUE FEVER is similar but does not usually show protein in the urine unless the urine is also bloody; also the bone pains of dengue are much worse. LEPTOSPIROSIS may be indistinguishable; treat for this if there is a question. RELAPSING FEVER also is similar but there is little or no protein in the urine. Other similar diseases are ARBOVIRAL FEVER, HEPATITIS, and the diseases listed on the chart in Index C-2 (general body pain), C-5 (fever and JAUNDICE), and C-9.

Bush laboratory: Bilirubin in the urine is quite common. There is always protein in the urine by the second day of illness. There may be blood in the urine on the third or fourth day.

Higher-Level Care. *Laboratory*: Sophisticated hospital laboratories can do blood tests or liver biopsies. *Facilities*: A level 4 hospital can render lifesaving care.

Treatment:

Prevention: Immunize. Excellent immunization is available. Immunity starts about 10 days after the injection. The immunization must be repeated every 10 years.

Patient Care: Same as HEPATITIS and, if necessary, HEMORRHAGIC FEVER. VITAMIN K injections may be helpful.

Regional Notes

Index O. East Asia

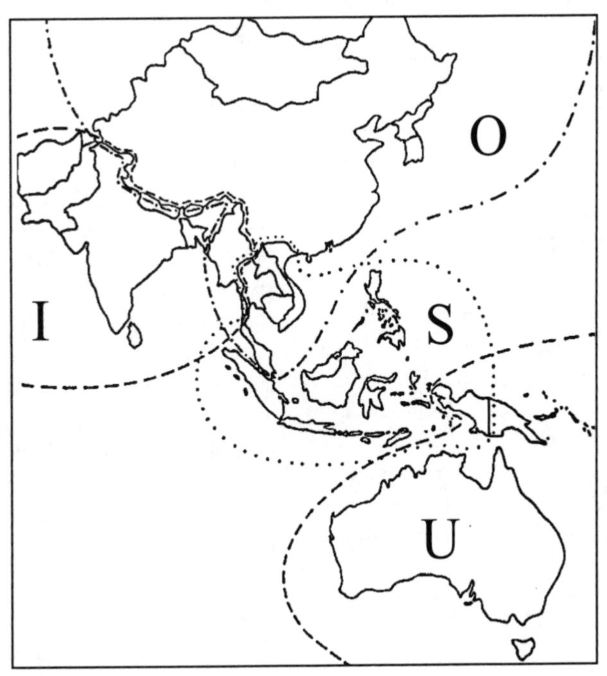

Index O: East Asia

ADDICTION

A regional example of uppers is Miang which is used in northern Thailand and is a cause of mouth CANCER. Betel nut (under PLANT POISONING) is also used regionally.

AMEBIC LIVER DISEASE

This is especially common in Taiwan, China, and Thailand. It is not common in Laos.

ANEMIA

Anemia due to red cell destruction, while most often due to MALARIA, may be due to THALLASEMIA in persons from northeast Thailand and adjacent areas. It may also be due to OVALOCYTOSIS in Malaysians. TROPICAL SPLENOMEGALY may cause this in scattered areas, and VISCERAL LEISHMANIASIS in China.

If the stool is positive for blood and the problem does not respond to treatment for HOOKWORM, consider SCHISTOSOMIASIS JAPONICUM in areas where that is prevalent.

ARTHRITIS

In China, RICKETS is a common and RHEUMATIC FEVER, an uncommon cause of arthritis; in Indochina, the situation is reversed.

ASCARIASIS

This is common in Laos.

ASTHMA

This is especially common in Indochina. The kind caused by little insects living in dust is common in China and Taiwan. It may be common elsewhere also.

BERIBERI

This is very common in agricultural workers in Malaysia.

BLADDER STONE

This occurs in this area.

BRAIN DAMAGE

Regional causes are Japanese B ENCEPHALITIS and SCHISTOSOMIASIS JAPONICUM.

BRUCELLOSIS

This is a problem in some areas of China.

CANCER

Cancer of the *mouth* is caused by the use of Betel nut or Miang (northern Thailand). (See PLANT POISONING.)

Cancer of the *nose and throat* is more common than average in this area, due to a virus.

Cancer of the *stomach* is quite common in the easternmost areas but the cause is uncertain.

Cancer of the *bile duct* (gallbladder area) is common in areas with LIVER FLUKE, especially in northeast Thailand.

Cancer of the *liver* is very prevalent in this area. It appears to be related to HEPATITIS B as well as PLANT POISONING (aflatoxin) due to sausage and moldy peanuts.

CANCRUM ORIS

This is rare in the region, except for areas of China with VISCERAL LEISHMANIASIS.

CHANCROID

This is particularly common in Korea and in Indochina. In Southeast Asia many strains of this are resistant to DOXYCYCLINE, SULFA, and COTRIMOXAZOLE. Most strains are sensitive to ERYTHROMYCIN, CHLORAMPHENICOL, CEFTRIAXONE (see CEPHALOSPORIN), CIPROFLOXACIN and other -oxacins.

CHICKEN POX

Similar regional disease: SPOTTED FEVER, rickettsiapox.

CHOLERA

This occurs mainly in epidemics in times of war, drought, or flood, although single cases occur here and there in Indochina. It is common in Malaysia but does not occur in Taiwan. It occurs from time to time in Korea and mainland China.

Similar regional disease: FOOD POISONING from rice.

CIRRHOSIS

Regional causes are SCHISTOSOMIASIS JAPONICUM (particularly in China) and INDIAN CHILDHOOD CIRRHOSIS.

CRETINISM

The first kind of cretinism[1] affects most cretins in Asia except for the Himalayan area where it affects only

[1] This refers to the description in the *Disease Index*.

50%. The second kind affects 50% of the cretins in the Himalayan area and rare cretins elsewhere in Asia.

CYSTICERCOSIS

It is very common in Korea and in China.

DENGUE FEVER

In Indochina this is very common. There are yearly epidemics in urban areas during the rainy season. The mosquitoes that carry the disease breed in house plants. In China there are also epidemics, especially in the south. DENGUE HEMORRHAGIC FEVER occurs throughout this area. See HEMORRHAGIC FEVER also.

DEPRESSION

An associated regional disease is LIVER FLUKE.

DIPHTHERIA

This is not common but it does occur sometimes in the crowded slum areas of Thailand and presumably other Asian countries.

DONOVANOSIS

Not common, but it does occur in this region.

DYSENTERY

Dysentery is uncommon in Taiwan. Amebic dysentery is generally very common in Indochina, but relatively uncommon in mainland China. Bacterial dysentery is common throughout Indochina.

Similar regional diseases: SCHISTOSOMIASIS JAPONICUM and PIG-BEL (uncommon).

ENCEPHALITIS

The only common kind of encephalitis in the southern part of this area is *Japanese B Encephalitis*. It occurs in China except for Xinging and Shanxi. There are yearly epidemics in Indochina, especially in northern Thailand, with most cases in July; it is carried by evening-biting mosquitoes. The disease occurs but is not so common in the rest of the area. About 40% of those who get the disease die from it and most of the rest have long-term disabilities.

Prevention: There is a good immunization available consisting of two injections, two weeks apart. It is available in Bangkok. Adult Westerners sometimes get allergic reactions to the immunization so they should stay near medical care for 2 weeks after receiving it.

Patients should be cared for under mosquito nets to avoid infecting the local mosquitoes and thus transmitting the disease.

Tick-borne encephalitis occurs in the northern part of this area, from 50° to 60° north latitude, extending south near the eastern coast, to Vladivostok. Treatment is supportive.

ENTERIC FEVER

Typhoid fever is not common in Taiwan. It occurs mainly from June to September in Korea. It occurs all year in Indochina. Paratyphoid is mainly from unsanitary food; it is not common in this area.

Similar regional disease: The second phase of SCHISTOSOMIASIS JAPONICUM, about 30-90 days after exposure, may resemble this. Consider this carefully, as the treatments are quite different.

FILARIASIS

Synonym: Elephantiasis, non-endemic.

This occurs in eastern China and in Sabah, Malaysia. It does not occur amongst the Ibans of Malaysia. There are two types of filariasis: Brugian and Bancroftian:

Brugian filariasis causes attacks that come and go, usually lasting just 4 days at a time. It often affects arms and breasts as well as legs but rarely genitals. It is found in the southeastern fourth China and the northern half of Vietnam. It is not found in Hainan.

Bancroftian filariasis often affects legs and the male genitals. It seldom or never affects breasts and arms. It is found in the southeast of China, and as far north along the coast as Qingdao. It is also found throughout Vietnam and on the island of Hainan.

FOOD POISONING

Gallbladder of raw fish: See separate entry below.

There are two kinds of food poisons that are peculiar to this area:

Rice that has stood at room temperature for a day or two grows bacteria that cause severe, watery diarrhea.

Raw shellfish (mussels, clams, and oysters) concentrate a toxin which causes symptoms within 30 minutes. It starts with tingling and numbness around the mouth first and then the limbs. Later, vomiting and uncoordination occur. Death is not uncommon. It initially appears similar to HYPERVENTILATION.

GALLBLADDER DISEASE

This is particularly associated with OVALOCYTOSIS (Malaysia), THALLASEMIA (northeast Thailand and adjacent areas), and LIVER FLUKE (northeast Thailand and the Far East). It is a common cause of ACUTE ABDOMEN in eastern Asia.

GALLBLADDER OF RAW FISH

This is from carp, which is a bottom feeder—caught with hooks or nets that have heavy weights. It is poisonous even after it is cooked. It is used in Asia as a Chinese traditional medicine for poor eyesight. It causes nausea, vomiting, diarrhea, abdominal pain, LIVER FAILURE, and KIDNEY FAILURE. For similar conditions see Protocol C-7.

Treatment: Not feasible in the village situation.

GIARDIASIS

In mainland China, it is not common but when it occurs symptoms tend to be severe.

GOITER

Regional, especially in lowland river deltas, inland, and high-altitude areas; rare to very common.

In Burma it is common both in lowland and hilly areas. It is also common amongst the Penans (nomads of Malaysia).

In mainland China, goiter due to IODINE excess occurs in the Kuitun-usum area and also in sea-coastal areas where people consume kelp salt and pickled vegetables.

HEART ATTACK

This is common in mainland China.

HEART FAILURE

This is common in mainland China. Regional diseases that are associated with it are SCHISTOSOMIASIS JAPONICUM and KESHAN DISEASE.

HEMORRHAGIC FEVER

In Indochina the most common cause is DENGUE FEVER in children and in expatriate adults. In the easternmost areas (the eastern parts of China and in Japan and Korea) it may be caused by an ARBOVIRAL FEVER associated with KIDNEY FAILURE; it is usually fatal.

Hemorrhagic fever occurs in Xinjiang Province, NW China.

HEPATITIS

Most local people have been exposed to hepatitis B prenatally or during childhood; it is a common problem in expatriates. It may be food- or water-borne in this area. Epidemics affecting nationals are usually water-borne hepatitis E in Burma, Thailand, southern China, and Malaysia.

Similar regional diseases: SCHISTOSOMIASIS JAPONICUM and LIVER FLUKE. LEPTOSPIROSIS (common in Malaysia and central Thailand) may be confused with this.

HIV INFECTION

A major epidemic has developed in Thailand. There is also a focus on the Thai-Burmese border, the "Golden Triangle".

HOOKWORM

This is generally common throughout this area. It is very common amongst agricultural workers, amongst the Ibans of Malaysia, and in Anhui Province of mainland China. In Cambodia, about 50% of the population is infected.

HYDATID DISEASE

Both kinds occur in Mongolia and also in north and north-west China: Gansu, Ningxia Hui, Qinghai, Sichuan, and Xingjiang; these are high-altitude areas in the Liupan mountains. Red foxes and small mammals are the hosts for the type transmitted by wild animal stool. It is not common but when it occurs it is very aggressive. Ordinary hydatid disease is between domestic dogs and sheep. Risk factors are poor hygiene, female gender, low income, limited education, lack of well water, and dog ownership.

This is not common, but it may occur in Indochina (Laos and Vietnam) and in the Himilaya area.

HYPERVENTILATION

Similar regional disease: FOOD POISONING. See the entry in this index.

INTESTINAL FLUKE

One kind is *echinostomiasis* which occurs in Taiwan and has minimal symptoms. It comes from eating inadequately cooked tadpoles, snails, fish, and frogs.

A second kind is *metagonimiasis* which is from eating raw fish. It is especially common in Korea. It provokes a high eosinophil count (hospital lab) and may result in HEART FAILURE. It may also invade the brain or spinal cord like SCHISTOSOMIASIS.

Another kind, *fasciolopsiasis*, is particularly common in Thailand amongst children who eat fresh-water plants. It is also common in Taiwan and the Far East generally. It is very common on the banks of large lakes with lotus plants and snails where there is sewage contamination of the water. In such areas up to 25% of the population may be infected.

The type of snail that carries the larvae of fasciolopsiasis. The diameter is about 1 cm.

JAUNDICE

The most common causes in this area are HEPATITIS, MALARIA, LEPTOSPIROSIS, AMEBIC LIVER DISEASE. Less common causes are LIVER FLUKE, INDIAN CHILDHOOD CIRRHOSIS, liver CANCER, and SCHISTOSOMIASIS JAPONICUM.

KATAYAMA DISEASE

This refers to the initial stage of SCHISTOSOMIASIS JAPONICUM (common) or HYDATID DISEASE (rare).

KESHAN DISEASE

Cause: Unknown
Very ill; Class 3; Mainland China
Age: Adults. **Who**: Women who have just given birth.
Onset: Very sudden.

Clinical:

This is a type of sudden, severe, HEART FAILURE (floppy type). It is almost invariably fatal.

Treatment: This should be done at a hospital, but the patient will probably die in any case. Treating it like ordinary HEART FAILURE might help temporarily.

KIDNEY FAILURE

Nephritic kidney failure is very common in Indochina.

A kind of ARBOVIRAL FEVER which can become HEMORRHAGIC FEVER is a cause of the *infective/toxic* type of kidney failure in the Far East.

OVALOCYTOSIS is a cause of the *hemolytic* type in Malaysia.

LARVA MIGRANS

In Sarawak (Borneo) and Thailand eating raw snail is a common source; in central and northern Thailand it comes from handling raw meat without gloves. This kind of deep larva migrans is called gnathostomiasis. It can cause very serious problems, including blindness.

Similar regional diseases: Deep larva migrans, if it is in the liver, may mimic LIVER FLUKE. In China, PARAGONIMIASIS may cause symptoms resembling skin-type larva migrans.

LEPROSY

This is very common throughout Indochina.

LEPTOSPIROSIS

This may occur in epidemics. It is common in Indochina and Korea. It occurs in mainland China and in Thailand. In Malaysia it is common in oil palm and rubber workers but not common in rice farmers.

LIVER FAILURE

Add the following regional causes:

Disease	Liver	Jaundice	Other
SCHISTOSOMIASIS JAPONICUM	Large, nontender	Rare/late	Big spleen, looks pregnant
LIVER FLUKE	Large, tender	Maybe	Burning pains

LIVER FLUKE

Synonyms: Chinese liver fluke, Clonorchiasis, Opisthorchiasis (this is the kind that occurs in Thailand and other parts of Indochina).

Present in Indochina, China, Korea, Hong Kong, Macao, Japan. In Laos, 36% of the population is infected.

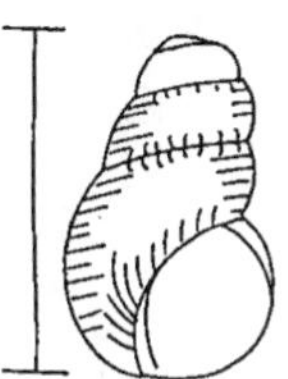

The kinds of snails that carry the liver fluke.
Lengths are 1-1.5 cm.

LYME DISEASE

This is known to occur in NE China, Eastern Russia, and in Japan.

MALABSORPTION

The following are regional causes. See Protocol C-14 for other causes.

Disease	Characteristics
CAPILLARIASIS	Northeast Thailand only; not generally common.
SCHISTOSOMIASIS JAPONICUM	Skin exposed to water with snails.
INTESTINAL FLUKE	Sometimes upper abdominal pains also.

MALARIA

The following areas have no malaria transmission at all: Brunei, Korea (N & S), Hong Kong, Japan, Macao, Mongolia, Singapore, Taiwan. Also reportedly there is no malaria transmission in the following areas, but check with local information. Malaria has been moving to higher elevations in many parts of the world, up to 2500 meters (8000 feet).

- Cambodia: Above 1500 m (5000 ft.)
- China: The north of the country, urban areas, and the south above 1500 m (5000 ft.)
- Laos: Vientiane
- Thailand: Bangkok and suburbs, Pattaya, Phuket

- Vietnam: Above 1500 m (5000 ft.); the Red and Mekong deltas.

One should keep in mind that, worldwide, malaria is entering areas where it previously was not transmitted. Therefore the areas listed above might be newly endemic areas. Seek local lore.

In the following areas, malaria is extremely common: Sarawak, Sabah, hilly border areas of Malaysia and of Thailand, and the southern half of China.

In southern China almost all the malaria is non-falciparum; in Indochina it is almost all falciparum. In Thailand it is almost all resistant to CHLOROQUINE and FANSIDAR. It is partly resistant to QUININE and there is some MEFLOQUINE resistance. Reportedly CHLOROQUINE plus CHLORPHENIRAMINE works well.

In Malaysia rural aboriginals are quite immune to falciparum after age 20, while town dwellers are more vulnerable in adulthood.

MALNUTRITION

Kwashiorkor occurs in the northern half of China. In Malaysia, marasmus is more common. Patients who have VISCERAL LEISHMANIASIS or SCHISTOSOMIASIS JAPONICUM are likely to have more problem with malnutrition.

MELIOIDOSIS

See SEPSIS. This is a form of SEPSIS that occurs in rural Indochina.

MENINGITIS

There have been meningococcal meningitis epidemics in Mongolia. This is the kind of meningitis with rapid onset and rapid spread throughout the community.

PARAGONIMIASIS

This is generally common throughout the area.

PELLAGRA

This is common in corn-growing parts of China.

PIG-BEL

This is not common but might occur in rural Asia.

PLAGUE

This is known to occur in Vietnam, Burma and mainland China.

PLANT POISONING

Add the following regional type:

Atriplicism: Caused by eating the leaves of a plant in China. The patient's hands itch and then develop large blisters. His fingers may become pale and develop GANGRENE. His face and eyelids swell and look bluish.

Treatment: Use only the routine treatment for any poisoning.

PNEUMOTHORAX

This is common in Asians.

POLIO

This is very common in Indochina, especially Laos; rare in Taiwan.

RABIES

This is a major problem in Thailand due to lack of routine immunization of dogs.

RELAPSING FEVER

This occurs on the Asian mainland only, not on any of the islands. It is not common.

RHEUMATIC FEVER

This is very common in Thailand and Mongolia; less so in mainland China and Taiwan.

RICKETS

This is particularly common in females and babies in Muslim cultures and in China.

SCHISTOSOMIASIS JAPONICUM

Cause: Worm

Synonyms: Bilharzia, Snail fever, Japonicum

Mildly ill to very ill; Class 2; Regional; this is particularly common in Fujian Province of China and generally in southern China, south of the Yangtze River and along both banks of the river. There are scattered areas between 22° and 32° North latitude, near and east of 100° longitude. It is also present in SEA. However, the disease has been eliminated from Japan. This description also applies to SCHISTOSOMIASIS MEKONGI.

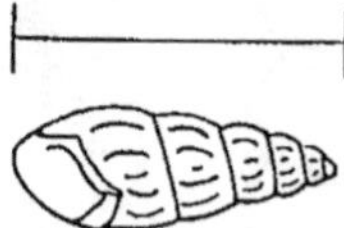

The type of snail that carries S. japonicum. Note the small hole and many swirls. Some have stripes and some do not. Length is about 0.7-1 cm.

Age: Any. **Who**: Skin exposed to water with infected snails. **Onset**: Beginning 3-7 weeks after exposure.

Clinical:

Initially: In Westerners this frequently starts as KATAYAMA DISEASE. Nationals skip this stage.

30 to 90 days after exposure: The patient may have lower-right abdominal pains with fevers, diarrhea or DYSENTERY, and cough. This stage can look just like ENTERIC FEVER. The patient is probably unable to work.

Three to five years later: The person has LIVER FAILURE with a large liver, large spleen, and an abdomen full of fluid so he looks pregnant. The liver enlarges before the spleen, the opposite of MALARIA. Frequently it is the left lobe which enlarges; this may be confused with splenic enlargement. The patient will have a decreased appetite and weight loss. Children grow poorly and they may have delayed sexual maturity. Alternatively, the patient may have chronic diarrhea, DYSENTERY, and MALABSORPTION (prompt, watery diarrhea whenever he eats anything).

Complications: The organism may invade the brain, causing paralysis, SEIZURES, crazy behavior, blindness, and possibly coma. It may invade the lung, causing RESPIRATORY INFECTION, and HEART FAILURE. These symptoms must be treated promptly on mere suspicion in anyone who has had any exposure during his or her lifetime. Be sure to use PREDNISONE as well as PRAZIQUANTEL. It may cause CANCER of the rectum.

Similar Conditions: *Fever and fatigue*: in the early stage resembles ENTERIC FEVER and SERUM SICKNESS. (KATAYAMA DISEASE probably is a type of SERUM SICKNESS).

Later stages are difficult to distinguish from LIVER FAILURE and MALABSORPTION from other causes; See Protocol C-14.

Brain effects sometimes resemble POLIO (paralysis), STROKE (paralysis), ENCEPHALITIS (seizures, crazy behavior), CYSTICERCOSIS (seizures).

Bush Laboratory: One can hatch the worm eggs and see the larvae using simple equipment. See Appendix 2 in Vol. I. This is more sensitive (more likely will be positive in the presence of the disease) than an egg search in a higher-level laboratory.

Higher-Level Care. *Laboratory*: The worm eggs can be found in the stool during the second stage of the disease. (Stool may be negative for eggs during the KATAYAMA phase.) The blood count may show increased eosinophils during the first and second stages only, in about ½ of the expatriates who get the disease.

Treatment:

Prevention: Use latrines; avoid exposure of skin to contaminated water; let a bucket of water without snails stand overnight before washing with it.

Patient Care: PRAZIQUANTEL. It is expensive but effective and safe enough to use even if you are not certain of the diagnosis. Occasionally patients get a severe allergic response (see ALLERGY) to the first dose of the drug. This is treated like any other ALLERGY, but do not stop the drug. It is due to dead and dying worms and will not recur as severely, with subsequent doses. If there are neurological symptoms (seizures, paralysis, loss of sensation, altered mental status), use DEXAMETHASONE, PREDNISONE, or PREDNISOLONE, as you would for MENINGITIS due to TB. In advanced liver disease PROPRANOLOL might be helpful. In either case seek professional medical advice. NIRIDAZOLE is an old, dangerous drug that should no longer be used. During the KATAYAMA phase it is essential to use PREDNISONE also. See the *Drug Index*.

Results: You should do repeat lab at 1, 3, and 6 months. Where schistosomiasis and HEPATITIS occur together, the prognosis is very poor.

SCHISTOSOMIASIS MEKONGI

Synonyms: Bilharzia, Snail fever

See SCHISTOSOMIASIS JAPONICUM. This disease is indistinguishable and the treatment is the same. The distinction is only academic.

Schistosomiasis mekongi is found on Khong Island in southern Laos, in fishermen on house boats near Kratie, east Kampuchea, and amongst the Orang Asli in Pahang and Perak States in Malaysia.

SCRUB TYPHUS

This occurs in the rural Asian and Pacific areas below 3800 m (12,500 ft.); it is most common in palm oil workers. It is rare in Sabah (Borneo). There are outbreaks during the spring and summer on Pington Island, eastern Fujian Province, PRC. It is present in a triangular area from Shanghai to Guangzhou along the coast, to 30° latitude, 110° longitude inland. It occurs in most of Taiwan, Vietnam, Cambodia, and Burma, in north and east Thailand, but little if any in Laos.

A form of scrub typhus found in Burma causes huge node swelling in the neck, resembling DIPHTHERIA.

SEIZURES

Regional diseases that may cause seizures are PARAGONIMIASIS, and SCHISTOSOMIASIS JAPONICUM.

SEPSIS

Melioidosis is a form of this that occurs in rural Indochina. There is a high death rate, especially in those with DIABETES or KIDNEY FAILURE.

SPOTTED FEVER (Tick typhus)

Tick typhus occurs in Mongolia and Siberia only. It is Siberian Tick Typhus. Rickettsial pox may occur in Korea.

SPRUE

This occurs in the entire area except for western China and Korea.

STROKE

Regional causes are SCHISTOSOMIASIS JAPONICUM and PARAGONIMIASIS. In China the problem is common and is usually due to HYPERTENSION.

STRONGYLOIDIASIS

This is very common in Indochina. The disease tends to persist in those who have had it; worms can be detected 30 years after last exposure.

Similar regional disease: SCHISTOSOMIASIS JAPONICUM in its initial stages.

SYPHILIS

In Thailand syphilis is common. Congenital syphilis is common in newborns.

TAPEWORM

The dwarf and rat tapeworms are common in Asia. Pork tapeworm is common in China, Taiwan, and Korea. Fish tapeworm occurs in Japan.

THALLASEMIA

In southern China, northeastern Thailand, and the surrounding areas this is quite common.

Similar regional diseases: VISCERAL LEISHMANIASIS, OVALOCYTOSIS.

TINEA

Tinea imbricate occurs in some coastal areas.

TOXEMIA

This is very common in China. In Malaysia it is more common amongst the Indians than Malays or Chinese, probably because of their depressed economic status.

TOXOPLASMOSIS

This is not common in China or Malaysia. There is a small risk in Thailand.

TREPONARID

This is found only in western China in this region.

TRICHINOSIS

This is common in mainland China. There have been small outbreaks in northern Thailand. It is rare to unknown in Muslim areas where pork is not used.

TRICHURIASIS

This is very common in Laos, amongst agricultural workers, in Ibans, and in urban slums of Malaysia. In many areas of China most people have this.

TROPICAL SPASTIC PARAPARESIS

This occurs in Japan. About 60% of the cases are females.

TROPICAL SPLENOMEGALY

According to some sources this occurs in parts of China, and according to other sources it does not occur at all in this area.

TUBERCULOSIS

This is known to be common in Burma, Cambodia, Laos, Sabah, Vietnam, Sarawak, and West Malaysia. In the Far East it is most common in Macau, Korea, Hong Kong, Japan, and Taiwan. Skin TB occurs in Malaysia.

Multiple drug-resistant TB is common in Korea.

TYPHUS

SCRUB TYPHUS is listed separately in the B Index. Tick typhus and Rickettsial pox are listed under SPOTTED FEVER.

Louse-borne typhus occurs in northern China and near the Himilaya area.

Murine typhus is common in China, Korea, and Thailand. It is most common in coastal areas, more during the summer than the winter.

VISCERAL LEISHMANIASIS

In China it is mainly in isolated, hilly, and dry areas north of the Yangtze River, in the northwest of the country. It is always below 200 meters (650 ft.) elevation except for Gansu Province where it may be found up to 1000 meters (3300 ft.). It does not occur in Indochina.

Age: Most less than 10 y.o.; in northwest China 95% are less than 5 years old; in the North Tarim River Valley most are less than 2 years old although parents may also be infected.

Clinical:

In China, some patients have darkening of their skin, HEART FAILURE, and nosebleeds. Their lymph nodes may be generally enlarged but their livers and spleens may be of normal size. In the North Tarim River Valley patients get bumps on their skin. The death rate is high there.

XEROPHTHALMIA

This is widespread in the rice-eating areas of Asia. In Thailand it is a rural but not an urban problem. In most of Asia there is a very high mortality rate for children who are blinded by this—up to 75% in the first 3 months after loss of vision. The deaths are mostly from infections because of the loss of immunity with this illness.

YAWS

Reportedly this does not occur in the Far East and it is uncommon in Indochina, occurring only in humid areas with grossly inadequate medical care.

Regional Notes

Index R. Mediterranean and the Middle East

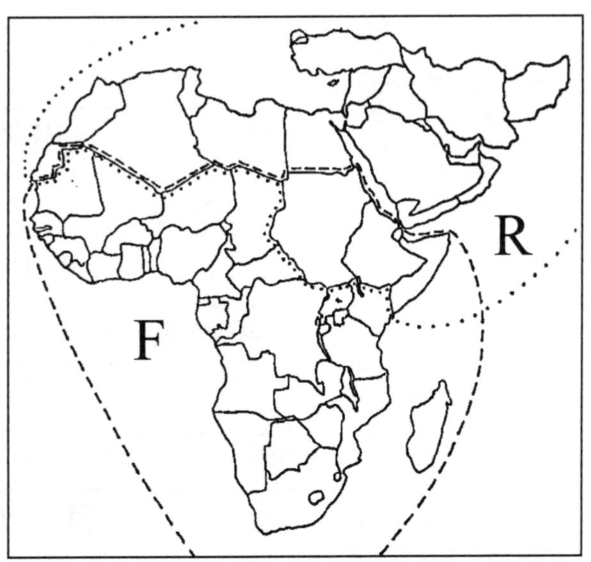

Index R: Mediterranean and Middle East

ADDICTION

Local types of uppers are Khat (mainly in eastern Ethiopia and adjacent Somali areas) and Betel nut (amongst the Indian population). (See PLANT POISONING).

AMEBIC LIVER DISEASE

This is particularly common in Algeria, Egypt, and in the Middle East south and east of Turkey. It is less common in southern Europe.

ANTHRAX

This is common in the Middle East in areas of animal husbandry, especially Iran and Iraq and northern Africa. It is most prevalent in late dry and early rainy seasons, in areas where the soil is neutral or alkaline.

ARBOVIRAL FEVER

Although it is not common, Rift Valley Fever occurs in Egypt, Sudan, Saudi Arabia, Yemen, and Somalia. It occasionally results in loss of vision or ENCEPHALITIS, or HEMORRHAGIC FEVER. It is carried by mosquitoes. The incubation period is 2-7 days. It is particularly common in times of flooding. The virus is considered a bioterrorist weapon. It may be directly contagious.

Also uncommon in this area is Kyasanur Forest Disease; see the description in the I regional index.

In this particular area, many of the arboviral fever cases have sand fly fever which is described below.

Sand Fly Fever

Cause: Virus

Moderately ill to very ill; Class 2; Regional, common throughout Egypt, Iran, and Iraq and along the west coast of Saudi Arabia, mainly June to August.

Age: Any. **Who**: Those bitten by sand flies. (This kind of sand fly feeds mostly on chickens, less on cows and horses, and only occasionally on humans. It bites at night and also 6:30-10:30 A.M.) See Volume I, Appendix 10. **Onset**: Very sudden, over hours, with a short incubation of 3-6 days.

Clinical:

Necessary: An initial fever with headache, eye pain, and general muscle pains, lasting 2-4 days. The liver and spleen are normal size and not tender. There is no rash.

Usually: The patient's eyes are red, the face is flushed, and the patient avoids light and eye movement because it causes more pain.

Commonly: The worst pain is in the low back. The patient may be depressed.

Sometimes: There is also nausea, vomiting, abdominal pains, and diarrhea. The neck may be stiff. The worst of the disease is over in a few days, but the patient does not feel healthy for weeks.

Complications: None

Similar diseases: See Protocol C-2.

Treatment: Keep the patient hydrated and well fed. Use ASPIRIN, ACETAMINOPHEN, or IBUPROFEN for pain. RIBAVIRIN may be helpful.

ASCARIASIS

This may exist, but is not likely to be a big health problem, in areas with less than 1200 mm rainfall per year. This includes most of this area except for parts of Italy, the Slavic countries, southern Turkey, and the area east of the Black Sea.

BELL'S PALSY

A regional cause of this is tick-borne RELAPSING FEVER, which is common throughout this area.

BERIBERI

This is very common in eastern Afghanistan but not common in Syria or the rest of the Middle East.

BLADDER STONE

This occurs in this area, especially in areas with SCHISTOSOMIASIS HEMATOBIUM.

BRAIN DAMAGE

The most likely local causes are HEAT ILLNESS and possibly SCHISTOSOMIASIS MANSONI.

BRUCELLOSIS

This is common in the northern half of Africa and the Middle East. It is especially common in Iran, Iraq, Kuwait, Jordan, Israel, the Red Sea area, and the Mediterranean. It is very common in the Van region of Turkey. In this area of the world it is related to milk and buttermilk more than cheese and raw liver. It is more prevalent in sheep and goats than in camels and cattle. Those who assist in the delivery of animals are particularly prone to getting the disease. In this area the disease affects children, causing MENINGITIS, paralysis, or uncoordination. In Jordan this occurs mostly from May to September. Most cases are caused by unpasteurized milk and milk products.

BURKITT LYMPHOMA

This is rare if it occurs at all in the Mediterranean and Middle East.

CANCER

The cancers that are common in most developing countries are common in this area also. In addition, bladder cancer is common in areas with SCHISTOSOMIASIS HEMATOBIUM, and cancer of the esophagus is common throughout this area. There is a cancer of the lymph nodes (lymphoma) that is locally common. It starts with large, painless lymph nodes, similar to TUBERCULOSIS. Skin cancer of the eyelids occurs in fair-skinned people in the desert areas in this region.

CAPILLARIASIS

This occurs in Egypt; a closely related disease occurs in Iran to some extent.

CHOLERA

In this area cholera generally occurs in Iraq and Iran only, mainly in epidemics in times of drought or flood.

CIRRHOSIS

This may be due to drinking too much ALCOHOL, to SCHISTOSOMIASIS MANSONI, HEMOCHROMATOSIS, or other diseases. It is worse with poor nutrition. See INDIAN CHILDHOOD CIRRHOSIS if the patient is a child of Indian ethnic origin.

CUTANEOUS LEISHMANIASIS

This is found throughout the area except for southeast Saudi Arabia, Oman, and UAE. In the Arabian Peninsula and along the north coast of Africa, it is almost all L. Major. In Turkey and the Balkans, it is almost all L. Tropica. In Israel, it is present along the Jordan River from the Dead Sea north for about 25 miles, about 5 miles on both sides of the river. In this area gerbils harbor the disease and the sand flies that breed in their burrows pass it on to humans. It also occurs in the northern Sinai area and the western Negev. There have been recent outbreaks in Tunisia and in western and SE Turkey. In rural desert areas the disease is maintained in the rodent population and the skin sores tend to be large and wet. In urban areas the sores are dry and crusted over; the disease is maintained in dogs and humans.

Who: Bitten by sand flies, in rural areas with gerbils and in urban areas with dogs. The flies bite especially at dusk but also throughout the night.

Treatment:

Prevention: Avoid contact with dogs; use insect repellants when such contact is unavoidable.

Patient Care: In Saudi Arabia add ZINC to the treatment and use it for 4 months.

DENGUE FEVER

This is a disease that is present almost worldwide but it reportedly is not found in this area except for Mogadischu, Somalia. There is potential of spreading.

DYSENTERY

Amebic dysentery is common in Algiers, and is uncommon in Saudi Arabia.

ELEPHANTIASIS, ENDEMIC

Synonym: Mossy foot

Endemic elephantiasis occurs in Ethiopia, Morocco, and perhaps elsewhere.

ENCEPHALITIS

Tick-borne encephalitis is found on the Balkan Penninsula and adjacent areas of Italy; it may also be found in other areas.

ENTERIC FEVER

Typhoid Fever, which is resistant to multiple drugs, is now common in Egypt. *Paratyphoid Fever* occurs in the Mediterranean area. In this area, there usually is fever plus some abdominal symptom. However, it may present as fever and cough, resembling BRONCHITIS or PNEUMONIA. This may resemble MENINGITIS or ENCEPHALITIS or it may cause just fever and crazy behavior.

Treatment: In this area where there is resistance to antibiotics, most respond to second- or third-generation CEPHALOSPORINs or CIPROFLOXACIN.

EPILEPSY

In this area it may be caused by ONCHOCERCIASIS.

FAVUS

Cause: Fungus

This is a fungal infection of the scalp which is common in the Middle East and the Mediterranean area. Initially it looks like TINEA. With time, round, bald patches develop and then yellow crusts appear in this area. The hair never grows back.

Treatment: GRISEOFULVIN. On day 1, shave the head and start the GRISEOFULVIN. On day 25 shave the head again. On day 31, the drug may be stopped. This should cure the problem. Check the person again on day 42. If there is any sign of the disease at that time, repeat the treatment.

FILARIASIS

Synonym: Elephantiasis, non-endemic.

This disease is present almost worldwide but it has, in the past, not been found in the Middle East and the Mediterranean areas except in eastern coastal Yemen and in coastal Turkey, opposite Cyprus. Recently it has been reported to be common in the southern Nile delta area of Egypt. It is carried there by Culex mosquitoes. See Volume I, Appendix 10.

GASTROENTERITIS

Similar regional diseases: PLANT POISONING due to Lolism.

GIARDIASIS

This is very common in the Middle East, especially in Algiers, Saudi Arabia, and Yemen in areas of poor sanitation.

GOITER

This is due to IODINE deficiency in mountainous areas of the eastern Mediterranean, southern Egypt, and Ethiopia.

GUINEA WORM

Cause: Worm.

Synonyms: Dracontiasis, Dracunculiasis.

Mildly to moderately ill; Class 1; Regional: occurs in Saudi Arabia and possibly in areas of Afghanistan adjacent to Pakistan, where water is obtained from wells into which people step. Old maps are not reliable and there are no new maps; the distribution is unknown because of conflict in the region, which excludes professional health care.

Age: Any. **Who**: Those who drink water contaminated with microscopic larvae. **Onset**: Variable; usually about 1 year after drinking infected water.

Clinical:

Necessary: A small bump forms, usually on the leg, but it may be elsewhere. This enlarges to become a blister. It is itchy and frequently burning; the pain is relieved by cold. When the blister breaks, one can see the end of the worm. A painful, open sore forms in place of the blister. There is only one worm per blister or sore and each worm is 30-70 cm (12-28 in.) long.

Maybe: The worm will discharge a milky fluid.

Complications: Secondary wound infection, OSTEOMYELITIS.

Similar Conditions: None except possibly in the very early stages.

Treatment:

Prevention: Encourage design of wells that eliminates the possibility of people climbing down into them. A simple sand filter works well to eliminate parasites from contaminated water. Use temphos (Abate) to treat affected water supplies.

Patient Care: The best treatment is for the worm to be surgically removed before the blister forms. This is a relatively easy procedure. It reduces the period of disability from weeks to two days. If you already know how to suture wounds, it would be feasible for you to learn how to do the procedure

Once the blister forms: Immerse the blister or sore in cold water. This makes the worm limp. Having the patient take IBUPROFEN helps also. Wind the worm on a small clean stick, a few centimeters a day, not so tightly that the worm breaks. This will gradually draw the worm out. (If the worm breaks, treat promptly with one of the medications listed below.) If the patient is bedridden anyway, keeping the area continually moist will hasten the worm expulsion (2 weeks vs. 2-3 months). Otherwise keep the area clean and dressed with ANTIBIOTIC OINTMENT to prevent infection. A number of different drugs are also useful, such as METRONIDAZOLE, TINIDAZOLE, MEBENDAZOLE, and THIABENDAZOLE.

HEMORRHAGIC FEVER

This occurs in Greece as well as other parts of the Mediterranean; it is not common. KIDNEY FAILURE is an occasional complication. It must be treated in a hospital.

Crimean-Congo hemorrhagic fever is a local form that is most common in northern Iraq and amongst Kuwaiti Bedouins. It also occurs in the Western Province of Saudi Arabia, the Mecca area. It is carried by ticks which live on domestic animals and bite humans who rest in shaded areas. It is also very contagious, being directly transmitted from patients to healthy people. Most cases occur from June to September. It looks very similar, in its early stages, to ARBOVIRAL FEVER caused by sand flies in this area. It can be distinguished by the fact that it has a slow pulse relative to the fever, and by the presence of protein and blood in the urine. It is potentially a bioterrorist weapon.

Treatment: RIBAVIRIN, with hospitalization. However, evacuation is not advisable; better to let the patient die than to start a worldwide epidemic.

HEPATITIS

Almost everyone has been exposed to *Hepatitis A* in childhood and is immune by adulthood.

Hepatitis B is more prevalent in Saudi Arabia than in any other part of the world, according to a Saudi medical journal.

Hepatitis C is most common in Turkey and in non-Bedouin Saudi Arabs.

Hepatitis is also common in Egypt, especially Hepatitis B and Hepatitis E. Gamma globulin from the States does not protect against Hepatitis E, but that from France does. Reportedly Hepatitis E does not frequently cause LIVER FAILURE in pregnancy in Egypt as it does elsewhere. Many cases are entirely without symptoms.

HIV INFECTION

It is reportedly very common amongst prostitutes in Djibouti and Addis Ababa. It is mostly an urban problem which is spreading to rural areas as a result of development and also armed conflicts.

HYDATID DISEASE

This is very common in the Middle East and arid northern Africa. Females are affected more than males and most are 50-60 years old. The liver is the most common organ affected, followed by lung, kidney, and spleen.

INTESTINAL FLUKE

In this area, this is Heterophyiasis which is prevalent in the Nile delta, Israel, Tunisia, Turkey, and the Port Said areas. It causes a high eosinophil count (hospital lab) but other diseases do also. *Complications*: HEART FAILURE or damage to the brain or spinal cord, similar to SCHISTOSOMIASIS.

IRITIS

This may be associated with ONCHOCERCIASIS on the Arabian Peninsula.

KATAYAMA DISEASE

Cause: Allergy/worm

This refers to the initial stage of SCHISTOSOMIASIS (either kind), GUINEA WORM, or HYDATID DISEASE. It is common with SCHISTOSOMIASIS MANSONI but rare with SCHISTOSOMIASIS HEMATOBIUM and the other diseases.

KIDNEY FAILURE

Additional regional causes:

Nephrotic type may result from SCHISTOSOMIASIS MANSONI.

Nephritic type is extremely common in the Middle East. It usually follows STREP THROAT.

Obstructive type: SCHISTOSOMIASIS HEMATOBIUM.

Hemolytic type: SICKLE CELL DISEASE.

KIDNEY INFECTION

Similar regional diseases: SCHISTOSOMIASIS HEMATOBIUM, SCHISTOSOMIASIS MANSONI.

KIDNEY STONE

Similar regional disease: SCHISTOSOMIASIS HEMATOBIUM.

LARVA MIGRANS

The deep type occurs in Israel, especially in the moister areas, and in the Mosul area of Iraq.

LEPROSY

This occurs in the area, but according to WHO statistics, it is not common in the region as a whole. Among these countries, it occurs mainly in Ethiopia, Yemen, and Egypt.

LEPTOSPIROSIS

This is not common in general in the Middle East. In Portugal, cattle get the disease as well as persons handling infected animals. It commonly results in a MENINGITIS-type illness which should be treated with antibiotics to cover both this and ordinary MENINGITIS.

LIVER FLUKE

Fascioliasis is present in some areas only, mainly those that raise sheep or cattle. It is particularly common in the Nile delta. It also occurs in Algeria, Morocco, Tunisia, Turkey, Iran, Iraq, Yemen, and Afghanistan.

Snail that carries the liver fluke. The length is about 1.4 cm.

LYME DISEASE

Lyme disease occurs in this area.

LYMPHOGRANULOMA VENEREUM

This is particularly common in northern Africa.

MALARIA

CHLOROQUINE-sensitive malaria occurs in Turkey, Iraq, Saudi Arabia, Egypt, and the islands of the Mediterranean.

CHLOROQUINE-resistant malaria occurs in Iran and Afghanistan; it is expected to spread rapidly. There has been a rapid increase in the amount of malaria in northern Afghanistan. This may spill over into Iran. In Afghanistan, most malaria is falciparum from September to November and most is non-falciparum from April to September.

The following areas reportedly have no malaria transmission at all: Bahrain, Cyprus, Israel, Jordan, Kuwait, Lebanon, Qatar, Maldives. Also reportedly free of malaria transmission are:

- Afghanistan: Kabul
- Iran: Areas in the northern part of the country above 1500 m (5000 ft.)
- Iraq: Over 1500 m (5000 ft.)
- Oman: Central area
- Saudi Arabia: Western part above 2000 m (6600 ft.)

One should note that the geographical extent of malaria transmission is expanding worldwide, and it is occurring at progressively higher elevations, in many areas up to 2500 meters (8000 feet). It is essential to seek local lore.

In Turkey and Iraq, there is no falciparum malaria. The malaria in Oman, Saudi Arabia, and Yemen is mostly falciparum. That in Iran and United Arab Emirates is about 1/4 falciparum. In the rest of the Middle East falciparum malaria is rare.

MALNUTRITION

Kwashiorkor is generally common in north Africa and the Middle East. In refeeding, one should note that camel milk has more vitamin C than milk of other sources.

MENINGITIS

In Kuwait this is not common; about 75% of the cases that occur in children are treatable with AMPICILLIN and CHLORAMPHENICOL. There have been meningococcal epidemics in Saudi Arabia. This is the form of meningitis with very rapid onset and rapid spread within the community.

Similar regional diseases: LEPTOSPIROSIS, BRUCELLOSIS, especially in children.

MONONUCLEOSIS

A very similar disease is a form of VISCERAL LEISHMANIASIS which occurs in Saudi Arabia. See the note under VISCERAL LEISHMANIASIS in this index.

MYCETOMA

This is common in Sudan.

MYIASIS

The Tumbu fly occurs in the Asia area of southwestern Saudi Arabia.

ONCHOCERCIASIS

This is present in Yemen at an altitude of 300-1200 m (1000-4000 ft.); in Wadis Ghayl, Rasyan, Zabid, Rima, Surdud, and possibly Siham and Harad; in Saudi Arabia near the wadis in the Asir region.

Eye symptoms are rare in the Middle East, but the skin symptoms are usually severe enough to prevent working.

Sowda is a form that is found in Yemen and northern Sudan. The skin becomes swollen and covered with scaly bumps. There is swelling of the lymph nodes, usually in the groin.

PELLAGRA

This occurs in the Black Sea area of Turkey and the corn-growing areas of Iran. It reportedly does not occur in Lebanon, Syria, or Iraq.

PELVIC INFECTION

Similar regional diseases: SCHISTOSOMIASIS HEMATOBIUM, SCHISTOSOMIASIS MANSONI.

PHIMOSIS

Similar regional disease: SCHISTOSOMIASIS HEMATOBIUM.

PLAGUE

This has been reported from Libya, Iran, Iraq, Asir area of Saudi Arabia, NW Yemen, and Western Sahara. There is a focus of infection in the Oran area of northern Algeria. It may occur elsewhere.

PLANT POISONING

Regional types are listed below:

Khat: A traditional drug used as a stimulant, it is widespread in the middle east and east Africa. The leaves and twigs of a Miraa tree are chewed or smoked or used for teas. It is an amphetamine. Some people become happy and gregarious; others become mellow. Repeated use may lead to ADDICTION. Treatment: Not required unless ADDICTION is a problem.

Lolism: Common in Africa and the Middle East, due to moldy wheat. Within 15 minutes the patient becomes dizzy, has a headache, slurred speech, trembling, and staggering. There may be diarrhea, vomiting, and abdominal pain. The patient may become unconscious or nearly so and remain that way about 10 hours. Treatment: Empty the stomach and give ACTIVATED CHARCOAL if possible.

Miscara: See Lolism, above.

Muiragi: See Khat, above.

POLIO

This was very common in Afghanistan, Yemen, Iraq, Ethiopia, Egypt, Lebanon, Pakistan, Somalia, and Oman. Recent worldwide immunization programs may have changed this. It is reportedly still common in areas of Iran and in the Iraq/Turkey border area. You can expect to see it wherever WHO personnel have not been welcomed.

PROCTITIS

Regional causes are SCHISTOSOMIASIS MANSONI and SCHISTOSOMIASIS HEMATOBIUM.

PROSTATITIS

Similar regional diseases: SCHISTOSOMIASIS MANSONI and SCHISTOSOMIASIS HEMATOBIUM

Q FEVER

This is present throughout the area except for Egypt, Israel, the Arabian Penninsula, and Syria where it is reportedly absent.

RELAPSING FEVER

Louse-borne is found mainly in the highlands of Ethiopia; it may occur elsewhere at times of war and social disruption. *Tick-borne* occurs in the Mediterranean area and Africa in general.

RHEUMATIC FEVER

This is common in Algeria, Egypt, Morocco, Iran, Cyprus, Ethiopia, and Kuwait.

RICKETS

This is particularly common in Muslim cultures, especially among women and babies, due to lack of skin exposure to the sun. It is widespread in the Middle East in Lebanon, Syria, Iraq, Saudi Arabia, Turkey, and Iran.

SCHISTOSOMIASIS HEMATOBIUM

Cause: Worm

Synonyms: Urinary bilharziasis, Snail fever, Bilharzia

Not ill to very ill; Class 2; Regional; this is especially frequent where there are dams and irrigation canals. It is present in the Nile Valley, in scattered areas of countries bordering the southern Mediterranean, scattered areas throughout central Sudan and northern Ethiopia. It also occurs in southern Somalia and adjacent Ethiopian border areas. It occurs in oases throughout the Arabian Penninsula and in a large area of Iraq and Syria. Over half the population may be affected in some areas. In the Taiz province of Yemen, Arab Republic, up to 90% of the people are infected in the western, southern, and northern parts of the province. All ages and both sexes are affected. The problem is less common, however, at higher than at lower altitudes.

Age: Any, but especially boys 5-15 y.o. who like to swim. **Who**: Skin exposed to water in which infected snails live. **Onset**: 10-12 weeks after exposure, then over days to weeks.

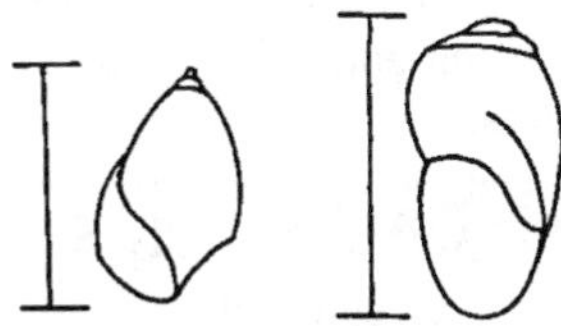

The type of snail that carries S. hematobium; note the large hole and 3 or 4 swirls. The length is about 0.7-1.5 cm.

Clinical:

➢ **Initially:**

Immediately after the exposure to contaminated water, mainly in expatriates there may be initial itching of the skin for 2-3 days. After the incubation period, Caucasians usually begin with KATAYAMA DISEASE: fevers, low abdominal pain, fatigue, and symptoms of ALLERGY. Nationals may skip these symptoms.

➢ **Later:**

Necessary: The patient develops bloody urine. Blood may be visible only or mainly at the end of urination. If it is not visible, a urine dipstick will demonstrate that it is present.

Usually: There is frequent urination and burning pain with urination. Nationals may have only bloody urine without other symptoms.

Maybe: There is kidney pain resembling KIDNEY STONE and leading to KIDNEY FAILURE. There may be swelling of the end of the penis and possibly bloody semen.

Occasionally: It can cause PROCTITIS or symptoms resembling SCHISTOSOMIASIS MANSONI.

➢ **Still later:**

The patient may have to urinate frequently and may dribble because the bladder becomes rigid; it cannot enlarge to hold its usual volume of urine.

Complications: Rarely this may cause problems with the spinal cord: sharp, shooting pains, weakness, numbness and tingling, inability to start urinating. Spinal cord schistosomiasis must be treated promptly with PRAZIQUANTEL and PREDNISONE, not waiting for lab results which may be falsely negative—do this with anyone who has had a prior exposure at any time in his/her life.

ANEMIA and weight loss are likely. The disease evidently contributes to MALNUTRITION since children show a growth spurt after treatment. Other complications are: VAGINITIS-type symptoms, bladder CANCER, KIDNEY INFECTION, inability to urinate, sores and growths on penis or in vagina, sterility in females, KIDNEY FAILURE, URETHRAL STRICTURE, and occasionally RESPIRATORY INFECTION from migrating worms. The bones may become thin and weak so fractures occur with minor injuries. Sometimes, after years, the worms invade the lungs, causing RESPIRATORY FAILURE and HEART FAILURE.

Females may develop PELVIC INFECTION and become at risk of CANCER. In both sexes the infection promotes the transmission of the HIV virus. In males an occasional complication is a BLADDER STONE; men with stones cannot urinate unless they jump up and down. Their urine may be bloody during the day and normal at night.

Similar Conditions: SEXUALLY TRANSMITTED DISEASES are the main point of confusion. URETHRITIS (visible pus from penis or female urethra), KIDNEY INFECTION (also nitrites and/or leukocytes in urine), KIDNEY FAILURE of other causes, ALLERGY (Hives) from other causes, PROSTATITIS (usually men over 50 y.o. only), TUBERCULOSIS of the genitals, FILARIASIS.

Bush Laboratory: Afternoon urine will test positive for blood (and protein) with a urine dipstick. One can hatch the worm eggs and see the larvae using simple equipment. See Appendix 2 in Vol. I.

Higher-Level Care. *Laboratory*: Eggs can be found with a microscope. The blood count may show increased eosinophils early in the disease, especially in expatriates; they may be absent later on.

Facilities: If there are any complications a level 4 or 5 facility is appropriate. In advanced disease biopsy, CT or MRI might be helpful.

Treatment:

Prevention: Use latrines, eliminate snails, avoid water exposure. Let a bucket of water stand overnight before using it for washing; be sure there are no snails in the water.

Patient Care: PRAZIQUANTEL; PREDNISONE or PREDNISOLONE along with the PRAZIQUANTEL might be helpful. Seek local medical advice. METRIFONATE is a cheaper alternative for widespread use. MEBENDAZOLE may work. NIRIDAZOLE is an old, dangerous drug that should no longer be used. Reportedly the antimalarial drug, ARTEMISININ (as artesunate), reduces the egg count by over 90%. Seek recent information.

Results: These should be evaluated at 3 and 6 months after treatment. Improvement starts after about one month.

SCHISTOSOMIASIS MANSONI

This is common along the Nile River Valley, in southern Sudan, and in central and western Ethiopia, especially along the Rift Valley. It is less common at higher than at lower altitudes. It also occurs in scattered locations within the Arabian Penninsula.

SCURVY

This is especially common in the Middle East in Lebanon, Syria, Iraq, Saudi Arabia, Iran, and northeast Turkey.

SEPSIS

This may be related to VISCERAL LEISHMANIASIS.

SICKLE CELL DISEASE

This occurs mainly in Africans and Blacks of African descent. A few scattered areas near the Persian Gulf and India and Pakistan also have the disease, but they do not have the severe symptoms of the African disease. In Saudi Arabia it occurs mostly in the Shi'i Muslims of the Qatif and Al-Hasa Oases; the ANEMIA is mild to moderate, leg ulcers are rare, and the spleen is large in adults. There is a form of severe sickle cell disease in Jizan, Quamfeda, Fayfa, and NW of Jeda, Saudi Arabia.

SPOTTED FEVER

Tick typhus occurs in areas adjacent to the Mediterranean, Black, and Caspian Seas. Other forms of the disease reportedly are not found in this region. In Israel, spotted fever is almost always found in teens or younger children. The best drugs in this area are: DOXYCYCLINE, CHLORAMPHENICOL, RIFAMPIN plus ERYTHROMYCIN, and possibly CIPROFLOXACIN or CLARITHROMYCIN. In any case it is important to treat until the fever has been absent for 3 days.

SPRUE

This is particularly common in the eastern coastal Mediterranean area and in Syria.

STROKE

This may be caused by SICKLE CELL DISEASE, SCHISTOSOMIASIS MANSONI, and SCHISTOSOMIASIS HEMATOBIUM, though rarely.

STRONGYLOIDIASIS

This is particularly common in Turkey and Iran.

Similar regional diseases: SCHISTOSOMIASIS MANSONI.

SYPHILIS

For endemic syphilis, see TREPONARID. This is common in the nomads of the desert areas of the Middle East.

TAPEWORM

Beef tapeworm occurs in Lebanon and fish tapeworm occurs in Israel.

TETANUS

Tetanus in newborns is very common in Iraq; there are many home births and immunization is uncommon.

TINEA

See FAVUS in this Index for a form of tinea that is peculiar to the Mediterranean and Middle East. Ordinary tinea also occurs in this area.

TOXOPLASMOSIS

This is a problem in Libya and in the mountainous areas of Iran.

TRACHOMA

This is common all over the Middle East, especially northern Africa and Saudi Arabia; more in low-income areas with dirt, flies, and overcrowding. It is less common amongst nomads and in sparsely-populated areas.

TREPONARID

Areas where this is found are amongst the Somali Bedoin of the north, the Bedouin of southern Arabia, and in northwest rural Pakistan.

TRICHINOSIS

This is rare to unknown in Jewish or Muslim areas where pork is prohibited.

TRICHURIASIS

This occurs in Yemen Arab Republic.

TROPICAL SPLENOMEGALY

Some sources say that it does not occur in the Middle East and other sources say that it does occur. It is rare if it occurs at all.

TROPICAL ULCER

Regional diseases that may appear similar or may cause this are SICKLE CELL DISEASE, CUTANEOUS LEISHMANIASIS, and GUINEA WORM.

TUBAL PREGNANCY

This may be caused by SCHISTOSOMIASIS MANSONI or SCHISTOSOMIASIS HEMATOBIUM.

TUBERCULOSIS

This is quite common in Iraq. In Israel (and presumably elsewhere) a large percentage of the TB involves the urinary system, the lymph nodes, and the bones. See the description under CANCER (in this index) of a form of that disease that can mimic lymph node tuberculosis. Also consider that in Saudi Arabia there is a form of VISCERAL LEISHMANIASIS that can mimic both MONONUCLEOSIS and lymph node tuberculosis.

TURISTA

In Egypt, it is most serious and prevalent in children below 24 months in the summer and autumn of the year. In Saudi Arabia, most diarrhea in children is due to a virus; it does not respond to antibiotics. If it continues in spite of ORS, ERYTHROMYCIN is the antibiotic most likely to succeed.

TYPHUS

Louse-borne typhus is at higher and cooler areas in Africa, Iraq, and Kuwait where there are crowding and body LICE. It occurs at some locations within the Balkan Penninsula and in Algeria.

Murine typhus, borne by rat fleas, is common amongst garbage collectors and others exposed to garbage in Egypt. There have been outbreaks in Kuwait. It occurs in Algeria and Morocco, as well as the Balkan Penninsula and the Sinai (and adjacent) areas.

URETHRAL STRICTURE

This may be caused by SCHISTOSOMIASIS MANSONI or SCHISTOSOMIASIS HEMATOBIUM.

URINARY OBSTRUCTION

This may be caused by SCHISTOSOMIASIS MANSONI or SCHISTOSOMIASIS HEMATOBIUM.

VAGINITIS

This may be caused by SCHISTOSOMIASIS MANSONI or SCHISTOSOMIASIS HEMATOBIUM.

VISCERAL LEISHMANIASIS

L. donovani, which affects both children and adults, occurs throughout this area. L. infantum, which affects mostly babies, occurs only along the Mediterranean rim in and west of the Balkans. The affected areas are constantly changing. This occurs in parts of Yemen, Arab Republic and in SE Turkey. Occasionally it is found in western Turkey. It is found in central Israel where dogs harbor the disease; sand flies carry it from the dogs to humans.

The parasite that usually causes CUTANEOUS LEISHMANIASIS will occasionally cause visceral leishmaniasis in Westerners in Saudi Arabia. It causes fatigue, fever, diarrhea, abdominal pains, and large lymph nodes.

In Israel most visceral leishmaniasis occurs in children under 6 years old, not in HIV-positive adults.

Visceral leishmaniasis in the presence of HIV INFECTION may be of sudden onset and rapid progression with a very bad prognosis.

XEROPHTHALMIA

This occurs in the Nile Valley, along the northwest coast of Africa, along the southeast coast of the Red Sea, in Syria, Iraq, Saudi Arabia, Turkey, Ethiopia, and Iran.

YAWS

This is a disease closely related to TREPONARID. It occurs mainly in the humid tropics; thus it is probably rare if it exists at all in the Middle East. At any rate, it is nearly indistinguishable from TREPONARID and is treated similarly.

Regional Notes

Index S. Southeast Asia

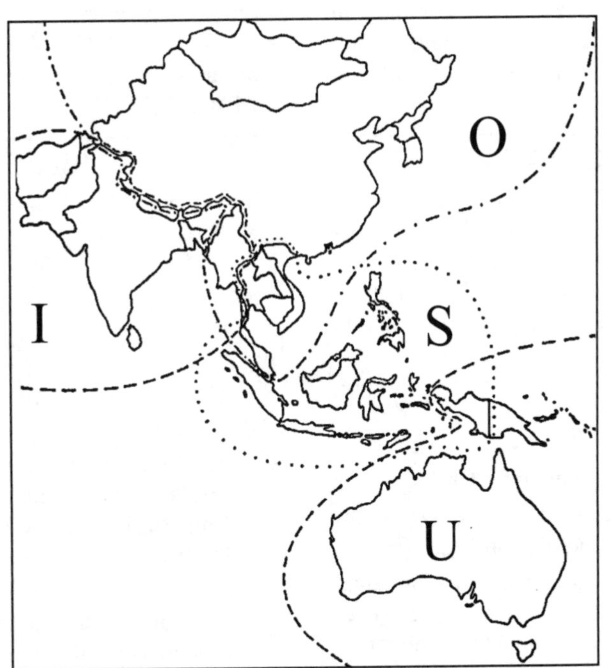

Index S: Southeast Asia

ACUTE ABDOMEN

Similar regional diseases: PIG-BEL may either mimic or cause this but it is rare except in Irian Jaya.

ADDICTION

Betel nut is used throughout Southeast Asia. See PLANT POISONING in the *Disease Index*.

AMEBIC LIVER DISEASE

This is common throughout Indochina, especially in Thailand. It is not common in Irian Jaya or Laos.

Similar regional diseases: In northeast Thailand LIVER FLUKE can appear quite similar.

ANEMIA

TROPICAL SPLENOMEGALY occurs in Vietnam and Irian Jaya. THALLASEMIA is extremely common in northeast Thailand and adjacent areas of neighboring countries. These both cause anemia due to red cell destruction.

ARBOVIRAL FEVER

The local forms of this are DENGUE FEVER, Japanese B Encephalitis, and Ross River fever. DENGUE FEVER is listed separately in the *Disease Index*; it may also develop into HEMORRHAGIC FEVER. For Japanese B Encephalitis, see the ENCEPHALITIS entry in this *Index*.

Ross River Fever

Cause: Virus

Synonyms: Ross River virus, Epidemic Polyarthritis.

Mildly to very ill; Class 2; Regional: It occurs in southern Vietnam, in the Mollucas, and in Irian Jaya.

Age: Any. **Who**: Mosquito-bitten, females more than males. The disease is transmitted both by Culex (evening biters) and Aedes (day biters). **Onset**: Unknown.

Clinical:

This causes a high fever with a severe ARTHRITIS that lasts for a long time (months to years) but eventually goes away. It is not known to cause problems in unborn babies.

Similar Conditions: See Protocol C-2.

Treatment:

Prevention: Since this is transmitted mostly by day and evening-biting mosquitoes, insect repellent during the day is helpful but bed nets at night do not help to prevent the disease except perhaps for those who go to bed very early.

Patient Care: ASPIRIN, ACETAMINOPHEN, or IBUPROFEN for the pain and fever. Antibiotics do no good at all.

ASCARIASIS

This is a problem all over the Southeast Asian area. Over 1/3 of the children are affected in Java and Floros. It is common in Laos and in peninsular Malaysia amongst Indian oil palm workers, affecting mainly children.

Similar regional diseases: Occasionally, when worms invade the gallbladder, the symptoms can mimic LIVER FLUKE.

BERIBERI

This is common in peninsular Malaysia and anywhere poor people eat a diet of white rice with little else.

BRAIN DAMAGE

The most common local cause is Japanese B ENCEPHALITIS.

BRUCELLOSIS

This occurs in the Philippines, and possibly elsewhere.

CANCER

Cancer of the *bile ducts* is common in northeast Thailand where LIVER FLUKE occurs.

Cancer of the *mouth* is relatively common in northern Thailand where Miang is chewed and where Betel nut is used.

Cancer of the *mouth and nose* affects the Indian population throughout this area. Also persons of southern Chinese descent are more susceptible than average to this.

Liver cancer is very common throughout this area; it is probably related to spoilage of grains and peanuts as well as to HEPATITIS B.

CEREBRAL PALSY

A local cause is JAPANESE B ENCEPHALITIS.

CHANCROID

Many cases in this area are resistant to DOXYCYCLINE, SULFA, and COTRIMOXAZOLE. They usually respond to ERYTHROMYCIN, CHLORAMPHENICOL, CEFTRIAXONE, and CIPROFLOXACIN (and other -oxacin drugs).

CHICKEN POX

In Southeast Asia, much of the adult population is not immune to chicken pox. In teenagers and young adults, there can be very serious complications, e.g. ENCEPHALITIS. Also chicken pox is very serious in pregnancy and amongst HIV-infected patients. When and if immunization is available, urge all acquaintances to be immunized.

CHOLERA

This occurs mainly in epidemics in times of drought or flood, except in Indonesia where it accounts for up to 50% of diarrhea cases in hospitals. It is relatively common all over Southeast Asia. The most common areas affected are Indonesia, Burma. Cambodia, and Malaysia.

CIRRHOSIS

Regional causes of this are SCHISTOSOMIASIS JAPONICUM and INDIAN CHILDHOOD CIRRHOSIS; also consider the worldwide causes.

CRETINISM

Of the two kinds of cretinism listed, it is the first kind which affects most cretins in this area.

CYSTICERCOSIS

This is very common in Irian Jaya and in Bali. STRONGYLOIDIASIS is also common in some areas there, so the treatment is quite problematic.

DENGUE FEVER

This is present throughout Southeast Asia. The distribution of the disease varies from year to year. It is especially common in Irian Jaya, and it occurs regularly in other parts of Indonesia. In Sarawak it is common inland but not on the coast. It occurs most commonly in July in Thailand and in November in the Philippines. HEMORRHAGIC FEVER is a common complication. In Cambodia, dengue and dengue hemorrhagic fever are reported from all areas. Malaysia reports yearly epidemics in all areas but the Federal Territory, Selangor, and Johor are most affected. In Vietnam, dengue is a major public health problem with most cases occurring in June.

DIABETES

This occurs as a complication of chronic PANCREATITIS in Indonesia.

DIPHTHERIA

This occurs throughout this area in the unimmunized, mostly with groups of cases appearing in crowded inner-city areas.

DONOVANOSIS

This is very common in Irian Jaya.

DYSENTERY

In Chiang Mai Province, Thailand, both types occur but bacterial is more common. Both kinds are common in Flores and central Java, Indonesia. In Thailand dysentery due to shigella is resistant to most antibiotics. (Symptoms are a high fever, prostration, and many very small diarrhea movements that look like plain blood) Seek professional care early.

Similar regional diseases: PIG-BEL in Irian Jaya. In other areas, consider PARAGONIMIASIS or SCHISTOSOMIASIS JAPONICUM.

ELEPHANTIASIS, ENDEMIC

Java, Indonesia, reportedly has an area of endemic elephantiasis (Mossy foot).

ENCEPHALITIS

Japanese B encephalitis (JBE) is the most common local cause of encephalitis. It occurs throughout this area but it is less common in southern than in northern Thailand. An immunization is available for this consisting of two injections, two weeks apart; it is available in Bangkok.

JBE is carried by Culex mosquitoes (see Volume I, Appendix 10). There is a 40% death rate with JBE and most of the survivors have significant long-term disabilities.

In certain areas, SCHISTOSOMIASIS JAPONICUM may also cause encephalitis.

ENTERIC FEVER

This is quite common in all Indochina. There are some abdominal symptoms present in almost all patients: nausea and vomiting; constipation; diarrhea; or abdominal pains. Occasionally it may cause isolated fever without other symptoms.

Similar regional diseases: See Protocols C-2 and C-9.

FILARIASIS

Synonym: Elephantiasis, non-endemic.

In this area, there are two types of filariasis: Bancroftian and Brugian.

Bancroftian filariasis occurs in Vietnam, Sumatra, Borneo, the southern half of the Philippines, and in the Indonesian islands directly east of Borneo, including Irian Jaya where it is very common. It does not occur in Java and the islands directly east of there. It more often affects the male genitals.

Brugian filariasis has largely the same distribution, but it does not occur in Indonesia east of Sulawesi. It often affects arms and breasts as well as the legs, but rarely the genitals.

FOOD POISONING

There are three kinds that are peculiar to this area:

Rice that has stood at room temperature for a day or two grows bacteria that cause severe, watery diarrhea.

Raw shellfish (mussels, clams, and oysters) concentrate a toxin which causes symptoms within 30 minutes. It starts with tingling and numbness around the mouth first and then the limbs. Later, vomiting and uncoordination occur. Death is not uncommon. It may appear similar to *HYPERVENTILATION.*

Gallbladder of Raw Fish: See the separare entry below.

GALLBLADDER DISEASE

Similar regional disease: LIVER FLUKE.

GALLBLADDER OF RAW FISH

This is from carp which is a bottom feeder, caught with heavy weights on lines or nets. The stuff is still poisonous if and when it is cooked.

It is used in Asia as a Chinese traditional medicine for poor eyesight, it causes nausea, vomiting, diarrhea, abdominal pain, LIVER FAILURE, and KIDNEY FAILURE.

Treatment: Not feasible in the village situation. Send out.

GASTROENTERITIS

Similar regional diseases: PIG-BEL (mostly Irian Jaya), CAPILLARIASIS (mostly the Philippines).

GIARDIASIS

This is generally common in Southeast Asia. In Chiang Mai Province, Thailand, it affects mainly younger children.

GOITER

This is common in the Penans of Sarawak. It generally occurs in lowland river deltas, in inland areas, and at higher altitudes. It is very common in the highlands of Irian Jaya.

HEART FAILURE

The most common regional causes are THALLASEMIA, RHEUMATIC FEVER, SCHISTOSOMIASIS JAPONICUM, and BERIBERI.

HEMORRHAGIC FEVER

This is almost all caused by DENGUE FEVER.

HEPATITIS

This is especially common in Indonesia where almost everyone has had the disease before 5 years of age. It may be transmitted prenatally from mother to baby. Hepatitis D is common.

Similar regional diseases: See the note under SPOTTED FEVER in this index. LEPTOSPIROSIS is as common as hepatitis in Malaysia and may be indistinguishable. Also consider SCHISTOSOMIASIS JAPONICUM, THALLASEMIA.

In some areas, hepatitis might be caused by Q FEVER rather than a virus. In this case the patient probably had close contact with newborn animals.

HIV INFECTION

This has become epidemic in Thailand, along the Thai-Burmese border area, and in Burma and Cambodia.

HOOKWORM

This is especially common in Sumatra and Java, Indonesia. About 50% of Cambodians are infected. It is also common in Chiang Mai Province, Thailand, affecting mainly 10-15 y.o. children. It is common in peninsular Malaysia amongst Indian oil palm workers, affecting mainly children. In Irian Jaya, hookworm is found everywhere but the infection is usually with only a few worms rather than many.

HYDATID DISEASE

This does not occur in the islands of Southeast Asia but may rarely occur in Indochina.

INTESTINAL FLUKE

One kind is echinostomiasis which occurs in Indonesia, Philippines, and Thailand and has minimal symptoms. It comes from eating inadequately cooked tadpoles, snails, fish, and frogs.

A second kind, fasciolopsiasis, is is particularly common in Kalimantan, Sumatra, and Indochina. It is found on the banks of large lakes with lotus plants and snails where there is sewage contamination of the water. In such areas up to 25% of the population may be infected. The most commonly affected plants are the water chestnut, water caltrop, and water hyacinth.

The type of snail that carries the larvae of the intestinal fluke. The diameter is about 1 cm.

Similar conditions: Also consider CAPILLARIASIS in the Philippines.

JAUNDICE

The most common regional causes are HEPATITIS, LEPTOSPIROSIS, LIVER FLUKE (in northeastern Thailand), and SCHISTOSOMIASIS JAPONICUM.

KATAYAMA DISEASE

In this area this is almost always due to the initial stage of SCHISTOSOMIASIS JAPONICUM.

KIDNEY FAILURE

The most common causes in this region are MALARIA, LEPTOSPIROSIS, and THALLASEMIA. OVALOCYTOSIS, in eastern Irian Jaya, causes kidney failure due to destruction of red blood cells.

LARVA MIGRANS

In this area, the deep type, gnathostomiasis, is caused by eating or handling raw or rare tadpoles, frogs, snakes, fish, chicken, slugs, or snails. Avoiding such infections involves using rubber gloves or tongs whenever handling raw meat. Such meats must be well cooked before they are eaten. These are very serious infections which must be treated by a physician. They are most common in Thailand.

LEPROSY

In this area leprosy is most common in Indonesia, Burma and Nepal; Thailand, Vietnam, Cambodia, and the Philippines have many patients also.

LEPTOSPIROSIS

This is generally common in this region. In Malaysia it is common around oil palm and rubber estates. It is not common on rice farms.

LIVER FAILURE

The most common causes are MALARIA, LEPTOSPIROSIS, HEPATITIS, ALCOHOLISM, and AMEBIC LIVER DISEASE. In Indian children, consider INDIAN CHILDHOOD CIRRHOSIS.

LIVER FLUKE

Synonym for the local form: Opisthorchiasis

This is common in Indonesia, NE Thailand, and Laos.

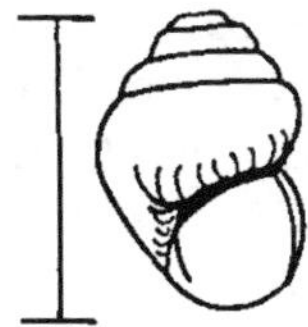

The kind of snail that carries the larva of the liver fluke; the height is about 1.5 cm.

In Thailand, symptoms of GALLBLADDER DISEASE are common. (See the illustration of the pain pattern in the main *Disease Index* under GALLBLADDER DISEASE.)

MALABSORPTION

The most common regional causes are GIARDIASIS and SPRUE. CAPILLARIASIS is a common cause in the northern coastal Philippines and northern Mindanao. Also see Protocol C-14.

MALARIA

The following areas reportedly have no malaria transmission. However, malaria has been moving to progressively higher elevations in recent years, in many areas as high as 2500 meters (8000 feet). Locally current information should be obtained:

- Cambodia: Above 1500 m (5000 ft.)
- Indonesia: Urban areas except for Irian Jaya
- Laos: Vientiane
- Philippines: Urban areas and areas above 1500 m (5000 ft.)
- Thailand: Bangkok and its suburbs; Pataya, Phuket.
- Vietnam: Above 1500 m (5000 ft.); the Red and Mekong deltas

Over all, about 1/2 to 2/3 of the malaria in this area is falciparum and it is almost all resistant to CHLOROQUINE and FANSIDAR. Non-falciparum malaria is becoming resistant to CHLOROQUINE, particularly in Indonesia and Burma.

Thailand: Most falciparum malaria is resistant to CHLOROQUINE, FANSIDAR and MEFLOQUINE; 85% of malaria is falciparum. There is some resistance to QUININE, but ARTEMISININ and QUINIDINE are very useful. HALOFANTRINE is dangerous. Daily DOXYCYCLINE works for prevention.

Near the *Thai-Burma border* there is a form of malaria that causes KIDNEY FAILURE of the nephrotic type. That kind of malaria is sensitive to CHLOROQUINE.

Malaysia: Resistance of falciparum to CHLOROQUINE is common, but less than half of the malaria is falciparum.

Indonesia: About 40% of the malaria is falciparum, and resistance is common.

Philippines: About 60% of the malaria is falciparum and resistance is common.

MALNUTRITION

This is particularly common in refugee camps where there is general malnutrition as well as specific vitamin deficiency diseases.

MEASLES

In Whites the rash is red spotted; in Blacks it is sandpapery, in Asians it has an intermediate appearance.

MELIOIDOSIS

See SEPSIS. This is a form of very serious SEPSIS found in Indochina and the Pacific.

PARAGONIMIASIS

This occurs in some areas of Southeast Asia. Exact distribution is unknown.

PIG-BEL

This is very common in Irian Jaya.

PLAGUE

This occurs in many areas of Vietnam, mostly January to April, and in Burma. There are occasional worldwide epidemics. It may occur anywhere.

PLANT POISONING

Add the following regional type:

Djenkol bean: Mainly in Indonesia and Malaysia, it is used as a food after being buried in the ground for 10 days and eaten when it sprouts. It is poisonous when eaten fresh. Sharp crystals form in the urine producing bloody urine, kidney pain (flanks), pain with urination, and sometimes KIDNEY FAILURE. *Treatment:* Empty the stomach, giving baking soda (sodium bicarbonate) in addition to ACTIVATED CHARCOAL. Watch for KIDNEY FAILURE.

PNEUMONIA

Very common in children, it accounts for about 50% of all infant deaths in the Philippines and Thailand. Also see the note under SPOTTED FEVER in this index.

PNEUMOTHORAX

This is a common problem in Asians.

POLIO

This is very common in the Philippines. The following countries also have a major problem with polio: Indonesia, Burma, Laos, Vietnam.

RABIES

This is not present in Irian Jaya, on Timor, Indonesia, or on Palawan, Philippines. It is a major problem in Thailand. Very few of their dogs are immunized so the disease spreads through the dog population and about 50 humans a year die as a result of rabid dog bites.

RHEUMATIC FEVER

This is very common in the Philippines.

RICKETS

This is particularly common in Muslim cultures.

SCHISTOSOMIASIS JAPONICUM

Cause: Worm

Synonyms: Bilharzia, Snail fever

Mildly ill to very ill; Class 2; Regional; It occurs in scattered areas throughout the southern Philippines, and near the Thai/Laos/Cambodia border area.

In Indonesia it is present only in the Napu and Lindu valleys of the Celebes. It is present in peninsular Malaysia, the north central area, around Kuala Lipis and Kuala Koyan. It does not occur in Thailand. (See SCHISTOSOMIASIS MEKONGI also.)

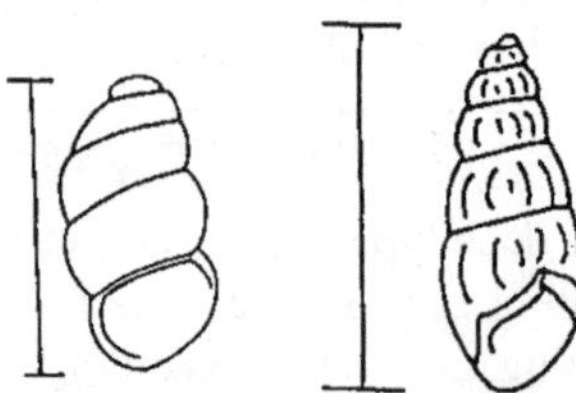

The kinds of snails that carry Schistosomiasis Japonicum. Note the small hole and many swirls. Some have stripes and some do not. Lengths are 0.5-1 cm.

Age: Any. **Who**: Skin exposed to water with infected snails. **Onset**: Beginning 3-7 weeks after exposure.

Clinical:

- **Initially:**

In Westerners this frequently starts as KATAYAMA DISEASE. Nationals skip this stage.

- **30 to 90 days after exposure:**

The patient may have lower-right abdominal pains with fevers, diarrhea or DYSENTERY, and cough. This stage can look just like ENTERIC FEVER. The patient is probably unable to work.

- **3 to 5 years later:**

The person has LIVER FAILURE with a large liver, large spleen, and an abdomen full of fluid so he looks pregnant. The liver enlarges before the spleen (the opposite of MALARIA) and frequently involves the left lobe of the liver which can mimic spleen enlargement. The patient will have a decreased appetite and weight loss. Children grow poorly and they may have delayed sexual maturity. Alternatively, the patient may have chronic diarrhea, DYSENTERY, and MALABSORPTION.

The organism may invade the brain, causing paralysis, SEIZURES, crazy behavior, blindness, and possibly coma. It may invade the lung, causing RESPIRATORY INFECTION, and HEART FAILURE. These symptoms must be treated promptly on mere suspicion in anyone who has had any exposure during his or her lifetime. Be sure to use PREDNISONE as well as PRAZIQUANTEL.

Complication: CANCER of the rectum.

Similar Conditions: *Fever and fatigue:* in the early stage resembles ENTERIC FEVER and SERUM SICKNESS. Later stages are difficult to distinguish from LIVER FAILURE and MALABSORPTION from other causes; see Protocol C-14.

Brain effects sometimes resemble POLIO (paralysis), STROKE (paralysis), ENCEPHALITIS (seizures, crazy behavior), CYSTICERCOSIS (seizures).

Bush Laboratory: It is possible to hatch the eggs and see the larvae that emerge, using simple equipment. See Appendix 2, Volume I. The hatching test is sensitive; it will most likely be positive in the presence of the disease. Take the stool sample between 10 AM and 2 PM.

Higher-Level Care. *Laboratory*: The worm eggs may be found in the stool, beginning sometime in the KATAYAMA phase and lasting into the full-blown disease. After the disease has become chronic, the eggs may be absent. A blood count may show many eosinophils early in the disease but it might not later on. There are also antibody tests. *Facilities*: If there are any complications it is mandatory to send out to a level 4 or 5 facility.

Treatment:

Prevention: Use latrines; avoid exposure of skin to contaminated water; let a bucket of water without snails stand overnight before washing with it.

Patient Care: PRAZIQUANTEL is effective and safe enough to use even if you are not certain of the diagnosis. For severe KATAYAMA, give PREDNISONE on days 1-5. Give PRAZIQUANTEL also on day 3. This will prevent worsening of the KATAYAMA DISEASE. Occasionally patients get a severe allergic response (see ALLERGY) to the first dose of the drug. This is treated like any other ALLERGY, but do not stop the drug. It is due to dead and dying worms and will not recur as severely, if at all, with subsequent doses. PREDNISONE or PREDNISOLONE along with the PRAZIQUANTEL might be helpful. In advanced liver disease PROPRANOLOL might be helpful. In either case seek professional medical advice. NIRIDAZOLE is an old, dangerous drug that should no longer be used.

If there are neurological symptoms (seizures, paralysis, loss of sensation, altered mental status), use DEXAMETHASONE or another corticosteroid, as you would for MENINGITIS due to TUBERCULOSIS.

You should evaluate the results of the treatment at 1, 3, and 6 months after giving the drug.

SCHISTOSOMIASIS MEKONGI

A disease nearly identical to SCHISTOSOMIASIS JAPONICUM, the differences being merely academic. It occurs in Cambodia, in two areas along the Mekong River. The symptoms and treatment are the same.

SCRUB TYPHUS

This is present throughout Thailand and east of there. It occurs in the northern Philippines, in peninsular Malaysia, in Sumatra, Java, scattered areas in Borneo, northern Sulawesi, and the northern half of Irian Jaya. This is most common in palm oil workers. It is rare in Sabah. Amongst the Khmer refugees in Thailand, it is the most common cause of general illness with fevers.

SEIZURES

Regional causes of seizures include Japanese B ENCEPHALITIS, PARAGONIMIASIS, and SCHISTOSOMIASIS JAPONICUM.

SEPSIS

Those particularly susceptible to sepsis include those with TROPICAL SPLENOMEGALY in Vietnam.

Melioidosis is a peculiar form of this which occurs in rural areas of Indochina as well as in northern Australia, between latitudes 20° North and 20° South, usually during 2 weeks following the onset of heavy rains, or else at other times with water exposure. The incubation period can be very long, a matter of years. It usually affects those in ill health otherwise: patients with DIABETES, CIRRHOSIS, KIDNEY FAILURE, or other chronic diseases. Most infections occur within 2 weeks of the onset of heavy rain, through exposure to water per occupation or recreation. This problem in someone with DIABETES or KIDNEY FAILURE frequently results in death.

SPOTTED FEVER

This probably does not occur in this area; at any rate it does not cause severe illness. A similar bacterial disease, Q FEVER, is found in pastoral areas of Indonesia except for Kalimantan and Irian Jaya. It causes a severe "flu" or PNEUMONIA or HEPATITIS.

SPRUE

This does not cause ANEMIA in this area. It is most common in Indochina, Indonesia, and the Philippines.

STROKE

This may be caused by SCHISTOSOMIASIS JAPONICUM.

STRONGYLOIDIASIS

This may cause SEPSIS in the presence of TROPICAL SPLENOMEGALY. It is common in Chiang Mai Province, Thailand, affecting mainly 10-15 y.o. children. It is relatively common all over Southeast Asia.

SYPHILIS

This is especially common in Thailand. Many Thai newborns have congenital syphilis.

TETANUS

This is a common cause of death in newborns in Indonesia.

THALLASEMIA

This is common throughout Indochina, mostly in people of Chinese and Malay origins. It is very common in NE Thailand and in refugees from neighboring areas. OVALOCYTOSIS, similar but less serious, is found mainly in Malaysia and in eastern Irian Jaya.

TINEA

Tinea imbricata occurs especially in Irian Jaya.

TOXOPLASMOSIS

This is generally less prevalent than average in cold or hot and arid regions, at high elevation, and in Malaysia. There is a small risk of acquiring it in Thailand. TROPICAL SPLENOMEGALY makes a person prone to developing the disease.

TRICHINOSIS

Generally not common in Indochina, but there are occasional outbreaks of the disease in northern Thailand. It has not been reported to occur in the Asian islands.

TRICHURIASIS

This is extremely common throughout this area, with more than 50% of the population affected in most of Laos, Indonesia, Malaysia, and the Philippines.

TROPICAL SPLENOMEGALY

This occurs mainly in Irian Jaya at 280-500 meters (900-1600 ft.). It also occurs in the Philippines and Vietnam.

TROPICAL ULCER

This is very common in the highlands of Irian Jaya.

TUBERCULOSIS

This is very common throughout this area; it affects about 10% of Cambodians. Reportedly, BCG immunization gives 83% protection against the disease in this area.

Similar regional disease: PARAGONIMIASIS

TURISTA

If diarrhea is severe, see CHOLERA.

TYPHUS

See TYPHUS or SCRUB TYPHUS in the main *Disease Index*. TYPHUS includes both *murine* typhus and *louse-borne* typhus. The known distribution of murine typhus is throughout peninsular SEA, the northern half of the Philippines, Sumatra, Java, and Sulawesi. It may occur elsewhere.

WHOOPING COUGH

This is extremely common in the Philippines.

XEROPHTHALMIA

This is especially common in rural peninsular Malaysia. In Thailand it is a rural, not an urban problem. In most of Asia there is a very high mortality rate for children who are blinded by this—up to 75% in the first 3 months. They die from infections due to the decreased immunity caused by the disease.

YAWS

In this area it is most prevalent in Cambodia, Indonesia, rural Kalimantan, on Sumatra, in the Moluccas, on Timor, and especially in Irian Jaya. In Irian Jaya it is most common in the lower-altitude highlands. It does not occur in Java.

Regional Notes

Index U. Australia and the South Pacific

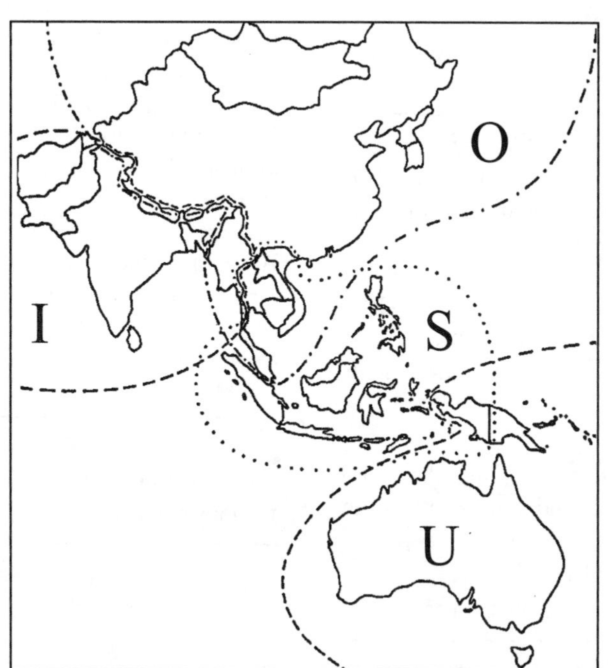

Index U: Australia and the South Pacific

ACUTE ABDOMEN

Similar regional disease: PIG-BEL.

ADDICTION

Uppers: Local examples are:

Betel nut is described under PLANT POISONING in the *Disease Index*.

Pituri, used by Australian aboriginals, has the effects of both uppers and outers. It is made from the stems and leaves of an erect shrub, 3-4 meters (9-12 ft.) tall, which is treated with ash. The drug causes hallucinations.

Downers: Local examples are:

Kava (also known as yanonga) is used in the south Pacific.

ALCOHOL is commonly abused by the Australian aborigines (amongst others).

Outers: The only example peculiar to the area is pituri, described above.

AMEBIC LIVER DISEASE

This is particularly common in Tutelle, Tuvalu, Wallis and Futuna Islands, New Caledonia, and Gilbert Island.

ANEMIA

Much of the anemia in pregnancy is due to MALARIA; it causes small babies but not premature births.

Anemia due to red cell destruction may be caused by the following diseases in this area:

- MALARIA
- OVALOCYTOSIS, especially along the north shore of Papua New Guinea and in the central highlands
- TROPICAL SPLENOMEGALY
- THALLASEMIA, common in New Guinea.

ANTHRAX

This is found in Australia, New Guinea, and Polynesia.

ARBOVIRAL FEVER; Ross River Fever

DENGUE FEVER, the most common, is listed separately in this *Index* and the *Disease Index*. *Murray Valley Fever* occurs in eastern Australia and on the island of New Guinea; it is a kind of ENCEPHALITIS and/or HEMORRHAGIC FEVER. (See the *Disease Index*.) *Ross River Fever* is also common, and is described below.

Ross River Fever

Cause: Virus

Synonyms: Ross River virus, Epidemic polyarthritis.

Mildly to very ill; Class 2; Regional; it occurs throughout this area except for the northern half of Western Australia.

Age: Any. **Who**: Mosquito-bitten.This is transmitted by both Culex (night-biters) and Aedes (day biters) **Onset**: Unknown.

Clinical:

This causes a high fever with a severe ARTHRITIS that lasts for a long time (months to years) but eventually goes away. It is not known to cause problems in unborn babies.

Similar conditions: See Protocol C-6.

Treatment:

Prevention: Since this is transmitted mostly by mosquitoes, insect repellent during the day is helpful as well as bed nets at night.

Patient Care: ASPIRIN, ACETAMINOPHEN, or IBUPROFEN for the pain and fever. Antibiotics do no good at all.

ARTHRITIS

A common local cause is Ross River Fever, a form of ARBOVIRAL FEVER. There is also a hereditary arthritis that occurs in this area. It affects few joints, usually asymmetrically. GOUT is common in some Pacific islands.

ASCARIASIS

This is common in New Guinea, and in many areas infections are heavy.

ASTHMA

In New Guinea and Australia, this is commonly caused by an insect that lives in house dust.

BRAIN DAMAGE

In this area, the most likely causes are cerebral MALARIA and Murray Valley fever (See ENCEPHALITIS).

BRUCELLOSIS

This occurs in Australia, New Zealand, and the Solomon Islands.

BURKITT LYMPHOMA

This occurs in New Guinea.

CANCER

BURKITT LYMPHOMA is a common type of childhood cancer.

Breast cancer is uncommon; it occurs more in the islands than elsewhere.

Cervical cancer is the most common cancer in females.

Liver cancer is the most common cancer in males.

Thyroid cancer is the second most common cancer in both sexes in Vanuatu. It is common throughout the Pacific area.

CHANCROID

This is common in all tropical parts of the Pacific area.

CHOLERA

This is generally common in Indonesia where it accounts for up to 50% of all diarrhea that is severe enough to send the patient to the hospital. It occurs in the Caroline Islands.

CRETINISM

This is particularly common in the central highlands of New Guinea.

CYSTICERCOSIS

This is very common in the highlands of New Guinea. It is the most common cause of SEIZURES that start during adult life.

DENGUE FEVER

This does not occur in New Zealand. It is common throughout most of the South Pacific, especially New Guinea. In Australia it is found mainly in North Queensland, also in the Torres strain area and in Queensland. It occurs in Fiji and New Caledonia. In Tonga and Vanuatu dengue is reportedly not common.

DIABETES

This is very common in the aboriginals in the Kimberly area.

DIPHTHERIA

Skin infections with diphtheria occur on the islands of the Pacific.

DONOVANOSIS

This is very prevalent in New Guinea, New Britain, and in Australia amongst the aboriginal population. In many areas it is the most common sexually transmitted disease.

DYSENTERY

Bacterial dysentery is particularly common in Australia. The southern coastal areas of New Guinea and surrounding islands have much amebic dysentery.

Similar regional disease: PIG-BEL.

EAR INFECTION, MIDDLE

Aboriginals in the Kimberly area frequently develop chronic middle ear infections caused by a peculiar germ that can be treated with SULFA, COTRIMOXAZOLE, DOXYCYCLINE, or ERYTHROMYCIN. It does not respond to other drugs.

In central Australia, the common germ responds well to AMPICILLIN and COTRIMOXAZOLE. The HIB immunization prevents it.

ENCEPHALITIS

Japanese B Encephalitis occurs in Australia (Torres Strait and Cape York Peninsula), Papua New Guinea and some Pacific Islands.

Murray Valley Fever is a local form of Encephalitis; see ARBOVIRAL FEVER in this *Index*, and also the *Disease Index*.

ENTERIC FEVER

In Papua New Guinea there are frequent complications as this affects the brain: deafness, uncoordination, and weakness that ascends from the feet upward. Seek professional medical care early.

ENTEROBIASIS

This is common in the area, with about half the adults infected.

FILARIASIS

Synonym: Elephantiasis, non-endemic.

Only the Bancroftian form is found in this area.

This is a major problem in the lower highlands of New Guinea. There is some spectacular swelling of legs and scrotums; reportedly some males carry their scrotums in wheelbarrows in front of them. It reportedly only rarely affects the breasts or arms.

The disease occurs mostly below 1200 meters (4000 ft.), mostly during the rainy season, mostly in heavily populated areas. It is present in most of the Pacific islands other than Australia and New Zealand. It is uncommon but not absent from American Samoa.

In French Polynesia it is very prevalent on Bora Bora, Maupiti, Kauehi, Kaukura, Taipivai, and Puamau. It is not common but it exists in New Caledonia. In Vanuatu, it is carried by the same species of mosquito that carries MALARIA. The disease is particularly common in the central and northern islands, especially the Torres Islands and the Cook Islands.

Prevention: IVERMECTIN is not quite as good as DEC for prevention but it is adequate if given twice a year.

FOOD POISONING

A form found in New Caledonia, New Zealand, and Polynesia is due to Ciguatera fish, causing vomiting and diarrhea as well as strange sensations (numbness and tingling), weakness, and possibly itching of the palms and soles.

Treatment: The same as general treatment for PLANT POISONING.

GALLBLADDER DISEASE

This may be caused by OVALOCYTOSIS.

GIARDIASIS

This is very common in Australian aboriginals.

GOITER

One finds this especially in inland and high altitude areas. It occurs in southeast Australia, in New Zealand and Tasmania. Scattered areas on the island of New Guinea are affected, as well as parts of New Britain and the northern portion of the Solomon Islands.

HEART FAILURE

Valvular failure is common in Tonga, as a result of RHEUMATIC FEVER and birth defects.

HEMORRHAGIC FEVER

This disease occurs, but is not common, in French Polynesia. When it occurs it is usually due to DENGUE FEVER or ARBOVIRAL FEVER (Murray Valley Fever).

HEPATITIS

This is extremely common in the south Pacific area. Almost all children have had hepatitis B before 10 years of age in Tonga and the aboriginal areas of Australia. It may be transmitted prenatally from mother to baby. Chronic hepatitis from this is common in Kiribati. Hepatitis B and D are more common in Nauru than anywhere else in the world. Hepatitis E is presently not known to occur here, but it will probably appear in time.

HIV INFECTION

This occurs in Australia. In Papua New Guinea there are many cases of (probably) falsely positive HIV tests. (This means that the blood test indicates the person has the disease when he really does not.) In comparison to the rest of the world, this region has the lowest HIV positive rate.

HOOKWORM

This is uncommon above 2000 meters (6600 ft.) elevation and in areas too dry for agriculture. It is common in New Guinea but people are not usually very sick with it. In Australia it occurs to a significant extent only in the Kimberly area.

HYDATID DISEASE

This is very common in the Collie area of SW Australia and in New Zealand. It does not occur in Tasmania. In this area only the kind transmitted by dogs occurs. You should only suspect the problem in areas where dogs are allowed to lick children's faces. Usually these are arid areas.

HYPERTENSION

This is especially common amongst aboriginals.

IMPETIGO

This is especially common in Australian aboriginals.

JAUNDICE

The most common regional causes are LEPTOSPIROSIS, HEPATITIS, MALARIA, THALLASEMIA, OVALOCYTOSIS.

KIDNEY FAILURE

Aboriginals have a high frequency of nephritic kidney failure, usually from CELLULITIS. OVALOCYTOSIS may cause hemolytic kidney failure.

LARVA MIGRANS

The deep type, acquired from eating raw snails, occurs in New Britain, Port Moresby, Lae, New Ireland, Bougainville Island, and the highlands of New Guinea. It may cause ENCEPHALITIS. It should be treated in a hospital.

LEPROSY

This is rare in New Zealand. It is common in New Guinea, in all the Pacific islands, and amongst aboriginal Australians in the North Territory. It is particularly common in French Polynesia, especially Gambier and the Southern Marquesas. About 60% is indeterminate or tuberculoid and about 40% lepromatous.

In this area leprosy might be acquired from using woven mats that have been used by leprous patients. The fine, rough strands inoculate the leprosy germ into the skin of the user. Presumably wearing thick clothing would prevent this.

Treatment: In Vanuatu and presumably surrounding islands, nationals have a very high rate (11%) of adverse reactions to DAPSONE. Their skin peels off and there is a high death rate. This occurs at 3-7 weeks after the beginning of treatment.

LEPTOSPIROSIS

This occurs in Australia. It is common in New Zealand. It is extremely common on Tahiti Island in French Polynesia, and in New Caledonia. It especially affects middle-aged farmers between March and May. In this area, about 1 in 4 cases is very serious, complicated by JAUNDICE and sometimes LIVER FAILURE, resulting in some deaths.

LIVER FAILURE

The most common regional causes are LEPTOSPIROSIS, HEPATITIS, ALCOHOLISM, and MALARIA.

LIVER FLUKE

The most recent information indicates that this cannot be acquired in the area. The few cases that have been reported have been from Australia, in persons who acquired the worm elsewhere.

LYME DISEASE

This is known to be in Australia, along the sea coast north of Sydney.

LYMPHOGRANULOMA VENEREUM

This occurs in warmer areas of the Pacific.

MALABSORPTION

The most common regional causes are GIARDIASIS, TRICHURIASIS, PIG-BEL, and STRONGYLOIDIASIS. Also see Protocol C-14.

MALARIA

This is widespread in this area; about 2/3 to 3/4 of the malaria in the South Pacific islands and Papua New Guinea is falciparum. In west-central Papua, over 50% of children less than 10 years old are affected. Those surviving to adulthood are immune to it. Some of the non-falciparum (as well as falciparum) malaria is resistant to CHLOROQUINE, particularly in Papua New Guinea.

Reportedly there is no malaria transmission in Australia. Other areas reportedly free of malaria transmission are:

- New Guinea: Above 1500 m (5000 ft.).
- New Zealand: Entirely.
- Vanuatu: Futuna Island.

However, it should be noted that malaria is now occurring at progressively higher elevations, in areas previously free of it. Therefore locally current information should be obtained.

In Vanuatu, about 88% of the malaria is resistant to CHLOROQUINE. In the Solomon Islands, 60-70% of the malaria is falciparum with resistance to CHLOROQUINE being very common. Some of the non-falciparum malaria has also become resistant to CHLOROQUINE. Resistance to FANSIDAR is widespread in PNG and presumably in Irian Jaya also.

In the Solomon Islands the situation is rapidly changing. It is important for expatriates to take prophylactic medication. Follow the advice of the British Embassy as to what to take and how much.

MALNUTRITION

Kwashiorkor is common in New Guinea. Australian aboriginals have stunted growth rather than skinny arms when they are malnourished. For them, measure their height and compare it to that of normally-nourished children of the same age and ethnic origin. When you are first in an area, measure the height of well-nourished children (as determined by normal hair color) of various ages to establish a standard.

Complications: PIG-BEL is a common complication of refeeding.

MEASLES

In PNG, measles accounts for about 1/3 of deaths in children in hospitals. Children should be immunized at 6 months of age.

PARAGONIMIASIS

This occurs in some areas of Papua New Guinea, the Solomon Islands, Western Samoa, and American Samoa.

PEPTIC ULCER

Similar regional diseases: PIG-BEL.

PIG-BEL

This is very common in New Guinea, especially the southern highlands

PLAGUE

This is not known to occur in this area. However, if there were a worldwide epidemic, there is nothing to prevent its occurrence.

PLANT POISONING

Plant poisoning due to Argemone oil occurs in the Pacific islands.

PNEUMONIA

This is by far the most common cause of death in New Guinea. A pneumonia that responds to AMPICILLIN but not PENICILLIN is common in aboriginal central Australia.

POLIO

This is particularly common on Wallis and Futuna Islands.

PYOMYOSITIS

This might be in the shoulder, arm, or back. It usually responds to ERYTHROMYCIN.

RABIES

This is present nearly worldwide, but reportedly does not occur on the island of New Guinea or in Australia.

RHEUMATIC FEVER

This is particularly common amongst aboriginal Australians, on the Cook Islands, in French Polynesia, on the Torres Straits Islands, in the Maoris of New Zealand, and in Tonga.

SCABIES

This is present worldwide, common everywhere, but especially in aboriginal Australia and highland New Guinea.

SCRUB TYPHUS

This occurs especially along the northeast coast of Australia, in Papua New Guinea, the eastern Solomon Islands, and Vanuatu.

SEIZURES

In New Guinea, the most common cause of seizures in adults is CYSTICERCOSIS.

SEPSIS

Patients with TROPICAL SPLENOMEGALY are prone to this.

A form of STRONGYLOIDIASIS in New Guinea causes overwhelming sepsis in babies.

Melioidosis is a peculiar form of sepsis which occurs in rural areas of Indochina as well as in northern Australia, around Darwin, in the aboriginal population, north of 20° latitude. Most infections occur within 2 weeks of the onset of heavy rains or at other times with water exposure. The incubation period can be very long, a matter of years. It usually affects those in ill health otherwise: patients with DIABETES, CIRRHOSIS, KIDNEY FAILURE, or other chronic diseases. This problem in someone with DIABETES or KIDNEY FAILURE frequently results in death.

SPOTTED FEVER

Tick typhus occurs in Queensland. It is usually a mild disease but might cause KIDNEY FAILURE, RESPIRATORY FAILURE or GANGRENE. It is occasionally fatal.

SPRUE

This might occur in northern Australia and possibly Papua, New Guinea.

STRONGYLOIDIASIS

Synonym: Swollen Baby Syndrome.

On the island of New Guinea, this is very common in the southern half of the island, from sea level to 1500 meters (5000 ft.). It causes an overwhelming infection (see SEPSIS) and death in children in the Gulf Provinces, known as Swollen Baby Syndrome. It is also common in aboriginals of the Kimberly area. It is particularly likely to cause SEPSIS in those who also have TROPICAL SPLENOMEGALY.

SYPHILIS

This is reportedly common in Fiji. All blood tests for syphilis will be positive in YAWS, which is very common in the island of New Guinea, and in TREPONARID, which occurs in central Australia.

TAPEWORM

Rat or dwarf tapeworm is common amongst the aboriginals of the Kimberly area and in the highlands of Papua New Guinea. Fish tapeworm occurs in Australia and New Guinea.

THALLASEMIA

This is very common all over the island of New Guinea.

TINEA

Synonym: Kaskad.

This is common in Australian aboriginals. Tinea imbricata (Kaskad) is very common below 1500 meters (5000 ft.) on the island of New Guinea.

TOXOPLASMOSIS

TROPICAL SPLENOMEGALY causes one to be more prone to this. In the Pacific area, it is very common in those who live with cats and it occurs, though less commonly, in those who live apart from cats.

TRACHOMA

This occurs in warmer parts of the Pacific area.

TREPONARID

This is found in central Australia. Though it is found only in dry areas, it is more common during the rainy season.

TRICHINOSIS

This is rare to non-existent in this area.

TRICHURIASIS

This is very common in Queensland but not in western Australia. Occurs commonly in New Guinea; may be very severe in some areas.

TROPICAL SPASTIC PARAPARESIS

This occurs on the Solomon Islands.

TROPICAL SPLENOMEGALY

This is common in New Guinea, especially in the upper Watut Valley, Morobe Province.

TROPICAL ULCER

This is common throughout the island of New Guinea. BURULI ULCERs are common in the Kumusi River area and in central Australia, but they occur throughout the region.

TUBERCULOSIS

This is common in the Pacific area except for Australia, New Zealand, Niue, and Guam.

TURISTA

In southwest Australia, GIARDIASIS and diarrhea responsive to ERYTHROMYCIN are common. In urban areas, a viral diarrhea that causes MALNUTRITION is common.

TYPHUS

Tick typhus is listed under SPOTTED FEVER; murine typhus and louse-borne typhus are described in the *Disease Index*; SCRUB TYPHUS is also a separate entry in this Index. Murine typhus outbreaks occur in Australia, along the eastern coast south of Rockhampton, and near the west coast of Western Australia.

WHOOPING COUGH

This is very common in the South Pacific.

YANONGA

See ADDICTION due to kava, in this Index. This is an alternative name.

YAWS

This is widespread in the Pacific islands and in New Guinea. It is common in aboriginal Australians. There have been mass outbreaks in the Solomon Islands and Vanuatu.

In ethnic groups where there is much promiscuity you should be reluctant to treat many people for yaws. If you do so, then the group, over time, will become vulnerable to SYPHILIS which has worse long term consequences.

Index to Volume II

B

C

D

E

I

J

K

Q

R

S

T

U

V